AFRO-AMERICAN HISTORY

Clio Bibliography Series

Abstracts from the periodicals data base of the
American Bibliographical Center

Eric H. Boehm, Editor

Users of the Clio Bibliography Series may refer to current issues of
America: History and Life *and* Historical Abstracts
for continuous bibliographic coverage of the subject areas
treated by each individual volume in the series.

Afro-American History

A Bibliography

Dwight L. Smith

EDITOR

INTRODUCTION BY

Benjamin Quarles

Santa Barbara, California
Oxford, England

Library of Congress Catalog Card Number 73-87155
ISBN Clothbound Edition 0-87436-123-0

American Bibliographical Center—Clio Press, Inc.
2040 Alameda Padre Serra
Santa Barbara, California

European Bibliographical Center—Clio Press
30 Cornmarket Street
Oxford OX1 3EY, England

Printed and bound in the United States of America

To all the scholars whose periodical articles
have given us a better understanding of
Afro-American history

CONTENTS

PREFACE

Afro-American History is the second volume in the Clio Bibliography Series published by the American Bibliographical Center. This series gathers abstracts taken from *America: History and Life* to produce special subject bibliographies of general and contemporary interest to researchers in history and the social sciences. The abstracts selected for inclusion in this bibliography were thus taken from a data base published quarterly since 1954.

Afro-American History is a selection of abstracts of articles published in literally hundreds of professional journals. Those 3,000 abstracts have been analytically classified and indexed to serve as a bibliographical reference tool and also to encourage casual browsing. It is significant that the researcher interested in Afro-American history now has access to a continuous and open-ended bibliography of the serial literature. Each new issue of *America: History and Life* will include additional abstracts of the new literature on the subject. Users of this bibliography are therefore encouraged to consult the indexes published with *America: History and Life* to update this special volume.

Afro-American History was initially prepared during the summer of 1972 when I served as consultant to the staff of the American Bibliographical Center in Santa Barbara, California. My assignment was to screen thousands of abstracts published in *America: History and Life* (Volumes 1 through 10, 1964-1972) and *Historical Abstracts* (Volumes 1 through 10, 1953-1964). (All of the latter abstracts have been published separately in *Volume 0, America: History and Life.*) As a result of that screening I selected the 2,274 abstracts which appear in this volume. I was also responsible for developing the detailed classification scheme used to categorize this otherwise amorphous mass of data. The final editorial preparation for the publication—indexing, copy preparation, and quality control—was accomplished during a second summer in Santa Barbara during 1973. The editorial responsibility for the finished product is shared by me and the indefatigable staff of ABC-Clio, Inc.

Several members of the staff merit special recognition for their special skills and for their unfailing good humor. Lloyd W. Garrison, the Managing Editor, provided editorial advice at each stage of the project. Mrs. Marsha J. McBaine, formerly Assistant Editor, *Historical Abstracts,* edited, classified, and indexed hundreds of abstracts to ensure uniformity of style and presentation. William H. Alexander, Department of History, University of California, Santa Barbara, provided expert advice concerning the classification scheme. Mrs. Lillian Kurosaka

Anderson and Miss Marcia Katz keyboarded, proofread, and verified editorial corrections and thousands of index entries. Miss Joan Haugh and Ms. Terry Simmerman copy read and proofed the final copy and Mr. William S. Rinaldo patiently completed the final layout. Ms. Barbara Monahan designed the type page, jacket, and cover. Mr. James R. Crane supervised the manufacturing process and provided liaison services with subcontractors. Ms. Rachel Hayes wrote the computer programs and supervised the machine processing which produced the photocomposition pages.

We are especially fortunate that Benjamin Quarles accepted a commission to write the introductory essay. His thoughtful prose places *Afro-American History* in a meaningful context by surveying and evaluating recent scholarship on the subject.

Finally, the publishers and I are indebted to the several hundred volunteer abstracters listed in this volume. Their descriptive summaries of the periodical literature abstracted in this volume provide a substance lacking in a mere listing of article titles. The efforts of the several abstracters who contributed fifty or more abstracts are worthy of this special acknowledgement.

DWIGHT L. SMITH

Miami University
Oxford, Ohio

INTRODUCTION

Benjamin Quarles, Morgan State College

Those interested in the reconstruction of the black past have been heartened in recent years by two not unrelated developments—the "legitimization" of black history as an academic discipline worthy of serious consideration, and the increasing availability of source materials necessary for a valid assessment of the black presence in America. By and large the scholarly community no longer resists the idea that black Americans have been instrumental in shaping this country's past to a degree hitherto not generally known or conceded. It is now taken for granted that blacks, and other minorities, "made history."

An enlightened awareness of the presence of blacks in American history is now less of a hurdle than the problem of source materials—the unearthing and making available of the hard facts, the retrieval of the relevant data. If the notion of no-black-history has been dispelled, the more mundane (but equally important) matter of provability still remains. The statement, "no documents, no history," remains as valid today as when it was coined more than seventy-five years ago. The definition of a document, or trace, is much more inclusive now than then, of course. And since then we have learned to be wary of calling certain races and groups "inarticulate," sensing that "the use of the term may express more of a hearing defect among historians than historiographical reality," as Jesse Lemisch has cautioned us.

If more abundant source materials in black studies are central to their coming of age, the marked increase of bibliographical tools in the field is a good omen. No longer need investigators feel that black history is terra incognita and that black figures must remain shadows in a mist. Periodical literature, including books comprised of several articles (the "festschriften"), are a major source of scholarly information, and hence the diffusion of such knowledge is a boon to researchers and other serious readers. For the past two decades the American Bibliographical Center, with headquarters in Santa Barbara, California, has addressed itself to this need, annually issuing a volume of concise, objective summaries of periodical literature concentrating on history and the related humanities and social sciences. Its success has been notable and the Center is now in the first rank in the field of historical bibliography worldwide.

After bringing out ten volumes of wide-ranging articles from over 2,300 international journals, the Center made a logical, almost inevitable, decision to bring out a number of special works, each devoted to a major topic area, its abstracts culled from the existing publications. Equally logical and perhaps equally inevitable, the editors decided that the second in this special abstracts series would focus on the Afro-American experience. The results we have before us. We may note two things about this compilation—its general nature and content, and its organization and utility.

Scope of this Work

This volume proposes to throw fresh light on the field of black history, revealing something of its depth and outreach by reprinting pertinent abstracts of articles which have made their appearance in the last two decades. We would naturally expect that this more recent time-span would be the most productive in any given field of knowledge. It has been of unusual importance in black history, this field having suffered considerable neglect. Hence in black history the periodic literature of more recent vintage is likely to be far more suggestive and pathbreaking than in those subject matter fields that hitherto have been more closely surveyed and intensively cultivated. An awareness of the presence of blacks has reached new heights in the period covered by this volume of abstracts. This increased interest in (or concern about) black Americans has been reflected in the world of scholarship. As a consequence we are now learning much that is new, and some of it likely to be arresting, in the whole field of black studies.

Embracing the gamut of human activities, the black past, like other fields of history, is richly grounded in the humanistic disciplines—art, music and literature. This orientation makes for an enlargement of vision. But if black history shares the common goals of all histories, it stands more to itself in evoking reactions based on considerations of race, color and ethnicity. Black history inevitably touches upon, when it does not directly relate to, a deep and complex social problem. Black history is likely to have a high "audience reaction" rating. Thus many of the articles abstracted in this compilation deal with black-white attitudes and behavior patterns in their many manifestations. We may be apprised, for example, of racial attitudes in American literature, of lawlessness and violence in black-white relationships, and that the boycott of segregated public accommodations and facilities was no invention of mid-twentieth century black activists.

As those who use this volume will quickly (and gratefully) discover, its outreach is broad. Its focus is America but on occasion we are taken to other lands. Indeed some of the summaries come from foreign language periodicals, including those in Japanese, Russian, Hungarian, Polish, French, Italian, Spanish, German and Dutch, which are likely to carry some such topic as "The Negro Problem in the United States." There are a number of abstracts on blacks in Canada and the attitudes toward them, cool more often than not. We may learn of British attitudes toward the Civil War, or the prejudices met by black British seamen in American ports during the nineteenth century. We may glean, if we choose, the views of Germans toward blacks in the post World War I period. One abstract gives a running glimpse of American blacks in Czarist Russia, including the famed Shakesperean actor, Ira Aldridge, about whom we could learn more in other of the summaries. One article tells us of the cordial reception "Porgy and Bess" received in New Zealand, as performed by a Maori cast; another piece points out that in Italy the stage version of "Uncle Tom's Cabin" has always been a great favorite, its popularity rising particularly in periods of political crises involving the exercise of freedom.

As to be expected, the geographical outreach of these abstracts embraces the ancestral homelands of the transplanted blacks—the west coast of Africa. For a given period we may learn the views of American blacks toward Africa and there are a number of pieces on the back-to-Africa proponent, the dynamic Marcus Garvey. We may meet other black emigrationists, some of them like Bishop Henry M. Turner who did not view Africa so much as heaven as he viewed America as hell.

The topics covered by the abstracts are almost as broad as life itself; indeed one piece bears the title, "Fertility Differentials in Detroit, 1920-1950," its burden that during this period the racial differentials tended "to converge." Black women in their myriad roles draw scholarly attention although the contemporary women's liberationist movement does not. To black men and women the battle of the sexes appears almost as a diversion in the light of the totality of problems they share in common because of color.

The Reconstruction period still retains a high interest, as judged by the number of abstracted articles devoted to it. As a rule the newer monographs absolve blacks from primary responsibility for the excesses that took place, and they give recognition to the not inconsiderable achievements of black legislators. This represents a revision of the image of the Reconstruction Negro as an illiterate incompetent, a willing pawn in the hands of corrupt and scheming politicians.

Recent political behavior by blacks is also of some scholarly interest, particularly for the years since the Voting Rights Act of 1965. As a number of articles suggest, the courts have left their benchmark on blacks, fixing their status and determining their legal and constitutional rights. Since the bulk of scholarly writing on blacks came during a decade characterized by racial violence, it is only natural that this phenomenon would claim scholarly interest. Many writers were attracted to riots, particularly to those of the 1960's. Their causes, as duly noted, were viewed differently by blacks than by whites, the former viewing racial outbreaks as the pent-up resentment against discrimination, and the latter viewing them as conceived by Communists and outside agitators moved by sinister or selfish motives.

This abstracts bibliography clearly bears out another central fact in black life and history—the truly astonishing variety of roles played by a host of individuals. Carrying hundreds of biographical and autobiographical articles, this compilation quickly dispels any notion that black Americans constituted a monolithic mass, thinking and acting alike. Aside from a common hatred of discrimination on the basis of color, a high degree of individualism permeated black life.

Hence in the recent periodical literature we must be prepared to meet figures like William Allen, a nineteenth century evangelist of the Society of Friends, or Peter W. Cassey, an Episcopal minister to his fellow blacks in early California. We will learn of achievers like Jeremiah B. Sanderson of New Bedford, Massachusetts, who went to California in 1854 and became a leading educator and churchman, and of slaveborn William Sanders Scarborough, who became a Greek scholar and president of Wilberforce University. Others among the many we would come across include a slave riverman who was a key figure in the local lumber industry, and a Nova Scotian black who won the Victoria Cross for his feats as a seaman during the Sepoy Mutiny in 1857.

The periodical literature reveals that blacks were engaged in a wider variety of economic activities than might have been expected. We are now much more familiar with Negro cowboys, and with the high incidence of blacks in the cattle industry generally, especially in Texas. Blacks engaged in the fur trade and were numbered among the "forty-niners" in gold rush California. We are now also told of the substantial quota of blacks in the antebellum New England whaling industry, some vessels being manned entirely by them, including the masters. Blacks in general, however, faced job discrimination and exclusion from labor unions, forcing many of them to become strike-breakers, as in the Hocking Valley, Ohio, coal mines in 1873.

In this compilation by Professor Smith the single topic receiving the most attention is slavery, a field worthy of attention because of changes in approach and substance and, equally important, the employment of newer research strategies. Slavery, as Staughton Lynd has pointed out, "is a key to the meaning of our national experience." It would seem proper, then, that a reevaluation of this important institution would be a first order of business.

Old questions in the scholarship of slavery loom large in the periodical literature, including such hardy perennials as the relative benignity of slavery in Latin America as against slavery in the United States, as to the profitability of slavery, and as to the validity of the "Sambo" personality of the slave, as theoretically advanced by Stanley Elkins. We are now given more rounded assessments of slavery in Atlantic diplomacy, particularly in the relationships between America and England. Historians, as we learn, are now more closely examining the slave in industry, one author holding that it owed its introduction therein to the practice of slave hiring, and another informing us that the hired slave ironworkers in Virginia were poorly fed and clothed. We are shown some of the pedagogical approaches to slavery. The geography textbooks written prior to 1830, for example, were antislavery. But by 1860 such sentiments had disappeared, book publishers wishing to push their wares in the South.

More and more we are beginning to see the slave in an active role, with a range or options wider than we had believed. Many of them found constructive outlets for their creative energies and social instinct. Slaves had their influence on the masters, four slave foods—the peanut, okra, cowpeas and sesame—crossing class barriers and finding their way to the white man's table. The ways in which the slave struck back come in for their share of attention; Eugene D. Genovese, for example, relates that the fine breeds of livestock imported into the South tended to deteriorate as a result of their mistreatment at the hands of slaves.

In their appraisals of slavery, many contemporary scholars make use of a source that had hitherto been somewhat suspect by their predecessors—the literature of the slave himself, including his songs and narratives, the latter comprising the tales of bondage and freedom written or narrated to ghost writers by former bondmen. To these must be added the interviews with ex-slaves, many of them held half a century or more after the end of slavery.

Those researchers into the African background of the transplanted slave must be particularly receptive as to less conventional sources. "The most spectacular feature of the new postwar boom in African history," writes Philip D. Curtin, "has been the development of new techniques for investigation, and the application of older techniques to the African past," the latter referring to better and more inclusive sources. The oral tradition is vital in the effort to throw light on early

Africa, the only clue in many instances. Used with proper professional safeguards, such nontraditional sources are already demonstrating their usefulness.

As one would learn from this collection of abstracted articles, the use of nonliterary sources in Afro-American studies is still quite infrequent. But in this field the use of conventional sources may bring an element of surprise to the reader, because unexpected. One might not have thought that there were in existence diaries of blacks, church records of black congregations, regimental records, travel accounts, photographs, electoral maps, and private papers, including Bible notations of births, marriages and deaths. As this volume clearly indicates, the sources for the study of black Americans are far richer than any but the professional bibliographers in the field might have sensed.

If the *Afro-American History* abstracts afford a richer understanding of the available documentation in the field, they also unveil many of the changes in our appraisals of persons and interpretations of events. Many of the articles in the compilation represent new attitudes toward old happenings. Other deal directly with the question of reappraisals, dwelling on the outmoded attitudes and frames of reference of earlier writers. The problem of objectivity in dealing with Negroes, as illustrated by the works of some historian (generally an earlier and more prominent one), or of some black-related occurrence, is a recurring theme in the current periodical literature. Perhaps with not too much surprise we learn that a given writer's achievement of objectivity was thwarted by his own background and the prevailing opinion of his day.

Many of these articles deal with one of the major curriculum changes in the sixties—the introduction of black studies programs. The prevailing opinion in the literature overwhelmingly supports this addition, although one author expresses some concern lest black studies fall under the control of lower-class militants "whose programs would not be intellectually valid." Another author had strong misgivings about giving blacks "any more prominence" in American history, holding that they had received as much credit as their contribution deserved.

Recent periodical literature has shown an increase in studies comparing blacks with other groups. One author, comparing and contrasting Negroes with immigrants, comes to the conclusion that the factor of race was crucial—the immigrant faced the problem of assimilation, to be sure, but this was hardly a hurdle when compared to the insurmountable wall of caste.

A further service of this volume of abstracts that might be mentioned is the helpful suggestions they contain as to sources to be seen and topics to be explored. One article, for example, bears the title, "Sources of the History of the Negro in Texas with Special Reference to their Implications for Research in Slavery." One writer informs us that "in many respects the history of Negroes in 19th century Cincinnati is yet to be written." An article, written by an authority on the abolitionist crusade, bears the title, "Slavery and Anti-Slavery: Subjects in Search of Authors." Those in search of leads as to sources and topics may find ore in such veins.

Use of This Work

This volume should prove of service to the scholar in compiling his bibliography, the professor in preparing his lecture, the advanced student in seeking a term topic, and the serious reader in general, not excluding those who like to browse. Its sheer volume of information is impressive—the essence of nearly 3,000 articles, gleaned from a harvest more than ten times that number, and published during the last two decades. These abstracts tell us not only what blacks have thought and said and done but of white reactions to their presence.

For readier reference this volume is divided into six chapters, each sub-divided in turn. In view of the wide-ranging nature of these abstracts, the first thing a reader should do on opening this book is to take a look at its organizational pattern. Otherwise he might feel that he has encountered an amorphous mass of data. The book's table of contents will dispel this feeling, providing a sense of direction as well as a point of reference.

As to be expected, the classification scheme is basically chronological, with the opening chapter furnishing an overview and giving the reader his bearings in general. The articles are numbered sequentially, each also bearing the name of its abstracter. (The staff of the American Bibliographical Center has issued a standing invitation to historians who might be interested in writing abstracts for their publications.)

The use of this volume is enhanced by its index, arranged in a threefold combination of author, topic and geographic location, and cross-referenced. Biographical entries are distinguished from those which are autobiographical. Broad topics, such as "Civil War" and "Racial Attitudes," carry subheads qualifying the subject matter into more explicit categories. A few of the entries carry an explanatory word, such as the labeling of the "Amistad" as a vessel, and Shadrach as a fugitive slave.

Affording new outlooks and acting as a catalyst, this abstracts bibliography on Afro-American history is a highly useful tool. The great majority of its summaries appear nowhere else in such a form. This compilation guides and suggests, whetting the appetite. It is timesaving, particularly in heading off the debilitating feeling that comes when a researcher realizes that he has been working on something that is already in print.

This volume itself is in no danger of falling into any such "lost motion" category. By dint of his skilled and diligent labors in a richly textured area of human behavior, Smith has produced an instrument of retrieval whereby a significant segment of the past takes on newer dimensions, providing a more proper perspective.

AFRO-AMERICAN HISTORY

LIST OF ABBREVIATIONS

A	Author-Prepared Abstract	*IHE*	Indice Histórico Español
Acad.	Academy, Académie, Academia	*Illus.*	Illustrated, Illustration
Agric.	Agriculture, Agricultural	*Inst.*	Institute, Institut, Instituto, Institutic
AIA	Abstracts in Anthropology	*Internat.*	International
Akad.	Akademie	*J.*	Journal, Journal-Prepared Abstract
Am.	America, American	*Lib.*	Library, Libraries
Ann.	Annals, Annales, Annual	*Mag.*	Magazine
Anthrop.	Anthropology, Anthropological	*Mus.*	Museum, Musée, Museo
Arch.	Archives	*Natl.*	National, Nationale, Nacional,
Archeol.	Archeology, Archeological		Nazionale
Assoc.	Association, Associate	*Phil.*	Philosophy, Philosophical
Asst.	Assistant	*Photo.*	Photograph
Biblio.	Bibliography, Bibliographical	*Pol.*	Politics, Political, Politique, Político
Biog.	Biography, Biographical	*Pres.*	President
Bull.	Bulletin	*Pro.*	Proceedings
Can.	Canada, Canadian, Canadien	*Pub.*	Publication
Cent.	Century	*Q.*	Quarterly
Coll.	College	*R.*	Review, Revue, Revista, Rivista
Com.	Committee	*Res.*	Research
Comm.	Commission	*S*	Staff-Prepared Abstract
Dept.	Department	*Sci.*	Science, Scientific
Dir.	Director, Direktor	*Secy.*	Secretary
Econ.	Economy, Economic,	*Soc.*	Society, Société, Sociedad, Societa
	Économique, Economico	*Sociol.*	Sociology, Sociological
Ed.	Editor	*Tr.*	Transactions
Educ.	Education, Educational	*Trans.*	Translator
Geneal.	Genealogy, Genealogical,	*U.*	University, Université, Università,
	Généalogique		Universidad, Universidade,
Grad.	Graduate		Universität
Hist.	History, Historical, Histoire,	*U.S.*	United States
	Historia, Historische	*Y.*	Yearbook

Abbreviations also apply to feminine and plural forms.
Abbreviations not noted above are based on *Webster's Third International Dictionary*
and the *United Stated Government Printing Office Style Manual*.

1

TRADITIONS IN AFRO-AMERICAN CULTURE

General History in the United States

1. Abbot, W. W. THE THIRTY-FOURTH ANNUAL MEETING OF THE SOUTHERN HISTORICAL ASSOCIATION. *J. of Southern Hist. 1969 35(1): 60-76.* Summarizes the meeting of the organization held in New Orleans, 6-9 November 1968, and gives brief synopses of the papers delivered at the 35 sessions. Panels on various historical topics were held in conjunction with the American Association for State and Local History, the Association for the Study of Negro Life and History, the Southern Conference on British Studies, and the American Studies Association. Of the 35 sessions, 11 were devoted to Latin-American history and non-American history. The "intensity of concern about contemporary problems" among historians was reflected in the "preoccupation with race and diplomacy," since 9 sessions were devoted to aspects of these two subjects.   I. M. Leonard

2. Adams, Richard P. SOUTHERN LITERATURE IN THE 1890'S. *Mississippi Q. 1968 21(4): 277-281.* In this decade the South was culturally and economically underdeveloped. Despite a brain drain of the best writers and a vassalage of southern writers to northern publishers, reviewers, and readers, out of the chaotic 1890's came significant foundations. Thomas Nelson Page so successfully popularized the sentimental myth of the South that everyone writing about the South since Page has had to do so with reference to his mythical values. Page anticipated William Faulkner in portrayal of his aristocrats as not only proud and brave but also narrow, inflexible, and pigheaded to the point of idiocy. Another predecessor to Faulkner in his representation of the ideal of chivalry is James Lane Allen. George Washington Cable was more realistic than Page in his handling of the weaknesses of the aristocratic character such as its tendency to ill-considered violence and susceptibility to corruption. Also, Cable apparently understood, as Page did not, the fact that the Yankees oppressed the aristocrats no more than the aristocrats oppressed the Negroes and poor whites. Mark Twain attacked the prewar southern ideal of chivalry and the institution of slavery in relation to the

aristocracy as well as the effects of miscegenation on individual personality and on social relations, thus anticipating a Faulkner theme. *The Awakening* (1899) by Kate Chopin is ahead of its time in its sympathetic treatment of a woman's sensuality, and ahead of Faulkner in sensitive exploration of cultural contrast between the Protestant morality of the rural mid-South and the relatively sophisticated mores of the Louisiana Creoles. The southern renaissance was partly based on an intense feeling of cultural disharmony and strain produced by the realization by sensitive southerners that their traditional way of life had been condemned by the world and by these southerners' need to communicate for the sake of understanding.   R. V. Calvert

3. Blake, Charles. OUR CONSTITUTION. *Negro Hist. Bull. 1960 23(8): 170, 183-185.* Analyzes the political and economic concepts in the Constitution and briefly traces the history of the struggle for Negro and labor rights.
                                                                      L. Gara

4. Bonner, James C. PLANTATION AND FARM: THE AGRICULTURAL SOUTH. *Writing Southern History: Essays in Historiography in Honor of Fletcher M. Green (Baton Rouge: Louisiana State U. Press, 1965): 147-174.* A conscious determination to maintain white supremacy is, according to Ulrich Bonnell Phillips, the central theme of the South's history. The Phillips-Gray-Dodd planter-poor white thesis was first seriously challenged by Frank L. Owsley and his students at Vanderbilt University, who, using exhaustively the voluminous manuscript census records, showed that the great mass of nonslaveholders were undeserving of being called "poor white." This group not only called attention to the yeoman farmer but also made historians aware of the value of these census records as source material. Frederick Jackson Turner's frontier hypothesis is seen as an agricultural interpretation of American history at a time when the country was fast entering an urban-industrial age. Joseph Schafer has shown that the trans-Mississippi cattle business had its forerunner in the southern Piedmont in the Revolutionary period. 109 biblio. notes.   E. P. Stickney

5. Brewer, William M. FIFTIETH ANNIVERSARY OF THE JOURNAL OF NEGRO HISTORY. *J. of Negro Hist. 1966 51(2): 75-97.* A plea for continued research and writing of Negro history, especially by Negro historians, and testimonial comments about the contributions made by *The Journal of Negro History* in its first 50 years of publication by Merle Curti, John Hope Franklin, Dwight L. Dumond, Benjamin Quarles, Kenneth M. Stampp, and 12 other historians.
                                                                      L. Gara

6. Brock, W. R. RACE AND THE AMERICAN PAST: A REVOLUTION IN HISTORIOGRAPHY. *History [Great Britain] 1967 52(174): 49-59.* A review article discussing recent works which reassess the "place of race in the American Past," notably: Kenneth M. Stampp, *The Eve of Reconstruction: America After the Civil War;* James M. McPherson, *The Struggle for Equality: Abolitionists and the Negro in the Civil War and Reconstruction;* David M. Rumers, *White Protestantism and the Negro;* Martin B. Duberman, ed., *The Anti-Slavery Vanguard: New Essays on the Abolitionists;* William Dusin Derre, *Civil War Issues*

in *Philadelphia;* Richard H. Scurll, *John P. Hale and the Politics of Abolition;* Otto H. Olsen, *Carpetbaggers' Crusade: the Life of Albion Winegar Tourgee;* Merlin Stonehouse, *John Wesley North and the Reform Frontier;* Charles L. Wagandt, *The Mighty Revolution: Negro Emancipation in Maryland 1862-1864;* Richard O. Curry, ed., *The Abolitionists: Reformers or Fanatics. American Problems Series;* Hugh D. Hawkins, ed., *The Abolitionists: Immediatism and the Question of Means;* John L. Thomas, ed., *Slavery Attacked: the Abolitionist Crusade;* Richard Nelson Current, ed., *Reconstruction 1865-71.* The reviewer stresses the recent favorable reevaluation of Radical Reconstruction, the reassessment of the abolitionists and their place in the American liberal tradition, the neglect of the Free Soil movement by historians, and the importance of changing economic and social habits in eroding the basis of slavery. In this field of historiography American historians seem to be committed to the proposition that racial inequality has been the great flaw in American civilization.   D. H. Murdoch

7. Brodie, Fawn N. THE POLITICAL HERO IN AMERICA: HIS FATE AND HIS FUTURE. *Virginia Q. R. 1970 46(1): 46-60.* Sees a number of threats to the political hero and his image in America. Threats include assassination (Lincoln, the Kennedys, King), disenchantment with synthetic heroes (Reagan), distortion by biographers and historians (Lincoln), telling everything (Franklin Delano Roosevelt), and psychoanalytical approach (Wilson). Jefferson is under attack because of his ambivalence, particularly on the subject of race. The author feels that, in the long run, heroes like Lincoln and Jefferson are secure because, if the student reads enough history, "he will learn that in a world governed so execrably for so many centuries, heroes of the magnitude of our greatest Americans - however diminished by accident, or weakness, or neurosis - shine very brightly in the galaxy of the world's great men."   O. H. Zabel

8. Brooks, Albert N. D. WHY NEGRO HISTORY ASSOCIATION? *Negro Hist. Bull. 1964 27(8): 189.* Argues that an understanding of the Negro's part in the American past is necessary for the Nation's welfare and security in the present.   L. Gara

9. Buchanan, William J. LEGEND OF THE BLACK CONQUISTADOR. *Mankind 1968 1(5): 21-25, 93.* In 1539 Estevancio de Dorantes, the Negro slave of a Spanish master, wandered through the lands of Nueva España. The folklore of the Zuni Indians contains a legend pertaining to his last journey. One of the survivors of the ill-fated Narvaez expedition of 1528, he wandered across Texas and New Mexico with Cabeza de Vaca. During the eight-year period of wandering, Estevan learned to speak at least six Indian languages. In the spring of 1539, Estevan was sent to the North to discover the "Cities of Gold." He soon began to assert himself at the expense of the friar with whom he was traveling. Now adorned with brightly colored plumes and practicing the weird ritual of a medicine man, he began to tell the Indians he met that he was a god, and he attracted a group of followers. From each group of new Indians which he met, he demanded and received women and gifts. Success clouded his judgment, and his arrogance with the Indians of Zuni led to his death in 1539. Illus.
                                                                    P. D. Thomas

10. Bucholz, Arden, Jr. CLIO AT THE LATIN SCHOOL OF CHICAGO: NEW APPROACHES. *Hist. Teacher 1969 3(1): 9-18.* Discusses the method of introducing students at the Latin School of Chicago to the study of history. The approach involves, first, a family history project in which the student finds out all he can about his family. The second project is an investigation of the student's family in its foreign setting. Other projects involve the investigation of topics pertaining to the American Civil War, comparative Negro history, and, especially, the history of the Latin School of Chicago. The students are taught to read and investigate critically, to discuss convincingly, and to write effectively. Although their attention span is somewhat limited, as is their level of abstraction, the better students, particularly, receive a solid grounding in the pursuit of historical knowledge.   C. W. Kennedy

11. Burke, Robert E. THE FIFTY-NINTH ANNUAL MEETING OF THE ORGANIZATION OF AMERICAN HISTORIANS. *J. of Am. Hist. 1966 53(2): 315-340.* The meeting of the organization, formerly known as the Mississippi Valley Historical Association, was held in Cincinnati 28-30 April 1966. Panels on various historical topics were held, some in conjunction with other groups dealing with specialized aspects of the discipline. Brief synopses are given of papers presented at the 32 sessions of the meeting. Of these, six sessions were devoted to reform movements and Progressivism, three to abolitionism and Reconstruction, three to urban history (including the Negro ghetto), and two on the New Deal.   K. B. West

12. Butts, R. Freeman. OUR TRADITION OF STATES' RIGHTS AND EDUCATION. *Hist. of Educ. J. 1959 10(1-4): 29-46.* Argues that from colonial times to the present the government has limited private education, that there should be strict separation of church and state in educational matters, that racial segregation in schools is a violation of the educational rights of Negroes, and that although American education is primarily a State and local responsibility, the States do not possess unlimited power over the schools and they cannot legally abolish their public school systems.   L. Gara

13. Caldwell, William. FRA ABRAHAM LINCOLN TIL MARTIN LUTHER KING [From Abraham Lincoln to Martin Luther King]. *Samtiden [Norway] 1963 72(10): 669-680.* The supporters of Lincoln were the representatives of big business who wished an economic halt to the development of the South and its expansion westward. They feared the absorption by the South and Britain of the economic role of the North; if the south had won it would have meant economic interests in the hands of southern industrialists. Northern victory meant no defeat of the southern aristocrat but only a temporary subordination which by use of the Ku Klux Klan and other devices southerners attempted to reduce or throw off. It is defeat of the southern Negro which lies back of frustration for blacks. After World War I and promises of new conditions leading to full equality, the Negro turned to other plans. One was Marcus Garvey's emigration ideas and his creation of an image of self-respect for the Negro. Because of his success he was charged with tax evasion and sentenced to three years in prison which destroyed his movement. Others, such as the Muslims and the Black Panthers, have contin-

ued to promote this idea of self-respect for the Negro. On the opposite side have been the American Nazis, the John Birch Society, the White Councils, America First, and other associations. this defeat of the southern for the Advancement of Colored People, the National Urban League, and various church groups of which Martin Luther King was a leader with his passive resistance and his speeding up of the movement toward the end of segregation. R. E. Lindgren

14. Calkins, David L. CHRONOLOGIC HIGHLIGHTS OF CINCINNATI'S BLACK COMMUNITY. *Cincinnati Hist. Soc. Bull. 1970 28(4): 344-353.* The story of Cincinnati's black community, in chronological highlights. Includes, for the 19th century, actions by whites which influenced black development in Cincinnati. Relates, for the post-World War II period, several black "firsts" in the city. Undocumented. H. S. Marks

15. Calkins, David L. 19TH CENTURY BLACK HISTORY: A BIBLIO-GRAPHIC ESSAY. *Cincinnati Hist. Soc. Bull. 1970 28(4): 336-343.* In many respects the history of Negroes in 19th-century Cincinnati is yet to be written. Existing sources and studies offer important and interesting insights, but reveal serious shortcomings. Existing source materials are primarily oriented toward the white community and only indirectly afford information concerning Negroes. Also, a susbstantial imbalance exists between scholarship efforts on pre- and post-Civil War topics; the pre-Civil War period is greatly favored. Two of the best sources for black history have been neglected - census population schedules and the local newspapers. 2 photos, 18 notes. H. S. Marks

16. Cave, Alfred A. MAIN THEMES IN RECENT SOUTHERN HISTORY. *Western Humanities R. 1966 20(2): 97-112.* Edward Alfred Pollard, in 1866, pictured the antebellum South as the seat of a noble and gracious civilization which was destroyed by a resentful North. Afterwards, Walter Lynwood Fleming, Ulrich Bonnell Phillips, Frank L. Owsley, and others offered variations on the defense of the southern cause. Wilbur J. Cash's *The Mind of the South* (New York: Knopf, 1940) surveyed the South's "characteristic vices," such as violence, intolerance, the doctrines of caste and class, and anti-intellectualism, and thus pointed the way for such historians as C. Vann Woodward and James W. Silver in rewriting the history of the South. Of the various interpretations which have been offered, the distinctiveness of the South is most plausibly explained in terms of slavery, the presence of the Negroes, and the attitudes toward race. A. Turner

17. Clark, John G. THE RACIAL LEGACY OF THE NINETEENTH-CEN-TURY SOUTH. *Midwest Q. 1965 7(1): 11-28.* Points out that since the Civil War poverty has replaced slavery as the major distinguishing feature between the South and the remainder of the Nation. Military reconstruction was not all black; it did much toward organizing public schools and various other social services. Separate but equal legislation forced the Negro to create a Negro community paralleling in every detail that of the dominant class. One point of view is advanced that the present Negro movement is inherently devoid of true revolutionary character because its members do not seek to remake the community, only

to join it. To this it is replied that when Negroes "join" the society, the society will be transformed, as any compound is with the addition of a new element. Sources quoted in the context.   G. H. G. Jones

18. Colvert, James B. VIEWS OF SOUTHERN CHARACTER IN SOME NORTHERN NOVELS. *Mississippi Q. 1965 18(2): 59-68.* While southern novelists have often examined qualities of a "socially undisciplined," impulsive South on a personal, subjective level, northern novelists have viewed such qualities symbolically for their larger social implications. Overtly critical of southern ideals, Henry James' *The Bostonians* (1886) and Nancy Hale's *Black Summer* (1963), with its picture of the repulsive yet dangerously attractive southerner, similarly conclude that "candid commitment to the basic facts of nature might be better than commitment to piety that abhors and fears them." Other less ambivalent expressions of the northern point of view include John William De Forest's *Miss Ravenel's Conversion* (1867) with its southerner as villain and Harriet Beecher Stowe's *Uncle Tom's Cabin* (1852) with its symbolical meaning of emancipation of instincts from Victorianism. In his meaning for the northern mind, the southerner has represented "experience freer and broader than the historically given attitudes of the North would allow."   R. V. Calvert

19. Cruden, Robert. JAMES FORD RHODES AND THE NEGRO: A STUDY IN THE PROBLEM OF OBJECTIVITY. *Ohio Hist. 1962 71(2): 129-137.* Represents an attempt to assess the possibility of achieving objectivity in the writing of history. The treatment of the Negro as found in the writings of James Ford Rhodes is made the basis for such an assessment. In his attempts to achieve objectivity Rhodes is shown to have failed because of his own background and the prevailing opinion of his day. The author concludes that until the historian can manage to avoid such influences, "it seems premature to talk of history as a genuinely scientific discipline."   S. L. Jones

20. Cunningham, George E. DEROGATORY IMAGES OF THE NEGRO AND NEGRO HISTORY. *Negro Hist. Bull. 1965 28(6): 126-127, 142-143.* After discussing the unfavorable images of Negroes which whites have accepted and summarizing some of the historical factors which contributed to the development of these images, the author pleads for Negroes to study their actual history and to take their rightful place in a new, integrated society.

L. Gara

21. Daniel, Walter G. NEGRO EDUCATION AND WELFARE ONE HUNDRED YEARS AFTER APPOMATTOX. *J. of Negro Educ. 1965 34(2): 103-105.* Comments on achievements of Negroes in the past century and proposes a program of goals for the remainder of the 20th century.   S. C. Pearson, Jr.

22. Davis, David Brion. VIOLENCE IN AMERICAN LITERATURE. *Ann. of the Am. Acad. of Pol. and Social Sci. 1966 364: 28-36.* "The frequency of fighting and killing in American literature is not necessarily proof of an unusually violent society, but literary treatments of violence have reflected certain historical condi-

tions and circumstances. The growth of popular literacy created a mass audience whose attention could best be held by suspense, surprise, and startling contrast. The Revolution provided a model for later fiction in which the hero's triumph was not a blow against authority but rather a defeat of the Tory, who defied the sacred rules of the compact. This convention gave expression to a fear of factionalism and anarchy, and to a desire to identify one's own interests with a tradition of self-sacrificing unity. The ideal of social unity might conflict with the ideal of a self-sufficient and self-relying individual, but later writers projected the image of the individualistic hero into the vacant spaces of the West, where his violent acts were devoid of social consequence. Although both proslavery and antislavery writers tended to see the Negro as a pacific being, he has become a focal point of violence in twentieth-century literature. In the twentieth century, American writers have assimilated the older traditions of individualistic and racial violence to an antirationalistic philosophy which looks on violence as a regenerative or creative force, or as a symbol of reality." J

23. Davis, John A. THE INFLUENCE OF AFRICANS ON AMERICAN CULTURE. *Ann. of the Am. Acad. of Pol. and Social Sci. 1965 354: 75-83.* "Africans have, since the early settlement of America, influenced the nation's language, manners, religion, literature, music, art, and dance. One of our most crucial urban problems, the Negro low-status family, may have African origins. In the realm of politics, the civil rights fight in America from its origin has been linked to the struggle for African freedom, and American Negro intellectuals have identified with African culture from the beginning of the formation of the International Society of African Culture and the American Society of African Culture. American Negro leadership has collectively thrown its considerable political weight on the side of African freedom, and black nationalist organizations have kept up a noisy gadfly agitation. In the midst of this, America must deal with a considerable African presence in the United Nations." J

24. Davis, Richard Beale. MRS. STOWE'S CHARACTERS-IN-SITUATIONS AND A SOUTHERN LITERARY TRADITION. *Essays on Am. Literature in Honor of Jay B. Hubbell (Durham: Duke U. Press, 1967): 108-125.* Harriet Beecher Stowe, in her two antislavery novels *Uncle Tom's Cabin* (1851) and *Dred* (1856), more than presenting "a peculiar variety of characters and their unusual tragic situations with a force as to indicate to later writers the potentialities of the plantation novel as a vehicle of depth and complexity and moral seriousness," actually marked "the definite beginnings of a literary tradition" by establishing varying patterns of characters-in-situations. George Washington Cable, Mark Twain, Robert Penn Warren, and William Faulkner, like Mrs. Stowe, "knew of their Southern situations partly by hearsay," but more than she, "they knew by experience." They followed her in "the writing of a story of their own land that moved them, a story told by placing human beings in situations." 10 notes.
C. L. Eichelberger

25. Davis, Sharon Carbonti. VERMONT'S ADOPTED SONS AND DAUGHTERS. *Vermont Hist. 1963 31(2): 122-127.* Third prize in State essay contest, on

seven notable Negro residents and natives. One of these, the Reverend Lemuel Hayes, was a Congregational minister; another, Sister St. Mary Magdalen, of the Congregation of Notre Dame, had been born on a Georgia plantation of a mulatto slave mother.   T. D. S. Bassett

26. Debouzy, Marianne. HISTORIQUE DU PROBLEME NOIR [History of the Negro problem]. *Ann.: Economies, Soc., Civilisations [France] 1966 21(3): 641-647.* The Negro problem is inseparable from nearly all the important events in the formation of the United States. The relationships between the past experiences of American Negroes and their present attitudes are discussed. Documented from printed sources.   R. Howell

27. Doderer, Hans. VON DER SKLAVEREI ZUR GLEICHBERECH-TIGUNG - EIN ÜBERBLICK ÜBER DIE GESCHICHTE DER NEGER IN DEN VEREINIGTEN STAATEN [From slavery to equal rights - a survey of the history of the Negroes in the United States]. *Geschichte in Wissenschaft und Unterricht [West Germany] 1964 15(1): 1-16.* Emphasizes 19th-century developments. Biblio.   B. K. Dehmelt

28. Duhamel, Jean. L'EVOLUTION DU PROBLEME NOIR AUX ETATS-UNIS [The evolution of the Negro problem in the United States]. *R. des Travaux de l'Acad. des Sci. Morales et Pol. et Comptes Rendus de ses Séances [France] 1964 117(2): 145-160.* Traces the evolution of Negro rights in America from colonial protests against slavery through emancipation and the "separate but equal" doctrine to the Supreme Court school decision of 1954 and the Civil Rights Act of 1964. As American Negroes acquire rights of citizenship and educational opportunity, they figure more prominently in finance, government, and the professions. The civil rights movement is an act of national conscience. It seeks, through complete social assimilation of the Negro, to make honorable amends for centuries of injustice.   J. R. Vignery

29. Durham, Philip and Jones, Everett L. SLAVES ON HORSEBACK. *Pacific Hist. R. 1964 33(4): 405-409.* Describes the life of the Negro cowboy in the Great Plains from 1850 to the 1870's. One in seven trailhands in the post-Civil War period was Negro.   J. McCutcheon

30. Eaton, Clement. RECENT TRENDS IN THE WRITING OF SOUTHERN HISTORY. *Louisiana Hist. Q. 1955 38(2): 26-42.* A brief study of the "new look" in the writing of southern U.S. history since 1945. There is a new interest in objective history writing concerning the South, particularly in relation to the Negro and a trend toward emphasis on economic, social, and cultural history rather than political and military history.   E. D. Johnson

31. Farley, Reynolds. THE URBANIZATION OF NEGROES IN THE UNITED STATES. *J. of Social Hist. 1968 1(3): 241-258.* Examines the process of urbanization of American Negroes and attempts to elucidate some factors responsible for the process. The distribution of Negro population has followed a

curious pattern. Originally brought to this country to work in cities as laborers or house servants in the 17th and early 18th centuries, the number of Negroes in cities grew until agricultural prosperity in the South opened a new niche for them as slaves in the plantation economy. The cotton gin and the settlement of the Gulf States after the American Revolution increased the need for slaves so that, by the Civil War, the black population was largely concentrated in rural southern areas. Lack of prosperity and industrialization in the post-Civil War South kept most blacks in the rural areas. European immigrants continued to occupy low skill jobs in the North, effectively blocking this opportunity for Negroes. Out-migration of blacks from the South began after the Civil War and a pattern was discernible by 1900. Practically all went to cities of the North and West. World War I and the declining need for agricultural workers encouraged out-migration. The Depression caused a slackening of the process, but World War II and the prosperity that followed caused resumption of pre-Depression trends. The result is that Negroes are more urbanized today than the white population, and the trend is likely to continue. 77 notes. **N. M. Drescher**

32. Fishel, Leslie H., Jr. THE NEGRO YESTERDAY AND TODAY: AN ESSAY REVIEW. *Wisconsin Mag. of Hist. 1965 48(4): 317-319.* Reviews Richard C. Wade's *Slavery in the Cities: The South 1820-1860* (New York: Oxford U. Press, 1964), *In their Own Words: A History of the American Negro, 1616-1865* by Milton Meltzer, ed. (New York: Crowell, 1964), and Thomas F. Pettigrew's *A Profile of the American Negro* (Princeton, N.J.: Van Norstrand, 1964). Wade's book explores the racial power struggle which existed in the cities of the South even before the Civil War, which was different from the situation in the rural areas. Meltzer's work collects the words which Negroes penned before the Civil War, which represent the pleadings and privations which illuminate the frustrations of being a Negro. Pettigrew's book synthesizes the recent scientific studies of the developing personality of the Negro. **H. A. Negaard**

33. Fisher, Marvin. MELVILLE'S "BELL-TOWER": A DOUBLE THRUST. *Am. Q. 1966 18(2, pt. 1): 200-207.* Regards "The Bell-Tower" as an important link between "The Paradise of Bachelors and the Tartarus of Maids" and "Benito Cereno." In all three works, Herman Melville explores "the natural law dooming masters to fall victims to their slaves," but in "The Bell-Tower" he attacks "unquestioning faith in technological progress" as well as the "domination of the processes of life and enslavement" of subordinate beings. The bell-tower itself symbolizes the wedding of religion and business, the bell and the clock, in "a monument to profit." Haman, a mechanical bell-ringer, rises in judgment against his "proud, god-rivaling artisan-inventor" and strikes him down in behalf of the forces of "natural law." In "The Bell-Tower" Melville asserts the transcendence of freedom over authority and condemns all forms of slavery, mechanical or otherwise. 5 notes. **R. S. Pickett**

34. Franco, José Luciano. LA PRESENCIA NEGRA EN EL NUEVO MUNDO. GLOSARIO AFROAMERICANO [The Negro presence in the New World. Afro-American glossary]. *Casa de las Américas [Cuba] 1966 6(36/37): 7-22.* Surveys numerous secondary sources on the importance and makeup of the

Negro element in the Western Hemisphere. The author estimates the number of slaves brought from Africa to America during the colonial era by the different European powers and indicates the African origins of the black descendants to be found in the various regions of the hemisphere. Comparing the cultural attitudes of a North American black scientist with a Guianese Duika oarsman and a Haitian peasant, the conclusion is reached that "the social environment in the making of the Black American is infinitely more potent than biological inheritance." A chart from M. J. Herskovits' *Man and His Works* is included. 35 notes.

C. J. Fleener

35. Franklin, John H. THE NEW NEGRO HISTORY. *J. of Negro Hist. 1957 42(2): 89-97.* Discusses the changes that have occurred in the last two decades in the writing, teaching, and study of the history of the Negro in the United States. "For the first time in the history of the United States, there is a striking resemblance between what historians are writing and what has actually happened in the history of the American Negro."

W. E. Wight

36. Gibson, Gail M. THE 1969 RESEARCH CONFERENCE AT MIDDLETOWN AND HARRISBURG. *Pennsylvania Hist. 1969 36(4): 451-472.* The Pennsylvania Historical Association's 1969 Research Conference was held at Middletown and Harrisburg during the weekend of 2-3 May. The status of papers of 20th-century governors was covered in detail, particularly the manuscripts of John S. Fisher and George Earle. Thomas Cochran discussed the problems involved in preserving and using business records. Several speakers provided information on "Problems and Source Materials in Negro History." The last session heard papers on "Who Needs a Biography." Emphasis was placed on scientists, physicians, artists, and labor leaders. Each paper is reported in considerable detail.

D. C. Swift

37. Glazer, Nathan. THE NEGRO AMERICAN. *Public Interest 1966 (3): 108-115.* A review and commentary on two issues of *Daedalus,* published in fall 1965 and winter 1966, which included 26 articles on the Negro American and the transcript of a conference in which some of the articles were discussed.

H. E. Cox

38. Gravely, William B. THE AFRO-AMERICAN METHODIST TRADITION: A REVIEW OF SOURCES IN REPRINT. *Methodist Hist. 1971 9(3): 21-33.* Lists the black leaders in abolitionist, educational, and civil rights movements that were influenced by Afro-American Methodism. The reprint series of various publishers include the careers of many of these men as well as source materials on the social and religious significance of the institutions of black Methodism in Afro-American history. The author reviews several of these reprints in the areas of biography, denominational history and protest literature. Undocumented, biblio.

J. K. Crane

39. Greene, Marc. RACE IN AMERICA: THE CENTURIES-OLD PROBLEM. *Q. Review [Great Britain] 1966 304(650): 353-364.* The thesis is that the

"problem of the coloured man," or what to do about and with him, was first faced by America in the Reconstruction period following the Civil War. The issue, then as now, is chiefly seen to be one of northern (and white) greed, expressed through political chicanery, since "it should be understood that the Negro problem in America, the racial conflict, beyond anything else is a problem of what part and how great a part he is going to play in politics." Supporting the analysis is the assertion that Negroes "in proportion to their total number, are no farther gone in extreme poverty than the whites in similar proportion."   R. G. Schafer

40. Hackney, Sheldon. SOUTHERN VIOLENCE. *Am. Hist. R. 1969 74(3): 906-925.* It has been known for some time that the South has had a peculiar pattern of violence: high rates of homicide and assault, moderate rates of crime against property, and low rates of suicide. Such factors as the frontier tradition, the presence of a large Negro population, poverty, the absence of cities, defeat in the Civil War, and economic underdevelopment have been frequently mentioned as possible causes for the South's pattern of violence, but none stands up as a valid explanation when closely examined. A multiple regression analysis of rates of violence and various measures of development suggest that the South is more violent than can be explained by current deviations from the national norms of education, wealth, and urbanization. Southern violence is a cultural trait. Though the reasons for the existence of this culture of violence have yet to be fully explored, much of it may be explained by the world view growing from the sense of grievances and persecution engendered by the historical experience of the South.   A

41. Henderson, George. NEGROES INTO AMERICANS: A DIALECTICAL DEVELOPMENT. *J. of Human Relations 1966 14(4): 535-549.* Analyzes the origin and use of the term "Negro" and structures the history of the American Negro into four "historical developmental stages," three of which have already been achieved. The achieved stages are, first, the predialectical stage of "Negroes," from 1619 to 1862; second, the thesis stage of "Negro Americans," 1863-1953; third, the present antithesis stage of "American Negroes." The synthesis stage, "the period when all citizens are accepted as 'Americans' without a racial prefix or suffix, has not become a reality." Before developing this dialectical structure, the author discusses the relevant thought of Hegel, William James, and John Dewey. Based on secondary sources.   D. J. Abramoske

42. Higginbotham, S. W. THE TWENTY NINTH ANNUAL MEETING. *J. of Southern Hist. 1964 30(1): 71-93.* On 7-9 November 1963 more than 700 persons heard the presidential address of Dr. James W. Silver of the University of Mississippi upon "Mississippi: The Closed Society." At scholarly sessions, 49 papers were read, covering the North Carolina Charter Tercentenary, historical writing, U.S. military history, elections, the Confederacy, southern urbanism, research and graduate study in the South, historians and the "new South," historical research and the law, religion in the South, economic history, historical uses of fiction, Appalachian America, Revolutionary history, and European and Latin American history.   S. E. Humphreys

43. Johnson, Oakley C. MARXISM AND THE NEGRO FREEDOM STRUG-
GLE, 1876-1917. *J. of Human Relations 1965 13(1): 21-39.* Describes the participation of Socialists in the struggle for Negro emancipation from about 1861 to
1917. "The work of Marx provided the basis for a sound and effective working-
class program on the Negro question....Inadequate use of this foundation was
made, however, by the Socialist Labor and Socialist parties through their doctrinaire positions of unreality about particular racial discriminations and injustices." Based on primary and secondary sources; 11 notes.   D. J. Abramoske

44. Klingberg, Frank J. CARTER GOODWIN WOODSON, HISTORIAN,
AND HIS CONTRIBUTION TO AMERICAN HISTORIOGRAPHY. *J. of
Negro Hist. 1956 41(1): 66-68.* Woodson supplied the scholarly ammunition for
a reevaluation of the role of the Negro in American life. Founder of the *Journal
of Negro History* and the *Negro History Bulletin,* he was a leader in finding facts
and in presenting them in books and monographs. Much work then and now has
been based on his pioneering.   W. E. Wight

45. Kmen, Henry A. REMEMBER THE "VIRGINIUS": NEW ORLEANS
AND CUBA IN 1873. *Louisiana Hist. 1970 1(4): 313-331.* Although New
Orleans had been too preoccupied with its own troubles to pay much attention
to the Cuban revolt that had begun in 1868, the Spanish capture of the *Virginius*
and the subsequent execution of several U.S. citizens who had been aboard
revived pro-Cuban sentiment in New Orleans. The *Virginius,* a former Confederate blockade runner, was owned and operated by Cuban rebels to bring materiel
and volunteers to their cause, but having U.S. registry, the vessel violated U.S.
neutrality laws. New Orleans newspapers fired the growing indignation in New
Orleans with stories of Spanish atrocities, ideological editorials, and economic
arguments against Spain. The ardor for Cuban independence or annexation affected Negroes and whites alike. Based on New Orleans newspapers; 55 notes.
R. L. Woodward

46. Kučera, Jaroslav. HISTORIE AMERICKÉ ARMÁDY, JEJÍ A TRADICE
A VOJENSKÉ DEDICTVÍ [Historiography of the American Army, its traditions and military heritage]. *Historie a Vojenstvi [Czechoslovakia] 1963 (2): 295-
318.* A critique of the themes and presentation of U.S. military history. Among
the major flaws are excessive attention to American past experience, disregard of
proved Soviet achievements, neglect of the military role of the common people,
exclusion of Negroes from American military history, and a tendency to justify
American claims to world domination. Based largely on recent articles in the
Military Review and on R. Ernest Dupuy's books, *Military Heritage of America*
(McGraw-Hill, 1956) and *The Compact History of the United States Army*
(Hawthorn Books, 1961).   R. E. Weltsch

47. Kugler, Ruben F. BIBLIOGRAPHY FOR AFRO-AMERICAN HIS-
TORY. *Social Studies 1969 60(5): 211-217.* Sets forth an annotated bibliography
designed for high school and college students and teachers, the general subject

of which concerns Afro-American history. Books, journals, pamphlets, and newsletters are listed along with their places of publication and organizational sponsors. L. Raife

48. Lash, John. A LONG, HARD LOOK AT THE GHETTO: A CRITICAL SUMMARY OF LITERATURE BY AND ABOUT NEGROES IN 1956. *Phylon 1957 18(1): 7-23.* A bibliography of social science literature written about and by Negroes in 1956, covering the period from approximately 1750 to the present. C. F. Latour

49. Le Riverend Brusone, Julio. AFROAMERICA [Afro-America]. *Casa de las Américas [Cuba] 1966 6(36/37): 23-31.* Traces the historical importance of Africa in the acculturation and development of the Western Hemisphere. The author progressively deals with the geographic distribution of Negro elements in America, the historical stages of black migrations, the areas in Africa from which the black man came, the slave era, the abolition of slavery, the repercussions of abolition, Negro influences in the hemisphere, and the integration of the Negro into the national life of the American nations. C. J. Fleener

50. Lee, Ulysses. THE DRAFT AND THE NEGRO. *Current Hist. 1968 55(323): 28-33, 47-48.* Surveying the status of the Negro in American military history, the author notes some improvement since World War II. Yet the disproportionate number of Negroes drafted into combat units and the high percentage of deaths suffered by Negroes constitute discriminatory treatment. B. D. Rhodes

51. Link, Eugene P. THE CIVIL RIGHTS ACTIVITIES OF THREE GREAT NEGRO PHYSICIANS (1840-1940). *J. of Negro Hist. 1967 52(3): 169-184.* Discusses the contributions of three Negro doctors to the struggle for civil rights. John Swett Rock (1825-66), illustrating the era of "individual assertion" of Negro demands by a small minority, overcame the obstacles of prejudice and dared to become a dentist, doctor, and lawyer who spoke in unequivocal terms of Negro rights and became the first Negro admitted to practice law before the U.S. Supreme Court. Daniel Hale Williams (1858-1931) represented a transitional time between the accommodation practices of Booker T. Washington and the more militant stance of W. E. B. Du Bois. While working in the South, Williams cooperated with Washington in order to get funds for hospital and nursing facilities but came increasingly to support the views of the Niagara Movement and the National Association for the Advancement of Colored People. Louis Tompkins Wright (1891-1952), symbolizing the more militant era, combined active participation in civil rights campaigns with his medical practice, fought racial discrimination in the American Medical Association, and became a chairman of the Board of Directors of the NAACP and editor of its magazine *The Crisis.* Documented; 29 notes. L. Gara

52. Logan, Frenise A. AN APPRAISAL OF FORTY-ONE YEARS OF THE JOURNAL OF NEGRO HISTORY, 1916-1957. *J. of Negro Hist. 1959 44(1):*

26-33. An analysis of 607 full-length articles appearing in the 42 volumes of the *Journal of Negro History* (ca. 1916-57). Virtually all significant work on Negro history has either appeared or been reflected in the *Journal.* The list of contributors includes almost everyone distinguished in the field, both Negro and non-Negro. A substantial number of papers have come from non-Negro historians. Despite the fact that 67 percent of all papers contributed deal with the period of sectional crisis, 1820-76, there is a growing interest in the history of the colored man outside the United States, with West Africa, the West Indies, and Brazil attracting the largest number of papers.   A

53. Mattingly, Paul H. USEFUL HISTORY AND BLACK IDENTITY. *Hist. of Educ. Q. 1970 10(3): 338-350.* Calls inadequate the juxtaposition of detached, "scientific" historical scholarship to historical writing as a deliberate instrument for ideological persuasion. Neither method focuses on historical change. Discusses Tamara Hareven's "Step-Children of the Dream" in the *History of Education Quarterly* (winter 1969). Hareven assesses historical documents from her own perspective without attempting to incorporate into her own view the views of the writers she criticizes. Hareven "psychologizes" history. Ralph Ellison avoided this danger in his *The Invisible Man* (New York: Signet Books, 1952). The historian's first loyalty must be to the changing language and values of the past. 7 notes.   J. Herbst

54. Meyer, Duane. THE CHARACTER OF MISSOURI HISTORY. *Missouri Hist. R. 1965 59(4): 464-469.* An author of a State history speaks his mind to a group of historians on the problems he has encountered in trying to do justice to Missouri. The paucity of material dealing with the history of Missouri since 1900 and the almost total absence of problem-oriented studies dealing with such topics as the Negro, immigration, urbanization, and the decline of the small farmer leave the author of a general Missouri history with too many gaps to fill.   W. F. Zornow

55. Munroe, John A. THE NEGRO IN DELAWARE. *South Atlantic Q. 1957 56(4): 428-444.* Traces the history of the Negro in the State of Delaware from the 17th century to 1957.   H. Kantor

56. Nash, Gerald D. RESEARCH OPPORTUNITIES IN THE ECONOMIC HISTORY OF THE SOUTH AFTER 1800. *J. of Southern Hist. 1966 32(3): 308-324.* Argues that overemphasis upon the revolution in race relations in the South has drawn attention away from a more fundamental revolution - the South's industrialization. The author asserts that an undue emphasis upon southern history before 1880 and upon political developments can distort the entire dimension of southern history. He pleads with students to devote a greater share of their energies to the last 75 years and to place a greater emphasis on the study of the process of industrialization, which brought about profound political and social change. He suggests numerous lacunae which need to be filled. Biblio. notes.   S. E. Humphreys

57. Neuffer, Claude Henry. FOLK ETYMOLOGY IN SOUTH CAROLINA PLACE NAMES. *Am. Speech 1966 41(4): 274-277.* Explains the origin of many strange South Carolina names. Bellyache Creek comes from the plantation it crosses, Belle Acres. The tract called Said Lands comes from a Negro corruption of the legal phrase "all the aforesaid lands," and We Creek belonged to a Negro who said "Das we [viz, 'our'] creek, suh!" A German settlement "zwanzig" miles from a major town is now Swansea. Based on the author's experience in South Carolina; 4 notes.   R. W. Shoemaker

58. Nevins, Allan. EL CENTENARIO DE LA EMANCIPACION [The centennial of the emancipation]. *Panoramas [Mexico] 1963 1(4): 37-52.* Written on the centennial of the Emancipation Proclamation, signed by President Abraham Lincoln on 1 January 1863. Mention is made of the high intelligence and good condition of the Negroes in the border States at the time of the Civil War as contrasted to the blurred intelligence and mistreatment of many of the Negroes of the deep South. The Union Army is generally praised for its kind and intelligent treatment of the Negroes, with General Ulysses Grant singled out for special honor. Taken in turn are the difficulties encountered in connection with the care of the Negroes after the Civil War, the building up of a new segregationist policy, the gradual improvement in the situation of the Negro, and the rapid changes resulting from President Harry S. Truman's orders to end segregation in the armed forces and to follow a policy of fair employment in all Federal agencies. The article was also published in the *Saturday Review* in English. 4 illus.
                                                S. E. Roberts

59. Newby, I. A. HISTORIANS AND NEGROES. *J. of Negro Hist. 1969 54(1): 32-47.* Endorses the recent upsurge of interest in Negro history which should furnish black youth with a sense of self-confidence and pride and make white youths aware of racism and its impact. The author read a number of standard syntheses of U.S. history and found that black Americans were treated in terms of "invisible man" history (completely ignoring black Americans), "spook" history (alluding to Negroes only as a background host for white history), "ghetto" history (discussing black Americans but in separate chapters), and "Sambo" history (based on racist assumptions about the black Americans). The historians reflected the society in which they lived and alternated between racism and paternalism, a situation which will be changed by the impact of recent events. 21 notes, including some comments about specific works mentioned in the article.
                                                L. Gara

60. Oppenheimer, Martin. CURRENT NEGRO PROTEST ACTIVITIES AND THE CONCEPT OF SOCIAL MOVEMENT. *Phylon 1963 24(2): 154-159.* The problem is to construct a conceptual model for analyzing modern Negro protest activity. History books treat protests as "accommodation" versus militancy, and relate changes to general socioeconomic climates. Still lacking is an overall history of Negro social movements probing 1) slavery and slave uprisings; 2) the post-Civil War "rural" period, extending into the present; and 3) the urban era, highlighting such movements as the NAACP, Garveyism, and Black Nationalism. Concepts which illuminate other movements do not aid analyses of Negro

protest; such concepts as "left," "revolutionary," and "ideology" confuse rather than clarify. Students of German nazism have better helped explain protest dynamics. Anthropologists offer useful categories of culture contact which help explain such disparate movements as the millenial and nativist phenomena. Slave, rural, and urban Negro protest movements can be seen through such common concepts as "revivalistic" (protesting against existing conditions), and "perpetuative innovative" (seeking new and ideal systems).   L. Filler

61. Osofsky, Gilbert. THE ENDURING GHETTO. *J. of Am. Hist. 1968 55(2): 243-255.* A study of Negro life in New York City, Philadelphia, and other communities in the early 19th century indicates that while segregated districts were not as solidly black as they have become in the 20th century, there were certain similarities in the status of blacks in these communities. The ghettos were not any more livable, healthful, or wholesome then than they are now. Violence, hideous tenements, poverty, de facto occupational segregation which left the Negro in the position of a propertyless proletariat, lack of relevant education, prejudice of immigrant groups, destructive behavior, a negative self-image - these are characteristics of the enduring ghetto. Based on secondary sources and printed contemporary works.   K. B. West

62. Patterson, Orlando. RETHINKING BLACK HISTORY. *Harvard Educ. R. 1971 41(3): 297-315.* Classifies American attitudes toward the Negro past, to examine the sociology of black historical knowledge. Distinguishes radical and conservative catastrophism, radical and conservative survivalism, and contributionism. Catastrophists view black history as a chronicle of horror; survivalists affirm continuity with the African past. Considers contributionism, with its theme of black contribution to world civilization, irrelevant and misleading. Only a small part of African history - that of the western Sub-Saharan coastal belt - is directly relevant to Afro-American experience. Asks for more study of the slavery period and greater utilization of nonliterary sources.
                    J. Herbst

63. Petrov, D. B. UROKI GRAZHDANSKOI VOINY V SSHA V SVETE SOVREMENNOSTI [The lessons of the Civil War in the United States in the light of the present]. *Voprosy Istorii [USSR] 1964 (1): 214-218.* Maintains that American historians have "falsified" the history of the Civil War by not giving the masses, especially the Negro, enough attention. Present Negro demonstrations clearly show that the American Negro was not given full freedom after 1863. Based on published U.S. and Soviet works; 23 notes.   A. Birkos

64. Redden, Carolyn L. THE AMERICAN NEGRO: AN ANNOTATED LIST OF EDUCATIONAL FILMS AND FILMSTRIPS. *J. of Negro Educ. 1964 33(1): 79-82.*

65. Richardson, Joe M. A NEGRO SUCCESS STORY: JAMES DALLAS BURRUS. *J. of Negro Hist. 1965 50(4): 274-282.* The mother of James Dallas Burrus (1846-1929) was a slave and his father was her white master. After the

Civil War, Burrus and his brother John entered Fisk University and were among the first Negroes to graduate from a southern college. Burrus taught mathematics at Fisk for several years, took graduate work at Dartmouth College, taught and managed the college farm at Alcorn Agricultural and Mechanical College in Mississippi, and in 1894 entered the real estate and drug business in Nashville. Although successful enough to bequeath nearly 120 thousand dollars to his Alma Mater, James Burrus died in the Jim Crow section of a Nashville streetcar.

L. Gara

66. Rodabaugh, James H. THE NEGRO IN THE OLD NORTHWEST. *In the Trek of the Immigrants: Essays Presented to Carl Wittke (Rock Island, Illinois: Augustana Coll. Lib., 1964): 219-239.* Studies the history of the Negroes in the first section in which the Federal Government prohibited slavery, the Old Northwest. Records show that Detroit had 129 Negro slaves in its population of 563 in 1706. In the early 1800's the Society of Friends was active in bringing in Negroes. The constitutions of five States denied them suffrage, and in 1848 Illinois and in 1851 Indiana adopted anti-immigration provisions in their constitutions. A counterforce to white Negrophobia was humanitarianism of sufficient strength to limit the enforcement of the "Black Laws." The earliest antislavery strength was among the New Englanders who settled the Western Reserve. Miami University became a vortex of the antislavery controversy. The underground railway brought 40 thousand to 50 thousand slaves across the Ohio. Negroes began to hold elective office. Their numbers have increased greatly since 1940 and, if this increase continues, the Negro vote in the Old Northwest, if organized and consolidated, could have remarkable political results. 79 notes.

E. P. Stickney

67. Rogge, Heinz. DIE AMERIKANISCHE NEGERFRAGE IN VERGANGENHEIT UND GEGENWART [The Negro problem in America: past and present]. *Geschichte in Wissenschaft und Unterricht [West Germany] 1958 9(9): 561-575, (10): 631-649.* The first part sketches the position of the Negro during the period of the settlement of America, under slavery, and during the Civil War, as well as movements to improve the Negro's lot and the social betterment of the Negro since 1940. In the second part, the author discusses the integration problem, southern reaction to it, and the cultural position of the Negro. Based primarily on works of American scholarship.

F. B. M. Hollyday

68. Sadik, Marvin S. PREVIEW: THE NEGRO IN AMERICAN ART. *Art in Am. 1964 52(3): 74-83.* Reviews the portrayal of the Negro in American painting, 1710-1963, by such artists as Ralph Earle, William Sidney Mount, Thomas Eakins, Reginald Marsh, Andrew Wyeth, and Jack Levine. Illus.

W. K. Bottorff

69. Schulte Nordholt, J. W. BEREDENEERDE BIBLIOGRAFIE OVER DE GESCHIEDENIS VAN DE NEGER IN DE V.S. [Critical bibliography of the history of the Negro in the United States]. *Kleio [Netherlands] 1966 7(2): 4-11.* This bibliography is divided into topical areas: general, slavery, Civil War, Reconstruction, 1877-1917, Negro protest, the sociological approach, and integration.

The author discusses a representative selection of works published in the United States since the 1880's, gives theses, and summarizes content of the major works.

D. Visser

70. Schulte Nordholt, J. W. EEN AMERIKAANS PROBLEEM HERZIEN IN OPDRACHT VAN DE TIJD. EEN BOEKBESPREKING [An American problem revised by the present time. A book review]. *Tijdschrift voor Geschiedenis [Netherlands] 1966 79(4): 418-438.* Demonstrates how modern historians, in the light of the present time which cries for equality and humanity, are at work to clear away the myths of the past. The author shows this through books about the South before the Civil War, the abolitionists, the Civil War, the Reconstruction period, the time from 1877 to 1917, the time after 1917, and the present.

G. van Roon

71. Schwartz, Jerome L. EARLY HISTORY OF PREPAID MEDICAL CARE PLANS. *Bull. of the Hist. of Medicine 1965 39(5): 450-475.* Describes and traces the development of the forms of prepaid medical care insurance from 1787 to 1929. "The first prepaid medical care plans were organized by fraternal societies and mutual benefit associations, which began to appear in the United States as early as 1787 with the formation of the Free African Society in Philadelphia. Initial health benefits provided by these associations were cash disability payments, aiming to replace a portion of the income lost during sickness. Later these employee groups, which had formed independent of employers, expanded the limited cash benefits into medical service programs....Around 1900, employee and industrial medical care plans were organized and later came to be known as 'contract practice.' The Workingmen's Compensation Laws, passed before World War I, stimulated the further development of prepaid plans. Remote areas in Washington, Oregon, Minnesota, and Pennsylvania, associated with lumbering, mining, and railroading industries, saw the founding of contract plans sponsored by industry, employees, physicians, hospitals, and medical societies. The early history of group insurance, private physician clinics, and hospital service plans laid the basis for the present day health insurance coverage under prepayment." 84 notes.

D. D. Cameron

72. Schwendemann, Glenn. NICODEMUS: NEGRO HAVEN ON THE SOLOMON. *Kansas Hist. Q. 1968 34(1): 10-31.* An account of a community in Kansas from the time it was founded by some former slaves from Kentucky then living in Topeka to the closing of the U.S. Post Office in 1953. Most attention is paid to the growth years through the 1880's when Nicodemus showed signs of developing into a commercial community of some importance. Biographies of some of the more prominent of the early settlers are sketched and evidence is offered in support of a contemporary appraisal that Nicodemus was "the bravest attempt ever made by people of any color to establish homes in the high plains of Western Kansas." Based on articles, local newspapers and manuscripts in the Kansas State Historical Society; illus., 83 notes.

W. F. Zornow

73. Shepperson, George. AFRICA AND AMERICA. *British Assoc. for Am. Studies Bull. [Great Britain] 1961 (3): 25-30.* Notes presented to the Third

Conference of African History and Archaeology at the London School of Oriental and African Studies July 1961 on the subject of American missionaries, trade, and particularly Negro relations with Africa in the 19th century, with a brief survey of recent writing on the subject.   D. McIntyre

74. Shepperson, George. NOTES ON NEGRO AMERICAN INFLUENCES ON THE EMERGENCE OF AFRICAN NATIONALISM. *J. of African Hist. [Great Britain] 1960 1(2): 299-312.* Observes that before the U.S. immigration controls of the 1920's, West Indians contributed a distinct element in the Negro-American interest and influence in Africa. Outlines the careers of Edward Blyden, Marcus Garvey, Albert Thorne and George Alexander McGuire. The role of Liberia prior to the Civil War is discussed, with particular reference to the influence of Martin R. Delany, the first Negro to be commissioned with field rank by President Lincoln. After the Civil War a few Negroes, such as Henry Turner, a Methodist bishop, and William Ellis, a stockbroker, suggested the "Back to Africa" ideal. After the First World War, Garvey's Universal Negro Improvement Association demanded "Africa for the Africans at home and abroad," and emergent African nationalism was influenced by the writings of Americans like W. E. B. Du Bois, one of the pioneers of the Pan-Africanist movement from the first conference in London (1900), and James Weldon Johnson, the Harlem journalist. In the later period, American influence was exerted through the African leaders educated in the United States (Nkrumah, Azikiwe, and Banda), the West Indian George Padmore, and the National Association for the Advancement of Colored People's lawyer, Thurgood Marshall.   W. D. McIntyre

75. Slawson, John. MUTUAL AID AND THE NEGRO. *Commentary 1966 41(4): 43-50.* "The idea of self-help or mutual aid as a means to further progress in securing full equality is not, to put it mildly, popular among Negroes." Negroes see emphasis on such ideas as "a diversionary tactic," intended (consciously or unconsciously) to divert attention from the question of discrimination and subjugation by whites to putative weaknesses of the Negro, and further implying "that the Negro bears an important share in the responsibility for his own plight." In addition, there have been many Negro efforts at self-help in the past, and the history of their failures is discouraging. The author examines the reasons for the failures, primarily that the Negroes as slaves had been purposefully prevented from developing any feeling of community or any communal institutions, and as free men were still often prevented and even, at best, not aided by any institutions such as the Federal Government which could have assured their success. Curiously, at present there are numerous self-help and mutual aid groups which refuse to discuss the subject with white liberals. Many such projects have received aid from white communities or institutions, and all should be encouraged.
A. K. Main

76. Smith, Frank E. VALOR'S SECOND PRIZE: SOUTHERN RACISM AND INTERNATIONALISM. *South Atlantic Q. 1965 64(3): 296-303.* Before World War II, the South had been a strong supporter of American internationalist policies, motivated early by slave expansionism and then by the need for export markets for staple goods. Southern senators were the strongest supporters of the

League of Nations. Although the south supported the Marshall Plan, since that time southern members of Congress have moved away from internationalist concepts to make the South a stronger center of isolationism than the Midwest. The major factor behind this change of attitude has not been southern industrialization and the need for protectionism, but racist sentiment based upon suspicion of the United Nations as a tool of newly emerging non-Western nations and foreign aid given to nonwhite countries. Racist domination of politics has also reduced the general quality of southern congressional representation.

J. M. Bumsted

77. Starobin, Robert. THE NEGRO: A CENTRAL THEME IN AMERICAN HISTORY. *J. of Contemporary Hist. [Great Britain] 1968 3(2): 37-53.* Negro history in the United States has been characterized until very recently either by traditionalism, which considered Negroes of little consequence to the American experience, or by revisionism, which emphasized that Negroes have made important contributions to American life. Within the last decade both groups have been challenged. The latest studies stress the centrality of institutions like slavery to long periods of American history and regard the Negro as the key to the meaning of the American experience. It is recognized that not all of American history, but rather long periods of it, have been largely shaped by the problem of slavery and of the freedmen. Some of the new revisionism, however, is characterized by elitism and political conservatism. Based on current literature on Negro history; 10 notes.   Sr. M. P. Trauth

78. Stuckert, Robert P. and Rinder, Irwin D. THE NEGRO IN THE SOCIAL SCIENCE LITERATURE: 1961. *Phylon 1962 23(2): 111-127.* Observes that recent writings no longer emphasize factors calculated to prove the human validity of Negroes, on the whole. Sociological emphasis is upon the study of systems, theory, and methodology. Historians treat the Negro in larger American contexts. The effort intended to overcome earlier tendencies to ignore the Negro has largely achieved its goal. Writings are reviewed or commented upon under the following headings: "General," "Historical Studies," "Community Studies," "Collective Behavior," "Housing," "Attitudes toward Desegregation," and "Civil Rights."   L. Filler

79. Thomas, Charles Walker. AMERICAN LANDMARKS CELEBRATION SEEKS TO PRESERVE NATION'S HERITAGE. *Negro Hist. Bull. 1964 28(1): 23-24.* Calls attention to the need and value of preserving landmarks of Negro history, as a part of our national response to the UNESCO sponsored "International Monuments Year."   L. Gara

80. Thomas, Charles Walker. ATLANTA IN RETROSPECT: REPORT ON THE 50TH ANNUAL MEETING. *Negro Hist. Bull. 1965 29(2): 29-30, 34.* A report on the 50th Annual Meeting of the Association for the Study of Negro Life and History (ASNLH) held at Atlanta University, Georgia, on 21-23 October 1965. The session opened with a memorial tribute to Carter G. Woodson, the founder of ASNLH. The featured address was delivered by Ralph McGill, a newspaper publisher and columnist, who pointed out that the system of segrega-

tion has so vitiated and distorted the history of the Southland and the Negro that really authentic history about these subjects must yet be written. "Mr. McGill's most significant contribution was perhaps the vigor with which he sought to infuse the Association with a sense of mission and obligation to write a scientific appraisal of a neglected aspect of the history of the United States." Lorenzo J. Greene, a professor of history at Lincoln University, Missouri, was elected President of ASNLH for the 1965-66 term. 2 photos.   D. D. Cameron

81. Thurston, Helen M. A SURVEY OF PUBLICATIONS ON THE HISTORY AND ARCHAEOLOGY OF OHIO, 1969-70. *Ohio Hist. 1969 78(4): 288-296.* Lists books, articles, and other materials under the headings of Archaeology, Arts and Crafts, Bibliography, Biography, Business and Industry, Education and Culture, Genealogy, Indians and the Wars, Literature, Local History, Miscellaneous, Ohio in the Wars, Politics and Government, Religion, Slavery, Civil War, Reconstruction, Urban History, and Theses and Dissertations on Ohio Subjects in Ohio Colleges and Universities.   S. L. Jones

82. Tindall, George B. SOUTHERN NEGROES SINCE RECONSTRUCTION: DISSOLVING THE STATIC IMAGE. *Writing Southern Hist.: Essays in Historiography in Honor of Fletcher M. Green (Baton Rouge: Louisiana State U. Press, 1965): 337-361.* In post-Reconstruction historiography the Negroes have suffered less from racial prejudice than from "a bias by omission." The Phelps-Stokes Fund was established at the Universities of Virginia and Georgia to stimulate investigation regarding the possibilities of the Negro in the South. The beginning of scholarly studies by Negroes came with W. E. B. Du Bois and Carter Goodson in the 1890's. The new Negro historiography paralleled the "great migration" from the South. It not only altered the static image, but also turned attention more strongly toward the Negro worker. In 1948 John Hope Franklin's *From Slavery to Freedom* (New York: Knopf) incorporated many results of the growing literature on Negro history. Recent studies of States in the 19th century and the biographical approach have both been fruitful. Great gaps in Negro historical scrutiny exist. 99 biblio. notes.   E. P. Stickney

83. Tindall, George B. THE BENIGHTED SOUTH: ORIGINS OF A MODERN IMAGE. *Virginia Q. R. 1964 40(2): 281-294.* One of the more long-lasting images of the South is that of the benighted South ruled by near barbarians. There is just enough truth in this that in the hands of a skillful propagandist it can be made to look like the whole truth. In the 1920's such propagandists appeared, led by Henry Louis Mencken. These men took the old abolitionist picture of the South and brought it up to date in such a way that the South has yet to overcome it. This is a survey of the efforts to create this image.   C. R. Allen, Jr.

84. Unsigned. FRANK J. KLINGBERG: A SELECT LIST OF PUBLICATIONS. *Negro Hist. Bull. 1957 21(3): 52-57.* Lists 18 books and 44 articles and monographs written by Frank J. Klingberg, former professor of history at the University of California at Los Angeles, along with excerpts from reviews of his books. Most of the titles relate to Negro history, slavery, abolition, or Anglo-American relations.   L. Gara

85. Unsigned. NEGRO HISTORY AND THE MODERN UNCLE TOM. *Negro Hist. Bull. 1964 27(6): 134-135.*

86. Unsigned. THE FAMILY OF PORTER WILLIAM PHILLIPS, SR. *Negro Hist. Bull. 1964 27(4): 81-84.* Genealogical article with biographical sketches. Illus.   S

87. Varenne, Lt. Col. LES NOIRS DANS LES FORCES ARMEES AMERI-CAINES [The Negro in the American armed forces]. *R. de Défense Natl. [France] 1968 24(12): 1873-1888.* Discusses the history of Negroes in the American armed forces, the question of segregation, and the problems to be found when the Negro will be demobilized. A number of actual integration problems remain in the armed forces.   J. J. Flynn

88. Wax, Darold D. THE NEGRO IN EARLY AMERICA. *Social Studies 1969 60(3): 109-118.* Asserts that an increasing interest in the American Negro demands a more accurate understanding of his role in America's past history. The author lists and evaluates the most important works written on the subject of the American Negro. His evaluations of these works as to their relative importance can serve as guidelines for interested persons who wish to gain a knowledge of the Negro's place in American history. 14 notes.   L. Raife

89. Weisbord, Robert G. THE BACK-TO-AFRICA IDEA. *Hist. Today [Great Britain] 1968 18(1): 30-37.* An analysis of the plans of white and Negro groups to encourage Negro immigration to Africa from America after 1816. The major figures discussed are Bishop Henry M. Turner, Martin R. Delany, and Marcus Aurelius Garvey. The emphasis is placed on the organization, plans, proceedings, and subsequent failures of the various groups. In assessing the response of the people to such plans, the author feels with Gunnar Myrdal that "it tells of a dissatisfaction so deep that it amounts to hopelessness of ever gaining a full life in America." Illus.   L. A. Knafla

90. Wesley, Charles H. CREATING AND MAINTAINING AN HISTORICAL TRADITION. *J. of Negro Hist. 1964 49(1): 13-33.* After discussing the uses of a historical tradition made by various minority peoples, the author traces the development of such a tradition by American Negroes. Prior to the Civil War, Negro conventions and individual Negroes protested the discrimination and mistreatment which their race suffered but only seldom did they resort to history in their statements. Some Negro authors, such as William Yates, William C. Nell, and William Wells Brown, called attention to past achievement in war and peace in answering those who argued along racial lines. These early works were followed by those of more careful Negro scholars and the work of the Association for the Study of Negro Life and History. More carefully researched and imaginative writing is needed in order to place the history of American Negroes in its proper position in the national past.   L. Gara

91. West, Earle H. SUMMARY OF RESEARCH DURING 1963 RELATED TO THE NEGRO AND NEGRO EDUCATION. *J. of Negro Educ. 1965 34(1): 30-38.* Provides summary and analysis of 58 doctoral dissertations completed in this field in 1963. Based primarily on *Dissertation Abstracts.*
S. C. Pearson, Jr.

92. West, Earle H. SUMMARY OF RESEARCH DURING 1964 RELATED TO THE NEGRO AND NEGRO EDUCATION. *J. of Negro Educ. 1966 35(1): 62-72.* Lists 80 dissertations reported to *Dissertation Abstracts* between August 1964 and August 1965: The dissertations are grouped into the broad categories of educational administration, higher education, history and politics, literature, psychology, secondary education, and sociology; annotations are provided.
S. C. Pearson, Jr.

93. Wiatr, Jerzy. O RASIZMIE W HISTORIOGRAFII AMERYKAŃSKIES [On racism in American historiography]. *Myśl Filozoficzna [Poland] 1956 2(22): 139-164.* Analyzes the crypto-racist and reactionary trend in American historiography as represented by Madison Grant, A. H. Stone, Henry William Elson, Allan Nevins, and Henry Steele Commager. These historians, whose theory of race is opposed by many anthropological and ethnological schools (e.g., Franz Boas, Otto Klineberg and F. H. Hankins), interpret American history on a nonclass basis, automatically excluding any allusion to the historical fact of the class struggle especially in the rise of abolitionism. They minimize the role of the Negro in American history, thus becoming apologists for the Ku Klux Klan. Final remarks deal with the fight against racism, conducted by American Marxist historians (W. Z. Foster and Herbert Aptheker) and by liberal historians such as Melville Jean Herskovits, J. H. Franklin, George Brown Tindall and James W. Silver. At the 1955 meeting of the American Historical Association there was much criticism of racist historiography.
G. Tietz

94. Wiebe, Robert. THE CONFINEMENTS OF CONSENSUS. *Tri-Q. 1966 (6): 155-158.* Testing American experience by a European gauge is an important contribution of the historians of consensus; however, existing differences must not be dismissed. Examples of the relevance of inner differences may be found in the ease and speed of American industrialization and in the peaceful processes of immigrant assimilation. While both reflect consensus, industrialization succeeded "because its millions of bitter enemies lacked the mentality and the means to organize an effective counterattack." In the second instance, immigrants and Negroes "have followed a hundred winding routes of their own, as groups and as individuals: and their pattern is a labyrinthine pluralism rather than so many markers along the way to a simple assimilation." In both instances "the absence of ideological debate, hard political battle, and armed conflict may indicate social distance and power differentials so great that they preclude any direct confrontation."
W. H. Agee

95. Woodson, June Baber. THE NEGRO IN DETROIT TO 1900. *Negro Hist. Bull. 1959 22(4): 90-91.* Discusses various aspects of Negro life in Detroit,

including population statistics as well as material on religion, education, mutual aid, Civil War service, and the political activity of the city's Negro residents. Undocumented.   L. Gara

96. Woodward, C. Vann. THE SOUTHERN ETHIC IN A PURITAN WORLD. *William and Mary Q. 1968 25(3): 343-370.* Discounts the "Janus-faced" myths of a distinctive southern culture. Determinants for southerners escaping the Puritan ethic are explained in the light of colonial origins, slavery, agrarianism, the plantation system, and precapitalistic society. An interpretation of postwar repressions and the Populist revolt substitute a mystique of "kinship, or clanship" for a hierarchical sense of community. The southern ethic is compared with the Puritan ethic. 55 notes.   H. M. Ward

97. Wright, J. Leitch, Jr. A NOTE ON THE FIRST SEMINOLE WAR AS SEEN BY THE INDIANS, NEGROES, AND THEIR BRITISH ADVISERS. *J. of Southern Hist. 1968 34(4): 565-575.* Suggests that the causes of the First Seminole War in 1817-18 were more complex than the traditional U.S. explanation. The Indians considered that part of their lands lay in the United States above the Florida boundary, that the Americans were the aggressors, and that, rather than making unprovoked attacks across the U.S. border, they were merely defending their homeland. Moreover, it seems apparent from the diplomatic exchanges between the United States, Britain, and Spain, that the United States was determined to have all of Spanish Florida. 26 notes.   I. M. Leonard

98. --. [FLANNERY O'CONNOR]. *Mississippi Q. 1968 21(4): 235-251.*
Montgomery, Marion. FLANNERY O'CONNOR AND THE NATURAL MAN, pp. 235-242. Interpreting Flannery O'Connor's symbols in her fiction is not an easy matter. She was concerned with the separation of the supernatural from the natural by the intellect, which (through its illusion of reality) led one to the devil's work. She attacked the natural, self-made man as an object of worship. For the natural man, in O'Connor's vision, a shocking revelation of the Hell he inhabits may set his soul ready in its desires for the terrors of mercy. Her characters, Asbury and Tarwater, can warn of the "terrible speed of Mercy" since they have confronted the dragon of death - not death of body, but of soul. Her vision of Hell is that of the modern heresy of the natural man with his fear of natural rather than spiritual death. Ultimately, what O'Connor does is affirm human nature transformed by the blessing of the incarnation. Based mainly on published material; 13 notes.
Byrd, Turner F. IRONIC DIMENSION IN FLANNERY O'CONNOR'S "THE ARTIFICIAL NIGGER," pp. 243-251. Carefully constructed, O'Connor's story "The Artificial Nigger " shows consummate artistry in the blending of classic literary allegory and theology, although the story is often misread at its most crucial point. Failure to detect the ironic mode as the basis of her technique has caused many to accept Mr. Head's judgment of his condition in the denouement as a true moment of grace, rather than as an extension of his stubborn, misguided omniscience. It is important for the reader to see the character Mr. Head not merely as O'Connor sees him but also as he sees himself; the reader must also interpret the action of the story and Mr. Head's conception of

his grandson through the grandfather's distorted vision. The reader can then accept the author's artistic irony. Based mainly on published material; 5 notes.

R. V. Calvert

99. --. [MELVILLE JEAN HERSKOVITS]. *Am. Anthropologist 1964 66(1): 83-109.*
Merriam, Alan P. MELVILLE JEAN HERSKOVITS, 1895-1963, pp. 83-90.
Moneypenney, Anne and Thorne, Barrie. A BIBLIOGRAPHY OF THE PUBLICATIONS OF MELVILLE JEAN HERSKOVITS, pp. 91-109.
A review and complete bibliography of Herskovits' work. His main interest was in the American Negro and his contributions to the field rank among the first. In the course of his work, Herskovits also studied the African and South American Negro. His broad interests included psychology, economics, education, and aesthetics, and he left lasting contributions in all fields, especially with respect to Negro cultures. The chronological bibliography includes 479 items.

A. Hopping

100. --. [MEMORIAL TO DR. ALBERT NEAL DOW BROOKS]. *Negro Hist. Bull. 1964 27(8): 186-199.*
Wesley, Charles H. TO US FROM FALLING HANDS, pp. 186-188. Reviews the accomplishments of Albert N. D. Brooks (1897-1964), Negro historian and educator, as secretary-treasurer of the Association for the Study of Negro Life and History and as editor of the *Negro History Bulletin.*
Unsigned. ON THE OCCASION OF AWARDING OF DOCTORATE DEGREE, p. 188. Publishes the citation read when Lincoln University gave Brooks an honorary degree in 1960.
Unsigned. WITH ALBERT N. D. BROOKS: UNFORGETTABLE SCENES FROM A FULL LIFE, pp. 192-193. Publishes several photographs depicting scenes from the life of Brooks.
Unsigned. RITES HELD FOR DR. BROOKS, p. 197. An obituary.
Unsigned. TEACHER AND PRINCIPAL, pp. 198-199. Remarks of appreciation for Brooks by three of his close associates.
Unsigned. DR. BROOKS SPEAKS ON RECONSTRUCTION. Summarizes Brook's views on Reconstruction in which he rejected the traditional view and emphasized the positive contribution of the Negroes and their betrayal by northern industrialists and politicians.

L. Gara

101. --. THE NEGRO IN ILLINOIS HISTORY. *J. of the Illinois State Hist. Soc. 1963 56(3): 431-624.*
Davis, Corneal A. and Robinson, William H. INTRODUCTION, pp. 431-432. As part of its program, the American Negro Emancipation Centennial Commission of Illinois, created to celebrate the centennial anniversary of the Emancipation Proclamation, has cooperated with the State historical society in this special issue of the *Journal.*
Horney, Helen and Keller, William E. THE NEGRO'S TWO HUNDRED FORTY YEARS IN ILLINOIS - A CHRONOLOGY, pp. 433-438. The 49 dates commence in 1712, when the French Government authorizied slave trade

in its colony of Louisiana. The last date, 1961, concerns the establishment of a Fair Employment Practices Commission in Illinois.

Meehan, Thomas A. JEAN BAPTISTE POINT DU SABLE, THE FIRST CHICAGOAN, pp. 439-453. Although the evidence is fragmentary, the first permanent settler of Chicago was probably a Negro with French or French colonial antecedents. Du Sable was a sincere Catholic and a man of means and culture.

Gertz, Elmer. THE BLACK LAWS OF ILLINOIS, pp. 454-473. The Illinois codes of behavior, legal and social, for slaves and free Negroes are traced from the days of the earliest French settlers to the Civil War period.

Strickland, Arvarh E. THE ILLINOIS BACKGROUND OF LINCOLN'S ATTITUDE TOWARD SLAVERY AND THE NEGRO, pp. 474-494. To a considerable extent Abraham Lincoln reflected the sentiment of central Illinois (a moderation of the extreme views of the southern and northern sections of the State) as to whether the State should have slavery, the moral issue of its justice or injustice, and the political and social status of free Negroes. How with this background he was later transformed into the "Great Emancipator" remains the complex question.

Watkins, Sylvestre C., Sr. SOME OF EARLY ILLINOIS' FREE NEGROES, pp. 495-507. Brief biographical sketches of a half dozen free Negroes. Some made contributions to improve the status of Negro rights in the State.

Gara, Larry. THE UNDERGROUND RAILROAD IN ILLINOIS, pp. 508-528. "Despicable slave-catchers" and "benevolent abolitionists" fill the romantic and traditional accounts of the underground railroad in Illinois. Although the historical picture is still incomplete, revisionist studies have already indicated the unreliable nature of tradition as a source of information.

Hicken, Victor. THE RECORD OF ILLINOIS' NEGRO SOLDIERS IN THE CIVIL WAR, pp. 529-551. With emphasis on the activities of Illinois Negro troops, the total national Negro contribution to the war effort is narrated.

Fisher, Miles Mark. NEGRO CHURCHES IN ILLINOIS: A FRAGMENTARY HISTORY WITH EMPHASIS ON CHICAGO, pp. 552-569. Denominational congregations of Negroes were organized as early as 1839. With fugitive slave and abolition controversies, racial as well as sectional cleavages resulted in the establishment of Negro sects. With the 1954 school desegregation decision, the current trend is to erase racial distinctions in denominational and congregational designations.

Lochard, Metz T. P. THE NEGRO PRESS IN ILLINOIS, pp. 570-591. Although the first Negro newspaper in the State was probably established in 1878, the history of the Negro press in Illinois is largely the story of the *Chicago Defender,* which first appeared in 1905. Its principal concern has been the achievement of social justice for the Negro in America.

Dilliard, Irving. CIVIL LIBERTIES OF NEGROES IN ILLINOIS SINCE 1865, pp. 592-624. Although much ground has been gained in the first century since the Emancipation Proclamation, the author asserts "much more remains to be won."   D. L. Smith

Political History

102. Baker, Riley E. NEGRO VOTER REGISTRATION IN LOUISIANA, 1879-1964. *Louisiana Studies 1965 4(4): 332-350.* A history of Negro voting in Louisiana. Voting statistics are analyzed and objectively diagnosed.

G. W. McGinty

103. Bennett, David H. THE ENIGMA OF AMERICAN EXTREMISM. *Centennial R. 1967 11(2): 198-219.* Discusses extremist movements in the American past with special reference to anti-Catholic and antialien political parties. Extremist movements in America have rested on a "subsoil of discontent, muted rage, and unhappiness." Recently extremism has turned to anticommunism and racism. The failure of the Communists in the United States came not because of the extremists but because the Communists could not make headway against the American consensus. Antialienism has been replaced by racist movements in which radical agitators work on the fringes of the black and white communities. Present-day political leaders do not try to force conformity as some did in the past, but rather seek a broad consensus based on compromise. The 1960's are difficult times and the future promises to be even more difficult. The extremist will always be with us even though his goals may change.   A. R. Stoesen

104. Bonner, James C. LEGISLATIVE APPORTIONMENT AND COUNTY UNIT VOTING IN GEORGIA SINCE 1777. *Georgia Hist. Q. 1963 47(4): 351-374.* Carefully surveys legislative apportionment and county unit voting in Georgia from 1777 to 1963, relating his analysis to national patterns in democratic procedures and to race relations.   R. Lowitt

105. Collins, Ernest M. CINCINNATI NEGROES AND PRESIDENTIAL POLITICS. *J. of Negro Hist. 1956 41(2): 131-137.* From the time of emancipation to 1932 the Negroes of Cincinnati supported the Republican Party. The economic aspects of the New Deal swung the Negro vote to the Democratic Party and they have continued to support it because of civil rights. If the Negro population of Ohio continues to increase at the 1930-50 rate, and the voting behavior of the Negroes in Cincinnati is duplicated in other cities of the State, the Republican Party will be forced to reappraise its political strategy.   W. E. Wight

106. Degler, Carl N. THE GREAT REVERSAL: THE REPUBLICAN PARTY'S FIRST CENTURY. *South Atlantic Q. 1966 65(1): 1-11.* Despite presidential victories in the years before 1896, the Republican Party was a minority party in terms of popular vote and control of Congress. For two generations after 1896, however, the party was the majority one. During this period of dominance it emphasized "positive action in behalf of Negro rights, economic growth, and the supremacy of the national authority." It was strong with farmers and in the urban

centers. But in the 1920's the party ignored its heritage and began to desert those positive principles which gave it mass appeal; today, it has become a minority party of negative action.   J. M. Bumsted

107. Diggs, Charles, Jr. NEGRO CONGRESSMEN. *Negro Hist. Bull. 1964 27(5): 114, 116.* Briefly discusses some of the contributions made by Negroes in the U.S. Congress from the era of Reconstruction to the present.
                                                                      L. Gara

108. Dumond, Dwight L. FOURTEENTH AMENDMENT TRILOGY IN HISTORICAL PERSPECTIVE. *Negro Hist. Bull. 1958 21(8): 192, 187-191.* Traces the American faith in natural rights protected by law back to the Declaration of Independence, the Constitution and the 14th Amendment. In the recent desegregation decisions the Supreme Court revitalized the 14th Amendment and broadened the judicial concept of equal protection under the law. Undocumented.
                                                                      L. Gara

109. Dykeman, Wilma. THE SOUTHERN DEMAGOGUE. *Virginia Q. R. 1957 33(4): 558-568.* Characterizes southern demagogues as men who were skilled in the use of words and adopted a distinctive manner of dress. The rural nature of the South, limited voting, and race are frequently mentioned as basic causes of southern demagoguery. The author believes that race is the one factor which holds together the whole fabric of southern politics.   W. E. Wight

110. Jackson, Carlton. THE WHITE BASIS SYSTEM AND THE DECLINE OF ALABAMA WHIGGERY. *Alabama Hist. Q. 1963 25(3/4): 246-253.* The White Basis system adopted by the Democratic Party in the Alabama Legislature in 1843 eliminated the three-fifths compromise of the Federal constitution. Enumerating only whites, the "white" counties of North Alabama gained an advantage in representation over the Black Belt. This, plus gerrymandering by the Democrats, kept the Whigs, a party which had as much as 45 percent of the voting population, powerless until the Civil War. Many unresolved questions concerning the White Basis system are enumerated. 16 notes.
                                                                 E. P. Stickney

111. Jackson, Joy J. REPORT ON THE TWELFTH ANNUAL MEETING. *Louisiana Hist. 1970 11(2): 177-179.* A discussion by the Program Chairman of papers presented at the 12th Annual Meeting of the Louisiana Historical Association, 13-14 March 1970. The three sessions were entitled: "Race, Class, and Third Party Conflict in Louisiana Politics since the Civil War," "The National Archives and Louisiana History," and "Louisiana and the Territorial Period."
                                                                 R. L. Woodward

112. Linden, Glenn M. A NOTE ON NEGRO SUFFRAGE AND REPUBLICAN POLITICS. *J. of Southern Hist. 1970 36(3): 411-420.* Using a series of roll-call votes in Congress during the years 1850-69 (from the 31st through the 40th Congresses), determines whether the Congressmen who voted for the 15th

amendment were acting consistently with their past public records. The author concludes that "Republican senators and representatives consistently voted in favor of measures for the improvement of the Negro's civil and political position in American society in the 1850's and 1860's." 15 notes.   I. M. Leonard

113. Lubell, Samuel. THE NEGRO AND THE DEMOCRATIC COALITION. *Commentary 1964 38(2): 19-27.* In contrast to the "image" projected by the Negro leaders, the Negro voter has been a loyal block voter, voting with the local machine. Discusses the reasons for this, how it has worked at various times, and how it has affected and is affecting various groups of white voters. Considers the effects of the CIO and the Negro intellectuals' swing away from their probusiness stance of the early twenties and before. Considers the effects of recent civil rights legislation and implementation and the personality of the president on voters' attitudes (especially southern voters), and closes with an unoptimistic glance toward the future.   E. W. Hathaway

114. Marbut, Frederick B. CONGRESS AND THE STANDING COMMITTEE OF CORRESPONDENTS. *Journalism Q. 1961 38(1): 52-58.* Traces the history of the five-man Standing Committee of Correspondents which supervises the press galleries in Congress. The committee, founded around 1877, worked out an agreement with the Speaker of the House and the Senate Rules Committee for regulating the press in its coverage of Congress. New regulations were adopted by the committee and accepted by the Speaker and Senate committee in 1947. In 1947 representatives of the Negro press and in 1949 reporters from the labor press were admitted to the press galleries for the first time. Representatives of government agencies are not permitted the use of the galleries.   L. Gara

115. McWhiney, Grady. WERE THE WHIGS A CLASS PARTY IN ALABAMA? *J. of Southern Hist. 1957 23(4): 510-522.* Shows that the common conception of the Whigs as a party of planters and slaveholders does not apply to Alabama, where the representatives of both the Whigs and the Democrats belonged to the same social classes.   P. Podjed

116. Moon, Henry Lee. NEGRO SUFFRAGE. *Natl. Civic R. 1970 59(5): 246-251.* One hundred years ago the 15th amendment was ratified, but this did not initiate Negro voting in the Nation, because Negro voting in the United States is older than the Nation, dating back to the colonial period. However, the South's subversion of the 15th amendment, after the restoration of the Confederacy in 1877, was intensified and continues today, though with vastly diminished force and effectiveness. The South used murder, intimidation, and refusal to register black citizens, regardless of their individual qualifications, as the means of maintaining the right to vote as the exclusive privilege of white men. The National Association for the Advancement of Colored People has spearheaded the long, hard struggle to regain the vote for black citizens, especially during the last half-century. Even today, the 1,500 elected black officials in the United States represent only .3 of one percent of the national total of more than 500 thousand officials, and the Negro population currently represents about 11 percent of the national total.   H. S. Marks

117. Morton, Peggy and Wood, Myrna. 1848 AND ALL THAT: OR THE NEW LEFT AND LABOR. *Horizons: The Marxist Q. 1968 25: 39-46.* Discusses New Left experiences in Canada and the United States. For the New Left, unlike the old left, organizing and community organizing are almost interchangeable terms. "The catch-phrase participatory democracy" gives an indication of the values supported by the New Left "a basically middle class and student movement." To the New Left the existing labor unions seem bureaucratic and conservative, thus they turned first to the "black people in the south, to minority groups, to the ghettoes." Class problems and the political organization of society as a whole lost their importance. Later, to reach more people, the New Left turned to the middle class and then to students specifically. The New Left is now coming to see that control of work and the products of labor must be the fundamental part of their organizational activities, but not with the emphasis of the establishment unions. The authors conclude that "Our major task should be to try and formulate a strategy that will enable us to test out new organizing ideas and areas around the most important factor in people's lives - their work."   W. E. Ratliff

118. Sisk, Glenn. THE NEGRO IN ATLANTA POLITICS (1870-1962). *Negro Hist. Bull. 1964 28(1): 17-18.* Briefly reviews the political activity of Negroes in Atlanta from the end of Reconstruction, when Negroes were gradually disfranchised, to 1962 when as a result of Supreme Court decisions and a new interest in politics an unprecedented 51 thousand Negroes had registered to vote.
                                                                            L. Gara

119. Smith, Frank E. THE DEMOCRATIC IDEA AND SOUTHERN CONGRESSIONAL POLITICS. *Mississippi Q. 1965 18(4): 223-230.* Because Deep South representation in the U.S. Congress for over a century has been dominated by the influence of racism, an assessment of democracy is impossible. In the postbellum South, two significant forces developed as a result of poor education of both Negroes and whites: 1) a landowner-banker-business group of leaders benefiting economically from cheap labor and 2) the unlettered and unskilled "poor white" group led to consider the Negro as competitor-enemy and willing to believe in "white supremacy." Most southern Congressmen, actually moderates by conviction, have been forced for 20 years to consider their chief responsibility in Congress to be continuing opposition to civil rights legislation. With the passage of such legislation in recent years, however, the disappearance of the race-dominated political straightjacket should see a vastly changed southern congressional representation. The combination of increased Negro voting and legislative reapportionment decisions of the courts promises great changes in southern politics. Subsidiary issues, such as foreign affairs, will indirectly feel racism as a force for years to come. Southerners' transfer of racism to interpreting international cooperation as an African or Mongolian threat has been reflected in increased southern unilateralism in congressional voting.   R. V. Calvert

120. Stenseth, Dagfinn. DEN AMERIKANSKE HØYESTERETT [The American Supreme Court]. *Internasjonal Politikk [Norway] 1960 (6): 133-138.* Discusses the role of the Supreme Court in American government and, particularly, the issues of segregation and race relations. recent views of the position of the

court and the judicial attitude on Negroes from the Dred Scott case to the present. He furnishes a brief survey of the court and its functions for an understanding of American government. R. E. Lindgren

121. Taylor, Joseph H. THE FOURTEENTH AMENDMENT, THE NEGRO, AND THE SPIRIT OF THE TIMES. *J. of Negro Hist. 1960 45(1): 21-37.* States that the 14th Amendment has gone through various stages of interpretation in keeping with the spirit of the times. From 1865 to 1882 the country was under the "spell" of the Civil War. There was sympathy for the lately emancipated freedmen, and the Supreme Court's decisions reflected this sympathy. From 1883 to 1937 the country was in the throes of rapid industrial growth and development. The Negro became the forgotten man during the course of the emphasis on moneymaking. Then came the New Deal, World War II, the United Nations, and the Declaration of Human Rights. The 14th Amendment is now being interpreted in the light of the emphasis on human rights, and once again it appears that it is being used as a shield and protector of the Negro, which many authorities claim was its original purpose. A

Social & Cultural History

122. Abrahams, Roger D. SOME VARIETIES OF HEROES IN AMERICA. *J. of the Folklore Inst. 1966 3(3): 341-362.* A discussion of representative hero stories in three American groups; the Negro, white rural folk communities, and urban popular culture, together with the view that heroic actions "reflect a view of life which is based upon contest values and a social hierarchy built on the model of a male-centered family." Although the three types differ "they all show the hero to be fixed permanently at the rebellious stage." They reflect cultural values and situations, and an understanding of them is of value in understanding the group. 32 notes. J. C. Crowe

123. Abrahams, Roger D. TRADITIONS OF ELOQUENCE IN AFRO-AMERICAN COMMUNITIES. *J. of Inter-Am. Studies and World Affairs 1970 12(4): 505-527.* Speaking is extremely important in Afro-American communities in the Western Hemisphere. There are two types of successful speakers. The first is the broad-talker who speaks informally and relies heavily on wit. The second is the good-talker who is elaborate, ornate, and grammatical. One or the other of these types is found from Philadelphia to the West Indies. This expressive culture was carried from Africa to the New World where it became mixed with European culture. At important community events such as weddings and baptisms, lengthy and eloquent orations are an integral part of the celebrations. Based on primary and secondary books and articles; 25 notes. J. R. Thomas

124. Asbell, Bernard. "A MAN AIN'T NOTHIN' BUT A MAN." *Am. Heritage 1963 14(6): 34-37, 95.* Attempts to produce the facts out of which the legend and the ballad of John Henry were produced. There was, apparently, a test of a steam drill against John Henry in which the machine failed. His death came later. Illus.
C. R. Allen, Jr.

125. Beja, Morris. IT MUST BE IMPORTANT: NEGROES IN CONTEMPO-RARY AMERICAN FICTION. *Antioch R. 1964 24(3): 323-336.* Reviews the treatment of the Negro in American literature and finds that it has been unreal. The American writer has been prevented from depicting the Negro honestly and as a person. Traditionally held concepts of the Negro's roles as a servant and sex symbol are examined.   D. F. Rossi

126. Bigglestone, W. E. OBERLIN COLLEGE AND THE NEGRO STU-DENT, 1865-1940. *J. of Negro Hist. 1971 56(3): 198-219.* Two years after Oberlin College was founded in 1835, its leadership decided to accept students without regard to race. Although this policy left the impression in some minds that Oberlin was a predominatly Negro college, its enrollment rarely averaged more than five percent black students. The school refused for the most part to become involved in overcoming racial discrimination practiced by surrounding societies and institutions, and the average Negro residing at the college found living conditions there difficult as a result. Some administrators and alumni also expressed hostility toward Oberlin's black students, and this aggravated their problems. Based mainly on primary sources; 78 notes.   R. S. Melamed

127. Billingsley, Andrew and Billingsley, Amy Tate. NEGRO FAMILY LIFE IN AMERICA. *Social Service R. 1965 39(3): 310-319.* The authors maintain that both the problems and the creative potential of Negroes are highly related to the economic, social, and psychological stability of Negro family life. Six crises for the Negro family have influenced its historical development: 1) from Africa to America, 2) from slavery to emancipation, 3) from rural to urban areas, 4) from the South to the North and West, 5) from negative to positive social status, and 6) from negative to positive self-image. Three patterns of Negro family life have emerged: patriarchal, equalitarian, and matriarchal. 15 notes.
D. H. Swift

128. Black, Isabella. BEREA COLLEGE. *Phylon 1957 18(3): 267-276.* Relates the background of the founding of Berea College in 1859, and its operation as an interracial college, until its transformation into an all-white "folkschool" in 1904 following the enactment of the Day Law, which prohibited "coeducation of the races" in Kentucky.   C. F. Latour

129. Chitty, Arthur B. ST. AUGUSTINE'S COLLEGE, RALEIGH, NORTH CAROLINA. *Hist. Mag. of the Protestant Episcopal Church 1966 35(3): 207-220.* Sketch of an Episcopal college (founded during Reconstruction days) and still operating as an institution of higher learning for Negroes. The author brings up to date the work of Cecil D. Halliburton, *A History of St. Augustine's College,*

1867-1937 (Raleigh, N.C.: 1937), and James H. Boykin's unpublished MS, "St. Augustine's College, 1938-1958." Appended is a list of "Colleges Suspected of Having Episcopal Connection." E. G. Roddy

130. Conley, Dorothy Ruth. NEGRO HISTORY LESSON PLAN. *Negro Hist. Bull. 1958 22(3): 64-67.* Presents a complete elementary school lesson plan which uses historical materials from the American Negro past to promote desirable racial attitudes. L. Gara

131. Cuban, Larry. JIM CROW HISTORY. *Negro Hist. Bull. 1962 25(4): 84-86.* Comments on history texts and courses which treat the Negro in a stereotyped fashion and imply that there is racial inferiority. Instead of a biased approach which reinforces prejudice he advises placing more emphasis on such topics as the diversity of American society, the various roles played by Negroes in American history, and the national, social, and economic setting of the Negro contribution. L. Gara

132. Davies, Vernon. FERTILITY VERSUS WELFARE: THE NEGRO AMERICAN DILEMMA. *Phylon 1966 27(3): 226-232.* Traces fertility trends among Negro Americans since about 1850 and compares them with trends among Caucasian Americans. A 1900 fertility ratio differential of Negroes and whites virtually disappeared by 1920 with a rapid decline in white mortality rates. From 1920 to 1935 crude birth rates of Negroes dropped 9.2 points, but from 1935 to 1955 they rose nine points. The fertility ratio acceleration from 1935 to 1955 was about 50 percent faster than for whites, in part because of a rapidly declining Negro mortality rate. Birth rates declined again after 1958, and by 1962 the birth rate for whites stood at 21.4 and for nonwhites at 30.5. The major contribution to the high fertility of Negroes derives from the rural South. Considering high fertility a major element in the etiology of poverty, the author recommends a population control program among rural Negroes of the South. Based on the U.S. Census of Population; 12 notes. S. C. Pearson, Jr.

133. Dundes, Alan. THE AMERICAN CONCEPT OF FOLKLORE. *J. of the Folklore Inst. 1966 3(3): 226-249.* The "American concept" of folklore should more appropriately be referred to as "some" American concepts of folklore. There are North American and South American as well as national concepts. In the United States, the term refers to both the materials studied and the study itself. In the *Journal of American Folklore* 1888, vol. 1, William Wells Newell listed collective aspects of the subject: 1) relics of Old English folklore; 2) lore of Negroes; 3) lore of the Indian tribes of North America; and 4) lore of French Canada, Mexico, and other special areas. These 19th-century aims are still the goals of most folklorists, with the addition of interest in the field of late immigrants and the study of any group of people "who share at least one common factor." Lore is generally explained as oral and spontaneous, but games and folk art exist, and folklore is often rewritten. The latter is especially noted in folklore "revivals." Historically, American folklore has relied heavily on imitation with the English theories and methods as models; it has shown historical bias and is now undergoing great changes. 43 notes, biblio. J. C. Crowe

134. Evans, Oliver. MELTING POT IN THE BAYOUS. *Am. Heritage 1963 15(1): 30-51, 106-107.* A survey of the various influences which made New Orleans the first melting pot in the United States. The author feels that the mixing of French, Spanish, Indian, Negro, and American cultures and blood before the Civil War produced a culture which was unique. The text is supplemented by sketches by A. R. Waud done in 1866.   C. R. Allen, Jr.

135. Fuller, Michael J. AFRICA AS SEEN BY WORLD HISTORY TEXT-BOOKS. *Social Educ. 1971 35(5): 466-477.* Points out cartographic, pictorial, and textual errors, distortions, and half-truths about Africa in world history texts commonly used in American high schools. Careful evaluation could prove instrumental in improving the quality of world history texts. At present there is no standard evaluation procedure. The National Council for the Social Studies and Social Education could do much to improve the quality of textbooks. Authors, editors, and publishers of textbooks, especially world history texts, could only respond positively to concerted professional criticism of their products. Illus., 40 notes.   D. H. Swift

136. Gans, Herbert J. REDEFINING THE SETTLEMENT'S FUNCTION FOR THE WAR ON POVERTY. *Social Work 1964 9(4): 3-12.* A hundred years ago the settlement house movement was established for the purpose of removing the deprivations of urban poverty. The European immigrant population has been replaced by Negroes, Puerto Ricans, and white Appalachians. The early success of the settlement house movement was due to the predominance of Jewish clients. The old settlement house movement wanted to change the slum-dwellers, not understand them, and to establish neighborhood democracy in the slums. Today, the settlement house must discover how socially mobile people can be helped in their efforts to become middle class. To achieve this goal, incomes have to be raised among the poor and racial discrimination has to be dealt with more forcefully than is now the case.   W. L. Willigan

137. Gérard, Albert. HISTORICAL ORIGINS AND LITERARY DESTINY OF NEGRITUDE. *Diogenes [France] 1964 48: 14-38.* Explores the shifting relationship between Africans and white men in the setting of colonial rule, particularly as expressed in literary form. The literature of negritude is compared with other, notably North American, literary expression by Negroes, and is placed in the perspective of a diversified attempt by Africans to secure for themselves by literary means a form of self-respect partly lost in the initial encounter with colonial rulers.   L. H. Legters

138. Grossack, Martin M., Blake, Elias, Jr., Chaves, Antonio F., and Roucek, Joseph S. CURRENT LITERATURE ON NEGRO EDUCATION. *J. of Negro Educ. 1965 34(1): 78-83.* Reviews the following books: *A Profile of the Negro American* (1964) by Thomas F. Pettigrew; *Crisis in Black and White* (1964) by Charles E. Silberman; *Cuba, the Economic and Social Revolution* (1964) edited by Dudley Seers; and *Contributions to Urban Sociology* (1964) edited by Ernest W. Burgess and Donald J. Bogue.   S. C. Pearson, Jr.

139. Hampton, Bill R. ON IDENTIFICATION AND NEGRO TRICKSTERS. *Southern Folklore Q. 1967 31(1): 55-65.* "Trickster is at one and the same time creator and destroyer, giver and negator, he who dupes others and is duped himself....He knows neither good nor evil yet he is responsible for both. He possesses no values...yet through his actions all values come into being." Stackolee, Brer Rabbit and John are forms of tricksters found in Negro literature, folktales, and life; all represent in varying guises efforts at identification, resistance, and winning. Special in the case of the American Negro are two severe ruptures of identity - from Africa to the New World and from the backward, rural South to urban and often urban-northern civilization. Lately, education and literacy caused the decay of the oral tale so that the most important models for identification now are in the mass media, such as Langston Hughes' character Simple. 34 notes, biblio.   H. Aptheker

140. Isaacs, Harold R. THE AMERICAN NEGRO AND AFRICA: SOME NOTES. *Phylon 1959 20(3): 219-233.* American Negroes have long been averse to giving positive recognition to Africa as the continent of their forebears. The present social and political upheaval in Africa is a challenge to American Negroes, as well as to white people. Interviews with American Negroes indicate that their attitude toward Africans - their acceptance of the stereotypes which white people created about African Negroes - affected their pride in their color and other attributes. There is only a meager literature on the American Negro-African relations, and enormous work is required to comprehend colonization movements, Liberia, Negro missions to Africa, and many other topics, ranging from earliest times to the present. In acquiring a new image of Africa, including the image of themselves which African Negroes are developing, the American Negro will acquire a new image of himself. Based on a paper read in New York, June 1959, at the Second Annual Conference of the American Society of African Culture.   L. Filler

141. Jones, Edward A. MOREHOUSE COLLEGE IN BUSINESS NINETY YEARS - BUILDING MEN. *Phylon 1957 18(3): 231-245.* Assesses the record of a liberal arts college for Negroes in the South.   C. F. Latour

142. Logan, Gwendolyn Evans. THE SLAVE IN CONNECTICUT DURING THE AMERICAN REVOLUTION. *Connecticut Hist. Soc. Bull. 1965 30(3): 73-80.* Discusses laws pertaining to the emancipation and military service of the six thousand Negroes in Connecticut during the American Revolution. The author concludes that, despite movements to end the slave trade and gradually free Negroes, severe black codes and other restrictions limited the freedom of Connecticut blacks. It is not clear how many Negroes who served in the Revolutionary armies received their freedom as a result. "That the ideals of the American Revolution and the practical...needs for fighting strength had helped bring about the emancipation of the Negro in Connecticut is not justified by the evidence." Biblio.   L. R. Murphy

143. Mathews, Marcia M. HENRY OSSAWA TANNER, AMERICAN ARTIST. *South Atlantic Q. 1966 65(4): 460-470.* The first American Negro artist to

win international acclaim, Tanner was unrivaled in the 19th century as a lyrical painter of Biblical themes. Son of a prominent Philadelphia African Methodist Episcopal Church minister, Tanner studied with Thomas Eakins and went to Paris in 1891, where he won the approval of Benjamin Constant. By the mid-1890's, Tanner was emphasizing Biblical paintings which were quite popular in the States. He remained in Paris, however, leaving it only briefly during World War I. Although Tanner may have been slighted critically in the United States because of his race, he himself always considered race incidental to talent and accomplishment. 8 illus., 5 notes.   J. M. Bumsted

144. Matras, Judah. SOCIAL STRATEGIES OF FAMILY FORMATION: SOME COMPARATIVE DATA FOR SCANDINAVIA, THE BRITISH ISLES, AND NORTH AMERICA. *Internat. Social Sci. J. 1965 17(2): 260-275.* Using census-type data on women classified by age at marriage and number of children born, the author estimates the numbers or percentages controlling or attempting to control fertility. For the United States, the tables show earlier marriage among rural groups than among urban, while in Canada urban-rural differences are nonexistent. In the 1940 U.S. Census data, Negroes married much earlier than whites with considerably less frequent practice of fertility control by Negroes, though over a period of years the Negro-white differences diminished. Some comparisons are given with field studies in the United States. 3 tables.
E. P. Stickney

145. Neyland, Leedell W. STATE-SUPPORTED HIGHER EDUCATION AMONG NEGROES IN THE STATE OF FLORIDA. *Florida Hist. Q. 1964 43(2): 105-122.* Florida's provision for higher education for Negroes started with the teacher training institutions of the 1880's, was continued through the all-Negro A. and M. University, to State financed scholarships to enable Florida Negroes to pursue graduate or professional work in other States. Now Florida Negroes seem assured of access on equal terms to all the public universities and junior colleges in Florida. Based on State papers, records of educational institutions, and secondary materials.   G. L. Lycan

146. Parsons, M. B. VIOLENCE AND CASTE IN SOUTHERN JUSTICE. *South Atlantic Q. 1961 60(4): 455-468.* Surveys the past of the American South, emphasizing the period since Reconstruction in relation to the race-caste system of justice and its concomitant violence. The author concludes that changes in southern society and politics are beginning to be reflected in southern justice and that the South may "become more like the nation" and its "archaic mechanisms of [white] monopolistic control of the law...will give way....But...the influence of the caste line in southern courts persists."   C. R. Allen, Jr.

147. Rose, Harold M. THE ALL-NEGRO TOWN: ITS EVOLUTION AND FUNCTION. *Geographical R. 1965 55(3): 362-381.* Identifies the phenomenon of the all-Negro town, breaks the towns into classes, and shows the relationship of the towns to their general environments. The author also examines the present and future development of the towns, particularly toward the suburban ideal. Maps, charts, and photos.   R. L. McBane

148. Rosenthal, Eric. THIS WAS NORTH LAWNDALE: THE TRANSPLAN-TATION OF A JEWISH COMMUNITY. *Jewish Social Studies 1960 22(2): 67-82.* A study of the sharp transition of a Chicago community from Jewish to Negro domination in 10 years. The author surveys both the roots and the results of this change. A. B. Rollins

149. Roundtree, John G. EDUCATION AND THE NEGRO. *Negro Hist. Bull. 1964 27(5): 106-108, 110.* Places educational opportunities for American Negroes in their historic setting of slavery, Reconstruction, and the crusade for free schools. The author concludes that segregated education is inferior, costly, and undesirable for the Nation; his recommendations include massive Federal aid for education. Based on secondary accounts. L. Gara

150. Shiel, John B. 175 YEARS IN ONE BOOK. *Long Island Forum 1970 33(3): 45-50.* Organized on 7 June 1794, the records of the Charity Society of Jericho and Westbury Friends are contained in a single ledger. The society was dedicated to the relief and education of the Negro, and it operated a number of schools for the education of Long Island's Negroes. After the Civil War, the society helped to support a number of southern Negro educational institutions. Today, its resources are used to support the Negro College Fund. 2 illus. G. Kurland

151. Simkins, Francis B. TOLERATING THE SOUTH'S PAST. *J. of Southern Hist. 1955 21(1): 3-16.* Southern historians should recognize the importance of the social hierarchy of their region and its distinctions of race and class. They might well focus on what is believed to have occurred as well as on actual events, including many aspects of legends, prejudices, and superstitions as part of an interpretation of the South. Historians should accept the values of the region and the time. D. Davis

152. Sisk, Glenn. THE NEGRO COLLEGES IN ATLANTA. *J. of Negro Educ. 1964 33(2): 131-135.* The author briefly discusses the histories of Atlanta University, founded in 1867, and Spelman College, founded in 1881. He relies on published histories of the schools, college catalogs, and other published material. S. C. Pearson, Jr.

153. Sisk, Glenn. THE NEGRO COLLEGES IN ATLANTA. *J. of Negro Educ. 1964 33(4): 404-408.* Briefly traces the history of Morris Brown College, Clark University, Gammon Theological Seminary, and the Atlanta School of Social Work; the affiliation of Atlanta University, Morehouse College, and Spelman College in 1929; and the formation of the Interdenominational Theological Center in 1961. Based on published histories, college bulletins, and catalogs. S. C. Pearson, Jr.

154. Smith, T. Lynn. THE CHANGING NUMBER AND DISTRIBUTION OF THE AGED NEGRO POPULATION OF THE UNITED STATES. *Phylon 1958 18(4): 339-354.* The Negro population of the United States is aging

rapidly. In 1900 only one Negro out of every 34 had passed his 65th birthday, whereas in 1950 the corresponding proportion was one out of 18. In 1960 there will be in the Nation about 1,150,000 Negroes of 65 years of age or more, and this number seems certain to increase steadily until the year 1990, when a small and temporary decrease should take place. The larger number of Negro babies born in the years 1875-84 in comparison with the births in the years 1865-74 is the principal cause of the increase, although lowered mortality of Negroes aged 55 or more accounts for about 30 percent of the gain.   A

155. Snoxall, R. A. AMERICA, ENGLAND AND AFRICAN LANGUAGES. *African Affairs [Great Britain] 1970 69(274): 64-66.* Discusses the teaching of African languages in the United States and England, including the teaching of Swahili at the University of California, Los Angeles. The author taught African languages in a number of schools in connection with the Oxford University Institute of Commonwealth Studies and the School of Oriental and African Studies. There was more demand for Swahili among caucasians than Negroes; it is difficult to find Negroes qualified to teach the language and some Negro students refuse to take the class unless it is.   N. E. Tutorow

156. Stokes, Maurice S. A BRIEF SURVEY OF HIGHER EDUCATION FOR NEGROES. *Social Studies 1964 55(6): 214-220.* A comprehensive, detailed survey of higher education for Negroes in the United States. The period from the establishment of Ashmun Institute in 1854 (now Lincoln University in Pennsylvania) to the year 1960, is covered. Phases of higher education included in the survey are: 1) total enrollment, 2) the type of legal control, whether public or private, 3) enrollment by sex, 4) decennial increases in number of institutions and increases in their enrollments, 5) patterns of curriculum development and organization, 6) types and levels of degrees granted and graduate research, 7) special educational features of curricula, 8) inter-institutional cooperation, and 9) business management and finance.   L. Raife

157. Thernstrom, Stephan. THE CASE OF BOSTON. *Massachusetts Hist. Soc. Pro. 1967 79: 109-122.* Analyzes social mobility in Boston since 1880 and reaches the conclusion that there never existed a rigid social structure in Boston that precluded mobility between classes. Despite the Brahmin influence, Boston's society was influenced by the same basic forces as in other American cities and a comparison of in and out migration shows a great deal more change and flux in population than commonly supposed. The author contends that there is more upward social mobility than there used to be and outlines some of the peculiar difficulties of the urban Negro in attempting to move upward under present circumstances. Based on quantitative analyses of Boston records and monographs on other cities; 12 notes.   J. B. Duff

158. Thorpe, Earl E. AFRICA IN THE THOUGHT OF NEGRO AMERICANS. *Negro Hist. Bull. 1959 23(1): 5-10.* Traces the attitudes of American Negroes toward Africa from colonial times to the present. Negroes have held diverse points of view ranging from a complete rejection of all things African to the black nationalism of the Marcus Garvey colonization movement. The author

detects a growing recognition of past African achievements and predicts that in the future, Afro-Americans will become even more devoted to their African homeland. L. Gara

159. Toll, William. THE CRISIS OF FREEDOM: TOWARD AN INTERPRE-TATION OF NEGRO LIFE. *J. of Am. Studies [Great Britain] 1969 3(2): 265-279.* "Endeavours to find substance in the accumulated academic literature in order to test an hypothesis suggested by E. Franklin Frazier: namely, that Negro patterns of life are adjustments to the unique environment of the New World that parallel white adjustments in almost every respect." Frazier argued that " while race prejudice has not been altogether a negligible factor, the general character of...Negro communities has been determined by the same economic and cultural forces that have shaped the organization of the community as a whole." In support of this thesis, a critique of the monographic literature published since the 1890's is presented. D. J. Abramoske

160. Truzzi, Marcello. THE 100 AMERICAN SONGBAG: CONSERVATIVE FOLKSONGS IN AMERICA. *Western Folklore 1969 28(1): 27-40.* Folksongs presently in the limelight are usually identified with "liberal" politics. This over-looks the folksongs and quasi-folksongs of the past that frequently identified their sentiments with the status quo. Lyrics of antiunion, anti-Chinese labor, Ku Klux Klan, southern proslave, oppressed Negro, oppressed minorities, antievolutionist, and fence-straddling songs are included as examples. The criterion for collection of folksongs should be historical accuracy, not propaganda. If the present bias in collecting continues then "the cultural diversity" of American song will be the last consideration of future historians. 24 notes. D. L. Smith

161. Unsigned. CURRENT LITERATURE ON NEGRO EDUCATION. *J. of Negro Educ. 1965 34(2): 178-183.* Reviews of John Wilson's *Education and Changing West African Culture;* John A. Carpenter's *Sword and Olive Branch: Oliver Otis Howard;* Milton M. Gordon's *Assimilation in American Life - The Role of Race, Religion, and National Origin;* Thomas F. Grossett's *Race - The History of an Idea in America;* Esther Raushenbush's *The Student and His Studies;* and E. Franklin Frazier's *The Negro Church in America.*
S. C. Pearson, Jr.

162. Weisenburger, Francis P. WILLIAM SANDERS SCARBOROUGH. *Ohio Hist. 1962 71(3): 203-226, 1963 72(1): 25-50.* Part I. "Early Life at Wilberforce," 1962 71(3): 203-226. A biographical study of Scarborough, who was born into slavery in Georgia in 1852. He acquired an education and graduated from Oberlin College in 1875. Following graduation he taught at Lewis High School, Macon, Georgia, at Payne Institute, Cokesbury, South Carolina, and at Wilberforce University, Wilberforce, Ohio. Scarborough went to Wilberforce as a teacher of the classics in 1877, and between 1908 and 1920 he was president of that institu-tion. Based mainly on an unpublished biography of Scarborough prepared by his widow and others, and material in the Scarborough Papers at Wilberforce Uni-versity.Part II."Scholarship, The Negro, Religion and Politics," 1963 72(1): 25-50.

Reviews Scarborough's writings, speeches, professional activities, and travels while he was on the faculty of Wilberforce University, and relates his career in the 1920's, when he was no longer a faculty member. In his scholarship Scarborough concentrated on classical languages and literatures, philology, and African languages and cultures. He also concerned himself with the problems of the Negro in the United States. He was a leader in the development of Negro education, advocating the attainment of a classical education by Negroes, in opposition to the emphasis on industrial education advocated by Booker T. Washington. Beginning in the 1880's Scarborough occupied a position of leadership in the African Methodist Episcopal Church, a position which occupied much of his time during the remainder of his life. Active in politics, Scarborough was recognized as a leader of the Republican Party both nationally and in Ohio. He participated in the Republican campaign in 1920, and, in the months which followed, he sought a Federal appointment. He was given a position in the Department of Agriculture which he occupied from November 1921 to 31 December 1923. At this post he was assigned the task of providing information to aid Negro farmers. In 1924 Scarborough returned to Wilberforce, Ohio, where he died on 9 September 1926.   S. L. Jones

163. Wesley, Charles H. DO NEGROES BELIEVE IN THEMSELVES? *Negro Hist. Bull. 1957 21(1): 2, 9-15.* Pleads for a renewed emphasis on the study and teaching of Negro history as an aid to better race relations. Such study should reveal the rich Negro background in African culture, call attention to the Negro contribution to America's heritage, and help give Negroes a faith in themselves as a distinct people.   L. Gara

164. Wilkerson, Doxey. THE GHETTO SCHOOL STRUGGLES IN HISTORICAL PERSPECTIVE. *Sci. and Soc. 1969 33(2): 130-149.* A historical survey of the American Negroes' various educational endeavors and restrictions, covering the years 1640-1960. The author finds that the development of black control over their own education is a part of the struggle for equality. Based mostly on secondary material; 45 notes.   R. S. Burns

165. --. [REEVALUATION OF SOUTHERN NOVELISTS, A SYMPOSIUM.] *Mississippi Q. 1967 20(2): 69-102.*
    Pugh, Griffith T. GEORGE WASHINGTON CABLE, pp. 69-76. A study of published works dealing with George Washington Cable reveals a high-water mark of interest in Cable in the decade of the 1880's, followed by a decline in interest until 1925 when reassessment was occasioned by his death. Since World War II interest in Cable has increased considerably. It has not been necessary to rediscover, reinterpret, or promote the author; the superficial view, however, has been that he was a talented fiction writer, sidetracked by his enthusiasm for social reform. Of course, there are critics who see Cable as a hero, losing as artist while gaining as human being. The opinion that he was realistic in his proposed solution to relations between Negro and white is questionable, since men do not behave in the unprejudiced way Cable wished. Reading his short stories, novels, and polemic works is still pleasurable and profitable.

Mason, Julian D., Jr. CHARLES W. CHESNUTT AS SOUTHERN AU-
THOR, pp. 77-89. Emphasizes the "Southernness" of Chesnutt in an effort to
correct the error of omission of the author from histories of southern literature.
Although Chesnutt was born in Ohio (1858), his parents were North Carolinians
who returned there in 1866. He therefore spent 17 formative years in the South.
The majority of his stories and articles deal with southern subject matter, and his
three novels reveal his concern for the welfare of the South. Chesnutt's straight-
forward subject matter, as well as his race (Negro), undoubtedly has prevented
his being claimed by the South along with many less important and less southern
writers. When remembered, it has been only as a local colorist or folklorist, not
as a novelist. 13 notes.

Watkins, Floyd C. THOMAS WOLFE, pp. 90-96. Both the greatest praise
and the most severe condemnation possible have probably already been written
about Thomas Wolfe, and a new and fair evaluation is still impossible. The
discipline of modern methods of criticism and Wolfe's art seem to move at cross
purposes. Further study is needed of Wolfe's humor and his use of folklore.
Critical description and knowledge of his style, rhetoric, and oratory are also
needed. Essential in evaluation of Wolfe is consideration of his variety and
artlessness. At his best he was able to portray human complexity and, at his worst,
he was creating only a simple and single tone. The contradictions and vacillations
in Wolfe's writing are almost unbelievable - from oversimplification to complexity
and from hatred to adoration, interspersed with objectivity. The truth about
Wolfe is complex. 11 notes.

Parks, Edd Winfield. JAMES BRANCH CABELL, pp. 97-102. This article was originally part of a symposium, "Re-Evaluations of Southern Novelists,"
presented by the Southeastern American Studies Association 12 November 1966.
One problem in the study of James Branch Cabell is the inability of his admirers
to agree on which of his books are his best. A majority of critics have apparently
preferred *Figures of Earth* (1921). Among Cabell's weaknesses are the elaborate
façades used for introductions, anagrammatic puzzles diverting much attention
from the story, and topical allusions which now require footnotes for younger
readers. On the positive side should be included the development of a valid
aesthetic for the philosophical romance - literature should present man as he
ought to be rather than as he is. Such virtues as "distinction and clarity...beauty
and sympathy...tenderness and truth and urbanity" Cabell's prose embodied, as
well as humanism and faith in man's indomitable will. The romance seems
banned from popular favor for all time, but perceptive readers will continue to
read Cabell as the writer of the best philosophical romances of this century. 10
notes.   R. V. Calvert

166. --. [SOUTHWESTERN FOLK HUMOR.] *Mississippi Q. 1964 17(2): 63-
122.*

Simpson, Lewis P. THE HUMOR OF THE OLD SOUTHWEST, pp.
63-66. Introduces four articles which were presented at the meeting of the American Studies Association of the Lower Mississippi in October 1963. The author
was chairman of the program.

Anderson, John Q. SCHOLARSHIP IN SOUTHWESTERN HUMOR -
PAST AND PRESENT, pp. 67-86. In analyzing criticism of the nature, influence, and significance of the humor of the Old Southwest, one discovers two

major theories: the environmental beginning about 1835, and the sociopolitical dating from the 1930's. The assumption that the humor of the Old Southwest was completely indigenous has been discounted, while attributing to it an ulterior motive of keeping a lower class in its place is falsely placing 20th-century thinking into the 19th century. The primary purpose of southwestern humorists was entertainment, and the merciless exposure of ignorance is characteristic of all great satirists. Scholarly investigation needs to be done of both the major and minor humorists with some concentration on literary influences. Still unanswered is the question of absence of influence of European romanticism. The folklore content of southwestern humor and the influence of oral folk tradition have not been fully evaluated. The humor of the Old Southwest, however, is well on the way toward full recognition as an important part of American literature. 50 notes.

Bettersworth, John K. THE HUMOR OF THE OLD SOUTHWEST: YESTERDAY AND TODAY, pp. 87-94. American as well as western and southern, the humor of the Old Southwest originated in human nature and included all social classes as objects of its satire, but the favorite was the yokel, a backwoodsman and usually a hunter. In the literary style of the polite essayist (usually Addisonian), writers undertook to record the humor of the southwestern rustic that they saw and heard. Developed by antebellum writers and essentially unchanged today, the formula for yokel humor assumes that the country yokel is per se very funny, even to himself, the object or perpetrator of some practical joke, a shark or completely gullible, profane, uncouth, with very poor grammar and spelling (if literate) and a ridiculous name. While the poor white was the object of laughter in the antebellum period, it was not until after the Civil War and emancipation that the Negro became a staple of southern humor. As was the case with other racial humor, Negro humor has been threatened with annihilation since the Negro's discovery that he is no longer funny to himself. With nationalization resulting in the threatened extinction of regional and class humor, only the southern yokel remains to be laughed at, until he perhaps achieves a similar fate.

Wheeler, Otis B. SOME USES OF FOLK HUMOR BY FAULKNER, pp. 107-122. Following a brief review of the origins and characteristics of American folk humor, an assessment is made of Faulkner's use of the materials and techniques of that humor in some of his novels and in such short stories as "Black Music," "Spotted Horses," and "Was," the last of which has frontier humor in an almost pure form. The Snopes stories are the chief repository of frontier humor in Faulkner's work. He modified folk humor for his purposes in four principal ways: justification by humor in expressing his comment on decadence, weakness, and foolishness; in the contrast of humorous qualities in the Snopes stories and such frightening elements as the demonic hero; by treating in a sophisticated manner material from folk humor tradition, with a resulting somewhat grotesque quality; and in "manipulation of the point of view," particularly well done in *The Town* (New York: Random House, 1957). With three narrators completing the ambivalent picture, both laughable and frightful at the same time, Faulkner did, as Malcolm Cowley said, actually "unite...three of the dominant trends in American literature from the beginning: that of the psychological horror story...and that of realistic frontier humor, with Mark Twain as its best example." 18 notes.

R. V. Calvert

Traditions in Afro-American Culture   45

167. --. [THE AMERICAN NEGRO COLLEGE.] *Harvard Educ. R. 1967 37.* Jencks, Christopher and Riesman, David. THE AMERICAN NEGRO COLLEGE. (1): 3-60. Considers the history (1865-1967), present status, and future prospects of the American Negro college. They rank it low in student aptitudes, faculty creativity, and intellectual and moral ferment, and characterize its atmosphere as repressive, monotonous, and conservative. The best colleges rank near the middle of all American universities. The authors conclude that for social and psychological reasons the Negro colleges, both private and public ones, are not likely to disappear through either dissolution or integration and are likewise not likely to change their present policies. The initiative for integration, if and when it comes to the public colleges, will have to come from the outside. Based on field work, interviews, and published sources; 57 notes.

Wright, Stephen J., Mays, Benjamin E., Gloster, Hugh M., Dent, Albert W., Jencks, Christopher, and Riesman, David. "THE AMERICAN NEGRO COLLEGE": FOUR RESPONSES AND A REPLY. (3): 451-468. All four responses to the Jencks and Riesman essay protest what they consider its unjustified slighting attitude and undocumented generalized changes presented in "journalese" rather than in the language of scholarship. They point out that Negro colleges are unfairly compared to colleges like Harvard and Oberlin; that no account is taken of their being underfinanced and attended by underprepared students; that the investigation lacked a solid research design and remained superficial; that evidence of the success or promise of Negro colleges is overlooked or dismissed. Jencks and Riesman reply that theirs was not a major research project but a chapter in a book on "many sorts of colleges and universities"; that they expected criticism; that they hope the Negro colleges will be strengthened in nonimitative ways. They suggest that the Negro colleges should carry out their own self-studies to convince others of their strength and achievement.

J. Herbst

Economic History

168. Bloch, Herman D. THE NEW YORK CITY NEGRO AND OCCUPATIONAL EVICTION, 1860-1910. *Internat. R. of Social Hist. 1960 5(1): 26-38.* Even before legal liberation (1827), free Negroes in New York dominated certain occupations similar to those learned under slavery and normally considered beneath the dignity of whites: as barbers, longshoremen, waiters, bootblacks, servants, laborers, etc. From 1840 to 1860 and especially from 1860 to 1910, the Negroes' occupational status regressed, although industrialization increased unskilled labor. White immigrants not only monopolized the new jobs but increasingly evicted Negroes from their traditional occupations. "Regardless of the social status of any white ethnic group, where the white man dominated the labor situation, he pushed his black brothers into jobs for which he did not care to compete." This economic subordination restricted the Negro's economic and social mobility and relegated him to an artificial and hereditary "helot status" long after liberation.

A. H. Kittell

169. Dowd, Douglas F. A COMPARATIVE ANALYSIS OF ECONOMIC DEVELOPMENT IN THE AMERICAN WEST AND SOUTH. *J. of Econ. Hist. 1956 16(4): 558-574.* Contends that the South, not the West, should be called an underdeveloped region. Western development cannot be called regional because it was too closely related to what happened in the East and overseas. The West was integrated into the Nation's economy, and even when the per capita income was lower than in the East, it was not "underdeveloped," since it was as fully exploited as contemporary technique allowed. The South, on the other hand, had the lowest per capita income, highest illiteracy rates and worst hygienic conditions of the country. The "industrial revolution" of the South in the 1880's was as one-sided as the agrarian development and did not make the South independent. Conditions could have been improved if Negroes and whites had combined their forces, but the race question prevented this. The author concludes that both the West and the South were short of capital and therefore economically dependent. Both were exploited, but the West was exploited because of its natural resources and the South because of its human resources in cheap labor. Finally, the South stood politically apart, while Westerners tried to improve their situation by ordinary political procedures.   D. van Arkel

170. Dummett, Clifton O. THE NEGRO IN DENTAL EDUCATION: A REVIEW OF IMPORTANT OCCURRENCES. *Phylon 1959 20(4): 379-388.* The prestige of medicine and the higher income resulting from its practice, have made it a more popular field for Negro professionals than dentistry. In 1840 the number of Negro dentists - all former apprentices, rather than dental school graduates - was estimated at 120. Since then, Howard University and Meharry Medical College have been responsible for educating most Negro dentists in the United States. Their number increased slowly: there were 478 in 1910, and 1,019 in 1920. "National Negro Health Week," instituted in 1916 by Booker T. Washington, helped focus attention on the need for dentists. The Class B status of the Negro dental college inspired Dr. Mordecai W. Johnson, new president of Howard, to insist, in 1926, that a first-rate dental college be established. By 1930 the number of Negro dentists was 1,773, but this was still inadequate, and the economic depression drastically affected the number of students entering dentistry. The achievement of Class A status by both Howard and Meharry, and other milestones offering dignity and competence to Negroes in the field - including some recognition by white dental associations - have not erased the fact that Negro dentists need more fully to appreciate their responsibilities to American dentistry and to the public.   L. Filler

171. Gross, James A. HISTORIANS AND THE LITERATURE OF THE NEGRO WORKER. *Labor Hist. 1969 10(3): 536-546.* Surveys the primary source literature on the Negro worker in America and suggests a number of topics for research. 33 notes.   L. L. Athey

172. Kemmerer, Donald L. THE CHANGING PATTERN OF AMERICAN ECONOMIC DEVELOPMENT. *J. of Econ. Hist. 1956 16(4): 575-589.* An analysis of the changes in the relations between land, labor, and capital throughout American history. As long as land was very cheap - the cost of the Louisiana

Purchase amounted to 3 cents an acre - labor was very expensive, thus stimulating slavery, and capital was extremely scarce. With the great wave of immigration, labor became cheap, while land became relatively scarce and therefore more expensive. Because much capital was needed for expansion, the government's main concern was to protect capital. The situation changed again after World War I, when immigration came to a standstill, and consequently the cost of labor rose. The price of land continued to rise, but capital was then abundant, and America became a creditor nation. The author shows how these changes affected economic theory of the various periods concerned. D. van Arkel

173. Klingberg, Frank J. THE ROLE OF THE NEGRO IN THE BUILDING OF THE AMERICAS. *Negro Hist. Bull. 1957 21(3): 51-52.* Emphasizes the important part played by Negroes in building the Americas, not only by immigration, but also through their economic contribution as a major source of labor.
L. Gara

174. Maxwell, Robert S. LUMBERMEN OF THE EAST TEXAS FRONTIER. *Forest Hist. 1965 9(1): 12-16.* The East Texas region, a timber region as large as Maine, was exploited mainly from 1865 to 1900. The first cut was longleaf pine, followed by shortleaf and loblolly pine, which also provided a second growth before 1965. Owners, both absentee and immigrant, and managers of business firms were usually from the northeastern United States and the Lake States, but the work forces were local whites and Afro-Americans. Henry J. Lutcher and G. Bedell Moore of Pennsylvania formed the L & M Company which invested in a variety of forest products and other industries between 1876 and 1965. John Henry Kirby invested in timber-related industries and organized the Kirby Lumber Company with the aid of eastern capital about 1900. William Joyce formed the Trinity County Lumber Company in 1890; by 1930, the company cut out and suspended East Texas operations, moving to the west coast and British Columbia. All three firms included railroad investment in their portfolio. The Texas lumber manufacturers organized themselves into a trade association. They cooperated on pricing and on political, legislative, labor, and wage policies without antitrust prosecution but violently and successfully opposed the organization of labor despite the best efforts of the Brotherhood of Timber Workers. 2 illus., 18 notes.
B. A. Vatter

175. Nicholls, William H. SOUTHERN TRADITION AND REGIONAL ECONOMIC PROGRESS. *Southern Econ. J. 1960 26(3): 187-198.* "Insofar as the New South has made material progress, it has done so *in spite of* the strongly inhibiting social, political, psychological, and philosophical elements in the Old South's cultural heritage." The major objective of this paper is to identify and analyze certain key noneconomic factors in the southern tradition which have offered formidable barriers to the material progress of the region and which, if ignored, will continue to do so. The author focuses his attention on five principal aspects of southern tradition: the dominance of agrarian values, the rigidity of the social structure, the undemocratic political structure, the weakness of social responsibility, and conformity of thought and behavior. He traces historically how and when each became an important part of the southern tradition and

analyzes carefully the deleterious effects of each on the rate of southern economic progress. He finds that the race issue has dominated all aspects of southern tradition and argues that southerners must at last face up to the question of whether they want material progress badly enough to give up race-oriented traditions which are inconsistent with it. The author presents a positive program for Southern economic development and appeals for a political and economic leadership courageous and responsible enough to enable the South to realize at last its full economic potential.   A

176. Pellegrin, Roland J. and Parenton, Vernon J. THE IMPACT OF SOCIO-ECONOMIC CHANGE ON RACIAL GROUPS IN A RURAL SETTING. *Phylon* 1962 23(1): 55-60. Technological change has been a major force in altering industrial and occupational composition in Bertrandville, a Negro community in Assumption Parish in rural south Louisiana. Sugarcane growers of Anglo-Saxon origin there developed the slavery system. Since emancipation, sugar production has been affected by mechanization and the development of insecticides and herbicides. Bertrandville Negroes used to suffer cyclical periods of employment and unemployment throughout the year. They are now much less affected by seasonal demands.   L. Filler

177. Rogers, William W. NEGRO KNIGHTS OF LABOR IN ARKANSAS: A CASE STUDY OF THE "MISCELLANEOUS" STRIKE. *Labor Hist.* 1969 10(3): 498-505. Assesses a strike by black members of the Knights of Labor against the Tate cotton plantation in Pulaski County, Arkansas. It was an effort by an all-black assembly to gain economic redress, but it was rapidly turned into a racial confrontation. Based on the Little Rock *Daily Arkansas Gazette;* 27 notes.   L. L. Athey

178. Smith, Wilson. WILLIAM PALEY'S THEOLOGICAL UTILITARIAN-ISM IN AMERICA. *William and Mary Q.* 1954 11(3): 402-424. Discusses the impact of Paley's *Moral Philosophy* and his *Natural Theology* on American thought. The former, stressing Locke's concept of property, was discarded under the influence of dogmatic abolitionism and the southern defense of slavery. The latter was standard reading in colleges in the antebellum period until John Fiske dealt it its death blow.   E. Oberholzer, Jr.

179. Street, James H. COTTON MECHANIZATION AND ECONOMIC DE-VELOPMENT. *Am. Econ. R.* 1955 45(4): 566-583. Analyzes the results obtained from a study of the causes that retarded the use of mechanized methods in cotton production in the Southern United States. The author distinguishes and discusses institutional, technological, and exogenous factors in the process of development. Institutional forces, chiefly slavery and a staple crop economy, retarded progressive changes. Technical inventions, originating from a variety of sources, coincided in their effects on harvesting, planting, and cotton weaving techniques. A high rate of population growth, in itself a result of previous technological influences, combined with a lag in institutional adjustments to inhibit economic improvement and the mechanization of agriculture. Biblio.
                                              R. Mueller

180. Unsigned. BROWN SKIN AND BRIGHT LEAF: THE STORY OF THE NEGRO'S ROLE IN THE TOBACCO INDUSTRY. *Negro Hist. Bull. 1955 19(1/2): 3-10, 27-33.* Sketches Negro contributions to American tobacco culture and the tobacco industry from its 17th-century beginnings to the present. The article was sponsored by the P. Lorillard Company and contains considerable advertising material.   L. Gara

181. Wheeler, James O. and Brunn, Stanley D. AN AGRICULTURAL GHETTO: NEGROES IN CASS COUNTY, MICHIGAN, 1845-1968. *Geographical R. 1969 59(3): 310-329.* "The century-old ghetto in southwestern Michigan suggests several parallels with urban-ghetto expansion and spatial structure. Once formed, the Negro farm group prospered for several generations, and it was not until after World War II that the agricultural land slowly began changing to white ownership. However, in the past ten years, owing principally to Negro migration from metropolitan areas such as Chicago, Negro farm ownership has increased, and the incipient fragmentation of the ghetto has been reversed. Although most Negro ownership is confined to the ghetto, there has been recent diffusion of black ownership to other parts of Cass County, and discrimination in the sale of farmland in the county seems to be less marked than in the past."
J

182. Whyte, Abbie. CHRISTIAN ELEMENTS IN NEGRO AMERICAN MUSLIM RELIGIOUS BELIEFS. *Phylon 1964 25(4): 382-388.* Traces and compares the history and some of the beliefs of the Moorish Science Temple and the Temple of Islam. Concludes that the sacred texts of these two Moslem groups are similar and seem to have been derived from the *Aquarian Gospel of Jesus the Christ,* a theosophist document written by Levi H. Dowling and first published in 1906.   S. C. Pearson, Jr.

Religion & the Churches

183. Allen, L. Scott. TOWARD PRESERVING THE HISTORY OF THE CENTRAL JURISDICTION. *Methodist Hist. 1968 7(1): 24-30.* The history of the Central Jurisdiction, the Negro portion of the Methodist Church, has been far reaching in its influence and significance. The author discusses the role of the Negro ministry, the laity, and Negro institutions in the Methodist Church from 1775 to the present.   H. L. Calkin

184. Berger, Monroe. DIE SCHWARZEN MUSLIMS [The Black Muslims]. *Monat [West Germany] 1965 17(198): 13-25, (199): 58-67.* Traces the influence

of Islam on the Negroes of Africa during medieval and early modern times and summarizes the evidence of Islam among slaves in America. The background of the Black Muslim movement in the United States in this century is then described. A predecessor was the Moorish Science Temple of America founded just before World War I by Timothy Drew. More directly connected with today's Black Muslims was the sect led by Wallace D. Fard in the early 1930's. After Fard disappeared in 1934, Elijah Poole (Elijah Muhammad) became the leader of some of Fard's followers and created the present Black Muslim organization whose ceremonies, customs, and religious beliefs are described.   D. H. Norton

185. Carroll, Kenneth L. QUAKERISM IN CAROLINE COUNTY, MARY-LAND: ITS RISE AND DECLINE. *Bull. of Friends Hist. Assoc. 1959 48(2): 83-102.* Traces the development of Quakerism in Caroline County from its appearance in 1727 until its disappearance in 1946. Quakerism in Caroline County reached its peak with the accession of the Nicholites, a similar sect, in 1798, and immediately thereafter. It began to decline in the 1840's because of emigration to the cities and to the West, especially Indiana, opposition to slavery, a rigid code of behavior, and the widespread appeal of Methodism. Four of the five meetings disbanded before the end of the 19th century, and the fifth in 1946. Based on the minutes of the monthly meetings of Friends in the Hall of Records, Annapolis, Maryland.   T. L. Moir

186. Carter, Paul A. RECENT HISTORIOGRAPHY OF THE PROTESTANT CHURCHES IN AMERICA. *Church Hist. 1968 37(1): 95-107.* Summarizes shifts in Protestant church history over the past 35 years and offers suggestions for future work in the area. The dominant position of neo-orthodox or liberal theology, the narrow definition of a Protestant "mainstream," and the virtual exclusion of groups such as Lutherans and Mormons from consideration have been challenged. The distinction between secular and religious histories of religion is no longer significant. Nonetheless the cleavage between religious history and church history or between the study of religion as a prophetic movement and religion as a series of institutions continues. While recognizing the values of a churchly history even of "religions of the Christian perimeter" the author cautions that some aspects of American religion such as Negro religion, New Thought, or "peace of mind" do not lend themselves to such treatment and that the tendency to speak of church rather than churches may mask a failure to appreciate the positive aspects of religious pluralism. Based on recently published literature in the field; 55 notes.   S. C. Pearson, Jr.

187. Christopher, Stefan C. THE NEGRO CHURCH IN THE U.S.A. *Organon 1971 2(2): 4-12.* The Negro church in the United States grew out of the environment and the institution of slavery, and is not linked directly to the "sect-like," the Negro churches were a response to their group's economic deprivation. The Negro, since he could not compete in the white world, would get along in the next world and in his own church. As white attitudes toward the Negro have softened,

Negro leadership, including Negro church leadership, has pushed forward not only in church matters but in the civil sphere as well. The result, which is inevitable, will be the incorporation of Black America into the white power structure. As this takes place membership in the Negro churches will decline. All forms of religious need will not disappear, however, and as the Negro is integrated into white society his religion will be indistinguishable from that of the general population. Based on primary and secondary sources. P. W. Kennedy

188. Denisoff, R. Serge. THE RELIGIOUS ROOTS OF THE AMERICAN SONG OF PERSUASION. *Western Folklore 1970 29(3): 175-184.* Many songs of propaganda and protest in America came originally from religious songs. Looks at the growth of early religious music as a means of communicating a message. Methodism and the frontier camp meeting created many of the methods later used by protesters. From these roots came Abolitionists, Grangers, and Populists. Eventually the labor movement adopted and rewrote familiar religious songs to make them a vehicle of protest. In such ways the Industrial Workers of the World (IWW) and the Communist Party of the early 20th century came to adopt protest songs as a key element in their fight to organize unskilled labor. The civil rights movement has used religious songs extensively. Compares the original hymns and the revised songs of persuasion. Based primarily on printed sources; 42 notes. R. A. Trennert

189. Drake, Richard B. THE GROWTH OF SEGREGATION IN AMERI-CAN CONGREGATIONALISM IN THE SOUTH. *Negro Hist. Bull. 1958 21(6): 135-137.* In pre-Civil War times some of the Congregational churches in the South practiced racial segregation. The integrated churches founded by the American Missionary Association during Reconstruction did not appeal to many Southern whites. Segregated Congregationalism of the post-Reconstruction period began in Georgia in the 1880's and by the end of that decade the National Council of the Congregational Church had accommodated itself to the Southern attitude on race and accepted a policy of segregation. L. Gara

190. Jason, William C., Jr. THE DELAWARE ANNUAL CONFERENCE OF THE METHODIST CHURCH, 1864-1965. *Methodist Hist. 1966 4(4): 26-40.* The background, establishment, growth, and eventual dissolution of the Delaware Conference of the Methodist Episcopal Church are recounted. The attempts to educate preachers, their influence on the Negro population, and their relationship with the white churches and the administrative organization are described. H. L. Calkin

191. King, Willis J. THE NEGRO MEMBERSHIP OF THE (FORMER) METHODIST CHURCH IN THE (NEW) UNITED METHODIST

CHURCH. *Methodist Hist. 1969 7(3): 32-43.* An account of the place the Negro has held in the Methodist Church from 1776 to 1939, including the acceptance of the Negro in an integrated church at first, the effect of division within the church over slavery in 1844, the establishment of all-Negro administrative organizations, the role of the Freedman's Aid Society and its successors, the issue of Negro membership in the Methodist union in 1939, and the establishment of a central jurisdiction based upon race rather than geography as was true of the white members of the church. 34 notes.   H. L. Calkin

192. Mounger, Dwyn M. RACIAL ATTITUDES IN THE PRESBYTERIAN CHURCH IN THE UNITED STATES. 1944-1954. *J. of Presbyterian Hist. 1970 48(1): 38-68.* Discusses racial attitudes of the southern Presbyterian Church in the United States through articles in two denominational journals, the conservative *Southern Presbyterian Journal* and the reform-minded *Presbyterian Outlook.* This church is the most regional of all major Protestant bodies in America, confined almost totally to the area of the old Confederacy and the border States. Traditionalists opposed the church's statements on social and political issues and defined the church's function as exclusively spiritual. These "preservers" relied heavily on Biblical passages to oppose integration and other measures of social reform. The "reformers" through the General Assembly and the Federal Council of Churches urged that the social gospel was an integral part of Christianity. Reformers saw the state replacing the church in the realm of morality and sought to reverse this trend. They insisted that church survival was dependent on a new policy responsive to social needs. The reformers, advocating gradualism in racial matters, grew stronger through the decade. They were successful in the General Assembly's Division of Christian Relations which issued two major statements in 1954, "The Church and Segregation," and "A Statement to Southern Christians." These reports opposed segregation and commended the Supreme Court's school desegregation decision, and were adopted by the church's General Assembly in 1954. Based on secondary sources; 139 notes.   S. C. Pearson, Jr.

193. Piper, John F., Jr. THE FORMATION OF THE SOCIAL POLICY OF THE FEDERAL COUNCIL OF CHURCHES. *J. of Church and State 1969 11(1): 63-82.* The Federal Council of Churches developed a social policy slowly - by action, by pronouncement, and by research and study. It was not tied to the member denominations since funds came primarily from individuals and denominations often appointed representatives to the council who were interested in the council's work. The author indicates the contours of its developing social policy up to 1916 by focusing on four aspects - economic problems, church-state relations, race relations, and international relations. It denounced selfish nationalism and promoted arbitration of international disputes. It called for protection of workers' health, abolition of child labor, and an equitable distribution of the industrial product. Also, it accepted a modified principle of church-state separation. With some difficulty, the council decided to work for social justice for Negroes and rejected racial separation. Based on published council reports and proceedings and on secondary works; 44 notes.   G. W. Hull

194. Rainwater, Percy L. INDIAN MISSIONS AND MISSIONARIES. *J. of Mississippi Hist. 1965 28(1): 15-39.* Describes the mission of the Reverend Joseph Bullen, a Presbyterian minister, at the Chickasaw Towns, 1799-1802; the development of the Federal policy encouraging agriculture and domestic manufacturing among Indians, which culminated in the enactment of "the so-called Civilization Law" of 1819; and the Presbyterian mission which the Reverend Thomas C. Stuart established in the Chickasaw nation in 1821. Bullen closed his mission because his assistants displeased the Chickasaw. By 1834 Stuart's mission converted more than a hundred Indians, Negroes, and whites and established schools which taught several hundred children. Based on secondary works and published diaries, letters, and Federal papers.   J. W. Hillje

195. Reese, Ruth. NEGERKIRKEN I USA [The Negro church in the United States]. *Samtiden [Norway] 1964 73(10): 584-591.* The author, a Negro singer, was born in Alabama, raised in Chicago, and studied music at Northwestern University. In 1963 she was awarded the "anniversary medal" of the Norwegian student association (Det norske studentersamfund). The article, which is related to the reoccurring acts of violence against Negro churches in the American South, is a brief survey of religious life among American Negroes since the arrival of slaves to the American Colonies. The Negro churches began to appear after the emancipation of the slaves in 1863. To the Negroes, the church became a place of emotional refuge where they felt temporarily secure from the psychological and material hardships they had to suffer during their daily lives in the white man's world. The Negro, who served as an officer in his church and who may have worked as a street cleaner during the rest of the week, achieved a sense of "high dignity" while on duty in his church. In addition to their religious functions, Negro churches also developed a variety of social functions, such as providing health care to the sick and the aged, aid to the unemployed, family guidance, and educational services to children and adults. A typical Sunday in a Negro church is described. Finally, the author makes some references to the civil rights movement since 1954, noting that the bombing of Negro churches consituted an attempt to strike at the vital nerve of Negro society, thereby apparently hoping to cripple the civil rights movement.   P. O. Jonsson

196. Reimers, David M. NEGRO BISHOPS AND DIOCESAN SEGREGATION IN THE PROTESTANT EPISCOPAL CHURCH: 1870-1954. *Hist. Mag. of the Protestant Episcopal Church 1962 31(3): 231-242.* Segregation along racial lines prevailed throughout the Episcopal Church in the later part of the 19th century, but the Sewanee proposal for the creation of separate Negro dioceses was rejected by the General Convention in 1883. The election of suffragans for Negro work was authorized in 1907, and two such bishops were elected in 1917 and 1918. In the 1940's and 1950's, the Episcopal Church in the South became effectively integrated.   E. Oberholzer, Jr.

197. Reimers, David M. THE RACE PROBLEM AND PRESBYTERIAN UNION. *Church Hist. 1962 31(2): 203-215.* Traces schisms in American Pres-

byterianism before the Civil War and discusses post-bellum efforts at reunion between the Presbyterian Church, U.S., and the Presbyterian Church, U.S.A. The Northern branch adopted a segregation system in 1904 in order to work in the South and to merge with the Cumberland branch. In 1929 and 1937, the Southern branch took the initiative in merger conversations, but the conservative elements in the South were able to defeat the union plan of 1954, which had been adopted by the General Assembly. The author suggests that antinorthern feeling combined with the earlier element of racial prejudice in causing the defeat of the plan by the presbyteries.   E. Oberholzer Jr.

198. Sherer, Robert Glenn, Jr. NEGRO CHURCHES IN RHODE ISLAND BEFORE 1860. *Rhode Island Hist. 1966 25(1): 9-25.* Compiles and states "all pertinent, available facts." Based on published source materials, newspapers, and secondary accounts.   P. J. Coleman

199. Sisk, Glenn N. CHURCHES IN THE ALABAMA BLACK BELT, 1875-1917. *Church Hist. 1954 23(2): 153-174.* Describes the life and work of the churches in the Black Belt of Alabama.   E. Oberholzer, Jr.

200. Thompson, Ernest Trice. PRESBYTERIANS NORTH AND SOUTH - EFFORTS TOWARD REUNION. *J. of Presbyterian Hist. 1965 43(1): 1-15.* Traces efforts to reunite Northern and Southern Presbyterian Churches since the Civil War. Such efforts began with an action of the General Assembly of the Northern Church in 1870, but the Southern Church was reluctant to move beyond very limited cooperation until 1917. The Southern Assembly approved the idea of organic union in 1929 and again in 1937, and it submitted a plan of union to the presbyteries for vote in 1954. Southern reaction to the *Brown vs. Board of Education of Topeka* decision defeated the plan, and the Southern Assembly dissolved its committee on union. However, sentiment for Presbyterian reunion in the South is again increasing. 18 notes.   S. C. Pearson, Jr.

201. Tokar, Elizabeth. HUMOROUS ANECDOTES COLLECTED FROM A METHODIST MINISTER. *Western Folklore 1967 26(2): 89-100.* Humor in the pulpit has been used since the beginning of Christianity. An important source of the illustrative joke is indigenous with the old-time Negro preacher. The Reverend Arthur L. Steinfeldt was in this tradition. Included here are several examples of anecdotes which he used as illustrations for his sermons and a number of "preacher tales" he did not consider suitable for use in sermons. 40 notes.
                                                                D. L. Smith

202. Trueblood, Roy W. UNION NEGOTIATIONS BETWEEN BLACK METHODISTS IN AMERICA. *Methodist Hist. 1970 8(4): 18-29.* Negroes have been a part of Methodist history in America since 1766. As early as 1787 they desired to have their own church organizations with black leadership. As a result, the African Methodist Episcopal Church, the African Methodist Episcopal Zion

Church, and the Christian Methodist Episcopal Church were established. During the past 100 years repeated efforts have been made to unite the three into a single church. Structural differences, personal pride and ambition, and failure to take the negotiations seriously are among the reasons union has not been accomplished. 22 notes.   H. L. Calkin

203. Williams, George Huntston. THE WILDERNESS AND PARADISE IN THE HISTORY OF THE CHURCH. *Church Hist. 1959 28(1): 3-24.* A discussion of the application of the Biblical motif of wilderness and garden in American history. The author traces the expression of the motif in the thought of the New England Puritans, Joseph Smith, the American Negroes, and leaders of American theological education; demonstrates its impact on American history; and relates the theme to the work of Frederick Jackson Turner and William Warren Sweet.
E. Oberholzer, Jr.

204. --. [ANGLICANISM, CATHOLICISM AND SLAVERY.] *Comparative Studies in Soc. and Hist. 1966 8(3): 295-330.*
Klein, Herbert S. Attempts to compare the slave systems of two colonial powers in the New World by studying "the relationship between infidel Negro and the Christian Church, in two highly representative colonies, those of Cuba and Virginia," and suggests that the weakness of the Anglican hierarchy in Virginia and the strength of the Catholic Church in Cuba "had a profound impact on the personality, social organization and even eventual assimilation of the Negro into Cuban and Virginian society." 124 notes.
Goveia, Elsa V. COMMENT, pp. 328-330. Suggests that the ratio of Negro slaves to white population was of greater significance in determining the treatment accorded to Negro slaves than the religion practiced in the colony. "The state of religion did not determine the state of slavery. It was the state of slavery which set limits to what the Catholics, Anglicans, or any of the other variety of Christians could hope to achieve." 3 notes.   R. D. Fiala

Contributions to American Culture

205. Alexander, Raymond Pace. STUDY OF NEGRO BLASTS RACIAL MYTHS: JUDGE ALEXANDER COMMENTS ON TEXTBOOKS IN LETTER TO THE PHILADELPHIA INQUIRER. *Negro Hist. Bull. 1964 28(1): 3-6.* Argues for school textbooks which depict the contributions of all peoples to the American past and reject all racial myths and stereotypes. The writings of Carter G. Woodson, William E. B. Du Bois, and other Negro scholars provide some of the essential material for teaching the Nation's history. They call attention to such formerly neglected items as the contribution of free Negroes to pre-Civil War American life and the accomplishments of Negro leaders during

the Reconstruction Era. A study of Negro history can help the Negroes better to understand themselves and the whites better to understand their country.

L. Gara

206. Austin, Gerlyn E. THE ADVENT OF THE NEGRO ACTOR ON THE LEGITIMATE STAGE IN AMERICA. *J. of Negro Educ. 1966 35(3): 237-245.* Traces the arrival of the Negro actor on the legitimate stage with the performance of Ridgely Torrence's *Three Plays for a Negro Theatre* in 1917. Early American drama introduced minor Negro parts as servants or comic relief figures, but such parts were generally played by whites. Negro minstrel companies emerged after the Civil War, and, by the turn of the century, Negro companies were departing from this form. By 1910 Negro companies playing before Negro audiences in Harlem were granted a new freedom, and in 1917 the Negro on the legitimate stage gained the serious attention of critics, the press, and the public. Only in the 1950's did the Negro receive nonracial roles in the American theater. Biblio.

S. C. Pearson, Jr.

207. Bardolph, Richard. SOCIAL ORIGINS OF DISTINGUISHED NEGROES. *J. of Negro Hist. 1955 40(3): 211-249.* Briefly outlines the social backgrounds and careers of some 50 outstanding Negroes who were born in the 18th and early 19th centuries - professional men, writers, preachers, and leaders of the abolition movement. Most prominent Negroes of the period appear to have held certain small but significant advantages over their less-favored kinsmen, and it was mainly the freeborn Negro, the fugitive, the manumitted, or the legally emancipated slave who gained a certain degree of eminence.

C. F. Latour

208. Bardolph, Richard. THE DISTINGUISHED NEGRO IN AMERICA, 1770-1936. *Am. Hist. R. 1955 60(3): 527-547.* Lists some 215 Negroes with careful bibliographical notes, including information on racial background, area of origin, education, and chief fields of activity. The method of selection and the changing character of Negro leadership, with reasons for the change, are discussed.

G. Rehder

209. Bardolph, Richard. THE NEGRO IN "WHO'S WHO IN AMERICA," 1936-1955. *J. of Negro Hist. 1957 42(4): 261-282.* A survey of the colored persons listed in *Who's Who in America,* used as an index of Negro eminence, concluding that religious leaders were the largest single group in 1936, but that educators led 20 years later. In other categories, persons achieved distinction chiefly in the Negro community rather than in American society as a whole.

W. E. Wight

210. Beaubien, Paul L. and Mattes, Merill J. GEORGE WASHINGTON CARVER NATIONAL MONUMENT: THE ARCHEOLOGICAL SEARCH FOR GEORGE WASHINGTON CARVER'S BIRTHPLACE. *Negro Hist. Bull. 1954 18(2): 33-38.* In 1952, after the purchase of the birthplace of George Washington Carver (1860-1943), a number of historians and archeologists under-

took to reconstruct it in its original form. The author reports on the results of the research for this project and on the inauguration of this national monument.

S

211. Blake, Emma L. ZORA NEALE HURSTON: AUTHOR AND FOLK-LORIST. *Negro Hist. Bull. 1966 29(7): 149-150, 165.* Hurston was born in Eatonville, Florida, on 7 January 1901, entered Howard University in 1919, transferred to Barnard College, and in 1929 received a bachelor's degree in anthropology. She was the first Negro woman to be awarded a Guggenheim Fellowship, which enabled her to gather material in the West Indies for future publications. "That Miss Hurston was a most versatile writer may be seen in the fact that in addition to her novels, definitive studies in anthropology, and autobiography, she wrote a number of short stories, a one-act play, two librettos, and many magazine articles. During the last years of her life she earned a precarious living as a substitute teacher at Lincoln Park Academy in Fort Pierce, Florida. She contributed to the local Negro paper, *The Chronicle,* and began work on a new novel which she never completed." She died on 3 February 1960. 2 photos.

D. D. Cameron

212. Bluestein, Gene. AMERICA'S FOLK INSTRUMENT: NOTES ON THE FIVE STRING BANJO. *Western Folklore 1964 23(4): 241-248.* Discusses the probable origin of the five-stringed banjo, asserting that the instrument made its way into the Western Hemisphere by way of the Negro slave trade. Also discusses the American refinements of the instrument and the methods of playing it. Documented, illus.

L. J. White

213. Bluestein, Gene. CONSTANCE ROURKE AND THE FOLK SOURCES OF AMERICAN LITERATURE. *Western Folklore 1967 26(2): 77-87.* An analysis of the method and approach of Constance Rourke is made in this review of her *American Humor, A Study of the National Character* (1931, reprinted in 1953 by Anchor Books). Her focus is on the folk sources of an American literary tradition and the role of humor in its development. She is preoccupied in offsetting the assertion that American civilization has little to offer in the fine arts. Her "characterological" studies identify the Yankee, the backwoodsman, and the Negro in the steady accretion of national characteristics of the emerging portrait of the American. After establishing these sources she turns to environmental and institutional forces. 9 notes.

D. L. Smith

214. Brown, Wesley A. ELEVEN MEN OF WEST POINT. *Negro Hist. Bull. 1956 19(7): 147-157.* Briefly reviews the role of Negro soldiers in wars in which the United States was a participant. Includes short biographies of the 11 Negroes who graduated from West Point as well as information about other Negroes who attended but did not graduate.

L. Gara

215. Bush, Joseph Bevans. DEATH OF LIZZIE MILES ENDS GREAT ERA OF BLUES SHOUTERS. *Negro Hist. Bull. 1963 27(3): 69.*

216. Clark, Rogie. WHAT IS NEGRO FOLKLORE? *Negro Hist. Bull. 1963 27(2): 40-41.* Emphasizes the significance of Negro folk music, which reflects the true spirit of Negro tradition and life, and pleads for preserving and perpetuating this valuable contribution to the world of music.   L. Gara

217. Clarke, John Henrik. THE ORIGIN AND GROWTH OF AFRO-AMERI-CAN LITERATURE. *J. of Human Relations 1968 16(3): 368-384.* Surveys the work of leading Afro-American writers from the mid-18th century to the present. The sophistication of the African heritage is emphasized. In all probability the first poem published by an American Negro was Jupiter Hammon's "An Evening Thought" (1760). Phyllis Wheatley (1753-84) became one of the best known poets of New England. After the American Revolution Prince Hall emerged as the accepted leader of Boston's blacks. Before the Civil War the main literary expression of the Negro was the slave narrative, the most famous of which was written by Frederick Douglass. During the Gilded Age and the Progressive Era Charles W. Chesnutt and Paul Laurence Dunbar were important. A Negro renaissance centered in Harlem during the 1920's. Most important is Richard Wright's work, particularly *Native Son* (New York: Harper, 1940). "Here, at last, was a black writer who wrote considerably better than many of his white contemporaries." Finally, in the 1960's there is James Baldwin, who "plays the role traditionally assigned to thinkers concerned with improvement of human conditions - that of alarmist." Now "it is time for the black writer to draw upon the universal values in his people's experience," just as Sean O'Casey did with the experiences of the Irish. An undocumented paper delivered at Savannah State College, Savannah, Georgia, on 16 April 1967.   D. J. Abramoske

218. Cotton, Lettie Jo. THE NEGRO IN THE AMERICAN THEATRE. *Negro Hist. Bull. 1960 23(8): 172-178.* Traces the history of the Negro character as portrayed on the American stage, and as it developed from the stereotype of the minstrel era to the present-day depiction of realistic human personalities. Includes material on some outstanding Negro producers, actors, and actresses, and comments on some of the discriminatory practices of the theater. Undocumented.   L. Gara

219. Destler, Chester McArthur. DAVID DICKSON'S "SYSTEM OF FARM-ING" AND THE AGRICULTURAL REVOLUTION IN THE DEEP SOUTH, 1850-1885. *Agric. Hist. 1957 31(3): 30-39.* Prior to the Civil War, David Dickson of Hancock County, Georgia, had made a fortune in cotton planting through what he claimed was an original system of farming. Basically, he practiced intensive rather than extensive cultivation. He emphasized close supervision of and development of skills among his slave laborers, soil improvement and fertility retention in his farms, use of fertilizer, self-sufficiency, and operation on a cash basis. After the Civil War, Dickson urged the use of Negroes as hired workers but changed to a tenancy system whereby the workers received a share of the crop. He continued to practice intensive agriculture and helped bring about an agricultural revival in the Deep South. Based on contemporary periodicals.   J (W. D. Rasmussen)

220. Dorson, Richard M. THE CAREER OF "JOHN HENRY." *Western Folklore 1965 24(3): 155-163.* Traces the story of the Negro hero, John Henry, from the quest for a full text of the ballad to its contribution to American literature, drama, art, and music. Relies on secondary sources. J. M. Brady

221. Durham, Philip. THE NEGRO COWBOY. *Am. Q. 1955 7(3): 291-301.* The Negro cowboy traveled West at the close of the Civil War and played a significant role in the development of the cattle industry, becoming a real part of the spirit of the West, but he does not appear in "Western Stories." He is included in western autobiography and in nonfiction works on the cowboy. The writer gives some possible reasons for his exclusion from "Western Stories." Ruby Kerley

222. Ernst, Robert. NEGRO CONCEPTS OF AMERICANISM. *J. of Negro Hist. 1954 39(3): 206-219.* Discussion of conceptions held in the last 150 years by prominent Negro individuals and groups concerning loyalty to and identification with the United States and American society. The colonization projects of the 19th century and the radical Pan-African movements were regarded by some as answers to the problems of inequality. Most of the movements, however, visualized education, social and political advances within the framework of American institutions and emphasized the loyalty and contribution of Negroes to the society. C. R. Spurgin

223. Evans, David. AFRO-AMERICAN ONE-STRINGED INSTRUMENTS. *Western Folklore 1970 29(4): 229-245.* Discusses a rare one-stringed musical instrument, sometimes called a "jitterbug," which is played by moving a bottle or some other object across a string mounted on a long board or wall. Lists all recorded knowledge of the instrument, which is best known among the black community in Mississippi. Comparisons taken from similar instruments in Africa and Mississippi lead to the conclusion that they are generally children's instruments designed to teach basic rhythms and patterns which will later be transferred to adult instruments. Research also seems to indicate that the African drummer did not reappear in Afro-American music because the "jitterbug" led to the adaptation of the guitar. Based on interviews and secondary sources; 30 notes, appendix. R. A. Trennert

224. Fowler, Robert H. THE NEGRO WHO WENT TO THE POLE WITH PEARY. *Am. Hist. Illus. 1966 1(1): 4-11, 52-55; (2): 45-51.* Part I. Relates the part played by Matthew A. Henson in the Peary expeditions to the North Pole. Historians have tended to underestimate the importance of Robert Peary's Negro assistant. The author attempts to present a more exact account of Henson's role. Born in 1866, Henson became acquainted with Peary in 1886 when he made his first trip with the noted explorer to Greenland. Perhaps Henson's greatest asset on these early explorations was his color. The Eskimos were drawn to him and taught him much of the Eskimo way of life. This knowledge proved extremely useful to Peary's expeditions. The various successes and failures of the two men are recounted until the start of the 1909 expedition. 10 illus. Part II. Recounts the final phase of Peary's last, and ultimately successful, expedition to the North

Pole. Matthew A. Henson, Peary's Negro assistant, claims that he was actually the first man to set foot on the North Pole. Peary had left orders for Henson to stop just short of the Pole so that he, Peary, could be the first man to arrive. However, Henson overshot his mark by two miles and actually reached the Pole before Peary. After 18 years of service with Peary, and agonizing periods of near starvation and overexhaustion, the search was finally over. Henson received relatively little credit for the part he had in the expeditions. Based on a personal interview with Matthew Henson two years before his death; map, 7 illus.

M. J. McBaine

225. Garrett, Romeo B. AFRICAN SURVIVALS IN AMERICAN CUL-TURE. *J. of Negro Hist. 1966 51(4): 239-245.* Although African survivals in American culture have diminished in the past century, some are still evident. Of the more than four thousand African words, names, and numbers still used by Negroes on the Georgia-South Carolina offshore islands, many have been incorporated into American speech. Negro spirituals and some of the most rhythmic New World dances have traceable African roots. African myths and folktales are preserved in American folklore. Among the African contributions to the New World diet are such items as black-eyed peas, watermelon, okra, cola drinks, and coffee. Mostly based on secondary material. L. Gara

226. Hurley, Neil P. TOWARD A SOCIOLOGY OF JAZZ. *Thought 1969 44(173): 219-246.* Suggests that jazz offers a valuable source of information concerning the changing position of Negroes in the United States. The author divides the history of American jazz into a series of stages which he labels primitive (to 1917), old time (1917-26), preclassical (1927-34), classical (1935-45), modern (1945-65), and Charlie Mingus (1965-present). He argues for a correspondence between a given stage of Negro jazz style and verbal content, a particular geographical focus of jazz music, and a particular degree of racial integration in the United States. Suggested are ways in which majority attitudes toward jazz have changed and the role of the mass media in effecting these changes.

J. C. English

227. Jackson, Marian. THE HISTORY AND SIGNIFICANCE OF NEGRO HISTORY WEEK. *Negro Hist. Bull. 1963 27(3): 70-72.* Reviews the career of Carter Goodwin Woodson, founder of the Association for the Study of Negro Life and History (in 1915), and evaluates the work of the association in calling the Nation's attention to the contributions of Negroes to the American past.

L. Gara

228. James, Milton M. BIOGRAPHICAL APPROACH TO THE STUDY OF NEGRO HISTORY. *Negro Hist. Bull. 1960 23(4): 74, 95.* Following a short introductory essay, presents a bibliography of 35 biographies and autobiographies of American Negroes. L. Gara

229. Jensen, Billie Barnes. ENTERTAINING THE 'FIFTY-NINERS. *J. of the West 1966 5(1): 82-90.* Uses entertainment to show how institutions and customs

of an older society were transplanted to the frontier but were conditioned by the frontier environment. Initially, the Colorado miners had only games, music, and hunting to occupy their leisure hours. When saloons were opened drinking and gambling became primary activities of the pioneer population. By the summer of 1859, the Cherry Creek settlements were growing rapidly and a theater was soon opened. The legitimate theater drew crowds in the last months of the year and so did another form of entertainment, the Negro minstrel show. Cultural organizations also flourished. In addition to lodges there were clubs established to provide entertainment and intellectual stimulus. Most residents found their social outlet in the bowling alleys and billiard saloons or at wrestling matches or horse races. These amusements helped the homesick miner to accept life on the frontier and to pass the long winter months when mining was impossible. Based on printed sources.   D. N. Brown

230. Johnston, Robert P. SIX MAJOR FIGURES IN AFRO-AMERICAN ART. *Michigan Academician 1971 3(4): 51-58.* Afro-American artists are seldom studied and the purpose of this essay is to briefly introduce six men and women who have made valuable artistic contributions. They are Robert S. Duncanson (1817-72), Edmonia Lewis (1843-ca. 1900), Jacob Lawrence (b. 1917), Hughie Lee-Smith (b. 1915), William E. Artis (b. 1914), and Romare Bearden (b. 1914). 5 illus., 21 notes.   E. M. Gersman

231. Josey, E. J. READING AND THE DISADVANTAGED. *Negro Hist. Bull. 1965 28(7): 156-157, 159.* Negro school libraries in the South are inadequate. "Many Negro young people desire to read about the Negro's contribution to America. Reading good books by and about Negroes, that may be supplied by the public library, many be the motivational force needed to stimulate disadvantaged youth to aspire to higher levels of achievement." Illus.
                                                                  E. P. Stickney

232. Martorella, Peter H. THE NEGRO'S ROLE IN AMERICAN HISTORY: GEORGE WASHINGTON CARVER - A CASE STUDY. *Social Studies 1969 60(7): 318-325.* Presents a detailed study of the achievements of an American Negro, George Washington Carver, who gained world fame and renown for his contributions to agricultural science. If such studies as this were made relative to the contributions of other black Americans, and were the results properly disseminated, they might enhance greater racial and cultural pride and ameliorate race relations in America. 48 notes.   L. R. Raife

233. McCree, Wade H., Jr. THE NEGRO RENAISSANCE IN MICHIGAN POLITICS. *Negro Hist. Bull. 1962/63 26(1): 7-9, 13.* Mostly a listing of Michigan Negroes who have held local, State, and national political offices from the era of Reconstruction to the present. Although the list is not complete, it bears out the author's thesis that Negroes have played an increasingly important role in Michigan politics and that they have done so as representatives of all the people in the State rather than as representatives of their race alone.
                                                                  L. Gara

234. McKinney, Harold. "NEGRO MUSIC": A DEFINITIVE AMERICAN EXPRESSION. *Negro Hist. Bull. 1964 27(5): 120-121, 126-127.* Describes blues and jazz as a combination of European and African music which has become the influential expression of American music on the international scene. Based on secondary accounts.   L. Gara

235. Mooney, H. F. POPULAR MUSIC SINCE THE 1920'S: THE SIGNIFI-CANCE OF SHIFTING TASTES. *Am. Q. 1968 20(1): 67-85.* The shifting tastes in popular music since the 1920's appear to be a continuation of major trends established in the previous 70 years. Among other things there were movements away from blandness, urbanity, and introspection; injection of Negroid influence; protest against traditional middle-class values; and reflection of contemporary youthful obsessions with sex, activism, and social problems. The transitions of the entire period are discussed with the final generalization that the outstanding trend in the 1950's and 1960's was a rejection of prettiness, over-refinement, academic orchestration and lyrics, smoothness, and subtlety. Even so, older values are sometimes included though engulfed in a pounding, shrieking sound. Based on published sources and examination of period music; 34 notes.
                                                                       D. E. Mayo

236. Post, Lauren C. JOSEPH C. FALCON, ACCORDIAN PLAYER AND SINGER: A BIOGRAPHICAL SKETCH. *Louisiana Hist. 1970 11(1): 63-79.* An interview with Joe Falcon (1900-65), taped five months before his death. Falcon, the first Louisiana acadian to make a commercial recording, was repre-sentative of the best of the Cajun musicians of southwest Louisiana. He comments in the interview with Post on his recording sessions, Cajun folksongs, Negro contributions, other musicians, "faisdodo" dance halls, and his wives. 6 photos, list of Falcon's commercial recordings.   R. L. Woodward

237. Savage, W. Sherman. GEORGE WASHINGTON OF CENTRALIA, WASHINGTON. *Negro Hist. Bull. 1963 27(2): 44-47.* Traces the career of George Washington (1817-1902), who was born in Virginia of a slave father and a white mother and who moved west as the ward of a white family, living for a time in Ohio, Missouri, and Illinois and finally settling in Washington, where he founded the city of Centralia. Documented.   L. Gara

238. Simms, David McD. THE NEGRO SPIRITUAL: ORIGINS AND THEMES. *J. of Negro Educ. 1966 35(1): 35-41.* Surveys recent literature on the Negro spiritual. In contrast to Miles Mark Fisher, author of *Negro Slave Songs in the United States* (New York: Citadel Press, 1964), Simms argues "that the Christian faith as the slave saw it was a decisive factor in the tonal development of the Spiritual." The author also considers the subject matter of the spiritual which he argues was drawn chiefly from "the Bible, the natural world and from personal experiences." He sees the restricted theological perspective of the spiritual as a reflection of the limitations of plantation preaching. He concludes that the great theme of the spirituals is "that every human being is a child of God and that all men are therefore brothers."   S. C. Pearson, Jr.

239. Soby, James Thrall and Friedlander, Lee. PHOTOGRAPHY: JAZZ. *Art in Am. 1963 51(4): 134-139.* Text and photographs interpreting the lives of several Negro jazz musicians. Illus. W. K. Bottorff

240. Spencer, Thomas E. ON THE PLACE OF THE NEGRO IN AMERICAN HISTORY. *Social Studies 1969 60(4): 150-158.* Presents a sound argument against the revisionists' clamor for giving the Negro a more prominent place in American history. The author asserts that the Negro has received a place in American history commensurate with his contributions to the growth and development of America and that the impact that he has exerted upon American history does not warrant a more deserving place for him. The author would strongly suggest leaving out of history books many Negroes whom revisionists and others, particularly Negroes, would include. The overriding importance of the individual's contribution to society should be the criterion upon which judgment should be based relative to history-book inclusion. L. Raife

241. Still, William Grant. MY ARKANSAS BOYHOOD. *Arkansas Hist. Q. 1967 26(3): 285-292.* A prominent Negro musician and composer recalls many of the people, scenes, incidents, and circumstances of his boyhood in Little Rock which he believes contributed to his subsequent accomplishments. Illus. B. A. Drummond

242. Trezise, Robert L. THE BLACK AMERICAN IN AMERICAN HISTORY TEXTBOOKS. *Social Studies 1969 60(4): 164-167.* Asserts that black Americans have been wrongfully omitted from American history textbooks and that school children never get to know anything of value concerning the contribution of the American Negro to the development of America. The author's assertions are based upon an investigation of 12 of the most widely used American history textbooks in the State of Michigan. The investigation was conducted by the Michigan Department of Education. L. Raife

Racial Attitudes & Policies

243. Arnoni, M. S. SPAGHETTI AND THE AMERICAN CIVILIZATION. *Minority of One 1968 10(3): 13-19.* The American Nation has consistently and self-righteously held itself in highest regard. Yet America was born too fast. The American future turned out to be oversized in relation to its past. According to the American myth, democracy was discovered in the United States. In reality, the American people were from the beginning uniform in their greed. American civilization has been and remains overwhelmingly materialistic and sensual. This is exemplified in the treatment of the Indian and in the maintenance of slavery. It is also manifested by expansion abroad, the current example of which is

Vietnam. In the American scale of values that which is not related to power and wealth is secondary. The supreme criterion is the advantage to be gained. This leads to frustration rather than gratification. Illus.   P. W. Kennedy

244. Bloch, Herman D. THE CIRCLE OF DISCRIMINATION AGAINST NEGROES. *Phylon 1955 16(3): 253-262.* Shows how social and economic discrimination of the New York City Negroes has affected their mode of life between 1624 and 1945. The whites' discrimination produced Negro reaction in the political realm. This in turn elicited the white man's intensified efforts to aggravate the Negro's social subordination. Thus, the discriminatory circle, from which the Negro can rarely extricate himself, consists of the following stages: 1) the Negro's subordination to the white man; 2) socioeconomic manifestations by whites limiting the Negro's social and economic opportunities; 3) restriction of the Negro's social mobility by economic discrimination (despite the rise of his economic status); 4) economic discrimination, primarily when competing for employment.
R. Mueller

245. Bogina, Sh. A. NEKOTORYE VOPROSY RAZVITIIA AMERIKAN-SKOI NATSII [Some issues in the development of the American Nation]. *Sovetskaia Etnografiia [USSR] 1968 (4): 52-64.* Outlines the basic elements in the formation of the American Nation in the 19th and 20th centuries, arguing that the immigration of large numbers of Europeans to America was "of colossal significance." Periods of major influx - their differences, similarities, and significance - are explored in detail. The author also discusses the various factors furthering and retarding the cultural assimilation process, the relationships between the immigrants and the receiving population (and the resulting personal and governmental discrimination), the relationships between the "new" and the "old" immigrants, and those between the newly arrived and the Negroes. The role of the labor movement in the cultural assimilation process is briefly explored. Based on American and Russian sources; 20 notes.   D. J. McIntyre

246. Brittain, Joseph M. SOME REFLECTIONS ON NEGRO SUFFRAGE AND POLITICS IN ALABAMA - PAST AND PRESENT. *J. of Negro Hist. 1962 47(2): 127-138.* Following the Civil War and until the return of white supremacy in 1875, Negroes participated actively in large numbers both as voters and as officeholders in Alabama politics. In 1926 the Negroes in Alabama started a campaign to regain their political rights, but such devices as the white primary, the poll tax and intimidation were used to prevent their success. In recent years a series of Supreme Court decisions, improved and determined Negro organization, and the support of the U.S. Department of Justice have enabled the Negro citizens to make some major political gains as the beginning of the realization of their full civil rights.   L. Gara

247. Brown, Willis L. REALTY, CHATTEL, OR PERSON: A CRITIQUE ON THE TAXONOMY OF THE NEGRO IN AMERICAN CULTURE. *Negro Hist. Bull. 1957 21(3): 59-61.* Reproduces and comments upon parts of five pre-Civil War documents, all of which accept the fact of Negro slavery, imply a degree of Negro inferiority, and are related to an economic consideration in the

form of the protection of a personal vested interest. The author concludes that antebellum southerners refused to classify Negroes as freeborn men and that this attitude has continued to the present. L. Gara

248. Burger, Nash K. TRUTH OR CONSEQUENCE: BOOKS AND BOOK REVIEWING. *South Atlantic Q. 1969 68(2): 152-166.* Discusses the problems of book reviewing, with particular reference to works on the South. Compares William Styron's *The Confessions of Nat Turner* (New York: New Am. Lib., 1968) and Stark Young's *So Red the Rose* (1934) and argues that Styron "failed to see the truth of the South whole" and that he perpetuated a "false and partial view." While Styron sees the South entirely through the race question, Young views "race relations as an aspect of Southern life." J. M. Bumsted

249. Bush, Joseph Bevans. IS AMERICA CHRISTIAN? *Negro Hist. Bull. 1964 27(7): 173, 178.* Briefly recites the abuses suffered by American Negroes in the past and suggests the changes necessary in American life to make the Nation truly Christian in its behavior. L. Gara

250. Degler, Carl N. A CENTURY OF THE KLANS: A REVIEW ARTICLE. *J. of Southern Hist. 1965 31(4): 435-443.* In the centennial year of the Ku Klux Klan, three books on its history were published. David M. Chalmers in *Hooded Americanism: The First Century of the Ku Klux Klan* (New York: Doubleday, 1965), combs the secondary literature and contemporary periodicals as no one has done before, but does little to analyze the myriad facts. He gives only one chapter to the Reconstruction period, the rest to the era since World War I. William Peirce Randel in *The Ku Klux Klan: A Century of Infamy* (New York: Chilton, 1965), devotes two-thirds of his book to the Reconstruction period, though omitting Alabama. His highly charged indignation over the Klan raises doubts as to the book's objectivity. Charles C. Alexander's *The Ku Klux Klan in the Southwest* (Lexington: U. of Kentucky Press, 1965) is a well-balanced, carefully documented study of the Klan in Arkansas, Texas, Louisiana and Oklahoma. The reviewer distinguishes between three different klans - that of the Reconstruction, the 1920's, and the present civil rights battle - and says it is wise to resist the temptation to lump them together. S. E. Humphreys

251. Draper, Theodore. THE FANTASY OF BLACK NATIONALISM. *Commentary 1969 48(3): 27-54.* Black nationalism in the United States is not new. It has taken two forms. First was migration or emigration, of white as well as black origin. The author traces the idea of emigration to Africa as a solution to the American race problem among such famous figures as Thomas Jefferson and Abraham Lincoln. The outstanding advocate for emigration among Negroes was Martin Robinson Delany (1812-85). The author gives Delany's background and philosophy and then traces the emigration idea through its various forms up to the present. The second form of black nationalism was the effort to create an independent Negro state within the boundaries of the United States. This also was an early white idea which the author describes historically. Today black nationalism is taking the form of the Black Muslim movement. The author concludes that

no leader has been able to define black nationalism. Detailed are some of the problems that have been produced by the fantasy of a black nation.

C. Grollman

252. Dumond, Dwight L. EMANCIPATION: HISTORY'S FANTASTIC REVERIE. *J. of Negro Hist. 1964 49(1): 1-12.* Briefly reviews the history of the denial of civil rights for Negroes, both before and since the Emancipation Proclamation. After refuting the idea that moderation or delay is justifiable, the author asserts that Americans are still in the depths of a reverie which fools them into trying to evade the issue of full equal rights which will no longer brook delay.

L. Gara

253. Eubanks, Thelma M. THE NEGRO TEACHER. *Negro Hist. Bull. 1964 27(5): 113.* Describes a supplementary textbook, *The Struggle for Freedom and Rights,* used in eighth grade American history courses in Detroit and discusses the role of the teacher as a promoter of freedom and human rights.

L. Gara

254. Farris, Charles D. THE RE-ENFRANCHISEMENT OF NEGROES IN FLORIDA. *J. of Negro Hist. 1954 39(4): 259-283.* Toward the end of the last century, the whites in the southern States succeeded in excluding the Negroes from political activity by means of regulations governing the electoral census and local administrative reforms. The author describes the controversy concerning this matter since 1885 in Florida. Between 1937 and 1947, new laws ended this situation.

S

255. Forbes, Jack D. RACE AND COLOR IN MEXICAN-AMERICAN PROBLEMS. *J. of Human Relations 1968 16(1): 55-68.* Demonstrates the fact that the reactions of white Americans to Mexican-Americans since the 1830's have been complicated by racist attitudes. In spite of this, the myth persists that "Mexican-Americans are 'Whites with Spanish Surnames' and that their problems are little if any different from those of Polish-Americans or Italian-Americans....Color prejudice against brown-skinned Mexican-Americans and Indian-Americans will not completely disappear, in the writer's opinion, until the brown-skinned Negro is also made a social equal of the white." Based on primary and secondary sources; 16 notes.

D. J. Abramoske

256. Franklin, John H. HISTORY OF RACIAL SEGREGATION IN THE UNITED STATES. *Ann. of the Am. Acad. of Pol. and Social Sci. 1956 (304): 1-9.* A brief historical account of the segregation of the Negro in the United States since 1787, with the main emphasis on the post-Civil War period, 1865-1956.

J. S. Counelis

257. Franklin, John Hope. THE DIGNITY OF MAN: PERSPECTIVES FOR TOMORROW. *Social Educ. 1964 28(5): 257-260, 265.* Address delivered to the 43d Annual Meeting of the National Council for the Social Studies, November 1963. The concept of the dignity of man in America is traced, from the Leyden

Agreement of 1618 through Thomas Jefferson, the Workingmen's Association of Philadelphia (1829), and Abraham Lincoln to the present day. The American idea is compared with its European counterparts, stressing the ideas of Locke and Rousseau. A sharp contrast is drawn between the evolving concept of the dignity of man and the practice of Negro slavery - a contrast which formed the beginning of "the loss of moral leadership on the part of the United States." Concludes that the outstanding failure of the United States in its second century of independence has been its present calculated denial of complete freedom to those emancipated a hundred years ago. M. Small

258. Fredrickson, George M. TWO SOUTHERN HISTORIANS. *Am. Hist. R. 1970 75(5): 1387-1392.* Reviews the work of Fletcher Melvin Green and David Morris Potter, both of whom have written extensively about the Old South. Potter and Green are alike in their freedom from a parochial view of their subject, but differ in their approaches and basic interpretations. Green is a skilled narrative historian who has interpreted the Old South as a basically democratic region; Potter is an analytical historian with interdisciplinary interests, who has described the South as perennially torn between aristocratic and democratic impulses. The reviewer suggests that in the Old South this conflict was resolved by the way in which concepts of racial hierarchy were incorporated into southern political and social thinking. A

259. Gohdes, Clarence. THE ATLANTIC CELEBRATES ITS HUNDREDTH BIRTHDAY. *South Atlantic Q. 1958 57(2): 163-167.* The *Atlantic Monthly* was projected in 1853 as an antislavery and literary mouthpiece of the "liberals" of New England. When its first number appeared in October 1857, under the editorship of James R. Lowell, it flourished primarily as a literary magazine. Since that time several radical shifts in editorial policy have taken place, and its survival at present is due to its very broad appeal. The centennial volume of selections from its contents corroborates the opinion that literature has been sacrificed for diversity. A

260. Greene, Marc T. BLACK VERSUS WHITE IN AMERICA. *Q. R. [Great Britain] 1956 294(609): 368-380.* Examines the race problem in America in its historical, sociological, and economic settings since the Civil War. Attempts to explain why the anti-Negro feeling in the American southern States is, after a century, as strong as ever. C. LeGuin

261. Grimshaw, Allen D. LAWLESSNESS AND VIOLENCE IN AMERICA AND THEIR SPECIAL MANIFESTATIONS IN CHANGING NEGRO-WHITE RELATIONSHIPS. *J. of Negro Hist. 1959 44(1): 52-72.* A chronological résumé of Negro-white violence throughout American history. The author begins with a reference to the lawless heritage of the United States, asserting that crime and social violence have been rampant throughout its history, race riots being only one of many manifestations of the conflict. Negro-white violence is dealt with by periods: 1640-1861, 1861-77, 1878-1914, 1915-29, 1930-41, 1942-45, and 1945 to date. The social forces and types of violence characterizing each period are described. R. E. Wilson

262. Gromov, Iu. A. "GRADUALIZM" - ORUDIE BOR'BY S OS-VOBODITEL'NYM DVIZHENIEM NEGROV V SSHA ["Gradualism" - as a weapon in the struggle against the Negro liberation movement in the United States]. *Novaia i Noveishaia Istoriia [USSR] 1968 12(5): 62-70.* Tracing treatment of the Negro in the United States from the latter part of the 19th century to the present, the author illustrates the way in which "gradualism" has been used to thwart the Negroes' aspiration for equality and liberation from social, political, and economic oppression. Particular detail is devoted to the period from 1954 to the present in this examination of white-Negro relationships in the United States. 32 notes.   E. B. Richards

263. Gross, Seymour L. THE NEGRO IN AMERICAN LITERARY CRITI-CISM. *R. of Pol. 1966 28(3): 273-292.* Traces developments in American literary criticism showing how, in the last one hundred years, the image of the Negro has "undergone an exquisite reversal." Whereas "our criticism began by locking the Negro into the fantasy construct of the stereotype so as to remove him from human consideration to a kind of psychological and moral no-man's land," it has emerged to embrace "a literary view of the Negro as a 'prototype' of the contemporary sense of existential dislocation." Documented.   Sr. M. McAuley

264. Hahn, Harlan. CIVIL LIBERTIES IN IOWA. *Ann. of Iowa 1965 38(1): 76-79.* Contends that Iowa possesses a record for protection of civil liberties that is unique in the Union. This record, however, is not without blemish as Iowa in the early 20th century legislated against "criminal syndicalism." A World War I governor practically required the use of English in Iowa schools. Yet Iowa is one of the few States that has neither required a loyalty oath of its employees nor attempted to regulate the nonviolent activities of so-called subversive groups. The author also notes that Iowa was one of the first States to pass a Civil Rights Act (1884) and that Iowa was among the first Northern States to enfranchise the Negro. He concludes that the State motto, "Our liberties we prize; our rights we will maintain," is a fitting one. 7 notes.   D. C. Swift

265. Hill, Herbert. STATE LAWS AND THE NEGRO: SOCIAL CHANGE AND THE IMPACT OF LAW. *African Forum 1965 1(2): 92-105.* Sketches the changes in the legal position of the Negro from the first arrival of slaves in 1619 to the present. Throughout the history of slavery in the United States the various State legislatures have been directly involved in the racial question. "The reversal of this process - the legal nullification of this extensive body of state statutes requiring the segregation of the races" - did not begin until the school segregation cases of 1954. The author discusses the various Federal and State commissions and laws that have been established to end discrimination, with particular attention to State fair employment practices commissions. The most advanced and complete State civil rights laws are in the area of employment. Thus, the legislatures that once used their powers to enslave and segregate the Negro are now major instruments in protecting the rights and equality of Negroes.
                                                             M. J. McBaine

266. Howarth, Herbert. T. S. ELIOT AND THE "LITTLE PREACHER." *Am. Q. 1961 13(2): 179-187.* Consists of a summary of the life of the Reverend William Greenleaf Eliot, drawn from the biography by Eliot's daughter-in-law, along with a comparison with his poet grandson T. S. Eliot. Despite their differing ideological outlooks, T. S. Eliot and his antislavery grandfather have several things in common. W. M. Armstrong

267. Johnson, Guion G. FREEDOM, EQUALITY, AND SEGREGATION. *R. of Pol. 1958 20(2): 147-163.* A review of the problem of racial segregation in the southern United States since the Civil War combined with a short social analysis of the problem. C. B. Joynt

268. Johnson, Guion G. SOUTHERN PATERNALISM TOWARDS NEGROES AFTER EMANCIPATION. *J. of Southern Hist. 1957 23(4): 483-509.* Describes the South's changing attitude toward the Negro in the period from emancipation to the present. Up to World War I, the paternalistic attitude was firmly entrenched in the South and served as a basis for segregation, but as a result of the two World Wars segregation theories had to be gradually abandoned. The author discusses various theories brought forth in this period about the "inferiority" of the Negro. P. Podjed

269. Kunkel, Paul A. MODIFICATIONS IN LOUISIANA NEGRO LEGAL STATUS UNDER LOUISIANA CONSTITUTIONS 1812-1957. *J. of Negro Hist. 1959 44(1): 1-25.* A review of the changes affecting the rights of Negroes under the 10 constitutions of Louisiana, 1812-1957. Special attention is given to the peculiarities arising from the incompatibility of Louisiana's French-Spanish legal background with Anglo-Saxon law and custom, and to the gradual withdrawal in the post-Reconstruction period following 1877 of the rights granted in the 1868 constitution under which the State had been readmitted to the Union. R. E. Wilson

270. Lipset, Seymour Martin. AN ANATOMY OF THE KLAN. *Commentary 1965 40(4): 74-83.* Places the three Ku Klux Klan organizations in historical perspective. The first Klan, formed in 1865, played a major role in restoring white supremacy to the South by intimidating the freed Negro slaves and their white supporters. The second Klan, founded in 1915 and dissolved in 1944, achieved a membership of six million between the years 1920-24. The third Klan, in reality a set of Klans formed since World War II, has not had the success of its predecessors because of better financed competition from other groups on the Right, although it still plays a role in many southern towns today. Recent books on the Klan movement do not shed much light on why the Klan declined so rapidly after 1924. "Perhaps the most interesting fact about Klan activity is that most of its vigilante violence was directed not against Negroes, Jews, Catholics, or the foreign-born, but rather against those involved in 'immoral' activities: adulterers, patrons of prostitutes, drunks, bootleggers, and the like....The Klan was, more than anything else, an instrument for restoring law and order and Victorian morality." D. D. Cameron

271. Logan, Rayford W. THE PROGRESS OF THE NEGRO AFTER A CENTURY OF EMANCIPATION. *J. of Negro Educ. 1963 32(4): 320-328.* Traces the place of the Negro in American life since emancipation. Deals with attempts to attain equal rights for Negroes by Federal, State, local, and nongovernmental action from Reconstruction to the present.   S. C. Pearson, Jr.

272. Lorch, Robert S. THE SOUTH AND THE SUPREME COURT. *Mid-Am. 1958 40(3): 139-162.* Through an examination of Supreme Court decisions, concludes that the highest tribunal of the United States has not been traditionally antisouthern (antagonistic to white supremacy). "Decisions burdensome to the cause of white supremacy and the Southern way of life have been rendered from time to time, but only in comparatively recent years have these outweighed in number and importance decisions tending in the other direction."
R. J. Marion

273. Lord, Walter. MISSISSIPPI: THE PAST THAT HAS NOT DIED. *Am. Heritage 1965 16(4): 4-9, 91-101.* The author, who wrote a book on the attempt of James Meredith to enter the University of Mississippi - *The Past That Would Not Die* (New York: Harper & Row, 1965) - here provides much of the background for understanding the hostility to the Negro in Mississippi. He focuses on the Mississippi experience of Reconstruction and its aftermath culminating in the establishment of a severe system of Jim Crow in that State. The increasing enforcement of that policy is traced to about 1950.   J. D. Filipiak

274. Mabee, Carleton. WOMEN AND NEGROES MARCH. *Midwest Q. 1966 6(2): 163-174.* Compares the early struggles of women's rights advocates with the demonstrations of Negro civil rights workers today. The author cites examples of similar newspaper statements on the inferiority of women and Negroes. He describes attacks on suffragist demonstrations, refusal of police protection, jailing, fines for obstructing traffic, and notes their similarities to incidents which have occurred in the integrationists' marches. The author conjectures that alarm and antagonism may be necessary before results can be obtained by the less shocking channels of discussion, press, and politics. Largely based on newspaper reports of the time.   G. H. G. Jones

275. Mabra, Fred J. MANPOWER UTILIZATION. *Military R. 1966 46(12): 92-97.* Traces the history of the utilization of Negro manpower in the armed forces of the United States through the early stages of the Revolutionary War, the Civil War, World Wars I and II, and to the present time. In 1866 the first legal steps were taken to establish the position of the Negro as a permanent part of the U.S. Army when a limited number of Regular Army units were designated for the enlistment of Negroes. In 1917 a special officers' training camp was established at Des Moines, Iowa. A total of 371,710 Negro troops, representing 10.7 percent of the U.S. forces, saw service during World War I. By January 1944 more than 500 thousand were in the Army. In 1946 a board headed by Lieutenant General Alvan C. Gillem, Jr. recognized both the responsibility and the right of the Negro citizen to take part in military service. In January 1950 all units, jobs, and schools were opened for assignment of personnel regardless of race, but the

new policy did not eliminate segregated units. In July 1951 it was announced that all segregated units in the Far East would be disbanded. Although the Army's policy of complete integration has been in effect since 1953, community acceptance of even a small number of Negro servicemen will continue to be a problem in some areas for the foreseeable future. Fig., 2 photos.   D. D. Cameron

276. Makavoff, Julian. AMERICA'S OTHER RACIAL MINORITY - JAPANESE AMERICANS. *Contemporary R. [Great Britain] 1967 211(1217): 310-314.* Compares the position of U.S. Orientals with U.S. Negroes, in particular considering the U.S.-born Japanese, or Nisei. Both Negroes and Nisei have rejected their land of origin for their land of birth. Nisei do not suffer racial discrimination on anything like the same scale as Negroes, due largely to their small numbers, wartime loyalty to the United States, high educational level, and good social behavior. Undocumented.   D. H. Murdoch

277. Mason, Alpheus Thomas. UNDERSTANDING THE WARREN COURT: JUDICIAL SELF-RESTRAINT AND JUDICIAL DUTY. *Pol. Sci. Q. 1966 81(4): 523-563.* Discusses and analyzes the "myth-shattering, precedent-breaking course" of the U.S. Supreme Court led by Chief Justice Earl Warren the past 14 years caught, as all of its predecessors, between the warring concepts of judicial duty and judicial self-restraint, dramatically illustrated by two historic examples - *Dred Scott vs. Sandford* (1857) and *Brown vs. Board of Education* (1954). The Dred Scott decision, in which the judges split nine ways, dealt a damaging blow to the Court's prestige; the Brown case, a unanimous decision, changed the image of America at home and abroad and sparked the Negro revolution, stimulating Congress to pass the first civil rights legislation in more than a century. The Warren Court, rousing bitter denunciation from those inclined to equate security with regression in its defense of basic freedoms, is stirring a powerful current in our politics but is in keeping with the principle that: "Judicial review, like the Constitution itself, affirms as well as negates, it is both a power-releasing and power-breaking function." Judicial review, as a barrier against governing, reached its high point in the middle 1930's, and, after the proposed "packing" of the Court in 1937, "a new era emerged stressing judicial duty and responsibility." The Warren Court is the fulfillment of the prognostications of Professor Edward S. Corwin, giving "voice to the conscience of the country," yet continually facing the confrontation of the basic constitutional verities - federalism and the Bill of Rights and the question of concern for the claims of economic dogma and political ideology. A host of Warren Court rulings reflect the shift of emphasis toward constitutional limitations and affirmations grounded in the Bill of Rights and away from federalism and separation of powers. Though the Warren Court, "in expanding the limits of freedom, in buttressing the moral foundations of society, in keeping open constitutional alternatives to violent change, brings us closer to the ideals we have long professed," history gives no guarantee for believing that it will not go too far. However, our system of government provides for dialogue, conflict, and opposition as corrective measures against judicial usurpation. Documented.   Sr. M. McAuley

278. McWilliams, Carey. ONE HUNDRED YEARS OF "THE NATION."
Journalism Q. 1965 42(2): 189-197. The *Nation* was established in 1865 by a
group of gifted men, Edwin L. Godkin, Anglo-Irish journalist; Frederick Law
Olmsted, architect of Central Park in New York; and Charles Eliot Norton,
Harvard scholar, with the Philadelphia abolitionist and philanthropist, James
Miller McKim, as backer. It was strongly revived under Oswald Garrison Villard,
who assumed the editorship in 1918. The thread of consistency that runs through
a century of its pages is not so much the "liberalism" that Godkin and Villard
espoused as idealism and refusal to "buy the official line" - its belief, as an
editorial in 1908 said, that "there is no force so potent in politics as a moral issue."
S. E. Humphreys

279. Meyer, Howard N. HISTORICAL BASIS OF EMANCIPATION, 1963.
Negro Hist. Bull. 1963 27(1): 4-6. Emphasizes the role played by distorted history
in perpetuating ideas of white supremacy and justifying policies of segregation.
School textbooks fail to call attention to the treatment of Negroes by the white
majority as well as the contributions of Negroes themselves to their struggle for
freedom. The author pleads for more accurate textbooks and teaching of Negro
history as an aid to achieving an integrated society.   L. Gara

280. Moore, John Hammond. JIM CROW IN GEORGIA. *South Atlantic Q.*
1967 66(4): 554-565. A study of acts, resolutions, and ordinances which Georgia
passed on segregation indicates no racial statutes from 1870 to 1890, increasing
numbers from 1890 to 1920, and then no perceptible change until Federal action
in the 1950's. Antebellum codes governing behavior of Negroes - both slave and
free - disappeared after Appomattox. By the beginning of the 20th century, a
Georgian Negro still faced few legal restrictions, but over the next half-century
Georgia enacted a number of Jim Crow laws and ordinances - although fewer
than one might expect. A combination of custom, State law, lethargy, and a
dedicated police force combined in most cities to assure segregation. After 1954,
Federal action forced Georgia to improve the legal status of her Negro citizens.
But though legally dead, it is too soon to dig Jim Crow's grave.
J. M. Bumsted

281. Nichols, Charles H. COLOR, CONSCIENCE AND CRUCIFIXION. A
STUDY OF RACIAL ATTITUDES IN AMERICAN LITERATURE AND
CRITICISM. *Jahrbuch für Amerikastudien [West Germany] 1961 6: 37-47.*
Examines the external picture of the Negro in the writings of Herman Melville,
Mark Twain, and William Faulkner "who, by general agreement, have seriously
interpreted the deepest concerns of our group life" and the Negro character as
"seen from within" in the novels of Richard Wright, J. Saunders Redding, and
Ralph Ellison. The ambivalent attitude of the first group of writers - in exposing
the guilt and cruelty of southern society and advocating simultaneously outspoken racist dogmas - and the reviews of their critics are presented as representative of the average American mind which refrains from attempting "to empathize
the experience of being a Negro in America," and has "the fear of an unknown
and chaotic world of unimaginable evil, its criminality, sex, violence, squalor -
a world damned and deserted by God, hopelessly beyond salvation," and whose

reaction thus results in "fear-guilt-hate." Only with the second group of writers does the "range, individuality and depth of the Negro character begin to appear in the Negro's picture of himself" gradually replacing the old image of the Negro based on fears and hatred.   G. Bassler

282. Nichols, Guerdon D. BREAKING THE COLOR BARRIER AT THE UNIVERSITY OF ARKANSAS. *Arkansas Hist. Q. 1968 27(1): 3-21.* An account of events and developments leading to the admission of the first Negro student since Reconstruction to the University of Arkansas. It is asserted that Arkansas was the first Southern State to admit Negroes and that it did so without any lawsuits. Undocumented.   B. A. Drummond

283. Nova, Fritz. DIE RASSENAUSEINANDERSETZUNG IN DEN VEREINIGTEN STAATEN VON AMERIKA [The race problem in the United States of America]. *Zeitschrift für Politik [West Germany] 1964 11(4): 323-331.* Reviews the attempts since the Civil War to deal with the race problem by constitutional amendments, the 1954 Supreme Court decision on school segregation, and the Civil Rights Bill of 1964. The author concludes that all of these are more or less unsuccessful paliatives, not solutions. Based on published sources; 40 notes.
                                                                          E. Ziemke

284. Owen, J. E. RACIAL ATTITUDES IN THE U.S. SOUTH. *Contemporary R. 1968 213(1228): 238-240, 262.* Discusses the causes of continuing racial tensions in the South. The social patterns that persisted through and after the Civil War were those of a caste system. Lying behind these rationalized attitudes toward inequalities are deep psychological drives, and the profit motive in cheap labor also buttresses supporters of the status quo. Southern reactions to changes in the racial situation are varied, but all show a tendency to blame the present unrest on northerners and agitators. Southern liberals provide some hope for a future which will show periodic violence on this issue for some time to come.
                                                                          D. H. Murdoch

285. Porter, Kenneth W. NEGROES AND INDIANS ON THE TEXAS FRONTIER, 1831-1876. *J. of Negro Hist. 1956 41(3): 185-214, (4): 285-310.* An examination of the relations between Negroes and Indians on the Texas frontier, revealing a "general pattern of mutual hostility similar to that which existed between Indians and white frontiersmen." Nevertheless, examples are "sufficiently numerous to demonstrate that the pattern of relations between Negro and Indian was not absolutely identical with that between white and Indian."
                                                                          W. E. Wight

286. Povey, John F. AMERICAN EDUCATION AND FRENCH ASSIMILATION: A COMPARISON. *Midwest Q. 1970 11(3): 265-279.* A comparison of American educational policy with French educational policy in Africa. The author points out that American policy of the late 19th and early 20th centuries was the result of the necessity of Americanizing the great tide of immigration in what was called the "melting pot." The United States did not take advantage of

the great cultural variety brought by immigration, but attempted to create a homogeneous society based on the assumption of the superiority of White Anglo-Saxon Protestantism. Immigrants were willing to change and accept this arrogant conception, but Negroes, Mexicans, and American Indians found it more difficult to reject their racial and cultural identity. French colonial administration in Africa printed instructions that it was essential to make the children understand the profound difference between the unstable and bloody past and the peaceful and fertile present due to a powerful and generous nation whose wars have been beneficial. The French emphasized that the native culture was abhorrent and obviously wrong. The author concludes that, when cultures meet, the interaction can move both ways and be a matter of mutual benefit rather than of conquest. Biblio. note.   G. H. G. Jones

287. Record, Wilson. NEGRO INTELLECTUALS AND NEGRO MOVE-MENTS IN HISTORICAL PERSPECTIVE. *Am. Q. 1956 8(1): 3-20.* The contention that the Negro intelligentsia tended to support egalitarian-integration movements while nonintellectual Negro leaders advocated subordination-separatist movements is supported by a survey of some pre-Civil War efforts by Negroes to change or abolish slavery, and by the protest activities of Negroes between the Civil War and World War I. The amount and kind of education for Negroes formed the basis of the Booker T. Washington-W. E. B. DuBois controversy; the Washington biracial system against the DuBois full citizenship policy.
                                                              R. Kerley

288. Reed, Germaine A. RACE LEGISLATION IN LOUISIANA, 1864-1920. *Louisiana Hist. 1965 6(4): 379-392.* Between 1864 and 1900 the legal status of Louisiana Negroes changed from slavery to freedom to citizenship to segregation. The whole of the segregation code was adopted between 1890 and 1920. Actual practice was often at variance with the State's organic law or statutes. Examples are given in the fields of education, public facilities, and transportation. Louisiana's separate coach law was reviewed by the Supreme Court *(Plessy vs. Ferguson,* 1896). For half a century after this the power of law supplemented tradition, public sentiment, and personal choice "in the maintenance of a rigid wall of separation between the...races." 73 notes.   E. P. Stickney

289. Riccio, Robert A. THE CRISIS IN RACE RELATIONS IN AMERICAN SOCIETY AS SEEN BY TWO NOVELISTS, WILLIAM FAULKNER AND JAMES BALDWIN. *Atenea [Puerto Rico] 1967 4(1): 41-53.* Summarizes and contrasts Faulkner's and Baldwin's views of race relations in the United States as seen in their writings. Explains myths and illusions Americans believe about themselves and their history since the Civil War. Compares the two novelists' views on the moral consequences of prejudice, the speed at which changes should be brought about, and the Negro's views of his own state as compared to the state of man. 16 notes.   C. J. Hoff

290. Robinson, Wilhelmena. THE NEGRO IN THE VILLAGE OF YELLOW SPRINGS, OHIO. *Negro Hist. Bull. 1966 29(5): 103-104, 110, 112.* The legacy of the Negro of Yellow Springs is not based on the institution of slavery in the

community but, rather, on the history of his escape from the shackles of bondage to an era where he found a sheltered haven for freedom. "By 1850 the Negro population in Ohio numbered 25,279 of whom 12,386 were native, and thousands of others came to the area through the activities of the antislavery societies, and astonishingly unbelievable, yet true, by a number of slave masters who brought their mixed families to the state for freedom, education and the beginnings of a new life." A spirit of cooperation engendered in the reception of freed Negroes set the keynote of the growth of racial tolerance among the two races. Bertha C. Hull, a Negro woman of Yellow Springs, was selected as the "Ohio Mother of the Year" in 1956. In 1965, James McKee was the first Negro to hold the office of Chief of Police in an Ohio community. 19 notes.   D. D. Cameron

291. Rosenbaum, Solomon. THE ORIGIN OF JUDICIAL SANCTION OF EDUCATIONAL SEGREGATION. *Negro Hist. Bull. 1955 18(4): 75-78, 80.* The first judicial decision on educational segregation in the United States is traced to the Massachusetts Supreme Judicial Court in 1849, and the evolution of judicial concepts on this issue in subsequent segregation suits is narrated. The author holds that the "separate but equal" compromise is legally invalid in the light of this evolution.   R. Mueller

292. Rutman, Darrett B. PHILIP ALEXANDER BRUCE: A DIVIDED MIND OF THE SOUTH. *Virginia Mag. of Hist. and Biog. 1960 68(4): 387-407.* Philip Alexander Bruce is described as a lawyer, businessman, and newspaper editor, not as a scholar. He believed that the superstructure of the antebellum South "rested...upon the mudsill of slavery," and expressed sadness that the Old South had passed; voiced the universal southern fear of the growing Negro population in the South; expressed partiality for the well-born and emphasized the southern (particularly the Virginia) tradition; and was anti-Negro, to whatever extent, and considered the Negro a problem. Yet he also voiced allegiance to, and optimism for, the New South, and failed to succumb to the notion that the Negro was inherently inferior or that the Negro presented a permanent problem.   J. H. Boykin

293. Sampson, R. V. RACE RELATIONS AND LAW IN THE UNITED STATES. *Q. R. [Great Britain] 1955 293(605): 363-376.* An examination of the historical background of the Negro problem, a dilemma inherited from the 19th century, growing out of a war which left a legacy of resentment. Emancipation left the South on the defensive; it logically culminated in the Supreme Court decision of 17 May 1954. Despite southern attitudes, the trend, due to socioeconomic, political, and educational changes, has been legally and actually toward ending racial segregation. The advance toward the Court's decision has been particularly steady since 1935.   C. LeGuin

294. Schloeder, Nicholas M. DECISION FOR NEGROES AND WHITES. *Negro Hist. Bull. 1961 24(7): 152-155.* The first part of the article traces the historical background of civil rights in the period following the Civil War and contrasts the moderate ideas of Booker T. Washington with those of the more militant W. E. B. DuBois. The second part analyzes current Negro attitudes in

terms of black nationalism, the fight for legal rights of the NAACP, and the nonviolent resistance of the freedom riders and sit-in demonstrators.

L. Gara

295. Tapia, Marian Lenci. SEPARATE BUT EQUAL: A REVIEW OF THE POLICY OF EQUAL PROTECTION IN U.S. PUBLIC EDUCATION 1896-1954. *Atenea [Puerto Rico] 1966 3(3): 81-87.* Explains how the U.S. Supreme Court changed its interpretations of the "separate but equal" doctrine set forth in *Plessy vs. Ferguson* (1896), which offered legal protection for segregation in education until 1954. The author cites important cases to show how, on the basis of the equal protection clause of the 14th amendment, the Court declared the doctrine invalid. *Missouri ex rel. Gaines vs. Canada* (1939) and *Sipuel vs. Board of Regents of Oklahoma* (1948) challenged equal protection under State laws. *Sweatt vs. Painter* (1950) challenged equality of facilities and established clear measuring criteria. *McLaurin vs. Oklahoma* tested "intangibles." Through *Brown vs. Topeka Board of Education* (1954) the doctrine itself was examined and, although it was not specifically overturned, the Court declared that it was inherently unequal due to social and psychological effects of segregation on education. Based on texts on constitutional law, U.S. Supreme Court Reports, and periodicals; 26 notes.   C. J. Hoff

296. Thompson, Charles H. THE CENTENNIAL OF THE EMANCIPATION PROCLAMATION. *J. of Negro Educ. 1963 32(1): 1-5.* The author cites instances in support of his thesis that the Negro's progress toward legal equality in America from 1863 to 1963 has come because of political expediency and the insistence of a few equalitarians.   S. C. Pearson, Jr.

297. Truzzi, Marcello. THE AMERICAN CIRCUS AS A SOURCE OF FOLK-LORE: AN INTRODUCTION. *Southern Folklore Q. 1966 30(4): 289-300.* The circus in the United States dates from 1793; its heyday lasted from 1871 to about 1915. It has been in severe decline lately. In 1903 there were about 100 circus companies, but only a dozen are active today. There is strict stratification among circus personnel between management and performers on the one hand and workingmen and roustabouts on the other. Within each are further stratifications, and racism is now common and more severe than it was 50 years ago (thus, Negroes as performers were then common and still appear in Europe but no longer in the United States). Sources of folklore come from 1) the techniques, 2) circus language, 3) legends, and 4) music and song of the circus. Details and examples of each are offered. 27 notes, plus interviews.   H. Aptheker

298. Vandersee, Charles. HENRY ADAMS AND THE INVISIBLE NEGRO. *South Atlantic Q. 1967 66(1): 13-30.* The answer to Adams' views on race are complex. He makes few references to Negroes in his published works, and not many more in his private writings. In England during the Civil War Adams mentioned the Negro mainly as an "issue" in diplomatic negotiations, and in 1865 he doubted the merits of Reconstruction, noting, "I fancy white is better breeding stock." This tinge of racism remained buried in his later years, though his only

contact with Negroes was through those who were servants. Adams' references to Negroes are characterized principally as indications of indifference. Based partly on unpublished correspondence; 52 notes.   J. M. Bumsted

299. Wechsler, Herbert. THE FUTURE OF POLITICAL AND INTELLEC- TUAL FREEDOM. *Virginia Q. R. 1970 46(3): 369-389.* Traces the history of the gradual application of the freedom and protections of the First Amendment through the 14th, to the States in which *Gitlow vs. New York* (1925) was a key decision. The author considers the content and scope of the protection guaran- teed. He examines freedom of speech, press, and religion, and also the extension of the franchise. The author concludes that "legal protection of the rights of conscience and expression and participation in the choice of those who exercise authority has reached its apogee in our time." Yet, it is ironic that at this very time the "significance of the entire legal effort is so violently challenged in the name of the blacks and of the poor." Our duty and purpose, therefore, is to defend those government and legal institutions which are responsive to just demands and not to permit the defense of freedom "to become the instrument of its impairment or subversion."   O. H. Zabel

300. Whipple, James B. SOUTHERN REBEL. *Phylon 1959 20(4): 345-357.* Southern attitudes with regard to segregation have experienced some change over the years. George Washington Cable was outstanding in his opposition to segrega- tion in the post-Civil War period. An ex-Confederate soldier and a loyal south- erner, he developed a liberal program whose sources were profound and complex. Cable's *The Silent South* (1885) demanded for the Negro civil equality and respect for his human dignity. It was repudiated by advocates of white suprem- acy, notably Henry W. Grady, spokesman for the "New South" - a South which was united on a segregation platform. Today there are many Souths. The Roman Catholic Church opposes segregation. The National Association for the Advance- ment of Colored People has led strong antisegregationist movements. Yet, on the other hand, Thomas R. Waring, editor of the Charleston *News and Courier,* is one among many who defend segregation with a firmness Grady did not possess. Violence remains a southern solution to the race question.   L. Filler

301. Woodward, C. Vann. THE QUESTION OF LOYALTY. *Am. Scholar 1964 33(4): 561-567.* The young southerner today is facing a crisis of identity arising from conflicts of loyalties. This is not the first such crisis. In the 1830's the Great Reaction redefined southern loyalty to exclude dissent. The author fears that a new effort is trying to restrict southern identity to conformity to an outmoded ethnic creed. "If this definition is allowed to prevail, it will be an evil day for the Southern heritage." The stereotype of a white South solidly united against justice and decent treatment for the Negro is a travesty upon the history of the South. We must move forward. Commencement address delivered at the College of William and Mary.   E. P. Stickney

302. Woodward, James E. THE NEGRO AND HIS STATUS IN AMERICA. *Negro Hist. Bull. 1962/63 26(1): 31-33, 50.* Begins by briefly tracing white attitudes toward the Negro while slavery was practiced in the United States. Most

whites, assuming that the Negroes were inferior, supported either slavery or colonization. Negro efforts to improve their own status included working within the abolition movement, slave revolts, and slave escapes. After a brief period of political rights during Reconstruction, Negroes were again relegated to second class citizenship. Twentieth-century movements to achieve equal rights include the National Association for the Advancement of Colored People, the Southern Christian Leadership Conference, and the Congress of Racial Equality. Undocumented. L. Gara

303. --. EMANCIPATION AND BEYOND. *J. of Human Relations 1964 12(1): 17-87.*

Walden, Daniel. THOREAU AND THE CONTINUING AMERICAN REVOLUTION, pp. 17-19. Emphasizes Thoreau's individualism.

Bernhard, Berl I. EQUALITY AND 1984, pp. 20-29. A commencement address delivered at Central State College, Wilberforce, Ohio, 2 June 1963. Summarizes the history of the Negro's changing status and insists that, although equal rights will soon have been won for all, "the struggle to close the gap between the proclamation of freedom and its practice" will continue.

Clarke, John Henrik. THE ALIENATION OF JAMES BALDWIN, pp. 30-33. A critical review of Baldwin's *The Fire Next Time* (1963).

Johnson, Oakley C. ONE YEAR IN THE DEEP SOUTH: A DOCUMENTARY OF SEVENTEEN YEARS EARLIER, pp. 34-49. Describes the author's experience in 1946-47 as a white English teacher at Talladega College, a school for Negroes in Alabama.

Tillman, James A., Jr. THE NATURE AND FUNCTION OF RACISM: A GENERAL HYPOTHESIS, pp. 50-59. A paper read before the National Conference on Religion and Race, Chicago, 14-17 January 1963. Racism developed in the Western world as a rationalization for the economic exploitation of non-Europeans. It survived as a defense mechanism for those who sought a "sense of identity and status in a highly fluid social system." "Lasting and meaningful changes in race relations cannot be achieved unless the majority-group American is given the psychosocial tools that will enable him to accept himself."

Gill, Robert L. LEGACY OF A CIVIL RIGHTS LAWYER, pp. 60-72. Recounts the achievements of George L. Vaughn, a Negro who was a pioneer St. Louis civil rights lawyer. Most important was Vaughn's fight against restrictive covenants, a struggle which climaxed in his argument before the U.S. Supreme Court in the case of *Shelly vs. Kraemer* in 1948.

Brooks, Maxwell R. THE MARCH ON WASHINGTON IN RETROSPECT, pp. 73-87. Discusses the events leading up to the march, in 1964, its organization, characteristics, and effects. It helped unify the civil rights movement and "captured the imagination and sympathy of people around the world." D. J. Abramoske

304. --. THE DEMOCRATIC IDEA AND THE DEEP SOUTH. *Mississippi Q. 1965 18(4): 201-222.*

Taylor, Joe Gray. HISTORICAL SURVEY, pp. 201-215. The antebellum Deep South, "that tier of states extending from South Carolina westward through Louisiana," was mainly a frontier. The combination of frontier influence and Jeffersonian ideas produced "free white adult male democracy." A partial answer to the question of how the plantation system could coexist with white democracy lies in the fact that the two-party antebellum Deep South actually exhibited some class conflict. Reaction against democratic ideas came with the reaction against abolitionism. Reconstruction regimes attempted to bring a northern conception of democracy to the former rebels. Tactics of force used to bring an end to Reconstruction largely became the normal procedure in southern politics for some time, under the concept of white supremacy. Early 20th-century southern reformers appealed to racial prejudice to gain popular support for their reforms. The spread of popular education in the Deep South, significantly affecting the Negro, also resulted in the commitment of the white intelligentsia to the democratic ideal. Based on published material; 32 notes.

Adams, Richard P. ACADEMIC REFLECTIONS, pp. 216-222. Statistics indicate that conditions of academic freedom and tenure, a significant aspect of the democratic idea, are worse in the South than in the United States as a whole. Since democracy provides for peaceful, systematic, and productive change and since institutions of higher learning are leaders of change, theirs is a vital role in this function of democracy. As active agents of change, institutions of higher learning come into conflict with those who dislike and resist change. The focus of this conflict at present is usually the problem or process of desegregation, actually only one aspect of a more complex problem, involving not just a region but mankind as a whole. It involves implementation of means to provide for all men a better life. Economic development, social reform, and extension of cultural activities, all needed in the Deep South, require enlightened social and political leadership with popular support. Most of all, individuals need courage to risk the displeasure of fellow citizens in advocating constructive programs which may not have popular support at the time.   R. V. Calvert

The Afro-American in Canada

305. Blakeley, Phillis R. WILLIAM HALL, CANADA'S FIRST NAVAL V. C. *Dalhousie R. [Canada] 1957 37(3): 250-258.* A brief biography of a Nova Scotian Negro who won the Victoria Cross for his feats as a seaman during the Sepoy Mutiny in 1857.   R. W. Winks

306. Davis, Morris. RESULTS OF PERSONALITY TESTS GIVEN TO NEGROES IN THE NORTHERN AND SOUTHERN UNITED STATES AND IN HALIFAX, CANADA. *Phylon 1964 25(4): 362-368.* The Tomkins-Horn Picture Arrangement Test was administered to white and Negro seventh, eighth, and ninth grade students in Halifax schools, and results were compared with data derived from administering the same test in the northern and southern United States as summarized in Bertram P. Karon's *The Negro Personality* (1958). The author concluded that "race by itself does not distinguish the Canadian groups psychologically; race plus economic differential has only a slightly greater distinguishing effect. Karon's major finding is confirmed: psychological

differences between whites and Negroes are not traceable to genetically transmitted racial characteristics but to social conditions, in particular to the (overtly or covertly) terroristic caste system of the American South." S. C. Pearson, Jr.

307. Hill, Daniel G. NEGROES IN TORONTO 1793-1865. *Ontario Hist. [Canada] 1963 55(2): 73-91.* The Negro community originated with the slaves of early settlers. The influx of fugitive slaves began in the 1830's and reached a peak in the 1850's. The integration of the Negroes into the white community is discussed and the development of abolitionist movements is noted. The author emphasizes the financial well-being of the Negroes and the growth of community churches and institutions. Based on a "recently discovered anti-slavery Negro weekly published in Toronto in the 1850's" and the unpublished family records of a Negro freedman; 63 notes.   J. M. E. Usher

308. Lubka, Nancy. FERMENT IN NOVA SCOTIA. *Queen's Q. [Canada] 1969 76(2): 213-228.* Discusses racism and its implications in Nova Scotia. Negroes have long been a part of the Province's population, but here, as elsewhere, ignorance and apathy have created racial problems. Under the leadership of H. A. J. Wedderburn, a Nova Scotian Human Rights Commission has been organized to deal with existing conditions and racist attitudes while simultaneously seeking improved social and economic status. The commission is especially active in Halifax, where the worst conditions exist, and its ultimate goal is simply a "decent life" for Negroes. 6 notes.   J. A. Casada

309. McCurdy, Alvin. HENRY WALTON BIBB. *Negro Hist. Bull. 1958 12(1): 19-21.* Reviews the character and achievements of Henry Bibb, a fugitive slave who escaped to Canada and became a successful newspaper editor and a promoter of Canadian colonization. The author makes a plea for improved racial understanding. Undocumented.   L. Gara

310. Pease, William H. and Pease, Jane H. OPPOSITION TO THE FOUNDING OF THE ELGIN SETTLEMENT. *Can. Hist. R. 1957 38(3): 202-218.* A case study of anti-Negro sentiment in Canada just prior to the American Civil War. The forms of anti-Negro sentiment detailed in this study establish the existence of a well-defined feeling in Canada against the Negro despite the legal safeguards which he enjoyed there. Although the Elgin Settlement (ca. 1849-69) provided a home for nearly one thousand Negroes and demonstrated their abilities, it failed to attack the basic problem, that of integrating one social group with another. Based on regional newspapers, church records, government documents and the William King Papers in the Public Archives of Canada.
                                                                        A

311. Pentland, H. H. THE DEVELOPMENT OF A CAPITALISTIC LABOUR MARKET IN CANADA. *Can. J. of Econ. and Pol. Sci. 1959 25(4): 450-461.* Analyzes the varying labor markets in Canada from 1688-1850, namely,

the slave, the feudal, and the capitalistic. The author's sketch of the capitalistic labor market is broken into three elements: 1) demand, 2) sources of supply, and 3) barriers to labor's escape from the market. B. W. Onstine

312. Rawlyk, George A. THE GUYSBOROUGH NEGROES: A STUDY IN ISOLATION. *Dalhousie R. [Canada] 1968 48(1): 24-36.* The "Loyalist Negroes" who settled in Nova Scotia after the American Revolution, received poor land in remote areas and were subject to discrimination by whites, but by the second generation the survivors had come to grips with the Nova Scotia environment. A handful of leaders appeared, notably Thomas Brownspriggs, one of the original settlers at Tracadie, followed by Dempsey Jordan, both schoolteachers. The Negroes were largely ignored by the Roman Catholic Church and the Anglicans but became an object of concern for Methodists and Baptists. The census report of 1871 is used to assess the position of the Negroes in Guysborough County, when their numbers stood at 747. The author comments on education provided for Negroes between 1790 and 1940. 19 notes. L. F. S. Upton

313. Reid, Patricia H. SEGREGATION IN BRITISH COLUMBIA. *Bull. of the United Church of Can. 1963 16: 1-15.* The issue of segregation arose in 1859-60 in a mission in British Columbia begun by the Congregational Unions in Canada and England. The first missionary, Reverend William F. Clarke, would have nothing to do with the "Negro corner" requested by some of his white parishioners. When his British colleague, Reverend Matthew Macfie, arrived shortly after Clarke, he began to hold separate services involving segregation of Negroes. Clarke's work for a time prospered, and a small church was erected. When the Colonial Missionary Society finally awakened to the situation, they upheld Clarke's position and recalled Macfie. Copiously documented from *The Canadian Independent Magazine.* E. P. Stickney

314. Weber, Ralph E. RIOT IN VICTORIA, 1860. *J. of Negro Hist. 1971 56(2): 141-148.* Much anti-Negro feeling existed on Vancouver Island after 1850. Most of the differences concerned the extension of voting privileges to the Negro immigrants of the region. Reproduces three newspaper selections from the *Colonist* of Victoria which illustrate the expectations and frustrations of Negroes on the island. 4 notes. R. S. Melamed

315. Wilson, Ruth Danenhower. NEGRO-WHITE RELATIONS IN WESTERN ONTARIO. *Negro Hist. Bull. 1955 18(5): 105-106.* Contrasting present-day racial discrimination in Dresden, Western Ontario, with earlier toleration, the writer sympathetically reviews the history of Western Ontario's Negro community since 1793. Discrimination originated during the mid-19th century out of religious friction, and later grew under the impact of housing, labor, and schooling issues. R. Mueller

316. Winks, Robin W. A HISTORY OF NEGRO SCHOOL SEGREGATION IN NOVA SCOTIA AND ONTARIO. *Can. Hist. R. 1969 52(2): 64-191.* Examines the rise of segregated schools for Negroes, especially in the 1850's, and

traces the attack upon such separate schools to their closing in the 1960's. Based on political and educational documents in the archives of Halifax, Ottawa, and Toronto.   A

317. Winks, Robin W. THE CANADIAN NEGRO: A HISTORICAL ASSESS-MENT. *J. of Negro Hist.* *1968 53(4): 283-300, 54(1): 1-18.* Part I. Scholars of Canadian life and history have found the social characteristics of Canadian Negroes as well as patterns of racial discrimination very similar to those in the United States. Canadians tend to blame the influence of the United States for any racial prejudice or discrimination which exists in their country. They are also ignorant of the plight of Negroes in Canada. Only in recent years has both scholarly and popular interest in the Canadian Negro made a limited amount of information available and this, combined with a series of events, has made visible the "invisible" black population of Canada. Part II. Negroes in Canada have been less aggressive in seeking their rights than those in the United States. Canadian black people are mostly nonmilitant, lacking both a national organization and a leader, permitting other groups to speak for them, and divided among themselves on the basis of the particular historical group to which they trace their ancestry. In general, white Canadians think of Negroes as Africans who should be left alone to develop in segregated communities. 11 notes.   L. Gara

2

THE BLACK EXPERIENCE IN COLONIAL AMERICA

African Origins & the Beginnings of Slavery

318. Ackerman, Robert K. COLONIAL LAND POLICIES AND THE SLAVE PROBLEM. *Pro. of the South Carolina Hist. Assoc. 1965: 28-35.* Discusses the problem of the large importation of Negro slaves into South Carolina during the early 18th century and the efforts of proprietors and later the royal government to curtail it so as to encourage compact settlements of relatively small land holdings, which would strengthen the defense of the colony and encourage trade.
                                                                                    J. W. Thacker, Jr.

319. Anderson, Robert L. THE END OF AN IDYLL. *Florida Hist. Q. 1963 42(1): 35-47.* For 131 years, Negro slaves from the English colonies and, later, the United States, fled to Florida and found a comfortable refuge among the Indians. They sometimes cooperated with Indian warriors in raiding Georgia plantations, until American forces occupied Florida.   G. L. Lycan

320. Andrews, Robert Hardy. THE FIRST AMERICAN FIGHT FOR CIVIL RIGHTS. *Mankind 1968 1(8): 8-9, 18.* In the spring of 1741 New York City witnessed an outburst of unrestrained hostility toward the Negroes in Manhattan. They were accused of theft and of planning to burn down the city. Protestants in the city resented the presence of the unemployed Irish Catholics and their mingling with the Negroes. While the details of the events of this year are obscure, it is known that a riot broke out and that 14 Negroes were burned at the stake, 20 were hanged in chains, and 71 were sold into slavery. Twenty-one white men and women who aided the blacks were arrested and tortured, and four white men were hanged.   P. D. Thomas

321. Annunziata, Frank. THREE THEORIES ON ANTI-SLAVERY IN CO-LONIAL AMERICAN LITERATURE. *Social Studies 1969 60(6): 250-257.* Presents documented evidence of antislavery sentiment, though such sentiments

were rare during the Colonial period of American history. The author interprets and comments on the works of antislavery leaders during the 18th century who found the practice inconsistent with biblical teachings as well as with political theories which extolled the rights of man. 48 notes. L. Raife

322. Babuscio, Jack. CREVECOEUR IN CHARLES TOWN: THE NEGRO IN THE CAGE. *J. of Hist. Studies 1969 2(4): 283-286.* Crèvecoeur's *Letters from an American Farmer,* published in 1782, picture a new nation in a new world having a new social system whose laws were those of a natural order and in which men were free and society was uninstitutionalized. But Letter IX describes Crèvecoeur's encounter with a Negro caged in a tree and being pecked to death by birds as punishment for a crime against the whites. Babuscio points out that the difference between social fact and ideal such as that which shocked Crèvecoeur ought also to shock today's romantics who conceive of democracy as a form of anarchic relationships. N. W. Moen

323. Bethke, Robert D. CHESTER COUNTY WIDOW WILLS (1714-1800): A FOLKLIFE SOURCE. *Pennsylvania Folklife 1968 18(1): 16-20.* The wills recorded in Will Books A (1714) through J (1800) have been examined to determine the kinds of information they give about Pennsylvania ways. Numerous excerpts from the provisions demonstrate the kinds of property, including slaves, which the widows held. Clothes, beds, and saddles seem to be most important. Discusses funeral arrangements. 60 notes, biblio. F. L. Harrold

324. Billias, George A. MISADVENTURES OF A MAINE SLAVER. *Am. Neptune 1959 19(2): 114-122.* Describes the voyage made by the schooner *Lynn* in 1795 from Kingston, Jamaica, to Savannah, Georgia, with a cargo of 70 slaves. In addition to hardships caused by foul weather, the slaves brought plague on board and conditions on the slaver were appalling. Based on the logbooks and papers of Samuel Patterson, a Maine master mariner. B. Waldstein

325. Boller, Paul F., Jr. GEORGE WASHINGTON AND THE QUAKERS. *Bull. of Friends Hist. Assoc. 1960 49(2): 67-83.* An account of the relations between Washington and the Quakers. Washington came gradually to respect, but not to share, the principles of the Friends. He did not sympathize with their pacifism during the Revolution, but he treated them with fairness and decency. After the war his sympathy increased, although he objected to their vigorous agitation on the antislavery issue. He approved of their efforts on behalf of the Indians. On the issue of war with France, he had a disagreement with the Quaker George Logan. Documented. N. D. Kurland

326. Boskin, Joseph. THE ORIGINS OF AMERICAN SLAVERY: EDUCATION AS AN INDEX OF EARLY DIFFERENTIATION. *J. of Negro Educ. 1966 35(2): 125-133.* Summarizes four recent works on the topic of slavery by Oscar and Mary Handlin, "The Origins of the Southern Labor System," *William and Mary Quarterly* 1950 (April); Carl N. Degler, "Black Men in a White Man's Country" in *Out of Our Past* (New York: Harper and Row, 1959); Stanley M.

Elkins, *Slavery: A Problem in American Institutional and Intellectual Life* (Chicago: U. of Chicago Press, 1959); and Winthrop Jordan, "Modern Tensions and the Origins of American Slavery" in *Journal of Southern History* 1962 28(1). The area of education as a significant index of early differentiation between slave and nonslave is analyzed. The author notes that 17th-century statutes concerned with education almost always omitted reference to "Negro" or "slave." He concludes that in this period during which the overriding objectives were survival and perpetuation of English culture the failure to provide for Negro education suggests that Negroes were regarded as uneducable. This attitude was reflected in laws equating the Negro as slave - meaning uncivilizable.   S. C. Pearson, Jr.

327. Bronner, Edwin B. INTERCOLONIAL RELATIONS AMONG QUAKERS BEFORE 1750. *Quaker Hist. 1967 56(1): 3-17.* The London Yearly Meeting (of British Friends) regarded the six American continental bodies and the smaller groups in the West Indies as subordinate. It sent an annual letter to each American yearly meeting and to Friends on each British island, expecting each to report. It also sent publications and traveling ministers, and sometimes expected monetary support from America. After the Philadelphia Yearly Meeting united the Quaker immigrants of the Delaware Valley in 1681, the English Friends approved of its attempt to become the American Quaker center. The plan of 1686 - to have the five other American yearly meetings, consisting mostly of converts, represented at Philadelphia - failed. Philadelphia sent more itinerant ministers along the seaboard than other American yearly meetings, and its 1719 discipline was influential. It failed to establish annual correspondence with them in the 17th century, and it was irregular in the 18th. Colonial American Friends sent money to each other for the relief of the persecuted and for building meeting houses. They exchanged publications and consulted, toward 1750, on the slavery questions.   T. D. S. Bassett

328. Bruns, Roger. ANTHONY BENEZET'S ASSERTION OF NEGRO EQUALITY. *J. of Negro Hist. 1971 56(3): 230-238.* Anthony Benezet (1713-84) was a Quaker schoolteacher who became the most prolific antislavery propagandist during the period of the American Revolution. He based his arguments against slavery on the unequivocal assertion that Negroes were biologically, morally, and intellectually equal to all other people. Some of his ideas about black culture, especially that in Africa, were simplistic and overdrawn, but it must be remembered that most opponents of slavery in his day still considered Negroes inherently inferior in almost every respect. 33 notes.   R. S. Melamed

329. Bumsted, John M. and Clark, Charles E. NEW ENGLAND'S TOM PAINE: JOHN ALLEN AND THE SPIRIT OF LIBERTY. *William and Mary Q. 1964 21(4): 561-570.* John Allen, who authored political pamphlets in pre-Revolutionary Boston, was an advocate of an American parliament as a counterpoise to the British Parliament. He was also a persistent critic of conditions in America ranging from slavery to religious taxation. Liberty and equality, to Allen, were derived fundamentally from the Scriptures.   H. M. Ward

330. Carroll, Kenneth L. WILLIAM SOUTHEBY, EARLY QUAKER ANTI-SLAVERY WRITER. *Pennsylvania Mag. of Hist. and Biog. 1965 89(4): 416-427.* A biographical sketch of William Southeby, early 18th-century antagonist of the Philadelphia Monthly Meeting on the question of slavery. His years in Cecil and Talbot Counties, Maryland, are touched upon, and his participation in Pennsylvania politics in the 1680's receives brief attention. The author deals mainly with Southeby's association with Philadelphia Quakerism, although his earlier activites as a Quaker in Maryland are also noted. His talent as a conciliator is described, as is his involvement in the Keithian controversy of the 1690's. Considerable emphasis is placed on his opposition to slavery and the reprimands which he received from the Philadelphia Monthly Meeting because of his published writings on the subject. Based on the Minutes of the Philadelphia Monthly Meeting, other Quaker documents, Maryland Land Records, and published sources, primary and secondary; 50 notes.   D. P. Gallagher

331. Cohen, Sheldon S. ELIAS NEAU, INSTRUCTOR TO NEW YORK'S SLAVES. *New-York Hist. Soc. Q. 1971 55(1): 6-27.* Elias Neau (1662-1722), a French Huguenot, settled in New York in 1691 and began a career in commerce. Captured and imprisoned by the French at sea in 1692, he was sentenced to the galleys for life, only to be freed after the Peace of Ryswick (1697). After his return to New York two years later, he prospered and spent the remainder of his life in humanitarian concerns, principally as catechist for New York City in connection with the Society for the Propagation of the Gospel in Foreign Parts. In this position he devoted much of his time to instruction, primarily religious, of the slave population. By his death a foundation for this type of activity had been well laid. Based on primary and secondary sources; 5 illus., 40 notes.

C. L. Grant

332. Craven, Wesley Frank. TWENTY NEGROES TO JAMESTOWN IN 1619? *Virginia Q. R. 1971 47(3): 416-420.* Explores the long-established "fact" that 20 Negroes, the first to reach this country, were delivered to Jamestown by a Dutch man-of-war in 1619. Captain John Smith, in his *Historie of Virginia* said there were 20, basing his comment on a still-extant letter of John Rolfe who said there were "20. and odd Negroes." Robert Beverley in 1705 added the information that these were the first Negroes to be "carried into the country." There is no evidence that the Dutch ship went beyond Cape Comfort. Other sources indicate that an English man-of-war, the *Treasurer,* with Negroes aboard arrived about the same time, but apparently took its Negroes to Bermuda. Discretion was used in reports because leaders of the Virginia Company feared that use of the colony as a base for privateering against the Spaniard and the West Indies would result in the king's displeasure. Negroes were in Bermuda as early as 1616; has historians' concern with the status of early Negroes resulted in failure to explore fully their first identification with the country?   O. H. Zabel

333. Cushing, John. THE CUSHING COURT AND THE ABOLITION OF SLAVERY IN MASSACHUSETTS: MORE NOTES ON THE "QUOCK WALKER CASE." *Am. J. of Legal Hist. 1961 5(2): 118-144.* Using unpublished court records and personal papers from various Massachusetts archives, the

author recounts the circumstances attending the abolition of Negro slavery in (1781) Massachusetts. The author concludes that the famous Quock Walker Case was only part of a series of litigations in which the abolition question was treated by the State courts, and that Chief Judge William Cushing does not completely deserve the reputation given him by historians as a champion of abolition.

N. C. Brockman, S.M.

334. Farnie, D. A. THE COMMERCIAL EMPIRE OF THE ATLANTIC, 1607-1783. *Econ. Hist. R. 1962 15(2): 205-218.* A synthesis of the state of Atlantic trade in the light of recent research (listed in an appended bibliography) which aims at fostering "discussion of the role of England in the growth of Atlantic trade during the two formative centuries." This is part of a great frontier movement, which found not gold but soil for the production of staples. The Dutch War of 1664-67 is "being seen as a turning point in history for it established English control over a complex of Atlantic trade." Sections are devoted to the nature and trends in the trade in cod and furs, tobacco, sugar, and slaves. The "Cisatlantic response" was the Americanization of English commerce and the development of a secular, commercial, sensate tradition. The revolt of the American colonies showed the dangers of settler-participation and of over-dependence on the American market.

B. L. Crapster

335. Giffen, Jane C. A SELECTION OF NEW HAMPSHIRE INVENTORIES. *Hist. New Hampshire 1969 24(1/2): 3-78.* Lists furniture, clothing, tools, utensils, livestock, slaves, real estate, pews, notes, and books (twice listed by title), for 12 families. All but two of the families were from Portsmouth; all but two were upper class; some were legatees. Based on provincial and Rockingham County probate records; brief biographical notes.

T. D. S. Bassett

336. Hast, Adele. THE LEGAL STATUS OF THE NEGRO IN VIRGINIA 1705-1765. *J. of Negro Hist. 1969 54(3): 217-239.* The slave in 18th-century Virginia was both a person and a nonperson at the same time. As a person, he was held liable for specific criminal acts and was a tithable individual in the revenue arrangements of the colony. As a nonperson, the slave was handled as property; he was part of his master's estate and could be inherited as real or personal property, bought or sold without consent, and taken for payment of debts. The slave after 1705 was forced to remain in bondage if he was not a Christian in his native land. After 1723 manumission was forbidden, except by public act. The author describes the situation of slaves in regard to marriage, court testimony, absence without permission, conspiracy, and possession of private property. Concerning his property status, the slave was considered a means of raising revenue, and in business dealings was legally the same as cattle. Owners who purchased slaves with hidden physical defects could sue for fraud. When dealt with in wills and estates, however, slaves tended to follow the law of real property rather than chattel ownership, but there was some confusion on this matter.Free Negroes were at times treated as white men when brought into court for debt or for bearing illegitimate children, but they were classified as Negro or

slave in regard to the militia, clergy, public officeholding, court testimony, and voting. Based on primary and secondary sources; 119 notes.

R. S. Melamed

337. Hoyt, Joseph B. SALEM'S WEST AFRICA TRADE 1835-1863 AND CAPTAIN VICTOR FRANCIS DEBAKER. *Essex Inst. Hist. Collections 1966 102(1): 37-73.* Discusses Salem's trade with West Africa, "a sort of last fling, a desperate attempt by men who had grown up in the maritime tradition to fight the inexorable forces that were strangling Salem's merchant marine." Early Salem trade with the area beginning in 1785 appears to have involved the slave trade, but public opinion drove the traders to search for other cargoes. Pepper was the first and only important item before 1835, when the official attitudes of European countries changed and trade was really opened up. The trade grew steadily, and the peak was reached in 1860. Most of the trade was monopolized by three merchants: Robert Brookhouse, Edward D. Kimball, and Charles Hoffman, but the author describes the trade through the life story of a typical ship captain, Victor Francis Debaker, born in 1818 in Nantes, France. His career began in Salem in 1837 as a mariner, and he advanced toward command as the trade grew. In the 1860's, he made a small fortune in the African trade, but he left it in 1863, about the time that Salem's overseas maritime activities ended for good. Annotated from unpublished papers. Maps and statistical appendix.

J. M. Bumsted

338. Ireland, Ralph R. SLAVERY ON LONG ISLAND: A STUDY OF ECONOMIC MOTIVATION. *J. of Long Island Hist. 1966 6(2): 1-12.* Slavery was introduced on Long Island, New York, perhaps as early as 1626. The slaves fulfilled the primary function of supplying cheap labor to the farmers of the region. In the absence of adequate numbers of indentured farm workers, the farmers were compelled to rely increasingly on slaves. Soon slave ownership became important in itself as a status symbol. Even ministers and Quakers owned slaves in the late 17th and early 18th centuries. It was not until the democratic foment of the Revolutionary era that moral objections were raised against slave ownership. The author asserts that many who supported emancipation in New York in the late 18th century did so not out of religious or ethical convictions, but rather because they desired to free themselves from an institution which was becoming too expensive to maintain.

J. Judd

339. Kates, Don B., Jr. ABOLITION, DEPORTATION, INTEGRATION: ATTITUDES TOWARD SLAVERY IN THE EARLY REPUBLIC. *J. of Negro Hist. 1968 53(1): 33-47.* Almost without exception American statesmen of the era 1770-1810 abhorred slavery, though only Benjamin Franklin advocated anything approaching immediate and complete emancipation. Social and political rather than economic considerations prompted their reluctance to foster immediate abolition. They feared the prospect of a racially integrated society and honestly believed that Negroes were morally and intellectually inferior to whites. Some favored programs of emancipation and colonization but these were objected to on the basis of an anticipated disaster from the loss of a labor supply, the enormity of financing such a venture, lack of agreement about the place to remove

blacks, and the reluctance of Negroes to leave the United States for some strange place. By rejecting integration and failing to agree on any method to end slavery, 18th-century Americans postponed solutions for later generations. Based on primary and secondary published works; 30 notes.   L. Gara

340. Kutler, Stanley I. PENNSYLVANIA COURTS, THE ABOLITION ACT, AND NEGRO RIGHTS. *Pennsylvania Hist. 1963 30(1): 14-27.* The "first statutory action against slavery in the United States" was the "Act for the Gradual Abolition of Slavery" by the Pennsylvania Legislature in 1780. Analyzes various court cases which "worked for the gradual abolition of slavery, but not for political and social equality....the major victory of the Negro was that he acquired a firm title to equal legal rights....The Negro's recourse to the courts protected, preserved, and advanced his freedom, and, in another century, is proving to be his most potent weapon in the quest for equality." 57 notes.
D. H. Swift

341. MacEacheren, Elaine. EMANCIPATION OF SLAVERY IN MASSACHUSETTS: A REEXAMINATION, 1770-1790. *J. of Negro Hist. 1970 55(4): 289-306.* Slavery was obscurely instituted in Massachusetts Bay a few years after the Colony was established, and its demise was equally obscure more than one hundred years later. It is still not clear why the Federal Census of 1790 failed to record any slaves in Massachusetts. The judicial and economic arguments of historians fail to provide a satisfactory answer to the problem; any solution must be found in local studies of the period. Concludes that evidence now indicates that the "peculiar institution" disintegrated in Boston because of the individual actions of both masters and slaves, and that the provisions of the Massachusetts Constitution of 1780 may have played a more important role than has been previously thought. 53 notes.   R. S. Melamed

342. Marshall, Peter. TRAVELLERS AND THE COLONIAL SCENE. *Bull. of the British Assoc. of Am. Studies 1963 (7): 5-28.* Describes the reactions of British, French, and American travelers during the 18th century to the 13 colonies. Such topics as the southern colonies, agriculture, religion, urban life, slavery, and the West are discussed. Based on secondary sources and published travel accounts.   D. J. Abramoske

343. McLoughlin, William G. and Jordan, Winthrop D., eds. BAPTISTS FACE THE BARBARITIES OF SLAVERY IN 1710. *J. of Southern Hist. 1963 29(4): 495-501.* Two letters from the Baptist association in South Moulton, Devon, England, to a Baptist Church at Ewhaw, near Charles Town, in the colony of South Carolina, replying to a question of the colonial congregation whether its members, as Christians, might comply with a South Carolina legal requirement that a master must castrate a slave who ran away for the fourth time for 30 days. The association found that compliance with the law was not a violation of proper conscience. Documented.   S. E. Humphreys

344. Middleton, Arthur P. THE COLONIAL VIRGINIA PARSON. *William and Mary Q. 1969 26(3): 425-440.* Explains the folklore behind the caricature of the down-to-earth Virginia parson in the 18th century. The typical Virginia cleric, on the contrary, was a member of the colonial aristocracy and usually well-to-do. Biographies of two contrasting clergymen, Jonathan Boucher and Devereux Jarratt, are sketched. Boucher, a High Churchman, appears more liberal-minded than is generally supposed, especially on tolerance and slavery. Jarratt, an Evangelical Anglican, is depicted as the more individualistic and open-minded of the two. Details are given of the training and rise to prominence of both men in the church. Note.   H. M. Ward

345. Miller, Randall M. THE FAILURE OF THE COLONY OF GEORGIA UNDER THE TRUSTEES. *Georgia Hist. Q. 1969 53(1): 1-17.* Argues that the Georgia colony was founded not primarily for philanthropic reasons but for purposes of mercantilism. Thus the Trustees laced their promotional tracts with economic arguments - the colony would create a new market, solve the unemployment problem in England, add to the productivity of the empire, and produce exotic crops hitherto obtainable only in the Orient. But the success of the Georgia experiment was compromised by prohibitions on slavery and on a fee simple land system. The Trustees gave in to the demands of the colonists on these two points by 1750. Only then, contends the author, did Georgia begin to prosper. Based largely on research in published primary material; 59 notes.   R. A. Mohl

346. Moulton, Phillips. JOHN WOOLMAN'S APPROACH TO SOCIAL ACTION - AS EXEMPLIFIED IN RELATION TO SLAVERY. *Church Hist. 1966 35(4): 399-410.* "Because of his concern for slaves, slaveholders, true religion, and society at large, and because he saw no realistic solution within the context of slavery, Woolman labored for its abolition." He spoke against slavery in Quaker meetings, in personal encounters with slaveholders, and through his published works. John Woolman's success derived from his integrity, emotional balance, love, and humility. Based on the published works of Woolman; 40 notes.   S. C. Pearson, Jr.

347. O'Brien, William. DID THE JENNISON CASE OUTLAW SLAVERY IN MASSACHUSETTS? *William and Mary Q. 1960 17(2): 219-241.* In spite of ambiguities in the records, a lack of newspaper references, and the clerk's insistence that no constitutional questions were decided, the evidence of Chief Justice Horace Gray's report of Chief Justice William Cushing's charge to the jury, that slavery was unconstitutional, cannot be refuted. The letter of the court clerk, Charles Cushing, does throw some doubt on the prevailing theories, however. Based on the records of the relevant trials and on hitherto unpublished correspondence between Jared Ingersoll and Charles Cushing.   E. Oberholzer, Jr.

348. Oedel, Howard T. SLAVERY IN COLONIAL PORTSMOUTH. *Hist. New Hampshire 1966 21(3): 3-11.* After the failure of Indian slavery and indentured servitude in the 17th century, Negro slaves, usually children, were brought from the West Indies for domestic service with the well-to-do. A third of the 150

in New Hampshire in 1721 were in Portsmouth; two-thirds of the 300 in 1775. The freedom clause in Article I of the 1783 New Hampshire constitution was interpreted to grant freedom to all slaves born thereafter; but many were emancipated and some ran away. The 1790 census listed 26 slaves and 76 free Negroes; a few slaves were left in 1840. Portsmouth merchants were never slavers. Based on family MSS., reminiscences, newspapers, and State documents.

T. D. S. Bassett

349. Palmer, Paul C. SERVANT INTO SLAVE: THE EVOLUTION OF THE LEGAL STATUS OF THE NEGRO LABORER IN COLONIAL VIRGINIA. *South Atlantic Q. 1966 65(3): 355-370.* Reviews the legal history of slavery in colonial Virginia to shed some light on the problem of the origins of racial slavery. By 1641, some Negroes were legally in a situation akin to slavery. By 1661, many Negroes were servants for life, and by 1670, most of the essentials of slavery were clearly established in law. From 1670 to 1705, Virginia developed a thorough legal statement of chattel slavery, and then mitigated this in minor details in the 18th century. It is clear that the development of chattel slavery was a gradual process, and equally apparent that the political leaders of the colony made no serious attempt to prevent or destroy the institution. 57 notes.

J. M. Bumsted

350. Rabe, Harry G. THE REVEREND DEVEREAUX JARRATT AND THE VIRGINIA SOCIAL ORDER. *Hist. Mag. of the Protestant Episcopal Church 1964 33(4): 299-336.* This 18th-century Virginian's *Autobiography* supplies much of the evidence upon which this study is based. The Reverend Devereaux Jarratt rose from the yeoman class to the gentry, eventually taking orders in the Anglican Church. For 38 years he served as pastor of Bath in Dinwiddie County, Virginia. Although a product of the "New Awakening," he contributed nothing original to theology. His working agreement with the Virginia Methodists collapsed when they broke with Anglicanism and organized the Methodist Episcopal Church in America. His attitude toward the War for Independence, the separation of church and state and the "leveling" of Virginia's social classes was typical of a man of his background and beliefs. Augustinian in his view of history, Jarratt's conservatism comes through in his writings. Convincing proof is offered that he was himself a slave-owner (and defender of slavery on Biblical grounds) despite his denials. The article is based on a master's thesis, Claremont College. Documented.

E. G. Roddy

351. Rankin, Hugh F. THE COLONIAL SOUTH. *Writing Southern Hist.: Essays in Historiography in Honor of Fletcher M. Green (Baton Rouge: Louisiana State U. Press: 1965); 3-37.* The colonial period of southern history has been constantly reevaluated. With the establishment of graduate schools in the South, historical curiosity began to be divorced from ancestor worship. Wesley Frank Craven's writings are a fundamental starting point for the study of the southern colonies. Many modern historians search for the roots of democracy in the political practices of the colonies. Inevitably the studies of slavery are controversial. The central theme of the literature of southern colonial history is a derivative

culture "undergoing environmental mutations." The nature of the sources has always limited the study of southern colonial culture to the upper classes. 100 biblio. notes. E. P. Stickney

352. Ruchames, Louis. THE SOURCES OF RACIAL THOUGHT IN COLONIAL AMERICA. *J. of Negro Hist. 1967 52(4): 251-272.* Racial thought in the English colonies in America was rooted in a long heritage of European racial thinking, ethnocentrism, and a history of slavery involving both Europeans and Africans. The author rejects Carl Degler's theory that racial prejudice led Englishmen to practice discrimination and that discrimination led to slavery. Rather it was the English experience with the slave trade, based on the assumption that Negroes were inferior creatures fit only for enslavement, that formed the English settlers' attitudes toward Africans in American colonies. Documented mostly by writings of other historians; 66 notes. L. Gara

353. Schmid, Hans. DIE VERSCHIEDENEN EINWANDERERWELLEN IN DIE VEREINIGTEN STAATEN VON NORDAMERIKA VON DEN ANFÄNGEN BIS ZUR QUOTENGESETZGEBUNG [The various waves of immigrants into the United States of North America from the beginning to the quota legislation]. *Hist. Jahrbuch [West Germany] 1965 85: 323-361.* Describes the ethnic, social, and religious composition of the large waves of immigrants who colonized the United States from prehistoric times (Indians and Eskimos) to the Johnson-Reed Act of 1924. In the 17th century the Anglo-Saxon element dominated but was surpassed in the 18th century by Africans, Scotch-Irish, and Germans. In the 19th century three waves can be distinguished: the five million who arrived between 1820 and 1860 were primarily Irish and South German, the bulk of the 10 million from 1860 to 1890 came also from Western and Northern Europe, but the 17 million between 1890 and 1920 were largely from Southern and Eastern Europe. The reasons for this emigration are discussed, also their forms and areas of settlement in the United States and their problem of assimilation. Based primarily on secondary sources; 81 notes. G. P. Bassler

354. Scott, Kenneth, ed. THE ARMS OF AMSTERDAM, AN EXTRACT FROM THE RECORDS OF THE GENERAL COURT OF VIRGINIA, 1664. *Virginia Mag. of Hist. and Biog. 1969 77(4): 407-440.* Reproduces the only known transcript - compiled in 1847 and placed in the New York Historical Society - of the affair of the *Arms of Amsterdam* (1661). While Englishman Robert Downman sailed as a privateer, bearing a letter of marque from Alfonso VI of Portugal and seeking Dutch merchant ships, the Portuguese and Dutch governments signed a treaty of peace. Also, separately, England agreed to deny assistance to Dutch or Portuguese privateers. Downman, however, captured a Dutch merchant-slaver and unloaded his cargo in Virginia. Justice was never rendered because England captured New Amsterdam while the case was under investigation. The 19 letters present the contestants' arguments. 19 notes. C. A. Newton

355. Spector, Robert M. THE QUOCK WALKER CASES (1781-83) - SLAVERY, ITS ABOLITION, AND NEGRO CITIZENSHIP IN EARLY MASSA-

CHUSETTS. *J. of Negro Hist. 1968 53(1): 12-32.* Argues that the Quock Walker cases in the Massachusetts courts were a part of a series of court decisions which brought about a "common law" of abolition rather than a new departure from legal tradition. Despite Section 91 of the Massachusetts *Body of Liberties* (1641) which prohibited slavery, economic considerations led to a growth of the institution in the colonial period. The Quock cases - *Walker vs. Jennison, Jennison vs. Caldwell,* and *Commonwealth vs. Jennison* - did not end discrimination against Negroes, which took numerous forms. Documented with legal records, manuscript and published materials; 101 notes.   L. Gara

356. Stange, Douglas C. "A COMPASSIONATE MOTHER TO HER POOR NEGRO SLAVES": THE LUTHERAN CHURCH AND NEGRO SLAVERY IN EARLY AMERICA. *Phylon 1968 29(3): 272-281.* The Lutheran Church throughout the American Colonies was eager to bring Negroes into the fold, with some success. At the same time it did not criticize slavery, making it clear that conversion did not also mean freedom. Thus, the author does not accept "the often repeated equation of several observers that a German equals an opponent of slavery," at least in the colonial period. "For from colonial Georgia to New York the Lutheran Church was intimately involved in the institution of slavery." Based on primary and secondary sources; 55 notes.   R. D. Cohen

357. Szasz, Ferenc M. THE NEW YORK SLAVE REVOLT OF 1741: A RE-EXAMINATION. *New York Hist. 1967 48(3): 215-230.* In 1740, New York City had a population of 12,000 people of whom 2,000 were slaves. During the winter and spring of 1740-41, an alleged slave plot to burn the city and murder its white inhabitants was uncovered by the authorities. Hysteria set in and, before reason returned to the city, 18 slaves and 4 whites had been hanged, 13 slaves burned at the stake, and 70 transported to the West Indies. Basing the article largely on the journal of Presiding Justice Daniel Horsmanden, the author concludes that the slave conspiracy thesis, resting upon the testimony of a female indentured servant, is not creditable. However, the author found that the white tavern-keeper accused of masterminding the servile insurrection was in fact the head of a criminal ring employing slaves to rob stores and houses. A conspiracy did exist in New York during the winter of 1740-41, but it was a conspiracy to rob rather than to overturn the established government. Based on primary and secondary sources; 53 notes.   G. Kurland

358. Towner, Lawrence W. THE SEWALL-SAFFIN DIALOGUE ON SLAVERY. *William and Mary Q. 1964 21(1): 40-52.* Presents a summary of Samuel Sewall's argument in *The Selling of Joseph: A Memorial* (Boston, 1700), and of John Saffin's response in *A Brief and Candid Answer to a Late Printed Sheet, Entitled, The Selling of Joseph* (Boston, 1701). Sewall opposed slavery as contrary to biblical teaching, uneconomic, and unethical. Saffin, whose position was shared by the Mathers, emphasized the conversion of slaves to Christianity, a theme Cotton Mather had been considering before Sewall's attack.
                                                              E. Oberholzer

359. Unsigned. A SLAVE MUTINY, 1764. *Connecticut Hist. Soc. Bull. 1966 31(1): 30-32.* Reprints two descriptions of a slave revolt aboard the brig *Hope* out of New London off the African coast in 1764. On 15 May 45 slaves mutinied, killed the captain, and took control of the vessel. The remaining whites soon suppressed the slaves, but the brig and its cargo were subsequently confiscated by Spanish officials in the West Indies.   L. R. Murphy

360. Waring, Joseph I. CORRESPONDENCE BETWEEN ALEXANDER GARDEN, M.D., AND THE ROYAL SOCIETY OF ARTS. *South Carolina Hist. Mag. 1963 64(1): 16-22, (2): 86-94.* Short biography of Alexander Garden explains his connection with the society. His report to the society, 20 April 1755, discusses chiefly slaves and the attitudes of planters toward machines, rice culture, sesame, and cotton. The use of potash is considered. The society's reply deals with grape culture. Correspondence begins again in April 1757 with Garden's annoyance that planters in South Carolina would plant only rice and indigo and not the exotic spices desired and recommended. Garden writes of the nature of the topography, grapes, and fear of the French. Imports and exports and their value are discussed and also the value of slave labor. Refers to his success with Henry Middleton, Christopher Gadsden, and others.   V. O. Bardsley

361. Wax, Darold D. GEORGIA AND THE NEGRO BEFORE THE AMERICAN REVOLUTION. *Georgia Hist. Q. 1967 51(1): 63-77.* Although British merchants and the imperial government have long been thought responsible for promotion of the American slave trade, the author contends that in the case of Georgia the colony's trustees enjoyed a free hand for two decades in fashioning a colonial establishment based solely upon white labor. Despite petitions from Georgia settlers and complaints in Parliament, the trustees enforced a ban on slavery, a policy embodied in legislation of 1735. Local advocates of slavery emphasized the necessity of Negro laborers in advancing the colony economically, while opponents focused upon the inhumanity of the institution and the dangers of slave revolts and conspiracies. The economic argument won out and the trustees authorized legislation of 1750 repealing the prohibition on slavery, which rapidly became an established institution in pre-Revolutionary Georgia. 44 notes.   R. A. Mohl

362. Wax, Darold D. NEGRO IMPORTS INTO PENNSYLVANIA, 1720-1766. *Pennsylvania Hist. 1965 32(3): 245-287.* The Negro slave trade remained small in Pennsylvania until 1729. After 1729 larger cargoes were imported and sold directly in the Philadelphia market. Several problems are involved in trying to estimate the extent of the slave trade due to the amount of smuggling and the vague terminology used to delineate the number of slaves (e.g., a parcel could mean as few as two or as many as 75 slaves). A list is given of Negro imports, containing the following information: importer's name, date, number of Negroes, where they were imported from, vessel, captain, and the source from which the information was derived. Not all information is available for each entry. Based on contemporary newspapers and manuscripts; 21 notes.   M. J. McBaine

363. Wax, Darold D. ROBERT ELLIS, PHILADELPHIA MERCHANT AND SLAVE TRADER. *Pennsylvania Mag. of Hist. and Biog. 1964 88(1): 52-69.* Robert Ellis, like other merchants, had first engaged in importing white servants; Negro trade was but one facet of his commercial activities. By 1725 he was well established as a Philadelphia merchant with ownership of a wharf near his house on Water Street. His correspondence illustrates the limited slave market which existed in Pennsylvania. Apparently after 1741 he was unsuccessful in having Negroes shipped north from Barbados. 75 notes.   E. P. Stickney

364. Wax, Darold D. THE DEMAND FOR SLAVE LABOR IN COLONIAL PENNSYLVANIA. *Pennsylvania Hist. 1967 34(4): 331-345.* The demand for Negroes in colonial Pennsylvania was restricted by the lack of plantation agriculture and the availability of skilled indentured servants. Most slaves were employed in agriculture, and it was rare to find more than four slaves on a farm. The second largest group of slaves was that of household servants. Slaves also were used in ironworks in considerable numbers and were found as sailors, sailmakers, bakers, masons, carpenters, shoemakers, butchers, tailors, millers, plasterers, painters, and stonecutters. Because the performance of extraordinarily heavy work was not required as on the southern plantation, Pennsylvania sought slaves between 12 and 20 years old so that they could be suitably trained and be productive for the longest possible time. Based on primary sources; 43 notes.
                                                                                        D. C. Swift

365. Wax, Donald D. NEGRO IMPORT DUTIES IN COLONIAL VIRGINIA: A STUDY OF BRITISH COMMERCIAL POLICY AND LOCAL PUBLIC POLICY. *Virginia Mag. of Hist. and Biog. 1971 79(1): 29-44.* Challenges the traditional assertion that British commercial interests defeated Virginia efforts to halt slave trade into the Colony by means of prohibitive imposts. A detailed summary of nearly three dozen colonial tariffs on Negroes shows that 1) only five met home office opposition; 2) the motive for tariffs was usually revenue for special projects such as the construction of the capitol, yet the fear of slave insurrection, over-extension of planters' credit, and a wish to increase the cash value of Negroes in Virginia all contributed to the tariff levies; and 3) scant evidence exists that humanitarian impulses worked. 66 notes.
                                                                                        C. A. Newton

366. Weir, Robert M. "THE HARMONY WE WERE FAMOUS FOR": AN INTERPRETATION OF PRE-REVOLUTIONARY SOUTH CAROLINA POLITICS. *William and Mary Q. 1969 26(4): 473-501.* South Carolinians had shaped a definite ideology concerning politics. The context of freedom under the British and South Carolina constitutional system was delineated. Absence of factions assured that the politician was checked at every turn by individual citizens. Affecting attitudes toward politics were economic prosperity, geographic location, Negrophobia, emulation of English ways, and religious dissent. The author's thesis simply is that Carolinians were developing "a country ideology" which transformed the character of local politics. There is comment on some of the particulars in the confrontation between "outsiders" (British placemen) and the representatives of internal interests. 62 notes.   H. M. Ward

367. Whitridge, Arnold. THE AMERICAN SLAVE-TRADE. *Hist. Today [Great Britain] 1958 8(7): 462-472.* A sketch of the history of the American trade in African slaves, from 1619 to 1861, with particular emphasis on the joint efforts of the British and American navies to suppress it after 1807. The author feels that if the American Government had cooperated fully with the British, the slave trade might have been suppressed earlier, and slavery in the Southern United States could not have survived without it.   E. D. Johnson

368. Willauer, G. J. PUBLIC FRIENDS REPORT TO LONDON YEARLY MEETING ON THEIR MISSIONS TO AMERICA, 1693-1763. *J. of the Friends' Hist. Soc. [Great Britain] 1968 52(2): 122-130.* An important source for knowledge of English and Irish Quaker ministers who went to the American Colonies is the London Yearly Meeting Minutes, a source up to now largely unexplored. In the period 1693-1763, 38 accounts of missions to America were received, representing the activities of about 50 men. The most valuable of these are 15 direct transcriptions of written statements. This source produced evidence of growth of Societies of Friends not only in New England and Rhode Island (the Puritan Colonies) but also in the Episcopalian Southern Colonies. A report of 1729 states that in Maryland, Virginia, and North Carolina, four, nine, and three new meeting houses respectively were built, as well as 40 more in the other Colonies. In addition to the spiritual growth of the Quaker movement in the New World and the missionary activities of the ministers, the minutes reveal the issues which troubled the Quakers, such as the Ranters, who were particularly strong in New England and Long Island. The Indians and later the Negroes also caused concern to the Friends. That the accounts decreased in detail and number toward the end of the period may have been due to the preoccupation of the London Yearly Meeting with affairs at home rather than to any falling off of zeal in the Colonies. 24 notes.   L. Brown

369. Woods, John A., ed. THE CORRESPONDENCE OF BENJAMIN RUSH AND GRANVILLE SHARP, 1773-1809. *J. of Am. Studies 1967 1(1): 1-38.* Reproduces a selection of unpublished letters exchanged between the English reformer, Granville Sharp, and Dr. Benjamin Rush of Philadelphia. Rush initiated the correspondence as a result of his acquaintance with Anthony Benezet, a pioneer opponent of slavery who had been writing to Sharp. The correspondents discussed three subjects at length: slavery and the slave trade, relations between England and America, and religion. Rush was especially interested in the "influence of physical causes upon the moral faculty." As for slavery, Sharp, for example, proposed a detailed scheme for compensated emancipation in the colonies. The events leading to the American Revolution were treated in some detail, both men condemning British policy. After the Revolution views were exchanged on the proper method of strengthening the American Episcopal Church. Such topics as the founding of Dickinson College, the danger of standing armies in America, and the personalities of George Washington, Thomas Jefferson, and James Madison were also discussed. The Rush-Sharp manuscripts annotated by the editor are in the possession of the Historical Society of Pennsylvania and Miss Lloyd-Baker of Hardwicke Court and were written in 1773-75, 1783-86, 1797, 1799, 1801, and 1809.   D. J. Abramoske

370. Wright, Louis B. ANTIDOTE TO ROMANTIC CONCEPTS OF COLO-NIAL VIRGINIA. *Virginia Q. R. 1966 42(1): 137-141.* A review essay of *The Diary of Colonel Landon Carter of Sabine Hall, 1752-1778,* edited by Jack P. Greene, (Charlottesville: U. Press of Virginia, 1964). A detailed social history of the daily life of a prominent Virginia aristocrat, it presents a remarkably complete picture of 18th-century Virginia agriculture, and describes intimate details of family life, slavery, and treatment of illnesses. While this 1,150-page diary is too gloomy and pessimistic, it provides an antidote to romantic notions of ease, luxury, and comfort surrounding 18th-century Virginia aristocrats. "A major contribution to the social history of the period."   O. H. Zabel

371. Zilversmit, Arthur. QUOK WALKER, MUMBET, AND THE ABOLI-TION OF SLAVERY IN MASSACHUSEITS. *William and Mary Q. 1968 25(4): 614-624.* Examines the pertinent facts of *Walker vs. Jennison, Jennison vs. Walker, Caldwell vs. Jennison, Brom and Bett vs. Ashley,* and *Commonwealth vs. Jennison.* The suit brought by Elizabeth Freeman (known as "Mumbet") in the *Brom and Bett* case led to a decision against slavery, and when the master accepted the decision, it is contended here, slavery was ended in Massachusetts. 23 notes.   H. M. Ward

The Elements of Black Society

372. Davis, Thomas J. THE NEW YORK SLAVE CONSPIRACY OF 1741 AS BLACK PROTEST. *J. of Negro Hist. 1971 56(1): 17-30.* In 1741 rumors spread that many of the two thousand slaves in New York City planned to burn the city and murder most of its nine thousand white inhabitants. Many have written off the episode as mass hysteria caused by a few scattered incidents, but the evidence could also indicate that the bondsmen were causing trouble to protest their condition. Unfortunately the words "slave revolt" bring more attention than the words "slave protest." After the conspiracy was disbelieved, many dismissed the problems of 1741 as insignificant. This attitude ignored their importance, for the bondsmen deliberately tried to better themselves and their position in society. 61 notes.   R. S. Melamed

373. Evans, Emory G., ed. A QUESTION OF COMPLEXION. *Virginia Mag. of Hist. and Biog. 1963 71(4): 411-415.* Reprints three documents in the Public Records Office [London] concerning the 1723 Virginia law depriving free Negroes and mulattoes of the franchise.   K. J. Bauer

374. Everett, Donald E. FREE PERSONS OF COLOR IN COLONIAL LOU-ISIANA. *Louisiana Hist. 1966 7(1): 21-50.* With few modifications, Negroes in Louisiana were governed by the *Code Noir* of 1724 until the acts of the territorial legislature of 1806-07 brought major revision. Even then, many of the original

provisions remained. This code placed only two restrictions on free Negroes: they could not shelter fugitive slaves and they had to show respect to former masters. In practice, however, despite substantial legal equality with whites, free blacks were frequently dependent on their white employers, even to the extent of self-imposed bondage in many cases. Free Negroes were often involved in criminal activities and in disputes with both blacks and whites. They also served in the military. Although condemnation of miscegenation occurred frequently, there was much libertinism between white men and colored women. The author relates a wide range of descriptions of free Negro life and society in colonial Louisiana. Based on records of the Louisiana Superior Council, legislation, and other colonial documents and published sources; 97 notes.   R. L. Woodward

375. Forbes, Jack D. BLACK PIONEERS: THE SPANISH-SPEAKING AFRO-AMERICANS OF THE SOUTHWEST. *Phylon 1966 27(3): 233-246.* Considers the prominent part played by Africans and Spaniards of part-African ancestry in the exploration and colonization of the Spanish empire in America. A study of records of Spanish-speaking towns in California leads the author to conclude that persons of part-Negro ancestry constituted at least 20 percent of the population in 1790. Over half of the population of such towns was non-Spanish. The records also suggest that as the status of persons improved in the community their race was sometimes changed from Negro to mulatto or from mulatto to Spaniard. This fact together with continuing miscegenation tended to obliterate both the memory and the physical characteristics of Negro ancestry in Spanish California. Racial attitudes of European and Anglo-American immigrants in the 19th century encouraged neglect of this theme and contributed to the myth of Castilian heritage among the upper class in California. Based largely on unpublished records of Spanish settlements in late 19th-century California in the Bancroft Library; 30 notes.   S. C. Pearson, Jr.

376. Haarmann, Albert W. THE SIEGE OF PENSACOLA: AN ORDER OF BATTLE. *Florida Hist. Q. 1966 44(3): 193-199.* Britain tried to hold Pensacola in 1781 by about two thousand men from her army and naval units of Negroes, Indians, German mercenaries, and local militia. Spain took the city with an attacking force of some eight thousand men: army, navy, French, Irish, Negro, and mulatto. Based on primary and secondary sources.   G. L. Lycan

377. Harris, Sheldon H. PAUL CUFFE'S WHITE APPRENTICE. *Am. Neptune 1963 23(3): 92-196.* Discusses the question of apprentices for sea service in colonial New England, with special reference to the apprentice of Paul Cuffe (1759-1817), Negro sea captain and merchant of Westport, Massachusetts. Main source is the indenture agreement in the New Bedford Free Public Library.   J. G. Lydon

378. Hershkowitz, Leo. TOM'S CASE: AN INCIDENT, 1741. *New York Hist. 1971 52(1): 63-71.* Reproduces the transcript of the trial of Tom, a Kingston (New York) slave, who was accused of attempting to rape and murder a white woman. At this time, hysteria gripped the State as the result of an alleged slave conspiracy uncovered in New York City, and Tom became the victim of the

general fear of slave insurrection. He was convicted and executed. Had times been more normal, the sentence would not have been so severe. The incident showed the precarious nature of the legal protection afforded slaves. Based on primary and secondary sources; illus., 12 notes.   G. Kurland

379. Holmes, Edward A. GEORGE LIELE: NEGRO SLAVERY'S PROPHET OF DELIVERANCE. *Baptist Q. [Great Britain] 1964 20(8): 340-351, 361.* Discusses the influence of George Liele on Negro Baptists in America and Jamaica. Liele was the first Negro to be ordained in the United States as a Baptist minister and formed the first Negro Baptist Church near Augusta, Georgia. Liele's life in the United States is surveyed. Following his removal to Jamaica in 1783, his activity among the slaves and his influence on the British Baptists in getting their aid are discussed. The reasons for his success in Jamaica are listed.
E. E. Eminhizer

380. King, David R. MISSIONARY VESTRYMAN. *Hist. Mag. of the Protestant Episcopal Church 1965 34(4): 361-368.* Biographical sketch of Elias Neau (1662-1722), Huguenot veteran of Louis XIV's galleys, convert to Episcopalianism and, by 1703, "one of the most prominent merchants" in New York City. In this year he offered his services to the Society for the Propagation of the Gospel as lay missionary to the thousand-odd Negro and Indian slaves of the city. For most of the remainder of his life he ministered to the spiritual and material needs of several hundred of these unfortunates. Despite their ignorance and the opposition of many of their masters to baptism, the missionary vestryman won the respect and confidence of his spiritual wards and the admiration of influential clergymen and colonial officials. Documented.   E. G. Roddy

381. Needler, Geoffrey D. LINGUISTIC EVIDENCE FROM [DR.] ALEXANDER HAMILTON'S "ITINERARIUM." *Am. Speech 1967 42(3): 211-218.* Comments on linguistic and dialect use in the northern colonies as observed by the Scottish-born Baltimore physician Alexander Hamilton (1712-56). Examples are given of proverbs and dialects (Scottish, Dutch, and Negro) recorded by Hamilton during a journey in 1744. Also included is "one of the earliest attempts to record the speech of a Negro, the first recorded dialogue between two Negroes, and possibly the only bilingual conversation of its kind ever recorded." Concludes with a glossary of 19 unusual Americanisms from the *Itinerarium* recorded "for the first time." Based on a reading of Hamilton's *Itinerarium; 10 notes.*
R. W. Shoemaker

382. Pilcher, George William. SAMUEL DAVIES AND THE INSTRUCTION OF NEGROES IN VIRGINIA. *Virginia Mag. of Hist. and Biog. 1966 74(3): 293-300.* Because he believed it his duty to teach the principles of Christianity to all, Samuel Davies, between his arrival in Hanover County, Virginia in 1748 and his departure in 1759 to become president of the College of New Jersey, "gradually assumed the role of pastor and educator of the Negro." He drew upon such English sources as the Society in London for Promoting Knowledge Among the Poor, and John and Charles Wesley, for the bulk of his support. Based on printed and manuscript sources; 35 notes.   K. J. Bauer

383. Sidwell, Robert T. "AN ODD FISH" - SAMUEL KEIMER AND A FOOTNOTE TO AMERICAN EDUCATIONAL HISTORY. *Hist. of Educ. Q. 1966 6(1): 16-30.* The "odd fish" is the designation bestowed on Samuel Keimer, Philadelphia printer, by Benjamin Franklin. The author feels that Keimer deserves some recognition for educational innovations he brought to the Colonies. In 1722 he attempted to open a reading school for male Negroes in Philadelphia; in 1726 he attempted to teach Hebrew through the pages of an almanac; and in 1728 he brought out an educational newspaper, the *Universal Instructor in All Arts and Sciences.* All these attempts came to nothing, chiefly because of Keimer's ineptness. Based chiefly on secondary sources.   J. Herbst

384. Twombly, Robert C. and Moore, Robert H. BLACK PURITAN: THE NEGRO IN SEVENTEENTH-CENTURY MASSACHUSETTS. *William and Mary Q. 1967 24(2): 224-242.* Puritan racial attitudes are demonstrated to have been no different from prejudices of white men elsewhere. Justice, however, was meted out equally to both races. Numerous criminal cases are cited. Punishments for crimes of violence, compared with later standards, were relatively light. Excepting militia service, no laws restricting Negroes were passed until the 1680's. Discriminating laws at the end of the century resulted not from the black man's presence but from experiences affecting social disorder. 34 notes.
H. M. Ward

385. Weatherwax, John M. LOS ANGELES 1781. *Negro Hist. Bull. 1954 18(1): 9.* A short description of the founding of Los Angeles in 1781 by 24 Mexican immigrant families on the orders of King Charles III of Spain. Twenty-six of the founders were of Negro origin. The only two whites were married to Indian women.   S

386. Weight, Glenn S. ANNIVERSARY OF PHYLLIS WHEATLEY REMAINS AN INSPIRATION TO ALL. *Negro Hist. Bull. 1962 25(4): 91-92.* A very brief sketch of the life of Phyllis Wheatley (1753?-84), the slave poetess of Boston whose verses astounded the literary world and went through numerous editions. She died in obscure poverty at the age of 31. Undocumented.
L. Gara

387. Willis, William S. DIVIDE AND RULE: RED, WHITE, AND BLACK IN THE SOUTHEAST. *J. of Negro Hist. 1963 48(3): 157-176.* Poses the thesis that hostility between Negroes and Indians in the Southeastern States during the colonial period was directly the result of white policy of divide and rule. Whites tried to prevent the mingling of Negroes and Indians. Indians were used to catch fugitive slaves and to put down slave rebellions; Negroes were used in military operations against the Indians. All these devices contributed to the mutual hostility which divided the two groups and prevented their combining in insurrection against the white man's rule. Most of the examples used relate to South Carolina. Documented.   L. Gara

388. Wright, Martha R. BIJAH'S LUCE OF GUILFORD, VERMONT. *Negro Hist. Bull.* 1965 28(7): 152-153, 159. Lucy Terry Prince, wife of Obijah Prince of Guilford, Vermont, is credited with being the first American Negro poet. Her poem "Bars Fight" (here given in full) describes an Indian raid on Deerfield in 1746. When she attempted, in vain, to secure the admission of her son to Williams College by appearing before its board, she was "one of the first American Negroes to attempt to break the color line in higher education." She won a case before the Supreme Court of the United States; her case against a neighbor's claim to some of their farm was handled by Isaac Tichenor who later became governor of Vermont. Lucy herself took over the arguments at length before the court in Vermont. Illus. E. P. Stickney

The American Revolution

389. Brown, Wallace. NEGROES AND THE AMERICAN REVOLUTION. *Hist. Today* 1964 14(8): 556-563. An analysis of British and colonial American usage of Negroes in the Revolutionary War. The Negroes were utilized more in the civilian services and the navy than in the army, and they received few tangible benefits from their participation. Illus. L. Knafla

390. Lutz, Paul V. A STATE'S CONCERN FOR THE SOLDIERS' WELFARE: HOW NORTH CAROLINA PROVIDED FOR HER TROOPS DURING THE REVOLUTION. *North Carolina Hist. R.* 1965 42(3): 315-318. North Carolina provided well for her troops in the American Revolution. They received cash bounties, after 1780 a slave "or the value thereof," clothing, food, and land (after 1782 from 640 to 1,200 acres depending on rank). The State attempted to mitigate against inflation in its compensation by valuing paper money in relation to specie. 11 notes. J. M. Bumsted

391. Ohline, Howard A. REPUBLICANISM AND SLAVERY: ORIGINS OF THE THREE-FIFTHS CLAUSE IN THE UNITED STATES CONSTITUTION. *William and Mary Q.* 1971 28(4): 563-584. The three-fifths clause did not derive from a sectional swap, as southern historians contend, or from a rejection of Revolutionary ideas, as the Progressive historians say. The clause instead resulted in a compromise of two political positions - those who wanted legislative supremacy and those who considered the people sovereign. Cites evidence that support of the three-fifths clause did not mean endorsement of slavery. Mentions writings of various nationalists and Anti-Federalists. 72 notes. H. M. Ward

392. Quarles, Benjamin. LORD DUNMORE AS LIBERATOR. *William and Mary Q.* 1958 15(4): 494-507. Dunmore's proclamation granting freedom to

slaves joining the Loyalist forces, which caused about 800 slaves to join the British side at the time and set the example for thousands of others, made him infamous in the eyes of the Patriots and a hero of the slaves.   E. Oberholzer, Jr.

3

SLAVERY & FREEDOM
(1783-1865)

The System of Slavery

393. Alford, Terry L. SOME MANUMISSIONS RECORDED IN THE
ADAMS COUNTY DEED BOOKS IN CHANCERY CLERK'S OFFICE,
NATCHEZ, MISSISSIPPI, 1795-1835 [SIC]. *J. of Mississippi Hist. 1971 33(1):
39-50.* A brief introduction of the data followed by a list of 187 manumissions
in Adams County, Mississippi, 1795-1855. The list includes the date of emancipation, the owner's name, and the name (and age if available) of the slave. "Emanci-
pations increased in Adams County in the early and middle 1830's." They
declined during and after the late 1830's. "A number of the manumittees were
young and healthy....Certain slaves were emancipated for outstanding service."
Owners who opposed slavery freed others. "Some slaves, after buying their own
way to freedom, became in turn slaveholders and emancipators themselves."
J. W. Hillje

394. Amacher, Anne Ward. MYTHS AND CONSEQUENCES: CALHOUN
AND SOME NASHVILLE AGRARIANS. *South Atlantic Q. 1960 59(2): 251-
264.* An analysis of the romanticized and inaccurate picture of John Caldwell
Calhoun drawn by the Nashville Agrarians, especially Allen Tate and Andrew
Nelson Lytle, concluding that their version of Calhoun is of interest to the
new-conservatives "who seemingly favor a social structure of more or less fixed
classes," and to those who would seek in the past a sanction for the "continued
fixing of the Negro at the bottom of the Southern social structure."
C. R. Allen, Jr.

395. Anderson, John Q. THE RICHMOND COMPILER, 1841-1844. *Louisiana
Hist. Q. 1956 39(4): 417-441.* A study of a rural newspaper published in the
village of Richmond, Madison Parish, Louisiana, in the 1840's. In an area of
cotton plantations and established slavery, the editorial policy of the *Compiler*
called for more of each, but also for roads, post offices, schools, and doctors for

the newly settled area. At the same time, its new items reflected the economic, social, and cultural conditions in the semifrontier society of its day.

E. D. Johnson

396. Arena, C. Richard. LANDHOLDING AND POLITICAL POWER IN SPANISH LOUISIANA. *Louisiana Hist. Q. 1955 38(4): 23-39.* A brief study of the power of the *cabildo,* the high court or council in the Spanish Government of Louisiana, ca. 1780-1800, with emphasis on its relationship to landholding, taxes, and treatment of slaves. Indicates that during the period covered the power of the *cabildo* increased gradually at the expense of the colonial governor. Based on Spanish colonial records and scholarly secondary studies.

E. D. Johnson

397. Arrington, Leonard J. and Haupt, Jon. INTOLERABLE ZION: THE IMAGE OF MORMONISM IN NINETEENTH CENTURY AMERICAN LITERATURE. *Western Humanities R. 1968 22(3): 243-260.* Statements made in America about Mormons have tended in recent years to be favorable. Quite the contrary was true in the 19th century. Fifty novels and tales of adventure about Mormons published in the second half of that century (listed at the conclusion of this essay) advance seven stereotypes or images which contributed to the public opinion of Mormons: the drunken, abusive husband; the white slave procurer; the seducer; the sinister secret society; the sinful, fallen city; the lustful Turk; and the cruel, lustful Southern slaveholder. Four of the earliest novels, published by women authors in 1855 and 1856, are analyzed in detail. 28 notes.

A. Turner

398. Atkins, Leah. THE FIRST LEGISLATIVE SESSION: THE GENERAL ASSEMBLY OF ALABAMA, HUNTSVILLE, 1819. *Alabama R. 1970 23(1): 30-44.* Following adoption of the State constitution (1819) the first General Assembly convened in Huntsville on 25 October 1819. It was charged with implementing the constitution of 1819, electing two U.S. Senators, and selecting the Secretary of State, State Treasurer, Attorney General, and Circuit Court judges. The assembly also dealt with such things as education, slavery, internal improvements, taxes, and salaries of State officials. The session lasted 44 days and saw the passage of 77 acts and nine resolutions. Based on various printed sources and the Tait, Walker, and Bibb papers located in the manuscript collections of the Alabama Department of Archives and History at Montgomery; 72 notes.

D. F. Henderson

399. Beatty-Brown, Florence R. LEGAL STATUS OF ARKANSAS NEGROES BEFORE EMANCIPATION. *Arkansas Hist. Q. 1969 28(1): 6-13.* A summary of those provisions of the constitutions of 1836 and 1861 and of the statutes, which define the legal status of Negroes in Arkansas. From 1849 on, the code governing Negroes and supporting slavery was strengthened repeatedly. The article includes reproductions of advertisements for runaway slaves. 34 notes.

B. A. Drummond

400. Beringer, Richard E. A PROFILE OF THE MEMBERS OF THE CON-
FEDERATE CONGRESS. *J. of Southern Hist. 1967 33(4): 518-541.* Using a
variety of sources but more than anything else the U.S. Census of 1860, the author
studies the personal, political, and economic background of the 267 members of
the provisional and First and Second Congresses of the Confederacy. The average
congressman was a man of some political experience, probably a Breckinridge
Democrat. He lived in a rural area away from the mountains, and, while he
practiced law, also had agricultural interests. He was born in one of the established seaboard States and had an estate worth between 40 thousand and 50
thousand dollars in 1860, an estate valuation much above the average. He owned
16 slaves, was between the ages of 30 and 60, a Protestant, and probably had some
college education. 8 tables, 27 notes. S. E. Humphreys

401. Bernstein, Barton J. SOUTHERN POLITICS AND ATTEMPTS TO RE-
OPEN THE AFRICAN SLAVE TRADE. *J. of Negro Hist. 1966 51(1): 16-35.*
In the 1850's, a minority in the slave States waged a campaign to reopen and
legalize the African slave trade. They argued that the slave trade was essential
to the perpetuation of slavery and that its revival would bring continued prosperity to the cotton region, particularly the Gulf States. Opponents maintained that
reviving the trade would depress the price of slaves, strengthen the northern
abolitionists, and contribute to the dissolution of the Union. The campaign failed
to attract any substantial support and, after secession became a fact, very few
southerners objected to that part of the Confederate Constitution which outlawed
foreign slave trade. Documented. L. Gara

402. Biehle, Reba Strickland. EDWARD OXFORD, PIONEER FARMER OF
MIDDLE GEORGIA. *Georgia Hist. Q. 1968 52(3): 187-198.* A biographical
treatment, based upon family papers and manuscript records, of a pioneer farmer
in post-Revolutionary Georgia. A typical "substantial farmer," or perhaps small
planter, Oxford owned as many as 12 slaves, but he also hired white labor and
had tenants. His cash crops were first tobacco and later cotton, and he manufactured and sold whiskey and brandy as well. Twice during his lifetime he moved
into frontier territory after Indian land cessions. It would appear that Oxford
achieved upward mobility as a result of these migrations, as he continually
improved his landholdings, his cash income, and his prestige and standing in the
pioneer community. 10 notes. R. A. Mohl

403. Blanks, W. D. CORRECTIVE CHURCH DISCIPLINE IN THE PRES-
BYTERIAN CHURCHES OF THE NINETEENTH CENTURY SOUTH. *J.
of Presbyterian Hist. 1966 44(2): 89-105.* Considers the use of corrective discipline by church sessions in the American South to enforce strict membership
requirements based upon the Westminster Standards. In cases of nonattendance
at worship, improper Sabbath observance, improper language, malicious gossip,
fighting, mistreatment of slaves, family conflict or premarital or extramarital
sexual relations, etc., members were tried and, if found guilty, admonished,
suspended, or excommunicated. Corrective discipline was designed to encourage

reformation of character, clear the name of those falsely accused, and protect the honor of religion. Based on manuscript session records and presbytery minutes. 75 notes.							S. C. Pearson, Jr.

404. Boney, F. N. DOCTOR THOMAS HAMILTON: TWO VIEWS OF A GENTLEMAN OF THE OLD SOUTH. *Phylon 1967 28(3): 288-292.* Thomas Hamilton, born shortly after the formation of the Federal Union, lived until a few years before the Civil War. While widely recognized as a skilled physician in Georgia, he was also a respected planter and a southern aristocrat in the fullest sense. Another portrait of the doctor-planter and sometime politician emerges from an unofficial, prejudiced remembrance of a fugitive slave named "Fed." The doctor cured the slave's master, Thomas Stevens, of an illness. In payment Stevens agreed to let him use Fed for an experiment he was conducting on the causes of sunstroke. The cruelty of the experiment is detailed in the account as is another experiment in which Hamilton attempted to determine how deep the black skin went. The author concludes that the account of the slave is true and that it is a reflection not only upon the doctor but also upon the southern society of which he was a respected member. Based on the Hamilton Papers located at the University of Georgia and on published sources; 4 notes.
								D. N. Brown

405. Boney, F. N. SOUTHERN SOJOURN: A YANKEE SALESMAN IN ANTE-BELLUM ALABAMA. *Alabama R. 1967 20(2): 142-154.* Excerpts from the papers of Miles E. Traver, a traveling salesman who toured the South in 1859 and 1860. Included are comments on terrain, profitability of slavery, and various costs, among which were ferriage, room and board, and freight. 10 notes.
								D. F. Henderson

406. Bradford, S. Sydney. THE NEGRO IRONWORKER IN ANTE BELLUM VIRGINIA. *J. of Southern Hist. 1959 25(2): 194-206.* Negroes supplied most of the labor used at charcoal furnaces and forges in Virginia even though ironmasters criticized their ability. Most of the slaves were hired, and the conditions of their life were oppressive: they worked hard, were poorly fed and clothed, and were separated from their families. The iron industry's continued reliance upon the Negroes in the 1840's and 1850's probably contributed to the failure of the ironmasters to adopt improved methods of production, and thus put them at an increasing disadvantage with regard to northern and British iron in these decades.
								S. E. Humphreys

407. Braverman, Howard. AN UNUSUAL CHARACTERIZATION BY A SOUTHERN ANTE-BELLUM WRITER. *Phylon 1958 19(2): 171-179.* Not all antebellum southern writers felt compelled to portray the Negro in the stereotyped pattern of contented servility. In his novel *Roanoke,* published in 1849, Calvin H. Wiley (1819-87), superintendent of the North Carolina educational system from 1852 to 1865, sympathetically portrayed a liberty-loving, articulate, and highly intelligent escaped slave. Based on the Wiley Papers in the archives

of the Historical Commission of North Carolina and the library of the University of North Carolina, and on contemporary regional newspapers.

A

408. Cadwallader, D. E. and Wilson, F. J. FOLKLORE MEDICINE AMONG GEORGIA'S PIEDMONT NEGROES AFTER THE CIVIL WAR. *Georgia Hist. Q. 1965 49(2): 217-227.* A collation of material found in manuscripts of the Georgia Writers Project of the Works Progress Administration relating to medicinal uses of plants by Piedmont Negroes after the Civil War.

R. Lowitt

409. Capers, Gerald M. THE RURAL LAG ON SOUTHERN CITIES. *Mississippi Q. 1968 21(4): 253-261.* Despite the lack of agreement among historians about what the South is and what made it the way it is, there can be no question that the South has been the most rural section of a nation rapidly becoming urbanized. The antebellum South's economic retardation and lack of diversification were not due to shortage of capital but rather to lack of incentive: investment in land and slaves was the traditional path to social prestige. The South's economic and spiritual alienation from other sections of the country was considerably enhanced by the Civil War, with physical destruction alone setting it back at least half a century. As the urbanization process continued, the successive frontiers and rural areas, with their lower per capita share of the national income, produced a rural lag, or economic drag, upon the cities. Economic forces in the late 19th century drove many rural southerners to cities where adaptation to the new life was very difficult. Vestiges of rural lag in most southern cities today are an indication of the continuing rural migration to urban centers with its continuing problem of adjustment. Documented by published material; 13 notes.

R. V. Calvert

410. Cardwell, Guy A. THE DUEL IN THE OLD SOUTH: CRUX OF A CONCEPT. *South Atlantic Q. 1967 66(1): 50-69.* Dueling in America lasted longer and was defended most vigorously in the antebellum South. Its continuation was related to frontier conditions and the concept of a cavalier southern gentleman. Nevertheless, most writers in the South opposed the duel and disassociated the defense of slavery from dueling as an institution. A southern gentleman should be a slaveholder and a Christian.

J. M. Bumsted

411. Chavis, John. FREEDOM VIA DETROIT. *Negro Hist. Bull. 1962/63 26(1): 30, 49.* Describes an incident in 1859 in which John Brown and some of his followers conducted 11 slaves from Missouri to Iowa where they were sent in a railroad freight car to Chicago, and later to Detroit and Canada. Based on secondary works.

L. Gara

412. Christensen, James B. NEGRO SLAVERY IN THE UTAH TERRITORY. *Phylon 1957 18(3): 298-305.* The first Negro slaves entered Utah in 1847, while

it was still a Mexican possession. The Mormon Church countenanced Negro slavery, in contrast to Indian slavery, on the basis of church doctrine, but allowed Negroes to become church members with inferior standing.   C. F. Latour

413. Chroust, Anton-Hermann. ABRAHAM LINCOLN ARGUES A PRO-SLAVERY CASE. *Am. J. of Legal Hist. 1961 5(4): 299-308.* Describes an 1847 case in which Abraham Lincoln argued for the continued slave status of a Kentucky slave who had been brought to Illinois by his master and kept there for a considerable time. Lincoln's argument, which he lost, is compared to an earlier similar case in which he had successfully argued the opposite position. Based on case records, documents from the Illinois State Historical Association, and secondary sources.   N. C. Brockman

414. Conrad, Alfred H., Dowd, Douglas, Engerman, Stanley, Ginzberg, Eli, Kelso, Charles, Meyer, John R., Scheiber, Harry N. and Sutch, Richard. SLAVERY AS AN OBSTACLE TO ECONOMIC GROWTH IN THE UNITED STATES: A PANEL DISCUSSION. *J. of Econ. Hist. 1967 27(4): 518-560.* A panel discussion arising out of a paper published in 1957 by Professors Conrad and Meyer which examined slavery as an obstacle to economic growth in the United States (see also abstracts 535 and 593). Ginzberg stated "The one thing we know about the American slave system is that it finally operated in such a way as to destroy the Union for a time. So some connection must be made between discussions of profitability and the destruction of the Union. Professor Conrad did mention that possibly slavery would have been profitable had it been contained in the original states, but we know that's just what the slave owners would not settle for....Slavery broke up the Union, it had to be expanded in order to stay profitable, and it was a poor way of raising the human resources of the region." Engerman observed: "The focus of the debate has become the question of Southern growth rates, the importance of the slave system in Southern growth before the Civil War and its lingering effects after the Civil War." Table.
D. D. Cameron

415. Conrad, Alfred H. and Meyer, John R. THE ECONOMICS OF SLAVERY IN THE ANTE BELLUM SOUTH. *J. of Pol. Econ. 1958 66(2): 95-130.* Takes issue with the often expressed viewpoint that slavery in the antebellum South was unprofitable. The demand for slave labor in the cottonbelt States insured returns for breeding operations on the less productive lands in the seaboard and border States. The authors further show that the maintenance of profits in the Old South depended on the expansion of slave agriculture into the Southwest. This is sufficient to explain the interest of the Old South in secession.   E. März

416. Coulter, E. Merton. FOUR SLAVE TRIALS IN ELBERT COUNTY, GEORGIA. *Georgia Hist. Q. 1957 41(3): 237-246.* Describes four slave trials held in Elbert County, Georgia, between 1837 and 1849. The minutes of these trials reveal a great deal about the legal status of the slaves during the quarter century preceding the Civil War and about the legal procedures applied to those charged with crimes. Based on a county record book.   R. Mueller

417. Coulter, E. Merton. SLAVERY AND FREEDOM IN ATHENS, GEORGIA, 1860-1866. *Georgia Hist. Q. 1965 49(3): 264-293.* A detailed account of life in Athens, Georgia, 1860-66, focusing largely but not exclusively on race relations.   R. Lowitt

418. Cross, Jasper W., ed. JOHN MILLER'S MISSIONARY JOURNAL - 1816-1817: RELIGIOUS CONDITIONS IN THE SOUTH AND MIDWEST. *J. of Presbyterian Hist. 1969 47(3): 226-261.* John E. Miller (1792-1847), a Presbyterian minister in the temporary employ of the New York Northern Missionary Society, maintained for the society a journal of his missionary tour of the South and West from 1 November 1816 to 14 May 1817. The manuscript journal, fully reproduced here, is in the possession of the Miller family. Miller traveled through Maryland, Washington, D.C., Virginia, the Carolinas, Georgia, Tennessee, Kentucky, and Ohio before returning to Pennsylvania. Miller noted the population, climate, and religious and social conditions of the communities which he visited. Many of his observations coincided with those of other early 19th-century visitors to the South and West. The moral, religious, and educational level of the South dismayed Miller. He was compassionate toward slaves and provided documentation for very early hostility of southern slaveholders toward religious instruction for the slaves. Less compassionate toward the Cherokee Indians, he termed them "an indolent, filthy, worthless set." Miller, though distressed by religious conditions in Nashville and particularly in Kentucky after the great western revivals, found conditions there more satisfactory than in the South. After talking with Gideon Blackburn (1772-1838), Miller claimed that there were no more than 10 or 12 regular preachers in the States of Indiana and Louisiana and the territories of Illinois, Missouri, and Mississippi. He encouraged the society to send missionaries into those areas. 58 notes.   S. C. Pearson, Jr.

419. Daniels, Jonathan. NEVER ALONE AT LAST. *Am. Heritage 1962 13(5): 28-31, 106-108.* Retells the story of Chang and Eng Bunker (died in 1874), the original "Siamese Twins," who married, brought up families and became prosperous slaveholding planters in the Old South. Undocumented, illus.
                                                                C. R. Allen, Jr.

420. Degler, Carl N. SLAVERY IN BRAZIL AND THE UNITED STATES: AN ESSAY IN COMPARATIVE HISTORY. *Am. Hist. R. 1970 75(4): 1004-1028.* Compares 19th-century slavery in the United States and Brazil in order to ascertain the extent to which the laws and practices of the state and the church in Brazil mitigated the impact of slavery upon Negroes. Contrary to the views of Frank Tannenbaum and Stanley Elkins, neither church nor state laws in Brazil differed in theory or in practice substantially from those in the United States. The admittedly greater amount of manumission of slaves and the arming of slaves in Brazil are best explained by differences in the economy, geography, and history of the two countries, rather than by differences in laws or in the attitudes of the church. Moreover, slave families were neither widely established nor protected in Brazil and, in general, slavery was physically harsher in Brazil than in the United States. The principal reason was that the persistence of the African slave trade in Brazil did not encourage good care as its early closing in the United States

did. Differences in the size and number of slave rebellions in the two countries also resulted from the fact that the slave trade in Brazil remained open after it was closed in the United States. Contrary to the situation in the United States, no racial defense of slavery developed in Brazil and blacks were used as slave catchers and overseers. Brazil, in short, did not develop that fear of blacks which, by the 19th century, was so characteristic of U.S. racial attitudes. The explanation for the differences in racial attitudes in contemporary Brazil and the United States is not to be found in the divergences in the law and practices of slavery as some historians have argued. Instead, differences in the institution of slavery were themselves a reflection of deeper social and cultural differences between the two societies.   A

421. Degler, Carl N. STARR ON SLAVERY. *J. of Econ. Hist. 1959 19(2):* *271-277.* A review of Chester G. Starr's article in the *Journal of Economic History* (March 1958) "An Overdose of Slavery," in which Starr enters a strong plea against comparing ancient and modern slavery. Documented.
                                                                    L. Adolphus

422. Dew, Charles B. TWO APPROACHES TO SOUTHERN HISTORY: PSY-CHOLOGY AND QUANTIFICATION. *South Atlantic Q. 1967 66(3): 307-* *325.* An evaluation of a few of the books and articles of Southern historians of the past 25 years who have used two new research tools: quantitative analysis and psychology. Quantification - the numerical summary of comparable data - has produced meaningful results in political history by destroying the cliché of the "Solid South." The Old South does not seem to have divided into parties based on economic characteristics. Work on the modern South has concluded that only on rare occasions is there a genuine southern solidarity. Quantification has proved less conclusive in analyzing the profitability of slavery. In the realm of psychology, much of the important work has been done in probing the mythology which has grown up around the South, especially the southern mind and slavery. Other attention has been focused on the psychology of the slaveholder and the slave.   J. M. Bumsted

423. Diamond, Sigmund. SOME EARLY USES OF THE QUESTIONNAIRE: VIEWS ON EDUCATION AND IMMIGRATION. *Public Opinion Q. 1963* *27(4): 528-542.* Traces various forms of compiling data on the basis of question-naires, beginning with the Domesday Book of William I in 1086. The article includes the efforts of Napoleon I between 1806 and 1812, Horace Mann, the founder of the American public school system (1839-44), as well as those favoring religious instruction for Negroes (1845).   B. E. Swanson

424. Dorsett, Lyle Wesley. SLAVEHOLDING IN JACKSON COUNTY, MIS-SOURI. *Missouri Hist. Soc. Bull. 1963 20(1): 25-37.* Documents and discusses in detail the characteristics and growth of slavery in a northern border county of Missouri in the four decades before the Civil War. Challenging earlier conten-tions that slavery was declining on the northern border of the South, the author points out that in 1860 slavery in this county was a thriving and profitable institution, despite mounting abolitionist and free Negro activity, increasing num-

bers of free-soil settlers, and the fact that the county was virtually surrounded by free territory. It is further demonstrated that this was a farm rather than a plantation area and that slavery was more a patriarchal and domestic than a commercial institution. R. J. Hanks

425. Dowty, Alan. URBAN SLAVERY IN PRO-SOUTHERN FICTION OF THE 1850'S. *J. of Southern Hist. 1966 32(1): 25-41.* The numerous novels written to answer *Uncle Tom's Cabin* by defending the institution of slavery might have been expected to mention the virtues of the Negro's life in urban centers of the South, as contrasted to the picture painted by Harriet Beecher Stowe of slavery on the plantations, but they did so scarcely at all. Whether the city provided contentment or provocation for the slave, it provided no scope for the talents of the proslavery propagandist. It meant a loosening of the slavery system and the offering of new horizons to the Negro. The city was part of a civilization the defenders of slavery were fighting. Documented. S. E. Humphreys

426. Drake, Frederick C. SECRET HISTORY OF THE SLAVE TRADE TO CUBA WRITTEN BY AN AMERICAN NAVAL OFFICER, ROBERT WILSON SCHUFELDT, 1861. *J. of Negro Hist. 1970 55(3): 218-235.* Presents a long letter from Schufeldt, a U.S. naval officer from 1839 to 1854, to Truman Smith, an American politician of limited national reputation. The letter, dated 6 January 1861, describes various facets of the slave trade carried on in American ships between Cuba and Africa. Schufeldt mentions that more Africans were landed on the island in 1860 than during the previous five years, and he estimates that their number exceeded 50 thousand since January 1860. The letter concludes with the observation that Spain has no interest in maintaining a permanent hold on the island, but simply seeks to drain as much gold as possible out of the country. 26 notes. R. S. Melamed

427. Drake, Winbourne Magruder. THE FRAMING OF MISSISSIPPI'S FIRST CONSTITUTION. *J. of Mississippi Hist. 1967 29(4): 301-327.* Describes and analyzes the immediate background and work of the 1817 constitutional convention of the Mississippi Territory, including the election of delegates, some characteristics of the delegates, and various parts of the constitution, such as the Declaration of Rights and provisions regarding slaves, revision, and the legislative, executive, and judicial branches. Focuses especially on areas where the recommendations of the drafting committee were revised and "on the liberal versus conservative or sectional rivalries which were reflected in the alteration or adoption of the various provisions." The author concludes that "the finished constitution was the product of a compromise between liberal and conservative forces, with the conservative predominating." Based largely on published and unpublished primary sources, particularly newspapers and manuscripts deposited in the Mississippi Department of Archives and History; 80 notes. J. W. Hillje

428. Duffy, John. A NOTE ON ANTE-BELLUM SOUTHERN NATIONALISM AND MEDICAL PRACTICE. *J. of Southern Hist. 1968 34(2): 266-276.* Analyzing the practice of medicine in Louisiana and Mississippi, the author

concludes that southern physicians, as did other southern professionals, provided intellectual justification for slavery. They did so by attempting to prove that southern medical practice was distinctive and that Negroes were anatomically and physiologically different from whites. 14 notes.   I. M. Leonard

429. Durden, Robert F. THE ESTABLISHMENT OF CALVARY PROTES-TANT EPISCOPAL CHURCH FOR NEGROES IN CHARLESTON. *South Carolina Hist. Mag. 1964 65(2): 63-84.* Shows the efforts by church leaders and slaveholders to establish a church for the blacks against opposition by those who feared that the Negro congregations would become " nurseries of self-government, in which the seeds of disloyalty and independence will be gradually sown to the ruin of the slave and the jeopardy of the master." An insurrection of slaves imprisoned in the city workhouse panicked the city in the summer of 1849, and an emotional by-product caused the gathering of a mob which threatened to destroy the "nigger church." However, after strict rules and regulations for the conduct of meetings were enacted, the church was finally completed and consecrated 23 December 1849. 49 notes.   R. S. Burke

430. Eaton, Clement. CLASS DIFFERENCES IN THE OLD SOUTH. *Virginia Q. R. 1957 33(3): 357-370.* Discusses the southern aristocracy, yeomanry, poor whites and slaves, and also briefly considers the businessman. "Southern society on the eve of the Civil War was, indeed, agrarian-minded and individualistic and very little troubled by class consciousness....There was no peasant psychology, therefore, among its people, even among the poor whites, and the middle class of landowning farmers was perhaps the freest and most self-respecting group in the world." Based on contemporary letters, diaries, and journals.
                    W. E. Wight

431. Eaton, Clement. SLAVE-HIRING IN THE UPPER SOUTH: A STEP TOWARD FREEDOM. *Mississippi Valley Hist. R. 1960 46(4): 663-678.* During the 1840's and 1850's, hiring rather than purchase of slaves became a common method of obtaining industrial and domestic labor in the Upper South. The effect was to "invisibly loosen the bonds of an archaic system" by giving the slave some economic bargaining power and a measure of independence. "Hiring was the main method of introducing the slave into southern industry and city life - an important step toward freedom."   D. R. Millar

432. Enkvist, Nils Erik. THE OCTOROON AND ENGLISH OPINIONS OF SLAVERY. *Am. Q. 1956 8(2): 166-170.* A study of Dion Boucicault's *Octoroon,* a play on slavery in the United States, and of its adverse reception in 1861 in England and its favorable reception in New York.   R. Kerley

433. Enloe, Louisa Dasher. SILAS DRAKE OF MARION COUNTY, MISSISSIPPI, AND HIS DESCENDANTS. *J. of Mississippi Hist. 1965 27(3): 268-284.* Largely genealogical information about Silas Drake (1765-1839) and his descendants. An ancestor of U.S. Senator John C. Stennis and a descendant of Thomas Drake, brother of Sir Francis Drake, Silas Drake settled in Mississippi about

1824, bequeathed 61 slaves, and was "the progenitor of a number of prominent Mississippi families" including those of Stennis, Hemingway, Brent, and Drake. Reprints Drake's will. Based on genealogies, published materials, county records, and Federal census records. J. W. Hillje

434. Erwin, Robert. THE SOUTHERN TRADITION OF FAILURE. *J. of Negro Hist. 1964 49(4): 256-263.* Describes the South as a kind of petty failure resulting from a rejection of major progressive tendencies in American life. When the trend was toward individual freedom, the South chose slavery; the South did not attract large numbers of foreign immigrants; it chose agriculture over industry, ignorance rather than education, and one-party government instead of a more open democracy. In order to contribute positively to history, the South of the future will first have to enter the mainstream of American life.

L. Gara

435. Evans, Robert, Jr. SOME ECONOMIC ASPECTS OF THE DOMESTIC SLAVE TRADE, 1830-1860. *Southern Econ. J. 1961 27(4): 329-337.* Basing his analysis on a wide variety of contemporary sources, the author examines in detail the economic aspects of the domestic slave trade in the southern United States. He concludes that the rates of return on capital invested in slave trading did not differ significantly from the returns to investments in slave holding, but that the incomes earned in slave trading were significantly higher than in alternative occupations. Hence he concludes that disapproval of the slave trader as such did not extend to the practice of lending capital to individuals engaged in the trade.

A. W. Coats

436. Feldmesser, Robert A. and Kelly, Paul E. SOCIOLOGY AND THE TEACHING OF AMERICAN HISTORY. *New England Social Studies Bull. 1965 22(2): 8-14.* As executive and associate directors of Sociological Resources for Secondary Schools, the authors emphasize the value of sociology for an understanding of the past and as an aid in the teaching of history. They demonstrate the usefulness of the sociological approach in exposition of the nature of Negro slavery in America prior to the Civil War and the role it played in causation of the war.

W. D. Metz

437. Fischer, Roger A. RACIAL SEGREGATION IN ANTE BELLUM NEW ORLEANS. *Am. Hist. R. 1969 74(3): 926-957.* Although many scholars have asserted that southern racial segregation originated in the period after Reconstruction, the system was widely practiced in southern cities, including New Orleans, long before the Civil War. Located in the heart of the deep South, New Orleans nevertheless was well known for its unusually lax race relations. Most of the city slaves hired out their services; some kept their own apartments. Several thousand free people of color lived lives virtually free of white control. Personal white authority over Negroes was virtually nonexistent. As a secondary line of defense for white supremacy, racial segregation was enforced in nearly all public contacts. Negroes were excluded from the schools and from hotels, restaurants, saloons, and ballrooms. Streetcars, hospitals, jails, and theaters segregated their colored patrons. The color line extended to the grave, as the cemeteries buried

whites and Negroes in different sections. Defiance of the color line was limited to such demimonde activities as gambling and prostitution, though increasing fears in the 1850's led whites to extend the color line to these activities as well. By the coming of the Civil War, the segregation system in New Orleans was as systematic and as rigid as the "Jim Crow" code that later developed throughout the South.   A

438. Fisher, Walter. PHYSICIANS AND SLAVERY IN THE ANTEBELLUM SOUTHERN MEDICAL JOURNAL. *J. of the Hist. of Medicine and Allied Sci. 1968 23(1): 36-49.* Suggests that historians pay greater attention to medical sources when writing about the history of American Negro slavery, particularly the writings of southern physicians in antebellum medical journals. The author then goes on to discuss the motives and profits involved in the medical care of slaves as well as the different type of medical practitioners caring for slaves. He concludes that one of the basic reasons for providing medical care for slaves was the large economic investment that this group represented. 54 notes.
G. N. Grob

439. Floan, Howard R. THE NEW YORK EVENING POST AND THE ANTE-BELLUM SOUTH. *Am. Q. 1956 8(3): 243-253.* A study of the role played by the New York *Evening Post* in the psychological conditioning for the Civil War. Its distinguished staff presented the South objectively with its frontier character, its labor problems, and social stratification. Three themes were stressed: distinction between slave power and southern society as a whole, success of slave power in national politics, and the effects of slavery on the moral fiber of southern society.
R. Kerley

440. Fogel, Robert W. and Engerman, Stanley L. THE RELATIVE EFFI-CIENCY OF SLAVERY: A COMPARISON OF NORTHERN AND SOUTH-ERN AGRICULTURE IN 1860. *Explorations in Econ. Hist. 1971 8(3): 353-367.* Offers "preliminary measures of the relative efficiency of input utilization in the agricultural sectors of the North and South in 1860. The principal instrument for measuring the level of efficiency is the geometric index of total factor productivity." The "computations reveal that it was the South, not the North, which was more efficient in the utilization of its resources." According to the index employed here, "productivity in agriculture was 9 percent higher in the South than in the North." Suggests "that the relative efficiency of southern agriculture is probably related to certain special features of the slave system" such as a more intensive employment of labor ("slaves worked more days per year, and perhaps more hours per day, than free farmers"), "the possibility that there were economies of scale in the slave sector of agriculture," and the possibility that "Plantation owners were able to shift part of the cost of maintaining the slave system for themselves to the community,....." Based on secondary sources; 2 tables, 12 notes, biblio.
C. J. Pusateri

441. Gara, Larry. FRIENDS AND THE UNDERGROUND RAILROAD. *Quaker Hist. 1962 51(1): 3-19.* Finds it to be a post-Civil War legend that the escape "system" was an articulated, nationwide, and centralized Quaker institu-

tion, based on a portrait of Simeon Halliday in *Uncle Tom's Cabin,* published reminiscences and activities of a few, including ex-Friends. Many Friends were moderate or wavering in support, or even hostile, and shared American views on racial inequality. They first supported the colonization movement. Help was local, sporadic, and limited to immediate relief plus guidance to the next safe stop. Wesleyan Methodists and Covenanter Presbyterians were equally favorable, and the role of free Negroes was large. Often fugitives had to depend on themselves alone. Documented by-product of the author's *The Liberty Line* (Lexington: U. of Kentucky Press, 1961).   T. D. S. Bassett

442. Gara, Larry. THE REAL STORY OF THE UNDERGROUND RAIL-ROAD. *Civil War Times 1964 3(5): 40-45.* Shows that most slaves escaped on their own initiative, mostly with help from free Negroes. Illus.

S

443. Gara, Larry. THE UNDERGROUND RAILROAD: A RE-EVALUA-TION. *Ohio Hist. Q. 1960 69(3): 217-230.* Suggests that the number of Negroes who moved to Canada along the underground railroad has been exaggerated, that the role of the abolitionists in the underground railroad has been overstated, and that the Negroes who escaped north through the underground railroad deserve more recognition for their aggressiveness and resourcefulness than they have received. The author believes that many of the mistaken impressions about the underground railroad derive from the fact that most studies of the institution have been based on abolitionist sources. Manuscript sources for the article include the Wilbur H. Siebert Collections in the Ohio Historical Society and the Houghton Library of Harvard University, the Weston Papers in the Boston Public Library, and the William Still Papers in the Pennsylvania Historical Society.

S. L. Jones

444. Gara, Larry. THE UNDERGROUND RAILROAD: LEGEND OR RE-ALITY? *Pro. of the Am. Phil. Soc. 1961 105(3): 334-339.* The legend of the underground railroad is a combination of fact and fancy. Many of the stories handed down by word of mouth had a factual basis, but frequent repetition has led to exaggeration and sometimes, in the annals of local history, fantasy has become fact. Far too much of the railroad's history rests upon the reminiscences of aged abolitionists written many years after the events. The railroad of historical reality existed, but it was markedly different from the institution of the popular legend. The legend has contributed to the idea that large numbers of slaves traveled to freedom on the line, and it has presented later generations with a distorted view of the workings of the underground railroad itself. The actual history of the institution is much more complex and even more interesting than the legend itself. Documented.   N. D. Kurland

445. Genovese, E. D. THE LOW PRODUCTIVITY OF SOUTHERN SLAVE LABOR: CAUSES AND EFFECTS. *Civil War Hist. 1963 9(4): 365-382.* Slavery was not only directly responsible for low economic output in the antebellum South, but was also directly a barrier to technological innovations that might have increased the output. The slave was an inefficient worker because of his general

poor health, owing to inadequate diet, and the lack of incentive and training. But beyond this, slavery affected adversely the entire economy of the South by its depressing influence on free labor, by inhibiting a needed division of labor on the plantation, and by diverting capital, which should have been invested in improved machinery and equipment, into slaves. Economic productivity could have been increased only by overthrowing the whole social order. Based on contemporary unpublished and published documents and statistical studies.

E. C. Murdock

446. Genovese, Eugene D. COTTON, SLAVERY AND SOIL EXHAUSTION IN THE OLD SOUTH. *Cotton Hist. R. 1961 2(1): 3-17.* Southern farming methods, including the use of slaves on large plantations, depleted the soil and prevented effective reclamation. Where reforms were introduced, slavery was eliminated or much of the slave force was sold. Based largely on State publications of the Old South. D. A. Stokes

447. Genovese, Eugene D. LIVESTOCK IN THE SLAVE ECONOMY OF THE OLD SOUTH - A REVISED VIEW. *Agric. Hist. 1962 36(3): 143-149.* Although livestock was abundant in the pre-Civil War South, there was a deficiency of meat and work animals. To a great extent this was because slaves tended to mistreat livestock. Fine breeds imported into the South generally deteriorated, instead of improving, the herd. Capital, as well as an appropriate labor force, was lacking for a livestock industry. W. D. Rasmussen

448. Genovese, Eugene D. MATERIALISM AND IDEALISM IN THE HISTORY OF NEGRO SLAVERY IN THE AMERICAS. *J. of Social Hist. 1968 1(4): 371-394.* A critical analysis of the major literature dealing with Negro slavery in the Americas from a hemispheric perspective, from 1967 to the present. Discusses the demand made by anthropologist Marvin Harris in *The Nature of Cultural Things* (New York: Random House, 1964) for a materialist alternative to the idealistic framework of Frank Tannenbaum, Stanley Elkins, Gilberto Freyre, and others. Tannenbaum first introduced the hemispheric perspective by showing that the current status of the Negro in the various societies of the Western Hemisphere has roots in the attitude toward the Negro as a slave, which reflects the total religious, legal, and moral history of the enslaving whites. In the process, he ignored the material foundations of each slave society, most particularly class relations. Later students have qualified his perspectives, but have worked within the framework of an "idealistic" interpretation. Harris, on the other hand, insists that material conditions determined social relations and necessarily prevailed over countertendencies in the historical tradition. Unfortunately, his work reveals him to be an economic determinist and, as such, ahistorical. By attempting to construct a materialism that bypasses ideological and psychological elements in the formation of social classes, he passes into a "variant of vulgar Marxism" and offers only soulless mechanism. 68 notes. N. M. Drescher

449. Genovese, Eugene D. THE NEGRO LABORER IN AFRICA AND THE SLAVE SOUTH. *Phylon 1960 21(4): 343-350.* Analyzes the argument that

Negro slaves in America worked poorly because of inherent indolence and beast-like incapacity and had to be trained to minimum effectiveness, and refutes it as resting on discredited grounds and sources. L. Filler

450. Goddard, John H. SOME LETTERS OF JAMES EPPINGER, 1832-1846. *Georgia Hist. Q. 1964 48(1): 85-103.* Letters present aspects of social and economic life during this period. Discussed are such items as agriculture, land speculation, slavery, Indian life, health, and business. R. Lowitt

451. Going, William T. PHILIP HENRY GOSSE ON THE OLD SOUTH-WEST FRONTIER. *Georgia R. 1967 21(1): 25-38.* Discusses the effect of English naturalist Philip Gosse's eight-month stay in Alabama (1838) on his career. Undecided over what to do with his life, he "tried the rough and impractical courses of teaching and preaching, but he discovered genuine satisfaction in [science] and drawing." He described the life he saw, especially slavery and lawlessness, and his writings "contributed significantly...to the historical record of what the Old Southwest frontier was like in 1838 as it began to fade into the settled environment of a Black Belt culture." His later work as a Plymouth Brother and his rebuttal of Darwin are possibly signs of a guilt feeling about not remaining in Alabama as a Methodist missionary. 7 notes. T. M. Condon

452. Goldman, Hannah S. THE TRAGIC GIFT: THE SERF AND SLAVE INTELLECTUAL IN RUSSIAN AND AMERICAN FICTION. *Phylon 1963 24(1): 51-61.* Significant parallels can be found in stories by Pavlov, Herzen, Ushakov, Odoyevsky, Dal, and Kukolnik, as compared with those by such writers as Richard Hildreth, Hattie Griffith, and E. C. Pierson, as well as Harriet Beecher Stowe's less-known *Dred [A Tale of the Great Dismal Swamp* (1856)]. Serfdom and slavery both were depicted as fostering misery. Gifted slaves and serfs often regretted having been able to emerge from their assigned low states. Russian novels were silent on the role of the Bible in the lot of the serf; it played a vigorous part in the American novels concerning slavery. L. Filler

453. Green, Charles. THE SECOND AMERICAN REVOLUTION. *Negro Hist. Bull. 1964 27(5): 103-105.* Reviews the subject of slave revolts with concentration on those led by Gabriel Prosser in 1800, Denmark Vesey in 1822, and Nat Turner in 1831. Based on secondary accounts. L. Gara

454. Griffin, Richard W. ANTE BELLUM INDUSTRIAL FOUNDATIONS OF THE (ALLEGED) "NEW SOUTH." *Textile Hist. R. 1964 5(2): 33-43.* An interest and participation in manufacturing developed in the South at the same time as in other sections of the United States. In every Southern State successful efforts were made to establish textile mills between 1807 and 1813. By the late 1830's the planter began to see the factory as a consumer of his cotton, as a place of employment of young and of superannuated slaves, and as a market for diversified farm products. By 1860 the South's share of the national textile industry had grown to between 20 and 25 percent. E. P. Stickney

455. Griffith, Benjamin W. A LONGER VERSION OF "GUINEA NEGRO SONG": FROM A GEORGIA FRONTIER SONGSTER. *Southern Folklore Q. 1964 28(2): 116-118.* Thomas H. Morgan lived in Macon County, Georgia, from 1829-51. During that period he collected songs and poems, including some by slaves. A six-stanza song, "The Negro and the Buckra Man," is published here - fascinating and ironical comments on various aspects of servitude.

H. Aptheker

456. Grover, Wayne C. GENEALOGICAL MATERIAL FROM UNITED STATES CENSUSES, 1790-1890. *Indiana Mag. of Hist. 1966 62(2): 157-158.* General announcement of microfilm copies of the original Federal population census schedules for 1800-90 which are now available for loan or purchase from the National Archives. These schedules contain a wealth of material of interest to genealogists, social historians, social scientists, and others interested in the American family, westward expansion, the status of free and slave labor, regional and local history, and immigration. Information given in these schedules becomes progressively more detailed in each successive census. From 1790 to 1840, only names of enumerated heads of families are listed, all others are recorded statistically. From 1850 on, census schedules record each person's age, occupation (if over 15), and place of birth. In 1870, if the parent of the person listed is of foreign birth, this is also noted. In 1880, schedules add the relationship of each individual to the head of the family. A card index to the 1880 census, broken down by States, and a special schedule supplementing the 1890 census giving information on Civil War veterans and their spouses, are also on microfilm and available for purchase or use.

J. Findlay

457. Hall, D. D., ed. A YANKEE TUTOR IN THE OLD SOUTH. *New England Q. 1960 33(1): 82-91.* Publishes entries from Charles William Holbrook's diary for the years 1850 to December 1852. After graduating from Williams College, Holbrook accepted a position as tutor on a North Carolina plantation. Holbrook, who was from Massachusetts, enjoyed the friendliness of the Southern people, but he deplored their "immorality" and hated slavery.

L. Gara

458. Halsey, Ashley, Jr. THE LAST AMERICAN SLAVE SHIP. *Civil War Times 1964 3(1): 18-21.* Relates the story of the purchase of the yacht *Wanderer* from L. O. Johnson of the New York Yacht Club by W. C. Corrie in 1858 and its conversion into a slave ship. The *Wanderer* made four successful and profitable trips past American and British patrols. The participants were caught and the *Wanderer* seized, but there was never any prosecution. Illus.

R. Strain

459. Hendrix, James Paisley, Jr. THE EFFORTS TO REOPEN THE AFRICAN SLAVE TRADE IN LOUISIANA. *Louisiana Hist. 1969 10(2): 97-123.* Although suggestions to reopen the African slave trade were heard in Louisiana as early as 1839, concrete proposals specifically related to the State were not made in the legislature until 1858. There followed a series of unsuccessful efforts to find a legal way of importing African laborers, but there was also considerable opposi-

tion. The author analyzes voting patterns on the issue. No simple pattern emerges from the study. To some, the effort was an honest attempt to alleviate the labor shortage; to others, it was a way to secession; to others still, it was a means of rebelling against the Buchanan administration. Based principally on records of the Louisiana legislature and contemporary newspapers; 87 notes.

R. L. Woodward

460. Henry, Bessie M. A YANKEE SCHOOLMISTRESS DISCOVERS VIRGINIA. *Essex Inst. Hist. Collections 1965 101(2): 121-132.* Biographical sketch of Abigail Mason of Salem, Massachusetts, as an introduction to the reprinting of a series of letters she wrote to relatives in the 1830's while serving as a schoolmistress on the plantations of the upper James River. The letters describe their author's views on dining customs (including Thanksgiving Virginia style), slavery, religious revivalism, and Christmas.   J. M. Bumsted

461. Hering, Julia F. PLANTATION ECONOMY IN LEON COUNTY, 1830-1840. *Florida Hist. Q. 1954 33(1): 32-47.* Provides a description of the cotton culture, slavery, land speculation, and banking practices in the Tallahassee area during the two decades preceding Florida's admission to the Union as a State. Based on court records, contemporary newspapers, and personal papers.

G. L. Lycan

462. Herndon, G. Melvin. SAMUEL EDWARD BUTLER OF VIRGINIA GOES TO GEORGIA, 1784. *Georgia Hist. Q. 1968 52(2): 115-131.* Surveys the career of a Virginia tobacco planter who migrated to upper Georgia in post-Revolutionary years. Butler's migration is representative of the exodus of planters from the older tobacco-producing counties of Virginia to new and more fertile Western lands. Virgin land was available in upper Georgia as Indian claims were eliminated, and the State's liberal land policy encouraged migration. Butler's move brought him prosperity and prestige. In Virginia he owned 13 slaves and 1,000 acres of land, but by his death in 1809 he had joined the ranks of the gentry, owning 35 slaves and more than 3,000 acres of tobacco land. Based largely on Butler family manuscripts; 76 notes.   R. A. Mohl

463. Higgins, W. Robert. CHARLES TOWN MERCHANTS AND FACTORS IN THE EXTERNAL NEGRO TRADE, 1735-1775. *South Carolina Hist. Mag. 1964 65(4): 205-217.* Lists 405 merchants, giving year of trading, number of cargoes, and duty paid. Sources are drawn from "Treasurer's Journals, Duties" in South Carolina Archives.   V. O. Bardsley

464. Holbrook, Abigail Curlee. COTTON MARKETING IN ANTEBELLUM TEXAS. *Southwestern Hist. Q. 1970 73(4): 431-455.* Traces the development of cotton-growing activities in Texas from the 1820's to the Civil War, including the small, independent farmers and merchants and the larger plantation owners with their slaves, enticed into Texas by Stephen Austin. Follows the growth of Texas from a Mexican Province to a Republic and then a State, and identifies the men most responsible for creating a viable cotton economy in Texas. Describes the

marketing, shipping, distribution, bankruptcies, and profits and losses and debts of the cotton growers, to illustrate how a frontier land soon became an integral part of an evolving industrial United States.   R. W. Delaney

465. Holmes, Jack D. L. THE ABORTIVE SLAVE REVOLT AT POINTE COUPEE, LOUISIANA, 1795. *Louisiana Hist. 1970 11(4): 341-362.* The abortive slave revolt at Pointe Coupée in 1795 reflected "various struggles between royalists and jacobins, Spaniards and Frenchmen, and between the blacks and whites." More than a third of the slaves in Louisiana were in the Pointe Coupée vicinity and conditions there were ripe for insurrection. Holmes details the revolt and its suppression under the orders of the Baron Francisco Luis Héctor de Carondelet, Governor of Louisiana, who "over-reacted" to the plot when he ordered the execution of 26 Negroes. The revolt led to a more comprehensive slave code, decreed by Carondelet, who tried to steer the "difficult course between what the Spanish law and humanity dictated, and the practical, and sometimes selfish desires of the Louisiana planters." This was neither the first nor the last Louisiana slave insurrection, but it simply proved once more that "the only way to avoid slave revolts was to eliminate the system of slavery which bred them." Based principally on manuscript sources in Spain and New Orleans; 75 notes, appendix.   R. L. Woodward

466. Hornick, Nancy Slocum. THE LAST APPEAL: LYDIA CHILD'S ANTI-SLAVERY LETTERS TO JOHN C. UNDERWOOD. *Virginia Mag. of Hist. and Biog. 1971 79(1): 45-54.* Brief biographical sketches of Lydia Maria Francis Child (1802-80) and John Curtiss Underwood (1809-73), a Virginian, precede reproduction of four letters from Child in 1860 on the mutually obsessive theme of abolition without southern secession.   C. A. Newton

467. House, Albert V. LABOR MANAGEMENT PROBLEMS ON GEORGIA RICE PLANTATIONS, 1840-1860. *Agric. Hist. 1954 28(4): 149-155.* In economic characteristics, the Georgia rice plantations had little in common with medieval manors or 17th and 18th-century plantations. The planters sent their rice into a competitive market with a goal of private profit. The slave labor was managed to provide for its most efficient and economical use. Within the limits of their resources and economic status, the Georgia rice planters managed their labor well. Based on published documents.   J (W. D. Rasmussen)

468. Hubbard, Eleanor. VERMONT'S UNDERGROUND RAILROAD. *Vermont Hist. 1965 33(2): 308-312.* Third prize essay on the underground railroad. Based on secondary works.   T. D. S. Bassett

469. Jackson, Donald. ON THE DEATH OF MERIWETHER LEWIS'S SERVANT. *William and Mary Q. 1964 21(3): 445-448.* Two letters from John Christopher Sueverman, a former slave, to Thomas Jefferson in 1810 tell of the destitution and the last illness of John Pernier (also known as Pirney, Pernia, and Pirny), also a former slave, who had been Lewis' servant.   E. Oberholzer

470. Jackson, James Conroy. THE RELIGIOUS EDUCATION OF THE NE-GRO IN SOUTH CAROLINA PRIOR TO 1850. *Hist. Mag. of the Protestant Episcopal Church* 1967 36(1): 35-61. General historical background of slavery in the South, particularly in South Carolina, followed by a discussion of the activities of the Episcopal Church in antebellum Charleston as it endeavored to bring religious instruction to the Negroes without violating the slave codes. By 1848 the church was fairly successful in helping the urban Negroes gain their religious rights. Based on secondary works; 82 notes.   E. G. Roddy

471. Jones, Archer and Hoepner, Paul H. THE SOUTH'S ECONOMIC IN-VESTMENT IN SLAVERY. *Am. J. of Econ. and Sociol.* 1967 26(3): 297-299. Examines the economics of slavery in the South. The authors disagree with the theory that, although profitable to the southern farmer, slavery was an "impedi-ment to the industrial development of the South." 6 notes.   D. F. Rossi

472. Jones, J. Ralph and Landess, Tom, ed. PORTRAITS OF GEORGIA SLAVES. *Georgia R.* 1967 21(1): 126-132, (2): 268-273, (3): 407-411, (4): 521-525, 1968 22(1): 125-127, (2): 254-257. Part I. Interviews ex-slaves in Georgia, 1936. Comments on their credibility, as the interviewer (Jones) was trying to find out about Negro life, and not trying to test a hypothesis. The first subject, Mary Gladdy (born about 1853), had experienced "visitations of the spirit" for over 20 years. She described slave religion, and life during the Civil War. Ella Hawkins (born about 1856) described the Civil War years, and how her brothers hid their owners' silverware and "treasures" from looting "Yankees." Note. Part II. In-cludes two 1937 interviews with the Reverend W. B. Allen (born about 1850). Covers slave traders, plantation life, the slaves' religious nature, patrols, and runaway slaves. Mentions the hours worked, "Yankees," overseers ("the regular run of them were trash"), punishment, and tortures. Part III. A portrait of "Uncle" Rias Body, a Georgia slave who was the property of Ben Body, a Harris County planter and an owner of some 80 slaves. Rias Body was born on 9 April 1849 near Waverly Hall, Georgia. The slaves were required to procure passes from their masters before they could go visiting or leave their homes. Negroes were auctioned off at the old slave mart by "speculators" for 400 dollars and up; women were sold for 600 dollars to one thousand dollars; black men well-trained in a special line of work often received a whipping as punishment, but because they were valuable property, "none was ever whipped to the point that he or she was incapacitated for work." The plantation slaves, whether they liked it or not, had to scrub themselves every Saturday night with a homemade lye soap. "In 1865 Yankee soldiers captured him, impressed him into Union service (much against his will), took him to Macon, and drilled him for two or three months. When the war ended he was released and came home." Rias Body said that slavery was both right and wrong: right because it raised the Negro from a savage state; wrong because it permanently established the Negro's inferiority. Part IV. Interviews Robert Kimbrough and Frances Kimbrough, ex-slaves (1936). Ro-bert's mother was auctioned in Broad Street, Richmond, in 1835, and he was born on a plantation in 1837. Discusses the war, "Yankee" thievery, foot-propelled cotton gins, and the lack of cruel punishment by owners. Frances Kimbrough remembered her owners with near-reverence, and had a strong superstitious bent. Part V. The story of "Mammy Dink" (Dink Walton Young, ca. 1840-1936)

touches on the familiar antebellum relationships between white and black children, the weekly slave diet on the Walton plantation, and the clothing and general treatment of the blacks by an apparently humane and compassionate white family. Part VI. Harriet Benton, of Columbus, tells how her father was sold into slavery and tells of her childhood days. Mary Carpenter, of Columbus, says that her owner protected her from a whipping by another planter and details ravages by the "Yankee" soldiers.   T. M. Condon, D. D. Cameron, and J. S. Pula

473. Jones, Robert Huhn. THE AMERICAN CIVIL WAR IN THE BRITISH SESSIONAL PAPERS: CATALOGUE AND COMMENTARY. *Pro. of the Am. Phil. Soc. 1963 107(5): 415-426.* A catalogue of British sessional papers, printed by order of the House of Commons or put before Commons by royal command, relating to the United States, 1861-65, compiled from the Readex Microprint Edition of the *British Sessional Papers,* Edgar L. Erickson, editor. Beyond the diplomatic exchanges between Britain and the United States there is comment concerning the American political system, much material on trade and shipping and the decline of the slave trade, as well as information on British colonies and their efforts to deal with a Negro-white problem.

R. G. Comegys

474. Jordan, Terry G. THE IMPRINT OF THE UPPER AND LOWER SOUTH ON MID-NINETEENTH CENTURY TEXAS. *Ann. of the Assoc. of Am. Geographers 1967 57(4): 667-690.* Establishes a dichotomy in the economic and social development of the American South. Using census data, the author determines that the settlement of Texas reflects this dichotomy. Distinct patterns based on differences of population origin and correlations with other cultural phenomena are identified. These included: 1) the occurrence and distribution of Negro slavery, 2) the cultivation of cotton, 3) the cultivation of wheat, 4) the cultivation of corn, 5) the cultivation of rice, 6) the cultivation of tobacco and hemp, 7) the use of draft animals, 8) the occurrence of food surpluses and deficiences, and 9) voting behavior on the issue of secession. 3 tables, 12 maps, 61 notes.   W. R. Boedecker

475. Joyaux, Georges J., ed. FOREST'S "VOYAGE AUX ETATS-UNIS DE L'AMERIQUE EN 1831." *Louisiana Hist. Q. 1956 39(4): 457-472.* Presents, with notes by the editor, extracts from a travel account written by P. Forest and published in Lyon, France, in 1834. The extracts deal with Forest's visit to New Orleans in 1831 and give his impressions of the climate, natural history, and social conditions there, with particular emphasis on slavery.   E. D. Johnson

476. Kaplan, Sidney, ed. BLACK MUTINY ON THE "AMISTAD." *Massachusetts R. 1969 10(3): 493-532.* Reproduces the entire text of John Warner Barber's *History of the Amistad Captives* (1840). Provides an explanatory essay. The *Amistad* was a Spanish slave ship captured by its inmates in 1839. It in turn was captured by the U.S. Navy off Montauk Point, Long Island, New York. The *Amistad* slaves were defended by John Quincy Adams; the U.S. Supreme Court awarded them their freedom. 5 illus.   G. Kurland

477. Kelley, Donald Brooks. HARPER'S FERRY: PRELUDE TO CRISIS IN MISSISSIPPI. *J. of Mississippi Hist. 1965 27(4): 351-372.* Describes the increasing fear and hysteria shown in the Mississippi press in the period from John Brown's raid in October 1859 until Mississippi seceded in January 1861. Both Whig and Democratic editors "filled their pages with reports of suspected servile revolts, violence or incendiary activity, and pleaded daily for increased vigilence against the ubiquitous enemy." Mississippians viewed all strangers with suspicion, tightened the slave code, and enacted a law compelling all free Negroes to leave the State by 1 July 1860 or be sold into slavery. Based on newspapers.

J. W. Hillje

478. Ketcham, Ralph L., ed. THE DICTATES OF CONSCIENCE: EDWARD COLES AND SLAVERY. *Virginia Q. R. 1960 36(1): 46-62.* Deals with the internal and external conflicts in the life of the prominent Virginian Edward Coles, a man "possessed of both slaves and the ideal that *all* men were free and equal." Incorporated are long excerpts from an unaddressed autobiographical letter dated April 1844, now in the possession of the Historical Society of Pennsylvania, tracing the stages by which Coles decided upon manumission, and the events which culminated in the final action. Included is a description of the reaction of the slaves on learning of their freedom. Not unaware of the genuine economic and social problems involved for white and Negro alike, Coles determined to take the slaves into the free territory of Illinois. Public service delayed his action until 1819. A letter from Thomas Jefferson to Coles (1814) gives the former's views on manumission. Coles' later career is noted.

C. R. Allen, Jr.

479. Kilson, Marion D. de B. TOWARDS FREEDOM: AN ANALYSIS OF SLAVE REVOLTS IN THE UNITED STATES. *Phylon 1964 25(2): 175-187.* Analyzes data from Herbert Aptheker's *American Negro Slave Revolts* (New York, 1943). Considers 65 revolts which are divided into three major types (systematic or rational, unsystematic or vandalistic, and situational or opportunistic), distinguished in terms of aims, preparation, area, number and nature of participants, and repercussions. The author observes that "slave revolts of all three types occurred throughout the slave period and in all the slave regions of the United States." Yet systematic revolts were most common in the pre-1776 and 1831-29 periods. Unsystematic revolts were predominantly a colonial phenomenon, and situational revolts were concentrated in the 1830-60 periods. Geographically, the revolts were concentrated in Virginia, Louisiana, and South Carolina, and within a few counties in these States, suggesting that certain socioeconomic variables facilitated their occurrence and recurrence in these areas in spite of their dependence on a catalyst in the form of an individual or individuals. The threat they posed to the slavocracy led to panic and mob vengeance, increased armed oppression of slaves, and establishment of legislative measures to prevent further outbreaks.

S. C. Pearson, Jr.

480. Kiple, Kenneth F. THE CASE AGAINST A NINETEENTH-CENTURY CUBA-FLORIDA SLAVE TRADE. *Florida Hist. Q. 1971 49(4): 346-355.* Recent research indicates that an extensive contraband slave trade to the United

States after 1808 probably did not exist. An account relied on as evidence by historians, Richard Drake's *Revelations of a Slave Smuggler* (1860), has been recently declared spurious by a historian of the slave trade. Records indicate that the slaver *Guerrero,* cited often as evidence of the Cuba-Florida slave trade, had plundered another ship of its slave cargo before fleeing from a British patrol schooner and running aground in the Florida Keys in 1827. The *Guerrero's* destination was evidently not Florida, but Havana. The very fact that such a commotion was created in St. Joseph, Florida, by the landing of the slave-ship *Emperor* in 1837 would indicate the uniqueness of such an event. Another fact usually overlooked is that Cuba had a shortage of blacks because of the sugar revolution and would hardly have been selling them. The price for slaves in the United States was about the same as it was in Cuba from 1808 until 1861. That a slave-trader would have risked capture carrying slaves from Cuba to Florida at no profit seems illogical. That a Cuba-to-Florida slave trade existed is probably only a myth. Based partly on unpublished Spanish records; 47 notes.

R. V. Calvert

481. Klein, Herbert S. NORTH AMERICAN COMPETITION AND THE CHARACTERISTICS OF THE AFRICAN SLAVE TRADE TO CUBA, 1790 TO 1794. *William and Mary Q. 1971 28(1): 87-102.* Because of the loss of trade within the British Empire, Americans had to seek new markets. After Spain opened the slave trade to all nations the United States gained a lucrative commerce. Because U.S. trade in slaves did not expand as much as the European trade, it approximated a local carrying trade. The author examines the effects of the slave trade on the population of Cuba. Cites extensive port records in Seville, Spain. 10 tables, 25 notes.

H. M. Ward

482. Korn, Bertram W. JEWS AND NEGRO SLAVERY IN THE OLD SOUTH, 1789-1865. *Pub. of the Am. Jewish Hist. Soc. 1961 50(3): 151-201.* This topic is broken down into the following subheadings: 1) Jews as planters and owners of slaves; 2) the treatment of slaves by Jews and attempts at emancipation; 3) Jews as taskmasters; 4) business dealings of Jews with slaves and free Negroes; 5) Jews as slavedealers; 6) cases of miscegenation involving Jews and Negroes, and 7) opinions of Jews about the slave system. Available secondary sources and primary materials, as found in archives and in contemporary newspapers, were utilized. It appears that opinions of Jews in the South about the system of slavery were to no appreciable degree different from those of their non-Jewish environment.

F. Rosenthal

483. Kugler, Ruben F. U. B. PHILLIPS' USE OF SOURCES. *J. of Negro Hist. 1962 47(3): 153-168.* Briefly reviews the criticism which current leading historians have made of the writings of Ulrich Bonnell Phillips concerning Negro slavery, and adds some information relating to Phillips' use of source materials. Using eight examples to prove the point, the author shows that Phillips cited writers to support an interpretation not supported in the original, quoted out of context, omitted a key sentence in at least one instance, and generalized from one

example. Phillips tended to use his sources in such a way as to produce a favorable impression of slavery and to picture the Negro as a willing chattel.

L. Gara

484. Kuhr, Manuel I. HOW GEORGE VEST CAME TO MISSOURI. *Missouri Hist. R. 1965 59(4): 424-427.* George Graham Vest was an important Missouri secessionist and a leading lawyer in that State for 50 years. While enroute from Kentucky to Santa Fe, where he hoped to open a law office, Vest paused in Georgetown, Missouri in July 1853 to defend a slave charged with rape and murder. His decision to remain in Missouri was prompted less by the fact that relatives of the victim lynched his client than it was by a desire to stand up to the men who threatened him with a similar fate for having the temerity to defend a Negro in court.

W. F. Zornow

485. Lahmeyer Lobo, Eulalia María. RIO DE JANEIRO E CHARLESTON S.C.: AS COMUNIDADES DE MERCADORES NO SECULO XVIII [Rio de Janeiro and Charleston, South Carolina: merchant communities of the 18th century]. *J. of Inter-Am. Studies and World Affairs 1970 12(4): 565-582.* Sociological studies have indicated that plantation economies that used slavery for labor and exported some of their produce created an elite merchant class that was distinct from the landed aristocracy and that was preoccupied with its own interests. Taking two such societies, Rio de Janeiro and Charleston, the author seeks to verify this thesis. In Rio de Janeiro he found that there were two separate influential classes - the rural aristocracy and the merchants - which had different interests and at times were in conflict. He also found that social status was difficult for the merchants to acquire but that the rural aristocracy automatically possessed it. In Charleston, there was a more harmonious relationship between the classes, with the merchant class having more social status than its counterpart in Brazil. Based on archival material, manuscripts, and official documents; 25 notes.

J. R. Thomas

486. Lander, Ernest M., Jr. THE DEVELOPMENT OF TEXTILES IN THE SOUTH CAROLINA PIEDMONT BEFORE 1860. *Cotton Hist. R. 1960 1(3): 88-100.* In 1816 a group of New Englanders opened a mill in the Spartanburg district, on the Tyger River. Until the depression following the Panic of 1837, a number of textile mills were built in the back country of the State. From 1838 to 1860 only six small mills were added. The first mills produced yarn, but by 1825 cloth was being manufactured. Only one plant employed slaves. Most plants operated 400 to 600 spindles. All were water driven. Only one mill made its proprietors wealthy.

D. A. Stokes

487. Lewis, Mary Agnes. SLAVERY AND PERSONALITY: A FURTHER COMMENT. *Am. Q. 1967 19(1): 114-121.* Refutes Stanley Elkins' thesis in *Slavery: A Problem in American Institutional and Intellectual Life* (Chicago: U. of Chicago Press, 1959) concerning the "Sambo" stereotype. Submissive personality traits were less pervasive than it appeared. "Selective inattention" to deviation on the part of slave owners and failure to observe that plentiful groups of "insignificant others" did exist for slaves has prevented Elkins and others from

seeing that a viable status-conferring society of other slaves had emerged. From this, owners received more trouble than compliance. The "Sambo" stereotype persisted only because whites wanted it to.   R. S. Pickett

488. Lewis, Roscoe E. THE LIFE OF MARK THRASH. *Phylon 1959 20(4): 389-403.* Mark Thrash was reputed to have been born a slave in Georgia in 1820, and was famous for his age and warm personality long before his death in 1943. His age was attested to by the U.S. Civil Service Commission. When interviewed in 1941, in his home in Georgia, he was in full control of his faculties, including his memory, which went back to his earliest years. Meanwhile, he received tourists with ease, his young wife receiving money offerings in his behalf. His memories went back to Nat Turner's Rebellion, and included tales of the Civil War, during which, he claimed, he had made contact with many of the famous protagonists. He also discussed his family and descendents, whose lives ramified into many ways and places. His story made up a career impressive for the scenes of slavery and freedom it included. The author made efforts to corroborate its details.   L. Filler

489. Lieber, Todd M. THE SIGNIFICANCE OF THE FRONTIER IN THE WRITING OF ANTEBELLUM SOUTHERN HISTORY. *Mississippi Q. 1969 22(4): 337-354.* Analysis of the work of several well-known historians of the South and of several college history textbooks reveals that Frederick Jackson Turner's ideas have not been as useful in interpreting the history of the antebellum South as might be expected. Historians have generally seen the frontier as only one of many factors which influenced the history of the South. Turner's hypotheses were chiefly valuable in pointing out new possibilities for research and examination. While Turnerian theories proved useful for the interpretation of the period up to 1820, other approaches - taking into consideration distinctive features of the region such as climate, the Negro, and the plantation system - were found to be more applicable to the period from 1820 to the Civil War. Based on published material; 32 notes.   R. V. Calvert

490. Luckingham, Bradford F. SCHOOLCRAFT, SLAVERY, AND SELF-EMANCIPATION. *J. of Negro Hist. 1965 50(2): 118-121.* Reprints Henry R. Schoolcraft's plan for the self-emancipation of slaves which he included in his *Travels in the Central Portions of the Mississippi Valley...in the Year 1821* (New York, 1925). Schoolcraft recorded his observations on slavery and emancipation during a visit to St. Louis. His plan included setting aside part of each work day for the slaves' own use, paying for work done during such periods and the gradual increase of free time until the slaves had fully purchased their freedom.
                                                                         L. Gara

491. Lythgoe, Dennis L. NEGRO SLAVERY AND MORMON DOCTRINE. *Western Humanities R. 1967 21(4): 327-338.* A survey of pronouncements on the subjects including some by Joseph Smith and Brigham Young. In spite of ambivalence or vagueness in some of the statements, Mormon doctrine has been close to the southern position on the Negro as bearer of the curse of Ham, slavery as a divine institution, intermarriage, abolition, and segregation, with States' rights

called in to support the position. Records show that at least two Negroes were admitted to the priesthood of the early Mormon Church, but the policy has since been firm that Negroes might become members but must be excluded from the priesthood. The church stressed the necessity for humane treatment of slaves. Besides published works, use has been made of files in the Church Historian's Office, Salt Lake City; 40 notes. A. Turner

492. MacMaster, Richard K. UNITED STATES NAVY AND AFRICAN EXPLORATION 1851-1860. *Mid-Am. 1964 46(3): 187-203.* In the decade before the Civil War American interest in Africa increased perceptively. The gradual decline of the slave trade contributed to the growth of legitimate commerce between West Africa and the United States and the extension of missionary activity to new centers. But little government support and the war cut these efforts off by the end of the decade. L. D. Silveri

493. Mahon, John K. BRITISH STRATEGY AND SOUTHERN INDIANS: WAR OF 1812. *Florida Hist. Q. 1966 44(4): 285-302.* Discusses the failure of a complex British scheme by officers operating in the Gulf of Mexico during the War of 1812 to conquer the southwestern part of the United States by means of an alliance with the Indians, escaped Negro slaves, Spaniards, and others. Based on British and American State papers, private papers, and secondary works. G. L. Lycan

494. Main, Jackson Turner. THE DISTRIBUTION OF PROPERTY IN POST-REVOLUTIONARY VIRGINIA. *Mississippi Valley Hist. R. 1954 41(2): 241-258.* Shows that a majority of the adult white males were not landowners, though the proportion of landless was not the same everywhere. Of the landowners, most were small farmers, 80 percent holding 200 acres or less. The distribution of slaves also varied greatly by section and the Fall Line, not the Tidewater, was the region of the largest estates. The physiography of Virginia was in a state of flux in the 1780's and 1790's. Based on annual compilations by the State of Virginia, begun in the years immediately following the close of the American Revolution. G. L. A. Reilly

495. Main, Jackson Turner. THE ONE HUNDRED. *William and Mary Q. 1954 11(3): 355-384.* A study of Virginia's hundred wealthiest men in the 1780's. These "one hundred" controlled only six percent of the land and six and one-half percent of the slaves. Large plantations were beginning to be divided. Entail and primogeniture, if ever frequently practiced, seem to have had little effect on landholding. Based on tax records; tables. E. Oberholzer, Jr.

496. Martin, Ida M. CIVIL LIBERTIES IN GEORGIA LEGISLATION 1800-1830. *Georgia Hist. Q. 1961 45(4): 329-344.* Examines Georgia legislation pertaining to freedom of religion, speech, press, assembly, and procedural due process between 1800 and 1830 and notes restrictions thereon, many of which were based on the State's police power to protect a society based on slavery and

cotton. Protection of individual rights was slow and subject to the will of the State legislature, against whose action appeal could be made only to the State courts.

R. Lowitt

497. Mathews, Donald G. THE METHODIST MISSION TO THE SLAVES, 1829-1844. *J. of Am. Hist. 1965 51(4): 615-631.* Surveys the extent of the Methodist Church's missionary work among slaves in the South during 1829-44. The author concludes the mission was a moral paradox in its extension of Christian and moral concern to the Negro and at the same time its underwriting of the status quo of the South's peculiar institution.   H. J. Silverman

498. McCorison, Marcus A. REPORT OF THE LIBRARIAN: ACQUISITIONS. *Pro. of the Am. Antiquarian Soc. 1965 75(2): 237-252.* A report given at the annual meeting held in Worcester of gifts and purchases of books for the society's collections. Among a total of 2,897 titles, 281 of which were printed before 1821, 66 of these were not recorded in bibliographies. The outstanding acquisition of the year was a 1786 edition of Daniel Boone's adventures. Books acquired also included other frontier narratives, almanacs, children's books, cookbooks, directories, newspapers, State documents, works of fiction, and additions to the Louisiana materials, including some Henri Remy manuscripts and a photostatic copy of the memoirs of Pierre Clement Laussat. Rare pamphlets and broadsides collected included an 1831 edition of a report on the Nat Turner insurrection in Virginia.   R. V. Calvert

499. McPherson, James M. BOOK REVIEW: "THE POLITICAL ECONOMY OF SLAVERY: STUDIES IN THE ECONOMY AND SOCIETY OF THE SLAVE SOUTH." *J. of Social Hist. 1968 1(3): 280-285.* The book, by Eugene D. Genovese (New York: Pantheon, 1965), deals with the impact of slavery on the economic and political structure of the antebellum South. He has two major theses: slavery was an inefficient, costly labor system that precluded modernization of the southern economy; and slavery formed the basis of a semifeudal society which differed so radically from the bourgeois capitalism of the North that it was in effect a separate civilization. In developing the first point, Genovese is convincing, but in dealing with the second, he is less so. He regards the Civil War as irrepressible, as a contest between two distinct social orders, dominated by ruling classes with antithetical interests. The reviewer states that three propositions suggested by the author but not proven leave him open to challenge. The first holds that slavery formed the basis of a noncapitalist social order; the second that the hegemony of large slaveholders determined the character of the South; and finally that, when insurrection came, the slaveholders knew what to do. Genovese's argument implies a belief in the power of rationality and in the ability of men to control the course of events. His work has broad scope and incisiveness. Its calm, restrained style emphasizes by contrast the bold controversial nature of its arguments. 11 notes.   N. M. Drescher

500. McPherson, Robert, ed. GEORGIA SLAVE TRIALS, 1837-1849. *Am. J. of Legal Hist. 1960 4(3): 257-284, (4): 364-377.* Prints court records involving

slaves, from Elbert County, Georgia. Both documents and summaries of cross examinations are given. The cases are all criminal, and include murder (of another slave), rape, breaking and entering, and arson.   N. C. Brockman

501. Meador, John. FLORIDA AND THE COMPROMISE OF 1850. *Florida Hist. Q. 1960 39(1): 16-33.* The Compromise of 1850, especially the admission of California as a free State and sectional resentments revolving around the Fugitive Slave Law, broke down the Whig Party in Florida, as it did in the Nation. Based on newspaper accounts, State papers, and secondary sources.

G. L. Lycan

502. Miles, Edwin A. THE MISSISSIPPI SLAVE INSURRECTION SCARE OF 1835. *J. of Negro Hist. 1957 42(1): 48-60.* The slave insurrection scare in Madison County, Mississippi, partially explains the southern opposition to the abolitionists in 1835 and the following years. "Although it seems likely that in this instance the fears of southern whites had been grossly exaggerated, their reaction was just as vehement as if the dangers had been real."

W. E. Wight

503. Miller, Lillian B. PAINTINGS, SCULPTURE, AND THE NATIONAL CHARACTER, 1815-1860. *J. of Am. Hist. 1967 53(4): 696-707.* Art in early 19th-century America was regarded as a necessary ingredient in the development of national character, a means of ultimately refining the crude, rough manifestations of what Europeans often saw as a crassly, almost brutally materialistic society, and a means of uniting a potentially divisive society around national symbols which translated certain principles and characteristics regarded as uniquely American by people especially in the Northeast and in the West. Accordingly, art was realistic only in the sense of meticulous rendering of detail, but was to represent idealized versions of people or of landscapes, inculcating values of freedom, optimism, rural life, energy, thrift, sobriety, heroism, health, and democracy. The art avoided depiction of real immigrants or of problems of industrialization, urbanization, slavery, or labor problems.   K. B. West

504. Miller, William L. A NOTE ON THE IMPORTANCE OF THE INTERSTATE SLAVE TRADE OF THE ANTE BELLUM SOUTH. *J. of Pol. Economy 1965 73(2): 181-187.* Attempts to determine the economic importance of the interstate slave trade of the antebellum South have sought to establish two main propositions: 1) this trade augmented the westward flow of population and made a net distribution to the movement of people from where they were less valuable to where they were more productive, 2) it brought profits to the planters in the older slaveholding States and thereby prolonged slavery by preventing voluntary manumission. The author endeavors to show that these two main propositions have not been substantiated and also provides evidence against them. The interstate slave trade was not essential for the perpetuation of slavery in the older Southern States. Though it may not have made a net addition to the westward movement of population, it did make a contribution to the slave-exporting States.

It provided the means of compensating these regions for the investment made in the slaves sold. There was no analogous offset for loss of whites through migration and for slaves who accompanied their masters.   H. Proschansky

505. Miller, William L. J. E. CAIRNES ON THE ECONOMICS OF AMERI-CAN NEGRO SLAVERY. *Southern Econ. J. 1964 30(4): 333-341.* In the course of a painstaking reexamination of John Elliott Cairnes' *The Slave Power,* originally published in 1862, many shortcomings are exposed, and the author concludes that Cairnes failed to examine the available evidence with sufficient care, mainly because he relied too heavily upon an a priori method.
A. W. Coats

506. Miller, William L. SLAVERY AND THE POPULATION OF THE SOUTH. *Southern Econ. J. 1961 28(1): 46-54.* A common belief has been that slavery prevented much immigration into the antebellum South and thereby kept population in that region sparse. Explicitly stated reasons have been that slavery is inherently repulsive and that it degraded labor. The important argument that it prevented accumulation and maintenance of nonhuman resources has been left implicit. Information from privately published sources and data from 1850 and subsequent censuses largely destroy this position. Instead of keeping population sparse in the South, slavery probably packed more people into that region than would have arrived in its absence.   A

507. Mitchell, Joseph. TRAVELLING PREACHER AND SETTLED FARMER. *Methodist Hist. 1967 5(4): 3-14.* Analyzes the 51 delegates from the slaveholding States to the 1844 General Conference of the Methodist Episcopal Church. These men, who were in support of James Osgood Andrew, were farmer-preachers. They were southerners first, farmers with families to support second, and theologically untrained ministers third. The author discusses their activities as preachers or holders of administrative positions in the Methodist Church and as farmers, their acquisition of land and slaves, and their financial status. Other biographical information on several is included. Based largely on U.S. census records and county record books; 50 notes.   H. L. Calkin

508. Moore, John H. SIMON GRAY, RIVERMAN: A SLAVE WHO WAS ALMOST FREE. *Mississippi Valley Hist. R. 1962 49(3): 471-484.* Numerous slaves were employed in the cypress lumber industry in the lower Mississippi in the antebellum era. Many of these Negroes assumed a position of importance, achieving a status of quasi-independence. Simon Gray's life is offered as an example of this genre of Negro. It is suggested that the role of the Negro in the pre-Civil War southern industry needs reexamination.   G. M. Gressley

509. Moore, John Hammond. A HYMN OF FREEDOM - SOUTH CAROLINA, 1813. *J. of Negro Hist. 1965 50(1): 50-53.* Publishes the words of a song which, according to the English abolitionist George Thompson, was used by slaves on an island near Charleston while planning an insurrection during the War of 1812. The rebellion, which depended upon cooperation from the British,

never took place, and the song was not written down until 1862 when a Presbyterian clergyman sent it to the historian Benson John Lossing.

L. Gara

510. Moore, Margaret DesChamps. PROTESTANTISM IN THE MISSISSIPPI TERRITORY. *J. of Mississippi Hist. 1967 29(4): 358-370.* Describes religious attitudes and Protestant religious activities in the Mississippi Territory, 1799-1817. "Free thought, skepticism, deism or indifference to religion were characteristic of the upper class" and inhabitants of the area were "far more interested in seeking riches in this world than in the next." The author focuses largely upon the Methodists, Baptists, and Presbyterians, the three leading denominations in the territory. Protestant ministers won converts, often promoted education, and had some influence in improving the treatment of slaves. Based largely on published secondary and primary sources; 47 notes. J. W. Hillje

511. Mörner, Magnus. DET JÄMFÖRANDE STUDIET AV NEGER-SLAVERIET I ANGLOAMERIKA OCH I LATINAMERIKA I AKTUELL FORSKNINGSDEBATT [Current research debates on the comparative study of Negro slavery in Anglo America and Latin America]. *Historiallinen Arkisto [Finland] 1968 63: 253-265.* Discusses recent research on slavery in the Americas. The contrast between Latin and Anglo-Saxon slavery posited by Frank Tannenbaum in *Slave and Citizen: The Negro in the Americas* (New York: Random House, 1947) can no longer be accepted. The nature of slavery seems to have varied widely in the Americas at various times and places, depending on local economic, political, and demographic circumstances. Much more detailed research remains to be done. 68 notes. R. G. Selleck

512. Morris, Richard B. THE MEASURE OF BONDAGE IN THE SLAVE STATES. *Mississippi Valley Hist. R. 1954 41(2): 219-240.* Applauds recent revisionism as to the role of plantation slavery in antebellum South but holds that it is as yet inadequate. Contends that conventional judgment of freedom and bondage by absolute standards errs in ignoring the fact that a large segment of the southern labor force of both races "operated under varying degrees of compulsion, legal or economic, in a twilight zone of bondage." Indentured servitude of the colonial pattern applied to whites in many areas prior to the war. Involuntary servitude, regardless of race, persisted even after the Civil War in maritime employment. The slave States often used compulsion in dealing with white vagrants or unemployed and the most cherished rights of personal security were weakly buttressed for all labor, white or Negro, free or slave. G. L. A. Reilly

513. Mount, Robert L. THE HINGE OF REFORM. *Mankind 1967 1(4): 46-48.* An examination of the events which led to the execution of Nathaniel Gordon, the only man legally executed for the crime of slave trading. Gordon was a New England sea captain who violated the Piracy Act of 1820, which made slave trading a capital offense, in order to make the easy money. Captured 50 miles off the coast of West Africa with a load of 897 slaves, Gordon was tried in New York. Found guilty, he was sentenced to hang. Illus. P. D. Thomas

514. Netenson, Walter F. SLAVERY IN THE 1850'S: THE RECOLLECTIONS OF AN ALABAMA UNIONIST. *Alabama Hist. Q. 1968 30(3/4): 219-227.* Wade Hampton Richardson's recollections on slavery during the 1850's and early 1860's. Richardson was an Alabama Unionist who joined the Union Army and eventually settled in the North. In the manuscript, written in the 1880's and printed here for the first time, Richardson describes the life of his family slaves along with some general observations on slave religion and Christmas activities.

E. E. Eminhizer

515. Nichols, Charles H. THE ORIGINS OF "UNCLE TOM'S CABIN." *Phylon 1958 19(3): 328-334.* An answer to the charge that *Uncle Tom's Cabin* has perpetuated race prejudice. Harriet Beecher Stowe's source was Richard Hildreth's *The Slave: or the Memoirs of Archy Moore* (1836). *Uncle Tom* used attitudes already common in America (Christianity, the sentimental picture of the family, the plantation myth) which appealed to its public. Based on slave narratives, contemporary reviews of the book, and biographies. A

516. Nichols, Charles H. WHO READ THE SLAVE NARRATIVES? *Phylon 1959 20(2): 149-162.* Slave narratives (the biographies and autobiographies of slaves) were largely propagated by abolitionists who edited, promoted, and distributed them after 1836. They are significant for their picture of slavery as seen by its victims and for their revelation of the mind of the enslaved. They were printed in large numbers and widely circulated. Harriet Beecher Stowe, Richard Hildreth, and Frederick Law Olmsted were among the best known 19th-century readers of these narratives. For some time after the Civil War such historians as Ulrich Phillips discredited the narratives and wrote with definite pro-slavery bias, but modern historians and commentators are turning again to the narratives for significant firsthand information on slavery. A

517. Oster, Harry. NEGRO HUMOR: JOHN AND OLD MARSTER. *J. of the Folklore Inst. 1968 5(1): 42-57.* Discusses the functional dynamics of tales of the master and slave variety. Humorous folktales of the "numbskull" variety "frequently appeal to the ordinary person's need to deaden the pangs of inferiority."

J. C. Crowe

518. Owsley, Frank L., Jr. ALBERT J. PICKETT: PLANTER-HISTORIAN OF THE OLD SOUTH. *Louisiana Studies 1969 8(2): 158-184.* A biography of one of the more successful Alabama planters before 1860. Pickett's father had considerable political experience in North Carolina before moving to Alabama in 1818, where he continued his interest in public affairs until 1837. Albert inherited an involvement in politics and expressed this interest publicly in 1832 at the age of 22. He was a follower of Andrew Jackson and expressed his nationalism in newspaper articles. He expressed his opinions, orally and in writing, on the leading issues of the day. These included the removal of the Indians, banking, commerce, transportation, education, and the importation of Negroes. His public activities led to an interest in Alabama history. His "Eight Days in New Orleans in February, 1847" was published in eight installments in the Montgomery *Daily Journal* as a test of his ability to write history. The acceptance prompted him to

write the *History of Alabama* (1847-51) and while gathering material he published essays which were later incorporated in the book. He realized the importance of advertising or remaining in contact with the public. His success encouraged him to undertake the history of the Southwest, which was approximately two-thirds finished when illness ended the project in 1857. His main occupation was farming, and he was one of of the largest planters in Montgomery and Autauga counties. His ideas and procedures on planting served as a pattern for others. Based on newspapers and personal letters; 125 notes.

G. W. McGinty

519. Pease, Jane H. A NOTE ON PATTERNS OF CONSPICUOUS CONSUMPTION AMONG SEABOARD PLANTERS, 1820-1860. *J. of Southern Hist. 1969 35(3): 381-393.* Questions the traditional assumption that planters consumed their resources in "riotous living" and examines "specific forms of conspicuous consumption." Among those discussed are extravagance in housing; excessive number of domestic servants (almost entirely slaves); hospitality to friends, relatives, and invited guests; entertainment; and high costs for education. Of these, the "strongest case for a distinctive pattern of conspicuous consumption lies in the numerous slaves used as nonprofit-producing domestic servants." Yet so many questions still remain unanswered - especially concerning the area of domestic servants - that the author concludes the evidence of southerners wasting potential savings for personal indulgences seems inconclusive. 47 notes.

I. M. Leonard

520. Peyer, Joan B. and Scott, Kenneth. GLIMPSES OF LONG ISLAND LIFE IN THE 1790'S. *J. of Long Island Hist. 1968 8(1): 26-56.* Excerpts from Long Island's first newspaper, *Frothingham's Long-Island Herald* (1791-98) treating "marriages and deaths, transportation and daily business activities, real estate sales and auctions, lost and found notices, including those of runaway slaves and apprentices, military reviews, celebrations, wind and weather, and other disasters." Each entry is identified by the day of the week as well as the date.

C. A. Newton

521. Phifer, Edward W. SLAVERY IN MICROCOSM: BURKE COUNTY, NORTH CAROLINA. *J. of Southern Hist. 1962 28(2): 137-165.* The history of slavery has been neglected by county historians. Likewise, historians of slavery have not adequately studied the large areas where staples were not produced, but where slavery nevertheless existed. Burke County, North Carolina, was located in the valley of the Catawba River, between two mountain ranges. Only 548 persons owned land, and only nine of these owned as many as 300 improved acres; 60 family heads owned 10 or more slaves. Of the 20 leading slaveowners, at least 13 had occupations not associated with agriculture. There were few public sales of slaves in the county except for settlement of estates. Slave hiring was a common practice in the county, and such hiring-out was conducted on a large-scale contractual basis during the gold rush of the early 1830's and during the railroad construction boom of the late 1850's.

S. E. Humphreys

522. Pickard, Kate E. R. THE KIDNAPPED AND THE RANSOMED. *Am. Jewish Arch. 1957 9(1): 3-31.* Peter Still, who had been kidnapped in childhood, bought his own freedom through the kindness of a Jewish merchant in Alabama and made his way back to Philadelphia. Three chapters reprinted from the recollections of a slave, first serialized in 1856 and republished in book form in 1941.   A. B. Rollins

523. Porter, Kenneth W. NEGROES AND THE SEMINOLE WAR, 1835-1842. *J. of Southern Hist. 1964 30(4): 427-450.* The Second Seminole War resulted from the decision to move the Seminoles from Florida. This decision was influenced by the presence and position of several hundred Negroes among the Seminoles, some of them slaves of the Seminoles or nominally free, but some of them runaways from white masters. The Negroes, fearful of being turned over to whites, strongly influenced the general Seminole decision to resist removal. These Negroes were shrewd and farsighted in their plans for resistance and active and aggressive in carrying them out. Once convinced, however, that the government was inflexibly determined on Seminole removal - and persuaded, too, that if they and the Indians surrendered, their own freedom and the lives of both races would be respected - they were almost as influential in persuading the more recalcitrant Indians to surrender as they had previously been in rallying Seminole resistance.   S. E. Humphreys

524. Price, John Milton. SLAVERY IN WINN PARISH. *Louisiana Hist. 1967 8(2): 137-148.* Contrary to general belief, the hill country of north central Louisiana did not show a strong antipathy to the plantation order and, in fact, contained a substantial number of slaves and slaveholders. Thirty-five percent of the households of Winn Parish held slaves, and 24 percent of the population were slaves. Nevertheless, the parish opposed secession, contributed little to the Confederate war effort, and welcomed Union victory. This reflected the fact that the region was not in the mainstream of Louisiana's economic and social activity and that it resented the aristocratic elements which dominated the State. Based on secondary accounts and on contemporary public records and travel accounts; tables, 25 notes.   R. L. Woodward

525. Proctor, William G., Jr. SLAVERY IN SOUTHWEST GEORGIA. *Georgia Hist. Q. 1965 49(1): 1-22.* A careful analysis, chiefly based on primary sources, of slavery in southwest Georgia for the period roughly from 1820 to 1860, testing the applicability of various theories regarding the nature of slavery.   R. Lowitt

526. Ravitz, Abe C. JOHN PIERPONT AND THE SLAVES' CHRISTMAS. *Phylon 1960 (4): 383-386.* The Reverend John Pierpont was a conspicuous literary, theological, and political figure whose verses and deeds elicited the admiration of the reformers of his time. Following graduation from Yale College in 1804, he thought of teaching and became a tutor to the children of a South Carolina planter, arriving in time for Christmas. He recorded in his journal notes which marked his vivid realization of the reality of slavery; in addition, his entries

include data of interest to the sociologist and folklorist. Within six months, he was thoroughly dissatisfied with the life about him, and developed the abolitionist views which he took north with him. L. Filler

527. Reinders, Robert C. SLAVERY IN NEW ORLEANS IN THE DECADE BEFORE THE CIVIL WAR. *Mid-Am. 1962 44(4): 211-221.* New Orleans was the greatest slave trading center in the South but also an extensive slave owning area in itself. Urban slavery, as in New Orleans, provided Negroes with a variety of experience lacking in the usual slave areas. They enjoyed greater freedom in action, work, and in their relationship with whites. It can probably be concluded that these slaves were contented without losing sight of the undoubted whetting of their appetite for freedom. L. D. Silveri

528. Reinders, Robert C. THE CHURCHES AND THE NEGRO IN NEW ORLEANS, 1850-1860. *Phylon 1961 22(3): 241-248.* In New Orleans about half the Negro population were communicants of the Roman Catholic Church. Catholics did not discriminate in church affairs, but followed the city's racial habits. Protestant denominations cooperated less. The Methodist Episcopal Church, South, was most active, but the Baptists, Protestant Episcopalians and Presbyterians also made limited efforts to serve Negroes. Lutherans, Unitarians, and others were largely indifferent. There were a few all-Negro religious organizations, which were ruled illegal in 1858. Voodoo had some social acceptability. Negro religious leaders made efforts to reassure the whites, endorsing slavery, for example. After the Civil War, Negroes set up their own churches, largely Baptist and African Methodist Episcopalian, identifying the old ones with slavery. The Catholics lost much of their following. Negroes sought integration in other areas, but felt freer in segregated churches. Only in the 20th century did Negro leaders see the need for leveling the walls between American Christians.
L. Filler

529. Richter, William L. SLAVERY IN BATON ROUGE, 1820-1860. *Louisiana Hist. 1969 10(2): 125-145.* Negro slaves were an important minority of antebellum Baton Rouge's population, which had reached only 5,428 by 1860. About a third of the whites in the town owned slaves, but few owned more than 10. Treatment and use of slaves was typical of other southern cities in most respects. Blacks were often involved in criminal activities, but court records indicate that free blacks were more often accused than slaves and that there were acquittals as well as convictions of both. White men living with colored women was a frequent scandal in the town. Although slavery was often unjust and harsh, the Baton Rouge slave had more opportunities for leisure time than his "country cousin." Dancing, gambling, racing, and drinking were popular diversions. Blacks attended both white churches and their own, as segregation was informal. "Slavery in Baton Rouge was a viable economic institution, growing with the town, and continually involving a stable one-third of the city's breadwinners." Based on Baton Rouge newspapers, other published sources, and municipal and parish records; statistical tables, 75 notes. R. L. Woodward

530. Rogers, George C., Jr. THE LETTERS OF WILLIAM LOUGHTON SMITH TO EDWARD RUTLEDGE, JUNE 6, 1789 TO APRIL 28, 1794. *South Carolina Hist. Mag. 1968 69(1): 1-25.* Presents an edited version of five letters written by Smith to Edward Rutledge (1749-1800) in 1789, upon whom he relied for advice during his first years in Congress. These letters reveal that "Smith was most perceptive in his forecast that the men who wished to strengthen the new government would do so by construing the powers described in the Constitution broadly. He therefore was in favor of adding the amendment that became the tenth, and he was apparently supporting this amendment in order to protect the interests of South Carolina, particularly her interest in slavery. At this point he was opposed to Hamiltonian constructions of the constitution." 88 notes.
D. D. Cameron

531. Rogers, George C., Jr. TWO JOSEPH WRAGG LETTERS. *South Carolina Hist. Mag. 1964 65(1): 16-19.* Two letters from Joseph Wragg of South Carolina to Isaac Hobhouse, a Bristol, England merchant prominent in the slave trade. The letters are concerned with such topics as proposed financial legislation which threatened business interests, the great demand for slaves, and problems arising out of legislation in Georgia concerned with trading with Indians. The first letter is located in the Bristol Archives Office and the second, in the Bristol Central Reference Library.
V. O. Bardsley

532. Rogers, Tommy W. D. R. HUNDLEY: A MULTI-CLASS THESIS OF SOCIAL STRATIFICATION IN THE ANTEBELLUM SOUTH. *Mississippi Q. 1970 23(2): 135-154.* Daniel R. Hundley, antebellum Alabama planter, lawyer, banker, and amateur sociologist, was an early exponent of a multiclass analysis of the antebellum South,exemplified by his *Social Relations in Our Southern States* (1860). Using horizontal as well as vertical status characteristics, Hundley identified seven distinct classes - southern gentleman, cotton snob, middle class, southern Yankee, southern bully, poor white trash, and Negro slave. Hundley made a considerable contribution toward understanding society in the antebellum South in the light of his objective of "understanding the types of men and women selected and shaped by a given society." Based mainly on secondary sources; 43 notes.
R. V. Calvert

533. Rose, Lisle A. A COMMUNICATION. *William and Mary Q. 1969 26(1): 162-164.* The assertion that race relations in the South deteriorated rapidly in the 1790's because of the Santo Domingo insurrection is borne out in white reaction to the Charleston slave conspiracy of 1797. Letters of South Carolina's Senator and Governor Edward Rutledge are cited as evidence. 4 notes.
H. M. Ward

534. Sanchez-Saavedra, E. M. "AN UNDISCIPLINED SET OF VAGA-BONDS." *Virginia Cavalcade 1969 18(4): 41-47.* Tells of the deterioration of the Richmond (Virginia) Public Guard between 1801 and 1807. Originally formed as a "protective measure against slave uprisings, invasions and other calamities," the guard fell so low as to be called "public banditti" in newspaper editorials.

After 1807, under new command, it was gradually rejuvenated, "becoming a showpiece of military efficiency until its dissolution in 1869."

R. S. Burke

535. Saraydar, Edward. A NOTE ON THE PROFITABILITY OF ANTE BELLUM SLAVERY. *Southern Econ. J. 1964 30(4): 325-332.* A detailed reexamination of the well-known article by Alfred H. Conrad and John R. Meyer on "The Economics of Slavery in the Ante-Bellum South," *Journal of Political Economy,* April 1958. The author concludes that Conrad and Meyer significantly overstated the financial returns to investment in slaves employed in cotton production after 1830, and that consequently the question of the general profitability of slavery needs to be reconsidered. A. W. Coats

536. Scarborough, William K. THE SOUTHERN PLANTATION OVERSEER: A REEVALUATION. *Agric. Hist. 1964 38(1): 13-20.* The myth of the general ineptness of the overseer was created by members of the planter community and perpetuated by writers whose chief insight into the character of the overseer was through the eyes of the employer. Despite the importance of the overseer to the plantation, his social position was low, he was usually underpaid for his responsibilities, suffered short and insecure tenure of position, was zealously criticized, and had difficulty in obtaining a clear understanding of his responsibilities. These conditions were created by his employer. In general overseers were better off and superior in their accomplishments on larger plantations, on those with absentee owners, on rice and suger plantations, and in the eastern as compared with the western part of the region. The worth and effectiveness of the overseer as an institution is shown by the persistence of the system throughout the antebellum period. W. D. Rasmussen

537. Seip, Terry L. SLAVES AND FREE NEGROES IN ALEXANDRIA, 1850-1860. *Louisiana Hist. 1969 10(2): 125-145.* Using Alexandria as a case study, tests the conclusions of Richard C. Wade's *Slavery in the Cities: The South, 1820-1860* (New York: Oxford U. Press, 1964). Wade studied the 10 largest cities of the antebellum South and assumed that urban patterns would be the same in smaller centers. Presenting a statistical profile of Negro activities in Alexandria, Seip admits that it may not be possible to generalize about small towns in the South. But, insofar as Alexandria was representative of such small towns, slavery and race relations possessed some characteristics of both the rural and more highly urban systems. Based on newspapers, census reports, and municipal, parish, and State records; 57 notes. R. L. Woodward

538. Shalhope, Robert E. EUGENE GENOVESE, THE MISSOURI ELITE, AND CIVIL WAR HISTORIOGRAPHY. *Bull. of the Missouri Hist. Soc. 1970 26(4): 271-282.* Eugene D. Genovese, in *The Political Economy of Slavery* (New York: Pantheon Books, 1965), contended that a class-conscious elite of planters ruled the South before the Civil War. Genovese's critics accepted most of his facts but not his interpretation; the debate over the book still persists. The author tests Genovese's thesis against the facts of slavery and politics in Missouri, 1840-65.

The facts in Missouri "substantiate much of what Genovese has written," but not Genovese's "Marxian analysis." Based on primary and secondary sources; 38 notes.   H. T. Lovin

539. Sigler, Jay A. THE RISE AND FALL OF THE THREE-FIFTHS CLAUSE. *Mid-Am. 1966 48(4): 271-277.* The three-fifths formula began as an attempt to equate slavery with property, a view not long held by many, and then was supported as a political and sectional solution to problems of power distribution. The formula disappeared after the Civil War, creating a need for a new power distribution.   L. D. Silveri

540. Sikes, Lewright. MEDICAL CARE FOR SLAVES: A PREVIEW OF THE WELFARE STATE. *Georgia Hist. Q. 1968 52(4): 405-413.* Contends that plantation owners in general provided excellent medical care for their slaves. Physicians were called in serious cases of sickness or injury, slave nurses and plantation infirmaries were maintained, and sick or weakened slaves were allowed periods of rest. The author argues that southern slaves received better medical care than did free Negroes in the North. Two reasons prompted plantation owners to assume such a paternalistic attitude: the need to preserve the slave as an economic investment, and the natural benevolence of the typical master, who assumed a parent role in his relationship to his slaves. 54 notes.   R. A. Mohl

541. Sinzheimer, G. P. G. THE ECONOMICS OF RUSSIAN SERFDOM AND THE ECONOMICS OF AMERICAN SLAVERY - A HISTORICAL COMPARISON. *Jahrbücher für Geschichte Osteuropas [West Germany] 1966 14(4): 513-528.* Traces both the circumstances and functions of slavery (serfdom) in the United States and Russia in a comparison of different modes of dealing with an essentially similar institution in two different societies. Based on original sources and secondary interpretation.   L. H. Legters

542. Sio, Arnold A. INTERPRETATIONS OF SLAVERY: THE SLAVE STATUS IN THE AMERICAS. *Comparative Studies in Soc. and Hist. 1965 7(3): 289-308.* The distinction is made between the slave as legal property and his position as an innately (racially) inferior being. This led to a dual position of the slave under the law. Contrary to the widely held conception, racial discrimination was present in Latin America as well as in the United States.
J (T. E. Gregory)

543. Sisk, Glenn. CONTEMPORARY SITUATION OF: "THE NEGRO IN ATLANTA." *Negro Hist. Bull. 1964 27(7): 174-176.* Reviews the status of the Negro population of Atlanta, Georgia from the time of slavery to 1872.
L. Gara

544. Sowder, William J. MELVILLE'S "I AND MY CHIMNEY": A SOUTHERN EXPOSURE. *Mississippi Q. 1963 16(3): 128-145.* Herman Melville's story, "I and My Chimney," indicates his interest in current affairs of his time. The story is an allegorical version of an accurate history of slavery in the South in the

late 18th and first half of the 19th century. In Melville's eyes, the Civil War was inevitable. A careful examination of the story's setting and of the narrator reveals that the chimney represented the South's "peculiar institution" and that the narrator was a southerner, rather than Melville himself, as critics have assumed. Nor should the narrator's wife be construed as Elizabeth Shaw Melville. In the characterization of the narrator's wife, who lived always in the future, Melville was criticizing the impractical liberal, incapable of realizing the complexity of a problem. The architect Scribe also reflected Melville's dislike of the liberal democrat with his belief in automatic progress and in money as the key to the solution of the slavery problem. Melville's tragic sense is most effectively reflected in the changing relationship between the conservative narrator and the liberal wife. The three characters meet their destruction in the chimney, just as the antebellum South suffered. 68 notes. R. V. Calvert

545. Stafford, Frances. ILLEGAL IMPORTATIONS: ENFORCEMENT OF THE SLAVE TRADE LAWS ALONG THE FLORIDA COAST, 1810-1828. *Florida Hist. Q. 1967 46(2): 124-133.* Despite prohibiton of slave importation by Congress in 1808 and further enforcement provisions in 1818 and 1820, inadequate equipment, money, and personnel, as well as individual and sectional indifference and human greed, prevented enforcement along the Florida coast. As early as 1810, Florida was a center for illegal slave importations, a regular route for smuggling Negroes into Southern States. Conscientious officials found it difficult to obtain cooperation from other not-so-conscientious officials. In 1828 Congress appropriated 30 thousand dollars for suppression of the slave trade, but no set policy was formulated regarding custody and care of Africans rescued from foreign ships pending their return to Africa. Based on printed documents and secondary works; 38 notes. R. V. Calvert

546. Stampp, Kenneth M. INTERPRETING THE SLAVEHOLDERS' WORLD: A REVIEW. *Agric. Hist. 1970 44(4): 407-412.* A review article on Eugene D. Genovese's *The World the Slaveholders Made* (New York: Pantheon Books, 1969). Outlines Genovese's general thesis and finds fault with the quantity and quality of the evidence used to support the book's arguments and with the general attempt to apply a Marxian interpretation to the southern slave system. Concludes that the antebellum South "is just about as unpromising a place for the application of a Marxian interpretation of history as one can imagine." Based on secondary sources; 3 notes. D. E. Brewster

547. Stange, Douglas C. OUR DUTY TO PREACH THE GOSPEL TO NEGROES: SOUTHERN LUTHERANS AND AMERICAN SLAVERY. *Concordia Hist. Inst. Q. 1969 42(4): 171-182.* Although Southern Lutherans were thoroughly committed to the maintenance of slavery, they did not entirely neglect the religious life of their slaves. No separate Negro Lutheran churches were founded, but as early as 1814 the North Carolina Synod declared that it was their duty to preach the Gospel to Negroes, and a protocol was formulated to determine the procedures for dealing with Negroes in Lutheran communities. Notable was the excellent work of a Lutheran pastor, John Bachman, with the Negro community in Charleston, South Carolina. Slavery was condemned by the Ger-

man Evangelical Lutheran Synod of Tennessee in 1822, but by the 1830's Southern Lutherans were attacking the northern abolitionists. The religious teaching
and baptizing of Negroes nonetheless continued. Southern Lutherans supported
the Confederacy during the Civil War and condemned the Emancipation Proclamation of 1863. Based on published primary sources; 68 notes.

D. J. Abramoske

548. Starobin, Robert. DISCIPLINING INDUSTRIAL SLAVES IN THE
OLD SOUTH. *J. of Negro Hist. 1968 53(2): 111-128.* While the discipline of
industrial slaves rested on violent coercion, other, less brutal methods, were
preferred and proved more effective. Among the more common disciplinary
methods were routinizing daily work, religious indoctrination, total control of
living and working conditions, and the pass and badge system. The use of rewards
and incentives, including small cash payments for special service, was also common. Such payments were part of a system of slave control and not considered
a step away from slavery by either the master or the slave. Capable and loyal slave
managers performed valuable services for their masters and gained a number of
rewards. Sometimes such slave managers were given their freedom but such acts
were a result of paternal recognition rather than a blow at the system itself. Based
mostly on manuscript sources; 39 notes.   L. Gara

549. Starobin, Robert S. THE ECONOMICS OF INDUSTRIAL SLAVERY IN
THE OLD SOUTH. *Business Hist. R. 1970 44(2): 131-174.* The most distinctive
aspect of southern industry was its wide and intensive use of slave labor. In the
1850's about five percent of the total slave population worked in industry, and
most industrial entrepreneurs employing slave labor enjoyed highly satisfactory
rates of return on their investments. The available evidence also indicates that
slave labor was not less efficient than the free labor available in the Old South.
Furthermore, slave ownership did not seriously lessen the mobility of labor, nor
did slavery inhibit investment in industrial enterprises. Indeed, many industries
were actually capitalized by transferring bondsmen from farming or planting to
manufacturing, milling, mining, and transportation. Slaveowners themselves, not
merchants or bankers, were the chief source of capital for industrial investment.
Southern industry failed to develop rapidly, not because of slavery, but because
of the limitations of southern markets, the difficulty of competing with northern
and foreign producers, and the ability of southern agriculture to outbid industry
for investment capital. Based on contemporary statistics and manuscript and
periodical sources; 4 tables, 96 notes.   C. J. Pusateri

550. Staudenraus, P. J. VICTIMS OF THE AFRICAN SLAVE TRADE, A
DOCUMENT. *J. of Negro Hist. 1956 41(2): 148-151.* A letter written in 1822
describing the sailing for Liberia of Negroes captured as they were being smug-
gled into South Carolina. The writer relates how slaves were captured in Africa
and gives a description of those about to sail.   W. E. Wight

551. Stein, Barbara H. BRAZIL VIEWED FROM SELMA, ALABAMA, 1867,
A BIBLIOGRAPHICAL SURVEY. *Princeton U. Lib. Chronicle 1966 27(2):
65-85.* Joel E. Mathews wrote a letter which was reprinted as a pamphlet on

Brazil in 1867. In it he commented upon the possibilities of the establishment and maintenance of a slave economy in Brazil similar to that which had been in the Southern States. Despite a foreboding that slavery would end soon in Brazil, he recommended that southerners emigrate. The question is raised: would Mathews have drawn the same conclusions had he read the then-current travel literature on Brazil? Those travel books are examined for their references to slavery, its similarity to the southern system, and its future. The conclusion is that they give no clear indication of an early end to slavery in Brazil. However, it did end in 1888. Illus., 46 biblio. notes.   D. Brockway

552. Steiner, Bruce E. A PLANTER'S TROUBLED CONSCIENCE. *J. of Southern Hist. 1962 28(3): 343-347.* Historians of southern slavery have said comparatively little on the subject of antebellum miscegenation. Of interest in this area are a testamentary letter and will codicil of Benjamin Watkins (1787-1825) in Chesterfield County, Virginia, in which he sought, with the anguish and remorse of a sensitive man, to make amends to a slave woman and her two sons by him, in a legal situation where manumission was difficult.
                                                                S. E. Humphreys

553. Stucky, Sterling. THROUGH THE PRISM OF FOLKLORE: THE BLACK ETHOS IN SLAVERY. *Massachusetts R. 1968 9(3): 417-437.* Challenges Stanley M. Elkins' contention that slavery was so dehumanizing that Negroes passively accepted their inferior social station. The folk song, which combined traditional African cultural patterns with Christian theology and contained double meanings and irony, was the major way Negroes resisted the dehumanization of slavery. The folk song enabled Negroes to fashion an ethos and set of values which preserved their essential humanity and enabled them to survive as spiritual beings in a slave society. Song was the one area in which blacks were not inferior to whites. Based on folk songs and secondary works; 55 notes.
                                                                G. Kurland

554. Suret-Canale, Jean. LE PROBLEME NOIR DANS L'HISTOIRE DES ETATS-UNIS [The black problem in the history of the United States]. *Pensée [France] 1966 (130): 105-109.* Herbert Aptheker's *History of the Blacks in the United States. Essays in the History of the American Negro* (New York: Internat. Publishers, 1945), and *Toward Negro Freedom* (New York: New Century Publishers, 1956) deal with problems found in trying to find accurate information about the blacks in America. The problem has been that blacks have been treated from the viewpoint of the slaveowner, and the southern regime has been pictured as a patriarchal and idyllic regime, one that has been good to the blacks and respondent to their hereditary incapacity. Aptheker shows in his two works that what was American slavery was a combination of the negative aspects of slavery with those of capitalistic exploitation. 8 notes.   D. F. Rossi

555. Suttles, William C., Jr. AFRICAN RELIGIOUS SURVIVALS AS FACTORS IN AMERICAN SLAVE REVOLTS. *J. of Negro Hist. 1971 56(2):*

97-104. African religious survivals were at the heart of slave unrest in the Americas, especially in the cases of Nat Turner and the Santo Domingo revolts. Based mainly on secondary sources; 30 notes.   R. S. Melamed

556. Szuhay-Havas, Ervin. ADALÉKOK AZ USA RABSZOLGATARTÓ ÁL-LAMAINAK GAZDASÁG- ÉS TÁRSA-DALOMTÖRTÉNETÉHEZ, 1790-1861 (NÉHÁNY Ú ÚJABB AMERIKAI STANDARD MUNKA BÍRÁLATÁVAL) [Data on the economic and social history of the slaveholding States of the United States, 1790-1861; with criticism of some newer American standard works]. *Századok [Hungary] 1959 93(5/6): 893-909.* Following criticism of contemporary American historiography, which is unable to deal correctly with the socioeconomic history of the South, outlines the mentality of the slaveholders and draws a picture of racism. The author devotes most attention to the historical development of the Negro question. Based on published sources.

F. Wagner

557. Takaki, Ronald. THE MOVEMENT TO REOPEN THE SLAVE TRADE IN SOUTH CAROLINA. *South Carolina Hist. Mag. 1965 66(1): 38-54.* The initial impulse to reopen the slave trade is attributed to the Free Soil controversy and to efforts to outnumber white settlers in newly-opened territory with "rudest Africans." Based on newspaper reports, census returns, journals, and secondary sources; tables.   V. O. Bardsley

558. Talmadge, John E. GEORGIA TESTS THE FUGITIVE SLAVE LAW. *Georgia Hist. Q. 1965 49(1): 57-64.* Relates "the affair of Dr. Collins' slaves" who escaped from Georgia to Boston and whose return to slavery, in accordance with the provisions of the 1850 Fugitive Slave Law, was thwarted by Theodore Parker and other Boston abolitionists. Despite this incident Dr. Collins and other Georgia conservatives voted at the Milledgeville Convention in 1850, with a large majority, a series of resolutions accepting the Compromise of 1850.

R. Lowitt

559. Thorpe, Earle E. CHATTEL SLAVERY AND CONCENTRATION CAMPS. *Negro Hist. Bull. 1962 25(8): 171-174.* Challenges the thesis set forth by Stanley M. Elkins in *Slavery: A Problem in American Institutional and Intellectual Life* which finds a parallel between the institution of Negro slavery and the Nazi concentration camps. According to Elkins the impact on the personalities of the slaves and inmates was much the same, in that both institutions created new, submissive character types. However, the institutions had many more differences than similarities: the question of acceptance and rebellion, the degree of totalitarianism involved, the threat of extermination, the emotional lives of the victims, and the importance of previous conditions of freedom or servitude. The author believes Elkins has accepted the "Sambo" character stereotype as the basis for his thesis.   L. Gara

560. Toplin, Robert Brent. PETER STILL VERSUS THE PECULIAR INSTI-TUTION. *Civil War Hist. 1967 13(4): 340-349.* Describes the nine-year (1845-

54) fight of slave Peter Still to win his own freedom and that of his family. Hired out to Tuscumbia, Alabama, merchants, Still was able to save enough money to buy his freedom for 500 dollars in 1849. It took five more years, however, to bring out his wife and three children. One escape effort was foiled after they had been brought to Indiana. Finally, Still was able to raise sufficient funds from northern antislavery sources to purchase his family. Still was reluctant to become an activist in the antislavery crusade for fear of the safety of other members of his family. He lived out his life quietly as a truck farmer near Burlington, New Jersey, where he died in 1868. Based on the Still Papers at Rutgers and Mrs. Kate Pickard's 1856 biography of Still.   E. C. Murdock

561. Troutman, Richard L. EMANCIPATION OF SLAVES BY HENRY CLAY. *J. of Negro Hist. 1955 40(2): 179-181.* Describes Henry Clay's benevolent attitude toward his slaves and his manumission of several of them between 1804 and 1844. An emancipation decree freeing two of his slaves is reprinted.
                                    R. Mueller

562. Troutman, Richard L. THE PHYSICAL SETTING OF THE BLUE-GRASS PLANTER. *Register of the Kentucky Hist. Soc. 1968 66(4): 367-377.* A description of the physical setting of planters in the bluegrass region of Kentucky. Most planters in this area did not have large slave holdings and large farms, because they did not rely on one staple crop but instead placed much of their land in pastures. Their homes built in Georgian, Gothic, or Greek Revival style were elegantly furnished. Woodland pastures or parks, sometimes stocked with deer, were common. The author has used primary materials which include contemporary magazines, U.S. census reports, and travel accounts; 39 notes.
                                    B. Wilkins

563. Unsigned. THE INEQUALITY OF REPRESENTATION IN THE GENERAL ASSEMBLY OF VIRGINIA: MEMORIAL TO THE LEGISLATURE OF THE COMMONWEALTH OF VIRGINIA, ADOPTED AT FULL MEETING OF THE CITIZENS OF KANAWHA. *West Virginia Hist. 1964 25(4): 283-298.* Document memorializing the Virginia Legislature to abate the grievances arising from inequality of representation (ca. 1841). Events leading to the disparity are recapitulated, and a warning is given to their "eastern brethren" to grant relief. Figures are cited showing the population of the western section to be greater than that of the eastern if slaves are excluded from the total. It is argued that slaves and farmers of the west cannot hold analogy to each other in the distribution of political rights and power and that the political community consists alone of the white population. It is claimed that the legislature should be reapportioned on the basis of white population and the western section be given equality with the east.   D. N. Brown

564. Upton, Mrs. R. Chester, ed. MINUTES OF THE ANTIOCH BAPTIST CHURCH, MARION COUNTY, MISSISSIPPI, 1828-1850: NATHAN SMART AND HOSEA DAVIS BIBLE RECORDS. *J. of Mississippi Hist. 1965 27(2): 191-209.* Excerpts from the minutes of the Antioch Baptist Church and brief entries regarding miscellaneous church business. Many names, many new

members (including a few Negroes), a number of letters "of dismission," and occasional disputes are mentioned. The Bible records are for the families of two members of the church. The Nathan Smart Bible records births (1749-1851), marriages (1826-72), and deaths (1836-1922). The Hosea Davis Bible records births (1799-1855), marriages (1822-74), and deaths (1838-80).

J. W. Hillje

565. Vanderhaar, Margaret M. A REEXAMINATION OF "BENITO CERENO." *Am. Literature 1968 40(2): 179-191.* The social meaning of "Benito Cereno" is not abolition, for Melville was repulsed by the Negro's capacity for mindless brutality. Rather, he depicts the theme of the corruption of both master and slave by slavery and the idea that good will without knowledge is ineffectual. 50 notes.   R. S. Burns

566. Voss, Stuart F. TOWN GROWTH IN CENTRAL MISSOURI, 1815-1880. AN URBAN CHAPARRAL. *Missouri Hist. R. 1969 64(1): 64-80, (2): 197-217, (3): 322-350.* Part I. The presence of the navigable Missouri River provided the means for opening Central Missouri to settlement at a time when the only other area of settlement was Saint Louis and the land adjacent to the Mississippi River. Such towns as Booksville, Arrow Rock, Rocheport, Smithton, Columbia, and Franklin, rose initially because they were centers of government or trade, which gave them an initial advantage over other towns. A river port with a county seat, with State and private institutions, and with terminal facilities for land transportation and trunk-line railroads usually grew in size and wealth. Based on census records, county and local histories, and articles; illus., photos, map, 36 notes. Part II. Urbanization in Central Missouri before the Civil War was stimulated by the transportation systems and traditional values of the region. Many towns prospered through trade with immigrants moving to California, Oregon, and Santa Fe, and through the sale of hemp, tobacco, cattle, mules, and slaves to the South. This trade also encouraged some manufacturing in the towns close to transportation. Inland towns continued to grow during the steamship era because they obtained valuable State institutions. The gentry that developed in the region shaped its traditions along southern lines and provided the State with much of its leadership. Based on census records, county and local histories, and articles; illus., 42 notes. Part III. The central Missouri towns began to lose their primacy during the 1850's when railroad construction enhanced the economic importance of other sections of the State. Wartime devastation added to the decline. After 1865 the central Missouri towns were shorn of their political, economic, and social importance. With capital and industry gone, they were unable to compete with Kansas City and Saint Louis. Skilled artisans coming to Missouri from Europe naturally settled where they could find work. In the struggle for survival, the only central Missouri towns able to keep going were those that retained large private and public institutions or built connecting lines to the main rail centers. By 1880 urban growth in central Missouri had stopped. Based on census records, county and local histories, and published articles; illus., 44 notes.

W. F. Zornow

567. Wade, Richard C. THE VESEY PLOT: A RECONSIDERATION. *J. of Southern Hist. 1964 30(2): 143-161.* Studies the reported plot said to have been led by Denmark Vesey for a slave rebellion in Charleston, South Carolina, during the summer of 1822, for which 35 Negroes were hanged and 37 transported out of the State. Deplores historians' acceptance of the official version of the plot and the judicial proceedings. The author utilizes documentary comparisons of two manuscript confessions with the published versions, criticism by Governor Thomas Bennett and his brother-in-law, Judge William Johnson, and letters by Johnson's daughter, Ana Hayes Johnson, as well as a consideration of social conditions in the city at the time, to argue that the plot existed largely in the minds of city officials, a frightened white community, and the special judges, who included Robert Y. Hayne. Documented. S. E. Humphreys

568. Wall, Bennett H. AFRICAN SLAVERY. *Writing Southern Hist.: Essays in Historiography in Honor of Fletcher M. Green (Baton Rouge: Louisiana State U. Press, 1965): 175-197.* Finds that far too much writing on slavery has been "an almost conditioned reflex to outside attacks" and has tended to ignore the economic, social, and psychological effects of the institution. An examination of general U.S. history textbooks shows a recent trend to minimize discussions of slavery as a social and economic system and to emphasize the political and propagandistic aspects. There is measurably less space devoted to slavery, the Old South, and the Negro in current texts than in those of a generation ago. The three important monographs on slavery by Ulrich Bonnell Phillips, Kenneth M. Stampp, and Stanley M. Elkins are compared. Phillips' argument that slavery was a declining institution has been both supported and denied by other scholars, whose views are summarized. 86 biblio. notes. E. P. Stickney

569. Wells, Tom Henderson. CHARLES AUGUSTUS LAFAYETTE LAMAR: GENTLEMAN SLAVE TRADER. *Georgia Hist. Q. 1963 47(2): 158-168.* A comprehensive biographical sketch focusing on Lamar's successful effort in 1858 to bring African slaves to the United States in defiance of the constitutional provision concerning the slave trade. R. Lowitt

570. Wells, Tom Henderson. MOVING A PLANTATION TO LOUISIANA. *Louisiana Studies 1967 6(3): 280-289.* Tells of the problems encountered in carving a plantation from the virgin wilderness of the northwest Louisiana hill section from 1853 to 1854. Transportation difficulties, overland and by water; the ravages of disease; the problem of procuring overseers for slaves; the clearing and cultivation of land; the privation, the isolation, and the scarcity of churches and education are described. 28 notes. G. W. McGinty

571. White, John. THE NOVELIST AS HISTORIAN: WILLIAM STYRON AND AMERICAN NEGRO SLAVERY. *J. of Am. Studies [Great Britain] 1971 4(2): 233-245.* Styron's novel, *The Confessions of Nat Turner* (New York: Random House, 1967), produced controversies primarily about the historical veracity of Styron's portrayal of the slave system and its effects on Negroes and southern whites. The author catalogs reactions to the novel in many quarters, ranging from scholars such as Comer Vann Woodward to Marxists such as Herbert Aptheker,

and to prominent American Negro writers and journalists. Styron enraged the latter two groups because he voiced anew the South's arguments in favor of slavery, depicted Negroes as typically playing the role of a "Sambo," and imputed psychosexual connotations to Nat Turner's behavior - an interpretation that especially annoyed Negro critics of the book. Yet Styron with remarkably few lapses pictured the slave system and black-white relationships much as the massive scholarship on slavery describes them. Collections of primary source materials likewise confirm Styron's accuracy. Based on primary and secondary sources; 29 notes.   H. T. Lovin

572. Whitridge, Arnold. ELI WHITNEY: NEMESIS OF THE SOUTH. *Am. Heritage 1955 6(3): 4-11.* Whitney's invention of the cotton gin was directly responsible for the rise of the "cotton kingdom" and the entrenchment of slavery in the Southern States of the United States. Yet, when the South turned its back on him and he was unable to secure a patent, Whitney returned to Connecticut, established a gun factory, and initiated a manufacturing process based on interchangeable parts. This new technique played a major role in the growth of northern industry. "It is one of the ironies of history that the man who inadvertantly contributed to the downfall of the South by his invention of the cotton gin should also have blazed the trail leading to the technological supremacy of the North."   A. W. Thompson

573. Whitten, David O. SLAVE BUYING IN 1835 VIRGINIA AS REVEALED BY LETTERS OF A LOUISIANA NEGRO SUGAR PLANTER. *Louisiana Hist. 1970 11(3): 231-244.* Negro plantation-owner Andrew Durnford wrote a series of letters to his New Orleans friend and factor, John McDonogh, while the former was in Virginia in 1835 buying slaves. The letters reveal details about slave prices, conditions, customs, transportation, and attitudes. Evidence that many slaves, or their descendents, were living in that vicinity in 1870 proves that the slaves were for use on Durnford's Plaquemines Parish plantation, St. Rosalie. Based on letters and other manuscripts in the Special Collections Division of the Tulane University Library, New Orleans; 22 notes.
                                                                              R. L. Woodward

574. Whitten, David O. TARIFF AND PROFIT IN THE ANTEBELLUM LOUISIANA SUGAR INDUSTRY. *Business Hist. R. 1970 44(2): 226-233.* In regard to profits and tariffs, the antebellum Louisiana sugar industry is a paradox. Although sugar planters were reputed to be among the most prosperous Southern slaveowners, they demanded and received a protective tariff for their product. The sugar cane industry of the 1850's was composed of a small number of planters capable of earning at least a normal profit, even at world sugar prices, and of a larger number of marginal planters subject to the vicissitudes of the domestic market and the protective tariff for their existence. Based mainly on historical statistics and secondary sources; 2 tables, 32 notes.   C. J. Pusateri

575. Wilson, L. W., ed. REMINISCENCES OF JIM TOMM. *Chronicles of Oklahoma 1966 44(3): 290-306.* A biographical narrative by the Negro Jim Tomm who was born a slave near Muskogee in 1859. Tomm describes his paren-

tage, life on the plantation, shoe and soap making, the log house with shake-shingle roof, and grinding corn and wheat. He describes also many of the events and battles during the Civil War, the Green Peach War between the Spieche and Checote factions, tribal laws and courts, hauling freight, toll bridges and ferries, steamboats, saltworks, ranches, churches and schools, Indian cooking and crafts, allotments, railroads, and the Snake uprising. His narrative reveals much of the life and many of the homely conditions of the period. Illus., 4 notes.

I. W. Van Noppen

576. Wilson, Mary Tolford. PEACEFUL INTEGRATION: THE OWNER'S ADOPTION OF HIS SLAVE'S FOOD. *J. of Negro Hist. 1964 49(2): 116-127.* Traces the gradual acceptance by the southern aristocracy of four food plants introduced into the South as items in the diets of their slaves. Okra, sesame, cowpeas, and peanuts all came to America from Africa, though the peanut had originally been transplanted there from South America. In the early 19th century these foods were being used by the masters as well as the slaves and by the time of the Civil War they had become familiar staples in the South.

L. Gara

577. Wilson, Prince E. BLACK MEN BEFORE THE CIVIL WAR. *Current Hist. 1969 57(339): 257-262, 305-306.* Until recently the role of the black American prior to the Civil War has been woefully neglected. Modern scholarship has made at least a beginning toward closing the gap.

B. D. Rhodes

578. Woodman, Harold David. THE PROFITABILITY OF SLAVERY: A HISTORICAL PERENNIAL. *J. of Southern Hist. 1963 29(3): 303-325.* Since before the Civil War, the question has been hotly argued whether slavery was profitable. Part of the difficulty lies in that two different questions have been discussed, and they are not necessarily related. Some have discussed whether it was profitable for the planter; others whether it was profitable for the South. New lines of research need to be explored. It is possible that the economics of slavery cannot even be discussed adequately in purely economic terms. Documented.

S. E. Humphreys

579. Woolfolk, George R. PLANTER CAPITALISM AND SLAVERY: THE LABOR THESIS. *J. of Negro Hist. 1956 41(2): 103-116.* Surveys the question "Was slavery profitable?" The major difficulty in earlier interpretation is held to be a tendency simply to equate "economic efficiency" with illusive dollar and cents "profits." Such an approach is said to defy all attempts at documentation and delineation. The basic questions should be: did planter capitalism based on slavery facilitate and successfully support or sustain an orderly pattern of economic existence? Could wealth be produced and exchanged creatively? Investigation of planter capitalism of the Long River counties of East Texas answers the question in the affirmative.

W. E. Wight

580. Woolfolk, George R. SOURCES OF THE HISTORY OF THE NEGRO IN TEXAS WITH SPECIAL REFERENCE TO THEIR IMPLICATIONS

FOR RESEARCH IN SLAVERY. *J. of Negro Hist. 1957 42(1): 38-47.* Reviews the materials in the various archival holdings of State, county, and local governments of Texas which can throw light upon the history of the Negro slave in that State. "Important as a species of wealth and undeniably a human being, the slave left a web of evidence that has much need of exploitation."   W. E. Wight

581. Woolfolk, George R. SOURCES OF THE HISTORY OF THE NEGRO IN TEXAS, WITH SPECIAL REFERENCE TO THEIR IMPLICATIONS FOR RESEARCH IN SLAVERY. *Negro Hist. Bull. 1957 20(5): 105-107, 112.* Discusses the need for continuing to locate private manuscripts bearing on Negro history and for supplementing such materials with the vast body of State and local archival materials which are already available but hardly touched. Such material should be used as an aid to an objective evaluation of slavery rather than for polemics.   L. Gara

582. Woolfolk, George Ruble. TAXES AND SLAVERY IN THE ANTE BELLUM SOUTH. *J. of Southern Hist. 1960 26(2): 180-200.* Pleads for consideration of issues arising out of taxation of slaves - on either the basis of poll or *ad valorem* - as clarifying some of the problems of public policy that arose between planters as a class and other whites whose political aspirations were divergent. The author seeks to show that taxes on slaves provided one of the fundamental sources of revenue to city, county, and State governments and one of the many instruments for regulating the socioeconomic aspects of the relations between the races. He suggests that such consideration will serve to place in proper focus the tendency to concentrate upon the plantation as the central institution in the agrarian society and may serve to open creative approaches to the main problems of antebellum history.   S. E. Humphreys

583. Wyllie, John Cook, ed. "OBSERVATIONS MADE DURING A SHORT RESIDENCE IN VIRGINIA" IN A LETTER FROM THOMAS H. PALMER, MAY 30, 1814. *Virginia Mag. of Hist. and Biog. 1968 76(4): 387-414.* Reprints with introduction and notes Palmer's letter originally printed in *The Historical Register of the United States,* III, pt. 1 (1814), pp. 53-76. Discusses such diverse subjects as local usage and pronunciation of words; tobacco; architecture; descriptions of towns, notably Richmond; banks; slavery; taxes; education; religion; and manufacturing. Illus., 39 notes.   K. J. Bauer

584. Yamamoto, Mikio. AMERIKA KYŪ-NAMBU NI OKERU HI-DOREI-SHOYŪ NŌMIN - DAI-NIJI AMERIKA KAKUMEI NO KŌZŌ HAAKU NO TAME NI [The nonslaveholding farmers in the "Old South" - toward understanding the framework of the "second American revolution"]. *Shirin [Japan] 1955 38(1): 21-34, (2): 23-41.* An attempt to clarify the position of nonslaveholders in the pre-Civil War period. Includes statistics showing this class to have been far more numerous than the slaveholders.   H. Imai

585. Yanuck, Julius. THOMAS RUFFIN AND NORTH CAROLINA SLAVE LAW. *J. of Southern Hist. 1955 21(4): 456-475.* Traces Thomas Ruffin's interpre-

tations of the North Carolina slave law during his service in the State Supreme Court. In his first opinion, *State vs. Mann,* Ruffin held that "the power of the master must be absolute to render the submission of the slave perfect." Cases cited show his judicial decisions were a mixture of strict construction of the law and generous concession, unless the safety of slavery was involved.

R. Kerley

586. Younger, Richard D. SOUTHERN GRAND JURIES AND SLAVERY. *J. of Negro Hist. 1955 40(2): 166-178.* A documented summary of various measures employed by southern grand juries during the first half of the 19th century to enforce legal limitation placed on Negroes and to combat insurrectionary and abolitionist attempts.

R. Mueller

587. Yzenbaard, John H. THE CROSSWHITE CASE. *Michigan Hist. 1969 53(2): 131-143.* A detailed narrative of *Giltner vs. Gorham et al.* (1848), in which the U.S. Circuit Court for Michigan decided against a group of antislavery citizens in Marshall who had obstructed the return of a Negro family, the Crosswhites, to its Kentucky master and helped them escape on the underground railroad to Canada. The author rejects the notion that there was a direct connection between the Crosswhite case and passage of the Fugitive Slave Act (1850). Based on primary and secondary sources; 5 illus., 37 notes.

J. K. Flack

588. Zelnik, M. FERTILITY OF THE AMERICAN NEGRO IN 1830 AND 1850. *Population Studies [Great Britain] 1966 20(1): 77-83.* "A comparison of the proportionate age distributions for Negroes enumerated in the decennial censuses of the United States: the first half of the 19th century indicates that by 1850, Negro fertility had apparently been declining for at least 20 years. This paper develops the relationship of the age distribution of a declining fertility population, where the decline has persisted for less than 25 years, to the stable population with the same current schedules of fertility and mortality. This relationship is used to estimate the Negro birth rate and total fertility as of 1850. In turn, these estimates and the relationship of the age distributions of two stable populations with different fertility are used to estimate the Negro birth rate and total fertility as of 1850." Based mainly on secondary sources; 20 notes.

J

589. --. OUR CONTACTS WITH AMERICAN INDIANS, POLYNESIANS, AND AFRICANS. *Pro. of the Am. Phil. Soc. 1963 107(2): 83-111.*

Hanke, Lewis. THE DAWN OF CONSCIENCE IN AMERICA: SPANISH EXPERIMENTS AND EXPERIENCES WITH INDIANS IN THE NEW WORLD, pp. 83-92. Considers the factors which influenced initial Spanish-Indian relations, noting that some early Spaniards anticipated the approach of modern anthropologists by giving serious attention to the nature of the various Indian cultures and by considering Indians as men who were not inferior but who were of equal ability with any other group of men. Many references to early Spanish sources and to scholarly articles.

Tolles, Frederick B. NONVIOLENT CONTACT: THE QUAKERS AND THE INDIANS, pp. 93-101. Traces the long history of nonviolent contact between Quakers and Indians, arguing that a theological concept, the Light Within, best explains Quaker behavior. Documented.

Dodge, Ernest S. EARLY AMERICAN CONTACTS IN POLYNESIA AND FIJI, pp. 102-106. A survey of early contacts between Americans (mostly New Englanders) and the islanders of Polynesia and Fiji. Certain homogeneous features of the two groups, as well as the easy-going disposition of the natives, promoted American influence. Documented.

Elkins, Stanley M. CULTURE CONTACTS AND NEGRO SLAVERY, pp. 107-109. Briefly compares and contrasts English Negro slavery with the Spanish and Portuguese system in Latin America and suggests that contrasts may have been derived from differences between English common law and Roman law which defined a slave as more than property, plus the influence of a powerful church and crown in Latin America.

Washburn, Wilcomb E. DISCUSSION OF THE SYMPOSIUM ON OUR CONTACTS WITH AMERICAN INDIANS, POLYNESIANS, AND AFRICANS, pp. 110-111.   R. G. Comegys

590. --. [RACE AND CLASS IN SOUTHERN HISTORY]. *Agric. Hist. 1967 41(4): 345-378.*

Genovese, Eugene D. RACE AND CLASS IN SOUTHERN HISTORY: AN APPRAISAL OF THE WORK OF ULRICH BONNELL PHILLIPS, pp. 345-378. Historian Phillips displayed an understanding of slavery as a social system. He appreciated the plantation as a community of unlike men trying to live together, and brilliantly described the slaveholding ruling class. His notion of white supremacy showed extraordinary insight, even though it requires modification. His work is an excellent introduction to southern history and especially to the problems posed by race and class. Based on Phillips' works.

Potter, David M., Stampp, Kenneth M., and Elkins, Stanley M. COMMENT, pp. 359-378.   W. D. Rasmussen

591. --. [SLAVERY: SELF-EMANCIPATION AND ABOLITIONISTS]. *J. of Negro Hist. 1965 50(2): 118-125.*

Luckingham, Bradford F. SCHOOLCRAFT, SLAVERY, AND SELF-EMANCIPATION, pp. 118-121. Reprints Henry R. Schoolcraft's plan for the self-emancipation of slaves which he included in his *Travels in the Central Portions of the Mississippi Valley...in the Year 1821* (New York, 1825).

Katz, William. ANOTHER SLAVE FREED, pp. 121-123. Reprints an 1859 account from the New York newspaper, *Anglo-African* which tells of a slave inventor who purchased his own freedom.

Kirkham, E. Bruce. A NOTE ON TWO ABOLITIONISTS AND A PEARL, pp. 123-125. Contrasts the propaganda use of the *Pearl* incident, involving an attempted escape of slaves, by William Lloyd Garrison in *The Liberator* and by Harriet Beecher Stowe in *A Key to Uncle Tom's Cabin* (1853).

L. Gara

592. --. [THE MURDER OF GEORGE WYTHE]. *William and Mary Q. 1955 12(4): 513-574.*

Boyd, Julian P. THE MURDER OF GEORGE WYTHE, pp. 513-542. A critical and historiographical analysis. Wythe's death was the aim of the murderer, who, ironically, escaped the gallows because the chancellor, although he favored emancipation, had continued the prohibition of Negro testimony against whites. The legend that a servant and prospective beneficiary under Wythe's will was the intended victim, originated in the 1850's and has been perpetuated since then. It was born of a desire to warn against racial hostility arising from excessive Negro freedom. Based on letters to Jefferson and other primary sources.

Hemphill, W. Edwin. EXAMINATIONS OF GEORGE WYTHE SWINNEY FOR FORGERY AND MURDER: A DOCUMENTARY ESSAY, pp. 543-574. George Wythe's death was premeditated by the chancellor's spend-thrift nephew, who sought to forestall discovery of his forgeries and to claim his inheritance prematurely. Though held for trial by the Hustings Court and indicted by the grand jury, Swinney was acquitted by the petit jury because of Wythe's forgiveness, while he was dying, incomplete autopsies, and the inadmissability of Negro evidence against whites. Legal loopholes enabled Swinney to escape conviction on the forgery charges. Based chiefly on records of hearings in the Hustings Court (1806). E. Oberholzer, Jr.

593. --. [THE PROFITABILITY OF ANTEBELLUM SLAVERY]. *Southern Econ. J. 1965 31(4): 365-383.*

Sutch, Richard. THE PROFITABILITY OF ANTE BELLUM SLAVERY - REVISITED, pp. 365-377. Claims that Edward Saraydar's "A Note on the Profitability of Ante Bellum Slavery" (see abstract 535) was vitiated by two sources of error. By failing to allow for the reproduction of the slave stock and by underestimating the average yield per hand, he tended to understate the rate of return to slaveowners and consequently failed to disprove the Alfred H. Conrad and John R. Meyer argument that slavery was at least as profitable as alternative investment opportunities. He also notes that even if slavery had been unprofitable in cotton production, it might still have been viable as an institution, since slaves had alternative uses. He estimates yields and rates of return for various parts of the South in 1849, 1859, and 1860.

Saraydar, Edward. THE PROFITABILITY OF ANTE BELLUM SLAVERY - A REPLY, pp. 377-383. Maintains that his earlier conclusions have not been vitiated by the criticisms of Richard Sutch since the critic had misunderstood the object of his original article. A. W. Coats

594. --. [THE STANLEY ELKINS THESIS.] *Civil War Hist. 1967 13(4): 293-339.*

Genovese, Eugene D. REBELLIOUSNESS AND DOCILITY IN THE NEGRO SLAVE: A CRITIQUE OF THE ELKINS THESIS, pp. 293-314. Challenges the Stanley Elkins thesis that the "Sambo" stereotype of the American Negro slave was due to the concentration camp character of plantation life. Elkins holds that in other countries, where the State, the church, and the laws afforded greater protections for the slaves, slaves were more rebellious, less docile, less like Sambo. The author argues that "Sambo existed wherever slavery existed," and that slaves were whatever they were - docile, rebellious, or in between - without reference to the institutional framework in which they lived. While Elkins "has raised the study of Southern slavery to a far higher level than ever before," he demonstrates both the advantages and disadvantages of psychology to the historian. Psychology can provide insights and suggest hypotheses, but it is no substitute for empirical investigation.

Fredrickson, George M. and Lasch, Christopher. RESISTANCE TO SLAVERY, pp. 315-329. An objection to the various methods of analyzing slave resistance. Those who argue that slaves were docile and those who argue that slaves were resistant rely chiefly on quantitative data which fails to answer the question. To clarify the matter the writers resort, like Stanley Elkins, to analogy, although they feel that Elkins' concentration camp figure is inappropriate. Instead of a concentration camp, they compare slavery to a prison. A prison system has many more of the variable factors - temperament of the guards and composition of the prison population - which existed under slavery but which did not exist in a Buchenwald. The prison analogy helps explain the major contradiction in the slave's behavior; his devotion, yet his noncooperation. It shows how "slaves could have accepted the legitimacy of their masters' authority without feeling any sense of obligation to obey it."

Kraditor, Aileen S. A NOTE ON ELKINS AND THE ABOLITIONISTS, pp. 330-339. Challenges the Stanley Elkins thesis that abolitionists were anti-institutionalists and the corollary - that they made slavery a "moral" issue. Actually, the great majority of abolitionists did work through such institutions as political parties and churches, trying to purify them and make them vehicles for emancipation. However, America in the mid-19th century was a fluid society, and, except for slavery, it possessed weak institutions. It was this anomaly of a rigid slave system in an otherwise unstructured society, not the abolitionists, that made slavery a moral issue.   E. C. Murdock

595. --. [THE STRUCTURE OF THE COTTON ECONOMY OF THE ANTEBELLUM SOUTH]. *Agric. Hist. 1970 44(1): 1-165.*

Gallman, Robert E. SELF-SUFFICIENCY IN THE COTTON ECONOMY OF THE ANTEBELLUM SOUTH, pp. 5-23. Large planters in the South tried to achieve self-sufficiency in basic foods. When they failed, the reason was not overproduction of cotton at the expense of food, but was due to developments that adversely affected the production of the staple crop as well as food. In developing his thesis, the author has compiled figures on human and animal food consumption on southern plantations. Based on manuscript census reports and plantation records; 7 tables, 31 notes.

Foust, James D. and Swan, Dale E. PRODUCTIVITY AND PROFITABILITY OF ANTEBELLUM LABOR: A MICRO-APPROACH, pp. 39-62. Concludes that slavery was profitable in the regions examined - Alluvial, Other New South, and Old South - and on farms in all slaveholding classes. Based on manuscript census reports; 8 tables, 27 notes, appendixes.

Wright, Gavin. "ECONOMIC DEMOCRACY" AND THE CONCENTRATION OF AGRICULTURAL WEALTH IN THE COTTON SOUTH, 1850-1860, pp. 63-93. Concludes that "there is little reason to reject the traditional view that the social implication of the slave-cotton regime was a highly unequal distribution of wealth," but warns the reader to be aware of the variety of possible comparisons and the different results they might yield. The author deals only with the cotton South and does not attempt to link agricultural wealth distribution and the production characteristics of cotton and slavery. Based on manuscript census reports; 10 tables, 33 notes, appendixes.

Parker, William N. SLAVERY AND SOUTHERN ECONOMIC DEVELOPMENT: AN HYPOTHESIS AND SOME EVIDENCE, pp. 115-126. Speculates as to the changes that would have resulted in the southern economy had slavery been abolished at the end of the 18th century. Appendix.

Engerman, Stanley L. THE ANTEBELLUM SOUTH: WHAT PROBABLY WAS AND WHAT SHOULD HAVE BEEN, pp. 127-142. A critique of the articles by Gallman and Parker. The author emphasizes the weaknesses of these two papers, but believes they provide information and ideas that will be of value to subsequent research. Based on secondary sources; table, 21 notes.

Genovese, Eugene D. COMMENTARY: A HISTORIAN'S VIEW, pp. 143-147. Discusses Parker's and Gallman's articles. Despite some reservations concerning these articles, the author is enthusiastic about the conclusions. He urges Parker, Gallman, and other economists to consider the broad implications of their strictly economic analyses. Undocumented.   D. E. Brewster

596. --. [WILLIAM STYRON'S "THE CONFESSIONS OF NAT TURNER" REVIEWED]. *South Atlantic Q. 1969 68(2): 167-187.*

Holder, Alan. STYRON'S SLAVE: THE CONFESSIONS OF NAT TURNER, pp. 167-180. With its historical overtones, Styron's *The Confessions of Nat Turner* (New York: Random House, 1967) has caused great controversy. Negroes have accused him of perpetuating a *Gone with the Wind* image of the South and are critical of the failure of Negroes in the novel to join in Turner's revolt. For Styron to find substance in Stanley Elkin's "Sambo" image hardly makes him a racist. More disturbing in the novel is Nat's alienation from his people and his distaste for them. How could he lead them? Equally dubious is the psychosexual explanation offered for Nat's behavior.

Durden, Robert F. WILLIAM STYRON AND HIS BLACK CRITICS, pp. 181-187. Black criticism of Styron's *Confessions of Nat Turner* includes issues of 1) the absence of Negro militancy, 2) Turner's sexual life, and 3) unhistorical Turner. The original 1831 confession of Turner serves as a rough basis for Styron's accounts. But the question is really larger. Should a novelist take an actual personage and event from history and scramble fact and fiction? Can a southern-born white speak for a militant black? 3 notes.

J. M. Bumsted

Slavery & Abolition as Public & Cultural Issues

Abbott, Richard H. see abstract 857.

597. Abzug, Robert B. THE INFLUENCE OF GARRISONIAN ABOLITIONISTS' FEARS OF SLAVE VIOLENCE ON THE ANTISLAVERY AR-

GUMENT: 1829-1840. *J. of Negro Hist. 1970 55(1): 15-28.* In 1829 William Lloyd Garrison warned Bostonian colonizationists that inaction on American slavery would eventually create a catastrophic race war. Garrison feared that within a century there would be 20 million blacks held in bondage, and he concluded that no country could successfully hold so many people as slaves. The only answer, Garrison ultimately concluded, was the immediate abolition of slavery, otherwise the vengence of Heaven would visit upon America. After 1834, however, Garrison and his fellow abolitionists concentrated more on the issue of civil liberties than violence, especially when it appeared that the slaves of the British Caribbean were being emancipated peacefully. Based mostly on primary sources; 67 notes.   R. S. Melamed

598. Allen, Carlos R., Jr., ed. DAVID BARROW'S "CIRCULAR LETTER" OF 1795. *William and Mary Q. 1963 20(3): 440-451.* The text of the letter from the Reverend Barrow, in which he justifies his departure from Virginia, with an introduction. The minister observes that he cannot support his family without keeping slaves, which he will not do. After affirming orthodox Christian doctrine, he states his "political creed," influenced by both Christianity (government is seen as a necessary evil, caused by original sin) and by the secular thought of his day, notably the Virginia Bill of Rights.   E. Oberholzer

599. Angle, Paul M. ILLINOIS: 1818. *Chicago Hist. 1968 8(6): 161-185.* Traces the process by which Illinois became the 21st State and conveys some impression of what the commonwealth was like in 1818. Although the Illinois Territory contained considerably less than the required population of sixty thousand for admission to the Union, in 1817 the territorial legislature inaugurated the movement for statehood. After the U. S. Congress approved an enabling act in April 1818, Illinois proceeded to draft a State constitution, copied in large part from the constitution of Indiana, Ohio, and Kentucky. In spite of the failure of the constitution to prohibit all forms of slavery, it was accepted by Congress and finally approved by President Monroe on 3 December. At that time conditions of life were primitive in Illinois. "Farming, the principal occupation of the inhabitants, was largely on a subsistence basis," a pattern which "would not change materially until the late '40s and '50s, when the Illinois and Michigan Canal and the new railroads offered cheap and fast transportation to markets." Based on Solon J. Buck's *Illinois in 1818* (1917); illus.   D. J. Abramoske

600. Angle, Paul M. MORRIS BIRKBECK: ILLUSTRIOUS ILLINOISAN. *Chicago Hist. 1967 8(5): 144-157.* Discusses the life of Morris Birkbeck (1764-1825), an English leaseholder who migrated to Illinois in 1817 and pioneered in the development of prairie farming. Birkbeck's books - *Notes on a Journey in America* (Philadelphia, 1817) and *Letters from Illinois* (1818) - "brought Illinois into notice not only in England but in the Eastern United States and in continental Europe as well." No less than 400 Englishmen were attracted to their southern Illinois settlement. William Cobbett, however, in his *A Year's Residence in the*

United States of America (New York, 1818, and London, 1819) attacked Birk-beck's alluring observations of frontier life, insisting, for example, that they were "calculated to produce great disappointment, not to say misery and ruin, amongst our own country people." Before his death in 1825 Birkbeck also served briefly as secretary of state of Illinois and played an important role in defeating the movement to make Illinois a slave State. Based on secondary and published primary sources. D. J. Abramoske

601. Arbena, Joseph L. POLITICS OR PRINCIPLE? RUFUS KING AND THE OPPOSITION TO SLAVERY, 1785-1825. *Essex Inst. Hist. Collections 1965 101(1): 56-77.* Rufus King of Massachusetts had a long history of opposition to the expansion of slavery and the slave trade. This stand was a product of moral conviction which coincided with the political realities of New England federalism. In 1785, King first opposed the extension of slavery into the Northwest Territo-ries, although he was willing "to suffer the continuance of slaves until they can be gradually emancipated in states already overrun with them." He did not press the issue very hard at this time, however. At the Constitutional Convention he indicated his opposition to slavery was based upon the political and economic advantages it gave to the South, and he was willing to compromise for political reasons. In 1817, he supported Senate action seeking abolition of the slave trade, and in 1819 spoke strongly for the antislavery amendment in the Missouri state-hood bill. In 1819, his arguments were political, economic, and humanitarian; the extension of slavery would adversely affect the security of the principles of freedom and liberty. After the Missouri Compromise he continued to support gradual emancipation in various ways. 82 notes. J. M. Bumsted

602. Armstrong, Maurice W. CORTLANDT VAN RENSSELAER: PRO-GRESSIVE CONSERVATIVE. *J. of the Presbyterian Hist. Soc. 1954 32(4): 213-240.* Excerpts from Cortlandt Van Rensselaer's (1808-61) writings are pre-sented showing his views on Christianity, education, various reform issues, and slavery. From these and from a review of his activities, the author considers him as representative of "progressive conservatism - a deep-running current in Ameri-can Presbyterianism." R. Mueller

603. Arnold, Dean A. THE ULTIMATUM OF VIRGINIA DISUNIONISTS: "SECURITY FOR SLAVERY OR DISUNION." *J. of Negro Hist. 1963 48(2): 115-129.* Challenges the thesis, popular with Civil War revisionists, that southern unionists were willing to make major concessions to prevent secession or war, but met with little cooperation from their northern counterparts. The author bases his conclusions on a study of Wyndham Robertson (1803-88), a Virginia unionist political leader. Robertson's loyalty to the Union was conditional to northern willingness to support and protect slavery. When he became convinced that slavery would not be perpetuated within the Union, he chose secession. Based on a study of the Robertson MSS. L. Gara

604. Bailor, Keith M. JOHN TAYLOR OF CAROLINE. CONTINUITY, CHANGE, AND DISCONTINUITY IN VIRGINIA'S SENTIMENTS TOWARD SLAVERY, 1790-1820. *Virginia Mag. of Hist. and Biog. 1967 75(3): 290-304.* John Taylor's defense of slavery reflected the fear of a bloody race war rather than an early statement of the slavery-State's right position. In this he mirrored the attitude of the thoughtful, pragmatic Virginia planters of the early national period. Based on Taylor's writings and monographic studies; 26 notes.

K. J. Bauer

605. Baltimore, Lester B. BENJAMIN F. STRINGFELLOW: THE FIGHT FOR SLAVERY ON THE MISSOURI BORDER. *Missouri Hist. R. 1967 62(1): 14-29.* As an outspoken member of the proslavery Platte County Self-Defensive Association, Stringfellow helped to define for many people the terms involved in the struggle over slavery in Kansas Territory. All his words and actions served to make others take an extreme stand in opposition to or in support of slavery. He knew that only the most vigorous support of slavery would insure its perpetuation. Based on newspapers, articles, monographs, and manuscripts in the State Historical Society of Missouri and the Kansas State Historical Society; illus., 68 notes.

W. F. Zornow

606. Barrett, C. Waller. JOHN GREENLEAF WHITTIER: THE 150TH ANNIVERSARY OF HIS BIRTH. *Pro. of the Am. Antiquarian Soc. 1957 67(2): 125-136.* In the 50 years since the 100th anniversary of his birth, Whittier's reputation has declined markedly, yet his contributions are far too significant to be forgotten. Joining the ranks of the abolitionists in 1833, Whittier played a decisive role in crystallizing wavering sentiments in the North and West against slavery. Through his poetry he aroused the moral indignation vital to the success of the cause, and through political maneuver he helped gain election of such antislavery leaders as Senator Charles Sumner. A second contribution made by Whittier was his evocative portrayal of the simple life of early rural New England, a significant component of the American experience. Finally, his poetry helped to preserve old tales and legends of the colonial period, adding to the richness of the American story.

W. D. Metz

607. Baylen, Joseph O. SUMNER AND LORD WHARNCLIFFE: SOME UNPUBLISHED LETTERS. *New England Q. 1962 35(3): 390-395.* Publishes two letters written by Charles Sumner to an English friend, John Stuart-Wortley, Lord Wharncliffe. In the letters Sumner commented on the election of 1852, Daniel Webster's foreign policy, and his own opposition to the Fugitive Slave Law.

L. Gara

608. Becker, Carl M. A BUCKEYE IN TENNESSEE: SOJOURN OF ALIENATION. *Tennessee Hist. Q. 1963 22(4): 335-346.* Finds that a move from Dayton, Ohio to Nashville, Tennessee, in July 1885, by Thomas Owen Lowe, 17-year-old bank clerk, brought northern and southern values into conflict for him and for his attorney father in Dayton - chiefly concerning slavery, egalitarian-

ism, and Fillmore, former Whig president, who was presidential candidate of the Know-Nothing Party in 1856. 42 notes chiefly cite unpublished letters located in the Dayton Public Library. W. A. Klutts

609. Beirne, Charles J. THE THEOLOGY OF THEODORE PARKER AND THE WAR WITH MEXICO. *Essex Inst. Hist. Collections 1968 104(2): 130-137.* Sketches Parker's background and theology in order to understand his attitude toward the Mexican War, which he opposed "intuitively" because it was another link in the chain enslaving the Negro. 28 notes. J. M. Bumsted

610. Bernard, Kenneth A. EMERSON AND SLAVERY - AND THE OTHER MAN. *Lincoln Herald 1956 57(4): 3-10.* A comparison of the writings and utterances of Ralph Waldo Emerson and Abraham Lincoln on the subject of slavery and its abolition. W. E. Wight

611. Berwanger, Eugene H. WESTERN PREJUDICE AND THE EXTENSION OF SLAVERY. *Civil War Hist. 1966 12(3): 197-212.* An account of the attempts to establish slavery in Illinois, Indiana, Kansas, California, and Oregon, in the 45 years prior to the Civil War. These efforts failed not so much because of antislavery, as of anti-Negro sentiments. The author points out that in the old Northwest as well as the new Far West dislike of the Negro was widespread and the people did not want them around, either as slaves or free persons. And since slavery would bring the Negro in, the exclusion of slavery would keep him out. Many Republican leaders capitalized on this feeling with great success, and protection of white labor was a more important concern to the party than uplifting the Negro. Based on contemporary newspapers and numerous primary and secondary sources. E. C. Murdock

612. Bierbaum, Milton E. FREDERICK STARR. A MISSOURI BORDER ABOLITIONIST: THE MAKING OF A MARTYR. *Missouri Hist. R. 1964 58(3): 309-325.* Starr, a Presbyterian minister, was a prominent abolitionist in western Missouri during the first year of the Kansas-Missouri conflict in 1854-55. He came to Weston in 1850 to serve as a pastor, but he soon became interested in the slavery issue and began to conduct a school for slaves. This project was soon abandoned, but after the passage of the Kansas-Nebraska Act (1854), Starr became active in a squatters' association to found Leavenworth. As the proslavery forces gained additional strength in western Missouri, Starr continued to assert that slavery was a moral and political evil. He left Weston early in 1855, after being warned or compelled to leave. A meeting at the Weston court house denounced ministers who opposed slavery, but the sentiments that were echoed from Starr's small pulpit were rapidly being repeated throughout the East. Based on local newspapers, histories, and the Starr Papers in the State Historical Society of Missouri. W. F. Zornow

613. Black, R. C., III. THOUGHTS ON THE CONFEDERACY. *Essays in Am. Historiography, Papers Presented in Honor of Allan Nevins, Donald Sheehan and Harold C. Syrett, eds. (New York and London: Columbia U. Press, 1960),*

pp. 20-36. Cites two sins committed by historians of the Confederacy: 1) extreme prejudice which made objective accounts impossible until about 1900, and 2) asking unnecessary questions, such as whether the Civil War was "irrepressible." Two fundamental questions must be asked about the Confederacy: why did it exist, and why did it fail? Black summarizes the views of writers on these questions and suggests that the Confederacy was "basically an effort to maintain a system of race control." R. Stone

614. Blue, Frederick J. THE OHIO FREE SOILERS AND PROBLEMS OF FACTIONALISM. *Ohio Hist. 1967 76(1/2): 17-32.* Shows how the factions in the Free Soil Party in Ohio interacted with the Democratic and Whig Parties after 1848 until the Kansas-Nebraska Act (1854) provided the stimulus for a union of antislavery men of all parties. Based on manuscript collections of Giddings, Chase, Sumner, and others. S. L. Jones

615. Boller, Paul F., Jr. CALHOUN ON LIBERTY. *South Atlantic Q. 1967 66(3): 395-408.* Although John C. Calhoun was fundamentally concerned with the question of liberty, he did not think in terms of the individual but of the community. The preservation of the community's liberty might require restriction of liberty for individuals; the right of free discussion was not central to his position. Under the pressure of events, Calhoun's conception of liberty became intertwined with local (sectional) liberty and slavery. In his *Disquisition on Government* (1850), Calhoun argued for his version of liberty. It was not a natural right, but a civil right created by those who were entitled to it - the better and abler in society. Negro slaves were too inferior to be considered within liberty as Calhoun expounded it. J. M. Bumsted

616. Booker, H. Marshall. THOMAS RODERICK DEW. *Virginia Cavalcade 1969 19(2): 20-29.* A biographical sketch of Thomas R. Dew (1802-46), emphasizing his views on slavery, free trade, and the Bank of the United States, and his influence on the mind of the South. His proslavery arguments were quoted throughout the region. Dew was a professor of political law at the College of William and Mary from 1826 to 1836 when he was elected president of the college, the first layman to hold the position. His most important work was *Review of the Debate [on the abolition of slavery] in the Virginia legislature of 1831 and 1832 (1832). Illus.* N. L. Peterson

617. Borchardt, Beatrice E. ARNOLD BUFFUM, BUOYANT ABOLITIONIST. *New-England Galaxy 1965 7(1): 23-30.* Traces the life of Arnold Buffum in his efforts at abolition. An account is given of his relationship with William Lloyd Garrison, his efforts to establish schools for the colored, his experiences as an abolitionist lecturer, his trips to Europe, and his final days at Eagleswood, a Utopian community near Perth Amboy, New Jersey. Pictures and mementos of abolitionist crusading are included. A. B. Lampe

618. Boyd, Willis D. THE AMERICAN COLONIZATION SOCIETY AND THE SLAVE RECAPTIVES OF 1860-1861: AN EARLY EXAMPLE OF

UNITED STATES-AFRICAN RELATIONS. *J. of Negro Hist. 1962 47(2): 108-126.* Traces the role of the American Colonization Society in resettling in Liberia the African Negroes captured on American slave ships in 1860 and 1861. The society acted as intermediary between the United States and Liberian governments and provided transportation for the Africans. In Liberia the problem of caring for and absorbing the new arrivals proved too great; many of them died and others lived in wretched poverty. The resettling of more than four thousand captives did facilitate the final breaking up of the slave trade and proved to be the last major undertaking of the Colonization Society. L. Gara

619. Bradley, A. Day. PROGRESSIVE FRIENDS IN MICHIGAN AND NEW YORK. *Quaker Hist. 1963 52(2): 95-103.* In 1839 Michigan Hicksite Quakers started a movement to change the church polity of Genesee Yearly Meeting, which also included Friends of Ontario and western New York. They objected to the power of ministers and elders and were active in antislavery and other reforms. With similar groups in New York State they opposed the disownment of the abolitionist Isaac Hopper. In 1848 they and a New York group of Progressive or Congregational Friends seceded. Small bodies also split off in North Collins and Marlborough, New York, but nearly all disappeared before the Civil War. Based on minutes in the Records Library of New York Yearly Meeting, New York City. T. D. S. Bassett

620. Bradley, L. Richard. THE LUTHERAN CHURCH AND SLAVERY. *Concordia Hist. Inst. Q. 1971 44(1): 32-41.* Reviews the nature of slavery and its ancient antecedents and scriptural defenses, before examining the attitudes of early American Lutherans toward the institution of slavery. Observes the contradiction implied when white Christians enslaved blacks under the guise of conversion. Examines the respective positions taken by different synods throughout the period 1790-1865, detailing the radical abolitionist Franckean Synod, which splintered from the Hartwick Synod of Albany, New York, in 1837. Concludes that the Lutheran Church was divided over the issue of slavery, due to a reflection of local attitudes, and to failing officially to be more evangelical in the entire matter of slavery. Based on records of minutes and proceedings of early American synods, and on secondary sources; illus., table, 61 notes. A. M. Brescia

621. Brauer, Kinley J. THE MASSACHUSETTS STATE TEXAS COMMITTEE: A LAST STAND AGAINST THE ANNEXATION OF TEXAS. *J. of Am. Hist. 1964 51(2): 214-231.* Describes the attempts of a group of anti-annexationists in Massachusetts, who organized the Massachusetts State Texas Committee, to prevent acceptance by the House of Representatives of the proslavery Texas constitution and to defeat the bill to admit Texas into the Union. The committee united various antislavery forces in Massachusetts into one unit, and the experience gained by its leaders, such as Charles Sumner, Charles Francis Adams, Henry Wilson, and John Gorham Palfrey, helped to forge a more permanent union of antislavery forces in the North. H. J. Silverman

622. Broderick, John C. THE PROBLEMS OF THE LITERARY EXECUTOR: THE CASE OF THEODORE PARKER. *Q. J. of the Lib. of Congress 1966*

23(4): 261-273. Against a background of enumerated 19th-century American literary executorships, reviews the problems of editing and custodianship of unpublished manuscripts, "particularly the conflict between a family's rights of privacy and a scholarly ideal of complete disclosure of a writer's literary remains." The attitudes and conduct of Mrs. Theodore Parker and her conflict with various publishers and executors over editions of the sermons and writings of Theodore Parker (1810-60) are detailed with quotations from the Parker Papers. There is a note describing the Library of Congress' Parker Papers, especially the correspondence with enumerated antislavery leaders. Illus., 16 notes.

H. J. Graham

623. Broussard, James H. SOME DETERMINANTS OF KNOW-NOTHING ELECTORAL STRENGTH IN THE SOUTH, 1856. *Louisiana Hist. 1966 7(1): 5-20.* Southern Whigs by and large drifted to the American (Know-Nothing) Party in the election of 1856, whereas Democrats remained loyal to their party. The American Party gained most among Unionist Whigs. States-rightist Whigs shunned the American Party, thereby enabling the Democrats to win most of the South. Whigs supported the American Party principally because of their desire to defeat the Democrats, their unionist sentiment, their antiforeign leanings, and the Know-Nothing neutrality on the slavery issue. Based principally on county election returns cited in W. Dean Burnham's *Presidential Ballots, 1836-1892* (Baltimore, 1955); 7 tables, 18 notes.

R. L. Woodward

624. Brown, A. Theodore. BUSINESS "NEUTRALISM" ON THE KANSAS BORDER: KANSAS CITY, 1854-1857. *J. of Southern Hist. 1963 29(2): 229-240.* Kansas City, Missouri, was incorporated in 1853 near two older communities it was soon to eclipse, Westport and Independence. With the opening of Kansas to settlement, it followed a different policy from the other two. Although the slave population of its county was about 17 percent and its population was proslavery, its business leaders nevertheless saw that their economic interests were linked to the development of Kansas, whether by pronorthern or prosouthern settlers. During the Kansas crisis they strove to maintain stable conditions in their community which were favorable to trade and immigration. Community leadership tried not to lose any opportunity of making money, though this meant exciting the hostility of Missourians around them.

S. E. Humphreys

625. Brown, Ira V. MILLER MC KIM AND PENNSYLVANIA ABOLITIONISM. *Pennsylvania Hist. 1963 30(1): 56-72.* A study of the history of Garrisonian abolitionism in Pennsylvania. Covers the period 1840-62, when James Miller McKim was the executive secretary and director of the Pennsylvania Anti-Slavery Society. The work of the society consisted largely of persuading northerners to stop condoning and supporting slavery. The abolitionist crusade was a religious movement. The optimistic McKim always believed that the antislavery cause would eventually win out. Illus., 52 notes.

D. H. Swift

626. Brown, Norman D. EDWARD STANLY: FIRST REPUBLICAN CANDIDATE FOR GOVERNOR OF CALIFORNIA. *California Hist. Soc. Q. 1968 47(3): 251-272.* After a political career in his native North Carolina, which he

represented as a Whig in Congress for several terms, Stanly retired from public life in 1853 and moved to California to practice law. To defeat the Know-Nothing ticket in San Francisco County he agreed to run for the State senate on the Whig ticket. The Republican Party was organized in California in 1856, and the following year Stanly, though a proslavery man, was nominated for governor. He repudiated all platforms and "went simply for a reformation of government affairs." In the campaign he denounced the Nebraska bill, argued against the Dred Scott decision, and upheld the power of Congress to legislate on territorial matters. Though he differed from the Republicans in his refusal to endorse the Wilmot Proviso or to disavow the admission of any future slave States, these differences did not commend him to his former friends of the American (Know-Nothing) Party; the result was that the Democrats won. In 1861 he favored Lincoln and the Union and in 1862 accepted Lincoln's appointment as Union Military Governor in North Carolina with the duty of promoting Unionist sentiment, a position which he held until the signing of the Emancipation Proclamation. After the war he supported Andrew Johnson. 82 notes.

E. P. Stickney

627. Brown, Richard H. THE MISSOURI CRISIS, SLAVERY, AND THE POLITICS OF JACKSONIANISM. *South Atlantic Q. 1966 65(1): 55-72.* Until the Civil War, the South controlled national politics in the United States, chiefly because it had a homogeneous electorate united by the institution of slavery. The country's first national political party - led by Jefferson and Madison - was an alliance of a southern minority with congenial interests outside the region. After the War of 1812, when the Republican Party became the party of the whole Nation, it ceased to be responsive to the South. The result was the Missouri crisis of 1819-20 which prefigured a political realignment of national parties. Before the crisis the ties between slavery, strict constitutional construction, and the Republican Party were implicit; after it they were explicit. Jacksonian strength came from the West and the old Republican areas of the South Atlantic States and New York.

J. M. Bumsted

628. Brown, William H. DAVID LAWRENCE MORRIL. *Hist. New Hampshire 1964 19(2): 3-26.* Biographical sketch of physician, Goffstown, New Hampshire preacher, Republican politician, and Concord newspaper publisher interested in the Sunday School movement. In Washington he opposed dueling, the foreign slave trade, and slavery in Missouri. Based on a diary during his 1802-11 pastorate; State documents while town representative (1808-16, speaker, 1816), State Senator (1823, president), and governor (1824-27); and *Annals of Congress* while U.S. Senator (1816-23).

T. D. S. Bassett

629. Brynn, Edward P. VERMONT'S POLITICAL VACUUM OF 1845-1856 AND THE EMERGENCE OF THE REPUBLICAN PARTY. *Vermont Hist. 1970 38(2): 113-123.* "Vermont Free Soilism, which began as the Liberty Party in 1840 and adopted new nomenclature in 1846," first eroded the Whigs, who were vague and mild on the antislavery issue. A coalition of Free Soilers and Democrats supported the Wilmot Proviso from 1849 to 1851. They capitalized on opposition to temperance and won State offices in 1853. Both hostility to

political bargaining and dissatisfaction at the failure to match parties with issues such as temperance provided the will to achieve political peace, through the 1854 coalition united by opposition to the Kansas-Nebraska Act (1854). This coalition survived and absorbed the American Party. After a decade of chaos, the coalition produced calm, cohesion, and a long-term Republican majority.

T. D. S. Bassett

630. Burke, Joseph C. MAX FARRAND REVISITED: A NEW LOOK AT SOUTHERN SECTIONALISM AND SLAVERY IN THE FEDERAL CON-VENTION. *Duquesne R. 1967 12(1): 1-21.* Attempts to show that the records of the American Constitutional Convention of 1787 which Max Farrand edited (published 1911-37) contradict the conclusions reached by Farrand the historian. In short, Farrand's conclusion that the issue of Western lands rather than the issue of slavery was the great concern of the convention reflected the viewpoint of his contemporaries rather than the viewpoint of the participants of the convention. 111 notes.

L. V. Eid

631. Burke, Joseph C. THE PROSLAVERY ARGUMENT AND THE FIRST CONGRESS. *Duquesne R. 1969 14(1): 3-15.* Although slavery was not a major issue in the First Congress, petitions from abolitionist groups hoping to excite the issues of both the slave trade and slavery aided development of the basic argument used in the defense of slavery when it became a major national issue. The shift from a pragmatic justification of slavery (used during the Constitutional Convention) to moral arguments for the justification of slavery came during the First Congress when the South responded to these abolitionist petitions. Southern Congressmen, especially William Smith of South Carolina, developed the basic arguments defending slavery as a "positive good" that were to be used later by John C. Calhoun and others. The emotional rhetoric of southern congressmen resulted in previously disinterested northerners becoming aware of the issue. The growing fear that even congressional discussion of antislave trade petitions might lead to decisions on slavery itself brought union between the upper and lower South. Based on the *Annals of Congress;* 54 notes.

M. R. Strausbaugh

632. Butcher, Philip. EMERSON AND THE SOUTH. *Phylon 1956 17(3): 279-286.* Ralph Waldo Emerson's antipathy toward the "peculiar institution" of the South led him into sympathy with the abolitionists. For him, the purpose of the Civil War was to bring an end to slavery, not to preserve a Union which countenanced slavery within its borders. Numerous extracts from his letters, from 1822 onward, are cited to show the development of his interest in the South and in the slavery question. His attitude to the South was that it, more than any other section of the nation, fell short of the ideal. His was primarily the position of an idealist, nor merely of a partisan social critic.

J. Erickson

633. Cain, Marvin R. LINCOLN'S VIEWS ON SLAVERY AND THE NE-GRO: A SUGGESTION. *Historian 1964 26(4): 502-520.* Suggests that an examination of Lincoln's view on slavery and race in terms of his personal thoughts rather than in the light of political consideration indicates that its antecedents

may have been "in Whiggish liberalism reminiscent more of the promise and humanitarianism of Jefferson rather than of the cold pragmatism of Clay." Documented. Sr. M. McAuley

634. Cardoso, J. J. HINTON ROWAN HELPER AS A RACIST IN THE ABOLITIONIST CAMP. *J. of Negro Hist. 1970 55(4): 323-330.* Hinton Rowan Helper (1829-1909) was a "middling" white from North Carolina, primarily known for *The Impending Crisis of the South: How to Meet It* (1857). This book proposed that slavery was the true cause of the South's backwardness, and that the only route to a progressive and truly democratic white southern society was the elimination of the "peculiar institution." Although Helper believed that Negroes were inferior and had to be proscribed from all sections of white society, he was always closely associated with northern abolitionists, who sincerely felt that he was one of their own. Helper himself tried to maintain independence from most abolitionists. He disliked both Lysander Spooner (1808-87), who justified (although he hoped to avoid) elimination of slavery by violence, and John Brown (1800-59). Nevertheless, the Lincoln administration refused to appoint Helper to any high office, since the public identified him too closely with abolition. 22 notes. R. S. Melamed

635. Cardoso, J. J. LINCOLN, ABOLITIONISM, AND PATRONAGE: THE CASE OF HINTON ROWAN HELPER. *J. of Negro Hist. 1968 53(2): 144-160.* At the request of Republican Party leaders, Hinton Rowan Helper prepared and supervised the publication of a compendium version of his controversial book *The Impending Crisis of the South* (1857). In choosing men for his cabinet, President-elect Lincoln was careful to avoid any who had endorsed Helper's book. Helper looked upon the 1860 Republican victory as a result of his work, and requested an important government post, attempting to use the influence of several men close to Lincoln to attain his goal. In November of 1861 Helper's efforts to get government patronage finally succeeded when he was appointed U.S. consul at Buenos Aires, a post he himself had suggested. Documented mostly with manuscript sources; 62 notes. L. Gara

636. Cardozo, Jack J. SOUTHERN REACTION TO HELPER'S "THE IMPENDING CRISIS." *Civil War Hist. 1970 16(1): 5-17.* Using contemporary newspapers and assorted documents, analyzes the southern response to Hinton Rowan Helper's famous book, *The Impending Crisis of the South: How to Meet It* (1857), which attacked the economics of slavery. Few southerners read the book or made a serious attempt to understand or logically answer Helper's charges; instead they responded emotionally by attacking Helper himself. Sincerely frightened by the book, authorities also went to great lengths to prevent its circulation in the South, and punished severely anyone caught either selling it or possessing it. E. C. Murdock

637. Carrigan, Jo Ann. YELLOW FEVER IN NEW ORLEANS, 1853: ABSTRACTIONS AND REALITIES. *J. of Southern Hist. 1959 25(3): 339-355.* Yellow fever swept through New Orleans in the summer of 1853, carrying off more than eight thousand of the inhabitants. Doctors were chiefly concerned with

means of treating the disease. Not knowing its cause or essential nature, they had to "travel blindfold," and employed every conceivable method from "doing nothing at all" to "the most potent remedies in heroic doses." Some persons died from too little medical attention and some from too much. Theories about the disease became involved with abolitionism and religion. At the end of the epidemic, a sanitary commission officially concluded that the disease was not contagious, that yellow fever differed from other fevers only in degree, and that a combination of local terrain and meteorological conditions was indispensable to the origin and transmission of the disease. But the speculation was philosophical rather than experimental.   S. E. Humphreys

638. Catton, Bruce. BLACK PAWN ON A FIELD OF PERIL. *Am. Heritage 1963 15(1): 66-71, 90-91.* This is not so much a biography of Dred Scott as it is an inquiry into the motives behind the case. The author argues that the case was pushed through the courts (even though Scott's owners intended to free him regardless of the outcome of the case) in order to get a clear-cut decision on many aspects of the case.   C. R. Allen, Jr.

639. Cave, Alfred A. THE CASE OF CALVIN COLTON: WHITE RACISM IN NORTHERN ANTISLAVERY THOUGHT. *New-York Hist. Soc. Q. 1969 53(3): 214-229.* Calvin Colton is best known as an early biographer of Henry Clay and the editor of the Kentuckian's papers. However, he also penned a number of antislavery tracts in the 1830's which, with his other writings, reveal that his opposition to slavery was accompanied by a strong belief in white superiority. Since the author believes that Colton's views were shared by a large segment of northerners in the antebellum period, such views must be considered "in any assessment of northern attitudes on the slavery issue." Based on primary sources; 8 illus., 20 notes.   C. L. Grant

640. Cecil, L. Moffitt. WILLIAM DEAN HOWELLS AND THE SOUTH. *Mississippi Q. 1967 20(1): 13-24.* The editorial work that Howells did for the *Ohio State Journal* revealed his antebellum animosity toward the South. Expressing regret, years later, he wondered how significant a part such irresponsible writing played in causing the outbreak of war. After the Civil War, Howells was still unable to regard the South with affection. Repelled by both slavery and war, Howells served as U.S. Consul at Venice, Italy, 1861-65, subsequently suffering guilt feelings for having avoided fighting. His writing for the next decade indicates that his sense of guilt intensified his bitterness toward the South. That Howells began in the 1870's to accept manuscripts from southern authors for the *Atlantic Monthly* is evidence more of his sound judgment than of any changed feelings toward the South. With very few exceptions, both the South and southern characters are excluded from Howells' fiction, and he was never able to maintain objectivity in considering the work of southern writers. His first trip to the South was made at age 77, by which time his attitude had become more tolerant (not sympathetic) toward the region. 30 notes.   R. V. Calvert

641. Chaney, William A., ed. A LOUISIANA PLANTER IN THE GOLD RUSH. *Louisiana Hist. 1962 3(2): 133-144.* Contains correspondence from Jesse

Holcomb Chaney, Louisiana planter and Methodist Episcopal lay preacher, who participated in the emigration to California, 1849-50. Writing to his oldest son, a student at Centenary College in Louisiana, Chaney makes interesting observations on "shipboard life, religious conditions on the ship and in California, the abolitionists at work in San Francisco, and wages and prices during the Gold Rush...[and] numerous references to Louisiana citizens in the emigration as well as at home." The correspondence, introduced by a brief biographical sketch of Chaney, does much to "demonstrate the impact which the rush made upon even the planter class."   D. C. James

642. Chaput, Donald. UNCLE TOM AND PREDESTINATION. *Negro Hist. Bull. 1964 27(6): 143.* Comments on the combination of sentimentality and Calvinist predestinarianism involved in the creation of Harriet Beecher Stowe's stereotype of a servile Negro, Uncle Tom.   L. Gara

643. Cheek, William F. JOHN MERCER LANGSTON: BLACK PROTEST LEADER AND ABOLITIONIST. *Civil War Hist. 1970 16(2): 101-120.* Laments the lack of recognition accorded to a number of outstanding black leaders of the 1850's, one of whom was Langston. Langston's Civil War and post-Civil War accomplishments have been acknowledged, but his energetic and far-ranging activities for Negro rights in Ohio before the Civil War have been overlooked. Well-educated and articulate, this "leading citizen" of Oberlin was the principal architect of the black convention movement and fought tirelessly for black voting rights and educational opportunities. He preached a doctrine of self-help to blacks, and argued that if moral suasion and political pressure failed to achieve their rights, active resistance to the white power structure was the only alternative. Based on primary sources.   E. C. Murdock

644. Choen, William. THOMAS JEFFERSON AND THE PROBLEM OF SLAVERY. *J. of Am. Hist. 1969 56(3): 503-526.* Historians have not paid sufficient attention to the anachronism of Jefferson denouncing slavery while continuing to hold slaves. Consistent in urging abolition of the slave trade, he would accomplish abolition gradually, would discourage the increase of free Negroes in the State, and would forbid slavery in western territories after an incubation period of 16 years. Jefferson believed Negroes to be inferior to whites in ability to reason and in physical attractiveness, and conjectured that they were generally an inferior race. They had a moral sense which made them men, but were a race so alien they could not coexist with whites on a basis of equality. In his own relations as a planter, Jefferson's self-interest played a large role and, in his work as diplomat, he had regard for the protection of slaveholders. As President he never forged a practical plan to abolish slavery and did nothing to jeopardize his position as a slaveholder. 77 notes.   K. B. West

645. Coggan, Blanche. THE UNDERGROUND RAILROAD IN MICHIGAN. *Negro Hist. Bull. 1964 27(5): 122-126.* Relates various incidents concerning the early antislavery movement and the underground railroad in Michigan as a territory and a State.   L. Gara

646. Cohen, Joel E. THE DRED SCOTT DECISION: BACKGROUND AND IMPLICATIONS. *Negro Hist. Bull. 1963 26(4): 145-147, 155.* Briefly reviews the background facts of Dred Scott's famous appeal for his personal freedom to the U.S. Supreme Court. While the majority decision upheld a conservative view of slaves as property, it also helped establish the court's power to declare congressional acts unconstitutional and to apply the due process clause of the 5th amendment to the substance of laws rather than to formal legal procedure. Based on secondary materials.   L. Gara

647. Colwell, James L. "THE CALAMITIES WHICH THEY APPREHEND": TOCQUEVILLE ON RACE IN AMERICA. *Western Humanities R. 1967 21(2): 93-100.* A review and assessment of the views on the race problem in America which Alexis de Tocqueville (1805-59) recorded in *Democracy in America* (1835). Tocqueville predicted that strong race prejudice would persist and that calamitous race warfare would result if any compromise were attempted in the South between the maintenance of slavery on the one hand and full intermingling of whites and blacks on the other. The author concludes that in this area Tocqueville's predictions were less accurate than in most others. Sources are *Democracy in America* and published comments on it; 40 notes.
                                                                           A. Turner

648. Conant, James B. MAN THINKING ABOUT MAN. *Am. Scholar 1964 33(4): 539-550.* Discusses two modes of thought, one typical of the natural scientist in his laboratory; the other typical of the logician, the legal scholar, and the philosopher concerned with ethical and religious problems. Examples are given of large-scale effects of writings of the latter type. Marxian dogma was formulated "at a time when the knowledge derived from the study of man as a part of nature was just beginning...its attitude toward science is dated about 1880." The alleged new scientific findings in anthropology were used to support anti-Semitism by the Nazis and human slavery in America in the Dred Scott decision. The author ends with a plea for a tolerant international community of scholars. Phi Beta Kappa oration at Harvard 9 June 1964.   E. P. Stickney

649. Cook, Fred J. THE SLAVE SHIP REBELLION. *Am. Heritage 1957 8(2): 60-64, 104-106.* Describes the rebellion of Negro slaves on the ship *Amistad* in 1839, as the slaves, led by one of their number, Cinqué, broke their chains and murdered some of their white captors and forced others to operate the ship. They finally arrived on Long Island believing themselves free. Soon, however, they found themselves charged with murder and piracy, complicated by salvage claims and diplomatic entanglements between the United States and Spain. In the United States the case evoked political animosity between President Van Buren and ex-President John Quincy Adams as the latter took up the cause of the *Amistad* Negroes before the Supreme Court, which held that they were free. They were educated, and finally returned to Sierra Leone in a fruitless search for their families. Undocumented; illus.   C. R. Allen, Jr.

650. Coulter, E. Merton. SEWARD AND THE SOUTH: HIS CAREER AS A GEORGIA SCHOOLMASTER. *Georgia Hist. Q. 1969 53(2): 147-164.* William

H. Seward, New York Governor, U.S. Senator, and Secretary of State under Lincoln and Johnson, is known as a leading Republican and abolitionist who coined the term "irrepressible conflict" to describe North-South differences. The author provides details on Seward's short experience as a teacher at Union Academy near Eatonton in western Georgia in 1819. Seward accepted the position while still a student at Union College in Schenectady, New York, apparently to escape an overbearing father. However, Seward's mother prevailed upon him to return after only a month of teaching. This experience may have played an important part in shaping Seward's image of the South in later years. 20 notes.

R. A. Mohl

651. Cox, Monty Woodall. FREEDOM DURING THE FREMONT CAMPAIGN: THE FATE OF ONE NORTH CAROLINIAN REPUBLICAN IN 1856. *North Carolina Hist. R. 1968 45(4): 357-383.* The fate of Benjamin Sherwood Hedrick (1827-86) of the University of North Carolina illustrates the state of public opinion and resulting pressure in North Carolina in 1856. Hedrick was a native North Carolinian, educated in the North, who taught agricultural chemistry at the university. In 1856 he was alleged to be supporting John C. Fremont for the Presidency and, in North Carolina, this was considered synonymous with rabid abolitionism. Hedrick admitted publicly that he opposed slavery in the abstract and its extension into the territories, but he defended it within the South's own borders. This position was unacceptable to opinion leaders in North Carolina, especially newspaper editors. In the ensuing crisis, Hedrick was dismissed for "political agitation." North Carolina in 1856 showed no respect for freedom of opinion or academic freedom. Illus., 176 notes, mainly from unpublished Hedrick papers.

J. M. Bumsted

652. Crandall, John C. PATRIOTISM AND HUMANITARIAN REFORM IN CHILDREN'S LITERATURE, 1825-1860. *Am. Q. 1969 21(1): 3-22.* American antebellum children's literature is analyzed in terms of its ideological characteristics. Ethnocentric writers, most of whom were less interested in literature than propaganda, offered a steady diet of nationalistic fare in which the young would have been unable to discern anything more than the glories of the status quo. Clergymen, educators, and others did not depict any flaws in American society. Poverty did not exist in stories written for such magazines as the *Juvenile Miscellany;* the travail which existed was regarded as either idiosyncratic failure or external taint. Although writers showed a mildly reform-minded bias on many issues, the concern of Temperance clearly dominated all others. The "Cold Water Army," which enlisted its greatest support in the 1840's, was a children's crusade of the first order. Pacifism ran a strong second to Temperance but, in the end, it became blunted by a strong Unionist sentiment. Antislavery attitudes, by contrast, were ambivalent; some reformers approached slavery with calculated moderation, while others clearly attacked it as immoral. The slave trade early received the brunt of the attack, but by the 1850's appeals to compromise and nationalism clearly crowded it for center stage. The tone of most of the writing was antipolitical, but a clear Whig bias occasionally showed through. National unity and a stable social order clearly took priority over other issues. 69 notes.

R. S. Pickett

653. Curran, Thomas J. SEWARD AND THE KNOW-NOTHINGS. *New-York Hist. Soc. Q. 1967 51(2): 140-159.* Following the elections of 1854, the Know-Nothing leaders in New York attempted to defeat Senator William H. Seward for reelection in January 1855. On several occasions, primarily in his apparent pro-Catholic leanings, Seward had alienated prominent Know-Nothings. However, largely through the efforts of Thurlow Weed, Know-Nothing efforts failed. Since Seward's antislavery activities more than outweighted his pro-Catholic associations, the results of the campaign were an indication that the Know-Nothings (officially The American Party) as a national party would be wrecked by the slavery question. Based on primary and secondary sources; 9 illus., 66 notes.   C. L. Grant

654. Currey, Cecil. QUAKERS IN "BLEEDING KANSAS." *Bull. of Friends Hist. Assoc. 1961 50(2): 96-101.* Quakers settled in Kansas Territory shortly after passage of the Kansas-Nebraska Act in 1854. Their aim was to witness against slavery and the resort to violence. They were occasionally in danger from the proslavery forces. Their pacifism was severely tested during the Civil War. Some of the young men did go into service and were read out of meetings. Documented.
                                                         N. D. Kurland

655. D'Elia, Donald J. DR. BENJAMIN RUSH AND THE NEGRO. *J. of the Hist. of Ideas 1969 30(3): 413-422.* From a decade before the Declaration of Independence to his death in 1813, Benjamin Rush was dedicated to the cause of Negro freedom. His "programs to help the Negro were carefully reasoned and planned," and were seemingly based on scientific evidence of the Negro's capacity for equal rights with whites. But Rush's humanitarian plans were "really the handmaid of his theology." The misery of slavery was, in his view, "a special means of salvation granted to Negroes by God."   W. H. Coates

656. Daly, L. J. SENATOR FROM ILLINOIS. *Hist. Bull. 1955 34(1): 22-33.* Reviews the life and social environment of Elias Kent Kane in Illinois during the period after 1814, when Kane settled in Kaskaskia as a lawyer. A leader of the proslavery faction, Kane was elected to the U.S. Senate in 1824. He died in 1835 while serving his second term as Senator.   W. J. Grattan

657. Daniel, W. Harrison. VIRGINIA BAPTISTS AND THE NEGRO IN THE ANTEBELLUM ERA. *J. of Negro Hist. 1971 56(1): 1-16.* As early as 1793 Virginia Baptists declared that hereditary slavery was not a moral or religious issue. Bondage was a political matter to Baptists; they felt that all questions and problems associated with the institution should be left to the politicians. Nevertheless, antebellum Negroes belonged to Baptist Churches in the Old Dominion, and lived under the same rules of church discipline. The Baptist Churches licensed and ordained numerous black preachers, but the practice began to decline in the early 19th century due to the growing fear that Negro preachers might encourage slave revolts. Ordination of black preachers ended entirely after Virginia adopted statutory prohibitions in 1832. Most black Baptists in antebellum Virginia belonged to mixed congregations, but a number of African Baptist Churches sprang up before 1860. These congregations lost most of their indepen-

dence after 1830 and were placed under the supervision of white Baptists due to fear and racism, yet the number of such churches trebled between 1830 and 1860. Based on primary sources; 72 notes. R. S. Melamed

658. Davis, David Brion. THE EMERGENCE OF IMMEDIATISM IN BRITISH AND AMERICAN ANTISLAVERY THOUGHT. *Mississippi Valley Hist. R. 1962/63 49(2): 209-230.* The definition of "immediatism" has been swathed in ambiquity in the history of antislavery thought. Immediatism as connoting contemporary consciousness of slave holding and intense feeling of moral commitment came in the early 1830's. Gradualism no longer seemed workable in an age of progress and of movements of natural rights. Immediatism represented a basic shift in ideology - now there would be no compromise with sin. Immediate emancipation, formerly an elusive goal, now became a compelling obligation. G. M. Gressley

659. Davis, Kenneth S. ELI THAYER AND THE KANSAS CRUSADE. *New-England Galaxy 1963 5(2): 23-33.* Eli Thayer (1819-99) did not organize the New England Emigrant Aid Company of Massachusetts as a benevolent institution but as a money making business. He was, however, attacking slavery in the process. He sought by colonization to make Kansas a laboratory demonstration of the inferiority of slave labor to free labor, a demonstration so convincing that the South's faith in slavery would be shaken. T. J. Farnham

660. Davis, Leona King. LITERARY OPINIONS ON SLAVERY IN AMERICAN LITERATURE FROM AFTER THE AMERICAN REVOLUTION TO THE CIVIL WAR. *Negro Hist. Bull. 1960 23(5): 99-101, 104, (6): 123-127, (7): 147-150.* The first part is mostly a discussion of the proslavery ideas of James Fenimore Cooper as expressed in his book *The American Democrat.* Cooper viewed slavery as a benevolent institution. He believed slavery was an internal institution within the States and that it would be unwise for Congress to amend the Constitution to abolish it. He recognized the importance of the racial factor and predicted that abolition of slavery would lead to a race war. In the second part the author discusses mainly the antislavery writings of John Greenleaf Whittier and James Russell Lowell. Whittier opposed the plan of the American Colonization Society to colonize the slaves and advocated immediate emancipation instead. In prose and poetry he argued that slavery was cruel, undemocratic, and harmful to the South. Lowell also argued against slavery and race prejudice. The antislavery viewpoints of Walt Whitman, William Cullen Bryant and Henry Wadsworth Longfellow are discussed in the third part. The author deals mainly with Whitman, whose argument against slavery was sentimental and without hostility to the slaveholder. Whitman alleged that slavery lowered the status of all labor and that the slave trade was the most abominable way to acquire money. He also sympathized with the plight of the fugitive slaves. The antislavery poems of Bryant and Longfellow were also sentimental. The author concludes with a short summary of all three parts. Documented with quotations and reference to secondary sources. L. Gara

661. Degler, Carl N. THERE WAS ANOTHER SOUTH. *Am. Heritage 1960*
11(5): 52-55, 100-103. Before the Civil War the South was not solid. The author
describes the dissent in the South, by Southern leaders and others, from the States
rights position, and deals with the minority parties of the Old South: the Whigs,
the Constitutional Union Party, etc. He discusses the Nullification theories of
John C. Calhoun and the rejection of these and other extremist theories by men
like James Madison, James L. Petigru, William G. Brownlow, John Bell, and
Howell Cobb. He also notes the organized opposition to slavery which existed in
the antebellum South. Undocumented, illus.   C. R. Allen, Jr.

662. Dement'ev, I. P. N. G. CHERNYSHEVSKY I KONSTITUTSIIA
DZHONA BRAUNA [N. G. Chernyshevski and John Brown's constitution].
Voprosy Istorii [USSR] 1959 (12): 137-144. An analysis of John Brown's document reveals that he had a high place in American abolitionist circles and that
his uprising was not of a spontaneous nature. Chernyshevski, who was deeply
interested in the American abolitionist movement and who wrote a newspaper
commentary on Brown's constitution, viewed the uprising as a qualitative growth
in the American antislavery movement. Through his study of Brown's "provisional" constitution, Chernyshevski became acquainted with American democratic ideals. Based on American and Russian published works.
                                                                    A. Birkos

663. Demos, John. THE ANTISLAVERY MOVEMENT AND THE PROB-
LEM OF VIOLENT "MEANS." *New England Q. 1964 37(4): 501-526.* An early
consensus among abolitionists opposing the idea of a violent overthrow of slavery
was beginning to break down by 1836. Like most of their reform colleagues, they
believed that policy must proceed from first principles. Their policy of nonresistance also typified the larger reform effort. The usual explanation of the division
between "political action" men and Garrisonian abolitionists emphasizes Garrison's repudiation of a proslavery Constitution and government. The actual basis
of his opposition to working within the American political system, however, was
nonresistance - the Constitution sanctioned the taking of life in war and capital
punishment. In the 1850's nonresistance completely collapsed and, by 1859, the
antislavery movement was almost as united in supporting forcible means as it had
been earlier in supporting pacifism. The decline of nonviolent abolitionism in the
late 1850's can be traced simply in the defections from the nonresistance movement. Growing receptivity to violence was influenced by passage of the Fugitive
Slave Law, reaction to the conflict over slavery in Kansas, and the growing
numerical strength of antislavery exponents. As large numbers of ordinary citizens belatedly became committed to antislavery, the scales were tipped in favor
of force. Based on newspapers, published letters, and secondary works; 79 notes.
                                                                    R. V. Calvert

664. Detweiller, Philip F. CONGRESSIONAL DEBATE ON SLAVERY AND
THE DECLARATION OF INDEPENDENCE, 1819-1821. *Am. Hist. R.*
1957/58 63(3): 598-616. Slavery was seldom debated in Congress before 1819,
and its relationship to the Declaration even less, but the Missouri question
brought it to the fore. Since the Constitution gave no convincing answers, anti-

slavery members resorted to the Declaration for an exact authority. The ensuing legalistic battle revolved chiefly around the "self-evident truth" that all men are created equal. The significance of the controversy lay in the attempt to fit the political principles of the Declaration to the requirements of a policy or belief and in demonstrating the growing disenchantment of southerners with Jeffersonian principles. Based mainly on the *Annals of Congress.*   J. P. Halstead

665. Dillon, Merton. THE FAILURE OF THE AMERICAN ABOLITION- ISTS. *J. of Southern Hist. 1959 25(2): 159-177.* Despite the 13th Amendment abolishing slavery, abolitionism must be regarded not as a triumph but as one of the major failures of American history. The abolitionists realized practically nothing of their program. The goals of the American Anti-Slavery Society were 1) to spread the doctrine of the sin of slavery, and 2) to eradicate the nearly universal prejudice against even the free Negro - thus, to effect a moral revolution in the country. The abolitionists believed the ending of prejudice had to precede the abolition of slavery. Slavery was eliminated by military and political forces (not moral or religious ones) in the Civil War, but racial prejudice was not. The abolitionists had failed to create widespread determination in any part of the nation to grant social or economic equality to the freedmen. At the meeting disbanding the society in 1870, one leading member cried out that the work was not done, "nor will it be done till the blackest man has every right which I, myself, enjoy."   S. E. Humphreys

666. Dillon, Merton L. THE ABOLITIONISTS: A DECADE OF HISTORI- OGRAPHY, 1959-1969. *J. of Southern Hist. 1969 35(4): 500-522.* Analysis of recent scholarship dealing with abolitionism and the nature of antebellum Amer- ica seems to confirm the conclusion that the abolitionists "always were a pro- phetic element operating in a deeply racist society whose inmost prejudices not even their most dedicated effort proved adequate to dispel." Consequently, they "appear only the more remarkable for bravery and clarity of vision as new accounts reveal the extent of racist views in American culture." However, one might "finally be forced to conclude, without astonishment or cynicism, that the abolitionists had indeed failed in their mission and that the crusade for justice which they waged before the Civil War must be renewed with every generation." 69 notes.   I. M. Leonard

667. Doherty, Robert W. SOCIAL BASES FOR THE PRESBYTERIAN SCHISM OF 1837-1838: THE PHILADELPHIA CASE. *J. of Social Hist. 1968 2(1): 69-79.* In addition to the traditionally accepted explanations for the splits in Protestant denominations, which centered on slavery and abolition, rising social heterogeneity among sects provided stimuli which encouraged schism. In addition, the author argues that rivivalism may have had more attraction for well-to-do sectors of the populace than it did for disinherited ones. Involved in the Presbyterian Schism (1837-38) were Charles Grandison Finney's "new mea- sures" and the milder Calvinism of Nathaniel William Taylor (1786-1858) and of Albert Barnes (1798-1870), as well as participation in nondenominational, benevolent organizations; continued cooperation with the Congregationalists; and the issues of slavery and abolitionism which added new fuel to old antago-

nisms. Growing social heterogeneity in Philadelphia produced divergent needs which could not be met effectively within a single, inflexible body of doctrine like Old School Calvinism. Without minimizing local factors and interpersonal conflict in the denomination, the author insists that the Jacksonian flux provided an environment which placed severe strain upon religious institutions and created high potential for conflict and schism. 23 notes. N. M. Drescher

668. Doty, Franklin A. FLORIDA, IOWA, AND THE NATIONAL "BALANCE OF POWER," 1845. *Florida Hist. Q. 1956 35(1): 30-59.* Debates in Congress and the territorial legislatures and correspondence among contemporary statesmen show how the problems of slavery and sectionalism caused long, heated controversies before these States - paired, one slave and one free - were admitted to the Union. G. L. Lycan

669. Downer, Alan S. THE DOWN EAST SCREAMER. *New England Q. 1969 42(2): 181-200.* Amos Angier Mann was an eccentric, self-proclaimed quack physician, a contributor to the Showhegan (Maine) *Democratic Clarion,* and the opinionated editor of *Mann's Family Physician and Weekly American Miscellany* from 1847. He was constantly in conflict with academically trained physicians and local politicians. He expressed controversial views on slavery, the potato rot, the Mexican War, and prohibition. Sued for libel and raided by local prohibitionists after 1851, Mann lived a long though tempestuous life as the "Down East Screamer." Based primarily on *Mann's Family Physician and Weekly American Miscellany;* 7 notes. K. B. West

670. Draughon, Ralph B., Jr. THE YOUNG MANHOOD OF WILLIAM L. YANCEY. *Alabama R. 1966 19(1): 28-40.* Born in South Carolina, Yancey was taken by his mother to Georgia in 1817. He received his first formal education at the Mount Zion Academy run by Nathan Beman. In 1821, Beman and Yancey's mother were married, and, in 1823, moved to Troy, New York. The couple did not get along well, especially after Beman became an abolitionist. Yancey's education was continued at various academies and at Williams College. He withdrew from college after three years, probably for financial reasons, and returned to the South, while he became one of the most vehement defenders of slavery. The South reacted strongly to the abolitionist movement, "but William Yancy reacted a great deal more strongly than most Southerners because he was spurred by his intense resentment of his stepfather." Based on printed sources and Yancey manuscripts in the Southern Historical Collection, University of North Carolina; 48 notes. D. F. Henderson

671. Duberman, Martin B. BEHIND THE SCENES AS THE MASSACHUSETTS "COALITION" OF 1851 DIVIDES THE SPOILS. *Essex Inst. Hist. Collections 1963 99(2): 152-160.* Analyzes the motions and actions of various politicians in Massachusetts, particularly Charles Francis Adams, in creating the 1857 coalition of Free Soil and Democratic Parties which elected Charles Sumner as senator in 1851. Many Free Soilers were uneasy about coalition with the

"pro-slavery" Democrats, and felt the coalition would - and did - destroy the morals of the Free Soil Party. Based largely on Charles Francis Adams' Diary.

J. M. Bumsted

672. Duberman, Martin B. SOME NOTES ON THE BEGINNINGS OF THE REPUBLICAN PARTY IN MASSACHUSETTS. *New England Q. 1961 34(3):. 364-370.* In September 1855, after several earlier attempts, Massachusetts political leaders who opposed Stephen A. Douglas' Kansas-Nebraska Act formed a coalition Republican Party in Worcester. The new party appealed to many who were opposed to any further extension of slavery, but the Know-Nothings also ran a candidate for governor and won the State elections of that year. The political events of 1855 in Massachusetts left the future still uncertain, and at that time it was doubtful that the Republican label could unite all those who opposed slavery.

L. Gara

673. Duberman, Martin B. THE ABOLITIONISTS AND PSYCHOLOGY. *J. of Negro Hist. 1962 47(3): 183-191.* Calls into question scholarship on the abolitionists which has characterized them as maladjusted individuals with eccentric personalities. Such a view overlooks the uniqueness of individuals and fails to take into account such relatively well-adjusted people as James Russell Lowell, Edmund Quincy, and Lydia Maria Child. In order to make meaningful generalizations about the abolitionists it is necessary for historians to use some of the newer findings in psychology and sociology and also to produce more biographical studies of individual reformers as a basis for such generalizations.

L. Gara

674. Dunson, A. A. NOTES ON THE MISSOURI GERMANS ON SLAVERY. *Missouri Hist. R. 1965 59(3): 355-366.* The repressive treatment that they had suffered in their own country made the German immigrants to America acutely aware of the inequities imposed upon slaves. The author reproduces many long excerpts on the evils of slavery from German books and such newspapers as *Anzeiger des Westens* and *Die Westliche Post.* These excerpts are reproduced in the original German, and each is followed by an English translation embodied in the text of the article. Proslavery elements in Missouri were very severe on Germans with the temerity to criticize slavery, but the German writers did not shrink from continuing their opposition.

W. F. Zornow

675. Eby, Cecil D., ed. THE LAST HOURS OF THE JOHN BROWN RAID: THE NARRATIVE OF DAVID H. STROTHER. *Virginia Mag. of Hist. and Biog. 1965 73(2): 169-177.* Reprints Strother's "The John Brown Raid. Notes by an Eyewitness and Citizen of the Invaded District." Strother, a resident of Martinsburg, Virginia reached Harpers Ferry shortly after Brown's capture. Notes, introduction.

K. J. Bauer

676. Eby, Cecil D., Jr. WHITTIER'S "BROWN OF OSSAWATOMIE". *New England Q. 1960 33(4): 452-461.* Explores the background of John Greenleaf Whittier's poem "Brown of Ossawatomie." Whitter, a pacifist Quaker, refused to

condone John Brown's violence at Harpers Ferry, but he pitied him as a human in distress. After Brown's execution Whittier wrote his poem which pictured the aged abolitionist stopping on his way to the gallows to kiss a Negro child. The incident was based on a false report of a New York *Tribune* correspondent. Ironically, the poem helped arouse emotions in North and South and contributed to the coming of the war which Whittier had hoped would be averted. Documented.   L. Gara

677. Ehrlich, Walter. WAS THE DRED SCOTT CASE VALID? *J. of Am. Hist. 1968 55(2): 256-265.* One important result of an intensive investigation of the sources of the famous Dred Scott Case is to show that Dred Scott was not owned by John Sanford, either personally or as part of an estate. This truth was not, however, appreciated by the attorneys of either side who proceeded as though Scott was in fact a slave owned by Sanford. Based principally on court and estate records and newspapers.   K. B. West

678. Eminhizer, Earl Eugene. ALEXANDER CAMPBELL'S THOUGHTS ON SLAVERY AND ABOLITION. *West Virginia Hist. 1972 33(2): 109-123.* Analysis of Campbell's lifetime hostility to slavery discloses considerable change in emphasis. Always he spoke as an individual and not for his church, claiming that only where the Bible spoke could the church speak. On humanitarian and liberal political grounds he sought as a delegate to the Virginia Constitutional Convention (1829) to abolish slavery, but the rise of abolitionism raised serious questions in his mind of political means and property rights. Particularly in the 1850's, as he attempted futilely to prevent the Disciples of Christ from severing on sectional lines over slavery, he urged moderation and scrupulous legality. Based largely on Campbell's newspapers; 74 notes.   C. A. Newton

679. Ewy, Marvin. THE UNITED STATES ARMY IN THE KANSAS BORDER TROUBLES, 1855-1856. *Kansas Hist. Q. 1966 32(4): 385-400.* U.S. forces in Kansas during the troublesome days that preceded the Civil War tended to follow a policy of neutrality in most cases. Three explanations are offered. Policy decisions were made in Washington where the authorities insisted upon a policy of strict neutrality by men in the field. Military officers in Kansas were aware that much of the trouble was motivated more by a desire for profit than by a desire to advance either freedom or slavery, and so they were very careful to see that the civilians who stood to profit did not provoke hostilities. Most of the professional soldiers in Kansas were devoted to the United States, and so they were able to rise above sectional interests or love for their own States to follow a policy that advanced national interests. Based on secondary works and material in the Kansas Historical Collections; 41 notes.   W. F. Zornow

680. Fairbanks, Jonathan L. FRIENDS IN WILMINGTON. *Quaker Hist. 1969 58(1): 31-40.* A building committee of bankers, merchants, and millers got plans and elevation drafted by Benjamin Ferris (1780-1867) for a new meeting house. Before the existing meeting house was torn down, Ferris sketched and described it in detail. Contracts were let early in 1816, and 123 Friends gave 13 thousand dollars and much labor to complete the building for use by 25 September 1817.

Ferris, a Philadelphia clockmaker in his youth, was (after 1813) a Wilmington druggist, bookkeeper, surveyor, and conveyancer. Chief contributor with William Gibbons to the proto-Hicksite side of the debate published as *Letters of Paul and Amicus* (1823), he also wrote for Gibbons' Hicksite *Berean.* He defended the Seneca Indians, lectured on phrenology, and promoted abolition and temperance, crowning his career with *A history of the original settlements on the Delaware* (1846). Gibbons (1781-1845), a Wilmington physician also on the building committee, founded and led the Delaware Academy of Natural Science (1827-45) and contributed a description of Friends to Daniel Rupp's religious encyclopedia of 1844. From a sesquicentennial address based mainly on secondary accounts.

T. D. S. Bassett

681. Farrison, W. Edward. A THEOLOGIAN'S MISSOURI COMPROMISE. *J. of Negro Hist. 1963 48(1): 33-43.* Examines the controversy which developed as a reaction to some statements which the former slave, William Wells Brown, included in his *Narrative of William W. Brown, a Fugitive Slave. Written by Himself* (Boston, 1847). Brown had cited alleged mistreatment of a female slave by her owner, Daniel D. Page of St. Louis. The Reverend Artemas Bullard, Page's pastor, defended Page, called Brown an impostor, and proved some of Brown's statements to be false. An exchange of letters in *The Congregationalist* between Bullard and Brown proved nothing. In the process, however, Bullard criticized the institution of slavery while defending slaveholders and thus reflected the same kind of thinking which produced the Missouri Compromise in the political sphere. Documented.

L. Gara

682. Fehrenbacher, D. E. LINCOLN, DOUGLAS, AND THE "FREEPORT QUESTION." *Am. Hist. R. 1961 66(3): 599-617.* "It seems reasonable to suggest that the famous exchange at Freeport is not the key to the historical significance of the great debates; that no great amount of cleverness or originality was required to draft the question; that Lincoln included it among his queries at the urging of his friends, rather than against their advice; that there was nothing very decisive about Douglas' reply at Freeport because he had already fully committed himself on the subject...; that Douglas' opposition to the Lecompton Constitution was the principal reason for his loss of standing in the South; and that the Freeport doctrine, for all the talk about it, was only a superficial factor in the disruption of the Democratic party." Based on contemporary newspapers, periodicals, and the printed correspondence of political leaders of the pre-Civil War period.

M. Berman

683. Fehrenbacher, D. E. LINCOLN, DOUGLAS, AND THE "FREEPORT QUESTION." *Am. Hist. R. 1961 66(3): 599-617.* Discusses the significance of the so-called "Freeport Question" concerning slavery in new territories. The author analyzes Stephen Arnold Douglas' statement on 27 August 1858 of popular determination as it influenced his political career and affected the split of the Democratic Party. In both cases the statement was of little importance. In contrast to the emphasis of many historians, Douglas' future and the party split were determined by previous and more significant factors. 59 notes.

W. A. Buckman

684. Fehrenbacher, D. E. THE ORIGINS AND PURPOSE OF LINCOLN'S 'HOUSE-DIVIDED' SPEECH (JUNE, 1858). *Mississippi Valley Hist. R. 1960 46(4): 615-643.* Rejects theories that Lincoln chose to speak his mind regardless of political consequences, or that he was gambling for the Presidency in 1860. Instead, reexamination of the speech and its origins proves that Lincoln intended to check possible Republican support for Stephen A. Douglas and the doctrine of popular sovereignty.   D. R. Millar

685. Fehrenbacher, Don E. LINCOLN AND JUDICIAL SUPREMACY: A NOTE ON THE GALENA SPEECH OF JULY 23, 1856. *Civil War Hist. 1970 16(3): 197-204.* Challenges the traditional view that Abraham Lincoln favored judicial disposition of the problem of slavery in the Territories. This view is based on a misreading of a reporter's summary of Lincoln's speech at Galena, Illinois, in the 1856 campaign. Lincoln in fact never supported judicial supremacy. He was opposed to court rulings - like the Dred Scott decision - which he felt did not reflect the thinking of a majority of the people. For him the Dred Scott opinion was not the final word on the subject. Lincoln's remarks following that decision demonstrated his belief in the ultimate authority of the people as interpreters of the Constitution. Based on primary and secondary sources.   E. C. Murdock

686. Fennimore, Jean Joy L. AUSTIN BLAIR: POLITICAL IDEALIST, 1845-1860. *Michigan Hist. 1964 48(2): 130-166.* Traces Austin Blair's political activities in the crucial years preceding the Civil War. During this period he served in both the Michigan House of Representatives and the State Senate. Blair consistently opposed slavery as an intolerable evil and espoused various humanitarian reforms. He was a Whig, a Free-Soiler, and figured prominently in the formation of the Republican Party. As a Republican candidate he was elected governor in 1860.   J. K. Flack

687. Field, Earle. CHARLES B. SEDGWICK'S LETTERS FROM WASHINGTON, 1859-1861. *Mid-Am. 1967 49(2): 129-139.* Charles B. Sedgwick, a prominent upstate New York attorney and abolitionist, served two terms as a Republican in the national House of Representatives from 1859 to 1863. His letters show that he was a determined foe of slavery who never would consider compromise on the matter. Until the firing on Fort Sumter, Sedgwick preferred the destruction of the Union to the continued association of free and slave States. The chief value of the letters is in the intimate glimpse of the life and opinions of an articulate participant. 18 notes.   L. D. Silveri

688. Filler, Louis. DYNAMICS OF REFORM; THE ANTISLAVERY CRUSADE, AND OTHERS: WITH SOMETHING ABOUT THE NEGRO. *Antioch R. 1967 27(3): 362-378.* Criticizes methods of writing about reform (especially abolitionism) that "fear that a respectful treatment of past unconventional causes or figures will lose us our control of present events and bring on modern catastrophes." The author seeks to interest historians not only in reform but in the society fostering it and its by-products. He points out that moral reform and political reform need one another to direct social unrest into adequate channels and he gives examples from many areas. 6 notes.   F. Harrold

689. Filler, Louis. GARRISON AGAIN, AND AGAIN: A REVIEW ARTI-
CLE. *Civil War Hist. 1965 11(1): 69-75.* An essay-review of two critical biographies - Walter M. Merrill's *Against Wind and Tide: A Biography of William
Lloyd Garrison* (Cambridge, 1963) and John L. Thomas' *The Liberator: William
Lloyd Garrison* (Boston, 1963) - which the author believes have added little to
Garrisonian historiography. If anything, they have further muddied the already
unclean waters. Why, it is asked, must we continue to tear down a major figure,
who admittedly had many shortcomings, but who remains the "leader or guiding
light of as brilliant a group of writers and agitators as America ever produced?"
Modern historians, unduly influenced by Gilbert Barnes' overdone criticism of
Garrison, need to take a fresh, fair look at the man. Once he is "in focus," fact
can be sifted from fiction, and the true Garrison, or something closer to it than
what we now have, will emerge.   E. C. Murdock

690. Filler, Louis. LIBERALISM, ANTI-SLAVERY, AND THE FOUNDERS
OF THE "INDEPENDENT." *New England Q. 1954 27(3): 291-306.* Drawn
largely from the files of the Congregational *Independent,* an American religious
paper founded in 1848, which promoted Congregational policy, attacked slavery,
and commented on a variety of social issues. Discusses the men who organized
this influential newspaper and the subtle shades of opinion which divided men
on religious liberalism and slavery. The *Independent* claimed a circulation of
45,000 in 1860 and more than double that after the war. Henry Ward Beecher
became a regular contributor.   D. Davis

691. Filler, Louis. SLAVERY AND ANTISLAVERY: SUBJECTS IN
SEARCH OF AUTHORS. *Ohio Hist. Q. 1960 69(2): 179-182.* Slavery and
antislavery have been inadequately appreciated as fields for research. Scholars
need to recapture awareness of their ramifications in colonization, sectionalism,
and civil liberties, as well as economic, moral, and political factors. Major figures
have been lost to study; even John Greenleaf Whittier's role in antislavery is
inadequately realized. Negro-white relations have been insufficiently considered.
The author suggests the organization of a permanent historical group to minister
to this academic need.   A

692. Finnie, Gordon E. THE ANTISLAVERY MOVEMENT IN THE UPPER
SOUTH BEFORE 1840. *J. of Southern Hist. 1969 35(3): 319-342.* Surveys and
evaluates the strength of the antislavery movement in the slave States of the upper
South (Delaware, Maryland, Virginia, North Carolina, Tennessee, Kentucky,
and Missouri). Rather than a widespread movement, the author concludes that
there was "at various times and places...a minute number of abolitionists who
advocated the immediate abolition of slavery, a few incorporationists who promoted the gradual abolition of slavery and the incorporation of the Negro in
American society, and a somewhat larger number of colonizationists who supported programs for gradual abolition when they were accompanied by the
immediate removal of the liberated Negro from the South." However, "at no time
in the history of the upper South did these persons represent more than a small
fraction of the white population." As for the small number of "feeble and thinly

scattered abolition societies" that existed in the upper South, they were "generally dominated by Southerners who urged that the Negro be removed from the South immediately upon manumission." 69 notes.   I. M. Leonard

693. Fladeland, Betty. WHO WERE THE ABOLITIONISTS? *J. of Negro Hist. 1964 49(2): 99-115.* Examines various charges which contemporaries and later writers have leveled against the abolitionists and concludes that each contains a germ of truth but none is valid when applied to all the abolitionists. Fanaticism, the goal of social equality for Negroes, eccentric behavior, disunionism, political opportunism, selfish considerations, violent language, and a martyr complex were all involved in the abolition movement but no single characteristic can be used to give an authentic picture of the whole movement. Diversity characterized the reformers; the only thing they had in common was a conviction in a common cause.   L. Gara

694. Flint, Allen. HAWTHORNE AND THE SLAVERY CRISIS. *New England Q. 1968 41(3): 393-408.* Hawthorne's response to the slavery crisis in America was one of anger, bewilderment, and critical curiosity. He evinced little concern for the Negro either as a slave or a free man, disliked slavery but took a rather detached view of it, and believed the Civil War would inevitably result in the breakup of the Union. As a democratic supporter of Franklin Pierce in the 1850's, he looked on with little understanding of the crucial issues involved in the breakup of the party system, feeling that reformist attempts to ameliorate the problem were bound to fail, and that only God could resolve the issues. He did not write during the Civil War, unable to formulate a real solution. Based on Hawthorne's letters and notebooks; 14 notes.   K. B. West

695. Foner, Eric. POLITICS AND PREJUDICE: THE FREE SOIL PARTY AND THE NEGRO, 1849-1852. *J. of Negro Hist. 1965 50(4): 239-256.* In 1848 the Free Soil Party, with a substantial contingent of discontented Democrats and Whigs in its ranks, emphasized that the Free Soil doctrine was advantageous for white northerners but failed to endorse equal rights for Negroes. Both political expediency and prejudice contributed to this position. In 1852, when the soilers were mostly Liberty Party men and abolitionists, the party again hedged on the question of full equality. Although a minority favored a less compromising stand, most Free Soil supporters continued to favor some form of racial separation as the most advanced position that the northern voters would accept.
                                                                         L. Gara

696. Foner, Eric. RACIAL ATTITUDES OF THE NEW YORK FREE SOILERS. *New York Hist. 1965 46(4): 311-329.* In the middle of the 19th century, most Americans believed that the Negro was destined to occupy a subordinate position in society. As a result, although great numbers of northerners condemned slavery during the 1840's, they opposed political and social equality for Negroes. In order to attract a wide following, leaders of the antislavery movement knew that they would have to divorce themselves from the idea of Negro equality. The leading organizers of the Free Soil Party came from the Democratic Party

in the State of New York. They had long been opposed to the granting of political rights to colored citizens, and they made their views prevail in the Free Soil Party.

B. T. Quinten

697. Foner, Eric. THE WILMOT PROVISO REVISITED. *J. of Am. Hist. 1969 56(2): 262-279.* In 1846 a group of Van Burenite Democrats, largely New Yorkers, sponsored the Wilmot Proviso, an attempt to stop the expansion of slavery into territories to be purchased from Mexico. The move was defensive in nature, an attempt to protect northern Democrats from the charge of acquiescing in a slave conspiracy to add more slave States. In New York especially, abolitionist sentiment was growing and Democrats were already under fire for supporting the South in the matter of the gag rule. Southerners would make no compromise to allow northerners to vote for Texas annexation and Van Buren came to believe that the northern Democrats were betrayed by Polk. Pushed by southern "aggression," Van Buren felt that the fragile coalition of his party was endangered. If accepted, he felt the Proviso might allow the party to survive. 67 notes.

K. B. West

698. Fornell, Earl W. AGITATION IN TEXAS FOR REOPENING THE SLAVE TRADE. *Southwestern Hist. Q. 1956/57 60(2): 245-259.* Discusses proslavery agitation in Texas newspapers, politics, and churches in 1857 and 1858.

J. A. Hudson

699. Fornell, Earl W. TEXANS AND FILIBUSTERS IN THE 1850'S. *Southwestern Hist. Q. 1956 59(4): 411-428.* Discusses Texas support of filibustering campaigns into Nicaragua. Texas support was aimed at establishing independent slaveholding States as a source of supply of cheap slave labor rather than at increasing southern representation in the national Congress.

J. A. Hudson

700. Franklin, William E. THE ARCHY CASE: THE CALIFORNIA SUPREME COURT REFUSES TO FREE A SLAVE. *Pacific Hist. R. 1963 32(2): 137-154.* Examines the legal arguments for and against freeing a slave brought to California by a citizen of Mississippi. Believes the decision was consistent with the views of Justice Burnett who disliked Negroes, slave or free, and wanted them barred from the community in which he lived.

J. McCutcheon

701. Freehling, William W. SPOILSMEN AND INTERESTS IN THE THOUGHT OF JOHN C. CALHOUN. *J. of Am. Hist. 1965 52(1): 25-42.* Discusses two aspects of John C. Calhoun's political thought which make him less of a thoroughgoing economic determinist than he has been considered. The first was his appreciation of the political power of antislavery ideology, and the second deviation was his concern for the dangers to democracy wrought by corrupt spoilsmen. The author concludes that these aspects of his thought are particularly revealing illustrations of his ambivalent attitude toward democracy.

H. J. Silverman

702. Furnas, J. C. PATROLLING THE MIDDLE PASSAGE. *Am. Heritage 1958 9(6): 4-9, 101-102.* Recounts the efforts of the United States to join the British in the suppression of the slave trade, which were impeded by the southern influence in the U.S. Navy. Undocumented, illus.   C. R. Allen, Jr.

703. Gara, Larry. A SOUTHERN QUAKER'S PLAN TO ABOLISH SLAV-ERY. *Quaker Hist. 1969 58(2): 104-107.* Prints an abridged letter of James Jones, member of the New Hope Monthly Meeting of Friends, Greene County, Tennessee, to his brother-in-law, John Ellis of Ohio, late in 1816. The letter reports the growth of Tennessee manumission societies to two hundred members within a year, and proposes to petition Congress to abolish the internal slave trade.
                                                        T. D. S. Bassett

704. Gara, Larry. HORACE MANN: ANTISLAVERY CONGRESSMAN. *Historian 1969 32(1): 19-33.* Explains how Mann, totally absorbed in educational reforms, became a member of Congress. The author outlines his service in the ranks of those members of the House of Representatives (1848-53) who opposed slavery in the territories. Based mostly on the Mann Papers in the Massachusetts Historical Society; 67 notes.   N. W. Moen

705. Gara, Larry. THE FUGITIVE SLAVE LAW IN THE EASTERN OHIO VALLEY. *Ohio Hist. 1963 73(2): 116-128.* Analyzes the effect of the Fugitive Slave Law of 1850 as enforced and interpreted in the eastern Ohio Valley. The author describes controversies and altercations which arose in the enforcement of the new law and shows how these incidents sometimes placed Ohio State officers in opposition to the U.S. Government. He concludes that in the Ohio Valley, as elsewhere in the Nation, the Fugitive Slave Law "contributed greatly to the increase in misunderstanding between the sections." Based on materials from Kentucky, Ohio, and Pennsylvania newspapers of the 1850's.
                                                        S. L. Jones

706. Gara, Larry. THE PROFESSIONAL FUGITIVE IN THE ABOLITION MOVEMENT. *Wisconsin Mag. of Hist. 1965 48(3): 196-204.* Professional fugitives (Negroes who had escaped from slavery and used their abilities to further the lot of their fellows) aided their cause in the following ways: 1) their unfavorable view of slavery helped to demolish the myth that the slaves were content and would remain so if not agitated by inflammatory ideas from the North; 2) their speeches, pamphlets, and other writings provided an example of Negro ability which could not be disputed; and 3) their speeches helped to personalize an issue that was often abstract and remote to men from the North. The author cites the works of Frederick Douglass, Henry Bibb, William Wells Brown, and others. Although these former slaves made a unique contribution to the abolition movement, they sometimes created problems for the abolitionists. Three of these are briefly discussed: 1) a few men proved to be imposters; 2) quarrels developed between the fugitives; and 3) their looking out for their own benefit first did not always aid the "cause." 3 illus., 4 photos, 29 notes.   H. A. Negaard

707. Gara, Larry, ed. BRILLIANT THOUGHTS AND IMPORTANT TRUTHS: A SPEECH OF FREDERICK DOUGLASS. *Ohio Hist. 1966 75(1):* *3-9.* An introductory note followed by the text of a speech by Frederick Douglass, as taken down by a reporter and printed in the Wilmington (Ohio) *Herald of Freedom* soon after it was given at a church meeting at Harveysburg, Warren County, Ohio, in the spring of 1852. Douglass attacked the support given to slavery by organized religion and the two major parties, concentrating particularly on the Whig Party. He asked for an end to northern subservience to the slave South. He contended that the Constitution was not necessarily a proslavery instrument. S. L. Jones

708. Gardner, Robert. A TENTH HOUR APOLOGY FOR SLAVERY. *J. of Southern Hist. 1960 26(3): 352-357.* John Leadley Dagg, former president of Mercer University at Penfield, Georgia, and a nationally known Baptist clergyman, defended slavery in his *Elements of Moral Science* (New York, 1859, 1860), but later writers consistently omit notice of him. He is found to be an accomodator of Christianity to the culture in which he lived, more of a scribe than an innovator. He took an attitude of Christian paternalism. The slave was a moral and immortal being (he did not say an intellectual one) and must be given opportunity, encouragement and instruction necessary to secure his eternal happiness. His rights were less in extent than those of free citizens, but no less sacred. An enlightened Christian community placed him "as a perpetual minor" under the guardianship of his master, who was entitled to fair profit, but would not exact undue labor or furnish substandard living conditions. S. E. Humphreys

709. Gatell, Frank Otto. CONSCIENCE AND JUDGMENT: THE BOLT OF THE MASSACHUSETTS CONSCIENCE WHIGS. *Historian 1959 21(1): 18-45.* Deals with the bolt of the Massachusetts "Conscience Whigs" from the Whig Party in 1848 in order to oppose the election of General Zachary Taylor, whose apparent lack of antislavery views was unsatisfactory to many New England Whigs. Failing to form an independent Whig movement, the "Conscience Whigs" joined the new Free Soil Party. The author presents the "Conscience Whigs" as a group movement in which no one figure predominated. E. C. Johnson

710. Gatell, Frank Otto. DOCTOR PALFREY FREES HIS SLAVES. *New England Q. 1961 34(1): 74-86.* Describes the procedure and incidents relating to the Reverend John G. Palfrey's freeing of 20 slaves he inherited from his father in 1843. The elder Palfrey had migrated to Louisiana in 1803 to become a planter, and the rest of the family, except John, went with him. John Palfrey inherited a third of his father's estate, including the slave property. Although he was not an extreme abolitionist, Palfrey refused to hold slave property, and he went to considerable expense and trouble to free his slaves and settle most of them in the North. L. Gara

711. Gatell, Frank Otto. POSTMASTER HUGER AND THE INCENDIARY PUBLICATIONS. *South Carolina Hist. Mag. 1963 64(4): 193-202.* Alfred Huger, Unionist postmaster at Charleston, South Carolina, was responsible for the safety of the mails, which included abolitionist and other tracts and literature

distasteful to his city and section. Included are six letters from Huger to Samuel L. Gouverner, postmaster at New York, in which Huger defends his section and its mores and quietly deletes offensive publications from distribution to protect other mail from attack. One letter from Gouverner to Huger assures him that no such material will be knowingly forwarded from New York.

V. E. Bardsley

712. Gates, Paul W. LAND AND CREDIT PROBLEMS IN UNDER-DEVELOPED KANSAS. *Kansas Hist. Q. 1965 31(1): 41-61.* In no State was speculation a more important factor in its development than in Kansas. Even the slavery controversy and the clash between border ruffians and Jayhawkers did not disrupt the flow of capital to Kansas. The existence of Indian lands in Kansas also provided speculators with unusual opportunities. Absentee ownership and high interest rates were among the more important problems faced by Kansans. Usury laws, occupancy laws, and taxation were effective weapons in the struggle to force land improvements or transfers of titles to residents. There was little abatement in the land and credit problem of territorial days during the decade after the Civil War. This subject is discussed in greater detail in the author's *Fifty Million Acres: Conflicts Over Kansas Land Policy, 1854-1890* (Ithaca, 1954).

W. F. Zornow

713. Geffen, Elizabeth M. PHILADELPHIA PROTESTANTISM REACTS TO SOCIAL REFORM MOVEMENTS BEFORE THE CIVIL WAR. *Pennsylvania Hist. 1963 30(2): 192-211.* Examines the reaction of Protestantism in Philadelphia to social reform movements including temperance, women's rights, prison reform, peace, and slavery in the period 1825-60. The author concludes that Philadelphia Protestants had no major objections to social reform movements, but insisted that such movements be controlled by those confirmed in the Protestant faith.

W. B. Miller

714. Genovese, Eugene D. A GEORGIA SLAVEHOLDER LOOKS AT AFRICA. *Georgia Hist. Q. 1967 51(2): 186-193.* A study of a short literary controversy in the antebellum South among correspondents to *The American Cotton Planter and the Soil of the South,* an agricultural journal edited by Noah B. Cloud. The controversy, stimulated by an editorial stand in 1859 favoring resumption of the African slave trade, centered on the African background of Negro slaves. One of the correspondents, "J.M.W.," a Georgia slaveholder, challenged the editorial suggestion that slavery was a civilizing agent and emphasized the advanced nature of African civilization and culture. Other writers, however, emphatically disagreed, and these latter views characterized southern opinion in general in the pre-Civil War period - opinions, says the author, hardly informed of the true nature of African society. Documented.

R. A. Mohl

715. Good, Donald G. ELISHA BATES AND SOCIAL REFORM. *Quaker Hist. 1969 58(2): 81-92.* A moderate, gradualist, antislavery writer (1817-24), Bates moved from Virginia to Mount Pleasant, Ohio, in 1817, and the next year bought Charles Osborn's weekly antislavery journal *Philanthropist.* He circulated his moralisms from Indiana to New York and Virginia, opposing coloni-

zation, the Missouri Compromise, the slave trade, and the free produce movement. Although he was clerk of the Ohio Yearly Meeting six times from 1819 to 1831, he aimed his journal beyond the Society of Friends to an evangelical Christian audience. In March 1821 he began publishing the monthly *Moral Advocate* which was against war, dueling, and capital punishment, and which advocated prison reform. He published a children's dictionary and a speller in 1821, and he helped administer Thomas Rotch's fund to educate poor children.

T. D. S. Bassett

716. Govan, Thomas P. WAS THE OLD SOUTH DIFFERENT? *J. of Southern Hist. 1955 21(4): 447-455.* Sectionalism as a divisive force in American history has had more importance as a subject for historians than it has had in the life of the Nation. At the time of the Civil War, the author sees the people not separated by differences in occupation and economic interest but unified by their common tradition and culture. The South, already questioning the principles of slavery, resented outside criticism. It blocked all action out of fear of the results of emancipation. The South's concern with maintenance of white supremacy identified it with all men of European origin who come in contact with large numbers of people of other origins.

Ruby Kerley

717. Graebner, Norman A. POLITICS AND THE OREGON COMPROMISE. *Pacific Northwest Q. 1961 52(1): 7-14.* A study of the political forces in the United States influencing decisions and actions in the compromise concerning the Oregon Territory in dispute with Great Britain. The author's picture of the tense factors includes the slavery question, factions within political parties, and personal ambitions.

C. C. Gorchels

718. Graebner, Norman A. 1848: SOUTHERN POLITICS AT THE CROSS-ROADS. *Historian 1962/63 25(1): 14-35.* Shows how the Whig and the Democratic parties both arrived at the crossroads of decision as to whether they would continue at all in the wake of the 1848 election. The Whig victory had been achieved by promising the North its way in Congress and in the Territories, and by reminding the South that Zachary Taylor was a slaveholder. It was unable to withstand sectional pressure, and was able to maintain a semblance of party unity solely on the principle of popular sovereignty in the Wilmot Proviso. The Democratic Party held two interpretations of this principle, and southern leaders regarded it as merely a program of procrastination. The post-election debate aggravated the sense of urgency among southern extremists to rally the South against the onslaught of northern power. Based on the John C. Calhoun Papers, South Carolinian Library; Thomas Butler King Papers, Southern Historical Collection, U. of North Carolina Library; James J. Hammond Papers, the John J. Crittenden Papers, and the Willie P. Magnum Papers in the Library of Congress.

Sr. M. McAuley

719. Grau, Richard. THE CHRISTIANA RIOT OF 1851: A REAPPRAISAL. *J. of the Lancaster County Hist. Soc. 1964 68(4): 147-175.* A reexamination of the forces which precipitated the bloody clash between a slave-owner, Edward Gorsuch, supported by Federal agents and the Fugitive Slave Act, and his slaves,

supported by fugitive slaves and Quaker sympathizers. Newspaper sentiments are analyzed. The results of the riot are seen as having great impact on the abolition movement. Maps, notes, biblio.   J. W. W. Loose

720. Green, Alan W. C. "JIM CROW," "ZIP COON": THE NORTHERN ORIGINS OF NEGRO MINSTRELSY. *Massachusetts R. 1970 11(2): 385-397.* Andrew Barton was the first to use a comic Negro character in his play, *The Disappointment* (1767). Negro comic relief proved highly popular, and by 1800 the happy-go-lucky, irresponsible, and foppish Negro was a standard stock character on the American stage. In the 1820's Thomas Dartmouth Rice invented the character "Jim Crow," and George Washington Dixon developed "Zip Coon," giving birth to the classic Negro minstrel. Both men were northerners, and Negro comic characters and minstrels were largely confined to the northern stage. Stage portrayal of Negroes reinforced white attitudes toward the black man, and satisfied the psychological need to feel superior to the incompetent figures performing on stage. "Jim Crow" and "Zip Coon" embodied the characteristics which white America wanted to see in American Negroes. Based on primary and secondary sources; 50 notes.   G. Kurland

721. Green, Fletcher M. NORTHERN MISSIONARY ACTIVITIES IN THE SOUTH, 1846-1861. *J. of Southern Hist. 1955 21(2): 147-172.* Describes the missionary activities of the northern churches in the slaveholding States beginning with the Amistad case (1839-41), which led to the formation of the American Missionary Association. In contrast to the American Board of Commissioners for Foreign Missions and the American Home Missionary Society, slaveholders were barred from membership in the association. The American Missionary Association, undertaking its own missionary work in the slaveholding States with such men as the Reverend John G. Fee, the Reverend George W. Bassett, and the Reverend Daniel Worth, developed into an abolitionist organization. The Southern Aid Society was formed in 1853 to "neither assail or defend slavery" but to preach the gospel. Failing as a peacemaker between the North and South, it was disbanded in the winter of 1860/61.   R. Kerley

722. Greene, John C. THE AMERICAN DEBATE ON THE NEGRO'S PLACE IN NATURE, 1780-1815. *J. of the Hist. of Ideas 1954 15(3): 384-396.* The leading advocate of the unity of the human race was the Reverend Samuel Stanhope Smith. His opponents were not necessarily defending slavery when they placed the Negro on a lower plane than the white. The Scriptures were involved in the controversy. Discussions of race formation in 1812-13 clearly anticipated Darwin in tentative suggestions about random variation and natural selection. Based on selections from a dozen American and English anthropological treatises, including those of Jefferson and Benjamin Rush.   W. H. Coates

723. Griffin, C. S. THE UNIVERSITY OF KANSAS AND THE YEARS OF FRUSTRATION, 1854-1864. *Kansas Hist. Q. 1966 32(1): 1-32.* The university that opened in Lawrence in 1866 was the product of many years of conflict. The factors that entered into the conflict included such things as rivalry between the advocates of public and private education, the efforts to make education an

element in the struggle between Free Staters and Proslaveryites, the rivalry between towns to become the site of a school, coeducation versus all-male education, an attempt to identify the college with a religious denomination, and an effort to create an educational system that met the qualifications imposed by the State constitution. Based on local newspapers, State records, and manuscripts at the University of Kansas and Kansas State Historical Society.

W. F. Zornow

724. Griffin, Clifford G. THE ABOLITIONISTS AND THE BENEVOLENT SOCIETIES, 1831-1861. *J. of Negro Hist. 1959 44(3): 195-216.* The story of the struggle which went on between abolitionist and anti-abolitionist factions to win control over and dictate policies of the three leading American Protestant benevolent societies during the three decades preceding the Civil War. Commercial and economic considerations, as well as political, moral, and religious ones, influenced the outcome, which was favorable for the abolitionists in one case, for the slavery interests in another, and resulted in a split in the third. The author concludes that as a result of this preliminary struggle, the Civil War would be fought largely as a Christian crusade. Sources include reports of missionary and benevolent societies and published works.

R. E. Wilson

725. Griffin, Clifford S. COOPERATION AND CONFLICT: THE SCHISM IN THE AMERICAN HOME MISSIONARY SOCIETY, 1837-1861. *J. of the Presbyterian Hist. Soc. 1960 38(4): 213-233.* Formed in 1826, the American Home Missionary Society proposed to coordinate the domestic missionary work of the Calvinist churches: Presbyterian, Congregational, Reformed Dutch, and Associate Reformed. Primary support came from the first two. When the Presbyterians split into Old and New Schools in 1837, the New School General Assembly voted its confidence in the Society, whereas the Old School rejected it completely. Despite efforts by Society officers for maintenance of true cooperation, intensifying denominationalism weakened the Society. In 1855 the General Assembly of the New School Presbyterians established a Church Extension Committee to supplement the work of the Home Missionary Society. Meanwhile, abolitionists, strong in the Congregational Church, in 1846 had established the American Missionary Association because of dissatisfaction with the equivocal position on slavery insisted on by the Presbyterians. By 1861 the combined effect of denominationalism and abolitionism was fully realized: the Presbyterian New School General Assembly created a Committee of Home Missions to satisfy its needs, and the American Home Missionary Society became the Congregational Home Society. Interdenominational cooperation had come to an end.

W. D. Metz

726. Griffin, J. David. HISTORIANS AND THE SIXTH ARTICLE OF THE ORDINANCE OF 1787. *Ohio Hist. 1969 78(4): 252-260.* Surveys monographic and textbook treatment of the question of the motivations for the adoption of the antislavery article of the Ordinance of 1787 from Richard Hildreth's discussion of the matter in 1849 to a monographic study by Jack E. Eblen on territorial government published in 1968, entitled *The First and Second United States*

Empires. Governors and Territorial Government, 1784-1912 (Pittsburgh, 1968). The author concludes that no adequate analysis of the problem has appeared.

S. L. Jones

727. Groff, Patrick J. THE ABOLITIONIST MOVEMENT IN HIGH SCHOOL TEXTS. *J. of Negro Educ. 1963 32(1): 43-51.* Survey of 18 American high school history texts, criticizing their generally unfavorable handling of abolitionists and abolitionism. The author based his criticism on various recently published works in the field but particularly on Dwight L. Dumond's *Antislavery.*

S. C. Pearson, Jr.

728. Guillory, James Denny. THE PRO-SLAVERY ARGUMENTS OF DR. SAMUEL A. CARTWRIGHT. *Louisiana Hist. 1968 9(3): 209-227.* In the two decades before the Civil War, southern physicians were involved in two separate campaigns which helped nourish a sense of southern nationalism: 1) to secure southern medical independence by convincing young southerners to attend southern medical schools and 2) to defend the contention that Negro slavery was morally right and socially and economically justifiable. The leader of such physicians in Louisiana was Samuel A. Cartwright, one of the most respected medical men in the State. Beginning in 1837 he attacked the abolitionists in articles and speeches, accusing them of being agents of British foreign policy. These articles in defense of slavery continued into the Civil War and included physical, moral, medical, and Biblical arguments. He particularly emphasized Negro physiological peculiarities and susceptibility to certain diseases. Cartwright played a major role in molding southern proslavery sentiment. Based chiefly on Cartwright's articles; 65 notes.

R. L. Woodward

729. Hale, Frank W. SALMON PORTLAND CHASE: RHETORICIAN OF ABOLITION. *Negro Hist. Bull. 1963 26(5): 165-168.* Outlines the pre-Civil War career of Salmon P. Chase (1808-73) who served in the U.S. Senate (1850-55) and as Republican Governor of Ohio (1855-59), emphasizing his role as the leading antislavery spokesman in Ohio. Based on secondary accounts.

L. Gara

730. Handlin, Oscar. EXPLOSION ON THE "PRINCETON." *Atlantic 1955 195(2): 63-68.* Examines the historical setting in which the death of Secretary of State Abel Upshur occurred. This brought to office John C. Calhoun, who abandoned the cautious policy of his predecessor and put the slavery issue in the spotlight in connection with the problem of annexing Texas. Thus, the issue of whether slavery was to expand together with the United States was clearly drawn.

H. C. Deutsch

731. Harrell, David E. JAMES SHANNON: PREACHER, EDUCATOR, AND FIRE-EATER. *Missouri Hist. R. 1969 63(2): 135-170.* Shannon was a distinguished teacher and influential preacher in the Disciples of Christ Church. A spirit of religious intolerance, an obstinate belief in his own views, and an absolute conviction that Negro slavery was an inevitable condition are shown to have

hampered his efficiency as a school administrator. Local political feuds, the slavery issue in Missouri, and the national issues associated with the Kansas-Nebraska Act made his years at the University of Missouri in Columbia between 1850 and 1855 particularly trying. The author takes the middle ground between Shannon's claim that his presidency of the university was a success and his critics' view that it was a total failure. The physical facilities and the academic program did not suffer in spite of deep religious and political struggles raging on campus and in the legislature during these years. Based on articles, newspapers, monographs, and the Shannon Papers in the Western Historical Manuscripts Collection, University of Missouri, and the Shannon collection at the Disciples of Christ Historical Society, Nashville, Tennessee; illus., 187 notes. W. F. Zornow

732. Harrell, David Edwin. PARDEE BUTLER: KANSAS CRUSADER. *Kansas Hist. Q. 1968 34(4): 386-408.* Pardee Butler is shown to have been one of the most prominent reformers in Kansas and a highly-respected preacher and organizer in the Disciples of Christ Church. Butler was a strong man who found himself drawn into every religious and reform issue that arose in Kansas during his 33-year association with the region. Abolitionism during the territorial period and prohibition during the years immediately after the Civil War were the dominant issues. Butler was attracted to both of them. Since it was in connection with these two reform movements that Butler left his greatest impression on the history of Kansas, the author limits his study to them. Based on local newspaper reports, religious periodicals, articles, recollections and other published writings by Butler; illus., 103 notes. W. F. Zornow

733. Harrell, David Edwin, Jr. THE SECTIONAL ORIGINS OF THE CHURCHES OF CHRIST. *J. of Southern Hist. 1964 30(3): 261-277.* The 20th-century Churches of Christ are the spirited offspring of the religious rednecks of the post-bellum South. The split between these rural, economically poor churches and the largely northern, urban, well-to-do Disciples of Christ - both groups being spiritual descendants of Alexander Campbell - has as a background the slavery dispute and the Civil War, but did not develop as a clear separation until the Reconstruction period and afterward. Indeed, because of the nebulous ecclesiastical organization, it was only the religious censuses of 1906-36 which actually made a clear distinction. Documented. S. E. Humphreys

734. Harris, Andrew, Jr. NORTHERN REACTION TO THE JOHN BROWN RAID. *Negro Hist. Bull. 1961 24(8): 177-180, 187.* Most northern reaction to the Harpers Ferry incident was moderate. Republican newspapers took pains to disassociate themselves from such violence, Republican politicians, including Lincoln, made it clear that they deplored the incident, and even many active abolitionists condemned Brown for his rash deeds. A number of Negro leaders and antislavery sympathizers hailed Brown as a liberator. A prolonged congressional investigation failed to reveal who had sponsored the raid. L. Gara

735. Hart, Charles Desmond. SLAVERY EXPANSION TO THE TERRITORIES. *New Mexico Hist. R. 1966 41(4): 269-286.* Born in Connecticut, educated

at Yale and the Litchfield Law School, Truman Smith served in the Connecticut legislature, the U.S. House, and finally the U.S. Senate. When he arose on 8 July 1850 all the great speeches on the compromise had been delivered. The heart of his speech was a definitive statement that "the natural limits of slavery expansion" had been reached in New Mexico and Utah. Portions of the speech reproduced in the article were taken from the *Congressional Globe.* 24 notes.

D. F. Henderson

736. Hart, Charles Desmond. THE NATURAL LIMITS OF SLAVERY EXPANSION: KANSAS-NEBRASKA, 1854. *Kansas Hist. Q. 1968 34(1): 32-50.* A study of the congressional debate on the Kansas-Nebraska bill of 1854 to sample public opinion on the limits of slavery expansion. The words of the 152 congressmen who debated on this issue during the winter and spring of 1854 are offered to show the various shades of opinion that developed during the discussion. The debate shows that there was a difference of opinion among congressmen from free States as to whether slavery would expand into this territory. The debate over slavery in the territories had concerned an area far removed from the States, but in 1854 the struggle for power in the territories assumed a new meaning when slavery was introduced in Kansas, a territory contiguous to the States. Based on the *Congressional Globe;* 67 notes.   W. F. Zornow

737. Hart, Jim Allee. JAMES REDPATH, MISSOURI CORRESPONDENT. *Missouri Hist. R. 1962/63 57(1): 70-78.* Deals with an aspect of the early career of James Redpath, who is best remembered as an editor of the *North American Review* and founder of the Boston Lyceum Bureau. After three years with the New York *Daily Tribune* and a southern tour to observe the evils of slavery, Redpath went to Missouri in 1855 to become the St. Louis *Daily Missouri Democrat's* "special correspondent" in Kansas Territory. The contents of many "J. R." letters, which appeared on the first and editorial pages of the *Democrat,* are described, insofar as they deal with Missouri places, personalities, and events. The text of these letters is taken directly from the newspaper, since neither Redpath, who wrote a book on his experiences, nor his biographer reproduced them.   W. F. Zornow

738. Harwood, Thomas F. THE ABOLITIONIST IMAGE OF LOUISIANA AND MISSISSIPPI. *Louisiana Hist. 1966 7(4): 281-308.* No other region of the South suffered so much vituperative abolitionist attack or furnished more material for such attack than Louisiana and Mississippi. The image that slavery was most oppressive in that region was already well set in the North when Harriet Beecher Stowe wrote *Uncle Tom's Cabin.* The author furnishes samples from this vast abolitionist literature relating to cruelty and oppression, the domestic slave trade, southern mores and life, and racial prejudice against the free Negro. He also gives examples of the optimistic belief that an antislavery sentiment was developing in New Orleans. 61 notes.   R. L. Woodward

739. Harwood, Thomas F. PREJUDICE AND ANTISLAVERY: THE COLLOQUY BETWEEN WILLIAM ELLERY CHANNING AND EDWARD STRUTT ABDY, 1834. *Am. Q. 1966 18(4): 697-700.* Discusses English visitor

E. S. Abdy's interview with the famed theologian Channing and speculates as to the importance of this confrontation as a factor in Channing's decision to take a strong stand against slaveholding. Abdy's penetrating questions might well have uncovered racial biases within the minds of a northern liberal such as Channing and motivated the latter to overcome his fastidious stance on social action. 9 notes; several of these contain further information on the dialogue and others refer to primary sources such as Abdy's *Journal of a Residence and Tour in the United States of North America, from April, 1833, to October, 1834,* 3 vols.

R. S. Pickett

740. Havas, John M. COMMERCE AND CALVINISM: THE JOURNAL OF COMMERCE, 1827-65. *Journalism Q. 1961 38(1): 84-86.* Traces the transformation of the New York *Journal of Commerce* from an evangelical newspaper emphasizing reform to a proslavery sheet. The paper was founded by Arthur Tappan in 1827 and published by his brother Lewis. In 1828 the Tappans sold the *Journal* and the new proprietors gave less attention to reform questions, supported sectional compromise, and defended slavery. During the Civil War the paper was branded a Copperhead sheet by its Republican opponents.

L. Gara

741. Haven, R., ed. JOHN BROWN AND HEMAN HUMPHREY: AN UN-PUBLISHED LETTER. *J. of Negro Hist. 1967 52(3): 220-224.* Gives the background and text of a letter of 18 April 1857 from John Brown to the Reverend Heman Humphrey, retired president of Amherst College, in which Brown optimistically reported on his plans to organize resistance to the proslavery government in Kansas and to raise the funds necessary for such a project.

L. Gara

742. Hayden, Roger. KETTERING 1792 AND PHILADELPHIA 1814. *Baptist Q. 1965 21(1): 3-20, (2): 64-72.* A series dealing with the influence of English Baptists on the mission movement among the Baptists in America. Part I. Deals with the role played by English Baptists through personal contact of missionaries sailing via America on their way to their field, and through printed matter of all kinds. The development of missions in England among Christians in general is reviewed with an emphasis on the Baptist. American mission societies are reviewed stressing the part played by Englishmen who had come to America following the formation of societies in England, and by publications. A discussion of the slavery issue as it related to missions at this time is included. Part II. Stresses the place of William Staughton as a connecting link between the English and American Baptists in mission work. Staughton's contribution in organizing the General Missionary Convention is indicated. There are long quotations and one letter in full dealing with the American Baptist mission organization.

E. E. Eminhizer

743. Hayne, Barrie. YANKEE IN THE PATRIARCHY: T. B. THORPE'S REPLY TO "UNCLE TOM'S CABIN." *Am. Q. 1968 20(2, pt. 1): 180-195.* Discusses 16 proslavery literary rebuttals, appearing around 1852-54, to Harriet Beecher Stowe's novel. Six of them were written by northerners, six by "native

Southerners," one by a southerner who lived in the North, and three by northerners "who had become Southerners by adoption." The author remarks that the
principal motivations behind these works seems to have been either a fear of
national disunity or regional sensitivity. Thomas B. Thorpe's *The Master's House*
(1853) is one of the most high-minded and complex of these books. Of all the
authors, only Thorpe depicts the slave master as a conscience-stricken character
and expresses doubts concerning the virtues of slavery. The novel's "chaotic
social breakdown" at the end reveals Thorpe's pessimism and perception of
impending national disaster. 22 notes.   R. S. Pickett

744. Heckman, Richard Allen. OUT-OF-STATE INFLUENCES AND THE
LINCOLN-DOUGLAS CAMPAIGN OF 1858. *J. of the Illinois State Hist. Soc.*
1966 59(1): 30-47. A considerable number of out-of-State politicians attempted
to affect the outcome of the 1858 senatorial election in Illinois through political
intrigue, letters, and speeches. Others went to Illinois to campaign actively for
one of the candidates. A principal threat to Stephen A. Douglas came from the
Democratic intraparty dispute over the Kansas proslavery Lecompton Constitution issue in which his position was challenged by President James Buchanan-led
forces. Horace Greeley, who led eastern Republicans in a pro-Douglas movement, caused considerable anxiety for both parties. Greeley was credited as a
major contributor to Abraham Lincoln's defeat in the election. Many other
prominent politicians of the day were involved directly or indirectly. Illus., 59
notes.   D. L. Smith

745. Heiss, Willard C. HIRAM MENDENHALL AND THE UNION HOME
COMMUNITY. *Bull. of Friends Hist. Assoc. 1955 44(1): 43-49.* Summary of a
speech eulogizing Hiram Mendenhall (1801-52), founder of an Indiana township
in 1836, which was dedicated to various reform movements, primarily abolitionism.   R. Mueller

746. Heiss, Willard C., ed. THE CHRONICLES OF JOHN AND ZA-
CHARIAH: AN INCIDENT IN THE HISTORY OF MIDWESTERN PRO-
GRESSIVE FRIENDS. *Bull. of Friends Hist. Assoc. 1957 46(2): 99-105.* Deals
with the state of affairs in Miami Monthly Meeting, Waynesville, Ohio, in 1846,
when the problem of slavery was before the Friends.   N. Kurland

747. Henig, Gerald S. THE JACKSONIAN ATTITUDE TOWARD ABOLI-
TIONISM IN THE 1830'S. *Tennessee Hist. Q. 1969 28(1): 42-56.* An evaluation
of the Democratic Party's hostility to, and a listing of the arguments against,
abolition. The author concludes that the chief motivation was the fear that an
antislavery crusade would provoke dissolution of the Union and bring on civil
war. Other arguments, with the names of the leading Jacksonians who endorsed
them, include the following: the danger to party unity, the constitutional protection of slavery, racial superiority, the benefits of slavery, the comparative evil of
the northern labor system, and the nationalistic opposition to the British antislavery agitation. The proslavery debaters listed are intellectuals and labor leaders,

from North and South, the unifying factors being their espousal of Jacksonian democracy and the rejection of abolition. Based mainly on primary sources; 62 notes. C. F. Ogilvie

748. Hickin, Patricia. JOHN C. UNDERWOOD AND THE ANTISLAVERY MOVEMENT IN VIRGINIA, 1847-1860. *Virginia Mag. of Hist. and Biog. 1965 73(2): 156-168.* A New York lawyer, married to a Virginian, John Curtis Underwood was an active abolitionist. In 1850, to prove the utility of free labor in the South, he moved to Virginia and established dairies and cheese factories employing only free men. These efforts failed. An inflammatory speech during the 1856 Republican convention earned him the enmity of his neighbors, and he left Virginia. In 1857 he promoted a scheme to colonize antislavery settlers in western Virginia. His main settlement at Ceredo (now in West Virginia) did not prosper. Nevertheless, Underwood did show that an antislavery man could speak out in antebellum Virginia. Based chiefly on Underwood's Papers in the Library of Congress. K. J. Bauer

749. Hillbruner, Anthony. THE LINCOLN-DOUGLAS DEBATES: A STUDY IN EQUALITY. *Lincoln Herald 1960 62(1): 3-12.* Concludes that Lincoln, though unwilling to espouse political and social equality for the Negro, was, at least on the slavery question, somewhat more equalitarian than Douglas. S. L. Jones

750. Hollcroft, Temple R., ed. A CONGRESSMAN'S LETTERS ON THE SPEAKER ELECTION IN THE THIRTY-FOURTH CONGRESS. *Mississippi Valley Hist. R. 1956 43(3): 444-458.* Reprint of 35 letters and short notes written by Edwin Barber Morgan (1806-81), a Republican Representative from New York. In these letters, which are dated between 28 November 1855 and 15 February 1856, Morgan describes his efforts in Congress to secure the Speaker's office for Nathaniel P. Banks of Massachusetts, who enjoyed the support of Know-Nothings and various factions of the Republican Party. These recently discovered letters provide evidence of the Republican Party's tenacious fight to stem the proslavery tide, which was growing during the Pierce administration. R. Mueller

751. Horner, Harlan Hoyt. THE SUBSTANCE OF THE LINCOLN-DOU-GLAS DEBATES. *Lincoln Herald 1961 63(2): 89-98, (3): 139-149.* The one theme Lincoln and Douglas discussed in their famous debates, when they stuck to the subject, was slavery in general, and especially in the Territories. Three positions advanced by Lincoln were controverted by Douglas: 1) that the Union could not endure as the fathers made it, divided into free and slave states; 2) that the Dred Scott Decision was not a sound doctrine; 3) that the Declaration of Independence included and meant Negroes as well as white men when it declared all men to be created equal. The principal substance of the debates hinged upon these three issues, though only about one-third of the time was given to their discussion. A

752. Horsnell, M. E. SPENCER ROANE AND THE PROPERTY OF RIGHTS: A POST-REVOLUTIONARY VIEW. *West Virginia Hist. 1969 30(4): 586-597.* A study of Roane's opinions as a member of the Virginia Court of Appeals between 1795 and 1822 reveals that the judge "does not fit the stereotype of the doctrinaire State-rights apologist." Roane not only opposed the establishment of any single church, but unlike Justice Joseph Story in *Terrett vs. Taylor* (U.S., 1815), he also disliked the establishment of multiple Christian churches via State protection of their property favors. For him separation of church and state was absolute and the church deserved no protection special to it. On slavery Roane hedged and vacillated; but in general he upheld a slave's right to freedom when that right did not contravene property rights or place an added welfare burden on society. 39 notes.   C. A. Newton

753. Howard, Thomas W. INDIANA NEWSPAPERS AND THE PRESIDENTIAL ELECTION OF 1824. *Indiana Mag. of Hist. 1967 63(3): 177-206.* Analyzes the opinions of Indiana newspapers concerning the candidates and the issues involved in the election of 1824, the "first true presidential contest" in the State. Studies attitudes toward William Harris Crawford, Henry Clay, John Quincy Adams, and Andrew Jackson. Notes that the prime issues for Indianans were slavery, the tariff, and internal improvements. Suggests that editorial policies of the newspapers studied reflected the political spectrum, but did not significantly affect the actual voting patterns in the State.   J. Findlay

754. Howard, Victor B. THE SLAVERY CONTROVERSY AND A SEMINARY FOR THE NORTHWEST. *J. of Presbyterian Hist. 1965 43(4): 227-253.* Traces the struggle in the Presbyterian Old School General Assembly over the establishment, location, and staffing of a northwestern seminary as a reflection of conflict on the slavery issue. The New Albany (Indiana) Theological Seminary was established by western synods in 1840. When the General Assembly in 1853 opened a seminary in Danville, Kentucky, northwestern synods were dissatisfied with the location and continued the New Albany seminary. In 1856 Professor Erasmus Darwin MacMaster and the directors at New Albany proposed moving the seminary to a more central location to serve northwestern synods. The school was moved to Chicago, and a struggle ensued between northwestern Free-Soilers under the leadership of MacMaster and conservatives under the leadership of Nathan Lewis Rice with the support of Cyrus McCormick for control of the school. In 1859 the seminary was placed under the control of the General Assembly and Rice was chosen professor of theology. MacMaster was restored to this post in 1866. While personal hostility between Rice and MacMaster contributed to the struggle, it was primarily a result of conflict over the slavery issue. Based on newspapers, letters, and church records; 154 notes.   S. C. Pearson, Jr.

755. Howe, John R., Jr. JOHN ADAMS'S VIEWS OF SLAVERY. *J. of Negro Hist. 1964 49(3): 201-206.* Although John Adams never gave much attention to the question of slavery, on a number of occasions he expressed his repugnance of it. He feared the possibility of a major slave insurrection but he did not find any acceptable solution for the South's dilemma. Adams rejected both immediate emancipation and colonization though he was convinced that the Federal Gov-

ernment had the power to prevent slave expansion and should use it if necessary. His attitudes toward slavery foreshadowed those of John Quincy Adams, his son.

L. Gara

756. Hubbell, John T. THREE GEORGIA UNIONISTS AND THE COMPROMISE OF 1850. *Georgia Hist. Q. 1967 51(3): 307-323.* Traces the influence of Alexander H. Stephens, Robert A. Toombs, and Howell Cobb upon the deliberations leading to the Compromise of 1850. Although Unionists, all three supported the compact theory of Union, advocated total State sovereignty, defended slavery, and insisted upon the doctrine of Federal nonintervention with regard to slavery in the territories (with the exception that the Federal Government was obligated to protect slavery there). In the event that Congress and the President would not support the southern constitutional position, these men were ready for secession. The Compromise of 1850, however, met their demands, and they actively worked for the Union. 44 notes.

R. A. Mohl

757. Huch, Ronald K. PATRIOTISM VERSUS PHILANTHROPY: A LETTER FROM GERRIT SMITH TO FREDERICK DOUGLASS. *New York Hist. 1968 49(3): 327-335.* During the winter of 1851-52, Lajos Kossuth, leader of the Magyar independence movement, visited the United States. Fearing that he would siphon off interest in the antislavery crusade, many abolitionists viewed his visit with mixed feelings. Frederick Douglass, the leading Negro abolitionist, wrote his close friend and fellow abolitionist Gerrit Smith, asking how he should receive Kossuth's American tour. Smith praised Kossuth as an unselfish patriot fighting to free an oppressed people but condemned his refusal to speak out against Negro slavery. It was Smith's conclusion that while Kossuth was a patriot he was not a philanthropist who would adopt all of mankind as his country. 3 illus., 10 notes.

G. Kurland

758. Hudson, Benjamin F. ANOTHER VIEW OF "UNCLE TOM." *Phylon 1963 24(1): 79-87.* "Uncle Tom" has come to connote a cowardly and contemptible character. A French critic in 1854 reviewing a play based on Mrs. Stowe's novel, saw him as a Stoic philosopher and likened him to Epictetus, who was patient, courageous, and resigned. The author of this article agrees, noting that goodness was a basic Stoic quality, and that the Uncle Tom of the novel was distinguished by goodness. His absolute Christian faith protected him and distinguished him from the Stoics. Although shoddy play productions helped demean Uncle Tom, his character merits appreciation.

L. Filler

759. Huff, Lawrence. JOSEPH ADDISON TURNER AND HIS QUARTERLY, "THE PLANTATION." *Georgia Hist. Q. 1970 54(4): 493-506.* An account of Joseph Addison Turner's proslavery publication, the *Plantation,* four numbers of which appeared in 1860. Written by Turner, a Georgian, but published in New York, the quarterly defended southern institutions, especially slavery, and promoted the development of southern literature. Includes several excerpts from Turner's editorials, poetry, and the political play, *Julius Sneezer,*

a parody of Shakespeare's *Julius Caesar.* Despite favorable reviews, the magazine ceased publication after the secession of South Carolina. Based on issues of the journal and correspondence of Turner; 57 notes.   R. A. Mohl

760. Hunter, Ethel A. THE TEN-FOOTERS OF NEW ENGLAND. *New-England Galaxy 1964 5(3): 41-46.* The ten-footers were backyard shops where 19th-century shoemakers plied their trade. These shoemakers were a hardy and independent lot. They were greatly interested in the philosophical problems of their times, especially slavery and abolitionism.   T. J. Farnham

761. Jacobs, Hubert, S.J. THE POTAWATOMI MISSION 1854. *Mid-Am. 1954 36(4): 220-236.* An introduction to an accompanying letter from Maurice Gailland, a Swiss Jesuit missionary assigned to the Mission of St. Mary, Kansas, to his former spiritual director in Rome, Franz Xavier Huber. The introduction describes the background of Jesuit missionary activity in the United States and relates how Father Gailland came to be assigned to this mission established for the Potawatomi Indians in Kansas. Discusses Gailland's missionary activities there and indicates where some of his letters have been published. The letter contains a brief account of the life and culture of the Potawatomi Indians. It mentions the controversy concerning slavery in the Territories and makes specific reference to the pending Kansas-Nebraska Act (1854).   R. F. Campbell

762. Jellison, Richard M. and Swartz, Phillip S. THE SCIENTIFIC INTERESTS OF ROBERT W. GIBBES. *South Carolina Hist. Mag. 1965 66(2): 77-97.* Much scientific investigation was carried on in the 19th century by gifted Charlestonians. One of these was Dr. Robert Wilson Gibbes whose first contributions were those associated with the identification of fossils. Gibbes had controversies with English authorities and sought support among his American colleagues. He suggested State support of science. His later studies, dealing with hybrids, brought forth his entrance into the Negro inferiority controversy. Based on letters and personal papers.   V. O. Bardsley

763. Jennings, Warren A. FACTORS IN THE DESTRUCTION OF THE MORMON PRESS IN MISSOURI, 1833. *Utah Hist. Q. 1967 35(1): 56-76.* Introduced into Jackson County, Missouri, in 1832 as an instrument for the propagation of the Mormon faith, the *Evening and Morning Star,* edited by William Wines Phelps, soon became a focal point of gentile opposition to Mormon settlement in the area. A major factor in gentile hostility was belief that the Mormons were agitating slaves and free Negroes. It was the publication in July 1833 of an article headed "Free People of Color" which precipitated the agitation which led to destruction of the newspaper's press by a gentile mob on 20 July 1833, a preliminary action in a series of events which led to the expulsion of the Mormons from the county in November 1833. Based in part on manuscript materials in the Office of the Historian of the Reorganized Church of Jesus Christ of Latter Day Saints and contemporary newspaper accounts.
                                                        S. L. Jones

764. Jervey, Edward D. LAROY SUNDERLAND: ZION'S WATCHMAN. *Methodist Hist. 1968 6(3): 16-32.* LaRoy Sunderland of New York City, a Methodist preacher, had a vital role in the abolitionist crusade. Through his publication, *Zion's Watchman,* his books, and his activities in various antislavery organizations from 1831 to 1842, he argued for the immediate abolition of slavery. His difficulties in his various activities, his statements and attitudes on slavery, and his trials for slander and falsehood are described. 71 notes.

H. L. Calkin

765. Johannsen, Robert W. STEPHEN A. DOUGLAS, "HARPER'S MAGAZINE," AND POPULAR SOVEREIGNTY. *Mississippi Valley Hist. R. 1959 45(4): 606-631.* A study of the historical setting of Stephen A. Douglas' essay in *Harper's Magazine,* September 1859, entitled "The Dividing Line between Federal and Local Authority: Popular Sovereignty in the Territories," including an analysis of Douglas' argument and the aftermath of the essay in American political discussion. The essay, in which Douglas attempted to construct a constitutional justification for his belief that the Territories of the United States were entitled to the privilege of self-government in all things pertaining to their local or domestic institutions, represented a significant stage in Douglas' development of "popular sovereignty" and resulted in an intense discussion of the issue of Congressional control over slavery in the Territories. The article not only aroused Republican opposition to Douglas' doctrine, but also deepened the split in the Democratic Party between the Douglas and Administration wings. Based on newspapers, contemporary pamphlets, and manuscripts, especially the Stephen A. Douglas Papers in the University of Chicago.

A

766. Johannsen, Robert W. STEPHEN A. DOUGLAS, POPULAR SOVEREIGNTY AND THE TERRITORIES. *Historian 1960 22(4): 378-395.* Depicts how "Douglas' concern for what he called popular sovereignty was as much a part of his devotion to western expansion as it was of his belief in democracy." While declining to consider the issue of slavery as a moral question, Douglas maintained that popular sovereignty was based fundamentally on moral right. The settlers in the four Territories enjoying this right - Utah, New Mexico, Kansas and Nebraska - recognized the serious limitations in Douglas' unwillingness to extend the principle to the popular election of territorial officials. By 1861 Douglas recognized the necessity for this extension, and modified his opinion in view of existing circumstances. Based on the Douglas Papers, University of Chicago Library, the *Congressional Globe,* and contemporary newspapers.

Sr. M. McAuley

767. Johannsen, Robert W. STEPHEN A. DOUGLAS AND THE SOUTH. *J. of Southern Hist. 1967 3(1): 26-50.* Stephen A. Douglas was as thoroughly national in his political ideals and actions as any man in his day, and he had sought to establish his political career upon a foundation of contact between North and South. Close personal friend of men from the South and husband of the daughter of a North Carolina planter, he became a plantation and slave owner (on behalf of his sons) by his wife's inheritance, but he took a pragmatic rather than a moral attitude toward slavery. His doctrine of popular sovereignty was

conceived as one upon which North and South might agree, as indeed they seemed to do for a while - though with differing interpretations of the doctrine. The Dred Scott decision, his opposition to the Lecompton Constitution, the Freeport doctrine, and his *Harper's Magazine* article in 1859 rendered him unacceptable to those who wielded political power in the South, but he did not give up hopes of healing the breach. Even after the Baltimore convention, he made two campaign trips into the South, perhaps not so much to promote his own election to the Presidency as to speak against the dissolution of the Union. After Sumter, he returned to Springfield depressed and worn out, filled with sadness, to tell his constituents that the Union must be preserved. 34 notes.

S. E. Humphreys

768. Johnson, William R. PRELUDE TO THE MISSOURI COMPROMISE. *New-York Hist. Soc. Q. 1964 48(1): 31-50.* Once the House of Representatives had passed the Tallmadge Amendment to the Missouri Enabling Act in February 1819, it began to consider a bill to create the Territory of Arkansas. Representative John W. Taylor of New York proposed an amendment to the bill similar to the Tallmadge Amendment. Although the amendment failed, the debates which followed indicated the reluctance of the House to interfere with slavery where it already existed and also facilitated the introduction of the idea of popular sovereignty.

C. L. Grant

769. Johnson, William R. PRELUDE TO THE MISSOURI COMPROMISE. *Arkansas Hist. Q. 1965 24(1): 47-66.* The debate in Congress over the proposed admission of Missouri as a State and the creation of Arkansas as a territory provided restrictionists an opportunity to try to limit slavery in these areas. John Taylor of New York led the fight for restricting slavery in Arkansas, while James Tallmadge of the same State spearheaded the same drive for Missouri. Although both were unsuccessful, Taylor's proposal of the line 36 degrees 30 minutes north latitude as a demarcation between free and slave States was later adopted as a major feature of the first Missouri Compromise. Based primarily on the *Annals of Congress.*

P. M. McCain

770. Jones, Stanley L. JOHN WENTWORTH AND ANTI-SLAVERY IN CHICAGO TO 1856. *Mid-Am. 1954 36(3): 147-160.* Discusses the political views and activities, 1836-56, of the prominent Chicago politician and newspaper editor. Conclusions are based on the political, economic, and social views expressed in his editorials. Stresses Wentworth's recognition that the political balance of power in northern Illinois was held by antislavery radicals. Insisting that northern Democrats must oppose southern economic "aggressiveness," including slavery, he called for a "fusionist" movement of all like-minded men. For this, Wentworth was called a traitor to the Democratic Party and was almost read out of its ranks.

M. J. Strahan

771. Jordan, Philip D. LINCOLN'S VIEWS ON MOB ACTION. *Lincoln Herald 1968 70(2): 73-76.* Contends that Lincoln in condemning mob action at Vicksburg and Saint Louis in a speech (1835) failed to discern the differing circumstances under which the two events occurred. The lynching of five gam-

blers in Vicksburg in 1835, the author asserts, was necessary "to achieve peace and social stability" when the city lacked "a sturdy social structure and...an effective police agency." Citizens of Saint Louis in 1836, however, in burning a Negro at the stake "without due cause, impeded the orderly process of law."

S. L. Jones

772. Kaplan, Sidney. TOWARDS PIP AND DAGGOO: FOOTNOTE ON MELVILLE'S YOUTH. *Phylon 1968 29(3): 291-302.* Living and writing before the Civil War, Herman Melville (1819-91) was strongly influenced by the anti-slavery movement and thus included many Negro characters in his writings. Within his own family Melville had had close contact with slaves, slaveholders, and slave traders; thus, the institution was not strange to him and, as he grew up, he witnessed the degraded condition of northern Negroes. Melville was well prepared to deal with the topic of the conflict of white and black early in his life. 43 notes.

R. D. Cohen

773. Karnback, William F. THE OLD DUTCHMAN: MARTIN KALB-FLEISCH OF BROOKLYN. *J. of Long Island Hist. 1969 9(1): 44-49.* Highlights of the political career of Kalbfleisch (1804-73). Within 30 years after his arrival in America in 1826, the Holland-born chemist held a number of small posts. By 1860 he won as a Democrat the mayoralty of Brooklyn. His career was marked by intense controversy, in part the result of his pro-union, anti-Negro, antiemancipation politics, and in part the result of his irascible temperament. He was elected to Congress in 1862 and to a second term as mayor in 1868, while in between victories he frequently led rump party opposition. 20 notes.

C. A. Newton

774. Kearns, Francis E. MARGARET FULLER AND THE ABOLITION MOVEMENT. *J. of the Hist. of Ideas 1964 25(1): 120-127.* "Margaret Fuller's aloofness towards the anti-slavery movement has been thoroughly exaggerated. Her cautious attitude towards partisans of that movement was caused not by her refusal to come to grips with the problems facing American democracy,...but resulted from the fact that her equalitarian principles, embracing the desire to liberate not only the Negro but also woman, were far more radical than those embraced by the more conservative reformers constituting the Abolition group."

W. H. Coates

775. Kennicott, Patrick. BLACK PERSUADERS IN THE ANTISLAVERY MOVEMENT. *Speech Monographs 1970 37(1): 15-24.* Describes the role of black speakers in the antislavery movement, identifies major black antislavery persuaders and the occasions at which they spoke, summarizes the major antislavery arguments they articulated, and renders a tentative assessment of their influence on the antislavery crusade. Although the activities of the white antislavery workers have in the past, received major publicity, the black abolitionist played a significant role in breaking the bonds of slavery. 68 notes.

D. R. Richardson

776. Koenig, Duane. THE EUROPEAN WORLD OF ALVAN STEWART, 1831. *Social Studies 1969 60(1): 23-33.* Presents a detailed analysis of the travels of Alvan Stewart, an American, in the year 1831. Some significant aspects of his life are that he turned abolitionist and temperance advocate and held views compatible with those of the common man. Quotations from Stewart's diary give valuable information concerning significant events in England and France. 20 notes.   L. Raife

777. Krug, Mark M. LYMAN TRUMBULL AND THE REAL ISSUES IN THE LINCOLN-DOUGLAS DEBATES. *J. of the Illinois State Hist. Soc. 1964 57(4): 380-396.* When the support of Lyman Trumbull, Republican senator from Illinois, was enlisted in behalf of Abraham Lincoln as he campaigned against Democratic Senator Stephen A. Douglas who was seeking reelection in 1858, Trumbull was regarded as the most able opponent of Douglas that could be found. The debates proved, however, that Lincoln was a match for Douglas. They revealed that Lincoln had far greater appeal than did Trumbull, that he could "stir men's souls to moral indignation." Most important was the national attention now focused on the inevitability of a conflict between freedom and slavery. Illus., 51 notes.   D. L. Smith

778. Lerner, Gerda. THE GRIMKE SISTERS AND THE STRUGGLE AGAINST RACE PREJUDICE. *J. of Negro Hist. 1963 48(4): 277-291.* Describes the efforts of Sarah and Angelina Grimké in combating prejudice against Negroes in the slave States of the South and later in the North. The Grimké sisters frequently spoke at public meetings on behalf of the colored people, wrote a number of tracts and pamphlets, and consistently acted upon their principles in their personal lives. As the only southern white women active in the antislavery movement, their example was influential. Documented with manuscript material.

L. Gara

779. Lewis, Gene D., ed. LINCOLN'S CINCINNATI SPEECH OF 1859. *Cincinnati Hist. Soc. Bull. 1965 23(3): 147-178.* Introduces a speech by Abraham Lincoln in Cincinnati on 17 September 1859. The series of speeches (of which this speech was a part) made for the Ohio elections and in opposition to Senator Stephen Arnold Douglas was more important than the more famous 1858 Lincoln-Douglas debates. Lincoln stressed the conservative side of the Republicans' approach to expansion and slavery, underlining that Douglas was the right candidate for expansion-minded and slave-owning Kentuckians, but not for the conservative, but free-soiler, people of Ohio. In this first run-in for the presidential election of 1860, the Republicans won; and Lincoln became more than a defeated Illinois politician. 4 illus., 15 notes.   T. M. Condon

780. Lewitt, Robert T. INDIAN MISSIONS AND ANTISLAVERY SENTIMENT: A CONFLICT OF EVANGELICAL AND HUMANITARIAN IDEALS. *Mississippi Valley Hist. R. 1963 50(1): 39-55.* In 1816, the American Board of Foreign Missions sent Cyrus Kingsbury to establish a mission among the Cherokees and Choctaws. As laborers on the missions Kingsbury used slaves

freely. This policy conflicted with the abolitionist sentiment on the American Board. Kingsbury elected to retain the slaves and thereby lost the abolitionist support to the North.   G. M. Gressley

781. Lightfoot, B. B. NOBODY'S NOMINEE: SAMPLE ORR AND THE ELECTION OF 1860. *Missouri Hist. R. 1966 60(2): 127-148.* An exciting gubernatorial race in Missouri accompanied the campaign to elect Abraham Lincoln to the Presidency in 1860. Sample Orr was an obscure politician who ran on the Constitutional Unionist Party ticket. He came within eight thousand votes of defeating the regular Democratic nominee, Claiborne Jackson. Orr's remarkable showing offers proof that most Missourians opposed secession and the agitation of the slavery question. Drawing on local newspaper reports of Orr's campaign, the author follows its progress from Orr's self-nomination in July to the final outcome in November.   W. F. Zornow

782. Lindsey, David. "THE ONLY SUBSTANTIAL DIFFERENCE": LINCOLN AND THE NEGRO. *Lincoln Herald 1966 68(2): 95-97.* Concludes that Lincoln believed in racial equality for his own time and that his attitudes toward slavery and the Negro support the contemporary civil rights movement.
S. L. Jones

783. Litwack, Leon F. THE ABOLITIONIST DILEMMA: THE ANTISLAVERY MOVEMENT AND THE NORTHERN NEGRO. *New England Q. 1961 34(1): 50-73.* Analyzes the attitudes of the abolitionists toward the northern Negroes and discusses the relationship between the two groups. Some abolitionists had race prejudice themselves, and others sometimes deferred to the prejudice of a majority of northern whites against social mingling of the races. Abolitionists did little to improve tangibly the economic lot of the Negroes, but they encouraged them to acquire status by acquiring wealth. Boston abolitionists did oppose segregated public schools, and their efforts contributed to the ending of the practice by legislation in 1855. The author concludes that though the abolitionists often had the prejudice of their time, they made significant contributions to the cause of freedom for the Negro in the North.   L. Gara

784. Lovejoy, David S. SAMUEL HOPKINS: RELIGION, SLAVERY AND THE REVOLUTION. *New England Q. 1967 40(2): 227-243.* Hopkins, minister at Great Barrington, Massachusetts (1743-ca.1770), and then in Newport, Rhode Island (1770-1803), opposed slavery vigorously. As with many others, his opposition to slavery was grounded on the principles of the Declaration of Independence, but Hopkins' opposition was also based on long-held religious convictions. A "new light" preacher influenced greatly by the work of Jonathan Edwards, he believed slavery contrary to the principles of "disinterested benevolence" put forward by Edwards in his *The Nature of True Virtue* (1775). He also pressed the well-established idea of a covenant between God and the nation, a covenant which was broken by the continued toleration of slavery. 23 notes.
K. B. West

785. Loveland, Anne C. EVANGELICALISM AND "IMMEDIATE EMAN-CIPATION" IN AMERICAN ANTISLAVERY THOUGHT. *J. of Southern Hist. 1966 32(2): 172-188.* Argues that the idea of "immediate emancipation" in the abolitionist movement emerged in the 1830's out of the evangelical movement in American Calvinist thought, particularly the theology of Charles Grandison Finney and Lyman Beecher, in respect to sin, ability, repentence, and benevolence. As the doctrine emerged, it was that the sin of slavery consisted primarily in allowing slavery to persist when it could be abolished; man's ability to abolish slavery determined his responsibility to do so; he could no more use gradualism in ending his sin in this respect than he could with leaving off alcohol, adultery, or stealing. The author specifically takes issue with the theory of Gilbert Hobbs Barnes in *The Antislavery Impulse* (New York, 1933), followed by several later writers, that the doctrine of immediate emancipation was a British import. Documented.   S. E. Humphreys

786. Lynd, Staughton. ON TURNER, BEARD AND SLAVERY. *J. of Negro Hist. 1963 48(4): 235-250.* Blames the neglect by American historians of slavery's great significance in U.S. history largely on Frederick Jackson Turner and Charles A. Beard. Turner's preoccupation with the frontier and his quasi-racial ideas of European superiority led him to minimize the importance of slavery. Beard's economic interpretation of the Civil War included slaveholders among agrarians in competition with northern capitalists, and underemphasized the role of slavery in bringing on the conflict. Beard failed to take note of abolitionist critics of the Constitution, and he considered them the product of a conflict between capitalist and agrarian interests. Because of the influence of Turner and Beard, historians have too long neglected slavery, which the author believes to be one of the distinctive themes of the American experience. Documented.   L. Gara

787. Lynd, Staughton. THE COMPROMISE OF 1787. *Pol. Sci. Q. 1966 81(2): 225-250.* Approaches the Northwest Ordinance adopted by the Continental Congress on 13 July 1787 as the product of sectional compromise; examines the problems of the Constitutional Convention which had, on 12 July 1787, adopted the three-fifths compromise; and submits that whether or not the ordinance was consciously intended to resolve the problems of the convention, it may have done so. The author sees the fugitive slave clause, unanimously adopted by both bodies, as a manifestation that the makers of both the ordinance and the Constitution were ready to compromise the concept that all men are equal. Documented.   Sr. M. McAuley

788. Maddox, Robert Franklin. THE PRESIDENTIAL ELECTION OF 1860 IN WESTERN VIRGINIA. *West Virginia Hist. 1964 25(3): 211-227.* Discusses the political situation in western Virginia with emphasis on the effect of the division of the Democratic Party into a minority group that was proslavery and a majority group favoring preservation of the Union. The author shows how this factionalism carried over into the State and national conventions, and how the majority of the Virginia delegates finally left the convention at Baltimore and supported John Cabell Breckinridge. A few gave their support to Stephen Doug-

las and even fewer joined to endorse John Bell. The Republicans in Virginia favored the nomination of William Henry Seward but supported Abraham Lincoln. The campaign in the State reflected the sectionalism and political diversity present before the conventions with the two major issues being states' rights and the Union. While Bell carried the State, Breckinridge won the most popular votes in the western section and would have won Virginia had the Democrats not split. The results show that western Virginians were unsympathetic to the abolitionist cause but were strongly for the Union. Primarily from published sources.

D. N. Brown

789. Maginnes, David R. THE CASE OF THE COURT HOUSE RIOTERS IN THE RENDITION OF THE FUGITIVE SLAVE ANTHONY BURNS, 1854. *J. of Negro Hist. 1971 56(1): 31-42.* Anthony Burns was arrested in Boston on 24 May 1854, an alleged fugitive slave. Two days later a group of Negroes, supported by a crowd of almost two thousand people, attacked the court house where he was held. They failed to free him, and he was subsequently returned to his master. The significance of the case is the rising consciousness of the Free Soilers on the fugitive slave issue and the fact that none of the rioters could be convicted in State or Federal courts despite the efforts of the Federal Government. 56 notes.

R. S. Melamed

790. Manierre, William R. A SOUTHERN RESPONSE TO MRS. STOWE: TWO LETTERS OF JOHN R. THOMPSON. *Virginia Mag. of Hist. and Biog. 1961 69(1): 83-92.* Thompson, a nationalist, felt compelled to defend the South from Mrs. Stowe's *Uncle Tom's Cabin* and *The Key to Uncle Tom's Cabin,* which she wrote to explain it. He wrote George Frederick Holmes, history professor at the University of Virginia, to write a "slashing" review of the book. As it was not received in October nor November, Thompson wrote his own "slashing" review. Two months afterwards, the Holmes article appeared in the *Messenger,* but his argument against the book was not impressive.

J. H. Boykin

791. Mansfield, Stephen. THOMAS RODERICK DEW AT WILLIAM AND MARY: "A MAIN PROP OF THAT VENERABLE INSTITUTION." *Virginia Mag. of Hist. and Biog. 1967 75(4): 429-442.* Dew joined the College of William and Mary faculty in 1826 as professor of law. His history course introduced the following year quickly became one of the most popular in the curriculum. He also wrote widely on economic matters, especially slavery. In 1836 he became president of William and Mary and greatly strengthened its faculty before accepting appointment in 1845 as professor of moral philosophy at the University of Virginia. Based on manuscript and printed sources; 61 notes.

K. J. Bauer

792. Marcus, Robert D. WENDELL PHILLIPS AND AMERICAN INSTITUTIONS. *J. of Am. Hist. 1969 56(1): 41-58.* The failure of noted abolitionists, including Phillips, to avoid war or to assure equality for the Negro, is often attributed to a nonprogrammatic, anti-institutional animus. It is true that Phillips used Garrisonian rhetoric, but he did so because he found that American institu-

tions gave him no leverage to move against slavery. He was faced with the challenge of moving an amorphous democratic mass and created the "institution" of a professional reformer asking probing questions in a dramatic fashion. Phillips posed a dilemma concerning the existence of a democratic union based on slavery, and saw the Constitution of 1787 as the cement of an infamous union. During Reconstruction he saw a necessity of revolutionary militancy to set up a Jeffersonian order in the postwar South, and became concerned with problems of monopoly, utilizing utopian political vehicles to repossess a bygone age and thus betraying his early role as radical critic. 93 notes.   K. B. West

793. Marsden, George. KINGDOM AND NATION: NEW SCHOOL PRES-BYTERIAN MILLENNIALISM IN THE CIVIL WAR ERA. *J. of Presbyterian Hist.* *1968 46(4): 254-273.* Millennialism constituted a major current in 19th-century American Protestant thought and contributed to the propensity of northern evangelicals to identify the Kingdom of God with the American nation. Many saw American progress as a sign of the second advent of Christ. While most New School Presbyterians were postmillennialists believing that Christ would come only at the end of a millennium of social reform and progress, a few were premillennialists expecting the return to precede the millennial age. Discussion of various views made millennial imagery familiar to most American Protestants. With the coming of the Civil War, New School Presbyterians used ideas of America's divine role in the coming millennium to vindicate the northern cause. The concept of a national covenant expressed the obligations of the Nation while the promise of a millennium embodied the hopes of the covenant-keeping people. The Confederate rebellion was pictured as a rebellion against God himself as well as a punishment by God for the sin of slaveholding, and the northern victory was identified with the welfare of the church and the progress of society toward a divine consummation. Based on published sermons, articles, and church records; 51 notes.   S. C. Pearson, Jr.

794. Mathews, Donald G. THE ABOLITIONISTS ON SLAVERY: THE CRITIQUE BEHIND THE SOCIAL MOVEMENT. *J. of Southern Hist.* *1967 33(2): 163-182.* Seeks to put aside the rhetoric of abolitionist agitation and to consider the abolition movement as a critique of slavery and in doing so finds that abolitionists actually held a balanced view of slavery. They are pictured as making a pioneering attempt to understand social determinism and at the same time to thwart it.   S. E. Humphreys

795. Mathews, Donald G. THE METHODIST SCHISM OF 1844 AND THE POPULARIZATION OF ANTISLAVERY SENTIMENT. *Mid.-Am. 1968 51(1): 3-23.* Examines the part played by the Methodist Episcopal Church in spreading the abolitionist message that slavery was a moral evil. As one of the major institutions of its day, this church provided both an organization and an effective source of communication for popularizing the slavery issue. When abolitionist activity disrupted the calm and unity of this group, the resultant schism provided a sounding board for antislavery activity. The stand taken by both sides

was based on a negative commitment in the slavery issue. Nonetheless this notion of evil when coupled with emotion became a crusade against slavery. Based on primary and secondary sources; 44 notes.   R. Eilerman

796. McFarland, Carl. ABRAHAM LINCOLN AND MONTANA TERRI-TORY. *Montana 1955 5(4): 42-47.* Describes the far-seeing achievements of Abraham Lincoln for the State of Montana, his concern for the development of mineral resources, his commendation of land grants to railroads, his interest in the territory as a settlement area, and the laws he signed for surveying the territory and for the care of the Indian tribes. The author recalls how the slavery question almost prevented the organization of the Territory of Montana. The Supreme Court finally ruled that Congress could not prohibit slavery in the territories, but that Negroes could not be citizens. After much controversy the Senate decided to adopt, by reference, the identical provisions of the Idaho territorial statue, a maneuver which obviated the necessity of including a "Negro clause," since there were no Negroes in Montana.   B. Waldstein

797. McKay, Ernest A. HENRY WILSON: UNPRINCIPLED KNOW NOTH-ING. *Mid-Am. 1964 46(1): 29-37.* Henry Wilson of Massachusetts, the "Natick Cobbler," though lacking financial means, possessed ability and ambition for political life. His strong antislavery feelings guided his career. Unsuccessful as candidate for governor of Massachusetts on the Free Soil ticket in 1853, he courted the support of the strong Know-Nothing Party in Massachusetts and was elected U.S. Senator two years later. However, his sentiments were not to be identified with this nativist movement.   L. D. Silveri

798. McManus, Edgar J. ANTI-SLAVERY LEGISLATION IN NEW YORK. *J. of Negro Hist. 1961 46(4): 207-216.* The American Revolution encouraged efforts to abolish slavery in New York. The New York Constitutional Convention of 1777 resolved that the legislature should take steps to abolish domestic slavery. Although in 1785 a majority of the legislators favored some kind of emancipation, their inability to agree on the question of suffrage for the freedmen made enact-ment of an emancipation measure impossible. Laws prohibiting the slave trade and encouraging private manumission were passed, and in 1799 the legislature added a *Gradual Manumission Act* to the State's statutes. In 1817 it enacted a general emancipation law to be effective in 1827. The New York movement for emancipation reflected the spirit of the times and cut across party and class lines.   L. Gara

799. McMillan, Malcolm C. WILLIAM L. YANCEY AND THE HIS-TORIANS: ONE HUNDRED YEARS. *Alabama R. 1967 20(3): 163-186.* Includes summaries of what historians have said about Yancey, a sketch of Yancey's life, and a call for a new biography. Any biographer of Yancey must try to resolve several puzzling questions: why Yancey could favor public educa-tion, women's rights, and prison reform, but still refuse equality of men; why Yancey opposed allowing representation on the basis of slave population but still defended the institution as a positive good. 72 notes.   D. F. Henderson

800. Mcmurtry, R. Gerald. LINCOLN AND FOSTER. *Lincoln Herald 1955 57(1/2): 18-22.* A character study of Abraham Lincoln and Stephen Collins Foster, showing their temperamental similarities, their attitude to the slavery question, and their influence, direct and indirect, on American history.

B. Waldstein

801. Mcpherson, Names M. THE FIGHT AGAINST THE GAG RULE: JOSHUA LEAVITT AND ANTISLAVERY INSURGENCY IN THE WHIG PARTY, 1839-1842. *J. of Negro Hist. 1963 48(3): 177-195.* Traces the activities and assesses the influence of abolitionist editor Joshua Leavitt as a special lobbyist in Washington in the 1840's. Leavitt encouraged antislavery Whig congressmen to push the slave issue on all occasions, even at the expense of party regularity. Although he met with initial opposition from some antislavery Whigs, his determination and persistence contributed to a change in the Whig ranks in the 1841-42 session of Congress, when John Quincy Adams and Joshua Giddings clearly broke with party unity and promoted a policy unacceptable to the Southern Whigs. As a leader of the informal antislavery committee in Washington, Leavitt contributed to the disintegration of the Whig Party and later to the formation of several new coalition parties. Documented.

L. Gara

802. Meerse, David E. BUCHANAN, CORRUPTION AND THE ELECTION OF 1860. *Civil War Hist. 1966 12(2): 116-131.* Suggests that corruption in the Buchanan administration - as publicized by congressional reports, Republican pamphlets and newspapers between 1857-60 - was a major issue in the 1860 election. Navy contract frauds, use of Federal monies to win elections, and defalcations by the New York City postmaster were but a few of numerous scandals which were effectively exploited by the Republicans against the Democrats in the summer of 1860. To safeguard themselves from similar attacks, the Republican National Convention bypassed William Seward as a presidential nominee because of his suspicious links with Thurlow Weed, and named "Honest Abe" Lincoln instead. Lincoln's record for honesty appears to have been almost as important as his stand on slavery and slavery extension as the reason for his nomination. The author does not say that corruption was the central issue in the 1860 election, but he points out that it was a major issue and that perhaps it has never been given proper recognition as such. Based on contemporary reports, pamphlets, letters, and newspapers.

E. C. Murdock

803. Melder, Keith. LADIES BOUNTIFUL: ORGANIZED WOMEN'S BENEVOLENCE IN EARLY 19TH-CENTURY AMERICA. *New York Hist. 1967 48(3): 231-254.* Surveys various women's benevolent associations in the eastern part of the United States from 1800 to the 1830's, and finds that they represented the female counterpart of the pervasive American desire to form voluntary associations for the accomplishment of a specific social goal. Working for the propagation of evangelical Christianity, for the abolition of prostitution and slavery, and for the amelioration of the condition of the poor, the helpless, and the insane, the women's benevolent movement was an important factor in the reformism of the Jacksonian era. Moreover, by giving women an important role

in the struggle for social betterment, the benevolent societies helped spur feminism and the later movement for women's rights. Based on primary and secondary sources; 81 notes.   G. Kurland

804. Melder, Keith E. FORERUNNERS OF FREEDOM: THE GRIMKE SISTERS IN MASSACHUSETTS, 1837-1838. *Essex Inst. Hist. Collections 1967 103(3): 223-249.* The arrival of the Grimké sisters - Angelina and Sarah - in Massachusetts in 1837 in the cause of antislavery soon changed into a much broader movement for female emancipation. The sisters were well-received by many in the State, especially women active in the growing lyceum movement of these years. But criticism, largely from clergymen, of women publicly preaching (even in opposition to slavery) forced the sisters to defend a woman's right to speak in public by extending the concept of equality to women. Several leading abolitionists supported them, and Angelina spoke before a special legislative subcommittee on behalf of antislavery and in defense of women's participation in the movement. In 1838, Angelina left Boston to marry Theodore Weld, and the sisters dropped from public view. But they left a legacy of division among reformers over the question of women's rights and awakened a previously dormant issue. Based mostly on unpublished manuscripts.   J. M. Bumsted

805. Merideth, Robert. A CONSERVATIVE ABOLITIONIST AT ALTON: EDWARD BEECHER'S NARRATIVE. *J. of Presbyterian Hist. 1964 42(1): 39-53, (2): 92-103.* Part I. Edward Beecher in 1830 became the first president of Illinois College in Jacksonville. By 1835 Beecher had abandoned gradualism as the proper approach to the destruction of slavery and had embraced Garrisonian abolitionism. By 1836 he had become the closest friend and associate of the abolitionist editor and Presbyterian minister, Reverend Elijah Lovejoy, killed by a mob while defending his press on 7 November 1837. This article traces Beecher's changing position, the relationship of his religious beliefs to his antislavery attitudes, and his involvement with Lovejoy. Beecher's *Narrative of Riots at Alton: in connection with the Death of Rev. Elijah P. Lovejoy* (1838) is a primary document, an eyewitness account, and is an eloquent defense of freedom of inquiry. Part II. Beecher's *Narrative* of Elijah P. Lovejoy's murder was an "interpretation, a theological analysis of a political tragedy." In it Beecher revealed himself as a theoretician of "conservative abolitionism" in sharp conflict with the radical abolitionism of William Lloyd Garrison. Beecher presented the concept of "organic sin" holding that slavery as a sin was one that "individuals in their individual capacity" could not commit but that the "body politic...the great omnipresent slaveholder" was the sinner. Thus it was the entire Nation that was responsible for Lovejoy's murder. His position was representative of a great body of American clergymen who strongly opposed slavery but refused to adopt a "fierce, fanatical and uncandid spirit" in attacking it. In 1835 they joined the American Union for the Relief and Improvement of the Colored Race, in 1840 they voted for James G. Birney and the Liberty Party, they broke away from the American Anti-Slavery Society in protest against Garrisonism, and formed the American and Foreign Anti-Slavery Society. They worked against slavery in the church, and in 1845 they supported the American Board of Commissioners for Foreign Missions against the attacks of the radical abolitionists.
                                                                          W. D. Metz

806. Merk, Frederick. A SAFETY VALVE THESIS AND TEXAN ANNEXA-
TION. *Mississippi Valley Hist. R. 1962 49(3): 413-436.* A nation-wide debate
took place on the admission of Texas to the Union in 1844. A conspiracy thesis
was fostered by John Quincy Adams. Robert J. Walker argued the safety valve
thesis, and John C. Calhoun fought for the slavery thesis. The safety valve thesis
dominated the debate because of its inherent appeal to leave the issue of slavery
in the hands of future generations.   G. M. Gressley

807. Montgomery, Horace. THE TWO HOWELL COBBS: A CASE OF MIS-
TAKEN IDENTITY. *J. of Southern Hist. 1962 28(3): 348-355.* Many historians
and all Library of Congress card entries except one have confused the Reverend
Howell Cobb (b. 1795) of Houston County, Georgia, an author of books on law,
religion and slavery, with Howell Cobb (b. 1815), Speaker of the U.S. House of
Representatives in the 31st Congress, Secretary of Treasury in the administration
of President James Buchanan, and president of the Provisional Congress of the
Confederacy in 1861-62. A summary of the life of the elder and more obscure
Cobb is given, along with a discussion of how the confusion of names was
something of a political embarrassment to the better-known Cobb, even in their
lifetimes.   S. E. Humphreys

808. Morrill, James R. THE PRESIDENTIAL ELECTION OF 1852: DEATH
KNELL OF THE WHIG PARTY OF NORTH CAROLINA. *North Carolina
Hist. R. 1967 44(4): 342-359.* The presidential election of 1852 in North Carolina
- as throughout the Nation - ended the Whig Party. The Southern Whigs forced
the party's candidate, General Winfield Scott, to endorse the Compromise of
1850. This made him unacceptable to many antisalvery advocates, but the last
minute nature of the endorsement also made southerners suspicious. The Whigs
in North Carolina could not produce united support for Scott, and key defections
cost him the State. The reality of the Whig collapse was somewhat cloaked by
the closeness of the vote in the State, but this was largely a factor of the obscurity
and lack of popular appeal of the Democratic candidate Franklin Pierce of New
Hampshire. Based largely on newspapers and unpublished sources; 70 notes.
                                                              J. M. Bumsted

809. Morrow, Ralph E. THE PROSLAVERY ARGUMENT REVISITED.
Mississippi Valley Hist. R. 1961 48(1): 79-94. Challenges the view that proslavery
propaganda was directed primarily at opinion outside the South. Instead, "every
major apology for slavery...explicitly showed concern for the state of southern
opinion," and "in the principal works produced after 1850, concern for the mind
of the slaveholder is as great if not greater than concern for any other element
of the southern population. Protestations of the 'positive good' of slavery measured not only the vigor of northern abolitionists' attacks but the anxiety over the
vulnerability of the South's psychological and intellectual armor."
                                                              D. R. Millar

810. Morton, Wesley. THE CENTRAL CHRISTIAN ADVOCATE OF THE
METHODIST EPISCOPAL CHURCH IN ST. LOUIS. *Methodist Hist. 1965
3(2): 39-49.* By 1849 there was a demand for a Methodist Episcopal Church

periodical to serve the States of Missouri, Iowa, Illinois, and Nebraska. The *Central Christian Advocate* was started in 1853 as a privately-sponsored endeavor but was a financial failure. The Methodist General Conference of 1856 undertook its publication as a church-sponsored periodical but financial losses mounted as subscribers were limited in number. One of the principal reasons for its lack of success is stated as being its middle-of-the-road position on slavery and similar questions. H. L. Calkin

811. Murdoch, Richard K. THE RETURN OF RUNAWAY SLAVES, 1790-1794. *Florida Hist. Q. 1959 38(2): 96-113.* Following its loss of prestige in the Nootka Sound controversy of 1790 with Great Britain, Spain agreed to return to the United States slaves that escaped to Florida, but stopped in 1794 when Spanish officials heard of Edmond Charles Edouard Genêt's plans for conquering Florida. Based on American and Spanish documents and secondary works.
G. L. Lycan

812. Murdoch, Richard K. THE SEAGROVE-WHITE STOLEN PROPERTY AGREEMENT OF 1797. *Georgia Hist. Q. 1958 42(3): 258-276.* The efforts of Georgia and the United States to reach agreement with Spanish authorities in East Florida for the return of runaway Negro slaves and stolen property resulted in an unofficial agreement in 1797. James Seagrove of Georgia, planter and land speculator, representing the United States, negotiated with Enrique White, the Spanish governor of East Florida, to settle this long-standing threat to the peace of the frontier. Based largely on unpublished official Spanish documents, a selection of which are printed at the end of the article. A

813. Murphy, Carol. TWO DESEGREGATED HEARTS. *Quaker Hist. 1964 53(2): 87-92.* Sarah Moore Grimké (1792-1873) and Angelina Emily Grimké (1805-79) were daughters of John Faucheraud Grimké, a Charleston, South Carolina slaveholder, revolutionary veteran, and judge. Raised Episcopalians, they became Friends soon after 1819. Years of inner conflict continued, for many Quakers were too rigid to accept these bright, energetic, and articulate women. Angelina first published her abolitionist views in 1835, and soon both sisters were writing and lecturing against slavery (a role new to women). Because Angelina married the non-Friend Theodore D. Weld "out of meeting" in 1838 (and Sarah attended the wedding), both were disowned and remained unaffiliated thereafter. Derived from Catherine H. Birney's *The Grimké Sisters* (1885).
T. D. S. Bassett

814. Myers, John. THE BEGINNING OF ANTISLAVERY AGENCIES IN VERMONT, 1832-1836. *Vermont Hist. 1968 36(3): 126-141.* "Vermont became the first state to readily accept abolitionist doctrines," not because its people were "intuitively anti-slavery," as local folklore has it, but because of the concerted efforts of Samuel J. May, Oliver Johnson, Orson S. Murray, and other agents of New England and American antislavery societies. Based on the proceedings of antislavery societies, Garrison correspondence, and local newspapers.
T. D. S. Bassett

815. Myers, John. THE MAJOR EFFORTS OF ANTI-SLAVERY AGENTS IN VERMONT, 1836-1838. *Vermont Hist. 1968 36(4): 214-229.* Shows the growth of abolitionist membership in 90 local societies to over eight thousand by 1838. Free Will Baptists, Baptists, and Connecticut Valley Methodists were most affected. Based on material from the archives of the American Anti-Slavery Society, the printed reports of the Vermont Anti-Slavery Society, and newspapers. T. D. S. Bassett

816. Myers, John L. ANTISLAVERY AGENCIES IN RHODE ISLAND, 1832-1835. *Rhode Island Hist. 1970 29(3/4): 82-93.* Examines the impact of local, national, and international speakers in rousing abolitionist sentiment. Argues that despite organizational, financial, and strategical difficulties, the controversial issue made some headway and that by 1835 it had been thrust into the arena of public discussion. Based on manuscripts, newspapers, annual reports, directories, and secondary accounts. P. J. Colenan

817. Myers, John L. ORGANIZATION OF "THE SEVENTY": TO AROUSE THE NORTH AGAINST SLAVERY. *Mid-Am. 1966 48(1): 29-46.* The Executive Committee of the American Anti-Slavery Society recruited agents, during 1836 and 1837, to travel throughout the North lecturing the public on antislavery themes. By 1837, antislavery auxiliaries had doubled to 1,006 and membership was estimated at 100 thousand. Lack of funds necessitated a drastic curtailment of this highly successful "agency" system. L. D. Silveri

818. Myers, John L. THE BEGINNING OF ANTI-SLAVERY AGENCIES IN NEW YORK STATE, 1833-1836. *New York Hist. 1962 43(2): 149-181.* Discusses the early tactics, successes, and failures of the abolitionist lecturers in New York State. Documented extensively from abolitionist journals and from manuscript sources. A. B. Rollins

819. Myers, John L. THE BEGINNING OF ANTISLAVERY AGENCIES IN NEW HAMPSHIRE, 1832-1835. *Hist. New Hampshire 1970 25(3): 2-25.* Antislavery agents, most of them second-rate speakers like Arnold Buffum, spent comparatively little time in New Hampshire until after the State Antislavery Society was organized at Concord in November 1834. By May 1835 the society had 10 locals (half a dozen with over 100 members), but met both a hostile press and much interference with its propaganda. Methodists provided much of the local leadership. 4 illus., 29 notes. T. D. S. Bassett

820. Myers, John L. THE MAJOR EFFORT OF ANTISLAVERY AGENTS IN NEW HAMPSHIRE, 1835-1837. *Hist. New Hampshire 1971 26(3): 3-27.* Gives detailed accounts of the travels and reception of George Storrs, David Root, Jonathan Hazelton, and David I. Robinson, agents of the American Anti-Slavery Society, who increased the number of New Hampshire antislavery societies from 42 to 70 between May 1836 and September 1837, and their membership from 2,500 to over four thousand. All but Root, a Congregational minister, were Methodist circuit riders of the New Hampshire Conference. They followed the

national strategy of cultivating the backcountry, with less attention to the cities. James G. Birney, who addressed the 8 June 1837 State convention at Concord, was afterwards "received" by President Nathan Lord of Dartmouth. The Panic of 1837 forced curtailment of activities just when the movement was changing character. New Hampshire remained cool to abolition, but its press and churches were less unfavorable in 1837 than they had been earlier.   T. D. S. Bassett

821. Myers, John L. THE MAJOR EFFORT OF NATIONAL ANTI-SLAVERY AGENTS IN NEW YORK STATE, 1836-1837. *New York Hist.* 1965 46(2): 162-186. Describes in detail the activities of abolitionist lecturers of the American Anti-Slavery Society in the years of their greatest effort.
A. B. Rollins

822. Nadelhaft, Jerome. THE SOMERSETT CASE AND SLAVERY: MYTH, REALITY, AND REPERCUSSIONS. *J. of Negro Hist.* 1966 51(3): 193-208. Traces the development of the myth that Lord Mansfield's 1772 decision in the case of James Somersett, a runaway slave, freed all the slaves on English soil, and considers its impact in the United States. Actually the decision only stated that a slave could not be shipped from England against his will, but an early English legal report and numerous American newspapers described the court's decision erroneously as one which freed fourteen thousand slaves and established the law of freedom. In America abolitionists and State courts drew upon the false interpretation of the Somersett Case for legal authority to free slaves who stepped upon free soil, and the issue added intensity to the already dangerous split between the sections in the 1850's.   L. Gara

823. Nichols, Roy F. THE KANSAS-NEBRASKA ACT: A CENTURY OF HISTORIOGRAPHY. *Mississippi Valley Hist. R.* 1956 43(2): 187-212. Shows how the early writing on the bill tended to be Northern in sympathy and hence very critical of Senator Stephen Douglas. A reaction that depicted Douglas as the champion of popular sovereignty soon set in. Both interpretations have brought many important materials to light, but these are still insufficient, since both tend to overestimate Douglas as a determining factor in the history of the bill. Attention should be focused on the disorganized state of American politics in that period. The significance of the episode lies in the fact that a bill meant to organize a territory became the instrument of disintegration and reorganization of the party system. The author discusses at length the complicated negotiations between various political groups that were needed to push the bill through the Senate and the House.   D. van Arkel

824. Nicolosi, Anthony S. GIFTS AND ACQUISITIONS. *J. of the Rutgers U. Lib.* 1965 28(2): 27-32. Notes on current acquisitions by the Rutgers University Library: books, newspapers, and manuscripts pertaining chiefly to New Jersey history, leaders, and institutions, including a complete file of the 52 numbers of *The New Jersey Freeman,* June 1844-March 1850, "the state's first anti-slavery newspaper," edited and printed by Dr. John Grimes of Boonton. Also added and

described is a collection of "approximately 100 letters of the Norwegian writer and Nobel prize winner, Sigrid Undset (1882-1949)" written principally during her residence in the United States, 1941-45.   H. J. Graham

825. Nogee, Joseph. THE PRIGG CASE AND FUGITIVE SLAVERY, 1842-1850. THE PRIGG CASE AND ITS CONSEQUENCES. *J. of Negro Hist. 1954 39(3): 185-205.* Deals with background data bearing on the U.S. Supreme Court decision in *Prigg vs. Pennsylvania* (1842) and subsequent measures in the pro-abolitionist northern States to circumvent the decision in the years 1842-50. The Fugitive Slave Act of 1783 was declared constitutional and states were forbidden to legislate on fugitive slavery. Some states, however, forbade their officials to fulfill their duties under the act, thus frustrating attempts to recapture fugitives.
C. R. Spurgin

826. Norton, Henry L., ed. THE TRAVELS OF THE MARSTONS. *J. of the Illinois State Hist. Soc. 1965 58(3): 279-300.* Edited by her grandnephew, Mrs. Margaret Marston Lawrence recounts in her memoirs principally the story of the 1849 migration of the Marston family to the United States. She was the eldest of the eight children of a comfortable middle-class family in England. Her father was a clothing manufacturer and shopkeeper. A Boonville, Missouri newspaper editor who was in England on business convinced the Marstons and another family that his home was a veritable Eden. The realities of a frontier community in a slave State were too much for the English families to tolerate. After several months they moved to Quincy, Illinois, and soon settled down with comfortable satisfaction. Illus.   D. L. Smith

827. Norton, Wesley. THE METHODIST EPISCOPAL CHURCH IN MICHIGAN AND THE POLITICS OF SLAVERY: 1850-1860. *Michigan Hist. 1964 48(3): 193-213.* Describes antislavery agitation by Methodist ministers and laymen in Michigan during the pre-Civil War decade. Resolutions passed by church conferences and editorials printed in church periodicals urged Methodists to exert political pressure in the crusade against slavery. The author concludes that "the Methodist Episcopal Church in Michigan was a major ally of the Republican Party from its birth through the crucial election of 1860."   J. K. Flack

828. O'Connor, Thomas H. NEW ENGLAND MILL MAGNATES AND THE SOUTH. *Textile Hist. R. 1964 5(2): 44-65.* The Civil War was not an "inevitable" clash of two divergent economic systems. In fact, the New England textile manufacturers consistently worked to prevent the disruption of the Union. They played a prominent part in public efforts designed to convince the South that abolitionists were not a true reflection of northern opinion. "A complementary economic system between North and South, a tolerant regard for the rights and privileges of the other, and a warm social relationship which augmented close economic ties" were contributions to national unity which Boston industrialists felt were jeopardized by the immoderate demands of the abolitionists. 83 notes.
E. P. Stickney

829. Oates, Stephen B. JOHN BROWN AND HIS JUDGES: A CRITIQUE OF THE HISTORICAL LITERATURE. *Civil War Hist. 1971 17(1): 5-24.* Reviews the major studies on John Brown, from those written by his colleagues to those by Oswald Garrison Villard (1910), Hill Peebles Wilson (1913), Robert Penn Warren (1929), James C. Malin (1942), and Allan Nevins (1950, in *Emergence of Lincoln,* volume 2). The early works "were either defenses or eulogies of Brown," and failed to come to grips with the whole man. Villard's book was careful and well-balanced, but the writer overlooked religion and environmental influences in the shaping of Brown's thought. Wilson and Warren condemned Brown as an unprincipled fanatic and criminal. Malin's work, purportedly the first scholarly treatment of Brown, viewed its subject as an insane, opportunistic, criminal, and not concerned with blacks but only with himself. Nevins got lost in a maze of fallacious psychoanalyzing over Brown's "insanity." Brown had his failings, but his good traits have too often been overlooked. He was an honest, sincere man, who dedicated his life to the extinction of that "sin against God" - Negro slavery. Based on primary and secondary sources.   E. C. Murdock

830. Oates, Stephen B. JOHN BROWN'S BLOODY PILGRIMAGE. *Southwest R. 1968 53(1): 1-22.* A popularized account of the genesis, execution, and significance of John Brown's attack on Harpers Ferry, Virginia, in October 1859. Based on Brown manuscripts in the Kansas State Historical Society, Topeka, and various printed works.   D. F. Henderson

831. Oates, Stephen B. TO WASH THIS LAND IN BLOOD...JOHN BROWN IN KANSAS. *Am. West 1969 6(4): 36-41, 6(6): 24-27.* Part I. Connecticut-born John Brown (1800-59) was raised in Ohio's Western Reserve to fear the Calvinist God and to hate slavery and its defenders. He memorized the entire Bible and aspired to become a minister, but an eye inflammation and a shortage of funds forced him to abandon this plan. Tragedy and failure were his lot: his first wife and two of their seven children died of emotional problems; seven of 13 children of his second marriage died in childhood; his tannery business was wiped out in the Panic of 1837, the first of a succession of failures of his business ventures. His life was a series of obsessions, not confined to slavery, which he pursued with single-minded determination. Increasingly Brown became involved in the anti-slavery movement. He worked in the Underground Railroad, opposed "black laws," attempted integration of a church he attended, and grew violent in his denunciations. He chided Negroes for passive submission to white oppression, exhorted others to kill anyone trying to enforce the Fugitive Slave Law, and even enlisted over 40 Massachusetts blacks in a mutual-defense organization. Until five of his sons who had moved to Kansas informed him that the territory was in danger of becoming a slave State, Brown had planned to migrate there to try land speculation. Believing in predestination, he felt that he was foreordained to come to grips with his destiny in Kansas. He moved there in 1855 and soon became a prominent figure in the momentous controversy to determine whether Kansas was to become a slave or a free State. 5 illus. Part II. When a Georgia contingent camped on Indian lands near Pottawatomie, Kansas Territory, John Brown was more than ever convinced that the slavery issue would soon erupt into full-scale war on the prairie. With the sacking of Lawrence by proslavers in May 1856, Brown became outraged at the seeming passive reaction of the free-staters and

the newly arrived Federal troops. He led his small party into proslave territory and murdered five people. Reciprocal reprisals and guerrilla war soon raged in southeastern Kansas. Brown evaded arrest and continued to lead others in what he regarded a holy war against slavery. As a new governor backed by Federal troops embarked on a program of pacification and the dispensing of evenhanded justice, Brown, his family, and close associates left Kansas. Convinced that his arrest had been ordered, sick with dysentery and fever, and filled with visions of a greater mission still to be accomplished, Brown planned extensive fund- and men-raising campaigns in the East. Adapted from a forthcoming biography. Illus., bilio. note.   D. L. Smith

832. Obermann, Karl. DIE AMERIKANISCHE ARBEITERBEWEGUNG VOR DEM BÜRGERKRIEG IM KAMPF FÜR DIE DEMOKRATIE UND GEGEN DIE HERRSCHAFT DER SKLAVENHALTER [The American labor movement before the Civil War in its fight for democracy and against the rule of slaveholders]. *Zeitschrift für Geschichtswissenschaft [East Germany] 1962 10(1): 103-135.* Following in large part Jeffersonian ideals, the first American labor organization was established with the founding of the Mechanics Union of Trade Associations in Philadelphia in the 1820's. Whereas in the 1840's the Utopian Socialist ideas of Robert Owen and François Fourier made a considerable impact upon American labor, the following decade saw the introduction of Marxist inspired Socialism, when Joseph Wedemeyer, a close friend of Marx and Engels, assumed a leading role in the American labor movement. The author concurs with the American historian F. J. Herriott that the antislavery sentiment among labor and the demands for "equal democratic rights for all nationalities" were key issues which induced organized Socialist labor to support the Republican Party in 1860. It was the latter labor group which proved of decisive significance in the Republican election victory and "for the victory of progressive bourgeois forces over slaveholders."   G. P. Blum

833. Oppenheimer, Eleonore. A GERMAN JEWISH EMANCIPATOR ON THE NEGRO QUESTION. *Negro Hist. Bull. 1954 18(1): 11.* As he wrote in the *Preussische Jahrbücher,* Gabriel Riesser was greatly upset when he saw Negro slaves in Washington during his trip through America in 1848. Subsequently, he added to his demands for social equality of Jews in Europe the same demands for Negroes.   S

834. Page, Elwin L. A FORGOTTEN FORERUNNER OF ABRAHAM LINCOLN. *Lincoln Herald 1963 65(4): 194-198.* Concludes that Jeremiah Mason (1767-1848), New Hampshire jurist and legislator, in his opposition to slavery extension during the Missouri Compromise debate, adopted attitudes similar to those of Abraham Lincoln. The analysis centers upon Mason's role in the adoption of resolutions by the New Hampshire legislature in protest against the Virginia Resolutions on the Missouri question.   S. L. Jones

835. Patton, James W., ed. LETTERS FROM NORTH CAROLINA EMIGRANTS IN THE OLD NORTHWEST, 1830-1834. *Mississippi Valley Hist. R. 1960 47(2): 263-277.* The letters illustrate the reasons for the heavy migration of

North Carolinians into the Old Northwest: 1) economic betterment due to richer soils and developed transportation facilities, 2) more responsive State and local governments, 3) absence of slavery (particularly important to Quakers), and others.   D. R. Millar

836. Pearson, Samuel C., Jr. FROM CHURCH TO DENOMINATION: AMERICAN CONGREGATIONALISM IN THE NINETEENTH CENTURY. *Church Hist. 1969 38(1): 67-87.* Traces the transition of American Congregationalism in the early 19th century from the status of New England establishment to that of national denomination. Congregationalists showed little interest in national ecclesiastical structures or vigorous competition with other religious groups at the beginning of the century. They cooperated with Presbyterians in the Plan of Union (1801) and with various churches in the work of the voluntary benevolent societies. However, the societies and the Plan of Union brought Congregationalists into intimate contact with other religious traditions. Out of this contact grew a denominational self-consciousness. Congregationalists came to see themselves theologically in conflict with conservative Calvinism as well as with Unitarianism and Universalism, institutionally in conflict with Presbyterian judicatories after the Presbyterian schism of 1837, and socially in conflict over national issues, principally slavery. Congregational self-consciousness focused on Congregationalism's liberal Calvinism (New England theology), congregational government, and commitment to abolition. In the West, where Congregational self-consciousness first emerged, a regional convention was held in 1846. A national convention met in 1852 at Albany, New York, abrogated the Plan of Union, and laid plans for strengthening the denomination. A National Council was held in 1865 and soon thereafter resulted in a continuing national ecclesiastical structure. Based on American Home Missionary Society letter files and published sources; 83 notes.   A

837. Pease, Jane H. THE ROAD TO HIGHER LAW. *New York Hist. 1959 40(2): 117-136.* Examines the evolution of William Henry Seward's antislavery ideas, which culminated in his "Higher Law" speech on the Compromise of 1850. From 1838 to 1850 moral conviction and humanitarianism increasingly overshadowed political considerations in Seward's attitudes toward the slavery issue and its attendant problems. Based primarily on private correspondence in the Seward Papers and Thurlow Weed Papers at the University of Rochester.
A

838. Pease, William H. and Pease, Jane H. ANTISLAVERY AMBIVALENCE: IMMEDIATISM, EXPEDIENCY, RACE. *Am. Q. 1965 17(4): 682-695.* Even though the abolitionists professed sympathy for the cause of the Negro, many were quite ambivalent when it came to describing the way and the time order in which he should be freed. Often, abolitionists tended to love the Negro in abstraction or ideal form, but not in reality. Also, in spite of their declarations for equality, abolitionists could not seem to contain their own senses of superiority toward Negroes. Sterotypic notions relative to Negroes being susceptible to disease as well as social control were widespread among reformers. They wished to mould the Negro into a pattern of middle-class respectability and were upset at

the protests of men such as Frederick Douglass and Henry Highland Garnet. Some reformers maintained the stance of "uplift" and the rhetoric of "the white man's burden" for the"downtrodden"; others eagerly sought martyrdom for themselves by espousing the cause of abolition. On the whole, antislavery advocates were torn between heartfelt concern and thinly veiled contempt. 53 notes.

R. S. Pickett

839. Pease, William H. and Pease, Jane H. BOSTON GARRISONIANS AND THE PROBLEM OF FREDERICK DOUGLASS. *Can. J. of Hist. 1967 2(2): 29-48.* Tension between Frederick Douglass and the Boston Garrisonians erupted as early as 1841 and was caused not by disagreement over political tactics but by the subtle racial prejudice of the "Boston Clique," who always considered the Negro as subservient, not equal, as "essentially a public exhibit in the antislavery crusade." Based on the abolitionist press and private papers; 51 notes.

F. J. McDonald

840. Pease, William H. and Pease, Jane H. FREEDOM AND PEACE: A NINE-TEENTH CENTURY DILEMMA. *Midwest Q. 1967 9(1): 23-40.* A study of Samuel Joseph May, a 19th-century pacifist and abolitionist, becomes strikingly contemporary in the light of present debate over the ethics of American activity in Vietnam and civil rights tactics here in the United States. During the 30 years preceding the Civil War, May was most vocal in his deep-seated commitment against war of any kind. He also joined openly with others in urging defiance of the law where slavery was concerned. When war came, he confronted in his own mind the conflicting demands of his nonresistance peace principles and his equally ardent demand that slavery must be abolished. The end which he sought demanded wholly incompatible means, and he found no consistent solution to his dilemma. A bibliographical note names as principal sources the May Collection of Papers at Cornell University and specific contemporary newspapers.

G. H. G. Jones

841. Pease, William H. and Pease, Jane H. SAMUEL J. MAY: CIVIL LIBER-TARIAN. *Cornell Lib. J. 1967 3: 7-25.* Discusses Samuel Joseph May, the Unitarian clergyman and civil libertarian whose library provided the foundation for Cornell University's Antislavery Collection. Covering the years from 1832 to 1861, the authors examine May's belief in spiritual freedom as the basis of civil liberty. The minister's convictions led him to champion unpopular causes of his day, such as pacifism, women's rights, and abolitionism. May defended Prudence Crandall whose school for young ladies in Canterbury, Connecticut, was attacked by local citizenry when she accepted a student who was part Negro. From 1835, when May was General Agent for the Massachusetts Anti-Slavery Society, until the Rochester Convention of 1861, when antiabolitionists seized the hall reserved by him for the antislavery groups, May often faced angry and violent mobs. At times, he had doubts about the wisdom of provocation in emotional times. The authors found, however, that May never wavered in defending the principle of civil rights. Based on primary and secondary sources;32 notes.

M. M. Williamson

842. Peltier, David P. NINETEENTH CENTURY VOTING PATTERNS IN DELAWARE. *Delaware Hist. 1969 13(3): 219-233.* Traces voting patterns in Delaware counties from 1811. Party loyalties in Delaware were well defined by geography, and party strength in the various hundreds was largely determined by economics, geography, tradition, and local party organization. Patterns of voting behavior which emerged in the 1830's remained visible throughout the remainder of the century. Continuity of party strength was a basic political factor in most hundreds during the 19th century. Only the tariff and slavery issues between 1840 and 1860 resulted in any substantial shift in party loyalties. Based on the reported returns of each hundred published in newspapers; 2 maps, 28 notes.   R. M. Miller

843. Perry, Lewis. ADIN BALLOU'S HOPEDALE COMMUNITY AND THE THEOLOGY OF ANTISLAVERY. *Church Hist. 1970 39(3): 372-389.* Examines the assumption that abolition was in its inception a religious movement rather than simply a movement of religious origins. Analyzes the theology of Adin Augustus Ballou (1803-90), a prominent abolitionist, Universalist, and the leading spokesman for the Hopedale Community at Milford, Massachusetts. Ballou struggled with a central problem of antislavery thought, that of the apparent contradiction between the movement's anti-institutionalism and the need for concerted popular action against slavery. His solution, communitarian separateness, was institutionalized in Hopedale Community. Objecting to all forms of coercion as contrary to divine government, Ballou became a spokesman for the New England Non-Resistance Society and elaborated a defense of nonresistance and of antislavery. Human, coercive governments, he argued, may be necessary in the short-run because of man's sin, but the redeemed should advance on the earth a kingdom of peace and righteousness that could supersede all such governments. The regenerate will voluntarily perform all noncoercive good works of existing governments. At Hopedale Ballou held to his principles of nonresistance against the steady drift of the abolitionist movement toward the use of political and police force. He searched there to discover ways of life whereby the regenerate could progressively redeem the world and usher in the millennium. Adopting a typological approach to the study of the Bible, "an infallible directory of religious faith and practice,"Ballou viewed the millennium as a future still hidden except in outline. Hopedale, with its principles of nonresistance (including antislavery), was a "presage" of this ultimately regenerated society. 54 notes.
                                                                          S. C. Pearson, Jr.

844. Perry, Lewis. VERSIONS OF ANARCHISM IN THE ANTISLAVERY MOVEMENT. *Am. Q. 1968 20(4): 768-782.* Agrees with Leo Tolstoy's contention that William Lloyd Garrison and his followers were not merely anarchistic in addition to being antislavery, but anarchistic *because* they were opposed to slavery. Organizations such as the New England Non-Resistance Society revealed the Christian base of this type of anarchism. The Garrisonians essentially repudiated "no-governmentism" in favor of an antinomian attack on "human pretentions to govern." They revered the "higher law" kind of government, yet their understanding of government was paradoxically joined with a vigorous denunciation of all authoritarianism. Linked with the Garrisonian's passionate desire to end slavery was a desire to terminate all forms of coercion and a preference of

non-resistance to disunionism. "Come-outerism" comprized another form of anarchism. Nathaniel P. Rogers, one of "come-outerism's" chief spokesmen, moved from a branch of anarchism which was based on religious authority, to the final extreme of anarchism which would not accept any leadership. In their quest for the millennium, the anarchists seemed to settle on two alternatives: the Hopedale Community and the Liberty Party. Adin Ballou and others opted for communitarianism, but the bulk of the anarchists chose the Liberty Party as a vehicle to express God's sovereignty over them. 35 notes.   R. S. Pickett

845. Pettit, Arthur Gordon. MARK TWAIN, UNRECONSTRUCTED SOUTHERNER, AND HIS VIEW OF THE NEGRO, 1835-1860. *Rocky Mountain Social Sci. J. 1970 7(1): 17-27.* Examines the cultural climate of Samuel Clemens' early life and delineates the forces that contributed to racial views which neither Clemens the private citizen, nor Mark Twain the public man and writer, would ever discard completely. 21 notes.   R. F. Allen

846. Pickard, John B., ed. JOHN GREENLEAF WHITTIER AND THE ABOLITIONIST SCHISM OF 1840. *New England Q. 1964 37(2): 250-254.* The first publication of the full text of a Whittier letter to his sister in 1840. The editor considers the third paragraph of this letter as most significant in indicating Whittier's opinions about the meeting of the American Anti-Slavery Society in New York on 12 May 1840, when William Lloyd Garrison forced a split in the organization by having Abby Kelley nominated for the business committee of the society. Whittier's letter indicates his loss of patience with Garrison and his increasing weariness with the mechanics of the reform movement. He had avoided the New York meeting rather than be forced to oppose Garrison, although Whittier was among the opposition in advocation of open political action. In this 1840 letter, Whittier humorously pictures Abby Kelley as the predatory Eve-Delilah female successfully conquering the established male superiority, represented by Amos A. Phelps, vigorous opponent of Garrison's leadership, who was voted down by the convention. Based on a manuscript in the editor's possession; 9 notes.   R. V. Calvert

847. Plummer, Mark A. LINCOLN'S FIRST DIRECT REPLY TO DOUGLAS ON SQUATTER SOVEREIGNTY RECALLED. *Lincoln Herald 1969 71(1): 27-32.* Contains the text and an introductory analysis of a reminiscence by Brinton Webb Woodward of an exchange of speeches by Stephen A. Douglas and Abraham Lincoln in Bloomington, Illinois, on 26 September 1854. The subject was the Kansas-Nebraska Act. Brinton's reminiscences are found to be at variance on several points with reports of the events and speeches of that day in Bloomington published in Illinois newspapers shortly after the exchange occurred.   S. L. Jones

848. Porter, Dorothy B. ANTI-SLAVERY MOVEMENT IN NORTHAMPTON. *Negro Hist. Bull. 1960 24(2): 33-34 and 41.* Depicts Northampton, Massachusetts as a town containing few slaves in the colonial period and as an important antislavery center in the 19th century. Sojourner Truth, Charles C. Burleigh, David Lee Child and his wife Lydia Maria Child were among the

antislavery reformers residing there. Northampton was the scene of a number of antislavery conventions and tradition credits it with considerable underground railroad activity. Documented. L. Gara

849. Posey, Walter B. PRESBYTERIAN CHURCH INFLUENCE IN LOWER MISSISSIPPI VALLEY. *J. of the Presbyterian Hist. Soc. 1955 33(1): 35-50.* Examines the activities and attitudes of the Presbyterian Church in the Lower Mississippi Valley in the beginning of the 19th century. The church contributed to the establishment of law and order, took a lead in establishing educational facilities, and supported the antislavery movement. It also engaged in missionary activities among the Indians but did not protest against the Indians' removal from their own land. Based on church records and published sources. S

850. Posey, Walter B. THE BAPTISTS AND SLAVERY IN THE LOWER MISSISSIPPI VALLEY. *J. of Negro Hist. 1956 41(2): 117-130.* Surveys the attitudes of the Baptist Churches toward slavery. The Baptists, in keeping with the language of the entire South, were sometimes apologetic for the slavery system, then tacitly acknowledged it, and finally made a defense on scriptural grounds. With these attitudes, the separation from the Northern Baptist Brethren was inevitable and came about in 1845 when the Southern Baptist Convention was organized. Based on printed sources. W. E. Wight

851. Pressly, Thomas J. BULLETS AND BALLOTS: LINCOLN AND THE "RIGHT OF REVOLUTION." *Am. Hist. R. 1962 67(3): 647-662.* In the 1840's and early 1850's Lincoln upheld the "right of revolution," expecting to use the concept to advance the cause of national independence and aid the extension of democracy. However, in the context of the mob violence and slavery disputes of the late 1850's, he opposed the use of force to effect social change and supported legal and orderly pressure for change. His inaugural address viewed the right of revolution as a moral right to be exercised only when orderly constitutional procedures broke down. His message to Congress of 4 July 1861 marked a further advance in his thought, for he now argued that the southern revolt was morally unjustified, making it the duty of the majority to fight in order to preserve the system of constitutional democracy. Based on an analysis of Lincoln's collected writings. M. Berman

852. Purifoy, Lewis M. THE METHODIST ANTI-SLAVERY TRADITION, 1784-1844. *Methodist Hist. 1966 4(4): 3-16.* The founding conference of American Methodism in 1784 castigated the institution of slavery in harshest terms. Rules for freeing slaves were adopted, but unpopularity led to suspension within a year. In 1796 another attempt to outlaw slavery among Methodists was made, but gradually restrictions were removed. Not until 1860 did the Methodist Church return to the strong antislavery position of 1784. Moral purpose in this cause was too weak and conservative tendencies were too strong to permit positive action at an earlier time. The abolitionists did, however, grow strong enough to trouble consciences of enough people to make the slavery question an issue of

major concern by 1844 and to precipitate the split in the church. Based largely on Methodist publications and writings of or about Methodist leaders. 46 notes.
H. L. Calkin

853. Purifoy, Lewis M. THE SOUTHERN METHODIST CHURCH AND THE PROSLAVERY ARGUMENT. *J. of Southern Hist. 1966 32(3): 325-341.* From its establishment in 1845 to the Civil War, the Methodist Episcopal Church, South, sought to "wash its hands" of the slavery question. Although it never repealed the inherited rules saying that slavery was an evil in a state where it was possible to free slaves, its leaders affirmed that slavery was sanctioned by Holy Scripture and thus was no sin, that it was a matter of state concern and none of the church's business. The view might have brought comfort and security had it been truly accepted, but the fury of Southern Methodist assault upon slavery's detractors gave proof that it was not accepted. Southern Methodists therefore came to the defense of the state, into whose hands the issue was supposed to have been committed, and the church thus became the most flagrant offender against its own precept that the strictest separation between political and ecclesiastical matters must be maintained. In the process of defending this very position, the church ended by subjecting itself completely to the state and identifying what was right and Christian with what was southern. Based largely on search through Methodist periodicals of the era.   S. E. Humphreys

854. Quarles, Benjamin. FREDERICK DOUGLASS: BRIDGE-BUILDER IN HUMAN RELATIONS. *Negro Hist. Bull. 1966 29(5): 99-100, 112.* Born a slave in Maryland, Douglass became one of the chief spokesmen of his day for the abolitionist movement. In 1845 he published his *Narrative of the Life of Frederick Douglass,* which became a best seller and was translated into French and German. His weekly newspaper, *The North Star,* began on 3 December 1847 and carried on its masthead the words "Right is of no sex." He held three Federal appointments: Marshal of the District of Columbia, Recorder of Deeds for the District, and U.S. Minister to Haiti. On 18 October 1965, the Commissioners of the District of Columbia dedicated a memorial bridge named in honor of the man who was himself a bridge-builder in human relations - between slavery and freedom, between Negroes and whites, and between struggle and success. 3 photos.   D. D. Cameron

855. Ratner, Lorman. NORTHERN CONCERN FOR SOCIAL ORDER AS CAUSE FOR REJECTING ANTI-SLAVERY, 1831-1840. *Historian 1965 28(1): 1-18.* Demonstrates the hypothesis that "in the 1830's a deep-rooted concern for social order explains at least in part the overwhelming rejection by many Northerners of anti-slavery," largely because of northern unpreparedness to face the task of ending slavery and its proud refusal to consider the problem with which the abolitionists confronted the Nation. Based on published sources and on the author's unpublished master's essay, "Anti-masonry in New York, An Aspect of Pre-Civil War Reform" (Cornell University, 1958) and his unpublished doctoral dissertation, "Northern Opposition to the Anti-Slavery Movement, 1831-1840" (Cornell University, 1961).   Sr. M. McAuley

856. Rawley, James A. JOSEPH JOHN GURNEY'S MISSION TO AMERICA, 1837-1840. *Mississippi Valley Hist. R. 1962 49(4): 653-674.* A close tie existed between English and American humanitarians. Joseph J. Gurney, English philanthropist and humanitarian, toured North America and the West Indies. Young America impressed Gurney. Judged by other British tourists, Gurney's approval of American civilization marked him as one of the more tolerant visitors. He inspired the American Quakers and gave a push to the abolitionist movement.

G. M. Gressley

857. Abbott, Richard H. YANKEE FARMERS IN NORTHERN VIRGINIA, 1840-1860. *Virginia Mag. of Hist. and Biog. 1968 76(1): 56-63.* Various groups of northern farmers were encouraged to settle in northern Virginia. However, when their notable success in revitalizing the abandoned tobacco and timber lands was used by abolitionists to attack slavery, the promoters lost interest. Based on contemporary newspapers and periodicals; 20 notes.

K. J. Bauer

858. Reardon, William R. and Foxen, John. THE PROPAGANDA PLAY. *Civil War Hist. 1955 1(3): 281-293.* After defining the term propaganda play, the authors use *Uncle Tom's Cabin,* the first effective propaganda play; *Bury the Dead, Waiting for Lefty;* and *One-Third of a Nation* "to clarify the form and end of the propaganda play."

W. E. Wight

859. Resh, Richard W. ALEXIS DE TOCQUEVILLE AND THE NEGRO: DEMOCRACY IN AMERICA RECONSIDERED. *J. of Negro Hist. 1963 48(4): 251-259.* After examining 35 travel accounts describing life in the United States between 1820 and 1832, the author concluded that many contemporary observers differed with Alexis de Tocqueville on slavery and the Negro. Like Tocqueville, the other writers recognized the danger that slavery posed to the Union and the unhappy lot of free Negroes in the North. Unlike Tocqueville, a number of the others rejected a concept of racial inferiority and recognized the exploitation of the slave system. Tocqueville's emphasis on theoretical social injustice contributed to his oversight of the plight of the individual Negro. Documented.

L. Gara

860. Richardson, Mary L. THE HISTORICAL AUTHENTICITY OF JOHN BROWN'S RAID IN STEPHEN VINCENT BENET'S "JOHN BROWN'S BODY." *West Virginia Hist. 1963 24(2): 168-175.* A comparison of the historical accuracy of John Brown's raid at Harpers Ferry as told by Benet with that of other historical accounts available.

M. M. Kanin

861. Riegel, Robert E. ABBY KELLEY. *New-England Galaxy 1965 6(4): 21-26.* Despite her abilities and good looks, Abby Kelley suffered as an extreme and doctrinaire abolitionist in a New England that was still marked by strong proslavery sentiment. In 1837 she decided to desert the comparative safety of teaching in order to devote all her efforts to freedom for the American Negro. After her

marriage in 1841 to Stephen Symonds Foster, a coworker for the cause, their home was a well-known station on the underground railroad. Abby was typical of the New England intellectuals who worked for reforms that would benefit others. On this basis she was an important factor in the ultimate success of the movement to free the slave. Illus.   E. P. Stickney

862. Roark, James L. GEORGE W. JULIAN: RADICAL LAND RE-FORMER. *Indiana Mag. of Hist. 1968 64(1): 25-38.* Describes the place of land reform in the public career of one of the best known abolitionists. Julian (1817-99) throughout his long political career sought to create in mid-19th-century America a nation of small landholders on the Jeffersonian model. He supported the Homestead bill in 1851. He linked land reform in the post-Civil War South to achievement of equitable relations for Negroes. In 1864 Julian proposed a major law that would confiscate land in the South and reallocate that land to Negroes and former Union soldiers. Following the defeat of that bill and of radical Reconstruction, Julian continued agitation for land reform in the Far West.   J. Findlay

863. Robertson, James I., Jr. THE BOOK THAT ENRAGED THE SOUTH. *Civil War Times Illus. 1969 7(9): 20-22.* Discusses the effects of the book, *The Impending Crisis of the South: How to Meet It,* by Hinton Rowan Helper (1829-1909). The book (1857) was the most damaging study of slavery after the publication of Harriet Elizabeth Beecher Stowe's *Uncle Tom's Cabin* (1852). Helper blamed the backwardness of the South on slaveowners and the slave system. He believed that the South was constantly falling behind the North in trade, business, culture, and society because of the single deterrent of slavery. Ironically, avid antislaveryites and Republicans passionately embraced Helper's book even though Helper himself was an expulsionistic Negrophobe. He hated slavery because he hated Negroes.   R. N. Alvis

864. Rogers, Tommy W. DR. FREDERICK A. ROSS AND THE PRES-BYTERIAN DEFENSE OF SLAVERY. *J. of Presbyterian Hist. 1967 45(2): 112-124.* Sketches the career and proslavery ideas of Frederick A. Ross. The son of a wealthy Virginia businessman, Ross settled in Tennessee where he bought a plantation and erected a fine home. After being converted by a Presbyterian pastor he was licensed to preach in 1825. He donated the Presbyterian Church in Kingsport, Tennessee, and regularly preached there without compensation. Upon suffering loss of his entire estate in 1850 Ross turned to the ministry as a source of income. He became pastor in Huntsville, Alabama, in 1853 and there published *Slavery Ordained of God* in 1857. He subscribed to the standard proslavery argument that slavery is biblically defensible and not itself a sin, but, unlike many advocates of slavery, he felt that discussion of the issue was beneficial in arresting the course of emancipation. When the General Assembly of the Presbyterian Church (New School) repudiated the biblical justification of slavery in 1857 Ross became active in the southern schism. Based on published sources and a manuscript autobiography; 55 notes.   S. C. Pearson, Jr.

865. Rogers, Tommy W. FREDERICK A. ROSS: HUNTSVILLE'S BELLIG-ERENT CLERGYMAN. *Alabama R. 1969 22(1): 53-67.* Sketch of Ross, pastor

of the Presbyterian Church, Huntsville, during most of the 1850's, arch defender of slavery, author of *Slavery Ordained of God* (1857), and proponent of southern nationalism during the Civil War. 46 notes.   D. F. Henderson

866. Roppolo, Joseph P. UNCLE TOM IN NEW ORLEANS: THREE LOST PLAYS. *New England Q. 1954 27(2): 213-226.* Discovers pro-Southern stage versions of *Uncle Tom's Cabin* in contemporary newspaper accounts. While New Orleans was angered by Mrs. Stowe's novel and the northern stage adaptations, the character of Uncle Tom was taken over as counterpropaganda. These plays were ineffective answers to the novel, however, and only served to emphasize the lines of division. Only the character of Uncle Tom himself, it appeared, could pass between the two regions as common currency.   D. Davis

867. Rose, Alan. THE IMAGE OF THE NEGRO IN THE PRE-CIVIL-WAR NOVELS OF JOHN PENDLETON KENNEDY AND WILLIAM GIL-MORE SIMMS. *J. of Am. Studies [Great Britain] 1971 4(2): 217-226.* Examines novels published before 1856 by two southern writers. Kennedy (1795-1870) and Simms (1806-70) were devoted to picturing favorably the society of the slaveholders; accordingly, they reacted as tension grew over the slavery issue before the Civil War. Their portrayal of Negroes, once totally benevolent, shifted with the growing social tensions to the point that Kennedy and Simms wrote about the "demonic malevolence of the Negro horde." They turned finally to themes of white invincibility, white suppression of Negroes, and the triumph of the slaveholding society. The image of Negroes then became that of an emasculated servant relegated to "harmless domesticity." Based on novels by Simms and Kennedy; 6 notes.   H. T. Lovin

868. Rosenberg, Norman L. PERSONAL LIBERTY LAWS AND SECTIONAL CRISIS: 1850-1861. *Civil War Hist. 1971 17(1): 25-44.* Surveys "personal liberty" legislation from the *Prigg v. Pennsylvania* (1842) case through the secession winter of 1860-61. The laws came in two big waves, the first following the Prigg ruling, which encouraged States not to assist Federal enforcement of the 1793 Fugitive Slave Law, and the second following the Kansas-Nebraska Act in 1854, which destroyed a three-year truce on the fugitive slave controversy. Personal liberty laws were important not for the help they gave runaway slaves but for their value as symbols to both sections. To the North, they represented a protest against the violation of individual liberties of black Americans; to the South, they represented northern defiance of constitutional obligations. Based on primary and secondary sources.   E. C. Murdock

869. Ruchames, Louis. PARALLELS OF JEWISH AND NEGRO HISTORY. *Negro Hist. Bull. 1955 19(3): 63-64, 66.* Discusses the role of American Jews in the abolitionist movement, their struggle for political and social equality, and their defense of free speech. Includes an appeal for continued extension of the rights of minorities in the United States.   L. Gara

870. Ruchames, Louis. RACE, MARRIAGE AND ABOLITION IN MASSA-CHUSETTS. *J. of Negro Hist. 1955 40(3): 250-273.* Describes the campaign by Massachusetts abolitionists to eliminate segregation and to assure equality of status for the Negro in marriage. The bill of 1705, forbidding mixed marriages, remained publicly unchallenged until William Lloyd Garrison and John P. Bigelow attacked it in 1831. Abolitionist agitation for its repeal reached a climax in 1840, but success was not achieved until 1843, following a Whig defeat and a Democratic victory in the election of 1842.   C. F. Latour

871. Ruchames, Louis. WILLIAM LLOYD GARRISON AND THE NEGRO FRANCHISE. *J. of Negro Hist. 1965 50(1): 37-49.* Rebuts the idea that William Lloyd Garrison was solely concerned with abolition and refused to support the cause of Negro suffrage after emancipation. Garrison felt very strongly that the cause of freedom for Negroes required Lincoln's victory at the polls in 1864 and he defended and explained the administration's attitude toward Negro suffrage. At no time did he reject the idea of Negro suffrage and after Lincoln's assassination he devoted much space in the *Liberator* to demands for it and other civil rights for colored Americans. Documented.   L. Gara

872. Rudolph, Frederick. STRADDLING THE LOG: MARK HOPKINS AND SLAVERY. *New England Social Studies Bull. 1959 16(2): 6-10.* Describes Hopkins' refusal to adopt an unequivocal stand in favor of abolition until after the beginning of the Civil War, and asserts that he thus "mirrored the view of his region and of the solid middle class," demanding "a fundamental regeneration of men before there could be a regeneration of society."   W. D. Metz

873. Russel, Robert R. WHAT WAS THE COMPROMISE OF 1850? *J. of Southern Hist. 1956 22(3): 292-309.* The author illustrates the lack of agreement on the provisions of the New Mexico and Utah Territorial Acts relating to slavery, from 22 college textbooks which give 12 substantially different descriptions of these provisions. He summarizes the slavery provisions and their intent and discusses them from the viewpoints of the proslavery and antislavery groups and the concessions of each.   R. Kerley

874. Russell, Robert G. PRELUDE TO THE PRESIDENCY: THE ELECTION OF ANDREW JOHNSON TO THE SENATE. *Tennessee Hist. Q. 1967 26(2): 148-176.* A discussion of Johnson's campaign for the Senate in 1856. The probability of a Democratic victory convinced him that it would be wise to resign the Tennessee governorship to make the race. He was supported by the rank and file but the party leadership had been antagonized by his opposition to aristocracy and to slavery. Johnson had to use political chicanery and to support his party enemies to insure his own election by the legislature. Democratic victories at the polls insured his election although there was some interparty opposition. Johnson's forces were even able to elect a successor for John Bell, whose Senate term was not to expire for two more years but before the next State legislative session. Johnson had set the course which he hoped would lead him to the Vice Presidency and, eventually, the Presidency. Documented, 129 notes.   C. F. Ogilvie

875. Russell, Robert R. CONSTITUTIONAL DOCTRINES WITH REGARD TO SLAVERY IN TERRITORIES. *J. of Southern Hist. 1966 32(4): 466-486.* Discusses four doctrines held and argued in the years before the Civil War regarding slavery in the territories: 1) the traditional and early prevailing view that Congress had complete or almost complete legislative power in the territories; 2) the Free Soil doctrine that the fifth amendment prohibited slavery in territories; 3) the Calhoun doctrine of "nonintervention" that the Federal Government in the territories was only the trustee or agent of the several sovereign States, obliged not to discriminate among the States and hence incapable of forbidding the bringing into any territory of anything that was legal property in any State, and 4) the Cass or "squatter sovereignty" doctrine, later accepted by Douglas, that the residents of territories had the right to decide for themselves. These four doctrines are discussed in terms of the Dred Scott decision and the 1860 party platforms. 46 notes. S. E. Humphreys

876. Russell, Robert Royal. THE ISSUES IN THE CONGRESSIONAL STRUGGLE OVER THE KANSAS-NEBRASKA BILL, 1854. *J. of Southern Hist. 1963 29(2): 187-210.* Although public lands policy, Indian policy, and railroad routes were involved in the struggle over the Kansas-Nebraska Bill, not more than five votes in the two houses of Congress combined were turned on the final vote by anything but the slavery issue. The slavery provisions were a compromise hammered out with great difficulty between a majority of Northern Democrats and nearly all southern members, Democratic and Whig. The Northern Democrats made great sacrifices of interests and principles and personal political advantage for the sake of party unity and sectional accommodation. The bill nevertheless fell short of meeting what the great majority of southern congressmen thought were the South's just demands. Based chiefly on congressional debates. S. E. Humphreys

877. Ryon, Roderick N. MORAL REFORM AND DEMOCRATIC POLITICS: THE DILEMMA OF ROBERTS VAUX. *Quaker Hist. 1970 59(1): 3-14.* Vaux, a wealthy, aristocratic Quaker, organized, spoke, and wrote against slavery and liquor, and for solitary confinement of convicts, free public schools, schools for defectives and delinquents, and the glorifying of Pennsylvania's bucolic, colonial, Quaker past. Opposed to universal suffrage and suspicious of politicians, he was forced to appeal for State support of reform because private aid fell short. After 1828 he felt that reformers had failed to change public opinion and joined the Jacksonians, becoming "The chief casualty of the Bank War in Philadelphia," shorn of institutional offices, and bewildered by partisanship. T. D. S. Bassett

878. Sahli, John R. THE SLAVERY ISSUE IN EARLY GEOGRAPHY TEXTBOOKS. *Hist. of Educ. Q. 1963 3(3): 153-158.* The author finds that American geography textbooks published before 1830 take a definite antislavery stand. By 1860 this sentiment had disappeared probably, he feels, because writers were anxious to have their books bought in the South. J. Herbst

879. Saitō, Makoto. J. C. KARUFŪN NI OKERU NASHONARIZUMU TO SEKUSHONARIZUMU [Nationalism and sectionalism in J. C. Calhoun]. *Kokka Gakkai Zasshi [Japan] 1961 74(11/12): 539-557, and 1962 75(1/2): 42-67. Parts 1 and 2.* Doubts whether nationalism and sectionalism in John Caldwell Calhoun should be treated as contradictions. The author intends through a study of Calhoun to explain the relationship between nationalism and sectionalism in American political history. When Calhoun acted as a nationalist in the War of 1812, he was fully aware of the interests of the section which he represented, the South characterized by the slave plantation. Calhoun could assert the interests of other sections and could thus act nationalistically, because his native state was also composed of several sections and his political behavior in his state was intersectional in miniature.   T. Miyake

880. Schapsmeier, Edward L. and Schapsmeier, Frederick H. LINCOLN AND DOUGLAS: THEIR VERSIONS OF THE WEST. *J. of the West 1968 7(4): 542-552.* Although very similar in their desire to remove the roadblock of slavery from the path of American development, the two men's enunciations of their ideal for the West were quite different. Douglas took the approach of popular sovereignty with the belief that the West would not choose to have slavery in the States which would be created there. Lincoln appealed to the "higher law" and took the approach that slavery could not be permitted in the West. They were both dedicated to the preservation of the Union and, had it not been for Douglas' untimely death, he might have been able to serve Lincoln and the Nation in that preservation.   R. N. Alvis

881. Schmidhauser, John R. JUDICIAL BEHAVIOR AND THE SECTIONAL CRISIS OF 1837-1860. *J. of Pol. 1961 23(4): 615-640.* A study of the relationship of the political and regional background of justices to decisionmaking during the sectional crisis which preceded the American Civil War. Supreme Court voting divisions involving slavery, the scope of the commerce clause, and the status of corporations were sectional. The 16 justices who participated in these decisions during the period 1837-60 generally divided on regional and party lines. Several exceptions, including Chief Justice Taney, exhibited a strong sense of institutional responsibility. Based on Supreme Court decisions, biographies, and secondary historical sources.   A

882. Schnell, Kempes. ANTI-SLAVERY INFLUENCES ON THE STATUS OF SLAVES IN A FREE STATE. *J. of Negro Hist. 1965 50(4): 257-273.* Prior to 1836 the courts of the northern border States protected the property claims of slaveholders traveling through or sojourning within their borders. Likewise, most of the slave States recognized the freedom of slaves granted by northern legal action. After 1836 abolitionist influence led northern courts gradually to reject all claims to slave property and northern legislatures to repeal sojourner protection laws. Most Southern States reacted by enacting laws forbidding free people of color to enter the States. Although the question affected relatively few individuals, it did symbolize a marked decline in mutual trust between the sections and a heightening of tension.   L. Gara

883. Schriver, Edward O. ANTISLAVERY: THE FREE SOIL AND FREE DEMOCRATIC PARTIES IN MAINE, 1848-1853. *New England Q. 1969 42(1): 82-94.* In 1848, leading Liberty Party men formed the Free Soil Party, which was united on two major principles - opposition to the extension of slavery and temperance reform. Changing its name to the Free Democracy Party in 1853, the group employed a newspaper, *The Portland Inquirer,* and State conventions to spread its message. It was not successful politically, never getting more than 14 percent of the total vote. However, it did elect some members to the State legislature and was able to combine with Whigs to elect Isaac Reed to the Congress. In 1855 they cooperated with some dissident Democrats and antislavery Whigs to elect Anson Peaslee Morrill to the Senate, a move that presaged the organization of the Maine Republican Party. 40 notes. K. B. West

884. Schwartz, Harold. FUGITIVE SLAVE DAYS IN BOSTON. *New England Q. 1954 27(2): 191-212.* Furnishes a picture of morally indignant Boston after the Fugitive Slave Law. Deeply aware of their history of resisting tyranny, Bostonians regarded the law as illegal and as an echo of British legislative oppression. However, in specific instances, they were inexperienced in extra-legal work before the Burns case. After 1854 the Vigilance Committee grew in power and effectiveness. The Fugitive Slave Law was nullified in Boston. Based largely on newspaper accounts and correspondence. D. Davis

885. Scott, Virginia. AN EARLY EPISODE OF BLACK RESISTANCE. *Pan-African J. 1970 3(3): 203-208.* There has been a century-long struggle by oppressed peoples to free themselves of Western control. An early instance of black resistance to slavery in the United States is presented in Harriet Beecher Stowe's novel *Dred* (1856). At the time of publication this book was almost as popular as *Uncle Tom's Cabin,* but it has since been relegated to obscurity by racist whites. The black rebel Dred is the most forceful figure in the abolitionist fiction of the 1850's. Mrs. Beecher authenticated her portrayal of Dred by invoking *The Confessions of Nat Turner,* in which he reveals that one of his chief followers was named Dred. Dred was the son of Denmark Vesey and an enslaved Mandingo woman. Early in youth he escaped from slavery to dwell in swamps along the southeast Atlantic shore where he led armed maroons until he was cut down in South Carolina's Great Dismal. E. E. Beauregard

886. Sevitch, Benjamin. THE WELL-PLANNED RIOT OF OCTOBER 21, 1835: UTICA'S ANSWER TO ABOLITIONISM. *New York Hist. 1969 50(3): 251-263.* Utica, New York, had traditionally been friendly to the cause of abolitionism, but in the mid-1830's fears of race amalgamation produced a general reaction against abolition and abolitionists. Utica was no exception to this rule, for on 21 October 1835 a mob led by Congressman Samuel Beardsley forceably broke up the New York State abolitionist convention and ransacked the offices of the *Utica Standard and Democrat.* The mob action had been carefully planned some four days earlier and had the support of Utica's leading citizens and elected officials. Based on primary and secondary sources; 3 illus., 51 notes. G. Kurland

887. Sewell, Richard H. JOHN P. HALE AND THE LIBERTY PARTY, 1847-1848. *New England Q. 1964 37(2): 200-223.* Serving as a Democratic Congressman from New Hampshire, John Parker Hale had publicly denounced the annexation of Texas in 1845 and proceeded to muster support of enough Independent Democrats, Whigs, and Liberty Party men to become, three years later, the first outspoken antislavery advocate elected to the Senate. Considering Hale's abolitionism moderate enough to attract men of antislavery principles away from the major parties, Liberty Party men began to consider him as a desirable presidential candidate possibility in 1846. Hale tardily and reluctantly accepted the Liberty Party nomination in January 1848, realizing that he might be throwing away his chances of nomination by a larger antislavery alliance later in the year. Despite Hale's broad popularity, Liberty Party leaders struck a bargain with the Barnburners, agreeing to back Martin Van Buren's nomination in return for Barnburner support of a "thorough Liberty platform," although most Liberty men were aware that the Van Buren advocates had no strong hatred of slavery. Hale worked hard to help the showing of the Free Soilers in the November election, and their strength at the polls was almost five times that of the Liberty Party in the 1844 election. Based partly on unpublished letters and diaries; 69 notes.   R. V. Calvert

888. Sheeler, J. Reuben. JOHN BROWN: A CENTURY LATER. *Negro Hist. Bull. 1960 24(1): 7-10, 15.* Depicts John Brown as a martyr to the causes of abolition of slavery and freedom for the economically oppressed classes. The author suggests that the same spirit that motivated John Brown also motivated various economic reformers and labor leaders after the Civil War and is a force today in the leaders opposing various forms of racial discrimination. Based on secondary material.   L. Gara

889. Sheeler, J. Reuben. THE SIGNIFICANCE OF ABRAHAM LINCOLN TO THE NEGRO. *Negro Hist. Bull. 1959 23(3): 57-59.* Depicts Lincoln as a practical and realistic political leader whose concept of democracy included freedom for the Negro.   L. Gara

890. Sherwin, Oscar. OF MARTYR BUILD: THEODORE PARKER. *Phylon 1959 20(2): 143-148.* A study of the Boston preacher Theodore Parker (1810-60) and what he stood for. The author deals with his liberal interpretation of Christianity, his simple and earnest preaching, his interest in the burning questions of social reform - intemperance, ignorance, the wrongs of woman, war, political corruption, and above all, slavery - the vilification he met with, and the courage he demonstrated. Based on biographies, historical works of the period and the *Liberator.*   A

891. Lanzinger, Klaus. UNTERSCHIEDE IM GEBRAUCH VON "SLAVE," SEINER WORTFAMILIE UND SEINER SINNVERWANDTEN IN DEN NORD- UND SÜD STAATEN VOR DEM BÜRGERKRIEG [Differences in the use of "slave," its family of words, and its synonymity in the northern and southern States before the Civil War]. *Jahrbuch für Amerikastudien [West Germany] 1962 7: 92-105.* Using the journal *The Pennsylvania Freeman*

and some Georgia "Plantation Books" the author traces the development and usages of the word "slave" and its compounds in America up to the 1860's as a supplement to sociological and historical scholarship.   G. Bassler

892. Short, Kenneth R. M. ENGLISH BAPTISTS AND AMERICAN SLAV-ERY. *Baptist Q. [Great Britain] 1964 20(6): 243-262.* Reviews relations between English and American Baptists, 1833-41, as they were affected by the abolition controversy. The English were concerned with pressing the Americans to take a stand for abolition in a letter in 1833 and through representatives sent to the Triennial Convention of 1835. The author discusses the representatives' problem in attempting to make their supporters in England understand that such a stand could not be taken by the Triennial Convention because of southern opposition to abolition. He points out the lack of understanding in regard to the effect of the American problem of abolition on the Baptists and how the issue would affect their national organization were it brought up by the English representatives.
E. E. Eminhizer

893. Shortreed, Margaret. THE ANTISLAVERY RADICALS: FROM CRU-SADE TO REVOLUTION 1840-1868. *Past and Present 1959 (16): 65-87.* An account of the ideas and objections of the Radical Republicans in the U.S. Congress prior to the beginning of Reconstruction. Their contribution to an-tisouthern thought and policy is outlined.   A. W. Coats

894. Sides, Sudie Duncan. SOUTHERN WOMEN AND SLAVERY. *Hist. To-day [Great Britain] 1970 20(1): 54-60, 20(2): 124-130.* Part I. Studies the attitudes of southern women toward slavery from 1810 to 1860. Reveals a picture "of squalor, discontent, annoyance, frustration, bitterness, self-pity." Women were continually wrapped up in racial problems they did not understand and did not want. Slavery was a white male policy foisted and imposed on an unwilling white female sex. Women, however, made little attempt to examine the deeper issues. Based on selected published letters and diaries; illus. Part II. The opinions of southern women toward slavery changed strongly after the Civil War. Slavery was thought a positive good for Negroes, and often a great hardship to white women. Slavery symbolized all the beauties of the past, the romantic past of the patriarchal society that was characterized by trust, tender affection, and provi-dence. White woman had come to reject the facts and reality of life, and a simple racist mentality permeated her attitudes and beliefs. Based on contemporary diaries, chronicles, memorials, and recollections; illus.   L. A. Knafla

895. Silbey, Joel H. THE SLAVERY-EXTENSION CONTROVERSY AND ILLINOIS CONGRESSMEN, 1846-50. *J. of the Illinois State Hist. Soc. 1965 58(4): 378-395.* Revisionist interpretation criticizes American historians for over-emphasizing and distorting pre-Civil War antislavery sentiment. Analysis of the political behavior of Illinois congressmen reveals that they refused to think and act in sectional terms despite the increasing bitterness over slavery. Some consis-tently supported one position or another, while others voted in no consistent

pattern. The Wilmot Proviso was appended to many bills, so they were frequently called upon to react to the issue. On other problems, such as internal improvements, tariff, and land policy, their voting was divided, usually along party lines. The author concludes that the differences among Illinois congressmen can be explained by the nature of national politics. At this level, other issues were considered more important than slavery extension; and there was a fear that absorption in the slavery question would threaten the success of other policies. Illus., 45 notes. D. L. Smith

896. Simkins, Francis B. ROBERT LEWIS DABNEY, SOUTHERN CONSERVATIVE. *Georgia R. 1964 18(4): 393-407.* Robert Lewis Dabney was a Virginia Presbyterian minister and a true southerner with strong antebellum conservative views. He deplored the action of the abolitionists and took a strong stand in justifying slavery by using the Bible scriptures. Under his leadership sectional reunion in the church was blocked during Reconstruction. H. G. Earnhart

897. Simon, Donald E. BROOKLYN IN THE ELECTION OF 1860. *New-York Hist. Soc. Q. 1967 51(3): 249-262.* In the election of 1860 Abraham Lincoln was unable to carry the city of Brooklyn. The campaign in the city centered on the issue of slavery with a majority of the voters apparently opposed to abolition. Victory for the Democrats was possible by fusion of anti-Negro sentiment (40 percent of the population was foreignborn), those fearful of the effect of a Republican victory on business, and those opposed to any interference with property. The result was an indication of the effect of urban conditions on political behavior. Based on newspapers and secondary sources; 5 illus., 31 notes. C. L. Grant

898. Simpson, Eleanor E. MELVILLE AND THE NEGRO: FROM "TYPEE" TO "BENITO CERENO." *Am. Literature 1969 41(1): 19-38.* Traces Herman Melville's attitudes toward Negroes in the light of literary conventions and, more importantly, thematic and artistic demands in *Moby Dick* and "Benito Cereno." R. S. Burns

899. Skelton, Lynda Worley. THE STATES RIGHTS MOVEMENT IN GEORGIA, 1825-1850. *Georgia Hist. Q. 1966 50(4): 391-412.* Analyzes the movement in Georgia as it was reflected in politics and related to matters such as Indian affairs, tariff policy, expansion, the U.S. Bank, slavery, and so forth. In almost every instance the doctrine was used in defense of economic interests and in no instance was it projected on a moral level. R. Lowitt

900. Skotheim, Robert Allen. A NOTE ON HISTORICAL METHOD: DAVID DONALD'S "TOWARD A RECONSIDERATION OF ABOLITIONISTS." *J. of Southern Hist. 1959 25(3): 356-365.* Considers an essay published in David Herbert Donald's, *Lincoln Reconsidered. Essays on the Civil War Era* (New York, 1956), which poses the question why the movement for immediate abolition of slavery emerged in the United States during the 1830's. Donald suggested the "status revolution" as the basic explanation and supported his social interpreta-

tion by a study of 106 leaders in the abolition movement. The author criticizes Donald's clarity; he also finds fault with the methodology, which he says is crucial to the validity of the entire thesis. For one thing, he finds that Donald concluded that abolition was a rural movement because only 12 percent of the leaders were born in cities. At the time of their birth, says his critic, only six percent of the U.S. population lived in cities; hence abolitionism could be argued to have been more urban than the nation as a whole.   S. E. Humphreys

901. Smiley, David L. CASSIUS M. CLAY AND JOHN G. FEE: A STUDY IN SOUTHERN ANTI-SLAVERY THOUGHT. *J. of Negro Hist. 1957 42(3): 201-213.* Referring to Cassius Marcellus Clay, Kentucky politician, and John G. Fee, Kentucky minister, the author demonstrates that the crusade against slavery was not carried by a homogeneous group of agitators, and also that it was not merely a religious movement for the moral reform of slaveholders. Clay was an advocate of free white labor and of an industrial economy, while Fee was a proponent of freedom, based on "the higher law," for an oppressed class. They thus reveal the division which weakened the emancipation effort.

W. E. Wight

902. Smith, Ellwood K. BACKGROUND AND CONSEQUENCE OF METHODIST UNION. *Methodist Hist. 1964 2(2): 1-30.* The questions of authority and race figured prominently in the debates and division of Methodism in the 18th and 19th centuries. They required serious attention as the Methodist Episcopal Church, the Methodist Episcopal Church, South, and the Methodist Protestant Church moved toward union in 1939. The causes, the background, and the actions leading to splits in the Methodist Episcopal Church in 1828 and 1844 are discussed. Numerous commissions were appointed, conferences held, proposals for union made and compromises suggested prior to acceptance by all three branches. 87 notes.   H. L. Calkin

903. Smith, Elwyn A. THE ROLE OF THE SOUTH IN THE PRESBYTERIAN SCHISM OF 1837-1838. *Church Hist. 1960 29(1): 44-63.* Demonstrates that doctrinal issues, not the slavery question, caused the schism, which after 1831 had been inevitable. Abolition was excluded from consideration in the General Assembly, and even without the South, the division would have occurred. The southern support of the Old School gave that group the victory in the 1830's. The sectional issue did not arise until the eve of the Civil War.

E. Oberholzer, Jr.

904. Smith, Harmon L. WILLIAM CAPERS AND WILLIAM A. SMITH, NEGLECTED ADVOCATES OF THE PRO-SLAVERY MORAL ARGUMENT. *Methodist Hist. 1964 31(1): 23-32.* William Capers of South Carolina and William Andrew Smith of Virginia were two clergymen from the Methodist Episcopal Church, South, who rose to repel the threat of abolition. Smith used a philosophical argument, supported by Scripture, which he applied to various contemporary associations such as church and state, master and slave. Capers devoted his energies to editorializing from a "firm Scriptural basis" on the

church-state relationahip as it pertained to slavery. There was an obvious parallel between John Calhoun's political thought and that of Capers and Smith, namely, the tenet of slavery as a positive good.   H. L. Calkin

905. Smith, James M. THE "SEPARATE BUT EQUAL" DOCTRINE: AN ABOLITIONIST DISCUSSES RACIAL SEGREGATION AND EDUCATIONAL POLICY DURING THE CIVIL WAR. *J. of Negro Hist. 1956 41(2): 138-147.* In a letter of a leading abolitionist written in 1864, the author finds an eloquent discussion, from the abolitionist viewpoint, of educational policy and the rights of a minority group four years before the adoption of the 14th Amendment. The general attack on separate educational facilities is held to parallel closely the line of reasoning of Chief Justice Warren and his fellow justices in repudiating the legalization of the prejudice of color.   W. E. Wight

906. Smith, Robert C. LIBERTY DISPLAYING THE ARTS AND SCIENCES: A PHILADELPHIA ALLEGORY BY SAMUEL JENNINGS. *Winterthur Portfolio 1965 2: 85-105.* Samuel Jennings, a Philadelphia painter who resided in London, in 1790 proposed to give a painting to the Philadelphia Library Company. Jennings' painting shows Liberty in the pose of a Yankee teacher with books in her hand, before a group of Negroes. The painting may well be the first one illustrating the rights of Negroes in America. The founders of the Library Company were involved in the early abolitionist movement; they suggested the topic for the painting. The original work was done in 1792 and was followed by a smaller version, the only difference being the inclusion of the British shield next to Liberty. Although the painting may not be great art, it is one of the first allegorical subjects executed by an American artist, and the first with an abolitionist message. Based on primary and secondary sources; 13 photos, 68 notes.   N. A. Kuntz

907. Smith, Robert P. WILLIAM COOPER NELL: CRUSADING BLACK ABOLITIONIST. *J. of Negro Hist. 1970 55(3): 182-199.* The antislavery movement had several outstanding Negroes that figured prominently in the abolitionist crusade. One of the most important though little known figures was William Cooper Nell, who engaged in journalism, lecturing, black conventions, history writing, and politics. Part of the reason for his eclipse was due to the fact that he lived and worked during the same period as Frederick Douglass. Like Douglass, Nell continued to work with the Garrisonians, even after the abolitionist movement began to split apart in the 1830's. Unlike Douglass, however, Nell always championed full integration and higher education for the Negro,and ardently fought Douglass on these points, for which Douglass bitterly attacked him as a "contemptible tool." Based mostly on primary sources; 75 notes.   R. S. Melamed

908. Smith, Warren Sylvester. "THE IMPERCEPTIBLE ARROWS OF QUAKERISM": MONCURE CONWAY AT SANDY SPRING. *Quaker Hist. 1963 52(1): 19-26.* In his early circuit-riding days the young Methodist preacher Conway stopped at Sandy Spring, Maryland where there was a meeting of Hicksite Quakers. His first visit impressed him so greatly that he was drawn back

repeatedly. This connection led to his separation from Methodism and entrance into Unitarianism. Though a Virginian, he became committed to a vigorous abolitionist view. Later he filled the pulpit of South Place Chapel in London for two decades. He had gone to London at the beginning of the Civil War to enlist support for northern abolitionists, although he regarded himself as a pacifist. 4 notes.   E. P. Stickney

909. Sowle, Patrick. THE NORTH CAROLINA MANUMISSION SOCIETY 1816-1834. *North Carolina Hist. R. 1965 42(1): 47-69.* Quakers in North Carolina had a long history of attempting to mitigate slaveholding by manumission, although State law made this difficult. In 1816, they founded the North Carolina Manumission Society to proselytize the people of the State, but quaker nonaggressive principles prevented the organization from ever becoming militant. The society later divided over the issue of manumission versus colonization, and by 1825 was captured by the colonizationists, who made some attempt to finance Negro colonization to Haiti and Liberia. But as the South became more belligerent in defense of slavery, the Quakers backed away from open antislavery activities, and many moved to the Midwest because of their passive opposition to the institution. The Manumission Society, while an interesting manifestation of southern antislavery sentiment, accomplished little. 128 notes.
                                                                      J. M. Bumsted

910. Speer, Michael, ed. AUTOBIOGRAPHY OF ADAM LOWRY RANKIN. *Ohio Hist. 1970 79(1): 18-55.* Consists of extensive excerpts from the autobiography of Rankin, abolitionist, educator, and frontier preacher and missionary. Location of the original manuscript is unknown. The excerpts published here are from a typed copy which is in the Ohio Historical Society Library.
                                                                      S. L. Jones

911. Spencer, Donald S. EDWARD COLES: VIRGINIA GENTLEMAN IN FRONTIER POLITICS. *J. of the Illinois State Hist. Soc. 1968 61(2): 150-163.* Contends that Cole's career in Illinois politics came to an early end because of the unpopularity of his antislavery stand.   S. L. Jones

912. Stange, Douglas C. BENJAMIN KURTZ OF THE "LUTHERAN OBSERVER" AND THE SLAVERY CRISIS. *Maryland Hist. Mag. 1967 62(3): 285-299.* Examines the *Lutheran Observer,* the most important Lutheran periodical in antebellum America, during the 25 years that Kurtz (1795-1865), edited it. He found himself between the proslavery feeling of Lutherans in the South and the antislavery feeling of Lutherans in the North. "His alliance with the advocates of American Lutheranism was evidence that he normally would have spoken to the slavery issue if the success of his paper and the unity of the church were not at stake." In 1858 Kurtz resigned and left his post to two associate editors, George Diehl and Frederick R. Anspach. The periodical printed but did not comment on the Emancipation Proclamation. In 1864, "when the Maryland state legislature made their state free, the *Observer* praised the event, [sic] it had done so little to bring about...." 67 notes.   D. H. Swift

913. Stange, Douglas C. BISHOP DANIEL ALEXANDER PAYNE'S PRO-
TESTATION OF AMERICAN SLAVERY, A DOCUMENT. *J. of Negro Hist.*
1967 52(1): 59-64. Reprints an 1839 statement by Daniel Alexander Payne, then
a Lutheran clergyman, protesting slavery. Payne's remarks, first published in *The
Lutheran Herald and Journal of the Franckean Synod,* were made in support of
a Franckean Synod Report on Slavery and amplified his major contention that
slavery should be opposed because it brutalizes man, destroys his moral agency,
and subverts the moral law of God. Payne, who helped draft the report, later
became a bishop of the African Methodist Church and president of Wilberforce
University.   L. Gara

914. Stange, Douglas C., ed. DR. SAMUEL SIMON SCHMUCKER AND THE
INCULCATION OF MODERATE ABOLITIONISM. *Concordia Hist. Inst. Q.*
1967 40(2): 78-83. Publishes a lecture on slavery delivered to the senior class of
Gettysburg Theological Seminary in August 1845 by S. S. Schmucker, influential
Lutheran spokesman for the antislavery cause. Slavery is condemned as an evil
institution for which, of course, no support can be found in the Bible. Compensated emancipation is advocated. According to the editor, Schmucker's moderate
views were probably heavily influenced by the writings of William Ellery Channing and Lydia Maria Child.   D. J. Abramoske

915. Stewart, James B. THE AIMS AND IMPACT OF GARRISONIAN ABO-
LITIONISM, 1840-1860. *Civil War Hist. 1969 15(3): 197-209.* Challenges the
theory that because of their extreme views, the Garrisonian abolitionists played
a minor role in the antislavery movement after 1840. While abjuring orthodox
political activity, they did bring heavy pressure to bear on many public figures,
pushing them toward a more advanced antislavery stance. In addition, they
armed the moderate antislavery crusaders with a needed vocabulary and with an
arsenal of arguments with which to battle the "slavocracy." Rather than an
impractical militant, Garrison and his followers were an important force in the
abolition achievements in the two decades before the Civil War.
                                                                    E. C. Murdock

916. Straka, Gerald M. THE SPIRIT OF CARLYLE IN THE OLD SOUTH.
Historian 1957 20(1): 39-57. Describes the well-known popularity of Thomas
Carlyle in the South following the publication of *Latter-Day Pamphlets* (1850),
which defended slavery. Less known is Carlyle's private repudiation of these
pamphlets and his assertion that although abolitionism was wrong, slavery was
not in accordance with natural law and that plans should be made for its gradual
extermination.   E. C. Johnson

917. Strassweg, Elga. THE KIDNAPPING OF HORACE BELL. *Indiana Hist.
Bull. 1969 46(8): 105-108.* In 1858 Horace Bell was kidnapped by a group of men
on the streets of New Albany, Indiana, and was taken to Kentucky where a
reward had been posted for his arrest. He had illegally freed his father and brother
from a Brandenburg, Kentucky, jail where they were held on a charge of enticing

Negroes away from their owners. Discusses the ensuing excitement on both sides of the Ohio River and Bell's eventual release. Includes two lengthy quotations from the New Albany *Daily Ledger.* D. H. Eyman

918. Straub, Jean S. ANTHONY BENEZET: TEACHER AND ABOLITION-IST OF THE EIGHTEENTH CENTURY. *Quaker Hist. 1968 57(1): 3-16.* Of a Huguenot family which moved from France to Holland, England, and America, Benezet spent over 40 years teaching in what became Penn Charter School and his own girls school in Philadelphia. He kept order without corporal punishment. In 1778 he published *The Pennsylvania Spelling Book* and a primer, and with the second editions in 1782 an essay on grammar. He disapproved of studying Latin, except for medicine, because of the Romans' heathen and militarist spirit. Lectures on useful sciences were to be copied into a bound notebook for permanent reference. He wrote several tracts against slavery, taught blacks in Philadelphia, and opposed recolonization in Africa. T. D. S. Bassett

919. Strickland, Arvarh E. NEGRO COLONIZATION MOVEMENTS TO 1840. *Lincoln Herald 1959 61(2): 43-56.* Analyzes the climate of opinion in which the American Colonization Society emerged and summarizes the history of that group up to 1840. Special attention is given to the very diverse opposition which the society encountered. The author concludes that the American Colonization Society "eludes evaluation," though it may be viewed as an agency which served progress as an "avenue of communication open between groups holding divergent opinions on vital issues." S. L. Jones

920. Strickland, Rex W. A DEDICATION TO THE MEMORY OF EUGENE CAMPBELL BARKER, 1874-1956. *Arizona and the West 1966 8(4): 301-304.* Texas born and Texas and eastern educated Eugene Campbell Barker spent his professional career at the University of Texas. His principal research interest was the history of his State, as biographer and editor of the papers of the leaders of the Republic of Texas. He was managing editor of the *Southwestern Historical Quarterly* for 27 years, president of the Mississippi Valley Historical Association, author of several textbooks for intermediate and secondary schools, and a stern but judicious taskmaster to his students. In his writings he destroyed the southern slave conspiracy hypothesis as an explanation for the acquisition of Texas and the Mexican Cession; he assessed the role of Texas in westward expansion and national development; and he pointed out that Mexican intransigency and oppression only partially explain the Texan Revolution and the Mexican War. Appended with a selected list of Barker's publications relating to the Southwest; illus. D. L. Smith

921. Stutler, Boyd B. ABRAHAM LINCOLN AND JOHN BROWN - A PARALLEL. *Civil War Hist. 1962 8(3): 290-299.* Lincoln's qualities contrasted sharply with those of Brown, but they also shared similarities. European liberals linked their names, and not entirely inappositely. Both were frontier-born, self-educated, and both hated slavery. Both died tragically. In methods, they differed. Brown's action at Harpers Ferry put the Republicans under fire. They repudiated him, but counterattacked by denouncing Missouri "Border Ruffians," for em-

ploying tactics similar to his. Lincoln avoided discussing Brown, so far as he could. Both accomplished their objectives, one in seeking the end of slavery, the other in seeking to preserve the Federal Union.   L. Filler

922. Stutler, Boyd B. THE HANGING OF JOHN BROWN. *Am. Heritage 1955 6(2): 4-9.* David Hunter Strother, correspondent for *Harper's Weekly,* gives an eyewitness description of the hanging of John Brown, 2 December 1859.
                                                                A. W. Thompson

923. Summers, Mary Floyd. POLITICS IN TISHOMINGO COUNTY, 1836-1860. *J. of Mississippi Hist. 1966 28(2): 133-151.* Describes county parties and State and Federal elections from 1836 to 1860 in Tishomingo County, a strongly Democratic county in northeast Mississippi. Political issues included the repudiation of State bonds, the annexation of Texas, and "the best means of preserving slavery." Unionist sentiment increased during the 1850's. In the election of 1860, John C. Breckinridge received 1,748 votes, John Bell, 1,412, and Stephen A. Douglas, 303. In the election for a State convention, the county by a more than two-to-one margin elected four delegates favoring "secession conditional upon all the southern states going out of the Union together" over a slate of delegates favoring "immediate and unconditional secession." Based on secondary works, newspapers, and material in the Mississippi Department of Archives and History.
                                                                      J. Hillje

924. Sutherland, Keith. CONGRESS AND THE KANSAS ISSUE IN 1860. *Kansas Hist. Q. 1969 35(1): 17-29.* The question of whether Kansas would be a free or slave State had been settled on the local level before 1860, but the issue remained alive on the national level. The argument centered around whether Kansas would be admitted to the Union in 1860, and whether admission would be granted before or after the presidential election. Each presidential candidate was forced to take a position on Kansas. The debate on the fourth enabling bill is shown to have had political implications in spite of the time devoted to boundary lines, Indian lands, and population requirements for admission to the Union. Both the Democrats and Republicans in Congress apparently were willing to use Kansas as a tool in the presidential election. Based on the *Congressional Globe,* newspapers, and manuscripts in the Library of Congress, the Kansas State Historical Society, the Massachusetts Historical Society, the University of Rochester, and the Indiana Historical Society; 28 notes.   W. F. Zornow

925. Sutton, Robert M. ILLINOIS' YEAR OF DECISION, 1837. *J. of the Illinois State Hist. Soc. 1965 58(1): 34-53.* Three episodes of 1837 mark a turning point in the history of the State of Illinois. Each met with initial failure and total misunderstanding. Within a generation each was regarded with a sense of accomplishment and enlightened understanding. The first: The Internal Improvements Act committed the State to river and road improvements and an unusually ambitious railroad building program which would, at the same time, give the State's economy a tremendous boost. The second: A transplanted Vermont blacksmith, John Deere, perfected a "self-scouring" steel plow that left a smooth cut and a well-turned furrow and shed the heavy sticky, black muck of the Illinois

prairies cleanly from its moldboard. The third: The moral convictions of an abolitionist editor, Elijah Parish Lovejoy, and his determination to exercise the freedom of the press at all costs, earned death for himself at the hands of a mob and martyrdom for the cause of abolitionism. Illus., 22 notes.

D. L. Smith

926. Swift, David E. SAMUEL HOPKINS: CALVINIST SOCIAL CONCERN IN EIGHTEENTH CENTURY NEW ENGLAND. *J. of Presbyterian Hist. 1969 47(1): 31-54.* Examines the antislavery activities of Samuel Hopkins (1721-1803) during and after the American Revolution. A student of Jonathan Edwards, Hopkins' earliest social concern was for fair treatment of Indians living near his parish. He argued for this on the basis that Christian compassion and expediency dictated fairness. When he transferred from a frontier to an urban parish, his concern for Negro slaves was similarly animated. In gaining an antislavery reputation during the Revolution, Hopkins exerted a great influence on his fellow clergymen, showing them the moral significance of the slave system. He was a leader in movements to send Negroes back to Africa while he educated some Negroes to be Christian missionaries there. The author uses some of Hopkins' writings and biographies about his subject. 52 notes.   D. M. Furman

927. Swisher, Carl B. DRED SCOTT ONE HUNDRED YEARS AFTER. *J. of Pol. 1957 19(2): 167-183.* The Dred Scott case and later similar cases are used to examine the character and processes of the American Government, particularly the position of the Federal judiciary. The author concludes that the Dred Scott case proves that the Supreme Court should articulate high constitutional ideals and not concern itself with solutions which can come only through political processes.   C. LeGuin

928. Tade, George T. THE ANTI-TEXAS ADDRESS: JOHN QUINCY ADAMS' PERSONAL FILIBUSTER. *Southern Speech J. 1965 30(3): 185-198.* Provides an account of an address-turned-filibuster. The article provides a clear statement of Adams' views on the annexation of Texas, slavery, and freedom of petition and debate. The author estimates the effectiveness of the address. 53 notes.   H. G. Stelzner

929. Talmadge, John E. BEN PERLEY POORE'S STAY IN ATHENS. *Georgia Hist. Q. 1957 41(3): 247-254.* Relates a youthful escapade of the journalist and newspaper publisher Ben Perley Poore which abruptly ended his management of the Athens (Georgia) newspaper *Southern Whig* and his stay at Athens. Poore was taken to court on the charge of having given on 30 January 1841 a party where Negro girls were entertained. The author disputes the authenticity of a published verdict according to which Poore was fined, and maintains that he was acquitted.   R. Mueller

930. Tate, Merze. SLAVERY AND RACISM AS DETERRENTS TO THE ANNEXATION OF HAWAII 1854-1855. *J. of Negro Hist. 1962 47(1): 1-18.* Intense political and economic difficulty led the king of Hawaii to consider

annexation to the United States in 1854-55. In opposing such a move the British consul general in Hawaii emphasized American race prejudice and the possibility that slavery would be exported to the islands. Pressure in the form of a threatened invasion from California only made the Hawaiian negotiators more cautious. A proposal that the United States should annex the kingdom as a state was rejected by the Hawaiian Government and most certainly would have met defeat in the U.S. Senate had it reached that point.   L. Gara

931. Thomas, Emory M. REBEL NATIONALISM: E. H. CUSHING AND THE CONFEDERATE EXPERIENCE. *Southwestern Hist. Q. 1970 73(3): 343-355.* The historical stance of Confederate nationalism is exemplified by the northern-born southern rebel, E. H. Cushing, editor of the Houston *Telegraph* and a strong proponent of a diversified economic nationalism for the South. Accepting the reality of slavery as the basis of southern life, Cushing pushed for a reopening of the slave trade to complement his vision of an independent and economically expanded South. Although he condemned the Constitutional Union ticket in 1858 on the grounds that it represented a revival of Whiggery, Cushing's economic posture was nothing if not Whig in tradition. Significantly, Cushing's definition of Whiggism meant government centralization, a concept which he had staunchly opposed until secession and the threat of defeat forced him to support the measures of Confederate centralization. A realist to the core, Cushing with his intense nationalism succeeded in transforming his entire political thought from an economic states' rightist position to support of a southern centralized and bureaucratic government.   R. W. Delaney

932. Thomas, John L. ROMANTIC REFORM IN AMERICA, 1815-1865. *Am. Q. 1965 17(4): 656-681.* The variety of reforms initiated during the Jacksonian era were fundamentally conservative attempts to arrest the leveling aspects of democracy and halt change in favor of an earlier standard of romantic individualism. Although movements could not be sharply delineated, the reformers moved through what might be regarded as several stages, i.e., the first stage was one in which benevolent societies with moral aims were undermined by romantic perfectionists, who, in turn, sought to revolutionize society through appealing to the individual conscience. Still moralists, the reformers brought to their work a sense of "psychological isolation": they disliked large-scale institutions and city life and clung to the nostalgia of rural existence. When the complexities of uplifting everyone became too great, they fled to different brands of perfectionism. Transcendentalism offered one form of escape and communitarian societies another. When they failed to recreate the extended family system in communitarianism, large-scale social reforms, such as abolitionism, offered the sole remaining hope of transforming society. When this occurred, individual perfectionism gave way to individualism qualified by social participation; participation in the antislavery crusade and the subsequent Civil War tended to reduce humanitarian alienation. 34 notes.   R. S. Pickett

933. Thurston, Helen M., compiler. A SURVEY OF PUBLICATIONS IN THE HISTORY AND ARCHAEOLOGY OF OHIO, 1967-1968. *Ohio Hist. 1968 77(4): 149-163.* A list of books and articles organized under the headings: Anti-

slavery Movement, Archaeology, Arts and Crafts, Bibliography, Biography, Business and Industry, Education and Culture, Genealogy, General, Indians and Indian Wars, Literature, Local History, Medicine, Miscellaneous, Ohio in the Wars, Politics and Government, Religion, Social History, Transportation, Travel and Description, and Theses and Dissertations on Ohio Subjects in Ohio Colleges and Universities. S. L. Jones

934. Tocqueville, Alexis de. THE NEGRO SLAVE IN AMERICA. *J. of Hist. Studies 1967 1(1): 86-98.* Tocqueville's portrayal of the Negro slave in America is as analytical and profound as it is descriptive and comprehensive. He found the Negro isolated and homeless - sold by Africa, repulsed by America. He compared the lot of the slaves with that of the Indian. He contrasted North and South, the fruits of free and slave labor, and the psychological impress of slavery upon black men and their owners. Tocqueville concluded that slavery was becoming uneconomical in America and was therefore diminishing, but that "slavery recedes, but the prejudice to which it has given birth is immovable." N. W. Moen

935. Trefousse, Hans L. BEN WADE AND THE NEGRO. *Ohio Hist. Q. 1959 68(2): 161-176.* A study of the attitude and prejudices of Senator Benjamin Franklin Wade of Ohio (1800-78). Evidence of private racial prejudice in the correspondence of a leading advocate of justice for Negroes raises the problem of motivation. Either Wade was a self-seeking hypocrite, anxious for votes in a radical constituency, or he himself was aware of the folly of his private outbursts. Wade's career and his own statements indicate that he was sincere. He did not believe that irrational private prejudices should influence rational public policy, and his radicalism hindered, rather than furthered, his career. Therefore, in spite of personal lapses, he remains one of the most important fighters for freedom during the middle period of American history. Based on newspapers, reminiscences, public records and the Wade Papers in the Library of Congress. A

936. Troxler, George. ELI CARUTHERS: A SILENT DISSENTER IN THE OLD SOUTH. *J. of Presbyterian Hist. 1967 45(2): 95-111.* Sketches the life of the Reverend Eli Caruthers of Guilford County, North Carolina. Educated at Princeton Seminary, Caruthers was ordained in 1821 by the Orange Presbytery. He was an advocate of the camp meeting and revival and a leader in local voluntary benevolent societies in Greensboro as well as pastor of churches in the area and a schoolmaster. In 1846 he moved to Alamance where he served the Presbyterian Church until his retirement. He published two volumes of the history of North Carolina during the Revolution and left an unpublished manuscript entitled "American Slavery and the Immediate Duty of Southern Slaveholders" written in the 1840's. In this work Caruthers vigorously attacked the institution of slavery and its defense on biblical grounds. He insisted that slaves must be freed before they could fully accept the Christian faith. In spite of his strong views, Caruthers did not speak out against slavery from the pulpit. He held no sympathy for the Confederate cause, retired in 1861, and died in 1865. Based on published and unpublished materials; 61 notes. S. C. Pearson, Jr.

937. Turner, Charles W. VIRGINIA STATE AGRICULTURAL SOCIETIES, 1811-1860. *Agric. Hist. 1964 38(3): 167-177.* The first State agricultural society in Virginia was organized in 1811, under the leadership of John Taylor, who was well known as an advocate of soil conservation. This society and its successors were reorganized at intervals. It was not until 1853 that a society with a definite, continuing program was established. A rival society, the Union Agricultural Society, was organized in 1857. These societies concentrated on attempting to get State aid for agriculture, advocating agricultural education, preserving slavery, and sponsoring State agricultural fairs.   W. D. Rasmussen

938. Tyson, Raymond W. HENRY WINTER DAVIS: ORATOR FOR THE UNION. *Maryland Hist. Mag. 1963 58(1): 1-19.* Henry Winter Davis is probably best remembered for the Wade-Davis Bill, which Lincoln pocket vetoed, and for the Wade-Davis Manifesto, of which the Baltimore congressman was the principal author. Less known today is his role as a superb orator for the cause of the Union and the abolition of slavery, both in the House of Representatives and on the stump. Davis' eloquence was, James A. Garfield once remarked, "clear and cold, like starlight." A little more than six months after the Civil War ended, the Maryland politician and one-time slaveholder died at the age of 48.
                                                                     W. L. Fox

939. Ulmer, S. Sidney. SUB-GROUP FORMATION IN THE CONSTITU-TIONAL CONVENTION. *Midwest J. of Pol. Sci. 1966 10(3): 288-303.* After some introductory remarks about the attempts to analyze the forces that produced the U.S. Constitution, with particular emphasis upon the work of Charles Beard, Forrest McDonald, Lee Benson, and Robert Brown, the author suggests the use of bloc analysis in understanding the voting behavior of representatives to the convention. The author concludes that there were cohesive blocs, upon which issue variation had little effect; and that distribution of property, economic interests of the delegates, and large State-small State dichotomy can not account for the voting groups revealed. However, it is pointed out that the investment in slavery could have been a contributing factor in the grouping of particular States. Ulmer suggests further research into this area, using the new quantitative techniques. 7 tables, 22 notes.   J. W. Thacker, Jr.

940. Unsigned. THE FIVE BRAVE NEGROES WITH JOHN BROWN AT HARPERS FERRY. *Negro Hist. Bull. 1964 27(7): 164-169.* Mostly concerns the role played by Sheilds Green, a fugitive slave, in the John Brown raid on Harpers Ferry. Green remained with Brown and was captured and hanged for his part in the raid.   L. Gara

941. Vacha, John E. THE CASE OF SARA LUCY BAGBY. *Ohio Hist. 1967 76(4): 222-231.* Describes reactions in Cleveland and elsewhere in the Western Reserve to the arrest and trial of Sara Lucy Bagby, escaped slave from Virginia, under the Fugitive Slave Law. The return of Sara Lucy Bagby to prison in Virginia without violent intervention in Cleveland was viewed as evidence of the

extent to which Republicans were willing to uphold the Fugitive Slave Law in order to preserve the Union. Based on contemporary newspaper accounts.
S. L. Jones

942. Van Horne, William E. LEWIS D. CAMPBELL AND THE KNOW-NOTHING PARTY IN OHIO. *Ohio Hist. 1967 76(4): 202-221.* Analyzes the difficulties experienced by Campbell as a leader in Ohio of the Know-Nothing Party in his attempts to maneuver politically upon the slavery question and achieve some measure of cooperation with the Republican Party. The author emphasizes Campbell's participation in national politics in this period. Based in part on the Campbell Papers in the Ohio Historical Society, the Chase Papers in the Library of Congress, and the Schouler Papers in the Massachusetts Historical Society.
S. L. Jones

943. Vaughter, Paul H., Jr. NOTES ON MISSISSIPPI HISTORY: THE NON-SLAVEHOLDER AND "FREE-LABOR" COTTON. *J. of Mississippi Hist. 1963 25(2): 112-122.* Includes editorials and letters written by agents of the Quakers' Free Produce Association in Philadelphia who went into Mississippi to buy free-labor cotton. The extracts are from the 1846-50 issues of the *Non-Slaveholder,* the association's official organ which was edited by Samuel Rhoads.
D. C. James

944. Wacholder, Ben Zion. SOME LEGAL AND POLITICAL VIEWS OF JUDAH P. BENJAMIN. *Hist. Judaica [France] 1956 18(1): 41-58.* Discusses Judah P. Benjamin's most famous cases and debates as a member of the New Orleans bar, as the leading Southern orator and defender of slavery in the U.S. Senate, and as British barrister and legal theoretician. In his liberal period in New Orleans, he argued eloquently that slavery was against the law of nature. In the Senate, he took the reverse position and became a leading Confederate politician, holding several positions in the Confederate government. After fleeing to England he published the *Treatise on the Law of Sale of Personal Property: with Special Reference to the American Decisions and the French Code and Civil Law,* well known as *Benjamin on Sales.* Based on the *Congressional Globe,* case records, articles in legal journals, etc.
D. B. Goodman

945. Wainwright, Nicholas B. SIDNEY GEORGE FISHER - THE PERSON-ALITY OF A DIARIST. *Pro. of the Am. Antiquarian Soc. 1962 72(1): 15-30.* Biographical sketch of Fisher (1809-71), descendant of an outstanding Philadelphia shipping merchant family, graduate of Dickinson College in 1828, lawyer who never practiced law, farmer, author, and diarist. Wrote numerous articles and books, including *The Law of the Territories* (1859), *The Laws of Race as Connected with Slavery* (1860), and *The Trial of the Constitution* (1862). Compiled a 70-volume diary (1834-71), the most complete and most revealing by a Philadelphian; covers personal life and lives of friends, but also includes valuable commentary on public affairs.
W. D. Metz

946. Walsh, Justin E. RADICALLY AND THOROUGHLY DEMOCRATIC:
WILBUR F. STOREY AND THE DETROIT "FREE PRESS" 1853 TO 1861.
Michigan Hist. 1963 47(3): 193-225. Examines the Detroit career of the Democracy's Northwest spokesman during the decade before the Civil War. Storey
acquired the *Free Press* when it was on the verge of failure and immediately
announced that the paper "will be radically and thoroughly democratic." Circulation swelled as the editor combined personal journalism with political partisanship. The "democratic" principles consistently expounded were racism and states'
rights. Negrophobia, in particular, dictated Storey's attitudes and policies. The
author corroborates the copperhead leader's "reputation for the sensational and
unsavory," and concludes that "he seemed incapable of political opposition on
a level above the most base." Based on the *Free Press* and includes quotations
from Storey's editorials.   J. K. Flack

947. Weiner, Gordon M. PENNSYLVANIA CONGRESSMEN AND THE
1836 GAG RULE:A QUANTITATIVE NOTE. *Pennsylvania Hist. 1969 36(3):
335-340.* It has been argued that the first major North-South division over slavery
was occasioned by abolitionist petitions to Congress and by southern efforts to
silence them. It has also been contended that Whigs used these debates to split
the Democratic Party along sectional lines. The author tests these views by
analyzing the votes of the Pennsylvania congressmen during the "gag rule"
controversy of 1836. Using 43 roll-call votes, the Pennsylvania delegation's pattern did not warrant the idea that the controversy divided Congress along North-
South lines. Congressmen showed some regularity as party members; yet,
Pennsylvania Whigs did not vote as a group often enough to support the view that
they were cooperating in a plan to split Democrats along sectional lines. 5 notes.
                                                                         D. C. Swift

948. Weisenburger, Francis P. LINCOLN AND HIS OHIO FRIENDS. *Ohio
Hist. Q. 1959 68(3): 223-256.* A comprehensive study of Lincoln's relations with
various citizens of Ohio during the early days of his political career and after his
election as President. The author considers the position and character of Lincoln
against the background of political intrigue, dissension over the slavery question
and the events of the Civil War. Based on extensive documents, journals, and
letters (sources given).   B. Waldstein

949. Wentworth, Jean. NOT WITHOUT HONOR: WILLIAM LLOYD GAR-
RISON. *Maryland Hist. Mag. 1967 62(3): 318-336.* A summary of Garrison's life
in Maryland and his work as editor of the *Liberator* in Boston. Examines the
motives of Garrison, the crusader who aroused the conscience of the Nation, and
the "attention-egoist" who some believe was a negligible figure in an irrelevant
movement. Defines the attitudes of later historians and biographers who tried to
place Garrison in retrospect as a factor in the slavery issue and as one of the
reasons for the Civil War. Garrison has eluded the grasp of all who have tried
to fit him into a current historiographical pattern or to explain his contributions
to history. 44 notes.   D. H. Swift

950. Whitaker, Cynthia. THE WHITE NEGRO: RUSSIAN AND AMERI-
CAN ABOLITION. *North Dakota Q. 1965 33(2): 32-37.* Traces similarities in
the Russian and American abolition movements in inception, argument, and
results. Censorship reduced the role of politics and religion in the Russian movement and made literary figures the chief agents of abolitionism. Despite the
circumlocutions necessary to outwit censorship, the Russian abolitionists utilized
essentially the same moral and economic arguments as did their American contemporaries. Based on contemporary and later published works.

J. F. Mahoney

951. Whitridge, Arnold. THE JOHN BROWN LEGEND. *Hist. Today [Great
Britain] 1957 7(4): 211-220.* An account and analysis debunking the "legend of
a noble soul battling against injustice and oppression" which "has had to be put
together out of the most unpromising materials." Brown was "a crack-brained
abolitionist" whom Abraham Lincoln, for example, disavowed.

W. M. Simon

952. Wiley, Earl W. LINCOLN AND THE FREEDOM RIDERS OF THE
1830'S. *Lincoln Herald 1967 69(2): 60-69.* Analyzes Lincoln's reaction to abolitionist and related antislavery agitations of the 1830's and concludes that the
moderate and conciliatory attitude toward the South displayed later in his career
was in evidence then. S. L. Jones

953. Wilson, L., Maj. THE CONTROVERSY OVER SLAVERY EXPANSION
AND THE CONCEPT OF THE SAFETY VALVE: IDEOLOGICAL CON-
FUSION IN THE 1850'S. *Mississippi Q. 1971 24(2): 135-153.* The debate over
the expansion of slavery into the Territories in the 1850's was characterized by
ideological confusion. Some proslavery spokesmen argued that lack of space for
expansion would make the press of population against available resources drive
down the value of labor and compel the release of slaves. Other proslavery
advocates believed that the slaveholding section could continue indefinitely without the safety valve of unsettled land; however, the end of the supply of free lands
would force conflict between labor and capital in the nonslave society, until
capital had won. Some antislavery proponents believed that open space was
essential for removal of surplus population. Ideological confusion was also apparent in the linking of policies formerly considered opposite ones - as was the case
relating to free homesteads and land grants made to railroads. While free homesteads were appealing as an escape from the evils of "civilization," railroad grants
were meant to encourage the spread of civilization. Confusion also existed as to
whether the lands actually belonged to the government or to the landless people.
Combining a high protective tariff with free homesteads represented another
ideological confusion. The high tariff was viewed by some to keep wages high
enough to prevent too many laborers from moving west; others thought wages
would be held up by the free homestead policy, which would draw off excess
labor. A pragmatic view of government, concerned only with the present and not
with future consequences of actions, was expressed in the Republican platform
of 1860, which became unified partly as a result of a common enemy, slavery
expansionists, who opposed both a higher tariff and free homesteads. The conflict

then became no longer one over how the future would be shaped but over who would shape it. Based partly on congressional records; 34 notes.

R. V. Calvert

954. Wilson, Major L. A PREVIEW OF THE IRREPRESSIBLE CONFLICT: THE ISSUE OF SLAVERY DURING THE NULLIFICATION CONTRO-VERSY. *Mississippi Q. 1966 19(4): 184-193.* During the period from 1828 to 1833, there was actually very little direct discussion of slavery as an issue in Congress. As the issue became involved in economic problems, however, discussions became more emotional. While "Nullifiers" attempted to explain the injustices of the tariff as resulting in the central government's transferring wealth from one part of the country to another, the opposing view held that inefficiency of slave labor was the chief reason for depression in the South. Arguments for slavery as a positive good began to develop locally in the South by the 1820's, with the nullification controversy providing the first national airing of such views. With the ideas about conflict set forth by John C. Calhoun in 1828, the analysis of the problem during the nullification controversy represented in itself another stage in the advancement toward a more fateful debate. Although peace came with compromise in 1833, the Nullifiers saw the lines of conflict drawn in the previous years as marking a clash between the planting States and the manufacturing States. 23 notes.

R. V. Calvert

955. Wilson, Major L. IDEOLOGICAL FRUITS OF MANIFEST DESTINY: THE GEOPOLITICS OF SLAVERY EXPANSION IN THE CRISIS OF 1850. *J. of the Illinois State Hist. Soc. 1970 63(2): 132-157.* Analyzes the positions adopted by Whigs, Democrats, and Free Soilers on the issue of slavery in the territories, and concludes that the Compromise of 1850 did not remove the major elements of conflict which this issue embraced. Based mainly on materials drawn from the *Congressional Globe.*

S. L. Jones

956. Wilson, Major L. MANIFEST DESTINY AND FREE SOIL: THE TRI-UMPH OF NEGATIVE LIBERALISM IN THE 1840'S. *Historian 1968 31(1): 36-56.* Analyzes the arguments of the champions of manifest destiny and the advocates of free soil, and finds that both exhibit a common cast of thought called negative liberalism. The latter is defined as seeking freedom by determined opposition to some presumed enemy or opposing tendency rather than in terms of a series of concrete, specific, positive objectives which, taken together, would constitute a program. Based mainly on the speeches and debates reported in the *Congressional Record.*

N. W. Moen

957. Wilson, Major L. OF TIME AND THE UNION: KANSAS-NEBRASKA AND THE APPEAL FROM PRESCRIPTION TO PRINCIPLE. *Midwest Q. 1968 10(1): 73-87.* Studies the Kansas-Nebraska Act (1854) and the debates over it in Congress. A key provision of the measure repealed the Missouri Compromise, which had for 34 years banned slavery in the North. By undoing an arrangement made by an earlier generation and sanctioned by the passing years, the repeal invited the protagonists in debate to seek some timeless principle by which to regulate slavery. It represented a movement from prescription to princi-

ple. In larger terms it was a movement from the laws of history to the laws of nature. The principle on which the Nation had been founded was freedom, but the free soil advocates favored freedom nationally and slavery locally.

G. H. G. Jones

958. Wilson, Major L. OF TIME AND THE UNION: WEBSTER AND HIS CRITICS IN THE CRISIS OF 1850. *Civil War Hist. 1968 14(4): 293-306.* Analyzes the nature of freedom as discussed in the Compromise debates of 1850. The first concept, espoused by Daniel Webster, viewed freedom as a goal to be achieved as soon as possible, but within the existing frame and without damage to the frame. The second concept, advanced by the Free-Soilers, held that freedom was an eternal absolute which had to be immediately proclaimed and sustained, whatever the price. Webster, arguing that history is a continuous unfolding process, objected to any sudden disruption of the process, as was demanded by antislavery forces. However, these forces remained unmoved by the historical process and they demanded freedom for the slaves. Webster won the battle of 1850, but lost the war of 1861-65, and Reconstruction was the price. Based on the *Congressional Globe* and secondary sources. E. C. Murdock

959. Wilson, Major L. THE BROKER STATE CONCEPT OF THE UNION IN THE 1840'S: A SYNTHESIS OF WHIG AND DEMOCRATIC VIEWS. *Louisiana Studies 1969 8(4): 321-347.* Discusses the various concepts of the nature of the Union set forth from 1830 to 1860, with emphasis on the "broker state" idea predominant in the 1840's, and how it conflicted with the corporate or federative views. The argument seems to be that if democracy in its first reading during the Age of Jackson was characterized by debate over the role of government in the lives of men, the "broker state" idea represented democracy in its second reading. At any rate, the "broker state" argument recorded the potent influence of the slavery issue. 65 notes. G. W. McGinty

960. Wittke, Carl. FRIEDRICH HASSAUREK: CINCINNATI'S LEADING FORTY-EIGHTER. *Ohio Hist. Q. 1959 68(1): 1-17.* A study of the career of a leading Forty-eighter in America, based largely on his personal papers. Hassaurek began his career as a radical journalist in Cincinnati, helped organize Freimänner Vereine, and was a leader in the cultural life of the city. He was an uncompromising opponent of slavery, an active worker for the new Republican Party, and U.S. minister to Ecuador by appointment from President Lincoln for his services in the campaign of 1860. He wrote several books on Latin-American themes, and edited the *Cincinnati Volksblatt,* a leading German-language newspaper, from 1865 to his death in 1885. A

961. Wolff, Gerald. THE SLAVOCRACY AND THE HOMESTEAD PROBLEM OF 1854. *Agric. Hist. 1966 40(2): 101-111.* Historians have long believed that southern opposition defeated the Homestead bill in 1854. However, careful analysis of voting records indicates that neither southern Senators nor members of the House of Representatives in 1854 were unified in their attitudes toward land-disposal policy. W. D. Rasmussen

962. Woodress, James. "UNCLE TOM'S CABIN" IN ITALY. *Essays on Am. Literature in Honor of Jay B. Hubbell (Durham: Duke U. Press, 1967): 126-140.* *Uncle Tom's Cabin* has been more continuously popular in Italy than elsewhere and has been constantly in print since 1852. "Three periods of maximum popularity...coincide with the emergence of major political crises" in Italy: during the Risorgimento in the early 1860's, during the Fascist era, and "after World War II, when liberty returned to Italy." A bibliographic listing of 67 Italian editions of *Uncle Tom's Cabin* is included.   C. L. Eichelberger

963. Wright, Edward Needles, ed. JOHN NEEDLES (1786-1878): AN AUTO-BIOGRAPHY. *Quaker Hist. 1969 58(1): 3-21.* Reminiscences of John Needles, written in 1872. Son of a Quaker boatbuilder, cabinetmaker, and farmer on the Eastern Shore of Maryland, Needles had sporadic schooling but a thorough woodworking apprenticeship. He tells how he prospered in Baltimore, in spite of the dull times during the War of 1812, unwise speculations in exports to South America and in Baltimore real estate, and a 13 thousand-dollar fire in 1838. He partly financed Benjamin Lundy's *Genius of Universal Emancipation,* an abolitionist newspaper published from 1821 to 1835. Sentences and paragraphs were arranged from the MS by the editor, who owns it, but otherwise the plain style of the text is reproduced, including the original spelling. 12 notes, biblio.
T. D. S. Bassett

964. Wyatt-Brown, Bertram. ABOLITIONISM: ITS MEANING FOR CONTEMPORARY AMERICAN REFORM. *Midwest Q. 1966 8(1): 41-55.* Discusses various attitudes toward abolitionists, beginning with the tradition that they plunged the Nation into the Civil War and the resulting Reconstruction. Historians pointed out that abolitionist propaganda to the effect that slaveholders were depraved and that slaves were docile helpless creatures led to the Nation's disillusionment with the freedmen. Historians emphasized the fact that abolitionists were self-righteous to the point of moral arrogance. Over 15 historians are cited who since the 1950's have added new dimensions to our understanding of the complexities of guilt feelings, described the work of individualists as compared to organizations, and compared English abolitionists to American ones. Agitators are seen as persuaders only, not lawmakers or policymakers. The abolitionists' concepts did not prepare them or anybody else for the racial prejudice and violence which followed emancipation.   G. H. G. Jones

965. Wyatt-Brown, Bertram. GOD AND DUN & BRADSTREET, 1841-1851. *Business Hist. R. 1966 40(4): 432-450.* A study of the founding by Lewis Tappan of the United States' largest credit-reporting agency. Tappan was often motivated by an evangelical Christianity, as is indicated by his interest in the American Missionary Association, the American Anti-Slavery Society, and the *National Era,* a reform journal of Washington, D.C.   J. H. Krenkel

966. Wyatt-Brown, Bertram. THE ABOLITIONISTS' POSTAL CAMPAIGN OF 1835. *J. of Negro Hist. 1965 50(4): 227-238.* Describes the American Anti-Slavery Society's 1835 campaign to bombard the American public, North and South, with a series of abolitionist pamphlets. Southern reaction included numer-

ous public rallies, the forming of vigilance committees, stealing and destroying mail bags containing the pamphlets, an economic boycott of New York merchants, and threats of legal action against Arthur Tappan, the society's president. Northern reaction was mixed but the campaign did succeed in focusing attention on the cause and arousing interest in the related question of constitutional liberties. The campaign helped prepare the North for a stronger antislavery position.

L. Gara

967. Wyatt-Brown, Bertram. WILLIAM LLOYD GARRISON AND ANTI-SLAVERY UNITY: A REAPPRAISAL. *Civil War Hist. 1967 13(1): 5-24.* Argues that the traditional view of Garrison as an extremist who would stop at nothing in his thirst to crush slavery is a misleading one. A truer view would show Garrison as a moderate, who never advocated violence or slave rebellion, who exercised a restraining influence on his more militant associates, and who never defied Federal (or any other) law. Unlike Thoreau, for example, Garrison always paid his taxes. Historians seem to have accepted the Garrison of the 1830's when his posture was most extreme and ignored the later Garrison which reflected a mellowing and stabilizing of his thought and words. In fact, Garrison turns out to be the real author of American nonviolence, from whom Thoreau, and in turn Gandhi and Martin Luther King, derived their philosophy. Based on primary and secondary sources.

E. C. Murdock

968. Zakharova, M. N. VOSSTANIE DZHONA BRAUNA I AMERIKAN-SKAIA BURZHUAZNAIA ISTORIOGRAFIIA [The revolt of John Brown and American bourgeois historiography]. *Novaia i Noveishaia Istoriia [USSR] 1960 (5): 112-125.* A survey of Brown's life up to the culmination of his activity, the revolt at Harpers Ferry, followed by a review of the literature on Brown. All the views of reactionary historians are refuted in E. Stone's book *Incident at Harper's Ferry. Primary Source Materials for Teaching Theory and Technique of the Investigative Essay* (New Jersey, 1956). Based also on numerous other works.

E. Wollert

969. Zanger, Jules. THE "TRAGIC OCTOROON" IN PRE-CIVIL WAR FICTION. *Am. Q. 1966 18(1): 63-70.* Describes the central role of the "tragic octoroon" as a fictional stereotype in antebellum abolitionist fiction. From R. Hildreth's *The Slave* (1836) to Harriet Beecher Stowe's *Uncle Tom's Cabin* (1852) and Dion Boucicault's *The Octoroon* (1859) over a dozen works featured the "tragic octoroon," a "beautiful young girl who possesses only the slightest evidences of Negro blood" and who is raised by and descended from white aristocracy on her father's side. In the standard account, the girl learns of her fate only upon her father's sudden death. She is then sold into slavery, victimized by an evil Yankee slave dealer and, if she manages to survive, rescued by a handsome young white aristocrat from the North. Southern apologists have regarded the octoroon plot as a means to gain support for abolitionism by appealing to "white sensibilities" and pro-Negro commentators have regarded it as "racial snobbery." Such charges fail to acknowledge the propaganda value and wide appeal of the plot. It appealed to northern notions of superiority and self-righteousness and showed the southerner's sin. The nightmarish reversal of the octoroon's situation

resembled, for some young middle-class women, the precariousness of their own existence. In order to illustrate contempt for Yankees who condoned slavery, the most evil beings in the books are Yankee overseers. As potential exploiters of the octoroon, these lowly creatures indicate the irrelevance of the "kindly master" myth. The shrewd, hard-driving overseer also had qualities about him which many would recognize as emerging cultural values in the North. Relevant novels are fully cited in the initial note. Critical works on American Negro fiction are cited thereafter. 5 notes. R. S. Pickett

970. Zeuner, Robert W. THE APPEAL TO CAESAR: A HISTORY OF THE METHODIST CHURCH PROPERTY CASE OF 1849. *Methodist Hist. 1969 7(2): 3-16.* Most property and funds owned by the Methodist Church were equitably divided between the northern and southern churches along strict geographical lines by 1848, following the split over the slavery issue. Division of the resources of the Methodist Book Concern was not easily agreed upon and led to the Methodist Church property cases. The author discusses the conditions leading up to the court cases, the arguments presented by both sides, and settlements handed down by the courts. Based in part on records of the U.S. Circuit Court for the Southern District of New York; 18 notes. H. L. Calkin

971. Zirker, Priscilla Allen. EVIDENCE OF THE SLAVERY DILEMMA IN "WHITE-JACKET." *Am. Q. 1966 18(3): 477-492.* The novel *White-Jacket* is explored and regarded as symptomatic of a contradiction in Herman Melville's mind between "militant egalitarianism" and pacifism. Although his libertarian impulse caused him to condemn class and racial exploitation, Melville temporizes by resorting to Negro stereotyping in some of his characterizations. He also avoids various opportunities to speak up on behalf of egalitarianism. Melville's desire to avoid class and sectional strife leads to ambivalence on the subject of social justice. Although he would eventually come to regard slavery as the greatest evil, in 1849 he felt it necessary to compromise for the sake of peace. 20 notes. R. S. Pickett

972. Zoellner, Robert H. NEGRO COLONIZATION: THE CLIMATE OF OPINION SURROUNDING LINCOLN, 1860-65. *Mid-Am. 1960 42(3): 131-150.* Relates the complexity of motivation surrounding Lincoln's scanty public utterances on Negro deportation and colonization. "In many cases, the surface altruism masked a pervasive and various self-interest" (ranging from fear of racial amalgamation to a means of increasing the nation's wealth). "It would, of course, be presumptuous to assign such motives to Lincoln where no proof exists. Nonetheless, an objective evaluation of his stand on the colonization issue cannot safely be made without a close scrutiny of the background against which he moved to solve, if he could, the 'Negro problem.'" R. J. Marion

973. Zorn, Roman J. THE NEW ENGLAND ANTI-SLAVERY SOCIETY: PIONEER ABOLITION ORGANIZATION. *J. of Negro Hist. 1957 42(3): 157-176.* Discusses the organization of the New England Anti-Slavery Society,

its gradual triumph over the American Colonization Society, and its reduction to an auxiliary position of the American Anti-Slavery Society.

W. E. Wight

974. Zuck, Lowell H. DIE AMERIKANISCHE ANTI-SKLAVEREIBEWEGUNG IN DEN KIRCHEN VOR DEM BÜRGERK-RIEGE [The American antislavery movement in the churches before the Civil War]. *Zeitschrift für Religions- und Geistesgeschichte [West Germany] 1965 17(4): 353-364*. Until 1830 slavery was generally opposed by Protestant Churches. Later, westward expansion and increasing influence of humanitarian reform caused a sharpening of the slavery issue between those for and against. After 1830, ministers of Christian denominations became extensive slaveholders and at the same time the literature of theological justification for slavery began to appear. The position of the churches centered about three parties: proslavery, abolitionist, and evangelical, the last of which condemned slavery as an institution but tread softly with slaveowners. Methodists were split over the issue in 1844 and formed Northern and Southern Conferences. Baptists saw similar schism in the same year. Presbyterians held together until 1857. Episcopalians and Lutherans split in the North and South after 1860 while Jews and Roman Catholics, having taken no clear stand on slavery, remained united religiously and divided politically. The division in churches prior to the Civil War was a major reason for making the war inevitable.

S. J. Miller

975. --. [THE BROADWAY JOURNAL]. *Bull. of the New York Public Lib. 1969 73(2): 74-113*.
Ehrlich, Heyward. THE "BROADWAY JOURNAL" (1): BRIGG'S DILEMMA AND POE'S STRATEGY, pp. 74-93. Concerns Edgar Allan Poe's connections with the *Broadway Journal,* the last of four magazines which he edited. Poe's letters shed little light on the magazine's brief history (January 1845-January 1846) and one must rely on the papers of Charles Frederick Briggs, organizer and founding editor. Poe's biographers either ignored Briggs' correspondence or dismissed certain economic details which Ehrlich believes are essential to an understanding of events leading to Poe's full control of the magazine. Contrary to the conclusion of most Poe biographers, the poet was not "the boss," with Briggs playing "second fiddle," and Poe did not have much to do with the "maneuvers" which resulted in his becoming editor and owner. Rather, Briggs was in charge of the magazine at the start and withdrew in July 1845 "after reaching an impasse with the publisher, John Bisco, over re-financing of the paper." The magazine's poverty caused Briggs to find another backer to fill Bisco's position, but when Bisco refused to leave, Briggs himself resigned. Bisco and Poe continued the magazine with Poe as editor. By October, however, Bisco evidently lost hope in the journal's possibilities for profit and Poe was left the sole owner as well as editor. Poe kept the magazine going apparently in order to promote interest in himself and his literary work. The author suggests that Poe had always hoped to establish an affluent journal but failing at that he used the *Broadway Journal* as a means to ensure his literary reputation. Based on unpublished manuscript materials, contemporary sources and secondary works; 86 notes.

Weidman, Bette S. THE "BROADWAY JOURNAL" (2): A CASU-
ALTY OF ABOLITION POLITICS, pp. 94-113. Contends that the *Broadway
Journal* of 1845 failed mainly because it became "a casualty of the troubling
political and moral issues of the day." Briggs, the founding editor, attempted to
prepare an audience for a national literature but only alienated most of the New
England abolitionists whom he had hoped to make contributors. By refusing to
make the magazine an organ of the reform movement, Briggs took "an unpopular, and some said, ambiguous stand on the issue of slavery." When Edgar Allan
Poe joined the magazine in March 1845, he further alienated abolitionists by his
outspoken southern bias. Ultimately the journal's "bright promise was dimmed
by clashes between Briggs and his assistant Poe, but quenched by the hostility of
an organized political faction." Based largely on unpublished manuscript materials and issues of the *Broadway Journal;* illus., 48 notes.   W. L. Bowers

976. --. THE FEBRUARY ISSUE: A DEDICATION TO CHARLES WES-
LEY. *Negro Hist. Bull. 1965 28(5): 99-104, 111-115, 119.*
    Unsigned. BRIEF BIOGRAPHY OF DR. CHARLES H. WESLEY, pp.
99-100. Reprinted from the Central State College *The Centralian,* 1 June 1964.
    Wesley, Charles H. THE GREAT MAN THEORY OF EMANCIPA-
TION, pp. 101-102, 111-115, 119.
    Biddie, Reginald F., Burgess, Quentin, and Page, William Allen. TRIB-
UTES TO DR. C. H. WESLEY, pp. 103-104.
    Biographical sketch, tributes, and a bibliography of the writings of Dr.
Charles H. Wesley, Negro historian and educator, on the occasion of his retirement as president of Central State College in Ohio. Wesley analyzes Abraham
Lincoln's antislavery views in terms of morality and politics and calls attention
to other individuals, white and colored, who also contributed to the abolition of
slavery in the United States.   L. Gara

977. --. THE ISSUE OF FREEDOM IN ILLINOIS. *J. of the Illinois State Hist.
Soc. 1964 57(3): 284-297.*
    Cassiday, John Thomas. UNDER GOV. EDWARD COLES, 1822-1826,
pp. 284-288. Edward Coles, the second governor of Illinois, pushed enlightened
ideas through a State legislature in which there was considerable proslavery
sentiment. The author credits Coles with saving Illinois from adopting a proslavery constitution in 1824. Illus., 11 notes.
    Hiller, Mary Jane. UNDER GOV. WM. H. BISSELL, 1857-1860, pp.
288-293. A Democrat turned Republican, William Bissell became his party's first
governor of Illinois. Although faced with a Democratic legislature, he succeeded
in preventing reapportionment legislation which would have given the proslavery
Democrats control of the State. Illus., 15 notes.
    Hartman, Linda. UNDER GOV. RICHARD YATES, 1861-1865, pp.
293-297. Richard Yates clearly stated the Republican position concerning secession of South Carolina in his January 1861 inaugural address, suppressed secession activities throughout southern Illinois, defeated a Copperhead move to adopt
a new State constitution, and vigorously pushed the State's war effort. Illus., 9
notes.   D. L. Smith

Slavery as an Internal Issue

978. Baur, John E. INTERNATIONAL REPERCUSSIONS OF THE HAITIAN REVOLUTION. *Américas 1969 25(4): 394-418.* The Haitian Revolution (1791-1804) had its first major external impact through refugees, the majority of whom were white. Thousands went to the United States, where they generally received sympathy and made important cultural and other contributions. Their influence was even greater in Louisiana, which received a large number both before and after annexation. Cuba, other West Indian islands, and even Venezuela absorbed refugees and benefited economically both from their technological innovations and from the interruption of Haitian competition through the revolution and its aftermath. The Haitian example and the resultant fear of slave uprisings directly influenced the policies of European power on such matters as abolition of the slave trade, and indirectly affected the later Spanish-American independence movement. The American nations hesitated to establish formal relations with Haiti even though the world's trading powers were active there. Destruction of French power in Haiti was an important cause of France's sale of Louisiana to the United States. The Haitian experience further contributed to the U.S. decision to abolish the slave trade. It was much cited by defenders of slavery, less often by opponents, and was well known to the black population, including leaders of several slave uprisings. Based on secondary sources; 103 notes.

D. Bushnell

979. Bondestead, Kjell. THE AMERICAN CIVIL WAR AND SWEDISH PUBLIC OPINION. *Swedish Pioneer Hist. Q. 1968 19(2): 95-115.* As one result of emigrant communications from America to Sweden and the reports of various travelers to America, two main views regarding American society were firmly established in Sweden by the beginning of the Civil War. The view expounded by the conservatives was that America was a horrible example of rule by the people. The liberal view was that America was a pattern for other societies to emulate. By the autumn of 1862 Swedish public opinion was near unanimous in its criticism of the aims of the Union, although the same opinion was vehemently against slavery. The liberal dissatisfaction with the Union is rooted in the fact that the war was not explained as a war to eliminate slavery and that the position of the South could be compared to European nations who were battling for their freedom against great odds. In the end, victory by the North secured the Swedish sympathies. 53 notes.

E. P. Costello

980. Brack, Gene M. MEXICAN OPINION, AMERICAN RACISM, AND THE WAR OF 1846. *Western Hist. Q. 1970 1(2): 161-174.* Mexican officials were well aware of the inadequacy and weakness of the nation's army and the emptiness of the treasury in the 1840's. They believed that Texas could not be recovered, that it was in the best interests of Mexico to preserve peace, and that war with the United States would be disastrous. Public opinion, however, was hostile to the United States and opposed the ceding of territory to her - the alternative to war. Mexicans closely related American expansionism to racism,

being aware of the state of the Indian and Negro in the United States. Knowing that Americans looked upon Mexicans as inferior, they feared the loss of Texas and California, as well as of other Mexican territory which would soon follow. For two decades the press had fed Mexicans a steady diet of American racism. The cumulative effect was a public opinion so rigidly opposed to American expansion that it forced Mexico into a war in 1846 that would not likely be won. 55 notes.

D. L. Smith

981. Brent, Robert A. MISSISSIPPI AND THE MEXICAN WAR. *J. of Mississippi Hist. 1969 31(3): 202-214.* Describes various aspects of the Mississippi relation to the Mexican War, including its original strong support for war, prewar attitudes of Mississippi newspapers, the policies of Mississippi Governor Albert Gallatin Brown, Mississippi officers in the war (notably Jefferson Davis and John Anthony Quitman). In addition, the author discusses attitudes regarding peace terms. There was much support for acquiring all of Mexico but a sharp split regarding the Treaty of Guadalupe Hidalgo. The Whig press supported the treaty while Democratic newspapers argued that the United States was not getting enough territory. Mississippians almost unanimously favored war because of support for Manifest Destiny and the belief that war was "an ideal way to expand slave territory." Based chiefly on newspapers; 35 notes.   J. W. Hillje

982. Brooke, George M., Jr. THE ROLE OF THE UNITED STATES NAVY IN THE SUPPRESSION OF THE AFRICAN SLAVE TRADE. *Am. Neptune 1961 21(1): 28-41.* Traces the disappointing results of American attempts to suppress this traffic. Use of the American flag as a protective cover for slaves was encouraged by U.S. refusal to grant Britain the right to search its vessels before 1862. Though branded as piracy in 1819, only spasmodic efforts were made to halt this trade down to 1839. Anglo-American tensions over the trade were eased somewhat by the Webster-Ashburton Treaty which established a permanent squadron. The government took greater interest in assisting legitimate trade to Africa at this time. The squadron was ineffective because it was often below strength and because of poor supply organization and antiquated vessels. In 1858 stronger forces were assigned and other changes saw improved effectiveness. Based mainly on Congressional and naval records.   J. G. Lydon

983. Carroll, Daniel B. HENRY MERCIER AND THE AMERICAN CIVIL WAR. *Diplomacy in the Age of Nationalism: Essays in Honor of Lynn Marshall Case (ed. by N. N. Barker and M. L. Brown): 109-123.* Traces the role and attitudes of Henri Mercier, French minister, during his diplomatic mission to the United States (1860-63). He disliked his appointment and constantly sought reassignment. Before the war he adopted southern views. American democracy did not impress him. Mercier respected northern military and economic power and warned his government of the need for future good relations with the North. He advocated an eventual tariff union between the North and South and even a dual republic with a common senate and defense forces to counter British power. Mercier opposed the French expedition into Mexico and preferred the gradual abolition of slavery. He urged the relaxation of the blockade (to help French

industries), Union adherence to maritime law, the release of James Murray Mason and John Slidell, and mediation (but not intervention) by France. 37 notes.

L. M. Case

984. Crook, D. P. PORTENTS OF WAR: ENGLISH OPINION ON SECESSION. *J. of Am. Studies [Great Britain] 1971 4(2): 163-179.* Discusses English opinion as expressed in "little journals" and by Walter Bagehot, writer Isabella Lucy Bird Bishop, and publishers Sir George Cornewall Lewis and William Harrison Ainsworth. They initially accused southern leaders in the United States of machinations to perpetuate slavery, and looked askance on the American abolitionists and the administration of James Buchanan. They applauded the Republican Party, the victor in the elections of 1860, and anticipated a "reform movement" that would find solutions to America's sectional controversies. English enthusiasm for the Republicans ebbed when Abraham Lincoln and Secretary of State William Henry Seward failed to prevent a civil war. English opinion - although still in sympathy with the North - opposed resort to war in the United States and preferred dissolution of the American union to armed coercion of the South by the North. Based on editorial expressions and other writings, mostly analyses of American political events, published in "little journals" in Great Britain; 56 notes.

H. T. Lovin

985. Duram, James C. A STUDY OF FRUSTRATION: BRITAIN, THE USA, AND THE AFRICAN SLAVE TRADE, 1815-1870. *Social Sci. 1965 40(4): 220-225.* Traces the conflict between Britain and the United States over Britain's attempt to suppress the Atlantic slave trade. Britain's method was developed by Foreign Minister Castlereagh between 1815 and 1823: a reliance on naval power and pragmatic diplomacy. American resistance grew out of traditional hostility to British interference on the high seas and out of the growing sensitivity of the American South after 1820 to any attack on slavery. The outbreak of the Civil War enabled Britain to conclude the Seward-Lyons Treaty with the United States, thereby achieving a mutual visit and search agreement and removing the last major obstacle to total suppression of the trade. Documented.

M. Small

986. Durden, Robert F. LINCOLN'S RADICAL REPUBLICAN ENVOY TO THE HAGUE AND THE SLAVERY QUESTION. *Lincoln Herald 1954 56(4): 25-33, 1955 57(1/2): 12-17.* The first article deals with the slavery question at the beginning of the 1860's. James Shepherd Pike, appointed by Lincoln as envoy to The Hague, was opposed to Lincoln's gradual policy of Negro liberation. Negotiations until 1864 between the U.S. and Dutch governments for a treaty relating to voluntary Negro emigration to Surinam were unsuccessful. The second article deals with the preparation of the treaty on emigration to Surinam. Pike suggested in 1862 a scheme for banishment to the southern States. The idea was not to be realized. Attention is drawn to Pike's divided attitude to the problem.

R. Chand

987. Harstad, Peter T. and Resh, Richard W. THE CAUSES OF THE MEXICAN WAR: A NOTE ON CHANGING INTERPRETATIONS. *Arizona and*

the West 1964 6(4): 289-302. In the wake of the Mexican War the abolitionist-inspired explanation of the conflict was that it represented the culmination of a long conspiracy on the part of the South to gain more land for slavery expansion and additional slave States. Subsequent interpretations, whether favorable or unfavorable to the Polk administration, couched in patriotic terms or advanced from some other point of view, were to be affected or colored by the abolitionist rationale. Not until the early years of the present century when they were conditioned by the debate over imperialism and the role of America in world affairs did historians in general discard the conspiracy thesis in favor of Manifest Destiny and the extension of national boundaries as the principal cause of the war. American historians still have not made any radical departure from this approach. Since, it is asserted, assumptions of historians are influenced by the society in which they live and by their own personalities, only future generations will be able to determine to what extent a new emphasis on economic and commercial factors as an explanation of the Mexican War reflect the attitudes of our own times. 33 notes.   D. L. Smith

988. Harwood, Thomas F. BRITISH EVANGELICAL ABOLITIONISM AND AMERICAN CHURCHES IN THE 1830'S. *J. of Southern Hist. 1962 28(3): 287-306.* One of the chief factors leading up to the crisis which divided major Protestant denominations in the period before the Civil War was the pressure from coreligionists in Great Britain who took strongly abolitionist attitudes. Specific references are made to such pressures upon American Baptists, Methodists, Presbyterians, and Quakers.   S. E. Humphreys

989. Henderson, Conway W. THE ANGLO-AMERICAN TREATY OF 1862 IN CIVIL WAR DIPLOMACY. *Civil War Hist. 1969 15(4): 308-319.* Traces the negotiations leading to the passage of the Anglo-American Treaty (1862), by which the United States gave Great Britain full authority to crack down on the trans-Atlantic slave trade when carried on by American ships. England had long sought such a treaty (the United States being the last holdout among major nations), but it was not until the South seceded from the Union and an antislavery administration was in power in Washington, that the United States was officially receptive to such an agreement.   E. C. Murdock

990. Jones, Horace Perry. SOUTHERN OPINION ON THE CRIMEAN WAR. *J. of Mississippi Hist. 1967 29(2): 95-117.* Focusing mainly on attitudes toward Russia and Britain, the author analyzed 95 articles which appeared in southern newspapers and periodicals during the Crimean War and concluded that 21 were "relatively neutral," 15 were pro-Allied, and 59 were pro-Russian. He agrees with Thomas A. Bailey that the South's attitude was more "anti-British than pro-Russian." Although the South sold much more cotton to Britain than to Russia, southerners were anti-British because of traditional anglophobia, alarm at possible British designs on Cuba, and resentment at British support of abolitionism. Based largely on southern newspapers and periodicals; 84 notes.
                                                            J. W. Hillje

991. Jones, Wilbur Devereux. THE INFLUENCE OF SLAVERY ON THE WEBSTER-ASHBURTON NEGOTIATIONS. *J. of Southern Hist. 1956 22(1): 48-58.* In presenting the Webster-Ashburton negotiations of 1842, which sought to settle the Maine boundary dispute and improve relations between the two countries, the author shows that the success of the negotiations was hindered by the strong British feeling against slavery and strong proslavery sentiment in Washington. Most of the minor problems were concerned with slavery: with the British release of the slaves on the *Creole* which was brought into Nassau, navigation of the Bahama Channel off the Florida coast, suppression of the African slave trade, and extradition. R. Kerley

992. Kliger, George and Albrecht, Robert C. A POLISH POET ON JOHN BROWN. *Polish R. 1963 8(3): 80-85.* The article cites and analyzes two poems on John Brown written by one of Poland's great poets, Cyprian Kamil Norwid (1821-83). The poems represent not only Europe's opinion of John Brown, but also Norwid's poetic style. According to the authors, "Norwid saw John Brown in relation to slavery in America, but more as a part of America, the symbol of freedom in the world." The poems are not easy to read in translation; but in the opinion of Messrs. Kliger and Albrecht, Norwid is not easy to read in his own native tongue. S. R. Pliska

993. Landry, Harral E. SLAVERY AND THE SLAVE TRADE IN ATLAN-TIC DIPLOMACY, 1850-1861. *J. of Southern Hist. 1961 27(2): 184-207.* The diplomatic victory won by the United States over Great Britain in respect to the West African slave trade, particularly in relation to Spanish Cuba, and the relaxation of British pressure that resulted, removed a cementing factor in the United States. The withdrawal of the foreign threat removed a common bond of North and South in the United States and had a serious and direct relation to the outbreak of the Civil War. This condition gives viability to the usually condemned memorandum of Secretary of State William H. Seward on 1 April 1861, propos-ing aggressive diplomatic action against Britain, France, Spain, and Russia. S. E. Humphreys

994. Langley, Lester D. SLAVERY, REFORM, AND AMERICAN POLICY IN CUBA, 1823-1878. *R. de Hist. de Am. [Mexico] 1968 (65/66): 71-84.* U.S. policy toward Cuba varied as opinions about slavery shifted. This is seen in the attitudes of John Quincy Adams, William James Calhoun, James Knox Polk, John Tyler, and Franklin Pierce. After the Civil War, the United States steadily pressed Spain to emancipate the slaves in Cuba. The conviction that all efforts were proving useless resulted in a willingness to resort to force in 1898. 28 notes. T. B. Davis

995. Long, Durwood. ALABAMA OPINION AND THE WHIG CUBAN POLICY, 1849-1851. *Alabama Hist. Q. 1963 25(3/4): 262-279.* The expansionist fervor of the 1840's led some citizens to agitate for the acquisition of Cuba. The decision of President Taylor to reverse the Democratic Party policy and return to a "let-alone" policy raised the question of how the slaveholding Southern Whigs would react. Which would they support - their party or filibustering to

"liberate" Cuba and form new slaveholding states which would send more senators in favor of slavery? The author concludes that the Southern Whigs were
mildly opposed to the acquisition of Cuba. Throughout these three years, the
Alabama Whigs fairly consistently followed the administration's neutrality policy. They were "more loyal to political and party principle than to immediate
economic interests." This fact is due to the control of the party in Alabama by
the commercial wing and not the slaveholding faction. Based on Federal documents and a wide range of Alabama newspapers; 59 notes.   E. P. Stickney

996. Maynard, Douglas H. THE WORLD'S ANTI-SLAVERY CONVENTION
[IN LONDON] OF 1840. *Mississippi Valley Hist. R. 1960 47(3): 452-471.* The
convention strengthened and enlarged the crusade against slavery by drawing
together into one combined effort the abolitionist forces of the mid-19th century.
Resolutions adopted by the convention reflect the influence of Joseph Sturge, who
believed that the slave trade could be ended only by abolition of slavery itself, and
that abolition should be realized only through religion and moral influence.
Although the refusal to admit women as delegates aroused considerable controversy, other issues (the role of the church and the endorsement of free labor as
means of combating slavery, etc.) were resolved amicably.   D. R. Millar

997. Merk, Frederick. DISSENT IN THE MEXICAN WAR. *Massachusetts
Hist. Soc. Pro. 1969 81: 121-136.* Reprinted in *Dissent in Three American Wars*
(Cambridge, Mass.: Harvard U. Press, 1970). Concentrates chiefly on political
opposition to the Mexican War with some reference to the dissent of literary
figures such as Ralph Waldo Emerson, Henry David Thoreau, and James Russell
Lowell. The political dissenters included conservative Whigs who criticized President James Knox Polk but voted supplies for the prosecution of the war; "conscience" Whigs and radical Democrats convinced that the administration hoped
to spread slavery into Mexico and Central America; and Southern Democrats
such as John Caldwell Calhoun, who doubted that a cause for war existed.
Concludes that the dissent prevented the treaty of peace with Mexico from being
even more harsh than it was. Based chiefly on newspapers and Federal and State
documents; 24 notes.   J. B. Duff

998. Murray, Alexander L. THE EXTRADITION OF FUGITIVE SLAVES
FROM CANADA: A RE-EVALUATION *Can. Hist. R. 1962 43(4): 298-314.*
Examines the claim that abolitionist agitation in 1842-43 induced the British
Government to exclude fugitive slaves from extradition under the Webster-
Ashburton Treaty. Research in Ottawa, Washington, London and Oxford shows
that the British Government realized late in the 1830's that strict adherence to
certain traditional legal rules would offer sufficient protection to the fugitive
slaves. This indirect protection, not the specific exemption of fugitive slaves which
the abolitionists demanded, continued to be British policy until American slavery
was abolished.   A

999. Rice, C. Duncan. THE ANTI-SLAVERY MISSION OF GEORGE
THOMPSON TO THE UNITED STATES, 1834-1835. *J. of Am. Studies [Great
Britain] 1968 2(1): 13-31.* Surveys the career of the British reformer, George

Thompson, and focuses on his 15-month visit to the United States in 1834-35. During his tours of New England, New York, and Pennsylvania, convinced abolitionists like William Lloyd Garrison welcomed him eagerly, "while the pro-slavery response was violent reaction to the whole idea of his interference from abroad." Although he thus did little more than confirm American attitudes toward slavery, Thompson did dominate "the connection between the extremist wings of the British and American anti-slavery movements," and after his return to Britain he assumed leadership of the extreme British opponents of slavery. His enthusiasm for his antislavery crusade in America illustrates "the mutual responsibility for each other's moral welfare felt by the British and American middle classes" during the antebellum period. Based on newspapers, published primary sources, manuscript collections, and secondary sources.   D. J. Abramoske

1000. Shively, Charles. AN OPTION FOR FREEDOM IN TEXAS, 1840-1844. *J. of Negro Hist. 1965 50(2): 77-96.* In 1839 Stephen Pearl Andrews moved from Louisiana to Texas where he became involved in a plan to attract free settlers and to abolish slavery. Andrews believed that cooperation with the British Government could help to accomplish his objectives. Although he found some Texans sympathetic to his program, others were strongly opposed, and twice he was expelled from Texas for his views. Andrews visited England to obtain support for Texas emancipation but a combination of circumstances led to a perpetuation of slavery in Texas rather than a decision in favor of human freedom. Documented.
L. Gara

1001. Suciu, I. D. THE ECHO IN ROMANIA OF THE USA CIVIL WAR. *R. Roumaine d'Hist. [Rumania] 1965 4(4): 739-763.* Contains the standard Marxian account of the causes of the American Civil War, but then goes on to describe the antislavery reactions of liberal Rumanians, such as Michel Kogălniceanu and Dimitrie Pop, and the publication in Rumanian of Harriet Beecher Stowe's *Uncle Tom's Cabin* in 1853. Most of this article contains quotations from contemporary Rumanian newspapers and journals in defense of the Union and in opposition to the Confederacy. Also discussed are the participation and observations of Rumanians in America during the war. This is the first English-language article to appear in this French-language journal.   S. D. Spector

1002. Sullivan, Harry R. THE SOUTH AND THE EMANCIPATION IN THE BRITISH WEST INDIES. *Georgia R. 1963 17(3): 259-270.* An examination of newspapers in the South during the English debate over emancipation of slaves in the British West Indies. The South's main concern was that British emancipation might prove a harbinger of the future.   H. G. Earnhart

1003. Taylor, Clare. NOTES ON AMERICAN NEGRO REFORMERS IN VICTORIAN BRITAIN. *British Assoc. for Am. Studies Bull. 1961 (2): 40-51.* American Negro speakers were much in demand at antislavery meetings in England. Beginning in the 1830's, this stream of visitors grew steadily in the 1840's, reached its peak in the early 1850's after the passage of the Fugitive Slave Act, and died away at the outbreak of the Civil War. Emphasis is placed on the division in American antislave ranks after 1840, which was reproduced in Britain, and the way in which the Negro speakers were in a sense reinforcing British upper-class anti-Americanism. Based largely on the Garrison papers in the Boston Public Library.   D. McIntyre

1004. Temperly, Howard. THE O'CONNELL-STEVENSON CONTRETEMPS: A REFLECTION OF THE ANGLO-AMERICAN SLAVERY ISSUE. *J. of Negro Hist. 1962 47(4): 217-233.* Describes the furor which arose in 1838 when Andrew Stevenson, American minister to Great Britain, demanded an explanation of Daniel O'Connell, an Irish reformer, of remarks the latter had made at a Birmingham antislavery meeting. O'Connell had reportedly referred to Stevenson as a slave breeder. Although the controversy did not result in a formal challenge, it led to prolonged newspaper discussion in Great Britain and America, a renewed effort of Congressman John Quincy Adams to end duelling in the United States, and a growing recognition that American slavery was out of step with changes taking place in other major nations.   L. Gara

1005. Urban, C. Stanley. THE AFRICANIZATION OF CUBA SCARE, 1853-1855. *Hispanic Am. Hist. R. 1957 37(1): 29-45.* Diplomatic pressure on Spain by France and Great Britain in the 1850's, coupled with the appointment of Juan M. Pezuela as Captain General of Cuba, caused slave-owning Cubans and pro-slavery southerners in the United States to believe the abolition of slavery in Cuba was at hand. Actions subsequently taken by Pezuela in Cuba reenforced this belief and caused Governor John Anthony Quitman of Mississippi to begin preparations for a filibustering expedition to Cuba. The Pierce administration proposal to buy Cuba, resulting in the Ostend Manifesto of 1854, aroused bitter northern opposition. The crisis passed when Spain recalled Pezuela, and Quitman abandoned preparations for the expedition.   R. B. McCornack

The Free Black Community

1006. Alford, Terry L. LETTER FROM LIBERIA, 1848. *Mississippi Q. 1969 22(2): 150-151.* After conversion to Methodism in 1832, Edward Brett Randolph of Columbus, Mississippi, decided to free his 21 slaves, valued at around 10,000 dollars. They sailed for Africa on the cargo vessel *Swift* in 1836. One manumittee Elisa Thilman wrote to her former owner from Greenville, Liberia, on 11 May 1848. Randolph apparently had also provided his slaves with education in Christian fundamentalism, since the writer consoles herself with her belief in God despite her difficulties. Describing her recovery from grave illness and declaring that her sister and her sister's children have all died, the letter writer feels isolated in the new African nation and requests that her former owner get a message to her mother, her father, and her sisters who are still in the United States to let them know that she is alive and to ask them to write to her. Elisa also sends her love to Virginia, the daughter of her former owner and closes by declaring "I remain Your Friend." The letter is in the Randolph-Sherman Papers (1813-1947) at the Mississippi State University; 6 notes.   R. V. Calvert

1007. Angle, Paul M. THE ILLINOIS BLACK LAWS. *Chicago Hist. 1967 8(3):* *65-75.* Traces the history of the Illinois black laws from their adoption in 1819 until their repeal in 1865. Although, as required by the Ordinance of 1787, the Illinois constitution of 1818 prohibited slavery, in 1819 the State legislature adopted a code designed to maintain Negro subservience. An attempt to legalize slavery did fail in the early 1820's, but the black code was strengthened in 1829 and 1845, and in 1853 the legislature prohibited free Negroes from entering the State. Among those who worked for the repeal of the legislation was John Jones, a wealthy Chicago Negro whose pamphlet, *The Black Laws of Illinois, And a Few Reasons Why They Should Be Repealed* (Chicago: Tribune Books and Job Office, 1864), is in the library of the Chicago Historical Society. Illus.
                                                                        D. J. Abramoske

1008. Armstrong, William M. THE FREEDMEN'S MOVEMENT AND THE FOUNDING OF THE "NATION." *J. of Am. Hist. 1967 53(4): 708-726.* The *Nation,* both in name and in its original aims, developed out of the concern of ex-abolitionists and supporters of the Freedmen's Bureau for establishing a journal devoted to supporting the interests of the black race. Ardent abolitionists contributed ideas and money, and Charles Eliot Norton brought supporters to the new journal. Edwin Lawrence Godkin was persuaded to become editor. Having earlier hoped to establish a weekly paper in conjunction with Frederick Law Olmsted, Godkin leaped at the opportunity, demanded autocratic authority over its editorial policy, and soon crossed swords with some of the abolitionists over the issue of Negro rights. The radicals lost a fight to control the editorial policy, and in 1866 Godkin took principal control of the *Nation.* Documented from private papers.   K. B. West

1009. Bell, Howard H. CHICAGO NEGROES IN THE REFORM MOVEMENT, 1847-1853. *Negro Hist. Bull. 1958 21(7): 153-155.* Chicago Negroes actively opposed discriminatory State laws, the constitutional clause of 1857 which provided a basis for preventing Negroes from coming into Illinois, and the Fugitive Slave Law of 1850. They participated in regional and national conventions and circulated petitions requesting the repeal of the Illinois black laws. Some also supported schools for Negroes, a Negro lyceum, and a Negro antislavery society.   L. Gara

1010. Bell, Howard H. EXPRESSIONS OF NEGRO MILITANCY IN THE NORTH, 1840-1860. *J. of Negro Hist. 1960 45(1): 11-20.* Shows the gradual development of militant utterances by northern Negroes concerning their increasingly difficult position in America during the two decades before the Civil War, and especially during the 1850's. Negro animosity was directed toward the Fugitive Slave Law, the semi-free status of Negroes, the Dred Scott decision, etc.

Based chiefly on abolitionist periodicals and official reports of State conventions, especially those of Ohio. Reference is made to the Canadian convention of 1853.

A

1011. Bell, Howard H. NATIONAL NEGRO CONVENTIONS IN THE MIDDLE 1840'S:MORAL SUASION VS. POLITICAL ACTION. *J. of Negro Hist. 1957 42(4): 247-260.* Examination of National Negro Conventions of 1841, 1843, 1847, and 1848 reveals a definite gain for independent Negro leadership. The author discusses the differences between the Garrisonian moral persuasionists and the political affiliationists, and the triumph of the latter. By 1847 "the National Negro Convention was once more the most powerful voice in Negro affairs - a voice that had a militant ring."   W. E. Wight

1012. Bell, Howard H. NEGRO NATIONALISM: A FACTOR IN EMIGRATION PROJECTS, 1858-1861. *J. of Negro Hist. 1962 47(1): 42-53.* Discusses the revival of Negro interest in emigration projects from 1858 to 1861. Although little actual emigration took place during those years, plans were made to colonize American Negroes in Haiti and other parts of the Western Hemisphere. Discouragement at the lack of progress in the area of civil rights, and a rising spirit of Negro nationalism contributed to the new attitude toward emigration. Frederick Douglass, William Wells Brown and some other Negro leaders endorsed the idea of founding a Negro nation which would be peopled at first by emigrants from the United States.   L. Gara

1013. Bell, Howard H. NEGRO NATIONALISM IN THE 1850'S. *J. of Negro Educ. 1966 35(1): 100-104.* Surveys the writings of Negro nationalists in the decade prior to the Civil War. "Negro Nationalism, always a minority movement, but ultimately a substantial minority," expressed "a pride in all things African, a sense of militant togetherness, a belief in the inherent superiority of the Negro, a religious sense of responsibility to the people of African descent, the doctrine of the natural right of the colored peoples to the tropics of the world, and - almost invariably - a belief in emigrating from the United States to create, or join, a Negro nation." With the coming of the Civil War organized emigration virtually ceased and the nationalist movement was absorbed into the Union cause.

S. C. Pearson, Jr.

1014. Bell, Howard H. NEGROES IN CALIFORNIA, 1849-1859. *Phylon 1967 28(2): 151-160.* During the period between 1849 and 1859 Negroes accounted for about one percent of the population of California. Of activity by free Negroes prior to 1854 little is known, but a society composed of at least 37 members existed in San Francisco in 1849. Early in their California history the Negroes encountered discrimination. In 1855 the Mayor of Sacramento vetoed a measure to authorize a school for Negroes. The majority of the City Council overrode the veto and the press denounced the mayor's action. Significant State conventions were held by Negroes in 1855, 1856, and 1857 in an effort to attack the problem of inequality before the law from the State level. Despite their protests little or nothing was accomplished in the matter of securing the right to testify in court. By the decade's end there were some hopeful signs. There was an indication of an organized effort to improve education in San Francisco. Still, Negroes had no right to testify in California courts and recognition of the right of suffrage was far in the future. Based on newspaper sources; 62 notes.   D. N. Brown

1015. Bell, Howard H. SOME REFORM INTERESTS OF THE NEGRO DURING THE 1850'S AS REFLECTED IN STATE CONVENTIONS. *Phylon 1960 21(2): 173-181.* Negro leaders first met in national convention in 1830 and every year thereafter till 1835; they then met in State conventions. By 1850 they could record gains in temperance and moral reform, education, the furtherance of vocational skills; but their social and political rights were few. The franchise was most energetically sought. Efforts in Connecticut and New Jersey were repulsed; internal feuds slowed efforts in Pennsylvania to retrieve the suffrage, lost in 1838. California Negroes concentrated on the right to exercise the oath in court. "Black laws" were the focus of attention in Illinois and Ohio. New York Negroes sought to influence the balance of power between Whigs and Democrats. Their New York State Suffrage Association was active in the presidential election of 1856, and the gubernatorial election of 1858. Ohio and Illinois Negroes also moved toward the Republican Party, while urging it toward a positive stand on Negro suffrage. Other campaigns included encouraging the acquisition of property, especially farms. The segregation of Negro children in schools was not a major concern. A representative press did interest some Negroes; *Frederick Douglass' Paper* did not fill their wants. *The Aliened American* and *The Mirror of the Times* were two attempts at helping the situation.
L. Filler

1016. Bell, Howard H. THE NEGRO EMIGRATION MOVEMENT, 1849-1854: A PHASE OF NEGRO NATIONALISM. *Phylon 1959 20(2): 132-142.* A survey of Negro interest in emigration from the free States of the North (and Maryland), 1849-54. Emigration interest was influenced by 1) increasing respect for Haiti and Liberia as independent Negro countries, 2) favorable reception of Negro leaders in Europe and increasing indifference shown them by antislavery audiences in America, 3) growing discontent due to the stringent Fugitive Slave Law of 1850, and 4) a growing sense of Negro nationalism, best exemplified in Martin R. Delany, who at this time planned to use Canada as a way station for migration to the Caribbean area to establish a Negro empire. Based on newspapers and periodicals, and on official reports of State, national, and international Negro conventions of the period.   A

1017. Bergman, G. M. THE NEGRO WHO RODE WITH FREMONT IN 1847. *Negro Hist. Bull. 1964 28(2): 31-32.* Reviews the contribution of Jacob Dodson, a Negro youth, who was with John C. Frémont on his famous ride from Los Angeles to Monterey, California in 1847 to confer with General Stephen Kearney on the capture of Los Angeles.   L. Gara

1018. Berkeley, Edmund, Jr. PROPHET WITHOUT HONOR. CHRISTOPHER MC PHERSON, FREE PERSON OF COLOR. *Virginia Mag. of Hist. and Biog. 1969 77(2): 180-190.* McPherson was born sometime before 1770 in Louisa County, Virginia, the son of a Scottish merchant and a slave. After some schooling he became a clerk and accountant for his owner, but received his emancipation in 1792. In 1799 he had a religious experience which convinced him that it was his mission to warn the world of impending doom, and he left the employ of his former master. Unable to get Government officials to take his warning seriously, he became a clerk in the High Court of Chancery in Richmond. He prospered but ran afoul of public opinion when he tried to open a night school for free men of color in 1811. Thereafter, harassed by various law suits, he gradually lost his fortune and turned increasingly to his religious mission. He died in New York in 1817. Based on Mcpherson's autobiography, contemporary documents, and newspapers; 32 notes.   K. J. Bauer

1019. Berwanger, Eugene H. THE "BLACK LAW" QUESTION IN ANTE-BELLUM CALIFORNIA. *J. of the West 1967 6(2): 205-220.* Emigration of free Negroes into the western territories was often discouraged by the adoption of "Black Laws" which usually curtailed civil rights and sometimes prevented their residence. In California civil rights restrictions were enacted but attempts at Negro exclusion failed. The author traces the various restrictions imposed upon Negro residents and the effect they had on migration. The conclusion is that attempts at Negro exclusion failed because of fear of congressional opposition, the more weighty problem of Chinese immigration, and the diverse character of the population. Documented from newspapers and other published primary and secondary sources; 39 notes.   D. N. Brown

1020. Bloch, Herman D. THE NEW YORK NEGRO'S BATTLE FOR POLTICAL RIGHTS, 1777-1865. *Internat. R. of Social Hist. 1964 9(1): 65-80.* Even though the first constitution of the State of New York (1777) did not formally forbid Negro suffrage, by 1809 restrictions were imposed and made more stringent after the emancipation of the Negro in the State in 1827. Before the passage of the 15th amendment, the New York legislature repeatedly approved amendments to reinstate Negro suffrage, but they were always rejected by the voters. Based on contemporary newspapers and published documents.

G. P. Blum

1021. Blodgett, Geoffrey. JOHN MERCER LANGSTON AND THE CASE OF EDMONIA LEWIS: OBERLIN, 1862. *J. of Negro Hist. 1968 53(3): 201-218.* Describes the events of 1862 when two Oberlin College coeds became seriously ill during a sleigh ride, presumably because of poison given them in spiced wine by their fellow-student Edmonia Lewis, a black girl. Most likely the poison was cantharides, or "Spanish Fly," a traditional aphrodisiac and also an irritant, which had been added to the girls' drinks to stimulate them sexually. Vigilantes brutally beat Edmonia Lewis, who was arrested but never brought to trial. At a preliminary hearing her lawyer John Mercer Langston demolished the case against her on the grounds of insufficient evidence. In Oberlin little was said publicly about the case, and, until Langston's autobiography appeared in 1894, none of the participants published an account of the incident. Edmonia Lewis later gained temporary renown as an artist and sculptor whose works were based on Indian and Negro themes. Based on primary and secondary sources; 32 notes.

L. Gara

1022. Bonekemper, Edward H., III. NEGRO OWNERSHIP OF REAL PROP-
ERTY IN HAMPTON AND ELIZABETH CITY COUNTY, VIRGINIA,
1860-1870. *J. of Negro Hist. 1970 55(3): 165-181.* Ownership of real property was
a badge of distinction between freemen and slaves in antebellum America, and
its possession was especially significant during the turbulent years of the Civil
War and Reconstruction. Studies the extent to which Negroes were able to
achieve the status of landowners in Hampton and Elizabeth City County during
the crucial decade 1860-70. Concludes that no revolutionary changes took place
in the pattern of living in the region, and that any increase in black landholding
resulted primarily from the efforts of northern missionaries and their supporting
organizations. Based mostly on primary sources; 46 notes.   R. S. Melamed

1023. Borome, Joseph A. ROBERT PURVIS AND HIS EARLY CHAL-
LENGE TO AMERICAN RACISM. *Negro Hist. Bull. 1967 30(5): 8-10.* An
account of the two moral victories over racism that marked the life of Robert
Purvis (1810-97), a person of "mixed ancestry and light skin." He outspokenly
President Andrew Jackson, "may well have been" the first American Negro to
advocated antislavery in the Northeastern States. Purvis, after the intercession of
crossing when, "passing" as white, he charmed the passengers, including Arthur
Peronneau Hayne (1790-1867) of South Carolina, and then revealed his ancestry.
Note.   D. H. Swift

1024. Boromé, Joseph A. WHEN FRENCH GUIANA SOUGHT AMERICAN
SETTLERS. *Caribbean Studies [Puerto Rico] 1967 7(2): 39-51.* In spite of a long
history of failure, new plans for colonization of French Guiana have been recur-
rent. In 1819 Pierre M. S. Catineau-Laroche of the French Foreign Ministry
presented a plan to introduce a hundred thousand poor French people into
Guiana over a 10-year period. The new governor of Guiana Pierre Clement de
Laussat criticized the scheme. Having served briefly as French prefect in Louisiana when it was ceded to the United States, Laussat was impressed by the
industrious westward movement of U.S. farmers. He proposed, over the doubts
of the French minister to the United States Hyde de Neuville, the emigration of
U.S. farmers to Guiana. Correctly recognizing that the opportunities in the
United States precluded enticement of U.S. farmers to emigrate to Guiana, Hyde
de Neuville suggested free Negroes as part of the American Colonization Society
program, but Laussat resisted that idea vehemently. In 1821 a few Irish immigrants to Norfolk, Virginia, went to Guiana and established Laussadelphie, but
within a year all had died or returned to North America. Some Frenchmen came
to the colonly under the Catineau-Laroche plan, but by 1826 Laussadelphie had
become a fiasco. Other colonization projects from 1606 to the present are discussed. Based on secondary and archival sources from the United States and
France; 43 notes.   R. L. Woodward, Jr.

1025. Bouise, Oscar A. THE NEGRO AND HIS IDEA OF RIGHTS: A
STUDY OF WHAT THE NEGRO CONSIDERED HIS RIGHTS AS DEM-
ONSTRATED IN HIS ORATIONS FROM 1780 TO 1840. *Negro Hist. Bull.
1962 26(2): 87-90.* A study of orations delivered by various American Negroes
from 1780 to 1840 revealed that natural, social, and civil rights provided the

major topics. Negro orators pointed out the discrepancy between American revolutionary statements and practices based on race prejudice. Speakers also called attention to slavery and discrimination as factors which limited the social rights of Negroes. The civil rights theme did not appear until 1813 and then emphasized the rights of citizenship and the injustice of a system of law which punished Negroes for crimes, but did not provide them with equal protection. Based mostly on published orations.   L. Gara

1026. Boyd, Willis D. JAMES REDPATH AND AMERICAN NEGRO COLONIZATION IN HAITI, 1860-1862. *Americas 1955 12(2): 169-182.* Redpath (a Scot) decried African colonization plans, preferring a Negro homeland in America. He feuded with many Negro leaders and often assailed the authorities in Washington, but did enlist Haitian official sponsorship. Between 1,000 and 2,000 colonists apparently went, attracted by promises of land on easy terms, draft-exemption, etc. They suffered severely from poor planning and inadequate local cooperation.   D. Bushnell

1027. Brown, Charles Sumner. THE GENESIS OF THE NEGRO LAWYER IN NEW ENGLAND. *Negro Hist. Bull. 1959 22(7): 147-152, (8): 171-177.* Part I. Includes brief sketches of the careers of three early Negro lawyers in Boston. Macon B. Allen practiced law in Boston from 1845 until the Reconstruction period, when he moved to South Carolina and held some minor appointive offices. Robert Morris served as a magistrate, fought unsuccessfully to desegregate the city schools, and played a leading role in the rescue of the fugitive slave Shadrach. Edwin Garrison Walker was elected to the Massachusetts legislature as a Republican in 1866 but he later joined the Democrats and became a leader in that party. Part II. Biographical information on 10 Negro lawyers who practiced their profession in New England. Attributes the larger number of Negro lawyers in Massachusetts to the State's earlier leadership in the abolition movement.
                                                              L. Gara

1028. Corbett, Demetrius M. TARAS SHEVCHENKO AND IRA ALDRIDGE (THE STORY OF FRIENDSHIP BETWEEN THE GREAT UKRAINIAN POET AND THE GREAT NEGRO TRAGEDIAN). *J. of Negro Educ. 1964 33(2): 143-150.* Traces this friendship from the first meeting of Aldridge and Shevchenko in St. Petersburg in 1858-59. Based on the *Reminiscences of Shevchenko and Ira Aldridge - The Negro Tragedian* by H. Marshall and M. Stock.   S. C. Pearson, Jr.

1029. Cox, H. E. JIM CROW IN THE CITY OF BROTHERLY LOVE: THE SEGREGATION OF PHILADELPHIA HORSE CARS. *Negro Hist. Bull. 1962 26(3): 119-123.* Shortly after horsecar lines began operating in Philadelphia in 1858, they adopted a policy of racial segregation. Negroes were permitted to ride only on the cars' front platforms. A poll of patrons indicated that the policy was favored by the majority of those who rode the cars. There were some persons who challenged the practice and in 1865 a committee was formed to force a change. Little was accomplished until 1867 when the State legislature passed a bill prohibiting the exclusion of Negroes from the Philadelphia horsecars. Documented.   L. Gara

1030. Curtiss, Mina. SOME AMERICAN NEGROES IN RUSSIA IN THE NINETEENTH CENTURY. *Massachusetts R. 1968 9(2): 268-288.* From the reign of Czar Alexander I through that of Czar Nicholas II, a small number of American Negroes served as servants of the Imperial Court. The first was Nelson, who came to Russia in 1809 as servant to John Quincy Adams. Nelson found Russia hospitable; a few of his countrymen followed him to Russia shortly. In 1858 Ira Frederick Aldridge, a famed Negro tragedian, toured Russia and won popular and critical acclaim. 8 illus., note.   G. Kurland

1031. Degler, Carl N. BLACK AND WHITE TOGETHER: BI-RACIAL POLITICS IN THE SOUTH. *Virginia Q. R. 1971 47(3): 421-444.* Argues that "a bi-racial politics has been at once a hope and a nightmare for the white South." After referring to the Reconstruction and Populist experiments, discusses the "largely forgotten" but "most successful instance of political cooperation between blacks and whites," the "Readjuster movement in Virginia during the 1880s under William Mahone...." Centering in Virginia and aimed at breaking the Bourbon hold on Virginia politics, the Readjusters, led by Mahone, called a biracial convention in 1879. Within three years they "captured the legislature, the governorship," the State's two U.S. Senate seats, and the majority of its congressional seats. They scaled down the State debt ("Readjusted" it), expanded social services, improved schools for both races, and abolished public whippings, the poll tax, and dueling. The reform accomplishments were praised in both North and South, but from 1883 on the racial issue was used effectively to defeat the Readjusters. In 1884 they joined the Republicans. Until his death in 1895 Mahone supported biracial politics, although his view toward blacks was always paternalistic. Perhaps the silence that has settled over Mahone and the Readjusters suggests the "threat to everything they stood for" which southern leaders saw in the Readjuster movement.   O. H. Zabel

1032. DeGrummond, Jane Lucas, ed. LUCINDA SPARKLE. *Louisiana Hist. 1961 2(3): 345-348.* Includes a letter which appeared in the *Louisiana Gazette,* 18 September 1810, addressed to the New Orleans city officials from a woman protesting the lack of a dignified promenade area where "nice girls" could parade their new clothes and "promote the cause of matrimony." The lady was objecting to the fact that the city's only public walks were the "stinkin' ol' streets" and the levee where "quadroons held sway."   D. C. James

1033. Dewey, Donald O. AN AMERICAN LIBERIA. *Pacific Hist. R. 1962 31(2): 179-182.* Presents an 1831 letter to James Madison by an "enterprising Southerner" suggesting a Negro colony "West of the Rocky Mountains" and also comments on Madison's views on Negro colonization.   R. Lowitt

1034. Doane, Gilbert H., ed. FOUR LETTERS PERTAINING TO THE REV-
EREND WILLIAM LEVINGTON, 1793(?)-1836. *Hist. Mag. of the Protestant
Episcopal Church 1963 32(1): 65-69.* Letters pertaining to a Negro desirous of
admission to the priesthood. These are now in the custody of the State Historical
Society of Wisconsin.   E. Oberholzer

1035. Ebner, Michael H. MRS. MILLER AND "THE PATTERSON SHOW":
A 1911 DEFEAT FOR RACIAL DISCRIMINATION. *New Jersey Hist. 1968
86(2): 88-91.* Concerns racial discrimination as practiced by a Paterson, New
Jersey, movie theater. A fine was levied, based on the New Jersey 1884 Civil
Rights Law, against the theater for charging blacks more than whites. 14 notes.
                                                         T. H. Brown

1036. Edwards, Frances. CONNECTICUT'S BLACK LAW. *New-England
Galaxy 1963 5(2): 34-42.* Discusses the attempt of Prudence Crandall (1803-89)
to establish a school for Negro girls in Canterbury, Connecticut. Local opposition
eventually forced the closing of the school, and Miss Crandall went to jail for
violating a law of the State of Connecticut which forbade schools such as hers.
                                                         T. J. Farnham

1037. Ege, Robert J. ISAIAH DORMAN: NEGRO CASUALTY WITH
RENO. *Montana 1966 16(1): 35-40.* The Indians who overran Major Reno's
original position in the Little Big Horn battle were surprised to find the body of
a Negro civilian. Sitting Bull identified him as Azimpa, a runaway slave who had
married a Sioux woman and lived at times among her people. Later he worked
around frontier army posts, where he was known as Isaiah Dorman. Apparently
he had accompanied General Terry's command as a guide and interpreter, in the
hope of meeting old friends among the Sioux.   S. R. Davison

1038. Farrison, William E. WILLIAM WELLS BROWN IN BUFFALO. *J. of
Negro Hist. 1954 39(4): 298-314.* Between 1836 and 1845, Brown created a Negro
movement in Buffalo which opposed the slave trade. He also organized a temperance movement among the Negroes.   S

1039. Fishel, Leslie H., Jr. WISCONSIN AND NEGRO SUFFRAGE. *Wisconsin Mag. of Hist. 1963 46(3): 180-196.* The question of Negro suffrage in Wisconsin became a subject of controversy even before the territory gained statehood.
The political aspects of the controversy as well as the legal questions of early
suffrage laws are studied.   W. F. Peterson

1040. Fisher, James A. THE STRUGGLE FOR NEGRO TESTIMONY IN
CALIFORNIA, 1851-1863. *Southern Calif. Q. 1969 51(4): 313-324.* A discussion of the 12-year struggle (1851-63) of California Negroes to gain the right to
testify "for or against white persons in state courts." During these years, Negroes
unavailingly petitioned the legislature to repeal anti-Negro testimony laws which
had been passed in 1850 and 1851. They also made speeches, held conventions,
and published editorials in the short-lived newspaper *The Mirror of the Times*

(San Francisco). Repeal of the laws finally came in 1863, probably due in large part to the humanitarian impulses toward Negroes generated by the Civil War, although the author suggests that the 12 years of Negro agitation also had some impact on legislative sentiment. Based on contemporary newspaper accounts, public documents, and secondary sources; 52 notes.   W. L. Bowers

1041. Foner, Philip S. JOHN BROWNE RUSSWURM, A DOCUMENT. *J. of Negro Hist. 1969 54(4): 393-397.* Russwurm was born of mixed racial parentage in Jamaica on 1 October 1799. At the age of eight he was sent to school in Quebec, and a few years later he settled in Maine with his father. In Maine Russwurm attended Bowdoin College, from which he became the first black graduate in 1826. After graduation Russwurm became convinced that Negroes had no future in the United States, and he subsequently moved to Liberia, where he lived until his death in 1851. The article includes a complete copy of Russwurm's commencement address given at the time he completed his academic studies. The address is entitled "The Condition and Prospects of Hayti" and extolls its people and the creation of its government. 2 notes.   R. S. Melamed

1042. Fornell, Earl W. THE ABDUCTION OF FREE NEGROES AND SLAVES IN TEXAS. *Southwestern Hist. Q. 1956/57 60(3): 369-380.* Discusses the kidnapping and the subsequent sale of free Negroes in Texas in the 1850's. Several cases are related to indicate some of the devices employed to acquire slave property. The legal and social position of the free Negro in Texas is briefly described.   J. A. Hudson

1043. Garvin, Russell. THE FREE NEGRO IN FLORIDA BEFORE THE CIVIL WAR. *Florida Hist. Q. 1967 46(1): 1-17.* After the Spanish in 1704 opened Florida to fugitive slaves from British plantations, Carolina and, later, Georgia were plagued with the problem of runaways. In 1740 British colonists destroyed the Negro fort three miles north of Saint Augustine. After the Revolution, several unsuccessful expeditions were made to capture runaway slaves living with or near the Creek and Seminole. Negroes joined the Indians in resistance against white penetration into Florida. Anti-immigration laws passed by the Florida legislature were not entirely effective in excluding new free Negroes. Laws limiting manumission were only partly successful. Regarded as a source of slave discontent, free Negroes were not allowed to vote or to serve on juries although they could own property. Florida law in 1842 required all free colored persons not in the territory before its cession to the United States to find a guardian and, in 1859, a master. The very little that is known about the free Negro in antebellum Florida indicates that anonymity served as part of the means of survival. 93 notes.   R. V. Calvert

1044. Geffen, Elizabeth M. VIOLENCE IN PHILADELPHIA IN THE 1840's AND 1850's. *Pennsylvania Hist. 1969 36(4): 381-410.* Violence was not unknown in Philadelphia before the 1840's and 1850's. The latter years, however, were particularly turbulent ones for the city because it was experiencing rapid growth and social change stimulated by industrialization and the immigration of large numbers of Irish Catholics. The problem of maintaining order was worsened by the fact that the Philadelphia area was divided into a number of separate jurisdictions. These areas were not unified until 1854. Anti-Negro riots in 1829, 1842, and 1849 had the effect of reducing the city's black population. Gangs, such as the Killers, Stingers, and Blood-Tubs, terrorized the citizenry. Workingmen with just grievances sometimes resorted to arson and rioting. The anti-Catholic riots of 1844 are described in detail. Finally, attention is given to the violent behavior of volunteer fire companies. Considerable background information is provided for each of these phenomena. Illus., 108 notes.   D. C. Swift

1045. Gloster, Jesse E. THE PROBLEM OF INSURANCE AMONG NEGROES PRIOR TO THE CIVIL WAR. *Negro Hist. Bull. 1963 27(2): 42-43.* Sketches insurance for American Negroes before the Civil War with mention of the roots of the insurance idea in African tribal culture, the early insurance services available to free Negroes, and the mutual aid societies formed secretly by the slaves. Documented.   L. Gara

1046. Hancock, Harold B., ed. WILLIAM YATES'S LETTER OF 1837: "SLAVERY, AND COLORED PEOPLE IN DELAWARE." *Delaware Hist. 1971 14(3): 205-216.* Reprints a letter by William D. Yates, a Negro agent for the American Anti-Slavery Society, in which Yates calculated that only one-twelfth of the State's population held any interest in slavery and that the institution was rapidly declining in Delaware. As such, Yates considered the State a critical testing ground for the role which whites would accord freedmen in society. Disappointment greeted Yates in Delaware as he discovered that race prejudice pervaded the State and that free Negroes were in a condition neither wholly free nor slave, yet subject to the disadvantages of both. Black Codes served to control the free Negro's mobility and denied him fundamental political, educational, and civil rights. In his concluding paragraph Yates raised a brief glimmer of optimism, observing that some free Negroes were landowners and tenants and had accumulated modest wealth and standing as a consequence of their mechanical skills and sober habits. 13 notes.   R. M. Miller

1047. Harding, Leonard. THE CINCINNATI RIOTS OF 1862. *Cincinnati Hist. Soc. Bull. 1967 25(4): 229-239.* Comparative prosperity during the Civil War hid from many "the downward trend in river commerce." Jobs were short on the levee, and fighting broke out between the Negro and Irish workers on 10 July 1862. On 12 July, the Cincinnati police were sent to Lexington to help protect it from the Confederate raider John Hunt Morgan, and the day after, four days of rioting started. Reviews the local newspapers' discussions of the causes of the riots, and concludes that a major result was the Negroes' loss of opportunity "to break into the mainstream of economic life." Photo, 28 notes.
T. M. Condon

1048. Heizer, Robert F. CIVIL RIGHTS IN CALIFORNIA IN THE 1850'S - A CASE HISTORY. *Kroeber Anthropological Soc. Papers 1964 31:129-137.* Presents the report of the case of *The People vs. Hall,* 1 October 1854, as determined by the Supreme Court of the State of California. The defendant, who had been previously convicted of murder on the testimony of Chinese witnesses, was cleared under extended interpretation of Sections 394 and 14 of the California Criminal Act. These sections state that the testimony of "Black, Mulatto or Indian" witnesses is not permissible in trying cases involving "White" defendants. The extension was made to include "Chinese" due to a suggested common origin of the Indian and Chinese "Races." The author includes some comments on racial discrimination and Indian indentureship in California. Based on primary and secondary sources; biblio. C. N. Warren

1049. Hill, Leonard U. JOHN RANDOLPH'S FREED SLAVES SETTLE IN WESTERN OHIO. *Cincinnati Hist. Soc. Bull. 1965 23(3): 179-187.* Relates the journey of Randolph's freed slaves in 1846. Released by his second will (of 1821), which a court found valid in 1845, nearly 400 set out by wagon in June 1846 for Cincinnati. From there they went by canal to Mercer County, where William Leigh had bought land for them. A white mob, however, forced them to leave. They moved toward Piqua, where local residents "brought them pails of soup daily." Violence drove them from Shelby County. They finally settled in Miami County. A certificate of freedom exists describing the members of the group. The 1850 census gives an idea of their numbers in Miami County. Reunions started in 1903. Many descendants remain. 2 illus., note. T. M. Condon

1050. Hoetink, Hermannus. "AMERICANS" IN SAMANA. *Caribbean Studies 1962/63 2(1): 3-22.* Under the Haitian occupation (1822-44) of the Spanish part of Santo Domingo, freed U.S. Negroes, particularly from the Baltimore and Philadelphia area, were encouraged to settle around and near Samaná Bay on the northeastern coast of Santo Domingo. For almost 140 years this fairly large group of settlers tilled the soil and grouped themselves in several scattered communities which resisted absorption into the predominantly Spanish and Catholic culture around them. Their Protestant religion and organized churches served to keep the group together. Some contact was sustained with English-speaking islands such as the Bahamas and the Virgin Islands. Also religious support from Protestant groups in Puerto Rico and the United States has been accepted in this century. The communities now show signs of integration into the Dominican way of life. More Spanish is being used instead of English and more youth are willing to marry persons of Spanish culture. J (T. Mathews)

1051. Howard, Lawrence C. A NOTE ON NEW ENGLAND WHALING AND AFRICA BEFORE 1860. *Negro Hist. Bull. 1958 22(1): 13-15.* Sketches the significant role that Negroes played in the American whaling industry. During most of the 19th century New England whalers frequented African waters and used Negroes in various capacities, ranging from deck hands to first mates. The number of AfroAmericans working on whaling ships increased after 1840, and some ships were entirely manned by Negro masters and crews. L. Gara

1052. James, Milton Morris. A NOTE ON RICHARD HUMPHREYS. *Negro Hist. Bull. 1959 23(1): 4.* Sketches the philanthropic work of Richard Humphreys, a Philadelphia Quaker whose will provided support for an Institute for Colored Youth and also a Shelter for Colored Orphans.   L. Gara

1053. James, Milton Morris. THE INSTITUTE FOR COLORED YOUTH. *Negro Hist. Bull. 1958 21(4): 83-85.* Relates the early history of the Institute for Colored Youth which grew out of a ten thousand dollar bequest for Negro education, contained in the will of Richard Humphrys, a Quaker businessman. After a slow and difficult start, the institute was moved from a farm to Philadelphia in 1852. Here the school prospered and in 1902 moved to Cheyney, Pennsylvania, where it eventually became a fully accredited teacher training institution.   L. Gara

1054. Jones, Louis C. A LEADER AHEAD OF HIS TIMES. *Am. Heritage 1963 14(4): 58-59, 83.* Describes the life of William Whipper, a well-to-do free Negro. In the 1830's he was editor of the Negro *National Reformer,* an abolitionist leader, supporter of Negro education, and champion of passive resistance as a means of achieving Negro rights. Portrait.   C. R. Allen, Jr.

1055. Kerber, Linda K. ABOLITIONISTS AND AMALGAMATORS: THE NEW YORK CITY RACE RIOTS OF 1834. *New York Hist. 1967 48(1): 28-39.* New York City in the 1830's had a well-developed "Jim Crow" system, and fear of social and economic advances by free Negroes ran deep. James Watson Webb, editor of the *Courier and Enquirer,* charged abolitionist leaders Arthur and Lewis Tappan with seeking race "amalgamation," and played upon the prejudice of the New York populace. Already frustrated by fraudulent municipal elections, labor trouble, incipient Irish-Nativist hostility, and dreading a possible cholera epidemic, an angry mob broke up an abolitionist meeting on 9 July 1834. For the next three days, white mobs murdered, burned, and looted in the Negro Five Points section of Manhattan. The mob was dispersed only when the militia was called out. Based on newspapers and secondary works; 22 notes.

                     G. Kurland

1056. Kirk-Greene, A. H. M. AMERICA IN THE NIGER VALLEY: A COLONIZATION CENTENARY. *Phylon 1962 23(3): 225-239.* Martin R. Delany's effort to organize a colonization movement to Nigeria, in the 1850's, is notable because, unlike other efforts, its aim was not to initiate compulsory rehabilitation of ex-slaves and Negroes rescued from slave ships. Delany's was an unconscious forerunner of Marcus Garvey's "Back to Africa" movement. At a Negro convention in 1858, he proposed an exploration of the Niger Valley in terms of its suitability for Negro emigration. He was later made head of an exploring party which drew up a treaty in 1858 between the chiefs of Abeokuta and the Negro commissioners. They returned with it to England where they formed the African Aid Society in behalf of the colonization plan. Delany drew up a report which was intended to begin organization of a colonization expedition in the United States, but the Civil War frustrated his plans.

                     L. Filler

1057. Klebaner, Benjamin Joseph. AMERICAN MANUMISSION LAWS AND THE RESPONSIBLITY FOR SUPPORTING SLAVES. *Virginia Mag. of Hist. and Biog. 1955 63(4): 443-453.* Reviews various pre-Civil War State laws pertaining to former owners' responsibilities regarding support of their indigenous or aged ex-slaves. C. F. Latour

1058. Langley, Harold D. THE NEGRO IN THE NAVY AND MERCHANT SERVICE 1798-1860. *J. of Negro Hist. 1967 52(4): 273-286.* Lack of statistical information along with an absence of a career enlisted naval service prior to the Civil War makes it difficult to write the history of the Negro contribution in the U.S. Navy and merchant fleet. Scattered references in diaries, journals, memoirs, and reports indicate that there were Negroes on virtually all naval and merchant vessels, that they got along well with other seamen, and that they sometimes met with discrimination from the officers. Documented with manuscript sources; 47 notes. L. Gara

Lanzinger, Klaus. see abstract 891.

1059. Lapp, Rudolph M. JEREMIAH SANDERSON: EARLY CALIFORNIA NEGRO. *J. of Negro Hist. 1968 53(4): 321-333.* Traces the movement and activities of Jeremiah B. Sanderson, a New Bedford free Negro. He went to California in 1854 where he became an outstanding leader as an educator and churchman. In the 1850's he was active in the Negro convention movement and after the Civil War he supported the movement for full civil rights. In all his activities he avoided controversy with other Negro leaders, working for harmony rather than dissension. He was killed in a railroad accident in 1875. Based on newspaper and manuscript sources; 49 notes. L. Gara

1060. Lapp, Rudolph M. NEGRO RIGHTS ACTIVITIES IN GOLD RUSH CALIFORNIA. *California Hist. Soc. Q. 1966 45(1): 3-20.* The activities of the small Negro population in early California bear witness to the inaccuracy of the idea that the American Negro did little in his own behalf. Slavery was unconstitutional in the new State. The free Negro told his black brother that in California he had a legal chance for freedom. After several cases in court, it became apparent that, at least in San Francisco and Sacramento, the California Negro had an increasing number of white friends. In 1855, the California Negroes held their First Colored Convention, organized by the Franchise League and mainly concerned with testimony rights in civil and criminal cases where white men were also involved. An anti-Negro immigration bill died in 1858. The decade of the 1860's saw the rise of the fortunes of the California Negro. "By the time of the Fourth Colored Convention of 1865," the testimony laws having been revised, "the Negro leadership was turning itself to the problems of education and suffrage." Based on official sources; 63 notes. E. P. Stickney

1061. Lapp, Rudolph M. THE NEGRO IN GOLD RUSH CALIFORNIA. *J. of Negro Hist. 1964 49(2): 81-98.* The gold rush brought several thousand slaves and free Negroes into California. They worked as miners, laborers, cooks, and in other service occupations. Some of those who came as slaves earned enough to purchase their own freedom. The pioneer society of California permitted a degree of freedom for Negroes not known in most other parts of the country, yet there were attempts to introduce slavery and to exclude free Negroes. In the courts Negroes were not allowed to testify against whites until 1863. Many of the California Negroes took advantage of the opportunities presented them for educational and economic advancement and they met in a number of conventions to demand improvement of their legal status.   L. Gara

1062. Loomis, Augustus W. SCENES IN THE INDIAN TERRITORY: KOWETAH MISSION. *Chronicles of Oklahoma 1968 46(1): 64-72.* In 1851, Augustus W. (Gustavus) Loomis published *Scenes in the Indian Territory* from his observations as an army commander in the area in the 1840's. Reprinted here is the portion dealing with a visit he made to the Kowetah Mission, near present Coweta, Oklahoma. Education, Negro interpreters, recreation, as well as a history of the mission are briefly described. 8 notes.   D. L. Smith

1063. Lumpkin, Katherine DuPre. "THE GENERAL PLAN WAS FREEDOM": A NEGRO SECRET ORDER ON THE UNDERGROUND RAILROAD. *Phylon 1967 28(1): 63-77.* William Lambert and George DeBaptiste were free Negroes who separately moved to Detroit in the 1840's. Both were leading Negro citizens of the city and were active figures in the antislavery movement. After the Civil War both described for publication a Negro secret order that had served as a branch of the underground railroad and had possibly been connected with John Brown. The author gives an account of the reminiscences which were published in Detroit newspapers and attempts to answer questions raised by the accounts. The conclusion is that, while such an organization did exist, it is impossible to establish how extensive it was and whether it reached out from Detroit and beyond. Based on materials found in the Burton Historical Collection of the Detroit Public Library; 38 notes.

D. N. Brown

1064. Mabee, Carleton. A NEGRO BOYCOTT TO INTEGRATE BOSTON SCHOOLS. *New England Q. 1968 41(3): 341-361.* From 1844 to 1855 Negro and white Garrisonians struggled for an end to segregated schools in Boston. They launched a boycott against Negro attendance at the Smith Grammar School, petitioned the State legislature, and instituted a court suit. The Garrisonians encountered obstacles from the racist Primary School Committee, segregationist blacks, and inactive Horace Mann, who was unwilling to compromise his public school mission. Aided by the 1854 victory of the antislavery (and anti-immigrant) Know-Nothing Party in Massachusetts, and by the popular outcry against the

Fugitive Slave Law, the legislature outlawed segregation in 1855 and Boston became the only large city to develop integrated schools: Leadership in the struggle was assumed by William Cooper Nell, a local Negro Garrisonian abolitionist.41 notes.   K. B. West

1065. Macmaster, Richard K. HENRY HIGHLAND GARNET AND THE AFRICAN CIVILIZATION SOCIETY. *J. of Presbyterian Hist. 1970 48(2): 95-112.* Discusses the founding of the African Civilization Society under the leadership of Garnet (1815-82). The revolutionary nationalist risings in 1848 led some in America's black community to hope to found a separate nation for their people. This aim was coupled with a desire to abolish slavery. Garnet, a black Presbyterian minister and editor, became a nationalist and abolitionist leader but rejected violence as a means to achieve his goals. Seeking alternatives, he joined the American Free Produce Association which boycotted southern goods to force an economic end to slavery. Thomas J. Bowen, former African missionary, influenced Garnet to found the African Civilization Society. The society hoped to create in Nigeria a Christian society of natives and black American emigrants which would grow cotton and other products to compete with American products. Such competition would result in lower prices and in eliminating the strongest support for slavery. The African settlement would thus be a Christian mission, an antislavery force, and a center of Negro nationality. However, many American blacks doubted the wisdom of colonization and believed primary attention should be devoted to America. Events in Africa and the Civil War destroyed the scheme. 78 notes.   S. C. Pearson, Jr.

1066. Meade, George P. A NEGRO SCIENTIST OF SLAVERY DAYS. *Negro Hist. Bull. 1957 20(7): 159-164.* Calls attention to the work of Norbert Rillieux (1806-94), engineer, scientist and inventor of the first practical multiple-effect vacuum evaporator, which was introduced in a Louisiana sugar factory in 1846. Rillieux, a quadroon, was born in New Orleans and moved to Paris about the time of the Civil War. He spent several years in Europe studying Egyptology and in 1881 patented a system for heating sugar beet juice with vapors in multiple-effect. Both of his major inventions involved principles now in universal use in the sugar industry. Reprint of an article from *Scientific Monthly* 1946 62: 317-326.
                                                                L. Gara

1067. Mohl, Raymond A. EDUCATION AS SOCIAL CONTROL IN NEW YORK CITY, 1784-1825. *New York Hist. 1970 51(3): 219-237.* In the half-century after the American Revolution, numerous primary schools were established in New York City. Most were church supported, and religion constituted a major portion of the curriculum. Founded for the education of the poor, Negroes, and Indians, they provided a basic education but stressed the inculcation of middle-class values and attitudes. The schools also found employment for their students as domestics or as apprentices in the trades. It was hoped that the schools could cure New York's poverty and social ills by training lower-class students to fit into a middle-class society. Social control and the prevention of social radicalism were the primary functions of the New York school system. Based on primary and secondary sources; 5 illus., 29 notes.   G. Kurland

1068. Muir, Andrew Forest. THE FREE NEGRO IN GALVESTON COUNTY, TEXAS. *Negro Hist. Bull. 1958 22(3): 68-70.* Discusses the fate of the small number of free Negroes in Galveston before the Civil War. After laws made residence for free Negroes illegal in Texas, some of them voluntarily became the nominal property of white masters in order to stay in the State. While some slaves were freed in Galveston, other free Negroes were enslaved both legally and illegally.   L. Gara

1069. Myers, John L. AMERICAN ANTISLAVERY SOCIETY AGENTS AND THE FREE NEGRO, 1833-1838. *J. of Negro Hist. 1967 52(3): 200-219.* Discusses the contribution of four agents of the American Anti-Slavery Society who in the years 1833-38 worked with free Negroes in the North and in Canada. John J. Miter and William Yates were assigned the area east of the Appalachian Mountains to encourage education, temperance, and general improvement of life among the colored population. Yates also published, in 1838, an important pamphlet, *Rights of Colored Men to Suffrage, Citizenship, and Trial by Jury in Philadelphia.* Augustus Wattles worked west of the Alleghenies and Hiram Wilson served the Negro colonists in Canada. Although the society had little money for this phase of its activity, the agents' assignments indicate a serious concern by the abolitionists for the welfare of free Negroes. Based on antislavery publications, newspapers, and manuscripts; 35 notes.   L. Gara

1070. Neyland, Leedell. THE FREE NEGRO IN FLORIDA. *Negro Hist. Bull. 1965 29(2): 27-28, 42-43, 45.* Gives a brief history of the free Negroes in Florida from 1830 to 1860, in which period the slave population increased from 15,500 to 61,745 while the free Negro population rose only from 844 to 932. "Despite the fact that repressive legislation was enacted quite prolifically after 1830, generally, free Negroes surmounted many obstacles and found noticeable outlet in the economic world. In the majority, free Negroes tended to be economically independent because from 1830 to 1860, a total of only 47 indigents were recorded. On the other hand, a considerable number were fairly substantial landholders or engaged in various remunerative business ventures." After Florida gained statehood in 1845, the free Negro was plagued with an increasing number of oppressive and inhumane ordinances and laws from both the municipal and State levels. "Even though the free Negro never numbered more than 832 in Florida, his very presence was a nemesis to the white members of the society." Biblio.
                                                                 D. D. Cameron

1071. Onderdonk, Henry, Jr. NOTES ON THE HISTORY OF QUEENS COUNTY. *J. of Long Island Hist. 1967 7(1): 53-76, (2): 36-56.* Part I. Reprints a manuscript deposited by Onderdonk, a late 19th-century local historian, in The Long Island Historical Society. It was originally entitled "Queens County in Olden Times." In 1865 the author published a different and much longer manuscript under the same title, thus the notes have been given a new title. They chronicle the political and social events from 15 January 1639 to 13 December 1781. Included are extracts from several journals, town records, and rolls. Part II. The entries cover the period from 1784 to 1852. Emphasis is on Tory difficulties, Negro crime, elections, extension of transportation facilities, deaths, and curiosities. A brief biographical sketch of Onderdonk's father concludes the notes. A lengthy comment on Onderdonk's sources, identifying them for the modern user, is added by John H. Lindenbusch.   C. A. Newton

1072. Pease, Jane H. and Pease, William H. BLACK POWER - THE DEBATE IN 1840. *Phylon 1968 29(1): 19-26.* In the 1830's white abolitionists in the United States held paternalistic attitudes toward Negroes and refused to accord them full equality within abolition societies. In 1840 black abolitionists initiated a debate over whether it was not preferable to organize separate black antislavery conventions in order to enable Negroes to become more active in the movement. In the end the separatists won and all-black conventions were organized, enabling Negroes to play a larger role in antislavery activities. What began as an effort by Negroes to gain basic civil rights through independent conventions became as well an appeal for direct action against the hard core of slavery. Based on newspapers and other primary documents; 23 notes.   R. D. Cohen

1073. Pease, William H. and Pease, Jane H. ORGANIZED NEGRO COMMUNITIES: A NORTH AMERICAN EXPERIMENT. *J. of Negro Hist. 1962 47(1): 19-34.* Discusses the functions and shortcomings of the organized Negro communities in the United States and Canada prior to the Civil War. The communities provided for mutual assistance, private land ownership, and political and educational experience in a rural, middle-class setting. Some of the promoters of such communities were interested in profits as well as service. Factors contributing to the failures of the communities included dishonesty and incompetence on the part of some leaders, and internal bickering. Because of their segregated nature, the communities' greatest shortcoming was their failure to prepare the Negro inhabitants for life in a fully free society.
                    L. Gara

1074. Perlman, Daniel. ORGANIZATIONS OF THE FREE NEGRO IN NEW YORK CITY, 1800-1860. *J. of Negro Hist. 1971 56(3): 181-197.* The antebellum free Negro was always attempting to improve his position, even though he faced enormous hardships and restrictions. In this regard, black social organizations aided the Negro in his efforts at self-improvement, but their exact number in New York City will forever remain undetermined because many societies died in their infancy and few that survived left any significant records. Black organizations in New York tended to develop along three general and uneven phases; mutual aid societies predominated from 1810 to 1830, literary organizations became strong in 1830-40, and the era of 1840-60 saw the rise of political action groups and national benevolent institutions. Based heavily on issues of the *Colored American* covering the years 1837-39; 88 notes.   R. S. Melamed

1075. Pih, Richard W. NEGRO SELF-IMPROVEMENT EFFORTS IN ANTE-BELLUM CINCINNATI, 1836-1850. *Ohio Hist. 1969 78(3): 179-187.* Shows how white discrimination prompted efforts by Cincinnati Negroes to establish businesses, schools, libraries, churches, Sunday schools, and other organizations and movements. Based mainly on newspapers.   S. L. Jones

1076. Poe, William A. LOTT CARY: MAN OF PURCHASED FREEDOM. *Church Hist. 1970 39(1): 49-61.* Cary (1780-1828) played a significant role in the colony of Liberia in its first decade. Cary was born in slavery and joined the First Baptist Church of Richmond, Virginia, in 1807. He subsequently learned to read and write and purchased freedom for himself and his family. With William Crane he formed the Richmond African Missionary Society and then announced his desire to become a missionary to Africa. Under the auspices of the American Colonization Society, the Baptist General Missionary Convention, and the Richmond Society Cary went to Africa in 1821. Before sailing he and other emigrants organized a church which became the First Baptist Church of Monrovia. After a short time in Sierra Leone, Cary went to Liberia and became an influential and stabilizing figure. He continued missionary work with both immigrants and natives, sought peace with indigenous tribes, sought to establish schools, and formed the Monrovia Baptist Missionary Society. Though he led opposition to Jehudi Ashmun and Colonization Society policies in 1823-24, he was subsequently reconciled to Ashmun and made vice agent for the colony. When Ashmun left Liberia in 1828 the whole responsibility for government of the colony fell on Cary until his untimely death later in that year. Based on published materials; 64 notes.   S. C. Pearson, Jr.

1077. Reese, James V. THE EARLY HISTORY OF LABOR ORGANIZA-TIONS IN TEXAS, 1838-1876. *Southwestern Hist. Q. 1968 72(1): 1-20.* Most labor activity in pre-Civil War Texas was spontaneous in response to a specific problem or promising situation which lasted only for the duration of the situation. Occasionally grievances were aired in public meetings, petitions, or in ethnic society clubs. First steps toward bona fide labor organizations came in the fifties when ethnic groups formed workingmen's associations to encourage the development of trades, instruction in English and arithmetic, and other benevolent activities. There is no evidence of organized labor activity during the Civil War. With printers in the forefront, several unions were established in the postwar years, including a small number of Negro labor groups. Few, if any, however, had sufficient strength to sustain a successful strike. Unionization accelerated in the seventies. The climax came in violent railway strikes in 1877 which ushered Texas into a new era of militant unionism. Railroads had broken the frontier pattern of isolated and self-sufficient agricultural communities and started the State toward a modern, although still primarily agricultural, economy. 71 notes.
                                                                       D. L. Smith

1078. Reinders, Robert C. THE FREE NEGRO IN THE NEW ORLEANS ECONOMY, 1850-1860. *Louisiana Hist. 1965 6(3): 273-285.* The free Negro in the 1850's in New Orleans held his own in the skilled trades, and the demand for common labor was great enough to prevent large-scale Negro unemployment. Negro businessmen had declined in number and prosperity since the 1830's. The one hope of security was land. Free Negro women owned real estate to a far greater extent than their white sisters. The 1850's was generally a period of white hostility, restrictive laws, and declining economic opportunities. Consequently most local free Negroes, rich and poor alike, were extremely pleased when the "Bluecoats" arrived in 1862. 52 notes.   E. P. Stickney

1079. Roy, Jessie H. NEGRO JUDGES IN THE UNITED STATES. *Negro Hist. Bull. 1965 28(5): 108-111.* Sketches the career of Miflin Wister Gibbs, born a free Negro in 1823 in Philadelphia, who had his own contracting business in that city. Gibbs went to California during the gold rush and later joined the gold rush to British Columbia. After the Civil War he moved to Arkansas where, in 1873, he became the first Negro judge when he was appointed municipal judge of Little Rock. L. Gara

1080. Ruchames, Louis. JIM CROW RAILROADS IN MASSACHUSETTS. *Am. Q. 1956 8(1): 61-75.* Public agitation about segregation on railroads in Massachusetts became an issue in 1841 with a series of incidents involving Negro and white leaders of the abolition movement. The author outlines some of these incidents and the arguments presented for legislative action to end segregation on the railroads. Despite legislative support the railroads were forced by public pressure to abandon their segregation policy. R. Kerley

1081. Ruchkin, Judith Polgar. THE ABOLITION OF "COLORED SCHOOLS" IN ROCHESTER, NEW YORK: 1832-1856. *New York Hist. 1970 51(4): 377-393.* Rochester's colored school was first opened in 1832. When the city began a free public school system in 1841, it assumed the cost of running the colored school but refused to permit Negro children to enroll at the white public schools. With the arrival of Frederick Douglass (ca. 1817-95) in Rochester in 1848, the movement for public school integration was resumed and, by 1850, some Negro children were being allowed to attend white schools. Rochester's colored school was disbanded in 1856 and its students transferred to white schools. However, this did not come about as the result of Douglass' efforts. It cost Rochester 30.77 dollars to maintain each student at the colored school while the cost of sending a white child to school was only 6.83 dollars per year. Rochester integrated its school system in the interests of economy rather than social justice. Based on primary and secondary sources; 7 illus., 42 notes. G. Kurland

1082. Savage, W. S. THE NEGRO COWBOY ON THE TEXAS PLAINS. *Negro Hist. Bull. 1961 24(7): 157-158, 163.* Discusses the contribution of Negro cowboys in Texas with special emphasis on "Eighty" John Wallace, Emanuel Organ, and Mathew "Bones" Hooks, who were all outstanding in their chosen work. L. Gara

1083. Seifman, Eli. THE UNITED COLONIZATION SOCIETIES OF NEW YORK AND PENNSYLVANIA AND THE ESTABLISHMENT OF THE AFRICAN COLONY OF BASSA COVE. *Pennsylvania Hist. 1968 35(1): 23-44.* The founding and development of the American Colonization Society are traced in considerable detail. Particular emphasis is laid on the abolitionists' challenge to the concept of colonization and other factors contributing to the decline of the society. As the society's influence waned, it fell into debt and it was decided that no further colonization ventures should be launched until the indebtedness was removed. Reacting against this decision, the New York unit of the society and Philadelphians known as the Young Men's Colonization Society of Pennsylvania decided in 1834 to establish independently another colony at Bassa Cove, 80 miles south of Monrovia. The parent society decided to assist the venture, but the colony was soon abandoned due to a raid by a local chieftain. When peace was restored, the Bassa Cove colony was reestablished and soon absorbed a neighboring settlement. In 1838 the American Colonization Society was reorganized into a federation of autonomous societies, and the errant New York and Philadelphia groups returned to the parent body. This reorganization also produced the Commonwealth of Liberia, of which the Bassa Cove settlement became the County of Grand Bassa. Based on primary sources; 54 notes.   D. C. Swift

1084. Sellers, James B. FREE NEGROES OF TUSCALOOSA COUNTY BEFORE THE THIRTEENTH AMENDMENT. *Alabama R. 1970 23(2): 110-127.* Contends that, while there may have been unrecorded cases that depict the lack of legal and economic rights under the law in regard to free Negroes, the record of "initiative and enterprise" written by men like Solomon Perteet (landowner, slave owner, and moneylender), Ned Berry (drayman and landowner), Zadock Love (landowner and slave owner), James Abbott (barber), Martin Greer, Jack Winn, and others, "should do much to break the stereotype of the free man of color as an outcast and a burden on the community." Based on Census Records, Tuscaloosa County Deed Records, Alabama State Tract Books, and Tuscaloosa County Circuit Court Records and Minutes; 66 notes.   D. F. Henderson

1085. Stange, Douglas C. BISHOP DANIEL A. PAYNE AND THE LUTHERAN CHURCH. *Lutheran Q. 1964 16(4): 354-359.* A biography of the educational and professional life of Daniel A. Payne (1811-93), who was probably the first Negro graduate of an American theological school. Supporting himself by menial tasks, he attended the Lutheran Theological Seminary at Gettysburg and was ordained a minister. Because the Lutheran Church had no congregation for him, he eventually joined the African Methodist Episcopal Church and later became a bishop. He was also the president of Wilberforce University, Ohio.
R. B. Lange

1086. Stange, Douglas C. LUTHERAN INVOLVEMENT IN THE AMERICAN COLONIZATION SOCIETY. *Mid-Am. 1967 49(2): 140-151.* The Reverend David Frederick Shaeffer of Maryland probably did more to further the aims of the American Colonization Society than any other Lutheran pastor. As editor of the *Evangelical Lutheran Intelligencer,* as president of the General Synod (1831 and 1832), and for many years its secretary, he was able to exert significant influence. Perhaps the main reason why the Colonization Society appealed to Lutherans during the years 1820 to 1830 was because it sought not to excite, but to reconcile. It afforded an opportunity to solve the Negro problem and in the process prevent divisions within the country and the church. 66 notes.
L. D. Silveri

1087. Stephenson, William W., Jr. INTEGRATION OF THE DETROIT PUBLIC SCHOOL SYSTEM DURING THE PERIOD, 1839-1869. *Negro Hist. Bull. 1962/63 26(1): 23-28.* Traces the early history of schools for Negro children in Detroit. In the 1830's such schools were held in various churches but seldom for a very long period of time. The following decade, separate free public schools were established for Negroes. In 1869 a colored parent, Joseph Workman, won a lawsuit in the Michigan Supreme Court which permitted him to enroll his child in a white school. The following year the Detroit Board of Education implemented the Workman decision by rescinding the rules and regulations which sustained racial segregation in the city's public schools. Based on newspapers and other contemporary sources.   L. Gara

1088. Sweat, Edward F. SOCIAL STATUS OF THE FREE NEGRO IN ANTEBELLUM GEORGIA. *Negro Hist. Bull. 1958 21(6): 129-131.* Although the few free Negroes in antebellum Georgia were assigned an inferior social position, they were permitted to own property, join the church, and marry legally. Laws making it illegal to teach Negroes to read and write were not enforced. A very small number of the free Negroes became wealthy and attained recognition and a social status not usually granted to people of their race.   L. Gara

1089. Talbert, Charles G. and Gregg, Clifford C. GEORGE MICHAEL BEDINGER, 1756-1843. *Register of the Kentucky Hist. Soc. 1967 65(1): 28-46.* Kentucky pioneer George Michael Bedinger had a varied career as an Indian fighter, Revolutionary War officer, surveyor, State legislator (1792-94), U.S. Congressman (1803-07), and successful businessman. On many issues he was far ahead of his time. Opposed to slavery, he supported the American Colonization Society which sought to send freed American Negroes to Liberia in Africa. Bedinger wanted the society's work to be subsidized by the U.S. Government. He favored internal improvements at public expense, especially the Maysville road, and was in favor of an amendment to the Constitution to abolish the electoral system, because it could defeat a candidate favored by a majority of the people. The two major sources were the Draper Manuscript Collection in the Wisconsin Historical Society and Danske Dandridge, *George Michael Bedinger: A Kentucky Pioneer* (Charlottesville, Virginia, 1909). Illus.   B. Wilkins

1090. Thompson, Erwin N. THE NEGRO SOLDIERS ON THE FRONTIER: A FORT DAVIS CASE STUDY. *J. of the West 1968 7(2): 217-235.* Gives an account of the Negro soldiers stationed at Fort Davis, Texas. The fort was established in 1854 and abandoned in 1862 during the Civil War. The first regulars to return in 1867 were Negroes. Between 1867 and 1885 all the regular colored units were stationed at Fort Davis at one time or another. Both their accomplishments as fighters and some comments on the social record are offered. Photographs of Fort Davis and a Remington sketch of an Apache scout and a Negro cavalryman are included.   R. N. Alvis

1091. Walker, Joseph E. A COMPARISON OF NEGRO AND WHITE LABOR IN CHARCOAL IRON COMMUNITY. *Labor Hist. 1969 10(3): 487-497.* Presents five wage tables of black and white workers in the Hopewell Village iron community in Berks County, Pennsylvania, between 1805 and 1853. Blacks were employed in significant numbers and there was less discrimination in the earlier years as compared to the later ones. Based on the Hopewell Village MSS; tables, 14 notes.   L. L. Athey

1092. Weeks, Louis, III. JOHN HOLT RICE AND THE AMERICAN COLO-
NIZATION SOCIETY. *J. of Presbyterian Hist. 1968 46(1): 26-41.* Reappraises
the role of the American Colonization Society (which tried to remove free
Negroes from the United States to Liberia) through a study of the career of John
Holt Rice, a Virginian and Presbyterian minister. Rice was a leader in the
establishment of the Union Theological Seminary in Virginia and edited *The
Evangelical and Literary Magazine.* He supported the ACS from its formation
in 1816 until his last illness in 1831. During these years he was subjected to
steadily increasing pressures because of his antislavery views. The author concludes that Rice, and presumably others, supported the ACS for the following
reasons: 1) it offered the only viable option to the status quo in Virginia, 2) the
support of the ACS by national bodies suggests an agreement by northerners and
southerners that the society offered a "way out," 3) Rice believed it would aid
the cause of antislavery, 4) he was misled by society propaganda, and 5) the
society's aims in Africa coincided with his own evangelicalism. The ACS may not
have been a complete failure as is often suggested and proslavery intimidation of
antislavery advocates may have been significant before 1831. Based on published
sources; 61 notes.   S. C. Pearson, Jr.

1093. White, Arthur O. THE BLACK MOVEMENT AGAINST JIM CROW
EDUCATION IN LOCKPORT, NEW YORK, 1835-1876. *New York Hist.
1969 50(3): 265-282.* In the mid-1830's, 188 of Lockport's 2,100 people were
Negroes, and the black community began to agitate for its own school. Without
benefit of public assistance, a black school was opened in 1840, but it faced
constant difficulties in attracting qualified teachers. Its academic standards generally were far below those of the white public schools and, when the black school
burned down in 1863, a movement began to integrate the public school system.
Lockport officials refused integration, but they did support a separate black
school which replaced the one destroyed by fire. In 1873 the Reverend C. W.
Mossell led a boycott of the black school and a series of sit-ins at the common
school to force integration. While Mossell's "confrontation" tactics failed, Lockport finally integrated its school system in 1876 because the cost of operating an
underattended all-black school was becoming prohibitive. There was no white
opposition to integration because the move was seen as economic. Based on
primary and secondary sources; 4 illus., 62 notes.   G. Kurland

1094. Wight, Willard E., ed. DOCUMENTS: TWO LETTERS FROM LIB-
ERIA. *J. of Negro Hist. 1959 44(4): 379-384.* The Methodist Episcopal Church
in the United States sent its first missionary to Liberia in 1835, 14 years after the
first shipload of emigrants left Boston to found the new colony for free Negroes.
The letters presented here are progress reports of a general nature (1849 and
1851) from Francis Burns, first missionary bishop, and John W. Roberts, his
successor. Both bishops were Negroes born in the United States. The letters are
in the James H. Weeks Collection, Southern Methodist University, Dallas, Texas.
                                                                       A. P. Tracy

1095. Woolfolk, George R. TURNER'S SAFETY VALVE AND FREE NE-
GRO WESTWARD MIGRATION. *Pacific Northwest Q. 1965 56(3): 125-130.*

Analyzes the migration of Negroes from areas east of the Mississippi River to trans-Mississippi Spanish borderlands in the framework of Frederick Jackson Turner's "safety-valve" theory, principally between 1850 and 1860.

C. C. Gorchels

The Civil War & Emancipation

1096. Abbott, Richard H. MASSACHUSETTS AND THE RECRUITMENT OF SOUTHERN NEGROES, 1863-1865. *Civil War Hist. 1968 14(3): 197-210.* Describes the rise and fall of efforts to recruit blacks in liberated Southern States to fill northern draft quotas. The idea originated in Massachusetts, where large numbers of factory operatives were being drained into the military. If former slaves would either volunteer or serve as substitutes for draftees, the problem could be solved. Incorporated in the July 1864 Amendment to the Enrollment Act, the "recruiting in Rebel states" proviso was an instant failure for reasons too numerous to list here. It was repealed in March 1865. Based on private papers and public documents.

E. C. Murdock

1097. Abzug, Robert H. THE COPPERHEADS: HISTORICAL APPROACHES TO CIVIL WAR DISSENT IN THE MIDWEST. *Indiana Mag. of Hist. 1970 66(1): 40-55.* Examines the theses of James Ford Rhodes, Allan Nevins, and other Civil War historians, with particular stress on Indiana and Midwestern writers. Hypothesizes that the common denominator of antiwar feeling among the extreme Peace Democrats was fear - fear of Negroes, abolitionists, industrialists, and tyranny. Based on secondary sources; 67 notes.

N. E. Tutorow

1098. Adams, Neal Monroe. NORTHERN NEGROPHOBIA DURING THE CIVIL WAR: AS REPORTED BY THE LONDON TIMES. *Negro Hist. Bull. 1964 28(1): 7-8.* Describes the reporting of the influential London *Times* of the attitudes of northerners toward the Negroes during the Civil War. According to the *Times,* northern sentiment was hostile toward Negroes and would not permit them to rise above the position of social outcast. Antislavery was a reaction to economic competition rather than a humanitarian concern. Lincoln was a moderate on the slavery question and he favored colonization as a follow-up of emancipation.

L. Gara

1099. Alford, Neill. THE INFLUENCE OF THE AMERICAN CIVIL WAR UPON THE GROWTH OF THE LAW OF DECEDENTS' ESTATES AND TRUSTS. *Am. J. of Legal Hist. 1960 4(4): 299-354.* Using contemporary legal documents and cases, presents four factors which determined the influence of the Civil War upon this branch of the law: emancipation of slaves, breakdown of local southern governments, population movements, and the loss of Confederate and

State currencies and credit. In the North, principal areas of doctrinal development were in charity law, informal wills of soldiers and sailors, and the question of whether grants and bounties were properly assets of decedents. Detailed discussion is also given to new policies regarding fiduciary problems.

N. C. Brockman

1100. Ambrose, Stephen E. BY ENLISTING NEGROES, COULD THE SOUTH STILL WIN THE WAR? *Civil War Times Illus. 1965 3(9): 16-21.* Patrick Ronayne Cleburne, one of two foreign-born generals in the Confederate Army, proposed to give up slavery in exchange for independence. He believed by enlisting Negroes, the South could still win the war. This idea was considered so revolutionary that Jefferson Davis asked him to keep it quiet. A generation passed before the full story was revealed when, at the death of a member of Cleburne's staff around 1890, a copy of Cleburne's letter was found, verified, and sent to the War Department for collection in the Confederate records. Illus.

E. P. Stickney

1101. Amundson, R. J. SANFORD AND GARIBALDI. *Civil War Hist. 1968 14(1): 40-45.* Narrates the efforts of an American diplomat Henry S. Sanford to secure the services of the Italian military hero Giuseppe Garibaldi as commander of the Federal forces around Washington in August 1861. Garibaldi declined the offer because he would not be given supreme power over all the armies with the authority to abolish slavery. The conclusion is that it was just as well for the Lincoln administration that Garibaldi did not accept the offer because he was too independent in thought and deed to have worked smoothly with the government. Based on the Sanford Papers in the National Archives.   E. C. Murdock

1102. Anderson, David D. EMERSON AND LINCOLN. *Lincoln Herald 1958 60(4): 123-128.* Ralph Waldo Emerson felt that human rights were more important than a mere political pact and that slavery, and not secession, was the true issue of the Civil War. Thus Emerson felt that Lincoln was not a representative man. He considered Lincoln timid, afraid to face the real issue and to prosecute relentlessly. As an intellectual, Emerson was suspicious of Lincoln's backwoods origin, but as time went on, the entries in his journal reflected a better understanding of the President. He later met Lincoln and came to consider him a "brave and just man." He later acknowledged Lincoln as the "Representative Man," the "Great Man" of his age. Biblio.   J. G. Turner

1103. Aptheker, Herbert. GRAZHDANSKAIA VOINA V SSHA [The Civil War in the United States]. *Novaia i Noveishaia Istoriia [USSR] 1961 (3): 88-96.* Centennial article describing the main causes of the American Civil War, its general course, and consequences in popular form. Stresses the part played in the Civil War by the Negro masses. No documentation with the exception of a concluding footnote from William Z. Foster's book, *The Negro People in American History.*   E. B. Richards

1104. Armstrong, Warren B. UNION CHAPLAINS AND THE EDUCATION OF THE FREEDMEN. *J. of Negro Hist. 1967 52(2): 104-115.* Discusses the contributions made by Union Army chaplains to the education of freedmen during the Civil War. Many chaplains, concerned about the freedmen's future, emphasized the importance of education and urged a national policy for such a program. Some taught freedmen in their spare time. In 1862 General Grant made Chaplain John Eaton responsible for the freedmen within Union lines in the Mississippi Valley. Eaton's assignment included directing such limited educational efforts as were being made, and in September of 1864 he was designated coordinator of all educational efforts under the War Department. Education of freedmen was never a major concern of the Union command, but the efforts and persistence of numerous chaplains guaranteed that for some of the former slaves the transition from slavery to life in a free society would be rendered less painful by attaining a rudimentary education.   L. Gara

1105. Ashcraft, Allan C., ed. MRS. RUSSELL AND THE BATTLE OF RAY-MOND, MISSISSIPPI. *J. of Mississippi Hist. 1963 25(1): 38-40.* Includes a letter written by Mrs. J. W. Russell, who lived on a plantation near Raymond, Mississippi, to her husband, who was in the Confederate ranks in Tennessee. The letter, dated 13 May 1863, one day after Ulysses S. Grant's victory at the Battle of Raymond, does not describe the fighting, but rather the confiscatory actions by Union troops passing the plantation and the reactions of the slaves, some of whom left to follow the Union forces but quickly returned, "saying they were tired of Yankees" already. The context of the letter is described in Ashcraft's brief introductory remarks.   D. C. James

1106. Becker, Carl M. PICTURE OF A YOUNG COPPERHEAD. *Ohio Hist. 1962 71(1): 3-23.* Reconstructs, from the man's personal papers, Thomas Owen Lowe's actions and attitudes during the Civil War. Lowe, a resident of Dayton, Ohio, became closely associated with the peace Democrats and ardently supported the war policies of Clement L. Vallandigham. Lowe blamed the abolitionists for the war and advocated a negotiated peace in which the independence of the Confederacy would be recognized. The Lowe Papers are in the Dayton Public Library.   S. L. Jones

1107. Bell, Howard H. NEGRO EMANCIPATION IN HISTORIC RETROSPECT: THE NATION, THE CONDITION AND PROSPECTS OF THE NEGRO AS REFLECTED IN THE NATIONAL CONVENTION OF 1864. *J. of Human Relations 1963 11(2): 221-231.* A paper read at the 47th Annual Meeting of the Association for the Study of Negro Life and History at Central State College, Wilberforce, Ohio, 25-27 October 1962. The National Negro Convention - which met at Syracuse, New York, 4-7 October 1864 - is described and the changing role and uncertain status of the Negro during the Civil War is stressed. A controversial issue was Negro nationalism, a survival of the antebellum decades. Based on newspapers, the *Proceedings of the National Convention of Colored Men,* and other sources.   D. J. Abramoske

1108. Bennett, N. R. AMERICANS IN ZANZIBAR: 1865-1915. *Tanganyika Notes and Records 1963 60: 49-66.* Preceded by two earlier articles on Americans in Zanzibar before 1865, this article concludes their activities on the island in the 19th century. After the Civil War the Americans who had previously dominated the trade of Zanzibar were beset by increased competition, problems associated with the abolition of the slave trade, and even natural disasters. The American traders overcame many of these difficulties largely because of the constant demand for American cloth until the European occupation of East Africa put an end to Zanzibar's importance. In 1915 the American consulate was closed and followed the main shift of commerce to the mainland.   R. O. Collins

1109. Berry, Mary F. NEGRO TROOPS IN BLUE AND GRAY: THE LOUISIANA NATIVE GUARDS, 1861-1863. *Louisiana Hist. 1967 8(2): 165-190.* During the Civil War the free Negroes of New Orleans continued their long tradition of military organization. A colored Confederate Native Guard was formed at the start of the war, its members possibly forced into service, but it was never used in regular service. General Benjamin Butler, Union military commander of New Orleans, organized a colored Federal Native Guard in 1862. It was used principally for guard duty and engineering tasks, although on its one combat mission it performed successfully. Based on records of the military units involved; 47 notes.   R. L. Woodward

1110. Bestor, Arthur. THE AMERICAN CIVIL WAR AS A CONSTITUTIONAL CRISIS. *Am. Hist. R. 1964 69(2): 327-352.* "Four irreconcilable constitutional doctrines were presented to the American people in 1860....They concerned a seemingly minor detail of the constitutional system. The arguments that supported the various positions were intricate and theoretical. But the abstractness of constitutional issues has nothing to do, one way or the other, with the role they may happen to play at a moment of crisis. The sole question is the load that events have laid upon them. Thanks to the structure of the American constitutional system itself, the abstruse issue of slavery in the territories was required to carry the burden of well-nigh all the emotional drives, well-nigh all the political and economic tensions, and well-nigh all the moral perplexities that resulted from the existence in the United States of an archaic system of labor and an intolerable policy of racial subjection."   M. Berman

1111. Bigelow, Martha M. VICKSBURG: EXPERIMENT IN FREEDOM. *J. of Mississippi Hist. 1964 26(1): 28-44.* Reevaluates the Federal Government's handling of the Negroes in the Vicksburg area 1863-65 as a significant harbinger of Reconstruction policies and programs, especially of the Freedmen's Bureau. Contraband camps, activities of freedmen's aid societies, use of Negroes in military preparations and engagements, religious and educational efforts, and the lessee system on abandoned plantations are all examined in the light of the government's pioneer experiment in coping with the sundry problems associated with the emancipation of large numbers of slaves in a combat zone. Stress is laid on the tremendous amount of suffering among the Negroes, especially on plantations operated by northern lessees.   D. C. James

1112. Bigelow, Martha Mitchell. FREEDMEN OF THE MISSISSIPPI VAL-LEY, 1862-1865. *Civil War Hist. 1962 8(1): 38-47.* The government had no established attitude toward Negro freedmen at the beginning of the war. In May 1861, Federal General Benjamin Franklin Butler declared escaped slaves to be contraband of war. In the Mississippi Valley, with its high concentration of slaves, a policy had to be developed. It was, slowly. John Eaton was put in charge of Negro affairs in much of Mississippi, Arkansas, Kentucky, Tennessee, and parts of Louisiana. He collected escaped slaves in camps, and worked to overcome prejudice against their use in Federal armies. The Emancipation Proclamation encouraged acceptance of Negroes for service as laborers and fighters, though menial work was emphasized.   L. Filler

1113. Blackburn, George M., ed. THE NEGRO AS VIEWED BY A MICHI-GAN CIVIL WAR SOLDIER: LETTERS OF JOHN C. BUCHANAN. *Michigan Hist. 1963 47(1): 75-84.* Eight letters from Captain Buchanan to his wife and mother reveal a firm opposition to slavery and a deep concern for the plight of Negroes. "There is in this Institution," he wrote, "an abject Servility, a Cringing, which may be likened to that of a whipped Hound." Even where slaves were treated with some degree of humanity he found the system "still repugnant to every feeling of justice and right in all its phases." Buchanan also recognized that what might be done for freed Negroes was an awesome question. He first considered Negroes unfit for combat duty and felt that their service would alienate "Union men." Later, however, he urged their enlistment into the army. The letters, written between 1861 and 1863 from Maryland, South Carolina, and Louisiana, are now part of the Bingham Papers in the Clarke Library.
                                                                        J. K. Flack

1114. Blassingame, John. THE SELECTION OF OFFICERS AND NON-COMMISSIONED OFFICERS OF NEGRO TROOPS IN THE UNION ARMY, 1863-1865. *Negro Hist. Bull. 1967 30(1): 8-11.* Investigates the system and selection procedure of the War Department for officers of Negro troops. A Board of Examiners tested candidates on loyalty, morality, health, intelligence, and knowledge of tactics for the units they expected to command. The system of training officers (Free Military School) was a harbinger of the present-day Officer Candidate School (OCS). The current emphasis on ability was the sole determinant in appointment and promotion in the armed forces. 33 notes.
                                                                        D. H. Swift

1115. Blassingame, John W. NEGRO CHAPLAINS IN THE CIVIL WAR. *Negro Hist. Bull. 1963 27(1): 23-24.* Briefly discusses the part played by Negro Civil War chaplains in fostering morale among the troops, providing religious leadership, and conducting literacy classes. Special attention is given to the work of Henry M. Turner, Samuel Harrison, and Garland H. White, though several other Negro chaplains are listed in the article. Documented with official records and secondary materials.   L. Gara

1116. Blassingame, John W. THE RECRUITMENT OF NEGRO TROOPS IN MISSOURI DURING THE CIVIL WAR. *Missouri Hist. R. 1964 58(3): 326-*

338. When Negroes were first recruited in Missouri, an effort was made to see that only the slaves of disloyal whites would be enlisted. By September 1863 there was strong pressure to recruit the slaves of loyal whites. In November this policy was approved, and a general recruitment began. There was little enthusiasm at first, but gradually many Missourians agreed that since the State quota was based on congressional representation, the recruitment of Negroes should also conform to the three-fifths rule. The system was chaotic and slow. The Radical Republicans fought to speed up enlistments, and the Negroes showed much willingness to serve. Missouri contributed a small total, however, a condition due to the indecision of the administration, the poorness of the recruitment system, and the opposition of the slaveholders. Based on newspapers, the Official Records, and Adjutant General's Office records in the National Archives.

W. F. Zornow

1117. Blassingame, John W. THE RECRUITMENT OF COLORED TROOPS IN KENTUCKY, MARYLAND AND MISSOURI 1863-1865. *Historian 1967 29(4): 533-545.* Faced with a lack of manpower, Lincoln wished to recruit Negro slaves from the border States to fight on the Union side during the Civil War. However, in so doing he risked alienating the slaveholders in those States; and, since his object was to save the Union rather than to abolish slavery, he did not want to free the slaves on the condition that they enlist. Radicals and slaveowners were in conflict on this issue. Radicals triumphed in Maryland and Missouri, but Kentuckians objected strongly to the end. Slaves enlisted mainly in order to gain emancipation. 41 notes.

F. J. Rossi

1118. Blassingame, John W. THE UNION ARMY AS AN EDUCATIONAL INSTITUTION FOR NEGROES, 1861-1865. *J. of Negro Educ. 1965 34(2): 152-159.* Thousands of Negroes received their first instruction in schools supervised or established by military authorities of the Union Army. "The educational ventures of the Union Army were important because they were forerunners of the Freedmen's Bureau, the United States Armed Forces Institute (ASAFI), adult education programs and...the origins of public school systems in the South," especially in Louisiana.

S. C. Pearson, Jr.

1119. Boney, F. N. THE CONQUEROR: SERGEANT MATHEW WOODRUFF IN WAR AND PEACE, 1861-1866. *Alabama R. 1970 23(3): 193-211.* Summarizes the activity of Sergeant Woodruff, Union infantryman from Missouri. The author reveals Woodruff's strong anti-Negro bias, the monotony and occasional hardship of an occupying army, and the final despair - desertion. Based on various sources including Woodruff's *Diary,* edited by Boney; 18 notes.

D. F. Henderson

1120. Boyd, Willis D. THE ÎLE A VACHE COLONIZATION VENTURE, 1862-1864. *The Americas 1959 16(1): 45-62.* Describes the effort to establish a colony of U.S. ex-slaves at Île à Vache, off the coast of Haiti, during the U.S. Civil War. The author discusses in greatest detail the prior negotiations and the later recriminations. Emigration was a solution to the Negro problem favored by

Lincoln himself, and various entrepreneurs were interested in this Haitian venture. About 450 Negroes went, but the colony failed because of poor organization, insufficient resources, and similar factors.   D. Bushnell

1121. Brogan, Sir Denis. THE DEBATE ON THE AMERICAN CIVIL WAR. *Pro. of the British Acad. 1963 49: 203-232.* The enormous costs of the war and its consequences in triumph and trauma have made it perhaps the central event in American experience, discussed in a huge literature of investigation and interpretation. The nature of the Union and the meaning of secession; the origin of the war and the question whether it was inevitable; the suggestions of underlying causes other than slavery; the reasons for the failure of the South: on these and related problems the author gives the views of recent historians and his own. Biblio.   H. D. Jordan

1122. Bryant, William Cullen, II, ed. A YANKEE SOLDIER LOOKS AT THE NEGRO. *Civil War Hist. 1961 7(2): 133-148.* Henry Martyn Cross, an 18-year old New Englander became a clerk with a Massachusetts regiment, and sailed with it to Hampton Roads, Virginia, then to Louisiana and Port Hudson. He began as a Unionist, contemptuous of Negroes. His letters to his parents reflected increasing regard for their industry and competence and displeasure with the contempt accorded them by Northerners as well as Southerners. He observed the varied qualities of the Negroes, from worthless "plantation darkey" to colored servant - "an intelligent, sad-looking man about thirty years old." Cross now felt he was fighting for freedom, not only the Union. At the Battle of Port Hudson they "mingled their blood with ours." Cross rose to captain and experienced capture and prison. Although he learned to respect ex-Confederates, he hoped they would freely give Negroes equal political rights.   L. Filler

1123. Buckmaster, Henrietta. ONE HUNDRED YEARS AGO. *New-England Galaxy 1963 5(1): 17-25.* Discusses the actions of Boston abolitionists during the three months between the announcement of the Emancipation Proclamation and its being made effective. Boston was the hub of antislavery agitation, and the leaders in Boston used all of their powers to see that President Lincoln did not go back on his pronouncement. There was great rejoicing in Boston when the proclamation was put into effect.   T. J. Farnham

1124. Byrne, Frank L. "A TERRIBLE MACHINE": GENERAL NEAL DOW'S MILITARY GOVERNMENT ON THE GULF COAST. *Civil War Hist. 1966 12(1): 5-22.* Discusses the Civil War activities of Maine prohibitionist Neal Dow, when he served as a military commander along the Gulf Coast in 1862-63. Stationed at Forts St. Philip and Jackson, Pensacola, and New Orleans, Dow, in his fanatical determination to punish rebels, emancipated slaves, imprisoned civilians, and stole (he called it confiscation) property. He justified many illegal acts on the grounds of military necessity, acting occasionally even in defiance of orders of his superiors. Sued for theft by a Mississippi plantation owner, Dow carried the case to the U.S. Supreme Court which in 1880 found for him in a split decision. The Dow experience demonstrates the problems of military rule in a nonwar zone. Based on Dow papers.   E. C. Murdock

1125. Cain, Marvin R. LINCOLN'S ATTORNEY GENERAL VIEWS THE SECESSION CRISIS: EDWARD BATES'S LETTERS TO WYNDHAM ROBERTSON. *Missouri Hist. Soc. Bull. 1964 21(1): 17-24.* Presents, with introductory comments, two previously unpublished letters (written 3 November 1860, and 23 February 1861) from Bates to his friend Robertson, ex-governor of Virginia, on the sectional crisis. A Missouri Unionist, Bates viewed the secessionist movement as the threat to the unity of the Mississippi Valley of a disloyal, conspiratorial minority in the Democratic Party pursuing a desperate policy doomed to failure. He felt no hesitation about the use of Federal coercive power. He predicted that the policy of Lincoln would be moderate and yet would not yield on the basic issues of slavery extension and preservation of the Union. Letters from Wyndham Robertson Collection, U. of Chicago. Also based on published sources; 11 notes.   R. J. Hanks

1126. Campbell, Alexander Elmslie. AN EXCESS OF ISOLATION: ISOLATION AND THE AMERICAN CIVIL WAR. *J. of Southern Hist. 1963 29(2): 161-174.* Analyzes and answers *An Excess of Democracy: The American Civil War and the Social Process* by David Donald (Oxford U. Press, 1960). Donald argued that efforts to avoid the crisis in the 1850's failed because "an excess of democracy" made the Nation "singularly ill-equipped to meet any shocks." The author argues that an excess of isolation allowed sectional differences to develop unchecked and prevented the Federal Government from developing adequately. The United States early became the most powerful State in the hemisphere while remaining insignificant in the world at large - facing no threat and posing none. Thus the unifying forces of national interest and a need for national defense were lacking. The institution of slavery set a historical trap, which could be sprung with devastating effect because of the country's isolation.   S. E. Humphreys

1127. Capers, Gerald M., Jr. CONFEDERATES AND YANKEES IN OCCUPIED NEW ORLEANS, 1862-1865. *J. of Southern Hist. 1964 30(4): 405-426.* First occupation commander of New Orleans after its capture in 1862 was Major General Benjamin F. Butler, who successfully subdued the city and its Confederates by stern measures but lost Abraham Lincoln's support because of criticism in Europe. The second commander was Major General Nathaniel P. Banks, who took a softer approach in the hope of organizing a pro-Union Louisiana government under Lincoln's 10 percent reconstruction plan. The third commander was Major General Stephen A. Hurlbut. The city was in a depression which began before its capture and was not relieved until after the fall of Vicksburg. Although there was declining antipathy, particularly after the opening of the Mississippi, the Latin Creoles of New Orleans generally refused to accept Yankee rule. Those who took positions in the Union government were largely northern-born men who had gone into business in New Orleans before the war. Life in the city changed considerably during the war, including the abolition of slavery in 1864.
S. E. Humphreys

1128. Carleton, William G. CIVIL WAR DISSIDENCE IN THE NORTH: THE PERSPECTIVE OF A CENTURY. *South Atlantic Q. 1966 65(3): 390-402.* During the Civil War, the older, larger, more diversified North had much more internal dissent than the South. Political leadership for the dissidents came from the Democratic Party and was mainly agrarian, civil-libertarian, and antiabolition. While the War Democrats supported the administration unreservedly, the Majority Democrats supported the war but attacked the administration on other issues. The third Democratic faction, the Peace Democrats, favored an end of hostilities and negotiation with the South. Dissent gave the Democrats political victories, slowed the movement to abolition (and laid the basis of opposition to Radical Reconstruction), and checked an overzealous military intervention in civil affairs. As for the Democrats' opposition to industrialization and centralization, this had little effect, but only because the North won a narrow victory over the South. The victory was largely a tribute to Lincoln's brilliant consensus politics which kept the North from fragmenting until victory could be achieved.

J. M. Bumsted

1129. Castel, Albert. CIVIL WAR KANSAS AND THE NEGRO. *J. of Negro Hist. 1966 51(2): 125-138.* The reputation of Kansas for radicalism concerning questions of abolition and Negro rights is only partially deserved. While a minority of settlers went to Kansas to assure its becoming a free State, most were either indifferent or hostile to the Negro. Kansas was the first State to raise Negro troops but it did so despite considerable opposition. After the war some Kansas communities had segregated schools and it was not until 1884 that the word "white" was removed from the voting provisions of the State constitution. Kansans were more willing to support the national program of Radical Republicanism than to implement progressive racial policies within the State's own borders.

L. Gara

1130. Castel, Albert. THE JAYHAWKERS AND COPPERHEADS OF KANSAS. *Civil War Hist. 1959 5(3): 283-293.* Describes the activities of the Jayhawkers, as well as the persecution of so-called Copperheads in the State of Kansas during the Civil War. Anyone suspected of rebel sympathies, of southern extraction, or with ties with southern church institutions was liable to be subjected to the harshest treatment by members of this passionately Unionist State with its fanatical hatred of the South and slavery. Such activities were a natural outlet for criminal elements and for reckless, violent frontier settlers. The worst consequence of these lawless activities was the detrimental influence on the relations between Missouri and Kansas. The Kansas State authorities made little effort to suppress these Jayhawkers, and Quantrill's murderous raid on Lawrence, Kansas, in August 1863 was direct retaliation for the Jayhawkers' marauding in the Missouri border counties.

B. Waldstein

1131. Catton, Bruce. CRISIS AT THE ANTIETAM. *Am. Heritage 1958 9(5): 54-57, 93-96.* A description of the Battle of Antietam, 17 September 1862, in the American Civil War, and its consequences, not the least of which was the creation of a favorable public opinion for the Emancipation Proclamation. Undocumented, illus.

C. R. Allen, Jr.

1132. Catton, Bruce. GLORY ROAD BEGAN IN THE WEST. *Civil War Hist. 1960 6(3): 229-237.* A tribute to the decisive part played by the Middle West in

determining the outcome of the Civil War. Although Virginia was the center of the stage, events in the Mississippi Valley, above all the capture of Vicksburg, were no less important. The author gives a detailed description of the major military engagements. Apart from the prowess of the Union armies of the West, the very character of the war was determined by the western armies. Although the westerner had no very strong feelings about the slavery issue, the army realized that the abolition of this institution would of necessity bring about the downfall of the Confederate economy, and this determined their actions. In this way, slavery was virtually abolished with the advance of the western armies.
B. Waldstein

1133. Catton, Bruce. LINCOLN'S DIFFICULT DECISIONS. *Civil War Hist. 1956 2(2): 5-12.* A speech delivered at the celebration of the 125th anniversary of Lincoln's arrival at New Salem, Illinois. The author traces Lincoln's important decisions, beginning with Fort Sumter. He sees the Emancipation Proclamation as the most momentous and difficult of all Lincoln's wartime decisions. "From the moment he signed this document it was certain that an incalculable new era would begin in American life....We have not yet come even moderately close to the realization of this ideal."
W. E. Wight

1134. Catton, Bruce. THE MOMENT OF DECISION. *Am. Heritage 1964 15(5): 48-53.* Examines presidential decisions to purchase Louisiana (Thomas Jefferson, 1803), defy South Carolina's attempt to nullify the Federal tariff (Andrew Jackson, 1832), issue the Emancipation Proclamation (Abraham Lincoln, 1862), prosecute the Northern Securities Company (Theodore Roosevelt, 1902), and order the use of the atomic bomb (Harry S. Truman, 1945). The ultimate decision is a lonely responsibility. Illus.
H. F. Bedford

1135. Cauthen, C. E. and Jones, Lewis P. THE COMING OF THE CIVIL WAR. *Writing Southern Hist.: Essays in Historiography in Honor of Fletcher M. Green (Baton Rouge: Louisiana State U. Press, 1965): 224-248.* After the early indictments and defenses, a more balanced treatment has become obvious. The transitional historians (1890-1930) opened the way for later pluralistic interpretations: Frederick Jackson Turner concluded that sectional schism came from many issues other than states' rights and slavery; Edward Channing concluded that slavery would eventually have disappeared; Ulrich B. Phillips was one of the first to say that the conflict of 1861 was not irrepressible. The flood of books in the 1930's gave much attention to the major causes of the war. The revisionists denied that the war had one fundamental cause. After World War II, new nationalists suggested that the issues of 1860 definitely were important enough to fight over and "implied that deemphasizing slavery as an un-compromisable moral issue amounted to condoning it." The involvement of these critics in the fight for Negro rights inevitably shaped their thinking about the Civil War. 101 biblio. notes.
E. P. Stickney

1136. Chenault, William W. and Reinders, Robert C. THE NORTHERN-BORN COMMUNITY OF NEW ORLEANS IN THE 1850'S. *J. of Am. Hist. 1964 51(2): 232-247.* Describes the Yankee influences in New Orleans as revealed by the community of northern-born businessmen who were leaders in the city's commerce and finance in the 1850's. These northern migrants brought elements of New England culture and attitudes, attitudes that were urban and national. The authors suggest that this Yankee background and business interest lay behind the city's later atypical response to the issues of slavery, secession, occupation, and Reconstruction.   H. J. Silverman

1137. Clebsch, William A. STEPHEN ELLIOTT'S VIEW OF THE CIVIL WAR. *Hist. Mag. of the Protestant Episcopal Church 1962 31(1): 7-20.* Elliott, first bishop of Georgia and presiding bishop of the Protestant Episcopal Church in the Confederate States, saw the Civil War as providential and replaced the "devil" theory by a "God" theory. It was a struggle for nationality, the antebellum government having defaulted in its national vocation. Although he opposed cruelty to slaves, Elliott regarded slavery as a means toward the civilization and Christianization of the Negro and considered the Emancipation Proclamation a calamity for the slaves.   E. Oberholzer, Jr.

1138. Coulter, E. Merton. ROBERT GOULD SHAW AND THE BURNING OF DARIEN, GEORGIA. *Civil War Hist. 1959 5(4): 363-373.* Describes the burning of the town of Darien, on the Georgia coast near the mouth of the Altamaha River, by Federal troops on 11 June 1863. Although the town was undefended and most of the inhabitants had taken refuge in a settlement about three miles away, the plundering Union troops, under the command of Colonel James Montgomery, ravaged the town and finally burned it to the ground. One of the units participating was the 54th Massachusetts Regiment, composed entirely of Negroes, except for its officers, and commanded by Colonel Robert Gould Shaw. The name of this officer was found subsequently in a ledger book which escaped the flames, and for some time Shaw was held responsible for the act of vandalism. In point of fact Shaw had protested violently against the action of his superior officer. His good name and his honor as a soldier and a Christian gentleman were later restored, and members of the Shaw family contributed generously to the rebuilding of the Episcopalian Church destroyed by the raiders. The burning of Darien led to the St. Albans Raid in October 1864, when a group of Confederate soldiers crossed from Canada into Vermont and occupied the town of St. Albans, inflicting much damage and plundering where they could. This action was designed to bring home to the northern people a realization of the kind of warfare they were inflicting on the South.   B. Waldstein

1139. Cullop, Charles P. EDWIN DE LEON, JEFFERSON DAVIS' PROPAGANDIST. *Civil War Hist. 1962 8(4): 386-400.* De Leon, son of a prominent South Carolina family, was a friend of Confederate President Jefferson Davis and persuaded him in 1862 that an effort was necessary to turn European opinion in favor of the Confederacy. Given 25 thousand dollars to attain this goal, De Leon sailed for England. Davis' Secretary of State Judah P. Benjamin was not pleased with the appointment, since De Leon superseded Benjamin's own friend, John Slidell. In England, De Leon found Henry Hotze, an Alabaman, excellently furthering the Southern cause with small finances, but through a strategic newspaper, the *Index*. In France, De Leon spent money freely to influence French opinion but encountered resistance in French distaste for the institution of slavery. He also opposed a Federal campaign to discredit Davis for his alleged role in a Mississippi bond repudiation in the 1840's. Nevertheless, he developed differences with Hotze and Slidell and offended Benjamin through unsystematic use of government funds. Davis agreed to his removal from office.

L. Filler

1140. Daniel, W. Harrison. SOUTHERN PROTESTANTISM AND THE NEGRO, 1860-1865. *North Carolina Hist. R. 1964 41(3): 338-359.* Using a great variety of unpublished Southern Protestant Church records and published sermons and church periodicals, the author treats the role of Negroes in the southern churches, the attitude of churchmen toward the institution of slavery and the war, and the use of religious training to counteract the Emancipation Proclamation by promoting loyalty to masters.   L. R. Harlan

1141. Davis, David Brion. ABOLITIONISTS AND FREEDMEN: AN ESSAY REVIEW. *J. of Southern Hist. 1965 31(2): 164-170.* Two new books have helped to bridge the gap that occurs in conventional historical periodization between the antislavery crusade, considered as ending in 1861, and the Reconstruction, beginning in 1865. James M. McPherson's *The Struggle for Equality: Abolitionists and the Negro in the Civil War and Reconstruction* (Princeton: Princeton U. Press, 1964) argues that abolitionists were farsighted enough to know that without political and economic power the Negro could never be truly free. He demolishes the stereotype that the abolitionist was content to abandon the Negro with the outbreak of war. He stresses the revolutionary implications of mass emancipation, the enrollment of freedmen in the Union Army, and the reformers' ideal of full social equality. Willie Lee Rose, in *Rehearsal for Reconstruction: The Port Royal Experiment* (Indianapolis: Bobbs-Merrill Company, 1964), studies the experiment of the abolitionist Gideonites with freedmen in the Sea Islands off Georgia, providing a subtle analysis of the diverse effects of slavery upon the Negro's personality and the difficulties he faced in adjusting to the uncertain policies of his new masters. She tells of inflated hopes and broken promises and a failure partly caused by the fact that the experiment was based on antebellum agricultural ideas. But Rose finds that the failure also was ultimately one of the American people, because the Nation was ready to use the Negro only in ways that seemed likely to bring the war to an end. By showing that many abolitionists were working for the same goals as the present proponents of civil rights, the two authors make it the more imperative for us to understand these crucial years in the history of the American Negro.   S. E. Humphreys

1142. Davison, Stanley R. and Tash, Dale. CONFEDERATE BACKWASH IN MONTANA TERRITORY. *Montana 1967 17(4): 50-58.* Throughout the sixties Montana territorial politics reflected feelings arising from the Civil War. Extreme viewpoints clashed as Radical Republicans in the Union League of America confronted unreconciled Democrats with a strong anti-Negro bias. The often cited pro-southern majority is found to have been a fact. The evidence exists in the files of newspapers from the period, cited extensively. Illus.

A

1143. Delaney, Norman C. LETTERS OF A MAINE SOLDIER BOY. *Civil War Hist. 1959 5(1): 45-61.* Excerpts from the letters of Charles Chase, a young private in the Union Army, written home between 1860 and 1864. The letters give his personal impressions of life in the army during the war, conditions, food, the characters and habits of his officers, and comments on the campaign, on the Negroes, on the actual fighting, etc. Chase was killed at Cold Harbor, Virginia, on 3 June 1864.   B. Waldstein

1144. Dement'ev, I. P. EVOLUTSIIA AMERIKANSKOI BURZHUAZNOI ISTORIOGRAFII GRAZHDANSKOI VOINY 1861-1865 GG [The evolution in American bourgeois historical research on the Civil War, 1861-65]. *Voprosy Istorii [USSR] 1958 (9): 135-151.* American historical research has produced the most contradictory opinions. They range from the recognition, at first, of the unavoidable character of the Civil War and its positive results to the theory, later on, of its senselessness and to the denial of its progressive historical significance; from the recognition of the important role of the masses, particularly the workers and Negroes, to the gross misrepresentation of their intentions. The author believes that American bourgeois historical research represents the deliberate application of a policy to the past. Based on works by Jefferson Davis, Alexander Stephens, John W. Draper, James Ford Rhodes, John W. Burgess, Frederick Jackson Turner, Avery Craven, Allan Nevins, and others.   E. Wollert

1145. Dodwell, H. B. AMERICAN CIVIL WAR. *Contemporary R. [Great Britain] 1965 206(1191): 192-204.* An undocumented, general account of the origins and course of the American Civil War. Tracing its genesis to the issue of slavery, the stages from 1780 to 1865 and the emergence of secession are outlined, and the cause of actual war is attributed to the attack on Fort Sumter. An account of the war itself covers the major campaigns and engagements.
                                                        D. H. Murdoch

1146. Edwards, John. AN ACCOUNT OF MY ESCAPE FROM THE SOUTH IN 1861. *Chronicles of Oklahoma 1965 43(1): 58-89.* Never before published, this narrative by a Presbyterian missionary begins on 11 May 1861 when a vigilance committee visited the Choctaw Reservation to check the allegiance of the missionaries and to warn those who were not willing to fight for the Confederacy to leave the Indian Territory. They believed that John Edwards was an abolitionist and threatened to hang him, but he convinced them that he had no objection to slavery so they merely commanded him to leave the Territory. Later, word came to him that the vigilance committee of Texans was coming to hang him. Most of the narrative relates the events of his escape as he and his family traveled first on horseback, then by wagon, boat, and train, eventually reaching Bath, New York. After the war he returned to minister to the Choctaw.
                                                        I. W. Van Noppen

1147. Ellis, Richard N. THE CIVIL WAR LETTERS OF AN IOWA FAMILY. *Ann. of Iowa 1969 39(8): 561-586.* Contains a selection of 17 Civil War letters among various members of the Simeon Stevens family of Oskaloosa, Iowa. The eldest son, Benjamin, author of 12 of the letters, enlisted in 1861 and fought with the 15th Iowa Volunteers at Shiloh and in the Vicksburg campaign. In 1863 he joined a new unit, the 19th Louisiana Infantry, African Descent - a black regiment which later became the 48th U.S. Colored Infantry and served at Vicksburg and in several Southern States. Despite a promise to his son that he would not enlist, Simeon volunteered and became ill and died in 1863. After the father's death, the second son, Stephen, enlisted and was captured during the Atlanta campaign of 1864. The letters are in the Iowa State Historical Museum and include valuable comments on the routine of army life and on the role of Negro troops in the Union Army. 18 notes.   W. R. Griffin

1148. Everett, Donald E. BEN BUTLER AND THE LOUISIANA NATIVE GUARDS, 1861-1862. *J. of Southern Hist. 1958 24(2): 202-217.* More than 1400 free Negroes were organized into the Louisiana militia by Governor Thomas O. Moore after May 1861. News accounts during that year and early 1862 indicate their loyalty to the Confederacy, but in April 1862 the Negro "Native Guards" refused to comply with orders to leave New Orleans with other Confederate forces when the city was occupied by Admiral David G. Farragut. Shortly afterward, Benjamin Franklin Butler, Union commanding general, received a visit from the officers of the Guards, who told him that they had not sympathized with the southern cause. In the autumn of 1862 Butler recalled them to duty with some white officers and some Negroes. He asked approval of the Department of War, but the latter took no action until after Butler had been relieved. In October Butler ordered Native Guards to assist in the defense of the Teche district, but Brigadier General Godfrey Weitzel refused to accept them under his command, believing they would not fight. Butler announced that only free Negroes would be recruited, but many of those enlisted were considered slaves by Confederate standards.   S. E. Humphreys

1149. Fahrner, Alvin A. WILLIAM "EXTRA BILLY" SMITH, GOVERNOR OF VIRGINIA 1864-1865: A PILLAR OF THE CONFEDERACY. *Virginia Mag. of Hist. and Biog. 1966 74(1): 68-87.* Attacks the contention that Smith, as governor of Virginia, contributed to the downfall of the Confederacy by an extreme insistence on states' rights. Although strongly states' rightist in principle, in fact "he was reasonably cooperative with the Davis administration." Smith's state forces made up of men not serving in the Confederate Army contributed to the military effort; his State-operated supply system provided goods essential to Virginia with a minimum of conflict with the central government; his power to exempt State officials from military service was carefully exercised, and he led the fight for enlisting Negro troops. Documented.   K. J. Bauer

1150. Fein, Isaac M. BALTIMORE JEWS DURING THE CIVIL WAR. *Am. Jewish Hist. Q. 1961/62 51(2): 67-96.* The Jews of Baltimore - a colony within the larger German colony - were mostly members of the Democratic Party and supported the status quo on the issue of slavery, but there were also significant spokesmen for the Republican and the secessionist attitudes. The author shows the positions of the four Baltimore rabbis - as the representatives of the Jewish community. Attention is also called to the problems of many of the more prominent families who were torn on this issue and had men on both sides. Based on extensive documentation from contemporary newspapers and collections.

F. Rosenthal

1151. Fen, Sing-Nan. CHARLES P. DAY, THE SUCCESSOR TO MARY S. PEAKE. *Phylon 1963 24(4): 388-391.* Charles P. Day taught Negroes in Hampton, Virginia, under the auspices of the American Missionary Association from 1862 to 1865. He is described as a "model missionary teacher."

S. C. Pearson, Jr.

1152. Fen, Sing-Nan. NOTES ON THE EDUCATION OF NEGROES IN NORTH CAROLINA DURING THE CIVIL WAR. *J. of Negro Educ. 1967 36(1): 24-31.* Traces the emergence of Negro education in North Carolina during the Civil War. Prewar hostility toward Negro education continued, and the Federally appointed Governor Edward Stanley closed the first schools in 1862. However, by March 1864 there were 11 schools with an enrollment of 2,300 to 2,400. These schools were established, supported, and staffed by northern freedmen's aid societies or by Negroes themselves; the role of white female teachers was most significant. In spite of hardships deriving from social hostility, military operations, sickness, poverty, inadequate supplies and facilities, and an inadequate understanding of the functions of education on the part of many students, the schools succeeded in establishing a new tradition of Negro education and in providing for Negro students a new relationship with white teachers. Based on published material and the American Missionary Association Collection at Fisk University; 33 notes.

S. C. Pearson, Jr.

1153. Fen Sing-Nan. NOTES ON THE EDUCATION OF NEGROES AT NORFOLK AND PORTSMOUTH, VIRGINIA, DURING THE CIVIL WAR. *Phylon 1967 28(2): 197-207.* Virginia law prior to the Civil War prohibited the educating of slaves and free Negroes. When Union troops occupied the area around Hampton Roads political factors made it difficult to establish schools north of the Roads, but as buildings were available in Portsmouth, missionary and educational work started there in 1863. The author contends that for both the freedmen and northern teachers the schools were more valuable for the fellowship and association they afforded than for any intellectual pursuit. He maintains that northern educators believed that Negro children could go through the common school routine with ease equal to that of white children. Their naïvety lay in their belief of individual salvation. Education was supposed to be the way to bring this about, but it proved to be a myth because freedmen in Virginia were suppressed under the collective strength of tradition and institutions with which the common school routine did not equip them to deal. Based on primary sources in the Fisk University Library; 44 notes.

D. N. Brown

1154. Floyd, Viola Caston. "THE FALL OF CHARLESTON." *South Carolina Hist. Mag. 1965 66(1): 1-17.* Reprints a communication of a reporter for the New York *Tribune* on the occupation of Charleston 18 February 1865. The report described the efforts to destroy all military installations and machines, two thousand bales of cotton, and boats. It reflects the general attitude toward Negroes and toward the white population.   V. O. Bardsley

1155. Foner, Philip S. ADDRESS OF FREDERICK DOUGLASS AT THE INAUGURATION OF DOUGLASS INSTITUTE, BALTIMORE, OCTOBER 1, 1865. *J. of Negro Hist. 1969 54(2): 174-183.* After a brief preface describing the dignitaries present, the article reprints in full Frederick Douglass' speech at the opening of the Douglass Institute in Baltimore, Maryland, on 1 October 1865. The address describes the condition of the Negro at the end of the Civil War. Douglass (1817?-95) concludes by stating that he hopes the institute will develop a sense of manhood and self-respect among the colored members in attendance. No mention is made in the speech, however, about Douglass' preference for the development of manual skills in Negroes rather than an emphasis on classical or liberal arts education. 10 notes.   R. S. Melamed

1156. Freehling, William W. THE EDITORIAL REVOLUTION, VIRGINIA, AND THE COMING OF THE CIVIL WAR: A REVIEW ESSAY. *Civil War Hist. 1970 16(1): 64-72.* Analyzes the four-volume edition, *Proceedings of the Virginia State Convention of 1861* (Richmond: Virginia State Lib., 1965), edited by George Reese. While it was unfortunate that Reese had inadequate funds to permit the proper annotation of the proceedings, the four volumes shed bright new light on the whole question of Civil War causation. The soul-searching and self-doubt evident in the convention over the future of slavery and the historic role of Virginia itself, make it clear that a fresh look at the South and its relations with Washington in the decade before the war is needed.   E. C. Murdock

1157. Gara, Larry. SLAVERY AND THE SLAVE POWER: A CRUCIAL DISTINCTION. *Civil War Hist. 1969 15(1): 5-18.* Points out the pre-Civil War distinction in the North between moral objections to slavery and political objections to the slave power. While the abolitionists opposed slavery on ethical grounds, most antislavery people - those active in the Free Soil and Republican Parties, for example - opposed the political power of the slaveowning interests rather than the institution itself. An understanding of this vital distinction is essential to an analysis of Civil War causation and also "helps explain how Americans could repress a rebellion led by a slave oligarchy and at the same time perpetuate a racist bias which a century later still plagues the nation." Based on primary and secondary sources.   E. C. Murdock

1158. Gara, Larry. THE FUGITIVE SLAVE LAW: A DOUBLE PARADOX. *Civil War Hist. 1964 10(3): 229-240.* Although the Compromise of 1850 was designed to ease sectional tensions, the effect of the Fugitive Slave Law was to worsen relations. "By recharging the highly emotional slavery debate, [it] helped to bring on the Civil War..." Further, in appealing for Federal assistance, states rightists were contradicting their own philosophy. The author points out that slaveowners were not really interested in capturing runaways, but rather in establishing the abstract constitutional principle of interstate rendition of "fugitives from labor." To maintain this right, they insisted on the Fugitive Slave Law.

This brought on the Civil War, which destroyed what was left of State sovereignty. Based on public and private documents and contemporary newspapers.
E. C. Murdock

1159. Gara, Larry and Boney, F. N. VIRGINIAN, SOUTHERNER, AMERICAN. *Virginia Cavalcade 1967 17(1): 11-19.* A biographical sketch of John Letcher (1813-84), governor of Virginia during the Civil War. Letcher, a Jacksonian Democrat, was interested in many reforms during the antebellum period, including the possibility of emancipation. A strong opponent of secession, he struggled to maintain a middle course in the face of growing extremism. In May 1859 he was elected 42d governor of Virginia, and in this position tried to avert the break-up of the Union. In the presidential campaign of 1860 he supported Stephen Douglas. When the Confederate government was organized he became a loyal supporter of Jefferson Davis. "Only a very few Southern governors stood so firmly behind their president, and many rebel states were never really incorporated into the Confederacy." Letcher's moderation prevailed during the era of Reconstruction also, and he advocated speedy reconciliation of the sections. Illus.
N. L. Peterson

1160. Gavronsky, Serge. AMERICAN SLAVERY AND THE FRENCH LIBERALS: AN INTERPRETATION OF THE ROLE OF SLAVERY IN FRENCH POLITICS DURING THE SECOND EMPIRE. *J. of Negro Hist. 1966 51(1): 36-52.* When the American Civil War broke out, French public opinion was antislavery. French editions of Harriet Beecher Stowe's *Uncle Tom's Cabin* and other antislavery writings as well as Victor Hugo's emotional reaction to the martyrdom of John Brown contributed to that sentiment. Emperor Napoleon III, however, viewed a southern victory or a mediated settlement as a possible aid to his Mexican policy. The liberal opposition capitalized on the popular dislike of slavery to frustrate the emperor's plan for recognizing southern independence and to polarize opinion against the domestic policies of the Second Empire. Documented.
L. Gara

1161. Gerhard, Dietrich. ABRAHAM LINCOLN, DIE VERFASSUNG UND DIE UNABHÄNGIGKEITSERKLÄRUNG [Abraham Lincoln, the Constitution and the Declaration of Independence]. *Jahrbuch für Amerikastudien [West Germany] 1966 11: 41-55.* Speech given at the annual meeting of the German Society for American Studies in Berlin on 11 June 1965. Shows that, contrary to the widely held 20th-century view of the almost irreconcilable polarity of the Constitution and the Declaration of Independence, these two documents were not considered as contradictory in mid-19th-century America. In Lincoln's thinking and acting both were harmoniously reconciled. While Lincoln's emergency measures to save the Union were derived from his deep loyalty to the Constitution, his attitude toward slavery was inspired by his faith in the ideals of the Declaration of Independence. To Lincoln, both documents were manifestations of the principle "freedom for all." Based on printed sources.
G. Bassler

1162. Goodell, Robert and Taylor, P. A. M. A GERMAN IMMIGRANT IN THE UNION ARMY: SELECTED LETTERS OF VALENTIN BECHLER.

J. of Am. Studies [Great Britain] 1971 4(2): 145-162. Valentin Bechler emigrated
from Germany to Newark, New Jersey, in 1856. He enlisted in the Union Army
and served until 1863, first in a New Jersey volunteer unit and later in a battery
of the New York Light Artillery. Reproduces the full text or excerpts from 21
letters written by Bechler in the Army. The letters deal mainly with the hardships
and loneliness of Civil War soldiering. They reflect Bechler's growing disenchantment with a war that he interpreted as one to ensure success for the abolitionists'
cause. Based on secondary sources and Bechler's letters, which are currently in
a privately-owned collection; 49 notes.   H. T. Lovin

1163. Haerdter, Robert. ABRAHAM LINCOLN. *Monat [West Germany] 1965
17(199): 29-36.* Sketches some of the significant events in Abraham Lincoln's
political career: the debates with Stephen Douglas, Lincoln's nomination and
election, the secession of the Southern States, the Emancipation Proclamation,
and Lincoln's assassination just as the Civil War ended. It was not Lincoln's
intention at first to deal with the slavery problem. The war began as a struggle
to preserve the Federal union, and only later did it become a war to free the Negro
slaves. Negroes were actually kept in subjection through the principle of "separate
but equal" well into the 20th century. Only with real equality for the Negro will
Lincoln's final aim be achieved.   D. H. Norton

1164. Ham, P. G., ed. THE MIND OF A COPPERHEAD: LETTERS OF
JOHN J. DAVIS ON THE SECESSION CRISIS AND STATEHOOD POLI-
TICS IN WESTERN VIRGINIA 1860-1862. *West Virginia Hist. 1962/63 24(2):
89-109.* Reviews the correspondence between John J. Davis and his fiancée, Miss
Anna Kennedy. They were the parents of John W. Davis, the 1924 Democratic
standard bearer for the Presidency. John J. Davis tried to convince his fiancée,
an avowed secessionist, that he was not hostile to the South or its institutions,
only to secession and rebellion. These letters contain valuable comment on the
secession crisis and movement for separate statehood in western Virginia, and
reveal the attitude and thought of a "Copperhead" or "Butternut" - who is a
conservative Union critic of radicalism and the Lincoln administration. Davis
doesn't fit the stereotype of a traitorous Copperhead with strong Confederate
sympathy. He opposed secession and called for suppression of the southern
rebellion. He equally denounced the Radical Republicans for perverting a struggle to save the Union into an abolitionist crusade to end slavery and subjugate
the South.   M. M. Kanin

1165. Hardeman, Nicholas P. BUSHWHACKER ACTIVITY ON THE MIS-
SOURI BORDER. LETTERS TO DR. GLEN O. HARDEMAN, 1862-1865.
Missouri Hist. R. 1964 58(3): 265-277. Hardeman typifies the contradictory
allegiances characteristic of Missourians during the Civil War. He was a successful farmer and slaveholder, but in 1862 he was commissioned as a surgeon in the
Union Army. He remained in this role until 1864. These letters, which cover the
period from October 1862 to January 1866, are concerned with numerous subjects. Most of them are written by Permelia Hardeman to her husband; they deal

with conditions at home and contain frequent references to the operations of Bushwhackers. The final letter concerns one of Hardeman's Negroes who was carried off during the Price Raid of 1864.   W. F. Zornow

1166. Harris, Sheldon H. JOHN L. O'SULLIVAN SERVES THE CONFEDER-ACY. *Civil War Hist. 1964 10(3): 275-290.* Sketch of the Civil War career of a man noted for his "Manifest Destiny" phrase. Although a radical northern Democrat, with heavy strains of Free-Soilism, O'Sullivan defected to the Confederacy early in 1862 and became an eloquent propagandist for the southern cause. The reason for this move was his belief in Negro inferiority and the slave system and his opposition to the "unconstitutional" efforts of the national government to overthrow that system. O'Sullivan, who spent most of the war looking after his unprofitable investments in Europe, in addition to writing a number of pamphlets, unsuccessfully sought to obtain Swedish ironclads for the Confederacy. Backer of lost causes, a failure in business, and with few resources, O'Sullivan, after the war, fell into obscurity and died some 30 years later. Extensive use of private papers and public documents.   E. C. Murdock

1167. Hatch, Carl E. EDITOR DAVID NAAR OF TRENTON: PROFILE OF THE ANTI-NEGRO MIND. *New Jersey Hist. 1968 (2): 71-87.* A discussion of the anti-Negro activities of David Naar (1800-83), owner and editor of the influential Democratic Party organ, the *Trenton Daily True American.* The "Ancillary, Military, Biblical, constitutional and economic" reasoning of David Naar during the Civil War is examined and explained. Concludes that "despite all the elaboration on Ancillary reasons, Naar's Anti-Negro mind was basically rooted in racism." 30 notes.   T. H. Brown

1168. Heckman, Richard Allen. BRITISH PRESS REACTION TO THE EMANCIPATION PROCLAMATION. *Lincoln Herald 1969 71(4): 150-157.* Concludes, on the basis of a study of British newspapers for the period October 1862, that newspapers of all shades of opinion were critical of Lincoln and the Emancipation Proclamation.   S. L. Jones

1169. Hernon, Joseph M. IRISH RELIGIOUS OPINION ON THE AMERICAN CIVIL WAR. *Catholic Hist. R. 1964 49(4): 508-523.* All the churches in Ireland supported Confederate independence. The author discusses the successful efforts of Confederate agents in winning the sympathy of the Catholic clergy, who were concerned about Union recruiting of Irishmen. Humanitarians in all the churches believed that the abolition of slavery would follow no matter what the result of the war and were more concerned about ending the horrible bloodshed. The complex views of Catholics, Presbyterians, and Quakers, reflected in the editorials, speeches, resolutions, and consular dispatches, are presented.
                                                                             A

1170. Hernon, Joseph M., Jr. BRITISH SYMPATHIES IN THE AMERCAN CIVIL WAR: A RECONSIDERATION. *J. of Southern Hist. 1967 33(3): 356-367.* Proposes revision of the standard interpretation of the British reaction to the American Civil War to show that hatred of democracy more than affinity with the southern aristocracy was a motive for upper-class sympathy with the South, and Britain's failure to recognize the Confederacy was due to the caution of Lord Palmerston, who was merely concerned with the enhancement of British power and defense of British interests. It is totally fallacious to believe that the Emancipation Proclamation effected a great change in British public opinion. Not until after the northern triumph was there overwhelming working-class acceptance of John Bright's abolitionist, prodemocratic interpretation of the war. Laborers, as was Gladstone, were converted by events on the battlefield and political expediency at home. Gladstone's opinion on the war reflects the evolution of British opinion from support for a nation struggling to be free, during the peak period of southern military success, to sympathy with the Union and the sudden realization that slavery, after all, was the principal issue in the war, following the triumph of northern armies and the assassination of Abraham Lincoln.

S. E. Humphreys

1171. Holliday, Joseph E. FREEDMEN'S AID SOCIETIES IN CINCINNATI, 1862-1870. *Cincinnati Hist. Soc. Bull. 1964 22(3): 169-185.* An account of the activities of various private societies which were formed in Cincinnati shortly after President Lincoln's preliminary Emancipation Proclamation on 22 September 1862, to aid future freedmen (contrabands). The first society to work almost exclusively for the refugees in the Mississippi Basin was the Cincinnati Contraband Relief Association, which was organized in November 1862. "The need for supplying the physical necessities of the refugees was one with which few humanitarians could quarrel, but some members believed that a broader program should be adopted - one that would educate the freedmen." The controversy that ensued led to the formation of the Western Freedmen's Aid Commission which concentrated its efforts on educational activities. "The private societies served a highly useful purpose in relieving the needs of refugee slaves in the months before the slow-moving federal government had matured its policies for them. Their contribution to the establishment of educational facilities for the freedmen, however, was their most enduring achievement." 3 illus., photo, 67 notes.

D. D. Cameron

1172. Hyman, Harold M. LINCOLN AND EQUAL RIGHTS FOR NEGROES: THE IRRELEVANCY OF THE "WADSWORTH LETTER." *Civil War Hist. 1966 12(3): 258-266.* While accepting Ludwell Johnson's "Wadsworth Letter" thesis, the author denies that the thesis is sufficient to show that Lincoln was not moving toward a full belief in Negro suffrage. Johnson contends that a January 1864 letter from Lincoln to General James S. Wadsworth, in which the President argues strongly for Negro suffrage, was spurious. If the Wadsworth letter were false, Johnson asserts, then Lincoln was not as progressive on the race question as many have contended. Hyman concedes the untrustworthiness of the Wadsworth letter, but holds that ample other evidence proves that Lincoln was evolving steadily into a racial egalitarian. Several examples of this evidence are cited.					E. C. Murdock

1173. Johnson, Ludwell H. LINCOLN AND EQUAL RIGHTS: THE AU-
THENTICITY OF THE WADSWORTH LETTER. *J. of Southern Hist. 1966
32(1): 83-87.* Considers the letter included on pp. 101-102 of Vol. VII of Roy P.
Basler's *Collected Works of Abraham Lincoln* (New Brunswick, New Jersey,
1953-55), which is supposed to have been written in January 1864 to Major
General James Samuel Wadsworth. The letter would be, if authentic, Lincoln's
strongest statement in favor of civil and political equality for Negroes. The
original of the letter does not exist and what is now presented as a single letter
has two separate sources, both secondary. The author argues that the first two
paragraphs are completely in agreement with Lincoln's public and private statements on Negro suffrage, but that the third paragraph does not ring true and the
fourth is clearly not authentic. Documented.   S. E. Humphreys

1174. Johnson, Ludwell H. LINCOLN AND EQUAL RIGHTS: A REPLY.
Civil War Hist. 1967 13(1): 66-73. In 1966 the author denied the authenticity of
the "Wadsworth Letter" in which Lincoln argued strongly for Negro suffrage
(see abstract 3:2411). Later in *Civil War History* (see abstract 4:2427) Harold
Hyman, while admitting that the Wadsworth letter was spurious, insisted that
other evidence confirmed the view that Lincoln was still moving steadily for a
full acceptance of Negro rights at the time of his death. In the present article
Johnson challenges Hyman's rebuttal. Rather than moving toward Negro
egalitarianism, Lincoln was merely reacting in different ways to special situations
according to the political pressures of the moment. The Louisiana situation, for
example - which Hyman stresses and where Lincoln's attitude on the race question was the most liberal - was such a special case. Based on primary and
secondary sources.   E. C. Murdock

1175. Johnson, Ludwell H. LINCOLN'S SOLUTION TO THE PROBLEM
OF PEACE TERMS, 1864-1865. *J. of Southern Hist. 1968 34(4): 576-586.*
To prevent losing control of the Republican Party to the Radical-led faction,
Lincoln sought to build a new conservative coalition which would include
Southerners and this necessitated ending the war through negotiations instead of unconditional surrender. Lincoln sought a middle course and this is
reflected in his development of terms for peace which the author tries to
reconstruct from the President's messages, correspondence, speeches, and
from contemporary accounts. In the broadest sense, he argues, Lincoln
"hoped to lead the North back to his original objective: the preservation of
the Union under the Constitution, with slavery (the root of disunion in Lincoln's view) an incidental casualty of the struggle." 25 notes.   I. M. Leonard

1176. Jones, Wilbur Devereux. BLYDEN, GLADSTONE AND THE WAR.
J. of Negro Hist. 1964 49(1): 56-61. Publishes parts of three letters of Edward
Wilmot Blyden, Negro author, Liberian diplomat, and nationalist, to William
Ewart Gladstone, then Chancellor of the Exchequer in Lord Palmerston's gov-
ernment. In the letters, written in 1861, the last two probably from the United
States, Blyden deplored racial discrimination in the United States and strongly
supported the British policy of neutrality concerning the Civil War.
                                                                        L. Gara

1177. Keene, Jesse L. SECTIONALISM IN THE PEACE CONVENTION OF 1861. *Florida Hist. Q. 1961 40(1): 53-81.* Heated arguments regarding slavery and proposals for avoiding conflict led to confusion and to the voting of resolutions by the convention that proved unsatisfactory to all concerned and unacceptable by Congress. Based on State papers, private papers, memoirs, newspapers, and secondary works.   G. L. Lycan

1178. Kirkland, Edward C. BOSTON DURING THE CIVIL WAR. *Pro. of the Massachusetts Hist. Soc. 1953-57 71: 194-204.* Describes the impact of the war upon Boston, especially on its young people and its Negro residents. Based on secondary sources and the Adams Papers at the Massachusetts Historical Society.
                                                                  N. Callahan

1179. Klement, Frank L. MIDWESTERN OPPOSITION TO LINCOLN'S EMANCIPATION POLICY. *J. of Negro Hist. 1964 49(3): 169-183.* Hatred of abolition and abolitionists was an important ingredient of midwestern Democratic politics long before the Civil War. The anti-abolition issues appealed to numerous Irish Americans, German Americans, and southern emigrants living in the Midwest. During the war many Democrats criticized any proposed step toward abolition and they severely censured Lincoln for issuing the Emancipation Proclamation. Clement Vallandingham labeled the Proclamation unconstitutional, unnecessary, and divisive. Democrats kept the issue alive in every election held during the war, and their refusal to accept the Emancipation Proclamation as a desirable reform contributed to the slow progress of civil rights after the war.
                                                                       L. Gara

1180. Kooker, Arthur R. ABRAHAM LINCOLN: SPOKESMAN FOR DEMOCRACY. *J. of the West 1965 4(2): 260-271.* Traces Lincoln's political life through his election as President and notes the many problems he had in dealing with Union generals. Lincoln's heroic stature rests on three broad principles which he stressed at every opportunity. These were his contention that the Nation was involved in a great moral struggle to abolish slavery, his insistence that the war was a struggle to renew the spirit of democratic government, and a hope for the future of mankind. Documented from published works; 44 notes.
                                                                  D. N. Brown

1181. Korusiewicz, Leon. PRZYCZYNY WOJNY SECESYJNEJ W HISTORI-OGRAFII AMERYKANSKIEJ [The causes of the secession war in the American historiography]. *Kwartalnik Historyczny [Poland] 1966 73(3): 673-687.* Informs Polish readers about specialized publications and detailed points of view on the Civil War. The survey starts with an analysis of the major publications which reflect the partisan points of view of the Confederates and the North. The "National School" brought forth a critical and objective assessment of various factors related to the war. The economic interpretations include the works of Charles Austin Beard and Vernon Louis Parrington. The works of Algie M. Simons, Karl Marx, Louis Hacker, Herbert Aptheker, W. E. B. Du Bois, and

Allan Nevins are given attention. Not only slavery but also the complex problem of racial adjustment and the adjustment of different civilizations to a common life played roles as causes of the Civil War. W. W. Soroka

1182. Krug, Mark M. THE REPUBLICAN PARTY AND THE EMANCIPA-TION PROCLAMATION. *J. of Negro Hist. 1963 48(2): 98-114.* Interprets the Emancipation Proclamation differently from some Civil War revisionists. Lincoln was not indifferent to the fate of the slaves. He was interested in correcting a moral wrong as well as in strengthening the military situation. Alleged radical pressures played virtually no part in the decision. All factions of the Republican Party approved the proclamation and recognized its great significance in changing the war aim. The proclamation was not a decisive factor in Republican setbacks at the polls in 1862, which can be explained by other factors. Based on primary source materials, mostly quotations from Lincoln and his contemporaries. L. Gara

1183. Land, Mary. "BLUFF" BEN WADE'S NEW ENGLAND BACK-GROUND. *New England Q. 1954 27(4): 484-509.* Uses manuscripts, local sources, and newspapers to trace the New England heritage of Ben Wade, Radical Republican Senator, abolitionist, and chairman of the powerful Committee on the Conduct of the War, which caused so much trouble for President Lincoln. Argues that despite Wade's freethinking doctrines, he was essentially a Puritan, whose absolutism contributed to his intolerance. With New England antecedents and a boyhood on the rough Ohio frontier, Wade was a dealer in absolutes, a radical reformer who completely disregarded the rights of his opponents. Orthodox only in his long record of obstructionism, he was picked by the Radical Republicans to succeed Andrew Johnson as President. D. Davis

1184. Large, David. AN IRISH FRIEND AND THE CIVIL WAR. *Bull. of Friends Hist. Assoc. 1958 47(1): 20-29.* An account of the opinions on the South and slavery of Joshua E. Todhunter, an Irish Quaker who did business in New York during the American Civil War, as revealed in letters written to Jonathan Pim in Dublin. Todhunter urged British intervention in favor of the South, arguing that southern independence was the only true means for attaining the eventual abolition of slavery and the protection of the Negro from the hostility of the white race in America. N. Kurland

1185. Lathrop, Barnes F. THE LAFOURCHE DISTRICT IN 1862: INVA-SION. *Louisiana Hist. 1961 2(2): 175-201.* Describes the invasion of the upper Bayou Lafourches region by Godfrey Weitzel's Union force of about three thousand men, 24-28 October 1862. The first part of the article delineates the troop movements of Weitzel's forces and those of the Confederates under Alfred Mouton. The culmination was a minor engagement at Georgia Landing or Labadieville, 27 October which Weitzel won. According to the author "the Lafourche district fell by this one fight." The latter part of the article concerns four documents - a letter, diary, journal, and essay written by members of sugar planter's families in the path of Weitzel's advance. They describe "the civilian upheaval produced by the coming of the Yankees and the attendant surge of the Negroes away from the plantations."   D. C. James

1186. Lee, R. Alton. THE CORWIN AMENDMENT IN THE SECESSION CRISIS. *Ohio Hist. Q. 1961 70(1): 1-26.* Analyzes the support given early in 1861 by Lincoln, William Henry Seward, and other moderate Republicans to the Corwin amendment, which would have protected slavery in the States against Federal interference. Traces the origin of the amendment to Seward, who, in turn, acted on instructions from Lincoln. It was first introduced in the House of Representatives by Charles Francis Adams, but the author concludes that "Adams' amendment came from Seward." Corwin's name is attached to the amendment only because he was the chairman of the House committee which approved it. The motive of the moderate Republicans in associating Lincoln and their party with the amendment was to prevent the secession of the border slave States.   S. L. Jones

1187. Lindsey, David. "SUNSET" COX, LEADER OF LINCOLN'S LOYAL OPPOSITION, 1861-1865. *Mid-Am. 1955 37(1): 3-30.* Describes the Congressional career of Samuel Sullivan Cox, Democrat from Columbus, Ohio, and leader of the moderate Democrats in Congress after 1861. He sought energetically to prevent secession and war. Unlike Clement L. Vallandigham, he gave qualified support to the Union war effort but simultaneously urged measures directed toward peace. He opposed confiscation and emancipation, but later supported (but did not vote for) the 13th Amendment. He consistently defended civil liberties in wartime and was a strong supporter of General McClellan as Presidential candidate in 1864. Based on the Cox Papers in the John Hay Library, Brown University.   R. F. Campbell

1188. Lottich, Kenneth V. THE CONNECTICUT RESERVE AND THE CIVIL WAR. *Hist. of Educ. J. 1957 8(3): 92-104.* Describes the Connecticut Reserve of Ohio as an important force for Puritanism, New England-type democracy, and abolitionism. The religious, social, and political ideas of New England which were transplanted to the West were perpetuated in the region's public schools. The ideas of the people of the Connecticut Reserve were in direct and fundamental conflict with those of the South, and the conflict was resolved only by the northern victory in the Civil War.   L. Gara

1189. Macmillan, Margaret B. MICHIGAN METHODISM IN THE CIVIL WAR. *Methodist Hist. 1965 3(2): 26-38.* Statistics reveal little of the patriotism or antislavery sentiment of Michigan Methodists during the Civil War. Brief accounts of three Methodists who served in the war are given to provide a clearer understanding of their role. John Harvey Faxon was an army private, James Shirley Smart served as a chaplain, and Seth Reed as a delegate to the U.S. Christian Commission. Using excerpts from their writings, their reactions to the war and the manner in which they participated are shown. Based largely on the

John H. Faxon Papers, Michigan Historical Collection of the University of Michigan, Ann Arbor, and the *Northwestern Christian Advocate.*

H. L. Calkin

1190. Maurer, Oscar. "PUNCH" ON SLAVERY AND CIVIL WAR IN AMERICA, 1841-65. *Victorian Studies 1957/58 1(1): 5-28.* In the 1840's *Punch* had a radical-humanitarian, anti-aristocratic bias, but by the 1860's the magazine had become much more conservative in its outlook. This change is shown clearly in its treatment of slavery and the American Civil War. Throughout the 1840's and 1850's, *Punch* satirized slavery along with other American failings, and sympathized openly with abolitionist opinion in the North. After the fall of Fort Sumter, however, it became outspokenly pro-southern. In opposing the North, *Punch* insisted that the war was being fought in the interests of a high tariff, rather than abolition. It claimed that emancipation was pure hypocrisy, and to the end prophesied the defeat of the North. Abraham Lincoln was vilified until his death, and then quite suddenly eulogized. On the basis of evidence taken from the diaries of some of the editors, the author suggests that this sudden about-face indicates that the editors were less wholehearted in their Southern sympathies than they believed their readers to be. D. Houston

1191. Mayhall, Mildred E. CAMP COOPER - FIRST FORT IN TEXAS TO FALL, 1861, AND EVENTS PRECEDING ITS FALL. *Texana 1967 5(4): 317-343.* Account of affairs on the West Texas frontier just before the Civil War. The people on the frontier were concerned about a wave of Comanche raids. The inhabitants of East Texas were concerned with the issues of slavery and secession. When the Texas legislature moved to secede, State troops moved on Camp Cooper, the key Federal fort on the frontier near the Brazos River. The fort was surrendered peaceably on 20 February 1861, almost two months before Fort Sumter's surrender. Presents the letters exchanged in the surrender. 36 notes.

W. A. Buckman

1192. McConnell, Roland C. FROM THE PRELIMINARY TO FINAL EMANCIPATION. THE FIRST HUNDRED DAYS. *J. of Negro Hist. 1963 48(4): 260-276.* A sample of opinion in the North, the Confederacy, and abroad on the preliminary emancipation of 22 September 1862 reveals widespread support in the North with a considerable dissenting minority. The hundred days between the preliminary and final proclamation gave the public an opportunity to debate the issues and voice objections, some of which caused modifications in the final document. The proclamation forced changes of both sections' war aims: the Confederacy added a defense of slavery to its struggle for independence and the North added abolition of slavery to its fight to preserve the Union. Documented mostly with manuscript and newspaper sources. L. Gara

1193. McGauge, James. LONG HOT SUMMER: 1863. *Mankind 1968 1(8): 10-17, 47-49.* By the summer of 1863, the pressures of the Civil War were beginning to make themselves manifest in New York City. Demands for an end to the war were increasing at a time when the Union Army needed more men. In July the War Department began to implement the provisions of the Enrollment and Conscription Act. On 11 July 1863 drawings for the draft began. The anti-draft sentiments of poorer citizens provoked them to loot and burn. As the frenzy of the mob continued, latent racial hatred became inextricably merged with the antidraft movement. Order was not restored until several regiments of Union troops were sent into the city. Illus. P. D. Thomas

1194. Mclaughry, John. JOHN WOLCOTT PHELPS: THE CIVIL WAR GENERAL WHO BECAME A FORGOTTEN PRESIDENTIAL CANDIDATE IN 1880. *Vermont Hist. 1970 38(4): 263-290.* Descended from lawyers who sided with New York in the New Hampshire Grants controversy, Phelps (1813-85) was a career Army officer who fought the Florida Indians, chaperoned Indian removal, and was brevetted captain for gallantry in the Mexican War. He resigned in 1859 and was appointed colonel of the 1st Vermont Regiment, spring 1861, and brigadier general in the Gulf Department under General B. F. Butler, December 1861-September 1862. His insistence that slaves who sought Union protection be freed and armed against the Confederacy led to his resignation, but when after the Emancipation Proclamation Governor Holbrook secured him the command of black troops he declined because of his scruple that the commission was not retroactive to his resignation. In his 22 years' retirement as a well-to-do bachelor (he married at 70 and had a son) he translated anti-Masonic tracts from the French and wrote texts and historical and polemical articles. He was regarded locally as eccentric if not lunatic, and ridiculed for accepting the presidential nomination of the American Party, opposed to secret societies, in 1880. He secured 707 votes. Based on secondary sources. T. D. S. Bassett

1195. Mcpherson, James. WAS WEST INDIAN EMANCIPATION A SUCCESS? THE ABOLITIONIST ARGUMENT DURING THE AMERICAN CIVIL WAR. *Caribbean Studies 1964 4(2): 28-34.* In 1861 the American abolitionists hoped to turn the Civil War into a crusade to free the slaves. From 1860 to 1863 they published studies to demonstrate the success of Negro emancipation in the British and French West Indies. They maintained that the abolition of slavery had proved socially beneficial to the Negro as well as profitable to the economy. The abolitionist evaluation of West Indian emancipation as a wise, safe, and successful policy has been largely confirmed by modern scholarship. One can surmise that their arguments must have played some part in convincing northerners that the abolition of slavery in America would be both safe and practicable. T. Mathews

1196. Mcpherson, James M. ABOLITIONIST AND NEGRO OPPOSITION TO COLONIZATION DURING THE CIVIL WAR. *Phylon 1965 26(4): 391-399.* At the beginning of the Civil War various colonization proposals were offered as solutions of the Negro question. Lincoln encouraged colonization of slaves who had come within Union lines and any free Negroes wishing to emigrate in a message to Congress in 1861. In 1862, with Lincoln's approval, Congress appropriated 600 thousand dollars to help finance voluntary emigration of freed Negroes, and Lincoln supported proposals for colonization in Central America. Negroes and abolitionists angrily opposed all such schemes. A group of 453 Negroes was colonized on Île à Vache near Haiti with government support in

1863, but the experiment was a disastrous failure. As Negroes entered the Union Army the clamor for colonization subsided, and in 1864 Congress repealed provisions of the legislation of 1862 appropriating funds for colonization purposes. Based on manuscript and published sources. S. C. Pearson, Jr.

1197. Monroe, Haskell. BISHOP PALMER'S THANKSGIVING DAY ADDRESS. *Louisiana Hist. 1963 4(2): 105-118.* Analyzes the Reverend Benjamin Morgan Palmer's famous fire-eating sermon of 29 November 1860 in the First Presbyterian Church of New Orleans. Palmer, who was born in South Carolina, was probably the second most influential Presbyterian minister in the South and was preaching to the third largest Presbyterian Church in the South at the time. His fervent defense of slavery as an institution sanctioned by the Scriptures led him to endorse secession as the will of God for a tormented South. His fiery sermon was widely reprinted across the South, and one New Orleans editor claimed that Palmer "has done more for the cause of secession in this state than any other man." D. C. James

1198. Monroe, Haskell. SOUTH CAROLINIANS AND THE FORMATION OF THE PRESBYTERIAN CHURCH IN THE CONFEDERATE STATES OF AMERICA. *J. of Presbyterian Hist. 1964 42(4): 219-243.* Traces the steps taken for the organization of the Presbyterian Church in the Confederate States under the leadership of the Reverend James Henley Thornwell, member of the faculty of Columbia Theological Seminary and pastor of the Presbyterian congregation in Charleston, South Carolina. Thornwell, Abner A. Porter (editor of the *Southern Presbyterian,* a denominational weekly), and their Presbyterian colleagues "tirelessly defended slavery" and sought before 1860 to reduce southern dependence on the North. When Lincoln was elected, they proclaimed that the time had come for secession and obtained from the Synod of South Carolina, at its meeting on 28 November 1860, a resolution supporting such action. After the fact of secession and the beginning of war, with South Carolinians still in the lead, plans were made for formal separation from the Presbyterian Church in the United States of America. In Augusta, Georgia in December 1861, "The General Assembly of the Presbyterian Church in the Confederate States of America" was organized, adhering both to the traditional conservative theology and the structure used by the denomination from which they separated. W. D. Metz

1199. Moser, Harold D. REACTION IN NORTH CAROLINA TO THE EMANCIPATION PROCLAMATION. *North Carolina Hist. R. 1967 44(1): 53-71.* Studies the reactions in North Carolina to Lincoln's Emancipation Proclamation which showed the southern nonslaveholding yeomen that they were fighting not for state's rights but for slavery, an institution in which they had no direct interest. To the accepted reasons for the Confederacy's defeat must be added the internal dissension that arose from the strong antislavery and antiplanter feelings of the small southern farmer and other nonslaveholders. During the spring and summer of 1863 the peace forces developed into a powerful faction that resulted in stronger accusations against slaveholders. In 1865 the General Assembly refused a measure to enslave free Negroes and to strengthen the State's patrol system to protect the whites from slave insurrections. As the war dragged on, over 100 thousand men deserted from the Confederate forces. Based on newspapers, *Official Records,* and secondary works; 83 notes.

E. P. Stickney

1200. Murray, Donald M. and Rodney, Robert M. COLONEL JULIAN E. BRYANT: CHAMPION OF THE NEGRO SOLDIER. *J. of the Illinois State Hist. Soc. 1963 56(2): 257-281.* Julian E. Bryant from Illinois championed recognition of liberated slaves and their use as soldiers in northern armies throughout the war.

D. L. Smith

1201. Murray, Robert B. THE END OF THE REBELLION. *North Carolina Hist. R. 1967 44(4): 321-341.* The date of the legal end of the Civil War - important for thousands of Americans pressing claims against the U.S. Government - was decided by the U.S. Supreme Court in 1869 in the case of *United States vs. Anderson.* This case has received little attention from historians despite its legal importance and the claimant's background as a free Negro from South Carolina. The court decided that the war had ended on 20 August 1866, the date on which President Andrew Johnson had proclaimed that the insurrection had ended. But of equal interest was the fact that the claimant was a Negro and was treated by the Court "as a complete equal without fanfare and without the benefit of constitutional amendment." 72 notes.

J. M. Bumsted

1202. Murray, Robert K. GENERAL SHERMAN, THE NEGRO, AND SLAVERY: THE STORY OF AN UNRECOGNIZED REBEL. *Negro Hist. Bull. 1959 22(6): 125-130.* Analyzes William Tecumseh Sherman's attitudes toward the Negro and slavery. Throughout his life Sherman believed in Negro inferiority and the desirability of white supremacy in the South. He supported the northern cause because of his belief in the Union, and he deplored all attempts to turn the conflict into an abolition crusade. After the Civil War Sherman supported Andrew Johnson's policies and opposed the Radical Republican program for Reconstruction.

L. Gara

1203. Myers, Richmond E. THE MORAVIAN CHURCH AND THE CIVIL WAR. *Moravian Hist. Soc. Tr. 1965 20(pt. 2): 226-248.* By numerous quotes from *The Moravian,* the *Salem Diary,* and the *Salem Memorabilia* the author is able to give a first-hand account of the Civil War in Pennsylvania, Maryland, and Salem, North Carolina. The position of the Moravian Church on slavery and pacifism is discussed, followed by the aforementioned quotes and including soldiers' letters home. The records of the Graceham, Maryland, church are especially important since it was located between lines.

J. G. Pennington

1204. Naylor, Robert A., ed. A MEXICAN CONSPIRATOR VIEWS THE CIVIL WAR. *Civil War Hist. 1963 9(1): 67-73.* The French, Spanish, and English agreement of 31 October 1861, to collect Mexican debts by force encouraged conservative Mexicans to hope for the overthrow of Liberal Benito Juarez' regime and the setting up of a new Mexican monarchy. They solicited views of the American situation from an intimate of theirs, then resident in New York -

Raphael de Raphael, a Spanish-born journalist. His 12 November 1861 letter judged northerners to be stupid, southerners weak. He predicted that the latter would have no choice but to battle desperately, prolonging the conflict. Unionists would be unable to enforce the Monroe Doctrine, and the Lincoln administration, thanks to its hatred of slavery, would not even oppose European intervention. Whether Raphael's analysis encouraged the conspirators to support Maximilian's abortive regime, the editor cannot say. L. Filler

1205. Nevins, Allan. A MAJOR RESULT OF THE CIVIL WAR. *Civil War Hist. 1959 5(3): 237-250.* Discusses the effect of the Civil War upon the character of the American people. The author sees the most important effect as the conversion of an unorganized nation into an organized nation reinforced by a new spirit of nationalism. The wartime activities of Quartermaster General Montgomery C. Meigs in organizing supplies for the Union forces played a highly important part in determining the structure of American life after the war. In allotting contracts he shaped government contract policy and began to organize government partnership with industry. Labor and transport, the postal system, agriculture, and the banking system were affected by the measures he introduced. The abolition of slavery and the triumph of the North were telling blows for the cause of liberalism throughout the world. They constituted a vindication of democracy and played a decisive role in the subsequent unification of Italy and Germany, in the stimulation of democratic currents in France and in the domestic politics of Britain (The Bill of Reform 1867). Despite the dangers of materialism introduced by large-scale organization, the advantages outweighed some of the negative factors. Barbara Waldstein

1206. Nevins, Allan. THE NEEDLESS CONFLICT. *Am. Heritage 1956 7(5): 5-9, 88-90.* Reviews the history of the conflict between the proponents and opponents of slavery in Kansas (1856-58) in relation to the question of the expansion of slavery into the Territories. The author holds that if President James Buchanan had acted more firmly "by grappling with disunion when it was yet weak and unprepared," the Civil War might have been avoided. This was a major failure in the history of American statesmanship. Undocumented, illus. C. R. Allen, Jr.

1207. Nichols, Roy F. A HUNDRED YEARS LATER: PERSPECTIVES ON THE CIVIL WAR. *J. of Southern Hist. 1967 33(2): 153-162.* Speech given at a meeting of the Southern Historical Association. The author raises a multitude of questions regarding the American Civil War, still unanswered as the centennial concludes, grouped around six points: 1) a restudy of the importance of slavery in precipitating the struggle; 2) the revival of the conspiracy concept; 3) the complexity of the dynamics that brought about the war and the many alternatives that were possible; 4) the possibility that the war, far from being inevitable, may actually have been accidental; 5) the objectives of the activists and how they sought to achieve their goals; and 6) whether the war, rather than being a unique event, was one phase of a long process which may still be continuing. S. E. Humphreys

1208. Noyes, Edward. THE NEGRO IN WISCONSIN'S CIVIL WAR EF-FORT. *Lincoln Herald 1967 69(2): 70-82.* Records the discriminations experienced by Negroes as civilians in Wisconsin and as troops serving under the State's colors during the Civil War. S. L. Jones

1209. Peeke, Carroll. DOCUMENTARY HISTORY OF THE AMERICAN CHURCH: BISHOP KIP AND THE DAY OF HUMILIATION AND PRAYER. *Hist. Mag. of the Protestant Episcopal Church 1965 34(2): 171-178.* The Right Reverend William Ingraham Kip, first bishop of California, was in Europe when President Andrew Johnson set aside 1 June 1865 as "A Day of Humiliation and Prayer" in memory of the martyred President Lincoln. The article consists of the text of Kip's sermon at Frankfort on the Main wherein he praises Lincoln, condemns slavery and calls upon all Americans to rebuild the Nation and to dwell henceforth in unity. During the war, Kip forbade any mention of the conflict in Grace Cathedral of San Francisco even though his sympathies were with the North. E. G. Roddy

1210. Peskin, Allan. THE HERO OF THE SANDY VALLEY: JAMES A. GARFIELD'S KENTUCKY CAMPAIGN OF 1861-1862. *Ohio Hist. 1963 72(1): 3-24, (2): 129-139.* Part I. Examines the role played by Garfield as commander of the 18th Brigade, which cleared a section of southeastern Kentucky of Confederate troops in a campaign conducted from December 1861 to mid-January 1862. Garfield had been appointed colonel in command of the 42d Ohio Volunteer Infantry, which he had recruited and organized in the fall of 1861. The article analyzes the strategic significance of the Sandy Valley operation and describes the operation itself both from the points of view of Garfield and of opposing Confederate General Humphrey Marshall. Part II. Though convinced that the war must result in the emancipation of the slaves, Garfield saw the necessity of following a moderate policy in the occupation of the Sandy Valley region. Difficulties in maintaining supplies, in fighting floods, and in coping with disease among the troops are described. The details of a minor battle at Pound Gap are also recounted. During this period Garfield was promoted to brigadier general, and in March 1862, shortly after the action at Pound Gap, he was ordered to report to Louisville for reassignment. Based on the Garfield and Marshall Papers. S. L. Jones

1211. Qualls, Youra. "SUCCESSORS OF WOOLMAN AND BENEZET": THE BEGINNINGS OF THE PHILADELPHIA FRIENDS FREEDMEN'S ASSOCIATION. *Bull. of Friends Hist. Assoc. 1956 45(2): 82-104.* An account of the leaders, aims, and activities during the first six months (November 1863-April 1864) of the association organized to assist the Negroes being freed by successes of the northern armies during the Civil War. The problem of how to help thousands of displaced, uneducated, poor, friendless Negroes was faced by a group of Friends, able Philadelphia leaders, inheritors of a tradition of benevolence toward the Negro. N. Kurland

1212. Quarles, Benjamin. THE ABDUCTION OF THE "PLANTER." *Civil War Hist. 1958 4(1): 5-10.* In 1862, a group of slaves in Charleston Harbor, South

Carolina, stole a Confederate transport. Instigator of the deed was Robert Smalls, a Negro who had learned boating and been part of the boat's slave crew. It gave itself over to Union ships maintaining the blockade of Southern ports and was taken to Port Royal, 60 miles away. The U.S. Congress quickly appraised the boat and made generous prize awards to Smalls and his associates. The *Planter* proved useful to Federal naval plans, as did its resourceful abductor.

L. Filler

1213. Quattlebaum, Isabel. TWELVE WOMEN IN THE FIRST DAYS OF THE CONFEDERACY. *Civil War Hist. 1961 7(4): 370-385.* Southern women approved of secession but were puzzled because the North would not permit it without bloodshed. They accepted slavery but deplored its cruel aspects. Some, like Betty Herndon Maury, found it difficult to repudiate the Union, but the greater number accepted allegiance to their states or the Confederacy. They hated Yankees, though they sometimes sympathized with Federal prisoners. Aside from their fears for friends and family, they enjoyed the earlier phases of the war. Hospital work chastened many, but few were able to perceive the larger issues of the national contest. L. Filler

1214. Raminov. THE AMERICAN CIVIL WAR (1861-1865). *J. of the United Service Inst. of India 1959 89(375): 177-183, (376): 261-276.* Part I. A broad introductory survey of the causes of the American Civil War, the effects of geography and politics on strategy, the personalities of the leaders, and the resolution of the problems involved. Slavery was not a major cause of the war. It was inevitable that the industrialized North would seek to enforce fiscal and tariff policies inimical to the feudal, cotton-growing South. In the fighting qualities of its troops, the South had the edge. The intelligence of the South was more effective. The South should have concentrated its main strategy in the West, but instead each side tried to capture the other's capital. When Grant at last secured the Mississippi and split the Confederacy, the war was won. The author follows the course of the war to 1861. Part II. This section consists of a factual narrative of military operations in the major battles of the Civil War. The author reads in the outcome of these engagements the folly of tailoring strategy to meet short-term political ends. He feels that the extraordinarily heavy losses were due to a lack of appreciation of the lethal power of the rifled musket in comparison to the old smoothbore. The desirability of flanking maneuvers over direct assaults against entrenched positions is also noted. M. Naidis

1215. Rand, Larry Anthony. AMERICA VIEWS RUSSIAN SERF EMANCI-PATION 1861. *Mid-Am. 1968 50(1): 42-51.* The emancipation of the Russian serf had a resounding effect upon the American people. Yet, not unlike the situation within Russia itself, opinion about Alexander II's actions was never unanimous. Although serfdom and slavery had things in common, there were always differences enough to keep American opinion on the question of emancipation divided. Based on newspaper and periodical accounts; 38 notes.

L. D. Silveri

1216. Rayback, Robert J. NEW YORK STATE IN THE CIVIL WAR. *New York Hist. 1961 42(1): 56-70.* Suggests three major revisions in the traditional picture of New York's relation to the war: that politicians such as William H. Seward and Martin Van Buren were interested largely in political advantage in espousing, late in life, the free-soil cause; that New York was largely responsible for the success of the Republican Party because of Thurlow Weed's expedient decision to merge the State's Whig Party with minority Republican elements in order to win elections; and that the State's support of both the war effort and Negro rights was considerably apathetic.   A. B. Rollins

1217. Reed, John Q. CIVIL WAR HUMOR: ARTEMUS WARD. *Civil War Hist. 1956 2(3): 87-101.* A study of the humor of Artemus Ward (Charles Farrar Browne), a humorist of the Civil War period, whose comments on the war and slavery rest "not upon any striking originality in his basic attitudes and opinions, but upon the vigor, freshness, and novelty of his expression."
W. E. Wight

1218. Reiger, John F. DEPRIVATION, DISAFFECTION, AND DESERTION IN CONFEDERATE FLORIDA. *Florida Hist. Q. 1970 48(3): 279-298.* Suffering by Florida families during the Civil War was widespread as a result of the blockade, of men leaving for the conflict, of Confederate impressment of provisions to supply troops, and of failure to plant food crops in preference to cotton or other money crops. Prices became exorbitant as early as January 1862 for both necessities and luxury items. Conditions were perhaps worst of all in south Florida. A compilation of soldiers' families, ordered by the governor in January 1863, revealed over 10 thousand persons (out of a total of over 78 thousand) in need of State aid. Besides widespread conditions of deprivation which tended to contribute to the antiwar feeling, high taxes, impressment, and conscription increased disaffection almost to revolt. More than 2,219 Florida Confederate soldiers were recorded as deserters. Conscription evaders and deserters joined forces to avoid arrest and some crossed Federal lines to enlist. Harsh methods of capturing Confederate deserters caused public sympathy for them. By spring of 1865, with most of east Florida in Union hands and the remainder of the State overrun with deserters, conscription evaders, refugees, and fugitive slaves, the desire for peace was all pervasive. Based partly on official Union and Confederate Army records and unpublished letters; 95 notes.
R. V. Calvert

1219. Reinders, Robert C., ed. A WISCONSIN SOLDIER REPORTS FROM NEW ORLEANS. *Louisiana Hist. 1962 3(4): 360-365.* Consists of a brief editorial introduction and one letter written by Captain Frank Dwight Harding, Fourth Wisconsin Infantry Regiment, New Orleans, to his father in Hudson, Wisconsin, dated 3 May 1862. The letter describes the trip aboard a Union transport up the Mississippi River after the successful passing of Forts Jackson and St. Philip, and the initial landing of Union troops in New Orleans. It includes accounts of the jubilant slaves along the banks and of the Confederate mutiny at Fort Jackson.   D. C. James

1220. Robbins, Gerald. THE RECRUITING AND ARMING OF NEGROES IN THE SOUTH CAROLINA SEA ISLANDS, 1862-1865. *Negro Hist. Bull. 1965 28(7): 150-151, 163-167.* When Major General David Hunter in 1862 became commander of the Department of the South, he declared the slaves freed and called for Negro volunteers to replace white soldiers being transferred to scenes of war. A letter from Hunter to Edwin M. Stanton read in Congress triggered a heated argument on arming slaves. The government refused payment for Hunter's colored recruits thus forcing him to disband them. A month later Brigadier General Rufus Saxton was authorized by Stanton to uniform and arm five thousand Negroes. These troops were sent into the coastal areas of Georgia and Florida on a raid which proved a success. Finally Abraham Lincoln's approval turned the tide and Saxton's regiment was officially inaugurated into the Army, 25 June 1863, under the command of Colonel William T. Higginson. 77 notes.   E. P. Stickney

1221. Robbins, Gerald. WILLIAM F. ALLEN: CLASSICAL SCHOLAR AMONG THE SLAVES. *Hist. of Educ. Q. 1965 5(4): 211-223.* Describes the work of Allen and his wife as teachers of the abandoned slaves on the Sea Islands off the coast of South Carolina. The report is based on contemporary sources and, primarily, on the William Francis Allen Papers at the State Historical Society of Wisconsin.   J. Herbst

1222. Robertson, James I., Jr. NEGRO SOLDIERS IN THE CIVIL WAR. *Civil War Times Illus. 1968 7(6): 21-32.* Americans of African descent made up 12 percent of Union forces. Of three premature attempts made early in 1862 to organize Negro units, two met with bitter disappointment. Several engagements in which Negro troops took part are described. About one-third of the 179,000 Negro troops were casualties. They suffered much from prejudice on the part of both Confederate and Union soldiers. Many were killed by their own side. In general, they made good soldiers.   R. N. Alvis

1223. Roper, Laura Wood. FREDERICK LAW OLMSTED AND THE PORT ROYAL EXPERIMENT. *J. of Southern Hist. 1965 31(3): 272-284.* After the capture of Port Royal and other South Carolina Sea Islands in 1861 more than eight thousand slaves were left behind in the flight of their masters. Frederick Law Olmsted sought to persuade the Lincoln administration, and particularly Secretary of War Edwin Stanton and Secretary of the Treasury Salmon P. Chase, to undertake a farseeing policy toward the Negroes there, that would protect them against hunger and disease and encourage them in self-support. Senator Lafayette S. Foster of Connecticut introduced a bill in Congress to achieve Olmsted's ends. In the showdown, however, neither Congress, Chase nor Stanton accepted the Olmsted plan and authorities at Port Royal groped for an effective plan until the enactment of the Freedmen's Bureau Act of 1865.
                                                                    S. E. Humphreys

1224. Rosenberg, John S. TOWARD A NEW CIVIL WAR REVISIONISM. *Am. Scholar 1969 38(2): 250-272.* First analyzes past generations of American historiographical revisionism, and then discusses some possible paths to be followed by a revised historiography of theamerican Civil War. Early revisionists such as Avery O. Craven and James G. Randall challenged the view of Charles Austin Beard and "nationalists" who had held that the war was an inevitable conflict between slavery and freedom. To do so, the revisionists were required to minimize slavery as a moral and political issue and stress emotionalism over largely symbolic issues. The interpretation enjoyed wide acceptance until the 1950's. In 1950 Kenneth M. Stampp pointed out that the war's end produced only rich victors and half-freed slaves. Soon after, historians reevaluated war and its uses in the light of the victory in World War II."New nationalists" such as Samuel Eliot Morison, Arthur M. Schlesinger, and Harold Hyman found the war a necessary step toward a better democracy. The impending "new revisionism," the author believes, will hold that the war was an unavoidable tragedy that cannot be justified by the meager gains that followed it. The postwar generation lacked moral conviction and gave power to Negroes only to preserve the hegemony of the Republican Party and the North. It would seem better if blacks had attempted to seize freedom. As it is, Negroes have gained little while the Nation has acquired a great "Treasury of Virtue," undeservedly.   T. R. Cripps

1225. Runkle, Gerald. KARL MARX AND THE AMERICAN CIVIL WAR. *Comparative Studies in Soc. and Hist. 1963 6(2): 117-141.* Surveys Marx' and Engels' views of the Civil War found in articles in the *New York Daily Tribune* (September 1861-January 1862) and the Vienna *Presse* (October 1861-November 1862) and in their correspondence; places these views in the theoretical Marxist assumptions, even though not expressed in these pieces; and notes certain errors of fact. The author also notes other errors of interpretation, which derive from the dialectical framework of Marx and Engels. They saw the war as a revolt of northern capitalism against the slaveholding aristocracy. The essential error, however, is the Hegelian one of mistaking the results of the war, which Marx clearly foresaw, for the cause of the war.   J. Harper

1226. Scott, Franklin D. AMERIKAN SISÄLLISSODAN MERKITYS [The meaning of the American Civil War]. *Historiallinen Aikakauskirja [Finland] 1958 56(3): 199-209.* Reviews the causes and impact of the American Civil War. The American nation was divided on two issues, the nature of the political federation and the principles of American social structure. Northern and southern States, respectively, evolved into distinct social, economic, and cultural communities which then clashed for control of the new West. Despite the northern victory, the issues of race relations and Federal vs. local jurisdiction remained unresolved, to reemerge with the 1954 Supreme Court decision on school integration. "The American Civil War is still alive today...because the disputes which caused it could not be erased by military victory."   R. G. Selleck

1227. Shapiro, Samuel. LINCOLN AND DANA. *Lincoln Herald 1958 60(4): 119-122.* Demonstrates Lincoln's ability to win friends and influence people even in dealing with minor officials. Charles Anderson Dana's low opinion of Lincoln was not improved by the issuance of the Emancipation Proclamation as he had been opposed to the antislavery legislation proposed by the radicals. Subsequent events altered Dana's contemptuous attitude toward Lincoln, who managed to win the respect and support of his patrician subordinate. Subsequently Dana contributed heavily to the Republican campaign chest. Lincoln's shrewd use of politeness and patronage won over this once scornful subordinate and demonstrated Lincoln's superb abilities as a master of men. Biblio.

J. G. Turner

1228. Shapiro, Samuel. THE RENDITION OF ANTHONY BURNS. *J. of Negro Hist. 1959 44(1): 43-51.* Recounts the incidents surrounding the arrest and trial of an escaped slave, Anthony Burns, in Boston in 1854, disturbing the superficial sectional calm which had followed the Compromise of 1850. Despite the efforts of the defense attorney, Richard Henry Davis, the court ordered Burns to be returned to his master in Virginia under the Fugitive Slave Law. The case was widely publicized in both North and South and aroused strong resentment in the North. Passage of the Kansas-Nebraska Act in the same year revived sectional animosity, and the Fugitive Slave Law and State personal liberty statutes stood as symbols of a deadlock to be washed away in the blood bath of the Civil War in the following decade. R. E. Wilson

1229. Shewmaker, Kenneth E. and Prinz, Andrew K., eds. A YANKEE IN LOUISIANA: SELECTIONS FROM THE DIARY AND CORRESPONDENCE OF HENRY R. GARDNER, 1862-1866. *Louisiana Hist. 1964 5(3): 271-295.* Written by Henry Rufus Gardner, a Union soldier who served in Louisiana, 1862-66. His principal combat experience was in the Teche campaign and in the siege of Port Hudson. After the war he remained for several years with the Quartermaster's Department in New Orleans and Brashear City, Louisiana. The selections are interspersed under topical entries such as army life, military operations, the Negro soldier, cotton speculation, and the New Orleans riot of 1866. They include 57 diary entries and 25 excerpts from letters to his parents. The originals are in the possession of Jean Gardner Groen, Oak Park, Illinois.

D. C. James

1230. Shosteck, Robert. THE JEWISH COMMUNITY OF WASHINGTON, D.C., DURING THE CIVIL WAR. *Am. Jewish Hist. Q. 1967 56(3): 319-347.* On the basis of census data, cemetery lists, and the records of the Washington Jewish congregations, a description of Jewish religious activities, social and cultural life, and economic status has been provided for the war years. In 1860 less than 200 Jews lived in the capital, which number increased rapidly throughout the war. Many of these newcomers remained highly transient. Simon Wolfe and other leaders of the community shared with their fellow citizens the prevailing hopes and attitudes toward the war and toward the basic issues of slavery and union. Jews served with Christians in the many home front welfare, nursing, and fund raising activities of the war years. F. Rosenthal

1231. Smith, Duane Allan. THE CONFEDERATE CAUSE IN THE COLORADO TERRITORY, 1861-1865. *Civil War Hist. 1961 7(1): 71-80.* Most Colorado settlers were Unionists. Negro slavery was not important in the Territory. Its Governor, William Gilpin, was ardently loyal to the Federal cause and labored to sustain it against southern sympathizers and Confederate guerrillas.

There were anti-Negro demonstrations and organized Confederate guerrilla raids, but the government they supported did not derive gold from their efforts nor territory. L. Filler

1232. Smith, Harold F. THE 1861 STRUGGLE FOR LEXINGTON, MISSOURI. *Civil War Hist. 1961 7(2): 155-166.* Missouri's importance to the North was emphasized by General John C. Frémont's appointment as western commander. Much of Missouri was proslavery. St. Louis was saved by the swift action of General Nathaniel Lyon and the fleeing of the pro-Confederate Governor, Sterling Price. When, however, Lyon met Price's forces at Wilson's Creek, unsuccessfully, the Federal drive to clear Missouri of Confederate sympathizers was slowed down. Price, in the southwest, determined to recapture the State, aimed at Lexington, largest city on the Missouri River between St. Louis and Kansas City, and moved northward in August 1861. Frémont proclaimed martial law, and Colonel James E. Mulligan of the 23d Illinois Volunteers was sent to defend Lexington. Though outnumbered, he ranged his troops within the city against Price's entering infantry and cavalry. These gradually invested Lexington, sealing off escape by boats, and in engagements over several days late in September defeated the besieged garrison, which surrendered some 3,500 men and considerable materiel. Northerners were disappointed, and responsibility for what was termed a disaster and disgrace was placed on Frémont. Price was unable to extend his victory, for lack of Confederate support and fear of Federal troops converging on the area. L. Filler

1233. Spalding, David, C.F.X. MARTIN JOHN SPALDING'S "DISSERTATION ON THE AMERICAN CIVIL WAR." *Catholic Hist. R. 1966 52(1): 66-85.* The Roman Catholic bishop of Louisville sent a confidential report to Rome in May of 1863 to enlighten the Holy See on the constitutional complexities of the Civil War and its true causes. It was primarily an indictment of the abolitionists, who, in Spalding's view, had captured the government and changed the goal of the war from the preservation of the Union, which he favored, to the immediate eradication of slavery, which he deemed a wanton violation of property rights. While he advocated gradual and compensated emancipation and sympathized with the views of the Peace Democrats, he urged a policy of noninvolvement for the American Catholic clergy. A

1234. Staudenraus, P. J. THE POPULAR ORIGINS OF THE THIRTEENTH AMENDMENT. *Mid-Am. 1968 50(2): 108-115.* Shows how, throughout the war years 1861-65, the rebellion made abolitionists of the great majority of Americans. From an early conciliatory attitude to protect slavery, many soon desired gradual emancipation as evidenced by piecemeal Congressional legislation (1862) dealing with the problem of freeing war "contraband" slaves. President Lincoln proposed gradual and compensated emancipation as well as colonization schemes; but when the 13th amendment passed the House on 30 January 1865 it took only until 18 December 1865 for 27 States to abolish slavery. Based primarily on Government documents and manuscripts; 23 notes. J. F. Scaccia

1235. Stein, Barbara H. O BRASIL VISTO DE SELMA, ALABAMA, 1867: UM LEVANTAMENTO BIBLIOGRAFICO [Brazil seen from Selma, Alabama, in 1867: a bibliographical survey]. *R. do Inst. de Estudos Brasileiros [Brazil] 1968 3: 47-63.* Surveys writings of Southerners interested in Brazil as a place of exile when slavery was abolished in the United States after the Civil War. The author also discusses earlier travelers' accounts (especially those of Americans, Englishmen, and Frenchmen) with which the ex-Confederates should have been familiar. Emphasized are those descriptions of Brazil dealing with slavery and race relations.the author compares and contrasts plantation systems of the two countries as seen by their respective contemporaries. Based on 19th-century travelers' accounts, many of which are available in the Princeton University Library; 46 notes. F. A. Dutra

1236. Stotts, Gene. THE NEGRO PAUL REVERE OF QUANTRILL'S RAID. *Negro Hist. Bull. 1963 26(5): 169-170.* Relates the story of an 18-year-old Negro servant's five-mile walk from a farmhouse to Eudora, Kansas, 20 August 1863, to warn the settlers there that a large Confederate raiding party was headed for Lawrence. Henry, the servant, accomplished his mission but two riders sent to warn Lawrence failed to reach their destination and the town was burned. L. Gara

1237. Straudenraus, P. J. OCCUPIED BEAUFORT, 1863: A WAR CORRESPONDENT'S VIEW. *South Carolina Hist. Mag. 1963 64(3): 136-145.* Noah Brooks, a correspondent for the Sacramento *Daily Union,* wrote the letter dated Beaufort, 17 June 1863, which was published in his paper during the following July. He opens his communication with a favorable description of the place, homes, and people. He contrasts with distinct disfavor the Negroes and Yankees who supplanted the local nabobs. Discussed are the old Episcopal Church, the "Grand Skedaddle" of the local gentry, the looting by Negroes and Yankees, the 1st South Carolina Regiment, commanded by Colonel T. W. Higginson, southern plantations in northern hands, and the military government. V. E. Bardsley

1238. Talmadge, John E. A PEACE MOVEMENT IN CIVIL WAR CONNECTICUT. *New England Q. 1964 37(3): 306-321.* At the Connecticut State Democratic convention in 1860, a conservative minority supporting John C. Breckinridge bolted and reassembled to nominate their candidate. The State's peace agitation was an expression of a resolute minority, many of whom apparently shared an anti-abolitionist feeling and grew bold following the Union defeat at Bull Run. As a whole, the State stood for war. With Governor William Buckingham's proclamation that the State would not hold sacred any "property used to subvert governmental authority," and the support by former peace newspapers of "constitutional war efforts," the peace movement died out in September 1861. The apparent reason that many people in Connecticut disapproved of the war lay in the fact that radical ideas stemming from Puritanism had not gained as much headway in the State as in other parts of New England, and editorial policy of the newspapers supporting peace served as a stimulus to stir these people to express their unpopular feeling in public protests. Based on letters in the Connecticut Historical Society, newspapers, and secondary sources; 69 notes.

R. V. Calvert

1239. Tarasova, V. M. DEKABRIST NIKOLAI TURGENEV I BOR'BA PRO- TIV RABSTVA V SSHA [The Decembrist Nikolai Turgenev and the struggle against slavery in the United States]. *Voprosy Istorii [USSR] 1963 (10): 209-212.* Notes the correspondence that took place between Nikolai Turgenev, Maria W. Weston, and Wendell P. Garrison from 1855 to 1865. It is pointed out that Turgenev deplored the fact that after Emancipation the exslaves did not receive any land or participate in government. Turgenev also was against the proposed scheme of sending freedmen to settlement colonies outside the United States. 16 notes.

A. Birkos

1240. Taylor, Joe Gray. SLAVERY IN LOUISIANA DURING THE CIVIL WAR. *Louisiana Hist. 1967 8(1): 27-33.* As Federal armies drew near, slavehold- ers in Louisiana had increasing difficulty holding their slaves on the plantations and getting work out of them. The immediate effect of the approach of Union troops was a slackening in work. Slavery became disorganized and inefficient. Slaves ran away by the thousands and demonstrated their desire for freedom above the security of the slave quarter again and again. They were a valuable source of information to the Federal troops. Instances of Negro violence toward whites increased, although they still were rare. In spite of their clear desire for freedom, Louisiana Negroes, and southern Negroes in general, failed to revolt against their masters during the Civil War. There were no real slave insurrections in Louisiana, and although many Negroes were enlisted in the Union Army, the evidence indicates that they were reluctant volunteers. Taylor suggests that the reason for this "may well have been the slave's realization that the attitude of the Northern soldier toward the Negro differed only in degree from the attitude of the master and the master's neighbors." Based principally on travel accounts and journals of northern soldiers; 15 notes.

R. L. Woodward

1241. Temkin, Sefton D. ISAAC MAYER WISE AND THE CIVIL WAR. *Am. Jewish Arch. 1963 15(2): 120-142.* Traces the political views of Wise, a prominent Cincinnati rabbi, from 1856 through 1863. Wise was first attracted by the Repub- lican Party. As secession became imminent, he refused to indulge in political preaching, but in other places made clear his acceptance of the right of secession, his yearning for peace, and his lack of concern over slavery. In 1863 he was sympathetic with Clement Vallandigham, perhaps partly because of that con- gressman's defense of Jewish rights. He toyed with running for the State senate on the Democratic ticket but was forced by his congregation to withdraw from the race. More research is needed before the patterns of Wise's thought can be firmly established from his erratic and shifting views and actions.

A. B. Rollins

1242. Temple, Wayne C., ed. AN ILLINOIS CAPTAIN IN THE SOUTH. *Lincoln Herald 1964 66(2): 97-102.* Contains the texts of letters from David Williams, Captain of Company C, 115th Volunteer Infantry Regiment, to John

Robert Corrie. While the letters reveal some aspects of camp life and military activity, in the main they deal with politics, abolition, and similar questions. The letters are now in the possession of Mr. and Mrs. Lester Linn Corrie, 302 West High Street, Urbana, Illinois.   S. L. Jones

1243. Thompson, William Y. SANITARY FAIRS OF THE CIVIL WAR. *Civil War Hist. 1958 4(1): 51-57.* The U.S. Sanitary Commission, organized in 1861, performed well, contributing 25 million dollars in services and goods. Their fairs helped provide this money. A pioneer venture was in Chicago, 27 October-7 November. Lincoln contributed for sale the original draft of the Emancipation Proclamation. Cities large and small emulated the Chicago Fair. The fair in Cincinnati was even more successful, selling letters of well-known personalities. The Boston Fair was staid but well received. Others in numerous cities presented individual novelties, famous personages, and striking profits.
                                                                   L. Filler

1244. Thorp, Robert K. THE COPPERHEAD DAYS OF DENNIS MAHONY. *Journalism Q. 1966 43(4): 680-686, 696.* Contains a summary biography of Dennis Mahony, "peace Democrat" and editor of the Dubuque *Herald,* focused particularly upon the time between Abraham Lincoln's election and the time Mahony was arrested (on no particular charges) and taken to Washington to be imprisoned for three months upon the authority of Secretary of War Edwin M. Stanton. Close study of Mahony's editorials indicates he was more misguided than disloyal, wrong on slavery but an honest critic of the Lincoln administration. He failed to understand that the people were willing to have their Constitution violated in order to win the war and preserve the Union. He was in step logically but out of step with the times - a conservative unable to hold back the tides of change. 16 notes.   S. E. Humphreys

1245. Thorpe, Earl E. THE DAY FREEDOM CAME. *Negro Hist. Bull. 1958 22(1): 10-12.* Discusses Negro reactions to freedom from slavery. Some successful runaway slaves described their contentment with their new life. Emancipation after the Civil War inspired celebrations, and freedmen sometimes left their former masters. Some former slaves recorded their preference for freedom even in a society which discriminated against them.   L. Gara

1246. Toppin, Edgar A. EMANCIPATION RECONSIDERED. *Negro Hist. Bull. 1963 26(8): 233-236.* Discusses the Emancipation Proclamation in terms of a number of complex factors including the significance of abolition in terms of American ideals of freedom, the mixed feelings on the question in the North, Lincoln's antislavery sympathies, Negro reaction to the proclamation, and its important contribution to the ultimate outcome of the Civil War. Based on published sources.   L. Gara

1247. Toppin, Edgar A. HUMBLY THEY SERVED: THE BLACK BRIGADE IN THE DEFENSE OF CINCINNATI. *J. of Negro Hist. 1963 48(2): 75-97.* Describes the contributions of Cincinnati's "Black Brigade" in preparing to defend the city against a possible Confederate attack in the summer of 1862. The brigade, comprised of Negro civilian laborers, worked along the Kentucky side of the Ohio River. Despite ridicule and a number of humiliating incidents, Cincinnati's Negroes served faithfully in the hard work of constructing roads and fortifications. A number of the brigade's members later joined military units when the Union Government began to recruit Negro soldiers. Documented.

L. Gara

1248. Unsigned. AN EYE WITNESS ACCOUNT OF THE OCCUPATION OF MT. PLEASANT. *South Carolina Hist. Mag. 1965 66(1): 8-14.* A letter from Henry Slade Tew (1805-84), mayor of Mt. Pleasant, South Carolina in 1865, to his daughter. Tew recounts in detail, the shock of the occupation by Union forces, gives credit generously to those who observed protocol, and makes observations on Negro reactions and behavior.

V. O. Bardsley

1249. Unsigned. IS THIS LT. JOHN CAMPBELL'S LETTER? *Ann. of Iowa 1969 39(7): 542-545.* Reproduces a letter sent to the Des Moines *Daily State Register* on 9 June 1863 by an unknown member of Company B, 5th Iowa Regiment, stationed near Vicksburg, Mississippi. It is possible that the letter which appeared in the newspaper on 23 June 1863 was from Lieutenant John Q. A. Campbell, since his diary [Edwin C. Bearss,"The Civil War Diary of Lt. John Q. A. Campbell, Company B, 5th Iowa Infantry," *Annals of Iowa,* 39(7): 519-541 (see abstract 8:1423)] mentions a letter sent to the Des Moines paper on 9 June. The correspondent discussed two major subjects - the haste with which Governor Samuel Jordan Kirkwood and other dignitaries left a gathering of troops which they were addressing when Confederates opened fire, and the question whether black soldiers in the Union Army would fight. The correspondent attributed the politicians' hasty departure to the feeling that their presence was drawing the enemy's attention and to a desire not to further endanger the Union troops. The heroic actions of newly enrolled colored regiments at the Battle of Milliken's Bend during extremely bloody hand-to-hand fighting seemed to convince the writer of the Negroes' bravery.

W. R. Griffin

1250. Unsigned. LEE BLAMED EWELL AND LONGSTREET FOR HIS FAILURE IN THE WILDERNESS. *Civil War Times Illus. 1966 5(1): 4-7.* Based on memoranda made by Colonel William Preston Johnston, professor at Washington College at the time Lee was president of the institution. The memoranda are based on conversations between the two men. In these Lee accused Lieutenant General Richard Stoddert Ewell of "vacillation" and Lieutenant General James Longstreet of being "often slow," and claimed to have recognized at the start of the war the necessity of the Confederacy's gradually emancipating the slaves and using Negroes as soldiers. The memoranda were found in the McCormick Library, Washington and Lee University, by professor emeritus of history W. G. Bean. Illus.

W. R. Boedecker

1251. Unsigned. UNBEKANNTE ARTIKEL VON KARL MARX ÜBER DEN BÜRGERKRIEG IN DEN USA [Unknown articles by Karl Marx on the Civil War in the United States]. *Beiträge zur Geschichte der Deutschen Arbeiter-*

bewegung [East Germany] 1959 1(2): 231-242. Includes commentary and text of four newspaper articles which Marx published in 1861 and 1862 in the Viennese journal *Presse.* Marx portrayed the American Civil War as a struggle between two social systems: the northern bourgeois capitalist system of wage labor and the southern system based on slave labor.   G. H. Davis

1252. Vandersee, Charles. HENRY ADAMS BEHIND THE SCENES: CIVIL WAR LETTERS TO FREDERICK W. SEWARD. *New York Public Lib. Bull. 1967 71(4): 245-264.* The self-deprecatory tone of the autobiographical *Education of Henry Adams* gives no indication of the attempts its author made to help his father, Charles Francis Adams, American minister to Great Britain, to keep England from aiding the South in the Civil War. While his father's private secretary, he secretly served as an anonymous London correspondent for the *New York Times* and sought to quell anti-British feeling in the North by showing readers that England was coming to accept the Unionist viewpoint. This article concerns a second way in which Adams tried to help his father: a series of letters that he wrote to Assistant Secretary of State Frederick William Seward in 1862 and 1863 suggesting policies which would aid the elder Adams. Since Seward was the son of Secretary of State William Henry Seward, there was little doubt about the potential influence he could have upon governmental policy. Ten of these letters exist in the William H. Seward Collection at the University of Rochester and are published here for the first time. In the letters Adams proposed that pamphlets be distributed in Europe to promote the Union cause, that a slave emancipation statement be made in 1862, that Negroes be assured "the rights of citizenship abroad," and that Union armies gain some victories with which to impress the English. The author considers the letters an interesting footnote to American diplomatic history and valuable documents of a man and an era. 60 notes.   W. L. Bowers

1253. Voegeli, Jacque. THE NORTHWEST AND THE RACE ISSUE 1861-1862. *Mississippi Valley Hist. R. 1963 50(2): 235-251.* In the Northwest, when the Civil War broke out, the opposition to slavery did not carry with it a commitment to equality for the Negro. Prominent northwestern Republicans were in the vanguard of the deportation movement. In Ohio, discriminatory anti-Negro laws continued to prevail. In the elections of 1862 the Democrats swept to victory in Congress. Elated Democrats from the Northwest hailed the elections as a repudiation of the emancipation heresy. Though many other factors inspired the political revolt against the party of Lincoln in the elections of 1862, many northwestern Republicans conceded the impact of the emancipation issue. 47 notes.   E. P. Stickney

1254. Wagandt, Charles L. ELECTION BY SWORD AND BALLOT: THE EMANCIPATIONIST VICTORY OF 1863. *Maryland Hist. Mag. 1964 59(2): 143-164.* "As in the nation, so in Maryland the war-time movement to free the slaves became a tool to overthrow the old social, economic, and political order. Of critical importance to the success of the campaign in Maryland was the election of November 4, 1863." Four Unconditional Unionists and one Democrat were elected to Congress while the emancipationists won 47 of the 74 seats in the Maryland House of Delegates.   W. L. Fox

1255. Wagandt, Charles L. THE ARMY VERSUS MARYLAND SLAVERY, 1862-1864. *Civil War Hist. 1964 10(2): 141-148.* Discusses wartime slavery in Maryland, where military officers relentlessly harassed slaveowners by: 1) refusing to restore fugitive slaves, 2) indiscriminately enlisting slaves whether of loyal or disloyal owners, and 3) releasing slaves from jail. The governor and others protested strongly to Lincoln, and although the President instructed Federal authorities to use common sense in the matter, the abuses continued. At length, with slaveowning influence declining steadily, slavery was abolished in Maryland in November, 1864. "To the Union army," concludes the author, "went considerable credit for the abolitionist victory." Published materials and State documents are the chief sources.   E. C. Murdock

1256. Wagandt, Charles L., ed. THE CIVIL WAR DIARY OF DR. SAMUEL A. HARRISON. *Civil War Hist. 1967 13(2): 131-146.* Excerpts from the wartime journal of Samuel A. Harrison who resided on Maryland's Eastern Shore. Although a Unionist, Harrison lived among many secessionists, and his journal clearly reflects the divided opinions and confused thoughts which prevailed in border State communities. His changing views and doubts about the Negro and his future pervade the entire document and afford a valuable insight into the thinking of an enlightened man on a "subject which has exercised and still occupies the best minds of the world."   E. C. Murdock

1257. Wainwright, Nicholas B. THE LOYAL OPPOSITION IN CIVIL WAR PHILADELPHIA. *Pennsylvania Mag. of Hist. and Biog. 1964 88(3): 294-315.* Both Republicans and Democrats were essentially loyal to the idea of the Union, but they differed in their interpretation of the Constitution. The Pennsylvania Democratic convention of 1862 put the blame for the war on northern abolitionists. In the campaign of 1864 the Democratic presidential candidate George B. McClellan was willing to continue slavery saying that "The Union is the one condition of peace." The Democratic Party declined because of the suspected loyalty of some of its leaders. After the assassination of Lincoln, *The Ace,* the Democratic newspaper in Philadelphia which had ridiculed Lincoln, editorialized: "No where...has sorrow for Mr. Lincoln's death been more unaffected and sincere than at this moment in the ranks of the great Democratic party." Based on manuscripts, diaries, and newspapers; 55 notes.   E. P. Stickney

1258. Wayland, Francis F., ed. FREMONT'S PURSUIT OF JACKSON IN THE SHENANDOAH VALLEY, "THE JOURNAL OF COLONEL ALBERT TRACY, MARCH-JULY 1862. *Virginia Mag. of Hist. and Biog. 1962 70(2): 165-194, (3): 332-354.* Tracy's journal is a detailed document describing the army in camp, marching, and fighting. The first part of the diary indicates that there were foreigners in the American army and gives bits of information to indicate rear guard action, destructiveness as well as tender care of enemy wounded, and the fact that 11 thousand Union troops at one time were pursuing over 14 thousand Confederates, although the Confederates did not know the Union forces were so small. The second part reveals the plan of operation, hunger and casualties, the everpresent mulattoes in the slaveholders household, general social information, and the events surrounding Frémont's resignation late in June 1862. J. H. Boykin

1259. Wesley, Charles H. THE CIVIL WAR AND THE NEGRO-AMERICAN. *J. of Negro Hist. 1962 47(2): 77-96.* Reviews the history of the Civil War Centennial plans and points out the glorification of the war and especially of the Southern cause and the commercialism which has characterized so much of the observance thus far. After a brief review of the plans of several minority groups, the author suggests some steps Negro Americans might take to improve the quality of commemorative events. They should carefully point out the true nature of the North and the South on the eve of the conflict, the major causes of the war, and the attitudes and acts of Negro Americans in the various States. Community meetings, museum exhibits, publication of Negro war records, and essay contests could implement the above ideas. The author closes with a plea that the commemoration be used to contribute to the realization of full freedom for the American Negro. L. Gara

1260. White, Lonnie J., ed. A BLUECOAT'S ACCOUNT OF THE CAMDEN EXPEDITION. *Arkansas Hist. Q. 1965 24(1): 82-89.* Much of a war is taken up in small engagements that never loom as significant turning points. Travel across country in the spring was hazardous for troops with equipment. Union columns from Fort Smith and Little Rock were expected to converge on Camden and then proceed to Shreveport. In the close fighting Negro troops demonstrated their courage and valor, but the Union forces found spring rains too strong a foe to do other than withdraw to Little Rock for better weather. This firsthand account is assumed to have been written by a white officer of a Negro regiment. It was originally published in the Lawrence, Kansas *Daily Tribune* on 15 February 1866. P. M. McCain

1261. Whitridge, Arnold. FANATICISM - NORTH AND SOUTH. *Virginia Q. R. 1962 38(3): 494-509.* Deals with the roles of extremists on both sides during the American Civil War and with their attitudes, which were built largely on erroneous facts. Exploring such issues as the fugitive slaves, slavery in the Territories, and the political developments, the author concludes that the war could have been avoided. He pays particular attention to the role played by Lincoln and Charles Sumner. Undocumented. C. R. Allen, Jr.

1262. Wight, Willard E. BISHOP VEROT AND THE CIVIL WAR. *Catholic Hist. R. 1961/62 47(2): 153-163.* Jean Marcel Pierre Auguste Verot, born in France in 1805, was named Bishop of Florida in 1857, and Bishop of Savannah in 1861. The author describes him as proslave, pro-Confederate, but greatly concerned about the material and spiritual welfare of the slaves, and relates Bishop Verot's problems as a bishop without access to Catholic publications, notably missals and the Baltimore catechism. Based on published biographies, professional journals, and newspapers. J. H. Boykin

1263. Wiley, Bell Irvin, ed. THE LETTERS OF WARREN AKIN, CONFED-
ERATE CONGRESSMAN. *Georgia Hist. Q. 1958 42(1): 70-92, 42(2): 193-214,
42(3): 294-313, 42(4): 408-427, 1959 43(1): 74-90.* Part I. Though Congressman
Warren Akin did nothing of importance during the 18 weeks he attended the
Congress at Richmond, his letters are important because of the extreme paucity
of surviving material on the Confederate Congress. The four letters reproduced
here are to Akin's wife and to a friend, and they deal mostly with personal
matters. However, they do indicate the extreme difficulties faced in Richmond,
and one contains an unusually flattering portrait of Jefferson Davis. Parts II-III.
Published here are letters by Akin to his wife during his absence from home while
he was in Richmond, Virginia, in December 1864 and January 1865. The letters
comment on events of the Civil War in the South and give a detailed account of
living conditions at that juncture, as well as expressing the writer's anxiety for
the future. Part IV. Letters written from Richmond, in January 1865 to members
of his family, while Sherman was marching through Georgia. They reflect conditions in the South in the last days of the Confederacy. Akin was anxious to pay
his debts before Confederate currency became entirely worthless and requested
his wife to dispose of his notes. He was also concerned about hiring out some of
his Negroes and the fact that others were not performing their chores as well as
when he was at home. Akin presents a favorable portrait of Jefferson Davis,
though he was pessimistic about the future of the Confederacy. Rumors of peace
talks and weariness with war permeate these letters. Part V. Letters from Akin
(January 1865, Richmond) to his wife delineating his life in the Confederate
capital and inquiring about his family, friends, slaves, etc., in Georgia.
R. Lowitt

1264. Williams, Lorraine A. NORTHERN INTELLECTUAL REACTION TO
THE POLICY OF EMANCIPATION. *J. of Negro Hist. 1961 46(3): 174-188.*
Describes northern reaction to the Lincoln-Frémont argument over emancipation, Lincoln's plan for compensated emancipation and colonization of the freedmen, the Emancipation Proclamation, and the 13th Amendment. The author
describes and quotes a variety of opinions on each of these events and concludes
that northern public opinion supported Lincoln's emancipation policy.
L. Gara

1265. Woodward, Isaiah A. LINCOLN AND THE CRITTENDEN COMPRO-
MISE. *Negro Hist. Bull. 1959 22(7): 153-154.* Discusses Lincoln's part in the
rejection of the proposed Crittenden Compromise which was designed to avert
civil war in 1860. Lincoln refused to yield on the question of opening any new
territory to slavery and the author believes his strong stand was a decisive factor
for the five Republican Senators on the compromise committee and therefore for
the ultimate rejection of the compromise itself.				L. Gara

1266. Woodward, Isaiah A. THE LIFE OF WILLIAM H. SEWARD AND HIS
ROLE IN THE CRISIS OF 1850 AND 1860. *Negro Hist. Bull. 1961 25(2):
27-31.* Briefly sketches the political career of William Henry Seward in New York
and in the United States Senate. During the crisis of 1850 Senator Seward opposed
compromise on the slavery question, but by 1860 he took a more conciliatory

position. As a member of the Committee of Thirteen, Seward was willing to support the Crittenden Compromise ideas until he consulted with President-elect Lincoln, who apparently persuaded him to reject any proposal which would further extend slavery in the Territories. Seward and his Republican colleagues voted against the compromise plan, and their decision contributed to a deepening of the sectional crisis which led to the Civil War. L. Gara

1267. Wooster, Ralph A. AN ANALYSIS OF THE MEMBERSHIP OF THE SECESSION CONVENTIONS OF THE LOWER SOUTH. *J. of Southern Hist. 1958 24(3): 360-368.* Census returns for 1860 on the 1,048 men who formed the secession conventions of the first seven States to secede show that there was little difference in places of birth and occupations of immediate secessionists and of those who favored some sort of delay. The secessionists were slightly wealthier and younger and held more slaves than their combined opponents, but the difference was not pronounced. In Louisiana and Mississippi, for example, the larger slaveholders favored delay. There was a slightly higher percentage of planters in the cooperationist faction than in the group of immediate secessionists.
S. E. Humphreys

1268. Wooster, Ralph A. THE SECESSION OF THE LOWER SOUTH: AN EXAMINATION OF CHANGING INTERPRETATIONS. *Civil War Hist. 1961 7(2): 117-127.* Northern writers during and after the Civil War believed secession was the result of a conspiracy by a few influential southern leaders. Horace Greeley, John W. Draper, Henry Wilson, and Hermann von Holst maintained this premise. James Ford Rhodes' *History of the United States,* though attributing secession exclusively to slavery, rejected conspiracy; secession reflected the popular will. Clement Eaton, Avery O. Craven, and Ulrich Bonnell Phillips also denied that conspiracy produced secession. Early in his history of the United States, Allan Nevins agreed, but later volumes discerned "a carefully planned conspiracy." David M. Potter believed secession not conspiratorial but unpopular. Secessionists had small majorities and would not sponsor popular referendums. However, large majorities were not necessary, a decade of controversy had defined a popular will in favor of secession. L. Filler

1269. Worley, Ted R. THE ARKANSAS PEACE SOCIETY OF 1861: A STUDY IN MOUNTAIN UNIONISM. *J. of Southern Hist. 1958 24(4): 445-456.* Union sentiment in seceded Arkansas was strongest in the upland counties of the northwestern and north central parts of the State, where few slaves were held. In November 1861, a secret organization was uncovered in some of these counties, and about 180 men were arrested, charged with disloyalty to the South, and impressed into the Confederate Army. Evidence now available indicates that the society was an organization for self-protection, a Unionist island of passive resistance, rather than an actively treasonable group. S. E. Humphreys

1270. Zorn, Roman J. JOHN BRIGHT AND THE BRITISH ATTITUDE TO THE AMERICAN CIVIL WAR. *Mid-Am. 1956 38(3): 131-145.* Shows how John Bright championed the Union cause during the American Civil War against predominating Confederate sympathies of British Government leaders. In his opposition to slavery, Bright was chiefly motivated by humanitarian sentiments which prompted him to work against his opponents' efforts to secure for the Confederacy British diplomatic recognition and the help of the British Navy to run the Union blockade of Confederate ports. Based on parliamentary records and contemporary newspapers. R. Mueller

1271. --. [HENRY BROOKS ADAMS]. *Arizona Q. 1968 24(4): 293-308, 325-341, 350-360.*
Vandersee, Charles. THE FOUR MENAGERIES OF HENRY ADAMS, pp. 293-308.
Martin, John S. HENRY ADAMS ON WAR: THE TRANSFORMA-TION OF HISTORY INTO METAPHOR, pp. 325-341.
Scheick, William J. SYMBOLISM IN THE EDUCATION OF HENRY ADAMS, pp. 350-360.
Focusing on Adams' letters and *The Education of Henry Adams,* these three authors examine different aspects of his writing technique. According to Vandersee, Adams used four different patterns of animal imagery in his letters. The first group consisted of ineffectual, weak, or mutilated animals, which Adams used in reference to himself. The second group of predatory and dangerous beasts referred to people in and around Washington. The younger generation - especially the daughters of his friends - were pictured as small and gentle animals. Adams also used "hog" or "pig" to refer to the general public. For the most part Adams "reserved his choicest beasts and fowls for the private enjoyment of his friends." Adams' meeting with the Italian revolutionary Garibaldi in 1860 and the American Civil War profoundly shocked him. Martin shows that both Henry Adams and his brother Charles Francis Adams, Jr., found their values changed by the Civil War (Charles had entered the Union Army, while Henry served as his father's secretary in London). Charles "moralized" the war as an effort to free the slaves, but Henry "began to see war in more universal, more metaphoric, terms associated with the naturalistic perspectives of late nineteenth century science." In particular Adams believed that the "illusions" of one generation led to the events of the next, and he used this theory to explain the causes of the War of 1812 in his *History of the United States.* War, used metaphorically, was the event which demolished the illusions of a generation. Thus Adams used war as a metaphor for historical change, particularly in *The Education.* The author, meanwhile, regards *The Education* as a "literary achievement and as a symbolic work of art" and discusses some of the symbols to be found in it. Boston, for example, stood for winter, confinement, school, and discipline, while Quincy symbolized summer, diversity, and naturalness. Washington, like Quincy, was a paradise. According to the author, "this recognition of Boston and Quincy as controlling organic symbols is necessary if one intends to comprehend and appreciate *The Education's* structure and theme." J. M. Hawes

1272. --. [RUSSIAN VERSION OF THE AMERICAN CIVIL WAR]. *Civil War Hist. 1962 8(4) 357-372.*
Stoflet, Ada M., translator. THE CIVIL WAR - RUSSIAN VERSION (I): FROM THE SOVIET ENCYCLOPEDIA, pp. 357-364. According to the Soviet *Entsiklopediia,* two social systems were in conflict: slavery versus free labor. Both sought to dominate the western territories. In 1854, the Republican Party was

formed, resisting westward expansion of slavery. The victory of Presidential candidate Lincoln in 1860 gave the signal for secession, despite northern material superiority in arms and materials. The influence of some big business interests economically tied to southern slaveholders prevented necessary military reforms in the North. Marx and Engels criticized northern strategy for failing to aim decisive blows at vital southern points. Northern workers and farmers served the Federal cause heroically, but the business class was concerned for its own aggrandizement. The English workingmen prevented their government from interfering with the course of the war. Progressive social reformers of all countries stepped forward in defense of the North.

Logsdon, Joseph A. THE CIVIL WAR - RUSSIAN VERSION (II): THE SOVIET HISTORIANS, pp. 365-372. The Civil War is the only American event which receives substantial attention in the official Soviet encyclopedia. In part, this is because it deals with origins of the modern race problem. The Soviet analysis follows that plotted by Marx and Engels, in their contemporary articles for the *New York Tribune,* the Vienna *Presse,* and their private correspondence. They saw the war as political and economic, rather than moral, and divided it into the "constitutional" (1861-62) and "revolutionary" (1863-65) periods. Their plan for splitting the Confederacy at Georgia curiously anticipated General William T. Sherman's 1864 march to the sea. Lenin's views on the war also influence Soviet historians. Robert F. Ivanov emphasizes the role of the masses in the conflict, more than the fathers of Communism preferred to do; they underscored class forces. D. B. Petrov, biographer of Lincoln, resorts to confused dialectics in order to explain his subject in Marxist terms. The South, too, is inaccurately seen as impelled to rebellion by slaveholders who "vigorously suppressed" the "people's movement" in their section. American historians are criticized, and even American Marxists corrected in favor of Soviet dogma.

L. Filler

4

RECONSTRUCTION & ITS AFTERMATH
(1865-1900)

The Reconstruction Period

1273. Abbott, Martin. FREE LAND, FREE LABOR, AND THE FREED-MEN'S BUREAU. *Agric. Hist. 1956 30(4): 150-156.* The Freedmen's Bureau was responsible for distributing confiscated lands to former slaves in 1865 until the program was stopped by President Andrew Johnson, who insisted upon the restoration of lands to their former owners. The bureau also endeavored for four years to establish an equitable system of contract labor. After that period, the free labor system was still full of imperfections even though bureau administration had been characterized by fairness, honesty and the protection of the rights of the freed worker. Based on documents in the National Archives.
J (W. D. Rasmussen)

1274. Abbott, Martin. FREEDOM'S CRY: NEGROES AND THEIR MEET-INGS IN SOUTH CAROLINA, 1865-1869. *Phylon 1959 20(3): 263-272.* Three months following Appomattox, a Negro group met in Charleston, South Carolina, to celebrate their freedom. During the next several years, Negroes met in convention and otherwise to frame appeals to white leaders of the State to grant them suffrage, to punish those who committed violence against them, and to respect their needs as workers and citizens. Negroes also organized to demonstrate their capacity to regulate their own affairs and to develop programs of cooperation with the white people. Creation of the State Republican Party in 1867 substantially ended their effort to operate meaningfully as a separate entity, but records refute the myth that the Negroes were wholly helpless and inarticulate in their own behalf.
L. Filler

1275. Abbott, Martin, ed. A NEW ENGLANDER IN THE SOUTH, 1865: A LETTER. *New England Q. 1959 32(3): 388-393.* Publishes a letter written by Captain Charles C. Soule, a Union Army officer, to General Oliver Otis Howard of the Freedmen's Bureau. Soule's letter gives an unfavorable impression of the new class of freedmen and calls attention to the complex human problems resulting from sudden emancipation. L. Gara

1276. Ahern, Wilbert H. THE COX PLAN OF RECONSTRUCTION: A CASE STUDY IN IDEOLOGY AND RACE RELATIONS. *Civil War Hist. 1970 16(4): 293-308.* An analysis of the 1865 Reconstruction proposal of General Jacob Dolson Cox (1828-1900) which would have located all Negroes in an autonomous State in the southeastern section of the country. Cox was no racist, but he was pessimistic about the prospects for an integrated American society after the Civil War. The choice, he felt, was between massive Federal intervention to protect the rights of the freedmen, on the one hand, or their total suppression on the other. Being strongly opposed to both, Cox suggested this scheme of domestic colonization. The plan itself was impractical and contradictory, but it showed the dilemma over the Nation's future which confronted throughtful liberals at the close of the war. Based on the Cox Papers. E. C. Murdock

1277. Aptheker, Herbert. AN UNPUBLISHED FREDERICK DOUGLASS LETTER. *J. of Negro Hist. 1959 44(3): 277-281.* Publishes for the first time a letter from Frederick Douglass (c. 1817-95), dated Rochester, New York, 14 June 1870. It presents Douglass' impressions of Hiram Revels, first Negro Senator in the United States, and contains a detailed account of Douglass' quite advanced views on religion. A

1278. Bacote, Clarence A. WILLIAM FINCH, NEGRO COUNCILMAN AND POLITICAL ACTIVITIES IN ATLANTA DURING EARLY RE-CONSTRUCTION. *J. of Negro Hist. 1955 40(4): 341-364.* Using the activities of Finch, first Negro elected to public office in Atlanta, as a framework, political activities in the city during early Reconstruction are surveyed with particular emphasis upon the important issues of the day: education of the poor, establishment of city water works, and legislation to benefit all citizens regardless of race. W. E. Wight

1279. Bell, John L., Jr. BAPTISTS AND THE NEGRO IN NORTH CAROLINA DURING RECONSTRUCTION. *North Carolina Hist. R. 1965 42(4): 391-409.* The emancipation of the Negro members of their churches forced the North Carolina Baptists to face similar problems to those of other denominations in the South. Since all agreed that the Negro was a permanent part of southern society, the church had to help make him a useful citizen through education and religious service. But with this went pressure to lead Negroes to form their own churches as quickly as possible, since the white Baptists' fixed purpose was to maintain a system of social inequality superseding any positive Christian duty to the Negro. The Negro sought some measure of equality and self-determination and collaborated in the separation of the two races into distinct churches, largely accomplished by 1875. Based on State denominational records; 94 notes. J. M. Bumsted

1280. Belser, Thomas A., Jr. ALABAMA PLANTATION TO GEORGIA FARM, JOHN HORRY DENT AND RECONSTRUCTION. *Alabama Hist. Q. 1963 25(1/2): 136-148.* Dent was an exception to the generalization that the years of Radical Reconstruction following the Civil War ruined the southern planter class. In 1866 he sold his plantation on Barbour Creek near Eufaula in order to get away from the low country where the many exslaves formed an undependable labor force. He immediately bought a 400-acre farm in the Piedmont region of Georgia. He was most successful with diversified farming, raising wheat, corn, oats, and rye in addition to cotton. In 1877 "If he were not the wealthy slave-owning planter of the ante-bellum days, he was still a man of property and substance....[having] successfully made the transition from the Old South to the New." 45 notes.   E. P. Stickney

1281. Blackburn, George M. RADICAL REPUBLICAN MOTIVATION: A CASE HISTORY. *J. of Negro Hist. 1969 54(2): 109-126.* Examines Michigan public opinion to determine why the Radical Republicans so violently opposed Andrew Johnson's Reconstruction program. Radicals of the Republican Party in Michigan tended to view adherents of the Democratic Party as supporters of "slave power" and "aristocracy," even after the Civil War ended. To Michigan Radicals, Reconstruction was an extension of the war, and the Radicals were determined not to lose the fruits of military victory. Both defenders and opponents of the Johnson Reconstruction program were split along party lines, partly indicating that their attitudes were politically motivated. Based on Michigan newspapers and the Zachariah Chandler and Austin Blair Papers; 57 notes.
                                                                    R. S. Melamed

1282. Boromé, Joseph A., ed. ROBERT PURVIS, WENDELL PHILIPPS, AND THE FREEDMEN'S BUREAU. *J. of Negro Hist. 1957 42(4): 292-295.* Wendell Phillips' reply to a letter from Purvis in which the latter had sought advice on whether to accept the position of Freedmen's Bureau Commissioner offered to him by President Andrew Johnson.   W. E. Wight

1283. Bratcher, John V., ed. A SOVIET HISTORIAN LOOKS AT RECONSTRUCTION. *Civil War Hist. 1969 15(3): 257-264.* A translation of an essay-review appearing in a Soviet historical journal of a book on Reconstruction written in 1958 by Soviet historian R. F. Ivanov, *The Negroes' Struggle for Land and Freedom in the South, U.S.A. (1865-1877)* [Moscow, 1958]. The reviewer observes that Ivanov has carefully exposed the shortcomings of American "bourgeois" historians who have dealt with the subject, and that includes practically everybody except the Marxists. The major weaknesses of American writers have been the failure to recognize the revolutionary character of the Civil War and Reconstruction, ignoring the role of the black in bringing about his own deliverance from bondage, and improper treatment of the land problem after the war.
                                                                    E. C. Murdock

1284. Brodhead, Michael J. ACCEPTING THE VERDICT: NATIONAL SUPREMACY AS EXPRESSED IN STATE CONSTITUTIONS, 1861-1912. *Nevada Hist. Soc. Q. 1970 13(2): 2-16.* Studies the various State constitutional expressions of the doctrine of national supremacy from the beginning of the American Civil War to the eve of World War I. Before the Civil War no State constitution touched on the question directly, but after 1865 nearly all of the Southern States and the new Western States incorporated some acknowledgement of Federal supremacy in their constitutions. The apparent acceptance of Federal supremacy by Southern States just after the Civil War is seen by the author as evidence that the South had accepted the verdict of the war and was more interested in taking up more vital matters, such as the status of the Negro. The Nevada constitution of 1863 incorporated the Federal supremacy principle, but this constitution failed ratification. The 1864 constitution of Nevada was accepted by the voters. The 1864 version contained and still contains what is the most all-encompassing statement of subordination to Federal power to be found in any of the State constitutions. Illus., photo, 37 notes.   E. P. Costello

1285. Brown, Arthur Z. THE PARTICIPATION OF NEGROES IN THE RECONSTRUCTION LEGISLATURES OF TEXAS. *Negro Hist. Bull. 1957 20(4): 87-88.* Reviews the constructive achievements of Negro members of the Texas Legislature from 1871 to 1895. Such Negro political leaders as Richard Allen and Matt Gaines identified themselves with regional economic interests and promoted legislation which served to benefit all elements in the State.

L. Gara

1286. Brown, Charles A. A. H. CURTIS: AN ALABAMA LEGISLATOR 1870-1876, WITH GLIMPSES INTO RECONSTRUCTION. *Negro Hist. Bull. 1962 25(5): 99-101.* Reviews the role of the Negro in post-Civil War Alabama politics and sketches the career of A. H. Curtis, who was born a slave and purchased his own freedom with money earned from various tasks. After the Civil War, Curtis served two terms in the Alabama Assembly and four years in the Senate. His interest in education led him to promote in the legislature the idea of a State normal school for Negroes and the founding of a Baptist school for colored students at Selma, Alabama.   L. Gara

1287. Brown, Charles A. JOHN DOZIER: A MEMBER OF THE GENERAL ASSEMBLY OF ALABAMA, 1872-1873 AND 1873-1874. *Negro Hist. Bull. 1962 26(3): 113, 128.* A sketch of the life of John Dozier (ca. 1800-ca. 1892), Negro Alabama legislator from 1872 to 1874, who was born a slave and emancipated by his owner. Based on information obtained from Dozier's descendants.

L. Gara

1288. Campbell, William A., ed. A FREEDMEN'S BUREAU DIARY BY GEORGE WAGNER. *Georgia Hist. Q. 1964 48(2): 196-214, (3): 333-360.* Part I. Short diary entries by a lieutenant and Civil War veteran, while he was stationed in Georgia, 1866-67. Illus. Part II. Covers Wagner's life during the year 1868 as a Union officer employed by the Freedmen's Bureau in Georgia.

R. Lowitt

1289. Carpenter, John A. ATROCITIES IN THE RECONSTRUCTION PE-
RIOD. *J. of Negro Hist. 1962 47(4): 234-247.* Questions the school of historical
interpretation which maintains that atrocities toward the freedmen in the Reconstruction period were fabricated for political purposes. Numerous agents and
assistant commissioners of the Freedmen's Bureau reported acts of violence,
including the murder of Negroes. The condition of the former slaves varied
considerably from place to place. Reports of widespread violence were exaggerated, but they had a basis in reality. Documented with Freedmen's Bureau
correspondence.   L. Gara

1290. Clark, John G. HISTORIANS AND THE JOINT COMMITTEE ON
RECONSTRUCTION. *Historian 1961 23(3): 348-361.* Offers some reflections
and evaluations concerning the treatment by historians of the Joint Committee
on Reconstruction, 1865-67. There are important deficiencies in Reconstruction
historiography. The attitudes of the northern Radical Republicans, the role of the
party machines regarding the freedmen, and the time when sincere affection for
the Negro disappeared into the maze of partisan politics are all questions requiring further investigation.   Sr. M. McAuley

1291. Coulter, E. Merton. AARON ALPEORIA BRADLEY, GEORGIA NE-
GRO POLITICAN DURING RECONSTRUCTION TIMES. PARTS I, II,
AND III. *Georgia Hist. Q. 1967 51(1): 15-41, (2): 154-174, (3): 264-306.* Part
I. An account of the early Reconstruction activities of Aaron Alpeoria Bradley,
radical Negro politican and demagogue. A runaway slave, Bradley returned to
Georgia at the end of the Civil War and quickly became a leading spokesman for
freedmen, advocating, for example, Negro rights to land under General Sherman's Special Field Order No. 15. After a short imprisonment for rabble-rousing
activities, Bradley was elected a delegate to the Georgia Constitutional Convention (1867-68) by Chatham County's Negro majority. His troublesome and contemptuous character and his irresponsible and incendiary statements brought
expulsion from the convention in February 1868. Documented largely from
newspapers and the journal of the Georgia Constitutional Convention. Part II.
Bradley declared himself a candidate for the Georgia State Senate. He was elected
handily in April 1868, largely because of his control of the Union League organization in Chatham County. His eligibility as a legislator was challenged, however, and he was expelled from the Senate soon after his election, as were two
other Negro Senators, on the grounds that Negroes were ineligible to hold office.
After a split with the Radical Republican organization in Georgia, he campaigned
unsuccessfully for Congress as an independent in the election of 1868. Negro riots
and violence marred the election, and Bradley fled the State as warrants sworn
out for his arrest charged him with inciting the rebellious outbreaks among the
freedmen. The author characterizes Bradley as a 19th-century "black power"
advocate. Documented. Part III. Bradley was restored to his seat in the Georgia
Senate in 1869 after a Federal law prohibited the exclusion of any legislative
member because of race. He promoted some humanitarian causes as a State
senator but also continued his radical and occasionally irrational activities, which
in turn led to a second expulsion from the senate in 1870. Bradley remained in
politics, however, running for Congress unsuccessfully in 1870, acting as spokesman for Chatham County's Negro voters, and disrupting the political scene

generally. The author agrees with a contemporary white editor's assessment of Bradley's career in Georgia Reconstruction politics: "he was a dangerous character in the demoralized times just after the war, and did much to provoke strife and to array the races." Documented, largely from newspaper sources and legislative documents.   R. A. Mohl

1292. Coulter, E. Merton. HENRY M. TURNER: GEORGIA NEGRO PREACHER-POLITICIAN. *Georgia Hist. Q. 48(4): 371-410.* Surveys the interesting and controversial career of Henry McNeal Turner, focusing particularly on his activities as a preacher and politician in Georgia during the Reconstruction era.   R. Lowitt

1293. Coulter, E. Merton. TUNIS G. CAMPBELL, NEGRO RECONSTRUCTIONIST IN GEORGIA, PARTS I AND II. *Georgia Hist. Q. 1967 51(4): 401-424, 1968 52(1): 16-52.* Part I. A study of Campbell's political career during the Reconstruction in Georgia. Born a free Negro in the North, Campbell accompanied Union troops to the South during the Civil War. Under the aegis of the Freedman's Bureau he became unofficial governor of Saint Catherines and adjacent islands off the coast of Georgia, where large numbers of freedmen had settled. Removed from this position in 1867, Campbell moved to McIntosh County on the mainland and began a career as a State politician. Supported by Negro majorities in the Second Election District, he served in the Georgia Constitutional Convention and the State Senate. Campbell was not a demagogue, but he supported legislation designed to aid freedmen and in 1870 testified before the congressional committee which wrote the Ku Klux Klan Act of 1871. Based on research in newspapers and legislative documents; 76 notes. Part II. Campbell established a political base in McIntosh County and the town of Darien, both of which had heavy Negro majorities. Negro votes secured him the position of justice of the peace and a term in the Georgia Senate, where he worked actively but unsuccessfully for unsegregated public education. An election dispute erased a victory in a campaign for the State House of Representatives in 1874. As a Negro radical Campbell incurred the wrath of white Georgians. Discredited by an investigation in the Georgia Senate, he was eventually arrested, tried, convicted, and imprisoned on a variety of charges relating to his activities as justice of the peace. The author contends that Campbell abused his political and judicial privileges, discriminated against whites in court cases, exercised "black power," and established a "reign of terror" in Darien. Based on research in newspapers and published State records; 88 notes.   R. A. Mohl

1294. Cox, John H. and Cox, LaWanda. ANDREW JOHNSON AND HIS GHOST WRITERS: AN ANALYSIS OF THE FREEDMEN'S BUREAU AND CIVIL RIGHTS VETO MESSAGES. *Mississippi Valley Hist. R. 1961 48(3): 460-479.* Compares the proposed drafts prepared for President Andrew Johnson's veto messages with the final versions as delivered, noting particularly Johnson's own contributions. Although Johnson's papers were mainly composed by William Henry Seward (Secretary of State), Henry Stanbery (Attorney General), and Gideon Welles (Secretary of Navy), they were very much his own. It was largely Johnson's own changes and insertions which revealed his recalcitrant attitude toward Negro rights, antagonized the Republican majority of Congress, and aroused the animosity resulting in his impeachment trial. Possibly greater deference on Johnson's part to Seward's political acumen and sensitivity to Republican attitudes might have helped solved the post-Civil War racial dilemma and spared the country a tragic experience.   R. E. Wilson

1295. Cox, LaWanda. THE PROMISE OF LAND FOR THE FREEDMEN. *Mississippi Valley Hist. R. 1958 45(3): 413-440.* An examination of Congressional intent behind the provision in the Freedmen's Bureau Act of 3 March 1865 that each male freedman be allotted 40 acres of abandoned or confiscated land for rental and future purchase. Legislators wished to avoid government paternalism and also the wartime abuse and exploitation of Negroes by northern lessees of southern land and by southern planters operating under military directives. Some desired to destroy large landholdings and substitute a small, owner-operated farm economy for the plantation system of the South. The author's findings constitute a revision of currently accepted interpretations of Republican motivation with respect to southern Reconstruction (these emphasize selfish economic and political aims) and show that national policy, as embodied in the act, was a commitment to freedom, equal status, and opportunity for landowner-ship for the southern Negro.   A

1296. Cox, LaWanda and Cox, John H. NEGRO SUFFRAGE AND REPUBLI-CAN POLITICS: THE PROBLEM OF MOTIVATION IN RECONSTRUC-TION HISTORIOGRAPHY. *J. of Southern Hist. 1967 33(3): 303-330.* Seeks revision of the thesis that political expediency was the principal motive for Republican sponsorship of Negro suffrage in the Reconstruction period. To the contrary, it is suggested that the Republican sponsorship was a risk, indeed a handicap to the party. The author cites figures of voting in counties of seven crucial Northern States with more than five percent Negro population for the remainder of the century to indicate that white votes lost generally exceeded the number of Negro votes gained. He concludes that motives of congressmen doubt-less were mixed, but that it is possible that party advantage actually was subordi-nated to principle. During the Civil War and Reconstruction, race prejudice was institutionalized in the Democratic Party and this very fact, plus the jibes of inconsistency and hypocrisy with which Democrats derided their opponents, may have helped to create the party unity that committed Republicans, and through them the Nation, to equal suffrage regardless of race.   S. R. Humphreys

1297. Crouch, Barry A. and Schultz, Leon J. CRISIS IN COLOR: RACIAL SEPARATION IN TEXAS DURING RECONSTRUCTION. *Civil War Hist. 1970 16(1): 37-49.* Using Texas as an example, the authors analyze Comer Vann Woodward's theory that true racial segregation in the South did not emerge until the 1890's. With respect to segregated education, urban ghettos, harsh vagrancy laws, political and social disabilities, and violent treatment, Texas Negroes were "put in their place" during Reconstruction, not in the 1890's.
                          E. C. Murdock

1298. Current, Richard N. CARPETBAGGERS RECONSIDERED. *A Festschrift for Frederick B. Artz (Durham: Duke U. Press, 1964): 139-157.* At the war's end the South beckoned to the Union soldier as a new frontier where many came as planters or as businessmen. Far more numerous than the few "political tramps who went south to make cynical use of the Negro vote and who continued to win both office and illicit gain" were the energetic men who invested in the South, who eventually got into politics, and whose behavior in office varied widely. Historical scholarship has given its sanction to the propaganda of the victorious side in the Reconstruction struggle; as with all propaganda, it was a mixture of truth and falsehood. Documented.   E. P. Stickney

1299. Curry, Richard O. DOCUMENTS: A NOTE ON THE MOTIVES OF THREE RADICAL REPUBLICANS. *J. of Negro Hist. 1962 47(4): 273-277.* Four previously unpublished letters by Radical Republicans from West Virginia reveal that their concern for subjugation of the South grew out of pragmatic political considerations rather than a humanitarian concern for the welfare of the Negroes. In 1862 Senator Waitman T. Willey supported colonization of the Negroes. Congressman Chester D. Hubbard believed that West Virginia's fate as a separate State required support of the Radical program. Archibald W. Campbell, editor of *The Wheeling Intelligencer,* viewed Negro suffrage as a technique to prevent the rebels from recapturing political power.   L. Gara

1300. Curry, Richard O. THE ABOLITIONISTS AND RECONSTRUCTION: A CRITICAL APPRAISAL. *J. of Southern Hist. 1968 34(4): 527-545.* To clarify why "white America" failed to provide an economic basis for Negro freedom during Reconstruction and to guarantee enforcement of the Negroes' political and legal rights, the author analyzes the recent treatments by historians of abolitionist ideology and attempts to resolve the interpretative contradictions. He strongly suggests that the abolitionists were by no means in agreement on these issues and were fundamentally convinced of the validity of the "dominant middle-class ideology of self help." Concluding that the "abolitionist response to emancipation has not received comprehensive historical interpretation," he calls for studies assessing the "ideological commitments which determined the positions abolitionists took on such issues as political activism, civil rights, freedmen's aid, confiscation, education, and race." 57 notes.   I. M. Leonard

1301. Davis, Curtis Carroll. VERY WELL-ROUNDED REPUBLICAN. *Virginia Mag. of Hist. and Biog. 1963 71(4): 461-487.* A physically imposing figure, John Sergeant Wise (1846-1913) was a son of Governor Henry A. Wise of Virginia. The Confederate veteran specialized in public utility law at Richmond, Virginia, 1867-88 and then moved to New York as a general counsel of the Edison Electric Company. Wise was an active Republican politician after 1869, largely because of the Negro question, and served one term (1883-85) in Congress.   K. J. Bauer

1302. Davis, Hugh C. EDWIN T. WINKLER: BAPTIST BAYARD. *Alabama R. 1964 17(1): 33-44.* Edwin Theodore Winkler (1823-83) was "a journalist, preacher, promoter of Christian education and denominational official." Winkler's views - as rabid as a prewar fire-eater's - on Radical Republicanism and the race problem after the Civil War are briefly presented. D. F. Henderson

1303. Dew, Lee Allen. THE RELUCTANT RADICALS OF 1866. *Midwest Q. 1967 8(3): 261-276.* Explores the personal racial attitudes of a selection of Radical Republican congressmen instrumental in the passage of the Civil Rights Act of 1866. Senator Lyman Trumbull of Illinois in his argument defined civil rights at length as what we would call today legal rights. Nowhere in the debates does Dew find specific mention of what we call social rights. Republican congressional leaders Trumbull, James Wilson Grimes, George Washington Julian, and William P. Fessenden are silent on the subject of racial integration. Schuyler Colfax, John Sherman, Carl Schurz, Henry Lane, and Robert Schenck were supporters of the Radical point of view of activists such as Charles Sumner and Thaddeus Stevens, but they do not speak of social equality. Even Sumner was said by Gideon Welles to love Negroes only in the abstract, not individuals. Thaddeus Stevens declared in Congress that colored men do not have the same intelligence as white men. Letters of another Radical Benjamin Wade are full of expressions of his low opinion of Negroes, and George Julian proclaimed that white people were socially, intellectually, and morally superior. The Radicals contributed much but they did not make the Negro a fully first class citizen.

G. H. G. Jones

1304. Dufour, Charles L. THE AGE OF WARMOTH. *Louisiana Hist. 1965 6(4): 335-364.* Presidential address to the Louisiana Historical Association. For a dozen years after 1865, Henry Clay Warmoth "was destined to play a leading role in the fantastic drama of Reconstruction, vilified by both the Democrats of Louisiana and a powerful faction of his own Republican Party." He was elected governor of Louisiana in 1867. "Charges of graft, swindles, bribery, extravagance, and waste were frequent." By 1872 the governor was opposed by the Custom House Gang, the Negroes "whom he had alienated by vetoes of civil rights legislation," and by the Democrats. He was finally impeached but before he could be tried his term as governor had expired. Frequent quotations are given from source material. E. P. Stickney

1305. English, Thomas H. THE OTHER UNCLE REMUS. *Georgia R. 1967 21(2): 210-217.* Describes Uncle Remus, "elder statesman of Atlanta's Negro community....Countenanced by the white folks as a general nuisance," and regarded by the urban Negroes as a white man's "nigger," he managed to hold his own. Joel Chandler Harris created the character in 1876, three years before he created the story-telling Uncle Remus. He "was intended to represent the essential Negro" and despised those Negroes who aped the white man's ways. The main problem dealt with in these Uncle Remus tales was adjustment to the new conditions following emancipation. T. M. Condon

1306. Feldman, Eugene. JAMES T. RAPIER, 1839-1884. *Negro Hist. Bull. 1956 20(3): 62-66.* A biographical sketch of James T. Rapier, son of an Alabama planter and a Negro mother. After college study in Canada and Scotland he returned to the United States at the end of the Civil War to become a significant Negro leader in Alabama during Reconstruction. He gained fame as a labor organizer, an editor and publisher, an official of the Alabama Republican Party, a delegate to the Alabama constitutional convention, and as a member of Congress. In Congress, from 1873 to 1875, Rapier championed antisegregation legislation.   L. Gara

1307. Fletcher, Marvin. THE NEGRO VOLUNTEER IN RECONSTRUCTION, 1865-66. *Military Affairs 1968 32(3): 124-130.* The availability of regiments of Negro volunteers with service time remaining prompted the Federal Government to use them as garrison troops in the South in 1865-66. Their presence caused friction with the local whites whose complaints led to the removal of the Negro troops. Based on newspapers, congressional documents, and monographs; 18 notes.   K. J. Bauer

1308. Gara, Larry. TEACHING FREEDMEN IN THE POST-WAR SOUTH, A DOCUMENT. *J. of Negro Hist. 1955 40(3): 274-276.* Quotes a letter dated 26 March 1867 from a Massachusetts businessman to an acquaintance in Newburyport describing the social ostracism experienced by a Newburyport woman teacher working in a Negro school in Gainesville, Florida.   C. F. Latour

1309. George, Joseph, Jr. "ABRAHAM AFRICANUS I": PRESIDENT LINCOLN THROUGH THE EYES OF A COPPERHEAD EDITOR. *Civil War Hist. 1968 14(3): 226-239.* An analysis of the writings and opinions of C. Chauncey Burr, who from 1863 to 1869 was the editor of *The Old Guard,* a bitterly antiadministration magazine published in New York City. Although an antislavery sympathizer in his earlier years, Burr for unknown reasons became an outspoken white supremacist by the time of the Civil War and was angrily opposed to emancipation. The author suggests that Burr's racial prejudice might supply a clue to Copperhead behavior generally. Based on material in the files of *The Old Guard.*   E. C. Murdock

1310. Granade, Ray. VIOLENCE: AN INSTRUMENT OF POLICY IN RECONSTRUCTION ALABAMA. *Alabama Hist. Q. 1968 30(3/4): 181-202.* Investigates the reason for violence in Alabama during Reconstruction. Several reasons are suggested: Alabama was still a frontier area; the people of the State were prone to violent action; fear of Negroes which came from the antebellum period; and reaction to the corruption and lawlessness of the military governments. The author points out that violence had been used by all sectors of the society and had cooled when Alabamians learned to use fraud at the ballot box.   E. E. Eminhizer

1311. Greene, A. C. THE DURABLE SOCIETY: AUSTIN IN THE RECONSTRUCTION. *Southwestern Hist. Q. 1969 72(4): 492-518.* Austin had a more stable and enlightened society during the Civil War and Reconstruction than did other cities in Texas. This was because Austin had opposed secession in 1861, was relatively stable economically, and was never endangered during the war. Also, with the complete collapse of civil government in Texas at the end of the war and the consequent looting by Confederate soldiers, Austin welcomed the return of U.S. rule and enjoyed good relations with Unionists and Federal troops. The customary acrimony toward Negroes and Radicals was not so evident in Austin, partly because the population was expanding and Austin enjoyed many local improvements including the building of sidewalks, bridges, and new buildings. In addition, the railroad and telegraph appeared during this time. Photos.

R. W. Delaney

1312. Gross, Theodore L. THE NEGRO IN THE LITERATURE OF RECON-STRUCTION. *Phylon 1961 22(1): 5-14.* Southern writers of Reconstruction were propagandists, who convinced American readers that carpetbaggers had misused the southern people and falsified their objectives. Most successful were local-color writers who emphasized their interest in reconciling North-South differences, and whose affectionate portraits of their locales won the interest of readers, while persuading them of the truth of what they wrote. Albion W. Tourgée, a northern humanitarian who lived in the South during Reconstruction, wrote fiction which sought to treat Negroes as individuals. Joel Chandler Harris, most popular of all southern fiction writers, limned the Negroes as misguided children in his Reconstruction novel, *Gabriel Tolliver* (1902). Thomas Nelson Page patronized the Negro, depicting him as a devoted slave or confused freeman. Page's *Red Rock* (1898) and *The Red Riders* (1924) reveal strong racist bias. Thomas Dixon's "trilogy of reconstruction," *The Leopard's Spots* (1902), *The Clansman* (1905) and *The Traitor* (1907) are a defense of the Ku Klux Klan. Lesser writers also depicted Negroes as ludicrous or as brutes, and their accounts affected those of such northern writers as Frank Stockton and Constance Fenimore Woolson.

L. Filler

1313. Gutman, Herbert G. DOCUMENTS ON NEGRO SEAMEN DURING THE RECONSTRUCTION PERIOD. *Labor Hist. 1966 7(3): 307-311.* Presents three documents from the Public Record Office in London, England, concerning problems faced by colored British seamen arriving in U.S. ports during the Reconstruction era. Pressures from American shipping masters and boarding-house keepers affected job opportunities of colored persons who were not American citizens.

L. L. Athey

1314. Gutman, Herbert G. ENGLISH LABOR VIEWS THE RECONSTRUC-TION: AN EDITORIAL IN THE BEE-HIVE (LONDON), SEPT. 26, 1874. *Labor Hist. 1968 9(1): 110-112.* Reprints an editorial from London's most important labor weekly which explains southern violence in the context of that region's history and is critical of those who question universal suffrage or support arguments for racial inferiority. The editorial is entitled "Whites and Blacks."

L. L. Athey

1315. Gutman, Herbert G. RECONSTRUCTION IN OHIO: NEGROES IN THE HOCKING VALLEY COAL MINES IN 1873 AND 1874. *Labor Hist. 1962 3(3): 243-264.* Improvements in transportation during the post-Civil War period made possible a national labor market as well as a national market for raw materials and manufactured goods. When the railroad came to the Hocking Valley of Ohio in 1869 the amount of coal shipped out of the valley increased from 105,000 tons in 1870 to one million tons in 1873. "The rapid expansion of the coal industry after 1869 made the 1873 depression even more difficult for the miners and operators." The miners were driven toward trade unionism and the operators to wage cutting. Announcement by the employers of a new contract on 1 April 1874, with sharply lower wages resulted in a miners' strike. In an effort to break the strike and the union, employers imported Negro workers from the South. The events in the Hocking Valley "should be viewed as part of a much larger social and economic process" as Negroes were used in other coal disputes during 1874. J. H. Krenkel

1316. Harlan, Louis R. DESEGREGATION IN NEW ORLEANS PUBLIC SCHOOLS DURING RECONSTRUCTION. *Am. Hist. R. 1962 67(3): 663-675.* "It is a fact not generally known even to historians that the New Orleans public schools during the Reconstruction period underwent substantial racial desegregation over a period of six and a half years, an experience shared by no other southern community until after 1954 and by few northern communities at the time. This essay is limited to a summary of the evidence that there was indeed desegregation in New Orleans in the 1870's and to an effort to explain it chiefly in terms of circumstances in New Orleans at the time." Based on manuscript letters and memoirs, official documents, and contemporary newspaper and periodical literature. M. Berman

1317. Harper, Alan D. WILLIAM A. DUNNING: THE HISTORIAN AS NEMESIS. *Civil War Hist. 1964 10(1): 54-66.* Though an important historian and political scientist, Dunning was also a confirmed racist, and his racist views have shaped the historical judgment on Reconstruction down to the present. Believing the Negro an inferior being, fit only for slavery and subjugation, Dunning insisted that the attempt to put him in a place of power was a monumental blunder, heroically resisted by the former white ruling class, aided by a courageous President, Andrew Johnson. Partly influenced by the prejudices of his southern students, but also conditioned by his own deeply-rooted anti-Negro feelings, Dunning painted a distorted picture of Reconstruction, but one difficult to erase. Unfortunately, "his prejudice has been a more potent force than his scholarship." Based on Dunning's published writings. E. C. Murdock

1318. Harris, William C. A RECONSIDERATION OF THE MISSISSIPPI SCALAWAG. *J. of Mississippi Hist. 1970 32(1): 3-42.* Based on Harris' "identification of 140 active scalawags," attempts to "delineate characteristics, attitudes, and motives of Mississippians who became scalawags and to describe some of the problems and vicissitudes involved in the organization of a viable white party in the state." The author challenges the blackguard, Whig, and Democratic interpretations of the scalawag. The chief weakness of both the Whig and Democratic schools is "their overemphasis on past political issues and allegiances." Representing a cross-section of Mississippi society, Mississippi scalawags "were products more of the convulsion produced by the Civil War and reconstruction than of past political or socio-economic ties." Most scalawags "were conservative in their political and social attitudes." They supported, "with differing enthusiasm," Negro political and legal rights, but strongly opposed social equality. Based on numerous published and unpublished sources, including manuscripts in the Library of Congress, the National Archives, and the Mississippi Department of Archives and History; 78 notes.   J. W. Hillje

1319. Harris, William C. FORMULATION OF THE FIRST MISSISSIPPI PLAN: THE BLACK CODE OF 1865. *J. of Mississippi Hist. 1967 29(3): 181-201.* In the postwar period Mississippi was the first Southern State to pass laws to define the Negro's position and to govern his conduct. The author describes the circumstances surrounding the enactment in Mississippi in 1865 of these acts which dealt with civil rights, apprenticeship, vagrancy, firearms, and misdemeanors, and which were collectively known as the Black Code. The code "actually represented a victory for the conservative or moderate plan in the legislature, although...some of its features, particularly the one prohibiting the leasing of country properties to freedmen, were unduly harsh and unwise....The whites of the plantation counties supported the moderate settlement, whereas the small farmers and poor whites of the hills and piney barrens opposed it." The Mississippi code became the first important propaganda weapon which the Radicals used to win northern public support for their Radical Reconstruction program. Based largely on newspapers and published public documents; 61 notes.
J. W. Hillje

1320. Harris, William C. HIRAM CASSEDY: A FORMER SOUTHERN NATIONALIST IN DEFENSE OF THE NEGRO IN MISSISSIPPI RECONSTRUCTION. *Louisiana Studies 1968 7(3): 252-258.* An account of how Mississippi planter Hiram Cassedy changed from an avid States' rights doctrinaire to a champion of the rights of the Mississippi Negro during Reconstruction. Similar individuals have received scant notice by historians, but indications are that many others followed a course similar, if not parallel, to that of Hiram Cassedy. A Cassedy letter of 16 December 1866 is reproduced. 16 notes.
G. W. McGinty

1321. Harrison, John M. DAVID ROSS LOCKE AND THE FIGHT ON RECONSTRUCTION. *Journalism Q. 1962 39(4): 491-499.* In concentrating upon the contributions of David Ross Locke (Petroleum Vesuvius Nasby) to the Union cause in the Civil War, historians have tended to overlook the part he played in the early stages of the fight on Reconstruction. In the crucial early months of 1866, just after he had assumed the editorship of the Toledo *Blade*, he was not the all-out spokesman of Radicalism he was to become. At that time he accused the Radicals of driving President Andrew Johnson and other moderates into the Democratic ranks. Rather than warring upon Johnson, he advised reminding him of his pledge to abolish slavery, establish suffrage, and guarantee the rights of the freedmen.   S. E. Humphreys

1322. Highsmith, William E. LOUISIANA LANDHOLDING DURING WAR AND RECONSTRUCTION. *Louisiana Hist. Q. 1955 38(1): 39-54.* Studies the effect of the Civil War and Reconstruction eras on Louisiana landholding. Louisiana was largely an area of sugar and cotton plantations in 1860, and, despite the freeing of the slaves, constant demands for land reforms, and the introduction of sharecropping, the plantation system survived. As of 1880, landholding by Negroes was still limited and that of white small farm owners was confined to the poorer lands in the northern and western parts of the State. Based on contemporary newspapers, family letters, and census statistics.   E. D. Johnson

1323. Hoeveler, J. David, Jr. RECONSTRUCTION AND THE FEDERAL COURTS: THE CIVIL RIGHTS ACT OF 1875. *Historian 1969 31(4): 604-617.* Weaknesses in previous legislation, effective resistance of the South, and growing apathy in the North led Congress to a final attempt to secure black civil rights. The act of 1875 was extensive. Enforcement was removed from the States and entrusted exclusively to the Federal courts. The author traces the five-year history of this act before it became law, and outlines its fate until 1883 when it was declared unconstitutional. Based on the *Congressional Record, Congressional Globe, The Nation,* and a number of secondary sources; 45 notes.
N. W. Moen

1324. Hoffman, Edwin D. FROM SLAVERY TO SELF-RELIANCE. *J. of Negro Hist. 1956 41(1): 8-42.* "A Record of Achievement of the Freedmen of the Sea Island Region," based with one exception upon printed sources. The author narrates the hopes and disappointments of the Negroes of the Sea Islands of South Carolina and Georgia as they gave "a remarkable demonstration of their ability to overcome the handicaps of a slave upbringing and to conduct themselves in the finest traditions of American Democracy."   W. E. Wight

1325. Hoffnagle, Warren. THE SOUTHERN HOMESTEAD ACT: ITS ORIGINS AND OPERATION. *Historian 1970 32(4): 612-629.* The reformers of the Reconstruction period realized that possession of political or social rights was only abstract unless accompanied by broad access to means of economic betterment. The Southern Homestead Act (21 June 1866) represented an effort to ensure that newly freed men in the South had the opportunities (which white men enjoyed elsewhere in the United States) to become independent small landowners. Relies on evidence from the *Congressional Globe* and the papers of the Freedman's Bureau in the National Archives to show how the dream collapsed in Southern States having adequate public lands, due to poor preparation, corruption, clumsy administration, and local opposition. 64 notes.   N. W. Moen

1326. Ivanov, R. F. NEGRITIANSKIE ORGANIZATSII V BOR'BE S PLANTATORSKOI REAKTSIEI V PERIOD REKONSTRUKTSII IUGA SSHA [Negro organizations in the struggle against the reactionary plantation-owners during the Reconstruction of the South of the United States]. *Novaia i Noveishaia Istoriia [USSR] 1958 2(1): 3-20.* The Reconstruction period was unable to give the Negroes anything beyond formal emancipation from slavery. According to Carl Schurz, "the planters keep on subduing their former slaves with brutal force." Using the tactics of class war, the Ku Klux Klan tried to organize pogroms against white Republicans and Negroes and to frustrate any democratization of the South. But the wealthy Republicans were also in favor only of gradual change in the South, the so-called "Prussian way." The Negroes therefore developed their own methods of resistance: they held mass meetings, collected signatures, presented petitions to the President and Congress, and founded political organizations. G. Liersch

1327. James, Parthena Louise. RECONSTRUCTION IN THE CHICKASAW NATION: THE FREEDMAN PROBLEM. *Chronicles of Oklahoma 1967 45(1): 44-57.* The Dawes Commission destroyed the Chickasaw Nation in 1894 by appropriating the land to individual tribal members. It was at this time that the problem of Chickasaw freedmen was solved. From the Civil War to 1894 much confusion existed with regard to the status of the freedmen. This made law and order in the Chickasaw Nation difficult. This confusion could have been avoided if the United States had acted to remove the freed slaves as the Chickasaw elected to have done under the treaty of 1866. But after the freedmen settled and built in the Nation they no longer wanted to move. The Chickasaw, however, were equally determined to move the black men for fear of losing control of their Nation. Fortunately for the Chickasaw, other Reconstruction problems were not so difficult. 50 notes. K. P. Davis

1328. Jaquette, Henrietta Stratton. FRIENDS' ASSOCIATION OF PHILA-DELPHIA FOR THE AID AND ELEVATION OF THE FREEDMEN. *Bull. of Friends Hist. Assoc. 1957 46(2): 67-83.* Describes the origins of the association and its activity to help provide education for freed Negroes in the South, 1864-72. Particular stress is placed upon the extent of cooperation with other groups and with such governmental bodies as the Freedmen's Bureau. N. D. Kurland

1329. Jervey, Edward D. MOTIVES AND METHODS OF THE METHODIST EPISCOPAL CHURCH IN THE PERIOD OF RECONSTRUCTION. *Methodist Hist. 1966 4(4): 17-25.* The Methodist Episcopal Church during the Reconstruction period actively supported "Radical Republican" legislation and worked fervently in the South to attain supremacy in Methodist affairs. Three conclusions are drawn: 1) The church through its freedman's aid did try to help the Negro toward self-sufficiency. 2) The church and its leaders sided with the "Radicals" on President Andrew Johnson's impeachment, not only out of a genuine concern that his policies would lead to a reestablishment of prewar southern power but also out of a concern for church property. 3) It seems likely that northern Methodists idealized the Negro too much. Based in part on Methodist periodicals and conference journals; 31 notes. H. L. Calkin

1330. Kelly, Alfred H. THE CONGRESSIONAL CONTROVERSY OVER SCHOOL SEGREGATION, 1867-1875. *Am. Hist. R. 1959 64(3): 537-563.* Chronicles the various efforts by Congress to enact compulsory desegregated schools into American law in the years of Reconstruction. All efforts foundered on the lack of public support and on direct opposition from the South. R. C. Raack

1331. Kincaid, Larry. VICTIMS OF CIRCUMSTANCE: AN INTERPRETA-
TION OF CHANGING ATTITUDES TOWARD REPUBLICAN POLICY
MAKERS AND RECONSTRUCTION. *J. of Am. Hist. 1970 57(1): 48-66.*
Reviews the historiography of Congressional Reconstruction policies and concludes that most historians, following a "New South" and "Progressive" orientation, have been interested in depicting Republican legislators as grasping political
opportunities, as being interested in upholding the dominance of the northeastern
business community, or, following World War II and the civil rights movement,
being interested in their vindication as sincere advocates of black rights. Such a
moralistic approach is inadequate. In the future more attention should be paid
to such problems as the organization and composition of the Republican Party,
the political ideas and activities of other groups in society, the specific processes
that produced important legislative decisions, and the implementation of and
compliance with these legislative decisions. Based on secondary sources; 47 notes.
K. B. West

1332. Kirkwood, Robert. HORACE GREELEY AND RECONSTRUCTION,
1865. *New York Hist. 1959 40(3): 270-280.* Sketches the program of "Universal
Amnesty-Universal Suffrage," of moderate reconstruction and reunion, which
Greeley advocated throughout the spring and summer of the last war year. The
publisher argued for economic rehabilitation, but against all forms of paternalism,
for political, but not social equality. Greeley argued that the freedmen had to
become "freemen" by being allowed "to take care of themselves" in a free labor
market. Suffrage could be restricted to those intellectually qualified, but restrictions had to apply equally to all people. Negroes and whites had to be free to
associate together or to refuse to "live on terms of social intimacy," as they chose.
A. B. Rollins

1333. Klein, Frederic Shriver. "OLD THAD" STEVENS. *Civil War Times 1964
2(10): 19-23.* The proposed programs of this controversial politician were far
ahead of his time. Stevens did not want the Negro forgotten just because slavery
had been abolished; he wanted economic opportunity for the freedmen through
land ownership. Stevens "deserves much more credit for emancipation than he
has received, and much less blame for the Reconstruction Era." Illus.
E. P. Stickney

1334. Krug, Mark A. FOR A FAIR DEAL IN THE TEACHING OF RECON-
STRUCTION HISTORY. *Social Educ. 1965 29(1): 7-14, 56.* Argues that high
school history textbooks oversimplify the Reconstruction period; this was not a
period in which the North viciously mistreated the South. The author also denies
that President Andrew Johnson attempted to carry on Lincoln's Reconstruction
policy. Lincoln at his death had no Reconstruction policy; his early 10 percent
plan had failed and he knew this. Johnson's plan stressed the role of the President
over that of Congress. Unlike Lincoln, Johnson was a believer in the principle of
white supremacy.
F. Rotondaro

1335. Krug, Mark M. ON REWRITING OF THE STORY OF RECON-
STRUCTION IN THE U.S. HISTORY TEXTBOOKS. *J. of Negro Hist. 1961*

46(3): 133-153. Analyzes the interpretation of the Reconstruction period found in high school U.S. history texts and concludes that most of these texts present the material in oversimplified terms which do not take much of the recent scholarship into account. Texts often overlook Abraham Lincoln's concern for creating a South loyal to the Union and his support for limited Negro suffrage. They fail to point out Andrew Johnson's political ineptitude, the wide assortment of opinions among the so-called Radicals, the importance of southern opposition to political rights for Negroes, the positive contributions of Negroes and of the Reconstruction governments, and the illegal violence of the Ku Klux Klan. The author concludes with a plea for rewriting the Reconstruction story as it appears in secondary texts.   L. Gara

1336. Linden, Glenn M. "RADICALS" AND ECONOMIC POLICIES: THE SENATE, 1861-1873. *J. of Southern Hist. 1966 32(2): 189-199.* Uses quantitative method in seeking to solve the old problem of "Who were the Radicals of the Reconstruction Congresses?" The author identifies 33 senators as "Radical," 28 as "Non-Radical" and 39 as "Unaligned" for the period from July 1861 through March 1873, in terms of their voting records in 82 roll calls on measures pertaining to Negroes and Reconstruction. Radicals are those who voted 75 percent or more of the time for measures of Radical policy. Continuation of the author's technique into the economic area shows that neither "Radical" nor "Non-Radical" senators voted alike on tariff, currency, and banking issues, but that senators from the same geographic section ("Radical" or "non-Radical") tended to vote together. Suggests that the definition of "Radicalism" should not specify a particular stand on economic questions.   S. E. Humphreys

1337. Lynd, Staughton. RETHINKING SLAVERY AND RECONSTRUCTION. *J. of Negro Hist. 1965 50(3): 198-209.* Takes issue with the "consensus" historians of slavery and Reconstruction who tend to blame the failure of Reconstruction on the psychological impact of the institution of slavery, on the slave, or on the political blundering of President Andrew Johnson, and with the view of historian Howard Zinn who alleged that Reconstruction failed because the Federal Government did not apply enough pressure on the South. Reconstruction's failure to guarantee Negro rights permanently stemmed from the government's refusal to give southern Negroes the land necessary to make them economically independent. Some abolitionists had argued the case for land distribution but their voices went unheeded. Based on several recent studies of slavery and Reconstruction.   L. Gara

1338. May, J. Thomas. THE FREEDMEN'S BUREAU AT THE LOCAL LEVEL: A STUDY OF A LOUISIANA AGENT. *Louisiana Hist. 1968 9(1): 5-19.* Details the 17-month term of W. H. Cornelius, representative of the five men who served as Freedmen's Bureau agents in Saint Martin Parish, Louisiana. Past historians have often cast such agents in the role of political liaison for the Radical Republicans to dominate Negro wards. The bureau agent was pictured as conspiring toward a complete reorganization of southern society. The records of the Saint Martin agent project a much different image. Only rarely do his reports refer to politics. Although concerned with achieving economic security for the freedmen, he believed that economic improvement could be obtained only through the rehabilitation of agriculture under the direction of white planters; his main interest was to guarantee a stable labor supply. Many of the services which Cornelius provided benefited the white man. The degree of control which the agent could exercise, although broad in theory, was limited in reality. Far removed from State officials and military contingents, he could ill afford to pursue a radical policy that would alienate the white community. More significantly, it was the policy of the bureau to work through existing political and judicial institutions, and these were controlled by southern whites. Usually, it was unlikely that the bureau agent would want to alienate the whites, since his own background was more similar to that of the whites than the blacks. Cornelius, by choice, favored the whites. Based on records of the Freedmen's Bureau of Saint Martin Parish; 31 notes. R. L. Woodward

1339. McDonough, James L. JOHN SCHOFIELD AS MILITARY DIRECTOR OF RECONSTRUCTION IN VIRGINIA. *Civil War Hist. 1969 15(3): 237-256.* A review of General John McAllister Schofield's administration of the military government of Virginia under the Reconstruction Acts (1867-68). Schofield ruled with a firm, but wise and impartial hand. Believing that the military reconstruction program was unduly harsh, he sought to moderate its worst features. The fact that he was criticized by conservative whites for supporting the radical cause on the one hand, and attacked by Radicals for thinking Negro suffrage premature on the other, suggests the middle course that Schofield steered. "In a difficult situation, he performed admirably." E. C. Murdock

1340. McKenna, Jeanne. "WITH THE HELP OF GOD AND LUCY STONE." *Kansas Hist. Q. 1970 36(1): 13-26.* An account of the election of 1867 in Kansas with special emphasis on the unsuccessful effort to secure the ratification of two amendments enfranchising Negroes and women. Samuel Newitt Wood (1825-91), the leading personality in the State legislature, is shown to have played a key role in the campaign. He made his major effort in support of woman suffrage by organizing a Kansas Impartial Suffrage Association and bypassing the local Republicans to work directly with powerful suffrage interests in the East. His motives were mixed. He may have wished to build a national political following or to sell land to eastern suffragists. Whether his motives were personal gain or lofty idealism, Wood gave himself unstintingly to the campaign. Based on local newspapers and manuscripts in the Kansas State Historical Society and the Library of Congress; illus., 46 notes. W. F. Zornow

1341. McPherson, James M. ABOLITIONISTS, WOMAN SUFFRAGE, AND THE NEGRO, 1865-1869. *Mid-Am. 1965 47(1): 40-47.* When the Civil War ended, many feminists wanted to unite the cause of the woman and the Negro and to work for the simultaneous elevation of both classes to civil and political equality. But because of the political exigencies of Reconstruction, most abolitionists desired to concentrate on the attainment of Negro suffrage while the opportunity was favorable and to postpone the drive for woman suffrage. The result was the schism of 1869 in the woman suffrage movement. L. D. Silveri

1342. Mcpherson, James M. COERCION OR CONCILIATION? ABOLI-
TIONISTS DEBATE PRESIDENT HAYES'S SOUTHERN POLICY. *New
England Q. 1966 39(4): 474-497.* Discusses the views of abolitionists toward the
Reconstruction policy of the Federal Government for several years prior to as
well as during the administration of Rutherford B. Hayes (from about 1870 to
1879). The increasing discontent of the North in the early 1870's toward Reconstruction alarmed the old-line abolitionists, but the mood of the voters could not
be squelched: in the election of 1874, the Democrats won control of the House
and reduced the number of Republicans in the Senate, thereby hastening the end
of Republican activity in the antislavery arena. But staunch abolitionists, notably
William Lloyd Garrison, Wendell Phillips, and John Greenleaf Whittier, supported the Reconstruction policy of the Grant administration. Hayes had been
convinced since 1875, however, that Grant's approach toward the South had to
be abandoned and hoped to substitute conciliation for coercion, believing that the
good will of southern whites would provide better protection for Negroes than
Federal troops. A majority of abolitionists failed to agree with this assessment and
spoke out, though without success, against Hayes' policies, but about 36 percent
of them shifted to support Hayes, thereby causing a decided division in their
ranks. Based primarily on the Garrison Papers in the Boston Public Library and
on other manuscripts, newspapers, and secondary materials; 53 notes.

W. G. Morgan

1343. Mcpherson, James M. GRANT OR GREELEY? THE ABOLITIONIST
DILEMMA IN THE ELECTION OF 1872. *Am. Hist. R. 1965 71(1): 43-61.*
Contrary to general belief, more than three-fourths of the former abolitionists
favored Ulysses S. Grant over his liberal Republican challenger, Horace Greeley,
despite the fact that such antislavery Republicans as Charles Francis Adams, Carl
Schurz, and Charles Sumner played an important part as supporters of Greeley
in the presidential election of 1872. Concerned for the welfare of the freedmen,
abolitionists were appalled by Greeley's formula for cooperation with "better
class" southern whites by granting amnesty to all Confederates and adopting a
hands-off policy toward the South, and they remained loyal to President Grant
in the belief that his southern policy promised the best protection for the Negro.
Most abolitionists believed that, moral suasion having failed earlier, true equality
could be achieved only through relentless law enforcement. This dilemma is still
with us. 59 notes.

E. P. Stickney

1344. Mechelke, Eugene R. SOME OBSERVATIONS ON MISSISSIPPI'S RE-
CONSTRUCTION HISTORIOGRAPHY. *J. of Mississippi Hist. 1971 33(1):
21-38.* Covers Mississippi Reconstruction historiography to 1965. Concludes that
"no such thing as Negro rule existed....Reconstruction government was not especially bad government. The record of the military in terms of office appointments
and other 'interference' was not bad; the record of the Freedmen's Bureau was
constructive; and the carpetbaggers and scalawags demonstrated themselves, for
the most part, to be rather creditable officials causing some, but not extensive,
extravagance and corruption....Bad economic conditions...cannot be completely,
or even largely, blamed upon the Republicans....The most significant conclusion
to be drawn, though, is the need to discontinue the use of the term *radical* as it
applies to the Reconstruction by Northerners, Negroes and scalawags in Missis-

sippi...there were no sweeping changes of a fundamental nature either in political activity or in the new status of the Mississippi Negro, who remained in essentially a servile state." Based on various secondary works; 72 notes.

J. W. Hillje

1345. Meier, August. NEGROES IN THE FIRST AND SECOND RECONSTRUCTIONS. *Civil War Hist. 1967 13(2): 114-130.* Questions whether the Civil War and Reconstruction ever brought about a real evolution in Negro rights. The abolition of slavery itself was not even an original war aim, and, although slavery was terminated, the rapid emergence of sharecropping, segregation, Jim Crow, and all the rest prevented any serious change from antebellum days. The postwar failure to respond to the Negro demands for education, civil rights, economic opportunity, and, above all, land, was a clear reflection of northern white indifference to the freedman. What little the Negro got - the 14th and 15th amendments and a couple of weak civil rights acts - were almost accidental bequests and were soon nullified by either the courts or the course of events. Still the amendments laid the groundwork for the civil rights revolution today, and with present-day white America far more conscious of Negro aspirations than was the Civil War generation, the author has real hope that this "second reconstruction" will bear honest fruit. Based largely on secondary sources.

E. C. Murdock

1346. Menard, Edith. JOHN WILLIS MENARD: FIRST NEGRO ELECTED TO THE U.S. CONGRESS; FIRST NEGRO TO SPEAK IN THE U.S. CONGRESS. *Negro Hist. Bull. 1964 28(3): 53-54.* Sketch of the public career of John Willis Menard (1838-93) who held several governmental positions and was elected to Congress from Louisiana in 1868. Menard's election was contested and even though he was not permitted to sit in Congress, his defense of his legal right to do so was the first speech made by a Negro in Congress.

L. Gara

1347. Milton, Nerissa Long. BLANCHE KELSO BRUCE. *Negro Hist. Bull. 1955 18(7): 168.* Biographical summary of Blanche Kelso Bruce (1841-98) lauding his civil service career and his achievements as U.S. Senator from Mississippi.

R. Mueller

1348. Morrill, James Roy III. NORTH CAROLINA AND THE ADMINISTRATION OF BREVET MAJOR GENERAL SICKLES. *North Carolina Hist. R. 1965 42(3): 291-305.* Moderate presidential Reconstruction in the South was terminated on 2 March 1867, when Congress passed over the executive veto an act dividing the region in five military districts, each headed by a military commander. The commander for the 2d Military District (North and South Carolina) was Brevet Major General Daniel E. Sickles, sympathetic to the South but impatient at white intransigence toward the Negro. Sickles' interference with State administration to speed racial integration - even outside the Reconstruction process - led to a clash between President Johnson and congress which resulted in a victory for Congressional authority but the removal of Sickles by the President. "Although Sickles' social and economic program created frictions which could have been avoided, in the last analysis it was the congressional reconstruction program itself, not Sickles' interpretation or implementation of it, which put a severe strain on the people of North Carolina." 65 notes.   J. M. Bumsted

1349. Morrow, Ralph E. NORTHERN METHODISM IN THE SOUTH DURING RECONSTRUCTION. *Mississippi Valley Hist. R. 1954 41(2): 197-218.* Methodists were the largest and wealthiest of the northern Protestant denominations. Though their war efforts were highly impressive, a greater challenge to the church was believed to lie in the incomparable proselyting opportunity to be found in the States of the defunct Confederacy. Patriotism and piety were to complement each other. Southern Methodists, however, proved wary of the overtures made to them, and this led Northerners to direct their main efforts toward the freedmen. Ministers who tried to integrate their congregations racially found the experiment a failure, and political alignment with the Radicals was of doubtful benefit to their mission. Eventually, the southern white reaction to the church was full of invective and led to social proscription. In appraising the consequences of its activity, the Church North was forced to conclude that, in general, the southern field had proved quite unrewarding.   G. L. A. Reilly

1350. Morton, Richard L., ed. LIFE IN VIRGINIA, BY A "YANKEE TEACHER," MARGARET NEWBOLD THORPE. *Virginia Mag. of Hist. and Biog. 1956 64(2): 180-207.* Presents the collected notes of a young woman from a prominent Philadelphia family, who served as a teacher during 1866-67 at Fort Magruder (near Williamsburg, Virginia), representing the Friends' Association of Philadelphia and Its Vicinity for the Relief of the Colored Freedmen. Miss Thorpe's notes emphasize sympathetically, if somewhat amusedly, the naïveté and cultural backwardness of her wards.   C. F. Latour

1351. Myers, John B. REACTION AND ADJUSTMENT: THE STRUGGLE OF ALABAMA FREEDMEN IN POST-BELLUM ALABAMA, 1865-1867. *Alabama Hist. Q. 1970 32(1/2): 5-22.* Discusses the main problems facing Negroes in Alabama after the Civil War. Emphasizes movement of blacks to the cities and the problems created by this movement. Indicates the government's role in bringing relief to those left homeless by the war; discusses government activities in feeding, clothing, and giving medical assistance.   E. E. Eminhizer

1352. Myers, John B. THE FREEDMAN AND THE LAW IN POST-BELLUM ALABAMA, 1865-1867. *Alabama R. 1970 23(1): 56-69.* A detailed analysis of the freedman in Alabama during the years 1865-67. The Alabama constitutional convention during Reconstruction failed to definitely recognize the legal rights of Negroes, leaving this task to the legislature. The legislature, meeting in November 1865, enacted a series of flagrantly discriminatory measures against freedmen. Governor Robert M. Patton vetoed these measures. The legislature made no attempt to override the veto; instead, it abandoned "open" discriminatory legislation in favor of covert acts, ultimately known collectively as the Black Code of Alabama. The final code contained "provisions for vagrancy, apprenticeship, enticing labor, and several other minor acts which did not overtly reveal racial discrimination." 52 notes.   D. F. Henderson

1353. Olsen, Otto H. RECONSIDERING THE SCALAWAGS. *Civil War Hist. 1966 12(4): 304-320.* Explores the roots of the Republican Party of North Carolina, founded in 1867, and concludes that it was largely an indigenous growth, incorporating prewar and wartime democratic, reformist, unionist, racial equality, and home rule elements. Its leadership was drawn from former Democrats of all stripes, former Whigs, former secessionists (not too numerous), and former antisecessionists. And the ultimate failure of North Carolina Republicanism was due not to its corruption, evil, extremism, or commitment to Negro equality, but to its idealism, conciliatory propensities, and lukewarm support of Negro suffrage. The party was too timid and reticent in fighting for what it believed and was soon destroyed. Based on primary and secondary sources.

E. C. Murdock

1354. Parker, Harold M., Jr. THE SYNOD OF KENTUCKY: FROM OLD SCHOOL ASSEMBLY TO THE SOUTHERN CHURCH. *J. of Presbyterian Hist. 1963 41(1): 14-36.* The Presbyterian Synod of Kentucky remained within the Old School Assembly during the Civil War, but endeavored to remain neutral in North-South controversies. When the Assembly in 1865 passed its "Reconstruction Resolutions" condemning slavery and secession, the Synod and the presbyteries within it protested vigorously. The resulting controversy led to the Gurley Order of 1868 by which the Assembly for all practical purposes exscinded the Synods of Kentucky and Missouri, and their formal dissolution was declared by the Assembly of 1867. By 1869 the Synod of Kentucky had united with the Southern Presbyterian Church.

W. D. Metz

1355. Partin, Robert. ALABAMA NEWSPAPER HUMOR DURING RECONSTRUCTION. *Alabama R. 1964 17(4): 243-260.* Case study of Alabama humor utilizing five Montgomery newspapers - the *Daily Mail, Weekly Mail, Daily Advertiser, Weekly Advertiser,* and the *Daily Post.* The subject matter included practically everyone: Negroes, whites, politicians, doctors, lawyers, husbands, wives, children, and even newspaper editors. Representative examples are included.

D. F. Henderson

1356. Pease, William H. THREE YEARS AMONG THE FREEDMEN: WILLIAM C. GANNETT AND THE PORT ROYAL EXPERIMENT. *J. of Negro Hist. 1957 42(2): 98-117.* Recounts the experiences of a northerner in an experiment in Negro rehabilitation on the Sea Islands of South Carolina, 1862-65.

W. E. Wight

1357. Peek, Ralph L. AFTERMATH OF MILITARY RECONSTRUCTION, 1868-1869. *Florida Hist. Q. 1964 43(2): 123-141.* Presents the desperate attempt of the "conservative" white people to wrest power from the northern-dominated government that was supported by Negroes and northern bayonets during the post-Civil War years, 1868-69. Based on State papers, newspapers, private correspondence, and periodical material.

G. L. Lycan

1358. Peek, Ralph L. CURBING OF VOTER INTIMIDATION IN FLORIDA, 1871. *Florida Hist. Q. 1965 43(4): 333-348.* Reconstruction acts of 1870 and 1871 failed to prevent intimidation and murder of Negroes and white Republicans in Florida but enabled Republicans to win the elections. Based on American State Papers, court reports, newspapers, and private correspondence.

G. L. Lycan

1359. Peek, Ralph L. ELECTION OF 1870 AND THE END OF RECONSTRUCTION IN FLORIDA. *Florida Hist. Q. 1967 45(4): 352-368.* Only 28 months after the end of military Reconstruction in Florida (July 1868), William Dunnington Bloxham, native conservative, was elected lieutenant governor, the first Democrat to win an important elective office, although he was delayed some 18 months before finally being inaugurated in June 1872. In the 1870 election, Republican tenure depended on Negro majorities in about 12 northern counties, and Democrats determined to win the lieutenant governorship, legislative seats, and one congressional seat by intimidating enough Negroes to affect the voting outcome. Despite the violence, since the Board of Canvassers ignored returns from nine counties in their official validation, Republican Samuel T. Day was elected, with Democrat Bloxham defeated. No official power came to the Democrats with Bloxham's delayed victory announced by the Florida Supreme Court in June 1872, but later events lend significance to the election. Republican hold on governmental power was uncertain after the 1870 election. The period 1873 to 1876 was marked by more cooperation between Democrats and Republicans. 73 notes.

R. V. Calvert

1360. Peek, Ralph L. MILITARY RECONSTRUCTION AND THE GROWTH OF ANTI-NEGRO SENTIMENT IN FLORIDA, 1867. *Florida Hist. Q. 1969 47(4): 380-400.* Anti-Negro sentiment of most white Floridians had crystallized by the end of 1867. Having failed to win the Negro as an ally, the Conservatives rejected him as a person, declaring their belief in his fundamental inferiority. There was no place for white Conservative Democrats in the political framework built by the Republican Party in 1867 with the Negro vote as its keystone. Disturbed by the postwar economic and social upheaval and viewing Negro ascendancy as a fundamental threat, Conservatives were convinced that their only solution lay in violent counterrevolution. Not only Southern Democrats but also southern loyalists and conservative Republicans felt an aversion to the Negro as a person and as a dominant political factor. The Negro was caught in a crossfire between contending factions. His greatest champion, the Radicals, suffered a shattering defeat in the final organization of the constitutional convention. Anti-Negro, anti-Reconstruction Southern Democrats aimed their main attack at the keystone of Republican strength - the Negro - as in 1868 they began to organize forces for open violence upon the resumption of civil government. Based partly on Freedmen's Bureau papers, Congressional records, and Republican Club minutes; 89 notes.

R. V. Calvert

1361. Perman, Michael. THE SOUTH AND CONGRESS'S RECONSTRUCTION POLICY. *J. of Am. Studies [Great Britain] 1971 4(2): 181-200.* In 1866 southern legislatures rejected the Howard Amendment (later known as the 14th

Amendment) to the U.S. Constitution. The South made numerous objections to the Howard Amendment. The South rampantly distrusted the Republican Party, and southern politicians and press alike suspected the alleged conciliatory intent of moderate Republicans. Southern legislatures likewise withheld approval from alternate plans that sought to find a middle ground between the Howard Amendment and southern desires. The South deliberately opted for the "immediate discomforts" of Negro suffrage and military occupation and hoped that its intransigence would over the long haul produce more advantageous terms of reconstruction for the South. of Congress and libraries in North Carolina, Mississippi, and Alabama; 54 notes.　　　　　　　　　　　　　　　　　　　　　H. T. Lovin

1362. Phillips, Paul David. WHITE REACTION TO THE FREEDMEN'S BUREAU IN TENNESSEE. *Tennessee Hist. Q. 1966 25(1): 50-62.* An account of the Freedmen's Bureau, established by Congress to be directed by the War Department for the purpose of serving as guardian of the four million freed Negroes in the transition from slavery to responsible freedom and citizenship. Most southern whites did not accept this "enlightened" view of the Negro's new status. Bureau schools between 1865 and 1870 caused violence and incendiary attacks across the State. In Memphis in the spring of 1866, the whites rioted for three days in the Negro community. The Ku Klux Klan became a system of terror against the freed Negroes. 76 notes.　　　　　　　　　　　　　　　D. H. Swift

1363. Pope, Christie Farnham. SOUTHERN HOMESTEADS FOR NEGROES. *Agric. Hist. 1970 44(2): 201-212.* An account of the Southern Homestead Act (1866). If judged in terms of its sponsors' aims, the act was a failure, primarily because it was based on two erroneous assumptions: 1) that the social institutions of the South could be changed by turning over the public domain of five Southern States to Negroes; and, 2) that the freedmen required nothing more than land to be transformed into prosperous, upstanding citizens. Based on congressional sources; 2 tables, 50 notes.　　　　　　　　D. E. Brewster

1364. Porter, Daniel R. GOVERNOR RUTHERFORD B. HAYES. *Ohio Hist. 1968 77(1-3): 58-75.* Concludes that during his three terms as governor Hayes's major achievements were the adoption of Negro suffrage in the face of apparent popular disapproval and the accomplishment of significant reforms in Ohio's penal and mental institutions. Based chiefly on newspaper materials.　　　　　　　　　　　　　　　　　　　　　　　　　　　　　　S. L. Jones

1365. Pressly, Thomas J. RACIAL ATTITUDES, SCHOLARSHIP, AND RECONSTRUCTION: A REVIEW ESSAY. *J. of Southern Hist. 1966 32(1): 88-93.* Publication in 1965 of Kenneth Milton Stampp's *Era of Reconstruction* (New York: Alfred A. Knopf) and reprinting in the same year of William Archibald Dunning's *Essays on the Civil War and Reconstruction* (New York: Harper and Row, originally produced between 1886 and 1904), demonstrate the great change that has occurred in 60 years in historical opinion concerning Reconstruction. Dunning disapproved of Radical Reconstruction, while recognizing some virtues in it. Stampp confidently praises Radical Reconstruction, while recognizing some tragic blunders in it. Both verdicts are based upon the best scholarship of their

times. What will be the verdict of historians 50 years hence? Would more systematic and comprehensive research, using quantitative techniques to supplement
traditional methods, help historians guard against potential distortions arising
from their own ideological convictions?   S. E. Humphreys

1366. Proctor, Samuel. YANKEE "SCHOOLMARMS" IN POST-WAR
FLORIDA. *J. of Negro Hist. 1959 44(3): 275-277.* Describes the difficulties
encountered by certain northern white women teachers sent to Florida after the
Civil War to organize schools for freed Negroes. The author includes the full text
of a letter sent by Harriet A. Barnes and Catherine R. Bent to Colonel Thomas
W. Osborn, Assistant Commissioner of the Freedmen's Bureau of Florida, reporting their progress and their problems arising mainly from hostility on the part
of white southerners. The original letter is in the War Records Office, National
Archives.   R. E. Wilson

1367. Reynolds, Donald E. THE NEW ORLEANS RIOT OF 1866, RECON-
SIDERED. *Louisiana Hist. 1964 5(1): 5-27.* Contrary to the traditional view of
the New Orleans riot of 1866 as the product of a Radical conspiracy (or the fear
of such a plot), Reynolds maintains that the riot probably resulted from "a
spontaneous explosion of racial antipathy on the part of the white mob. The
whites appear to have rioted, not because they believed the convention could
accomplish what it proposed, but because of that which was proposed." The
Louisiana whites' expression of racism through violence aided the Radical Republican efforts to gain control of Reconstruction and to bring Negro suffrage.
Based on a variety of primary and secondary materials, including the testimony
in *House Reports,* 39 Cong., 2 Sess., No. 16.   D. C. James

1368. Richards, Ira Don. LITTLE ROCK ON THE ROAD TO REUNION,
1865-1880. *Arkansas Hist. Q. 1966 25(4): 312-335.* The Civil War left 4,135
graves in Little Rock's cemeteries but it had not battle-scarred the community.
Many northern soldiers remained and influenced the city's life. Local politics fell
into Radical Republican hands which exploited the Negro vote. Democrats did
not gain control of local government until 1875. As late as 1880 there was a
Republican majority in the presidential races. Railroads, which soon tied the city
to larger centers, proved also to be avenues for the spread of epidemics. During
the 1870's strict quarantines were placed on travelers from Memphis to prevent
yellow fever outbreaks. Based primarily on current newspapers.
                                                                        P. M. McCain

1369. Richardson, Joe M. AN EVALUATION OF THE FREEDMEN'S BU-
REAU IN FLORIDA. *Florida Hist. Q. 1962/63 41(3): 223-238.* The Freedmen's
Bureau made a serious attempt in Florida to feed needy Negroes and whites,
1865-67, to induce the Negroes to work for a living, to encourage white men to
give the freedmen a fair chance, to inspire mutual confidence between the races,
and to introduce a public school system. Based on Congressional documents,
newspapers, personal correspondence, memoirs, and secondary material.
                                                                        G. L. Lycan

1370. Richardson, Joe M. FLORIDA BLACK CODES. *Fla. Hist. Q. 1969 47(4): 365-379.* In 1865, many Floridians retained a hope that they might receive some compensation for their freed slaves or that a system of apprenticeship would be established, since they believed rigid controls necessary to force former slaves to work. White Floridians of every economic and social class considered the Negro inferior and criminally inclined. The Florida Legislature in late December 1865, controlled by former slaveholders and ex-Confederates, passed legislation attempting to separate the two races and placing the Negro in a distinctly inferior position by identifying anyone with one-eighth or more Negro blood as a "person of color." Some of the black codes were not enforced because of Freedmen's Bureau interference. Usually demanding costs in advance from Negroes, courts assessed freedmen large fines for petty offenses while either ignoring or lightly punishing white outrages against Negroes. Passage of the black codes insured intercession by the Federal Government, ultimately resulting in the Reconstruction Acts of 1867 and the Florida constitution of 1868 overturning the black codes. Based on Congressional and Florida legislative records, contemporary newspapers, Freedmen's Bureau records, and unpublished letters; 44 notes.

R. V. Calvert

1371. Richardson, Joe M. JONATHAN C. GIBBS [CA. 1827-74]: FLORIDA'S ONLY NEGRO CABINET MEMBER. *Florida Hist. Q. 1964 42(4): 363-368.* Describes some of the life and works of one of Florida's most successful educators. Documented.

G. L. Lycan

1372. Richardson, Joe M. THE FREEDMEN'S BUREAU AND NEGRO LABOR IN FLORIDA. *Florida Hist. Q. 1960 39(2): 176-184.* In Florida the Freedmen's Bureau used the vagrancy laws and other coercive means to compel the Negro, just after the American Civil War, to live up to his labor contracts, thus helping the defeated southern planter more than the Negro who had so recently obtained his freedom. Based on reports of Congressional committees, newspapers, and private papers.

G. L. Lycan

1373. Richardson, Joe M. THE NEGRO IN POST CIVIL-WAR TENNESSEE: A REPORT BY A NORTHERN MISSIONARY. *J. of Negro Educ. 1965 34(4): 419-424.* A letter written by Mrs. Caroline A. S. Crosby from Nashville on 1 May 1866 is reproduced and edited. Mrs. Crosby, from Pepperell, Massachusetts, was a representative of the American Missionary Association responsible for distribution of books, food, and clothing to the freedmen as well as for instruction in Fisk School. The letter, addressed to the Reverend Michael E. Strieby, secretary of the AMA, "presents an eyewitness view of Negro religion, education, destitution, and family life in post Civil-War Tennessee."

S. C. Pearson, Jr.

1374. Richardson, Joe M., ed. THE MEMPHIS RACE RIOT AND ITS AFTERMATH: REPORT BY A NORTHERN MISSIONARY. *Tennessee Hist. Q. 1965 24(1): 63-69.* An "eyewitness, though not unbiased" letter of 21 May 1866 from Ewing O. Tade, of the American Missionary Association, to the Reverend Michael E. Strieby, New York, on events of 1-3 May 1866. Based chiefly on published sources; 22 notes.

1375. Riddleberger, Patrick W. THE RADICALS' ABANDONMENT OF THE NEGRO DURING RECONSTRUCTION. *J. of Negro Hist. 1960 45(2): 88-102.* An analysis of the changing attitudes of Radical Republicans toward the Negro during Reconstruction, especially after 1872. Emphasis is placed on those Radicals and former abolitionists - like George Washington Julian (1817-99), Carl Schurz (1829-1906), and Horace Greeley (1811-72) - who went into the Liberal Republican movement in 1872. An explanation of their abandonment of the Negro is sought in their declining political fortunes and the consequent compromise with southern conservatives, changing social theory, and changing concepts of reform. Based on manuscript collections and published works of several political leaders and on newspapers and periodicals of the era.

A

1376. Roberts, Derrell. ROBERT TOOMBS: AN UNRECONSTRUCTED REBEL ON FREEDMEN. *Negro Hist. Bull. 1965 28(8): 191-192.* During the war Robert A. Toombs had been a critic of Jefferson Davis, even to the point of opposing a bill to conscript slaves into the Confederate Army in March 1865. Like other southerners he feared a Federal land policy. He had a low opinion of northern carpetbaggers. He declared that no political party would receive his support if it recognized the 14th and 15th amendments. When testifying before a congressional investigating committee in 1876 he said that he and other legislators got elected "by carrying the black vote by intimidation and bribery." 8 notes.

E. P. Stickney

1377. Rogers, William W., ed. FROM PLANTER TO FARMER: A GEORGIA MAN IN RECONSTRUCTION TEXAS. *Southwestern Hist. Q. 1969 72(4): 526-529.* Thomas E. Blackshear was a member of a distinguished Georgia family, and was a planter, State legislator, and Major-General of the State militia during the Indian wars. When Georgia became more populated, Blackshear moved to Texas where he acquired sizable land holdings. He did not serve in the Civil War, but four of his sons served in the Confederate Army. This letter of 11 February 1867 shows Blackshear's racial bias, but it also shows that he realized the old plantation system could no longer continue. It is a lucid contemporary proposal for the revival of agriculture in postbellum Texas.   R. W. Delaney

1378. Rosen, F. Bruce, ed. A PLAN TO HOMESTEAD FREEDMEN IN FLORIDA IN 1866. *FLorida Hist. Q. 1965 43(4): 379-384.* A letter, with editorial comments, from Colonel Thomal W. Osborn to General Oliver Otis Howard, 1 January 1866, recommending that all of Florida south of 28 degrees latitude be bought by the U.S. Government, reduced to a territorial status politically, and given to the Negro freedmen as homesteads. Sources: Osborn's letter, personal papers, State papers, biographical material, secondary works, and newspapers.

G. L. Lycan

1379. Russell, James F. S. PRESIDENT ANDREW JOHNSON. *Hist. Today [Great Britain] 1954 4(9): 618-626.* Disputes the general belief that Johnson's tenure of office was a national disaster. Sketches his early life and political career, then concentrates on the Civil War period. His belief in white supremacy was secondary to his belief in democracy, which he saw as the cause of the North, so that he became the only Southern senator to defend the cause of the Union. It was ironic that he was elevated to the Presidency of a northern and predominantly Republican government. This inevitably led to the conflict culminating in his impeachment. However, his conciliatory policy would have been preferable in the long run to that of the radicals and "carpetbaggers." Also discusses the reasons for his continuing unpopularity.   W. M. Simon

1380. Scroggs, Jack B. CARPETBAGGER CONSTITUTIONAL REFORM IN THE SOUTH ATLANTIC STATES, 1867-1868. *J. of Southern Hist. 1961 27(4): 475-493.* Under Congressional Reconstruction, new constitutions were adopted in Virginia, the Carolinas, Georgia, and Florida in 1867-68. Northern ("carpetbag") influence was dominant or important in the northern three, while conservative forces controlled the latter two. A comparison is thus possible. In all five States, there was a sweeping extension of the franchise and of officeholding opportunities and enlargement of the principles of earlier bills of rights. All adult men, including the Negro, got the right to vote and hold office. In Virginia and North and South Carolina, representation was for the first time based entirely upon population, and most State and local offices were made elective. In Georgia and Florida, in an effort to maintain white supremacy, legislatures were apportioned to benefit the white conservatives, and the governor was given broad appointive power. The carpetbagger, as opposed to Negro legislators, showed no enthusiasm for economic democracy, such as debt repudiation or property confiscation might have represented, convinced that the same industry and commerce which had transformed the North would revolutionize the South.

S. E. Humphreys

1381. Scroggs, Jack B. SOUTHERN RECONSTRUCTION: A RADICAL VIEW. *J. of Southern Hist. 1958 24(4): 407-429.* Study of correspondence between Southern Radical Republicans and national Radical leaders reveals a more complicated evolution of the movement than historians have hitherto been aware of. Difficulties of adjusting the interests of the previously politically submerged class of native whites, the Negroes, and the recently arrived northerners plagued the party from its victory in 1867 until its overthrow in 1876, and contributed much to its downfall. There was lack of cooperation between the leading Radicals of the South and the Congressional Radicals. National leaders refused to become involved in the party splits in southern States and left the intrastate difficulties to be solved by local leaders. The southern Radicals became increasingly a burden and embarrassment to the national party. Personal ambition and differences in ideology worked to produce antagonistic groups within the party in each of the South Atlantic States, and astute conservative politicians proved adept at widening the gaps, which ultimately proved disastrous in all the States studied.

S. E. Humphreys

1382. Sefton, James E. A NOTE ON THE POLITICAL INTIMIDATION OF BLACK MEN BY OTHER BLACK MEN. *Georgia Hist. Q. 1968 52(4): 443-448.* Presents evidence that in the Reconstruction South, Republican Negroes interfered with the voting rights of Democratic Negroes. In many areas of the

South the Democratic Party made many overt attempts to win the support of black voters. While not denying white intimidation of blacks by such groups as the Ku Klux Klan, the author contends that Republican blacks carried out intimidating activities of their own, utilizing institutions such as the Union League Clubs and the local militia. 5 notes.   R. A. Mohl

1383. Sefton, James E. IN SEARCH OF A SYNTHESIS FOR RECONSTRUC-TION: AN ESSAY REVIEW. *Georgia Hist. Q. 1969 53(4): 470-475.* Reviews Avery Craven's new study, *Reconstruction: The Ending of the Civil War* (New York: Holt, Rinehart and Winston, 1969). Craven's purpose was to show how and why basic problems were avoided and left to future generations for solution. One of his central themes was that democracy was on trial during Reconstruction, that Americans were struggling with the problem of achieving a balance between freedom and equality. Sefton questions whether freedom and equality were anti-thetical, or if political figures of the time believed them to be antithetical. An answer to this question, he says, might help explain radical republicanism. Sefton criticizes Craven for a deterministic view of Reconstruction - that the problems were insoluble. Monographs on individual States during Reconstruction have made generalization difficult, and it may be impossible to find an adequate basis for a Reconstruction synthesis. 14 notes.   R. A. Mohl

1384. Sefton, James E., ed. CHIEF JUSTICE CHASE AS AN ADVISER ON PRESIDENTIAL RECONSTRUCTION. *Civil War Hist. 1967 13(3): 242-264.* Reprints and comments on seven letters sent by Chief Justice Salmon P. Chase to President Andrew Johnson in May 1865 from the Carolinas and Florida. The documents contain Chase's impressions of southern thinking and his recommen-dations for Reconstruction policy. His strongest recommendation, that of Negro suffrage, was not incorporated in Johnson's plan of Reconstruction announced 29 May, although "some of the procedural details" seemed to reflect Chase's thinking. The author suggests that the chief justice's strong personal commitment to Negro suffrage caused him to believe that it was really desired, when, in fact, there was strong opposition to it in both the North and the South. While the letters apparently carried little weight with the President, it is contended that they deserve more consideration than historians have so far given them.
E. C. Murdock

1385. Shapiro, Herbert. THE KU KLUX KLAN DURING RECONSTRUC-TION: THE SOUTH CAROLINA EPISODE. *J. of Negro Hist. 1964 49(1): 34-55.* In South Carolina the Ku Klux Klan acted against Negroes and whites who befriended them with threats, beatings, murder, and, in one instance, a mass lynching. The Klan was widespread and attracted upper-class members and conservative political leaders who condoned its excesses in the interest of southern home rule. Although mild action by the Federal Government destroyed the Klan, it was effective as an agent acting to prevent Negroes from voting, to destroy the Negro militia, and to strengthen the morale of southern conservatives.
L. Gara

1386. Shepperson, George. THE AMERICAN NEGRO AND AFRICA. *British Assoc. for Am. Studies Bull. 1964 (8): 3-20.* An abbreviated version of an Edinburgh "Town and Gown" lecture delivered 3 March 1964. The complicated interaction between Negro Americans and Africans is discussed. Although from the time of the founding of the American Colonization Society in 1817, the majority of colored Americans have had little commitment to Africa, a minority of American Negro intellectuals have helped to stimulate the growth of African nationalism. Others have been active in educational and missionary work in Africa. Africans have also attended American universities. After World War II the balance tipped, and Africa, "in an age of independence, began to influence the Negroes of America more than they influenced Africa." Documentation available upon request.   D. J. Abramoske

1387. Shofner, Jerrell H. POLITICAL RECONSTRUCTION IN FLORIDA. *Florida Hist. Q. 1966 45(2): 145-170.* An analysis of Florida politics during the Reconstruction era showing that the Democrats of the 1890's in calling for white solidarity to prevent a return to Negro dominated days of Reconstruction were distorting the history of Florida. White Floridians were not helpless under a corrupt government of outsiders supported by ignorant Negro voters until 1876. Moderate Republicans gained control of the government and should bear the responsibility for the chaos and inefficiency of the period, while Democrats as a limiting factor on Republican policymakers should share the blame. Florida came nearer to having an operating two-party system in 1876 than it has had since. 56 notes.   R. V. Calvert

1388. Singletary, Otis A. THE NEGRO MILITIA DURING RADICAL RECONSTRUCTION. *Military Affairs 1955 19(4): 177-186.* The Negro southern State militias were organized in 1867 as the military support for the Radical State governments. Lacking adequate Federal support and effective leadership the militia proved ineffective. It provoked strong opposition among the whites as both a racial and a political force. Although the whites used various forms of intimidation, including violence and assassination, the death blow came in the form of the White Leagues or Rifle Companies. Those political, military organizations were dedicated to both the destruction of the Negro militia and the restoration of white political control.   K. J. Bauer

1389. Singletary, Otis A. THE TEXAS MILITIA DURING RECONSTRUCTION. *Southwestern Hist. Q. 1956/57 60(1): 23-35.* In spite of Federal laws prohibiting the formation of militia forces in the southern States, General Edmund J. Davis, radical governor of Texas from 1870 to 1874, organized a "Negro militia," so-called although both races participated, in Texas in 1870. The author traces the activities of the Texas militia and its influence on State politics from its organization to its abolition in 1874.   J. A. Hudson

1390. Sinkler, George. RACE: PRINCIPLES AND POLICY OF RUTHERFORD B. HAYES. *Ohio Hist. 1968 77(1-3): 149-167.* Views Hayes's policy as based on his belief that the Negro must be given equal rights though inherent differences between the races did exist. As President, Hayes is seen as coming with little hesitation or difficulty to a policy of leaving the problem in the hands of Southern State officials, believing that they would keep their promises to recognize Negro rights.   S. L. Jones

1391. Sisk, Glenn N. NEGRO CHURCHES IN THE ALABAMA BLACK BELT 1875-1917. *J. of the Presbyterian Hist. Soc. 1955 33(2): 87-92.* A regional study of the role of religion and of the formation of Congregational Churches in Alabama during the Reconstruction period. Extensive documentation.
R. Mueller

1392. Smith, Thomas H. OHIO QUAKERS AND THE MISSISSIPPI FREED-MEN - "A FIELD TO LABOR." *Ohio Hist. 1969 78(3): 159-171.* Shows how Ohio Quakers, searching for a program to aid freed slaves, turned to education. After a brief trial in Tennessee, they concentrated their efforts on Jackson, Mississippi. These efforts were sustained until 1875, though the approaching end of Reconstruction often made it difficult to carry on. In 1875 the school in Jackson was abandoned and Ohio Quakers shifted their attention to other concerns, such as international peace, temperance, and the condition of the American Indian. Based mainly on Freedmen's Bureau Records in the National Archives, on the Minutes of the Ohio Yearly Meeting of the Society of Friends, and on contemporary newspapers.   S. L. Jones

1393. Sowle, Patrick. THE ABOLITION OF SLAVERY. *Georgia Hist. Q. 1968 52(3): 237-255.* An account of southern attitudes and policies toward freedmen in the early period of Reconstruction. Most southerners accepted emancipation realistically but disagreed about the place of the free Negro in southern society. The author adheres to the view that slavery, more than simply a labor system, was an institutionalized method of race control. With emancipation, southerners recognized the necessity for new techniques of race control - techniques implemented with the passage of Black Codes in every Southern State. Southern leaders favored Andrew Johnson's plan of Reconstruction because it allowed Southern States to deal with the Negro without "Yankee" interference. Based largely upon research in newspapers and other primary sources; 61 notes.
R. A. Mohl

1394. Sowle, Patrick. THE PLACE OF THE NEGRO IN THE DEFEATED CONFEDERACY, 1865. *Studies in Hist. and the Social Sci.: Essays in Honor of John A. Kinneman (Normal, Illinois: Illinois State U., 1965): 97-109.* In the realignment of society and economy at the close of the war, the freed Negro suddenly occupied positions of power. His inexperience led to permanent disruption of the "once-pleasant association" between former owners and their slaves. While the policies of President Johnson would have generally been palatable, too many Federal practices were easily associated with "carpetbaggers," "scalawags," and the Negro. The Negro was the only one to remain a scapegoat for many of the postwar ills of the region. Many southerners felt that this deteriorated relationship was "a domestic problem" and best handled without northern interference. 61 notes.   F. W. Soady, Jr.

1395. Sproat, John G. BLUEPRINT FOR RADICAL RECONSTRUCTION. *J. of Southern Hist. 1957 23(1): 25-44.* During the American Civil War, Secretary of War Edwin McMasters Stanton created the American Freedmen's Inquiry Commission to investigate the problem of refugee Negro slaves within Union lines. Under the chairmanship of Robert Dale Owen and with the encouragement of Senator Charles Sumner, the commission exceeded its original orders and outlined a virtual blueprint for reconstructing the southern States during and after the war. A comparison of its reports with subsequent Congressional action on reconstruction indicates that Radical Republican leaders were strongly influenced by the commission's findings and recommendations. Based on AFIC documents and papers, the Official Records of the Rebellion, and the personal papers of Stanton, Sumner, and other Radical leaders.　　　　　　A

1396. St. Clair, Kenneth E. MILITARY JUSTICE IN NORTH CAROLINA, 1865: A MICROCOSM OF RECONSTRUCTION. *Civil War Hist. 1965 11(4): 341-350.* Employing the experience of North Carolina as typical of all states, the author surveys the problem of military justice in the South during the early months of Reconstruction. The problem was complicated by two factors: 1) the absence of any precedents, and 2) the conflict in authority between the military commander, provisional governor, and head of the Freedmen's Bureau in North Carolina. Crimes committed by soldiers, as well as those by civilians, became the centers of dispute between these three administrators, as they held widely-diverging views on both the seriousness of various offenses and the extent of the punishments to be imposed. Disagreement was most rife in cases involving Negroes accused of crime. Although the record of military government in this first year was "uneven," it was still satisfactory, and "some valuable experience had been gained in martial law." Based on North Carolina and Federal archival sources.　　　　　　E. C. Murdock

1397. Stampp, Kenneth M. THE TRAGIC LEGEND OF RECONSTRUCTION. *Commentary 1965 39(1): 44-50.* The Dunning interpretation had been written at a time when "xenophobia had become almost a national disease," when Negroes and immigrants were being lumped together as unassimilable aliens. Moreover a rising spirit of nationalism stimulated a desire for sectional reconciliation, part of the price of which was a virtual abdication of Federal responsibility for the protection of the Negro's rights. Numerous social scientists supplied racists with a seemingly respectable scientific argument. When social scientists later revised their notions about race, historians became "increasingly critical of the Dunning interpretation of reconstruction." The legend of Reconstruction had serious consequences in that it influenced the political behavior of many white men, North and South.　　　　　　E. P. Stickney

1398. Surrency, Erwin. THE LEGAL EFFECTS OF THE CIVIL WAR. *Am. J. of Legal Hist. 1961 5(2): 145-165.* Discusses such specific legal problems as the validity of Confederate statutes, contracts involving Confederate money, and the manumission of slaves. Concludes that the U.S. Supreme Court provided much-needed guidance to the State courts, which tended to be harsh in their judgments during the Reconstruction period.　　　　　　N. C. Brockman, S.M.

1399. Sweat, Edward F. FRANCIS L. CARDOZA - PROFILE OF INTEG-
RITY IN RECONSTRUCTION POLITICS. *J. of Negro Hist. 1961 46(4): 217-
232.* Describes the political career of Francis Louis Cardoza, who was born a free
Negro in Charleston, South Carolina in 1837 and became an important figure in
his native State's Reconstruction government. Cardoza, who was well educated
and became a conservative political leader, served in the South Carolina Constitutional Convention of 1868 and later as Secretary of State and Treasurer. As a
political leader he was competent and served with a sense of integrity. When the
Democrats again won control of the State in 1876 they indicted Cardoza along
with other Reconstruction figures for misuse of office. The trials were primarily
of a partisan nature and Cardoza was pardoned before his sentence was executed.
Cardoza's public career helps to refute the charge that the Negroes in Reconstruction government lacked intelligence and a sense of public responsibility.
L. Gara

1400. Sweat, Edward F. SOME NOTES ON THE ROLE OF NEGROES IN
THE ESTABLISHMENT OF PUBLIC SCHOOLS IN SOUTH CAROLINA.
Phylon 1961 22(2): 160-166. Negroes played a decisive role in laying the foundations for free, tax-supported schools in South Carolina. When the Federal Government overthrew the first, all-white post-Civil War government, 76 among the
members of the Constitutional Convention of 1868 were Negroes, many of them
illiterate. These, however, voted under the direction of their more educated
leaders. The latter included Francis Louis Cardoza, reared in the North and
educated abroad, who headed the education committee. Its problem was to
discard older "free" schools, which were really pauper schools, in favor of schools
built with funds raised by direct taxation. The committee's three white men and
five Negroes provided a report which broke with antebellum presumptions and
stipulated that schooling was to be compulsory. The committee did not emphasize
integrated schools but equal opportunities, though integration seems to have been
expected. Although the Reconstruction government was overthrown, the return
of white supremacy did not destroy the work of the convention. No new constitutional convention was held until 1895, and the constitution of the Reconstructionists continued to be the State's basic law, with the provision for public education
continuing to remain essentially unaltered. However, education did in time come
to mean education for the white majority of the State, despite the fact that the
meagre State funds for Negro schools were implemented by those of philanthropic foundations.   L. Filler

1401. Swidler, Arlene. BROWNSON AND THE "WOMAN QUESTION."
Am. Benedictine R. 1968 19(2): 211-219. After his conversion to Roman Catholicism in 1844 following a career in the Protestant ministry, Orestes A. Brownson
used his fame as a writer and editor to propagate his new faith. Brownson
emerged quite early as an antifeminist and expressed his view that suffrage was
a civil right. This argument was largely nullified in 1870 with the passage of the
15th amendment giving suffrage to all Negro males. After this, Brownson based
his arguments largely on religious grounds and, in his last years, saw the Catholic
Church as the one bulwark against the "shameful" women's rights movement.
By this time, his views were too rigid to adjust to changing social conditions and
his opinions on suffrage became irrelevant. 40 notes.   E. J. O'Brien

1402. Swinney, Everette. ENFORCING THE FIFTEENTH AMENDMENT, 1870-1877. *J. of Southern Hist. 1962 28(2): 202-218.* The three Enforcement Acts of 1870-71 represented the response of the U.S. Grant administration to the challenging by the South of the radicals' Reconstruction program. At the time, measures to protect the constitutional rights of the Negro, particularly the franchise, were much needed, and the laws were essentially sound. They worked fairly well for three or four years, although shortage of troops, money, and courts plagued law enforcement officers from the beginning. After 1874, the acts were virtually dead, by a combination of southern intransigence and northern apathy, increased by depression. In its determination to win home rule, the South was willing to face the prospect of race war; the North was not. But the failure of the policy does not mean the laws were iniquitous; the Civil Rights Acts of 1957 and 1960 return to the 1870 principles, and the 1961 Civil Rights Commission report goes beyond them.   S. E. Humphreys

1403. Taylor, Joe Gray. NEW ORLEANS AND RECONSTRUCTION. *Louisiana Hist. 1968 9(3): 189-208.* The presidential address at the 10th annual Louisiana Historical Association meeting in New Orleans 15 March 1968. New Orleans is different from the rest of the South, but the reaction of that city to defeat and Reconstruction was like the South in general and rural Louisiana in particular. New Orleanians gave little support to emancipation proposals and none whatsoever for Negro civil rights. Friction between Negroes and whites increased, as did hatred by New Orleans citizens for northerners. The riot of 1866 led to the 14th amendment and to the Reconstruction Acts of 1867, but there is no evidence that anyone in Louisiana realized that actions of Louisianans were to any extent responsible for Reconstruction legislation. The author details Reconstruction administrations of the city and the development of segregation practices. Although there are some exceptions noted, it is concluded that "cosmopolitan" New Orleans was as racist in its attitudes during Reconstruction as were the rural districts of Louisiana, and it was the scene of much anti-Negro and anticarpetbagger violence. Based on a wide variety of manuscripts, newspapers, and secondary sources; 57 notes.   R. L. Woodward

1404. Trefousse, Hans L. THE MOTIVATION OF A RADICAL REPUBLICAN: BENJAMIN F. WADE. *Ohio Hist. 1964 73(2): 63-74.* Summarizes the unfriendly treatment previously accorded Wade by historians and argues that this treatment is, in fact, unjustified. The author concludes that Wade was not a demagogue but rather a sincere politician, that he was not an ambitious opportunist in politics but a man who adhered to his beliefs even when he knew them to be unpopular, that he was not vindictive in his political actions, and that he was not in any special way the agent of powerful businessmen. He is seen as motivated by opposition to slavery, loyalty to the Whig and Republican parties, and "devotion to a Hamiltonian concept of the relations between government and industry." Footnotes cite manuscripts (particularly Wade Papers in the Library of Congress), newspapers, the *Congressional Globe,* and other materials.
S. L. Jones

1405. Trelease, Allen W. WHO WERE THE SCALAWAGS? *J. of Southern Hist. 1963 29(4): 445-468.* Disputes David Donald's contention that white Republicans of the Reconstruction period in the South were predominantly "old-line" Whigs who accepted Negro suffrage in the hope of controlling the votes of the former slaves. The author uses statistical methods in counties where the Republican vote in 1872 exceeded the Negro population and obtains findings which seem to indicate identification of prewar Whigs with postwar Republicans only in Tennessee, North Carolina, and to some extent in Virginia. The same statistics, and maps based upon these statistics, seem to show that "the great majority of native white Republicans" were hill-country farmers. Documented.
                                                                                                S. E. Humphreys

1406. Uzee, Philip D. THE BEGINNINGS OF THE LOUISIANA REPUBLICAN PARTY. *Louisiana Hist. 1971 12(3): 197-211.* Beginning in 1863, New Orleans Unionists led by Thomas J. Durant, working to restore civil government to Louisiana and with the backing of military authorities, organized the Republican Party in Louisiana. They allied themselves with Negroes and northern Radicals and, under the leadership of Durant's successor, Henry C. Warmouth, controlled the Reconstruction government of the State from 1868 to 1877. They achieved some progress in economic rehabilitation, education, and civil and political rights for Negroes, but were also associated with fraud, corruption, and violence. Based on primary and secondary sources; 4 photos, 67 notes.
                                                                                                R. L. Woodward

1407. Vincent, Charles. NEGRO LEADERSHIP AND PROGRAMS IN THE LOUISIANA CONSTITUTIONAL CONVENTION OF 1868.*Louisiana Hist. 1969 10(4): 339-351.* Negro delegates to the Louisiana constitutional Convention in 1868 generally were not of a revolutionary nature, as has been charged. They served commendably and succeeded in gaining many rights and privileges for Negroes. The Constitution of 1868 provided for all persons to enjoy equal rights and privileges, integrated schools, a new suffrage law, an end to the "Black Code" of 1865, and representation in the legislature on the basis of total population. Negro delegates were not hostile toward whites, but simply fought to establish legislation equitable to all.Based on the *Journal of the Proceedings of the Convention for Framing a Constitution...* (New Orleans, 1867-68). 44 notes.
                                                                                                R. L. Woodward

1408. Voight, Gilbert P. A SOUTH CAROLINA NEGRO PARADISE. *Negro Hist. Bull. 1958 22(1): 7-9.* Describes the predominantly Negro Beaufort County, South Carolina, in the period following the Civil War. A combination of cheap land, good schools, and competent political leadership enabled the freedmen to become successful yeoman farmers. The antebellum plantation paradise became a kind of Negro paradise where the former slaves learned to live responsible lives on their own resources.   L. Gara

1409. Wagstaff, Thomas. CALL YOUR OLD MASTER - "MASTER": SOUTHERN POLITICAL LEADERS AND NEGRO LABOR DURING PRESIDENTIAL RECONSTRUCTION. *Labor Hist. 1969 10(3): 323-345.*

Southern political leaders during presidential Reconstruction held attitudes of a property-owning class which affected their view of Negro labor. The rights of class gave them natural authority over their labor force and the natural right to exercise the powers of government. Northern and southern conservatives differed little in their attitudes toward class, and had they applied their economic and class logic consistently, they might well have disarmed President Andrew Johnson's opponents and made his reconstruction policy a success. Based on southern newspapers, MSS of southern political leaders, and a wide range of secondary sources; 55 notes. L. L. Athey

1410. Walden, Daniel. W. E. B. DU BOIS: PIONEER RECONSTRUCTION HISTORIAN. *Negro Hist. Bull. 1963 26(5): 159-160, 164.* A discussion of W. E. B. Du Bois' contributions to Reconstruction scholarship, with emphasis on his views concerning the positive aspects of Negro participation in the government of that era. L. Gara

1411. Warren, Hanna R. RECONSTRUCTION IN THE CHEROKEE NATION. *Chronicles of Oklahoma 1967 45(2): 180-189.* The Ridge faction of the Cherokee Nation in Oklahoma joined the Confederacy in the Civil War. After 1863, the Ross faction repudiated their southern commitments, freed their slaves, and supported the Union. When the Ross faction confiscated the Ridge faction's property during the war, the long-standing bitterness between the two groups increased. This hampered Federal treatymaking efforts and caused considerable hardship to the Indians in the winter of 1865-66. The northern group signed the Reconstruction Treaty of 1866 and the southern element accepted the terms without signing. It was a year later before harmony was restored and 1870 before all the legal technicalities were resolved. The status of their former Negro slaves remained a touchy question. 40 notes. D. L. Smith

1412. Webb, Ross A. BENJAMIN H. BRISTOW: CIVIL RIGHTS CHAMPION, 1866-72. *Civil War Hist. 1969 15(1): 39-53.* A review of the achievements and disappointments, in the field of civil rights, of Benjamin H. Bristow (1832-96) who served as U.S. attorney for Kentucky (1866-69) and as U.S. Solicitor General (1870-72). In the first role, Bristow's hardest struggles came in cases involving the Civil Rights Act of 1866 and, although there were setbacks, "Kentucky was one of the few states where the...act was adequately sustained." As Solicitor General, he was principally and successfully engaged in enforcing the Enforcement Acts of 1871-72. However, as the spirit of the times and the courts hardened against Federal intervention in behalf of Negro rights, Bristow became disillusioned and resigned his post. Based on primary sources. E. C. Murdock

1413. Weisberger, Bernard A. THE DARK AND BLOODY GROUND OF RECONSTRUCTION HISTORIOGRAPHY. *J. of Southern Hist. 1959 25(4): 427-447.* Since 1939 a revision has been going on in historical thinking regarding the Reconstruction period of American history, 1865-77. Yet the revision has been reflected entirely in articles, and the only full-length scholarly treatment of the period in the last two decades has rejected the revisionist point of view. Most textbooks likewise hold to the stereotypes regarding the "scalawags" and "carpetbaggers" and the evil of Negro enfranchisement. The author argues that: 1) white historians have avoided grasping the nettle of the race conflict fearing their own emotional involvement; 2) it is time to take a fresh look at the image of "abnormal corruption" of the period; 3) the period should be studied as an episode in the decline and fall of American States, rather than as a conspiracy to overthrow sound constitutional arrangements; 4) historians should escape from obsolete ideas of economics and see the period as one in which a new agrarian-industrial capitalism emerged; and 5) more sociological and psychological insights should be applied to the study of Reconstruction.   S. E. Humphreys

1414. Weissbuch, Ted N. ALBION W. TOURGEE: PROPAGANDIST AND CRITIC OF RECONSTRUCTION. *Ohio Hist. Q. 1961 70(1): 27-44.* Demonstrates the relationship between Tourgée's own experiences with Reconstruction in the South and his analysis of it in his two novels, *A Fool's Errand* (1879) and *Bricks Without Straw* (1880). Tourgée, a native of Ohio, went to North Carolina in 1865 and lived there until 1879, when he moved to New York. Tourgée was hostile to the southern aristocracy and severely critical of the northern Reconstructionists. He agreed with the objectives of the latter group, but thought their methods wrong. Though he later changed his mind, he believed at the time he wrote these two novels that education was the solution to the Negro's problem.
                                                                    S. L. Jones

1415. Wesley, Edgar B. FORTY ACRES AND A MULE AND A SPELLER. *Hist. of Educ. J. 1957 8(4): 113-127.* After the Civil War the Federal Government failed to give the freedmen the land, farm equipment, and education promised them. The short-lived Freedmen's Bureau provided some schools for Negroes, and northern philanthropists and teachers supplemented the program of the government, but during the Reconstruction period only about 10 percent of southern Negro children ever attended a school. Federal neglect continued after Reconstruction, when the Negroes were again made the wards of their former owners.   L. Gara

1416. Wharton, Vernon L. RECONSTRUCTION. *Writing Southern Hist.: Essays in Historiography in Honor of Fletcher M. Green (Baton Rouge: Louisiana State U. Press, 1965): 295-315.* In the historiography of southern Reconstruction, William Dunnington Bloxham has not received proper attention. Among historians of the William Archibald Dunning type the scholarly and objective works by Clara Mildred Thompson on Georgia and by Ella Lonn on Louisiana are remarkably temperate. With acceptance of the belief that Radical Reconstruction had been a tragic error came the rehabilitation of Andrew Johnson who, after 1920, emerged as hero and martyr. In 1938 Francis B. Simkins pointed out that the main issue of Reconstruction was the race question, and in 1940 the *American Historical Review* published the controversial and influential paper by Howard K. Beale "On Rewriting Reconstruction History." Both were challenges for new basic research. In 1959 Carl N. Degler came to the blunt conclusion that "the tragedy of Reconstruction is that it failed." 72 biblio. notes.
                                                                    E. P. Stickney

1417. White, James B. CHANGING INTERPRETATIONS OF THE NEGRO IN THE RECONSTRUCTION GOVERNMENTS. *Negro Hist. Bull. 1958 22(2): 31-34.* Calls attention to a variety of historical interpretations of the part that Negroes played in Reconstruction governments. Most recent studies are less biased'than the earlier ones, and they are less likely to reflect partisan and regional prejudices. The newer monographs do not blame the Negroes for the excesses of Reconstruction and often recognize their positive achievements.

L. Gara

1418. Wiggins, Sarah Woolfolk. THE "PIG IRON" KELLEY RIOT IN MO-BILE, MAY 14, 1867. *Alabama R. 1970 23(1): 45-55.* "In May 1867 Judge William Darrah Kelley of Philadelphia began a speaking tour through several of the former Confederate states." Judge Kelley was intent on laying the foundations of the Republican Party in the South. His appearance in Mobile on 14 May 1867 sparked the only major riot in Alabama during Reconstruction. A predominately Negro crowd of approximately 4,000, many carrying clubs and firearms, assembled to hear Kelley at 8:00 p.m. Although heckled, Judge Kelley was able to speak for about 20 minutes. What followed is subject to various interpretations. A shot was fired toward the speaker's stand and horses attached to the ambulance of the 15th U.S. Infantry were frightened and started to run through the crowd. The crowd immediately panicked and, before order was restored, one white and one black were dead and 20 people were wounded. Based on manuscript collections and newspapers; 36 notes.

D. F. Henderson

1419. Wiggins, Sarah Woolfolk. UNIONIST EFFORTS TO CONTROL ALA-BAMA RECONSTRUCTION 1865-1867. *Alabama Hist. Q. 1968 30(1): 51-64.* Discusses the attempt of Alabama unionists to control Alabama politics following the Civil War. The author considers their failure to do this as caused by the congressional Reconstruction policy, which disenfranchised many voters, and the Republican Party's attempt to control the State through the Negro. This last factor put the power back into the hands of the black belt, something which the unionists wanted to avoid.

E. E. Eminhizer

1420. Wight, Willard E., ed. NEGROES IN THE GEORGIA LEGISLATURE: THE CASE OF F. H. FYALL OF MACON COUNTY. *Georgia Hist. Q. 1960 44(1): 85-97.* Documentary evidence which reveals how the Georgia Legislature removed its Negro members in 1868 by means of parliamentary legerdemain.

R. Lowitt

1421. Wight, Willard E., ed. RECONSTRUCTION IN GEORGIA: THREE LETTERS BY EDWIN G. HIGBEE. *Georgia Hist. Q. 1957 41(1): 81-90.* Higbee, a school teacher in Georgia but a staunch Unionist, describes in these letters the opposition to Reconstruction. He particularly complains about northern military personnel, sent to protect the Unionists and the freed slaves, who actually sided with the conservative southerners. The bribes and acts of violence employed by opponents of the new State Constitution of 1868 are also mentioned.

D. van Arkel

1422. Williams, Burton J. RELIGION AND RECONSTRUCTION: A CLER-IC'S CONCEPTION. *Methodist Hist. 1971 9(3): 45-52.* Cyrus R. Rice was a clergyman of the Methodist Episcopal Church, South, who transferred to the Methodist Episcopal Church in 1865. On 23 June 1865 he addressed the Baldwin City, Kansas, District Conference on "Reconstruction of the Rebel States." In this speech, which is reprinted here, Rice discussed the meaning of secession and rebellion, the status of the seceded States, the chance of revival of slavery, the need for reconstruction, possible changes in the Constitution, and the reconstruction of the churches. The manuscript address is in the Kansas Methodist Historical Library at Baker University. 19 notes. H. L. Calkin

1423. Wood, Forrest G. ON REVISING RECONSTRUCTION HISTORY: NEGRO SUFFRAGE, WHITE DISFRANCHISEMENT, AND COMMON SENSE. *J. of Negro Hist. 1966 51(2): 98-113.* Rejects the traditional view of Reconstruction on the matters of wholesale disfranchisement of whites in order to assure Negro supremacy in the Southern States. In the five States with available statistics, white disfranchisement did not give colored voters a majority. More important than disfranchisement in giving control to the Radicals was the refusal of many Southern whites to register or to vote. Despite frequent statements to the contrary, southern Negroes did not hold the balance of power nor did colored office holders control the political machinery of the Southern states during Reconstruction. L. Gara

1424. Woodward, C. Vann. SEEDS OF FAILURE IN RADICAL RACE POLICY. *Pro. of the Am. Phil. Soc. 1966 110(1): 1-9.* Examines Radical racial policies during the Civil War and Reconstruction in light of the generally antagonistic attitude of many northern people toward the Negro. Noting the fear of the North that large numbers of Negroes would flee into their section from the South, the author indicates that much of the motivation behind civil rights legislation and the Constitutional amendments during this period stemmed from a desire to allay such doubts and to keep Republicans in office in both sections. This ambivalent and partisan attitude carried the seeds of failure of the overall policies toward the freedmen, though the author concedes that the "Second Reconstruction" owes much of its impetus to the "First." The article is based on various primary and secondary sources; 31 notes. W. G. Morgan

1425. Worthen, Edward H. A DIFFERENT KIND OF YANKEE CONQUISTADOR. *Vermont Hist. 1969 37(4): 272-276.* Fernando Cortez Willett (1842-75), born in Bakersfield, Vermont, into a hop-raising Congregationalist family with an antislavery Wesleyan grandfather, left Williams College in 1862 and served nine months in the 13th Vermont Regiment. In his printed Williams Class Day oration (1865) he urged equality for freedmen and the poor. Principal at Bakersfield Academy and Evansville (Indiana) High School, he went to Colorado for his consumption, wrote a travel guide, prepared for the ministry at Lane Theological Seminary in Cincinnati, Ohio, and died as secretary to John U. Foster, Minister to Mexico. T. D. S. Bassett

Post-Reconstruction Political Realignments

1426. Bacote, Clarence A. NEGRO OFFICEHOLDERS IN GEORGIA UNDER PRESIDENT MC KINLEY. *J. of Negro Hist. 1959 44(3): 217-239.* Summarizes how President William McKinley, the archconservative 30 years removed from the idealism of the early Republican leaders like Charles Sumner (1811-74) and Thaddeus Stevens (1792-1868), dealt with the Negro's aspirations for Federal officeholding in Georgia. Although Negroes represented 90 percent of the party's strength in the State, they received only about five major appointments and a few minor ones on the State level. On the other hand, white Republicans, Democrats, and Populists were appointed to all of the Federal marshalships in addition to nearly five hundred post office jobs. Despite the Negro's loyalty to the party on the national level, McKinley did not intend to oppose the central position of white southerners, namely, "white supremacy." Based on both white and Negro regional papers.   A

1427. Casdorph, Paul Douglas. NORRIS WRIGHT CUNEY AND TEXAS REPUBLICAN POLITICS, 1883-1896. *Southwestern Hist. Q. 1965 68(4): 455-464.* From 1883 to 1896, Texan-born Negro Norris Wright Cuney was the Republican Party leader in his State. From his appointment in 1871 as sergeant-at-arms of the State legislature, lawyer Cuney's professional political career was in the ascendancy. His control of the Negro element in the State party gave him control of the entire party. National Republican success in the election of 1888 gave Cuney the position of collector of customs in Galveston, one of the most important Federal positions in the South. The growing white-colored breach in the State party, his relationships with leaders of the national party, and Republican defeat in national elections had much to do with the downfall of Cuney. 62 notes.   D. L. Smith

1428. Cheek, William F. A NEGRO RUNS FOR CONGRESS: JOHN MERCER LANGSTON AND THE VIRGINIA CAMPAIGN OF 1888. *J. of Negro Hist. 1967 52(1): 14-34.* Describes the Virginia political campaign of 1888 which resulted in the election to Congress of John Mercer Langston, the only Negro who successfully challenged both Democratic and Republican organizations. From 1879 to 1885 Virginia was controlled politically by William Mahone's Readjuster (later Republican) Party which practiced a liberal racial policy and won the support of the Negro voters. Although the Democrats gained control of the State in 1885, Mahone remained a powerful influence in the Fourth Congressional District. When Langston decided to run for Congress he was opposed by Mahone who forced Langston to run as an independent. Obvious fraud by all parties and contested votes threw the election decision into the House of Representatives, which finally decided for Langston. Documented with newspaper and manuscript sources.   L. Gara

1429. Davis, Hugh C. HILARY A. HERBERT: BOURBON APOLOGIST. *Alabama R. 1967 20(3): 216-225.* Congressman from Alabama (1876-93) and

Secretary of the Navy under Grover Cleveland, Herbert was a leading apologist of the Bourbon "regimes of the post-Reconstruction South." "Redemption" meant a return to the equality of States, not of individuals. He disliked centralization of power in the Federal Government, and in particular the Republican Party. Likewise he disliked the Farmers' Alliance-Populist program because it was socialistic. Toward the Negro, he adopted the position of race paternalism, trying to prove that racial equality "was impossible because of the natural inferiority of the Negro." Based on speeches and two books, *The Abolition Crusade and Its Consequences* (1912) and *Why the Solid South* (1890), by Herbert; 20 notes.
D. F. Henderson

1430. De Santis, Vincent P. THE REPUBLICAN PARTY AND THE SOUTHERN NEGRO, 1877-1897. *J. of Negro Hist. 1960 45(2): 71-87.* The tragic story of how the Republican Party instead of protecting the southern Negro and looking after him as the ward of the Nation, deserted him and left him as the ward of the dominant race in the South. In part this abandonment of the Negro was beyond the control of the Republicans, but it was also a part of a well-planned policy that the Republicans had worked out for the South in the post-Reconstruction years. This abandonment caused the Negro to become suspicious and critical of the Republican Party. Yet for all his misgivings and hostility, the Negro preferred Republicans to Democrats. Based on various manuscript and newspaper sources.   A

1431. Drake, Richard Bryant. FREEDMEN'S AID SOCIETIES AND SECTIONAL COMPROMISE. *J. of Southern Hist. 1963 29(2): 175-186.* Numerous freedmen's aid societies were established at the end of the Civil War to work with the government's Freedmen's Bureau and Radical Republicans for education and equality of Negroes. But in the 1870's, as the politicians gradually abandoned the Negro to the political tutelage of the New South's leaders, the zeal of the various freedmen's aid societies waned and they too began to seek accommodation with southern whites. Nonsectarian societies showed this compromise first, then the societies related to churches which were strongly represented in both North and South, and finally the Congregationalist society, and the American Missionary Association. By accomodation with the South, under the leadership of General Samuel C. Armstrong, principal of Hampton Institute, the association in turn got southern acceptance and effective support for its Negro colleges - Hampton, Atlanta, Fisk and Talladega. In 1875, Frederick Douglass asserted the Negro had been "more injured than benefitted" by the freedmen's aid societies.
S. E. Humphreys

1432. Folk, Patrick A. "OUR FRANK": THE CONGRESSIONAL CAREER OF FRANK H. HURD. *Northwest Ohio Q. 1969 41(2): 45-69, 1970 42(3): 47-63.* Part I. Gives a brief account of Hurd's boyhood years between 1840 and 1861 before concentrating on his role as a leader in the Ohio Democratic Party during the Civil War and Reconstruction. Deals primarily with the national campaign of 1872 and the local campaigns of 1872 and 1874 in Ohio. Hurd is shown to have been an opponent of the 13th, 14th, and 15th amendments, since he regarded them as unconstitutional because some States had been coerced into accepting them. He continued to play a prominent role in the party after moving to Toledo in 1869. He opposed the "New Departure" which advocated that the Democrats accept the outcome of the war. After losing out during the Liberal-Republican campaign in 1872, Hurd eked out a slight victory in a gerrymandered district in 1874 in spite of vigorous opposition from Republican orators and newspapers. Based on local newspapers, articles and local histories; 219 notes. Part II. Deals with activities in connection with the Pacific railroad, the resumption of specie payment and the Alabama claims as issues that came before the 44th Congress, and his work as a member of the House judiciary committee; but emphasizes his role during his disputed presidential election of 1876. In speeches before the House, Hurd tried to demolish the arguments in support of counting electoral votes from Louisiana and Colorado. Based on secondary sources; 154 notes. W. F. Zornow

1433. Gardner, Robert Wallace. A FRUSTRATED MINORITY: THE NEGRO AND NEW YORK CITY POLITICS OF THE 1880'S AS TYPIFIED BY THE MAYORALTY ELECTION OF 1886. *Negro Hist. Bull. 1966 29(4): 83-84, 94.* Describes and comments on the Negro vote in New York City in the 1880's, which at that time was not considered important by either the Republican or the Democratic Party. The Negro vote (about 1.6 percent of the total vote) overwhelmingly supported the Republican Party until the late 1880's. In the mayoralty contest of 1886, Abram Hewett (Democrat) was elected with 90 thousand votes; Henry George (Union Labor) received 68,140 votes; and Theodore Roosevelt (Republican) had 60,435 votes. Some prominent Negroes viewed this election as a key to greater recognition for the race and claimed that colored men could make their influence felt by voting the Democratic ticket and by helping to increase the majority of the party whose condidate was certain to be elected in any event. Black men realized that their Republican vote meant little and that they were not needed by the party. 29 notes. D. D. Cameron

1434. Going, Allen J. THE AGRARIAN REVOLT. *Writing Southern Hist.: Essays in Historiography in Honor of Fletcher M. Green (Baton Rouge: Louisiana State U. Press, 1965): 362-382.* Finds that interpretations of Populism during the past 70 years have swung full circle from distrust to approval and back to adverse criticism. An increasing number of favorable treatments came in the 1930's of which the earliest was Hicks' *The Populist Revolt.* The works of Beard, Parrington, Virginius Dabney, C. Vann Woodward, Daniel M. Robison, and others were beginning to show that the southern agrarian revolt, rather than being a Western import, had origins and dynamics of its own. They indicated a need "for further study of the internal frictions beneath the solidarity of the post-Reconstruction South." More recent interpretations are those by Fred A. Shannon (1957) and by Theodore Saloutos (1960). Negro-Populist relationships have been subject to varying interpretations. Hofstadter has recently stressed the latent nativism of the southern agrarian organizations. 80 biblio. notes. E. P. Stickney

1435. Graves, John William. NEGRO DISFRANCHISEMENT IN ARKANSAS. *Arkansas Hist. Q. 1967 26(3): 199-225.* Discusses the impersonal social forces of the last decade of the 19th century and the early years of the 20th century which resulted in the disfranchisement of a majority of Negroes in Arkansas. The three major instruments by which this was accomplished were: the Election Law of 1891 which gave absolute control over election machinery to the Democratic Party, the poll tax amendments adopted in 1892 and 1908, and the white primary of the Democratic Party which was ordered to be used throughout the State by the State Democratic central committee in 1906. 112 notes.   B. A. Drummond

1436. Gutman, Herbert G. PETER H. CLARK: PIONEER NEGRO SOCIAL-IST, 1877. *J. of Negro Educ. 1965 34(4): 413-418.* Sketches the political and economic transformation of Peter H. Clark, principal of the Colored High School of Cincinnati and until 1877 a member of the Republican Party. Clark joined the Workingmen's Party of the United States in 1877 thereby probably becoming the first American Negro socialist. In the fall of 1877 Clark was nominated for the office of State superintendent of schools by the Workingmen's Party. The text of his speech of 22 July 1877 before a group of striking Cincinnati railroad workers is reproduced from the *Cincinnati Commercial* as an illustration of Clark's political and economic ideas.   S. C. Pearson, Jr.

1437. Ingle, H. Larry. A SOUTHERN DEMOCRAT AT LARGE: WILLIAM HODGE KITCHIN AND THE POPULIST PARTY. *North Carolina Hist. R. 1968 45(2): 178-194.* Not all Southern Populists were agrarian radicals. Many disclaimed radical inclinations and argued principally in terms of replacing government by the few with government by the many. William Hodge Kitchin is an example of this point of view. Kitchin fought for the Confederacy, rising to the rank of captain. After the war, he attacked the established white ruling class in North Carolina, using the rhetoric of democracy in the service of white supremacy (a term he is alleged to have invented). By the late 1880's he broke with the Democratic Party and joined the Populists, where he had a better chance for leadership and influence. In the party, he attempted to preserve conservative principles. Kitchin's populism was not radical, but a mixture of white conservatism and opportunism. 97 notes.   J. M. Bumsted

1438. James, Joseph B. SOUTHERN REACTION TO THE PROPOSAL OF THE FOURTEENTH AMENDMENT. *J. of Southern Hist. 1956 22(4): 477-497.* Surveys the reaction of such southern States as Texas, Georgia, Arkansas, Florida, and Alabama to the Fourteenth Amendment. Rejection by eight southern States led to a movement to submit a more acceptable counterproposal with the backing of President Johnson leading to limited suffrage for freedmen and omission of the disqualification section.   R. Kerley

1439. Lasch, Christopher. THE ANTI-IMPERIALISTS, THE PHILIPPINES, AND THE INEQUALITY OF MAN. *J. of Southern Hist. 1958 24(3): 319-331.* Southern Democrats almost unanimously condemned the annexation of the Philippine Islands to the United States in 1899, on the ground that Asians, like Negroes, were innately inferior to whites and could not be assimilated to American life. This argument, however, brought forth none of the angry rejoinders from the North that would have been made two decades earlier. The North had receded far from its mid-century racial liberalism. This change was partly the result of Darwinism. At the turn of the century, the very men who had previously been active in the antislavery and other "liberal" causes acquiesced in the anti-Jeffersonian policy of imperialism, just as they acquiesced in other illiberal actions, namely, the first serious restrictions on immigration and the South's successful reelimination of the Negro from white society. S. E. Humphreys

1440. Lawrence, Alexander A. SOME LETTERS FROM HENRY C. WAYNE TO HAMILTON FISH. *Georgia Hist. Q. 1959 43(4): 391-409.* Publishes correspondence between the Georgian Henry C. Wayne (1815-83), who during the Reconstruction period became a Republican, and the Secretary of State, Hamilton Fish. It deals in part with topics that are still current - the race question in the South and the problem of establishing the Republican party there. The letters bear witness to Wayne's difficulty as a conservative southerner who had affiliated himself with the Republican Party. R. Lowitt

1441. Logsdon, Joseph. AN ILLINOIS CARPETBAGGER LOOKS AT THE SOUTHERN NEGRO. *J. of the Illinois State Hist. Soc. 1969 62(1): 53-64.* James Shaw, who spent the years 1865 to 1873 in Alabama as an editor of Republican newspapers, defended Negro suffrage and the general course of radical reconstruction in that State at a time when opinion had moved overwhelmingly to the support of Johnson's antiradical policy. Shaw expressed his opinion in an article published in the Aurora (Illinois) *Daily Beacon-News* 31 July 1915 and reprinted here. S. L. Jones

1442. Lowitt, Richard, ed. DAVID M. KEY VIEWS THE LEGAL AND POLITICAL STATUS OF THE NEGRO IN 1885. *J. of Negro Hist. 1969 54(3): 285-293.* David McKendree Key (1824-1900) was a prominent figure during the Compromise of 1877. A former Confederate officer and an active politician in his native State of Tennessee, he was appointed to several different posts by President Rutherford B. Hayes. His speech on the legal and political status of the Negro was given before the Tennessee Bar Association on 2 July 1885 and is reprinted in full at the end of the editor's introduction. The speaker bypassed the issue of voting rights, which he felt was not material to the State of Tennessee, but rather concentrated on the problems of segregation and social equality. He maintained that the Negro was free and therefore must be treated in public with a respect due to any free man, even though he personally believed in the superiority of the white race. 4 notes. R. S. Melamed

1443. Meier, August. THE NEGRO AND THE DEMOCRATIC PARTY 1875-1915. *Phylon 1956 17(2): 173-191.* Studies the attempts of nominally Republican Negro leaders either to come to an understanding with the Democrats or to maintain political independence. Particular attention is paid to the movements of the 1880's, and those between 1908 and 1912. Corruption and poor policy is seen as motivating Negro disaffection in the 1880's; indifference and even hostility under Roosevelt and Taft, coupled with Democratic sympathy, were the forces at work in the second period. The first attempt failed due to the increasing restriction of the franchise in the South. The second ended in disillusionment with Wilson. Attention is devoted to the role of the Negro opponents of Booker T. Washington in this struggle.   J. Warnock

1444. Saunders, Robert M. THE TRANSFORMATION OF TOM WATSON, 1894-1895. *Georgia Hist. Q. 1970 54(3): 339-356.* An account of Georgia Populist Thomas Edward Watson's move to the political right after his third defeat as congressional candidate in 1895. Becoming increasingly conservative, Watson attacked Roman Catholics, Jews, labor, radicals, Socialists, Democrats, and, more particularly, men like Jacob Coxey and Henry George. He also became a thorough racist, abandoning his former position of moderation on the Negro question. The transformation of the mid-1890's prepared the way for Watson's notorious role in the early 20th century. Based on newspapers and the Watson Papers; 94 notes.   R. A. Mohl

1445. Shafner, Jerrell H. and Rogers, William Warren. JOSEPH C. MANNING: MILITANT AGRARIAN, ENDURING POPULIST. *Alabama Hist. Q. 1967 29(1 and 2): 5-37.* Reviews the activities of J. C. Manning as a populist leader in Alabama, especially during the elections from 1892 to 1896. The discussion points out that Manning differed from many populist leaders in that he retained his views throughout his life. His chief hope was to gain free election and majority rule in Alabama. The illegality of the elections of 1892 and 1894 are pointed out. Stressed also is the fact that Manning wanted to keep the franchise for everyone and that he was of the opinion that the Constitution of 1901 was really an attempt on the part of the Democratic Party to keep power so as to prevent needed reform. The Negro and white supremacy were means to this end. Manning's books on needed social reform are reviewed briefly.   E. E. Eminhizer

1446. Singletary, Otis A. THE ELECTION OF 1878 IN LOUISIANA. *Louisiana Hist. Q. 1957 40(1): 46-53.* Although the withdrawal of Federal troops from Louisiana in April 1877 is usually considered to have ended Reconstruction in that State, it was not until after the elections of November 1878 that white supremacy and the Democratic Party were firmly in control. Political fraud and violence won the election for the Democrats. Based on contemporary newspapers and documents.   E. D. Johnson

1447. Sivachev, N. V. NEGRITIANSKII VOPROS V RABOCHEM DVIZHENII SSHA (1919-1939 GG.) [The Negro question in the U.S. labor movement (1919-39)]. *Voprosy Istorii [USSR] 1966 (8): 47-61.* Discusses the process of proletarianization of American Negroes after World War I through migration northward, increased employment in industry, and urbanization. The stand of the Communist Party of the United States and of the leadership of the Socialist Party on the Negro question is described. The fate of the Negroes during the depression years, the activities and errors of the American Working Negro Congress, and the entry of Negroes into the organized labor movement, especially the Congress of Industrial Organizations (CIO), are depicted. 58 notes.   B. V. Maciuika

1448. Smith, W. Calvin. THE RECONSTRUCTION "TRIUMPH" OF RUFUS B. BULLOCK. *Georgia Hist. Q. 1968 52(4): 414-425.* An account of the Reconstruction government of Georgia Governor Rufus B. Bullock. A split in the Republican Party in 1868 prevented Bullock from dominating the State legislature. Thus thwarted, Bullock appealed successfully to the War Department, President Grant, and Congress. Grant and the Congressional Radicals fell in with Bullock's plan because of their wish that Georgia ratify the 15th amendment. A purge of the State legislature restored Bullock and his wing of the Republican Party to power, but the governor's policies alienated moderates and contributed to Democratic success in the election of 1870, thus ending Reconstruction in Georgia. 42 notes.   R. A. Mohl

1449. Steelman, Joseph F. VICISSITUDES OF REPUBLICAN PARTY POLITICS: THE CAMPAIGN OF 1892 IN NORTH CAROLINA. *North Carolina Hist. R. 1966 43(4): 430-442.* In the face of cleavages in the Democratic ranks, the Republicans of North Carolina in 1892 sought in vain to unite their own party. On the State level Republican Party leaders resented the Negro aspirations of leadership in local politics. Negro spokesmen maintained that the Negro voter held the balance of power in the party and therefore should receive proper consideration. When the vote was cast, the decline of Republican support in the Coastal Plain and Piedmont areas suggested "that conflicting attitudes on party strategy, the denunciation of the chairman and the state ticket, and the particularly bitter attacks upon Negro Republicans influenced a shift to the other parties in this campaign and election." Undoubtedly many Negro Republicans voted for Democrats or Populists. In the opinion of one member of the Republican National Committee in New York "the Republican leaders threw away the great opportunity of their lives...to eliminate the color line." Based on the Grimes Papers and the Ransome Papers, both at the University of North Carolina; the Josephus Daniels Papers at the Library of Congress; the Edward Chambers Smith Papers at Duke University; and many newspapers; 74 notes.

E. P. Stickney

1450. Tunnell, T. B., Jr. THE NEGRO, THE REPUBLICAN PARTY, AND THE ELECTION OF 1876 IN LOUISIANA. *Louisiana Hist. 1966 7(2): 101-116.* Investigates the loyalty of Negro voters to the Republican Party in the election of 1876. The author refutes the interpretation that Negroes defected from the Republican Party because of white terrorist intimidation. Instead, Negroes in Louisiana voted the Democratic ticket because of the long-standing intraparty feud between supporters of ex-Governor Henry Clay Warmoth and the Custom-House faction, the failure of Republican incumbents to make good their promises to the Negro community, widespread corruption of local Republican officials, and the vigorous Democratic campaign to woo Negroes away from their traditional alliance with Republicans. Based principally on records of the committees investigating the election of 1876; 69 notes.   R. L. Woodward

1451. Uzee, Philip D. THE REPUBLICAN PARTY IN THE LOUISIANA ELECTION OF 1896. *Louisiana Hist. 1961 2(3): 332-344.* Analyzes the gubernatorial campaign and election of 1896 in Louisiana when Democrat Murphy J.

Foster defeated J. N. Pharr, a Fusionist candidate. Pharr represented a coalition of Republicans, Populists, and sugar planters defecting from the Democratic ranks. The election is important as the last major opposition by the Republican Party in Louisiana. Also, "it was in 1896 that the issue of the buying and controlling of Negro votes came to a head and many leaders came to believe that only by eliminating the Negro vote could fair and uncorrupt elections be held in Louisiana." The disfranchisement movement culminated in the anti-Negro suffrage clauses of the 1898 constitution. Based mainly on newspapers and the William E. Chandler Papers, Library of Congress.   D. C. James

1452. Ward, Judson Clements, Jr. THE NEW DEPARTURE DEMOCRATS OF GEORGIA: AN INTERPRETATION. *Georgia Hist. Q. 1957 41(3): 227-236.* A summary of political developments in Georgia between 1872, the year in which the Democratic Party regained control of all three branches of the State government, and 1890, when the Farmers' Alliance captured the Democratic Party. This meant a "new departure," since the party now combined political conservatism with the vigorous promotion of new financial, agrarian, industrial, and trading enterprises. The "New Departure" Democrats thereby made Georgia's reconciliation with the North easier and contributed to the State's economic rehabiliation. Their dedication to white supremacy and States' rights, however, retarded the liberal evolution of the State and confined its political life to bigoted single-party control, from which Georgia politics has suffered up to the present.
R. Mueller

1453. Welch, Richard E., Jr. THE FEDERAL ELECTIONS BILL OF 1890: POSTSCRIPTS AND PRELUDE. *J. of Am. Hist. 1965 52(3): 511-526.* A reinterpretation of the Federal Elections Bill of 1890 based on the recently opened papers of Senator George F. Hoar of Massachusetts, floor manager for the bill in the Senate. The author suggests the bill was not the result of Republican bloody-shirt politics but was inspired by a wish to validate the principles of national citizenship and the 15th amendment and by a desire to undermine Democratic control of southern politics, thereby enhancing the position of the Republican Party. He interprets the bill's defeat more as the acceptance of Negro subjugation than as the culmination of sectional reconciliation.
H. J. Silverman

1454. Wilhoit, Francis M. AN INTERPRETATION OF POPULISM'S IMPACT ON THE GEORGIA NEGRO. *J. of Negro Hist. 1967 52(2): 116-127.* Lists and analyzes conclusions drawn from the Georgia election of 1892 which led to defeat of the Populist program and to the return of Georgia Populist leaders to a policy of excluding Negroes from political life rather than trying to win their support. Among the conclusions are the lack of class consciousness among the poor in Georgia, the importance of race in the State's politics, the continued tension between rural and urban areas, the fragile nature of southern liberalism, the tendency of bigotry to spread from one area of human relations to another, and the crucial importance of politics in determining the Negro's status in the South.   L. Gara

1455. Williamson, Edward C. THE CONSTITUTIONAL CONVENTION OF 1885. *Florida Hist. Q. 1962/63 41(2): 116-126.* Formal eradication of the carpet-bag constitution of 1868 and its replacement by that of 1885, returning power to local areas and placing the government in the hands of the white people of Florida. Based on Florida State papers, private papers, secondary works, and newspapers.   G. L. Lycan

Racial Attitudes & Policies

1456. Albrecht, Robert C. THE POLITICAL THOUGHT OF DAVID A. WASSON. *Am. Q. 1965 17(4): 742-748.* Regards the Reverend David Wasson, Transcendentalist clergyman and poet-essayist, as a well-known and ardent proponent of conservative thought. Wasson based his writings on a belief in the "basic equality of men and their potentiality for spiritual growth," but tempered his ideas with notions about the unequal "spiritual development of men" and the supremacy of a "higher law" than majority rule. Universal suffrage bothered Wasson; he would deny it to Negroes, women, and recent immigrants. Wasson regarded the 17th-century Puritan commonwealth as the ideal political state; it held within it a unity of religion and community. Wasson felt that a state governed by moral authority would be the solution of the dilemma of liberal Christianity and liberal politics. 13 notes.   R. S. Pickett

1457. Ander, O. Fritiof. THE SWEDISH-AMERICAN PRESS IN THE ELECTION OF 1912. *Swedish Pioneer Hist. Q. 1963 14(3): 103-126.* The ties which the Swedish American press had developed with the Republican Party over the question of slavery following the Civil War were strengthened over the years. However, 1912 proved a year of changing support. In a study of Swedish American newspapers it was found that the Progressive Party of Roosevelt had more appeal. Several papers also supported Wilson over the Republican Taft for the Presidency. The main reasons for the shift to the Progressives are seen to be the popularity of Roosevelt and the freshness of a party which had no past record to defend.   W. F. Peterson

1458. Bacote, Clarence A. NEGRO PROSCRIPTIONS, PROTESTS AND PROPOSED SOLUTIONS IN GEORGIA, 1880-1908. *J. of Southern Hist. 1959 25(4): 471-498.* Following Reconstruction in Georgia, the Negro was not only the victim of political disfranchisement and educational discrimination, but also suffered humiliation in the form of "Jim Crow" laws, lynching, and the convict lease system. These forms of racial proscription brought forth numerous protests from Negroes, but to no avail. Convinced of the futility of striving for first-class citizenship in such an environment, some Negro leaders proposed three avenues of escape, namely: 1) return to Africa; 2) exodus to the North; and 3) colonization in the frontier West.   S. E. Humphreys

1459. Bernstein, Barton J. CASE LAW IN "PLESSY V. FERGUSON." *J. of Negro Hist. 1962 47(3): 192-198.* Examines the cases cited in the *Plessy vs. Ferguson* decision of 1896 and concludes that the decision constituted bad law and was unsupported by precedent. The cases cited were distorted beyond their original significance in order to sanction the "separate but equal" doctrine expressed in this decision.   L. Gara

1460. Bernstein, Barton J. PLESSY V. FERGUSON: CONSERVATIVE SOCIOLOGICAL JURISPRUDENCE. *J. of Negro Hist. 1963 48(3): 196-205.* Proposes that the *Plessy vs. Ferguson* decision of 1896 was just as much an example of sociological jurisprudence as the 1954 decision in the *Segregation Cases* which overruled the separate but equal doctrine. In legalizing segregation, the court mistakenly contended that the practice was consistent with custom or tradition, basing its decision partly on contemporary doctrines of racial inferiority which reinforced the practice. The effect of the decision was to assure that segregation would be practiced and to give added weight to concepts of racial differences which undergird it. Documented.   L. Gara

1461. Berrier, G. Gail. THE NEGRO SUFFRAGE ISSUE IN IOWA-1865-1868. *Ann. of Iowa 1968 39(4): 241-261.* Edward Russell, editor of the Davenport *Gazette,* was the leading advocate of Negro suffrage in Iowa. In 1865 he maneuvered the State Republican convention into endorsing this reform. Some Republicans refused to campaign on this platform, while others pointed out that the Negro would not vote until after two successive legislatures voted to submit a constitutional amendment to the people. A number of Republicans mollified popular fears with the assertion that the Negro was inherently inferior to whites and would never accomplish social equality. Democrats argued that a Republican victory would invite Negro migration to Iowa. In 1868 the suffrage amendment was carried by 56.5 percent of the vote while General Grant garnered 62 percent of the Iowa vote in the presidential contest. Based on newspapers and secondary materials; illus., 65 notes.   D. C. Swift

1462. Betts, John R. THE NEGRO AND THE NEW ENGLAND CONSCIENCE IN THE DAYS OF JOHN BOYLE O'REILLY. *J. of Negro Hist. 1966 51(4): 246-261.* Reviews the activity of Boston editor John Boyle O'Reilly as a defender of social equality and full civil rights for Negroes. From the time of his arrival in America in 1870 until his death in 1890 O'Reilly fought against racial prejudice as well as for Irish freedom. His paper, the Boston *Pilot,* focused attention on racial incidents, gave much space to colored Americans, reported the struggle for freedom of the Irish and the Negro as a mutual one, and editorially counseled the victims of racial injustice to resist their oppressors even with violence if necessary. Documented with numerous quotations from O'Reilly's editorials and other writings.   L. Gara

1463. Bloch, Herman D. THE NEW YORK AFRO-AMERICAN'S STRUGGLE FOR POLITICAL RIGHTS AND THE EMERGENCE OF POLITICAL RECOGNITION, 1865-1900. *Internat. R. of Social Hist. [Netherlands] 1968 13(3): 321-349.* Emancipation and passage of the 14th amendment did not assure Afro-Americans in New York State of unrestricted manhood suffrage before 1870. After the adoption of the 15th amendment they won full voting rights; however, they failed to build an effective position of political strength which would have helped them to promote social equality during the postbellum decades. They did not muster the kind of united political effort that would have been necessary to break Afro-American ideological ties with the Republican Party in order to exploit the opportunities for advantageous political action in the two-party system of New York State. Afro-Americans were outnumbered by whites, lacked experience and resources to support a strong organization of their own as well as an independent press, and constantly encountered de facto racism condoned by New York State's ineffectual laws. Based on published sources.

G. P. Blum

1464. Bovee, John R. "DOCTOR HUGUET": DONNELLY ON BEING BLACK. *Minnesota Hist. 1969 41(6): 286-294.* Analyzes *Doctor Huguet* (New York: Arno Press), a novel written in 1891 by Ignatius Donnelly (1831-1901), whose political career overshadowed his literary endeavors. Summarizes the plot and compares its concern for Negroes with similar sentiments that Donnelly expressed in Congress during Reconstruction. Although the novel had little literary merit, Donnelly effectively showed, through the experiences of a white man who became black, the horror of being a Negro in the South in the late 19th century. Donnelly improperly blamed carpetbaggers rather than southern planters for the Negroes' backwardness at emancipation and generally regarded Negroes as physically and intellectually inferior to whites. He nevertheless called for equal protection for Negroes under the law, abhorred white violence against Negroes, stressed brotherhood, and emphasized the value of nonviolence and political power as tools for Negroes to ameliorate oppressive conditions. Based on Donnelly's publications and personal papers, the *Congressional Globe,* and selected secondary sources; illus., 20 notes.

G. R. Adams

1465. Boyd, Willis Dolmond. NEGRO COLONIZATION IN THE RECONSTRUCTION ERA 1865-1870. *Georgia Hist. Q. 1956 40(4): 360-382.* Reviews the efforts made by the American Colonization Society immediately after the Civil War to interest the emancipated Negroes and government and private groups in furthering increased Negro emigration to Liberia as a long-term solution of the American race problem. The whites, however, regarded the society more with good-humored indulgence than as an organization capable of doing great harm or great good for the country, and the Negroes showed a singular lack of enthusiasm for moving to Africa. By 1870, the ambitious plans of the society were clearly doomed.

C. F. Latour

1466. Brewer, James H. EDITORIALS FROM THE DAMNED. *J. of Southern Hist. 1962 28(2): 225-233.* Despite the bitter climate of the disfranchisement era, Richmond's leading Negro newspaper conducted a militant crusade for preservation of equal rights. The editor and publisher of the Richmond *Planet* was John Mitchell, Jr., who had been a member of the city's common council for two years, an alderman for eight, and twice a delegate to national Republican conventions. In his attempt to stem the tide of reaction, the editor tended to indulge and cater to conservative Virginians, because he saw no likelihood of obtaining help from the northern liberals or the Federal Government. He expressed willingness to accept literacy tests, if they were applied equally against both races.

S. E. Humphreys

1467. Butcher, Philip. MARK TWAIN'S INSTALLMENT ON THE NATIONAL DEBT. *Southern Literary J. 1969 1(2): 48-55.* Though probably less "desouthernized" than William Dean Howells thought him to be, Twain nevertheless considered Negroes to be "people who had been wronged by his [Twain's] forebears and were still unjustly treated by his contemporaries." Among the ways in which Twain tried to make amends for his ancestors was his virtually anonymous assistance to black students, particularly to Warner Thornton McGuinn whom he helped through Yale Law School and who later had a distinguished legal career. For Twain, the McGuinn case was "an installment on what he regarded as both a personal and a national debt." Based on published sources, the Twain Papers, and letters to the author; 14 notes.   J. L. Colwell

1468. Caldwell, Dan. THE NEGROIZATION OF THE CHINESE STEREOTYPE IN CALIFORNIA. *Southern California Q. 1971 53(2): 123-131.* White Californians between 1848 and 1890 systematically converted their image of the Chinese in their midst into that of the Negro. This "negroization" process involved seeing the Chinese as possessing the same characteristics as Negroes, e.g., degraded, filthy, intellectually inferior. Using articles and cartoons from magazines of the period, shows the evolution of the Chinese stereotype to the point at which it took on all aspects of the "negroid" stereotype. Based on contemporary sources; 5 illus., 32 notes.   W. L. Bowers

1469. Chafe, William H. THE NEGRO AND POPULISM: A KANSAS CASE STUDY. *J. of Southern Hist. 1968 34(3): 402-419.* Seeking to explain why populism failed as a biracial movement, the author analyzes the "attitudes, aspirations, and concerns" of the Negro community in Kansas, and concludes that the Negro and white Populists actually did not share a common self-interest. Whereas whites were primarily concerned about economic issues, Negroes sought security against prejudice and violence as well as stability and status from the white community. This divergence of interest prompted Negroes to support the rich and wellborn white class that had traditionally befriended them. Thus, it is important "that historians concerned with Negro-white relations look at the Negro as an active participant instead of as a passive observer and recognize that the Negro's peculiar history and experience have given him a set of assumptions, perceptions, and interests which may be quite distinct from those of his white counterpart." 68 notes.   I. M. Leonard

1470. Chellis, Barbara A. THOSE EXTRAORDINARY TWINS: NEGROES AND WHITES. *Am. Q. 1969 21(1): 100-112.* Analyzes Mark Twain's farce entitled "Those Extraordinary Twins" and his novel *Pudd'nhead Wilson* (1894). A number of ambiguities appear in the work, but the protagonist becomes the spokesman for Twain's view of slavery and the human condition. Although Roxy allows her son to become a "white man" and unknowingly corrupts him, she eventually emerges as a heroine who has compassion for both those who suffered from the slave system and those who were demeaned by it. 13 notes.

R. S. Pickett

1471. Clancy, John J. A MUGWUMP ON MINORITIES. *J. of Negro Hist. 1966 51(3): 174-192.* Pictures Edwin L. Godkin, founder of the *Nation,* as a life-long admirer of English aristocratic ideals. Godkin viewed an America which he thought lacked a genteel tradition and stability. In his publication he opposed many American reform movements and held low opinions of Indians, Negroes, Irish Catholics, and immigrants who were not Anglo-Saxons. He supported Chinese exclusion, Radical Reconstruction, and Civil Service reform which he hoped would place a small minority of well-educated men in government jobs.

L. Gara

1472. Claude, Richard. CONSTITUTIONAL VOTING RIGHTS AND EARLY U.S. SUPREME COURT DOCTRINE. *J. of Negro Hist. 1966 51(2): 114-124.* Reviews some significant Supreme Court decisions on voting rights. Prior to 1884 the court tended to view the right to vote as State-derived rather than federally-derived, but in that year *Ex Parte Yarbrough* acknowledged the Constitution as the source. The decision also recognized the power of Congress to protect voters in congressional elections and contributed legal groundwork to the voting provisions in recent civil rights legislation.

L. Gara

1473. Cross, Joseph W. SEGREGATION IN REVERSE: ST. LOUIS, 1873. *J. of Negro Hist. 1969 54(2): 183-186.* Presents documents, written during the period 1870-73, which represent orders from the Roman Catholic Archdiocese of Saint Louis to the effect that certain churches in the area were to be used exclusively by Negroes, with whites completely excluded from the premises, except under rare mitigating circumstances. The documents consist of an extract of one letter from the Archbishop of St. Louis, full reproductions of a statement by Father Patrick John Ryan, a letter by Father I. Panken, and one endorsement by Father Joseph G. Zealand, President of Saint Louis University. 8 notes.

R. S. Melamed

1474. Cunningham, George E. CONSTITUTIONAL DISENFRANCHISE-MENT OF THE NEGRO IN LOUISIANA, 1898. *Negro Hist. Bull. 1966 29(7): 147-148, 158-160, 166.* Between 1888 and 1898 the Negro voter roll in Louisiana dropped from 128,150 to 12,902 as a result of violence, intimidation, and conspiratorial, fraudulent manipulation of suffrage laws. Aware of this, the 134 delegates who met in the Mechanics Institute building in New Orleans for the Louisiana Constitutional Convention of 1898 organized their convention not only to disenfranchise Negroes, but also to eliminate violence as a perpetual device to maintain white rule. By 1898, after disenfranchisement, the number of white voters increased from 74,133 to 125,437, while the number of Negro voters declined from 12,902 to 5,320. With the loss of the Negro vote, political power shifted to the whites in the predominantly political parishes. 7 notes.

D. D. Cameron

1475. Cunningham, George E. THE ITALIAN, A HINDRANCE TO WHITE SOLIDARITY IN LOUISIANA, 1890-1898. *J. of Negro Hist. 1965 50(1): 22-36.* In the 1890's Italian immigrants in Louisiana were not easily assimilated into the rest of the white population and on two separate occasions Italians, suspected of murder but not convicted by ordinary processes, were lynched by mobs. When the State tried to disfranchise Negroes through a proposed discriminatory suffrage amendment, Italians joined Populists to defeat the measure. In the constitutional convention of 1898 the political machine of New Orleans prevented Louisiana's grandfather clause from being applied to Italians in the State. Eventually Louisiana's Italians identified themselves with the older white residents and gradually gained acceptance by that method. Documented.   L. Gara

1476. Daniel, Pete. UP FROM SLAVERY AND DOWN TO PEONAGE: THE ALONZO BAILEY CASE. *J. of Am. Hist. 1970 57(3): 654-670.* From 1885 to 1907, the State of Alabama developed a contract labor law which stipulated that a laborer who received a monetary advance on a salary for a labor contract but left his job without repaying the money could be punished just as if he had stolen the money. Laws did not provide for the introduction of evidence from a defendant and the prosecution was not required to prove fraud. These omissions were widely regarded as an attempt to trap Negroes into debt peonage, and an effort was made to have the laws declared unconstitutional. Judge William Holcombe Thomas and other whites in Montgomery, Alabama, led the effort. Booker T. Washington took part, although his support was kept secret. Washington furnished important contacts in the North, including Theodore Roosevelt and the Justice Department. The U.S. Supreme Court overturned the law in *Bailey vs. Alabama* (1911). 89 notes.   K. B. West

1477. Daniel, W. Harrison. VIRGINIA BAPTISTS AND THE NEGRO, 1865-1902. *Virginia Mag. of Hist. and Biog. 1968 76(3): 340-363.* Virginia Baptists of the 1865-1902 period continued to believe that the Negro was the least competent of men and utterly unqualified for the franchise. The majority were dedicated to complete, but paternalistic, segregation and white supremacy despite numerous statements of concern for the Negro's spiritual and educational welfare. Based on church records and newspapers; 78 notes.   K. J. Bauer

1478. Dethloff, Henry C. THE ALLIANCE AND THE LOTTERY: FARMERS TRY FOR THE SWEEPSTAKES. *Louisiana Hist. 1965 6(2): 141-159.* In the election of 1892 the lottery issue involved an attempt to break the "money-monopoly," and to end machine control and fraud and corruption in government. It assumed that destruction of the lottery run by the Louisiana Lottery Company would restore "white supremacy," alleviate the lot of farmers, clear the path for progressive city government in New Orleans, and clear out of the State the last vestiges of Radical rule. The defeat of the lottery bill accomplished none of these things. It only increased urban and rural reform frustration and led to more violent revolts in 1896. 73 notes.   E. P. Stickney

1479. Dethloff, Henry C. and Jones, Robert R. RACE RELATIONS IN LOUISIANA, 1877-98. *Louisiana Hist. 1968 9(4): 301-323.* The authors survey the historical literature on the Negro in Southern States during the post-Reconstruction period, noting the dearth of such study on Louisiana. The Negro in Louisiana during this period enjoyed neither social nor political equality with whites, and he was subject to violence, discrimination, economic coercion, and political trickery. Nevertheless, he possessed greater political, social, and civil rights before 1898 than at anytime thereafter until the1950's. Negroes were also active in the organized labor movement in this period. Jim Crow legislation and practices began in the 1890's, climaxing in the Constitutional Convention of 1898. Based on newspapers, published records, secondary sources, and MSS in libraries of the University of Southwestern Louisiana, Tulane University, and Louisiana State University; 97 notes.   R. L. Woodward

1480. Dykstra, Robert R. and Hahn, Harlan. NORTHERN VOTERS AND NEGRO SUFFRAGE: THE CASE OF IOWA, 1868. *Public Opinion Q. 1968 32(2): 202-215.* Examine the Negro suffrage question in Iowa in 1868 when 66.5 percent of the voters approved the issue after rejecting it by a margin of 85.4 percent in 1857. Extension of the franchise was a frequent referendum issue in the 1860's, because State legislators were reluctant to decide such a burning political issue themselves. Since Iowa was the only State in 1868 (a presidential election year representing a peak time for voting on Negro suffrage) to adopt franchise extension by means of a single, uncomplicated referendum, the authors select Iowa for study to illuminate postwar popular attitudes toward Negro rights in the North. An analysis of county and township election returns and census reports shows a strong correlation between voting for the Republican candidate for President (Grant) and voting for Negro suffrage. Rural workers in prosperous areas who had least to fear from economic displacement voted for Negro suffrage. Immigrants, who were usually Democrats and who, as common laborers, felt their jobs threatened by Negroes, voted against Negro suffrage in Iowa. 4 tables, 37 notes.   D. J. Trickey

1481. Erickson, Leonard. TOLEDO DESEGREGATES, 1871. *Northwest Ohio Q. 1968/69 41(1): 5-12.* Negro schools were made possible in Ohio by a law of 1849, but the Negro school in Toledo was quite inadequate. The move to desegregate schools in Toledo developed into a two-phase fight: the first phase began in April 1869 and ended with no progress toward desegregation; the second phase began in January 1871 with a court case instituted by a Negro who said his daughter was physically unable to walk to the Negro school. The matter was settled in June when the school board voted to desegregate Toledo's schools. Contemporary observers said the action came in response to an expression of popular will at the school board election in 1871. Popular opinion was not clearly expressed in 1871, but it undoubtedly played a role. Conscience, economic good sense, and a desire to end another relic of slavery probably also helped to end segregation in schools. Based on monographs, articles, newspapers, State and local laws, and educational records; 46 notes.   W. F. Zornow

1482. Fertig, Walter L. MAURICE THOMPSON AS A SPOKESMAN FOR THE NEW SOUTH. *Indiana Mag. of Hist. 1964 60(4): 323-330.* Considers the efforts of a minor writer of the post-Civil War period to effect a reconciliation of North-South differences in his literary work. Born in Indiana, transplanted southerner during the war, resident of Hoosierland in postwar years, Maurice Thompson revealed in his public writings attitudes toward the Negro and the "Lost Cause" which coincided with dominant southern feelings and underscored the need for understanding and acceptance of the South's actions in the war. Expresses the feeling among northern writers late in the 19th century of the need to end divisions between the sections by accommodating more nearly to prevailing southern attitudes.   J. Findlay

1483. Fischer, Roger A. A PIONEER PROTEST: THE NEW ORLEANS STREET-CAR CONTROVERSY OF 1867. *J. of Negro Hist. 1968 53(3): 219-233.* New Orleans streetcars continued to practice racial segregation immediately following the Civil War just as they had in the period prior to the conflict. Negro demands that discrimination in the cars cease met with opposition from the streetcar companies and from white passengers. However, demonstrations and reaction which brought the city to the brink of race war finally resulted in an official end to the policy of segregation in 1867. In 1902, segregation in the New Orleans cars was again introduced by State law.   L. Gara

1484. Fishel, Leslie H. THE GENESIS OF THE FIRST WISCONSIN CIVIL RIGHTS ACT. *Wisconsin Mag. of Hist. 1966 49(4): 324-333.* After an introduction depicting the state of civil rights for Negroes in the North, particularly in Wisconsin, the author enumerates events leading up to the passage of the Civil Rights Act (1895) and mentions some of its consequences. Describes the part played by legislators, judges, the press, and Wisconsin Negroes, emphasizing Judge Daniel Johnson and William T. Green. 3 photos, 31 notes.
                                                              H. A. Negaard

1485. Fisher, John E. ATTICUS HAYGOOD AND NATIONAL UNITY. *Georgia Hist. Q. 1966 50(2): 113-125.* Surveys and documents the efforts of Atticus Haygood, Bishop of the Methodist Episcopal Church, South, in 1865-96, to promote national unity, racial equality, and amity, especially among white people in the South.   R. Lowitt

1486. Fowler, Wilton B. A CARPETBAGGER'S CONVERSION TO WHITE SUPREMACY. *North Carolina Hist. R. 1966 43(3): 286-304.* One of the leading carpetbag politicians of South Carolina was Daniel Henry Chamberlain, a New Englander who was an officer in a predominantly Negro regiment and moved to the South after the Civil War. He served as South Carolina's attorney general from 1868 to 1872 and as Republican Governor of the State from 1874 to 1877, losing his office as a result of the Compromise of 1877. In South Carolina, Chamberlain was a strong supporter of Negro rights, but he later became a white supremacist, a result of his conversion to states' rights, laissez-faire, and evolution. By 1896, liberty meant the right to save oneself from the rising tide of equality. Chamberlain justified white supremacy by arguing that, in evolutionary terms, the Negro obviously belonged to a lower and inferior social order. 69 notes.
                                                              J. M. Bumsted

1487. Franklin, John Hope. JIM CROW GOES TO SCHOOL: THE GENESIS OF LEGAL SEGREGATION IN SOUTHERN SCHOOLS. *South Atlantic Q. 1959 58(2): 225-235.* Describes the development of segregation in the 19th century. The author notes that in the pre-Civil War North, segregation existed in militias and schools. He contends that the roots of segregation are in the concept of Negro inferiority, held even by the opponents of slavery, and that segregation first existed in those places which had abolished slavery because segregation was not necessary for "race discipline" where slavery existed. Most schools established by the Freedmen's Bureau were segregated. Segregation was pushed at various times during Reconstruction by different groups: "the Southern white irreconcilables, the Negroes who wanted an education more than they wanted integration," Radicals who saw in segregation an extension of northern practices, and foundations such as the Peabody Fund, which used its grants to push segregation and denied them to States which integrated schools.   C. R. Allen, Jr.

1488. Gaston, Paul M. THE "NEW SOUTH." *Writing Southern Hist.: Essays in Historiography in Honor of Fletcher M. Green (Baton Rouge: Louisiana State U. Press, 1965); 316-336.* Here the term "New South" is used to describe: 1) the ideology worked out by means of the post-Reconstruction years, and 2) the "point of view of historians of a later period whose interpretations reflected the ideas of the original New South crusaders." A New South creed emphasized the concept of the triumph over adversity. A characteristic representative of the New South school, Paul Herman Buck, developed the theme of national reconciliation. The new historians found that "one-partyism, white supremacy, patriotism, morality in government, and the industrial revolution were all part of one pattern." In 1951, C. Vann Woodward revealed a politics of class and interest that exploited race and tradition to maintain its hold over the region; the reality of this revisionist version was "low wages, lack of opportunity, and poverty." 73 biblio. notes.
E. P. Stickney

1489. Gatell, Frank Otto, ed. THE SLAVEHOLDER AND THE ABOLITIONIST: BINDING UP A FAMILY'S WOUNDS. *J. of Southern Hist. 1961 27(3): 368-391.* Series of letters exchanged between two brothers, John Gorham Palfrey (1796-1881), Massachusetts Unitarian minister, editor, historian, and Free Soil politician, and William Taylor Palfrey (1800-68), Louisiana planter and Congressman, between the end of the Civil War and the Louisianian's death, in which the family's wounds were still apparent, but in which the healing process was well under way.   S. E. Humphreys

1490. Gatewood, Willard B. KANSAS NEGROES AND THE SPANISH-AMERICAN WAR. *Kansas Hist. Q. 1971 37(3): 300-313.* The war with Spain came just as Kansas Negroes faced an uncertain future, but the war seemed to offer some hope that it might lead to better times. Negroes joined the 23d Kansas, an all-black regiment, with expectation that the imperial venture might improve their economic position and demonstrate their willingness to be valuable citizens. The results were far from encouraging; the blacks did not improve their position but learned only that this "is a world of deception." Some Negroes appreciated the new empire as a possible refuge from the oppressive atmosphere at home.

Perhaps such a possibility offered the only hope of Negroes to share in the fruits of imperialism. The deteriorating status of blacks in America prompted many schemes for emigration, and probably in no other State did such projects elicit more discussion among Negroes than in Kansas. Based on secondary sources; illus., 66 notes.   W. F. Zornow

1491. Gatewood, Willard B., Jr. NEGRO TROOPS IN FLORIDA, 1898. *Florida Hist. Q. 1970 49(1): 1-15.* The Spanish-American War (1898) brought mixed reactions among Negro Americans. Some enthusiastically supported the war effort: those who saw the black man's participation in the war as a chance to raise his status at home, and those who thought the opening of Cuba and the Philippines to American influence an economic opportunity for Negroes. A highly vocal anti-imperialist element of black citizens, however, envisioned little chance of improvement in a transfer from Spanish to American rule, in view of the lynchings, disfranchisement, and segregation in the United States. The majority of Negroes took neither stand, but simply considered military service an obligation of citizenship. The Jim Crowism encountered by the Negro troops in Florida on the trip to and from Cuba belied the prediction that their war record would justify their title to all citizenship privileges. The Negro soldiers were inclined to defy regional race customs and discrimination. This was called disturbance of peaceful race relations, and became justification for lynching Negroes. The stationing of so large a contingent of Negro soldiers in the South, therefore, helped to end any remaining internal resistance to racism. Based partly on regimental records, National Archives; 56 notes.   R. V. Calvert

1492. Gianakos, Perry E. THE SPANISH AMERICAN WAR AND THE DOUBLE PARADOX OF THE NEGRO AMERICAN. *Phylon 1965 26(1): 34-49.* Notes two paradoxes in the relationship of the Spanish-American War to the position of American Negroes. "On the one hand, there was a widespread sympathy for down-trodden peoples abroad (the Cubans, in this instance); but on the other hand, while there was sympathy for the white, down-trodden farmers, Populists and workers at home, there was a noticeable lack of sympathy for the down-trodden peoples of color at home." Yet in the popular literature of the war "the image of the Negro is almost universally favorable; while sympathy may have been denied him at home, it was not denied him while serving his country abroad." Documented by quotations from published literature of the period.
                                                                         S. C. Pearson, Jr.

1493. Gravely, William B. HIRAM REVELS PROTESTS RACIAL SEPARATION IN THE METHODIST EPISCOPAL CHURCH. *Methodist Hist. 1970 8(3): 13-20.* A reprint of a letter (from Hiram Rhoades Revels, Negro Methodist preacher and U.S. Senator from Mississippi, 1870-71) first published in *The Southwestern Advocate* (New Orleans) on 4 May 1876. In the letter Revels (1822-1901) argued against separating the Methodist Episcopal Church by color. The author provides background data on Revels' life and on the attitudes of the church on separation into black and white conferences. 19 notes.
                                                                         H. L. Calkin

1494. Graves, John William. THE ARKANSAS SEPARATE COACH LAW OF 1891. *J. of the West 1968 7(4): 531-541.* Uses the example of the Arkansas Separate Coach Law to demonstrate that many of the segregation laws and practices grew up in the late 19th century. It is suggested that the political pressures brought about by the depression of 1888 as well as other economic factors were largely responsible for the upsurge in segregation laws. The passage of this law saw the beginning of the polarization of the races in Arkansas.

R. N. Alvis

1495. Gross, Theodore L. THOMAS NELSON PAGE: CREATOR OF A VIRGINIA CLASSIC. *Georgia R. 1966 20(3): 338-351.* Reviews the work of Page, a southern writer. His "evocation of life in Virginia before the war still remains as a standard of its kind." Discusses several stories published in *In Ole Virginia* (1887), especially "Marse Chan." Page found that "he was in effect a leader of the whole Southern school of local color fiction." *In Ole Virginia* was "preeminently the Virginia classic." The Negro narrator is often, however, the only credible character, the white gentlemen and ladies being too idealized. "A leading Southerner in Washington society during the 1890's," Page was Ambassador to Italy, 1913-19. Page was well received by critics, although in 1907 one report claimed that "the South has outgrown Mr. Page." T. M. Condon

1496. Haller, John S. CIVIL WAR ANTHROPOMETRY: THE MAKING OF A RACIAL IDEOLOGY. *Civil War Hist. 1970 16(4): 309-324.* Analyzes the impact of Civil War anthropometry on postwar racial attitudes. The major wartime studies of the physical dimensions of black troops compared to white troops became the basis for various "scientific" theories of black physical and mental inferiority which flourished for several generations. Although the Civil War gave the slaves their freedom, it also supplied anthropometric justification for keeping them "in their place" when they were supposedly free. Based on primary and secondary sources. E. C. Murdock

1497. Haywood, Charles. NEGRO MINSTRELSY AND SHAKESPEAREAN BURLESQUE. *Folklore and Soc.: Essays in Honor of Benjamin A. Botkin (Hatboro, Pennsylvania: Folklore Associates, Inc., 1966): 77-92.* A discussion of the development of theatrical Negro stereotypes beginning with "Jim Crow" created by Thomas Dartmouth Rice of the Southern Theatre in Louisville, Kentucky, in 1828. Such other characters as "Zip Coon," "Dandy," and the "Broadway Swell" became the typical Negroes in the minstrel shows of the 19th century. From 1850 to 1870 Shakespeare enjoyed great popularity on the American stage, and his plays "offered the minstrelmen rare opportunities for 'hilarious parody and uproarious delineating.'" Thus, the American audience saw the Negro as a theatrical comic personality. 31 notes. J. C. Crowe

1498. Hixon, William B., Jr. MOORFIELD STOREY AND THE STRUGGLE FOR EQUALITY. *J. of Am. Hist. 1968 55(3): 533-554.* Storey, one of the cofounders of the National Association for the Advancement of Colored People, based his championship of Negro rights on the concept of "equality before the law," a concept associated with Charles Sumner. As a young man, Storey had served as a secretary to Sumner and the relations between the two men had been quite friendly. However, for three decades after leaving Sumner, Storey was a Mugwump crusading for clean government, low tariff, and anti-imperialism. His defense of the Negro was most pronounced in the period 1899-1900 as a result of his opposition to racist arguments employed in the decision to annex the Philippines. As legal council for the NAACP he successfully attacked the Oklahoma "grandfather clause," the "all-white primaries of a one-party South," and municipal residential segregation ordinances. In addition, he wrote letters, speeches, and articles attacking the concept of Negro inferiority and defending the Negro's role in Reconstruction. Based partly on unpublished Storey letters; 89 notes.   K. B. West

1499. Jager, Ronald B. CHARLES SUMNER, THE CONSTITUTION, AND THE CIVIL RIGHTS ACT OF 1875. *New England Q. 1969 42(3): 350-372.* In his defense of the constitutionality of civil rights legislation, Sumner (1811-74) emphasized the social desirability and necessity of such legislation, understating common law precedents and legal logic. The law needed to take into account a new force of black people with the vote, whose rights needed protection. Although the Supreme Court was to declare the Civil Rights Act of 1875 unconstitutional in 1883, Sumner in 1874 had reason to believe that the 14th amendment was intended to protect people against abuses by individuals as well as by States, and that the civil rights bill could stand a constitutional test. In his emphasis on the need for legislation to reflect changing social needs, Sumner anticipated the legal opinions of Justice Louis Dembitz Brandeis and the Supreme Court ruling in *Brown vs. Board of Education of Topeka* (1954). 90 notes.

K. B. West

1500. James, Parthena Louise. THE WHITE THREAT IN THE CHICKASAW NATION. *Chronicles of Oklahoma 1968 46(1): 73-85.* After 1871, the influx of whites into the Chickasaw Nation in Oklahoma posed a threat. Civil War veterans leased land from the Chickasaw or hired themselves out to the Indians as laborers. As with the emancipated Negroes in their midst, the whites as citizens were not subject to the jurisdiction of the Indians. The Chickasaw were fearful of the time when they might be outnumbered. Their one hope, they believed, was allotment of their lands to individuals. Legal technicalities prevented this in the 1870's. 70 notes.   D. L. Smith

1501. Jones, Alan. THOMAS M. COOLEY AND THE INTERSTATE COMMERCE COMMISSION: CONTINUITY AND CHANGE IN THE DOCTRINE OF EQUAL RIGHTS. *Pol. Sci. Q. 1966 81(4): 602-627.* Analyzes the development of the attitudes of Thomas McIntyre Cooley, "whose 1887 appointment to the Interstate Commerce Commission gave dignity and distinction to the inception of federal regulatory action." He wrestled with the varying implications of the doctrine of equal rights dealing with the danger of corporate power, with the balance of public interest and private rights, with the relationship of property rights to the police power of the State, and with the respective roles of courts, legislatures, and administrative agencies. During the four years he served the ICC, Cooley applied the equal rights philosophy stated in his *Treatise on Consti-*

tutional Limitations (1868) in cases ranging from discrimination favoring the Standard Oil Company to discrimination against Negroes by offering them inferior accommodations. Cooley sought to broaden the powers of the ICC and to develop the meaning of the Interstate Commerce Act by applying public education, administrative interpretation, and statistical analysis to the American railroad problem, and by urging the "due process of law" did not of necessity imply judicial process. During these years the Federal courts began to stifle the process of developing regulation by commission. Cooley's attitudes, well-meaning and democratic as they were, reflected the basic ambiguities inherent in the American doctrine of equal rights. Yet he deserves credit for also illustrating the adaptability of the doctrine to the changing times. He believed in the future rather than the past, in defense of the public interest rather than the protection of private right, and in the ideal of more humane equality in preference to unfettered liberty. Based on the Thomas M. Cooley Papers, manuscripts in the historical collections and the law library, University of Michigan, and on published material.

Sr. M. McAuley

1502. Kahn, Maxine Baker. CONGRESSMAN ASHLEY IN THE POST-CIVIL WAR YEARS. *Northwest Ohio Q. 1964 36(3): 116-133, (4): 194-210.* Part I. John Ashley was associated with the antislavery movement in Ohio before the Civil War. As a member of Congress during the war he played a particularly important role. In 1862 he introduced a bill to abolish slavery in the District of Columbia, and during the following year he introduced the 13th amendment. An effort is made to show that Ashley was largely responsible for the amendment, since it seemed to be a logical outgrowth of his earlier proposal to abolish slavery in Washington. Based on newspapers, government documents, and biographies. Part II. Ashley delivered a series of speeches throughout the West shortly after the Civil War ended. He bore down on the need to enfranchise the Negroes, by arguing that the few trustworthy whites in the South needed help from every possible source, if they were to reconstruct their States. Ashley became a greater champion of Negro suffrage in 1866 and made it the key issue in his campaign for reelection that year. His campaign is described in detail. Ashley again spoke of Negro suffrage after his reelection, but he soon became diverted by the efforts to impeach the president. Based on local newspaper accounts, biographies, and government documents.

W. F. Zornow

1503. Kaplan, Sidney. ALBION W. TOURGEE: ATTORNEY FOR THE SEGREGATED. *J. of Negro Hist. 1964 49(2): 128-133.* Discusses the role of Albion W. Tourgée, author of the Reconstruction novel *A Fool's Errand* (1879), as attorney for Homer A. Plessy, whose refusal to accept racial segregation resulted in the Supreme Court decision *Plessy vs. Ferguson,* giving the court's approval to the separate but equal doctrine. Justice John M. Harlan dissented and a number of his ideas were borrowed from Tourgée's arguments. Tourgée insisted that equality was in accord with the Declaration of Independence, and that the Louisiana segregation law was a kind of class legislation pinning a badge of servitude and inferiority on the Negro. Tourgée's arguments were unacceptable to the majority of the court in 1896 but provided the basis for the court's rejection of the separate but equal doctrine more than half a century later.

L. Gara

1504. Kelley, Robert. THE THOUGHT AND CHARACTER OF SAMUEL J. TILDEN: THE DEMOCRAT AS INHERITOR. *Historian 1964 26(2): 176-205.* Analyzes Tilden as a Jacksonian thinker, traces possible influences - both psychological and sociological - and shows the evolution of his liberalism through the Civil War period to his presidential campaign of 1876. Key points are his obsession with corruption as produced by Whig-Republican concepts of business-government linkage; anti-Negro prejudice and Darwinist racism; and economic ideas. Naturalism and statistics permeated his world view. Documented from published sources and from the Tilden Papers, Manuscript Division, New York Public Library.   A

1505. Kenneally, James J. WOMAN SUFFRAGE AND THE MASSACHU-SETTS "REFERENDUM" OF 1895. *Historian 1968 30(4): 617-633.* After the Civil War, feminists believed that women's rights would march hand in hand with Negro freedom because the objectives of each group rested on the common denominator of equality before the law without distinction as to sex or color. When the 14th amendment proved to contain the word "male," movements were founded to secure votes for women in State elections. The author tells of suffrage agitation in Massachusetts, culminating in a referendum on the question, the only one in a large Eastern State before 1915. Based on newspapers and the papers of various Massachusetts suffrage organizations held in the Houghton Library at Harvard University and the Massachusetts Historical Society in Boston.
                                                                       N. W. Moen

1506. Lesourd, Jean-Alain. LA QUESTION NOIRE AUX ETATS-UNIS DE 1860 A 1914 [The Negro question in the United States from 1860 to 1914]. *Information Historique [France] 1960 22(4): 159-162.* A summary of the main facts of Negro history from the Civil War to World War I, based on writings of Franklin Frazier, Rayford Logan, C. Vann Woodward, Alain Locke, W. E. B. Du Bois, Margaret Butcher, and Frank Schoell.   G. Iggers

1507. Lopez, Claira S. JAMES K. VARDAMAN AND THE NEGRO: THE FOUNDATION OF MISSISSIPPI'S RACIAL POLICY. *Southern Q. 1965 3(2): 155-180.* Although primarily concerned with the welfare of the whites, James Vardaman used the issue of race to his political advantage and as governor of Mississippi initiated a number of "progressive" reforms. He believed the Negro was inferior and thus should be placed in subservience to the white man. This attitude carried no hate with it, however, and he instituted no program against the Negro. His writings and speeches crystallized Mississippi views on race. The author has made extensive use of the files of the Jackson, Mississippi, *Weekly Clarion Ledger.*   D. A. Stokes

1508. Mandel, Bernard. SAMUEL GOMPERS AND THE NEGRO WORK-ERS, 1886-1914. *J. of Negro Hist. 1955 40(1): 34-60.* Describes the evolution of Gompers' views on the Negro question which illustrates his transition from a militant labor agitator to a conservative bureaucrat. He began with a relatively advanced attitude toward Negro workers, advocating their free admission to the unions. Under the pressure of opposition from union leaders he retreated to a policy of "Jim-Crowism." Based on Gompers' correspondence in the American Federation of Labor archives and published sources.   S

1509. Mcpherson, James M. ABOLITIONISTS AND THE CIVIL RIGHTS ACT OF 1875. *J. of Am. Hist. 1965 52(3): 493-510.* Describes the work of the abolitionists as early as 1863 to incorporate the Negro's freedom and equal rights into the law of the land. The Civil Rights Act of 1875 was the culmination of their efforts, but their high hopes for racial justice were betrayed by the moral indifference and political sordidness of the post-Civil War era. The author concludes that the Civil Rights Act was doomed to impotence from the outset and it had become unenforceable even before the Supreme Court declared it unconstitutional in 1883.   H. J. Silverman

1510. Moore, Jack B. IMAGES OF THE NEGRO IN EARLY AMERICAN SHORT FICTION. *Mississippi Q. 1969 22(1): 47-57.* Without popular civil rights pressure, early American short fiction writers were dramatizing Negro problems. Their image of the Negro determined generally by a hatred of slavery, mostly anonymous but probably eastern writers employed a sentimental style in presenting the Negro as an attractive, decent human being with a soul. Neither professionals nor artists, these early writers produced no masterpieces while attacking slavery vigorously, and they occasionally distorted reality. A dignified, human image of a recognizably oppressed group in American society evolved in one decade. Based on periodicals of the 1790's; 2 notes.   R. V. Calvert

1511. Morrison, Joseph L. MAIN CURRENTS IN "BRANN'S ICONO-CLAST." *Journalism Q. 1963 40(2): 219-227.* William Cooper Brann (1855-98) within three years attracted a nationwide circulation of 100,000 for a personal publication of harangue and vituperation. The author finds that humor was a characteristic and primary part of his writing, though he deprecated humor; he excelled in ridicule and wrote numerous effective parodies of Old Testament stories. He showed religious tolerance, but at the same time castigated religion. He was completely irrational toward Negroes. He attacked newspapers, their publishers, and their society pages. He took a dark view of the American economic system and of politics and politicians. He was puritanic in morals, but no respecter of persons. Based on an analysis of Brann's writings.

S. E. Humphreys

1512. Norris, Marjorie M. AN EARLY INSTANCE OF NONVIOLENCE: THE LOUISVILLE DEMONSTRATIONS OF 1870-71. *J. of Southern Hist. 1965 32(4): 488-504.* "Ride-ins" conducted without violence by Negroes on Louisville streetcars 30 October 1870 and 11-13 May 1871 were buttressed by a Federal District Court decision and finally resulted in intervention by the city's mayor. They brought integration permanently on the city's transportation lines and helped develop among the Negroes an early faith in moral resistance doctrines. 74 notes.   S. E. Humphreys

1513. Owens, Harry P. THE EUFAULA RIOT OF 1874. *Alabama R. 1963 16(3): 224-238.* Relations between Negroes and whites had deteriorated rapidly between 1870 and 1874 in Eufaula, Alabama. The first open violence occurred during a local election in February, 1874. During the general election in October, a full-scale riot, involving an undetermined number of whites and approximately 1500 Negroes left 75 men wounded, 12 of whom were whites. The Negroes left town and made no effort to return to the polls. The riots at Eufaula and nearby Spring Hill, where a number of ballots were destroyed, gave the election to the Democrats. The Barbour County grand jury and a national congressional committee investigated the riots, the former absolving the whites, the latter exonerating the Negroes. D. F. Henderson

1514. Palmer, Paul C. MISCEGENATION AS AN ISSUE IN THE ARKANSAS CONSTITUTIONAL CONVENTION OF 1868. *Arkansas Hist. Q. 1965 24(2): 99-126.* The debate over possible constitutional prohibition against mixed marriages permitted delegates to vent their prejudices before adoption of a compromise which opposed "all amalgamation" but left to the State assembly enactment of a law to govern the problem. Based primarily on the debates of the convention. P. M. McCain

1515. Peek, Ralph L. LAWLESSNESS IN FLORIDA, 1868-1871. *Florida Hist. Q. 1961 40(2): 164-185.* In their desperate attempt to regain control of local and State government in Florida following the Civil War, the white people resorted to such widespread violence that 153 people - mostly Negroes and whites who supported Negroes - were killed in Jackson County alone. Based on contemporary newspapers, reports of the U.S. Congress, publications of the Freedmen's Bureau, and secondary works. G. L. Lycan

1516. Peoples, Morgan D. "KANSAS FEVER" IN NORTH LOUISIANA. *Louisiana Hist. 1970 11(2): 121-135.* A short, but lively, migration of freed Negroes from the lower Mississippi Valley to Kansas occurred in 1879-80. A U.S. Senate committee investigated the mass immigration, but its conclusions simply reflected party-line positions. The Democrats blamed Republicans for luring the Negroes to States where they were fighting for continuance of Republican strength. The Republicans accused southern white Democrats of imposing intolerable hardships upon the freedmen, forcing them to flee. The reasons for the exodus were several: blacks were ill treated, although their condition was better than in much of the rest of the South; white political domination had been achieved in 1878 by much terrorism of the blacks; a yellow fever epidemic in 1878 had added to the turmoil; blacks complained of sexual outrages against their women by the whites; educational facilities for the blacks were nonexistent or inadequate; and propaganda encouraging the immigration was effective in Louisiana, sponsored by civil rights groups, the railroads, and Kansas land interests. Negroes found Kansas as difficult as the South, and no more than a third of the immigrants remained there. A majority of those leaving returned to their old homes in the lower Mississippi Valley. Based principally on *Senate Reports* and Louisiana newspapers; 6 photos, 72 notes. R. L. Woodward

Reconstruction & Its Aftermath

1517. Pettit, Arthur G. MARK TWAIN AND THE NEGRO, 1867-1869. *J. of Negro Hist. 1971 56(2): 88-96.* Samuel Langhorne Clemens had two distinct personalities: that exhibited in his writings as Mark Twain, and that found in his private life. During 1867-69, Clemens began to alter his public references to Negroes. After 1867, for instance, he never used the word "nigger" in his public writing without quotation marks - except for his *Huckleberry Finn* stories, in which the author was not the narrator. Much of Clemens' deletion of unfavorable references on race were due to outside pressures; he wished to sell his books to northern Yankees, and he courted favor from the Stalwart faction of the Republican Party. In private, though, he remained an unreconstructed southerner when it came to referring to Negroes. Based on Clemens' private letters and public writing; 18 notes.   R. S. Melamed

1518. Pettit, Arthur G. MARK TWAIN'S ATTITUDE TOWARD THE NEGRO IN THE WEST, 1861-1867. *Western Hist. Q. 1970 1(1): 51-62.* The climax of Samuel Langhorne Clemens' personal race prejudice occurred during the years 1861-67 when he was in Nevada, California, and Hawaii. Also, in these years he assumed Mark Twain as his nom de plume as "white spokesman for the foolish, half-witted, slaphappy 'darky' of longstanding minstrel tradition." His racist views can be traced at least as far back as his boyhood apprenticeship to his hometown newspaper. When he went to Nevada in 1861 he found it expedient to become a "Unionized Southerner," but he did not feel compelled to change his convictions about blacks. Although a piece which he composed for a Virginia City paper while drunk showed his true feelings and forced him to flee from California, he continued to use the press as an outlet for his views. When he went to Hawaii as correspondent for a Sacramento paper, he referred to the natives as "niggers." Clemens' western experience reveals the distance he had yet to travel before he became basically liberal in his attitudes about blacks. Returning to the East in 1867, he began to evaluate his extreme feelings and soon launched a new career of liberal lip service to blacks. Most, but not all, of his violent prejudice was left behind in the West. 19 notes.   D. L. Smith

1519. Phillips, James R. PHILLIPS BROOKS: SPOKESMAN FOR FREEDOM. *Negro Hist. Bull. 1963 27(1): 10.* A brief note on Phillips Brooks (1835-93) as a spokesman for abolishing slavery and later for opposing race prejudice and granting freedmen and other Negroes full legal and social equality.
L. Gara

1520. Pollack, Norman. IGNATIUS DONNELLY ON HUMAN RIGHTS: A STUDY OF TWO NOVELS. *Mid-Am. 1965 47(2): 99-112.* Donnelly's novels *Doctor Huguet* (1891) and *The Golden Bottle* (1892) testify that he had a dream not of the denial but of the affirmation of man, whether Negro or white, Christian or Jew; not a society based on authoritarian principles but its very opposite, the realization of human dignity and human rights.   L. D. Silveri

1521. Rubin, Louis D. SOUTHERN LOCAL COLOR AND THE BLACK MAN. *Southern R. 1970 6(4): 1011-1030.* Compares major white, 19th-century southern authors and their respective attitudes toward the role of the black man in regional literature. Notes changing status patterns and interpretations and the modification of southern racial concepts. Concludes that a writer can more easily transcend the social barriers created by his environment, enabling himself to champion the cause of all social underdogs and to finally portray the Negro as a human being possessing dignity and equal worth.   R. W. Dubay

1522. Rubin, Louis D., Jr. THE DIVISION OF THE HEART: CABLE'S "THE GRANDISSIMES." *Southern Literary J. 1969 1(2): 27-47.* "The Grandissimes [1880], George W. Cable's best novel, a work of social observation of Southern society unsurpassed in its time, and the first novel by a Southerner to deal seriously with the relationships of white and Negro, remains even so a deeply flawed work." In support of this view, the author asserts that its hero, Frowenfeld, represents too well Cable's own emotional succumbing to the attractions of Louisiana's Creole society, while remaining intellectually a social critic far in advance of his time who campaigned heroically but futilely to awaken the Nation to the South's denial of the freedmen's civil rights and humanity. "He never brought the two impulses together, never attempted to realize and to delineate the contradictions and cruxes involved in their presence within a single sensibility, his own."   J. L. Colwell

1523. Rudwick, Elliott M. and Meier, August. BLACK MAN IN THE "WHITE CITY": NEGROES AND THE COLUMBIA EXPOSITION, 1893. *Phylon 1965 26(4): 354-361.* Traces the restricted role of the Negro in the World's Columbian Exposition from his exclusion from the commission planning the fair and from the Board of Lady Managers to the scarcity of Negro exhibits and the declaration of a Jim Crow day. Frederick Douglass was the featured speaker on Colored Jubilee Day and "made it crystal-clear that for Negroes the fair symbolized not the material progress of America, but a moral regression - the reconciliation of the North and South at the expense of Negroes."   S. C. Pearson, Jr.

1524. Sanders, Albert N. JIM CROW COMES TO SOUTH CAROLINA. *Pro. of the South Carolina Hist. Assoc. 1966: 27-39.* Traces the development of the Jim Crow laws in South Carolina, concentrating on the relative lateness of their passage and the reasons for them. Between 1876 and 1898, the so-called Hamptonite solution was in effect, appointing Negroes to office, allowing them to vote and cooperating with them generally in return for their support. The situation changed when Benjamin Ryan Tillman started his rise to power in the late 1880's. The key fight over Jim Crow legislation ended in 1898 with the passage of a law requiring the railroads in South Carolina to provide separate coaches for each race on passenger trains. The author concludes that by 1917 Jim Crow laws were generally accepted in South Carolina. Based on primary and secondary material; 82 notes.   J. W. Thacker, Jr.

1525. Saunders, Robert. SOUTHERN POPULISTS AND THE NEGRO 1893-1895. *J. of Negro Hist. 1969 54(3): 240-261.* The Populists maintained token Negro participation in their top party machinery but had little black influence on the local level in the South. Only in Virginia was any black grass roots campaign attempted, but even there it was stillborn. No evidence exists of Negro attendance at State or local Populist conventions except in the heavily black-populated South after 1892, and even there it was done on an "at large" basis rather than by assigning black delegates to particular districts for fear of being attacked by the Democrats as a "Negro dominated party." The State Populist Party platforms occasionally had planks of interest to Negroes, on election laws, on the convict lease system, and on schools, but only the Georgia Populists mentioned all these subjects at the same time. The Populists never seriously questioned the issue of fraudulent elections involving restriction of Negro suffrage, and thus threw away any chance of achieving power with the aid of black voters. 69 notes.   R. S. Melamed

1526. Simms, L. Moody, Jr. A NOTE ON SIDNEY LANIER'S ATTITUDE TOWARD THE NEGRO AND TOWARD POPULISM. *Georgia Hist. Q. 1968 52(3): 305-307.* Traces the southern Populist attitude toward the Negro to an essay by Sidney Lanier entitled "The New South." Published in 1880, this essay advocated that the political unity of the small farmers of the South, black and white alike, was more important than maintaining the tradition of racial antagonism. By the 1890's, southern Populists, especially Tom Watson, successfully promoted these same ideas. 9 notes.   R. A. Mohl

1527. Simms, L. Moody, Jr. CHARLES FRANCIS ADAMS, JR. AND THE NEGRO QUESTION. *New England Q. 1968 41(3): 436-438.* By 1900, Adams was depicted as a man who had repudiated his earlier idealism on behalf of the Negro and, under the influence of his study of the works of Charles Darwin, had concluded that the Negro was inferior to the white man in the qualities of individuality and self-reliance that were necessary for him to succeed in white America. Having been guaranteed the rights of citizenship by the Federal Government, Negroes should expect no favors, but should work out their own destiny. Based on Adams' writings; 9 notes.   K. B. West

1528. Simms, L. Moody, Jr. THOMAS UNDERWOOD DUDLEY: A FORGOTTEN VOICE OF DISSENT. *Mississippi Q. 1967 20(4): 217-223.* Thomas Underwood Dudley, Episcopal bishop of Kentucky, was one of a small group of late 19th-century southerners who dissented from the majority view that the Negro should be entirely removed from politics and a completely segregated society created. Openly rejecting such ideas, Dudley asked, instead, in an article in the *Century Magazine* in 1885, "How shall we help the Negro?" His answer was that it was the duty of every American to help uplift the Negro and prepare him for responsible citizenship. He saw segregation and political disfranchisement as negative solutions, to result only in continued and increased degradation and decay for the Negro. Emphasizing the Golden Rule and the concept of the fatherhood of God and the brotherhood of man, Bishop Dudley insisted that southern whites should first help the Negro by treating him justly as a freeman. Then, they should sympathize with the Negro, encouraging him by example on a neighborly basis, rather than officially, with churches serving as the best place for such interaction. Doubts held by Dudley regarding the Negro's ability to improve significantly in morality and his fear of miscegenation did not undermine his conviction that elevation of the Negro was in the interest of both races. Based on published material; 25 notes.   R. V. Calvert

1529. Sinkler, George. BENJAMIN HARRISON AND THE MATTER OF RACE. *Indiana Mag. of Hist. 1969 65(3): 197-214.* Discusses the official relationship of Harrison to the Negro during the 1888 presidential campaign and during his term in office. A plea for racial equality was an integral part of his inaugural address. Harrison refused to blame the Negro for his poverty and lack of education. He also rejected the idea that southerners alone should work out the problems of race relations. He advocated the Negro franchise and, in 1884, had supported the Blair Education Bill. As President, Harrison supported Negroes in their bid for patronage. Each major incident involving Negroes with which Harrison was concerned during his Presidency is detailed. The author concludes that "Harrison exerted greater leadership, no matter how unsuccessful, in matters of race than any of the post-Reconstruction Presidents prior to the twentieth century." Based on primary sources; 61 notes.   N. E. Tutorow

1530. Smith, Claude P. OFFICIAL EFFORTS BY THE STATE OF MISSIS-SIPPI TO ENCOURAGE IMMIGRATION, 1868-1886. *J. of Mississippi Hist. 1970 32(4): 327-340.* Traces the history of Mississippi's modest and relatively unsuccessful efforts to strengthen its economy by attracting immigrants. Under a new constitution ratified in 1869, the State established a Department of Immigration; but the legislature abolished it in 1886. The department secured reduced railroad rates for immigrants and distributed various publications, including maps and over 50 thousand copies of German, Swedish, and English editions of a handbook. But the campaign failed, for in 1870 the State had 11,171 aliens; in 1880, 9,210; and in 1890, 7,952. While the State may have abolished the department partly because the North and West offered greater opportunities for immigrants, the most important factor may have been "that once the whites had complete social, political, and economic control over the Negro, it was no longer necessary to import laborers." Based on various published primary sources; 56 notes.   J. W. Hillje

1531. Somers, Dale A. A CITY ON WHEELS: THE BICYCLE ERA IN NEW ORLEANS. *Louisiana Hist. 1967 8(3): 219-238.* Of the sports that attracted 19th-century Americans, none enjoyed greater popularity than cycling. The author traces the history of the bicycle and its rather slow acceptance in New Orleans, beginning in the 1860's but unenthusiastic until the 1880's. The organization of an elite social group, the New Orleans Bicycle Club, stimulated greater interest, but the admission of Negroes by the club's national affiliate, the League of American Wheelmen, retarded the club's activities in the 1890's. Meanwhile, other cycling clubs had been organized. State and municipal legislation affecting bicycling is discussed as is the cyclists' role in promoting better streets and highways. Also discussed are promotional efforts to sell bicycles. Overcoming early opposition, female cyclists increased in numbers in the 1890's. Cycling reached its peak of popularity in New Orleans in 1895 and 1896. The electric streetcar and the automobile caused its decline thereafter. Based principally on contemporary articles in New Orleans newspapers and bicycling publications; 81 notes.   R. L. Woodward

1532. Talbott, F. SOME LEGISLATIVE AND LEGAL ASPECTS OF THE NEGRO QUESTION IN WEST VIRGINIA DURING THE CIVIL WAR AND RECONSTRUCTION. *West Virginia Hist. 1962/63 24(1): 1-31, (2): 110-133, (3): 211-247.* Part I. Reviews the factors that made the pattern of slavery in West Virginia different from its eastern portion. This is a documented account of the popular and legislative struggle to improve, as well as to deny, certain civil rights of the freed Negro. By 1868 the Negroes in West Virginia had many rights added to their freedom from slavery which were not theirs either under the Virginia Code of 1860, or in the new State of West Virginia before 1863. These rights included permission to leave and return to the State, the right to assemble, permission and provision for an education, trial and punishment in the same manner as whites, and marital rights. Part II. Reviews the debate and legislative battles regarding the establishment of free public education for the Negro in West Virginia. The legislature of 1863 laid the statutory foundation for a system of free public education in West Virginia. Despite bitter opposition for free education for the Negro, the legislature established an almost-equal education for Negro children. Among the problems was the securing of satisfactory teachers for the colored schools and the ever present problem of bringing together sufficient colored children to provide a reasonably satisfactory school with the funds availabe. The author also reviews the opposition to Negro suffrage. Closely interrelated with the Negro suffrage question in West Virginia was the subject of the disfranchisement of the thousands of ex-Confederates in West Virginia. Included are excerpts from speeches, editorials, and letters giving contrasting viewpoints on Negro suffrage. A letter from Robert E. Lee indicates concern that the noneducated, newly freed Negro would certainly become a victim of the demagogue. Part III. Describes the heated controversy in the West Virginia Legislature over the ratification of the 15th Amendment. Strong opposition existed among West Virginians to the granting of the franchise to the Negro while there were still white West Virginians who were denied the vote because of their service in the Confederate forces. This controversy became more heated over a similar franchise amendment to the West Virginia constitution. Seething and protracted debate developed over the consideration of an amendment to the State constitution which entitled "the male citizen of the state to vote at all elections" and whether the word "white" should be inserted before male. Adoption of the amendment excluding the word "white" was overwhelming. In the Constitutional Convention of 1872 the question of qualifying Negroes to hold public office and to serve as jurors arose. The controversy over granting these privileges solely to white male citizens continued. The effort to limit solely to whites was defeated and thus "by 1872, to the people of West Virginia the Civil War was over and the Negro question was a dead issue."   M. M. Kanin

1533. Theisen, Lee Scott. THE FIGHT IN LINCOLN, N.M., 1878: THE TESTIMONY OF TWO NEGRO PARTICIPANTS. *Arizona and the West 1970 12(2): 173-198.* Two rival groups, struggling for economic and political dominance of Lincoln County, New Mexico, plunged the area into lawlessness in 1878.

Murders, embezzlement charges, and terror prevailed. A new sheriff, who was also made a deputy U.S. marshal, enlisted the aid of Federal troops from nearby Fort Stanton to serve warrants for the arrests of several persons who had taken refuge in a fort-like home in Lincoln. The decisive week of 15-19 July 1878 in the Lincoln County War was brought to a climax when the sheriff set fire to the house. As its occupants fled the blaze, several of them were killed by the posse. The widow of the slain leader brought charges against the Army colonel who refused to intervene to save the men. Some 60 witnesses were heard in the subsequent court of inquiry at Fort Stanton in 1879. The author presents the testimony of two Negroes, who were employees of the captured party and had been present for most of the fight. Aside from the details of the affair which their statements contain, the documents are commentaries on frontier justice, western attitudes about race, and the prevalent mores of the day. Illus., map, 24 notes.

D. L. Smith

1534. Thompson, William Fletcher, Jr. PICTORIAL IMAGES OF THE NE-GRO DURING THE CIVIL WAR. *Wisconsin Mag. of Hist. 1965 48(4): 282-294.* During the period between the introduction of illustrated journalism to the United States (1857) and the advent of news photography in the 1890's, artists and cartoonists "enjoyed a unique opportunity to shape the public mind." The new illustrated weeklies supplied their readers with the then unprecedented volume and variety of news pictures at a low purchase price. The author contends that this was a great influence in shaping the widespread view of the Negro as one of several stereotype characters, which lasted down to the time of the golden age of the moving pictures. Even reform-minded editors like George William Curtis of *Harper's Weekly* failed to give their readers a true image of the Negro because they viewed the Negro not as an individual or even as part of a distinct cultural group, but rather as "an abstraction, an issue, a problem to be met through paternal efforts of benevolent white leadership." The work of several cartoonists is mentioned, especially the work of Thomas Nast. 9 illus., 26 notes.

H. A. Negaard

1535. Toppin, Edgar A. NEGRO EMANCIPATION IN HISTORIC RETRO-SPECT: OHIO, THE NEGRO SUFFRAGE ISSUE IN POSTBELLUM OHIO POLITICS. *J. of Human Relations 1963 11(2): 232-246.* Reconsiders "Ohio's sluggish progression toward impartial suffrage" from 1803 to 1870. The author focuses on the years from 1865 to 1870 and especially on the gubernatorial election of 1865, the real significance of which "most observers have overlooked." When timid Unionists, in the interest of party harmony, attempted to avoid the issue of Negro suffrage during the pre-election campaign, they surrendered the initiative to Democratic racists who began building "the sentiment that would so decisively defeat Negro suffrage two years later." A paper read at the 47th Annual Meeting of the Association for the Study of Negro Life and History at Central State College, Wilberforce, Ohio, 26 October 1962. Extensively documented.

D. J. Abramoske

1536. Vaughn, William P. PARTNERS IN SEGREGATION: BARNAS SEARS AND THE PEABODY FUND. *Civil War Hist. 1964 10(3): 260-274.*

An account of efforts to improve southern education through a one million dollar grant of George Peabody in 1867. Dr. Barnas Sears supervised the disbursing of the Peabody Fund until his death in 1880. He carried out his duties with dedication and good judgment but accepted the southern position in race relations, contending that integrated schools would drive the whites away and thus destroy the public school system. By continuing the separate-but-equal program, Negroes got an education consistent with their needs and abilities. The author holds that by using Peabody money as a billy-club to insure segregated schools, Sears did much to postpone and make more painful the inevitable day when segregated schooling would have to end. Based on Peabody Trustee Reports, J. L. M. Curry Papers (Library of Congress), and contemporary public records and newspapers.

E. C. Murdock

1537. Vaughn, William P. SEPARATE AND UNEQUAL: THE CIVIL RIGHTS ACT OF 1875 AND DEFEAT OF THE SCHOOL INTEGRATION CLAUSE. *Southwestern Social Sci. Q. 1967 48(2): 146-154.* Traces the attempt by Senator Charles Sumner of Massachusetts to secure passage of a civil rights bill containing a school desegregation clause. Less than a year after Sumner's death in March 1874, the Civil Rights Act of 1875 was signed by President Grant, but without the school desegregation clause. Threat of a Democratic filibuster led by southerners, and fear that such a clause might mean an end to the newly formed public school system in the South, prompted the deletion. 37 notes.

D. F. Henderson

1538. Weaver, Valeria W. THE FAILURE OF CIVIL RIGHTS 1875 - 1883 AND ITS REPERCUSSIONS. *J. of Negro Hist. 1969 54(4): 368-382.* The Civil Rights Act of 1875 climaxed the efforts of Radical Republicans to prevent discrimination against Negroes. In general, however, the law was disregarded with impunity throughout the country, and the number of cases brought before the courts under the act diminished rapidly by the 1880's. In 1883 the U.S. Supreme Court declared the public accommodation sections of the law unconstitutional, and attempts to pass a new and revised version were met with presidential passivity and insufficient support in Congress. State civil rights acts fared a little better on the topic of public accommodations, especially in those places where black political power was influential. But, even on a State level, enforcement could prove to be a difficult and exhausting experience. Thus, the Civil Rights Act (1875), the State civil rights acts, and the Interstate Commerce Act (1887) had no real measurable effect on racial discrimination in public accommodations, amusement, conveyances, or in the choosing of juries. The failure lay primarily in the courts and the enforcement of the law rather than in the provisions of the particular acts. Based mostly on State court citations; 85 notes.

R. S. Melamed

1539. Weiss, Nathan. GENERAL BENJAMIN FRANKLIN BUTLER AND THE NEGRO: THE EVOLUTION OF THE RACIAL VIEWS OF A PRACTICAL POLITICIAN. *Negro Hist. Bull. 1965 29(1): 3-4, 14-16, 23.* Despite Major General Butler's early proslavery record in the years that followed the Civil War, he rendered valuable service to the Negro's cause. Although many of his "radical" reforms (on labor, finance, monopoly, and woman suffrage) proved to be either beneficial or harmless, his liberal interpretation of the doctrine of social equality with relation to the Negro marks him as a man whose beliefs were far in advance of his time with regard to the racial question. After Butler entered Congress, he became the most ardent advocate of Negro equality in the House of Representatives and was mainly responsible for the passage in Congress of a Civil Rights Act (1875). This act provides that "all persons within the jurisdiction of the United States (shall) be entitled to full and equal enjoyment of accommodations, facilities and privileges of inns, public conveyances, theatres, etc." When Butler became Governor of Massachusetts, he appointed the first Judge of Irish descent in the Bay State, and the first Negro to the judiciary of the Commonwealth. 57 notes.   D. D. Cameron

1540. West, Earle H. THE PEABODY EDUCATION FUND AND NEGRO EDUCATION, 1867-1880. *Hist. of Educ. Q. 1966 6(2): 3-21.* As the fund's general agent, Barnas Sears was chiefly responsible for a policy that gave disproportionately small aid to Negro schools. Although believing in racial equality and in the need for popular support of a public education system, Sears accepted and supported racially segregated schools. While he channeled aid to Negro schools through the Freedmen's Bureau, he supported a separate, private white school system in Louisiana. Unintentionally, yet undeniably, Sears helped to strengthen segregation and discrimination in the South. Based on both manuscript and printed sources.   J. Herbst

1541. Westin, Alan F. RIDE - IN. *Am. Heritage 1962 13(5): 57-64.* Traces the first efforts of southern Negroes to break the segregation barriers, beginning in 1871 and lasting nearly two decades, and culminating in a series of Supreme Court decisions which held the Civil Rights Bill of 1875 to be invalid. Undocumented, illus.   C. R. Allen, Jr.

1542. Williams, Edward C. THE ALABAMA ELECTION OF 1874. *Alabama R. 1964 17(3): 210-218.* In the Alabama State elections of 1874, the planter-merchant classes of the Black Belt counties were determined to oust the Republicans. Through a combination of old line Whigs, former Douglas Democrats and Breckenridge Democrats, and a platform calling for economy in government and white supremacy, the Republicans were defeated and George Smith Houston elected governor.   D. F. Henderson

1543. Williamson, Edward C. BLACK BELT POLITICAL CRISIS: THE SAVAGE-JAMES LYNCHING, 1882. *Florida Hist. Q. 1967 45(4): 402-409.* After 1876, with appointment of key county officials by the Governor, Democrats controlled the election machinery in Republican-voting Madison County, Florida. In the 1880 election, intimidation, coercion, and disputed returns resulted in a congressional investigation into voting irregularities with two Negro lieutenants, Charles Savage and Howard James, of Republican county boss, Dennis Eagan, reluctantly testifying. Savage, accompanied by James, charged attorney Frank Patterson with election fraud. A confrontation with Savage the following day resulted in Patterson's death. Arrested on complicity, Eagan was released because of the death sentence on Savage and James, who were transferred to Tallahassee to await outcome of an appeal. Then, in August 1882, as the Hamilton County sheriff and four guards came through the town of Madison with Savage and James, an unmasked mob easily boarded the train and riddled the prisoners with bullets after overcoming the guards. Despite eyewitness testimony identifying mob leaders, a coroner's jury decided that the lynchers were unknown parties. Since Madison County officials decided against pressing for a trial while Governor William D. Bloxham refused to replace appointed county officials, the lynching of the two Negro Republicans remained an unpunished crime. 32 notes.

R. V. Calvert

1544. Wyatt-Brown, Bertram. THE CIVIL RIGHTS ACT OF 1875. *Western Pol. Q. 1965 18(4): 763-775.* For almost five years Senator Charles Sumner labored for the passage of this act. The bill was used as a football by both political camps. As introduced by Sumner, it would have outlawed segregation and discrimination in all public relationships, from churches to schools to jury boxes. Gradually emasculated, the section on schools was omitted. In addition, punitive provisions were minimal and, above all, the bill (and the act as passed) required that the initiative for the enforcement had to come from the Negro complainant. The death of Sumner in 1874 did add momentum to passage of the bill in a much watered-down version as a memorial to the Massachusetts Senator. 86 notes.

H. Aptheker

1545. Wynes, Charles E. BISHOP THOMAS U. DUDLEY AND THE UPLIFT OF THE NEGRO. *Register of the Kentucky Hist. Soc. 1967 65(3): 230-238.* Thomas Underwood Dudley, southern born, Virginia educated, Protestant Episcopal Bishop of Kentucky, was long an advocate of equal rights for Negroes. In the mid-1880's he called for an end to the separation of the races because he felt it would hinder the uplift of the Negro. He further stated that the white South must solve the Negro problem itself and not wait for the courts to do it. Based mainly on an article Dudley wrote for *The Century* in 1885; 32 notes.

B. Wilkins

1546. Wynes, Charles E. LEWIS HARVIE BLAIR, VIRGINIA REFORMER. *Virginia Mag. of Hist. and Biog. 1964 72(1): 3-18.* Blair was a member of one of Richmond's most prominent families, a Confederate veteran, and a successful businessman whose book *The Prosperity of the South Dependent upon the Elevation of the Negro* (Richmond: Everett Waddey, 1889) capped a long career as a heretic in relation to his background. Late in life, for reasons that are not clear, Blair reversed himself to accept the conventional southern position on race.

K. J. Bauer

1547. Olenick, Monte M. ALBION W. TOURGEE: RADICAL REPUBLICAN SPOKESMAN OF THE CIVIL WAR CRUSADE. *Phylon 1962 23(4): 332-345.* Civil War soldier, Reconstructionist judge, writer, editor, and lawyer, Tourgée fought for Negro equality. As a Radical judge in North Carolina, he roused southern hatred because of the sentences he imposed on Ku Klux Klan members. His novel, *The Invisible Empire* (1879), denounced this terrorist organization.

The overthrow of Reconstruction forced him to leave the South, and his most famous novel, *A Fool's Errand* (1879), recapitulating his experiences, sold almost 200 thousand copies and was hailed as a new *Uncle Tom's Cabin*. Other writings, public speaking, and other efforts continued Tourgée's campaign in behalf of the Negroes. Although his arguments favoring equality were rejected in the famous case of *Plessy vs. Ferguson* (1896), they were finally accepted in *Brown vs. Board of Education* (1954).   L. Filler

Development of an Afro-American Community

1548. Aptheker, Herbert. DU BOIS ON DOUGLASS: 1895. *J. of Negro Hist. 1964 49(4): 264-268.* Publishes the text of an address which William Edward Burghardt Du Bois delivered on 9 March 1895 as a young instructor at a Wilberforce University memorial service for Frederick Douglass. Du Bois dealt with the topic "Douglass as a Statesman." He depicted Douglass as a genuine leader who was ahead of his time in advocating the abolition of slavery, the use of Negro troops in the Civil War, immediate enfranchisement, and freedom, integrity and honesty in diplomatic relations.   L. Gara

1549. Broderick, Francis L. GERMAN INFLUENCE ON THE SCHOLARSHIP OF W. E. B. DUBOIS. *Phylon 1958 19(4): 367-371.* Two years (1892-94) of study under Gustav Schmoller at the University of Berlin led W. E. B. DuBois to abandon institutional history for sociology. Based on DuBois's early books and the unpublished DuBois papers.   A

1550. Brown, Charles A. LLOYD LEFTWICH, ALABAMA STATE SENATOR. *Negro Hist. Bull. 1963 26(5): 161-162.* Sketches some highlights of the career of Lloyd Leftwich (1832-1918), who was born a slave in Alabama and served in the senate of that State from 1872 to 1876. The article contains information about some of Leftwich's descendants and is based mostly on interviews with members of the family.   L. Gara

1551. Brown, Charles A. WILLIAM HOOPER COUNCILL: ALABAMA LEGISLATOR, EDITOR AND LAWYER. *Negro Hist. Bull. 1963 26(5): 171-172.* A brief sketch of William Hooper Councill (1849-1909), who was born a slave and after the Civil War achieved considerable success as an educator (president of Alabama A. and M. College, 1875-1909), lawyer, editor, and member of the Alabama House of Representatives (1870-72). The sketch includes data obtained from some of Councill's descendants as well as information about them.   L. Gara

1552. Butcher, Philip. GEORGE W. CABLE AND GEORGE W. WILLIAMS: AN ABORTIVE COLLABORATION. *J. of Negro Hist. 1968 53(4): 334-344.*

Discusses the relationship between the former Confederate George Washington Cable(1844-1925) and George Washington Williams (1849-91), a noted Negro minister and author of *History of the Negro Race in America, 1619-1880* (1882). After corresponding, the two writers met in Worcester, Massachusetts, but Cable's offer to have some of Williams' orations distributed among members of a literary club came to nothing. Cable and Williams shared a concern for civil rights, a recognition of the importance of Negro history, and an active interest in founding an association for its study. 16 notes.   L. Gara

1553. Calista, Donald J. BOOKER T. WASHINGTON: ANOTHER LOOK. *J. of Negro Hist. 1964 49(4): 240-255.* Reassesses Booker T. Washington's moderate views in light of the plight of southern Negroes at the time of his greatest influence. By the mid-1890's, earlier hopeful signs for an improved status for Negroes had disappeared. Depression and a resurgence of intense racism throughout the Nation led many Negroes to despair of bettering their lot. Washington spoke for economic gains and denied that southern Negroes desired immediate social equality. Both southern whites and Negroes found his point of view useful. Washington, however, never rejected full equality as an ultimate goal, and just prior to his death he wrote an article in which he vigorously attacked segregation as an unjust institution which further widened the breach between the races. Documented with a variety of sources.   L. Gara

1554. Cook, Mercer. BOOKER T. WASHINGTON AND THE FRENCH. *J. of Negro Hist. 1955 40(4): 318-340.* Surveys the French interest in Washington, founder of Tuskegee Institute, and in the school itself. The article is based on a study of French journals, French books on America, and some portions of the Washington manuscripts in the Library of Congress. The author concludes that despite some Frenchmen who wrote of the usual stereotype Negro, the traditional French sympathy for the Negro was not altered.   W. E. Wight

1555. Daniel, Pete and Kaugman, Stuart. THE BOOKER T. WASHINGTON PAPERS AND HISTORICAL EDITING AT MARYLAND. *Maryland Historian 1970 1(1): 23-29.* Outlines the history and scope of the Booker T. Washington Project sponsored by the University of Maryland and the National Endowment for the Humanities. Indicates the advantages of editorial training for graduate programs in history. 8 notes.   G. O. Gagnon

1556. Drake, Donald E., II. MILITANCY IN FORTUNE'S NEW YORK AGE. *J. of Negro Hist. 1970 55(4): 307-322.* Timothy Thomas Fortune founded and edited *The New York Age* during the 1880's. This newspaper stood out as an uncompromising and independent voice of Negro militance in a period known for "accommodation" by the Negro community. Fortune built the *Age* into the leading Negro newspaper in the United States, but its circulation never exceeded ten thousand. The *Age* gave the Republican Party "its Civil War and Reconstruction dues," and supported the use of political power by Negroes whenever possible. Fortune opposed emigration to Africa; instead he supported the creation of a Negro State in the Oklahoma Territory. Strong emphasis on racial pride underscored most of the militance expressed in the *Age;* Fortune insisted that Negroes needed to develop their own separate culture. In his later years Fortune grew so disillusioned that he took up writing pamphlets for Marcus Garvey's Back to Africa Movement. 53 notes.   R. S. Melamed

1557. Dunnigan, Alice E. EARLY HISTORY OF NEGRO WOMEN IN JOURNALISM. *Negro Hist. Bull. 1965 28(8): 178-179, 193, 197.* The first Negro newspaper was *Freedom's Journal,* New York City, 1827, while the first Negro paper to be published in the South was the *Colored American,* started in Augusta, Georgia in 1865. Frederick Douglass started the *New National Era* in Washington, D.C. soon after the Civil War. With the upsurge of Negro papers throughout the Nation in the 1870's came an increased number of new journalists including many Negro women writers. The names and achievements of 19 such Negro women are given in some detail. Many wrote for religious papers.
E. P. Stickney

1558. Flynn, John P. BOOKER T. WASHINGTON: UNCLE TOM OR WOODEN HORSE. *J. of Negro Hist. 1969 54(3): 262-274.* Booker T. Washington seems to have epitomized the model of the Protestant ethic man, and many of his actions should be viewed in this light. His secularized asceticism, however, was criticized. Washington played host to many Social Darwinists of his day and sometimes borrowed from their ideas, especially in regard to his emphasis on a technical rather than a liberal arts education for young black people. Washington believed that the Protestant ethic and Social Darwinism provided the best means for the materialistic advancement of colored people, which to him was more important than a drive for political rights. It is within this context that one must judge whether Booker T. Washington was an Uncle Tom or a wooden horse. Based mostly on secondary sources; 38 notes, biblio.   R. S. Melamed

1559. Foner, Philip S., ed. IS BOOKER T. WASHINGTON'S IDEA CORRECT? *J. of Negro Hist. 1970 55(4): 343-347.* Presents two documents, one from *The Christian Recorder* (28 November 1895) and the other from the *Voice of Missions* in Atlanta (December 1895), which give the earliest known criticism by Negroes of the ideas of Booker T. Washington. Both excerpts claim that Washington's views are degrading for Negroes.   R. S. Melamed

1560. Gatewood, Willard B. WILLIAM D. CRUM, A NEGRO IN POLITICS. *J. of Negro Hist. 1968 53(4): 301-320.* Sketches the political career of William Demos Crum (1859-1912), a wealthy Negro physician of Charleston, South Carolina, who was active in the Republican Party. A prominent physician with moderate views on any question touching race, Crum was highly regarded by the white community until President Benjamin Harrison appointed him postmaster of Charleston in 1892. White opposition to the appointment was so extreme that Harrison withdrew Crum's name. Similar opposition arose when President Theodore Roosevelt named Crum collector of the Port of Charleston, but Roosevelt did not back down and after several years the Senate confirmed his appointment. Crum resigned following William Howard Taft's election and became minister

resident and consul general to Liberia, a much safer post from the standpoint of the cautious Taft administration. Based on newspaper and MS. sources; 48 notes.
L. Gara

1561. Gottschalk, Jane. THE RHETORICAL STRATEGY OF BOOKER T. WASHINGTON. *Phylon 1966 27(4): 388-395.* Examines the Sunday evening talks by Washington at Tuskegee Institute which were subsequently published as *Character Building* (1902). The author describes these talks as homilies preaching hard work and social virtues as the means to achievement of the goal of respect and cooperation of whites. The talks were simple, direct, conversational, and paternal. They were filled with practical admonitions and personal anecdotes, and they emphasized the virtues of labor at the expense of those of the intellect. 12 notes.
S. C. Pearson, Jr.

1562. Harlan, Louis R. BOOKER T. WASHINGTON AND THE KANAWHA VALLEY 1875-1879. *West Virginia Hist. 1972 33(2): 124-141.* Surveys Booker Taliaferro Washington's public career in his boyhood home of Malden, shortly after he graduated from Hampton Institute. As a teacher, lay church leader, active community spokesman, and (briefly) political speechmaker urging that the capital be moved to Charlestown, Washington gained the self-confidence and perspective that guided him the rest of his public life. Based on newspapers; 46 notes.
C. A. Newton

1563. Harlan, Louis R. BOOKER T. WASHINGTON AND THE WHITE MAN'S BURDEN. *Am. Hist. R. 1966 71(2): 441-467.* Washington's principal life commitment to the spreading of the educational system and social philosophy of Tuskegee Institute led him to encourage American Negro enterprise and philanthropy in Africa but to reject the proposals of emigrationists, visionaries, and missionaries. In Africa, he supported the principle, if not all of the practices, of colonialism. In Togo, South Africa, and the Congo, he was quick to remind white men when they neglected the responsibilities of power. In Liberia he offered a form of Negro nationalism and self-government, while the power, both political and economic, went to American officials and international bankers. His extensive correspondence with African nationalists was initiated by them but he made no concessions to them. Based on the Booker T. Washington Papers, Library of Congress; 106 notes.
E. P. Stickney

1564. Hudson, Gossie Harold. AN UNPUBLISHED LETTER WRITTEN TO PAUL LAURENCE DUNBAR, 1894. *J. of Negro Hist. 1970 55(3): 215-217.* Presents a letter written by Rebekah Baldwin to Dunbar (1872-1906) on 18 July 1894. In the letter Baldwin admonishes Dunbar to work harder on his poetry, and questions him as to why he writes literature so "wildly" while he corresponds with her in only a reserved fashion. Note.
R. S. Melamed

1565. Ketchum, Richard M. FACES FROM THE PAST - VIII. *Am. Heritage 1962 13(6): 10-11.* Sketch of Booker T. Washington, Negro educator. Portrait.
C. R. Allen, Jr.

1566. Larson, Charles R. THE NOVELS OF PAUL LAURENCE DUNBAR. *Phylon 1968 29(3): 257-271.* Analyzes the novels of Paul Laurence Dunbar (1872-1906), the first Negro American to undertake seriously the career of a man of letters. Although not considered an outspoken advocate of Negro rights, the author believes that during Dunbar's late and brief (five-year) career as a novelist he did demonstrate concern for racial issues. The author discusses each of the four novels Dunbar wrote. *The Uncalled* (1898) was a promising first novel and contained many of the important themes of his later fiction. The last novel, *The Sport of the Gods,* was the most important. In it he used Negroes as his major characters, treated their problems with sympathy, and seemed to call upon them to organize to obtain their rights. 13 notes.   R. D. Cohen

1567. Lewis, Elsie M. THE POLITICAL MIND OF THE NEGRO, 1865-1900. *J. of Southern Hist. 1955 21(2): 189-202.* A small group of Negro leaders launched the philosophy of equality and human rights at the close of the Civil War. During the war, the National Convention of Colored Men established the National Equal Rights League with provision for State and local organizations to unify thought and action of the Negroes. Following the failure of the national government to guarantee their political and civil rights, some leaders advocated that the Negro must become an independent force in politics.
R. Kerley

1568. Love, Rose Leary. [GEORGE WASHINGTON CARVER]. *Negro Hist. Bull. 1967 30.*
GEORGE WASHINGTON CARVER - A BOY WHO WISHED TO KNOW "WHY?", (1): 13-15. Summarizes the boyhood of George Washington Carver (1864-1943). Surveys his early character training and environment. Describes the depth and intelligence of his personality.
GEORGE WASHINGTON CARVER - THE BOY WHO WANTED TO KNOW WHY?, (2): 15-18. Traces Carver's school years at Neosha, Missouri, and Fort Scott, Kansas. Describes his jobs after high school in and around Minneapolis, Kansas. Carver bought a laundry but later decided to sell his interest and further his education. After an unsuccessful attempt to enter Highland University, he took out a land claim, built a sod house, and farmed 160 acres. He then worked at a hotel in Winterset, Iowa, and entered nearby Simpson College. He was then 25.
"BOY WHO WISHED TO KNOW WHY" GEORGE WASHINGTON CARVER, (3): 15-19. Discusses Carver's attendance at Iowa State College and his early contributions to science there. Booker T. Washington recruited Carver for Tuskegee Institute in Alabama. Describes Carver's improvement of soil and crops, particularly his sweet potato and peanut research. George B. Love wrote of Carver, "He gave himself to build for others."   D. H. Swift

1569. Meier, August. BOOKER T. WASHINGTON AND THE TOWN OF MOUND BAYOU. *Phylon 1954 15(4): 396-401.* Describes the town of Mound Bayou in Mississippi as typical of those segregated Negro communities that turned from the ideal of political and constitutional rights to the ideologies of economic advancement, self-help, and racial solidarity. In spite of the help received from northern philanthropies and Booker T. Washington at Tuskegee Institute, the town never fulfilled its mission of justifying the "advantages of the disadvantages" in segregation. The community was doomed to failure because self-help and racial solidarity were not a sufficient base upon which to build a successful economy and community.   R. Hyman

1570. Meier, August. NEGRO CLASS STRUCTURE AND IDEOLOGY IN THE AGE OF BOOKER T. WASHINGTON. *Phylon 1962 23(3): 258-266.* The view that Negroes would advance in status by encouraging thrift, industry, and racial solidarity antedated Washington's leadership in Negro affairs. Frederick Douglass militantly espoused such middle-class proposals in the 1840's and 1850's. Later, they served Negro businessmen who could ask economic support from others of their race. Negro businessmen identified with banks, cemetery and realty associations, insurance enterprises, and retail and service establishments solicited Negro support. Newspapermen, undertakers, some barber and retail establishments, physicians, and lawyers increasingly served their segregated constituents. Such Negro elements came to constitute not only an economic elite among Negroes, but a social elite, in New Orleans, Charleston, Nashville, and in cities of the New South as well as the North.   L. Filler

1571. Meier, August. TOWARD A REINTERPRETATION OF BOOKER T. WASHINGTON. *J. of Southern Hist. 1957 23(2): 220-227.* Though outwardly an accommodator who appeared to accept disfranchisement and segregation and deprecated agitation and political activity, covertly Washington was active in politics, financed a legal attack on disfranchisement and various efforts against segregation, and in other ways worked to undermine the American race system. Based on the Booker T. Washington Papers, Library of Congress.
                                                                         A

1572. Olsen, Otto H. ALBION W. TOURGEE AND NEGRO MILITANTS IN THE 1890'S: A DOCUMENTARY SELECTION. *Sci. and Soc. 1964 28(2): 183-207.* In 1891 Albion W. Tourgee, in the columns of the widely read Chicago Republican newspaper *Inter Ocean,* launched the National Citizens' Rights Association in behalf of Negro rights. From 1881 to 1897 he was "the most militant, vocal, persistent, and widely heard advocate of Negro equality." The greatest success of the NCRA was in securing the adoption of a resolution denouncing segregation by the General Conference of the Methodist Episcopal Church in 1892. The association brought a case *(Plessy vs. Ferguson)* to the Supreme Court only to end in failure in 1896. Includes selections from the hundreds of letters written by Negroes to Tourgee in support of the NCRA.   E. P. Stickney

1573. Poxpey, C. Spencer. THE WASHINGTON-DU BOIS CONTROVERSY AND ITS EFFECT ON THE NEGRO PROBLEM. *Hist. of Educ. J. 1957 8(4): 128-152.* Traces the roots of the feud between Booker T. Washington and W. E. B. Du Bois to their clashing personalities, their different backgrounds and training, and their programs for improving the lot of the American Negro. The author places the controversy in the setting of Reconstruction and the era which followed it. He concludes that both leaders contributed to racial progress and that the controversy itself helped call attention to the problem.   L. Gara

1574. Redkey, Edwin S. BISHOP TURNER'S AFRICAN DREAM. *J. of Am. Hist. 1967 54(2): 271-290.* Henry McNeal Turner (1834-1915), bishop of the African Methodist Episcopal Church, identified himself with the cause of Negro emigration to Liberia and Africa generally and for that purpose associated himself with the American Colonization Society, generally in bad odor with his fellows. His decision was based largely on a profound disillusionment with and contempt for the white American society and a belief that Negroes could not obtain the respect of that society unless they demonstrated a capacity for self-government and independence and developed pride in being black. Turner believed that his own career of frustration had shown that was unlikely in America, but the right kind of American Negro leadership could transform Liberia and all of Africa into a black state that could command respect and pride in self. A bitterly contentious man, few endorsed Turner's views but they link the pre-Civil War colonization movement with Marcus Garvey's movement. Documented.
K. B. West

1575. Scheiner, Seth M. EARLY CAREER OF T. THOMAS FORTUNE, 1879-1890. *Negro Hist. Bull. 1964 27(7): 170-172.* Reviews the early career of Negro journalist, Timothy Thomas Fortune, who advocated a course of political independence for American Negroes. At various times Fortune supported the Democrats, the Republicans, and the Prohibitionists. His independent attitude caused Fortune to break openly with the policies and leadership of Booker T. Washington with whom he had been closely associated.   L. Gara

1576. Slavens, George Everett. THE MISSOURI NEGRO PRESS, 1875-1920. *Missouri Hist. R. 1970 64(4): 413-431.* Of the 64 Negro papers published in Missouri since Reconstruction, only 16 are now available for examination. Most of the papers were published in St. Louis and Kansas City, the two cities with the largest Negro population, but Negro papers were published in 11 other towns. Most of the papers lasted only a short time; only three papers published in 1920 survived to the present. For some unknown reason the papers usually ceased publication at a peak of circulation. Most of the papers merely carried information of interest to the Negro community and no serious effort was made to provide essential news coverage. Most of the editors were gradualists where race relations were concerned, but they rallied to present a more activist front against moves to increase segregation in the State. The issue of most concern to the editors was politics, which meant an all-out commitment to the Republican Party. Based on newspaper files and annual newspaper registers; illus., 47 notes.
W. F. Zornow

1577. Stange, Douglas C. A NOTE ON DANIEL A. PAYNE. *Negro Hist. Bull. 1964 28(1): 9-10.* Sketches the career of Daniel Alexander Payne (1811-93), outstanding Negro educator, president of Wilberforce University, bishop of the African Methodist Episcopal Church, and man of letters.   L. Gara

1578. Thornbrough, Emma L. BOOKER T. WASHINGTON AS SEEN BY HIS WHITE CONTEMPORARIES. *J. of Negro Hist. 1968 53(2): 161-182.* With very few exceptions, white Americans of his own generation extolled Booker T. Washington as the spokesman for his race. Among the factors upon which his reputation rested were his stories and humorous references based on a stereotype of Negroes, his acceptable views on education, and his apparent rejection of political activity and the ideal of social equality for Negroes. Some of his activities, such as his accepting President Theodore Roosevelt's highly publicized invitation to dine at the White House, seemed to belie part of his teachings, and there was considerable ambiguity concerning his ultimate goals. The author believes that in honoring Washington, whites were assuaging guilt feelings over racial discrimination in a way that permitted them to continue such discrimination with a clear conscience. Documented mostly with newspaper sources; 50 notes.   L. Gara

1579. Thornbrough, Emma Lou. AMERICAN NEGRO NEWSPAPERS, 1880-1914. *Business Hist. R. 1966 40(4): 467-490.* A study of weekly American Negro newspapers at the turn of the century examines the problems of organizing and of financing.   J. H. Krenkel

1580. Thornbrough, Emma Lou. THE NATIONAL AFRO-AMERICAN LEAGUE, 1887-1908. *J. of Southern Hist. 1961 27(4): 494-512.* The National Afro-American League (later Council) was an important predecessor of the National Association for the Advancement of Colored People in seeking civil rights for Negroes. It was organized in 1890 in Chicago in pursuance of an 1887 call by Timothy Thomas Fortune (1856-1928), editor of a New York Negro newspaper. After one year, he became its president, but allowed the league to become defunct in 1893 for lack of support. He called the movement premature. In 1898 it was revived as the National Afro-American Council. Bishop Alexander Walters of the African Methodist Episcopal Zion Church was president for seven terms and then Fortune became president. Early in the revival, W. E. B. Du Bois was prominent in the organization. In control behind the scenes was Booker T. Washington, who had become an intimate friend of Fortune. After attacks upon Washington, particularly by Monroe Trotter, and after failure to get financial support, Fortune resigned in 1904, but Walters sought to keep the council alive. Du Bois founded the Niagara Movement. In 1909, Walters and Du Bois participated in the call for the establishment of the NAACP, but neither Fortune nor Washington took part.   S. E. Humphreys

1581. Thorpe, Earl E. FREDERICK DOUGLASS, W. E. B. DUBOIS AND BOOKER T. WASHINGTON. *Negro Hist. Bull. 1956 20(2): 39-42.* Discusses similarities in the ideas associated with Douglass, Du Bois and Washington. All three shifted from an emphasis on moral values to an emphasis on pragmatism. They all had faith in education as a force for bettering human relations, they all recognized the importance of economic forces, and they all had a fundamentally positive attitude toward the South. Each of these leaders made a unique contribution toward the common goal of eradicating race prejudice.   L. Gara

1582. Thorpe, Earl E. WILLIAM HOOPER COUNCILL. *Negro Hist. Bull.* *1956 19(4): 85-86, 89.* Discusses the career and ideas of the Alabama ex-slave educator, William Hooper Councill (1848-1909), founder and for 35 years president of the Alabama Agricultural and Mechanical College.   L. Gara

1583. Turner, Darwin T. PAUL LAURENCE DUNBAR: THE REJECTED SYMBOL. *J. of Negro Hist. 1967 52(1): 1-13.* Discusses the rejection by students and critics of Paul Laurence Dunbar (1872-1906) as a symbol of the intellectual potential of American Negroes. Such scholars have mistakenly assumed that all of Dunbar's writing has perpetuated stereotypes based on plantation folklore and minstrel show psychology. In his earlier fiction Dunbar protested racial injustice in both the North and the South, though he created comic Negro characters and, especially in his later writings, revealed an ignorance of slavery as an institution. His shortcomings were shared by many of his contemporaries and his literary reputation and role as a social critic should not be beclouded because of them. Documented.   L. Gara

1584. Urofsky, Melvin I. BLANCHE K. BRUCE: UNITED STATES SENATOR, 1875-1881. *J. of Mississippi Hist. 1967 29(2): 118-141.* Traces the long and distinguished career of Blanche Kelso Bruce, U.S. Senator from Mississippi, 1875-81, "the only Negro yet to serve a full term as U.S. Senator," and "the first Negro to hold so many high public offices and honors." Born a slave in Virginia, Bruce received a good education and in 1868 moved to Mississippi, where he rose through a series of local, State, and national public offices. "He concerned himself with practically any problem that affected the Negro" and he was particularly interested in "the idea of resettlement in Africa." As Senator he introduced a number of bills, some designed specifically to aid Negroes, but he did not present any bills of national significance which became law. As Senator he ranked with most of his white colleagues "in ability, honesty, and performance" and he "did as well as any Negro could possibly have done, and better than most." Based on various secondary sources, the *Congressional Record,* and the Bruce Papers; 61 notes.   J. W. Hillje

1585. Wahle, Kathleen O'Mara. ALEXANDER CRUMMELL: BLACK EVANGELIST AND PAN-NEGRO NATIONALIST. *Phylon 1968 29(4): 388-395.* One of the 19th-century leaders of the back-to-Africa movement was the Reverend Alexander Crummell (1819-98), Anglican minister and pan-Negro nationalist. A free black living in the North, he experienced considerable discrimination in his early years. He was ordained in 1844 and later received a bachelor's degree from Queens College, Cambridge University. In 1853 he became a missionary in Liberia and remained there for 20 years. He attempted to reform Liberian society, hoping it would attract Negro immigration from the United States. Crummell believed in racial identity and solidarity. Finally discontented with Liberia, he returned to the United States in 1873 where he continued as a spokesman for black nationalism and self-help. Based on primary and secondary sources; 53 notes.   R. D. Cohen

1586. Walden, Daniel. THE CONTEMPORARY OPPOSITION TO THE PO-
LITICAL AND EDUCATIONAL IDEAS OF BOOKER T. WASHINGTON.
J. of Negro Hist. 1960 45(2): 105-115. It was Booker T. Washington's belief that
he could serve his people best by promoting industrial education and not preaching social equality. For this temperate attitude he won commendation from the
southern press, but incurred no little criticism from more militant Negro leaders
who urged an all-out struggle for electoral, educational, and social equality. His
more outspoken critics, such as John Hope, Monroe Trotter, and especially W.
E. B. Du Bois, blamed Washington's attitude for the disenfranchisement of the
Negro, Jim Crow laws, the decline of Negro colleges of higher education, and the
firmer establishment of color caste in the South. Based on published materials,
particularly the books of Washington and Du Bois.   R. E. Wilson

1587. Wamble, Gaston Hugh. NEGROES AND MISSOURI PROTESTANT
CHURCHES BEFORE AND AFTER THE CIVIL WAR. *Missouri Hist. R.
1967 61(3): 321-347.* Drawing on the records of 35 local churches, diaries,
correspondence, and selected newspapers, the author examines the role played by
Negroes in Missouri Protestant churches before and after the Civil War. Before
the war the Negroes and whites enjoyed a common religious experience, a fact
borne out by the congregational records. After the war the Negroes separated to
form their own congregations. Without completely rejecting racial segregation as
a cause of the development, the author maintains that a more plausible explanation lies in the fact that Negroes were anxious to form their own congregations
as a way of demonstrating the freedom they had won during the war. Illus., 113
notes.   W. F. Zornow

The Social & Economic Situation

1588. Amundson, Richard J. HENRY S. SANFORD AND LABOR PROB-
LEMS IN THE FLORIDA ORANGE INDUSTRY. *Florida Hist. Q. 1965
43(3): 229-243.* Henry S. Sanford, pioneer orange grower, finding local laborers,
white and Negro, unreliable, resorted to importing Swedes. They worked well but
were undependable beyond the one year contracted for, so he finally resorted to
importing Negroes from north Florida and Georgia. Sources: *Sanford Papers* and
secondary works.   G. L. Lycan

1589. Black, Paul V. THE KNIGHTS OF LABOR AND THE SOUTH, 1873-
1893. *Southern Q. 1963 1(3): 201-212.* The rural South helped transform the
Knights of Labor from a craft union into a multipurpose organization. Southern
members of the order acquiesced to some degree in the national policy of interracial cooperation, and Negroes were admitted to membership in Southern assemblies. The Knights of the trans-Mississippi South were heavily committed in the
strikes conducted by the organization against Jay Gould's railroads. The organization was active in southern politics and in 1886 scored a number of successes

in the Southeast. As the organization declined in other sections during the late 1880's, it made striking membership gains in the South. The author has gleaned most of his material from monographs. D. A. Stokes

1590. Bloch, Herman D. LABOR AND THE NEGRO 1866-1910. *J. of Negro Hist. 1965 50(3): 163-184.* In the years after the Civil War the top leaders of all the national unions disavowed a policy of racial discrimination but permitted its practice on the local level. The National Labor Union contained many unions that excluded Negroes, even though such exclusion conflicted with stated national policy. From 1870 to 1876, when the Knights of Labor was a significant union, Negroes did join locals, some of which were mixed and some completely colored. The national leaders of the American Federation of Labor spoke even more strongly against discrimination, but member unions continued the practice. Negroes had little opportunity to join unions in the period prior to 1910. When they did it was often because they offered competition to skilled, organized workers and could best be controlled by absorbing them into the organization. Documented. L. Gara

1591. Brewer, H. Peers. THE PROTESTANT EPISCOPAL FREEDMAN'S COMMISSION, 1865-1878. *Hist. Mag. of the Protestant Episcopal Church 1957 26(4): 361-381.* The principal work of the commission, formed in response to the plight of the liberated slaves, was in the field of Negro education. The author concludes that while the commission's motives were good, the haste with which it was organized precluded a plan of action and resulted in a lack of financial support. E. Oberholzer, Jr.

1592. Butler, Jon. COMMUNITIES AND CONGREGATIONS: THE BLACK CHURCH IN ST. PAUL, 1860-1900. *J. of Negro Hist. 1971 56(2): 118-134.* St. Paul contained some black residents ever since its founding, but the overwhelming majority of them were male until the 1950's. As a consequence, the black churches of St. Paul never developed into distinct community institutions with a strongly positive relationship between themselves and the surrounding populace. The congregations served only a relatively small proportion of the Negro population in any direct manner. Unfortunately, no direct assessment of their impact on the values and behavior of the city's unmarried blacks is possible because these men left little historical documentation about themselves. Based primarily on Minnesota church newspapers and church records; 71 notes. R. S. Melamed

1593. Clark, John G. RADICALS AND MODERATES ON THE JOINT COMMITTEE ON RECONSTRUCTION. *Mid-Am. 1963 45(2): 79-98.* Most Republicans, including radicals and moderates, feared that if the southern representations were allowed in Congress at the conclusion of hostilities they would coalesce with the Democrats and control the government. This meant, for the Republicans, assumption of the Confederate debt, the restoration of slavery under a less odious name, and the return of the leaders of the rebellion to power. Emphasis is placed upon the undoubted sincerity of many Republicans in this belief. L. D. Silveri

1594. Clary, George E., Jr. SOUTHERN METHODISM'S "UNIQUE ADVEN-TURE" IN RACE RELATIONS: PAINE COLLEGE, 1882-1903. *Methodist Hist. 1971 9(2): 22-33.* Paine College, in Augusta, was founded to provide educational opportunities for black people. It was related to the Methodist Episcopal Church, South, a white church, and the Christian Methodist Episcopal Church, a black church. The school, first known as Paine Institute, was started with great enthusiasm in 1882. The next year the race question was raised, and the proposed school came under attack in the church press. The school was financially weak for a number of years. In 1888 a black was elected to the faculty against outspoken opposition. During the 1890's the school developed into a "college" at least in name. Biblio. H. L. Calkin

1595. Destler, Chester McArthur. THE POST-BELLUM SOUTH: LETTERS AND DOCUMENTS. *Georgia Hist. Q. 1962 46(1): 79-94.* A group of letters that add to existing knowledge of the human, racial, social, educational, economic and political life of people of moderate means in Georgia and South Carolina during the last years of the 19th century, 1866-97. R. Lowitt

1596. Doherty, Herbert J., Jr. VOICES OF PROTEST FROM THE NEW SOUTH, 1875-1910. *Mississippi Valley Hist. R. 1955 42(1): 45-66.* Though industry, a late arrival in the South, was accompanied by many of the same socioeconomic problems that it had brought to the North, there were other urgent and uniquely southern problems. In general, these were caused by postwar economic chaos and by the presence of the freed Negro. An ex-slave, Timothy Thomas Fortune, emerged as a full-fledged social and economic critic. He was hopeful for the solution of southern problems by racial cooperation. James Captain Powell pointed up the evils of the convict lease system, which was also criticized and publicized by George Washington Cable. Cable evidenced his distress over the lot of the Negro. Walter Hines Page pleaded for decent education for both races. All these critics were looked upon by their southern contemporaries as "crackpots" and trouble-makers. They do, however, show that the historian of the South must not ignore the existence of reform currents, however weak, in that region. G. L. A. Reilly

1597. Durham, Philip and Jones, Everett L. NEGRO COWBOYS. *Am. West 1964 1(4): 26-31, 87.* More than five thousand Negro cowboys went up the trails from Texas in the years after the Civil War. Nearly all the pioneer cattlemen employed some Negroes. Like their white counterparts, thousands did their jobs and drew their pay without making even local history unless they got their names in the paper for disturbing the peace. Most of them disappeared when the trail drives were over and the dust settled. The Owen Wister-Zane Grey West includes whites of all kinds, Indians, and Chinese, but the Negro cowboy has been "fenced out." Anecdotal account excerpted from a forthcoming book of the same title. Biblio. note, illus. D. L. Smith

1598. Eckert, Edward K. CONTRACT LABOR IN FLORIDA DURING RE-CONSTRUCTION. *Florida Hist. Q. 1968 47(1): 34-50.* Since revisionist historians pointed out the lack of significant change in local economic and social conditions in an otherwise comparatively progressive postbellum South, the existence of debt peonage in Florida during Reconstruction could only be assumed because of scarcity of records. An 1873 ledger kept by an Alachua County cotton planter, John Haile, however, provides proof that enormous profitability was possible through contract, semipermanent labor enabling the owner to operate his farm with a guaranteed, inexpensive work force. Haile's records show that he was able to keep his contract hands in a continuing state of debt to himself by keeping credit charges one year in arrears while reflecting current indebtedness of the workers to his plantation store. Fear of the power of the law should they break a contractual obligation, as well as ignorance about how to go about leaving and where to go, kept the Negroes on the plantation. Thus they were bound to the soil as effectively as they had been before the Civil War. Based on an unpublished journal, county records, and published works; 64 notes.   R. V. Calvert

1599. Estes, Phoebe Beckner. THE REVEREND PETER VINEGAR. *Southern Folklore Q. 1959 23(4): 239-252.* The life and activities of Alexander Campbell Vinegar, nicknamed "Peter" (1842-1905), a Negro Baptist preacher and revivalist of great renown in and around the area of Lexington, Kentucky from the 1880's until his death. His sermons were attended by thousands, white and Negro, and were the sources of many folk-sayings and tales. The author suggests that Vinegar's importance merits further study. Based on interviews and contemporary newspapers.   H. Aptheker

1600. Fishel, Leslie H., Jr. REPERCUSSIONS OF RECONSTRUCTION: THE NORTHERN NEGRO, 1870-1883. *Civil War Hist. 1968 14(4): 325-345.* Studies the sources of the failure of Negro leadership in the North during Reconstruction. Because of declining interest from whites, bitter internal disputes among the elite, an emerging black caste system based on color, disagreement over the wisdom of integration, and a blindness to the growing needs and problems of Negroes in an urban environment, northern leaders lost control. The resulting vacuum paved the way for the ignored, chaotic ghetto of the 20th century. Based on contemporary newspapers and periodicals.   E. C. Murdock

1601. Fleming, Elvis Eugene. CAPTAIN NICHOLAS NOLAN: LOST ON THE STAKED PLAINS. *Texana 1966 4(1): 1-13.* Captain Nicholas Nolan, in search of marauding Comanches, led a detachment of Negro cavalrymen and a group of buffalo hunters into the Staked Plains of northwest Texas and eastern New Mexico in the summer of 1877. Although the expedition became lost and suffered from lack of water, it indirectly removed the last major Indian impediment to settlement of the area.   W. Elkins

1602. Going, Allen J. THE REVEREND EDGAR GARDNER MURPHY: HIS IDEAS AND INFLUENCE. *Hist. Mag. of the Protestant Episcopal Church 1956 25(4): 391-402.* A brief, documented discussion of E. G. Murphy's work (1869-1913) in the fields of child labor, education (including his leadership in the Southern Education Board), and Negro-white relations in the South. Murphy was a progressive and exemplified the ideal of the social gospel.
                                                      E. Oberholzer, Jr.

1603. Grob, Gerald N. ORGANIZED LABOR AND THE NEGRO WORKER, 1865-1900. *Labor Hist. 1960 1(2): 164-176.* While labor leaders at the national level generally took a stand against racial discrimination, union members often opposed the admission of Negroes into their organizations. During the 1860's, even though the National Labor Union declined to recognize a color line, its affiliates allowed exclusion or separate unions for Negroes. In the early 1880's the Knights of Labor became the dominant labor organization. Although Terence Vincent Powderly, head of the Knights, consistently proposed unionization of Negro workers, "he was at the same time prevented by pressure from the rank and file from vigorously enforcing his equalitarian views." When the American Federation of Labor emerged as the leading organization after 1886, its leader, Samuel Gompers, proclaimed that there should be no distinction between white and Negro workers. Though Gompers vigorously attempted to induce affiliates of the A.F. of L. to accept Negro workers, he eventually succumbed to pressure and in 1900 suggested that the Negroes should organize their own unions.   J. H. Krenkel

1604. Gutman, Herbert G. BLACK COAL MINERS AND THE GREEN-BACK-LABOR PARTY IN REDEEMER, ALABAMA: 1878-1879. *Labor Hist. 1969 10(3): 506-535.* Presents 26 selected and edited letters from black and white coal miners who lived in the Birmingham steel region of Alabama. They provide a description of the new Alabama working class and its living and working conditions. Based on letters taken from the *National Labor Tribune* of Pittsburgh; 6 notes.   L. L. Athey

1605. Harris, Andrew. DEARFIELD, A NEGRO GHOST TOWN IN WELD COUNTY, COLORADO. *Negro Hist. Bull. 1963 27(2): 38-39.* Briefly describes Dearfield, Colorado, a Negro community founded and promoted by O. T. Jackson around the turn of the 20th century and abandoned within a decade after a combination of depression and drought discouraged its settlers. Documented with newspaper material.   L. Gara

1606. Herndon, Jane. HENRY MC NEAL TURNER'S AFRICAN DREAM: A RE-EVALUATION. *Mississippi Q. 1969 22(4): 327-336.* Turner's vision of an African nation of American Negroes represented an early example of Negro nationalistic thought. In Turner's projected African nation, the Negro's potentialities would be exemplified and the belief in black inferiority discredited, so that self-respect might be engendered among Negroes. The unfortunate fact was that those who wished to go to Africa could not finance their emigration, and Congress refused to appropriate any money, despite Turner's many petitions. While he advocated the return of only two or three million successful Negroes with necessary financial resources, that group was unwilling to exchange security for uncertainty in an undeveloped land. Making four trips to Africa in the 1890's, Turner wrote letters describing and praising the continent in the *Voice of Missions* and other publications, but the failure of the few Negroes who attempted settlement in Liberia discouraged further efforts. Turner stimulated an interest in the

American Negro's African heritage and helped awaken Negro racial pride. Based partly on the monthly *Voice of Missions* (1893-1900); 20 notes.

R. V. Calvert

1607. Hopkins, Richard J. OCCUPATIONAL AND GEOGRAPHIC MOBILITY IN ATLANTA, 1870-1896. *J. of Southern Hist. 1968 34(2): 200-213.* In trying to suggest whether Atlanta, Georgia, and other southern cities developed in a similar way between 1870 and 1896 and had the same basic social organization as cities in other sections of the country, the author adopted the methodological approach used by Stephan Thernstrom in his analysis of Newburyport, Massachusetts, *Poverty and Progress: Social Mobility in a Nineteenth Century City* (Cambridge: Harvard U. Press, 1964). Census statistics, provided in six tables, seemed to indicate that the prospects for achieving higher occupational position were more favorable for foreign immigrants in southern cities than in other sections of the country precisely because of the presence of a large body of Negroes in low-status manual occupations. In short, "race consciousness removed Southern Negroes farther from the mainstream of urban occupational mobility than nativist prejudice moved immigrants in Northern and Western cities." 16 notes. I. M. Leonard

1608. Killian, Lewis M. THE AMBIVALENT POSITION OF THE NEGRO IN THE SOUTH 1867-1900. *Negro Hist. Bull. 1960 23(4): 81-86.* Compares the lot of Negroes in the South during the Reconstruction period with their present status. After the abolition of slavery, the freedmen received temporary political rights, but about the turn of the century they were disfranchised, segregated, and subjected to economic discrimination. The author pleads for a settlement based on racial justice, rather than an abandonment of Negro rights in the interest of peace, as was the case in the earlier era. L. Gara

1609. Kraditor, Aileen S. TACTICAL PROBLEMS OF THE WOMAN-SUFFRAGE MOVEMENT IN THE SOUTH. *Louisiana Studies 1966 5(4): 289-305.* A discourse on the women's suffrage movement in the South that begins with a statement of conditions that delayed the movement a generation after it appeared in the Northeast. Five reasons that Clement Eaton suggested in his *The Freedom-of-Thought Struggle in the Old South* (New York: Harper, 1964) for the weakness of the women's rights movement in the middle of the 19th century are given. Then the observation is made that the rise of a women's rights movement is dependent on "a group of educated, capable women who need outlets for their energies" and "a lack of such outlets that are socially acceptable." Southern women had special problems caused by four circumstances peculiar to their region: 1) the South was the most conservative region with regard to the woman's role, 2) the South was a one-party section, 3) the states' rights shibboleth created special problems for a movement to amend the Federal Constitution, and 4) the Negro question. Each of the four circumstances is discussed. 28 notes.

G. W. McGinty

1610. Lewis, Roscoe E. THE LIFE OF PRISCILLA JOYNER. *Phylon 1959 20(1): 71-81.* A case study of an American ex-slave born in 1858 and interviewed when she was 95. The fact that she was the mulatto child of a white mother and a Negro father, was verified by original census records for 1860 in the National Archives, Washington, D.C. Records show she had two older white half-sisters and two younger white half-brothers. While such relations during slavery have been reported, this is one case which has been positively authenticated.

A

1611. Littlefield, Daniel F., Jr. and Underhill, Lonnie E. NEGRO MARSHALS IN THE INDIAN TERRITORY. *J. of Negro Hist. 1971 56(2): 77-87.* It is little known that several of the lawmen in Indian Territory (now Oklahoma) during the late 19th century were Negroes. Their duties pertained to the regions occupied by the Five Civilized Tribes - the Cherokee, Choctaw, Creek, Chicasaw, and Seminole - and were used by the Indian Police and the U.S. Marshal's office. The Indians preferred the black law officers, who unlike the white officials had lived all or most of their lives among the Indians and Indian freedmen. A fee system and the lack of available courts also made the Indians distrust white officers. Based mostly on Indian newspapers of the region, and on secondary sources; 45 notes.   R. S. Melamed

1612. Logan, Frenise A. FACTORS INFLUENCING THE EFFICIENCY OF NEGRO FARM LABORERS IN POST-RECONSTRUCTION NORTH CAROLINA. *Agric. Hist. 1959 33(4): 185-189.* In 1890, 64.6 percent of the total Negro population in North Carolina was employed in agricultural pursuits. Some white landlords and employers, particularly in areas with large Negro population, asserted that Negro tenants and farm laborers were unreliable and inefficient. In areas where the Negro percentage of the population was small, the honesty, thriftiness, and reliability of the Negro tenants and farm hands was emphasized. Evidence indicates that in areas of heavy Negro population, employers paid Negroes wages substantially lower than those paid to whites, that there was an emphasis on the mortgage and lien bond system with all its abuses, and that wages were often partially paid in supplies.   J (W. D. Rasmussen)

1613. Marcus, Irwin M. THE SOUTHERN NEGRO AND THE KNIGHTS OF LABOR. *Negro Hist. Bull. 1967 30(3): 5-7.* Discusses some of the factors responsible for the desire of many Negroes to affiliate with the Knights of Labor. The social programs of the Knights attracted many Negroes. The Knights provided the mutual benefit and social features of national fraternal orders: functions usually neglected by trade unions. The order offered Negroes an opportunity to obtain leadership positions. The Knights demonstrated their policy of labor solidarity by the use of strikes to increase the wages and decrease the work week of Negro workers. 15 notes.   D. H. Swift

1614. Millet, Donald J. SOME ASPECTS OF AGRICULTURAL RETARDATION IN SOUTHWEST LOUISIANA, 1865-1900. *Louisiana Hist. 1970 11(1): 37-61.* The Civil War disrupted agriculture in southwestern Louisiana because the emancipation of the slaves caused labor difficulties. When the wage system failed, farmers turned to share cropping. Cotton made a more rapid recovery in the postwar period than sugar, the latter requiring expensive machinery. Overproduction and the depression of the 1870's led to a decline in cotton prosperity, but sugar recovery occurred in the 1890's, surpassing prewar levels, and rice also became important. Corn, grown mostly for subsistence, was not so greatly affected as the other crops. Other crops grown in the region were Irish and sweet potatoes, vegetables, and fruits, especially oranges. By the end of the century, land values, (a reliable indication of prosperity) had increased perceptibly. There was also rising interest in scientific cattle breeding. Based principally on Louisiana newspapers and census reports; 102 notes. R. L. Woodward

1615. Mitchell, Broadus. ECONOMICS IN THE SOUTH. *Current Hist. 1957 32(189): 267-272.* The cotton economy of the Old South tended to discourage venture capital in favor of bank and mortgage loans, which stifled economic development. With increasing industrialization following the economic crises of the 1870's, southerners felt more bound to defend their economic superiority against the Negro. This helps to explain why the economic progress of the South has been slow in the period from 1815 to 1890. C. F. Latour

1616. Montgomery, Horace. A BODY SNATCHER SPONSORS PENNSYL-VANIA'S ANATOMY ACT. *J. of the Hist. of Medicine and Allied Sci. 1966 21(4): 374-400.* A study of the origins of the passage of a statewide anatomy law in 1883. Although Pennsylvania was preeminent in medical education, it was slow in passing an anatomy act. The passage of an act in 1883 resulted from the work of William James McKnight, a member of the State Senate, a practicing physician, and a convicted former grave robber. The immediate background of the act of 1883 was the disclosure in late 1882 of an organized gang of grave robbers in Philadelphia, where a number of medical schools were located. The grave robbers were especially active in a Negro cemetery, which caused considerable unrest in the Negro community. 69 notes. G. N. Grob

1617. Neary, Margaret. SOME ASPECTS OF NEGRO SOCIAL LIFE IN RICHMOND, VIRGINIA 1865-1880. *Maryland Historian 1970 1(2): 105-119.* A description of the social, charitable, religious, and military organization which provided the 28 thousand Richmond Negroes with a separate, highly structured, and well-organized program of social activities. Based on newspapers, unpublished theses, and secondary sources; 41 notes, 4 appendixes.

G. O. Gagnon

1618. O'Donnell, James H., III, ed. A FREEDMAN THANKS HIS PATRONS: LETTERS OF TAYLOR THISTLE, 1872-1873. *J. of Southern Hist. 1967 3(1): 68-84.* Taylor Z. Thistle, a Missouri mulatto, was one of the freed slaves trained for the Baptist ministry at the Nashville Normal and Theological Institute. While he was at the institute he wrote letters regarding himself to Olive W. Cushing, a member of the Baptist Church at Scituate, Massachusetts, who collected money in that church to support him. Seven letters of Thistle to Miss Cushing, two letters to Miss Cushing by Daniel W. Phillips, who founded the institute, and two endorsements on Thistle's letters by Phillips and Alanson P. Mason of the American Baptist Home Mission Society are reproduced from the Cushing Family Papers in the Duke University Library. 24 notes. S. E. Humphreys

1619. Oetgen, Jerome. THE ORIGINS OF THE BENEDICTINE ORDER IN GEORGIA. *Georgia Hist. Q. 1969 53(2): 165-183.* Describes the activities in the 1870's and 1880's of the Catholic order in Savannah and on the islands off the coast of Georgia. Missionary efforts were centered at the Isle of Hope near Savannah, where a monastery and an agricultural-manual labor school were established for freedmen. Churches and schools were also built in the city for blacks and whites. The leading spirit in the missionary work was Father Oswald Moosmueller, O.S.B., who sparked the enterprise between 1877 and 1887. The monastery and school eventually failed, largely because of lack of interest in Catholicism and farming among the Negro inhabitants of the Isle of Hope. The author likens the Benedictine activities to the efforts of Spanish missionaries to convert the Indians on the same land in the 16th century. Based on research in Benedictine archives at St. Vincent Archabbey in Latrobe, Pennsylvania; 37 notes.   R. A. Mohl

1620. Phillips, James R. THE LITTLE-KNOWN NEGRO ROUGH RIDERS. *Negro Hist. Bull. 1963 27(3): 59.* Brief description of the contributions of Negro troops to the fighting in Cuba during the Spanish-American War.
                                                                                              L. Gara

1621. Polos, Nicholas C. SEGREGATION AND JOHN SWETT. *Southern California Q. 1964 46(1): 69-82.* From 1863 to 1867 John Swett was California's fourth superintendent of public instruction. Being a strong Union man, he argued that: 1) for self-preservation every representative government should provide for the education of every child; and 2) the property of the State should be taxed to pay for that education. He was ahead of his time; not till 1886 did the NEA give attention to race education. Based on newspapers, journals of the Senate and Assembly, and statutes of Swett's two administrations.   E. P. Stickney

1622. Porter, Kenneth O. NEGRO LABOR IN THE WESTERN CATTLE INDUSTRY, 1866-1900. *Labor Hist. 1969 10(3): 346-374.* Surveys the occupations which Negroes held or to which they could aspire in the cattle industry. Although seldom attaining the position of foreman or trail boss, the Negro laborer was probably less discriminated against in the cattle industry than in any other industry. The services of the eight or nine thousand Negroes were definitely needed for the success of the trail drives and the work of the ranches. Based on the archival files of J. Frank Dobie and on numerous primary and secondary sources; 91 notes.   L. L. Athey

1623. Riddleberger, Patrick W. GEORGE W. JULIAN: ABOLITIONIST LAND REFORMER. *Agric. Hist. 1955 29(3): 108-115.* George W. Julian of Indiana carried on an attack from 1863 to 1871 in Congress against the landed aristocracy of the South and against land monopoly and speculation. He had an unrestrainable urge for controversy which kept him from accomplishing some of his objectives. Based on published and unpublished documents.
                                                                             J (W. D. Rasmussen)

1624. Ridout, Lionel Utley. THE CHURCH, THE CHINESE, AND THE NEGROES IN CALIFORNIA, 1849-1893. *Hist. Mag. of the Protestant Episcopal Church 1959 28(2): 115-138.* A survey of the Episcopal Church's mission to the Chinese and Negroes in California. In spite of the devoted work of the Reverend Edward W. Syle as missionary to the Chinese and of the Reverend Peter W. Cassey, a Negro minister, the Episcopal Church was unsuccessful in its efforts to work with the two groups. Bishop Kip's one failure was his neglect of the Chinese settlers.   E. Oberholzer, Jr.

1625. Rogers, Benjamin F. FLORIDA SEEN THROUGH THE EYES OF NINETEENTH CENTURY TRAVELLERS. *Florida Hist. Q. 1955 34(2): 177-189.* Portrays the climate, scenery, negro and white residents, and possibilities of economic development as seen, chiefly, by northern and foreign tourists.
G. L. Lycan

1626. Rogers, William W. THE NEGRO ALLIANCE IN ALABAMA. *J. of Negro Hist. 1960 45(1): 38-44.* Negro alliances or farmers' cooperative unions flourished briefly in Alabama, as elsewhere in the South, from 1887 to 1891. Despite opposition from Bourbon Democrats as well as some conservatives within the ranks of the white alliances, Negro alliances generally had the strong sympathy and support of the white alliances, with which they cooperated in promoting causes of mutual interest. The importance of both white and Negro alliances declined sharply after 1891 when they began to neglect their economic programs and became involved in politics. Based on contemporary press reports.
R. E. Wilson

1627. Roy, Jessie H. COLORED JUDGES: JUDGE GEORGE LEWIS RUFFIN. *Negro Hist. Bull. 1965 28(6): 135-137.* Brief sketch of Lewis Ruffin (1834-86), Massachusetts legislator, lawyer, and pioneer civil rights worker, who became the State's first Negro judge.   L. Gara

1628. Ryon, Fred L. WILLIAM ALLEN, NEGRO EVANGELIST OF THE SOCIETY OF FRIENDS. *Bull. of Friends Hist. Assoc. 1958 47(2): 94-105.* An account of the Quaker religious activities of William Allen (d. 1898), an ex-slave who was active in Indiana, Ohio, New York and Canada. Based on the author's acquaintance with Allen.   N. Kurland

1629. Saloutos, Theodore. SOUTHERN AGRICULTURE AND THE PROBLEMS OF READJUSTMENT: 1865-1877. *Agric. Hist. 1956 30(2): 58-76.* The complex problems of agricultural readjustment in the southern United States after the Civil War, including landholding, social classes, staple production, the place of the Negro, credit, and markets are summarized and discussed. The author concludes that the problems defied solution. The article is based on printed sources.   J (W. D. Rasmussen)

1630. Savage, W. Sherman. THE NEGRO PIONEER IN THE STATE OF WASHINGTON. *Negro Hist. Bull. 1958 21(4): 93-95.* Tells of the work and contributions of the small number of Negroes who migrated to the Territory and State of Washington. L. Gara

1631. Schwendemann, Glenn. THE "EXODUSTERS" ON THE MISSOURI. *Kansas Hist. Q. 1963 29(1): 25-40.* In 1879 many Negroes migrated to Kansas. It was difficult to find places for them to settle. Kansas City, Kansas refused to receive them, and Kansas City, Missouri was outside the State. Consequently they moved from St. Louis to Wyandotte, where they were received cordially. Several local committees were established to assist them in finding permanent settlements and jobs. Many settled at Lawrence, Leavenworth, Topeka, and Atchison, although the latter town was criticized for not taking its share. The migration died down during the summer, but during the winter of 1879-80 the State was deluged by another crowd of immigrants from Texas. Based on local newspapers. W. F. Zornow

1632. Seifman, Eli. EDUCATION OR EMIGRATION: THE SCHISM WITHIN THE AFRICAN COLONIZATION MOVEMENT, 1865-1875. *Hist. of Educ. Q. 1967 7(1): 36-57.* After a review of early attempts at the colonization of American free Negroes in America or Africa and of the founding of the American Colonization Society in 1816, the author discusses developments within that society after the Civil War. Through the efforts of the Reverend John B. Pinney, the New York State branch of the Colonization Society in 1869 shifted its emphasis from colonization to aid for public education in Liberia. This brought conflict with the national parent society and schism within the State, where the supporters of colonization rallied around the Reverend John Orcutt and in November organized a rival branch under the presidency of Samuel Finley Breese Morse. At the 1870 meeting of the national society delegates from both State branches were seated, yet the conflict between them persisted. The American Colonization Society was dissolved after 1900, yet the New York State Colonization Society continues to promote education in Liberia today. Based on published proceedings and publications; 82 notes. J. Herbst

1633. Sisk, Glenn N. CRIME AND JUSTICE IN THE ALABAMA BLACK BELT, 1875-1917. *Mid-Am. 1958 40(2): 106-113.* According to official State of Alabama reports, crime in the Black Belt before 1917 was highest among the Negro population, and justice, largely left to the discretion of the counties until State reform laws were passed in the early 1900's, was impeded by substandard prison conditions, unreasonable penalties, and a system of convict-lease to private contractors. R. J. Marion

1634. Sisk, Glenn N. FUNERAL CUSTOMS IN THE ALABAMA BLACK BELT, 1870-1910. *Southern Folklore Q. 1959 23(3): 169-171.* Comments on customs among both Negro and white men and women. Based on interviews, contemporary sources, and secondary works. H. Aptheker

1635. Sisk, Glenn N. SOCIAL ASPECTS OF THE ALABAMA BLACK BELT, 1875-1917. *Mid-Am. 1955 37(1): 31-47.* A survey of social conditions. The period 1865-1900 saw a movement of the white population from the Black Belt to towns and cities. This trend was offset in some degree by the growth of small communities and by nonsouthern immigration. In spite of individual instances of business and professional success, most Negroes remained very poor and inferior in the opinion of the whites. White supremacy dominated social relations. Based largely on local newspapers.   R. F. Campbell

1636. Smythe, Donald. JOHN J. PERSHING AT FORT ASSINIBOINE. *Montana 1968 18(1): 19-23.* John J. Pershing, future commander of the American Expeditionary Force in World War I, was stationed in 1895 at Fort Assiniboine in northern Montana. As lieutenant of a troop of the 10th Cavalry, a Negro regiment, he carried out orders to gather and deliver to the international border a number of Cree Indians for deportation to Canada. His management of this difficult assignment won commendation from his superiors. 16 notes.
                                                                S. R. Davison

1637. Spalding, David, C.F.X. THE NEGRO CATHOLIC CONGRESSES, 1889-1894. *Catholic Hist. R. 1969 55(3): 337-357.* "At the prompting of Daniel A. Rudd, a Negro publisher, annual congresses for Negro Catholics were held in Washington, D.C., Cincinnati, Philadelphia, Chicago, and Baltimore. With each congress the delegates became more critical of the discrimination practiced against their race by the white populace in general and the Catholic Church in particular. A mood of optimism during the first three congresses gave way to a growing frustration. Soon after the establishment of a permanent organization, the movement collapsed for reasons not apparent but in some way related to the triumph of political and Catholic conservatism in the United States."
                                                                              J

1638. Tate, Merze. DECADENCE OF THE HAWAIIAN NATION AND PROPOSALS TO IMPORT A NEGRO LABOR FORCE. *J. of Negro Hist. 1962 47(4): 248-263.* Prior to and following the U.S. annexation of the Hawaiian Islands, American officials were concerned about the constant decline of the native Hawaiian population. Planters imported Japanese, Chinese, and Portuguese contract laborers to work the sugar fields. Efforts were also made to encourage immigration from the United States, but plans to attract American Negroes to the islands always met with determined opposition from the whites there who based their arguments on racial grounds. Documented with material from the Archives of Hawaii and other sources.   L. Gara

1639. Thelen, David P. and Fischel, Leslie H., Jr. RECONSTRUCTION IN THE NORTH: THE "WORLD" LOOKS AT NEW YORK'S NEGROES, MARCH 16, 1867. *New York Hist. 1968 49(4): 405-440.* Reprints the text of the New York *World's* 1867 in-depth survey of the socioeconomic and political conditions of New York City's Negro population. It generally finds the city's 10 thousand Negroes on the lowest rungs of the economic ladder, but holds that their crime rates and standards of morality and personal cleanliness compare favorably with those of whites in similar socioeconomic conditions. The *World's* analysis, judged by the standards of the age, was remarkably accurate and objective. 5 illus., 36 notes. G. Kurland

1640. Thompson, Edgar K. NAVASSA: A FORGOTTEN ACQUISITION. *Am. Neptune 1966 26(3): 171-176.* Deals with the acquisition of this Caribbean island during a period of heavy demand for guano fertilizer in the 1850's, under the Guano Act of 1856. The author also gives details of a riot there in 1889 by Negro contract laborers digging guano, in protest against inhuman treatment. Five whites were killed and nine Negroes. The laborers involved were convicted of murder and their appeal that the island was not American territory failed. Temporarily abandoned, the island was used by Cuban gun runners in the 1890's and a lighthouse erected there in 1913 which the U.S. Government still maintains. Haiti periodically protests our sovereignty. Illus. J. G. Lydon

1641. Tribe, Ivan M. RISE AND DECLINE OF PRIVATE ACADEMIES IN ALBANY, OHIO. *Ohio Hist. 1969 78(3): 188-201.* Reviews the history of private academies in the Ohio town of Albany, concentrating mainly on their operation and financing, their contributions to Negro education, and the influence exerted on them by Oberlin College. Based on the Salmon P. Chase Papers in the Library of Congress and on published materials. S. L. Jones

1642. Unsigned. THE GOODRIDGE BROTHERS: SAGINAW VALLEY PHOTOGRAPHIC HISTORIANS. *Michigan Hist. 1969 53(3): 240-246.* Biographical and descriptive information accompany eight late-19th-century photographs (five depicting aspects of the lumbering industry) from the work of Glenalvin, William, and Wallace Goodridge, the sons of a Maryland slave who migrated to Michigan and, between the 1860's and the turn of the century, maintained a photographic studio in East Saginaw. Lumbering, street scenes, and Great Lakes shipping were their favorite subjects. 11 notes. J. K. Flack

1643. Utley, Robert M. "PECOS BILL" ON THE TEXAS FRONTIER. *Am. West 1969 6(1): 4-13, 61-62.* William R. Shafter had risen to the brevet rank of brigadier general in the Michigan Volunteers in the Civil War. Under the 1869 reorganization of the Army he was commissioned a lieutenant colonel of infantry. His assignment was to one of four Negro regiments garrisoning the little frontier forts of the West and fighting hostile Indians over the next three decades. Except for a brief period in Dakota, Pecos Bill Shafter's role in the opening of the West was played out largely on the sterile frontiers of Texas and Mexico. Ironically, one minority (black troops) was being used to subjugate another minority (Indians). This was compounded by the increasing employment of Indian scouts by the Army against the Indians. The use of black troops was "a calculated humiliation" against conquered Texans but it was turned to discrimination against the blacks who for nearly two decades were left to police the most disagreeable sectors of the American frontier. Tough, aggressive, and persevering, Shafter enjoyed the respect, if rarely the affection, of his troops and fellow officers. Although his racism was barely concealed, he still proved an effective commander of Negro troops. Shafter was one of the frontier Army's more effective leaders. Heretofore this has been largely unknown and his chief claim to fame has been that of a caricatured figure in the Spanish-American War. 7 illus., map, biblio. note.

D. L. Smith

1644. Vaughn, William P. WEST POINT AND THE FIRST NEGRO CADET. *Military Affairs 1971 35(3): 100-102.* James Webster Smith (1850-76) entered West Point in 1870, the first Negro to do so. Subjected to much cadet harassment from the beginning he was convicted during the spring of 1871, by a court martial, of conduct unbecoming an officer. The sentence of dismissal was reduced to repeating the plebe year. He was dropped from the roles in 1874 for academic deficiencies. Based on West Point records and contemporary newspapers; 4 notes.

K. J. Bauer

1645. Walters, Ronald. POLITICAL STRATEGIES OF THE RECONSTRUC-TION. *Current Hist. 1969 57(339): 263-268, 301.* In terms of unresolved human problems, there are many similarities between the present and the Reconstruction period. A solution to the problems remaining from Reconstruction will not be found until the black community organizes effectively.

B. D. Rhodes

1646. Westerman, George W. HISTORICAL NOTES ON WEST INDIANS ON THE ISTHMUS OF PANAMA. *Phylon 1961 22(4): 340-350.* British West Indians have lived in the Isthmus since 1849, when some of them came to help build the Panama railroad. De Lesseps's French canal project later brought up to 20 thousand more, nine-tenths of them Negroes; they were later incorporated into the labor forces set up by the U.S. Government for building the Panama Canal. They varied in physique, complexion, and mannerisms, though all spoke English and lived separately from the natives. Overpopulation of the Islands brought more - members of the "better classes" as well as peasants - to gain from further canal construction work. They concentrated in urban areas, where they maintained churches, modest schools, and social life, through rigorous and often inhumane work conditions. Often discriminated against, they helped themselves through voluntary associations. Their services to Panama have received some recognition, though more has been merited.

L. Filler

5

AFRO-AMERICAN SOCIETY IN THE TWENTIETH CENTURY

Racial Attitudes & Segregation

1647. Abernethy, Lloyd M. THE WASHINGTON RACE WAR OF JULY, 1919. *Maryland Hist. Mag. 1963 58(4): 309-324.* In Washington, D.C., during a four-day period - 19-22 July 1919 - "a full scale race war fed by the passions and prejudices of both whites and Negroes resisted the efforts of public authorities to restore order." The city's population had risen from 359,997 in 1916 to 455,428 in 1919. A large number of the new residents, both Negro and white, came from the South. Competition for jobs and the failure of the city's major newspapers to take "any definite action to ease the growing tension between the whites and the Negroes" were important causes of this "race war."   W. L. Fox

1648. Alexander, Charles C. WHITE-ROBED REFORMERS: THE KU KLUX KLAN COMES TO ARKANSAS, 1921-22. *Arkansas Hist. Q. 1963 22(1): 8-23.* In 1920 Edward Young Clarke and Elizabeth Tyler entered into a business partnership with William Joseph Simmons, founder of the Ku Klux Klan. "Partly because of Clarke's propagandizing, but largely because of the passions of the people who joined it," the Klan became the primary outlet for hatred of Catholics, Jews, Negroes, foreigners, radicals, as well as bootleggers, adulterers, and other "objectionable" types. Eventually anti-Catholicism obscured all other prejudices. In Klan history in Arkansas it is surprising that, considering the social acceptability of violence against Negroes, only a few were assaulted. Based on an unpublished doctoral dissertation, University of Texas, 1962; 34 notes.
                                                              E. P. Stickney

1649. Aptheker, Herbert. THE NEGRO COLLEGE STUDENT IN THE 1920'S - YEARS OF PREPARATION AND PROTEST: AN INTRODUC-TION. *Sci. and Soc. 1969 33(2): 150-167.* Finds parallels between grievances and movements of blacks on campuses today with blacks in the 1920's. Argues that the seeds of today's activism were planted just after World War I. 29 notes.

R. S. Burns

1650. Ashby, Darrell LeRoy. WILLIAM E. BORAH AND THE POLITICS OF CONSTITUTIONALISM. *Pacific Northwest Q. 1967 58(3): 119-129.* Senator William Edgar Borah, powerful Congressman from the State of Idaho, was once considered by political experts to be an outstanding "moral and intellectual leader" in the U.S. Senate. Covering essentially the period of 1925 to 1928, the author says that Borah's moral force was eroded by what is termed Borah's "double constitutional standard" in vigorously supporting the cause for prohibition against liquor "while rationalizing away the failures of the states to enforce the rights of Negroes." The descriptions of Borah's activities as a political leader and interpreter of the U.S. Constitution are well documented.

C. C. Gorchels

1651. Bailes, Sue. EUGENE TALMADGE AND THE BOARD OF REGENTS CONTROVERSY. *Georgia Hist. Q. 1969 53(4): 409-423.* Summarizes a 1941 controversy stemming from Governor Eugene Talmadge's attempts to purge the University of Georgia of Communists, "foreigners" (non-Georgians), and subscribers to racial equality. The Governor reacted to charges made by a disgruntled faculty member that the dean of the University's College of Education advocated bringing blacks and whites together in the classroom. The accusing professor had earlier been dismissed from her position for incompetence. Talmadge used the occasion to make a general attack on the university. The Board of Regents at first refused Talmadge's demands for dismissal of offending faculty members, but after the Governor restructured the board, the dismissals took place. In response to this "unprecedented and unjustifiable political interference," the Southern Association of Schools and Colleges revoked the accreditation of 10 Georgia colleges and universities. Talmadge's successor, Ellis Arnall, won the election on a campaign of removing the university from political machinations, and accreditation was restored in 1943. Based mostly on newspapers and periodicals; 81 notes.

R. A. Mohl

1652. Bailey, Kenneth K. SOUTHERN WHITE PROTESTANTISM AT THE TURN OF THE CENTURY. *Am. Hist. R. 1963 68(3): 618-635.* In 1900 most southerners belonged to explicitly southern denominations that were rigidly segregated along racial lines. Although sectarian debate often raged fiercely, "on such precepts as heaven and hell, God and Satan, depravity and redemption, there was little dispute. Few Southerners doubted the literal authenticity of the Scriptures or the ever presence of God in man's affairs." Poverty of resources limited both church life and ministerial training. Southern seminaries shared with the laity a distrust of scholarship and theological innovation. Few showed any interest in the application of Christian teaching to the life of society. Religious thought continued to stress individual regeneration and "although camp meetings have been generally supplanted by more decorous indoor services, most Southern congregations still sponsored special evangelistic campaigns each year." Based on printed primary sources.

M. Berman

1653. Bell, Wendell and Willis, Ernest M. THE SEGREGATION OF NEGROES IN AMERICAN CITIES: A COMPARATIVE ANALYSIS. *Social and Econ. Studies 1957 6(1): 59-75.* Presents the findings of a preliminary study in a comparative framework of the differential residential segregation of Negroes in American cities. Only three variables appeared to be related to Negro segregation: region, proportion of the total population represented by Negroes, and the size of the Negro population. In 22 central cities of "standard metropolitan area" the U.S. census figures showed that the nonwhite population increased by 58 percent while the white population decreased almost two percent from 1940 to 1950. The findings suggest the likelihood that the Negro became increasingly segregated from 1940 to 1950. Without some kind of "preventive planning," residential segregation can be expected to increase for cities in the Northeast, North Central, and Western regions of the United States. References, statistical table.   E. P. Stickney

1654. Bloch, Herman D. CRAFT UNIONS: A LINK IN THE CIRCLE OF NEGRO DISCRIMINATION. *Phylon 1958 18(4): 361-372.* This historical study has two objectives: to reveal why socioeconomic discrimination is an independent variable affecting the Negro's mode of life, and how some craft unions have influenced the operation of this variable. The author's test case is craft union-Negro relations in New York City for the period from 1866 to 1945. The total historical process is a circle from which the Negro occasionally has been able to extricate himself. Four factors explain the operation of the circle: 1) Negro subordination to the white man, 2) socioeconomic manifestations - the Negro is assigned social and economic status, 3) economico-social discrimination - the Negro's social mobility is limited despite a rise in his economic status, and 4) "purely economic" - concerned with competition for jobs. Each of these factors inherent in the data permit some formalization.   A

1655. Bloch, Herman D. THE EMPLOYMENT STATUS OF THE NEW YORK NEGRO IN RETROSPECT. *Phylon 1959 20(4): 327-344.* Although Negroes accounted for at least 25 percent of consumer trade in Harlem, New York, in the 1920's, Negroes were seldom hired as workers there. Subsequent developments continued to show patterns of discrimination. Devious methods were utilized by some New York employers to restrict their personnel to white persons, despite the training, competence, and other qualities of Negro applicants. Others sought to restrict Negroes to menial jobs. In addition, the Negro was not only last hired, but the soonest separated from his position. As a result, he was kept in a state of frustration which, according to his temperament, bred bitterness, hatred, or apathy. The basic purpose of discrimination was economic: the Negro's low status helped control the demands of white workers, even though the overall income of white people was much higher than that of Negroes. The latter have responded to conditions in several ways: by acting as strikebreakers, by passing as white, by exerting economic and political pressure when possible, and by such actions as the Harlem riot of 1935. Legal protection and economic prosperity are necessary to the social advance of the Negro.   L. Filler

1656. Bloomfield, Maxwell. DIXON'S "THE LEOPARD'S SPOTS": A STUDY IN POPULAR RACISM. *Am. Q. 1964 16(3): 387-401.* Thomas Dixon, Jr. ex-actor, lawyer, preacher, and propagandist, called forth the spectre of the "black peril" in *The Leopard's Spots* (1902) his first and most successful "mob novel." In true Muckraker fashion Dixon tapped the antidemocratic vein running just below the surface of the Progressive mind, i.e. the belief in the superiority of Anglo-Saxon middle-class civilization. He warned that the "amoral" and "inferior" Negro, through social equality and eventually miscegenation, would destroy the Progressive dream. R. S. Pickett

1657. Blum, Eleanor. MEMORIES OF A MISSISSIPPI CHILDHOOD. *Antioch R. 1965 25(2): 248-266.* An account of the author's life in Mississippi in the 1920's and early 1930's. She discusses the mores, education, culture, economics, and the Negro question as she experienced them. D. F. Rossi

1658. Blumenthal, Henry. WOODROW WILSON AND THE RACE QUESTION. *J. of Negro Hist. 1963 48(1): 1-21.* Despite Woodrow Wilson's vague pre-election assurances given to American Negroes, the Wilson administration actually set back the cause of civil rights for colored Americans. Wilson defended the status quo for Negroes partly because he believed that their lot could only be gradually improved through education, vocational training, and improved economic opportunities, and partly because he shared the assumptions of racial inequality which most Americans held to be true. Political expediency also led Wilson to emphasize domestic reforms other than Negro rights. Well documented. L. Gara

1659. Boller, Paul F., Jr. PURLINGS AND PLATITUDES: MENCKEN'S AMERICANA. *Southwest R. 1965 50(4): 357-371.* Samples from Henry L. Mencken's "Americana" on religion, high culture, the 18th amendment, and the American Negro. The name "Americana" was not applied until 1922, but the department had originated in the *Smart Set* in 1914. D. F. Henderson

1660. Brack, Harold A. ERNEST FREMONT TITTLE: A PULPIT CRITIC OF THE AMERICAN SOCIAL ORDER. *Q. J. of Speech 1966 52(4): 364-370.* A description of the social issues dealt with by Ernest Fremont Tittle from the pulpit. As the pastor of the First Methodist Church in Evanston, Illinois, Tittle drew national attention as he spoke his mind on issues concerning such matters as international peace organizations, the Ku Klux Klan, military training in high schools and colleges, free speech, war and peace, race relations, and slum clearance. His basic principle was that "the preacher must be granted the full right to declare the Counsel of God as he understands it," and he was, as a result, denounced by such groups as the Paul Reveres, the American Legion, and the *Chicago Tribune.* The author declares that although Tittle's sermons concerned social issues, his preaching was basically God-centered. The primary sources are the texts of Tittle's sermons; 42 notes. M. A. Hayes

1661. Brewer, James H. THE WAR AGAINST JIM CROW IN THE LAND OF GOSHEN. *Negro Hist. Bull. 1960 24(3): 53-57.* Describes the boycott used by the Negro population of Richmond, Virginia, to oppose the policy of racial segregation put into effect on the city streetcars in 1904. John Mitchell, Jr., editor of the Richmond *Planet,* organized the resistance which contributed to the ultimate bankruptcy of the street car company. The success of the boycott was nullified by a Virginia law of 1906 which required separation of the races in street cars. Documented.   L. Gara

1662. Brittain, Joseph M. THE RETURN OF THE NEGRO TO ALABAMA POLITICS, 1930-1954. *Negro Hist. Bull. 1959 22(8): 196-199.* Traces the movement to disfranchise Negroes in Alabama after the return of ex-Confederates to power in 1880, and the opposition to it. Persistent efforts and a series of legal victories enabled a minority of Negroes to circumvent various discriminatory devices. By 1954 approximately fifty thousand Negro voters were registered in Alabama.   L. Gara

1663. Burnside, Ronald D. RACISM IN THE ADMINISTRATIONS OF GOVERNOR COLE BLEASE. *Pro. of the South Carolina Hist. Assoc. 1964: 43-57.* Traces the element of racism in the administrations of Coleman Livingston Blease (from 1911 to 1915) and its effect on race relations in South Carolina. Blease's racial views were based on his belief in the innate inferiority of the Negro race and the Negro's low moral nature. Although Blease did not create the race issue, he exploited it to his political advantage and made no effort to improve race relations in the State. Moreover, his inflammatory speeches in defense of lynching were damaging to law and order.   J. W. Thacker, Jr.

1664. Carrott, M. Browning. THE SUPREME COURT AND MINORITY RIGHTS IN THE NINETEEN-TWENTIES. *Northwest Ohio Q. 1969 41(4): 144-156.* The Supreme Court of Chief Justice William Howard Taft usually curbed the activities of labor and radical political organizations; but, during an era of general intolerance, it used its great power to support the personal liberties of ethnic, religious, and racial groups in a series of cases between 1923 and 1927 involving parochial schools, foreign-language instruction, and the right of Negroes to vote. Sensing that it was a period of unrest, the justices tried to create a new political base by favoring those increasingly active minority groups whose moderate leadership and opposition to the Klan made them appear useful allies in the struggle for stability. Based on biographies, monographs, articles, Government reports, and the Taft Papers in the Library of Congress; 55 notes.
                                                    W. F. Zornow

1665. Carter, Everett. CULTURAL HISTORY WRITTEN WITH LIGHTNING: THE SIGNIFICANCE OF "THE BIRTH OF A NATION." *Am. Q. 1960 12(3): 347-357.* Examines the cultural and artistic significance of the 1915 David Lewelyn Wark Griffith film, *The Birth of a Nation,* and concludes that as motion picture art, it fails of greatness. Technique without content is not enough. By drawing a grossly inaccurate and inflammatory stereotype of the Negro, the film "instead of attempting to reach a whole vision, sinewed with moral responsibility," sought only to satisfy a jaded popular appetite. Based on a study of the film, secondary sources, and Thomas Dixon's *The Clansman,* the novel on which it was based.   W. M. Armstrong

1666. Carter, Hodding. THE FORGIVEN FAULKNER. *J. of Inter-Am. Studies 1965 7(2): 127-148.* The author recalls some of the foibles of Faulkner when he encountered him in a literary colony in the French Quarter of New Orleans. In addition he examines Faulkner's racial views as expressed in published letters to the editor of the Memphis *Commercial Appeal.*   J. R. Thomas

1667. Carter, Wilmoth A. NEGRO MAIN STREET AS A SYMBOL OF DIS-CRIMINATION. *Phylon 1960 21(3): 234-242.* The Negro, like other ethnic and racial groups, has adjusted to urban life in specific, group-oriented fashion, and his "Main Street" has been a shopping and social center, a service and cultural area. Raleigh, North Carolina, provided data for the following description. In the 1880-90 period, Negro barbers, shoemakers, butchers, and others served Negroes and white people on downtown "front streets." There was a limited amount of forced segregation. In the 20th century, white realtors increasingly would not rent to Negroes, who migrated to streets segregated for Negroes. There was fluctuating segregation and minimum discrimination, 1865-75; fixed segregation and heightened discrimination, 1875-1910; persistent segregation and lessened discrimination, 1910-1930's; and a "sloping" segregation and a less obvious discrimination since then. The depression of the 1930's modified white policy, since white people sought Negro patronage, and this process has continued. Negro "Main Street" persists because discriminatory policies are still pursued.

L. Filler

1668. Celarier, Michelle. A STUDY OF PUBLIC OPINION ON DESEGRE-GATION IN OKLAHOMA HIGHER EDUCATION. *Chronicles of Oklahoma 1969 47(3): 268-281.* Deals with three court cases involving desegregation in Oklahoma higher education between 1946 and 1955. Ada Lois Sipuel (later Mrs. Fisher) applied for admission to the Oklahoma University School of Law in 1946 and was denied on the basis of race. Public opinion was mixed, with Oklahoma University students having the most liberal outlook. In 1948, George W. McLaurin, a black man with a master's degree from Kansas University, applied for admission to Oklahoma University. Whereas Mrs. Fisher had not been admitted and a separate black law school had been provided, McLaurin was eventually admitted. By 1948 public opinion had apparently become more cognizant that desegregation was inevitable. The famous *Brown vs. Board of Education of Topeka* case (1954) all but ended segregation in Oklahoma higher education, at least on an enforced basis. In all cases, the public seems to have feared racial intermarriage as the final result of desegregation. Opinion gradually changed to a grudging acceptance. Based on sources from four public and two college newspapers; 44 notes.   K. P. Davis

1669. Clayton, Bruce L. THE RACIAL THOUGHT OF A SOUTHERN INTELLECTUAL AT THE BEGINNING OF THE CENTURY: WILLIAM GARROTT BROWN. *South Atlantic Q. 1964 63(1): 93-103.* In understanding the South's racial thought at the turn of the 20th century, an analysis of the writings of William Garrott Brown - a humane, conscientious, and emancipated southerner - is instructive. Brown saw the South as politically retarded and undemocratic because of the Negro, and he hoped Negro disfranchisement would enable the white South to divide politically and restore the two-party system. He also supported gradual improvement of the Negro's lot through education and employment in the needed new southern industrial expansion. He opposed abridgement of the Negro's right to work in the South. But Brown was a man who thought of the Negro problem only in white man's terms. 22 notes.

J. M. Bumsted

1670. Cripps, Thomas. PAUL ROBESON AND BLACK IDENTITY IN AMERICAN MOVIES. *Massachusetts R. 1970 11(3): 468-485.* In the 1920's and 1930's, American Negroes were disgusted with the image of Negroes in Hollywood movies and made Negro-oriented films in various east coast studios for showing in segregated and ghetto movie theaters. However, the noted Negro actor Paul Robeson in the years 1924-44, attempted to make movies for general viewing which portrayed Negroes realistically and sympathetically. He made a dozen such films, but only *Emperor Jones* was a popular success, and his efforts ended in failure. Concludes that Robeson failed because white America would only accept Negroes in the subservient and comic role offered by Hollywood. Based on primary and secondary sources; 41 notes. G. Kurland

1671. Cripps, Thomas R. THE REACTION OF THE NEGRO TO THE MOTION PICTURE "BIRTH OF A NATION." *Historian 1962/63 25(3): 344-362.* Analyzes the unsuccessful fight of American Negroes against an artistically superb film released in 1915, based on Thomas Dixon's fiery novel, *The Clansman,* and reflective of the deep hostility toward Negroes, particularly in the deep South. "For Negroes, their failure in the fight against *Birth of a Nation* was another reminder that the scant progress made in the Roosevelt years was not necessarily inevitable and that the Wilson era was a time of troubles characterized by a Jim Crow Federal Government, lynching, and the seed-time of a new Ku Klux Klan. The controversy also demonstrated the seriousness with which films had come to be regarded both as creators and reflectors of opinions and attitudes after only two decades of existence." Based on the author's correspondence with Mrs. Thomas Dixon; on Thomas Dixon's "Southern Horizons: An Autobiography," a manuscript in possession of Mrs. Dixon, Raleigh, North Carolina; on the Booker T. Washington Papers, Library of Congress; and on contemporary periodicals and extensive published sources. Sr. M. McAuley

1672. Cripps, Thomas R. THE UNFORMED IMAGE: THE NEGRO IN THE MOVIES BEFORE "BIRTH OF A NATION." *Maryland Historian 1971 2(1): 13-26.* Characterization of Negroes in films prior to "Birth of a Nation" was varied. Often, Negroes were portrayed sympathetically due to the need for audiences in urban areas and to the urban location of most filming. The turning point was the concomitant development of David Wark Griffith's dominant style and the migration of the film industry to California - away from the polyethnic North. In the sterile atmosphere of Hollywood, Negroes were utilized only as comic relief. The southern mystique prevented use of Negroes as heroes; the National Association for the Advancement of Colored People (NAACP) prevented their use as villains. Based on films, personal papers, and secondary sources; photos, 51 notes.   G. O. Gagnon

1673. Crowe, Charles. RACIAL MASSACRE IN ATLANTA SEPTEMBER 22, 1906. *J. of Negro Hist. 1969 54(2): 150-173.* The Atlanta riot of 1906 was a representative riot of the Progressive era and, like most southern riots of the time, contained more barbarous atrocities and paternalistic rescues of servants than did the northern disorders. Before the riot began, there had been months of intense political campaigning in which Negro baiting was a prominent feature. The newspapers of the area fully sympathized with the politicians and further inflamed white public opinion as a result. The riot lasted five days and 26 people were killed - one white and 25 blacks. Part of the article was presented in a paper at the annual meeting of the American Historical Association in Toronto on 29 December 1967. 20 notes.   R. S. Melamed

1674. Crowe, Charles. RACIAL VIOLENCE AND SOCIAL REFORM - ORIGINS OF THE ATLANTA RIOT OF 1906. *J. of Negro Hist. 1968 53(3): 234-256.* Describes Georgia progressives as political leaders whose program of reform government always included anti-Negro measures which they frequently linked with popular goals such as clean franchise or antialcoholism. The racism of the reformers and their editor allies contributed to the bloody race riot in Atlanta in 1906, which in turn strengthened the forces making for prohibition and political repression of the black man. Violence against Negroes was tacitly accepted by nearly all southern leaders as a last resort to maintain white supremacy, and the progressive reformers were no exception.   L. Gara

1675. Crowe, Charles. TOM WATSON, POPULISTS, AND BLACKS RECONSIDERED. *J. of Negro Hist. 1970 55(2): 99-116.* Thomas Edward Watson, a political leader of agrarian malcontents in Georgia at the turn of the 20th century, maintained his devotion to white supremacy throughout his entire political career, but he did make a few token concessions to Negroes during the 1890's. Some of his positions can be explained by the fact that he had an extremely secure and loyal following of people who were willing to tolerate his eccentricities because they were certain of his racist ideology and regional loyalty. Many of Watson's deviations can also be traced to his hatred of all things Wilsonian, and the acceptance of his strange ideas was frequently due to the ignorance of his audience and the fact that he wrapped them in "Dixie cellophane." Based mostly on primary source materials; 23 notes.   R. S. Melamed

1676. Cuban, Larry. A STRATEGY FOR RACIAL PEACE: NEGRO LEADERSHIP IN CLEVELAND, 1900-1919. *Phylon 1967 28(3): 299-311.* Despite the fact that Cleveland was regarded as a mecca for Negroes in the early years of the 20th century it was only in the most narrow sense a promised land. Negroes were separated residentially and socially from the white community. Negroes were forced to reside in less healthy areas, stood a greater chance of being arrested than their white counterparts, and found work available only in unskilled and service occupations. Why, asks the author, was there less racial strife in Cleveland than in other American cities? He concludes that it was because the Negro leadership practiced accommodation with the whites. They preached that protest on the part of the Negro community was unrealistic because economic and political ties with the whites were too important to be jeopardized by agitation. Thus, the accommodationist pattern of responses by conservative Negro leaders helped to maintain peace. Based on published sources; 42 notes.

D. N. Brown

1677. Dalfiume, Richard M. "THE FORGOTTEN YEARS" OF THE NEGRO REVOLUTION. *J. of Am. Hist. 1968 55(1): 90-106.* The war years of 1939 to 1945 constitute the watershed in recent Negro history. It was then that the seeds of protest movements were sown. The morale of the Negro at the beginning of the war was low, reflecting his experiences in World War I and the discrimination practiced in industrial employment and in the armed forces. The slogans of the war and the exaltation of democracy were seen as rank hypocrisy and provoked cynicism among many Negroes who were isolationist or even pro-Axis in their sentiments. At the same time there was hope that something good for Negroes might come out of the war and a determination to right existing wrongs. This resulted in protest movements symbolized by the March on Washington Movement, the growth of the National Association for the Advancement of Colored People, growing militancy of the Negro press, and a determination to bring race relations into conformity with the creed of democracy. Documented from the Negro press and government reports.

K. B. West

1678. Daniel, Pete. BLACK POWER IN THE 1920'S: THE CASE OF TUSKEGEE VETERANS HOSPITAL. *J. of Southern Hist. 1970 36(3): 368-388.* Examines an early instance of Negro militancy in Alabama. In this case, the "NAACP [National Association for the Advancement of Colored People], the National Medical Association, the black press, [President] Warren Harding, and especially [Robert Russa] Moton and [Frank T.] Hines had triumphed over the determined southern whites and their allies, black and white, in the Veterans Bureau. Surprisingly, the whites in Alabama and especially in Tuskegee quietly accepted the all-black hospital. Against militant blacks aided by the power of the federal government, they had little choice, even in Alabama, even in the 1920's." 89 notes.

I. M. Leonard

1679. Davenport, F. Garvin, Jr. THOMAS DIXON'S MYTHOLOGY OF SOUTHERN HISTORY. *J. of Southern Hist. 1970 36(3): 350-367.* A close textual analysis of Dixon's novels suggests that he "saw in the South's grim experience during the Civil War and Reconstruction a lesson in the realities of history which might be used to preserve and strengthen the values and aspirations of the Nation. At the turn of the century white America was beset by many threats to its cultural innocence, including industrialism, irresponsible capitalism, urban squalor and poverty, new theories of politics and morals, and, of course, Negro equality. In creating his own mythological response to these problems, Dixon began with the theme of Union, defined as provincial, white Jeffersonian democracy, and then incorporated what he saw as the South's uniqueness. This theme of uniqueness centered around a way of life which had resisted corruption either by the materialism of the urban-industrial North or by the new and dangerous social and political philosophies. With this uniqueness and with the wisdom gained through the struggles under the burdens of defeat, privation, and the Negro threat to white innocence, Dixon suggested that the South could and would embark upon a great mission to preserve those basic American values which seemed threatened on every side....The mission was to lead the nation away from all the threats to its innocence, and primarily away from what Dixon saw as the dangers of racial equality." 37 notes.   I. M. Leonard

1680. DeGraaf, Lawrence B. THE CITY OF BLACK ANGELS: EMER-GENCE OF THE LOS ANGELES GHETTO, 1890-1930. *Pacific Hist. R. 1970 39(3): 323-352.* Studies the origins and growth of the black ghetto, since 1900 the largest in California. Describes the ghetto as it was both before and after the great migration from the South which started in 1915, and the gradual increase of restriction to and deterioration of the area. Covers the housing situation and the relationship with other minorities, both major factors in the distinctive nature of the black ghetto in Los Angeles. 113 notes.   E. C. Hyslop

1681. Downes, Randolph C. NEGRO RIGHTS AND WHITE BACKLASH IN THE CAMPAIGN OF 1920. *Ohio Hist. 1966 75(2/3): 85-107.* Describes how Warren Harding handled the race issue among key groups of Negro and white voters in the presidential campaign of 1920. Harding, taking a moderate course and carefully aligning himself with moderate Negro leaders, concentrated his campaign for Negro votes in the North and emphasized as campaign issues Republican support for antilynching legislation and against Democratic mistreatment of Negroes in the occupation of Haiti. In Oklahoma, which seemed to be swinging to the Republican Party, he courted white votes at the risk of alienating militant northern Negroes by speaking against the use of force to achieve racial equality. The author suggests that Democratic publication of rumors that Harding had Negro ancestors created a reaction sympathetic to Harding and took much of the sting out of the white backlash which appeared in northern areas. Based mainly on the Harding Papers in the Ohio Historical Society.
                    S. L. Jones

1682. Dreer, Herman. REV. GEORGE E. STEVENS, PIONEER CHAMPION OF INTEGRATION. *Negro Hist. Bull. 1956 19(5): 99-101.* Describes the activities of Reverend George E. Stevens, for 35 years the pastor of Central Baptist Church in St. Louis, as a leader in the integration movement. He succeeded in campaigns against restoring segregated streetcars in St. Louis and Kansas City in 1907, and against extension of racial segregation in public education in St. Louis.   L. Gara

1683. Durham, Frank. THE REPUTED DEMISES OF UNCLE TOM: OR, THE TREATMENT OF THE NEGRO IN FICTION BY WHITE SOUTH-ERN AUTHORS IN THE 1920'S. *Southern Literary J. 1970 2(2): 26-50.* Discusses the "New Negro" as portrayed in the 1920's by authors from a region whose inhabitants "have rather loudly proclaimed that they alone 'know' the

Negro and hence are best fitted to deal with him in both life and letters." Traces the background of 19th-century literary racial stereotypes and illustrates "a serious and conscious attempt on the part of Southern writers to present the Negro in new ways." Draws on Thomas Sigismund Stribling's *Birthright* (1922), Hubert Anthony Shands' *White and Black* (1922), DuBose Heyward's *Porgy* (1925), and Julia Mood Peterkin's *Scarlet Sister Mary* (1928). 31 notes.

J. L. Colwell

1684. Dwyer, Norval. THE CAMP UPTON STORY, 1917-1921. *Long Island Forum 1970 33(1): 6-10, (2): 31-34, (3): 54-57.* Part I. Camp Upton, located near Yaphank on Eastern Long Island, was one of 16 training camps set up in the spring and summer of 1917 to muster draftees into the National Army. Designed to process 40 thousand men, the camp's construction was delayed almost three months due to the difficulties of clearing the sandy soil, and to the problems posed by poison ivy and mosquitoes. The problem of attracting capable workmen was compounded by the fact that the camp was guarded by a Negro regiment; white laborers, resenting Negro supervision, often clashed with the guards. Based on local newspaper accounts, army reports, and oral recollections; 2 illus. Part II. After much delay, Camp Upton finally opened in September of 1917 and received its first recruits from New York City. The major concern of the camp's commanding officer, Major-General J. Franklin Bell (1856-1919), was to protect the surrounding Long Island community from the rowdyness of the recruits. Under army orders, 39 neighboring saloons were closed down and no liquor was permitted within five miles of the camp. Gambling and illicit sex were harshly punished and, on the whole, camp discipline was quite good. Recruits from New York's tough Hell's Kitchen and Gas House gangs agreed to temporary truce so that they might concentrate on fighting the Kaiser. The only problem involving Camp Upton was the sabotaging of a troop train in November 1917, which killed one soldier and injured 15. 2 illus. Part III. Under the command of General J. Franklin Bell the 77th Division was trained in the art of trench warfare. In March 1918, the Division was sent to France where it fought with gallantry in the Battle of the Argonne Forest. Ninety officers and two thousand men were killed and several thousand more were wounded. While the 77th was fighting in France, Irving Berlin's "Yip, Yip, Yaphank," based on his experiences at Camp Upton, was being performed on Broadway. 2 illus.

G. Kurland

1685. Eastman, Joel W. CLAUDE L'ENGLE, FLORIDA MUCKRAKER. *Florida Hist. Q. 1967 45(3): 243-252.* Historians dealing with the first decade of the 20th century, while thoroughly covering the national level, have failed to consider the State and local level of muckraking journals. Careful study of one Florida muckraker and his publishing enterprise reveals that regional and State muckraking wielded considerable influence. Evidence of this significance can be found in the comparatively wide circulation of Claude L'Engle's *Sun,* the success of the journal's muckraking exposures, the impact of the publication on Florida politics, and L'Engle's subsequent election to Congress. In general, following the main pattern of national muckraking magazines, the *Sun* nevertheless revealed certain peculiarities; it was very pro-Union, with a southern and Progressive racial bias, and it was violently anti-Theodore Roosevelt. 24 notes.

R. V. Calvert

1686. Eighmy, John Lee. RELIGIOUS LIBERALISM IN THE SOUTH DUR-
ING THE PROGRESSIVE ERA. *Church Hist. 1969 38(3): 359-372.* The Social
Gospel movement emphasized Christianizing the social order. Though primarily
a northern, urban, industrial phenomenon, the movement also existed in the
South. There it addressed not only urban and industrial problems but also the
older problems of poverty, racial injustice, and illiteracy. Southern churchmen
were active in various crusades to reform agriculture, prisons, public health, and
education, but gave their most massive support to the prohibition cause. The
Southern Sociological Congress, founded in 1912, offered considerable clerical
leadership and a social program for the region. The congress became a rallying
point for social Christianity. Many churchmen objected to the new emphasis, but
others offered vigorous support. The Presbyterian, Southern Baptist, and Methodist Churches, while ambivalent, accepted some aspects of social Christianity.
Based on published materials; 53 notes.   S. C. Pearson, Jr.

1687. Fish, John O. SOUTHERN METHODISM AND ACCOMMODATION
OF THE NEGRO, 1902-1915. *J. of Negro Hist. 1970 55(3): 200-214.* Immediately after the Civil War, the Methodist Episcopal Church, South, saw vast
numbers of its Negro members leave to join other denominations. Generally this
was due to the fact that Southern Methodism was willing to acknowledge the
Negro's emancipation, but refused to accord the black man a position of social
equality within the church. Southerners in general thought that race questions
were problems pertaining to the proper treatment of inferior and subordinate
people, not matters dealing with the Christian religion. To Southern Methodists,
the refusal of Negro social recognition betrayed neither a defective social conscience nor a limited Christian brotherhood. Throughout the Progressive era,
Southern Methodists maintained distinctions between a "black brother in Christ"
and "white brother in Christ." Based on primary and secondary sources; 52 notes.
                                                                    R. S. Melamed

1688. Fleming, Robert E. IRONY AS A KEY TO JOHNSON'S "THE AUTO-
BIOGRAPHY OF AN EX-COLOURED MAN." *Am. Literature 1971 43(1):
83-96.* James Weldon Johnson's 1912 novel (New York: Hill and Wang, 1960)
is rightfully praised for its objective presentation of Negro manners in America.
But an awareness of the ironic tone reveals the novel's unity in its study of a
marginal man who narrates the story of his own life without fully realizing the
significance of what he tells his readers. The subtle use of irony was a major
change of direction for black novelists from heavy-handed propagandistic techniques. 6 notes.   R. S. Burns

1689. Flynt, Wayne. DISSENT IN ZION: ALABAMA BAPTISTS AND SO-
CIAL ISSUES, 1900-1914. *J. of Southern Hist. 1969 35(4): 523-542.* During the
Progressive era "many influential Baptist leaders and pastors in Alabama were
forcefully committed to progressive social ideas [in the fields of education, labor
relations, use of convict labor, poverty, child labor, public health, and even the
"Negro Question"] and championed them with a courage and candor not subsequently excelled and perhaps not since equaled in the state." 79 notes.
                                                                    I. M. Leonard

1690. Flynt, Wayne. THE NEGRO AND ALABAMA BAPTISTS DURING THE PROGRESSIVE ERA. *J. of the Ala Acad. of Sci. 1968 39(2): 163-167.* At the turn of the 20th century, Baptists constituted one-half of the white population in Alabama. Baptist leaders and clergymen writing in their denomination's official organ, *The Alabama Baptist,* during the Progressive era (1900-07), reflected a strong element of racism, advocating white supremacy in education and politics. Some clerical leaders challenged the worst aspects of racism (such as lynching practices) more frequently than did any other southern professional group. Concludes that Alabama Baptists are partly responsible both for Alabama's present racial dilemma and for the humanity necessary for its solution. 11 notes.   Sr. A. Doyle

1691. Forrey. Robert. NEGROES IN THE FICTION OF F. SCOTT FITZGERALD. *Phylon 1967 28(3): 293-298.* Fitzgerald had a fascination with the rich which is reflected in his novels. The social status he envied required not only money but also the type of security that came from a very old and very white American family. To be at the bottom of his society was to be dark-skinned and poor. Thus, Fitzgerald's Negroes are generally menial characters who are referred to in a disparaging manner. On the question of race Fitzgerald does not belong in the liberal tradition in American letters. The author concludes that it was only near the end of his life that Fitzgerald began to outgrow his bias although he realized as early as 1925 that it weakened his work. In his final, unfinished novel, *The Last Tycoon,* Fitzgerald was able to introduce a Negro at an important point without any of the accouterments of racism. Based on published sources; 27 notes.   D. N. Brown

1692. Gatewood, Willard B. BOOKER T. WASHINGTON AND THE ULRICH AFFAIR. *J. of Negro Hist. 1970 55(1): 29-44.* In 1911 Booker T. Washington was physically attacked in New York City by Henry Albert Ulrich. Ulrich claimed that he beat Washington because he caught him looking through a keyhole in a local apartment building. Washington went to the police and had Ulrich arrested, but after many delays in setting a trial date, he was found innocent of the charges. Many people offered Washington aid and support, including some of his most militant black critics. There was a temporary reconciliation between Washington and his opponents and, after the verdict of innocence, he left the court stating that he would only go out when accompanied by a companion. Many Negro observers on the scene were perturbed by the way Washington used "round about methods" to handle the situation, and the affair only deepened the conviction of his opponents that his ways were becoming increasingly less effective. Based mostly on primary sources; 52 notes.   R. S. Melamed

1693. Gatewood, Willard B. THEODORE ROOSEVELT AND THE INDIANOLA AFFAIR. *J. of Negro Hist. 1968 53(1): 48-69.* Discusses the political repercussions of the "Indianola Affair," which grew out of Theodore Roosevelt's defense of Mrs. Minnie M. Cox, longtime postmistress of Indianola, Mississippi, who was a Negro. Anti-Negro sentiment revolving around Mrs. Cox became a major issue in the State political campaigns of 1903, and, when whites demanded the removal of Mrs. Cox, Roosevelt moved to close down the post office instead. In 1904 he reopened the office with a white postmaster. Victory for the whites however was not complete, for the new postmaster was a longtime defender of Mrs. Cox and the postal facility was reopened as a fourth-class office rather than a third-class one as it had been previously. Based on manuscript and newspaper sources; 44 notes.   L. Gara

1694. Genovese, Eugene D. THE SIGNIFICANCE OF THE SLAVE PLAN-TATION FOR SOUTHERN ECONOMIC DEVELOPMENT. *J. of Southern Hist. 1962 28(4): 422-437.* Takes issue with historians who would revise the concept that plantation slavery was responsible for the economic woes of the antebellum South. Argues that plantation slavery so limited the purchasing power of the region that it could not sustain much industry. That industry which could be created usually lacked a home market of sufficient scope to permit large-scale operation; cost of production, therefore, was often too high for competition with northern firms drawing upon much wider markets. Without enough industry to support urbanization, a general and extensive diversification of agriculture was impossible. The low level of demand was sufficient to retard economic develop-ment.   S. E. Humphreys

1695. Gill, Robert L. THE NEGRO IN THE SUPREME COURT - 1940. *Negro Hist. Bull. 1965 28(8): 194, 197-200.* In the 24 years ending May 1939 only 13 cases in which the NAACP was interested came to the Supreme Court, but in 1940 six such cases were presented to the court in each of which the association was successful. The 1940 decisions dealt with forced or extorted decisions, restric-tive covenants in land leases, the denial of equal pay to school teachers because of race or color, and the exclusion of Negroes from grand juries because of race or color. The cases are described, with quotations from the decisions of Justice Hugo La F. Black or Justice Harlan F. Stone. 7 notes.   E. P. Stickney

1696. Goldman, Eric F. SUMMER SUNDAY. *Am. Heritage 1964 15(4): 83-89.* Describes the lynching of a Negro accused of murder in Coatesville, Pennsylva-nia, in 1911. In an epilogue the author suggests that social changes and the uncertainties that accompanied industrialization, new immigrants from Europe, and Negro immigrants from the South, all combined to challenge and worry older residents of northern communities. Those in Coatesville relieved their hostility by violence. Illus.   H. F. Bedford

1697. Graham, James D. NEGRO PROTEST IN AMERICA, 1900-1955: A BIBLIOGRAPHICAL GUIDE. *South Atlantic Q. 1968 67(1): 94-107.* In the period under consideration, the expression of Negro protest was mainly through writing. The author lists and discusses some 60 works.   J. M. Bumsted

1698. Greenbaum, Fred. THE ANTI-LYNCHING BILL OF 1935: THE IRONY OF "EQUAL JUSTICE - UNDER LAW." *J. of Human Relations 1967 15(3): 72-85.* Traces the history of the Anti-Lynching Bill introduced in the U.S. Senate in 1934 and 1935. In spite of the urging of Walter White of the National

Association for the Advancement of Colored People, Mrs. Eleanor Roosevelt, and the bill's cosponsors - Edward Prentiss Costigan of Colorado and Robert Wagner of New York - President Roosevelt refused to give the bill his full support, and the Senate adjourned without considering it in 1934. The bill was debated in 1935, but Southern Senators used the filibuster and their knowledge of parliamentary tactics to prevent its passage. The arguments for and against the bill are summarized. Based on manuscripts, *The New York Times,* and other published primary sources.   D. J. Abramoske

1699. Hager, William M. THE PLAN OF SAN DIEGO: UNREST ON THE TEXAS BORDER IN 1915. *Arizona and the West 1963 5(4): 327-336.* A 1915 irredentist plot, the "Plan of San Diego," so dubbed because the border town of San Diego, Texas, seemed to be the center of much of what transpired, is still an enigma as to its conspirators and precisely how it fitted into the troubled times along the Mexican-American border. The ambitious plan envisioned conquering California, Arizona, New Mexico, Colorado, and Texas, and creating an "independent Mexican republic" which would later ask for annexation by Mexico. After that the revolutionaries would seize Utah, Wyoming, South Dakota, Nebraska, Kansas, and Oklahoma, from which an independent republic would be created to serve as a buffer between Mexico and "the damned big-footed creatures of the north." Apparently the latter was to become a Negro republic. The plan was discovered before it could hatch. Rather than "a grand design" as it was regarded at the time, the author concludes that it was a stratagem to camougflage border raids with constitutionality and to earn American recognition for Mexican revolutionist Venustiano Carranza. Based on government documents, newspaper reports, and monographic studies; 39 notes.   D. L. Smith

1700. Hamilton, Holman. THE SIXTY-FIRST ANNUAL MEETING OF THE ORGANIZATION OF AMERICAN HISTORIANS. *J. of Am. Hist. 1968 55(2): 349-368.* The meeting was held in Dallas on 18, 19, and 20 April 1968. One hundred and ninety-seven participants representing 115 universities and colleges participated in 47 sessions that were largely dominated by themes of revisionism in certain areas: the FDR "purges" of 1938, the role of Western farmers in expanding governmental power, the Indian policy of Andrew Jackson, the predominance of conservative attitudes in the 1930's, the American Revolution as conspiracy, the Negro revolution in World War II, changing views on Daniel Webster. Many papers also reflected the concern of some historians for the future of history as a discipline relevant to contemporary social problems and to high school students, and an interest in a comparative framework for aspects of the history of the United States.   K. B. West

1701. Hare, Nathan. THE DAY THE "RACE WAR" STRUCK CHICAGO. *Negro Hist. Bull. 1962 30(6): 123-125.* Analyzes the factors which led to the Chicago race riot of July 1919. The author concludes that such violence is the result of long-time frustrations and anxieties in both of the groups involved and the eventual placing of all blame on a scapegoat. In this instance, newspaper headlines fanned the fire of racial prejudice, the police failed to protect the minority group, and ordinary citizens committed deeds of violence which would have been out of character for them under normal conditions.

L. Gara

1702. Harper, Glenn T. "COTTON TOM" HEFLIN AND THE ELECTION OF 1930; THE PRICE OF PARTY DISLOYALTY. *Historian 1968 30(3): 389-411.* In 1928, the test of a true Democrat was support for (Alfred Emanuel) "Al" Smith. His opposition to rum, Romanism, and liberal views on race questions prevented Senator James Thomas Heflin, elected to public office by Alabamians for 40 years, from meeting this test. He urged Alabama to vote for Herbert Hoover. The author reports how the Democratic Party of Alabama disciplined the Senator for his apostacy. Based on contemporary press accounts, the *Congressional Record,* and A. B. Moore's *History of Alabama* (University of Alabama, 1934).   N. W. Moen

1703. Harrell, James A. NEGRO LEADERSHIP IN THE ELECTION YEAR 1936. *J. of Southern Hist. 1968 34(4): 546-564.* At the 1936 National Negro Congress, held in Chicago, Negro leaders evaluated the impact upon the Negro of the New Deal. In so doing, they exposed their basic positions toward the Negro race's relationship to American society. Three distinct interpretations of the Negro's present and future status in America were revealed which approximated accommodation to segregation (espoused by the "most notable Negro conservative of 1936" W. E. B. Du Bois), protest (led by the NAACP which represented the nonpartisan protest forces between Democrat and Republican partisans), and revolution (led by A. Philip Randolph and Ralph J. Bunche). These three basic positions "have continued to present the significant alternatives available to Negro spokesmen as they face new situations in American life." 53 notes.

I. M. Leonard

1704. Hausdorff, Don. TOPICAL SATIRE AND THE TEMPER OF THE EARLY 1930's. *South Atlantic Q. 1966 65(1): 12-33.* A good deal can be learned about the popular temper through magazine humor, since humorists seek to be topical. In the early 1930's, the older 1920's humor still prevailed. Economic radicalism was spoofed, as were politicians, advertising, city life, and intellectuals; women were foolish and Negroes were idlers. But a new style was growing which emphasized economy of drawing, precision in language, and the one-line caption. This style was led by *The New Yorker.* Villains tended to disappear, scapegoats vanished, and the emphasis was on ordinary people caught in the complexities of society. Tolerance and sophistication were emphasized. 20 notes.

J. M. Bumsted

1705. Haydorn, Heinz-Joachim. SCHWARZ UND WEISS IN USA [Black and white in the United States]. *Frankfurter Hefte [West Germany] 1955 10(11): 787-800.* An appraisal of the Negro's response during the past 30 years to discrimination by whites and to discriminatory attitudes of various Negro groups toward each other. Based on Richard Wright's *12 Million Black Voices* [Schwarz unter Weiss] (Frankfurt/Main: Europäische Verlagsanstalt, 1952).

R. Mueller

1706. Heckman, Richard Allen and Hall, Betty Jean. BEREA COLLEGE AND THE DAY LAW. *Register of the Kentucky Hist. Soc. 1968 66(1): 35-52.* Founded shortly before the Civil War, Berea College in Kentucky began admitting Negro students in 1866. Despite outside pressures, Berea maintained an integrated student body - more Negro than white - until the 1890's. However, in 1904 Carl Day, a State legislator, influenced by prejudice against Negroes prevalent in the State, secured passage of a bill which prohibited Negroes and whites from being educated together under the same roof. The law was obviously aimed at Berea. Questioning the constitutionality of the law, Berea went to court, but lost finally in 1908 when the U.S. Supreme Court upheld the validity of the Day Law. The rumor that William G. Frost, president of Berea, was instrumental in drafting the Day Law is rejected by the authors. Based on primary sources, especially newspapers, college records, and the Day Law File in the Berea College Library; 91 notes.   B. Wilkins

1707. Hefley, J. Theodore. FREEDOM UPHELD: THE CIVIL LIBERTIES STANCE OF "THE CHRISTIAN CENTURY" BETWEEN THE WARS. *Church Hist. 1968 37(2): 174-194.* Standing within the muckraking-progressive tradition, *The Christian Century* under the editorship of Charles Clayton Morrison reflected a lively interest in the problems of civil liberties in the interwar period. It supported freedom of speech, press, and radio as well as labor's right to strike. It championed the cause of Sacco and Vanzetti and rejected notions of a Red menace in America. It supported academic freedom and opposed the smear tactics of the House Committee on Un-American Activities. But the *Century* was not always consistent when its own values were endangered. It sometimes supported film censorship and was unconcerned for the constitutional rights of bootleggers and gamblers. Its mild Anglo-Saxonism was reflected in condescension toward Jews and Negroes. However, its attitude toward Negro rights became significantly more liberal during these years. Based on editorial material in the nondenominational weekly; 59 notes.   S. C. Pearson, Jr.

1708. Hixson, William B., Jr. MOORFIELD STOREY AND THE DEFENSE OF THE DYER ANTI-LYNCHING BILL. *New England Q. 1969 42(1): 65-81.* Storey was a legal and constitutional conservative, but his role as defender of civil rights and president of the National Association for the Advancement of Colored People brought him into some conflict of roles when he confronted the Dyer Anti-Lynching Bill. At first, Storey was convinced that the bill involved the Federal Government in an unconstitutional effort to protect civil liberties against individual actions subject to the sole jurisdiction of States. However, the palpable unwillingness of State authorities to stop lynching or to take criminal action against mobs led Storey to conclude that the 5th and 14th amendments gave the Federal Government power to protect Negroes from murderous mobs and a negligent State authority. His views of constitutional law seemed to be taking a more flexible course, but his views more completely reflect the views of his earlier Radical Republican acquaintances. 57 notes.   K. B. West

1709. Hoffman, Edwin D. THE GENESIS OF THE MODERN MOVEMENT FOR EQUAL RIGHTS IN SOUTH CAROLINA, 1930-1939. *J. of Negro Hist.*

1959 44(4): 346-369. The impressive gains made by Negroes of South Carolina during World War II and the postwar decade were achieved through a movement of mass militancy which had its origin in the Great Depression. The early 1930's were times of complete white supremacy, economic exploitation, sharecropping, chain gangs and lynchings. The election of Roosevelt gave impetus to efforts toward improvement. "In the Thirties trends were established...that were to make...history in the field of equal rights." Based on interviews, Negro publications, newspaper reports, and minutes of meetings.   A. P. Tracy

1710. Holmes, William F. WHITECAPPING: AGRARIAN VIOLENCE IN MISSISSIPPI, 1902-1906. *J. of Southern Hist. 1969 35(2): 165-185.* Lashing out against depression, poverty, and exploitation, small farmers in southwestern Mississippi formed secret terrorist clubs known as Whitecaps to reduce "the influence of merchants over farm lands, to control Negro labor, and to keep the Negro in his 'place.'" Because these "nightriders discouraged merchants and industrialists from doing business in the state, and...threatened to drive away Negro laborers," respectable citizens moved to stamp out the movement in the early years of the 20th century. Interestingly, though James Kimble Vardaman's "Negro-baiting campaign" of 1903 seemingly gave support to the terrorists, as governor he "worked...conscientiously against whitecapping" to prevent its economic threat to Mississippi. 92 notes.   I. M. Leonard

1711. Holt, Wythe W., Jr. THE VIRGINIA CONSTITUTIONAL CONVENTION OF 1901-1902. A REFORM MOVEMENT WHICH LACKED SUBSTANCE. *Virginia Mag. of Hist. and Biog. 1968 76(1): 67-102.* The Constitutional Convention of 1901-02 was called primarily to disfranchise Negro voters but it was also seen by many as a vehicle for reform. It failed in the latter effort largely because the reformers lacked ideological unity. Based on the proceedings of the convention plus published and unpublished studies; 150 notes.   K. J. Bauer

1712. Jack, Homer A. LILLIAN SMITH OF CLAYTON, GEORGIA. *Christian Cent. 1957 74(40): 1166-1168.* Study of the life of a missionary to China who returned to Georgia, was shocked by the ambiguities of the southern way of life and, after publication of *Strange Fruit* in 1944, became "the most widely read writer on race relations in the world."   S. E. Humphreys

1713. Jensen, Joan M. APARTHEID: PACIFIC COAST STYLE. *Pacific Hist. R. 1969 38(3): 335-340.* Analyzes the role of municipal ordinances and restrictive covenants as a means to maintain racial segregation. These methods started in California at the end of the 19th century (aimed against the Chinese) and culminated in the Proposition 14 battle in 1967. The methods have affected all minority groups. Historians have done little to document the origins of the specific means used to maintain and increase residential discrimination. Based on primary sources; 8 notes.   E. C. Hyslop

1714. Johnson, Evans C. OSCAR UNDERWOOD AND THE HOBSON CAM-
PAIGN. *Alabama R. 1963 16(2): 125-140.* The death of Senator Joseph Forney
Johnston in August 1913 gave representatives Oscar W. Underwood and Richmond Pearson Hobson opportunity to run for the vacant seat. Prohibition was
the principal factor in the race. Underwood was a local optionist, Hobson a
Prohibitionist. Religion, the Negro question, labor, and conservation served as
additional issues. The campaign was bitter and expensive, costing each candidate
over ten thousand dollars. Underwood won surprisingly easily, securing 62 percent of the total vote.   D. F. Henderson

1715. Kazin, Alfred. H. G. WELLS, AMERICA AND "THE FUTURE." *Am.
Scholar 1968 37(1): 137-144.* An inquiry into H. G. Wells' travel book on America *The Future in America: A Search After Realities* based on a trip made in
1906. Wells criticized America for its failure to attain its possibilities, unlike other
English travelers who sought only failure to live up to "democratic" pretensions.
At the same time, Wells was struck by the power and liveliness of America while
also noting its hatred of Negroes, its conformity, and its technological hardware.
Yet at the same time he also fretted over the masses of immigrants that he saw
coming through Ellis Island and worried that they might alter the essence of
America. By the time of his 1935 visit to America, Wells wanted to see even more
that America was developing into a rational state and thus praised both Franklin
Roosevelt and Joseph Stalin for their gestures in that direction. But Wells may
have died believing that human reason was still immature. The author draws
upon Wells' own books, Henry James's *The American Scene,* and other personal
views of America.   T. R. Cripps

1716. Kelleher, Daniel. ST. LOUIS' 1916 RESIDENTIAL SEGREGATION
ORDINANCE. *Bull. of the Missouri Hist. Soc. 1970 26(3): 239-248.* Neighborhood improvement groups in St. Louis federated into the United Welfare Association, joined with the St. Louis Real Estate Association in a drive to impose
racially segregated neighborhoods in St. Louis. The segregationists finally won
the day in the St. Louis municipal election of 1916. Details the activities of the
antisegregationists who successfully prolonged the time before legally-mandated
segregation was imposed in St. Louis and then carried their fight to the courts,
which toppled the St. Louis segregation ordinance. Based on newspapers and
magazines and on manuscripts in the St. Louis Public Library; 57 notes.
                                                                    H. T. Lovin

1717. Kelley, Donald Brooks. DEEP SOUTH DILEMMA: THE MISSISSIPPI
PRESS IN THE PRESIDENTIAL ELECTION OF 1928. *J. of Mississippi Hist.
1963 25(2): 63-92.* Twenty-seven Mississippi newspapers representing 25 towns
and cities are cited in this analysis of the dilemma that Mississippi citizens faced
in deciding between Herbert Hoover and Alfred Smith in the 1928 presidential
campaign. The author maintains that "the moral crusade to perpetuate white
supremacy by supporting the Democratic Party clashed with the equally militant
determination to preserve a close-knit Anglo-Saxon, Protestant and agrarian
America by repudiating the Democratic nominee."   D. C. James

1718. King, William E. CHARLES MC IVER FIGHTS FOR THE TARHEEL NEGRO'S RIGHT TO AN EDUCATION. *North Carolina Hist. R. 1964 41(3): 360-369.* Correspondence between Charles Duncan McIver, president of the State Normal and Industrial College, and his distant cousin, John McMillan McIver, during the local taxation campaign for public schools in North Carolina in 1902. The former, a member of the Southern Education Board and leading champion of public education, argues eloquently against division of school funds according to the tax payments of the two races and in favor of full inclusion of Negro children in public school opportunities. For McIver, at least, the often abused term "universal education" included Negroes. Quoted in full from the Charles Duncan McIver Papers at Greensboro.					L. R. Harlan

1719. Kirby, Jack Temple. CLARENCE POE'S VISION OF A SEGREGATED "GREAT RURAL CIVILIZATION." *South Atlantic Q. 1969 68(1): 27-38.* There was an agrarian rural progressivism in the South. Its outstanding spokesman was Clarence Poe (1881-1964), whose principal reform proposal was racial segregation. Poe was an energetic moralist with an all-encompassing social conscience. Most of his reform ideas came from visits to Great Britain and familiarity with South African "reform" currents which were emphasizing proto-apartheid. Poe wanted white farmers to give up using Negro labor. He was favorably disposed to Negroes - so long as "racial integrity" was preserved. He never achieved his ambitions of total separation of the races. 29 notes.
					J. M. Bumsted

1720. Levenstein, Harvey A. FRANZ BOAS AS POLITICAL ACTIVIST. *Kroeber Anthrop. Soc. Papers 1963 29: 15-24.* The involvement of Franz Boas in political issues in the popular arena began with an article on the Negro problem in 1904 and continued until his death in 1942. It is likely that the source of his strong liberal attitude was a liberal Jewish upbringing. A moot point is whether his anthropological interests led to his political involvements or vice versa. His involvement began with the issue of racism; with the advent of World War I and then again with the rise of Hitler in Germany, he broadened his scope to argue against nationalism and to advocate a world state without political boundaries. Unfortunately, although his arguments against racism and nationalism were cogent, his understanding of the sources and programs for solution of these problems was inadequate. Based on primary sources; 6 notes, biblio.
					C. N. Warren

1721. Levine, Daniel. GOMPERS AND RACISM: STRATEGY OF LIMITED OBJECTIVES. *Mid-Am. 1961 43(2): 106-113.* Disagrees with the thesis that Samuel Gompers' racism clearly compromised his principles. The author rather sees the labor leader rigidly applying his main theory "that a hard core of tough troops should be used against limited objectives": the eight-hour day, high wages and better working conditions. In this context Gompers viewed racial equality as a possible deterrent to the realization of these primary goals. Based largely on the *American Federationist* and the Gompers' Letterbooks in the Washington, D.C., headquarters of the AFL-CIO.					R. J. Marion

1722. Logue, Cal M. RALPH MC GILL: CONVICTIONS OF A SOUTHERN EDITOR. *Journalism Q. 1968 45(4): 647-652.* Analyzes the late Ralph McGill's writings and speeches to define his stand on human rights and to determine his basic beliefs. The views in his Atlanta *Constitution* columns changed considerably since the 1930's when he advocated separate but equal treatment of Negroes. Between the late 1940's and early 1950's he tried to convince his readers that the South could learn to live with the inevitable social change, predicting the 1954 Supreme Court desegregation ruling. After that decision he emphasized compliance with legal and moral law, arguing that segregation was wrong. Basic to his views was the importance of legal, feasible, southern-based, moral solutions. He believed that education is important for the individual and the community, that all should share equal rights, and that the South should ensure the rights of its own citizens. Based on primary sources; 36 notes.   K. J. Puffer

1723. Mcdonald, James L. REACTIONARY REBELS; AGRARIANS IN DEFENSE OF THE SOUTH. *Midwest Q. 1969 10(2): 155-170.* Discusses Allen Tate, John Crowe Ransom, Donald Davidson, Robert Penn Warren, the Southern Agrarian movement, and the New Criticism movement. The author considers the Agrarians of the 1930's to be the spiritual fathers of the segregationists of the 1960's. He believes the agrarian program was above all else a defense of the Old South in opposition to those who would modernize it. The Agrarians wrote biographies of southern heroes and idealizations of the Civil War, and they maintained justification of the southerner's treatment of the Negro. They enunciated the myth of White Supremacy and Negro docility at being allowed to live as an inferior in the white man's world. The Agrarians are now somewhat elderly and have abandoned their militant sectionalism, but their writings of the 1930's remain as formal stylized arguments and appeals for the southern status quo. Select biblio.   G. H. G. Jones

1724. Meier, August. BOYCOTTS OF SEGREGATED STREET CARS, 1894-1906. A RESEARCH NOTE. *Phylon 1957 18(3): 296-297.* Briefly notes the circumstances of Negro boycotts of segregated street cars in Atlanta (1894, 1900), Augusta (1898), Jacksonville (1901), Columbia (1903), New Orleans, Mobile and Houston (1904), and Austin and Nashville (1906).   C. F. Latour

1725. Meier, August and Rudwick, Elliott M. EARLY BOYCOTTS OF SEGREGATED SCHOOLS: THE EAST ORANGE, NEW JERSEY, EXPERIENCE, 1899-1906. *Hist. of Educ. Q. 1967 7(1): 22-35.* Middle- and upper-class Negro protest began in East Orange when, in 1899, the Board of Education set up an ungraded class for "backward colored pupils" at Eastern Elementary School. By 1901 white children were also assigned to this class. Yet in 1905 separate classes for backward colored children reappeared, now in two elementary schools. A Negro boycott of these schools led to the opening of private schools in two Negro churches. The Board of Education made assignment to the special classes dependent upon examination, and by 1906 the Negro protest movement collapsed, having achieved only a reduction in the number of Negro students in the special classes. The author attributes the collapse of the protest to the fading of white support and to disagreements between "respectable" Negroes and lower-class migrants from the South. Based mainly on newspaper files; 50 notes.   J. Herbst

1726. Meier, August and Rudwick, Elliott M. EARLY BOYCOTTS OF SEG-REGATED SCHOOLS: THE ALTON, ILLINOIS CASE, 1897-1908. *J. of Negro Educ. 1967 36(4): 394-402.* In 1896 the Alton city council abolished neighborhood school districts making possible segregated education. Opposition within the Negro community was led by Scott Bibb, a fireman in a local glass-works. When in the fall of 1897 his two older children were reassigned to an all-Negro school, Bibb together with other Negro manual workers organized an effective boycott of the Jim Crow schools. The boycott lasted throughout the school year but gradually declined in strength. Nevertheless, several families kept their children out of public schools through 11 years of litigation. Decisions against the plaintiffs in five jury trials were appealed to the Illinois Supreme Court. Finally on the fifth appeal in 1908 the Illinois Supreme Court agreed that the plaintiffs could not receive a fair trial in circuit court and instead of ordering another trial directed Alton officials to admit the Bibb children to their old school. The threat of racial violence was used to emasculate even this decision, and another boycott was organized in the fall of 1908. This boycott failed, and even Bibb enrolled his younger children in the segregated school. Segregated education continued in Alton in open defiance of the court decision of 1908 until the early 1950's. Based on newspaper accounts and legal opinions; 45 notes.
                                                                S. C. Pearson, Jr.

1727. Meier, August and Rudwick, Elliott. EARLY BOYCOTTS OF SEGRE-GATED SCHOOLS: THE CASE OF SPRINGFIELD, OHIO, 1922-23. *Am. Q. 1968 20(4): 744-758.* Discusses the school boycott in Springfield, Ohio, as an example of "non-violent direct action" in response to widespread entrenchment of northern school boards. A historical account of Springfield's response to the school segregation issue reveals that "political cleavage" played a major role in the actions of the Negro community itself; supporters of the Republicans chose to adopt a clearly segregationist stance in what had earlier been an open school system. The participants in the boycott identified with the Democrats, thus illus-trating the historical shift in politics regarding race relations. Since the National Association for the Advancement of Colored People was immobilized by polar-ization among Negro leaders, an organization known as the Civil Rights Protec-tive League was activated to combat the segregationist strategy which the school board had adopted in 1920. The league picketed and boycotted the Fulton School, which had become all black under the school board edict; the league's goal was to take the case to court. Although leading school board officials were eventually exposed as members of the Ku Klux Klan and although Judge Frank N. Krapp ruled in the league's favor, the school board was able to maintain an essentially segregated school system. Based on interview data and primary printed sources; 72 notes.   R. S. Pickett

1728. Meier, August and Rudwick, Elliot M. NEGRO PROTEST AT THE CHICAGO WORLD'S FAIR, 1933-1934. *J. of the Illinois State Hist. Soc. 1966*

59(2): 161-171. Reviews the portrayal of Negro contributions to American life in the exhibits and activities of the World's Fair. Major emphasis is given to discrimination in employment and in restaurant service. The conclusion is that discrimination in service was in the main removed during the second year of the Fair as a result of Negro political action. Based on contemporary newspaper accounts.

S. L. Jones

1729. Meier, August and Rudwick, Elliott. THE BOYCOTT MOVEMENT AGAINST JIM CROW STREETCARS IN THE SOUTH, 1900-1906. *J. of Am. Hist. 1969 55(4): 756-775.* In the early years of the 20th century, boycotts against segregated streetcars broke out in many cities throughout the Old Confederacy. The result of new laws compelling racial separation, these protests were led largely by Negro editors, small businessmen, and some clergymen. They were opposed by many important Negro ministers, including many Baptists, who urged accommodation to the new laws. The protests were conservative in attempting to preserve a nonsegregated status quo, in the absence of direct confrontation with whites, and in the nonviolent course advocated by the leaders. The boycotts were successful in getting large numbers of Negroes to refrain from riding the cars and in stimulating some short-lived self-help transportation companies. However, they uniformly failed to procure repeal of the degrading laws. They are significant as tactics most useful in an era of white hostility and general Negro accommodation. Based mostly on newspapers; 97 notes.

K. B. West

1730. Meier, August and Rudwick, Elliott. THE RISE OF SEGREGATION IN THE FEDERAL BUREAUCRACY, 1900-1930. *Phylon 1967 28(2): 178-184.* Segregation in the Federal bureaucracy is a well-known aspect of President Wilson's administration. Generally forgotten has been that this was a Republican as well as a Democratic policy. Segregation in Federal agencies began during the administration of Theodore Roosevelt and took various forms. Negroes were generally required to work in separate rooms. Segregated lockers, washrooms, and lunchrooms were widespread. Under Taft, segregation was extended even further and such was likewise the case when Wilson assumed the Presidency. During the campaign of 1920 Harding pledged to Negro leaders that the practice would be ended by executive order, but the order was never issued. During the Coolidge administration protests intensified but the situation became worse and Hoover ignored the problem while receiving Negro delegations who came to see him about persistent discrimination. The authors conclude that Wilson has been unfairly assailed as the architect of segregation in government offices. Documented from published sources; 38 notes.

D. N. Brown

1731. Meredith, H. L. AGRARIAN SOCIALISM AND THE NEGRO IN OKLAHOMA, 1900-1918. *Labor Hist. 1970 11(3): 277-284.* Surveys the relationship between the Negro and the Socialist Party in Oklahoma. The party split on the question of Negro suffrage, although the official position was to encourage Negroes to vote Socialist. The passage of the Grandfather Clause (1910) reduced the Negro vote, and the Green Corn Rebellion (1917) destroyed the Socialist Party. Based on census reports, newspapers, and the files of the Socialist Party of America; 32 notes.   L. L. Athey

1732. Miller, Robert Moats. THE PROTESTANT CHURCHES AND LYNCHING, 1919-1939. *J. of Negro Hist. 1957 42(2): 118-131.* Concludes that the "record of the Protestant churches was spotted, but on the whole their concern with lynching was both deeper and more widespread than commonly believed." Based on primary sources.   W. E. Wight

1733. Miller, Robert Moats. THE ATTITUDES OF AMERICAN PROTES-TANTISM TOWARD THE NEGRO. *J. of Negro Hist. 1956 41(3): 215-240.* Using printed minutes, church publications, and both published and unpublished studies of the church's relation to the Negro, the author finds a vast gulf between the Christian creed and the actual deeds of Protestants. In spite of the interest of a few in racial justice, American Protestantism "all too often accommodated itself to prejudice at the peril of its own soul" and "came increasingly to the recognition that a segregated church *content* in its segregation was wrong." W. E. Wight

1734. Miller, Robert Moats. THE SOCIAL ATTITUDES OF THE AMERI-CAN EPISCOPAL CHURCH DURING TWO DECADES, 1919-1939. *Hist. Mag. of the Protestant Episcopal Church 1956 25(2): 162-192.* Based mainly on church periodicals, the article examines the church's position on war, labor, civil liberties, and race relations. In the 1920's the Episcopal Church was not as sensitive to these problems as were some other churches, but social Christianity was not dead. In the 1930's the church swung to a position somewhat left of center. In the area of Negro relations, the church's action lagged behind its profession.   E. Oberholzer, Jr.

1735. Miller, Robert Moats. THE SOCIAL ATTITUDES OF THE AMERI-CAN METHODISTS, 1919-29. *Religion in Life 1958 27(2): 185-198.* Analyzes Methodist thought on war and peace, civil liberties, race relations, labor, and the issue capitalism vs. collectivism. Methodists supported World War I, the League, the World Court, and disarmament. Although many southern ministers joined the Ku Klux Klan, the church generally opposed both it and lynchings. Japanese exclusion, Ford's "Protocols of Zion," and race discrimination were opposed, but Southern Methodists tended to favor justice for Negroes within the framework of segregation. The social creed of 1908 was endorsed. Generally, Methodism was strongly conservative, but a strong undercurrent of Social Christianity continued in the North. Undocumented.   E. Oberholzer, Jr.

1736. Miller, William D. RURAL VALUES AND URBAN PROGRESS: MEMPHIS, 1900-1917. *Mississippi Q. 1968 21(4): 263-274.* Despite prospects of a new era for Memphis at the turn of the century, the city seemed to retrogress in certain areas of social experience for the next two decades. Its sin-center image, acquired early in its history, stood on a solid basis of factual evidence by 1900, with a significant number of the city's residents believing they were achieving status by ordering their lives in accord with this myth. Granted respectability by the academic community, the dogma of Anglo-Saxon supremacy was widely accepted. In the South, the doctrine became highly formalized and invested with feudal values, including conformity to a prescribed code of conduct for Negroes and with the press continually emphasizing the doctrine. Punishment for nonconformists was violence and death. Other feudal survivals were the "unwritten law" regarding womanly honor permitting blood revenge and the code of honor involving autonomy in personal deportment and including the duel as last resort. Based on newspapers, census statistics, crime reports, and other published material; 37 notes.   R. V. Calvert

1737. Miner, Ward L. THE SOUTHERN WHITE-NEGRO PROBLEM THROUGH THE LENS OF FAULKNER'S FICTION. *J. of Human Relations 1966 14(4): 507-517.* A reading of William Faulkner's works would indicate that the South does not have the human resources to solve the problem of racial tension. Faulkner's white man suffers from a "legacy of guilt and destructiveness" and "lacks the ability of being realistic, let alone honest, in his relations with Negroes." The Negro is idealized by Faulkner. Although they "inevitably share with their white neighbors a too easy dependence on violence," Negroes are the "carriers of effective religious values." "Patient suffering is the black man's foreseeable lot; Faulkner can see little else."   D. J. Abramoske

1738. Moellering, Ralph. LUTHERANS ON SOCIAL PROBLEMS, 1917 TO 1940. *Concordia Hist. Inst. Q. 1969 42(1): 27-40.* Reviews Lutheran thought on a variety of social questions from 1917 to 1940. During the 19th century, when most Lutherans were farmers or small-town people, urban problems were likely to be considered inexplicable or thought of in moralistic terms. In the 20th century, though some Lutherans supported the reform programs of such figures as Theodore Roosevelt and Woodrow Wilson, there was much conservatism in the Lutheran churches. The weakness of the Lutheran approach was that "it was filled with pious platitudes which would remain meaningless until they were applied to specific, concrete proposals for remedial action." The suffering of lower classes, it was suggested in 1917, was due to their "personal failings." Nevertheless, some did support the labor movement; as early as 1919 Lutherans were called to make the Gospel relevant for "an age of labor"; and during the 1930's many Lutherans supported New Deal programs. Although Lutheran attitudes toward Jews and Negroes were predominantly negative, there were those who acted on the assumption that "the Good Samaritan knows no discrimination in color and race." Based on theses, Lutheran periodicals, and other published sources; 47 notes.   D. J. Abramoske

1739. Moore, John Hammond. SOUTH CAROLINA'S REACTION TO THE PHOTOPLAY, "THE BIRTH OF A NATION." *Pro. of the South Carolina Hist. Assoc. 1963: 30-40.* After discussing the almost hostile reception in South Carolina of Thomas Dixon's novel and play, *The Clansman,* from which *The Birth of a Nation* was made, the author traces the reaction to the film. Ten years before the film was made, Dixon's touring company of the play stirred the opposition of the South Carolina press by the controversial thesis that "The Ku Klux Klan saved the South from the Negro, scalawag, and carpetbagger." In spite of the lingering feud between the writer and the Columbia *State's* editor, the film received almost unanimous approval all over South Carolina but, unlike in the rest of the Nation, did not produce much support for the revived Klan. Because of the widespread objection to Dixon and the local scene of his work, his name and the locale of the film were not emphasized in the advertising in South Carolina.   J. W. Thacker, Jr.

1740. Moore, R. Laurence. FLAWED FRATERNITY: AMERICAN SOCIAL-IST RESPONSE TO THE AMERICAN NEGRO, 1901-1912. *Historian 1969 32(1): 1-18.* Uses a number of contemporary Socialist journals and records of the proceedings at national conventions to show that, although the delegates who established the Socialist Party of America in 1901 also passed a resolution on the plight of the American Negro, the party during the next decade did nothing to extend this original commitment or to fight for black Americans. This failure cannot be blamed on the right or left wing. The author finds that interest in the matter was restricted to only a few. For the Negro, the Socialist part in efforts for civil rights was like other aspects of American life, a matter of separate and more or less equal. 46 notes.   N. W. Moen

1741. Morrison, Joseph L. JOSEPHUS DANIELS AND THE BASSETT ACA-DEMIC FREEDOM CASE. *Journalism Q. 1962 39(2): 187-195.* Northerners have found it difficult to understand how Josephus Daniels, so "progressive" on such issues as trusts, public education, and political reform, could have been so "reactionary" as to lead the hue and cry for the dismissal of John Spencer Bassett, a professor at Trinity College (now Duke University), for having written in 1903 that Booker T. Washington was "the greatest man, save General Lee, born in the South in a hundred years." But the episode concentrated within itself too many political passions, prejudices, and emotions for unalloyed reason to have pre-vailed.   S. E. Humphreys

1742. Morrison, Joseph L. THE OBSESSIVE "MIND" OF W. J. CASH. *Virginia Q. R. 1965 41(2): 266-286.* Analyzes the development of Wilbur J. Cash's idea, his articles for Henry Mencken's *American Mercury,* and the influence of Dr. Broadus Mitchell. "The near pessimism that has helped 'Mind [of the south]' to hold up so well stems not from the agrarian concern with the rise of industriali-zation but from realizing that the future would try the South's capacity for adjustment - and Cash had his eye clearly on the Negro question - beyond anything it had accomplished in the past." Based on important new findings: extensive interviews and correspondence with his family and friends and use of the papers of Howard W. Odum, Lillian Smith, Jonathan Daniels, and Alfred A. Knopf, besides Cash's own autobiographical sketch.   E. P. Stickney

1743. Murray, Hugh T., Jr. THE NAACP VERSUS THE COMMUNIST PARTY: THE SCOTTSBORO RAPE CASES, 1931-1932. *Phylon 1967 28(3): 276-287.* Examines the charge that the Communist Party sought to sacrifice the nine young Negroes who allegedly raped two white prostitutes near Scottsboro,

Alabama, in 1931 in order to make martyrs for the cause of Communist propaganda. Eight of the boys were quickly found guilty and all but the youngest were sentenced to die in the electric chair. Before this case the International Labor Defense, a Communist front organization, had been inactive in the defense of Negroes, but it won out in its struggle with the National Association for the Advancement of Colored People in the fight to represent the youths' appeals. The ILD promoted mass public appeals for justice as well as engaging in the legal efforts to secure a reversal of the convictions. The author notes that this was the first time such widespread mass efforts had been staged on behalf of Negro rights, and the NAACP opposed them. The author concludes that the Communists did not attempt to make martyrs of the Scottsboro boys, but instead saved them from a bungling defense and initiated a mass movement on behalf of the Negroes. Largely based on published sources; 68 notes.   D. N. Brown

1744. Newby, I. A. STATES' RIGHTS AND SOUTHERN CONGRESSMEN DURING WORLD WAR I. *Phylon 1963 24(1): 34-50.* Southern congressmen during World War I wittingly helped undermine states' rights principles by supporting administration wartime measures. They played dominant roles in Congress. They included reactionaries and progressives. Acts which affected states' rights included the Conscription Act, the Espionage Act, the Lever Food Control Act, and the Railroad Act, among others. Most remarkably, southerners approved efforts to prevent Senate filibustering which interfered with the passage of war measures, believing white supremacy would survive their opportunism.
                                                                        L. Filler

1745. Osborn, George C. THE PROBLEM OF THE NEGRO IN GOVERNMENT, 1913. *Historian 1961 23(3): 330-347.* Delineates the nature of the Negro problem in the civil service at the beginning of Wilson's administration and depicts the administration's policy of segregation, despite agitation on the part of the National Association for the Advancement of Colored People and the National Negro Press Association and their supporters. During the Wilson years the Negroes actually lost ground in their struggle for equal recognition by the national government. Relies particularly on the Woodrow Wilson Papers, Library of Congress, and the Oswald Garrison Villard Papers, Harvard University.
                                                                  Sr. M. McAuley

1746. Osofsky, Gilbert. RACE RIOT, 1900: A STUDY OF ETHNIC VIOLENCE. *J. of Negro Educ. 1963 32(1): 16-24.* Racial violence marked the formative years of the northern Negro communities (1890-1910). In New York City the arrival of Negroes heightened tensions between the Irish and Negro communities, and a fatal knifing of a policeman by a Negro and a subsequent fight between a Negro and a white near the scene of the dead policeman's home set off a race riot on 15 August 1900. Police brutality against the Negro community was unchecked and unpunished, though it was later made a political issue by the Republican Party.   S. C. Pearson

1747. Paszek, Lawrence J. NEGROES AND THE AIR FORCE, 1939-1949. *Military Affairs 1967 31(1): 1-9.* No Negroes served in the Air Corps prior to

1941 because of the impossibility of forming all-Negro units. After the passage of the Selective Service Act in 1940 the Air Corps began accepting Negroes and forming Negro units but only about 145 thousand served in the Army Air Forces at the peak in World War II. Lack of skills and education limited most Negroes to transportation, base defense, and supply units. Although four all-Negro fighter squadrons saw action during the war, difficulties in securing sufficient competent personnel prevented the four all-Negro bomber squadrons from reaching the front. Problems of finding sufficiently trained Negroes to man all-Negro units intensified in the postwar period and were not overcome until the 1949 decision to integrate all Air Force units. Based mainly on Air Corps and Air Force records; 28 notes.   K. J. Bauer

1748. Porter, Kenneth. RACISM IN CHILDREN'S RHYMES AND SAY-INGS, CENTRAL KANSAS, 1910-1918. *Western Folklore 1965 24(3): 191-196.* Concerned mainly with the term "nigger." The article is based on the sayings and rhymes which the author heard and used as a child.   J. M. Brady

1749. Reagan, Hugh D. RACE AS A FACTOR IN THE PRESIDENTIAL ELECTION OF 1928 IN ALABAMA. *Alabama R. 1966 19(1): 5-19.* Three issues were important in this campaign - religion, prohibition, and white suprem-acy. By the end of the campaign, however, both loyal Democrats and the Republi-cans were placing most emphasis on white supremacy. It was this emphasis that saved the loyal Democrats. "Otherwise, Al Smith might have been defeated in Alabama." Based principally on newspapers.   D. F. Henderson

1750. Record, Wilson C. THE DEVELOPMENT OF THE COMMUNIST POSITION ON THE NEGRO QUESTION IN THE UNITED STATES. *Phy-lon 1958 19(3): 306-326.* The theoretical and program position of the Communist Party on the Negro question in the United States bears little resemblance to the earlier formulations of Karl Marx. Major changes in the Communist approach were initiated by Lenin and carried forward by Stalin, who, at the Sixth World Congress of the Communist International, dictated adoption of the "separate nation" thesis. In the United States during the past 30 years, the Communist position on the Negro question has vacillated between observations of this ideo-logical dictate on the one hand and building an effective Communist following among the Negroes on the other.   A

1751. Reichard, Gary W. THE ABERRATION OF 1920: AN ANALYSIS OF HARDING'S VICTORY IN TENNESSEE. *J. of Southern Hist. 1970 36(1): 33-49.* "The Harding victory in Tennessee was the first fissure in the Solid South after 1876, and certainly some of the forces at work represented serious disloca-tions in the political life of the state. In many ways, however, Tennessee politics were unchanged in 1920 from those of previous state party battles. The Negro tended to be suppressed in the cotton belt in the West and in rural Middle Tennessee as he had been before. The three Grand Divisions [of the State - East Tennessee, Middle Tennessee, and West Tennessee] remained loyal to their tradi-tional majority parties. The rural areas generally tended to be more strongly Republican than the urban areas. Indeed, the change in Tennessee voting behavior in 1920 appears to have been more a difference in degree than a difference in kind....from the perspective of nearly half a century, then, the Republican victory of 1920 in Tennessee appears to have been only the result of forces peculiar to that election rather than the beginning of a coherent trend in the politics of the state." Based on primary and secondary sources; 63 notes.

I. M. Leonard

1752. Rice, Roger L. RESIDENTIAL SEGREGATION BY LAW, 1910-1917. *J. of Southern Hist. 1968 34(2): 179-199.* Traces the evolution of residential segregation laws (the first of which was passed by the Baltimore City Council in December 1919), focuses on the legal opposition to this and other similar laws in cities of the South and Southeast by the National Association for the Advancement of Colored People, and discusses the origins and subsequent applications of the Supreme Court's Buchanan vs. Warley decision in 1917 which rendered such laws unconstitutional. 60 notes.

I. M. Leonard

1753. Rudwick, Elliott M. OSCAR DE PRIEST AND THE JIM CROW RESTAURANT IN THE U.S. HOUSE OF REPRESENTATIVES. *J. of Negro Educ. 1966 35(1): 77-82.* Surveys the attempt of Oscar DePriest, the first Negro Congressman since 1900, to open a House public restaurant to Negroes during his tenure as a Republican Congressman from Chicago from 1929 to 1935. When his private secretary was ejected from this restaurant in 1934, DePriest introduced a resolution requesting the House to investigate the authority for this action taken by order of Representative Lindsay C. Warren of North Carolina. The resolution was pigeonholed in the Rules Committee, and a month later DePriest began obtaining signatures to a petition to circumvent the committee. After Howard University faculty and students resorted to direct action to assert their right to use the restaurant, DePriest, though at first furious at the students, defended their action on the floor of the House and sufficient signatures were secured to bring the resolution before the House. The House voted to appoint a committee, and this body split along party lines with the majority of three Democrats voting to uphold racial segregation. With DePriest's defeat in the 1934 election the matter was dropped.

S. C. Pearson, Jr.

1754. Rudwick, Elliott M. W. E. B. DUBOIS AND THE UNIVERSAL RACES CONGRESS OF 1911. *Phylon 1959 20(4): 372-378.* The precursor of world conferences on races met at the University of London in 1911. It aroused the hopes and expectations of W. E. B. Du Bois, American Negro leader, whose radical approach to the Negro problem worried Booker T. Washington, famous head of Tuskegee Institute, in Alabama, a moderate and practical educational enterprise. The conference itself attracted distinguished scientists. Du Bois was encouraged by the creation of an "international committee" charged with advancing world peace through interracial cooperation. The conference failed to explore the implications of imperialism, and though it offered scientific proofs of race equality, it accomplished little and was not followed up by further conferences; World War I ended plans for a second conference. Du Bois was affected by the idealism which pervaded the meetings in London, inspired by his multiracial associations, and encouraged in an international outlook. His talents as propagandist, rather than administrator, were given scope.   L. Filler

1755. Salmond, John A. THE CIVILIAN CONSERVATION CORPS AND THE NEGRO. *J. of Am. Hist. 1965 52(1): 75-88.* Describes the assistance and treatment received by Negroes from the CCC during its nine-year existence. The author concludes that the CCC did fulfill at least some of its obligations toward unemployed American Negro youth. While much was accomplished, there was much that could have been done.   H. J. Silverman

1756. Scheiber, Jane L. and Scheiber, Harry N. THE WILSON ADMINISTRATION AND THE WARTIME MOBILIZATION OF BLACK AMERICANS, 1917-1918. *Labor Hist. 1969 10(3): 433-458.* Argues that the U.S. entry into World War I dramatically changed the Wilson administration's attitude toward black America. The policy changes favoring blacks were strictly wartime measures for the mobilization of black manpower in aid of the war effort - nothing more. Although many blacks believed that their cooperation in the war effort would help secure improvements within the United States, Wilson's administration never committed itself to relieving the unjust conditions in which black Americans lived. Based on the Wilson Papers, the NAACP Papers, and the Newton D. Baker Papers, plus a wide range of secondary sources; 82 notes.
                    L. L. Athey

1757. Scheiner, Seth M. PRESIDENT THEODORE ROOSEVELT AND THE NEGRO, 1901-1908. *J. of Negro Hist. 1962 47(3): 169-182.* Theodore Roosevelt's policies toward the American Negroes were based primarily on political considerations. Personally, Roosevelt believed the Negro inferior and thought only certain Negroes should be permitted to vote. Early in his administration, policy toward the Negro was based on an appeal to northern Negro votes. However, when Roosevelt discovered that such incidents as inviting Booker T. Washington to dinner and the appointment of Negroes to Federal jobs resulted in loss of support in the South, he changed his practices. In his speeches, too, Roosevelt became increasingly "moderate" on the race question during his second administration.   L. Gara

1758. Scott, Anne Firor. AFTER SUFFRAGE: SOUTHERN WOMEN IN THE TWENTIES. *J. of Southern Hist. 1963 30(3): 298-318.* Although southern women have an impressive record of accomplishment since the effective date of the 19th amendment, the high expectations of those who led the suffrage movement did not come to pass. The number of women in public life is probably no greater today than in 1925. There has been a strong reluctance upon the part of political leaders to give the women any real voice in party decisions or any real places on the tickets. Women have worked effectively in party organizational work and can possibly lay claim to having decided the outcome of some elections. Even more real are their achievements, through such organizations as the League of Women Voters and the Young Women's Christian Association, in influencing public policy on such subjects as female and child labor, unionization, and racial matters. Documented. S. E. Humphreys

1759. Seawright, Sally. DESEGREGATION AT MARYLAND: THE NAACP AND THE MURRAY CASE IN THE 1930'S. *Maryland Historian 1970 1(1): 59-73.* A close examination of the maneuvering and incidents leading to *University of Maryland vs. Donald G. Murray* (1935). Some individuals, among them Charles Hamilton Houston of the NAACP (National Association for the Advancement of Colored People), decided that Maryland was an ideal State in which to challenge "separate but equal" educational facilities. Thurgood Marshall played a significant role in constructing the carefully prepared NAACP test case. In the initial case and the subsequent appeal, University of Maryland lawyers argued that the State had adequately provided "separate but equal" facilities - which was patently false. The significance of the favorable decision was that the color bar had been broken at one southern professional school and that "separate but equal" had been interpreted relative to a specific program. The courts' decision also motivated an improvement in Negro educational facilities throughout the South and was an important preparation for the Brown decision of 1954. Primarily based on NAACP records; 38 notes. G. O. Gagnon

1760. Sherman, Richard B. JOHNSTOWN V. THE NEGRO: SOUTHERN MIGRANTS AND THE EXODUS OF 1923. *Pennsylvania Hist. 1963 30(4): 454-464.* Summarizes a particular local racial problem in Pennsylvania as a by-product of "the vast migration of Southern Negroes to the North during and shortly after the First World War....community apathy and demagogic leadership resulted in misfortune for many of the newcomers" in Johnstown during 1923. "...the plight of the Negroes in Johnstown provided another illustration of the fact that the northern migration had made the racial issue" a national problem. The racial problems "called for intelligent and courageous planning. They could not be solved by drift and inaction." 39 notes. D. H. Swift

1761. Sherman, Richard B. REPUBLICANS AND NEGROES: THE LESSONS OF NORMALCY. *Phylon 1966 27(1): 63-79.* Traces the Republican Party position on such topics as antilynching legislation, participation of Negroes in party affairs, control of the Ku Klux Klan, Federal protection of the right to vote, and appointment of Negroes to government offices. The Republican Party was divided by the tension between idealism and political expediency in the 1920's and was unable to commit itself clearly either to Negro rights or to rebuilding the party in the white South. Based on published sources; 53 notes.
S. C. Pearson, Jr.

1762. Sherman, Richard B. THE HARDING ADMINISTRATION AND THE NEGRO: AN OPPORTUNITY LOST. *J. of Negro Hist. 1964 49(3): 151-168.* In the presidential election of 1920 many Negroes supported Warren G. Harding in the hope that a return of the Republicans to power would end some of the policies of racial discrimination associated with the Wilson administration. Although President Harding extended mild support to pending Federal antilynching legislation and to the idea of establishing an interracial commission to study race relations, nothing came of either proposal and discrimination practiced in various Federal agencies continued. Harding faced pressures from both pro-Negro and southern elements and as a result he gave little but vague promises to those who favored an improvement in race relations.					L. Gara

1763. Simms, L. Moody, Jr. CARL SCHURZ AND THE NEGRO. *Missouri Hist. Soc. Bull. 1969 25(3): 236-238.* A revisionist interpretation in David W. Southern's *The Malignant Heritage: Yankee Progressives and the Negro Question, 1901-1914* (Chicago, Loyola U. Press, 1968) holds that Carl Schurz changed his earlier abolitionist attitudes about the Negro. Basing his judgment on an article which Schurz published in 1904, two years before his death, Southern concludes that Schurz' approach to race relations was somewhat reversed. The present author maintains that his revisionist interpretation is a misinterpretation of Schurz' article. 12 notes.					D. L. Smith

1764. Simms, L. Moody, Jr. JOSIAH ROYCE AND THE SOUTHERN RACE QUESTION. *Mississippi Q. 1969 22(1): 71-74.* In the title essay of *Race, Questions, Provincialism, and Other American Problems* (1908), scholastic idealist Josiah Royce suggested a course of action designed to mitigate racial tensions in the southern United States. He advocated inclusion of the Negro in a program of development of community spirit and challenged white southerners to inculcate among Negroes a feeling of oneness with their community. This could be done by encouraging Negro self-respect and pride in furthering good social order. To alleviate racial friction, Negroes should be given an increasingly responsible part in administration and policing of their own race. If the accidental were not confused with the essential, Royce believed, Americans would soon see that an apparently overwhelming race-problem was actually a "perfectly curable" situation. Based on published material; 8 notes.					R. V. Calvert

1765. Simms, L. Moody, Jr. PHILIP ALEXANDER BRUCE AND THE NEGRO PROBLEM, 1884-1930. *Virginia Mag. of Hist. and Biog. 1965 75(3): 349-362.* In his widely hailed *The Plantation Negro as a Freeman* (New York, 1889), Philip Bruce described the free Negro as the chief stumbling block to the economic recovery of the South. By the time that his *Rise of the New South* (New York, 1905) appeared, his views had begun to change. While still believing in the inherent inferiority of the Negro as a worker, he admitted that the Negro no longer constituted such a heavy brake on the southern economy. In the mid-1920's he looked toward the eventual rise of the Negro to the level of the whites. Based on Bruce's writings, contemporary sources, and monographs; 65 notes.					K. J. Bauer

1766. Simms, L. Moody, Jr. WILLIAM DORSEY JELKS AND THE PROBLEM OF NEGRO EDUCATION. *Alabama R. 1970 23(1): 70-74.* Notes the radical views of Governor William Dorsey Jelks on Negro education. In a 1907 essay entitled "The Acuteness of the Negro Question," Jelks adopted the view that "book learning" encouraged and increased criminality in the Negro. Thus, Jelks and other extremists maintained that the Negro's literary education must be limited to the barest fundamentals. 17 notes.   D. F. Henderson

1767. Sitkoff, Harvard. THE DETROIT RACE RIOT OF 1943. *Michigan Hist. 1969 53(3): 183-206.* Studies the causes, character, and consequences of racial violence in Detroit during the early summer of 1943. Tensions had been building for several years and the riot came as no surprise. Still, city, State, national, military, and local police officials proved evasive and inefficient - even negligent - when the crisis struck. Virtually all public officials believed the Negro was solely responsible for the disorders, took refuge in self-serving explanations of what happened, and chose to ignore the vicious and tragic portents for the future. Based on primary materials in the Library of Congress, the National Archives, the Franklin D. Roosevelt Library, the Michigan Historical Collections, and the Columbia University Oral History Center, as well as a wide range of contemporary published sources; 8 illus., 46 notes.   J. K. Flack

1768. Smith, William H. WILLIAM JENNINGS BRYAN AND RACISM. *J. of Negro Hist. 1969 54(2): 127-149.* Bryan was inconsistant and paradoxical in his attitudes toward race. His attitude regarding some minorities was rather broadminded, but regarding others (especially Negroes) his attitude approached that of a strict segregationist. Bryan was not unique in his failure to relate racial ideas with the contemporary emphasis on democracy and rule by the people; many of his fellow Progressives shared the same contradiction. Bryan's anti-Semitic attitude toward Jews was superficial at most; and on the subject of Orientals he was somewhat ambivalent, except in the matter of immigration to which he strenuously objected. William Jennings Bryan had very little to do with the Ku Klux Klan and did not sympathize with its program of racial and religious intolerance toward Jews and Roman Catholics. As for North American Indians, Bryan felt that they had potential equal to that of any other race. However, in regard to Negroes, Bryan accepted the contemporary race relations as they then existed, and was opposed to any concept of social equality between the white and black races. The author concludes by mentioning that the source of Bryan's racial attitudes is still controversial, Bryan himself claiming that they were formed before he lived in the South. 66 notes.   R. S. Melamed

1769. Snell, William R. FIERY CROSSES IN THE ROARING TWENTIES: ACTIVITIES OF THE REVISED KLAN IN ALABAMA, 1915-1930. *Alabama R. 1970 23(4): 256-276.* Reviews the activities of the revised Ku Klux Klan in Alabama, including membership drives and initiations, objectives, and activities. The objectives of the Alabama Klansmen varied. Among the areas stressed were education, anti-Catholicism, enforcement of laws and strict morals, and racial purity. In some areas the Klan exercised a great deal of political influence; but, where political activity failed, the Klan was not above using illegal means, such as flogging. The revised Klan reached its peak in 1925 when it had over 115 thousand members in Alabama; by 1930 it had only 1,349 members. "The decision to enter politics and the propensity toward violence started the order on its road to oblivion; and continuous feuds in the state and national orders aided in wrecking the organization." Based on various newspapers; 34 notes.

D. F. Henderson

1770. Steelman, Joseph F. THE TRIALS OF A REPUBLICAN STATE CHAIRMAN: JOHN MOTLEY MOREHEAD AND NORTH CAROLINA POLITICS, 1910-1912. *North Carolina Hist. R. 1966 43(1): 31-42.* The appointment of Morehead as State chairman representing rising business and commercial interests in the State was interpreted as a sign of a rejuvenation of the Republican Party in the South. But Morehead faced the political ineptitude of Taft, division within his party, and skillful campaign tactics by the Democrats, who turned the 1910 campaign from economic issues to charges of fraud and alleged Republican support of the franchise for Negroes. The Democrats won easily. In 1912 the Republican Party in North Carolina was virtually destroyed by the national schism between Taft and Roosevelt. Based mainly on unpublished papers; 61 notes.

J. M. Bumsted

1771. Taylor, A. Elizabeth. THE WOMAN SUFFRAGE MOVEMENT IN MISSISSIPPI, 1890-1920. *J. of Mississippi Hist. 1968 30(1): 1-34.* Describes the woman suffrage movement in Mississippi from 1890, when a State constitutional convention considered the subject, until 1920 when the Federal amendment for woman suffrage was ratified. The author focuses primarily upon the activities of the Mississippi Woman Suffrage Association, organized in 1897 and which throughout its history was affiliated with the National American Woman Suffrage Association. The State organization engaged in various pressure group activities but achieved limited political success. The Mississippi Legislature several times defeated proposals for woman suffrage, as in 1920 when it rejected the proposed Federal amendment. In 1920, however, the legislature approved a resolution to give women the right to vote by amending the State constitution. Although this plan received more favorable than unfavorable votes in the November 1920 elections, it failed because it did not receive a majority of all votes cast. Opponents of woman suffrage often argued that it would be dangerous because it would give Negro women the right to vote. Based on various primary sources including newspapers; 143 notes.

J. W. Hillje

1772. Thornbrough, Emma Lou. SEGREGATION IN INDIANA DURING THE KLAN ERA OF THE 1920'S. *Mississippi Valley Hist. R. 1961 47(4): 594-618.* Klan influence may have played some part in the tightening of racial barriers in the 1920's, but it does not appear to have been the prime mover. Actually, the rapid influx of Negroes from the rural South into urban centers of a State where there had always been a tradition of racism seems to offer a sufficient explanation of the demand for segregation. The same attitudes among the people of Indiana which caused them to embrace the Klan caused them to favor separation of the races. Although Klan propaganda may have intensified race feeling, it is still conceivable that the segregation measures which were adopted in the 1920's might have been adopted if the Klan had not existed.

D. R. Millar

1773. Thornton, J. Miles, III. ALABAMA POLITICS, J. THOMAS HEFLIN, AND THE EXPULSION MOVEMENT OF 1929. *Alabama R. 1968 21(2): 83-112.* In order to maintain power, at the turn of the century the Bourbon elite of Alabama had to eliminate the Negro from politics while admitting to power the excluded white groups "from whose ranks dissident movements had time and again arisen." During the twenties, the whites, predominantly from northern Alabama, became restless under Bourbon rule and thus revolted. Using the Ku Klux Klan as their vehicle, in 1926 they elected a governor, various local officials, and a number of Congressmen. During the presidential campaign of 1928 the Klan and its ally the Anti-Saloon League mounted a major political effort, led by the State's senior U.S. Senator J. Thomas Heflin, to oppose Al Smith, the Democratic presidential candidate. The effort was almost successful. Smith carried the State by only seven thousand votes. Feeling endangered, the Bourbons thus began a movement to expel from the party those who had supported Hoover in 1928. In December 1929 the State Democratic Executive Committee approved an expulsion resolution. "The demonstration that the Bourbons could still effectively discipline protesters who transgressed the borders of the status quo ended, for the present, all North Alabama ambitions in that direction." Based on the Heflin Papers in the University of Alabama Library and various newspapers; 89 notes.   D. F. Henderson

1774. Toppin, Edgar A. A HALF-CENTURY OF STRUGGLE FOR EQUAL RIGHTS, 1916-1965. *Negro Hist. Bull. 1965 28(8): 176-177, 188-189, 197.* Quotes President Lyndon B. Johnson: "There is no part of America where the promise of equality has been fully kept." The author adds that "the Negro has come a long way when his cause is adopted so ardently by...a native of a former Confederate State." To focus only on still exisiting inequalities is to have a distorted perspective. President Woodrow Wilson defended and extended segregation practices in government offices. Changes such as a decline in lynchings, the modern Ku Klux Klan, urbanization and Negro migration, the leadership culminating in the National Association for the Advancement of Colored People, the trend in Negro votes from Republican to Democratic, and the fluctuating economic status of Negroes are surveyed. 16 notes.   E. P. Stickney

1775. Toppin, Edgar A. WALTER WHITE AND THE ATLANTA NAACP'S FIGHT FOR EQUAL SCHOOLS, 1916-1917. *Hist. of Educ. Q. 1967 7(1): 3-21.* Walter White, an Atlanta insurance company cashier, was instrumental in organizing the fight of the Atlanta National Association for the Advancement of Colored People (NAACP) for improvement of the "separate but equal" public schools for Negroes and for the establishment of Negro high schools. In 1916-17 during White's residence in Atlanta, the fight did not move beyond attempts to mobilize public opinion. In 1918 and 1919 an organized Negro boycott thwarted a bond issue for schools and led to a new and successful issue in 1921, followed in 1924 by the opening of the first public high school for Negroes in the city. The author criticizes the work of the Atlanta NAACP for its appeal to middle-class sentiment and its reliance on the small group of Negro professional men and businessmen. Based on published sources and research in the NAACP archives; 46 notes.   J. Herbst

1776. Tuttle, William M., Jr. LABOR CONFLICT AND RACIAL VI-
OLENCE: THE BLACK WORKER IN CHICAGO, 1894-1919. *Labor Hist.*
1969 10(3): 408-432. Labor conflict in Chicago between the white rank and file
and their black counterparts retarded unionization and set a pattern for race
relations. Negro distrust of unions and white workers, the economic advantages
to be accrued by nonunion workers, the manipulation of black workers by management, and the hatred of black workers by whites, produced 25 years of violence
and influenced the bloody race riot of 1919. Based on newspspers, public documents, and files of the U.S. Department of Labor in the National Archives; 79
notes.   L. L. Athey

1777. Tuttle, William M., Jr. VIEWS OF A NEGRO DURING "THE RED
SUMMER" OF 1919 - A DOCUMENT. *J. of Negro Hist. 1966 51(3): 209-218.*
Publishes a letter written shortly after the bloody Chicago race riots of 1919 by
Stanley B. Norvell, a Negro war veteran, explaining the causes of the riots. In
his letter Norvell pointed out the lack of understanding by whites of the sentiments and aspirations of American Negroes. Education and the experience of the
recent war had led Negroes to reject continued submission to discrimination and
segregation. Instead of equal treatment Negroes wanted the same treatment in all
areas of life, and when their hopes were unfulfilled they became enraged and
turned to violence as an outlet for their frustration.   L. Gara

1778. Vander Zanden, James W. THE IDEOLOGY OF WHITE SUPREM-
ACY. *J. of the Hist. of Ideas 1959 20(3): 385-402.* The major premises of the
segregationist position, stemming from the antebellum period, are: "1. Segregation is part of the natural order and as such is eternally fixed. 2. The Negro is
inferior to the white or, at the very least, is 'different' from the white. 3. The
breakdown of segregation in any of its aspects will inevitably lead to racial
amalgamation, resulting in a host of disastrous consequences."
                                                                  W. H. Coates

1779. Voss, Carl Hermann. THE LION AND THE LAMB: AN EVALU-
ATION OF THE LIFE AND WORK OF STEPHEN S. WISE. *Am. Jewish*
Archives 1969 21(1): 3-19. A biographical analysis, from first-hand knowledge,
of Rabbi Wise's humanitarian,social, and organizational concerns. Among these
were the American Civil Liberties Union, American Jewish Congress, and the
National Association for the Advancement of Colored People, which he helped
found. A life-long Zionist, rabbinic leader, founder of New York's Free Synagogue, and president of the Jewish Institute of Religion, Wise worked also with
Christian theologians on behalf of labor's rights, in opposition to political corruption, and for other social reforms.   J. Brandes

1780. Walden, Daniel. RACE AND IMPERIALISM: THE ACHILLES HEEL
OF THE PROGRESSIVES. *Sci. and Soc. 1967 31(2): 222-232.* Segregation and
colonialism are essentially the same; this point is seen in America's "Manifest
Destiny" of the mid-19th century and the rhetoric of Progressive spokesmen

during the early 20th century. Progressivism was not revolutionary; it embodied the traditions of the "White Anglo-Saxon Protestant." 29 notes.

R. S. Burns

1781. Ware, Gilbert. LOBBYING AS A MEANS OF PROTEST: THE NAACP AS AN AGENT OF EQUALITY. *J. of Negro Educ. 1964 33(2): 103-110.* While the National Association for the Advancement of Colored People is best known for its legal activities, the author defends its record in lobbying for a Federal antilynching law, an FEPC, antipoll tax legislation, and against the confirmation of a Supreme Court justice considered hostile to Negroes and the Senate rule permitting the filibuster. Based on records of legislative committee hearings, NAACP annual reports, and various published works. S. C. Pearson, Jr.

1782. Warnock, Henry Y. ANDREW SLEDD, SOUTHERN METHODISTS, AND THE NEGRO: A CASE HISTORY. *J. of Southern Hist. 1965 31(3): 252-271.* In the July 1902 issue of *Atlantic Monthly* (pp. 65-73), the Reverend Andrew Sledd, professor of Latin at Emory College (then located at Covington, Georgia, now Emory University at Atlanta), published an article, "The Negro: Another View," accusing the South of dehumanizing the Negro and demanding that he be treated with courtesy and equality in public places. He particularly attacked the South for lynchings. Sledd was the son-in-law of Bishop Warren A. Candler of the Southern Methodist Church, former president of Emory College. Mrs. W. H. Felton, later to be the first woman senator in the United States, furiously attacked Sledd in the columns of the Atlanta *Constitution* (3 August 1902), perhaps partly as a roundabout way of attacking Bishop Candler, who had often criticized her views. On subsequent days, numerous news stories, editorials, and letters appeared in various Georgia papers and on 12 August the executive committee of Emory College trustees accepted Sledd's resignation, although he returned in 1914 to the college's Candler School of Theology and achieved a national reputation in biblical scholarship. It appears that he gave in with questionable haste, that the college officials handled the matter too precipitately, and that if both he and they had waited a little longer his departure might not have been necessary. But the case also shows there was not only extreme prejudice on racial matters, but that even in 1902 there was a moderate undercurrent of southern thought, especially within the Southern Methodist Church. A year later, John Spencer Bassett of Trinity College (now Duke U.) wrote in the *South Atlantic Quarterly*, that Booker T. Washington was the second-ranking citizen of the 19th-century South. He was similarly criticized but retained his position. S. E. Humphreys

1783. Warnock, Henry Y. SOUTHERN METHODISTS, THE NEGRO, AND UNIFICATION: THE FIRST PHASE. *J. of Negro Hist. 1967 52(4): 287-304.* Traces the various moves toward the 1939 merger of the Northern and Southern Methodists and the Methodist Protestant Church, with emphasis on the question of the place of the Negro in the united church. From 1911, when the merger was first seriously proposed, it was clear that the southern church was willing to accept Negroes in a united church and that the northern church was willing to accept segregation. Eventually the Negro achieved what amounted to proportional representation in the general church conference. From this study the southern church appears to be moderately progressive and willing to adjust rather than a bulwark of opposition to the unification movement. Documented with various church reports, newspapers, and a few manuscript sources; 45 notes.

L. Gara

1784. Wesley, Charles H. W. E. B. DU BOIS - THE HISTORIAN. *J. of Negro Hist. 1965 50(3): 147-162.* Describes William E. B. Du Bois as a historian whose writings were professedly biased in favor of the Negro. His book *The Suppression of the African Slave Trade to the United States of America, 1638-1870* (1895) earned him a reputation as a historian. Shortly afterwards Du Bois concerned himself with sociological as well as historical questions. He became preoccupied with questions of race and racism and drew upon his creative imagination and considerable literary skill to present the plight of the American Negroes to the world of letters. Mostly based on the writings of Du Bois.   L. Gara

1785. Whatley, Larry. THE WORKS PROGRESS ADMINISTRATION IN MISSISSIPPI. *J. of Mississippi Hist. 1968 30(1): 35-50.* Describes the operations of the WPA in Mississippi from its origin in 1935 to its end in 1943. Described are various classes of projects, including public buildings, parks and recreational facilities, conservation, sewers and other utility projects, airports and transportation, white collar projects, sewing and canning, health and sanitation, and highways, roads, and streets. The Mississippi Legislature passed several laws dealing with the WPA and there was some political controversy over the organization. "The majority of Mississippians favored the W.P.A., [but] there was strong opposition to the program." Although racial discrimination on WPA projects was prohibited, in Mississippi Negroes had separate projects and "there was probably little or only token integration." WPA projects in Mississippi were revolutionary in that women were given "the same rights and benefits as men." Based on various primary sources, chiefly newspapers and WPA publications; 104 notes.

J. W. Hillje

1786. Wilson, Harold. THE ROLE OF CARTER GLASS IN THE DISEN-FRANCHISEMENT OF THE VIRGINIA NEGRO. *Historian 1969 32(1): 69-82.* Discusses the conviction of Carter Glass (1858-1946) that the Negro is inferior to the white race, and that the male voters among what amounted to one-third of Virginia's population should be largely disenfranchised. The author shows how Glass worked diligently to influence the State Democratic Party and the State legislature to call for a constitutional convention (1901), and describes how Glass labored to secure a frame of government which incorporated his views. He was so successful that the new constitution denied the vote to about 50 percent of those who formerly exercised it. It also created an electorate which made Virginia virtually a one party State and sent Glass to Washington for a career in Congress. Not until the Eisenhower-Stevenson campaign in 1952 did more Virginians go to the polls than in the presidential election of 1888, the last under the former constitution. 84 notes.   N. W. Moen

1787. Wolters, Raymond. SECTION 7A AND THE BLACK WORKER. *Labor Hist. 1969 10(3): 459-474.* The black worker was not aided by the operation of Section 7a of the National Industrial Recovery Act. In fact, the American Federation of Labor between 1933 and 1935 organized some shops at the expense of Negro labor. Although the Urban League and the National Association for the Advancement of Colored People tried to get the AFL leadership to enforce the stated principle that there should be no discrimination on the basis of race, the AFL did little. When the NAACP and the Urban League attempted to obtain a provision in the National Labor Relations (Wagner) Act to prevent unions from discriminating on the basis of race, they were defeated by the AFL. Based on the files of the NAACP and the Urban League; 26 notes. L. L. Athey

1788. Worley, Lynda F. WILLIAM ALLEN WHITE: KANSAN EXTRAOR-DINARY. *Social Sci. 1966 41(2): 91-98.* A study of the origins and nature of the progressivism of William Allen White (1868-1944). White's parents brought to him a heritage of New England puritanism (father) and midwestern abolitionism (mother), both of which prepared his mind for the progressivism of Theodore Roosevelt. White saw progressivism as a manifestation of abolitionist principles in an industrial age. By 1901 he had shed his conservatism of Populist days and launched into a crusade against the "bond-holding aristocracy" and "Jim Crow" legislation, at the same time that he supported prohibition, direct legislation, and suffrage for women. Drawn largely from White's publications. M. Small

1789. Worthman, Paul B. A BLACK WORKER AND THE BRICKLAYERS AND MASONS' UNION, 1903. *J. of Negro Hist. 1969 54(4): 398-404.* Many building trades unions in the United States were desegregated at the turn of the 20th century. One of the most integrated unions, at least by the provisions of its constitution and regulations, was the Bricklayers and Masons' International Union, formed in 1865. Robert Rhodes was a black member of this union when he tried to gain employment in 1903 in Indianapolis, Indiana. The local in Indianapolis, however, refused to require its members to work with Rhodes and prevented his securing meaningful employment. Rhodes appealed to the international headquarters, but received only partial satisfaction. Eventually, Rhodes had to find employment elsewhere in a nonunion environment. Several letters are reprinted from the *38th Annual Report of the President and Secretary of the Bricklayers and Masons' International Union of America, 1903,* illustrating the lack of union interest in enforcing the nondiscriminatory provisions of its bylaws and constitution. R. S. Melamed

1790. Wyman, Walker D. and Hart, John D. THE LEGEND OF CHARLIE GLASS. *Colorado Mag. 1969 46(1): 40-54.* Charlie Glass was a Negro cowboy and top foreman, in the twenties and thirties, of the Lazy Y Cross Ranch of Oscar L. Turner in western Colorado and eastern Utah. He became involved in the cattlemen-sheepmen wars and killed a Basque sheepherder in 1921. In the trial he was acquitted of the murder charge. However, in 1937 he was killed in a truck accident under peculiar circumstances which suggest foul play by two transient sheepherders. Based largely on newspaper accounts and interviews; illus.

O. H. Zabel

1791. Wynes, Charles E. THE EVOLUTION OF JIM CROW LAWS IN TWENTIETH CENTURY VIRGINIA. *Phylon 1967 28(4): 416-425.* Virginia, like other Southern States, entered the 20th century without rigid, caste-like segregation established and maintained by State law. In 1900 the first statewide segregation law was enacted. It required railroads to furnish separate or partitioned cars for the two races. Until 1944 Virginia added to the long list of segregation laws. The greatest number of these were enacted during the 1920's and 1930's. The explanation for this is that earlier the Negro had been disfranchised by the new State constitution of 1902, but by the 1920's white southerners knew their world was changing because many of their institutions were under attack from within and without. Segregation laws were falling before the Federal courts and southern Negroes were attacking the constitutionality of white primaries. White Virginians responded by demanding more comprehensive statutes regulating contact between the races, and politicians acted. Despite efforts of a small number of white Virginians to bring about repeal of these laws in the 1950's, political leaders refused to face reality. Virginia's inability to solve her racial problems without pressures from Federal law was not, concludes the author, due to any innate conservatism of her people or even devotion to the "Southern way of life" but can be assigned to the myopia of her political leaders. Based on published sources; 30 notes.   D. N. Brown

1792. Wynes, Charles E. THE REVEREND QUINCY EWING: SOUTHERN RACIAL HERETIC IN THE "CAJUN" COUNTRY. *Louisiana Hist. 1966 7(3): 221-228.* Biographical sketch of a Napoleonville, Louisiana Episcopal clergyman who attacked the widely-held southern concept of Negro inferiority in "The Heart of the Race Problem," *Atlantic Monthly,* Vol. 103, March 1909. He argued that the real race problem was not Negro inferiority, but rather the white man's effort toward and anxiety over maintaining the Negro in a position of inferiority. Based on Ewing's article and on correspondence and interviews with Ewing's relatives and associates.   R. L. Woodward

The Social, Political, & Economic Situation

1793. Adelman, Lynn. A STUDY OF JAMES WELDON JOHNSON. *J. of Negro Hist. 1967 52(2): 128-145.* Reviews the career of James Weldon Johnson (1871-1938) as a moderate Negro leader whose work paved the way for more militant voices after his death. After a sheltered middle-class childhood in Jacksonville, Florida, Johnson attended Atlanta University where he first confronted the race question. Following graduation he taught school, started a short-lived newspaper, studied law and practiced it briefly, joined his brother in a song writing partnership, and held two consular posts. While serving with the State Department he began writing poetry and fiction with predominantly racial themes, and after returning to the United States he became editor of the *New York Age,* America's leading Negro newspaper. In 1916 Johnson became field secretary for the National Association for the Advancement of Colored People, starting a 15-year career as a leader in that association. As a leading Negro spokesman he helped educate the public to the need for antilynching legislation and building up the NAACP as a powerful, nationwide organization in the vanguard of the struggle for civil rights. L. Gara

1794. Allswang, John M. THE CHICAGO NEGRO VOTER AND THE DEMOCRATIC CONSENSUS: A CASE STUDY, 1918-1936. *J. of the Illinois State Hist. Soc. 1967 60(2): 145-175.* Shows that the vote in five Negro ghetto areas in Chicago did not move decisively into the Democratic column until the election of 1936 and even then generally exceeded 50 percent in the mayoral but not in the presidential balloting. The persisting loyalty of Negro voters to the Republicans is explained in large part by reference to William Hale Thompson's leadership and popularity, while the move in the 1930's to the Democrats is seen principally as the result of the special efforts of Anton J. Cermak and Edward J. Kelly to attract the Negro vote. S. L. Jones

1795. Aptheker, Herbert. LENIN, NATIONAL LIBERATION, AND THE UNITED STATES. *New World R. 1970 38(1): 159-167.* Examines the writings of Lenin on national liberation and specifically on the "exquisite torment" suffered by black Americans, dating from Lenin's 1913 essay "Russians and Negroes" and his "Capitalism and Agriculture in the United States" (1917). The author gives special attention to the contemporary labors of William Edward Burghardt Du Bois and the influence that each man may have exerted on the other. Appended are documents containing comments on Lenin by Black Americans including Du Bois, the Garvey movement (the Universal Negro Improvement Association), W. A. Domingo, Claude McKay, Edwin Brooks, Paul Robeson, and poems by Langston Hughes and Richard Wright.
J

1796. Aptheker, Herbert, ed. DU BOIS ON JAMES WELDON JOHNSON. *J. of Negro Hist. 1967 52(3): 224-227.* A testimonial address delivered by W. E. B. Du Bois at a dinner given 14 May 1921 to honor James Weldon Johnson upon his retirement as executive secretary of the National Association for the Advancement of Colored People. After reviewing Johnson's career as lawyer, poet, and diplomat, Du Bois commented on his personality and his significant contributions to the NAACP. L. Gara

1797. Arden, Eugene. THE EARLY HARLEM NOVEL. *Phylon 1959 20(1): 25-31.* Paul Laurence Dunbar's *The Sport of the Gods* (1902) was the earliest serious novel about Negro life in New York. Starting in the 1920's an enormous Harlem literature developed. It was at first romantic, as exemplified by Carl Van Vechten's *Nigger Heaven* (1926), and then later became realistic, as in Countee

Cullen's *One Way to Heaven* (1932), depicting tensions in the "black ghetto." Current Harlem fiction tends toward sensationalistic accounts of teenage gang life.   A

1798. Beck, Earl R. GERMAN VIEWS OF NEGRO LIFE IN THE UNITED STATES, 1919-1933. *J. of Negro Hist. 1963 48(1): 22-32.* Concludes that many of the German travelers who visited the United States and later recorded their experiences believed that the position of the Negro in American society constituted the Nation's most pressing social issue. The visitors from Germany noted the inconsistency of American democratic ideals and the denial of civil rights to Negroes, the economic improvement of Negroes, the lack of a rational basis for racial segregation and discrimination, the desirable effects of racial mixture, and the contributions of Negroes to American music and dance. Based on original published sources.   L. Gara

1799. Belles, A. Gilbert. THE COLLEGE FACULTY, THE NEGRO SCHOLAR, AND THE JULIUS ROSENWALD FUND. *J. of Negro Hist. 1969 54(4): 383-392.* The Rosenwald Fund was created in 1917 by Julius Rosenwald, president of Sears, Roebuck and Company, for the improvement of education and race relations. After much success, it was finally dissolved in June of 1948. The fund was used to subsidize public school and county libraries and to further the work of individuals and organizations devoted to encouraging racial understanding. The fund was also to aid the appointment of Negro professors to otherwise all-white faculties of colleges and universities. Some of the most creative work of the fund was accomplished under the direction of Fred G. Wale during the 1940's. Based primarily on the correspondence of Fred G. Wale; 27 notes.   R. S. Melamed

1800. Bittle, William E. and Geis, Gilbert L. RACIAL SELF-FULFILLMENT AND THE RISE OF AN ALL-NEGRO COMMUNITY IN OKLAHOMA. *Phylon 1957 18(3): 247-260.* The establishment of Boley, an all-Negro community in east-central Oklahoma, toward the beginning of the 20th century was at first greeted with enthusiasm and considerable good will by both whites and Negroes. Only after admission of Oklahoma Territory as a State, when it became obvious that the Negro community held the political balance of power in Okfuskee County, did the whites combine to destroy the voting power of the Oklahoma Negroes. Disheartened and disillusioned, many of them emigrated to the Gold Coast after 1910.   C. F. Latour

1801. Blair, John L. A TIME FOR PARTING: THE NEGRO DURING THE COOLIDGE YEARS. *J. of Am. Studies [Great Britain] 1969 3(2): 177-199.* Discusses President Calvin Coolidge's handling of the Negro vote and the erosion of Negro support for the Republican Party during the 1920's. Coolidge was sympathetic and open to Negro appeals and spoke out strongly in favor of racial justice. Beyond that, however, not much was done. The President knew very little about Negroes, was reluctant to rock the boat, and naïvely thought "that you need only point out a man's error for him voluntarily to tread the path of the enlightened." Negro leaders, largely loyal to the Republicans, warned of growing unrest. Though still suspicious of the Democratic Party, significant numbers had decided it was time to leave the Republican Party by 1928. Based on newspapers and the Coolidge Papers.   D. J. Abramoske

1802. Brandfon, Robert L. THE END OF IMMIGRATION TO THE COTTON FIELDS. *Mississippi Valley Hist. R. 1964 50(4): 591-611.* The rich land of the Yazoo-Mississippi Delta was at the end of the 19th century a leading plantation area where the introduction of immigrant labor would benefit the cotton-dominated economy. By 1903, 52 Italian families were working on one plantation. In 1904-05 the Italian ambassador was a guest of the Southern Railroad. The few Italian immigrants that came were disappointed by the inability of a tenant to gain economic independence. By replacing the Negro in the same type of work and under the same conditions, the Italians assumed the status of Negroes. After 1910 their small number declined rapidly. 53 notes.
        E. P. Stickney

1803. Brewer, James H. ROBERT LEE VANN, DEMOCRAT OR REPUBLICAN: AN EXPONENT OF LOOSE LEAF POLITICS. *Negro Hist. Bull. 1958 21(5): 100-103.* Robert Lee Vann, the influential editor of the *Pittsburgh Courier,* advocated "loose leaf politics," under which the Negroes would refrain from giving unquestioned support to either the Democrats or the Republicans but would bargain for advantages from both parties. He supported Franklin Roosevelt in 1932 and 1936, but by 1940, the year in which he died, had thrown his support to Wendell Wilkie.   L. Gara

1804. Brewer, James H. THE GHOSTS OF JACKSON WARD. *Negro Hist. Bull. 1958 22(2): 27-30.* Describes the municipal election of 1900 in Richmond, Virginia, in which the Democrats used a combination of forgery and fraud to defeat the Republican Negroes of Jackson Ward as a first step toward depriving them of the right to vote and hold office.   L. Gara

1805. Broderick, Francis L. DU BOIS AND THE DEMOCRATIC PARTY, 1908-1916. *Negro Hist. Bull. 1957 21(2): 41-44.* Describes W. E. B. Du Bois' shifting political tactics and Negro reaction to them during the Progressive period. On grounds of expediency, Du Bois advised Negroes to support the Democrats in 1888, later gave lukewarm endorsement to Theodore Roosevelt, and returned to the Democratic fold in the national elections of 1908 and 1912. Quickly disillusioned with Wilson, he opposed him in 1916 and supported Warren Harding in 1920. For the next 16 years, DuBois refused to back either major party.   L. Gara

1806. Brooks, Albert N. D. H. COUNCILL TRENHOLM: MARTYR ON ALABAMA RACIAL TIGHTROPE. *Negro Hist. Bull. 1963 26(8): 230-232.* A brief sketch of the life of H. Councill Trenholm (1900-63), prominent Negro educator from Alabama. Trenholm's activities included serving for 38 years as president of Alabama State College, vice president of the Association for the Study of Negro Life and History, and a member of the board of directors of the American Teachers Association.   L. Gara

1807. Butcher, Philip. W. S. BRAITHWAITE'S SOUTHERN EXPOSURE: RESCUE AND REVELATION. *Southern Literary J. 1971 3(2): 49-61.* An account of the 10 years, 1935-45, that William Stanley Beaumont Braithwaite (1878-1962), the black poet and critic, spent on the faculty of Atlanta University. A native of Boston, he frequently contributed to the Boston *Transcript*. Braithwaite was the first anthologist to provide book form for work by Robert Frost, Edwin Arlington Robinson, Amy Lowell, Wallace Stevens, and others. Unable to earn a living by this work in the Depression, he steeled himself to teach in the South despite his total lack of formal education beyond elementary school. He was one of the first Altanta University professors to interest students in scholarship on black subjects, and found much satisfaction in his work prior to his retirement to Harlem. 19 notes.   J. L. Colwell

1808. Cantor, Louis. A PROLOGUE TO THE PROTEST MOVEMENT: THE MISSOURI SHARECROPPER ROADSIDE DEMONSTRATION OF 1939. *J. of Am. Hist. 1969 55(4): 804-822.* On 10 January 1939 motorists in the "bootheel" area of southeastern Missouri were greeted by a roadside demonstration of hundreds of sharecroppers who camped there for three or four days before being dispersed by State police. The action was organized by Owen H. Whitfield, a Negro preacher and leader of the Southern Tenant Farmers Union. The demonstrators protested bad conditions in the area and, particularly, mass evictions of tenants by landlords who did not wish to share parity checks with them. The demonstration provoked initial local hostility, but attained widespread sympathetic publicity. It had an immediate effect in providing federally-financed low-rental housing for cropper families, but did nothing to change the unfairness of Agricultural Adjustment Administration legislation. The demonstration revealed conflicts over Communist attempts to dominate the STFU. 94 notes.
                                                                  K. B. West

1809. Carnegie, Mary Elizabeth. THE IMPACT OF INTEGRATION ON THE NURSING PROFESSION: AN HISTORICAL SKETCH. *Negro Hist. Bull. 1965 28(7): 154-155, 168.* The Negro nurses in 1908 banded together into the National Association of Colored Graduate Nurses. Its archives contain invaluable information on the history of its struggle for integration. The association was dissolved in 1951 after the American Nurses' Association agreed to admit Negroes. The author details the ways in which "prejudice in nursing is being exposed, identified, and dealt with," as well as the extent to which Negro nurses are achieving recognition by holding important positions in a profession "further along the road to complete integration than any other profession" in the United States. Illus., 9 notes.   E. P. Stickney

1810. Chaffee, Mary Law. WILLIAM E. B. DU BOIS' CONCEPT OF THE RACIAL PROBLEM IN THE UNITED STATES. *J. of Negro Hist. 1956 41(3): 241-258.* Describes Du Bois' break with the philosophy of Booker T. Washington, his leadership of the National Association for the Advancement of Colored People and his withdrawal from that organization in 1934. His present radical position of complete socialization "has alienated him from the majority of Negro intellectuals" but "his latter-day extremes can hardly nullify the constructive influence of his earlier career." Based on the writings of Du Bois and some of his contemporaries.   W. E. Wight

1811. Chaffin, Glenn. AUNT TISH: BELOVED GOURMET OF THE BITTER ROOT. *Montana 1971 21(4): 67-69.* Appreciative account of Tish Nevins, born a slave in 1862, who went to Montana's Bitter Root Valley in 1899 as housekeeper for a motherless family. In later years she operated a boarding house in Hamilton, serving food whose fame extended beyond the State. Stresses the high character and lovable personality of a humble lady who recognized her limitations but refused to regard herself as "disadvantaged." Illus.   S. R. Davison

1812. Chalmers, David. THE KU KLUX KLAN IN POLITICS IN THE 1920'S. *Mississippi Q. 1965 18(4): 234-247.* During the decade of the 1920's the Ku Klux Klan was a very real force in American politics, marching, electing, and sometimes terrorizing from Maine to California. Although this wave of the "politics of hate and fear" has not had important lasting influence in American public life, during the 1920's the Klan aided in electing 16 U.S. Senators (nine Republicans and seven Democrats) and 11 governors (six Republicans and five Democrats), with an undetermined number of Congressmen as members of the hooded order. During the decade the Klan aided American nativism and a "persistent, underrated anti-Catholicism" was still a political factor in 1960. Such negativism toward outsiders and change did not survive as a potent political movement. Despite political power and some impressive successes, the Klan lacked the leadership required to perpetuate any such political force. The major result of Klan political activities, besides encouraging nativist sentiments, perhaps was reaction occurring in the urban revolution of the New Deal. Many large nonsouthern cities by 1924 were experiencing declining Republican pluralities. Although the extent of Klan operation in American cities is not generally recognized, the organization probably helped shift many ethnic (including Negro) city votes to the Democratic column. A potent force in national party politics in 1924, the Klan had almost disbanded by election time in 1928, mainly because of "its own ineptness and seaminess" but partly because of pessimism running counter to the prevailing American mood. Partly based on unpublished documents and manuscripts; 47 notes.   R. V. Calvert

1813. Clum, John M. RIDGELY TORRENCE'S NEGRO PLAYS: A NOBLE BEGINNING. *South Atlantic Q. 1969 68(1): 96-108.* Torrence's *Three Plays for the Negro Theatre* (produced together in New York in 1917) were the first attempts on stage to present Negroes as humans. The production, with an all-Negro cast, was in a legitimate theater. Torrence used Negro dialect and music, although the plays were not socially conscious. Critics were enthusiastic about the plays but not the players. This may have hampered success of the production, although America's declaration of war, occurring a day after the plays opened, was probably more significant. 13 notes.   J. M. Bumsted

1814. Cole, Howson W., ed. LIFE IN THE CAMP LEE SOLDIERS' HOME, "A LETTER OF BENJAMIN J. ROGERS, DECEMBER 27, 1904." *Virginia Mag. of Hist. and Biog. 1962 70(4): 468-470.* Describes the home, with its two physicians, two nurses, and a half-dozen Negro men and women, and its two hundred inmates, as it existed in December 1904. There were 20 dormitories, a chapel, and other facilities.   J. H. Boykin

1815. Coulter, E. M. A GEORGIA LAWYER AND HIS NEGRO CLIENT: A STUDY IN BLACK AND WHITE. *Georgia Hist. Q. 1969 53(3): 305-320.* A study of the case of Thad Boyd, Jr., a Negro convicted of murdering a brother-in-law in a family argument in 1902. Defended by white lawyer Edward K. Lumpkin of Athens, Boyd served 12 years of a life term before being paroled in 1915. The author contends that the white lawyer took an unusual interest in the case and worked continuously to free Boyd and to reform the Georgia prison system. Based largely on newspaper research and the Boyd-Lumpkin correspondence; 15 notes.   R. A. Mohl

1816. Davis, Arthur P. I GO TO WHITTIER SCHOOL. *Phylon 1960 21(2): 155-166.* The author's recollections of Whittier School, in Hampton, Virginia, which he attended from 1912 until 1918. At Whittier, a training school for Hampton Institute students preparing to be teachers, he received a superior grammar-school education, especially for a Negro child. The white school, Symes-Eaton, though the oldest free school in America, dating from 1635, offered a less adequate educational program. Whittier was a New England missionary outpost, and carried on the stern tradition it inherited.   L. Filler

1817. Deighton, H. S. LES NEGRES ET LA DEMOCRATIE AMERICAINE [The Negro and American democracy]. *Politique Etrangère [France] 1954 19(3): 275-290.* A discussion of the past and present status of the Negro and of the progress achieved during the past 20 years toward securing equal rights for him. Despite the progress achieved, the Negro remains an underprivileged minority which is, however, absolutely nationalist American in its sentiments. The continuation of the present favorable development depends to some extent on the economic situation.   S

1818. Dowie, J. Iverne. THE AMERICAN NEGRO: AN OLD IMMIGRANT ON A NEW FRONTIER. *In the Trek of the Immigrants: Essays Presented to Carl Wittke (Rock Island, Illinois: Augustana Coll. Lib., 1964): 241-260.* Negroes are America's latter-day immigrants, and the decade of the 1920's was their frontier period. "The story of the Negro during World War I parallels the story of the immigrants who came over at an earlier time to build our railroads and dig our mines when the supply of native labor was inadequate." In the 1920's writers "were putting in words the thoughts which present-day Negroes are framing in action." Included is the text of a letter from Harlem showing the extent to which Harlem in the 1920's represented a "chance." 45 notes.
                                    E. P. Stickney

1819. Eagle, Joanna. THE ARTISTIC ODYSSEY OF A BLACK PAINTER FROM THE RURAL SOUTH. *Smithsonian 1971 2(8): 34-39.* Discusses the life and work of William H. Johnson, an American painter. Johnson was born in Florence, South Carolina, in 1901. He decided to become an artist and went to New York in 1918. By 1921 after working at a variety of odd jobs he was able to attend the National Academy of Design. There he worked with Charles Hawthorne, who arranged for Johnson to go to Europe, where he was influenced by the work of the Russian-French expressionist, Chaim Soutine. When he returned to the United States in 1929, he won a competition held in New York by the Harmon Foundation, an organization devoted to helping black artists. In Florence, soon afterward he was arrested while painting the *Jacobia Hotel,* probably because the subject had become a brothel. After this incident he did not return to the South for 14 years. Johnson went back to Europe and married Holcha Krake, a Danish weaver and ceramicist 15 years his senior. In 1938, because of the rumblings of World War II, the Johnsons returned to the United States. He found employment with the WPA Fine Arts Project and taught at the Harlem Community Arts Center. He now began to "paint my people" and developed a new style. His wife died in 1943, and he became mentally ill soon after. He died after spending 23 years in a New York State mental hospital in 1970. Illus.

J. M. Hawes

1820. Eaton, Dorothy S. ANNUAL REPORT ON ACQUISITIONS: MANUSCRIPTS. *Q. J. of the Lib. of Congress 1965 22(4): 319-335.* Materials added during the year 1964 are noted and characterized briefly under the headings: personal papers (including families, Presidents of the United States, cabinet members, members of Congress, the Supreme Court, armed forces, writers, artists, scientists, other public figures); archives (of organizations - including the NAACP, Atlantic Union, the Democratic congressional caucus 1916-25, 1933-57 from the papers of the late Clarence Cannon); and reproductions (including information on current interlibrary copying and loan). H. J. Graham

1821. Ellison, Ralph. ON BECOMING A WRITER. *Commentary 1964 38(4): 57-60.* Recollections and comments on growing up as a Negro in Oklahoma in the years between World War I and the Great Depression with some observations on writing and a certain acerbity toward "friends of the Negro" and others.

E. W. Hathaway

1822. Farr, Finis. "JEFF, IT'S UP TO YOU." *Am. Heritage 1964 15(2): 64-77.* Jack Johnson was the first Negro to win the world heavyweight boxing crown. Many whites felt that this ex-drifter and criminal had to be stopped. Jim Jeffries had retired a couple of years before undefeated. He was now encouraged to return to the ring and teach Johnson a lesson and at the same time defend the honor of the white race. The author traces the history of the Johnson-Jeffries fight. He concludes that Johnson was needed to gain the Negro recognition in boxing which later made the appearance of Joe Louis and Cassius Clay possible.

C. R. Allen, Jr.

1823. Fishel, Leslie H., Jr. THE NEGRO IN THE NEW DEAL ERA. *Wisconsin Mag. of Hist. 1965 48(2): 111-126.* Franklin Delano Roosevelt and his New Deal agencies, the National Association for the Advancement of Colored People (NAACP), the Communists, the widespread publicity of the Scottsboro case, the national Urban League, the mass migration of the Negro to Northern cities as a result of the World War II industries, the war itself, the loosening hold of the Negro church, and the increased educational opportunities for Negroes are discussed as elements which made the 20 years between F.D.R.'s inauguration and the eve of the Supreme Court's desegregation decisions the most revolutionary two decades in the history of the American Negro up to that time. "The essay was taken from a chapter in the book, *The American Negro, a Documentary Story,* by Mr. Fishel and Benjamin Quarles." 11 illus., 31 notes.

H. A. Negaard

1824. Flynt, Wayne. FLORIDA LABOR AND POLITICAL "RADICALISM," 1919-1920. *Labor Hist. 1968 9(1): 73-90.* Surveys the wave of strikes and violence which swept Florida in 1919 and helped cause the identification of union activity with extremism. Strikes and violence among cigar workers, phosphate miners, firemen, and other laborers plus the rise of union activity was identified as radical. The unrest of 1919 laid the base for labor's strenuous political effort in Florida in 1920. Based on newspapers, articles, and archival material of the U.S. Shipping Board; 58 notes.

L. L. Athey

1825. Fogel, David. SOCIAL WORK AND NEGROES. *Phylon 1957 18(3): 277-285.* Reviews the history of social welfare work for Negroes, which began during World War I, as recorded in the *Proceedings* of the National Conference on Social Welfare.

C. F. Latour

1826. Foner, Philip S. THE IWW AND THE BLACK WORKER. *J. of Negro Hist. 1970 55(1): 45-64.* The "Wobblies" (Industrial Workers of the World) took a strong stand against racial discrimination, but did little to organize Negro workers during the first four years of its existence. Beginning in 1910, the IWW made a determined effort to recruit black members, but made little headway because most of its appeals failed to recognize that Negroes faced a race problem in America. Statements by the IWW that Negroes could cure their troubles through the abolishment of the wage system fell on deaf ears, and the only area where the Wobblies made any advances in black membership were among longshoremen and lumber workers. Based on primary and secondary sources; 53 notes.

R. S. Melamed

1827. Fullinwider, S. P. JEAN TOOMER: LOST GENERATION, OR NEGRO RENAISSANCE? *Phylon 1966 27(4): 396-403.* Biography of Jean Toomer, American Negro writer of the "lost generation." The grandson of P. B. S. Pinchback, Toomer developed an intense concern for the human condition from his childhood experiences. After revolting against his family and feeling his intellectual world collapse, Toomer developed the theme of alienation or "frigidization of the self." He urged fusion of intellect and emotion in a retreat from the outside world to isolation and subjectivity. For a time Toomer viewed the southern Negro folk spirit as an identity-giving absolute, and this theme pervades *Cane* which he published in 1923. Subsequently he rejected this theme and after a mystical religious experience in 1926 became a propagandist for a religious answer to the condition of alienation. Toomer continued to write, but his work became smug and dead, and he was no longer able to find a publisher. Based on the Toomer Papers in Fisk University Library and published sources; 22 notes.

S. C. Pearson, Jr.

1828. Fulmer, John L. STATE PER CAPITA INCOME DIFFERENTIALS: 1940 AND 1950. *Southern Econ. J. 1955 22(1): 32-47.* Using census data, the author tested four factors in a regression analysis with State per capita incomes, comparing regression coefficients for 1940 and 1951, both statistically and in a dynamic analysis of both years compositely. The conclusion was that all factors changed from 1940 to 1950, toward less agriculture, greater percentage of population employed relatively fewer Negroes, and a higher level of education. Differences between States increased with respect to the first and fourth factors, but considerably decreased with regard to the second and third. In general State per capita incomes increased.

A. W. Coats

1829. Gardner, Bettye and Thomas, Bettye. THE CULTURAL IMPACT OF THE HOWARD THEATRE ON THE BLACK COMMUNITY. *J. of Negro Hist. 1970 55(4): 253-265.* The Howard Theatre, in the heart of the black community of Washington, D.C., gave performances from 1910 through the 1960's. Few black Washingtonians of any class or age failed to attend or at least hear of the theater during that era. The chief attractions were vaudeville, musicals, stock company productions, and an occasional circus. When the theater was not in use the community used the building for variety programs, testimonials, concerts, and church meetings. In the late 1920's and early 1930's famous bands and amateur night contests were introduced with great success. By the 1950's the elite of the Negro community had moved away from the neighborhood and the better black performers began to find more profitable the more elegant, racially integrated establishments elsewhere in the area. Based mostly on primary sources and interviews; 31 notes.

R. S. Melamed

1830. González, José Luis. LOS PRIMEROS NOVELISTAS NEGROS NORTE AMERICANOS [The first Negro North American novelists]. *Casa de las Americas [Cuba] 1966 6(36/37): 98-114.* Sketches the late 19th- and early 20th-century literary careers of Paul Laurence Dunbar, Charles W. Chesnutt, and James Weldon Johnson, placing them in the context of their time and position within United States society. He uses W. E. B. DuBois' term "talented tenth" to describe these authors' black bourgeois backgrounds and to explain their efforts to maintain and improve their status within a race-conscious society. The themes and subject matter of their various works are interpreted in terms of the author's thesis. 27 notes.

C. J. Fleener

1831. Gordon, Rita Werner. THE CHANGE IN THE POLITICAL ALIGNMENT OF CHICAGO'S NEGROES DURING THE NEW DEAL. *J. of Am. Hist. 1969 56(3): 584-603.* The rapidly increasing Negro population of Chicago was traditionally Republican because of its hatred of the Democratic Party and because of the beneficence of a Republican machine which, under William Hale Thompson, obtained Negro support. This support slipped some during the administration of Herbert Hoover, who was widely believed to be "lily white" in his policies. Negroes also suffered disproportionately from the Depression. Nonetheless, they supported the Republicans in 1932 because Franklin D. Roosevelt was an unknown with a Texan as running mate, and because Anton Joseph Cermak had not impressed them while mayor. Support for the Democrats increased as New Deal programs, especially the Works Progress Administration, benefited Negroes, and because Mrs. Roosevelt and Harold Ickes proved sympathetic. Chicago Negro politicians found the Democratic Party a vehicle for advancement. The percentage of Negroes supporting Democrats increased in 1940 and 1944. Table, 116 notes.   K. B. West

1832. Grantham, Dewey W., Jr. THE SOUTH AND THE RECONSTRUCTION OF AMERICAN POLITICS. *J. of Am. Hist. 1966 53(2): 227-246.* The South has undergone a profound political transformation since 1929, a transformation resulting from the impact of New Deal and Fair Deal programs and the concomitant influence of Federal power; the nationalization and urbanization of the Democratic Party, depriving the "Solid South" of some of its political advantage; the industrialization and urbanization of the South itself; and the power of the Negro voter and Negro leadership buttressed by Federal power. This "revolution" manifests itself in the increased power of urban voting groups, the increased strength of a Republican Party based on conservative urban whites and rural white supremacists, the development of issue-oriented elections and of program-oriented southern governors, and perhaps in the growing impotence of the southern Democratic-Republican coalition in the U.S. Congress.   K. B. West

1833. Green, G. N. REPUBLICANS, BULL MOOSE, AND NEGROES IN FLORIDA, 1912. *Florida Hist. Q. 1964 43(2): 153-164.* Describes the incredibly confused process by which the pro-Roosevelt Negroes of Florida in 1912 were excluded from the list of Roosevelt delegates and were so antagonized that many of them turned against the Republican Party and cast their votes for Wilson. Based on newspapers, Republican Party records, private papers, and secondary material.   G. L. Lycan

1834. Greene, Lorenzo J. DR. WOODSON PREPARES FOR NEGRO HISTORY WEEK, 1930. *Negro Hist. Bull. 1965 28(8): 174-175, 195-197.* Excerpts from the diary of a Carter G. Woodson protege, who had done much of the field work for the study of the Negro church by the Association for the Study of Negro Life and History. By 1930 he was a dedicated employee of the association. The diary of the meetings in January 1930 to prepare for the first celebration of Negro History Week throws light upon the problems and the personalities involved. The highlight was to be the presence of four Negro congressmen, three of whom had served in the 1870's and 1880's while the fourth, Oscar De Priest of Chicago, was the first Negro to sit in Congress since 1901.   E. P. Stickney

1835. Hagedorn, Hermann. WORDS FOR TODAY - BY THEODORE ROOSEVELT. *New York Times Mag. 1957 27(October): 11, 78-79.* On the occasion of the 100th anniversary of Theodore Roosevelt's birth, presents a series of quotations of his views on such subjects as Americanism, national character, power, the Square Deal, labor unions, and the Negro.   R. J. Marion

1836. Holmes, Eugene C. ALAIN L. LOCKE AND THE ADULT EDUCA-TION MOVEMENT. *J. of Negro Educ. 1965 34(1): 5-10.* Locke's interest in adult education found early expression in several journal articles, and in 1924 he was a delegate to the first Conference on Adult Education called by the Carnegie Foundation. His interest in the movement continued, and in 1945-46 he served as president of the Adult Education Association of America. He edited a series of *Bronze Booklets* which were published by the Associates in Negro Folk Education and which significantly contributed to adult education for and about Negroes in America. Biblio.   S. C. Pearson, Jr.

1837. Jackson, Miles M., Jr., ed. LETTERS TO A FRIEND: CORRESPON-DENCE FROM JAMES WELDON JOHNSON TO GEORGE A. TOWNS. *Phylon 1968 29(2): 182-198.* Introduces 23 letters from James Weldon Johnson (1871-1938) to George A. Towns (d. 1960), written over the period 1896-1934. Among his many accomplishments, Johnson served as Executive Secretary of the National Association for the Advancement of Colored People from 1920 to 1938. Towns, a schoolmate of Johnson's, was for 27 years a professor of English at Atlanta University. The letters concern mostly personal matters and give a good insight into Johnson's life, personality, and ideas. 49 notes.   R. D. Cohen

1838. James, Felix. THE TUSKEGEE INSTITUTE MOVABLE SCHOOL, 1906-1923. *Agric. Hist. 1971 45(3): 201-209.* Discusses efforts by Tuskegee to teach improved agricultural techniques and homemaking skills to Negro farmers and their families through a movable school which took instructors and demon-strations to the farmers. The school led to improved farming practices, encour-aged the black farmer's attachment to his home, helped disseminate knowledge of home economics, and stimulated tenants to purchase land. To a certain extent, the movable school also led to an improvement in race relations. Based on newspapers and the files of the Tuskegee Institute Experiment Station; 48 notes.
D. E. Brewster

1839. James, Milton M. LESLIE PINCKNEY HILL. *Negro Hist. Bull. 1961 24(6): 135-138.* A short biographical sketch of Leslie Pinckney Hill, Negro educator and writer. Hill was born in Lynchburg, Virginia, and attended public school in East Orange, New Jersey. From high school he entered Harvard, where he earned his B.A. and M.A. degrees. He taught three years at Tuskegee Institute, served five years as principal of Manassas Industrial Institute, and in 1913 he became principal of Cheyney Training School of Teachers in Pennsylvania. Un-der his guidance Cheyney became a fully accredited teachers college. Leslie P. Hill also wrote poetry and prose. Three of his poems are included in the article.
L. Gara

1840. Janifer, Ellsworth. SAMUEL COLERIDGE-TAYLOR IN WASHING-
TON. *Phylon 1967 28(2): 185-196.* Taylor was born in London in 1875, the son
of a native African physician. He did not live to see his youthful promise develop
into genius. Much of what he wrote is immature, but some is superb and makes
a decisive contribution to English musical literature. Taylor became the first
Negro composer to win international recognition. He was especially significant
to the American Negro to whom he became a symbol of rare pride and cultural
fulfillment. His compositions were performed in various American cities before
he went to Washington, D.C., in 1904 to conduct a festival of his works. The
author details this and subsequent visits of Taylor to the United States. He
concludes that Taylor showed that no ethnic group had a monopoly upon musical
genius, and that his visits were a symbol of hope to aspiring Negro American
composers who were struggling to assert their individuality in the face of racial
prejudice. Based on published sources; 19 notes.   D. N. Brown

1841. Josey, E. J. EDWARD CHRISTIAN WILLIAMS: A LIBRARIAN'S
LIBRARIAN. *J. of Lib. Hist. 1969 4(2): 106-122.* A brief biographical study of
this important though little-known Negro librarian based on personal papers and
interviews with onetime associates. Educated at Western Reserve University,
Williams (1871-1929) worked first as a librarian there, attended the New York
State Library School, and then returned to Western Reserve, where he taught and
later served as university librarian. From 1909 to 1916 he served as principal of
a District of Columbia Negro high school and thereafter held the post of librarian
of Howard University until his death. Quotes Williams' writings to discuss the
problems he faced as a teacher and librarian and comments on his views on the
question of race. 33 notes.   V. S. Ekrut

1842. Maunder, Elwood R. GO SOUTH YOUNG MAN: AN INTERVIEW
WITH J. E. MC CAFFREY. *Forest Hist. 1965 8(4): 2-18.* J. E. McCaffrey
received his first education in forestry at the New York State Ranger School.
Almost all his forest work experience was in the southern United States, but
World War I service in wood procurement in France brought him in contact with
a tradition of forest management 100 to 300 years old. McCaffrey, who retired
from the International Paper Company in 1964, was first employed by them in
1928, when he worked briefly on the north shore of the Gulf of St. Lawrence in
Canada. Earlier, between 1919 and 1928, McCaffrey had various managerial jobs
in the southern woods in mechanized steam railroad logging and sawmilling.
Logging crews were mainly Negro, with a sprinkling of whites, especially in
managerial positions, although the dangerous job of recruiting labor from other
companies was usually done by an especially skilled Negro logger. Research and
development investments in the paper and pulp industry have been small. Since
the future may show paper products created from synthetics, however, research
and development have become more important. McCaffrey believes that much
more must be invested in forest-related scientific research and that foresters,
chemists, and biologists must work together in order to communicate and inspire
one another. 9 illus.   B. A. Vatter

1843. Mayer, A. and Klapprodt, Carol. FERTILITY DIFFERENTIAL IN DETROIT: 1920-1950. *Population Studies 1955 9(2): 148-158.* "Surveys the pattern of differential fertility in a highly industrialized city between 1920 and 1950. In general, fertility differentials between whites and non-whites are tending to converge. Economic differentials are decreasing also, but not as markedly. Yearly birthrates, even when nuptiality is considered, are not an effective measure of these increasingly small differentials in fertility." J

1844. Mcconnell, Roland C. A SMALL COLLEGE AND THE ARCHIVAL RECORD. *J. of Negro Educ. 1963 32(1): 84-86.* Discusses the uses of the Papers of Emmett J. Scott (1873-1957) which are preserved in Soper Library at Morgan State College. The papers provide a record of Scott's work as secretary to Booker T. Washington, secretary of Tuskegee Institute, Howard University, and the Southern Education Foundation, and his work in the War Department, Republican National Committee, Sun Shipbuilding Co., and Washington, D.C. Board of Indeterminate Sentence and Parole. A Preliminary Inventory of the Scott Papers prepared by McConnell is available from the College librarian.
S. C. Pearson, Jr.

1845. McKelvey, Blake. CITIES AS NURSERIES OF SELF-CONSCIOUS MINORITIES. *Pacific Hist. R. 1970 39(3): 367-381.* Shows the various means by which minority groups in the United States have asserted their own identity and have participated actively in the life of their chosen city. Summarizes the history of the Irish, German, Jewish, Spanish-American, Oriental, Polish, and Italian migrations' adjustment and their maintenance of independence. This process culminated in the black migration from the South and the resultant poverty programs, many of which sought "maximum feasible participation" to encourage expression of identity. 26 notes. E. C. Hyslop

1846. McLemore, Nannie Pitts. JAMES K. VARDAMAN, A MISSISSIPPI PROGRESSIVE. *J. of Mississippi Hist. 1967 29(1): 1-11.* Describes Vardaman's support of reforms and the achievement of some reforms in Mississippi, partly through his efforts as governor from 1904 to 1908. Vardaman advocated prohibition, direct primaries, election of judges, higher pay for judges, and the establishment of industrial schools for Negroes and juvenile delinquents. While he was governor, Mississippi constructed new school buildings, increased teacher salaries, and prohibited the use of convict labor on any lands except those owned by the State. A new governing board for the penitentiary was established, as well as agricultural experiment stations, a Department of Agriculture and Immigration, and a State Livestock Sanitary Board. The most singificant reform was in penal administration. As U.S. Senator, 1913-19, Vardaman consistently supported the Wilson administration until he opposed a diplomatic policy which he felt would lead the United States into World War I. Based on State publications and secondary sources; 23 notes. J. W. Hillje

1847. Meier, August and Rudwick, Elliot. HOW CORE BEGAN. *Social Sci. Q. 1969 49(4): 789-799.* The Congress of Racial Equality (CORE) emerged from Fellowship for Reconciliation(FOR) in 1942 and 1943 through the activities of six members of its Chicago chapter who were particularly concerned with race relations. These six, including James Farmer, and the 50 charter members of the Chicago Committee on Racial Equality, the next formal step, were united in their Christian-Gandhian pacifism. The whites, however, tended to be concerned as much for proving the methods while the Negroes thought increasingly in terms of the results. Their early efforts included a roller rink, a private housing unit near the University of Chicago, and several downtown restaurants. Strikingly, in retrospect, they seemed as concerned for the conversion of the individual as for the removal of the barrier. Based on interviews, manuscripts, and secondary materials; 32 notes.   M. Hough

1848. Meyer, Howard N. HOW J.F.K.'S GRANDFATHER FOUGHT THE GRANDFATHER CLAUSE. *Negro Hist. Bull. 1963 27(2): 27.* Briefly relates how in 1901 Congressman John F. Fitzgerald, President Kennedy's maternal grandfather, supported an amendment to a reapportionment bill which attempted to limit the representation of any state denying Negroes to the vote. Although the amendment was based on a clause of the 14th Amendment, only three Congressmen supported it. It was not until 1917 that its target, southern grandfather clauses, was eliminated by a Supreme Court decision.   L. Gara

1849. Miller, Ratner A. COMPONENTS OF LABOR FORCE GROWTH. *J. of Econ. Hist. 1962 22(1): 47-58.* Suggests that contrary to popular opinion the migration of southern Negroes into northern industrial centers between 1920 and 1950 did not serve as the primary source of labor, which in the period 1890-1920 was supplied by foreign immigration; rather it was the increasing use of female labor that took up the slack created by immigration restriction. The "paper is based on data assembled from Censuses of Population by the University of Pennsylvania's Population Studies Center."   E. Feldman

1850. Miller, Sally M. THE SOCIALIST PARTY AND THE NEGRO, 1901-1920. *J. of Negro Hist. 1971 56(3): 220-229.* The Socialist Party was founded in 1901 and obtained the greatest number of votes of any party on the left in a presidential election when Eugene Debs ran for that office in 1912. The Socialists took little note of the Negro until the United States entered World War I, and then they viewed him primarily as an oppressed member of the working class rather than as a man subject to the effects of great racial prejudice. Few Negroes joined the party, primarily because the black community in America at the turn of the 20th century was more interested in obtaining its fair share from the system rather than in abolishing capitalism. As a result, the Socialists were as invisible to the Negro as the Negro was invisible to their party. 25 notes.
R. S. Melamed

1851. Mitchell, Bonnie. WISCONSIN NAACP MARCHES 50 YEARS. *Wisconsin Then and Now 1968 15(4): 1-3.* Surveys the Wisconsin National Association for the Advancement of Colored People since its inception in Beloit in 1919. In 1953 the three chapters at Beloit, Milwaukee, and Madison formed the State Conference of the NAACP to push for major reforms in education, housing, and

jobs. In 1966 a State fair housing law was passed and new approaches were implemented by the State Employment Service as a result of their efforts. Illus.
                                                                    D. P. Peltier

1852. Neyland, Leedell W. THE EDUCATIONAL LEADERSHIP OF J. R. E. LEE. *Negro Hist. Bull. 1962 25(4): 75-78.* Briefly sketches the career of John Robert Edward Lee (1864-1944), whose 20-year service as president of Florida A. and M. College for Negroes resulted in accreditation, a better faculty, increased enrollment, and an improved physical plant.   L. Gara

1853. Olson, James S. ORGANIZED BLACK LEADERSHIP AND INDUSTRIALISM: THE RACIAL RESPONSE, 1936-1945. *Labor Hist. 1969 10(3): 475-486.* Organized black leadership was at first skeptical about the Committee on Industrial Organization and industrialism. Blacks had migrated to northern cities during World War I and had been alienated by the American Federation of Labor's "opposition to industrial unionism." The C.I.O. was the "long-sought-after viable alternative to industrial paternalism." Between 1936 and 1945 the achievements of the C.I.O. in organizing black and white workers without discrimination largely persuaded the black leadership to accept the organization and to identify with the theme of racial and labor solidarity. Based on black newspapers and periodicals; 50 notes.   L. L. Athey

1854. Osborn, George C. WOODROW WILSON APPOINTS ROBERT H. TERRELL JUDGE OF MUNICIPAL COURT, DISTRICT OF COLUMBIA. *Negro Hist. Bull. 1959 22(5): 111-115.* Discusses Woodrow Wilson's reappointment of Robert H. Terrell as a judge of the Municipal Court of the District of Columbia. Terrell, a Republican and a Negro, received support from lawyers and businessmen who petitioned Wilson to reappoint him. Despite opposition from James Kimble Vardaman and Hoke Smith enough Democrats joined the Republican minority in the Senate to confirm Wilson's reappointment of Terrell.
                                                                    L. Gara

1855. Osofsky, Gilbert. A DECADE OF URBAN TRAGEDY: HOW HARLEM BECAME A SLUM. *New York Hist. 1965 46(4): 330-355.* During the 1920's, the Negro population of Harlem in New York City vastly increased. At the same time, most whites migrated from Harlem into other boroughs. Many West Indian Negroes were among those moving into Harlem, and they quickly antagonized the native American colored population. High rents and low salaries led to congested and unsanitary conditions. Some of the migrants lacked elementary training in the most simple processes of good health and sanitation. With a death rate of 42 percent greater than the remainder of New York City, Harlem became a center for quack healers. A large number of "storefront" churches were established, but most of the ministers were probably charlatans of some kind. Harlem was one of the leading prostitution centers of Manhattan throughout the 1920's.   B. T. Quinten

1856. Osofsky, Gilbert. PROGRESSIVISM AND THE NEGRO: NEW YORK, 1900-1915. *Am. Q. 1964 16(2, part 1): 153-168.* Negro migration to northern cities from the 1890's to World War I did more than arouse racial antagonism; it also motivated nonpolitical progressives such as Victoria Earle Matthews, Francis A. Kellor, and Mary White Ovington to spearhead labor and housing reforms. Ovington and labor reformer William Lewis Buckley also helped to found the NAACP, and in 1906 Buckley and others created the Committee for Improving the Industrial Condition of the Negro in New York. This organization later merged with others to form the National Urban League.

R. S. Pickett

1857. Osofsky, Gilbert. SYMBOLS OF THE JAZZ AGE: THE NEW NEGRO AND HARLEM DISCOVERED. *Am. Q. 1965 17(2, Part 1): 229-238.* Harlem emerged into the limelight of the 1920's as the embodiment of hedonism and liberal culture. As the supposed home of the "New Negro," Harlem received the attention of white thrill-seekers and literati alike. Enthusiasm waned, however, with the advent of the Great Depression. Harlem as artistic capital and "erotic utopia" vanished as the Harlem "already known to stolid census-takers, city health officers and social workers" came into the unrelieving and unflattering light of the 1930's. Documented, 43 notes.

R. S. Pickett

1858. Paetel, Karl O. NAACP: DIE SELBSTWEHR DER AMERIKANI-SCHEN NEGER [NAACP: the self-defense of the American Negroes] *Deutsche Rundschau [West Germany] 1961 87(6): 505-511.* Deals with the roots of the National Association for the Advancement of Colored People, founded in the early 20th century.

G. Schoebe

1859. Paisley, Clifton L. VAN BRUNT'S STORE, IAMONIA, FLORIDA, 1902-1911. *Florida Hist. Q. 1970 48(4): 353-367.* In 1902, Richard F. Van Brunt (d. 1914) opened his country store in Iamonia, Florida, a crossroads rural community 18 miles north of Tallahassee and one mile south of the Georgia State line. Most of Van Brunt's customers were black, since the Negro population considerably outnumbered the white. Customers came to socialize, make business deals, and collect their mail in Van Brunt's post office, as well as trade with the storekeeper. Recorded purchases of farm equipment reveal that farm technology had advanced very little since the 1880's. One-horse plowing was still apparently common. Most purchased items included corn, salt pork, sugar, lard, coffee, syrup, rice, flour, cloth, shoes, guns, shells, and medicines. Northerners attracted to the area by hunting and fishing opportunities and the winter climate had begun buying land and became Van Brunt customers too. Most business was on credit, with cotton most often used to settle accounts. The necessity of hauling the cotton to Georgia to market it caused Van Brunt to eventually decide to close his Iamonia store and open a business at Miccosukee on the Florida Central Railroad in January 1912. By this time, cotton production was declining in importance and was being supplanted by quail raising. Based on unpublished account books at Florida State University; 3 illus., map.

R. V. Calvert

1860. Palmer, Dewey H. MOVING NORTH: MIGRATION OF NEGROES DURING WORLD WAR I. *Phylon 1967 28(1): 52-62.* Preceding World War I and continuing throughout World War II an exodus of Negroes from rural to urban areas and from South to North and West occurred. The exodus, at first welcomed by southern whites, began when the Negro learned of greater economic opportunities in northern industries. While increased economic opportunity was the primary inducement to migrants, social and political freedom were also attractions. The continuing migration during the war years caused concern on the part of southern whites on the loss of their labor force. States began to legislate against labor recruiters and efforts were made to convince the Negro that he would be better treated in the South. Migration continued during and after the war and was an important factor in bringing the question of civil rights into national politics. The national political activity of Negroes grew and the lack of civil rights was made an important issue in America. Based on published sources; 82 notes.   D. N. Brown

1861. Peavy, Charles D. FAULKNER'S USE OF FOLKLORE IN "THE SOUND AND THE FURY." *J. of Am. Folklore 1966 79(313): 437-447.* Points out a number of southern regional and Negro folk beliefs used by William Faulkner in *The Sound and the Fury* (1929). Among these are the jimson-weed as a sex symbol, the narcissus as the plant of nemesis, the cornflower as the symbol of innocence, the screech owl as a symbol of death; the jaybird's connection with the devil, the superstition against naming a child for a dead person, and the "Christmas gift" game. 30 notes.   E. P. Stickney

1862. Polreichová, Helena. TŘÍDNÍ SLOŽENÍ ČERNOŠSKÉHO OBYVA-TELSTVA VE SPOJENÝCH STÁTECH AMERICKÝCH 1910-1960 [Class structure of the Negro population in the United States of America, 1910-60]. *Československý Časopis Historický [Czechoslovakia] 1964 12(1): 84-110.* Investigates the social stratification, agricultural as well as industrial proletariat, unemployment, and many related questions of the Negroes, frequently with official statistical publications. The Negro bourgeoisie has gradually lost its significance, as has the agrarian proletariat generally. But the Negro industrial proletariat, though the most important part of the Negro population, cannot lead the Negro movement because of the oppressive racial discriminatory policy of the white Americans. Present-day Negro leadership is composed of the intelligentsia, religious leaders, and militant students. Based on American monographic and periodical literature.   F. Wagner

1863. Presley, James. THE AMERICAN DREAM OF LANGSTON HUGHES. *Southwest R. 1963 48(4): 380-386.* Analysis of the "American Dream" expressed by Langston Hughes (1902-67) - part Indian, Negro, and Caucasian - in his poetry and prose. For Hughes the "Dream" does exist. "And the Dream *must* be fulfilled."   D. F. Henderson

1864. Puth, Robert C. SUPREME LIFE: THE HISTORY OF A NEGRO LIFE INSURANCE COMPANY, 1919-1962. *Business Hist. R. 1969 43(1): 1-20.* The story of the Supreme Life Insurance Company, now the third largest black insurance firm in the United States, is traced from the company's establishment by Frank L. Gillespie in Chicago in 1919 as Liberty Life Insurance, through its reorganization under its present name in 1929, to the 1960's. The author concludes that the company owes its existence to the original refusal of white insurance firms to sell to Negroes. With improving Negro mortality rates and rising incomes, however, white competition has appeared since World War II. As a result, the company's future and that of other black insurance companies is not bright as long as they remain restricted to the Negro market. The author sees an irony in the fact that a Negro life insurance firm faces a struggle ahead because of improvements in the economic and social positions of Negroes as a whole. Based on company records and personal interviews; illus., 100 notes.

C. J. Pusateri

1865. Record, Wilson C. INTELLECTUALS IN SOCIAL AND RACIAL MOVEMENTS. *Phylon 1954 15(3): 231-242.* Analyzes crucial differences between white and Negro intellectuals and their involvement in social and civic reform movements during the 1930's. The author contends that differences between Negroes and whites in their participation in reform movements are chiefly rooted in and determined by society's attitude toward race characteristics.

R. Mueller

1866. Record, Wilson C. NEGRO INTELLECTUAL LEADERSHIP IN THE NATIONAL ASSOCIATION FOR THE ADVANCEMENT OF COLORED PEOPLE: 1910-1940. *Phylon 1956 17(4): 375-389.* The rising Negro leadership of the NAACP since its inception has 1) gained for it the support of the rank and file Negro elements in all parts of the United States; 2) enabled this movement to work in close liaison with other reform movements such as feminism; and 3) won over enlightened white civic leaders in the South. Lists NAACP leaders. Based on original documentation.

R. Mueller

1867. Rehkopf, Charles F. THE EPISCOPATE OF BISHOP JOHNSON. *Missouri Hist. Soc. Bull. 1963 19(3): 231-246.* Bishop Johnson was Episcopal Bishop Coadjutor of Missouri from 1911 to 1923 and diocesan from 1923 until his retirement in 1933. A brief introduction on his early life and ministry on the frontier is followed by an account of his relationship with the diocesan, Bishop Tuttle, and of the former's efforts to deal with and improve the organization and administration of the diocese. Particularly interested in the expansion of mission and educational activities, Bishop Johnson eschewed theological and doctrinal disputes. Brief mention is made of the problem of administering Negro congregations and of the tentative effort to create a racial episcopate. Also included is a bibliography and lists of parishes and missions in the Diocese of Missouri.

R. J. Hanks

1868. Robbins, Gerald. ROSSA B. COOLEY AND PENN SCHOOL: SOCIAL DYNAMO IN A NEGRO RURAL SUBCULTURE, 1901-1930. *J. of Negro Educ. 1964 33(1): 43-51.* The author traces the impact of Miss Cooley's educational philosophy on Penn School, an institution founded on St. Helena Island,

South Carolina, in 1862. Miss Cooley came to Penn School from Hampton Institute with an interest in "education for life" and in improving social conditions in the community. Based on published materials.   S. C. Pearson, Jr.

1869. Romero, Patricia. THE EARLY ORGANIZATION OF THE RED-CAPS. *Negro Hist. Bull. 1966 29(5): 101-102, 114.* The first recorded reference to a Redcap was on Labor Day in 1890 when James Williams, a porter in New York's Grand Central Station, tied a piece of red flannel around his black cap to be more easily identified. Before long, other porters adopted this mode of identification. The first efforts to launch a national organization of Redcaps began in the Northwestern Station in Chicago in 1937 under the leadership of Willard Saxby Townsend, who had been born and raised in Cincinnati, Ohio. The first convention of Redcaps was held at the Harrison Hotel in Chicago on 1 June 1937, with over 100 delegates representing 1,100 Redcaps in terminals and stations in every part of the United States. "The year 1937 brought significant gains in organization to the Redcaps although no relations had been established between the railroads. Even dissention between the two races did not hamper overall efforts to enlist Redcaps to support the new international brotherhood." 12 notes.
D. D. Cameron

1870. Roy, Jessie H. COLORED JUDGES: JUDGE ROBERT H. TERRELL. *Negro Hist. Bull. 1965 28(7): 158, 162.* Robert H. Terrel graduated from Harvard Law School in 1884, the third Negro to graduate from Harvard and the first to do so *cum laude.* After teaching in Washington he began a law practice in partnership with John R. Lynch, former Negro congressman from Mississippi. He served as judge of the Municipal Court of Washington, D.C. under Presidents Theodore Roosevelt, William H. Taft, Woodrow Wilson, and Warren G. Harding. His most famous case was the "Ball Rent Act." Twice reversed by the Court of Appeals, his decision was upheld by the Supreme Court. Illus.
E. P. Stickney

1871. Rudwick, Elliott M. EAST ST. LOUIS AND THE "COLONIZATION CONSPIRACY" OF 1916. *J. of Negro Educ. 1964 33(1): 35-42.* The East St. Louis race riot of 1917 is traced to Democratic Party charges of a "colonization conspiracy" to bring Negroes from the South to East St. Louis and other sections of Illinois in order to bolster Republican power in the 1916 election. Similar charges of conspiracy were made in Indiana and Ohio, though none of the charges was substantiated. The anti-Negro propaganda of the election campaign soon found economic expression and erupted in violence in July 1917. The article is based on contemporary newspaper accounts.   S. C. Pearson, Jr.

1872. Rudwick, Elliott M. THE NIAGARA MOVEMENT. *J. of Negro Hist. 1957 42(3): 177-200.* Traces the history of the Niagara Movement (1905-10), a precursor of the National Association for the Advancement of Colored People. The author describes the roles of William E. B. Du Bois in leading the movement and of Booker T. Washington in opposing it. "The Niagara men (and their friends in other equal rights organizations) did promulgate a set of blueprints which were to be guides...after the N.A.A.C.P. appeared on the scene."   W. E. Wight

1873. Russell, Francis. THE FOUR MYSTERIES OF WARREN HARDING. *Am. Heritage 1963 14(3): 4-9, 81-86.* Deals with these allegations about President Warren Harding: 1) that he had Negro blood, 2) that he was father of an illigitimate daughter, 3) that he met death by murder or suicide rather than a heart attack, and 4) that his widow behaved curiously in the destruction of the President's correspondence.   C. R. Allen, Jr.

1874. Scheiner, Seth M. THE NEW YORK CITY NEGRO AND THE TENE-MENT, 1880-1910. *New York Hist. 1964 45(4): 304-315.* Traces the changing patterns of Negro residence in Manhattan before World War I. Based on contemporary periodicals.   A. B. Rollins

1875. Scrimsher, Lila Gravatt, ed. THE DIARIES AND WRITINGS OF GEORGE A. MATSON, BLACK CITIZEN OF LINCOLN, NEBRASKA, 1901-1913. *Nebraska Hist. 1971 52(2): 133-168.* Excerpts from the diary and autobiography of George A. Matson (1849-1913) covering the period 1869-85 and delineating his successful efforts to obtain an education and his subsequent career as barber, schoolteacher, and clergyman, chiefly in Ohio and Missouri.
                                                                                R. Lowitt

1876. Semonche, John E. THE "AMERICAN MAGAZINE" OF 1906-15: PRINCIPLE VS. PROFIT. *Journalism Q. 1963 40(1): 36-44.* The *American Magazine* was founded by John S. Phillips, Ida M. Tarbell, Ray Stannard Baker, Lincoln Steffens, William Allen White, Finley Peter Dunne, John M. Siddall, and others of the muckraker tradition after a break with *McClure's Magazine* in 1906. It had financial help from William Kent, millionaire reformer from California, and had an outstanding series on the Negro and a controversial one on the Mexico of Porfirio Diaz, and took part in the opposition to President William Howard Taft. Financial difficulties, particularly lack of capital, plagued the group, which finally sold out to the Crowell Company, which began to moderate the muckraking slightly, so that most of the original group resigned in 1915 and the Crowell management created a different kind of magazine under Siddall.
                                                                                S. E. Humphreys

1877. Singh, Baljit. THE SURVIVAL OF THE WEAKEST: A CASE HIS-TORY OF THE LIBERIAN CRISIS OF THE 1930'S. *J. of Human Relations 1966 14(2): 242-260.* In 1930 an international commission of inquiry (Johnson-Christy Commission), which had been appointed by the League of Nations to investigate conditions in Liberia, issued a shocking report confirming "the existence of slavery, forced labor, exploitation of native tribes, and financial corruption." Protracted negotiations were conducted between Liberia and the League between 1930 and 1934. The United States was particularly interested in the labor and financial disputes because of the Liberian investments of the Firestone Rubber Company. It was not until after Franklin D. Roosevelt "decided that American aid to Liberia would please all political factions among the Negro citizenry" that Liberia's time of troubles came to an end. Based on League of Nations documents, newspapers, and other primary sources.   D. J. Abramoske

1878. Smith, T. Lynn. THE REDISTRIBUTION OF THE NEGRO POPULA-
TION OF THE UNITED STATES, 1910-1960. *J. of Negro Hist. 1966 51(3):*
155-173. Prior to 1910 the vast majority of Negroes lived in the South, mostly
in the rural sections. After World War I, Negroes flocked from the South to a
few of the larger industrial cities of the North. This northward migration slowed
down in the depression years of the early 1930's, only to resume again on a larger
scale in 1938. Less spectacular were the movements of colored people from the
rural South to southern towns and cities, which resulted in nearly a third of all
American Negroes living in urban areas of the South by 1960, and to west coast
cities during and after World War II. The exodus of Negroes from the rural South
continued and accelerated after 1950, resulting in a change in the distribution of
Negroes in southern rural areas, with the largest percentage in Mississippi and
North Carolina by 1960. Based on census reports; 2 maps, 4 tables.
L. Gara

1879. Stearns, Marshall and Stearns, Jean. AMERICAN VERNACULAR
DANCE: THE WHITMAN SISTERS. *Southwest R. 1966 51(4): 350-358.* The
Whitman sisters - Mabel, Essie, Alberta, and Alice - trouped the country from
1903 to 1943. Consisting of from 20 to 30 performers, their troupe was the highest
paid act on the Theater Owners Booking Association circuit, and perhaps the
greatest incubator of dancing talent for Negro shows in the country.
D. F. Henderson

1880. Stearns, Marshall and Stearns, Jean. FRONTIERS OF HUMOR:
AMERICAN VERNACULAR DANCE. *Southern Folklore Q. 1966 30(3): 227-*
235. Discusses the content and underlying meaning of humor and songs offered
by Negro duets - man and woman - in vaudeville and nightclub performances
during the first half of the 20th century. Since the performers were generally
Negro men and women performing for their own people, the subtlety and candor
were great; some of the best-known teams are described and sections of their
songs reproduced.
H. Aptheker

1881. Steelman, Joseph F. JONATHAN ELWOOD COX AND NORTH
CAROLINA'S GUBERNATORIAL CAMPAIGN OF 1908. *North Carolina*
Hist. R. 1964 41(4): 436-447. Predictions that Negro disfranchisement would
permit meaningful two-party division of whites along economic and ideological
lines were too optimistic. The Republican Party did not gain in white voters what
it lost in Negro voters and remained rent with personal factions obsessed with
patronage. National party pressure in 1908 dictated a ticket of businessmen
headed by Jonathan Elwood Cox, furniture manufacturer. Refusal of local professional politicians to support Cox, and his own political ineptitude, limited Republican gains in this year when a State reform Democratic administration had made
enemies. Cox' Papers are the most important of several manuscript sources.
L. R. Harlan

1882. Stevens, David H. LIFE AND WORK OF TREVOR ARNETT. *Phylon*
1955 16(2): 127-140. A biographical account on Trevor Arnett (1870-1955),
which includes a description of his achievements as secretary and, later, president

of the General Education Board of the Rockefeller Foundation, in furthering the work of Negro colleges in the South and of denominational colleges.

S

1883. Taeuber, Irene B. DEMOGRAPHIC TRANSITIONS AND POPULA-TION PROBLEMS IN THE UNITED STATES. *Ann. of the Am. Acad. of Pol. and Social Sci. 1967 369: 131-140.* "The development, growth, and transformation of the population of the United States were unique in the late settlement; the vast, rich, and sparsely settled area; and the immigrant formation. There were demographic transitions rather than a unidirectional process. Birth rates were very high in the colonial and early national periods, declined in rural areas and cities alike to the 1930's, and then rose substantially, only to decline again for roughly a decade now. The occupational movements from agricultural to professional and related activities, the advances of education to high levels, and the changes from rural to urban and then to metropolitan residence underlay the demographic transitions. A generation ago the problems appeared those of decline; a decade ago the problems seemed to be those of a rapid growth that would eventually press on resources, economy, and social facilities. Today assessments of the future are conjectural. The major population problems are those of metropolitan agglomeration, particularly the differentiations of central cities and outer areas; the swift movements of the disadvantaged Negro population into central cities; the massive irregularities in age changes introduced by the changing birth rates of past years; and the adjustments to exodus from the Deep South and the mid-continent and influx to Florida, the Southwest and California. The most intricate problem is the reconciliation of the ideals of family size prevalent in the generally affluent population with the economic, social, and political developments that are muted and eventually jeopardized by continuing increases in numbers." J

1884. Thomson, Keith W. and Durham, Frank. THE IMPACT OF "PORGY AND BESS" IN NEW ZEALAND. *Mississippi Q. 1967 20(4): 207-216.* With only three of its roles sung and acted by imported American Negro artists, the George Gershwin-DuBose Heyward-Ira Gershwin opera, *Porgy and Bess* (1935), played triumphantly for four months in New Zealand. The predominantly Maori cast, including New Zealand's most famous singer Inia Te Wiata as Porgy, took the production to Australia under sponsorship of the Australian Elizabethan Theatre Trust, and the opera was selected as the major production of the 1966 Adelaide Festival of the Arts. While objections have been voiced for very different reasons to the novel, *Porgy* (1925), later made into a play, and the opera, *Porgy and Bess,* and no production of either the play or the opera has been staged in Heyward's native city of Charleston, Heyward's primary aim was not one of social protest but rather of creating a work of art. Most New Zealanders (as well as most Americans and other nationalities) have accepted the work on Heyward's terms. The favorable reception of the Maori production of the opera has resulted in considerable discussion in New Zealand of maintaining a Maori acting and opera company, for which native works could be written. R. V. Calvert

1885. Tinsley, James A. ROOSEVELT, FORAKER AND THE BROWNS-VILLE AFFRAY. *J. of Negro Hist. 1956 41(1): 43-65.* Theodore Roosevelt ordered the dishonorable discharge of a brigade of U.S. Negro soldiers suspected of terrorizing for 10 minutes a section of Brownsville, Texas, on 13 August 1906. Senator Joseph Benson Foraker of Ohio led the fight to reverse this order. The author believes that Roosevelt was motivated by "perhaps a sort of unconscious compensating impulse for the earlier Booker T. Washington dinner" and his impatience at the law's slowness.   W. E. Wight

1886. Toppin, Edgar A. THE NEGRO IN AMERICA: 1901 TO 1956. *Current Hist. 1969 57(339): 269-274, 307.* From 1890 to 1910 the status of black Americans declined drastically under the assault of disfranchisement, segregation, and lynching. Thereafter, the black man began a long upward struggle for equality. Basic factors in the climb were a shift of the black population northward from the rural South and a resumption of the quest for equal rights.
                                                                        B. D. Rhodes

1887. Tucker, David M. BLACK PRIDE AND NEGRO BUSINESS IN THE 1920'S: GEORGE WASHINGTON LEE OF MEMPHIS. *Business Hist. R. 1969 43(4): 435-451.* Argues that black businessmen often have been unjustly maligned by liberal intellectuals for having ruthlessly exploited their race for the benefit of a pitifully small Negro middle class. Since the black masses were, and would continue to be, laborers, it was said that social reform and not black capitalism should have been the goal. This leftist position, however, creates a certain distortion by dismissing the black businessmen without ever really considering that, as racial leaders, they might have been worth what they cost their race in higher prices. In the urban South, black capitalists appear to have provided the most aggressive local leadership, and this was the case in Memphis where the positive role of black business was exemplified by George Washington Lee, an articulate and shrewd insurance executive. If businessmen are not generally thought of as intellectuals today, the Negro businessman of the 1920's was often an exception. Negroes who went into business generally did so precisely because few other white collar positions gave them as much, if any, freedom for independent thought and action. As a writer and orator, George Lee articulated the need for developing black business and black pride as a detour to full equality; racial chauvinism would emancipate the Negro from the sense of inferiority bequeathed to him. Based mainly on published sources; 38 notes.   C. J. Pusateri

1888. Tuttle, William M., Jr. CONTESTED NEIGHBORHOODS AND RACIAL VIOLENCE: PRELUDE TO THE CHICAGO RIOT OF 1919. *J. of Negro Hist. 1970 55(4): 266-288.* Covers the problems of an expanding black community in Chicago prior to the race riot of 1919. Several serious incidents occurred for two years before the outbreak of mass violence. An extreme shortage of housing for Negro migrants and returning Negro servicemen caused the incidents. Some leaders thought that the problem might be relieved by a large-scale summer construction program, but this failed to materialize when Chicago's contractors locked out the city's building tradesmen. Seven explosions and six hot weeks preceded the riot. Many Negroes repeatedly advocated arming themselves that summer. 41 notes.   R. S. Melamed

1889. Unsigned. PROFILE OF THE NAACP. *Negro Hist. Bull. 1964 27(4):* *74-76.*

1890. Watson, Richard L., Jr. THE DEFEAT OF JUDGE PARKER: A STUDY IN PRESSURE GROUPS AND POLITICS. *Mississippi Valley Hist. R. 1963 50(2): 213-234.* In 1930 Hoover nominated Judge John J. Parker of North Carolina to succeed Edward T. Sanford on the U.S. Supreme Court. Parker's rejection by the Senate is historically significant. As Parker had upheld the use of the injunction, his rejection symbolized labor's resurgence. In his campaign for governor in 1920 Parker had declared the Negro unready for politics, with the result that the National Association for the Advancement of Colored People used its pressure to defeat the confirmation of his nomination, thus achieving one of its first important victories. Parker's defeat reflected a growing opposition to the predominant philosophy of the Supreme Court, raised questions about the role of pressure groups, and demonstrated how an apparently routine appointment can become a personal campaign for office. 83 notes.
E. P. Stickney

1891. Welden, Daniel, ed. THE PROBLEM OF COLOR IN THE TWEN-TIETH CENTURY: A MEMORIAL TO W. E. B. DU BOIS. *J. of Human Relations 1966 14(1): 2-179.*
Anonymous. RACISM: THAT OTHER FACE OF NATIONALISM, pp.2-16.
Roucek, Joseph. THE CHANGING RELATIONSHIP OF THE AMERI-CAN NEGRO TO AFRICAN HISTORY AND POLITICS, pp. 17-27. Dis-cusses Western concepts of African culture and history and the changing atti-tudes of the American Negro toward Africa. The development of African nationalism, the growth of a scientific body of knowledge of Africa's culture and history, and the increased importance of international relations for the United States are among the factors stressed to explain the new, more posi-tive attitudes among American Negroes. 5 notes.
Walden, Daniel and Wylie, Kenneth. W. E. B. DU BOIS: PAN-AFRICANISM'S INTELLECTUAL FATHER, pp. 28-41. Examines the role played by the Negro Socialist, W. E. B. Du Bois, in the Pan-African Movement and assesses his impact on the eventual growth of African nationalism. Believing that the vanguard of any movement to free Africa from colonialism must begin in the New World, Du Bois was especially active in the early days of Pan-Africanism. He was the spirit behind the first important Pan-African Conference in 1919; he influenced the course of the 1921 conference; and he provided the intellectual justification for the Pan-African program as it later developed. Un-documented.
Du Bois, William Edward Burghardt. PROSPECT OF A WORLD WITHOUT RACE CONFLICT, pp. 42-54. Writing in 1944, the author surveyed and commented on the universal practice of white exploitation of the colored races. To deal with the challenge of racial injustice the author insisted that we

must "have wide dissemination of truth" because "careless ignorance of the facts of race is precisely the refuge where antisocial economic reaction flourishes." In addition, "we need organized effort to release the colored laborer from the domination of the investor." Permanent international peace will not be achieved unless exploiting investors are driven from their hideout behind race discrimination.

Thompson, Daniel C. THE RISE OF THE NEGRO PROTEST, pp. 56-73. "Examines the Negro protest movement in terms of its essential nature, techniques, and consequences." From colonial times to the present Negro aspirations for human fulfillment - the desire for new experience, security, recognition, and response - have been frustrated by the wide variety of repressive measures adopted by the white community. Negroes have protested through indirect verbal protest, direct verbal protest, and direct action. This protest movement has not taken the form of radicalism. Negroes accept traditional American ideals and values. The movement has fostered racial unity and pride, created an increasingly favorable public opinion, and resulted in solid political action. 8 notes.

Watson, Bruce. THE BACKLASH OF WHITE SUPREMACY: CASTE STATUS AND THE NEGRO REVOLT, pp. 88-99. Reviews the changing pattern of European and American racism from ancient times to the present. "We created the American Negro to do our dirty work for us, and we have used him as a status marker ever since we freed him; and now that status has become the dominant value in our society, our need for him has become extremely acute." 12 notes.

Hale, Frank W. FREDERICK DOUGLASS: ANTISLAVERY CRUSADER AND LECTURER, pp. 100-111. A biographical sketch of Frederick Douglass, 1817-95. Douglass' experience as a slave in Maryland and his career as a northern abolitionist are described. 7 notes.

Bontemps, Arna. A TRIBUTE TO DU BOIS, pp. 112-114. Focuses on Du Bois' life as a student at Fisk University in the 1880's.

Walden, Daniel. W. E. B. DU BOIS'S ESSENTIAL YEARS: THE LINK FROM DOUGLASS TO THE PRESENT, pp. 115-127. Relates the thought and career of Du Bois to the current Negro protest movement and compares his work to that of Frederick Douglass and Booker T. Washington.

Hughes, Langston. A PRAYER, pp. 128-130. Comments on a prayer written by Du Bois in 1906 at the time of the Atlanta race riots and notes its relevance to the violent attacks on civil rights workers and Negroes in the 1960's.

Miller, Henry. "W. E. B. DU BOIS," FROM PLEXUS, pp. 131-136. Records the author's impressions of Du Bois.

Du Bois, William Edward Burghardt. CREDO, pp. 137-138. Writing in 1904, Du Bois affirmed his belief in man, liberty, God, and the Devil.

Du Bois, William Edward Burghardt. BEHOLD THE LAND, pp. 139-145. In an address delivered in 1946 to the Southern Youth Legislature, the author advised southern youth to remain in the South and accept the challenge of southern racism.

Wilkins, Roy. A TRIBUTE, pp. 147-148. Extols Du Bois as the father of the current Negro protest movement.

Apctheker, Herbert. DU BOIS: THE FINAL YEARS, pp. 149-155. An evaluation of Du Bois emphasizing the community and growth of his career from the time of his educational work in Atlanta until his final years as a Communist scholar in Ghana.

Golden, L. Hanga and Melikian, O. WILLIAM E. B. DU BOIS: SCIEN-
TIST AND PUBLIC FIGURE, pp. 156-168. Examines Du Bois' career from a
Marxist viewpoint. In his early writings, for example, "Du Bois somewhat over-
rated the importance of pigmentation in human relations and at the same time
underrated the antagonism between labor and capital." Two of his books, *John
Brown* (1909) and *Black Reconstruction* (1935), "lack class analysis." Du Bois'
attitudes toward the inevitable collapse of capitalist imperialism and the successes
of socialism are also discussed.

Melish, William Howard. ONE OF "THE GREAT COMPANIONS," pp.
169-170. An extract from a Du Bois memorial address delivered in Ghana in
1963.

Johnson, Lyndon Baines. TO FULFILL THESE RIGHTS, pp. 172-179.
An address delivered at a Howard University Commencement, Washington,
D.C., 4 June 1965. Although during recent years some significant progress has
been made in finally freeing American Negroes, the condition of black men in the
United States is still grim. The walls of separation are still intact and rising. The
economic gulf between white and black is widening. The causes of these depressing conditions are discussed. The Johnson administration pledges itself to attack
racial injustice, and a call is issued for a White House conference on this subject.

D. J. Abramoske

1892. Wertz, Irma Jackson. PROFILE: LANGSTON HUGHES. *Negro Hist.
Bull. 1964 27(6): 146-147.* Discusses the various literary contributions of Langston Hughes (b. 1902), famous Negro poet, novelist, and historian.

L. Gara

1893. Wesley, Charles H. OUR FIFTIETH YEAR. *Negro Hist. Bull. 1965 28(8):
172-173, 195.* This year marks the half century of the Association for the Study
of Negro Life and History which was organized by Dr. Carter Goodwin Woodson
in 1915. Woodson graduated from Berea College, did graduate work at the
University of Chicago, and received his Ph.D. in history from Harvard. He
published *The Education of the Negro Prior to 1861* (1915) and the first issue
of the *Journal of Negro History* (1916). The *Negro History Bulletin* first appeared in 1935.

E. P. Stickney

1894. Wharfield, H. B. A FIGHT WITH THE YAQUIS AT BEAR VALLEY,
1918. *Arizoniana 1963 4(3): 1-8.* Escaping notice because of World War I struggles at the time, the skirmish of 9 January 1918, west of Nogales, Arizona,
involved Troop "E" of the Negro 10th U.S. Cavalry under Captain Frederick H.
L. Ryder and a band of some 30 Yaquis. Text of a letter of reminiscence by Ryder
is included. Documented, illus.

E. P. Stickney

1895. Williams, Delores M. MUSIC ON THE STRECKENFUS STEAMERS.
Bull. of the Missouri Hist. Soc. 1968 24(3): 241-247. The Streckenfus Line,
founded by John Streckenfus, built an enviable reputation based on the operation
of excursion vessels on the Mississippi River between St. Louis and New Orleans.
That repute derived largely from the line's tradition of offering patrons the best
in music. Several entertainers - notably Charles Mills, Louis Armstrong and

Walter Pichon - performed aboard Streckenfus steamers enroute to national fame. Based on interviews and secondary source materials; 23 notes.

H. T. Lovin

1896. Williams, Robert Lewis, Jr. THE NEGRO'S MIGRATION TO LOS ANGELES, 1900-1946. *Negro Hist. Bull. 1956 19(5): 102, 112-113.* Describes Negro migration to Los Angeles and the adjustment of the migrant to his new environment. Recent large increases in the Negro population of Los Angeles have come from nearby States with large Negro populations. Most migrants were middle-class Negroes from urban areas who were primarily interested in security and a new experience. In Los Angeles there developed segregated housing, many occupational changes, a lessening of church influence, changed leisure habits, modified racial attitudes, and gradual increases in political activity.

L. Gara

1897. Williams, T. Harry. THE GENTLEMAN FROM LOUISIANA: DEMA-GOGUE OR DEMOCRAT. *J. of Southern Hist. 1960 26(1): 3-21.* Huey P. Long stands without a rival as the greatest of southern mass leaders. "He asked the Southern United States to turn its gaze from 'nigger' devils and take a long, hard look at itself. He asked people to forget the past, the glorious past and the sad past, and address themselves to the present. There is something wrong here, he said, and we can fix it up ourselves. Bluntly, forcibly, even crudely, he injected an element of realism into Southern politics." Not without reason did one of his unfavorable critics say that Long was the first southerner since Calhoun to have an original idea, the first to extend the boundaries of political thought. Above all, he gave the southern masses hope. He did some foolish things and some wrong things. There is a tragedy in the story, and perhaps it is not entirely his fault that he did not become the South's peerless Progressive. Perhaps the lesson of Long is that if in a democracy needed changes are denied too long by an interested minority, the changes, when they come, will come with a measure of repression and revenge. Perhaps the gravest indictment that can be made of southern politics in recent times is that the urge for reform had to be accomplished by pressures that left in leaders like Long a degree of cynicism about the democratic process.

S. E. Humphreys

1898. Williamson, Hugh. THE ROLE OF THE COURTS IN THE STATUS OF THE NEGRO. *J. of Negro Hist. 1955 40(1): 61-72.* Examines several decisions rendered by U.S. courts in cases involving discrimination against Negroes between 1900 and the present. These cases involved questions such as the Negro's position in the labor unions, his exclusion from certain residential districts, and discrimination in public transportation and public education. In all these cases, the courts upheld the principle of equality of civic and political rights, thereby playing an important role in the emancipation of the Negro.

S

1899. Wiseman, John B. RACISM IN DEMOCRATIC POLITICS, 1904-1912. *Mid.-Am. 1968 51(1): 38-58.* Describes the race question in Democratic politics during the years 1904-12. The author explains how the commitment of Southern

Democrats to racist policies sapped the party of its national strength and appeal and inhibited its revitalization during this period. When dissension within the Republican Party brought the Democrats success in the 1910 elections, northern Democrats and the more liberal element of Southern Democrats were able to break the hold of racism on the party. This tendency toward moderation and modernization continued through Woodrow Wilson's first term as President. In the election of 1916 the party was free to choose a more progressive platform. Based on primary and secondary sources; 82 notes.   R. Eilerman

1900. Woodard, James E. VERNON: AN ALL NEGRO TOWN IN SOUTH-EASTERN OKLAHOMA. *Negro Hist. Bull. 1964 27(5): 115-116.* A sketch of the town of Vernon, Oklahoma, which was founded by Negroes from the South in 1911 and which currently contains only a small remnant of its earlier population. Undocumented.   L. Gara

1901. Worthman, Paul B. BLACK WORKERS AND LABOR UNIONS IN BIRMINGHAM, ALABAMA, 1897-1904. *Labor Hist. 10(3): 375-407.* Argues that between 1897 and 1904, the growth of Birmingham's labor movement stimulated efforts to organize black workers. Despite racial hostility, the industrialists' exploitation of race hatred, and the advice of some leading clergymen to Negroes that union organization was evil, black workers were organized and interracial cooperation did exist. The collapse of black labor unions after 1904 was a result of employer attacks, lack of support from the American Federation of Labor, and lost strikes. Based on newspapers, the Gompers correspondence, and censuses; 107 notes.   L. L. Athey

1902. Zangrando, Robert L. THE NAACP AND A FEDERAL ANTILYNCH-ING BILL, 1934-1940. *J. of Negro Hist. 1965 50(2): 106-117.* Describes the campaign of the National Association for the Advancement of Colored People (NAACP) for Federal antilynching legislation from 1934 to 1940, when the organization concentrated on congressional lobbying. The NAACP campaign included sending witnesses to congressional hearings, a petition and letter-writing campaign, an art exhibit, and providing legislators with facts and statistics. Two bills sponsored by the NAACP passed the House of Representatives only to be killed in the Senate. The campaign, however, acted as a deterrent to lynching, publicized the work of the NAACP, and helped prepare the way for public acceptance of Negro rights. Documented.   L. Gara

1903. --. [NEGROES AND NEW DEAL RESETTLEMENT]. *Agric. Hist. 1971 45(3): 179-200.*
      Holley, Donald. THE NEGRO IN THE NEW DEAL RESETTLEMENT PROGRAM, pp. 179-193. Traces the history of several New Deal resettlement programs as they affected Negroes. The Division of Subsistence Homesteads and the Federal Emergency Relief Administration helped lay the groundwork for a liberal resettlement program, but in themselves accomplished little. The resettlement administration and especially its successor, the Farm Security Administration (FSA), were responsible for most of the resettlement benefits for Negro farmers. The FSA programs brought substantial gains to some Negro sharecrop-

pers and tenants, but dealt timidly with racial problems and did little in the long run for the majority of Negro tenants and day laborers in the South. Based mainly on records in the National Archives; 42 notes.

Nipp, Robert E. THE NEGRO IN THE NEW DEAL RESETTLEMENT PROGRAM: A COMMENT, pp. 195-200. Criticizes Holley for assessing New Deal resettlement efforts by current standards instead of in the context of the times. Stresses the importance of congressional opposition to resettlement programs and the fact that before the New Deal, social programs were not thought to be the responsibility of government. The Farm Security Administration broke ground for current Farmers' Home Administration programs.

D. E. Brewster

1904. --. [THE HAMPTON INSTITUTE STRIKE OF 1927]. *Am. Scholar 1969 38(4): 668-684.*

Graham, Edward K. THE HAMPTON INSTITUTE STRIKE OF 1927: A CASE STUDY IN STUDENT PROTEST, pp. 668-682.

Mead, Margaret. POSTSCRIPT: THE 1969 DEMONSTRATIONS, pp. 682-684.

Graham relates the story of the Hampton protests of 1927 and the administration's mistakes and rigidity. Mead admires the school for having remembered and learned from the 1927 strike and thus avoiding a major confrontation in 1969. The earlier strike emerged from a long tradition of repressive social rules, bad teaching in a proud school just emerging from academy to collegiate status, and the naïveté of an orthodox northern preacher who had been Hampton's president - James Edgar Gregg. After the first stage of the strike, ostensibly over keeping the lights on during a movie, the president denied the students any rights of appeal or other due process; suspended the leaders, many of whom went onto distinguished careers; and gave out false press releases which papered over the deep-seated causes of unrest in a year that had seen an epidemic of protests in black colleges. Mead praised the Hampton trustees and administration for avoiding such a disaster in 1969, but expressed concern over the seeming inability of institutions to achieve resolutions of problems of governance or achieve an emotional catharsis. Based mostly on primary sources.

T. R. Cripps

1905. --. [WOODROW WILSON AND NEGRO APPOINTMENTS]. *J. of Southern Hist. 1958 24(4).*

Wolgemuth, Kathleen Long. WOODROW WILSON'S APPOINTMENT POLICY AND THE NEGRO, pp. 457-471. Many Negro leaders, such as W. E. B. Du Bois of the National Association for the Advancement of Colored People and Bishop Alexander Walters of the National Colored Democratic League, worked strenuously for the election of Woodrow Wilson as President in 1912. They expected reward in terms of patronage for Negroes. The only Negro Democrat appointed to office, however, was James L. Curtis, named minister to Liberia in 1916. The nomination of A. E. Patterson as registrar of the Treasury was withdrawn at the nominee's request in the face of opposition. Wilson reappointed one Negro, Robert H. Terrell, as a municipal judge in the District of Columbia, and allowed six Negroes to keep the consular positions they held in previous administrations. In 22 cases where posts had previously been held by Negroes, Wilson named white appointees. This pleased Southern Democrats, but it persuaded Negro leaders that further support of the Democratic Party at that time was senseless.

Osborn, George C. WOODROW WILSON APPOINTS A NEGRO JUDGE, pp. 481-493. In his reappointment of Robert H. Terrell as municipal judge in the District of Columbia, President Woodrow Wilson realized that he was flying in the face of opposition of important Southern Democrats. He counted upon support of northern Democrats and northern Republicans (Terrell was a Republican) to win approval of the nomination. The strategy was successful; Terrell was confirmed, 39 to 24.   S. E. Humphreys

The Pan-African Impulse & Other Cultural Perspectives

1906. Bittle, William E. and Geis, Gilbert L. ALFRED CHARLES SAM AND AN AFRICAN RETURN: A CASE STUDY IN NEGRO DESPAIR. *Phylon 1962 23(2): 178-196.* This effort at return to Africa was notable in being Negro-conceived and Negro-implemented throughout. Its strength derived from the presence, particularly in Oklahoma, of all-Negro settlements, such as Boley, which had grown, from the viewpoint of white neighbors, alarmingly large. The whites moved rapidly and successfully to disenfranchise the Negroes, and by physical threats and social and economic action reduced them to ignominious status. Hence, they were ready and receptive when Sam, a Gold Coast native who came to the United States in 1911 and engaged in business, came among them and agitated for a return to Africa. He stirred Negroes in Oklahoma, and also in Kansas, Texas, and Arkansas. Many were roused to hope and efforts of organization. One product was a tent colony at Weleetka, Oklahoma, where they lived in sordid circumstances while waiting for Sam to consummate his shallow plans. Finally, in 1914, he led a group of some 60 Negroes by boat from Galveston, Texas, leaving hundreds waiting behind. The ship experienced a poor voyage, non-cooperation from the British officials at the Gold Coast, sickness, demoralization, and deaths. Their leader fled. The few who survived to come home brought news which ended the enterprise. But though Sam was an inadequate leader, he briefly gave his followers something to live for.   L. Filler

1907. Cahnman, Werner J. IN MEMORIAM: WILLIAM EDWARD BURGHARDT DU BOIS, 1868-1963. *Am. Sociol. R. 1964 29(3): 407-408.* William Du Bois, sociologist and historian, left his mark as a scholar, a propagandist, and an organizer. His controversy with Booker T. Washington revealed the alternatives before the American Negro. Du Bois was the first to raise the banner of the Negro revolt. In 1961 as an act of defiance he joined the Communist Party. He was many years ahead of his time as co-founder of the Pan-African Congresses. He was the first Negro elected to the National Institute of Arts and Letters, was editor of *Crisis,* and author of 19 books. "He never bartered the goal of liberty against the wages of expedience." E. P. Stickney

1908. Contee, Clarence G. THE EMERGENCE OF DU BOIS AS AN AFRI-CAN NATIONALIST. *J. of Negro Hist. 1969 54(1): 48-60.* Discusses W. E. B. Du Bois' participation in the Pan-African Conference of 1900 held in London. The conference gave Du Bois (1868-1963) his first opportunity to act directly on behalf of African nationalism. The conference aimed to protest the treatment accorded Negroes in Western and colonial parts of the world and to bring all people of African descent closer together. It was dominated by delegates from the United States and Great Britain, and the nonrevolutionary resolutions reflected the moderate, middle-class attitudes of those attending. The conference intro-duced the term "Pan-African" and generated the hopes of black men for im-proved conditions everywhere. It was also an important experience for the 32-year-old Du Bois who continued to foster the ideas of Pan-Africanism in the 1920's and until his death in 1963. Based partly on Du Bois' writings; 50 notes. L. Gara

1909. Cooper, Wayne. CLAUDE MC KAY AND THE NEW NEGRO OF THE 1920'S. *Phylon 1964 25(3): 297-306.* The author traces the career of the poet and novelist Claude McKay, one of the first creative writers to give expres-sion to the new spirit awakened in American Negroes in the 1920's. McKay contributed poetry to *The Liberator* which he also helped edit in the early twenties and identified himself with the radical-bohemian set in Greenwich Vil-lage. He toured Russia and associated himself with various Communist groups but never fully accepted their ideology and was attacked by American Commu-nists in the 1930's. He identified with the common Negro to whom he attributed an uninhibited creativity and joy in life lost by Europeans and other Americans and produced three novels reflecting his interest in the Negro folk. In his poetry he best expressed the new Negro's determination to protect his human dignity, his cultural worth, and his right to a decent life. S. C. Pearson, Jr.

1910. Du Bois, William Edward Burghardt and [Regina de Marcos, trans.]. LOS COMBATES ESPIRITUALES DE LOS NEGROS DE NORTEAMERICA [The spiritual battles of North American Negroes]. *Casa de las Americas [Cuba] 1966 6(36/37): 142-146.* A selection from Du Bois' 1903 novel *The Souls of Black Folks.* The question the author asks himself is "How can I be Negro?" He indicates that there is a schizophrenic problem in being both American and black because these two attributes are viewed as mutually exclusive by white Ameri-cans. He concludes that these elements must be amalgamated if the American Dream is to be achieved. "The keystone of the aspirations of this great republic is simply the Negro Problem." C. J. Fleener

1911. Efrat, Edgar S. INCIPIENT PANAFRICANISM: W. E. B. DU BOIS AND THE EARLY DAYS. *Australian J. of Pol. and Hist. 1967 13(3): 383-393.* A critical assessment of the career of William Edward Burghardt Du Bois to the 1940's. Brought up in well-to-do, middle-class rural New England, Du Bois did not become aware of his Negro separateness until he attended Fisk University in the 1880's. He retained a "romantic and primitive" view of the African colonial world. As chairman of the Resolutions Committee of the 1900 Pan-African Conference in London he drafted a prophetic document about the role of race conflict in the 20th century. He was founder of the Niagra Movement, later the National Association for the Advancement of Colored People of the United States, but while Negroes who migrated to the northern cities in World War I encountered growing violence, Du Bois was immersed in international Negro movements. During the Versailles Peace Conference the Pan-African Congress proposed that an Ethiopian utopia should be created in the former German colonies in Africa. In the 1930's the Pan-African movement petered out, and when from the late 1940's an emergent black Africa became a reality Du Bois became a Communist. The author concludes that "objective evaluations of Du Bois are hard to come by" and he provides some interim bibliographical comments. Documented from Du Bois' writings.   D. McIntyre

1912. Elkins, W. F. MARCUS GARVEY, THE "NEGRO WORLD," AND THE BRITISH WEST INDIES, 1919-1920. *Sci. and Soc. 1972 36(1): 63-77.* Immediately after World War I black solidarity challenged white supremacy in the British West Indies. Great quantities of propaganda literature, such as the *Negro World* from New York City, which carried the views of Marcus Garvey, had been shipped to the West Indies and Africa. Most of the British colonies banned the *Negro World.* A survey of events in British Honduras, British Guiana, the Windward Islands, and other colonies in connection with its suppression suggested the power of the new national and social consciousness. In the Panama Canal Zone, where thousands of British Afro-West Indians worked, the American Government responded to the growth of Garveyism by moving to keep Garvey out of the Canal Zone. He was brought to trial and deported because of his radical ideology, not because of wrongdoing. 30 notes.   E. P. Stickney

1913. Elkins, W. F. "UNREST AMONG THE NEGROES": A BRITISH DOC-UMENT OF 1919. *Sci. and Soc. 1968 32(1): 66-79.* A British document of October 1919 points to broad currents of Afro-American nationalism and socialism in the United States which was infiltrating the West Indies. Heretofore unpublished, the document is from the British National Archives. 6 notes.
                                                                    R. S. Burns

1914. Fein, Charlotte Phillips. MARCUS GARVEY: HIS OPINIONS ABOUT AFRICA. *J. of Negro Educ. 1964 33(4): 446-449.* Garvey was a Jamaican Negro agitator. His career as founder of the Universal Negro Improvement Association is outlined, and it is suggested that his theory about Africa may be summarized in two assumptions: "First, he believed that African civilization was the first of all world civilizations to develop beyond the primitive stage, and that it had attained unscaled peaks before the rapacious Europeans destroyed and plundered it. Second, he held that there was nothing inherently inferior about the African race, which, given time, proper aid, and education, would rise again to untold splendor." Based on published materials in the Schomburg Collection, New York Public Library.   S. C. Pearson, Jr.

1915. Gold, Joseph. THE TWO WORLDS OF "LIGHT IN AUGUST." *Mississippi Q. 1963 16(3): 160-167.* An attempt to synthesize various criticisms of *Light in August* (1932) and to point the way toward new approaches to the Faulkner novel. To understand the role of the character Joe Christmas it is necessary to view him as only half of a composite picture - the hero is the reflector of society's perversions. A critic of his shaping forces, he is also a symbol for humanity. Faulkner uses the South's race conflict as a symbol for modern human disintegration. The isolation of Joe Christmas results from his refusal to be accepted either as black or as white rather than as he is really - a mixture. The character Lena Grove embodies all elements missing from modern society and represents an alternative to Joe Christmas and his world by the acceptance of all with an innocent viewpoint, judging others by her own goodness. The character Byron Bunch, not bound by the past, compelled by love to become involved with Lena, also attempts to help Christmas, although it is too late. Christmas has already become the animal hunted by the society that has formed him. Faulkner's ending of the novel indicates his belief in man, however. 8 notes.   R. V. Calvert

1916. Irele, Abiola. NEGRITUDE OR BLACK CULTURAL NATIONALISM. *J. of Modern African Studies [Great Britain] 1965 3(3): 321-348.* Negritude is a philosophy seeking both freedom from white domination and contempt and compensation for that domination and humiliation. Negritude's background included black subcultures in the United States, Brazil, and Cuba but more significant was the post-World War I American Negro renaissance which influenced black intellectuals in the Caribbean and France. Because of American occupation in 1915, Haitian intellectuals sought a "national soul" in Haiti's African heritage, thereby becoming negritude's first poets. Bergsonism, surrealism, Marxism, and *littérature engagée* made possible negritude's progressive formulation but revisionistic anthropology pointedly provoked the black counteroffensive in Paris before World War II. Documented.   E. E. Beauregard

1917. Kimmey, John L. THE GOOD EARTH IN "LIGHT IN AUGUST." *Mississippi Q. 1964 17(1): 1-8.* One of William Faulkner's fundamental themes - man's relationship with the natural world - is the chief concern of *Light in August* (1932), while miscegenation, white southern Protestantism, and suggestions of the Christ story are all auxiliary elements. The major theme is presented in a beginning contrast between the destructive wastefulness of the lumber mill and the purposeful fruitfulness of Lena Grove, who has a faith in the "immemorial earth" not found in the other characters. With a feeling for nature similar to Lena's but lacking her unwavering faith, Byron Bunch is connected with the earth through the determination binding him to Lena. Lucas Burch, Joanna Burden, and Joe Christmas are alienated from the good earth while Hightower alternately hates, fears, and flees the natural world. Hightower's regained faith is part of Lena's good earth. References to the season and the light (and contrasting dark) reinforce the major theme. Faulkner's remark that the book title denoted a time older than Christian civilization indicates that the author intended to go beyond the Christ story in the theme. 5 notes.
R. V. Calvert

1918. Langley, J. Ayo. CHIEF SAM'S AFRICAN MOVEMENT AND RACE CONSCIOUSNESS IN WEST AFRICA. *Phylon 1971 32(2): 164-178.* Account of the enterprise of Chief Alfred Sam of the Gold Coast to bring New World Negroes back to Africa. Discusses the prophets of the movement and the opposition. Most of the migrant volunteers were Oklahoma farmers. In 1914 the company ship set sail for Africa, but too much dreaming and not enough planning and organization proved fatal to the expedition. 51 notes. W. A. Buckman

1919. Parker, John W. BENJAMIN BRAWLEY AND THE AMERICAN CULTURAL TRADITION. *Phylon 1955 16(2): 183-194.* A biographical account of Dr. Benjamin G. Brawley (1882-1939), the American Negro writer, scholar, teacher, and apostle of good will among the races, with quotations from his writings. S

1920. Partington, Paul G. "THE MOON ILLUSTRATED WEEKLY" - PRECURSOR OF THE "CRISIS." *J. of Negro Hist. 1963 48(3): 206-216.* Relates the brief history of *The Moon Illustrated Weekly,* published in Memphis, by W. E. B. Du Bois in 1905-06. The magazine was Du Bois' personal project though he had previously described his publication plans to a number of people from whom he sought financial and other support. The magazine found few subscribers, mostly in Memphis and Atlanta, and ran into financial trouble immediately. However, it was the first attempt at a quality Negro weekly magazine and in its pages were items concerning the struggle for equality and freedom, Africa, and the Niagara movement. The journal gave Du Bois his first editorial experience and was the precursor of the much more successful *Crisis.* Documented. L. Gara

1921. Rogers, Benjamin F. WILLIAM E. B. DU BOIS, MARCUS GARVEY, AND PAN-AFRICA. *J. of Negro Hist. 1955 40(2): 154-165.* The sincere struggle of W. E. B. Du Bois for Negro civil rights in the United States and his futile attempts to unite the Negroes of the world are favorably compared with the radical and extravagant schemes of Marcus Garvey for Negro colonization in Africa during the early 1920's. R. Mueller

1922. Starling, Lathan, Sr. and Franklin, Donald. THE LIFE AND WORKS OF MARCUS GARVEY. *Negro Hist. Bull. 1962/63 26(1): 36-38.* Depicts Marcus Garvey as a 20th-century savior and his Universal Negro Improvement Association as a panacea for the problems of the American Negro. Many of the concepts of current African nationalism, the struggle for Negro rights, and the Black Muslim movement stem from Garvey's teaching. Undocumented. L. Gara

1923. White, Gavin. PATRIARCH MC GUIRE AND THE EPISCOPAL CHURCH. *Hist. Mag. of the Protestant Episcopal Church 1969 38(2): 109-141.* An account of George Alexander McGuire (1866-1934), able Negro clergyman, who became chaplain-general of Marcus Garvey's Universal Negro Improvement Association and founder of the African Orthodox Church. His primary object, the foundation of a church for all peoples of African descent (both in Africa and elsewhere), failed. But his church, the A.O.C., has survived. 115 notes.

E. G. Roddy

6

THE CONTEMPORARY SCENE
(Since 1945)

Racial Conflict & the Civil Rights Movement

1924. Amaker, Norman C. THE 1950'S: RACIAL EQUALITY AND THE
LAW. *Current Hist. 1969 57(339): 275-280, 300-301.* The school segregation
cases decided by the Supreme Court at the beginning of the decade were a first
step of major significance in breaking down the legal basis of the caste system.
When the Court ordered desegregation to proceed with "all deliberate speed" the
responses varied from outright defiance to the use of evasive tactics and delay.
The courts, applying the logic of the school cases, subsequently established the
principle of nondiscrimination in the use of all governmentally connected facilities.
B. D. Rhodes

1925. Arnez, Nancy L. A THOUGHTFUL LOOK AT PLACEMENT POLI-
CIES IN A NEW ERA. *J. of Negro Educ. 1966 35(1): 48-54.* Considers the
problems of the selection of Negro personnel for predominantly white schools and
white personnel for predominantly Negro schools. Statistics for 1964-65 show a
decided increase in teacher integration since 1960-61 largely as a result of the
transfer of highly qualified Negro teachers into integrated schools. The author
expresses concern that Negro communities may not receive their fair share of
talented teachers and administrators, Negro and white, to replace those lost
through this process. She surveys several programs for the recruitment and
training of teachers for culturally deprived children and encourages intensified
efforts in this area.
S. C. Pearson, Jr.

1926. Axon, Gordon V. THE UNITED STATES TODAY. *Q. Review [Great
Britain] 1967 305(652): 144-152.* The United States is an immensely wealthy and
powerful nation, and one in which domestic and foreign policies are controlled
by wealth. Internally, despite professions of democracy, money is the key to
political power, education, draft deferment, decent jobs, housing, and legal rights.
This fact produces social injustice, racism, riots, and crime. Externally, the at-

tempt to preserve economic privilege abroad makes the United States blind to the reality of social revolution and unresponsive to an accommodation with the USSR and China. The prognosis for breaking the power of wealth in American society is not good.   K. B. West

1927. Back, Kurt W. SOCIOLOGY ENCOUNTERS THE PROTEST MOVE-MENT FOR DESEGREGATION. *Phylon 1963 24(3): 232-239.* Considers why social scientists did not assess the importance of the nascent protest movement against segregation in America and discusses a theory of race relations which will lend itself to more accurate observation in the future.   S. C. Pearson, Jr.

1928. Baker, James T. THOMAS MERTON'S RESPONSE TO AMERICA, THE GRIM REAPER OF VIOLENCE. *Religion in Life 1971 40(1): 52-63.* To Thomas Merton, American society's violent past molded its personality and nature. The most visible sign was racial segregation and discrimination. In his writings he warned of the violence he saw coming because of that situation. The antidote, he felt, was a nonviolent response such as that of Martin Luther King, Jr. and especially of Gandhi. Details aspects of Gandhi's teachings important from Merton's point of view. Merton's idealism may prove to be of lasting value. 24 notes.   D. Brockway

1929. Baker, Leonard. COMPLIANCE. *Am. Educ. 1965 1(6)Sept.: 24-26.* Survey of the effect of guidelines for desegregation of southern school districts formulated by the U.S. Office of Education in compliance with Section 601 of the Civil Rights Act of 1964. Concludes that either out of respect for law or Federal financial aid "the South intends to fulfill its commitment to desegregated schools." Illus.   W. R. Boedecker

1930. Barker, Lucius J. THIRD PARTIES IN LITIGATION: A SYSTEMIC VIEW OF THE JUDICIAL FUNCTION. *J. of Pol. 1967 29(1): 41-69.* The value of third-party intervention in litigation has been proven by recent court decisions which have had an effect reaching far beyond the parties immediately involved. The two chief examples of this are *Brown vs. Board of Education of Topeka* (1954) which ordered an end to public school segregation, and *Baker vs. Carr* (1962) which brought about a reapportionment of State legislatures. Third parties usually enter the judicial process by initiating litigation or filing *amicus curiae* briefs. The effect has been the creation of a "judicial forum much more accessible to individuals who raise issues of broad-scale significance." Attempts to stop or hamper the efforts of third parties, such as Virginia's "massive resistance" of the mid-1950's, have failed. While most of the third-party efforts have had beneficial results, they lead the courts into functions that are essentially legislative in nature. On the other hand they have made the executive and legislative branches more responsive to the needs and problems of the present. With the latter development, the courts will no longer be involved in policymaking functions and will return to their traditional role of measuring actions by legal and constitutional standards. 114 notes.   A. R. Stoesen

1931. Bartholomew, Paul C. THE SUPREME COURT OF THE UNITED STATES, 1964-1965. *Western Pol. Q. 1965 (4): 741-754.* This Court disposed of 105 cases. The cases with the most substantive qualities to them included several in the broad category of civil liberties. In *Zemel vs. Rusk* the Court upheld the Secretary of State's refusal to validate a passport for tourist travel in Cuba. In *U.S. vs. Seeger* 10 persons involved in three cases, having been convicted of refusing to submit to army induction, found their convictions reversed. Though belonging to no orthodox religious sect, the Court held that their religious belief opposing war was valid and that therefore they were entitled to exemption. Certain free speech and press cases were adjudicated by the Court. In *Lamont vs. Postmaster General of the U.S.* the requirement that the recipient of overseas Communist mail specifically tell the postmaster that he desired such mail was held invalid. In *Garrison vs. State of Louisiana* a conviction of the New Orleans district attorney under the State's criminal defamation statute was held invalid. In *Cox vs. Louisiana* restrictions on picketing and demonstrating were held invalid although such regulations connected with proximity to a court were upheld. Film censorship powers by a State were limited in *Freedman vs. Maryland,* while in *U.S. vs. Brown* that portion of the Landrum-Griffin Act that barred Communists from serving as officers or employees of a trade union was held unconstitutional. Wide use of search and seizure in *Stanford vs. Texas* - again involving a Communist - was held invalid; as was warrantless arrest, in a case, *Beck vs. Ohio,* involving the driver of an automobile. Prohibition of self-incrimination was successfully invoked against use of a tape recording in *Griffin vs. California.* In *Swain vs. Alabama* the Court ruled that a fair trial for a Negro did not require that Negroes be represented in proportion to the population numbers in jury selection. In *Turner vs. Louisiana* it was held that a defendant did not receive a fair trial since two of the sheriffs who testified against him were for three days in close contact with the jury trying him. The first test of the sweep of the 24th amendment - outlawing poll taxes - was successful in *Harman vs. Forssenius.* In Louisiana a requirement that voter registrants interpret constitutional clauses to the satisfaction of registrars was held invalid in *Louisiana vs. U.S.* A Florida law in effect making criminal cohabitation between a Negro and a white couple was held invalid in *McLaughlin vs. Florida,* since only such couples were punished. On the basis of Congress' right to regulate interstate commerce, the public accommodations and service - in hotels and restaurants - section of the Civil Rights Act of 1964 were held valid. Some extension of State power resulted from *U.S. vs. California,* where the State's rights to inland waters were upheld and where such waters were for the first time actually defined.

H. Aptheker

1932. Bartley, N. V. LOOKING BACK AT LITTLE ROCK. *Arkansas Hist. Q. 1966 25(2): 101-116.* Preparation for a token desegregation in Little Rock was carried out more among the civic leaders whose children would not as likely be attending Central High as the new Hall High. Because of the scheduled shift to a city-manager plan in November 1957, Little Rock's lameduck city government had virtually left desegregation arrangements to School Superintendent Virgil Blossom. As a small militant opposition began to arise, on a number of occasions school authorities sought, from Governor Orval E. Faubus, a public statement promising to maintain order. Prior to his intervention Faubus had sought to avoid involvement in the desegregation question, holding that it was a local problem. The author suggests that the conditions described by school officials in requesting aid from the governor played a significant part in serving as a basis for his action in calling out the National Guard. He had previously sought unsuccessfully to obtain assurances from the Federal Government that it would maintain order.

P. M. McCain

1933. Bickel, Alexander M. THE CIVIL RIGHTS ACT OF 1964. *Commentary 1964 38(2): 33-39.* Describes President Kennedy's early attitudes on civil rights, the effect of the Birmingham demonstrations, the story of the bill on its way through Congress, and the provisions of the bill itself, with some comments on probable ramifications. Concludes with an estimate of the outlook for the future. The cause of civil rights will triumph because this statute represents the passing of the point of no return.

E. W. Hathaway

1934. Billington, Monroe. PUBLIC SCHOOL INTEGRATION IN OKLA-HOMA, 1954-1963. *Historian 1964 26(4): 521-537.* Following the Supreme Court decision 17 May 1954, declaring State-supported segregated schools Oklahoma's integration of Negro students and teachers with whites made a reasonably adequate start, but slowed down considerably by 1958, and had made only limited progress by 1963. The greatest single problem stemming from integration has been the failure to employ Negro teachers in the integrated schools. Based predominantly on periodical sources, Oklahoma statutes, and material from the Files of the State Superintendent of Public Instruction, Oklahoma City.

Sr. M. McAuley

1935. Bloombaum, Milton. THE CONDITIONS UNDERLYING RACE RIOTS AS PORTRAYED BY MULTIDIMENSIONAL SCALOGRAM ANALYSIS: A REANALYSIS OF LIEBERSON AND SILVERMAN'S DATA. *Am. Sociol. R. 1968 33(1): 76-91.* "A portion of [Stanley] Lieberson and [Arnold R.] Silverman's data on the underlying conditions of race riots [see abstract 3:605] was reanalyzed, using a recently developed technique of nonmetric data analysis. Multidimensional scalogram analysis (MSA) was applied to data on nine demographic conditions characterizing 24 cities in which Negro-white race riots occurred and 24 matched cities in which riots did not occur. Riots and controls are effectively partitioned with only 19 percent error in a two-space, even though no one of the underlying conditions is strongly related to the occurrence of riots. The nine conditions are also shown to reflect time and regional differences; the MSA distinguished between Northern pre-World-War-II and Southern post World-War-II cities."

J

1936. Bohn, Stanley. TOWARD A NEW UNDERSTANDING OF NONRESISTANCE. *Mennonite Life 1967 22(1): 14-17.* Discusses the author's experiences in the civil rights movement in the 1960's. As a white member of the National Association for the Advancement of Colored People in Kansas City, Kansas, he was able to mediate between whites and Negroes. The relationship between the idea of nonresistance and the author's Mennonite religious orientation is explored. A belief in nonresistance should not lead to neutrality or noninvolvement. Reconciliation is possible only if one has chosen sides and stood with the oppressed. When the author sold his home in a white community to a Negro family, he endured a great deal of harassment. Within a year, however, the whites became reconciled to the presence of Negroes in their midst.

D. J. Abramoske

1937. Bolner, James. DEFINING RACIAL IMBALANCE IN PUBLIC EDU-CATIONAL INSTITUTIONS. *J. of Negro Educ. 1968 37(2): 114-126.* Surveys legislative, executive, and judicial interpretations of "racial imbalance" and offers suggestions. While the Massachusetts legislature and the New York City Board of Education have employed formulas expressing percentage figures, most northern legislative and executive definitions have been less precise as have been most Federal and State judicial definitions. There is no official Federal definition. The author concludes that racial imbalance may be defined in terms of: 1) only nonwhite concentrations of a specified intensity, 2) nonwhite and white concentrations of specified intensities, or 3) a "community ratio" rule whereby the nonwhite percentage (maximun and/or minimum) for public educational purposes is related to the nonwhite proportion of the population. While expressing preference for the latter approach, the author also suggests an optimum nonwhite percentage range between 20 and 45 percent. 32 notes.   S. C. Pearson, Jr.

1938. Bolner, James. MR. CHIEF JUSTICE FRED M. VINSON AND RA-CIAL DISCRIMINATION. *Register of the Kentucky Hist. Soc. 1966 64(1): 29-43.* Examines the impact of Chief Justice Vinson on the constitutional problem of racial discrimination, with emphasis placed on the areas of housing and education. The "Vinson Court" has been noted for its illiberalism and "McCarthyism," but the author contends that Vinson "held no radical views on any subject," that he acted with "calm good sense" in racial discrimination controversies, and that his court "prepared the way for the decision in the 1954 *School Desegregation Cases.*" Documented.   J. F. Cook

1939. Borch, Herbert von. AMERICA REACHES THE LIMITS OF POWER. *Am.-German R. 1969 35(3): 1-5.* Comments on the domestic conflict within the United States during the 1960's as well as America's failure in foreign policy. The increase in Negro militancy and antiliberal New Left movements, revelations of failures to meet the needs of the poor, and the Vietnamese War all reveal that America has reached the limits of its power. Illus.   G. H. Davis

1940. Boskin, Joseph. THE REVOLT OF THE URBAN GHETTOS, 1964-1967. *Ann. of the Am. Acad. of Pol. and Social Sci. 1969 382: 1-14.* "The revolt of the urban ghettos in the mid-1960's was in large part the consequence of a dichotomy in the thinking of Caucasians regarding the city. Accepting the city as a source of work but rejecting it as a desirable place to live, whites moved out to the suburbs and left the inner city to the underclasses. The minority groups, on the other hand, initially sought socioeconomic salvation within the city; it was, in the words of biographer Claude Brown, the 'Promised Land.' Instead, the ethnic groups suffered confinement to the ghettos and restricted opportunities within the city. The ghetto enclave produced a consciousness of experience among its residents, of which a sense of entrapment was an integral aspect. The more than one hundred major riots which ensued between 1964 and 1967 were spontaneous outbursts of hostility toward ghetto conditions and toward those who perpetuated the environment. A high level of support, demonstrated in both attitude and action, prevailed during the revolts. Significantly, the two institutions which represented the white establishment, the police and businesses, were singled out for attack. Largely ignored were libraries, schools, and civic buildings. The riots were thus the result of an ecological malaise in American society which had prevailed for decades prior to the assaults of the ghettos in the 1960's."

J

1941. Boskin, Joseph and Philson, Victor, M.D. THE LOS ANGELES RIOT OF 1965: A MEDICAL PROFILE OF AN URBAN CRISIS. *Pacific Hist. R. 1970* 39(3): 353-365. Analyzes the treatment of the injured in the Watts riot of 1965, based on an investigation of emergency room records. Describes the manner in which patients were brought to the hospitals, the number of patients treated, and by whom. The statistics indicate that the published figures of the number wounded were inflated, and included all those brought into hospitals for treatment, not just those injured in the riot. 20 notes.   E. C. Hyslop

1942. Bosmajian, Haig A. THE RHETORIC OF MARTIN LUTHER KING'S LETTER FROM BIRMINGHAM JAIL. *Midwest Q. 1967 8(2): 127-143.* Analyzes King's most eloquent statement of his case and cause in this public letter of 1963, considering it in the great tradition of the famous letter of Emile Zola in 1898 and that of Thomas Mann of 1937. While he was imprisoned for civil rights demonstration, eight clergymen wrote a letter to the newspaper urging the Negro community to withdraw support from the civil rights demonstrations, and the famous "Letter from the Birmingham Jail" was his answer to them. Using the form of refutation known as the Method of Residues, he points out in detail that the Negro community was deprived of all avenues of action except demonstration. He identifies the actions and principles of the civil rights movement with various men of renown, philosophers, theologians, and other historical figures. A feeling of good will pervades the letter, and there is some humor, as in the quotation of the elderly woman who said, "my feets is tired, but my soul is rested." He points out that the power structure of the South is consoled by the church's silent and often vocal sanction of things as they are, and puts his hope outside the church, in God and America.   G. H. G. Jones

1943. Breslow, Paul. A RETURN TO THE WINDY CITY. *Twentieth Cent. [Great Britain] 1966 175(1030): 27-39.* An analysis of the Chicago race riots and of crime as an aspect of Chicago society. The author, a British observer who spent part of the summer of 1965 in Chicago, presents a description of student life and society at the University of Chicago.   L. Knafla

1944. Brogan, D. W. THE STUDENT REVOLT. *Encounter [Great Britain] 1968 31(178): 20-25.* Comments on the causes and nature of student revolt in the United States. The political role of the university has a long history, but the scale of the present disturbances is unprecedented. Hostility to the Vietnam War is genuine and general, but the most immediate response is provoked by the race issue; with the mingling of these protests the structure of university government has been attacked. The author examines student leadership and ideas as well as popular reactions.   D. H. Murdoch

1945. Busch, Joel H. DIE REVOLUTION DER AMERIKANISCHEN NE-GER [The revolution of the American Negroes]. *Politische Studien [West Germany]* 1965 16(164): 680-684. The Negro revolution has passed from its first phase (spontaneous action by certain groups and classes) to the second phase of collective struggle instead of individual action. The masses are now mobilized in the struggle for equality, but the discipline of the mass movement is quite remarkable. The Negro movement, however, is threatened by such problems as declining average incomes among Negroes, high unemployment, de facto school segregation, and growing Negro slums, and it appears uncertain as to how long Negro leaders will be able to prevent an explosion among their people.
                                                                        R. V. Pierard

1946. Cagle, Lawrence T. and Beker, Jerome. SOCIAL CHARACTERISTICS AND EDUCATIONAL ASPIRATIONS OF NORTHERN, LOWER-CLASS, PREDOMINANTLY NEGRO PARENTS WHO ACCEPTED AND DE-CLINED A SCHOOL INTEGRATION OPPORTUNITY. *J. of Negro Educ.* 1968 37(4) 406-417. A survey of Negro families in a medium-sized northern city who accepted or refused the bussing of their elementary school children to predominantly white, middle-class schools. The authors found no distinctive differences in the social or economic characteristics of those families who accepted bussing and those who refused. 3 tables, 28 notes.   B. D. Johnson

1947. Clarke, James W. and Sole, John W. HOW SOUTHERN CHILDREN FELT ABOUT KING'S DEATH. *Trans-action* 1968 5(10): 35-40. A statistical study of the reaction of southern children to the assassination of Martin Luther King, Jr. The study sought to discover how children reacted, whether their responses were similar to those regarding the John F. Kennedy assassination, whether there were racial differences in the reaction, and to what extent the reaction reflected their parents' opinions. The study discovered that Negroes were more shocked than whites, that white females were more shocked than white males, and that white parents whose occupations were professional, managerial, or proprietory were more concerned than parents whose occupations were clerical or involved sales or manual labor. Among Negro children, the higher the level of education the greater the tendency to blame the event on a racist white society. More than half the Negro children expressed a desire for "extra-legal revenge on King's assassin." 2 photos, 10 tables.   A. Erlebacher

1948. Cleghorn, Reese. 1968: A TIME FOR REDISCOVERY. *J.: Division of Higher Educ. United Church of Christ* 1968 7(1): 1-10. Briefly reviews the Civil Rights activities in the South in the early 1960's. It was a time of high ideals, with the young, both black and white, in the forefront. By 1967, however, the idealism and steam appeared to have left the movement, to be replaced by apparent apathy, especially in the Negro colleges. In 1968 the effort was revitalized with a different emphasis, but again having college youth in the vanguard. Unfortunately, the naked violence of Orangeburg, South Carolina, and Memphis, Tennessee, had replaced the righteous nonviolence of Selma and Birmingham, Alabama. The Civil Rights movement as a separate national force is dead. The movement should become a "people development" movement which could help everyone.

C. W. Ohrvall

1949. Coles, Robert. CHILDREN AND RACIAL DEMONSTRATIONS. *Am. Scholar 1964 34(1): 78-92.* The author, a child psychologist, has studied not only white and Negro southern children in newly desegregated schools, but also young persons who have taken part in racial demonstrations and sit-in movements. Sees similarities between such children and "children who have endured the special hells of our modern civilized world," i.e., British children under the blitz, children in Nazi-occupied Europe, and children who survived the atomic bomb. Concludes that many of the youths who take an active part in racial demonstrations are better integrated than other youths psychologically as well as racially because they act out of moral convictions, and in a spirit of sensitivity and thoughtfulness. "Whatever their motives, these hopeful children of the sit-ins are not willing to accept the prevailing values of a segregated society. They are committed to action, dedicated to affirming new values. They have not been the first Negro youths to dream of freedom, to want cafeteria coffee, to covet revenge. If they are white, they are not the first youths to flout powerful customs and try to build their very own."

D. D. Cameron

1950. Compton, Neil. CONSENSUS TELEVISION. *Commentary 1965 40(4): 67-72.* The author, who is the TV critic for *Commentary,* states that the viewer of American TV programs is left with two strong impressions: "first, the great networks seem to express a massive political consensus; second, they are commercial to a degree which even an outsider used to television advertising finds overwhelming." He concedes that news bulletins about battles, air raids, or government shake-ups are, on the whole, honestly handled by all three networks, but he is not favorably impressed by most of the occasional public-affairs specials. "The apolitical, undialectical attitude of the U.S. networks towards the news extends beyond the touchier aspects of foreign policy. The fight for civil rights is now part of the consensus, so the subject takes second place only to Vietnam in the amount of time devoted to it and the degree of commitment expressed.... During the past five or six years we have seen the television news on all three networks become personalized, packaged, and merchandised, and competing for high ratings as though it were a quiz show or a situation comedy....The networks have so brainwashed viewers into accepting their version of the upper-middle-class, non-denominational suburban family of television serials as the reality of life in America, that any departure from the stereotype is regarded as libelous or subversive." Only a decline in the power of the advertising industry will permit the establishment of a publicly owned, nonprofit radio and television service.

D. D. Cameron

1951. Cooper, David. "NOBODY WANTED SCHOOL DESEGREGATION." *Am. Educ. 1967 3(6): 2-4.* Describes the manner in which one southern county board of education managed a program of school desegregation. The procedure adopted included a two-week institute, financed by a Federal grant, for Negro and white educators, and an intensive program of public appearances by the board chairman and the district superintendent of schools. "A good part of the success lay in the fact that what happened was not just a desegregation program. The county school system was already embarked on a massive consolidation program and a program of school construction designed for greater efficiency and better schools." 3 photos.   W. R. Boedecker

1952. Dabney, Virginius. THE PACE IS IMPORTANT. *Virginia Q. R. 1965 41(2): 176-191.* Late in 1964 the Gallup Poll showed 49 percent of Negroes everywhere favored gradualism. Richmond is one of the best examples of constructive interracial achievement in a southern city. Its Negroes have shown how to get results without violence: suits in courts, peaceful picketing, and "selective buying." "Massive resistance" made for the smoothness of Virginia's reluctant acquiescence in the Federal court desegregation decisions after all legal maneuvers had been exhausted. Allan Nevins and Arnold Toynbee are quoted as saying that complete integration will mean racial amalgamation.   E. P. Stickney

1953. Daniel, Walter G. EDUCATION AND CIVIL RIGHTS IN 1965. *J. of Negro Educ. 1965 34(3): 197-203.* Summarizes the contents of this yearbook number of the *Journal.* The editor indicates three major purposes of the yearbook: "(1) to define the nature of the problems associated with achieving equal educational opportunity for all Americans, with special reference to the disadvantaged population composed mostly of Negroes; (2) to evaluate the current trends and strategies for providing educational opportunity and intergroup cooperation; and (3) to make suggestions for future improvement."   S. C. Pearson, Jr.

1954. Danzig, David. RIGHTISTS, RACISTS, AND SEPARATISTS: A WHITE BLOC IN THE MAKING? *Commentary 1964 38(2): 28-32.* Discusses the attitudes of various white groups toward civil rights for Negroes in general (as expressed in Federal legislation) and in particular (at the local level, in such issues as sending your own child to an integrated school or having Negroes move into your block). Considerable discrepancies are found, even among the liberals, whose "gradualism" is not well received by the more militant Negro leaders who would like their "Freedom Now." The author views with concern the possibility of a "White Bloc" (noting Italian and Polish districts supporting the "backlash"), and feels that the Negro is entitled to the benefits that other minorities have obtained in the wake of the New Deal.   E. W. Hathaway

1955. Danzig, David. THE MEANING OF NEGRO STRATEGY. *Commentary 1964 37(2): 41-46.* The emergence of Negro communal solidarity enables Negroes to use political pressure tactics for achieving their legitimate share of the goods of American society. The use of such power by ethnic, religious, and racial groups is not new in the United States. However, it represents a radical departure from the traditional civil rights conception by liberals who espoused the gradual admission of deserving Negroes into the larger society. Today, mounting Negro populations and concentrations in large northern cities and tensions created by their unfavorable economic positions increase demands from Negroes for pressure tactics and account for the developing rudimentary group coherence and indigenous leadership among Negroes. J. J. Appel

1956. Danzig, David and Field, John. THE BETRAYAL OF THE AMERICAN CITY. *Commentary 1968 45(6): 52-59.* To control riots in the cities, police power is now minimized and replaced with rigid curfews, speedy arrest, and the use of Negro groups who isolate the few active rioters. Many Negroes, however, feel that the whites will not change their attitude unless force is applied, while whites consider the use of force necessary to maintain stability. Congress passed only six bills to aid the cities. The employment and housing programs begun by government and private industry are too small to have much effect. The Federal Government should spend much more money on the problems of the cities than the present administration is doing. Because of the refusal of Congress to face the problem, more violence can be expected. C. Grollman

1957. Decter, Midge. THE NEGRO AND THE NEW YORK SCHOOLS. *Commentary 1964 38(3): 25-34.* Reports on the attitudes and goals of various groups concerned with integration in the New York schools, suggesting that some of these may be impracticable. Describes the various plans offered to correct the condition, the types of opposition met with, and other practical aspects of the problem. E. W. Hathaway

1958. Demerath, N. J., III, Marwell, Gerald, and Aiken, Michael T. CRITERIA AND CONTINGENCIES OF SUCCESS IN A RADICAL POLITICAL MOVEMENT. *J. of Social Issues 1971 27(1): 63-80.* Investigates the factors underlying the subjective sense of success and failure in a particular event in political activism. Focuses on 49 local projects in the South in which white student civil rights workers with the Southern Christian Leadership Conference took part in 1965. The purpose of this political activism was voter registration. However, success was also measured by the degree of project cohesiveness, the building of black organizations, and the sense of personal satisfaction which the volunteers felt as individuals. Concludes that one of the biggest distinctions between Old and New Left concerns the means-end concept of the movement itself. The older liberal perspective regarded movements as a means to societal ends, while the New Left's more radical view seeks to change society into a continuing mass movement in its own right. 3 tables, note, biblio. R. J. Wechman

1959. Determan, Dean W. and Ware, Gilbert. NEW DIMENSIONS IN EDUCATION: TITLE VI OF THE CIVIL RIGHTS ACT OF 1964. *J. of Negro Educ. 1966 35(1): 5-10.* Considers the application to programs in higher education of the provision that no person on the ground of race, color, or national origin may "be excluded from participation in, be denied the benefits of, or be subjected to discrimination under any program or activity receiving Federal financial assistance." To counteract the danger of uneven enforcement of Title VI, a standard "Assurance" form has been developed for use by all colleges and universities receiving or applying for aid which commits the institution to make no distinction on the ground of race, color, or national origin in its practices relating to the admission and treatment of students. The extent of coverage of the Title VI Assurance, obligations of the institutions, and procedures for enforcement are described.

S. C. Pearson, Jr.

1960. Donadio, Stephen. BLACK POWER AT COLUMBIA. *Commentary 1968 46(3): 67-76.* The gymnasium issue at Columbia University originated in 1961 when Columbia leased part of a park to construct a gymnasium which was to be used also by the neighboring residents, mostly Negroes. The Negroes at first approved, but as criticism was directed at the project by militants, dissatisfaction spread within the community. Demonstrations were held against the proposed gymnasium. Opposition also grew on the campus. The Negro students barricaded Hamilton Hall on 24 April 1968. The whites were forced to be equally militant. There were many causes of the riot, but race was the basic issue. The black cause won sympathy from the press, faculty, and administration. The author concludes that the events at Columbia have far-reaching implications for future protest movements.

C. Grollman

1961. Doyon, Jacques. LA MARCHE DE SELMA [The Selma March]. *Esprit [France] 1965 33(7/8): 161-168.* Describes the civil rights demonstration which began in Selma, Alabama and ended at the capitol, Montgomery, in March 1965. All types of Americans and many foreigners participated. The relationships between the marchers were friendly and cordial. The demonstrators were surrounded by a hostile crowd of whites. The impressive, nationwide support of Negro rights marked a turning point in the history of the Negro in America.

Mother M. H. Quinlan

1962. Dugger, Ronnie. THESE ARE THE TIMES: ON BEING A SOUTHERN LIBERAL. *Commentary 1964 37(4): 40-45.* The author recounts his experiences in and private reactions to the racist society of his home State. Concludes that southern liberal whites who have hitherto privately accepted the Negroes' demands for civil rights as morally right will be called upon to "risk everything," even life itself, as they declare their beliefs openly.

J. J. Appel

1963. Dunn, James R. TITLE VI, THE GUIDELINES AND SCHOOL DESEGREGATION IN THE SOUTH. *Virginia Law R. 1967 53(1): 42-88.* Analyzes the background and context of Title VI of the Civil Rights Act of 1964 which "provided that discrimination in federally assisted programs must cease, or those programs would no longer be federally assisted." Examines the Guidelines issued by the U.S. Office of Education in 1965 "which incorporated freedom of choice as one acceptable type of desegregation plan[,]" followed by a new set of Guidelines in 1966 "which included a test of effectiveness for the free-choice plans and required measurable progress in faculty desegregation." Concludes that "The administrative standards for school desegregation under Title VI and the 1966 Guidelines are consistent with current decisions of the federal courts which require that school officials take affirmative steps to desegregate the schools previously operated on a legally segregated basis. Whether in a judicial or an administrative context, the constitutional duty is the same: public schools in the

South formerly segregated by law must be desegregated in fact, and this duty extends equally to students and faculty....When student desegregation does not result from the efforts of the pupils and their parents under freedom-of-choice plans, and the dual system effectively continues under its own momentum by virtue of former official sanction and continuing social pressures, school authorities must change to non-racial attendance zones or some other affirmative means of pupil assignment." 212 notes.   D. D. Cameron

1964. Eckstein, George Günther. ASPEKTE DER GEWALT: NIMMT DIE AGGRESSIVITÄT ZU? [Aspects of power: is there increasing aggression?]. *Frankfurter Hefte [West Germany] 1969 24(11): 798-806.* A survey of social unrest in the United States from the early 1950's, with general commentary on the "sit-ins," the civil rights movement of 1964, the crisis in the cities, the black revolt, and student unrest. The author is particularly interested in identifying the group and revolutionary character of unrest, violence, and dissent, and in ascertaining the role of the mass media, the concept and practice of power, and the political implications of new group movements.   R. Heywood

1965. Eckstein, Günther. DIE NEUE LINKE IN DEN USA [The "New Left" in the United States]. *Frankfurther Hefte [West Germany] 1968 23(3): 181-188.* A discussion of the "New Left" movement in the United States, beginning in 1958, generated primarily from college campuses, and representing a varied response to three problems: Negro rights, education at the multiversity, and the war in Vietnam. The author is primarily concerned with the two most important groups of the New Left: Students for a Democratic Society (SDS), and the Student Nonviolent Coordinating Committee (SNCC). The role and concerns of these two groups and their relationship with the Black Power movement are discussed.   R. W. Heywood

1966. Eldridge, Mary N. EARL WARREN: DEFENDER OF HUMAN RIGHTS. *Negro Hist. Bull. 1967 30(5): 11-13.* Traces the early life and later political career of Earl Warren. Analyzes the monumental 1954 Supreme Court decision of *Brown vs. Board of Education of Topeka;* and outlines the philosophy of Justice Warren's views on social issues. Warren feels "there was no protection of minority groups by the executive or legislative branches of the government for so many years that the Court had to right the situation through broad interpretations of the Constitution." Warren believes that significant cases dealing with urban problems and the attack on poverty will be brought before the Court for years to come.   D. H. Swift

1967. Emmerich, Oliver. THE DEMOCRATIC IDEA AND THE SOUTHERN JOURNALIST. *Mississippi Q. 1965 18(4): 231-233.* The democratic idea of freedom of the press, meaning freedom of information to the people, is tested more often than is perhaps realized in America. In emotionally tense times, as in present-day Mississippi, the press has to determine how responsibility and effectiveness can be achieved simultaneously. During the "Ole Miss" crisis, Governor Ross Robert Barnett proved how irresponsibility can be temporarily highly effective. More than editorial courage is involved in a newspaper's responsibility, however. When emotionalism is more pronounced than reason, it helps to understand the historic significance of racial problems and to comprehend the difficulties involved. Non-Southern understanding and sympathy for Southerners who are working for the democratic idea in the South and actually making progress would help considerably.   R. V. Calvert

1968. Fabius. AMERIKAS VIETNAMPOLITIK AM WENDEPUNKT [A turning point in America's Vietnam politics]. *Schweizer Monatshefte [Switzerland] 1968 48(2): 159-161.* Analyzes tne first stages of the peace negotiations between the United States and North Vietnam following President Johnson's broadcast of 31 March 1968. The problem of division within America's social order, the assassination of Martin Luther King, and the economic crises of the winter of 1967-68 are all discussed and placed in perspective against the "peace" efforts in the Far East. In a far broader view than simply trying to negotiate a settlement, the United States is seen as a great power searching for a new identity in the world.   J. F. Dawson

1969. Feagans, Janet. ATLANTA THEATRE SEGREGATION: A CASE OF PROLONGED AVOIDANCE. *J. of Human Relations 1965 13(2): 208-218.* Surveys the progress made toward desegregation of Southern theaters and describes how Atlanta's downtown movie houses were desegregated in 1962. While this continues at a snail's pace, at least one opinion poll and two surveys reveal that "a more favorable attitudinal climate exists in support of theatre desegregation than most southern communities are willing to acknowledge or accommodate."   D. J. Abramoske

1970. Feagin, Joe R. and Sheatsley, Paul B. GHETTO RESIDENT APPRAISALS OF A RIOT. *Public Opinion Q. 1968 32(3): 352-362.* The shooting of a Negro boy in New York in July 1964 by a white policeman precipitated a riot that began in Harlem and spread quickly to Brooklyn's Bedford-Stuyvesant sections. Presents assessments by Bedford-Stuyvesant residents of the causes, purposes, participants, and effects of the riot. Uses a probability sample with quotas to insure sufficient representation of employed females and younger males. Responses to the question of the real cause of the riot indicate that many saw the riot as a protest against white police, white discrimination, or deprivation of Negroes by whites. These responses contrast strikingly with white interpretations of similar riots which show belief in Communist conspiracy and outside agitators. 3 tables, 13 notes.   D. J. Trickey

1971. Flacks, Richard. REVIEW ARTICLE. "THE CONFLICT OF GENERATIONS: THE CHARACTER AND SIGNIFICANCE OF STUDENT MOVEMENTS." *J. of Social Hist. 1970 4(2): 141-153.* In *The Conflict of Generations: The Character and Significance of Student Movements* (New York: Basic Books, 1969), Lewis S. Feuer attempts to compare 19th- and 20th-century student movements in both developing nations and advanced industrial societies. The breakdown of generational equilibrium is due to "de-authoritization," in which the younger generation becomes disillusioned with the older generation. Students tend to represent themselves as morally superior to their elders, destined to effect social change, being at one with the impoverished. Frustrated idealism becomes destructive. Feuer's bias against the younger generation is evidenced in discussions on events surrounding Martin Luther King's march in Selma, Alabama, in 1965, the teach-ins of 1965, and the Berkeley situation. In spite of its bias, the book contains important insights, although Feuer locates the cause of student revolutions in psychological problems of youth, rather than in an inadequate social system. An alternative to Feuer's argument is suggested, which stresses the primacy of social, cultural, and historical factors in influencing student movements.   K. A. Chauvin

1972. Flowers, Richmond M. A NEW BRAND OF SOUTHERN POLITICS. *Colorado Q. 1968 16(3): 243-254.* Government is made up of people, not law, and in the South people (the Order) continually have clashed with law over segregation in recent years. This is unfortunate because it is not right. Civil rights is the correct thing to do; civil rights is a movement to elevate Negroes to equal rights and to integrate Negroes into the mainstream of American life. Considerable obstructions to this goal exist, e.g., when Negroes simply reject U.S. laws. Another serious problem is the injection of the Vietnam issue into civil rights by irresponsible leaders.   B. A. Storey

1973. Fogelson, Robert M. WHITE ON BLACK: A CRITIQUE OF THE MCCONE COMMISSION REPORT ON THE LOS ANGELES RIOTS. *Pol. Sci. Q. 1967 82(3): 337-367.* Reconsiders the investigation by the McCone Commission into the Watts riots of August 1965 asserting that evidence accumulated by the commission was evaluated in the light of preconceptions which caused it to derive erroneous analyses from untenable assumptions and, therefore, to offer incomplete explanations and inadequate recommendations. The author concludes: "Not until white America abandons the preconceptions about rioting, law-enforcement, slums, and ghettos which misled the McCone Commission will it recognize the riots of the nineteen-sixties for what they were - articulate protests against genuine grievances in the Negro ghettos." Documentation based on extensive published sources; on unpublished material prepared for the U.S. Office of Economic Opportunity; on "The 1960's Riots: Interpretations and Recommendations," a report prepared by the author for the President's Commission on Law Enforcement and Administration of Justice, December 1966; on a statement transcribed from a NAACP Seminar, Columbus, Ohio, 2 April 1966; and on the McCone Commission Report and information in the McCone Commission Archives, California State Library, Sacramento, and in the UCLA Library; 75 notes.
                                                        Sr. M. McAuley

1974. Franklin, John Hope. A CENTURY OF CIVIL WAR OBSERVANCE. *J. of Negro Hist. 1962 47(2): 97-107.* Earlier observances of the Civil War were characterized by an emphasis on national unity and a spirit of restraint and reserve. The centennial observance has evoked unprecedented enthusiasm with emphasis on reliving the events rather than facing up to the implications of the conflict in terms of our expressed ideals and goals. In observing the Civil War,

Americans should recognize their failure to grant the full emancipation to the Negro which should have followed naturally the abolition of slavery.

L. Gara

1975. Frazier, Thomas R. AN ANALYSIS OF NONVIOLENT COERCION AS USED BY THE SIT-IN MOVEMENT. *Phylon 1968 29(1): 27-40.* There are two needs that must be dealt with in a conflict situation, the instrumental needs of resolving the conflict and the expressive needs of the participants. The use of nonviolent coercion in the southern sit-in movement in 1960 fulfilled both of these needs. The author discusses the philosophy behind nonviolent coercion, emphasizing the contributions of Gandhi and Martin Luther King, Jr., and its application during the early sit-in movement in 1960. The role of the Congress of Racial Equality (CORE) is briefly discussed. The author concludes that nonviolent coercion has been effective on several fronts in breaking traditional patterns of behavior in the South. Based on primary and secondary sources; 41 notes.

R. D. Cohen

1976. Fuller, Hoyt W. THE MYTH OF THE "NEW NEGRO." *Southwest R. 1963 48(4): 353-357.* Maintains that there is nothing "new" about the young militant Negroes who are pushing for Negro equality in the United States. The old Negroes desired equality and rights also. The fact that the world has "at last challenged the concept of white supremacy" explains the relative success of the young Negroes.

D. F. Henderson

1977. Gaston, Paul M. SPEAKING FOR THE NEGRO. *Virginia Q. R. 1965 41(4): 612-618.* Reviews seven of the more than 50 books on civil rights resulting from the turmoil of the summer of 1965. These books are representative, as the quality is uneven and emphasis is heavy on Mississippi. Reviewed are Russell H. Barrett's *Integration at Ole Miss* (Chicago: Quadrangle, 1965), Walter Lord's *The Past That Would Not Die* (New York: Harper and Row, 1964), Robert Canzoneri's *"I Do So Politely": A Voice from the South* (Boston: Houghton-Mifflin, 1965), William McCord's *Mississippi: The Long, Hot Summer* (New York: W. W. Norton and Co., 1965), Elizabeth Sutherland's (ed.) *Letters from Mississippi* (New York: Harper and Row, 1965), John Ehle's *The Free Men* (New York: Harper and Row, 1965), and Robert Penn Warren's *Who Speaks for The Negro?* (New York: Random, 1965).

O. H. Zabel

1978. Gill, Robert L. SHAPING THE NEGRO REVOLUTION THROUGH COURT DECISIONS 1964-1966. *J. of Human Relations 1967 15(4): 423-442.* Reviews recent decisions of the U.S. Supreme Court on such matters as the Civil Rights Act of 1964, breach of the peace cases, the exclusion of Negroes from jury service, miscegenation, educational segregation, legal attacks upon the National Association for the Advancement of Colored People, disfranchisement of Negroes, and criminal law. "In the period from 1964-1966, we find emerging from federal legislative, executive orders, and judicial processes, an expanding body of Civil Rights and related Common Law...purposely directed toward the realization of a single class of citizenship in the United States with equality of opportunity for all. Never before in American history has so profound and revolutionary a change been effected as quickly and as bloodlessly." Based on Supreme Court decisions; 52 notes. D. J. Abramoske

1979. Gill, Robert L. THE NEGRO IN THE SUPREME COURT, 1954-64. *Negro Hist. Bull.* *1964 28(3): 51-52, 65-67, 1965 28(4): 86-88, (5): 117-119.* The author assumes that the decade 1954-64 constituted a turning point in the second American revolution, the movement to bring full freedom to all Americans, and discusses the more significant Supreme Court decisions affecting this revolution. The third part reviews major civil rights cases decided by the U.S. Supreme Court from 1954 to 1964. During this decade the court has consistently struck down State and local laws which imposed a policy of segregation in publicly owned or operated facilities. Concludes with a comment on the need for the protection of the voting rights of Negroes and for the complete legal equality which the American heritage and the Christian religion promise. L. Gara

1980. Glazer, Nathan. THE NEW LEFT AND ITS LIMITS. *Commentary 1968 46(1): 31-39.* Defines the radical Left as those who believe that something is fundamentally wrong with American society which can be righted only by a radical change. The New Left argues that people for reasons of security, prestige, duty, etc. have been trapped into serving big and powerful institutions. The author shows that in all industrially advanced societies problems have become more technical and less political, and he uses the Negro and his struggle for equality as an example. C. G. Lauritsen

1981. Glenn, Norval D. THE ROLE OF WHITE RESISTANCE AND FACIL-ITATION IN THE NEGRO STRUGGLE FOR EQUALITY. *Phylon 1965 26(2): 105-116.* Argues that "the fate of Negro Americans has been and remains largely in the hands of the dominant white population." Of various explanations of white action and policy toward Negroes such as self-interest (perceived and/or objective), values and morals, and emotion, self-interest is most important. Though many whites have come to support the Negro cause out of self-interest, Negro and white interests remain opposed in many ways. Force rather than persuasion will be necessary to destroy white resistance and make possible further gains by Negroes. S. C. Pearson, Jr.

1982. Goldbloom, Maurice J. THE NEW YORK SCHOOL CRISIS. *Commentary 1969 47(1): 43-58.* Schools today are sick, and Negro schools in particular need drastic improvements. To improve teaching, it is necessary to eliminate the present education course requirements for teaching positions. Schools have been improved by the use of the More Effective Schools Program and the Responsible Environment (better known as the "talking typewriter"). Instead of expanding such programs, the New York Board of Education has produced gimmicks. The resentment and frustration of the Negroes errupted at Intermediate School 201 in Harlem. The author gives details on the causes, issues, and consequences of the outbreak. He feels community control of schools is a gimmick which will be approved by the upper class since it will not entail increasing expenditures and taxes, and by the Negroes since it offers them the simulacrum of power.

C. G. Lauritsen

1983. Gray, Charles H. A SCALE ANALYSIS OF THE VOTING RECORDS OF SENATORS KENNEDY, JOHNSON AND GOLDWATER, 1957-1960. *Am. Pol. Sci. R. 1965 59(3): 615-621.* Using the Guttman scaling technique to determine public postures and possible changes of the candidates as the 1960 campaign approached, all their roll-call votes in the 85th and 86th Congresses are analyzed. More than 70 percent of their votes were significant in ideological meaning. Scales were constructed for domestic economic welfare, agricultural price support, civil rights, foreign military aid, and public power. John F. Kennedy was generally the most liberal, Lyndon B. Johnson moderate, and Barry M. Goldwater strongly conservative. The most marked shift was in civil rights, with Kennedy moving to a strong pro position, Johnson becoming slightly more liberal, and Goldwater moving closer to the die-hard southern stand. Graphs.

H. G. Warren

1984. Greenberg, Jack. THE CIVIL RIGHTS ACTS OF 1964-1965. *African Forum 1966 1(3): 91-104.* Discusses the major events leading to the passage of the Civil Rights Act of 1964 and the Voting Rights Act of 1965. The author pays particular attention to the school segregation cases of 1954 and how they paved the way for later significant legislation. In discussing the 1964 act, the author feels that probably the most important section is that stating, "Federal funds cannot be given to any program or activity that discriminates against persons on grounds of race." He feels that much of the existing discrimination could be curtailed if the government (particularly the Department of Health, Education, and Welfare) would use its legal power to discontinue Federal aid to programs that continue to practice racial discrimination. The 1965 voting act sought to eliminate various loopholes that allowed voting discrimination to continue even after the passage of the 1957, 1960, and 1964 acts. The Civil Rights Commission found in late 1965 that compliance with the act was still not complete in some Southern States.

M. J. McBaine

1985. Greene, Marc T. AMERICA: THE UNCERTAIN FUTURE. *Quarterly R. [Great Britain] 1964 302(640): 222-233.* A listing of the various problems facing the United States, including the safety of the President, relief of poverty, unemployment, ill-health, crime, excessive government spending, civil rights for Negro citizens, moral laxity, "flagrant dishonesty in business concernments," suppression of religion, the uncertainty of the American labor situation, and the distressed position of the white collar worker.

R. G. Schafer

1986. Griessman, B. Eugene. TOWARD AN UNDERSTANDING OF URBAN UNREST AND RIOTING. *J. of Human Relations 1968 16(3): 315-332.* Discusses rioting as an ancient form of human behavior and reviews several theories of social conflict that aid in the understanding of urban unrest and rioting in the 1960's. Robert E. Park related social conflict to interaction patterns and social change. Gustave Le Bon viewed riots as a form of collective behavior. Karl

Marx saw revolution resulting from the continued degradation of the proletariat, whereas Alexis de Tocqueville linked revolution with "improved" conditions. Revolutions, according to James C. Davies' recent suggestions, are most likely to occur when a prolonged period of economic and social development is followed by a short period of sharp reversal. The special characteristics of urban life are viewed as forming a setting in which rioting is likely to occur. Relative deprivation is looked upon as a significant dynamic element, and Negro racial militancy is interpreted within the large theoretical framework of social conflict. Finally, positive functions of social conflict are suggested as relevant considerations in predicting what might occur as an aftermath of the riots. 31 notes.

D. J. Abramoske

1987. Griffin, Leland M. THE RHETORICAL STRUCTURE OF THE "NEW LEFT" MOVEMENT: PART I. *Q. J. of Speech 1964 50(2): 113-135.* Within the development of the "New Left" movement are the "peace" and "civil rights" movements; and in considering their development the author repeatedly cites their "aggressive orators": James Baldwin, Erich Fromm, Michael Harrington, A. J. Muste, Bayard Rustin, Harvey Swados, Norman Thomas, C. Wright Mills, to name but a few. The author also traces the inception and development of some of the "New Left" groups, i.e., War Resisters' League, Student Nonviolent Coordinating Committee, Turn Toward Peace, and the Congress of Racial Equality. The rhetorical structure of the entire movement is examined via a Burkeian (Kenneth) analysis. Multiple sources are used, chiefly those pamphlets, journals, and books of the "New Left" movement itself. *New America* and *Liberation* are the two most reoccurring sources. 99 notes.

M. A. Hayes

1988. Hahn, Harlan. GHETTO SENTIMENTS ON VIOLENCE. *Sci. and Soc. 1969 33(2): 197-208.* Most ghetto residents of untroubled areas supported the radical objectives of violence. The author bases his argument on the report of the Kerner Commission on Civil Disorders and finds the pacific conclusions of the report fallacious. 21 notes.

R. S. Burns

1989. Harding, Vincent. WHERE HAVE ALL THE LOVERS GONE? *Mennonite Life 1967 22(1): 5-13.* Reprinted from *New South* 1966 21(1). From the beginning of the Negro freedom movement in the 1950's, "it was clear that a majority of those who accepted a nonviolent approach were ready to turn to other means if it did not work." Much of the utopian vigor of the civil rights movement has been undermined by the "friendly" intervention and programs of the Federal government. The quest for political and economic power has become more important than "the task of redemption through suffering and dogged loving." Violence is built into the American grain far more deeply than nonviolence. 5 notes.

D. J. Abramoske

1990. Hatchett, John F. THE NEGRO REVOLUTION: A QUEST FOR JUSTICE? *J. of Human Relations 1966 14(3): 406-421.* Analyzes the concept of justice in relation to the contemporary revolt of the Negro. Although the focal point of the civil rights movement tends to be the achievement of equality, "what the Negro *really* wants at bottom is justice and the concomitant sense of dignity it accords one." As a result of an increasing sense of frustration, alienation, and despair, the Negro revolution is moving in the direction of a more volatile expression. "It is time to demand just treatment and to fight, if necessary." 27 notes.   D. J. Abramoske

1991. Height, Dorothy I. A TIME TO LISTEN: CIVIL RIGHTS AND THE MASS MEDIA. *Southwest R. 1968 43(3): 221-235.* Chastises the mass communications media for failing to contribute to human understanding. Instead of ameliorating racial conflict, they have tended to thrive on it, to use snappy phrases such as "Black Power" to portray a very complex movement. There has been progress, but its extent will in part be determined by the degree that "every one of the media of communications we touch shall help to create a climate in which the stress is not just on 'law and order' but on justice and equality."
D. F. Henderson

1992. Henderson, George. LEGAL ASPIRATIONS AND SUCCESSES IN THE AMERICAN NEGRO REVOLUTION. *J. of Human Relations 1965 13(2): 185-195.* "Many aspects of the Negro's level of aspiration in seeking legal equality do not conform to psychological theories of aspiration." Past successes do not account for the high level of legal aspirations. They are to be explained by such factors as "the group definition of 'law' and favorable sources of law." 18 notes.   D. J. Abramoske

1993. Henderson, George. UNDERSTANDING THE NEGRO REVOLT. *Social Studies 1967 58(4): 145-153.* Cites poverty, discrimination, mistreatment, and general neglect of social, economic, and political problems of Negroes by the power structure as bases for the revolt. An understanding of the Negro's problems will help others to rationalize the Negro's motives. To many Americans the word Negro carries with it connotations of inferiority, automatically engendering prejudiced feelings about the Negro as a class and as an individual, without allowing the mind to reflect upon logical premises concerning the true character of Negroes on the basis of individual merit. 29 notes.   L. Raife

1994. Henkin, Lewis. THE UNITED NATIONS AND HUMAN RIGHTS. *Internat. Organization 1965 19(3): 504-517.* Surveys the place of human rights in the U.N. scheme. "The achievements have been modest, subtle, gradual." The Universal Declaration of Human Rights is reflected in the constitutions of the new nations and "may perhaps be credited also with influencing nations with... more developed traditions of freedom" to adopt the Convention for the protection of Human Rights and Fundamental Freedoms (1950). The United Nations has been a major instrument in "the inevitable demise of white racism....Even the United States Civil Rights Act of 1964 owes its existence in some measure to the subtle influences of United Nations concern to end racial discrimination."
E. P. Stickney

1995. Himes, Joseph S. THE FUNCTIONS OF RACIAL CONFLICT. *Social Forces 1966 45(1): 1-10.* "Social conflict is revealed as both natural and functional in human society. Conflict is called 'realistic' when rationally determined means are used to achieve culturally approved ends. In the field of Negro struggle, legal redress, political pressure and mass action meet these defining criteria of realistic conflict. This study examines some of the social functions of conflict as here defined. It is asked: does realistic conflict by Negroes have any system-maintaining and system-enhancing consequences for the larger American society? The analysis revealed that realistic racial conflict (1) alters the social structure, (2) extends social communication, (3) enhances social solidarity, and (4) facilitates personal identity." J

1996. Hines, Ralph H. and Pierce, James E. NEGRO LEADERSHIP AFTER THE SOCIAL CRISIS: AN ANALYSIS OF LEADERSHIP CHANGES IN MONTGOMERY, ALABAMA. *Phylon 1965 26(2): 162-172.* Analyzes the continuities and discontinuities of leadership surrounding the social crisis occasioned by the Montgomery bus boycott from 1955 to 1957. The authors found that protest leaders who replaced accommodation leaders during the crisis were in turn replaced by accommodation leaders within 18 months after the bus boycott. They suggest that leadership in the social crisis may be a correlate of the changing conditions of the community as well as a factor in the process of change itself and that when "the social situation approaches reconciliation, protest leadership seems no longer desirable or necessary." S. C. Pearson, Jr.

1997. Hixson, William. THE NEGRO REVOLUTION AND THE INTELLECTUALS. *Am. Scholar 1964 33(4): 581-593.* The intellectual community, while not reinforcing the educated public's racial prejudices, has reinforced its conservatism with the result that revolution has seldom been in such disfavor as since World War II. The intellectuals' view of America as an orderly society with a high degree of equality and pluralism has made the Negro's task of articulating his aims to the educated public more difficult. Unless present interpretations are reevaluated, "their public, faced with increasingly 'revolutionary' demands, will regard the Negro movement as challenging everything 'American'" - and the commitment to American ideals, still shared by Negroes, the white public, and the intellectuals, will be destroyed. E. P. Stickney

1998. Hunter, Charlayne A. ON THE CASE IN RESURRECTION CITY. *Trans-action 1968 5(10): 47-55.* A study of some of the problems and tensions which occurred in Resurrection City, Washington, D.C., during the 1968 Poor People's campaign. The author especially notes the interrelations and tensions between urban and rural oriented blacks. Also sketched are the particular contributions of Resurrection City leaders such as Hosea Williams and the Reverend Jesse Jackson. Among the most moving experiences were the constant demonstrations at various Federal bureaus and departments. Resurrection City made the poor visible, but it is arguable whether it was effective. The rural blacks learned enough to move toward a more militant stance on issues concerning their welfare. The greatest success of the campaign was in demonstrating what the system had done to the black population of the United States. 4 photos.
A. Erlebacher

1999. Hurtig, Serge. LES NOUVEAUX ASPECTS DU PROBLEMS NOIR AUX ETATS-UNIS [New aspects of the racial problem in the United States]. *Pol. Etrangère [France] 1963 (6): 477-492.* Estimates that demands for racial equality finally achieved primary political importance in the summer of 1963. The possibility of new political alignments on ideological bases has arisen; hence President Kennedy's fatal attempt to retain the loyalty of Texas. Economic and social changes are needed, for which opinion is not yet ready. Because of the long-range internal crisis, American foreign policy may fall into isolationism or into hyperactivity, diverting public opinion.   J. E. Helmreich

2000. Iakovlev, N. N. O NEKOTORYKH PROBLEMAKH VNUTRENNEI POLITIKI SSHA [Some problems of internal politics of the United States]. *Prepodavanie Istorii v Shkole [USSR] 1965 (1): 3-15.* Discusses the economic, social, and political situation in the United States from the early 1950's to 1964. The author attempts to show that although American economic growth has been steady during the Eisenhower, Kennedy, and Johnson administrations, economic life has been artificially supported by huge expenditures for armaments. The American economy has not fully solved the problem of unemployment. Socially, desegregation has not proceeded quickly enough as evidenced by Negro demonstrations, and American labor is still subjected to the monopolistic interests of big business which has the support of the Federal Government. Through a study of recent American history, historians can better appreciate the value of Soviet constructive labors. Based on American and Soviet published works; 39 notes.
                                                                    A. Birkos

2001. Jackman, Norman and Dodson, Jack. NEGRO YOUTH AND DIRECT ACTION. *Phylon 1967 28(1): 5-15.* Examines the tactics employed by the Congress of Racial Equality (CORE) in recruitment, leadership, and organization goals. An examination of CORE files and interviews with group leaders and field workers reveal that recruitment of young Negroes has generally been impeded by the entrenched Negro power structure, whose members feel that CORE may diminish their power by attracting young people; and that local CORE chapters are occasionally hampered by internal dissension occasioned by a leadership which sometimes seeks personal aggrandizement. The organization's field representatives are especially effective in capitalizing on the discontent of young Negroes and giving it direction. The greatest problems facing CORE are maintaining a nonviolent position and the absence of long-range goals. Based on files, interviews, and published sources; 7 notes.   D. N. Brown

2002. Jackson, George L. CONSTRAINTS OF THE NEGRO CIVIL RIGHTS MOVEMENT ON AMERICAN MILITARY EFFECTIVENESS: A SURVEY. *Naval War Coll. R. 1970 22(5): 100-107.* Since 1964 every phase of American life has been affected by the Negro civil rights movement. The movement has affected the military establishment, and senior officers should recognize how it has constrained the use of military power in the execution of foreign policy. Riots and urban disturbances have required more frequent use of military forces to quell riots and have thus brought the military into a greater interplay in domestic life. Morale within the military establishment has been adversely affected, thus constraining military effectiveness. While we should give due recognition to the goals of the movement, the United States must not allow its capability of deterring a potential aggressor to decline. Based on secondary sources; 20 notes.

A. S. Birkos

2003. Johnson, Gerald W. WETHARRYNGTON: SCHOLIA ON HANNAH ARENDT. *Am. Scholar 1964 33(2): 202-210.* An answer to Hannah Arendt's article, "Man's Conquest of Space." *American Scholar,* Autumn 1963, concentrates on three issues before American public opinion today: the Cold War, the civil rights agitation, and unemployment as a function of a lagging economy, and argues "that the debate on each of these is thinner than the personality of Eichmann." The term "war" presumes victory or defeat. We could benefit not by Russia's defeat but by her transformation so that the two countries might divert their resources to something better than armament. As regards the Negroes, it is shadowboxing to concentrate on social status rather than the basic issue of liberty. As to unemployment, the subject is obscured "by a fog of words" when we should be applying the energy released by technology to stimulate the economy to create new jobs faster than automation can abolish old ones. The author concludes that even shadowboxing is taking action, if not so committed as "Wetharryngton" of the Chevy Chace ballad, who, when both his legs were gone, knelt and fought on his knees.

E. P. Stickney

2004. Johnson, Oakley C. NEW ORLEANS STORY. *Centennial R. 1968 12(2): 193-219.* An account of the author's experiences (1947-51) as professor of English at Dillard University in New Orleans. He describes student problems, attitudes, and performance, with quotations from their work. During Henry A. Wallace's Progressive Party campaign of 1948, the major efforts in Louisiana involved voter registration and the dissemination of information. These were only partially successful. The author was also active in the Louisiana branch of the Civil Rights Congress which sought to expose acts of violence toward Negroes. In 1949, Johnson was called before a Federal Grand Jury investigating Communist activities under the Smith Act. Nothing came of this proceeding except that the Dillard administration asked Johnson to sign a resignation, which they promised not to use unless it became "necessary." The fact that he was a white professor in a southern Negro college made him suspect and caused the administration some difficulties. Matters came to a head in 1951 when Johnson sent copies of an article he had written dealing with unequal justice in rape cases to two white members of the Dillard Board of Trustees. His contract was not renewed. He understood the Dillard administration's dilemma and left without bitterness. Some students wanted to come to his support, but Johnson advised them to take their risks "in defense of a Negro leader or for the sake of a vital principle directly applicable to themselves."

A. R. Stoesen

2005. Jones, Juanita DaLomba. HE WHO PERPETRATES (MY DAY AS A PICKET FOR FREEDOM). *Phylon 1963 24(3): 290-299.* The author relates her experiences as a participant in a group picketing restaurants for service.

S. C. Pearson, Jr.

2006. Kaiser, Ernest. RECENT LITERATURE ON BLACK LIBERATION STRUGGLES AND THE GHETTO CRISES. *Sci. and Soc. 1969 33(2): 168-196.* A survey of books, articles, and monographs on numerous aspects of the black civil rights movement from 1966 to 1969.   R. S. Burns

2007. Kazin, Michael. SOME NOTES ON S.D.S. *Am. Scholar 1969 38(4): 644-655.* A brief survey of the growth of the American student movement from the civil rights and "North Student" movements of the early 1960's to the self-consciously revolutionary SDS (Students for a Democratic Society) movement. The author first discusses the Greensboro, North Carolina, lunchcounter sit-ins which led to the formation of the Student Non-Violent Coordinating Committee. When the southern black students proselyted on northern campuses, the newly formed SDS departed from its older advisers (Michael Harrington, Norman Thomas, and Bayard Rustin) and followed the counsel of Tom Hayden's 1962 "Port Huron Statement" which excoriated American society while describing a democratic vision of a society in which people participated at all levels in their government. The SDS concentrated on action and community organization rather than Marxist theorizing, hoping to avoid the sectarian squabbling of the Old Left. Mildly supporting Lyndon B. Johnson in 1964, SDS grew larger and rejected conventional politics soon after the bombing of North Vietnam. When Stokely Carmichael became head of SNCC, SDS quickly followed his advice to white radicals to organize the white working class. Support for the Black Panther Party's stress on community action also gained SDS support, as did black studies and other university programs. Because the SDS split in 1969, a clear identity awaits future developments. Based largely on James O'Brien's pamphlet *A History of the New Left, 1960-1968* (Boston: New England Free Press, 1968).
T. R. Cripps

2008. Keniston, Kenneth. HEADS AND SEEKERS: DRUGS ON CAMPUS, COUNTER-CULTURES AND AMERICAN SOCIETY. *Am. Scholar 1968/69 38(1): 97-112.* Reports on drug use in American universities, focusing on both patterns and motives. The author's use of Gallup Polls and other data minimizes the incidence of campus drug use but finds the following distinct patterns: high use at elite schools and among liberal arts students; major usage among two groups, "heads" (frequent use by student members of a "counter-culture") and "seekers" (students who express philosophical yearnings for "meaning"). Both groups tend to reject what they see as hypocrisy and irrelevance in middle-class American life, while at the same time they become suspicious of careerism in their own universities and thus appear to reject intellect and to opt for an experiential life of immediacy. Their rejection of conventional society is encouraged by: 1) "stimulus flooding" - a numbing brought on by overcommunication by mass media; 2) "automatic affluence" - the indifference to economic pursuits as life goals, wealth having already been achieved by parents; and 3) "social and political disenchantment" - brought on by the apparent barrenness of political life, its presumed corruption, coincident with the growing racial exclusivity of the civil rights movement. The result is a campus culture that encourages personal small-group relationships, internalized drug experiences, and the rejection of deferred gratification in favor of immediate sensation.   T. R. Cripps

2009. King, Martin Luther, Jr. LETTER FROM A BIRMINGHAM JAIL. *Negro Hist. Bull. 1964 27(6): 156.* A letter reprinted from *Time* magazine.

S

2010. King, Martin Luther, Jr. LETTRE DE LA PRISON DE BIRMINGHAM [Letter from Birmingham jail]. *Esprit [France] 1964 32(1): 3-20.* The response of the Negro leader of the nonviolent movement for civil rights to the Alabama clergymen who blamed him and his followers for lack of Christian spirit. King points out that the Negroes can wait no longer for justice to be done and that his movement is intended to get the desired results but without violence. He emphasizes the Christian spirit of prayer and self-restraint in which their work is undertaken, and he urges that the churches come to the aid of justice.

Mother M. H. Quinlan

2011. King, Martin Luther, Jr. NONVIOLENCE THE ONLY WAY. *Indo-Asian Culture [India] 1964 13(1): 54-62.* An explanation of the philosophy of resistance by nonviolence, and of the reasons why King believed nonviolence to be the best tactic to use in the struggle to obtain civil rights for the Negroes of the United States. The article is published in an issue which is devoted to remembrance and appreciation of Jawaharlal Nehru, the late Indian leader.

A. K. Main

2012. Kizer, George A. FEDERAL AID TO EDUCATION: 1945-1963. *Hist. of Educ. Q. 1970 10(1): 84-102.* During the Truman administration (1945-52) the issues of Federal aid to private schools and the use of revenues from off-shore oil lands for educational purposes were the chief controversial questions. The first one resulted in stalemate; the second in a presidential veto of a bill intended to give part of these revenues to the States. Only two bills were passed - one providing for Federal aid to school construction, the other for compensation of educational expenses incurred in federally impacted areas. During the Eisenhower years, as a consequence of the 1954 desegregation decision of the Supreme Court, the opposition to Federal aid came from conservative Republicans and southern segregationists. In 1961, during President Kennedy's administration, education aid bills were again defeated on both the race and the religious issues. No change occurred in this controversy during the remainder of the Kennedy Presidency. 91 notes.

J. Herbst

2013. Knoll, Erwin. TEN YEARS OF DELIBERATE SPEED. *Am. Educ. 1964 1(1): 1-3.* Reviews efforts to implement the Supreme Court's *Brown vs. Board of Education* decision. "Because *de jure* school desegregation in the South is far from an accomplished fact, the region has not yet been confronted with the even more complex issue facing the North - *de facto* segregation based on discrimination in housing." Undocumented, illus., graph.

W. R. Boedecker

2014. Krause, P. Allen. RABBIS AND NEGRO RIGHTS IN THE SOUTH, 1954-1967. *Am. Jewish Arch. 1969 21(1): 20-47.* An ordained Reform rabbi, the author investigated the participation of Southern rabbis in the Negro civil rights movement through questionnaires, taped interviews, and correspondence (all now on file at the American Jewish Archives, Cincinnati). Though allowing for differences, the southern Christian reaction to the civil rights movement was often marked by "sullen defiance." As less than one percent of the population, many Jews in the South were only "frightened friends," few daring to be active integrationists. In some cases, rabbis active in the civil rights movement found themselves subjected to recriminations and "harassing acts" (such as a 1958 dynamite blast which caused 200 thousand dollars damage to an Atlanta synagogue). Reform rabbis generally have "played a respectable, if not overly important role" in the civil rights movement in the South.   J. Brandes

2015. Lanier, Nancy I. USIA'S COVERAGE OF CIVIL RIGHTS, 1963-65. *Journalism Q. 1967 44(2): 333-337.* Compares U.S. Information Agency reporting of 18 specific racial incidents with that of *The New York Times.* The theme stressed most often by the USIA was found to be the actions and reactions of the U.S. Government, with extensive coverage concentrated upon public reactions. Much background material was used and integration, biracialism, and interracial cooperation were stressed. Less attention was given to violence than in the *Times.* A careful balance was achieved between telling the truth and fulfilling the mission of a government spokesman. Documentation is in the articles and broadcasts themselves.   S. E. Humphreys

2016. Lassale, Jean-Pierre. LES DEVELOPPEMENTS RECENTS DU PROBLEME NOIR AUX ETATS-UNIS [Recent developments of the Negro problem in the United States]. *R. Internat. de Droit Comparé [France] 1964 16(3): 515-544.* At the beginning of the 20th century, Negro leaders hoped to solve the problem of race relations in the United States by raising the economic and cultural level of the Negroes. Today, there are two other plans: 1) that of a small minority, which seeks Negro autonomy, and 2) that of the great majority, whose goal is speedy integration, no longer through court action but through nonviolent social action. The Supreme Court has carried the principle of desegregation beyond the public educational system to other social areas in which there is some form of State action. In addition, congressional and presidential action has been necessary to protect Negro suffrage and to expedite integration of schools and public accommodations involved in interstate commerce. 67 notes.
                                                          J. S. Gassner

2017. Laue, James H. THE MOVEMENT: DISCOVERING WHERE IT'S AT AND HOW TO GET IT. *Urban and Social Change R. 1970 3(2): 6-11.* The civil rights movement of the early 1960's made some gains for blacks, such as desegregation of public accommodations and registration of black voters in the South. But it did not solve the black's fundamental socioeconomic problems. It did, however, sanction "protest as a legitimate activity for large groups of Americans who have heretofore been apolitical." Moving beyond the tactics and goals of the civil rights movement, the current "movement" demands "that significant group gains in a pluralistic society come not from the benevolence of the rulers, but from organization, negotiable power, self-advocacy, and confrontation." Its goals are more radical today, and its most important tactic is the use of the radical reform caucus within existing institutions and organizations. Also important is the new emphasis on ageism and sexism. 3 illus., 7 notes. R. D. Cohen

2018. Laursen, Johannes. NEGERSPØRGSMÅLET I USA [The Negro question in the United States]. *Økonomi og Politik [Denmark] 1964 38(1): 3-11.* Summary of events from 1954 to 1964 with some comments. R. E. Lindgren

2019. Lees, John D. THE IMPLEMENTATION OF THE CIVIL RIGHTS ACT OF 1964 - TITLE VI AND THE USE OF FEDERAL FUNDS. *British Assoc. for Am. Studies Bull. [Great Britain] 1965 (11): 16-23.* The Civil Rights Act of 1964 is proving more effective in combating discrimination than the presidential orders, departmental regulations, and court rulings that have been relied on since 1946. Under Title VI of the act every Federal agency providing financial assistance through grants, loans, or contracts, is required to eliminate discrimination in these programs on the grounds of race, color, or national origin. The impact of Title VI on Federal hospital and farm programs is discussed in detail. Based on published government documents; 10 notes.
D. J. Abramoske

2020. Leonard, Edward A. NONVIOLENCE AND VIOLENCE IN AMERI-CAN RACIAL PROTESTS, 1942-1967. *Rocky Mountain Social Sci. J. 1969 6(1): 10-22.* Contends that, after a period of nonviolence, racial protests seem to have returned to the traditional pattern - a pattern of violence accompanied by little real progress. The author tries to answer two questions: Why did a six-year period of large-scale protests (1960-65) go by without significant violence by Negroes? And why did nonviolence turn so quickly to violence just at the time that its efficacy was seemingly being proven beyond doubt? 27 notes.
R. F. Allen

2021. Lictman, Allan. THE FEDERAL ASSAULT AGAINST VOTING DIS-CRIMINATION IN THE DEEP SOUTH: 1957-1967. *J. of Negro Hist. 1969 54(4): 346-367.* The voting discrimination against Negroes, which began in the post-Reconstruction period of U.S. history, lasted well into the 20th century. As late as 1956 only 19 percent of the Negroes in Mississippi, Alabama, Louisiana, and Georgia were registered to vote, while 76 percent of the eligible white popula-tion was listed on the voting rolls. Congress finally responded to this situation in 1957 by adopting a voting rights act and by establishing the Civil Rights Division of the Department of Justice. The author traces the efforts of the Assistant Attorney Generals in the Civil Rights Division to eliminate unconstitu-tional denials of the right to vote from December 1957 through December 1967. During the first seven years of this period, the division did not succeed in securing the ballot for the southern Negro, but it did establish a factual record in the courts which provided the basis for the Voting Rights Act (1965). After the passage of this act, much resistance to the registration of Negroes in the South melted away, and the Division then concentrated on enforcement of school desegregation. Based on primary sources and oral interviews; 99 notes. R. S. Melamed

2022. Lieberson, Stanley and Silverman, Arnold R. THE PRECIPITANTS AND UNDERLYING CONDITIONS OF RACE RIOTS. *Am. Sociol. R. 1965 30(6): 887-898.* "The immediate precipitants and underlying conditions of 76 race riots in the U.S. between 1913 and 1963 are examined, using journalistic accounts and census data. The precipitants tend to be highly charged violations of one racial group by the other - rape, murder, assault, and police brutality. Since many of these precipitants are normally dealt with by established community institutions and because the response is not restricted to the alleged aggressor, various underlying conditions must be present. Hypotheses derived from earlier case studies and texts on collective behavior are examined to determine why riots occur where they do rather than in other cities of comparable size and location. Occupational and municipal government characteristics influence the occurrence of riots; demographic and housing characteristics do not. Riots seem most likely to occur in communities where institutional malfunctioning, cross-pressures, or other inadequacies are such that the city is unable to resolve racial problems."
J

2023. Lloyd, K. URBAN RACE RIOTS V. EFFECTIVE ANTI-DISCRIMINATION AGENCIES: AN END OR A BEGINNING? *Public Administration [Great Britain] 1967 45(spring): 43-53.* Urban race riots in the United States are the result of community failures in intergroup relations, yet it will be at least a decade before American institutions adjust to the Negro revolution. Practical alternatives to 10 years of race riots are therefore essential. It is here suggested that one stop-gap alternative could be "the effective public administration of widely suggested community anti-discrimination agencies." Analysis of existing Federal, State, and municipal agencies over the last 20 years teaches important lessons, the most significant being the necessity of developing effective prevention programs at the community level. The author concludes that "all community institutions - political, governmental, economic, educational, religious and family - must undergo basic long-range changes if the American dilemma in race relations is to be solved." Based on printed and secondary sources.
D. H. Murdoch

2024. Logan, Rayford W. AN ASSESSMENT OF CURRENT AMERICAN INFLUENCE IN AFRICA. *Ann. of the Am. Acad. of Pol. and Social Sci. 1966 366: 99-107.* Assessments of current American influence in Africa are hazardous. The fact that U.S. commitments are worldwide means that Africa has to compete for attention. Among liabilities are the sensitivity of African diplomats and American support of dictators such as Salazar. The recent disenchantment of most African nations with the Soviet Union, Red China, and Nationalist China may be counted a major victory for the United States. African leaders are becoming more realistic in assessing neocolonialism. Scholarly knowledge about Africa has increased rapidly and a number of organizations interested in Africa are attacking the inequalities imposed upon most American Negroes. On the domestic scene the Achilles heel of our foreign policy is the "Negro Problem." Unfortunately our information agencies apparently fail to offset the propaganda in Africa of our adversaries. Many Africans are more aware of Watts and other violent eruptions and the acquittal of many whites tried for murder in civil rights cases than they are of the progress in desegregation and discrimination. Our greatest current liabilities are Rhodesia and South Africa. E. P. Stickney

2025. Lopez Morales, Eduardo E. VOCES DE PROTESTA DE LOS NEGROS EN ESTADOS UNIDOS [Voices of protest among Negroes in the United States]. *Casa de las Americas [Cuba] 1966 6(36/37): 183-185.* A review of the Spanish translation of W. Haywood Burns' volume of the above title. The reviewer scores Burns for missing the basic problem facing the Negro in the United States: "it is not merely an ethnic crisis, even though on the surface it might seem that, but it has its basis in the capitalist exploitative system....[This economic system] having achieved its most reactionary and frankly Fascist level, now incorporates racial theories to maintain its predominance." Aside from this basic flaw, the volume is favorably reviewed. C. J. Fleener

2026. Lytle, Clifford M. THE HISTORY OF THE CIVIL RIGHTS BILL OF 1964. *J. of Negro Hist. 1966 51(4): 275-296.* Discusses the major factors which led to the passage of the 1964 Civil Rights Act. Pressure for effective civil rights legislation resulted from a series of freedom rides, sit-ins, and school crises which made Americans aware of the extent of racial discrimination. In Congress a bipartisan coalition overcame a number of institutional legislative barriers including the House Rules Committee and the southern filibuster. Prodded by the massive March-on-Washington, moderates in Congress joined more determined advocates of civil rights to pass the most comprehensive bill of its kind in history. Documented. L. Gara

2027. Mabee, Carleton. THE CRISIS IN NEGRO LEADERSHIP. *Antioch R. 1964 24(3): 365-378.* Discusses Negro leadership and the mistrust by middle-class Negroes of their leaders. The author gives a history of the demands of Negro leaders for equality and discusses the views of the optimistic school of Negroes concerning civil rights. D. F. Rossi

2028. Mabee, Carleton. VOTING IN THE BLACK BELT: STUDENT NON-VIOLENT COORDINATING COMMITTEE IN TENNESSEE AND MISSISSIPPI. *Negro Hist. Bull. 1963 27(3): 50-56.* Discusses the significant role of voter registration in the civil rights movement and relates in detail some of the major obstacles confronting those who are working on this program in Mississippi. L. Gara

2029. Manley, J. F. THE U.S. CIVIL RIGHTS ACT OF 1964. *Contemporary R. [Great Britain] 1965 206(1188): 10-13.* Analyzes the political problems involved in effecting the passage of the Civil Rights Bill (H.R. 7152), successfully to become the 1964 Civil Rights Act, with particular reference to the battle in the Senate. Undocumented. D. H. Murdoch

2030. Mann, Pete. "I GUESS WE'RE JUST IMPATIENT." *Am. Educ. 1966 2(3): 5-7.* Describes the peaceful desegregation of the Volusia County, Florida, public schools through the development of teacher-training programs designed to improve the quality of education in all of the district's schools. The program, "Personal Responsibility for Individual Development through Education" (PRIDE), included a demonstration school, reading center, observation program, instructional services, and a variety of inservice activities. Illus.

W. R. Boedecker

2031. Marx, Gary T. A DOCUMENT WITH A DIFFERENCE, "REPORT OF THE NATIONAL ADVISORY COMMISSION ON CIVIL DISORDERS." *Trans-action 1968 5(9): 56-58.* A review of the *Report of the National Advisory Commission on Civil Disorders.* The reviewer feels the most significant part of the report is its recommendations. No nation deserves freedom unless it can reach the causes of racial disorder. That part of the report which deals with what happened and why it took place is not new but merely a restatement of earlier reports. The facts of each riot, the similarities, and the differences are carefully noted, but there is little awareness of the relationship of the riot to the interaction between the black ghetto and the police. The reviewer differs with the Commission's conclusion that riots cannot bring about social change. In some instances the riots have led to an opening of communication which could lead to change. The work of this Commission will not be doubted or differed with by many. The Report tended to ignore the connection between the Vietnam War and the 1968 riots. A significant proportion of race riots have taken place during or immediately before or after wars. The conclusion of the Commission is a call to work for a national priority on the elimination of the causes of the riots.

A. Erlebacher

2032. Materassi, Mario. JAMES BALDWIN, UN PROFETA DEL NOSTRO TEMPO [James Baldwin, a prophet of our time]. *Il Ponte [Italy] 1966 22(3): 359-369.* Based on a conversation with James Baldwin when he was in Florence, Italy, in December 1965 for a fund-raising campaign for Negro civil rights. The author discusses some of Baldwin's writings and asserts that the Negro writer is one of those contemporary American novelists who are most deeply rooted in the traditions of the United States.

C. F. Delzell

2033. McCain, Ray. SPEAKING ON SCHOOL DESEGREGATION BY ATLANTA MINISTERS. *Southern Speech J. 1964 29(3): 256-262.* Describes the rhetorical efforts by Atlanta ministers to put desegregation into effect on 30 August 1961. The author analyzes sermons which developed the issue and concludes that the effort by the ministers contributed to the maintenance of order. 7 notes.

H. G. Stelzner

2034. McCoy, Donald R. and Ruetten, Richard T. THE CIVIL RIGHTS MOVEMENT: 1940-1954. *Midwest Q. 1969 11(1): 11-34.* Studies the Negro rights movement, pointing out its weakness before the 1930's and the legislation which brought about the great change between the years 1940-54. Franklin D. Roosevelt, and especially Eleanor Roosevelt, had principally a psychological effect on civil rights but the first government action was forced by A. Philip Randolph's "March on Washington Movement." To avoid the movement, Mr.

Roosevelt issued Executive Order 8802 which halted discrimination on all new defense contracts. The author traces the legislation and Supreme Court decisions through 1954 when progress slackened and little more happened. After moving ahead thus far, the expectations of Negroes were not met and the result was frustration. The author concludes that continuing unemployment, segregation, and discrimination underlie the frustrations causing the unprecedented abrasive civil rights movement of the 1960's. References to specific legislation.

G. H. G. Jones

2035. McKelvey, Blake. ROCHESTER'S NEAR NORTHEAST. *Rochester Hist.* *1967 29(2): 1-23.* Traces the history of the area in Rochester chosen for inclusion in the Demonstration Cities project. It has been a section of continued flux, swept by successive waves of new peoples from the original Irish settlers through the Germans and the East European Jews to the more recent Negro immigration. The city was perennially slow to recognize and deal with the problems of this district and what was done always turned out to be too little, too late. Pent-up frustrations in the Negro community exploded in the evening of 24 July 1964. The author (who wrote before the 1967 riots which also centered in the same neighborhood) ends on a note of hope that the Demonstration Cities project would help to settle some of the difficulties of a historically problem-ridden region of downtown Rochester. J. J. McCusker

2036. McLean, George A. MISSISSIPPI: THE CRISIS IN REVIEW. *South Atlantic Q. 1966 65(2): 279-288.* Review essay by a leading Mississippi newspaper published *(Tupelo Daily Journal)* of recent literature on the civil rights movement in Mississippi. Books reviewed include Walter Lord, *The Past That Would Not Die* (New York: Harper & Row, 1965); William Bradford Huie, *Three Lives for Mississippi* (New York: Trident Press, 1965); Russell H. Barrett, *Integration at Ole Miss* (Chicago: Quadrangle Press, 1965); Robert Canzonari, *I Do So Politely* (Boston: Houghton Mifflin, 1965); and *Letters from Mississippi.* The reviewer sees indications of subtle changes under way in Mississippi but emphasizes that reform must come gradually through persistent and patient effort rather than overnight. J. M. Bumsted

2037. Meier, August. NEGRO PROTEST MOVEMENTS AND ORGANIZATIONS. *J. of Negro Educ. 1963 32(4): 437-450.* Discusses the role of NAACP, CORE, SCLC, and SNCC in the period from 1950 to 1963.

S. C. Pearson, Jr.

2038. Merton, Thomas. DIE SCHWARZE REVOLUTION IN AMERIKA [The Black revolution in America]. *Dokumente [West Germany] 1964 20(2): 132-138.* Criticizes the white American's failure "to think black," i.e., to grasp the true dimensions of the American racial problem as experienced by the Negro. While the blacks want to offer to the whites a true message of salvation, the latter are so blinded that they overlook the dangerous risk of disregarding this offer. The black message, as put forth by Martin Luther King, James Baldwin, and others is God's message calling on white society to repent before it is too late and to atone for its manifold sins committed in the past against the "lower races" in many parts of the world. Undocumented except for two long quotations from James Baldwin's *The Fire Next Time.*   G. P. Bassler

2039. Meyer, Philip. AFTERMATH OF MARTYRDOM: NEGRO MILI-TANCY AND MARTIN LUTHER KING. *Public Opinion Q. 1969 33(2): 160-173.* Since *The Miami Herald* had conducted a survey designed to measure militancy and readiness for violence before the assassination of Martin Luther King, Jr., "a base was available for a pretest-posttest design to test the theory that the King assassination caused increased Negro militancy." Survey results did not support this hypothesis; in fact, King's death may have strengthened "the militant middle" and the cause of nonviolence. Since 55 percent of the survey area residents in the original sample said they read *The Miami Herald* regularly, the original survey itself "may have encouraged the expression of Negro militancy along conventional lines," by making Negroes aware of how widely their views were shared. 530 Miami Negroes were originally surveyed and a subsample of 186 were re-interviewed. 5 tables, 22 notes.   D. J. Trickey

2040. Millard, Thomas L. THE NEGRO AND SOCIAL PROTEST. *J. of Negro Educ. 1963 32(1): 92-98.* Argues that protest should not be an end in itself, that "the Negro must ultimately reject the increasing obsolescence of protest per se and seek his fulfillment in the virile standards of his own resources and creativity," and that "preparing the Negro for participation in first class citizenship is perhaps the greatest dilemma facing Negro leadership with the possible exception of his segregated existence - the very thing he is trying to overcome."
                                                                        S. C. Pearson, Jr.

2041. Misner, Gordon E. THE RESPONSE OF POLICE AGENCIES. *Ann. of the Am. Acad. of Pol. and Social Sci. 1969 382: 109-119.* "Police response to the protest of the 1960's has not been monolithic. Although one can and must generalize, it must be borne in mind that police response not only has varied geographically, but has also been affected by differences in administrative style among agencies within certain regions and by the time factor: the results of one confrontation can have either a positive or negative effect on police procedures in a later one. Although the substance, tactics, and strategies of protest movements have changed, police agencies are precisely those institutions most resistant to change in operating procedures and administrative styles. One reason for this conservatism is lack of experience in dealing with mass protest groups; another is the long-standing hostile relationship between police agencies and minorities, civil rights groups, and social protest in general, a relationship which indicates that police reflect the basic conservatism of much of the public. The confrontations between police and Negro-protest-movement groups during the struggle for civil rights illustrate the problem, especially those which occurred during the period of nonviolent direct action and during the sporadic riots in various urban ghettos from 1964 to 1968. That effective police action can prevent the eruption of violence without interfering with the rights of individual citizens was proven by the success of police strategy in dealing with protest groups at the Republican

National Convention in 1964. Generally, however, the usually conservative operating posture of the nation's police when dealing with protest groups reflects the posture of the political system itself."   J

2042. Morsell, John A. LEGISLATION AND ITS IMPLEMENTATION. *J. of Negro Educ. 1965 34(3): 232-238.* Discusses legislation in the Southern States designed to prevent or make difficult integration of schools, legislation in Northern States designed to prevent or discourage segregation and discrimination, and Federal legislation in the Civil Rights Act of 1964 designed to protect the rights of all citizens in education.   S. C. Pearson, Jr.

2043. Moynihan, Daniel P. THE PRESIDENT AND THE NEGRO: THE MOMENT LOST. *Commentary 1967 43(2): 31-45.* "It appears that the nation may be in the process of reproducing the tragic events of the Reconstruction: giving to Negroes the forms of legal equality, but withholding the economic and political resources which are the bases of social equality." In June 1965 President Johnson gave an address at Howard University which was revolutionary in its scope and new proposals to go beyond the issue of legal civil rights for Negroes to find ways of bringing them into the mainstream of American society. This new departure was influenced primarily by a report prepared by the author for the Department of Labor, entitled *The Negro Family: The Case for National Action* ("Moynihan report"). The report spoke of the paramount importance of somehow reforming Negro family life by providing "the economic stability that was clearly the basis of family stability." Unfortunately, the civil rights movement seized upon the Moynihan report rather than the initiative offered by the President, and found in its emphasis upon the poor family life of lower-class Negroes a kind of condescending racism. A tremendous furor developed, and, as a consequence, the movement was unable to take advantage of the opportunity offered; instead, the conference called by the President, "To Fulfill These Rights," was spent in ratifying old clichés which accomplished nothing. Meanwhile, the Watts riots had destroyed the image of the nonviolent, suffering, and deserving Negro, and the 1966 elections closed the doors on further progress at this time.
A. K. Main

2044. Murphy, Walter F. DEEDS UNDER A DOCTRINE: CIVIL LIBERTIES IN THE 1963 TERM. *Am. Pol. Sci. R. 1965 59(1): 64-79.* Examines decisions of the Supreme Court on civil liberties, divisions among the justices, doctrinal implications, and possible political effects. Under "Deeds," are considered cases in criminal justice, freedom of expression and association, apportionment, and discrimination against insular minorities. The latter term applies to generally beleaguered minority groups. Decisions were heavily libertarian, strongly supporting civil rights; Justices John Harlan and Hugo Black were less libertarian than their associates, but these libertarians control the Court. Urban political power and Negro political influence will increase. Documented, tables, 103 notes.   H. G. Warren

2045. Mutignon, Pierre. LE PROBLEME NOIR AUX ETATS-UNIS DEPUIS LE CIVIL RIGHTS ACT DU 2 JUILLET 1964 [The Negro problem in the

United States since the Civil Rights Act of 2 July 1964]. *R. Internat. de Droit Comparé [France] 1966 18(3): 669-699.* The gaps in previous legislation and judicial decisions led to the Civil Rights Act of 1964 and the Voting Rights Act of 1965. The former strengthened Negro suffrage in the South, provided for desegregation of public facilities, gave the U.S. Attorney General increased power of enforcement, extended the life of the Civil Rights Commission, and forbade discrimination in labor relations. Its constitutionality was upheld in two U.S. Supreme Court decisions. The Voting Rights Act, which restricted the use of the literacy test under certain conditions and provided for Federal registration of colored voters, was subsequently upheld by the Supreme Court. An attempt to circumvent the 24th amendment was struck down by the Supreme Court, which nullified the poll tax for State elections in a later decision. 73 notes.

J. S. Gassner

2046. Myers, Frank E. CIVIL DISOBEDIENCE AND ORGANIZATIONAL CHANGE: THE BRITISH COMMITTEE OF 100. *Pol. Sci. Q. 1971 86(1): 92-112.* Analyzes and compares the composition and behavior of civil disobedience groups in Britain and America. The groups discussed are the British Committee of 100, founded 22 October 1960, which was the rebellious offspring of the Campaign for Nuclear Disarmament (CND), organized in 1958, and the Direct Action Committee against Nuclear War (DAC), formed in 1957 as a pacifist group pledged to civil disobedience, and the Student Nonviolent Coordinating Committee (SNCC) and the Congress of Racial Equality (CORE) in the United States, both of which developed in the early 1960's as challengers to the National Association for the Advancement of Colored People (NAACP). Concludes that 1) groups adopting illegal actions as explicit tactics normally originate as factions of larger protest organizations, 2) such groups tend, with the passage of time, to draw younger rather than older persons into positions of leadership, and 3) they are likely, at least in the eyes of their followers, to fall below expectations in achieving their aims. 36 notes.   D. D. Cameron

2047. Nelson, Harold A. ON LIBERALS AND THE CURRENT RACIAL SITUATION. *Phylon 1964 25(4): 389-398.* Recent attacks by Negroes and some white liberals on "white liberals" encouraged the author to consider several facets of the present racial struggle which he feels are often neglected.

S. C. Pearson, Jr.

2048. Oppenheimer, Martin. INSTITUTIONS OF HIGHER LEARNING AND THE 1960 SIT-INS: SOME CLUES FOR SOCIAL ACTION. *J. of Negro Educ. 1963 32(3): 286-288.* During 1960 sit-ins tended to occur most often and to have the greatest chance of success in urban areas with a Negro institution of higher education and with a lower percentage of Negro population.

S. C. Pearson, Jr.

2049. Oppenheimer, Martin. THE SOUTHERN STUDENT MOVEMENT: YEAR I. *J. of Negro Educ. 1964 33(4): 396-403.* Traces the background for the sit-in movement, its critical period of development from February through October 1960, and its institutionalization thereafter. "The Southern Negro Sit-In

Movement thus passed through a life-cycle similar to that found in many other movements, from an informal, less organized form to a formal, structured form."

S. C. Pearson, Jr.

2050. Oppenheimer, Martin. THE SOUTHERN STUDENT SIT-INS: INTRA-GROUP RELATIONS AND COMMUNITY CONFLICT. *Phylon 1966 27(1): 20-26.* Discusses sociological theories of conflict in terms of the southern sit-in movement of 1960. The author believes that singing, joking, and worship serve to unify the sit-in movement and to provide an avenue for expression of hostility. He traces interactive relationships from the emergence of conflict through a series of unfolding stages: the incipient stage characterized by spontaneity, the counter-active phase with the emergence of concensus among whites for dealing with Negroes, the *détente* or cooling-off period, the reorganizational stage, and the slowdown phase. Based on data used in a 1963 University of Pennsylvania dissertation; 11 notes.

S. C. Pearson, Jr.

2051. Orbell, John M. PROTEST PARTICIPATION AMONG SOUTHERN NEGRO COLLEGE STUDENTS. *Am. Pol. Sci. R. 1967 61(2): 446-456.* "The data on which the present study is based are drawn from a survey of Negro college students conducted in 1962, about two years after the sit-in movement began, by Professors Donald R. Matthews and James W. Prothro....The data suggest that at least two college variables have a significant impact on protest, independent of all other factors....the manner in which the college is supported - by state or private finance - and its quality....As might be expected, the data leave no doubt that the higher quality colleges recruit from the higher status part of the Negro population, but they also show that such high status is strongly associated with protest participation....The data also confirm the suspicion that most high-quality Negro colleges in the South are private and that most low-quality ones are state-run....by focusing on one factor - the structure of intergroup relations - some advance can be made toward integrating various theoretical propositions about the origin of the Negro protest movement." 6 tables, 41 notes.

D. D. Cameron

2052. Page, Benjamin. EL MOVIMIENTO ESTUDIANTIL EN LOS ESTADOS UNIDOS [The student movement in the United States]. *Casa de las Americas [Cuba] 1967 7(43): 13-24.* At the present time, American students have lost their characteristic apathy and entered into political action. They have become, for the first time, dissatisfied with "the American way of life." This is a result of two developments: the rebellion of white, middle-class youth against the ideals, values, and modes of their class; and the blacks, traditionally excluded from the middle class of America, have formed liberation movements. These two factors have developed independently and have not yet realized their areas of common interest. The author predicts that these youth movements will merge and grow, and he views these events as excellent portents for the future.

C. J. Fleener

2053. Paige, Jeffery M. POLITICAL ORIENTATION AND RIOT PARTICIPATION. *Am. Sociol. R. 1971 36(5): 810-820.* "The relationship between political trust, political efficacy and riot participation is analyzed in a survey of 237 black males in Newark, New Jersey. Self-reported riot participants are more likely to be found among the dissident - those high on political efficacy but low on political trust, rather than among the alienated - those who are both distrustful and ignorant of government. When compared to civil rights activists and voters, rioters are similar in their generally higher levels of political information but lower in trust of the government. Rioting appears to be a disorganized form of political protest rather than an act of personal frustration, or social isolation, as has been suggested in some past research." J

2054. Paletz, David L. and Dunn, Robert. PRESS COVERAGE OF CIVIL DISORDERS: A CASE STUDY OF WINSTON-SALEM, 1967. *Public Opinion Q. 1969 33(3): 328-345.* Study of press coverage of a 1967 four day riot in Winston-Salem, precipitated by the death of a Negro who had been hit on the head with a billy club while attempting to flee arrest. The tone for the reporting by the *Winston-Salem Journal* was set months before the riot when city officials were quoted as saying trouble was more likely to come from "thugs and hoodlums" who see a chance to profit from looting than from Negroes staging a racial protest. "The fact that Negroes were rioting was never mentioned in a headline,..." though highway patrolmen and National Guardsmen were called in before the riot was quelled. The *Journal* appeared motivated by a desire to curb violence and reduce racial tension; however, in diminishing riots the news media does not "contribute to an understanding of the nature of Afro-American grievances or of conditions in that community." 56 notes.   D. J. Trickey

2055. Palmer, R. Roderick. "THE NEGRO'S QUEST FOR FREEDOM AND THE GOOD LIFE." *J. of Negro Educ. 1965 34(1): 11-16.* Urges the combination of the science of social action with the instinct for social action in order that the attainment of civil rights by American Negroes may lead to "the long-term harvest of social, political, and economic reforms made possible by the possession and use of those rights." Such reforms will create an interracial community in the United States.   S. C. Pearson, Jr.

2056. Pastusiak, Longin. DYSKUSJA WOKOL USTAWODASTWA PRZE-CIW "BUNTOM" W USA [Discussion of the antiriot legislation in the United States]. *Państwo i Prawo [Poland] 1968 23(11): 797-801.* Assumes that a campaign against all leftist and liberal elements is mounting. Symptomatic of it is a number of legislative proposals in Congress dealing with the problem of riots and related matters. Among them are: a bill which defines treason in the time of peace; an antiriot bill by Representative William C. Cramer of Florida adopted by the House of Representatives; and an antiriot rider by Senators Frank Lausche and Strom Thurmond to a civil rights bill. The author believes that there is a sufficient number of antiriot laws on the statute books. Quoting the arguments of the oppositon, he maintains that the fallacious premise of the present antiriot legislative proposals is the equation of the struggle of the Negroes with the racist, extremist organizations. Instead of pacifying, the present antiriot legislation may further antagonize the racial groups. Note.   T. N. Cieplak

2057. Pastusiak, Longin. O SYTUACJI SPOLECZNEJ W USA [On the social situation in the United States of America]. *Nowe Drogi [Poland] 1968 22(233): 130-143.* Maintains that the present social crisis in the United States is a result of complex causes, old and new. Its intensification coincided with the escalation of the war in Vietnam. The latter is also responsible for other ills such as the loss of powers by Congress, acute political division in the country, and the fiasco of the Great Society. An increased number of protesters and a radicalization of their programs are characteristic of the recent stage of the crisis. "Resurrection City" and the stormy conventions of some of the Negro organizations prove this. The growth and the radicalization of the student movement in the 1960's is attributed to the expansion of the institutions of higher learning and the militarization of most scientific research. Platforms of both national parties are believed to be too general to provide adquate recommendations for the future solution of this crisis. 17 notes. T. N. Cieplak

2058. Patrick, Clarence H. DESEGREGATION IN A SOUTHERN CITY: A DESCRIPTIVE REPORT. *Phylon Q. 1964 25(3): 263-269.* A description of the modification in traditional patterns of accommodation between Negroes and whites in Winston-Salem, North Carolina. After a community race relations survey was made in 1946 a bi-racial council was established; and from 1946 to 1960 numerous and significant changes were made in customs involving interracial relations, without incident. Since the beginning of sit-in protests in 1960 many additional changes have taken place, and Winston-Salem remains a community in which desegregation is generally well accepted and racial conflict is minimal. S. C. Pearson, Jr.

2059. Peiser, G. L'AIDE AMERICAINE A L'AFRIQUE NOIRE [American aid to Black Africa]. *Ann. Africaines [Senegal] 1965: 95-120.* American aid to Black Africa represents a small percentage of the total American aid program and of all external aid to the area during the period 1946-65. The author discusses some of the reasons for this: the lesser strategic importance of Africa, the preponderant role played by former colonial powers of Europe, and the neutralist and state socialist policies of some African States. American aid has concentrated in education, agriculture, and health, and particularly in English-speaking countries. Beginning with President Kennedy and his Secretary of State for African Affairs G. Mennen Williams, American interest and aid to Africa increased, and the United States departed from its earlier policy of viewing neutralism as immoral. Negro protests in America are related with African independence movements, and American Negroes are seen taking an increasing interest in Africa. Based on Agency for International Development reports. Tables list American economic and military aid for each Black African country from 1946 to 1964. 17 notes. B. Harris

2060. Petrof, John V. THE EFFECT OF STUDENT BOYCOTTS UPON THE PURCHASING HABITS OF NEGRO FAMILIES IN ATLANTA, GEORGIA. *Phylon 1963 24(3): 266-270.* A survey of 594 Negro families in

Atlanta, Georgia, disclosed that after a student boycott of downtown merchants many Negro families failed to return to previous shopping patterns and that their expenditures in downtown Atlanta decreased significantly.   S. C. Pearson, Jr.

2061. Pettigrew, Thomas F. ACTUAL GAINS AND PSYCHOLOGICAL LOSSES: THE NEGRO AMERICAN PROTEST. *J. of Negro Educ. 1963 32(4): 493-506.* Surveys gains of the Negro population in the 1950's and notes that they appear significant only when compared with previous Negro conditions. The author suggests that the Negro protest will continue to grow in intensity and depth.   S. C. Pearson, Jr.

2062. Pfautz, Harold W. THE NEW "NEW NEGRO": EMERGING AMERI-CAN. *Phylon 1963 24(4): 360-368.* During and since World War II there has emerged a new "New Negro" in open revolt against the social patterns of segregation and discrimination. The author concludes that conflict is necessary for assimilation and that "the new 'New Negro' was not only born in conflict, but he will continue to mature only in the crucible of conflict. Sociologically speaking...conflict is inherently a socializing process."   S. C. Pearson, Jr.

2063. Piety, Harold R. REVOLUTION COMES TO EAST ST. LOUIS. *FO-CUS/Midwest 1968 6(42): 12-17.* Studies the organization and activity of militants in East St. Louis, particularly the foundation of the Black Economic Union. The use of terrorism by the militants has led to a hardening of attitudes both among whites and among black militants. 3 illus.   R. Howell

2064. Pinard, Maurice, Kirk, Jerome, and von Eschen, Donald. PROCESSES OF RECRUITMENT IN THE SIT-IN MOVEMENT. *Public Opinion Q. 1969 33(3): 355-369.* Negroes are often a minority in "their" movements and the most deprived are essentially absent from the ranks. One reason for the reluctance of the deprived to join movements is the absence of some radical ideology to translate grievances into political action, but once the deprived join they are among the most active members. The authors distributed questionnaires to some 500 to 600 members of civil rights organizations staging "a demonstration at eating places along U.S. Route 40 between Baltimore and Wilmington [in 1961]," getting 60 to 80 percent response. The data supported their hypotheses; "alienation rooted in deprivation leads to retreatism,...[while] alienation rooted in ideology will produce rebellious tendencies,...." 6 tables, 30 notes.   D. J. Trickey

2065. Polgar, Denes. AMERIKAI PROBLEMAK AZ ELNOKVALASZTAS UTAN [American problems after the presidential elections]. *Társadalmi Szemle [Hungary] 1964 19(12): 79-82.* A discussion of problems facing President Johnson after his victory. Among these domestic problems: the dollar flow, the balancing of the budget, the depression expected to take place in May 1965, the Negro and civil rights question, the crime wave, the plight of the farmers, increased Social Security benefits, and the war on poverty. No meaningful solution can be found to these problems unless the government cuts back military spending significantly and shuts down many of its bases located in foreign countries. In foreign affairs a general change in the Vietnamese, Chinese, Atlantic, Latin-American, and African policies needs to be made. Although the author holds it unlikely that Johnson will makes these changes, he expects the President to continue the policy of peaceful coexistence.   I. Volgyes

2066. Ponder, Henry. AN EXAMPLE OF THE ALTERNATIVE COST DOC-TRINE APPLIED TO RACIAL DISCRIMINATION. *J. of Negro Educ. 1966 35(1): 42-47.* Surveys the loss to downtown merchants in Petersburg, Virginia, during a six-week "economic withdrawal" by Negroes. The author assumes that the withdrawal was 80 percent effective and that downtown merchants sustained a loss in business of 1,296,745 dollars as the alternative cost of discrimination. He concludes that the businessmen of Petersburg and elsewhere have more to gain from integration than they stand to lose because of it.   S. C. Pearson, Jr.

2067. Porambo, Ron. NOT WHEN THEY DID HIM LIKE THAT. *Washington Monthly 1971 3(8): 40-48.* Describes the lack of real change in Newark since the riots in 1967. Despite the election of a black mayor and a massive influx of money, the situation of the blacks and the poor has not changed. Centers on two killings in the city, the reaction to them by the press and administration, and the attitude of the people concerned.   S. R. Duguid

2068. Puryear, Paul L. EQUITY POWER AND THE SCHOOL DESEGRE-GATION CASES. *Harvard Educ. R. 1963 33(4): 421-438.* In implementing the Supreme Court decision on school desegregation, Federal courts have been hesitant to order school boards to take positive action to eliminate all forms of segregation, and have frequently contented themselves with a board's action to allow individual students to escape segregation. The courts' caution plus the magnitude of the problem account for the slow pace of desegregation in the South. Nevertheless, the courts have barred the States' police power as a means of avoiding desegregation, when used to evade desegregation, and have encouraged boards to adopt the "track system" to avoid lowering of academic standards. Private school systems which receive public support through tuition grants or other means have been under attack by the courts.   J. Herbst

2069. Racine, D. A. HOWARD, LA PLUS GRANDE UNIVERSITE NOIRE AMERICAINE [Howard, the largest American black university]. *Esprit [France] 1969 37(5): 776-789.* The 1969 actions of Howard University students against the administration featured many of the same slogans of world student unrest - more autonomy, more student responsibilities for administrative decisions, and a larger role in deciding their own destinies. Because Howard University is the largest black university in the United States, the demonstrations had a great significance for black American views of the United States as a whole, and for the black generation conflict.   G. F. Jewsbury

2070. Randolph, A. Phillip. FROM CIVIL RIGHTS TO SOCIAL REVOLU-TION. *J.: Division of Higher Educ. United Church of Christ 1968 7(2): 12-16.* The civil rights revolution is a deepening crisis for the movement and the movers.

The change in aim has resulted in a proliferation of "movements," leaders, slogans, and doctrines. This has caused an uncoordinated effort so weakened as to lose effectiveness. No one group has the answer, and even the power of the vote is only the beginning of the effort. The young black potential leader should reject the revolutionary and the concept of black separatism, and should work on the proposition that change can be made through the democratic process.

C. W. Ohrvall

2071. Rathbun, John W. MARTIN LUTHER KING: THE THEOLOGY OF SOCIAL ACTION. *Am. Q. 1968 20(1): 38-53.* Examines the theological basis for King as a social reformer. His ideas, which are legitimately intellectual, are derived from four sources: the Social Gospel of Walter Rauschenbusch, the Protestant Neo-Orthodoxy of Reinhold Niebuhr and Paul Tillich, Personalism taught at Boston University, and Gandhi's concept of nonviolent love. King's synthesis of these four sources supported his civil rights activities. He was a fundamentalist, but this was severely modified by his background and education. Laws may be broken, said King, if they are unjust laws which do not conform to eternal, natural law. Jesus, said King, was a true revolutionary who brought peace as a "presence of justice" instead of an "absence of tension." The church also must be revolutionary to counteract evil and bring about social justice. King's theology of social action foresaw complete, unprejudiced equality based on natural rights and privileges. Based on published materials; 30 notes.

D. E. Mayo

2072. Reichman, Stanley. TEACHING ABOUT CIVIL RIGHTS AND THE LOS ANGELES RIOTS. *California Social Sci. R. 1965 5(1): 11-13.* High school students in California have received dogmatic and extremely simplified answers to the problems posed by the Los Angeles riots of 1965. Teachers have the responsibility of reminding their students that "truth is an elusive quarry, especially truth in the political-economic-social order...the Negro minority is in a very different and far more complex position in American society than were the other minorities that were eventually assimilated."

F. Rotondaro

2073. Remington, Robin Alison. MOSCOW, PEKING AND BLACK AMERICAN REVOLUTION. *Survey [Great Britain] 1970 (74/75): 237-252.* Discusses the differences and reasons for these differences in the attitudes of Moscow and Peking toward black Americans. China's attitude is designed as a "stick with which to beat the Soviets" and as an integral part of the revolutionary image China hopes to project toward the Third World. The Soviets, being more cautious, did not shift their position from self-determination to black integration until 1962. In illustrating the changes in attitudes, the author focuses on the Black Power movement, the riots in the summer of 1967, and the assassination of Martin Luther King., Jr. In conclusion, notes that the argument is a small part of the old Lenin-Roy debate and that both countries put their self-interest first. Moreover, the danger is not that blacks contact Moscow and Peking, but that this contact will be magnified out of proportion and will create the very conditions that will tend to increase such contact. 50 notes.

R. B. Valliant

2074. Riddick, Floyd M. and Zweben, Murray. THE EIGHTY-EIGHTH CONGRESS: SECOND SESSION. *Western Pol. Q. 1965 18(2, pt. 1): 334-349.* This session convened 7 January 1964 and the hope and aim were for an early adjournment to make ready for the party conventions. Adjournment did not come, however, until 3 October, one month before the general election. President Lyndon Johnson laid before the Congress a very ambitious program and urged its speedy enactment. Only part of the program was enacted and little of it within his suggested time schedule. His suggestions included measures devoted to poverty, health, transportation, foreign aid, and appropriations related specifically to Vietnam. The political and organizational structure of the two Houses remained almost identical with that of the previous session. The Civil Rights Act of 1964 - finally enacted - was the most debated bill in history - 10 days in the House and 82 in the Senate. In connection with it, cloture was invoked successfully - for the first time in connection with civil rights and the sixth time in history. Certain Senate rule changes - aimed at speeding procedure and releasing time for committees - were made. The Congress agreed on appropriations of over 94 billion dollars plus 11.8 billion dollars permanent appropriations; the total was 4.1 billion dollars below administration requests. Almost all of the President's 55 thousand appointments were approved by the Senate. As a whole, Congress approved 57.6 percent of the administration's 217 legislative proposals, including civil rights, tax reduction, and antipoverty. On the other hand, foreign aid was cut nearly eight percent, medicare did not pass, efforts to change the immigration quota system were thwarted, water pollution control failed, and extension of minimum wages was defeated. The President signed 408 measures into public law and 195 into private law. Three tables elucidate the text, as follows: 1) A comparison of activities of 1st and 2nd sessions of the 88th Congress; 2) Pages of debate in the *Congressional Record,* from minimum of three to maximum of one thousand or more devoted to bills debated, from the 85th through the 88th Congress; 3) Attendance, through vote records, divided by Republicans and Democrats, in 1962, 1963, and 1964, the data showing small variation, from a low of 79 percent to a high of 87 percent. 130 notes.   H. Aptheker

2075. Riddick, George E. BLACK POWER IN THE WHITE PERSPECTIVE. *Mennonite Life 1967 22(1): 29-35.* Discusses the Negro freedom movement and the current position of Negroes in American life. Economically, educationally, and politically the Negro is still tragically behind his white contemporary. No serious observer of the urban Negro ghetto "can seriously entertain anything less than the possibility of a total conflagration" in the immediate future. Negroes understand that frequently the white establishment "does nothing apart from the presence of substantial conflict which in effect bargains the community into a crisis." The author concludes with observations on the role of the Christian churches in the racial struggle. "The church is not under obligation to support every segment of the black power movement," but it must accept the idea of creative conflict and allay the fears of the white community.
                    D. J. Abramoske

2076. Roberts, Adam. MARTIN LUTHER KING AND NON-VIOLENT RESISTANCE. *World Today [Great Britain] 1968 24(6): 226-236.* After Gandhi, Martin Luther King, Jr., was the most important proponent of nonviolent action in this century. In the origins of nonviolent resistance, the 1955 bus boycott in Montgomery, Alabama, was the crucial event. Nonviolent resistance requires a degree of unified organization and leadership to be effective; in this respect, the local and accidental beginnings of the civil rights movement have been a source of weakness. There is speculation on both the nature of the civil rights movement and the future of nonviolent resistance after the assassination of King. Documented from printed sources, including King's works.   R. Howell

2077. Rose, Arnold M., special ed. THE NEGRO PROTEST. *Ann. of the Am. Acad. of Pol. and Social Sci. 1965 357: 1-126.*

Rose, Arnold M. THE AMERICAN NEGRO PROBLEM IN THE CONTEXT OF SOCIAL CHANGE, pp. 1-17.

Thompson, Daniel C. THE RISE OF THE NEGRO PROTEST, pp. 18-29.

Hill, Herbert. RACIAL INEQUALITY IN EMPLOYMENT: THE PATTERNS OF DISCRIMINATION, pp. 30-47.

Sindler, Allan. PROTEST AGAINST THE POLITICAL STATUS OF THE NEGRO, pp. 48-54.

Murray, Pauli. PROTEST AGAINST THE LEGAL STATUS OF THE NEGRO, pp. 55-64.

Cothran, Tilman C. THE NEGRO PROTEST AGAINST SEGREGATION IN THE SOUTH, pp. 65-72.

Miller, Loren. THE PROTEST AGAINST HOUSING SEGREGATION, pp. 73-79.

Batchelder, Alan B. ECONOMIC FORCES SERVING THE ENDS OF THE NEGRO PROTEST, pp. 80-88.

Record, Jane Cassels and Record, Wilson. IDEOLOGICAL FORCES AND THE NEGRO PROTEST, pp. 89-96.

Morsell, John A. THE NATIONAL ASSOCIATION FOR THE ADVANCEMENT OF COLORED PEOPLE AND ITS STRATEGY, pp. 97-101.

Young, Whitney M. THE URBAN LEAGUE AND ITS STRATEGY, pp. 102-107.

Dunbar, Leslie W. THE SOUTHERN REGIONAL COUNCIL, pp. 108-112.

Rich, Marvin. THE CONGRESS OF RACIAL EQUALITY AND ITS STRATEGY, pp. 113-118.

Laue, James H. THE CHANGING CHARACTER OF THE NEGRO PROTEST, pp. 119-126.

To the social scientist - but not to the ordinary Negro - the effect of the organized protest movement and of the social changes operating throughout American society has been to bring about changes generally in accord with the major goals of the movement. Even if deliberate discriminations are eliminated, the Negro has the handicaps of past discriminations to contend with, as well as the changes wrought by automation and the slowness of schools in teaching for a society in rapid change. "The conflict between the Negro protest and its reaction will generate more violence," often irrational. The major change of the past decade is a shift of initiative from the hands of a relatively few professional desegregationists to large numbers of average citizens who are now willing to confront the segregated system through direct action. The movement is now turning to an essential political phase, requiring the major civil rights groups to coordinate their programs. E. P. Stickney

2078. Rudwick, Elliott M. FIFTY YEARS OF RACE RELATIONS IN EAST ST. LOUIS: THE BREAKING DOWN OF WHITE SUPREMACY. *Midcontinent Am. Studies J. 1965 6(1): 3-13.* Traces the history of the Negro movement for equality in East St. Louis, from the bloody race riots of 1917 to the nonviolent demonstrations of the present decade. The race riots of 1917 were initiated by white supremacists who resented the Negro for political and economic reasons, and from that time until the 1950's, the memory of that riot was used to keep Negroes on the defensive. The Negro is on the offensive today through the use of various nonviolent techniques which lessen the possibility of race riots and provide for the rectification of grievances. Racial violence will reoccur only when reasonable alternatives are exhausted, and then will be led by Negroes rather than whites. B. M. Morrison

2079. Rustin, Bayard. FROM PROTEST TO POLITICS: THE FUTURE OF THE CIVIL RIGHTS MOVEMENT. *Commentary 1965 39(2): 25-31.* Asserts that the civil rights movement is now (and should be) moving from the stage of single-issue protest, during which the legal foundations of racism crumbled, to the stage of the exertion of political power, during which the Negroes must present a truly radical program to effect a "qualitative transformation of fundamental institutions." Negroes cannot obtain equality within the present framework of political and economic relations; therefore, they must press for "full employment, abolition of slums, the reconstruction of our educational system, new definitions of work and leisure." Negroes cannot achieve this alone. They must create an effective political majority from the available progressive forces - Negroes, organized labor, liberals, and religious groups. R. J. Moore

2080. Rustin, Bayard. THE WATTS "MANIFESTO" AND THE MC CONE REPORT. *Commentary 1966 41(3): 29-35.* The Watts riots of August 1965 in Los Angeles were in many ways a "manifesto" of the American Negro community, bringing to light for the first time the massive despair and hatred that continue to brew in northern ghettos despite civil rights legislation and the "war on poverty." The report prepared by the commission under the direction of John A. McCone attempted to answer the "manifesto" constructively. The McCone Report "is a bold departure from the standard government paper on social problems," going beyond the "mere recital of statistics" to discuss the real problems - unemployment, inadequate schools, dilapidated housing. Unfortunately, after this optimistic beginning, the report fails to propose any real solutions, instead hopefully recommending "existing programs which have already shown themselves to be inadequate." The results of such lack of vision "may very well continue to teach impoverished, segregated, and ignored Negroes that the only way they can get the ear of America is to rise up in violence." A. K. Main

2081. Sargent, Lesli W., Carr, Wiley, and McDonald, Elizabeth. SIGNIFICANT COVERAGE OF INTEGRATION BY MINORITY GROUP MAGAZINES. *J. of Human Relations 1965 13(4): 484-491.* Reports the results of two content analysis studies. Comparing the use of photographs in *Life* and *Ebony* in January 1962 and December 1963, the authors found that both magazines were favorable to integration but that *Life* presented a much more graphic picture of integration violence than did *Ebony*. "It appears that *Ebony* does not propose to build up the Negro as a martyr in the integration struggle and is not attempting to incite violence." In a second study of racial coverage in two Catholic journals, *America* and *Commonweal*, it was found that following the publication of *Pacem in Terris* (1965) the encyclical of Pope John XXIII, "there was a significant increase in the percentage of magazine space devoted to the subject and a highly significant increase in the magazines' advocacy of social justice ideas expressed in the Pope's message." 4 notes.   D. J. Abramoske

2082. Scoble, Harry M. THE MC CONE COMMISSION AND SOCIAL SCIENCE. *Phylon 1968 29(2): 167-181.* Analyzes the McCone Commission report on the Watts riots in Los Angeles in August 1965. Often following major social catastrophes, Americans turn to a special commission to study the causes and recommend policies in order to prevent a recurrence. According to the author, the McCone Commission was very superficial in its approach, for it refused to look for or find any psychological, sociological, or political meaning in the Watts riots, but approached them only "through middle-class and legalistic perspectives." The commission's analysis of the facts was highly subjective and biased; for example, the data was seriously distorted concerning the number of participants. Part of the problem was that the commission was asked to prepare a report within one hundred days. More important, the commission sought simple answers in order to "preserve as nearly as possible the existing distribution of power." It essentially blamed the disturbances on criminal elements within the Negro community. 27 notes.   R. D. Cohen

2083. Scott, Alan. TWENTY-FIVE YEARS OF OPINION ON INTEGRA- TION IN TEXAS. *Southwestern Social Sci. Q. 1967 48(2): 155-163.* Beginning in 1946 the Texas poll began sampling public opinion on civil rights. The analysis of poll results reveals that although Texas has moved fairly rapidly in the field of school integration, public attitudes have not changed as significantly as previously thought. In 1961, 54 percent of whites favored integration, yet in 1965, 70 percent of the whites said integration had been moving too fast. It is predicted that by 1970 the integration "in the elementary and secondary schools would be complete and total."   D. F. Henderson

2084. Scott, Joseph L. SOCIAL CLASS FACTORS UNDERLYING THE CIVIL RIGHTS MOVEMENT. *Phylon 1966 27(2): 132-144.* Reports the find- ings of a survey of Negro heads of households in a small, predominantly segre- gated, south central Indiana town. Younger Negroes were more militant integrationists. Integrationists tended to be better educated and higher paid, to hold better jobs, and to have musical, religious, and food preferences associated with middle-class whites. The author believes that militant integrationists have been striving to participate in middle-class life and are motivated by the inability to realize this aspiration in a segregated society. 16 notes.   S. C. Pearson, Jr.

2085. Sémidéi, Manuela. LA POLITIQUE AMERICAINE APRES LES ELEC-TIONS [American policy after the elections]. *R. Pol. et Parlementaire [France] 1966 68(773): 13-26.* Interprets the 1966 legislative election results as ambiguous and contradictory. The Negro question was uppermost in the voters' minds but its impact varied sectionally. In general the election was a conservative reaction, which means a slowdown in both the Great Society and civil rights but no shift in foreign policy. The Democrats face further political problems in the South; the Republicans, though gaining, are divided by personalities. Illus.
     T. D. Lockwood

2086. Shaffer, J. SATYAGRAHA'S TWENTY-FIFTH ANNIVERSARY IN THE UNITED STATES. *United Asia [India] 1965 17(1): 5-7.* Explores use of spiritual force as a successful rational base for bringing about the Negro revolution in the United States along lines similar to those of the "revolution without war" in India as led by Gandhi.   R. E. Frykenberg

2087. Shanor, Donald R. SOUTHERN EDITORS AND SELMA. *Journalism Q. 1967 44(1): 133-135.* Of 170 southern newspapers examined, those supporting the Selma marchers, totaling 60, ran 72 nationally syndicated columns agreeing with their views and 10 opposing them. The 57 newspapers opposed editorially to the Selma march used 31 columns that disagreed with their own views and 29 that agreed. Throughout the South there was ample exposure to the columnists' opinions on Selma's week of crisis.   S. E. Humphreys

2088. Shaskolsky, Leon S. THE NEGRO PROTEST MOVEMENT - REVOLT OR REFORM? *Phylon 1968 29(2): 156-166.* Analyzes "whether the present attempt by Negroes to achieve the social status, the share in the political power, and the economic opportunities so long denied them is likely to follow the traditional form of gradual minority penetration into the dominant strata of the society or whether these are unique factors in the present process which might result in a departure from the normal development." The author argues for the latter view. American society is different today, particularly since personal advancement on a large scale is no longer possible. Thus the Negroes' problems are group problems, demanding large-scale structural changes in society. Negroes, further, are set apart by their color, unlike previous minority groups. Whether Negroes will turn to traditional reform or revolt to change society "may well depend," the author concludes, "not on the program presented by those seeking power but on the response evoked in those possessing it." Based on secondary sources; 13 notes.   R. D. Cohen

2089. Sherman, Jimmie. FROM THE ASHES: A PERSONAL REACTION TO THE REVOLT OF WATTS. *Antioch R. 1967 27(3): 285-293.* A first-person narrative of a native of the Watts area of Los Angeles outlining the early frustration of his ambition and his reaction to the riot of 1965 which led him to become a professional writer and playwright. Included is some of his poetry.

F. Harrold

2090. Silver, James W. MISSISSIPPI: THE CLOSED SOCIETY. *J. of Southern Hist. 1964 30(1): 3-34.* Since the 1850's, Mississippi has been growing toward a "hyper-orthodox social order in which the individual has no option except to be loyal to the will of the white majority," which has subscribed to an inflexible philosophy not based on fact, logic, or reason. Especially in times of stress the orthodoxy becomes more rigid, more removed from reality, and the conformity demanded of it more extreme. This closed society, operating efficiently and almost automatically, as if it were some malicious Frankenstein monster, had no way of avoiding the fatal confrontation with the Federal Government at the University of Mississippi in 1962.

S. E. Humphreys

2091. Skolnik, Jerome. STUDENT PROTEST. *AAUP Bull. 1969 55(3): 309-326.* Campus demonstrations have risen since 1964. Forty percent of all students support "activist" values. Historically, student movements arise in periods of painful social transition. But the activism of the 1960's has unique qualities: it is more widely distributed and more militant than formerly, and it integrates local student concerns with broad social issues. Phases in the American movement include: 1) free speech and civil rights in the South; 2) resistance to war in Vietnam and to the draft; 3) attack on campus authoritarianism; 4) widening of antiauthoritarianism to include general distrust of the "establishment" on every level; and 5) black student and Third World protest. Fragmented by huge enrollments and disciplinary specialization, colleges and universities are in a crisis. They must alter governance to accommodate academic autonomy with broadened public responsibilities. 51 notes.

L. G. Geiger

2092. Smart, M. Neff. BLUE MONDAY: AN AMERICAN TEACHER IN ETHIOPIA. *Western Humanities R. 1964 18(3): 255-263.* A Fulbright lecturer in journalism at Haile Selassie I University relates how he found it impossible to explain to students and faculty members, or even to discuss with them, the errors they found in a *Time* magazine report from Africa or the news reports of the mass arrests of freedom marchers in Jackson, Mississippi.

A. Turner

2093. Smith, D. H. THE RHETORIC OF RIOTS. *Contemporary R. [Great Britain] 1968 213(1233): 178-184.* A historical account of the Negro protest movement in America from 1955 to date, stressing the pivotal importance of the summer of 1965 in providing a new dimension to the already developed nonverbal rhetoric of protest - the "rhetoric of riots." At present the new aggression is directed inward at the black ghetto, but will soon "spill over the ghetto walls and burn white America" unless laws are passed and enforced abolishing institutional racism. 7 notes.

D. H. Murdoch

2094. Smith, Frank E. THE EMERGING SOUTH. *Virginia Q. R. 1965 41(2): 161-175.* The positive benefit of the 1964 presidential campaign was the impetus toward a two-party system in the South. The South has begun to respond to national issues, though the "bitter-end Deep South opposition to racial change" will still hinder economic and social progress. The failure of those in responsible positions to respond to peaceable, rapid compliance with the school desegregation decision is in large part due to the failure of President Eisenhower to take decisive action to support the law and the court. The Negroes spoke out for full rights "only when they were shamed by the courageous dedication of the...sit-in movement." An indictment must be returned against the churches and newspapers for failure to assume leadership.   E. P. Stickney

2095. Smith, Ralph V. BEHIND THE RIOTS. *Am. Educ. 1967 3(10): 2-4, 31.* Examines the Detroit riot from the perspective of a member of a team of investigators in the midst of a sociological study of the city when the disorder began. Evidence is found to support a compression-dispersion theory. The Detroit ghetto represents a compressed discontent and compressed Negro interaction. Rather than finding signs of decreasing segregation, the evidence indicated an increasing trend. Despite this, the Detroit Negro continued to view education as his hope for a better future. Excerpted from an oral presentation based on a report entitled "Community Interaction and Racial Integration in the Detroit Area." 5 photos.
                                                                 W. R. Boedecker

2096. Snider, Howard. SEPARATE AND UNEQUAL: A SUMMARY OF THE REPORT OF THE NATIONAL ADVISORY COMMISSION ON CIVIL DISORDERS AND SOME OBSERVATIONS. *Mennonite Life 1968 23(3): 100-103.* Summarizes and comments on the *Report of the National Advisory Commission on Civil Disorders* (New York: The New York Times Company, 1968). Following the widespread disorders of 1967 in the Negro urban ghettos, this special presidential commission investigated 75 major and representative incidents in which the destruction of property and life occurred. The characteristics of the riots, their causes, and the commission's recommendations for alleviating ghetto unrest are discussed. Except for attempts to increase police efficiency, little has been done to implement the commission's recommendations. "The question must be raised as to whether the present social system is plastic enough to make the modifications necessary to the realization of common opportunity. The power structure's commitment to the myth of the American ideal of equality is so great that it is probably incapable of entertaining even in an elemental way structural changes that are necessary for practical realization of the ideal."   D. J. Abramoske

2097. Soderbergh, Peter A. THE NEGRO REVOLUTION AND THE YEAR OF DECISION: 1963-1964. *Social Sci. 1965 40(2): 86-93.* Analyzes the Negro revolution of the 1960's in terms of "classical" revolutionary patterns. Whereas there is nothing in American history which serves as a precedent, the Negro struggle for civil rights is following a pattern which more violent and far-reaching revolutions than our own have previously followed. The first stage of the Negro revolution came between 1954 and 1961, when intellectual and liberal minorities upheld the Supreme Court's desegregation decision. In 1961 the second stage began - "sit-ins," passive resistance, boycotts, outbreaks of violence in Mississippi and Alabama - an end to the "cold war," as it were. We are on the brink of the third stage of revolution, in which a "transfer of power" will be effected if the Federal Government chooses to continue to back the Negro claim. However, that third stage could end in open violence if Washington adopts conservative policies. In the end, it will be up to the great majority of white Americans to determine which road the revolution will take.   M. Small

2098. Spilerman, Seymour. THE CAUSES OF RACIAL DISTURBANCES: TESTS OF AN EXPLANATION. *Am. Sociol. R. 1971 36(3): 427-442.* "The adequacy of a recently proposed explanation for the location of racial disorders during the 1960's is evaluated in this paper. Two approaches to evaluation are used: (1) The proportion of variation accounted for by the variables assumed to be related to the occurrence of disorders is compared with an estimate of the 'maximum explanable proportion of variation,' and (2) the structural equation derived from an analysis of the 1961-67 disorders is used to predict the locations of the 1968 disturbances. The conclusions from these investigations support the proposed explanation only with respect to the non-South, but indicate that the distribution of disorders among southern cities has been converging during the late 1960's to the pattern which has been prevalent in the non-South throughout this decade. This finding is interpreted as evidence of the decreasing importance of regional cultures as an intervening factor in the development of black solidarity."   J

2099. Starr, Roger. JOHN V. LINDSAY: A POLITICAL PORTRAIT. *Commentary 1970 49(2): 25-42.* Describes Lindsay's progenitors, education, and political career. Lindsay graduated from Yale and served in the Navy during World War II. He subsequently became a lawyer and showed an interest in politics by joining a Republican Club. Elected to the House of Representatives, Lindsay worked for civil rights for American Negroes and for those issues which affect freedom of speech, discrimination in immigration, and unfair restrictions on employment. Some of the problems facing Lindsay as mayor of New York and his solutions are discussed. Concludes that Lindsay's political future is uncertain.
                                                                C. Grollman

2100. Steamer, Robert J. PRESIDENTIAL STIMULUS AND SCHOOL DESEGREGATION. *Phylon 1963 24(1): 20-33.* Eisenhower as President, it is said, failed to rise to the spirit of the Supreme Court decision of 1954. Kennedy better appreciated the duty laid upon the President by his office. His strategy was to press foreign and domestic programs before entering civil rights controversies. His programs, including antirecession and welfare measures, aided the Negro. He created a moral tone which furthered the cause of Negro equality. Kennedy opposed segregation at federally-sponsored meetings, made statements opposing discrimination, and made Negro appointments.   L. Filler

2101. Sullivan, Neil V. A CASE STUDY IN ACHIEVING EQUAL EDUCATIONAL OPPORTUNITY. *J. of Negro Educ. 1965 34(3): 319-326.* Summarizes the history of the Free Schools in Prince Edward County, Virginia, which were operated in 1963-64 to provide education for Negroes and those whites willing to participate in this venture in a county where all public schools had been closed for four years in defiance of Federal court orders to desegregate. After considering successful practices in the Free Schools, the former superintendent of these schools suggests ways in which other school systems may provide equal educational opportunity for all children.   S. C. Pearson, Jr.

2102. Thompson, Daniel C. CIVIL RIGHTS LEADERSHIP (AN OPINION STUDY). *J. of Negro Educ. 1963 32(4): 426-436.* Reports a 1962 survey of opinions of civil rights leaders in which they dealt with questions of citizenship, employment, and education and evaluated the civil rights movement.
                                                                    S. C. Pearson, Jr.

2103. Trilling, Diana. ON THE STEPS OF LOW LIBRARY: LIBERALISM AND THE REVOLUTION OF THE YOUNG. *Commentary 1968 46(5): 29-55.* Compares the uprising at Columbia University with the march on the Pentagon. The former was an improvisational act; the latter was a symbolic enterprise. The students in both cases took the moral stance of blamelessness. The Columbia students did not need revolutionary ideology since they believed they bore no responsibility for what they did. Those students inside the building were frightened of police brutality. Those outside, such as the author who is a faculty wife, were worried that the ghetto might join the revolt. The author feels that the problems and advantages of Columbia are the problems and advantages of the United States. She concludes with a discussion of the role of the faculty, white students, black students, administration, and trustees during the uprising.
                                                                    C. Grollman

2104. Tunc, André. LE VINGT-QUATRIEME AMENDEMENT A LA CONSTITUTION DES ETATS-UNIS [The 24th Amendment to the Constitution of the United States]. *R. Internat. de Droit Comparé [France] 1964 16(2): 371-372.* The effects of the 24th amendment will be limited because 1) only five States still have the poll tax, 2) it applies only to Federal elections, and 3) there are many other ways of excluding the Negroes from the suffrage. Nevertheless, it is a step in the right direction and it may have a valuable educational and psychological effect. 7 notes.   J. S. Gassner

2105. Ulmer, S. Sidney. SUPREME COURT BEHAVIOR IN RACIAL EXCLUSION CASES: 1935-1960. *Am. Pol. Sci. R. 1962 56(2): 325-330.* Seeks to find whether inferences about Supreme Court behavior in cases involving exclusion of Negroes from jury service in State courts from 1935 to 1960 "can be sharpened by a shift from the traditional method of analysis." The author offers two hypotheses, with two conditions each, for the court's decisions in this area.
                                                                    B. W. Onstine

2106. Unsigned. JAMES FARMER OF CORE. *Negro Hist. Bull. 1964 27(7): 160-161.* A brief sketch of James Farmer, national director of the Congress of Racial Equality (CORE), and description of its program of nonviolent direct action to end racial discrimination.   L. Gara

2107. Unsigned. LE PROBLEME NOIR AUX ETATS-UNIS [The Negro problem in the United States]. *R. de Défense Natl. [France] 1963 19(8/9): 1352-1365.* Reviews the Negro problem through the eyes of the white, Negro, and political elements in the United States. Discusses the work of Truman, Eisenhower, and Kennedy on civil rights and lists the international reaction to the Birmingham disturbances. The conclusion calls for some positive action by the United States to retain its influence in world affairs.					J. J. Flynn

2108. Unsigned. MARTIN LUTHER KING, JR.: MAN OF 1963. *Negro Hist. Bull. 1964 27(6): 136-137.* A summary of the *Time* story which announced its choice of King as the man of the year for 1963 and summarized his role of leadership in the Negro revolution.					L. Gara

2109. Unsigned. WALTER WHITE'S CRUSADE. *Freedom and Union 1955 10(5): 15-16.* Reprint of editorials in the *Washington Evening Star,* the *Baltimore Sun,* and *The New York Herald Tribune* on the death of Walter White (21 March 1955), extolling his crusade for Negro rights.					R. Mueller

2110. Useem, Michael and Marx, Gary T. MAJORITY INVOLVEMENT IN MINORITY MOVEMENTS: CIVIL RIGHTS, ABOLITION, UNTOUCHABILITY. *J. of Social Issues 1971 27(1): 81-104.* Compares the abolition and civil rights movements in the United States and the movement to abolish untouchability in India. When conflict of an ideological nature emerged, there was a tendency for insiders to see themselves as more radical and committed than outsiders and as more eager to bring about change immediately rather than gradually, less willing to compromise, and more willing to use noninstitutionalized means of protest. 2 notes, biblio.					R. J. Wechman

2111. Van Zanten, John W. COMMUNIST THEORY AND THE AMERICAN NEGRO QUESTION. *R. of Pol. 1967 29(4): 435-456.* Examines the Soviet estimate of the significance and meaning of the Negro "revolution" in America, concentrating on the period since 1953 and emphasizing the theoretical treatment. The author shows that after Stalin's death the Communist analysis shifted from the frontal assault technique of exacerbating existing contradictions in racial relations to a more subtle gradualism echoing the Marxian tenet that capitalism can collapse only when it has reached its final point of development. Noting that currently "the Soviets have accepted a view of the Negro problem which inherently carries with it a cautious vote of confidence in the American social system," the questions are raised of priority in the sequence of Communist thinking, recognition of changed conditions on tactical goals, and the implications of the current policy of the CPUSA to exert united efforts to superintend the radicalization of the Negroes by infiltrating existing organizations and seeking to guide the evolving civil rights movement which seems to contain inherent tendencies in accord with Soviet ideology. The signs of Communist recognition of the viability and resiliency of the American social fabric are clearly indicated by the gradual acceptance by the CPSU of the CPUSA views on the Negro problem, viewing the

Negro situation more in the light of class rather than race conflicts and regarding it as a social question. Documented from sources in Russian and in English; 42 notes. Sr. M. McAuley

2112. Walker, Jack L. PROTEST AND NEGOTIATION: A CASE STUDY OF NEGRO LEADERSHIP IN ATLANTA, GEORGIA. *Midwest J. of Pol. Sci. 1963 7(2): 99-124.* Describes the political attitudes and goals of a group of Negro civic leaders in Atlanta, Georgia. It inquires into the motives of the sit-in demonstrators involved in the controversy over lunch counter segregation which lasted from March 1960 until September 1961. The differences between attitudes and socioeconomic factors as well as the goals and tactics of the various Negro leaders are examined. Finally, the author speculates about the future development of the Negro community in Atlanta. B. W. Onstine

2113. Walker, Jack L. THE FUNCTIONS OF DISUNITY: NEGRO LEADERSHIP IN A SOUTHERN CITY. *J. of Negro Educ. 1963 32(3): 227-236.* Studies the sit-in controversy in Atlanta, Georgia, noting the emergence of new, more militant Negro leadership in the South, which the established leadership has often resisted. "A Negro community in a Southern city is likely to be more effective in eliminating the institutions of segregation if it has both conservative and protest elements within its leadership." Protest leaders precipitate tension through direct action while conservative leaders maintain channels of communication with the white community. S. C. Pearson, Jr.

2114. Warren, Robert Penn. TWO FOR SNCC. *Commentary 1965 39(4): 38-48.* A report on interviews with two activists in the Student Non-Violent Coordinating Committee. The topics for discussion include attitudes toward violence, Martin Luther King, Jr., Negro-white cooperation, the Negro identity, the Negro stereotype, and opportunism. An excerpt from the author's new book, *Who Speaks for the Negro?* (New York: Random House, 1965). R. J. Moore

2115. Weber, Paul J. and Lavalette, Henri de. REFLEXIONS SUR LES EMEUTES AUX ETATS-UNIS [Reflections on the riots in the United States]. *Etudes [France] 1967 327(November): 451-461.* Argues that just because the condition of the blacks in the United States is better than it has ever been before, they are now rising up to protest against the very real discrimination which they suffer in matters of schooling, housing, social acceptance, and economic opportunity. The bitterness of their protest is associated with their history of slavery with its ill effects on family life and the consequent psychic disorders. 11 notes. Sr. M. H. Quinlan

2116. Weinberg, Carl. EDUCATION LEVEL AND PERCEPTIONS OF LOS ANGELES NEGROES OF EDUCATIONAL CONDITIONS IN A RIOT AREA. *J. of Negro Educ. 1967 36(4): 377-384.* Following the Watts riot 106 Negroes in the area were interviewed on the subject of race relations and conditions of Negro life in Los Angeles. Education appears to mediate for Negroes their hostility toward the white power structure and discrepancies in the world of opportunities. Those with greater education perceived greater Negro opportunities in education and employment and felt the riot less justified. Social distance, however, proved a more significant variable in differentiating the population on these issues. Differences were also found to be no more important than general uniformities. Thus while a significant relationship was found between educational attainment and feelings that the riot was justified, only 12 percent of the total group disapproved of the riot. 5 notes.   S. C. Pearson, Jr.

2117. Weiss, Samuel A. DILEMMAS OF NEGRO MILITANCY. *Midwest Q. 1967 9(1): 97-107.* Examines and comments on James Farmer's book, *Freedom - When?* (New York: Random House, 1965). CORE's (Congress of Racial Equality) policy under Farmer, its former national director, was to resist actively but nonviolently. However, its philosophy of nonviolence and integration was and is being increasingly questioned by young militants. The rise of Black Power militancy and attacks on the doctrine of nonviolence as ineffectual show that either white power yields to just demands made nonviolently or violence will erupt. While violence is self-defeating, concessions have been speeded by riots in the ghetto. The NAACP (National Association for the Advancement of Colored People) still maintains that color is irrelevant, but CORE emphasizes race differences. Integration presupposes the dissolution of the Negro community into the white majority, while separation emphasizes the right to exist separately as a Negro.   G. H. G. Jones

2118. Wilber, Leon A. CONSTITUTIONAL DECISIONS OF THE UNITED STATES SUPREME COURT IN THE OCTOBER 1964 TERM. *Southern Q. 1966 4(2): 172-206.* During the 1964-65 session of the court, the justices decided 40 constitutional cases, seven of which laid down new principles. The 1964 Civil Rights Act was upheld, a section of a congressional act of 1959, barring Communists from holding offices in labor unions, was struck down, and a 1961 decision which had applied Federal standards of search and seizure to State officials was held not to be retroactive.   D. A. Stokes

2119. Wilkerson, Doxey A. SCHOOL INTEGRATION, COMPENSATORY EDUCATION AND THE CIVIL RIGHTS MOVEMENT IN THE NORTH. *J. of Negro Educ. 1965 34(3): 300-309.* Suggests that the supposed antagonism between integration and compensatory education is more apparent than real and that a synthesis of the two in "quality integrated education" is desirable and dependent upon wisely directed pressures by the civil rights movement.   S. C. Pearson, Jr.

2120. Wilson, James Q. and Wilde, Harold R. THE URBAN MOOD. *Commentary 1969 48(4): 52-61.* There is a strong current of popular opinion running against some trends in social change. The polls show that crime in the streets and Negro riots are seen as serious menaces. The American political system does not quickly or accurately mirror changes in public opinion at the local level. The election for mayor in Los Angeles, Minneapolis, Detroit, and New York is discussed in detail. Although the liberal mayors of the 1960's have been defeated or have retired, the authors conclude on an optimistic note.

C. Grollman

2121. Wiltner, Charles L. PRIDE AND PROGRESS. *Am. Educ. 1966 2(9): 23-25.* Reviews the record of desegregation in the public school system of Atlanta. The process occurred in two parts, the first involving the resolution of the legal conflict between the State and Federal Governments, the second concerning the mechanics of desegregation. The author sees the achievement of desegregation as the result of cooperation between parents, pupils, school administrators, community leaders, city officials, and the police force. 3 photos.

W. R. Boedecker

2122. Wisdom, John Minor. GUIDELINES ON TRIAL. *Am. Educ. 1967 3(3): 18-20.* Excerpts from the majority decision in a case which consolidated the appeals of seven cases from two States. The decision sustained and reinforced the U.S. Office of Education's guidelines for the desegregation of schools, finding they "are constitutional and are within the statutory authority created in the Civil Rights Act of 1964." Taken from the court's "slip" decision.

W. R. Boedecker

2123. Wynes, Charles E. EQUALITY IN AMERICA. *Virginia Q. R. 1964 40(4): 641-644.* A discussion of three books on racial equality in the United States. Included are Benjamin Muse's *Ten Years of Prelude* (1964); Alan P. Grimes' *Equality in America* (1964); and *Assimilation in American Life* (1964) by Milton M. Gordon.

J. Frazier

2124. Zangrando, Robert L. FROM CIVIL RIGHTS TO BLACK LIBERATION: THE UNSETTLED 1960'S. *Current Hist. 1969 57(339): 281-286, 299.* In the early years of the decade an entirely new set of forces was mobilized on behalf of minority group rights: joint initiative by field workers and local residents, direct action by blacks and whites, and some involvement by the Federal Government. By 1965, however, mistrust had replaced harmony within the civil rights movement due to a combination of political expediency, white racism, and the diversion of energy produced by the Vietnam War.

B. D. Rhodes

2125. Zangrando, Robert L., Yeh, Stephen H. K., and Brooks, A. Russell. LITERATURE OF RACE AND CULTURE. *Phylon 1964 25(3): 307-313.* Reviews of the following books: *Race and Radicalism: The NAACP and the Communist Party in Conflict* (1964) by Wilson Record, *Assimilation in American Life* (1964) by Milton M. Gordon, *Intermarriage* (1964) by Albert I. Gordon, *Women in the New Asia* (1963) edited by Barbara Ward, *Mine Eyes have Seen the Glory: A Novel of the New American Revolution* (1964) by Tristram Coffin, and *The Premier* (1964) by Earl Conrad.

S. C. Pearson, Jr.

2126. Zangrando, Robert L. THE DIRECTION OF THE MARCH. *Negro Hist. Bull. 1963 27(3): 60-64.* Discusses the August 1963 civil rights march in Washington in terms of its place in the broader movement and relates it to the history of the civil rights struggle which began around the time of World War I.

L. Gara

2127. --. [BLACK AMERICA]. *Soc. Sci. Q. 1968 49(3): 433-741.*

Glenn, Norval D. THE KERNER REPORT, SOCIAL SCIENTISTS, AND THE AMERICAN PUBLIC: INTRODUCTION TO A SYMPOSIUM, pp. 433-437. Following a brief résumé of the conclusions of the commission, the author summarizes the other papers of the symposium and predicts that the Kerner Report "is largely irrelevant to the course of race relations in the United States, or it may even tend to increase violence." 15 notes.

Meier, August and Rudwick, Elliott. NEGRO PROTEST AND URBAN UNREST, pp. 438-443. Two major points of the Kerner Report are examined: "the treatment of the causes of the riots of the 1960's and the historical sketch of the Negro protest movement." The cause of the riots was not simply white racism but rather the thwarting of rapidly rising expectations and the failure quickly to achieve full equality and racial justice. 2 notes.

Mack, Raymond W. OF WHITE RACISM AND BLACK MOBILIZA-TION, pp. 444-447. Attempts to answer the question of why black Americans, who have been oppressed for 300 years, suddenly turned to violent protest in the 1960's. Pointed out are four variables which differentiate black Americans today from their forefathers: educational mobility, increased expectations, social organization to protest the discrimination, and migration and dislocation. 4 notes.

Edwards, G. Franklin and Jones, Clifton R. THE COMMISSION'S RE-PORT: SOME SOCIOLOGICAL AND POLICY CONSIDERATIONS, pp. 448-452. Contends that the primary value of the report is that it "calls attention to the national significance of the problem of civil disorders and their underlying causes." The authors optimistically predict that the existing structure will be changed at many levels to solve the problems. 9 notes.

Prestage, Jewel L. BLACK POLITICS AND THE KERNER REPORT CONCERNS AND DIRECTION, pp. 453-464. Attempts to relate the report to several theories and research findings in the following three areas of political science: political socialization, democratic theory, and black political strategy. 47 notes.

Ginzberg, Eli. THE ECONOMIST WHO CHANGED HIS MIND, pp. 465-468. The author, in testifying before the Kerner Commission, stressed the need for expanded government programs "aimed at improving the preparation of Negro children and young for work and life, and the concomitant need for an expanded and strengthened manpower policy that would provide jobs for many Negroes who are currently out of the labor force, unemployed or underemployed." He now feels that this approach is too limited and short term in nature. Only by exorcising racism from American life, can the "many necessary and essential programs of specific assistance to the Negro community have some prospect of succeeding."

Akins, Carl. THE RIOT COMMISSION REPORT AND THE NOTION OF "POLITICAL TRUTH," pp. 469-473. Deals with the notion that the "truth" found in any report is based upon political acceptability rather than objectivity.

Many people expected the Kerner Report to be a "whitewash" to express "political truth." It did not, but the boldness of the report appears largely to have been a failure. 9 notes.

Geschwender, James A. CIVIL RIGHTS PROTEST AND RIOTS: A DISAPPEARING DISTINCTION, pp. 474-484. Concerned with the proper label for recent urban disorders, whether they are merely hostile outbursts or segments of a social movement. The author concludes that the disorders are creative rioting falling "clearly within the evolutionary pattern of the civil rights movement, a social movement which may or may not eventually become revolutionary." 52 notes.

Sears, David O. and Tomlinson, T. M. RIOT IDEOLOGY IN LOS ANGELES: A STUDY OF NEGRO ATTITUDES, pp. 485-503. Attempts to dispel three widely held myths about the Negro community's response to riots: that the riots are participated in and viewed favorably by only a tiny segment of the Negro community, that most Negroes see the riots as purposeless, meaningless, senseless outbursts of criminality, and that Negroes generally believe that no benefit will result from the riots. Based on data obtained from interviews conducted with three samples of respondents in Los Angeles County in late 1965 and early 1966; 11 tables, 22 notes.

Downes, Bryan T. SOCIAL AND POLITICAL CHARACTERISTICS OF RIOT CITIES: A COMPARATIVE STUDY, pp. 504-520. Following a brief examination of the nature of the hostile outbursts of 1964-68, the author analyzes some of the characteristics of cities (pop. 25,000 and over) experiencing racial violence since 1964. He concludes that the "environmental context one finds in cities in which hostile outbursts took place tends to be quite different from that found in communities in which no incidents occurred." Moreover, contextual differences tend to be further accentuated in those cities in which more violent outbursts occurred. 6 tables, 32 notes.

Orum, Anthony M. and Orum, Amy W. THE CLASS AND STATUS BASES OF NEGRO STUDENT PROTEST, pp. 521-533. Analyzes the question: to what extent is the participation of Negro college students in the Negro protest movement a response to economic or status-related deprivation? It was discovered that the several major interpretations of the growth of the Negro protest movement fail to explain student participation in those activities. Based on the responses of 3,500 seniors at Negro colleges who graduated in the spring of 1964; 7 tables, 39 notes.

Holloway, Harry. NEGRO POLITICAL STRATEGY: COALITION OR INDEPENDENT POWER POLITICS?, pp. 534-547. Proposes three alternatives for Negro political strategy: formation of a liberal coalition to unite Negroes with "underdog" whites, development of a conservative coalition to unite Negroes with "the better sort of white," and a policy of independence and pragmatism in which ad hoc coalitions are accepted but continuing coalition ties are rejected. The analysis focuses on three locales where the alternatives are used: Houston and the liberal coalition, Atlanta and the Conservative Coalition, and Memphis and Independent Power Politics. 25 notes.

Ippolito, Dennis S., Donaldson, William S., and Bowman, Lewis. POLITICAL ORIENTATION AMONG NEGROES AND WHITES, pp. 548-556. Reports "the inter-racial differences in advocacy of public or private implementation and federal involvement in programs to aid the handicapped, and, finally, the correlates of the sub-groups advocating various types of implementation and involvement." Most Negroes and whites accepted the relevance of the program and supported its objectives, but three-fourths of the Negroes favored governmental implementation, while nearly a majority of the whites favored private or "mixed" implementation. Data collected from personal interviews in Petersburg, Virginia, and Norfolk, Virginia, in 1967; 7 tables, 11 notes.

Hirsch, Herbert and Donohew, Lewis. A NOTE ON NEGRO-WHITE DIFFERENCES IN ATTITUDES TOWARD THE SUPREME COURT, pp. 557-562. Focuses on race as a variable in attitudes toward governmental institutions. Reveals that Negroes evaluated the Court more positively and less negatively than whites, even when geographic area, education, income, political party identification, and sense of political efficacy were controlled. Data used compiled from the University of Michigan Survey Research Center post-election study of the 1964 Presidential election; 6 tables, 8 notes.

Price, Daniel O. OCCUPATIONAL CHANCES AMONG WHITES AND NONWHITES, WITH PROJECTIONS FOR 1970, pp. 563-572. Examines the occupational characteristics of white and nonwhite males and females from the period 1920 to 1960, using Federal census data. Through extrapolation of trends, occupational distribution for 1970 is projected. 14 figures, table, 2 notes.

Straits, Bruce C. RESIDENTIAL MOVEMENT AMONG NEGROES AND WHITES IN CHICAGO, pp. 573-592. Using data compiled on 839 white and 721 nonwhite household heads, contends that the higher incidence of residential mobility among Negroes is a consequence of factors that, for the most part, affect only Negroes, "including occupational and residential discrimination, the Negro housing market, and family and employment instability." 6 tables, 37 notes.

Gottlieb, David and Campbell, Jay, Jr. WINNERS AND LOSERS IN THE RACE FOR THE GOOD LIFE: A COMPARISON OF BLACKS AND WHITES, pp. 593-602. Investigates two questions, "(1) What do poor youth want? and (2) What is the impact of race on the social factors that appear to facilitate or block attainment of their expressed goals?" Comparison is between a group of low-income male students who were in three different eastern high schools (winners) and a select group of Job Corps trainees (losers). It is concluded that poor youth in general aspire to middle-class affluence. Racial prejudice has compounded the burden on black youth. "The white Loser has apparently introjected his failure and lowered his sights, while the black Loser retains his aspirations and very likely projects his failure onto the injustice of the system." 10 tables, 8 notes.

Cartwright, Walter J. and Burtis, Thomas R. RACE AND INTELLIGENCE: CHANGING OPINIONS IN SOCIAL SCIENCE, pp. 603-618. After surveying the historical background leading to an emphasis on race and intelligence, the authors review the changes which have occurred in the experts' opinions, possible reasons for these changes, and the degree of disagreement which persists. 74 notes.

Stafford, James E., Cox, Keither K., and Higginbotham, James B. SOME CONSUMPTION PATTERN DIFFERENCES BETWEEN URBAN WHITES AND NEGROES, pp. 619-630. Proposes the basic question, "Does a Negro market really exist?" The specific purpose of the paper was "to determine if there existed between Negroes and whites consumption-pattern differences which were not accounted for by income differentials, and to specify, where possible, the nature of possible origin(s) of those differences." Variations in consumption of five product categories evaluated were found between Negroes and whites. Most of these differences could be explained in terms of income or sociodemographic variations, but several were explainable in terms of purely "racial" influences.

Sommers, Montrose S. and Bruce, Grady D. BLACKS, WHITES, AND PRODUCTS: RELATIVE DEPRIVATION AND REFERENCE GROUP BEHAVIOR, pp. 631-642. Compares white and black responses to product symbolism: "That is, produces are said to symbolize action or activity patterns." Q-sort methodology is applied to measuring the relative deprivation experienced when comparisons are made; 7 tables, 15 notes.

Sturdivant, Frederick D. and Wilhelm, Walter T. POVERTY, MINORITIES, AND CONSUMER EXPLOITATION, pp. 643-650. Attempts to test the hypothesis that residents of the ghetto pay more for their consumer goods than do other Americans. Using three couples with similar credit profiles - one white, one Negro, and one Mexican-American, and three shopping districts - it was discovered that the average price asked of the three couples for a given product "was always higher in the disadvantaged-area stores than in the control area.... The total cost, or the credit price averaged higher in the poverty areas as well." 2 tables, 10 notes.

Schulz, David A. VARIATIONS IN THE FATHER ROLE IN COMPLETE FAMILIES OF THE NEGRO LOWER CLASS, pp. 651-659. Describes and analyzes some of the variations in the husband-father role in Negro families. Based on a study of 10 lower-class Negro families, it is concluded that the male's status depends not only upon his income and his willingness to share that income with the family but also upon the degree of his "adherence to the norms of monogamous marriage, his ability to cope with the harsh realities of the ghetto, and his capacity to be a pal to his children." 17 notes.

Feagin, Joe R. THE KINSHIP TIES OF NEGRO URBANITES, pp. 660-665. Various studies have indicated important kinship ties among urban dwellers. Using data collected in connection with an evaluation study of a low-income housing demonstration program in Boston's Roxbury Negro ghetto, the author corroborates and amplifies the earlier studies. Data revealed that the majority of Negro respondents had relatives in the Boston area. Approximately one-half depended on relatives for aid in moving to their present address. 4 tables, 13 notes.

Eighmy, John Lee. THE BAPTISTS AND SLAVERY: AN EXAMINATION OF THE ORIGINS AND BENEFITS OF SEGREGATION, pp. 666-673. A rather weak attempt to justify the Baptist's defense first of slavery and then of segregation. Separation in religion led to an independent Negro church, and the growth of that church "must stand as one of the most enduring accomplishments of the Reconstruction period." 29 notes.

Hadden, Jeffrey K. IDEOLOGICAL CONFLICT BETWEEN PROTESTANT CLERGY AND LAITY ON CIVIL RIGHTS, pp. 674-683. Explores the attitudes of Protestant clergy and laity toward civil rights and the attitudes of laity toward the involvement of clergy in civil rights. It is concluded that the clergy are, in general, sympathetic toward the movement to achieve social justice for the Negro, but are far from unanimous. The laity believe that the clergy "should speak out on moral issues, but specifically, they reject clergy involvement in the civil rights struggle." Finally, "those who never attend church express somewhat less prejudicial sentiment than those who do attend." Based on a survey of Protestant ministers in six major denominations conducted early in 1965 and a survey of the American lay public's attitudes toward involvement of the clergy in civil rights conducted early in 1967; 4 tables, 8 notes.

Cramer, M. Richard. FACTORS RELATED TO WILLINGNESS TO EXPERIENCE DESEGREGATION AMONG STUDENTS IN SEGRE-GATED SCHOOLS, pp. 684-696. Concerned with the measurement at one point in time of a single index of a key dependent variable in the desegregation process: "attitudes about desegregation." Attempts to use a group of other factors as predictors of differentiation in these attitudes, in particular leadership and inno-vation-potential dimensions. 5 tables, 14 notes.

Jeffries, Vincent and Morris, Richard T. ALTRUISM, EGOISM, AND ANTAGONISM TOWARD NEGROES, pp. 697-709. Presents data on the relationship between the values of altruism and egoism and the level of antago-nism toward Negroes. "Altruism is associated with a lower level of antagonism and a higher level of solidarity toward Negroes than is egoism." Based on 583 interviews conducted in Los Angeles; 4 tables, 22 notes.

Conway, M. Margaret. THE WHITE BACKLASH RE-EXAMINED: WALLACE AND THE 1964 PRIMARIES, pp. 710-719. Examines the results of the Wisconsin, Indiana, and Maryland primaries in relation to several recent studies on the nature of the white backlash and concludes that the middle-class electorate hypothesis, suggested by Michael Rogin, appears appropriate in Wis-consin, but that a pattern of working-class electorate backlash - a hypothesis proposed by Seymour Martin Lipset - is applicable in Maryland and Indiana. 5 tables, 19 notes.

Van der Slik, Jack R. CONSTITUENCY CHARACTERISTICS AND ROLL CALL VOTING ON NEGRO RIGHTS IN THE 88TH CONGRESS, pp. 720-731. Measures and explains recent roll call voting on questions of Negro rights in the House of Representatives. Using 5 roll call votes, and 21 constituency variables, it is concluded there were substantial correlations between Negro rights support and constituency characteristics, but the "covariation producing these correlations is mostly regional in nature." 3 tables, 17 notes.

Hart, Charles Desmond. WHY LINCOLN SAID "NO": CONGRES-SIONAL ATTITUDES ON SLAVERY EXPANSION, 1860-1861, pp. 732-741. Discusses why Lincoln refused to support the Crittenden Compromise, intro-duced in Congress on 18 December 1860, which proposed extending the Missouri Compromise to the Pacific coast. The chief fear by Lincoln and Republican congressmen was that, under such a settlement, slavery might have been extended to Central and South America. 45 notes.   D. F. Henderson

2128. --. "BLACK POWER": TWO VIEWS. *Commentary 1966 42(3): 35-46.*
Rustin, Bayard. "BLACK POWER" AND COALITION POLITICS, pp. 35-40. "Black power" is the slogan of a new militant movement in the struggle for Negro rights, produced by the fact that despite all of the liberal legislative and judicial action in the past decade, "Negroes today are in worse economic shape, live in worse slums, and attend more highly segregated schools than in 1954." Many Negroes have lost faith in the civil rights movement, basically a white liberal movement, and have turned instead to the only thing they have left, their community and its potential power, if organized. The author sees this movement

as self-defeating, springing first from a defeatist conviction that the Negro community can never achieve equality through integration into American society, but feels that it must inevitably grow unless the liberal establishment, including moderate civil rights leaders, will apply enough effort to win more than the paper gains of the past.

Danzig, David. IN DEFENSE OF "BLACK POWER," pp. 41-46. The civil rights movement has mostly dissolved, its place being taken now by a Negro movement with specifically Negro-oriented goals which go beyond the idea of equality before the law of all citizens which was the major goal of white civil rights workers, to the ideal of making the Negro equal in socioeconomic terms as well. "Black power" expresses the determination to achieve this goal through group solidarity in the community, rather than simple absorption of Negroes into the white community one-by-one, which is all the civil rights legislation has been able to offer. The author feels however that the aims of the movement still cannot be realized without the help of white liberals; he foresees possible local coalitions to accomplish socioeconomic goals, just as the national coalition accomplished legis-lative-judicial goals.   A. K. Main

2129. --. [DEATH OF ROBERT KENNEDY]. *Trans-action 1968 5(8): 3-6.*
Horowitz, Irving L. KENNEDY'S DEATH - MYTHS AND REALI-TIES, pp. 3-5. Contends that there are five myths resulting from the death of Senator Robert Kennedy. The first is that assassination has become infectious and contagious in America. The second is that violence has increased as the nearness to change has quickened. Third, the contention that there will always be violence and that therefore gun control laws are without utility. Fourth, the argument that there are no possible conspiracies involved with Senator Kennedy's assassination. Senator Kennedy's death was connected with a political issue. Finally, the notion that dramatic deaths like that of Senator Kennedy radically affect the course of history.

Gans, Herbert J. WHY DID KENNEDY DIE?, pp. 5-6. Suggests some tentative answers to the question "Why did Kennedy die?" His basic contention is that Robert Kennedy's death, just as that of Martin Luther King, Jr., Medgar Evers, and John F. Kennedy, was to slow down the present process of social change in America. Robert Kennedy was a leader in this process. To say that our society is sick is an insufficient answer. The way to deal with political assassination is for our society to accept the reality that a great deal of social change must come about in a very short time.   A. Erlebacher

2130. --. FIRST CONFERENCE ON VIOLENCE. *J. of Human Relations 1965 13(3): 383-428.*
Unsigned. SUMMARY OF SESSIONS, pp. 385-408. The participants of this informal conference sponsored by Brandeis University discussed such topics as "spontaneous and 'senseless' violence in modern cities or suburbs"; the political impact of organized violence; the treatment of criminals and their brutalization through imprisonment; the disastrous effect of the growing impersonalization of contemporary American society; ways and means of strengthening police departments, the legal profession, and social agencies; and the feasibility of a domestic peace corps to work with slum dwellers. "As the Conference proceeded, semantic issues were left behind, and problems of practical

control and management of violence in current American society received concentrated attention." In part as a result of proposals made during the conference, Brandeis University is establishing a permanent Institute on Violence.

Long, Norton E. POLITICAL VIOLENCE, pp. 409-417. Although not denying the importance of psychological factors in explaining violence, the author "would attribute more explanatory power to the existence of socially and even organizationally violent roles and occasions for their activation. If this view is correct, Klan violence is less due to peculiar psychological propensities of Klansmen than to the socially sustained role structure." Violence is not necessarily pathological. "The example of race relations and labor suggests that violence is importantly a means of communication among parties."

Menninger, Karl. TOWARD THE UNDERSTANDING OF VIOLENCE, pp. 418-426. The word violence should not be used as an equivalent to lawlessness. "We are denouncing *violence* when I think we mean to denounce *destructiveness,* which usually today is non-violent." Sigmund Freud's dual instinct theory is accepted. "Our task is to eliminate as far as we can, to control, to harness, to sublimate, to direct our own aggressive impulses and that of our colleagues away from the enjoyment of causing pain in other people. I do not believe there is such a thing as good aggression." Violence is probably always motivated; there is no such thing as "senseless violence."

Rankin, J. Lee. A CLOSING STATEMENT, pp. 427-428. Presents the author's general reflections on the conference and on his experience working with the Warren Commission's investigation of President John F. Kennedy's assassination. D. J. Abramoske

2131. --. [RACE AND EQUALITY IN AMERICAN EDUCATION]. *J. of Negro Educ. 1968 37(3): 185-339.*

Thompson, Charles H. RACE AND EQUALITY OF EDUCATIONAL OPPORTUNITY: DEFINING THE PROBLEM, pp. 191-203. The author accepts the Coleman Report's definition of equality of educational opportunity as being based on the achievement levels of the students James S. Coleman, et al., *Equality of Educational Opportunity* [Washington, D.C.: U.S. Government Printing Office, 1966]. The difference between the achievement levels of the average white and average Negro students at grade 12 is the degree of inequality of educational opportunity. The Coleman Report noted that Negroes in predominantly white schools "achieve at a higher level than those in all Negro or predominantly...Negro schools." This is apparently due to the "social class climate" rather than race alone. To put all students in predominantly middle-class schools, however, would require massive integration because only 25 or 30 percent of Negroes can be classified as middle-class. Compensatory programs to raise the achievement levels of slum and ghetto children would cost a minimum of 5 billion dollars a year for the next five years. The predominantly Negro colleges and universities are in a transitional stage of compensatory education. Most educators see a need to restructure the educational system in order to effect desegregation, but many parents fear this. The author indicates that a wholly new approach to education may be needed. 42 notes.

West, Earle H. PROGRESS TOWARD EQUALITY OF OPPORTUNITY IN ELEMENTARY AND SECONDARY EDUCATION, pp. 212-219. Negro youths today are completing secondary school at a rate close to that of whites. This is especially true in the metropolitan central cities, but the largest disparity is in the rural South. Negroes are lagging further behind, however, in the percentages of each group going to college. In spite of this fact, there is little good vocational education available for these Negro high school students. There is also little in the way of post-high school educational opportunity for Negroes as compared to whites. The desegregation rate in the South increased rapidly following the 1964 Civil Rights Act and the 1965 Elementary and Secondary Education Act, but faculty desegregation has lagged behind. In the northern cities, however, school segregation has increased due to residential isolation. 27 notes.

Willie, Charles V. NEW PERSPECTIVES IN SCHOOL-COMMUNITY RELATIONS, pp. 220-226. School administrators must now learn to work with and relate to the subdominant power groups as well as with the dominant power groups in the community. A decentralized school system would give more power to these subdominant groups. 20 notes.

Shulman, Lee S. NEGRO-WHITE DIFFERENCES IN EMPLOYABILITY, SELF-CONCEPT, AND RELATED MEASURES AMONG ADOLESCENTS CLASSIFIED AS MENTALLY HANDICAPPED, pp. 227-240. Results of a five-year study of the vocational development of teen-agers classified by the public schools as Educable Mentally Handicapped. One-third of these were Negroes. It was found that the retarded Negroes were more employable than the retarded whites. The Negroes, tending to come from lower-class, culturally disadvantaged homes had more normal lives than the retarded middle-class white adolescents whose parents expected more. Social and economic class were the determining factors. The standard IQ tests predict the employability of the middle-class children, but tests such as the Purdue Pegboard give a more realistic indication of the vocational educability of lower-class children. 2 figs., 3 tables, 2 notes.

Poussaint, Alvin F. and Atkinson, Carolyn O. NEGRO YOUTH AND PSYCHOLOGICAL MOTIVATION, pp. 241-251. Three motivational factors are studied: self-concept, patterned needs, and society's rewards. The Negro's self-concept has been very poor, based on the reactions of white society and older Negroes. The patterned needs include the need for achievement, the need for self-assertion or aggression, and the need for approval. The Negro youth has, however, been patterned in the past to be unaggressive and unassertive in order to gain approval. The authors suggest that Negroes do better in an integrated school because it approximates the situation in the outside, predominantly white, society. In this situation the Negro's sense of control over his environment and therefore his achievement and level of self-assertion rise. The rewards of society have not been constant for Negroes, and therefore these external rewards are poor motivators. 45 notes.

Cameron, Howard K. NONINTELLECTUAL CORRELATES OF ACADEMIC ACHIEVEMENT, pp. 252-257. Reviews recent studies on the validity of tests of nonintellectual traits (self-concept, achievement motivation, personal adjustment, etc.) as predictors of academic success. Table, 19 notes.

Manning, Winton H. THE MEASUREMENT OF INTELLECTUAL CAPACITY AND PERFORMANCE, pp. 258-267. Tests are vital in our educational system. They function for the students (guidance, equivalency certificates, and as part of the learning process) and for the institutions (for selection, prescriptions for educational treatments, and evaluation of their programs). Lower-class

Negroes tend to be hostile toward tests as symbols of inequality of educational opportunity. Differences in white and Negro scores on such tests have been blamed on the differences in environment and schools and on a built-in middle-class bias in the tests. Current tests have proved to be good predictors of academic achievement within certain situations; e.g., for Negroes in a predominantly Negro college. He suggests that a basic problem is the lack of "formal language" among disadvantaged youths which hampers their reasoning abilities. New studies of language and cognitive development are needed. 40 notes.

Gordon, Edmund W. and Jablonsky, Adelaide. COMPENSATORY EDU-CATION IN THE EQUALIZATION OF EDUCATIONAL OPPORTU-NITY, pp. 268-290. The first section reviews various compensatory programs (i.e., programs aimed at raising disadvantaged children to a level at which they can be educated by current methods). These include programs for pre-schoolers, drop-outs, and high school graduates in need of occupational training. However, while these programs increased greatly the quantity of effort, the methods used were largely the same old methods of traditional pedagogy. The authors recommend 10 criteria for consideration in developing a program of compensatory education. The second part of this article is sub-titled: "An Organizational Model for Compensatory Education." This model deals largely with the disadvantaged at the preschool and primary levels, and with students of all classes at the upper levels. A full program of compensatory education for the disadvantaged would cost about 101 billion dollars. 2 tables.

Mahan, Thomas W. THE BUSING OF STUDENTS FOR EQUAL OP-PORTUNITIES, pp. 291-300. "Busing" is defined in this article as including programs in which ghetto children are transported to essentially white schools and placed in classes where they are less than 25 percent of the class. The case studies discussed are those programs in Boston, Hartford, Rochester, and White Plains. Most ghetto parents approved of these programs, as did most of the white parents involved in the programs. The children in Hartford and White Plains were closely observed and it was shown that the ghetto children increased achievement and there was no loss to the white students. Children tend to follow the examples of the majority, and the ghetto children worked to meet the achievement levels of the majority in their classes - the middle-class whites. The busing costs about 250 to 270 dollars per child for tuition and transportation, but the major obstacle is political. Busing appears to be an effective method of moving toward equal educational opportunity. 2 tables, biblio.

Fischer, John H. SCHOOL PARKS FOR EDUCATIONAL OPPORTU-NITY, pp. 301-309. The school park would be a campus complex in which thousands of children - middle-class and ghetto - would go to the same campus. These parks, whether for kindergarten through grade 12 or on a k-4-4-4 basis, would have a student body of not less than 15,000 each. These parks should be arranged to integrate different races and social classes. The advantage of size would result in more efficient, economical, and better education for all. Such parks would cost about 50 million dollars, and considerable Federal support would be necessary. 8 notes.

Barros, Francis J. EQUAL OPPORTUNITY IN HIGHER EDUCA-TION, pp. 310-315. In today's technological society education is vital, but equal opportunity for higher education does not yet exist. Various reports that many Negro colleges are inferior are quoted. It is necessary for colleges actively to recruit disadvantaged youths, regardless of their test scores or past academic achievements, and give them the necessary compensatory training. Extensive Federal support is needed to provide higher education for these disadvantaged students. 11 notes.

Stembridge, Barbara Penn. A STUDENT'S APPRAISAL OF THE ADEQUACY OF HIGHER EDUCATION FOR BLACK AMERICANS, pp. 316-322. Negro colleges are inadequate because they try to copy inadequate white models, do not challenge their students enough, and stifle their faculties. The author's plan for elimination of these inadequacies involves a study of the functions of these institutions and how well they are performed, an evaluation of current standard measurements for human potential and achievement, the establishment of black community two-year colleges which would offer work toward transfer to four-year colleges, terminal work, and adult education. 9 notes.

Hayes, Charles L. INSTITUTIONAL APPRAISAL AND PLANNING FOR EQUAL EDUCATIONAL OPPORTUNITY, pp. 323-329. There are two fundamental problems facing Negro colleges today: students are tending to avoid small colleges, and Negro colleges are not producing the young leaders needed today. These small colleges have great financial needs, but they must realistically study themselves and then plan. The small colleges should cooperate with each other, but only if it is beneficial. There is no virtue in being small; these colleges must exploit their size. They can be more flexible, more innovative, and more alert to students' needs than large universities. There is opportunity for the creation of "a genuinely complete community of scholars" in these small colleges.

Cooke, Paul Phillips. EQUAL EDUCATIONAL OPPORTUNITY: SOME FINDINGS AND CONCLUSIONS, pp. 330-339. Summarizes the papers in this special number and makes two major conclusions. Equal educational opportunity does not exist in the United States and will not exist in this generation. Unless this country can provide full and equal employment opportunity and the chance for self-pride, disadvantaged children will lack the motivation to achieve in school. Therefore equal educational opportunity cannot exist under the present economic and social conditions. B. D. Johnson

2132. --. [RACE AND RACISM, THE NEGRO AND POVERTY, IN AMERICA TODAY]. *J. of Human Relations 1969 17(2): 162-278.*

Jenkins, Carl S. HAT, pp. 162-172. "A strong genetic basis can be attributed to an animalistic territorial response in man. This might be called the 'HAT' Syndrome - Human Animal Territorial Syndrome, a carry-over from evolutionary man. It has been known for a long period that the animal world is territorial in nature....It is easy to see a real application to man. Villages compete against villages...countries against countries....This is essentially what has happened in the present racial confrontation in the United States. Black families, confined to ghetto areas by force and economic rule for over two hundred years, have finally staked out their territory to repel the white invaders....Open housing and its fierce resistance is evidently a manifestation of territorialism....If we might project this thought further, then, open housing and what it means is a necessity for a working democracy. It is necessary for these people to think that their territory consists of a wider area." Based on published sources; 2 notes.

Olsen, Edward G. RACISM, A MODERN INVENTION, pp. 173-184. Defines the terms "race" and "racism," traces the origins of racism to the 16th century, summarizes 19th-century racist thought, and analyzes the theory and significance of racial segregation in America today. The prospects for the future are bleak "unless White America realizes and responds democratically now to the first law of history: *without justice there will be no law and order except in a semimilitary and dictatorial state."* 6 notes.

Groves, Harry E. THE REVOLT OF BLACK STUDENTS, pp. 185-197. "The black student is caught up in all of the forces that are applicable to students in general. But the fact of his race is an additional dimension of enormous significance." Even more than the white student, the black student is concerned over the war in Vietnam, the values and priorities of a racist society, and the need to reform American universities. The revolution of black students has been entirely justified. There remains only the question of tactics. Continued student pressure in the form of demonstrations and other similar actions may well be self-defeating.

Joynes, Thomas J. NEGRO IDENTITY - BLACK POWER AND VIO-LENCE, pp. 198-207. Discusses race relations in the United States from the point of view of psychodynamics. Political unity among Negroes is in many respects a fine goal, but it is as likely of fulfillment as white unity. There is a great deal of apathy among Negroes. Circumstances compel them to think in terms of individual survival. Black violence is not constructive, but the avenues for action do not lead anywhere else. "Given the opportunity, Negroes react like other Americans when they see a chance to distinguish themselves....Society has not provided its black citizens with the tools of strong ego construction....One has to know who one is before being able to accept differences with equanimity, and this idea of knowing who one is, and being aware of possibilities and alternatives in behavior and expression, is not part of the thinking of most Negroes." There is little hope of improvement in race relations in the United States, because Americans have selective hearing, selective eyesight, and they suffer from a rigidity of values.

Relyea, Harold C. BLACK POWER AND PARALLEL INSTITU-TIONS: IDEOLOGICAL AND THEORETICAL CONSIDERATIONS, pp. 208-223. Discusses the meaning and significance of the term "Black Power" and its implication in the development of economic, political, and educational institutions controlled by Negroes. 27 notes.

Parker, Yvonne. RACIAL PREJUDICE - THE CAUSE AND THE CURE, pp. 224-235. "The growing child learns to behave primarily by following the modes and models of behavior around him....By the time he is told for the first time that 'Negroes are inferior,' he is *already* convinced of it." Reform of customary community practices is the key to the prevention of prejudice. Based on the author's personal experiences.

Hazel, David W. and Ratkowski, Alex. RESPONSES TO "RACIAL PREJUDICE - THE CAUSE AND 'THE CURE,' " pp. 236-241. Criticizes the preceding article as sincere but simplistic.

Harper, Dean. THE OTHER WAR, pp. 242-259. Assesses the progress made by three battles against poverty in the United States. Two of these battles are being fought by the Government in the form of public welfare and the educational programs developed by the Office of Economic Opportunity. Public welfare was not designed as a weapon against poverty. A major weakness of the Economic Opportunity Act (1964) was the failure to provide for an adequate evaluation of the effectiveness of new programs - Job Corps, Neighborhood Youth Corps, Work-Study Programs, Project Head Start, and Upward Bound.

Saul Alinsky has developed a third alternative - the organization of the poor in their own communities. Mention should also be made of attempts minimally to train and employ the poor as "indigenous social workers." There is little hard evidence that any of these tactics are effective; indeed, "probably there will never be good evidence that a particular program is effective." Three principles now have widespread support in a revised battle plan on poverty: the Federal Government should promote economic growth more vigorously, there should be greater emphasis on job creation, and everyone should be assured a minimum level of income.

Ashbrook, James B. "A NEW DAY HAS TAKEN PLACE": AN INTERPRETIVE DESCRIPTION OF THE CRISIS IN BLACK AND WHITE, pp. 260-278. Tells the story of race relations at Colgate Rochester Divinity School from the first phase, Blind Integration (1958-60), through the phase of Cooperative Civil Rights (1961-64), to a period when the black students expressed their anger openly and defiantly, deliberately cutting themselves off from the whites. In 1967-68 the school moved "from resegregation with abusiveness to a resegregation with abrasiveness." Based on the author's personal experiences.

D. J. Abramoske

2133. --. SYMPOSIUM: HUMAN RIGHTS. *J. of Phil. 1964 61(20): 628-645.*
Wasserstrom, Richard. HUMAN RIGHTS, AND RACIAL DISCRIMINATION, pp. 628-641. Attempts to delineate one set of arguments for natural rights. Concludes that two rights, well-being and freedom, can be justified as natural, and that these are being denied southern Negroes.

Feinberg, Joel. WASSERSTROM ON HUMAN RIGHTS, pp. 641-645. Wasserstrom fails to distinguish between one man's right and another's resultant obligations. The latter is obligated not to interfere with the former's exercise of his right; he is not obligated to "give" the right to him. Otherwise, agrees with the paper.

J. Hines

2134. --. [THE ANTIOCH REVIEW]. *Antioch R. 1965/66 25(4): 496-486, 1966 26(1): 120-127.*
Bixler, Paul. QUANDARIES OF A QUARTERLY, pp. 469-486. The former librarian and editor of the *Antioch Review* writes of the history of the review since its founding in 1940. The political situation at the time of its inception is examined, as are the editorial viewpoints since 1940. Note.

Champney, Freeman. ANNIVERSARY THOUGHTS FROM A FOUNDING EDITOR, pp. 120-127. Recalls various events such as the Depression; the rise of fascism in Spain, Italy, and Germany; the growing attraction of Marxism in the 1930's; the desegregation efforts in the South; the Bay of Pigs episode; and Black Power.

D. F. Rossi

2135. --. [THE GRIPES OF ACADEME]. *North Am. R. 1969 6(2): 16-33, 46-61.*
Preis, Julie. UW: THE UNREVOLUTIONARY PRESENT, pp. 16-20. A view of the February 1969 clash between the Black Student Alliance and the

University of Wisconsin administration, which involved police and National Guardsmen. The author criticizes the administration for being repressive and self-righteous.

Young, H. Edwin. A CHANCELLOR'S PRESS CONFERENCE, pp. 21-25. A copy of the press conference between Chancellor Young and the press, with the exception of three minor, noted deletions.

Light, D. W., Jr. and Feldman, David. BLACK AND WHITE AT BRANDEIS, pp. 25-29. Describe the black-white problems at Brandeis University, which led to the black's 11-day occupation of Ford Hall. Basic to the whole situation is the cultural gap between black students and the schools that recruit them. The authors state that Brandeis' Afro-American Society felt compelled to act because of broken promises and unfulfilled new needs. They briefly describe President Abram's use of both ultimatum and stand-off strategies, and end by posing the four main issues revealed by the crisis.

Rainey, Thomas B. and Small, Bunny. THE DUKE CRISIS: "IT AIN'T OVER" pp. 30-33, 46. A description of a demonstration at Duke University in the spring of 1968, known as the Duke Vigil. The authors criticize the power structure in which decisionmaking power rests with big-business trustees, far removed from education and moral commitment.

Unger, William. CONFRONTATION: ONE YEAR LATER, pp. 46-48. Describes the sit-in at Trinity College, including the naïveté of student leaders as they tried to unite the students and protest reasonably.

Greason, A. L., Jr. PROTEST AND REACTION: STUDENTS AND SOCIETY IN CONFLICT, pp. 48-53. Evaluates current student unrest in America, emphasizing the loss of center on campuses, which has resulted in the existence of extremes only. Student involvement on all levels of the university and in society is the only way to solve the current situation.

Reid, John. THE STRUGGLE AT HARVARD, pp. 54-58. Presents six demands the Students for a Democratic Society (SDS) made to the Harvard administration after seizing a building. The author, a radical, admits mistakes but claims that the movement is gaining strength not only among students but among the working people of the Cambridge area.

S. L. McNeel

Racial Attitudes & the Pattern of Discrimination

2136. Akar, John T. AN AFRICAN VIEWS AMERICA. *Mennonite Life 1967 22(1): 19-23.* A friendly critique of America by an African intellectual who finds both Russia and the United States confusing and in many ways repellent. Russians talk of anticolonialism, for example, but they oppress Eastern Europe. American foreign policy is objectionable, too, especially in Vietnam. Africans think of America as decadent, a society which makes heroes of its football players and ignores its poets. It is a sex- and dollar-oriented civilization. But most disturbing of all is its racism.   D. J. Abramoske

2137. Appel, John J. AMERICAN NEGRO AND IMMIGRANT EXPERI-
ENCE: SIMILARITIES AND DIFFERENCES. *Am. Q. 1966 18(1): 95-103.*
Reminds those who would compare the history of Negro and immigrant experience, that the critical factor is race. Although immigrants faced problems of
assimilation, they were not blocked by caste status. "Cultural memories" also
differentiated Negroes from immigrants. For the Negro, historical experience
denied American ideals. Often in competition with the Negro, urban immigrants
sometimes feared or exploited the Negro in order to elevate themselves. Despite
the vicissitudes they encountered, most immigrants have either made it out or
have been helped out of the ghetto. Those who failed to make it were largely
hidden from view. In the case of the Negro, failures take place in the broad
daylight of current publicity. Basic goals, e.g., jobs, decent housing, and equal
opportunity, are still often out of range for Negroes. In order to gain his share,
the Negro may resort, as the immigrant has done before him, to ethnic chauvinism. 4 notes.   R. S. Pickett

2138. Babow, Irving. RESTRICTIVE PRACTICES IN PUBLIC ACCOMMO-
DATIONS IN A NORTHERN COMMUNITY. *Phylon 1963 24(1): 5-12.* Deals
with San Francisco, in which one out of five residents is "nonwhite." Places of
public accommodation play a major role in its economy. Despite gains made in
recent years, Negroes experience restrictions, as do Orientals and Filipinos on
occasion. Mexican Americans and Jews are rarely restricted. Those who do not
employ "nonwhites" in public contact jobs also discourage "nonwhite" clientele.
Exclusion, segregation, discourtesy, and quotas are among methods employed by
a relatively small percentage of keepers of restaurants, motels, hotels, taverns, and
other establishments.   L. Filler

2139. Bahr, Howard M. and Gibbs, Jack P. RACIAL DIFFERENTIATION IN
AMERICAN METROPOLITAN AREAS. *Social Forces 1967 45(4): 521-532.*
"A theory on the interrelations among four forms of racial differentiation is
formulated and tested, using data from the 1960 United States Census for a
random sample of 33 Standard Metropolitan Statistical Areas. The findings
generally support the theory with respect to interrelations among educational,
occupational and income differentiation. The relation of residential differentiation to the other three forms of Negro-white differentiation is not close, which
indicates that residential differentiation may not be as 'basic' to other forms of
racial differentiation as is commonly believed."   J

2140. Banks, James A. DEVELOPING RACIAL TOLERANCE WITH LIT-
ERATURE ON THE BLACK INNER CITY. *Social Educ. 1970 34(5): 549-552.*
Believes it is imperative that white suburban children, who are described as
"culturally sheltered," develop positive attitudes toward people who have different racial and cultural backgrounds. An attitude of tolerance and/or understanding for differing ethnic origins is a vital necessity in today's "highly

polarized" American society. Factual descriptions of urban riots do not deeply arouse the emotions of white children since these "incidents seem remote from their lives and experiences." Literature, however, can be a vehicle to acquaint youngsters with different racial and ethnic groups and to develop tolerance. By reading novels about black people, white children can come to know them as human beings and develop emotional awareness of their problems. 7 notes.

G. D. Doyle

2141. Banta, Thomas J. THE KENNEDY ASSASSINATION: EARLY THOUGHTS AND EMOTIONS. *Public Opinion Q. 1964 28(2): 216-224.* A study, designed on the day of the assassination, analyzes interviews with 114 people completed within nine hours of the time each first heard the news. The diffusion of news was such that 22 percent were mass-media-informed. "Over twice the percentage of Republicans as of Democrats showed complete belief in the first reports heard. This should be interpreted as Democratic *disbelief.*" In their imputation of blame Republicans in the sample tended to protect the right wing and the conservative, while Democrats showed concern for protection of the Negro.

E. P. Stickney

2142. Barcus, F. Earle and Levin, Jack. ROLE DISTANCE IN NEGRO AND MAJORITY FICTION. *Journalism Q. 1966 43(4): 709-714.* Fiction containing both Negro and non-Negro characters was coded in high-circulation, "majority-oriented" magazines (19 stories) and Negro-oriented magazines (15 stories) in respect to the expectation of intimacy between the characters. The two groups revealed almost identical patterns of "social distance," but they may come from different sources. The majority stories ignored racial conflict and civil rights struggles and the social distance seemed to have been the reflection of traditional patterns of race relations in American society and of exclusion of Negroes from status reserved for "whites only." The Negro magazines' stories focused upon the tension in Negro-white relations, dealing primarily with the reality of racial inequality in the context of the recent social revolution. 3 tables, 11 notes.

S. E. Humphreys

2143. Baron, Harold M. BLACK POWERLESSNESS IN CHICAGO. *Trans-action 1968 6(10): 27-33.* A study of the extent of black exclusion from policy-making positions in Chicago and of the areas in which blacks do participate in the policymaking process. Of 10,997 policymaking positions in the public and private sector, blacks occupied only 285. The highest percentages of blacks were in government, public education, and unions; the lowest percentages were in business corporations and universities. Even in public life blacks seldom hold positions in sectors which lack a black constituency. In the politics of Cook County the black organization operated as a "submachine" of the Cook County Democratic organization. The author thinks the best way to increase the number and power of blacks in decisionmaking is to unify the black constituency. In order to do this it must develop its own set of goals and policies. 3 charts, photo.

A. Erlebacher

2144. Belvin, William L., Jr. THE GEORGIA GUBERNATORIAL PRIMARY OF 1946. *Georgia Hist. Q. 1966 50(1): 36-53.* Careful analysis of the primary campaign in which Eugene Talmadge, though losing in popular votes, nevertheless won the gubernatorial nomination for a fourth term owing largely to his racist appeal to rural voters and to the operation of the county unit system.
R. Lowitt

2145. Billington, Monroe. FREEDOM TO SERVE: THE PRESIDENT'S COMMITTEE ON EQUALITY OF TREATMENT AND OPPORTUNITY IN THE ARMED FORCES, 1949-1950. *J. of Negro Hist. 1966 51(4): 262-274.* Discusses the contribution of President Harry S. Truman's Committee on Equality of Treatment and Opportunity in the Armed Forces toward ending racial segregation in the U.S. military establishment. The President asked the committee for concrete results and within a year and a half the racial policies of the Air Force, the Navy, and the Army were genuinely liberalized. The Army was the most reluctant branch of the military services to modify its policies but the committee persisted until its proposals were accepted. After the Army agreed to desegregate, only the National Guard units in the Southern States remained segregated. Based on manuscript sources.
L. Gara

2146. Billington, Monroe. PUBLIC SCHOOL INTEGRATION IN MISSOURI, 1954-64. *J. of Negro Educ. 1966 35(3): 252-262.* Considers the process of desegregation in Missouri schools in the decade after the Supreme Court's *Brown vs. Board of Education of Topeka* decision with particular attention to the St. Louis and Kansas City areas and to six southeastern counties which together contain the majority of Missouri Negroes. While Missouri indicated its intention to implement the decision and integration seemed rapid at first, the process of integration had virtually halted by 1958; and by 1964 less than half of Missouri's Negro pupils were attending classes with whites. The impact of urban housing patterns and the integration of teachers are discussed. 52 notes.
S. C. Pearson, Jr.

2147. Birenbaum, William M. WHOSE LAW AND ORDER? SEGREGATION AND THE ABUSE OF DUE PROCESS ON THE AMERICAN CAMPUS. *J.: Division of Higher Educ. United Church of Christ 1969 7(7): 3-6.* A new kind of learning community, able to carry out education for freedom, is the crucial issue today. But, "The hard line - not reform or even reconsideration - is what is being preached by liberal university professors, conservative governors and state legislators, and the President of the United States." This formidable power bloc will succeed in suppressing the students and the radical faculty. A new program could be instituted to integrate new knowledge into the school curriculum and thus achieve aspirations which the United States claims to cherish. Draws on a theme in the author's book, *Overlive: Power, Poverty and the University* (New York: Dell Publishing Co.).
C. W. Ohrvall

2148. Black, Isabella. RACE AND UNREASON: ANTI-NEGRO OPINION IN PROFESSIONAL AND SCIENTIFIC LITERATURE SINCE 1954. *Phylon 1965 26(1): 65-79.* Surveys scientific and professional literature of the decade since the Brown vs. Board of Education decision and concludes that anti-Negro opinion is widespread therein and offers a barrier to speedy integration of southern schools and to elimination of discrimination in education, jobs, and housing in the North. S. C. Pearson, Jr.

2149. Blake, Elias, Jr. COLOR PREJUDICE AND THE EDUCATION OF LOW INCOME NEGROES IN THE NORTH AND WEST. *J. of Negro Educ. 1965 34(3): 288-299.* Observes that color prejudice is the norm in American society and that higher education and income levels do not necessarily result in a greater willingness to have intimate or long-term social relationships with Negroes. Thus acceptance of the fact of color prejudice "may be the first step toward at least starting a dialogue within the educational profession," dealing with interpersonal relationships between Negro and white teachers, the perception of students by teachers related to their reactions to skin color differences, feelings about white-Negro differences, the role of the teacher's race in affecting student performance, and intraracial dimensions of color prejudice among Negro staff members. Documented. S. C. Pearson, Jr.

2150. Blumberg, Leonard. SEGREGATED HOUSING, MARGINAL LOCATION, AND THE CRISIS OF CONFIDENCE. *Phylon 1964 25(4): 321-330.* Considers present racial relationships in the United States in a political context and reports a study of recent trends in racially segregated housing in Atlanta, Philadelphia, and Pasadena as illustrations of the process which is being used by Negroes to raise the level of tension in the white population to the point where it will delegitimize the discrimination and shift its evaluation of the Negro population. The author concludes that present racial relationships evidence a crisis of confidence on the part of Negroes in the American political process which, if long continued, may reduce "the probability that viable re-definitions can be reached within the framework of the revolutionary democratic ideology of 'liberty, equality, and fraternity.'" S. C. Pearson, Jr.

2151. Blumberg, Leonard and Lalli, Michael. LITTLE GHETTOES: A STUDY OF NEGROES IN THE SUBURBS. *Phylon 1966 27(2): 117-131.* Traces the Negro and white population ratios for the out-county area of Philadelphia for the period 1930 to 1960 and characterizes Negro suburban ghettos on the basis of 379 interviews in 6 areas. The data suggest that the segregated Negro community is a composite of "black bourgeoisie" and "respectables," that residents are actively in pursuit of the dominant values of American society, and that they identify highly with the suburbs in general and their own locality in particular in community terms. Racial segregation continues and is relatively effective in the area. S. C. Pearson, Jr.

2152. Blume, Norman. CLERGYMEN AND SOCIAL ACTION. *Sociol. and Social Res. 1970 54(2): 237-248.* "This study of ministerial behavior patterns in an open housing pledge card campaign in the Toledo, Ohio, area found that the clerics who involved themselves more actively in the campaign included those whose attitudes concurred with this effort, were reared in a region considered to be more sympathetic to integrated living, were younger, whose congregations supported and did not oppose involvement in the campaign, and who were by religion of the liberal Protestant, Jewish, Bahai, and Unitarian faiths. On the other hand, the congregation's organizational structure, the socioeconomic structure of the congregation, neighborhood proximity to the black ghetto, and the integration of the congregation seemed to have little impact on the involvement of the individual clergyman. Moreover, the Catholic, Lutheran, Baptist, and Presbyterian clerics tended to abstain from involvement in this program of social action." J

2153. Boesel, David, Berk, Richard, Groves, W. Eugene, Eidson, Bettye, and Rossi, Peter H. WHITE INSTITUTIONS AND BLACK RAGE. *Trans-action 1969 6(5): 24-31.* At the request of the National Advisory Commission on Civil Disorders (the Kerner Commission) the authors surveyed the reasons for black outrage concerning white institutions. In 15 northern cities they interviewed men and women working for large firms, retail merchants, public schools, welfare departments, police departments, and in politics. The views of various white groups toward blacks and their struggle seem to vary with whites' concepts of their own experiences with blacks and their preconceptions about blacks. Employers show aversions to hiring blacks, ghetto merchants fear thievery and competition, teachers are appalled at the physical condition of slum schools, social workers sympathize with black causes but still feel they have a responsibility to "teach the poor how to live," police feel that Negroes are favored, and black political workers lack the means to make the larger community respond to black needs. Many of the white responses result from the rising of the Negro against the dominant white institutions in the ghetto. The excesses and the inadequacies are more apparent than ever. The institutions must be reformed or the black community will make it more difficult for them to function at all. 3 photos, biblio.
A. Erlebacher

2154. Bogardus, Emory S. COMPARING RACIAL DISTANCE IN ETHI-OPIA, SOUTH AFRICA, AND THE UNITED STATES. *Sociol. and Social Res. 1968 52(2): 149-156.* "Three extensive racial distance studies are compared in this article. These investigations were made in widely separated regions of the world, namely, Ethiopia, South Africa, and the United States. The results of these studies are comparable chiefly because all made use of the same Ethnic Distance Scale for measuring racial reactions." J

2155. Bolner, James. TOWARD A THEORY OF RACIAL REPARATIONS. *Phylon 1968 29(1): 41-47.* Examines certain aspects of the attempt to render legitimate and orderly the assimilation of Negroes through benign racial treatment. There are two justifications of racial reparations: 1) payment to nonwhites who have been injured by racial discrimination; and 2) prevention of further disorder by financially assisting nonwhites. That is, there is both a moral and a practical justification. The author offers criticisms of both approaches, emphasizing the fact that they are forms of racism. He also defends such policies by noting that nonwhites have a legitimate claim to such reparations and that the implementation of reparations programs by the executive and legislative branches of the Central Government would probably not be blocked on constitutional grounds by the judiciary because of the establishment of precedent in other areas affecting racial matters, such as civil rights, voting, housing, etc. Based on primary and secondary sources; 31 notes.   R. D. Cohen

2156. Bone, Robert A. THE NOVELS OF JAMES BALDWIN. *Tri-Q. 1964 1: 3-20.* As "the most important Negro writer to emerge during the last decade," James Baldwin "has succeeded in transporting the entire discussion of American race relations to the interior plane," which "is a major breakthrough for the American imagination." *Go Tell It on the Mountain* (New York: Grosset and Dunlap, 1953), his best novel to date, is a novel of the great migration of Negroes to the North. Based on primary sources; photo, 14 notes.   W. H. Agee

2157. Bowers, David R. A REPORT ON ACTIVITY BY PUBLISHERS IN DIRECTING NEWSROOM DECISIONS. *Journalism Q. 1967 44(1): 43-52.* Managing editors of 613 evening daily newspapers rated the activity of their publishers in directing use or nonuse, content, or display of news. Findings were that: 1) the closer the geographical proximity of subject matter, the more active is the publisher in news direction; 2) the larger the circulation of the newspaper, the less active is the publisher in news direction; 3) publisher activity is higher in areas which conceivably might affect newspaper revenue than in social issues such as politics, race, religion, labor, or war; 4) publisher activity is higher in areas involving themselves and their personal activity than in most social issues, but this activity is not as high as in areas which might conceivably affect revenue; 5) publisher activity has no particular variation from one geographical region to the next, although in most categories it is less in New England; 6) publisher activity regarding news of local race or racial issues is highest in States with the greatest proportion of Negroes; 7) publisher activity appears to be less prevalent in use or nonuse of news than in content or display of news, especially in larger newspapers, and 8) more publishers' directions are expressed than implied when specific news stories are concerned. It is suggested that the smaller percentage of involvement by publishers of dailies with large circulations should be examined closely by those who criticize bigness in the American press. 6 tables, 5 notes.
                                                                S. E. Humphreys

2158. Bowman, Lewis. RACIAL DISCRIMINATION AND NEGRO LEADERSHIP PROBLEMS: THE CASE OF "NORTHERN COMMUNITY." *Social Forces 1965 44(2): 173-185.* "This is a report of recent research in *Northern Community,* a New England city where Negroes constitute a relatively minor portion of the total population. Although not as spectacularly evident as in many Southern communities, or in other Northern communities of greater Negro concentrations in the total population, problems of discrimination in employment, housing, and school facilities do exist in *Northern Community.* Concomitant problems of Negro leadership appear to be compounding the problems of racial discrimination, or at least to be making the search for solutions to the problems more difficult."   J

2159. Brooks, Thomas R. "NEW YORK'S FINEST." *Commentary 1965 40(2): 29-36.* Discusses the reasons why a New York City Council subcommittee has recommended "that the Council set up its own committee to review the findings of the Police Department's Civilian Complaint Review Board," and why "the whole notion of civilian review of police behavior is distasteful to the police themselves." After considering the increase in the number of New York City policemen (now one policeman for every 330 citizens), their wage scale (6,647 dollars for the first year rising to 8,098 dollars after three years of service), their ethnic background (mainly Irish and Italian, with very few Negroes or Puerto Ricans), and the recruits' reasons for joining the police force (a steady job with security), the author attributes the occasional outbursts of senseless police brutality to the fact that police work is routine, frustrating, and boring, and thus makes for quick tempers. "Obviously, much can be done by the Department to improve relations with the city's minority groups, but just as obviously little will be done unless enough political pressure for improved policies is built up."

D. D. Cameron

2160. Brown, Claude. SATURDAY NIGHT IN HARLEM: A MEMOIR. *Commentary 1965 40(1): 47-53.* A recollection of the violence of Saturday nights in the New York ghetto, and of the surprises - such as finding one's father out with another woman or learning that one's brother is on dope.

R. J. Moore

2161. Brunn, Stanley D. and Hoffman, Wayne L. THE SPATIAL RESPONSE OF NEGROES AND WHITES TOWARD OPEN HOUSING: THE FLINT REFERENDUM. *Ann. of the Assoc. of Am. Geographers 1970 60(1): 18-36.* "The white and Negro response to the 1968 open housing referendum in Flint, Michigan, is used to investigate spatial variations in attitudes. Simple and stepwise multiple regression models were utilized that incorporated measures of income, education, housing, and distance. Separate analyses were made for the white and Negro voting behavior. For the white population it was hypothesized that a positive vote would be associated with high median incomes, high median education levels, high median housing values, and increased distances from the edge of the nearest Negro ghetto and nearest Negro precinct. This hypothesis was rejected. For the Negro precincts it was postulated that the variations in income, education, and housing value would not account for differences in the vote owing to the crucial nature of this issue. This was accepted." J

2162. Buck, Joyce. THE EFFECTS OF NEGRO AND WHITE DIALECTAL VARIATIONS UPON ATTITUDES OF COLLEGE STUDENTS. *Speech Monographs 1968 35(2): 181-186.* An experimental examination of the influence of dialectal variations in Negro and white speakers. The results indicated that: 1) subjects' attitudes were more favorable toward standard dialect of both Negro and white speakers than toward nonstandard dialect, 2) subjects preferred the nonstandard dialect of the Negro speakers to the nonstandard dialect of the white speakers, 3) all standard dialect speakers were considered to be more competent than nonstandard speakers, 4) Negro and white standard speakers were not perceived as being more trustworthy than the white nonstandard speakers, and

5) Negro and white standard dialect speakers were not perceived as being more trustworthy than the nonstandard Negro speakers. 23 notes.

D. R. Richardson

2163. Burns, Haywood. THE RULE OF LAW IN THE SOUTH. *Commentary 1965 40(3): 80-90.* The author points out that despite the guarantees of the U.S. Constitution and Federal law, "Negroes in the South (and whites working with them) have been repeatedly deprived of their rights both by private individuals and by state and local officials. Because they have failed to act effectively in many such instances,the President and the Department of Justice have not been fulfilling their constitutional and other legal obligations." Although under Title 18, Section 594 of the U.S. Code there are criminal penalties of up to a thousand dollars fine and one year in jail for "whoever intimidates, threatens, coerces or attempts to intimidate...any other person for the purpose of interfering with the right of such other person to vote or to vote as he may choose," these provisions have rarely been implemented by the Justice Department, "and potential Negro voters remain intimidated by the quite justified fear that they will be beaten, their homes bombed, their families threatened, or their livelihoods destroyed....The standard rebuttal of Justice Department spokesmen like Robert Kennedy and Burke Marshall has been to assert that 'We have no national police force,' and to disclaim responsibility for the protection of citizens' rights on the grounds that such protection would upset federal-state relations." The author makes constructive suggestions for the reevaluation, improvement, and revision of the Federal law enforcement system in the South. "Confronted by its Constitutional duty and backed by a growing consensus on civil rights, the Executive has enough power to establish the rule of law in the South." D. D. Cameron

2164. Byrne, Donn and Andres, David. PREJUDICE AND INTERPERSONAL EXPECTANCIES. *J. of Negro Educ. 1964 33(4): 441-445.* A group of 70 students at the University of Texas was given a test designed to measure anti-Negro prejudice and another designed to ascertain expectancies with respect to the consequences of interactions between whites and Negroes. Results suggested "that individuals high in anti-Negro prejudice express expectancies of a lower ratio of positive to negative reinforcements as a consequence of Negro-white interactions than do individuals low in prejudice." S. C. Pearson, Jr.

2165. Campbell, Ernest Q. NEGROES, EDUCATION, AND THE SOUTHERN STATES. *Social Forces 1969 47(3): 253-265.* "The educational attainments of Negroes in the southern states are, compared to whites, exceedingly poor, and justly a condition for national concern and remediation. But evidence is presented that interracial differences in educational facilities and accomplishments are not decidedly more pronounced in the South than in the nation, and the question of why this fact has been largely hidden is discussed. The argument is advanced that educational competence rather than educational facilities is a more appropriate measure of opportunity. It is suggested that strategies for remediation must focus on desegregation, on the reprofessionalization of teachers, on creating a sense of efficacy in students, and on reducing the influence of educationally impoverished homes. There is a discussion of authenticity as an issue for white southerners and for Negroes, and a concluding section discusses current tensions between scholarly analysis and social action in the conduct of sociologists."

J

2166. Carleton, William G. KENNEDY IN HISTORY: AN EARLY APPRAISAL. *Antioch R. 1964 24(3): 277-299.* A "historical appraisal of John Fitzgerald Kennedy written less than a year after his death." The author traces Kennedy's voting record in Congress, his views on foreign policy, his attitude toward the Negro, and his attitude toward Senator Joseph McCarthy. The author discusses the issues of the 1960 presidential campaign and Kennedy's foreign policy while in office. 10 notes. D. F. Rossi

2167. Carter, Hodding. OUR TOWN IS CONSERVATIVE. *Virginia Q. R. 1965 41(2): 202-206.* Describes the voluntary desegregation of the schools in Greenville, Mississippi, anu gives many other examples to show "that Greenville is not Mississippi - save geographically." The town is conservative in the concept of noblesses oblige which "entails a sense of personal responsibility for keeping alive the best that has been handed down, including commitment to a goal of civil decency and responsibility." Justice, too, has been even-handed and color blind, but among the churches only the Roman Catholic and the Episcopal have admitted Negro worshippers. E. P. Stickney

2168. Chace, James. DECLINE AND FALL RIVER: REHABILITATING THE WHITE GHETTO. *Interplay 1969 3(4): 40-43.* Fall River is an industrial city of poor, white, lower-middle-class workers who have suffered because of the decline of the textile industry in New England. Various urban rehabilitation projects are underway there, but directors of the programs have run into problems in cooperating with the national government, such as difficulty in getting home improvement loans approved quickly. This is "a classic case of confrontation between the community and the government." The white working class distrusts the national government, there is widespread fear that blacks will settle in white neighborhoods, and slum owners are able to exploit minority ethnic groups who have no choice but to accept substandard housing. A greater degree of total community control of urban rehabilitation is necessary. Illus., photo.

J. A. Zabel

2169. Clark, Kenneth. FOLKLORE OF NEGRO CHILDREN IN GREATER LOUISVILLE REFLECTING ATTITUDES TOWARD RACE. *Kentucky Folklore Record 1964 10(1): 1-11.* Samples of Negro songs, chants, and sayings collected by a recorder on playgrounds are used to support the thesis that "folklore which reflects belief in Negro inferiority will, at the very least, have the effect of reinforcing the dominant white attitudes in the minds of Negro children who keep this verbal play in circulation." J. C. Crowe

2170. Cleary, Robert E. GUBERNATORIAL LEADERSHIP AND STATE POLICY ON DESEGREGATION IN PUBLIC HIGHER EDUCATION. *Phylon 1966 27(2): 165-170.* Discusses the role of the governors in Mississippi,

Georgia, and North Carolina in desegregation in higher education, concluding that the political structure in Mississippi is the least well-organized of these three States to choose a goal and accomplish it. The leaders of Georgia and particularly of North Carolina are in a better position to achieve accepted objectives. Mississippi has followed a policy of massive resistance while Georgia, with its more organized system, followed a somewhat more liberal course; and North Carolina, with its most structured politics, followed a still more liberal course. 6 notes.

S. C. Pearson, Jr.

2171. Cohen, David K. EDUCATION AND RACE. *Hist. of Educ. Q. 1969 9(3): 281-286.* Raises questions for the future historian of urban education. Asks why schools were chosen as the vehicle for integration, why compensatory education was relied on to eliminate poverty-created disparities among children, how politics affects urban education, and why there is such a strong belief that education can overcome poverty and disparities in achievement. Also suggests that such questions can be asked fruitfully only when one questions prevailing assumptions.

J. Herbst

2172. Cohnsteadt, Martin L. A NEW KIND OF ADULT EDUCATOR IN INTERGROUP RELATIONS. *J. of Human Relations 1964 12(3): 351-357.* A paper presented to the Great Lakes Regional Conference, National Association of Intergroup Relations Officials, Chicago, Illinois, 23 June 1962. Discusses the functions and challenges facing intergroup relations workers, also referred to as Urban Extension Agents. In a pluralistic society, they seek, for example, "to interpret each group to the other and to mediate between conflicting interests." Emphasizes the need to understand the social structure of both the majority culture and the subcultures. The article is particularly relevant to race relations. Four scholarly works are cited.

D. J. Abramoske

2173. Colemen, A. Lee. THE RURAL-URBAN VARIABLE IN RACE RELATIONS. *Rural Sociol. 1965 30(4): 393-406.* Explains the relationship between rural sociology and race relations. Race relations by tradition have been formulated as an "urban" phenomenon. Although rural society has been away from the mainstream of the civil rights movement, a great deal of social change is currently taking place in rural America: in voting registration, public school desegregation, and public accommodations desegregation. In the past, the Department of Agriculture has not been receptive to the idea of research in race relations in rural areas. This is no longer the case. Race relations is a fertile area for future research. 38 notes.

A. S. Freedman

2174. Cone, J.H. BLACK CONSCIOUSNESS AND THE BLACK CHURCH: A HISTORICAL-THEOLOGICAL INTERPRETATION. *Ann. of the Am.*

Acad. of Pol. and Social Sci. 1970 387: 49-55. "Black consciousness as expressed in Black Power is the most significant reality of the black community. Though the phrases 'Black Power' and 'black consciousness' are relatively new, the reality that they symbolize is rooted in the past. Black consciousness is the black community focusing on its blackness in order that black people may know not only why they are oppressed, but also what they must do about that oppression. Because there always have been black people who have resisted the white definitions of blackness, it is appropriate to say that black consciousness is as old as black slavery. It is not possible to enslave a people because they are black and expect them not to be aware of their blackness as the means of liberation. It is Black Power's emphasis on liberation that makes it unquestionably a manifestation of God's work in America. The Christian Gospel is a gospel of liberation. The pre-Civil War black churches recognized this, and that was why they refused to accept an interpretation of Christianity that was unrelated to civil freedom. Unfortunately, the post-Civil War black churches forgot about this emphasis and began to identify religion with piety. But the rise of Black Theology in the black churches is a renewal of the pre-Civil War emphasis. It is not certain whether the major black denominations will respond positively by reordering their structures in the light of Black Power. What is certain is the black community's awareness of its blackness as the only tool for liberation. And unless the black churches redefine their existence in the light of the fathers who fought, risking death, to end slavery, the judgment of God will descend upon it in the persons of those who affirm with Brother Eldridge Cleaver: 'We shall have our manhood. We shall have it or the earth will be leveled by our attempts to gain it.'"

J

2175. Conyers, James E. and Kennedy, T. H. NEGRO PASSING: TO PASS OR NOT TO PASS. *Phylon 1963 24(3): 215-223.* Groups of Negro and white college students ranked in order of importance incentives for Negroes passing or not passing as whites. Negroes ranked incentives or reasons for passing in the following order of importance: 1) to secure equal cultural, social, and recreational advantages; 2) to secure economic advantages; 3) love or marriage; 4) psychic thrill in fooling whites; 5) lack of identification with Negroes; 6) feeling of importance; and 7) to hide one's past life. Whites ranked incentives for passing in the same order except for a reversal of position for items 4) and 5). Negroes listed incentives or reasons for not passing in the following order: 1) pride in being a Negro; 2) reluctance to cut ties with family and friends; 3) refusal to face the problem; 4) desertion of Negro cause; 5) would make one feel nervous and suspicious; 6) greater in-group esteem by remaining Negro; 7) risk would be too great; 8) would involve too much well thought out, calculated planning; and 9) life would be too lonely as a white. Whites arranged these incentives in the following order of significance: 2), 1), 3), 4), 5), 8), 6), 7), and 9).

S. C. Pearson, Jr.

2176. Cornelius, Paul. INTERRACIAL CHILDREN'S BOOKS: PROBLEMS AND PROGRESS. *Lib. Q. 1971 41(2): 106-127.* Discusses the reasons racial minorities have been inadequately represented in children's books, and considers what has happened in the past five years to redress the situation. Focuses upon factors which created interest in the problem of racial imbalance in children's books and those which impeded publication (until recently) of interracial children's books. Describes and evaluates recent publications for teenagers from minorities, and reviews the activities of the Council on Interracial Books and the impact of recent Black Power advocates. Based on secondary sources; 27 notes.

C. A. Newton

2177. Cosman, Bernard. REPUBLICANISM IN THE SOUTH: GOLD-WATER'S IMPACT UPON VOTING ALIGNMENTS IN CONGRES-SIONAL, GUBERNATORIAL, AND SENATORIAL RACES. *Southwestern Soc. Sci. Q. 1967 48(1): 13-23.* A detailed look at the impact of the Goldwater outcome upon pre-1964 voting alignments. Analysis is subdivided between urban and rural, and between Deep South (South Carolina, Georgia, Alabama, Mississippi, and Louisiana) and non-Deep South (Virginia, North Carolina, Texas, Arkansas, Florida, and Tennessee). Conclusions: 1) In the non-Deep South, Republicans may be expected to do better in their traditional domain and in the cities than in the countryside and black belts. 2) In the Deep South, Republican voting will continue at relatively high levels in traditional domain, and "among upper-status white urbanites as well as among black-belt white voters," if the party continues to "appeal to economic conservatism...and maintaining the racial status quo." 8 notes.

D. F. Henderson

2178. Cox, Keith K. CHANGES IN STEREOTYPING OF NEGROES AND WHITES IN MAGAZINE ADVERTISEMENTS. *Public Opinion Q. 1969/70 33(4): 603-606.* The author studied advertisements to determine whether there has been any change in the stereotyping of the occupational role of Negroes in general magazine advertisements since 1949-50. Two occupational categories were used: "Above skilled labor" - entertainment, sports, professional, business man, student, idle, clerical - and "below skilled labor" - maid, cook, servant, waiter, porter, butler, chauffeur, cowboy, farmer, soldier, African, Island laborer. In the 1949 study, advertisements with Negroes comprised .57 percent of all ads, and in 1967-68, 2.17 percent of all ads. While there was only a slight shift in the "above skilled" labor category of whites, there is a major shift in the "above skilled" labor category for Negroes (from 6.1 percent in 1949-50 to 71.3 percent in 1967-68). In 1949, no ads portrayed Negroes as professionals, businessmen, students, or clerical workers, while 21 percent did so in 1967-68. 2 tables, 4 notes.

D. J. Trickey

2179. Crain, Robert L. and Rosenthal, Donald B. COMMUNITY STATUS AS A DIMENSION OF LOCAL DECISION-MAKING. *Am. Sociol. R. 1967 32(6): 970-984.* "We hypothesize that the higher the socioeconomic status of the population of a community, the greater the level of citizen participation in day-to-day community decision-making. The main effect of this seems to be to increase the power of the citizens vis-à-vis the local government and the elite; in turn, this leads to high levels of controversy, decentralization of decision-making power, and a tendency toward immobility on the part of the government. The relationship is curvilinear at the extreme upper end of the distribution; very high-status cities demonstrate a more tightly organized and more potent decision-making structure, similar to low status cities. Data are used from national surveys of urban renewal, school desegregation, bond referenda, fluoridation controversies, politicalparty structures, Negro registration in the South, election contests, and civil rights movements." J

2180. Cripps, Thomas R. THE DEATH OF RASTUS: NEGROES IN AMERI-CAN FILMS SINCE 1945. *Phylon 1967 28(3): 267-275.* Sees a private censorship code among American motion picture producers which over the years has proscribed depicting all the vicious elements of the Negro stereotype and has tolerated the ridiculous elements. Thus through the 1930's and 1940's only racial comics such as Rochester crept into American films. From 1945 through 1954 films depicted Negroes as social problems. After 1954, Negro roles showed emerging characters which still retained a hint of the subservient Rastus, but in the 1960's the varied themes have seen the beginnings of a fully articulated character. The first intimations of the end of the Negro stereotype were seen in the anti-Fascist war movies. Shortly after this vogue ended, the cycle of racial message movies began. This spent itself and a new character was created: a Negro who cannot be fulfilled without the self-sacrifice or support of white men. It is in the art movie where one currently finds the most sensitive view of Negroes in American life because they attempt to deal with reality seriously. Based on published sources; 21 notes. D. N. Brown

2181. Crockett, George W., Jr. RACISM IN THE LAW. *Sci. and Soc. 1969 33(2): 223-230.* Law and order rhetoric has often masked antiblack racism. However, three positive developments hint at an end to racism in the law: 1) black self-awareness, 2) identification of blacks and poor whites as a single class - the poor, and 3) an establishment frightened enough to want reform. R. S. Burns

2182. Croussy, Guy. IL Y A LES BLANCS ET LES NOIRS, PROMENADES A NEW YORK [There are whites and Negroes: strolls in New York]. *Esprit [France] 1965 (3): 502-513.* A French observer's impressions of Negro-white relations in the poorer sections of New York City. Race relations, tense between members of the working class, are amicable in the entertainment world. The Black Muslims have no striking popularity with the city crowds but are doing an important preparatory work among students, workers, and youth in general, convincing them of the Negro's superiority and of his right to autonomy in face of white society. Mother M. H. Quinlan

2183. Cutright, Phillips. NEGRO SUBORDINATION AND WHITE GAINS. *Am. Sociol. R. 1965 30(1): 110-112.* Discusses Norval Glenn's data on "Occupational Benefits to Whites from the Subordination of Negroes" *(American Sociological Review, June 1963).* The research indicates that "the white population, Northern and Southern, derives occupational and income gains that are directly associated with the proportion of Negroes in the labor force." Thus in the northern cities with growing Negro populations whites may be expected to increase their resistance to equal employment opportunities; whites in the South to continue their patterns. E. P. Stickney

2184. Dalfiume, Richard M. THE FAHY COMMITTEE AND DESEGREGATION OF THE ARMED FORCES. *Historian 1968 31(1): 1-20.* The increasing importance of the Negro vote, the encouragement of white liberals, and the embarassment of U.S. race problems in the Cold War were among factors leading President Truman to issue an executive order ending segregation in the armed forces and creating a committee, later called the Fahy Committee, to implement the policy. The committee encountered little resistance from the Navy and Air Force. The author chronicles the committee's ultimately successful struggles with the Army. Based principally on armed forces records in the National Archives and on the Truman and Fahy Papers in the Harry S. Truman Library; 47 notes. N. W. Moen

2185. Davis, F. James. THE EFFECTS OF A FREEWAY DISPLACEMENT ON RACIAL HOUSING SEGREGATION IN A NORTHERN CITY. *Phylon 1965 26(3): 209-215.* A study of the actions of 177 families displaced by clearance for freeway construction in St. Paul, Minnesota. The clearance increased the density of nonwhite concentration and extended the boundaries of the nonwhite area, for a much smaller proportion of nonwhites, as compared with whites, were relocated outside the nonwhite area. However, direct discrimination did not appear to account entirely for the increase in racial housing segregation. Much "was evidently due to fear of discrimination outside of the nonwhite area, and to in-group cohesiveness in the face of potential discrimination." S. C. Pearson, Jr.

2186. Davis, James C. CLEVELAND'S WHITE PROBLEM: A CHALLENGE TO THE BAR. *J. of Human Relations 1967 15(4): 395-410.* Discusses the failure of the city of Cleveland to alleviate its racial troubles. The central difficulty is the inability of white voters in Cleveland's "nationality wards" to understand the variety of factors - the absence of a Negro family unity, for example - which makes it impossible for the isolated Negro community to solve its problems. It is not true that Negroes are confronted with exactly the same situation previously overcome by white immigrant groups. The creation of an environment in which the Negro can have a fair chance is the responsibility of the white population. Cleveland's political leaders are reluctant to support special programs in Negro areas, however, because of opposition from white voters. Unless the city's legal profession stops wasting its time criticizing the politicians and helps find a solution to Cleveland's white problem, "it must necessarily follow that the opportunities for the profitable practice of law in Cleveland will soon be materially foreshortened." An address before the meeting of the Cleveland Bar Association, 13 March 1967. D. J. Abramoske

2187. De Shazo, Elmer Anthony. AN EQUAL OPPORTUNITIES COMMITTEE AT WORK IN TEXAS. *Social Sci. 1966 41(2): 99-106.* A firsthand account of the reaction of a small town in a rural county in central Texas to the Supreme

Court's desegregation decision. The study concentrates on the activities of an equal opportunities committee established by the San Marcos, Texas, city council in 1963.   M. Small

2188. Deane, Paul C. THE PERSISTENCE OF UNCLE TOM: AN EXAMINATION OF THE IMAGE OF THE NEGRO IN CHILDREN'S FICTION SERIES. *J. of Negro Educ. 1968 37(2): 140-145.* Children's fiction series dominate reading between the second and sixth grades. Several of these are examined for their presentation of the Negro, and the author concludes that, while dialect disappeared in the 1950's, these children's books continue to portray the Negro in inferior positions and with personality traits and general character used a half century ago. With the exception of three individual books he finds that the Negro is not allowed to develop as a real person. Instead he is revealed as a century-old cliché. 5 notes.   S. C. Pearson, Jr.

2189. DeBerry, Clyde E., Fashing, Joseph, and Harris, Calvin. BLACK POWER AND BLACK POPULATION: A DILEMMA. *J. of Negro Educ. 1969 38(1): 14-21.* A study made in 1966 of the racial situation in Eugene, Oregon, to test the hypothesis that integration was easier and more likely with a small black population. Eugene had only 92 black families. The questionnaire-interviewer approach was used. There is no residential segregation in Eugene, but this is due to Negro insistence on good housing when the formerly black areas were destroyed for public works projects and urban renewal following World War II. Eugene is not a city of open occupancy, however, and discrimination exists in employment.   B. D. Johnson

2190. Dentler, Robert A. COMMUNITY BEHAVIOR AND NORTHERN SCHOOL DESEGREGATION. *J. of Negro Educ. 1965 34(3): 258-267.* School segregation remains pronounced in the North, and minority segregated public schools there tend to have poorer facilities, less qualified staff, and poorer programs of instruction than majority segregated schools. Yet the priority given to desegregation is still in flux, and "the actual net rate of Northern urban and suburban desegregation per year approximates zero." The root of the problem in the North is the neighborhood school which provides competitive advantage for some clients and an acceptable handicap for others. The organization of the school systems contributes to the general difficulty experienced in effecting change. Population movement and shifting public attitudes contribute to lessening of segregation, but greatest change takes place only where it is supported by the educators themselves.   S. C. Pearson, Jr.

2191. Dodson, Dan W. SCHOOL ADMINISTRATION, CONTROL AND PUBLIC POLICY CONCERNING INTEGRATION. *J. of Negro Educ. 1965 34(3): 249-257.* Argues that the chief lesson learned about the American school system since 1954 is its relationship to the power order as the "instrumentality through which the mythologies of such power structure are inculcated." Thus the challenge to schools is a challenge to the power structure of the community in which the school leadership generally protects the interests of the power structure. Formal statements of policy seldom accomplish as much change as they seem to suggest. The author doubts if the social order would support a school which "did too good a job in eradicating prejudices from the minds of the children" and proposes that some self-segregation of minority groups may be necessary in order to generate power with which to force restructuring of race relations.   S. C. Pearson, Jr.

2192. Domenach, Jean-Marie. LES ETATS-UNIS SOUS NIXON [The United States under Nixon]. *Esprit [France] 1969 37(11): 612-628.* Discusses the United States in the first two years of the Nixon administration. The author is struck by the increasing mechanization of the country, curious at the calm in the black ghettos, shocked by the continued lack of gun control, intrigued by the social conflict between old and young, puzzled by the drug scene, and interested by the great changes in recent years. The central American problem is more moral or spiritual than political or economic. Neither the Left nor the Right seems capable of solving the general malaise surrounding the Nation. Takes comfort that in reaching the moon, America renews its dissatisfaction with earthly things. The United States, despite the Vietnam War and its peculiar problems, poses to the French people the problems of France's future.   G. F. Jewsbury

2193. Duncan, Beverly and Duncan, Otis Dudley. MINORITIES AND THE PROCESS OF STRATIFICATION. *Am. Sociol. R. 1968 33(3): 356-364.* "Data concerning educational and occupational achievement, and the influence thereon of social and national origin, are presented for a 1962 sample of native American non-Negro males, ages 25-64, whose family heads had been pursuing a nonfarm occupation when the respondent was 16. There are substantial differences among national-origin groups with respect to both educational and occupational achievement. Allowance for inter-group differences in social origin, by partial regression techniques, reduces the range of difference with respect to educational achievement, and with respect to occupational achievement, by about one-third. The national-origin classification is much less important as an explanation of the variance among respondents with respect to their education and occupation than with respect to the education and occupation of their family heads. In this sense a "melting-pot" phenomenon obtains in America. Once equated with respect to starting point in the social structure and educational attainment, the occupational achievement of one national-origin group differs little from that of another. The experience of non-Negro minorities, as revealed by these data, would argue against the existence of pervasive discrimination on purely ethnic grounds. The notion of equal opportunity irrespective of national origin is a near reality, the outstanding exceptions being the over-achievement of Russian-Americans and the under-achievement of Latin-Americans. This finding contrasts sharply with the evidence, based on the same mode of analysis, of discrimination against the American Negro."   J

2194. Duncan, Otis Dudley. DISCRIMINATION AGAINST NEGROES. *Ann. of the Am. Acad. of Pol. and Social Sci. 1967 371: 85-103.* "The functions of indicators to measure fullness of participation of minorities in American society can best be understood by relating them to strategic junctures in the socioeco-nomic life cycle. Data for Negroes, in particular, reveal the operation of two types of handicaps - those common to all members of the society subject to disadvantages of background or misfortune, and those specific to minority status. To distinguish between them, and thus to measure progress in reducing discrimination, requires not only comprehensive time series but also methods and models suited to the analysis of causal sequences. Despite the growing fund of valuable indicators of the status of 'nonwhite' Americans, a number of statistical hazards must be circumvented before reliable inferences and realistic recommendations become possible. In reaching interpretations in this field, social science should operate as a 'third force,' complementing the work of policy-makers and program-administrators, on the one hand, and civic action groups on the other. Present knowledge is inadequate to the task of formulating specific proposals for redirecting trends. It could rapidly become more nearly adequate with the availability of sufficient resources for research, full cooperation of official statistical agencies, freedom to investigate so-called sensitive problems, and concerted attempts to improve analytical and interpretive models. For the moment, we can only be sure that formidable obstacles remain in the way of achieving freedom from discrimination."   J

2195. Dure, Leon. VIRGINIA'S NEW FREEDOMS. *Georgia R. 1964 18(1): 3-16.* Sees the Supreme Court decision of 1954, Brown vs. Board of Education, as lacking any firm principle. For this reason it has been possible for the State of Virginia to skirt this decision by "developing" new freedoms - individual freedom of association and individual liberty in education. Other freedoms are suggested - "freedom of welfare and taxes."   H. G. Earnhart

2196. Eckhardt, William. PREJUDICE: FEAR, HATE, OR MYTHOLOGY? *J. of Human Relations 1968 16(1): 32-41.* Analyzes prejudice "as a function of dedication to the aristocratic myth of superiority whose most fundamental effect in our culture has been to reduce the average Negro's purchasing power to one-half that of the average white person. Effective remedial action would seem to require further dedication and actualization of the democratic myth of equality and an economic subsidy to equalize the Negro's purchasing power. This ideological or mythological interpretation of prejudice denies that emotional factors such as fear or hate are the primary determinants of prejudice, but it does not deny that they may play a secondary role in many cases, and especially in cases of extreme prejudice which would probably include the core group of dedicated leaders (sociopathic personalities) and devoted followers (psychoneurotic personalities)." Based on recent studies of the authoritarian personality, the radical right, and fascism.   D. J. Abramoske

2197. Eddy, Elizabeth M. STUDENT PERSPECTIVES ON THE SOUTHERN CHURCH. *Phylon 1964 25(4): 369-381.* Presents a descriptive account of the attitudes of 374 male northern and southern freshmen students in a large Ivy League college toward integration of a northern and southern church. The majority of respondents belonged to a church and "appeared to be committed to a church in which color *per se* is of less importance than other factors." Opposition to integration of the northern church was considerably less than to integration of the southern church on the part of both northern and southern students.

Student attitudes reflect not only an orientation toward secular values but also the student's conception of religion. Students more amenable to secular values are less anti-Negro than students oriented toward fundamentalist values but more anti-Negro than students oriented toward modernist religious values.

S. C. Pearson, Jr.

2198. Elhorst, Hansjorg. TWO YEARS AFTER INTEGRATION: RACE RE-LATIONS AT A DEEP SOUTH UNIVERSITY. *Phylon 1967 28(1): 41-51.* In 1964, after a court order, Louisiana State University was integrated on the undergraduate level. On the surface everything remained calm, but the personal experience of the first Negro students was less pleasant. Insults and threats were everywhere encountered and a few incidents of physical violence occurred. Barely one-fourth of the approximately 80 Negro students who entered the university in 1964 were still studying there in 1966, but this study attempts to compare the recent situation with that of the past. It covers the social contacts of Negro students, the discrimination they encounter, and the attitude of staff and adminis-tration. Replies to the questionnaire showed that the majority of the Negro students were still absolutely excluded from all social groups on the campus and they felt discrimination in almost all aspects of college life except the classroom. A majority believed faculty and administration friendly and helpful. Most be-lieved that the relationship between Negro and white students would improve. Tables.

D. N. Brown

2199. Epstein, Joseph. TWO SOUTHERN LIBERALS. *Commentary 1964 38(6): 73-74, 76, 78.* A review of *Mississippi: The Closed Society* (1964) by James W. Silver and *A Time to Speak* (1964) by Charles Morgan, Jr. The two authors are relatively recent examples of a new type of southern gentleman which has arisen in the past few years - a type which isn't measured "by the old standards of lineage and wealth" but which, nonetheless, "*is* driven by the old ideals of courage, integrity, and honor." The stories of this educator from Mississippi and this lawyer from Alabama illustrate the southern tragedy. The South, because it is as yet unencumbered by a crystalized industrialism, has the opportunity to establish the good society which men have dreamed about for America. But the South repudiates the dream by the rejection of such men as Silver and Morgan.

R. J. Moore

2200. Erskine, Hazel. THE POLLS: SPEED OF RACIAL INTEGRATION. *Public Opinion Q. 1968 32(3): 513-524.* A collection of public opinion polling questions based on nationwide samples of opinion taken during the 1960's, some of them broken down according to regions, politics, occupations, income, age, religion, or sex, reflecting opinions on the rate at which racial integration should be progressing. Survey results are reprinted from the Gallup Poll and the Ameri-can Institute of Public Opinion, the Harris Survey and Louis Harris and Asso-ciates, and the Survey Research Center, University of Michigan.

D. J. Trickey

2201. Fairlie, Henry. ANGRY BLACKS, GUILTY WHITES, THREATENED JEWS. *Interplay 1969 3(1): 25-28.* Anti-Semitism is a distinct type of prejudice not limited to particular times and places, and is more prevalent now than at any time since 1945. Anti-Semitism results from the white liberal's guilt feelings about his relations with Negroes; the Jew becomes a scapegoat. Disenchantment with the role of the State of Israel is a contributing factor. The danger exists of making anti-Semitism respectable.   J. A. Zabel

2202. Formby, John. THE EXTENT OF WAGE AND SALARY DISCRIMINATION AGAINST NON-WHITE LABOR. *Southern Econ. J. 1968 35(2): 140-150.* The cost of discrimination in economic terms is the net value of output to the whole economy which is foregone because of the resultant misallocation of resources. Market discrimination against nonwhites is measured by the net wage and salary income differentials between perfectly substitutable white and nonwhite labor. Basing his analysis on the U.S. census data for 1950 and 1960, the author concludes that the extent of wage and salary discrimination adjusted for price changes increased from 4 billion dollars in 1949 to 6.6 billion dollars in 1959, i.e. an almost 20 percent increase in per capita income (from 750 to 896 dollars). The extent of discrimination in absolute terms rose in the South far more than in the North, although it decreased for females in the North and West.
                                                               A. W. Coats

2203. Forslund, Morris A. AGE, OCCUPATION, AND CONVICTION RATES OF WHITE AND NEGRO MALES: A CASE STUDY. *Rocky Mountain Social Sci. J. 1969 6(1): 141-146.* The author is concerned with the differences in the probability of conviction by age and occupation level for white and Negro males respectively, and whether or not these differences are similar for the two racial groups. The data were drawn from the police blotters of Stamford, Connecticut, during the period from 1958 through 1961, excluding motor vehicle violations. 4 tables, 5 notes.   R. F. Allen

2204. Frank, Joseph. LEMMINGS AND MOLES. *Massachusetts R. 1970 11(2): 398-400.* Two years after the release of the report of the Kerner Commission, its recommendations still have not been implemented. American Negroes are developing a political split personality. On the campus, they demand separation (special admissions policies, Black Studies, black-only dormitories, etc.); in society at large, they demand full integration. Black separation on the campus can lead only back to the ghetto or to mass suicide. Negroes should coalesce with poor and liberal whites, and advance by appealing to the guilty conscience of white America. Note.   G. Kurland

2205. Friedman, Murray. IS WHITE RACISM THE PROBLEM? *Commentary 1969 47(1): 61-65.* Accusing the whites of racism obscures the true complexities of our social situation. The United States has diverse ethnic, religious, and racial groups. Ethnic self-confidence and self-assertion are becoming more intense. The "Black Power" movement is only one manifestation of this. Other myths are that we are a nation of individuals rather than of groups and that racial and ethnic conflicts have nothing but bad results. Group collisions are present now because of the problem of control of city schools. There is a need for enormous sensitivity and the development of procedures that will protect the interests of the conflicting groups. Effective bargaining cannot take place until we get beyond simplistic slogans and appeals to the American creed.   C. G. Lauritsen

2206. Garrison, Karl C., Jr. THE BEHAVIOR OF CLERGY ON RACIAL INTEGRATION AS RELATED TO A CHILDHOOD SOCIALIZATION FACTOR. *Sociol. and Social Res. 1967 51(2): 209-219.* "Behavior on integration of a population of white Protestant clergymen was found to be related to the presence or absence of childhood experiences with nonwhites. where parish-situational norms were neutral or unfavorable to activist behavior, among at-titudinally 'concerned' clergy, those with childhood experiences with nonwhites were more likely to engage in activist behavior than those without these experi-ences. In the type of parish situation presumably least favorable to activist behav-ior, some behavioral differential related to childhood experiences with nonwhites was also found among attitudinally 'unconcerned' clergy."   J

2207. Geschwender, James A. NEGRO EDUCATION: THE FALSE FAITH. *Phylon 1968 29(4): 371-379.* While there is a widespread belief that increased educational opportunity is the surest method of securing economic and social progress for Negroes, the author produces evidence of a contrary nature. Accord-ing to one study of the period 1940-60, while both Negroes and whites made educational gains, "whites were twice as successful as Negroes in translating gains in higher education into gains in better jobs." Other studies document the fact that Negroes are overrepresented in operative occupations at all educational levels, while underrepresented in craft and sales occupations. Thus, while educa-tional opportunities for Negroes increase, racial discrimination continues to bring about occupational inequalities, at least up to 1960. 2 tables, 15 notes.
R. D. Cohen

2208. Geyer, Hans-Martin. DER SIEGER IM WAHLKAMPF UM DIE USA-PRÄSIDENTSCHAFT [The victor in the electoral struggle for the U.S. presi-dency]. *Deutsche Aussenpolitik [East Germany] 1965 10(1): 47-53.* Analyzes the U.S. presidential elections of 1964 from a Communist point of view. Attributes President Johnson's victory to the high economic prosperity and the "consolida-tion of the democratic forces" from labor unions to Negro organizations against the "Fascist" threat contained in Senator Goldwater's Republican platform. Documented.   G. Bassler

2209. Gibbs, Jack P. OCCUPATIONAL DIFFERENTIATION OF NEGROES AND WHITES IN THE UNITED STATES. *Social Forces 1965 44(2): 159-165.* "Crude and standardized measures of the occupational differen-tiation of Negroes and whites are reported for each of the United States. The standardized measure eliminates the influence of the occupational structure on the amount of differentiation. Although there is considerable variation in the crude measure from state to state, the differences are not consistent with what is generally believed about racial differentiation in the United States and its connection with prejudice. The standardized measures show that a substantial amount of the differences among states is due to variation in occupational structure." J

2210. Glazer, Nathan. AMERICA'S RACE PARADOX. THE GAP BETWEEN SOCIAL PROGRESS AND POLITICAL DESPAIR. *Encounter [Great Britain] 1968 31(181): 9-18.* Though the economic and social status of the American Negro is improving, racial violence and extremism are increasing at the same time. Three answers have been postulated: repression, increased social improvement, and separate political power and existence for the Negro. The last position makes use of the "colonial" analogy assuming that Negroes are deliberately excluded from the whole of a U.S. society of European "settlers." This outlook underrates the tremendous power of American society to incorporate new groups, one of which eventually will be the Negro. D. H. Murdoch

2211. Glazer, Nathan. BLACKS, JEWS AND THE INTELLECTUALS. *Commentary 1969 47(4): 33-39.* Discusses whether Jews are threatened by black anti-Semitism. For most American Negroes there is as yet no reason to equate anti-whitism with anti-Semitism. Nevertheless, younger black militants have spread anti-Semitism which has been abetted by Jewish intelligentsia. What is to be done? Jews should relearn the experiences of nazism. They should not give black anti-Semitism the circulation that they are at present. They should educate those who sympathize with the militant blacks on the less desirable aspects of their programs. Finally, Jews should end financial support to such groups. C. G. Lauritsen

2212. Glazer, Nathan. NEGROES AND JEWS: THE NEW CHALLENGE TO PLURALISM. *Commentary 1964 38(6): 29-34.* Asserts that Negro-Jewish relations are undergoing considerable change due to the new nature of the demands which Negro leaders are making of American society. Traditionally Negro and Jewish leaderships have cooperated to achieve mutual gains, despite the fact that the masses of Negroes bore ill feelings toward the Jews as exploiters. In recent years, however, much of the Negro leadership has adopted the antipathy of their constituents to Jews because the latter have not been amenable to the Negro's assertion that equality means not just equality of opportunity but equality of results. Similarly, many Jews have disapproved of the Negro demands which threaten the existence of ethnic and religious groups which persist in white America as distinctive communities. Demolition of these communities may be necessary to obtain full equality for the Negro, but that solution would create a far different environment from the one in which we now live. R. J. Moore

2213. Glazer, Nathan. THE GHETTO CRISIS. *Encounter [Great Britain] 1967 29(170): 15-22.* A discussion of the implications of the American Negro's entry into a phase of extreme radicalism, stressing the domination of extremism, the emergence of near-revolutionary tactics, the minor nature of the backlash at this stage, and the difficulties of establishing substantial reforms. D. H. Murdoch

2214. Glenn, Norval D. THE RELATIVE SIZE OF THE NEGRO POPULA-
TION AND NEGRO OCCUPATIONAL STATUS. *Social Forces 1964 43(1):
42-49.* "The hypothesis that the relative size of the Negro population and Negro
occupational status are inversely related was not supported by a study of the
populations of the 151 SMA's that had 100,000 or more people in 1950. However,
this finding was not constructed as a refutation of the widely held belief that
discrimination against a minority varies directly with the relative size of the
minority population. Rather, it was concluded that 'overflow' of Negroes into
intermediate-level occupations offsets any greater discrimination in those localities where the relative number of Negroes is large."   J

2215. Goldbloom, Maurice J. IS THERE A BACKLASH VOTE? *Commentary
1969 48(2): 17-26.* Challenges the interpretation of the 1968 elections as a general
swing to the Right. The author believes that the candidates who won stressing
"law and order" would have won regardless of the reaction to black militancy
and student disorders. Those who habitually vote for liberal candidates still do.
To prove his case, the author discusses the issues in Los Angeles, Minneapolis,
and New York. In each casethe backlash vote was small. Also discussed are the
less well-publicized primaries in New Jersey and Montana, which also show no
swing to right-wing sentiment. The author concludes that the swing to the Right
may still occur in future elections, but that the end of the Vietnam War should
lead people to vote for their hopes rather than their fears.   C. Grollman

2216. Goodman, Paul. THE EMPTY SOCIETY. *Commentary 1966 42(5): 53-
60.* A general survey of modern American society, which has become increasingly
tightly organized and rigidly formulated since World War II, serving the god of
a technologically oriented efficiency to the point of denying any human values
which may conflict. It shows two major tendencies: "to expand, meaninglessly,
for its own sake; and...to exclude human beings as useless." The relation of the
society to the people who compose it is increasingly a matter of what use the
people are to the purposes of the society; thus, college students, whose training
will be necessary to run the society, are deferred from the draft, "while farm boys,
Negroes, and Spanish Americans are drafted because they are otherwise good for
nothing....War is not regarded as a dread emergency, in which each one does his
bit, but as part of the ongoing business of society, in which fighting and dying
are usual categories of the division of labor....people...can mathematically be
dispensed with." Opposing this monolithic social machine, "there is only the
tradition of America, populist, pluralist, and libertarian." The author ventures no
opinions as to which will prevail.   A. K. Main

2217. Gould, William B. LABOR ARBITRATION OF GRIEVANCES IN-
VOLVING RACIAL DISCRIMINATION. *Arbitration J. 1969 24(4): 197-227.*
"Traditionally, labor arbitration is thought of as a private process, 'essentially
tailored to the needs of the parties.' But Title VII of the Civil Rights Act of 1964
imposes obligations which can not always be satisfied by interpretation of collective bargaining agreements alone. New concepts and procedures are required,
including, on occasion, the right of interested third parties to intervene in grievance arbitration. After citing the case law on the right of grievants to assert claims

of discrimination in all forums, the author concludes: 'It is too late for those involved in arbitration, or for the trade union movement generally, to complain about the limited regulation by public law concepts. If ever there was an area in which the value of consensual arrangements is clearly outweighted, it is found in the attempt to eliminate the systematic discrimination which government, unions, and employers historically have practiced against the Negro worker."

J

2218. Grafton, Thomas H. AN ATTITUDE SCALE ON ACCEPTING NE-GRO STUDENTS. *Social Forces 1964 43(1): 38-41.* "A Thurstone-type scale of 20 items was constructed for the purpose of measuring attitudes among the all-white students of a Southern college for women on the hypothetical question of accepting a Negro student. The scale items appear on the whole, to meet the statistical specifications in regard to consistency of response and 'equal intervals' as usually defined for tests of this sort. When the scale was administered to 280 students out of a student body of 504, Southern students were found to be significantly more opposed than border and Northern students. Freshmen were more opposed than older students, but at only the .10 level of confidence."

J

2219. Greeley, Andrew M. A NOTE ON POLITICAL AND SOCIAL DIF-FERENCES AMONG ETHNIC COLLEGE GRADUATES. *Sociol. of Educ. 1969 42(1): 98-103.* Reports data gathered by the National Opinion Center in 1968 from a subsample of 1961 college graduates. Indicates that even among young people with a college education, ethnic background continues to be a strong predictor of attitudes and behavior, but that wide divergencies exist among the ethnic groups within the Protestant, Catholic, and Jewish traditions. In many instances the differences among groups within the traditions are greater than the differences among the religions themselves. The results should cause social scientists to reexamine their idea that ethnicity is no longer an important variable in American society. The seven tabulated results of responses to the questionnaire were: Political Affiliation by Father's Ethnic Background, Percentage Liberal, Racial Attitudes, Support of Student Militancy, High on Federal Aid to Colleges, Artistic and Reading Habits, and Career Choices (Academic, Private Business or Corporation). Classifies 11 groups: Protestant (English, Irish, German, Scandinavian), Catholic (Irish, German, Italian, Polish), Jewish (German, Polish), and Black. 7 tables.   D. D. Cameron

2220. Green, Gordon C. NEGRO DIALECT, THE LAST BARRIER TO IN-TEGRATION. *J. of Negro Educ. 1963 32(1): 81-83.* The American Negro can help himself "gain status as a fellow citizen with equal rights and responsibilities" by taking "special pains to see that he and his children destroy this last chain that binds him to the past, the Negro dialect."   S. C. Pearson, Jr.

2221. Green, Jerome. WHEN MORAL PROPHECY FAILS. *Catalyst 1969 (4): 63-78.* Some contradictions and inconsistencies regarding change and the recent impact of race relations relate to the "explosion of collective action of Negro Americans for fuller integration in American society." Gunnar Myrdal's theory of moral prophecy, as cited in *An American Dilemma* (New York: Harper and Row, 1967), errs in that it is essentially "virtue of necessity." Believes that "good will not triumph over evil" and that the moral prophetic mystique should be discarded because it has proven useless in helping to understand social change. Examination of "the pursuit of self interest" and the "struggle for power" is a far more accurate gauge in predicting future changes in the relation of whites and Negroes.   P. A. Proett

2222. Greenwood, Michael J. A NOTE ON INCOME DIFFERENCES, JOB VACANCIES AND WHITE-NONWHITE INTERSTATE MIGRATION. *Rocky Mountain Social Sci. J. 1970 7(2): 17-21.* Analyzes characteristics of white and nonwhite migration during 1955-60. Net migration of both whites and nonwhites tended toward high-income States, but the tendency for the net movement of nonwhites was higher. Discrimination against nonwhites is least in States with relatively high levels of nonwhite income, while discrimination tends to be relatively great in those States whose nonagricultural employment volume is expanding rapidly. Based on the 1960 U.S. Census; 2 tables, 5 notes.
                                                                A. P. Young

2223. Guild, June Purcell. WHO IS A NEGRO? *J. of Negro Educ. 1964 33(1): 83-85.* Concerned with the disparity between biological and legal definitions of Negro in America and particularly with State statutes forbidding the marriage of a Negro to a person of another race.   S. C. Pearson, Jr.

2224. Harding, Vincent. ALIENS IN OUR LAND. *J.: Division of Higher Educ. United Church of Christ 1968 7(2): 6-11.* Discusses directions America and its black citizens might take. The not-too-probable ideal is an open America, with liberty and justice for all. The second possibility is the status quo. The third possibility is the continual buying off of the cream of black intellectuals, thus dividing the black community. The fourth possibility is the creation of Bantu-like cities with limited black control. The fifth and wildest possibility is a separation which would create a kind of black nation within the United States. The need to build a multiracial, pluralistic society is urgent but may not be possible.
                                                                C. W. Ohrvall

2225. Hare, Nathan. CONFLICTING RACIAL ORIENTATIONS OF NEGRO COLLEGE STUDENTS AND PROFESSORS. *J. of Negro Educ. 1965 34(4): 431-434.* Examines conflicts in enthusiasm for discussing the subject of race in predominantly Negro college classrooms. A questionnaire completed by 67 students indicated that "they hold a general impression that professors devote an excessive amount of time to such considerations." The more optimistic the student was with respect to the possibility of complete integration, the greater was his tendency to regard professors as devoting too much time to the subject of race. Also, students with greater general knowledge of racial information were less receptive to racial discussions by professors. Students rated textbooks more favorably than professors on their treatment of race.   S. C. Pearson, Jr.

2226. Hatcher, Richard G. THE BLACK ROLE IN URBAN POLITICS. *Current Hist. 1969 57(339): 287-289, 306-307.* Although black political power is today visible and meaningful in urban America, it is under attack from those who advocate tactics of "disannexation" and "metro government." The isolated salients established by black political action must be protected now if blacks are to retain any degree of social equity.   B. D. Rhodes

2227. Heiberg, Inge. JAMES BALDWIN - NEGERFORFATTER OG DIKTER [James Baldwin - Negro author and poet]. *Samtiden [Norway] 1965 74(5): 280-287.* The personal life and intellectual development of Baldwin is examined on the basis of the following works: *Notes of a Native Son* (New York: Dial, 1963), *Go Tell It on the Mountain* (New York: Dell, 1970), *The Amen Corner* (New York: Dial, 1968), *Blues for Mr. Charlie* (New York: Dial, 1964), and *The Fire Next Time* (New York: Dell, 1970). Much of his literary production has taken the form of an effort to come to terms with himself as a Negro and an American, and also to reconcile himself to his hate-filled relationship with his stepfather. By leaving the United States in 1948, he came to understand his identity as an American, meaning that even as a Negro he could not be anything but an American even if he hated his native land. He also learned in Europe that the psychic ordeal that he had faced in connection with his life in Harlem did not vanish simply through his exodus from the United States. Baldwin's mission as a writer is interpreted as being one of creating "possibilities for identification between men with skins of different colors," a problem that is not unique to the United States but which affects the entire world.   P. O. Jonsson

2228. Heifetz, Robert. THE PUBLIC SECTOR, RESIDENTIAL DESEGREGATION, AND THE SCHOOLS: A CASE STUDY FROM BUFFALO, NEW YORK. *Urban R. 1968 2(4): 30-33.* The impact of activities of urban agencies in the public sector can continue segregation. The experience of Buffalo shows that urban renewal and relocation projects perpetuate the pattern of community segregation, whereas public agencies could have fostered greater integration if they had sought to follow such an idea. The result caused a continuation of school segregation and decreased the opportunity for greater equality of education. Likewise, the welfare department, which pays rent for dependent children, did not follow a policy of integration and thus aided school segregation. Unless city agencies pursue a policy of integration they will fail to solve the problem of the intercity. 19 notes.   H. B. Powell

2229. Helbich, Wolfgang J. DIE KRISE DER BÜRGERRECHTS-BEWEGUNG IN DEN VEREINIGTEN STAATEN. DIE ZWEITE PHASE DER NEGEREMANZIPATION 1954-1966 [The crisis of the civil rights movement in the United States. The second phase of Negro emancipation 1954-66]. *Europa-Archiv [West Germany] 1967 22(10): 359-368.* Discusses the white backlash as seen in the congressional elections of 1966 and sees 1966 as the end of the second phase of emancipation for the Negro. The progress made since 1954 in the fields of voting, school desegregation, and open desegregation in hotels, restaurants, and other public facilities is detailed. The author outlines the methods used by the different civil rights groups. 9 notes.   D. F. Rossi

2230. Heller, Celia Stopnicka and Pinkney, Alphonso. THE ATTITUDES OF NEGROES TOWARD JEWS. *Social Forces 1965 43(3): 364-369.* "Data from the recent *Newsweek* Poll of American Negroes are analyzed. Specifically, those data are examined which deal with the attitudes of Negroes toward the role of Jews in the cause of Negro rights. In general, it was found that Negroes have relatively favorable attitudes toward Jews. Although a plurality gave 'not sure' responses, few voiced negative feelings."   J

2231. Henderson, Donald. MINORITY RESPONSE AND THE CONFLICT MODEL. *Phylon 1964 25(1): 18-26.* Argues that the application of the conflict model of society, rather than the equilibrium model, to the area of race relations is useful. Describing American race relations as built on a system of constraint, the author briefly considers adjustive, protest, maintenance, and synthesis groups working in this area.   S. C. Pearson, Jr.

2232. Hendon, William S. DISCRIMINATION AGAINST NEGRO HOME-OWNERS IN PROPERTY TAX ASSESSMENT. *Am. J. of Econ. and Sociol. 1968 27(2): 125-132.* Compares property tax assessments of Negro and white homeowners in Fort Worth, Texas, during the period 1958-63. Concludes "that discrimination exists in the property tax between White and Negro homeowners. The Negro homeowner pays more taxes per dollar of tax base than does his White counterpart." Urges that more studies be undertaken so that "the work of the appraisers in the field" can be more consistent. 6 tables.   D. R. B. Ross

2233. Hero, Alfred O., Jr. SOUTHERN JEWS, RACE RELATIONS, AND FOREIGN POLICY. *Jewish Social Studies 1965 27(4): 213-235.* Interviews and opinion surveys of Jews in the South indicated that they tended to be less in favor of racial integration and more conservative on foreign policy issues, such as economic cooperation, than their coreligionists in the North. However, they were also much less likely to be strongly segregationist or racist than white southern gentiles. Jewish liberalism on the issues of race and international policy was modified by anxiety over unfavorable public reaction, especially in smaller and isolated communities. Rejection of domestic equalitarianism and liberal interna-tionalism was prevalent among recent converts into the Episcopal or Presbyterian elite.   J. Brandes

2234. Hickerson, Nathaniel. SOME ASPECTS OF SCHOOL INTEGRATION IN A CALIFORNIA HIGH SCHOOL. *J. of Negro Educ. 1965 34(2): 130-137.* Presents an abstract of a doctoral dissertation prepared for the University of California, Berkeley. The author compared Negro and non-Negro students rela-tive to their assignments and participation in several areas of a high school in the San Francisco Bay area. The school was found to mirror the relations of the community to its Negro population. The high school, "wittingly or unwittingly, apparently does little to encourage its non-Negro students to alter the image of Negroes created by practices and customs common to the community."
                                                       S. C. Pearson, Jr.

2235. Himmelfarb, Milton. IS AMERICAN JEWRY IN CRISIS? *Commentary 1969 47(3): 33-42.* Those who feel that American Jews have become conservative are wrong. The author uses data from public opinion polls to prove that Jews have supported liberal candidates even in recent times. He says that Negroes have made enemies of the whites generally and of Jews specifically. Allies against Negro anti-Semitism are not going to come from the liberal or radical Left. The author describes the different kinds of Jews and their reaction to Negro complaints. He concludes that Jews do not lack the instinct of self-preservation, but that they now need luck.   C. G. Lauritsen

2236. Hines, Ralph H. SOCIAL DISTANCE COMPONENTS IN INTEGRA-TION ATTITUDES OF NEGRO COLLEGE STUDENTS. *J. of Negro Educ. 1968 37(1): 23-30.* Reports the findings of a study designed to measure social distance components in integration attitudes of 995 Negro college students who were from predominantly Negro colleges. The results indicate that Negro college students show a general preference for whites over other racial-ethnic groups in most crucial situations. However, certain areas of the interactive rating scale reveal ethnocentric tendencies involving race pride and racial identification. As social interaction moves from group activities to interpersonal relationship, am-bivalence toward other Negroes is dissipated, and whites became the least desir-able objects of preference. Next to other Negroes, minority groups who are themselves the object of prejudice and discrimination are preferred in such situa-tions. 20 notes.   S. C. Pearson, Jr.

2237. Hodge, Robert W. and Treiman, Donald J. OCCUPATIONAL MOBIL-ITY AND ATTITUDES TOWARD NEGROES. *Am. Sociol. R. 1966 31(1): 93-102.* "Two models of the relationship between occupational mobility and attitudes toward Negroes are examined: (1) an additive model which implies that individuals form their attitudes by striking an average between the views appro-priate to their class of origin and those appropriate to their class of destination; and (2) an interaction model according to which occupational mobility creates abnormal strain which is manifested in greater hostility toward Negroes than would be expected from additive effects alone. To assess the two models, previous empirical materials are reviewed and new data from a representative national sample of the adult white population of the U.S. are analyzed using a dummy variable multiple regression procedure. Strong support is found for the additive model, and little or no support for the interaction model."   J

2238. Hofstetter, C. Richard. POLITICAL DISENGAGEMENT AND THE DEATH OF MARTIN LUTHER KING. *Public Opinion Q. 1969 33(2): 174-179.* King's "assassination was a stimulus that led...to...[political] disengage-ment[,]" a process that "occurs when normally positive and latent diffuse sentiments toward the political system...become negative." Since the "assassina-tion occurred approximately midway through the interviewing phase of a survey project concerning electoral behavior in Central Ohio[,]" responses of individuals "interviewed before the assassination were compared with [those of] respondents interviewed following King's death in order to ascertain the impact of this event on political disengagement." King's assassination produced strong alternations in

Negroes' affective ties to the political system. Positive affect increased, contrary to expectation, for the National Association for the Advancement of Colored People and for Negroes as a group. Overall affect became more negative toward police, whites, national politicians, and Richard M. Nixon, while attitudes toward the Republican Party, the Democratic Party, and Lyndon B. Johnson changed little. Some 182 white and 27 Negro respondents were interviewed before the assassination, and 156 white and 29 Negro respondents after the assassination. Table, 13 notes.   D. J. Trickey

2239. Holl, Karl. DIE JOHN BIRCH SOCIETY: EIN FAKTOR DER AMER-ICANISCHEN INNENPOLITIK [The John Birch Society: a factor in American domestic politics]. *Politische Studien [West Germany] 1966 17(169): 579-587.* An analysis of the Birch Society by a German scholar who studied in the United States. The society's ideology draws upon the strong American feelings of individualism and anti-communism. As its program is deliberately vague, it gives easy answers to problems. Its stand on the race question and governmental centralization attracts the sympathy of many Americans who are not members. The menace of the ideology lies in its tendency to label any political or social change as communist-inspired and in its isolationism. Its antidemocratic organizational structure is highly effective for carrying out its tasks. In spite of the small membership, the group is quite well financed. Its strategy is to capture key positions in the two major parties, especially the Republican. Although the society is similar to the Communists in its organization and tactics, moderate elements in American society counteract its danger. Based on Birch literature and interviews; 14 notes.   R. V. Pierard

2240. Hough, Richard L., Summers, Gene F., and O'Meara, James. PARENTAL INFLUENCE, YOUTH CONTRACULTURE, AND RURAL ADOLES-CENT ATTITUDES TOWARD MINORITY GROUPS. *Rural Sociol. 1969 34(3): 383-386.* Analyzes two independent sets of data concerning students' and parents' attitudes toward four minority groups: Latin Americans, Germans, Negroes, and Jews. The parents' data were collected from 1,096 households in two rural counties - one undergoing industrial expansion and the other a relatively stable community centered around a county seat service city. The youth data were obtained from questionnaire responses by 738 students in consolidated high schools in the two counties. The authors conclude that a youth subculture, or "contraculture," does not exist; that adolescent peers are no more in agreement regarding social distance than are their parents and reflect the attitudes of their parents; and that the parents' attitudes toward minority groups determine their children's attitudes. This article is a revision of a paper presented to the Midwest Sociological Society, April 1968, in Omaha. Table, note, biblio.
                                                                  D. D. Cameron

2241. Howard, David H. AN EXPLORATORY STUDY OF ATTITUDES OF NEGRO PROFESSIONALS TOWARD COMPETITION WITH WHITES. *Social Forces 1966 45(1): 20-26.* "There has been considerable speculation regarding the significance of the component competition in the race attitudes of Negroes and whites. However, empirical research in the field has neglected exploration of the significance of this factor. In the present report, attitudinal responses of 100 male Negro physicians, dentists, lawyers and public school teachers toward open competition reveal ambivalence about the matter. While they tend to accept the idea of open competition, they are considerably less than enthusiastic." J

2242. Howe, Harold, II. NATIONAL IDEALS AND EDUCATIONAL POLICY. *Urban R. 1968 2(4): 22-24.* The ideal of equality is the standard for determining educational policy. While some advocates maintain that compensatory education (providing the best educational service for nominally segregated ghetto schools) will provide equality of opportunity, others argue that complete desegregation is the solution. For the present both approaches must be used, but ultimately complete integration is the only answer. Local boards of education, State departments of education, and the Federal Government must work toward this goal. H. B. Powell

2243. Hughes, Everett C. RACE RELATIONS AND THE SOCIOLOGICAL IMAGINATION. *Am. Sociol. R. 1963 28(6): 879-890.* "The situations in which race relations occur are of such variety that they furnish a laboratory for many sociological problems. Social and economic changes call inter-racial arrangements and status bargains into question. The two great cases of this on this continent are the relations of French with English Canadians and of Negro with White Americans. Both have given rise to new, massive movements for change of status; but the changes sought are not the same. The Negroes want to disappear as a group; the French Canadians, to be more distinct. To understand such movements and to predict their occurrence and outcome require full use of the sociological imagination and of a variety of methods of research." J

2244. Husson-Dumoutier, Alain. MOI QUI VOULAIS DEVENIR NOIR... [I who wanted to become a Negro...]. *Esprit [France] 1964 32(1): 21-23.* Presents the reflections of a young American Jew of Russian immigrant extraction who fell in love with a Negro girl, middle class like himself, but finally did not marry her. He explains his own and his parents' lack of racial prejudice, describes his upbringing in an integrated section of Chicago, and then indicates he could not come to the point of marrying the Negro, whom he really loved, because they both knew that their children would not be accepted by his family or by hers, that they would not fit into any circle of friends, and that in the social conditions existing in the United States where "there are no hedges between gardens or between families" they would never be able to find a place. Mother M. H. Quinlan

2245. Inger, Morton and Stout, Robert T. SCHOOL DESEGREGATION: THE NEED TO GOVERN. *Urban R. 1968 3(2): 35-38.* Studies the decisionmaking process in eight cities affected by one of the main issues facing school boards during the 1960's, desegregation. While each city had its share of desegregation opponents, those cities where the school board assumed the responsibility of desegregation as a moral and educational obligation had the least controversy. On the other hand, cities that left the integration decision up to the public had heated fights. It is the duty of school boards to assume public responsibility in making a positive decision to integrate schools.   H. B. Powell

2246. Jackson, Jacquelyne Johnson. AN EXPLORATION OF ATTITUDES TOWARD FACULTY DESEGREGATION AT NEGRO COLLEGES. *Phylon 1967 28(4): 338-352.* Analyzes replies given by Negro faculty members to a questionnaire distributed at an annual meeting of a predominantly Negro association. Thirty-three Negro faculty members responded. Twenty-nine of these were males, all were born in Southern States, and the majority were assistant or associate professors, with no teaching experience on the faculty level in any white institution. The study of attitudes held by Negro faculty members toward desegregation of their facilities revealed that they favored the addition of white faculty members, but that they were concerned about the qualities possessed by white teachers, effects upon faculty morale, salaries, the allocation of power positions, and the effects upon the Negro teacher market. 4 tables.   D. N. Brown

2247. Janes, Robert W. and Byuarm, Samuel W. THE EFFECT OF A VOLUNTARY COMMUNITY IMPROVEMENT PROGRAM ON LOCAL RACE RELATIONS. *Phylon 1965 26(1): 25-33.* Reports the results of a study by a university community development agency of the impact on race relations of a voluntarily undertaken community improvement program in a northern town of 3,400. While partially successful, the program after five years had failed "to encourage an improved identification by the local population with their community" or "to provide motivation for more effective working together to meet community problems and to develop and recruit new leaders and talent which would serve to enhance community life." The program further "had made no change in the pattern of race relations except, perhaps, to maintain a feeling on the part of a number of Negroes of continued exploitation at the hands of the local white majority."   S. C. Pearson, Jr.

2248. Johnson, David W. RACIAL ATTITUDES OF NEGRO FREEDOM SCHOOL PARTICIPANTS AND NEGRO AND WHITE CIVIL RIGHTS PARTICIPANTS. *Social Forces 1966 45(2): 266-272.* "In this study the experimenter investigated the racial attitudes of (1) a group of Negro children and teenagers who were participating in a Freedom School where they were being taught Negro history and (2) a militant interracial civil rights group of teenagers. The results indicate that the groups studied have positive attitudes toward Negroes, despite the fact that they perceive 'most whites' as having negative attitudes toward Negroes. This finding suggests that a re-evaluation of the literature on the self-attitudes of Negroes is needed, with finer lines of differentiation being drawn between Negroes from different backgrounds and from different groups within the Negro community."   J

2249. Justman, Joseph. CHILDREN'S REACTION TO OPEN ENROLLMENT. *Urban R. 1968 3(2): 32-34.* Open enrollment offers one way of helping to meet the problem of school desegregation. Black parents may transfer their children to white schools, and whites may send their children to black schools, to help achieve a greater racial balance among all schools. Deals with how well open enrollment children and resident children adjust to each other. Group size plays a part in the adjustment. School principals will not have an easy time making the procedure work. H. B. Powell

2250. Kain, John F. HOUSING SEGREGATION, NEGRO EMPLOYMENT, AND METROPOLITAN DECENTRALIZATION. *Q. J. of Econ. 1968 82(2): 175-197.* Evaluates the hypothesis that racial segregation in the housing markets affects the distribution of Negro employment and reduces Negro employment opportunities. Postwar suburbanization of employment has seriously aggravated the problem. Data on place of work and place of residence were obtained from the home interview surveys of the Detroit Area Traffic Study in 1952, the Chicago Area Traffic Study in 1956, the census, and other published materials. T. Hočevar

2251. Kane, Richard D. STUDENTS REACT TO A WHITE MAN TEACHING BLACK HISTORY. *Social Studies 1970 61(7): 318-323.* Asks whether a white man can qualify to teach black history notwithstanding acceptable academic preparation. The implications are that much irrationality and prejudice block acceptance of the white man by certain black students in some areas of the United States. To this position, many historians have replied that race is not necessarily a factor in determining successful black history instruction. L. R. Raife

2252. Keeley, Benjamin J. REACTIONS OF A GROUP OF WHITE PARISHIONERS TOWARD THE ACCEPTANCE OF A NEGRO AS PASTOR. *Sociol. and Social Research 1971 55(2): 216-228.* "Data obtained from the pulpit committee of a white, liberal, middle class church seeking a new minister are used to examine thirteen hypotheses which suggest a number of personal and social characteristics differentiating those white church members who react positively to extending a call to a Negro minister from those who react negatively." J

2253. Kelly, Walter J. HISTORICAL PERSPECTIVES ON RACISM. *Hist. Teacher 1969 2(4): 27-30.* Discusses the third annual Conference on Afro-American History, at the University of Illinois, 7 November 1968. Teachers of history "must develop courses and materials based on historically valid approaches so that the field will not go by default to those whose sense of outrage and grievance has outstripped their rational judgment." D. J. Engler

2254. Killens, John Oliver. BROADWAY IN BLACK AND WHITE. *African Forum 1966 1(3): 66-76.* Reviews the success of Negro actors and playwrights from 1958 to 1966. The author discusses the careers of such stars as Sidney Poitier and Harry Belafonte and their contribution to theater in the United States. Even though there are many Negroes in the film, television, and theater industries in the United States, "the accomplishments of the Negro artists in the performing and dramatic arts are infinitesimal in comparison to what they would be if show business in America were free of racial prejudice."   M. J. McBaine

2255. Killian, Lewis M. and Grigg, Charles M. COMMUNITY RESISTANCE TO AND ACCEPTANCE OF DESEGREGATION. *J. of Negro Educ. 1965 34(3): 268-277.* The present situation and immediate prospect for the Negro in American society is unclear, for there are evidences of advance in such accomplishments as the passage of the Civil Rights Act of 1964 and of failure to effect material improvement in economic and educational opportunity or in residential desegregation and to eliminate the threat of violence by adequate and equal police protection. The author insists that effective and lasting reform depends upon "acceptance by individual citizens of the spirit as well as the letter of the law."
                                                                     S. C. Pearson, Jr.

2256. King, Albion Roy. A WHITE PHILOSOPHER IN A SOUTHERN GHETTO. *J. of Human Relations 1968 16.*
    I. ON GETTING ALONG IN THE SOUTH, (3): 401-409. Reports on the author's experiences during his recent residence of five months in a college town in Mississippi. In order to avoid embarrassment neither the name of the town nor of the Negro college at which the author taught is mentioned. The town's pattern of race relations, the nature of the Negro ghetto in which the author lived, and the changing racial attitudes of whites and blacks are among the topics discussed. Northern reformers who attempt to help the southern Negro are likely to find "among the colored people a deep unconscious aversion to being dominated by white opinion. At the worst such Northern invasion consolidates the white community in bitter opposition." The white closed society has built a tremendous storehouse of resentment among southern colored people. "And a sad part of it is that so few of them realize how it happened and the explosive quality of it."
    II. ON THE PROBLEM OF MISCEGENATION, (4): 547-555. "The white fear of amalgamation of the races seems groundless. There will continue to be pressure to make intermarriage legitimate, and it is simple justice, for the white man is not going to enforce his laws on miscegenation any more than he will enforce the prohibition law, and for the same reason - cultural patterns are stronger than law....The closed society operates with especial tightness in some Protestant church circles....The white churches in the South are in pathetic decline." It is in the Negro churches that faith and hope are electric. The position of the Negro has improved somewhat in politics and in education, and the State government has curtailed the reign of terror. Economic pressure and the work of the churches may contribute to further progress in race relations.
                                                                     D. J. Abramoske

2257. Kozol, Jonathan. HALLS OF DARKNESS: IN THE GHETTO SCHOOLS. *Harvard Educ. R. 1967 37(3): 379-407.* A firsthand account of conditions in a de facto segregated school in the metropolitan area of Boston, which is excerpted from the author's *Death at an Early Age* (Boston: Houghton Mifflin, 1967), introduces the reader to the squalor, injustice, and moral rottenness that passes for public education in the segregated schools of one of America's large urban centers. The author draws a frightening profile of "the dedicated senior teachers [who] are a sacrosanct entity in American opinion," and whom he charges with perpetuating, profiting from, and apologizing for the ghetto school systems. Based on personal experience. J. Herbst

2258. Kriegel, Leonard. UNCLE TOM AND TINY TIM: SOME REFLEC-TIONS ON THE CRIPPLE AS NEGRO. *Am. Scholar 1969 38(3): 412-430.* Discusses the role of the cripple in American life. From childhood through maturity, from onset of crippling disease to final acceptance of its permanent result, the author finds that the closest analog to the life of the cripple is the life of the Negro in America. The most significant factor in the equation is that determination of identity and expectation are in the hands of "others," those outside of life, those with power, the superior beings, the "normal" people; that is, white people. T. R. Cripps

2259. Langendorf, Richard. RESIDENTIAL DESEGREGATION POTEN-TIAL. *J. of the Am. Inst. of Planners 1969 35(2): 90-95.* "Assuming that desegre-gation is a desirable long-range goal, this paper examines the potential for reasonable progress toward that goal, using data from eleven of the twelve largest metropolitan areas in the U.S. First, a Negro working-class income group is identified as possible candidates for desegregation. Second, suburban housing costs are compared with the ability of ghetto residents to pay. Although present new suburban housing is too expensive for most working-class Negroes, neither costs of existing housing nor current income levels appear as significant restric-tions on Negro suburbanization. Furthermore, existing federal housing aids can facilitate construction of suburban law and moderate income housing. Given commitment to use of existing tools, a substantial amount of desegregation can now occur within the existing suburban housing supply." J

2260. Lee, George A. NEGROES IN A MEDIUM-SIZED METROPOLIS: ALLENTOWN, PENNSYLVANIA - A CASE STUDY. *J. of Negro Educ. 1968 37(4): 397-405.* A study made from interviews with approximately one-half of the Negro families, 20 Negro teenagers, and 7 Negro leaders in Allentown, Pennsyl-vania, during 1965 and 1966. The Negro population is small. Approximately two-thirds of the recent arrivals came from the South. Residential discrimination was found and is a major reason for the lack of a strong Negro middle class. These Negro professionals tend to go where there is more opportunity for good housing and more social life for them. The Negro unemployment rate is very high because of the lack of skills. The school is the least discriminatory place, but many Negroes get little encouragement from home to continue their educations. The Negro remains stigmatized because of his color, education, occupation, and level of aspiration. 2 tables, 29 notes. B. D. Johnson

2261. Lekachman, Robert. DEATH OF A SLOGAN - THE GREAT SOCIETY 1967. *Commentary 1967 43(1): 56-61.* Lyndon Johnson's coalition of big busi-nessmen, trade unions, liberal intellectuals, white ethnic minorities, and Negroes began to disintegrate before the 1966 election. Trade unions did not do as well as corporations during the Johnson years. Social welfare did poorly because

Americans preferred reduction in taxes to social improvements. The Great Society was further weakened because it was impossible to accommodate both the Vietnam War and the race issue. The author notes that social welfare is the easiest area in which to reduce spending since welfare programs are least protected by bureaucratic and congressional interest; also, those who are aided have small influence in elections. The white backlash further reduced aid to the Negro, particularly in poverty programs and housing proposals. The author concludes that programs such as education will continue because they aid the prosperous. The Great Society has not redistributed the Nation's income; instead, it raised the prestige of the business community and failed to halt racism and poverty.
C. Grollman

2262. Lerner, Michael. RESPECTABLE BIGOTRY. *Am. Scholar 1969 38(4): 606-617.* Argues that "liberal-to-radical" students and university faculty display "respectable bigotry" when they fail to comprehend and include in their canon of acceptable underdogs the fears and motives of the lower-middle classes. In effect, a rash of "Polish jokes," ridiculing of recent Italian political candidates, and condemnation of police and National Guardsmen as "pigs" are all little more than evidences of upper-class elitist class-bigotry. Added to the pattern is a tendency for upper-class university elitists find common cause with lower-class ghetto blacks, admire their patois, and emulate their music; on the other hand, they find representatives of the class that separates them (i.e., the white lower-middle class) reprehensible and crude, especially in their political style, as is exemplified by the Chicago police, Mayor Daley, and the reaction of people in Cicero, Illinois, to Martin Luther King's march through their neighborhoods. The consequences of this upper-class bigotry the author finds "tragic"; Americans were prevented from developing electable alternatives to Richard Nixon and George Wallace. A Nixon alliance seems, then, contingent on upper-middle-class ability to deal with or not to deal with its own bigotry before it is able to deal with lower-middle-class bigotry.
T. R. Cripps

2263. Levenson, Bernard and Mcdill, Mary S. VOCATIONAL GRADUATES IN AUTO MECHANICS: A FOLLOW-UP STUDY OF NEGRO AND WHITE YOUTH. *Phylon 1966 27(4): 347-357.* Reports the results of a study of Negro and white graduates of vocational schools in Baltimore, Maryland. Earnings records of a sample of graduates of classes 1956 to 1960 were examined. The median earnings of Negro graduates ranged from 45 to 55 percent of those of white graduates, and length of time in the labor market made no appreciable difference. No factors other than discrimination in industry could be found to explain the different levels of earnings. Based on records of the Social Security Administration; 18 notes.
S. C. Pearson, Jr.

2264. Levine, Richard H. THEY MADE A BETTER SCHOOL. *Am. Educ. 1969 5(9): 8-10.* A brief description of the efforts of the Providence school district to end de facto school segregation. The core of the program involved busing children into a former neighborhood school in the black ghetto. The former school was converted into a model school featuring innovative and experimental programs. Although it remained a neighborhood school, white children could attend if their parents would agree to bus them, and many parents agreed. Black children were also free to attend schools in white neighborhoods. Based on interviews with individuals involved in the program; 4 photos.

W. R. Boedecker

2265. Lightfoote-Wilson, Thomasyne. INSTITUTIONAL ACCESS: THE ROAD TO NATIONAL INTEGRATION. *J. of Human Relations 1968 16(3): 343-353.* Discusses the problem of Negro-white relations, criticizes the simplistic solutions supplied by journalists like Joseph Alsop, and offers suggestions for the improvement of race relations and the education of minority groups. Institutional access and participation are defined and considered essential keys "for disentangling the knotty course toward national integration." Contrary to the views of Mr. Alsop, whites are moving to the suburbs not to find quality education but to escape reality, difficulty, and Negro participation. The school is an essential institution for the development of a more democratic society. Teachers who are unable to react positively to their minority-group students should be fired. All students should have an opportunity to participate in activities that relate to a larger group. Schools must facilitate identification with the social system by, for example, studying ethnic contributions made by all Americans. The curriculum should be responsive to student preferences. Based on recently published works and the author's experience as a teacher in California during the academic year 1966-67.

D. J. Abramoske

2266. Link, Ruth. AMBASSADOR HOLLAND AND THE SWEDES. *Crisis 1971 78(2): 43-48.* Discusses the nature and causes of demonstrations against American Ambassador Jerome Holland, a black, on his arrival in Sweden in April 1970. Ambassador Holland was met at the airport by a supporter of the National Liberation Front (NLF) who called him a murderer (due to U.S. involvement in Vietnam) and told him to go home. In the first few days in Stockholm, American Negro supporters of the NLF demonstrated against Holland, calling him a "house nigger." Newspapers all over Sweden editorialized against this "intolerable and irresponsible behavior." Holland said he did not object to demonstrations against the United States, but felt he was being attacked personally. He did not hide in the embassy, but journeyed out to meet the people. People in the United States received the mistaken impression that Sweden was a racist country. The author finds it ironic that this impression was caused by American Negroes in Sweden. Sweden is the most American-oriented country in Europe and also the least racist, as Ambassador Holland soon found out. Everywhere he went he met Swedes who treated him with respect and who were outraged by the demonstrations. Holland now believes the majority of Swedes are pro-American and pro-Negro, although they are obviously disappointed in the American involvement in Vietnam.

R. L. Nix

2267. Linn, Lawrence S. VERBAL ATTITUDES AND OVERT BEHAVIOR: A STUDY OF RACIAL DISCRIMINATION. *Social Forces 1965 43(3): 353-364.* "The present study in attempting to measure the relationship between racial attitudes and overt behavior asked *Ss* to pose for a photograph with a Negro of the opposite sex. Discrepancies between verbal attitudes and subsequent overt behavior involving those attitudes was found in 59 percent of the cases. The relationship between attitude (prejudice) and behavior (discrimination) is seen to be a function of the level of social involvement with the attitude object as well as the amount of prior experience with it. One implication of the study is that statements of predictions of racial behavior based on attitude measurements have little reliability unless first validated empirically."   J

2268. Lombardi, Donald N. FACTORS AFFECTING CHANGES IN ATTITUDES TOWARD NEGROES AMONG HIGH SCHOOL STUDENTS. *J. of Negro Educ. 1963 32(2): 129-136.* Based on research conducted for a doctoral dissertation at Fordham University in 1958-59. Students' attitude changes are significantly related to the educational level of the mother and to declines in their own academic success. Other variables studied were found not to be significantly related to attitude change.   S. C. Pearson, Jr.

2269. Lowe, Gilbert Antonio. A STUDY OF JAMAICAN STUDENTS AT HOWARD UNIVERSITY, 1961-1962. *J. of Negro Educ. 1964 33(4): 450-453.* One hundred forty-two of a total of 205 Jamaican students enrolled at Howard University were studied through questionnaires, interviews, and school records. The study revealed that the subjects experienced considerable upward social mobility, though the selective process is related to their studying abroad, and to the fact that the subjects' parents, in terms of occupation and education, were superior to the majority of Jamaican adults. The subjects experienced little alienation from home ties and associated their major problems in the United States with employment and racial discrimination.   S. C. Pearson, Jr.

2270. Lurie, Melvin and Rayack, Elton. EMPLOYMENT OPPORTUNITIES FOR NEGRO FAMILIES IN "SATELLITE" CITIES. *Southern Econ. J. 1969 36(2): 191-195.* In place of the policy of "suburbanization" which has been advanced as a solution to the problem of racial segregation in employment, the author proposes that some Negro families should move to small industrial satellite cities near metropolitan areas. The policy should be designed to disperse the central city residents by a chain migration system. The recommendation is based on an interview study of Negro families in Middletown, Connecticut, in 1964.   A. W. Coats

2271. Mack, Raymond W. STUDENT IDEOLOGIES, CAMPUS UNREST, AND SOCIAL CHANGE. *Northwestern Report 1969 4(3): 24-28.* College students view higher education as an inalienable right, not as a privilege to be earned, and they take affluence for granted, seeing it as the natural order of things. Politically, college students can be divided into four broad groups. The conservatives, the overwhelming majority, do not seek any fundamental social changes and merely want to acquire a secure niche in life. The idealistic reformers, the liberals of the previous generation, sincerely want to improve society, but reject the older liberalism as ineffectual. This group is susceptible to the destructive radicalism of the New Left, and university administrators must seek to work with the idealists and channel their reform efforts into constructive paths. The blacks are interested solely in winning social and economic opportunity for their own people. The New Left, which claims a monopoly on truth, asserts the right to suppress all those who disagree with its methods and goals. 2 illus.

G. Kurland

2272. MaKaroff, Julian. AMERICA'S OTHER RACIAL MINORITY: WHY JAPANESE-AMERICANS FARE BETTER THAN US NEGROES. *Eastern World [Great Britain] 1966 20(11/12): 17-18.* Orientals make up about .5 percent of America's population. Most of them are descendants of those who immigrated in large numbers before the Immigration Act of 1924. A short history of Japanese Americans is given, with a description of the present circumstances of the half-million Nisei, or second-generation Japanese Americans. They have fared better in American society than Negroes because of their smaller numbers relative to whites and their higher educational and cultural level. During World War II, all Japanese Americans were placed in relocation camps, but some were subsequently allowed to take part in the Allied war effort, fighting in both Europe and Asia. They were of considerable help in deciphering Japanese military codes.

A. K. Main

2273. Makaroff, Julian. AMERIKAS UNBEKANNTE RASSENMINDER-HEIT: JAPANISCH-AMERIKANER [America's unknown racial minority: the Japanese Americans]. *Politische Studien [West Germany] 1968 19(181): 577-580.* The one-half million Japanese-Americans have no ties with their Japanese heritage and feel themselves fully to be American. In comparison to Negroes, the Nisei experience little racial discrimination today, although before World War II the situation for them was much less favorable. The loyalty which the Nisei demonstrated in the war did much to enhance their position in America.

R. V. Pierard

2274. Marcuse, Peter. INTEGRATION AND THE PLANNER. *J. of the Am. Inst. of Planners 1969 35(2): 113-117.* "Segregation is increasing in American cities, and recent city plans fail to grapple realistically with the problem. Serious questions are being raised, by both whites and blacks, as to whether integration in housing is either a strategically wise or a theoretically valid objective. The alternative of improving the ghetto is often put forward. A commitment to *freedom of choice* requires both some integrated housing and such action in the ghetto as its residents desire. An aggressive role for planners in fostering integration, coupled with assistance to the ghetto in formulating its own plans and achieving the power to implement them, is recommended." J

2275. Marshall, Ray. SOME FACTORS INFLUENCING THE UPGRADING OF NEGROES IN THE SOUTHERN PETROLEUM REFINING INDUS-TRY. *Social Forces 1963 42(2): 186-195.* "Efforts to upgrade Negroes in the petroleum refining industry, which is concentrated in the Southwest, started long before the end of World War II, but reached a peak of activity in the economic and social ferment following 1950. This paper examines in detail some of the efforts to eliminate segregated seniority lines in the petroleum refining industry and concludes that a number of forces have been required to break down formal job segregation in this industry, but that the extent to which employment patterns actually change will depend upon such factors as: economic conditions; the attitudes of management, white workers, and the union; the particular promotion system involved; the initiative and organization of the Negroes involved and the kinds and amount of power they can bring to bear on management, unions, and white workers."   J

2276. Marshall, Ray. THE NEGRO AND ORGANIZED LABOR. *J. of Negro Educ.* 1963 32(4): 373-389. Discusses racial discrimination within the labor movement and possible means of eliminating such discrimination.
S. C. Pearson, Jr.

2277. Martin, Charles E. THE PATH TO INTEGRATION. *Am. Educ.* 1968 4(8): 25-27. The efforts to desegregate public schools in the 14 years since the Supreme Court decision is the "pursuit of a false goal" in which "our concentration on rationalized mechanics, freedom of choice, and letter-of-the-law statistics has not produced appreciable changes in our classrooms or equalized educational opportunities. The schools of this country are a system devised by society, and education is a vital component of total social direction. Therefore the only proper issues for our consideration in this matter are the provision of equal educational opportunity for all students in an integrated school society and the exercise of educational leadership for the eventual integration of the broader society which created our educational system and gives reason for being." Based on an address given at a conference of Kentucky school superintendents.   W. R. Boedecker

2278. Martin, Patricia. TEACHING IN A SEGREGATED SCHOOL. *Mennonite Life* 1967 22(1): 37-39. Discusses the author's experience teaching kindergarten in two Negro public schools in Kansas. Although the first school was as well financed and equipped as middle-class schools in the community, it was in fact not equal to the white schools. The Negro parents were unable to cooperate as effectively as parents in white areas. There was a large teacher turnover. The Negro students were culturally disadvantaged. The second school was much worse because of inadequate facilities. "School administrations will be most influenced to change by pressure from parents, both black and white together, who desire their children be trained to live in an integrated, democratic society."
D. J. Abramoske

2279. Matthews, Donald R. and Prothro, James W. STATEWAYS VERSUS FOLKWAYS: CRITICAL FACTORS IN SOUTHERN REACTIONS TO BROWN VS. BOARD OF EDUCATION. *Essays on the Am. Constitution: A Commemorative Volume in Honor of Alpheus T. Mason (Englewood, N.J.: Prentice-Hall, Inc., 1964): 139-156.* In contrast to the border States, the South has been characterized by only token segregation. Demographic factors - especially urbanism, Negro and white income, and Negro education - account for much of the variation in school desegregation. The relative importance of demographic and political factors varies from one issue to another. "As school desegregation passes the threshold of legitimacy in the South, it will become more and more responsive to political manipulation." The authors suggest that the proportion of issues in which stateways outweigh folkways is one indication of the degree to which that society has attained democracy. 6 tables, 37 notes.

E. P. Stickney

2280. Mccain, R. Ray. REACTIONS TO THE UNITED STATES SUPREME COURT SEGREGATION DECISION OF 1954. *Georgia Hist. Q. 1968 52 (4): 371-387.* Analyzes southern response to the historic 1954 Supreme Court decision in *Brown vs. Board of Education of Topeka,* which overturned the separate but equal clause of *Cumming vs. County Board of Education* (1899). Four border States (Delaware, Maryland, West Virginia, and Missouri) and Washington, D.C., took immediate steps to comply with the court's decision. Seven Southern States (Arkansas, Florida, Kentucky, North Carolina, Oklahoma, Tennessee, and Texas) maintained a status quo on desegregation in 1954 but indicated that plans for integrated education could eventually be formulated. Alabama and Virginia seemed determined on an evasive course. Georgia, Louisiana, Mississippi, and South Carolina seemed unalterably opposed to implementation of the Court's ruling, and the legislatures of these States were granted authority to abolish the public school systems, if necessary, to maintain segregation. Based on research in newspapers, periodicals, and the reports of State study commissions; 66 notes.   R. A. Mohl

2281. Mcdill, Mary Sexton, Stinchcombe, Arthur L. , and Walker, Dollie. SEGREGATION AND EDUCATIONAL DISADVANTAGE: ESTIMATES OF THE INFLUENCE OF DIFFERENT SEGREGATING FACTORS. *Sociol. of Educ. 1968 41(3): 239-244.* "A regression equation relating Negroes' verbal achievement to the proportion Negro in their schools, taken from the Coleman report, is applied to data on school composition in Baltimore and Baltimore suburbs. This allows estimation of the educational disadvantage due to different segregating influences. For Baltimore Negroes as a group, the most important local segregating influences are the city-suburban boundary and the private-public school system boundary. Segregation within the city public school system does not account for much of the educational disadvantage."

J

2282. McGill, Ralph. LOOK AWAY, LOOK AWAY. *Massachusetts Hist. Soc. Pro. 1966 78: 50-62.* Discusses the harmful effects of the southern segregation system not only upon its most obvious victim, the Negro, but upon poor whites as well. While not deprecating the "considerable gains" made since 1956, the author warns that much of the progress has been confined to the Negro middle class. In the South and in the North, civil rights legislation has not yet done much for the poor, Negro or white. 8 notes.   J. B. Duff

2283. McGill, Ralph. THE HUMAN CONDITION. *Social Educ. 1964 28(2): 64-67.* Selects as the one major phenomenon of our country since 1945 the astonishing mobility of the population, especially the South's outmigration. "When it is considered that it was not until after 1945 that the deep-South States began programs of building high schools for Negro pupils, the acuteness of the regional problems becomes better understood. The net result is that both races have suffered discrimination in education." McGill notes the fact that most new jobs in recent decades are in the service category. Lee Oswald's "many rejections are common to the school dropout groups in American society." (Walter E. Myer Lecture at the 43d annual meeting of the National Council for the Social Studies at Los Angeles, November 1963.)   E. P. Stickney

2284. McGraw, B. T. EQUAL OPPORTUNITY IN HOUSING - TRENDS AND IMPLICATIONS. *Phylon 1964 25(1): 5-17.* The author cites statistics to illustrate the difficulty which the nonwhite experiences in seeking access to urban housing in the United States today and traces recent trends toward providing equal opportunity in housing.   S. C. Pearson, Jr.

2285. Meagher, Sylvia. TWO ASSASSINATIONS. *Minority of One 1968 10(6): 9-10.* An indictment of the racism and inhumanity of American society which made possible the assassinations of John F. Kennedy and Martin Luther King, as well as the killing of innocent people abroad, especially in Asia. Assassination with impunity is inherent in the American way. It is sanctioned by the Establishment, and is intensified by pronouncements by local and Federal authorities who always try to establish the role of the lone, deranged murderer in political assassinations.   P. W. Kennedy

2286. Meer, Bernard and Freedman, Edward. THE IMPACT OF NEGRO NEIGHBORS ON WHITE HOME OWNERS. *Social Forces 1966 45(1): 11-19.* "The purpose of this study was to test the hypothesis that equal-status contact between Negroes and whites in a predominantly white middle- to upper-middle-class neighborhood would lead to a reduction of prejudice. The results suggest that equal-status contact in one area (in this case residential) does lead to a reduction of prejudice in that area (Negroes were more accepted as neighbors), but this change does not necessarily generalize to other areas of interpersonal contact. However, when residential contact leads to more intimate types of interactions, a more extensive reduction in prejudice may follow."   J

2287. Melish, Ilene H. ATTITUDES TOWARD THE WHITE MINORITY ON A BLACK SOUTHERN CAMPUS: 1966-1968. *Sociol. Q. 1970 11(3): 321-330.* An analysis of black students' attitudes toward their white colleagues at a small, rural southern college (unnamed) where there were only 12 or 13 whites per semester out of a total student population of roughly 600. The study was done during the transition years 1966-68 which saw the rise of "black power." "Although one of the major results of this study was the discovery of the presence of a minority of approximately 10 percent of black students who were hostile toward their white colleagues, the prime finding was that during the transition period the overwhelming feeling of blacks about whites at the College was one of *difference,* of *foreignness.*" About one-third of the black students desired a larger white enrollment. There was much racial friction at the college, particularly since two-thirds of the faculty was white. 4 tables, 2 notes.   R. D. Cohen

2288. Mercedes, Sister Maria. INTEGRATION: CONTRAST IN FREE-DOMS. *Liberal Educ. 1964 50(3): 367-374.* Views integration as a process to be distinguished from desegregation. The former "refers more truly to the spirit of the principle, and desegregation to the letter, but that where the spirit is not lived there will be, in fact, an inability to live up to the letter." Describes the attitudes of men toward the issue as falling along a continuum from segregation, or hate, to integration, or love. The author sees most people, a majority of whom are white, as falling between the two extremes. The white in this group, as well as all blacks, will be brought freedom as a result of integration. The challenge for implementing integration is a moral obligation placed upon each individual and institution. The college and university should assist white students to develop an appreciation of the feelings of others, a sensitivity to their special sufferings and needs, a greater awareness of the obligations of justice and charity. 3 notes.
W. R. Boedecker

2289. Metzger, Walter P. THE CRISIS OF ACADEMIC AUTHORITY. *Daedalus 1970 99(3): 568-608.* Discusses the growing resistance to academic authority and regulations, both nonviolent and violent. Major problems alienating students from the university are the disparate relationships between academic and nonacademic persons, as well as the exploitation of the disadvantaged by the university (e.g., the events at Columbia University in April 1968). In this connection, what students want is to be able to control decisions that affect their lives and to discontinue inequities against the poor, Negroes, women, and students. What is needed is a reordering of roles (i.e., academic roles), proper instruction, and allowing authority to be retained by the university as a resource, not as an issue. 11 notes.
A. Krichmar

2290. Mitchell, John N. and Finch, Robert H. SCHOOL DESEGREGATION POLICY, 1969. *Current Hist. 1969 57(339): 303-305.* Concerns the policies of the Nixon administration in the field of school desegregation. Indicates that the law of the land will be upheld in the South without the use of unrealistic deadlines. Announces a substantial program to attack de facto segregation in the North. A joint statement issued on 3 July 1969.
B. D. Rhodes

2291. Mogulof, Melvin B. BLACK COMMUNITY DEVELOPMENT IN FIVE WESTERN MODEL CITIES. *Social Work 1970 15(1): 12-18.* An in-depth analysis of five western cities programs with predominantly black neighborhoods is presented for the purpose of ascertaining if their decisionmaking structure is adversary or coalition. Data is submitted to support the observation that the decisionmaking structure in the five cities was adversary. The author concludes that this form of decisionmaking power is conducive to program efforts which are racially separatist. Table, 5 figs., 6 notes.
W. L. Willigan

2292. Molènes, Charles Melchior de. L'EGALISATION RACIALE AUX ETATS-UNIS [Racial equalization in the United States]. *R. Pol. et Parlementaire [France] 1967 69(780): 79-86.* Over the last 15 years the United States has made considerable progress in moving toward true integration. The Supreme Court decision of 1954 illustrates effective judicial intervention, the election of Negroes to high office is another step forward, and even Adam Clayton Powell's notoriety cannot diminish his congressional prominence. But, the author concludes, there still remains inequality before the law: local administration has yet to observe in all respects the civil rights of Negroes.   T. D. Lockwood

2293. Molotch, Harvey. RACIAL INTEGRATION IN A TRANSITION COMMUNITY. *Am. Sociol. R. 1969 34(6): 878-893.* "An attempt is made to record conditions under which various forms of racial integration occur in a changing community and the relationship between those conditions and the means by which members of the two races attempt to cope with the challenges of sharing biracial social environments. Racial headcounts are reported for various kinds of social settings and impressions are provided of the nature and differential consequences on blacks and whites of biracial interaction in such environments. Racial integration is found to be very limited in frequency and intensity, despite biracial propinquity. It is especially limited in those circumstances where interpersonal behavior is ordinarily informal, spontaneous or intense. Transracial solidarity occurs only in circumstances in which cross-racial cues of similarity, reliability and trust are strong relative to other opportunities for social solidarity.   J

2294. Morgenthau, Hans J. THE COMING TEST OF AMERICAN DEMOCRACY. *Commentary 1964 37(1): 61-63.* The achievement of equality for the American Negro and the realization of full employment in a sound social and economic order are two grave, interrelated issues threatening the stability of American democracy. Even if American Negroes are accorded full legal and social equality in the foreseeable future - an unlikely condition in view of the persistence of social segregation patterns in American society - their position as unskilled laborers in a contracting labor market and the resentment of large numbers of white unemployed will continue to be sources of alienation and incentives to violence. Anarchic, largely unreported violence born of resentment already terrorizes many American streets and schools. Only a revolution in American economic practice and social organization can avoid the danger of government by force to contain the inflammatory mixture of racial discontent and economic deprivation.   J. J. Appel

2295. Morrill, Richard L. THE NEGRO GHETTO: PROBLEMS AND ALTERNATIVES. *Geographical R. 1965 55(3): 339-361.* Examines the nature of the ghetto and pinpoints four forces which hinder change: namely, prejudice against Negroes, Negro characteristics, discrimination by the real-estate industry, and legal and governmental barriers. The author explains the Negro movement using Seattle as an example, and proposes alternatives to present patterns of ghetto expansion. Maps and charts.   R. L. McBane

2296. Morris, J. LETTER FROM CRANBURY, N.J. *Encounter [Great Britain] 1967 29(171): 9-12.* A personal note on a small American farming town - Cranbury, New Jersey. The author traces the impact of major trends in the period 1954-67, particularly the color problem, changes in the social structure, growing urbanization, and economic expansion.   D. H. Murdoch

2297. Morris, Richard T. and Jeffries, Vincent. VIOLENCE NEXT DOOR. *Social Forces 1968 46(3): 352-358.* An exploratory study based on samples of six Los Angeles communities, primarily white, after the Watts upheaval of 1965. Questions were derived from Robin M. Williams' *Strangers Next Door* (New York: Prentice-Hall, 1964), where social distance between whites and Negroes is scaled. Another consideration of this report was the extent of "antagonism." There were more "egoistic" than "altruistic" respondents. Findings indicate that voluntary contact between whites and Negroes is related to "low antagonism," whereas involuntary contact is not. There are many unknowns. Implications are not clear. It appears that racial attitudes are more basic and stable than reactions to a single event. 10 tables. A. S. Freedman

2298. Mortimer, M. ANATOMY OF AMERICAN ASSIMILATION. *Q. R. [Great Britain] 1966 304(647): 11-16.* For a long time the United States has sought to provide "a pattern for almost every form of racial assimilation and integration." However, Americans have not solved the problem of assimilating the Negro. This is a difficult matter due to the large numbers, the exceptional "visibility," the unique circumstance of forced migration, the failure to develop community strength, and the lack of a cohesive cultural background of the Negroes. Since World War II the problem has become more urgent, with the militant Negro leaders by-passing the traditional paths of economic and educational equality to press for immediate legal and political equality. Legal gains have not provided a complete solution: it is suggested that separation (but not the forced kind of South Africa), rather than assimilation, might provide real equality for Negro Americans. R. G. Schafer

2299. Mouledous, Joseph C. FROM BROWDERISM TO PEACEFUL CO-EXISTENCE: AN ANALYSIS OF DEVELOPMENTS IN THE COMMUNIST POSITION ON THE AMERICAN NEGRO. *Phylon 1964 25(1): 79-90.* Surveys the impact of shifting ideology within the Soviet Union on the American Communist Party's position on the Negro question from 1941 to 1964. This position is traced from the party's assertion that American Negroes in the Black Belt constitute a separate nation and should have the right of self-determination through Browder's argument for full integration of the Negro into American life, a later reemphasis on the former position, and a decisive abandonment of the slogan of self-determination in 1956. S. C. Pearson, Jr.

2300. Mühlen, Norbert. IM SÜDEN DER USA: EINE REISE DURCH MISSISSIPPI UND ARKANSAS [In southern United States: a journey through Mississippi and Arkansas]. *Monat [West Germany] 1966 18(208): 5-16.* After giving his personal reaction to life in the Southern States as he found it in some of the towns, the author gives a summary account of the race troubles of the past years and of the present improved situation. M. Petrie

2301. Muir, Donal E. and McGlamery, C. Donald. THE EVOLUTION OF DESEGREGATION ATTITUDES OF SOUTHERN UNIVERSITY STUDENTS. *Phylon 1968 29(2): 105-117.* A statistical study of desegregation attitudes at the University of Alabama in 1963 and 1966. Six different tables are presented which offer statistical information in the following areas: general white attitudes toward Negroes and desegregation, role-set analysis, analysis of reference group materials, reference group partialled by own attitude, own attitude about segregation-integration by school and class year, and analysis of Shaffer Hypothesis materials. The authors conclude that "there seems little question that the University of Alabama student body is increasingly adopting attitudes compatible with integration." The change is apparently due to growing patterns of desegregation throughout the Nation and to the positive desegregation experiences of the University of Alabama. 6 tables, 8 notes.   R. D. Cohen

2302. Mullen, James H. RACIAL TENSIONS ON CAMPUS. *Pan-African J. 1970 3(1): 30-33.* Racial tensions in America are crucial today. Even though the term "race" should be eliminated, the problems resulting from differentiating followmen on some basis would remain. Racism, compounded by the "generation-gap," has produced human estrangement. Racism estrangement dwells on the campus, which is a microcosm of society at large. Jersey City State College attacks racism estrangement by significantly recruiting students and faculty from minority groups, by offering a black studies program, and by an ethnic studies institute. The resulting danger of polarization must be overcome in the college by finding the sources of the *elán vital* so as to "begin to understand the mystery of unity in difference, understanding in uncertainty and even love in antipathy."
E. E. Beauregard

2303. Müller, Günther. SCHWERPUNKTVERLAGERUNG IN DEN USA [A shift in the center of gravity in the United States]. *Politische Studien [West Germany] 1964 15(158): 693-695.* A commentary on the up-coming American election in November 1964, which expresses considerable apprehension about Senator Goldwater and the resurgence of right-wing activity. The author feels that the political weight in the United States has swung to the right and he shows considerable concern about American social and racial problems.
R. V. Pierard

2304. Murrell, Glen. THE DESEGREGATION OF PADUCAH JUNIOR COLLEGE. *Register of the Kentucky Hist. Soc. 1969 67(1): 63-79.* Racial segregation in Kentucky's public educational institutions was maintained through the enforcement of the Day School Law of 1904. The author describes the efforts of the Paducah Chapter of the National Association for the Advancement of Colored People beginning in 1949 to desegregate Paducah Junior College. After several lawsuits and much legal maneuvering, Paducah Junior College was ordered in January 1952 by the U. S. District Court to desegregate its facilities. The first Negro students enrolled in June 1953, almost a year before the U. S. Supreme Court ruled that racial segregation violated the Constitution. Based on letters, court records, newspapers, and interviews; 76 notes.   B. Wilkins

2305. Nelson, Harold A. THE RE-EDUCATION OF SOCIOLOGISTS: A NOTE ON THE IMPACT OF DR. MARTIN LUTHER KING, JR. AS EDUCATOR. *J. of Human Relations 1968 16(4): 514-523.* One of the valuable contributions of Martin Luther King, Jr., was to confront sociology with the realities of ethnic relations and thereby to demonstrate to sociologists that many of their conceptualizations were outmoded, naïve, and irrelevant. King challenged sociologists to "act as morally committed, emotionally involved revolutionaries." The civil rights movement undermined "vague theories of gradualism built upon a faith that somehow, inexorably, 'things were getting better.'...Dr. King gave life and graphic illustration to the fact that ideas, values, and ethics may stand as the dynamic element in change." His career forces reconsideration of traditional theories of leadership and education.   D. J. Abramoske

2306. Olsen, Marvin E. ALIENATION AND POLITICAL OPINIONS. *Public Opinion Q. 1965 29(2): 200-212.* Considers the relation of alienation toward such issues as governmental action programs, racial integration, freedom of speech, and international organization, each of which is found to be an area where alienation has important effects. Alienation is defined as an attitude of separation or estrangement between oneself and some salient aspect of the social environment. Occupational level is found to have a close inverse relationship to alienation. Moreover, nonalienated people were found to be unfavorable to increased domestic action but favorable to foreign aid, while alienated persons took directly opposite stands. Data for this research analysis were taken from the 1958 Detroit Area Study of the University of Michigan. 4 tables, 14 notes.
    E. P. Stickney

2307. Orbell, John M. and Sherrill, Kenneth S. RACIAL ATTITUDES AND THE METROPOLITAN CONTEXT: A STRUCTURAL ANALYSIS. *Public Opinion Q. 1969 33(1): 46-55.* The authors investigate the relationship between racial hostility and metropolitan living and apply a technique which brings individual and contextual variables together in the same analysis. For the urban situation, "area status and racial composition interact in their impact on white racial attitudes, and...whites of similar status differ in their attitudes toward blacks when they live in areas of different status." 3 tables, 15 notes.
    D. J. Trickey

2308. Patten, Thomas H., Jr. THE INDUSTRIAL INTEGRATION OF THE NEGRO. *Phylon 1963 24(4): 334-352.* Studies the relationships between social causation, social change, and social action as they affect the industrial integration of the Negro. In order to achieve integration "more is dependent upon Negroes making an all-out effort through organized leadership groups than in depending upon the existing industrial institutional structure to change by itself or through discontinuous, spontaneous collective behavior."   S. C. Pearson, Jr.

2309. Peck, Sidney M. and Rosen, Sidney. THE INFLUENCE OF THE PEER GROUP ON THE ATTITUDES OF GIRLS TOWARD COLOR DIFFERENCES. *Phylon 1965 26(1): 50-63.* Considers the extent to which their peer group influences the attitudes of six- and eight-year-old white girls toward Negro youngsters. The material is based on a study among children in Milwaukee, Wisconsin, into whose neighborhood Negroes were beginning to move. It was found that the girls "were aware of color differences; that they rigidly preferred white to Negro children; that they categorically excluded Negro youngsters from private fun clubs; and that they were influenced markedly by their peers in the acceptance and rejection of colored children."   S. C. Pearson, Jr.

2310. Pettigrew, Thomas. SCHOOL INTEGRATION IN CURRENT PER-SPECTIVE. *Urban R. 1969 3(3): 4-8.* Public education in the United States since 1954 has become more segregated, particularly in northern cities, due to two factors: separation of schools according to social class structure, and racism. Public schools reflect separation by social classes far more than racism. That a large majority of Negroes are in the lower class while whites make up the middle class has caused segregation. Other factors tending to increase segregation are white central-city parochial schools and the rezoning of school districts according to social classes. Discusses ways to counter the current trend and advocates integration as essential to preserve American democracy.   H. B. Powell

2311. Pfautz, Harold W. THE POWER STRUCTURE OF THE NEGRO SUB-COMMUNITY: A CASE STUDY AND A COMPARATIVE VIEW. *Phylon 1962 23(2): 156-166.* The manner in which a sub-community organizes itself will help determine its power to make demands on the dominant group. The power structure of the Negro community in Providence, Rhode Island, is contrasted with that of "Regional City" - a traditional Deep South urban situation - and "Pacific City." This latter is a relatively new and dynamic Northwest coast urban situation, lacking sub-community identity and organization. In Providence, a younger generation revolt caused some promising developments, in terms of Negro wants. Nevertheless, Negro status in the city keeps it closer to the traditional southern pattern, than to the west coast pattern. This is partly because (as appended tables indicate) the Providence community is not united as a power structure, partly because protest takes place within the status quo: a situation which makes for moderate actions.   L. Filler

2312. Piedmont, Eugene B. CHANGING RACIAL ATTITUDES AT A SOUTHERN UNIVERSITY: 1947-1964. *J. of Negro Educ. 1967 36(1): 32-41.* Reports and discusses results of surveys of student opinion toward Negroes at the University of Virginia conducted by a local human relations organization in 1947-48, 1957, and 1963-64. The first two surveys were limited to graduate and professional students while the third included undergraduates. In 1947-48 no Negroes had been admitted to the University, and there was little concern about integration. The second survey followed the 1954 Supreme Court decision and was conducted in the midst of Virginia's massive resistance. A few Negroes were enrolled in the University after 1951. The surveys indicate that an increasing proportion of students had favorable attitudes toward Negroes as students and as professors and that attitudes of graduate students were more favorable than those of undergraduates. Unfavorable feelings were more common than feelings that action should be taken to exclude Negroes. Student opinion was more favorable toward Negroes on campus than off campus, and student status was a better predictor of attitude than residence or region.   S. C. Pearson, Jr.

2313. Pilling, Patricia L. SEGREGATION: COTTAGE RENTAL IN MICHI-GAN. *Phylon 1964 25(2): 191-201.* Describes an attempt of two women, one Negro and one white, the latter accompanied by her three children, to find cottage accommodations for a week-long summer vacation in southwestern Michigan. Though Michigan in 1962 had an equal accommodations law, separate letters to 16 resorts produced four replies indicating only one vacancy (not for the date requested) for the Negro and ten replies indicating eight vacancies for the white. Accommodations were eventually secured near Jackson, Michigan, through inquiry among friends.   S. C. Pearson, Jr.

2314. Pinkney, Alphonso. PREJUDICE TOWARD MEXICAN AND NEGRO AMERICANS: A COMPARISON. *Phylon 1963 24(4): 353-359.* Basing his article on findings of the staff of Cornell Studies in Intergroup Relations in a 1952 study of a western city, the author declares that "the pattern of prejudice toward Negro and Mexican Americans in this community is essentially the same. The differences which exist are in the degree to which the respondents expressed prejudice toward these two minorities. In this respect the differences are often great...There is considerably less prejudice expressed toward Mexican than toward Negro Americans."   S. C. Pearson, Jr.

2315. Plastrik, Stanley. CONFRONTATION IN PITTSBURGH. *Dissent 1970 17(1): 25-31.* Focuses on the difficulties of the Black Construction Coalition (BCC) in Pittsburgh in integrating the construction unions there - one example of the larger problems facing construction unions nationally. One such problem is the reluctance of those unions to increase their recruitment and update their methods in the face of both the technological revolution now underway in the building industry and the critical mass-building needs of the country. Predicts that this resistance will increase government intervention, which can only hurt the union cause.   W. L. Hogeboom

2316. Powledge, Fred. SEGREGATION, NORTHERN STYLE. *Am. Educ. 1966 3(1): 1-5.* Discusses de facto school segregation. The practice "is really a problem of urban areas whether they be in the North or the South." De facto segregation is seen as the product of housing discrimination, in turn contributing to the Negro unemployment crisis as well as further housing discrimination. Six frequently employed techniques used to eliminate the practices are considered. None have been successful in the large urban centers. More progress has been made in a few suburban school districts throughout the country. Illus.
                                                                    W. R. Boedecker

2317. Proctor, Samuel. THE COLLEGE AND THE URBAN COMMUNITY: RACIAL INSULARITY AND NATIONAL PURPOSE. *Liberal Educ. 1969 55(1): 78-85.* In the 1950's it was hoped that integration of public schools would decrease prejudice. But such optimistic hopes have proven unfounded. The militant blacks have turned against the "system" because it has been out of their reach. Therefore, these young blacks must be trained for the management level where they would bring fresh insights into policy making.   C. G. Lauritsen

2318. Reddick, L. D. WHAT NOW DO WE LEARN OF RACE AND MI-
NORITY PEOPLES? *J. of Negro Educ. 1965 34(3): 367-376.* Suggests that
Federal agencies have generally avoided the issue of race on the domestic scene
though there is a present tendency for the government to assume more responsibility in this area. States are also dealing more affirmatively with intergroup
relations, and schools and educators have expressed growing concern for the
history of minorities and the scientific study of race. Television has contributed
to the dissemination of responsible information about race and minorities, and
creative writers and artists in the Negro community have encouraged a new pride
in "Negroness." S. C. Pearson, Jr.

2319. Reid, Inez Smith. THE CONFLICT OVER DECENTRALIZATION:
THE EDUCATIONAL SYSTEM OF NEW YORK CITY. *Pan-African J. 1969
2(1): 69-93.* Decentralization places much power in local school boards. Blacks,
Puerto Ricans, and their sympathizers use decentralization to attack the "normal
American political process" and de facto segregation in New York City schools.
Decentralization involves the struggle between power holders (Council of Supervisory Associations, Board of Examiners, United Federation of Teachers, and
other labor unions) and power seekers (Board of Education, Superintendent of
Schools, Mayor, and community groups). Illustrations of this power struggle
include: in the transfer of teachers, the triumphs of the United Federation of
Teachers over the Ocean-Hill Brownsville Demonstration Project; in the selection
of demonstration principals, victory by the Council of Supervisory Associations
over Ocean-Hill Brownsville, Superintendent of Schools, and Board of Education.
The mass media inflamed passions through a black writer and organization, the
United Federation of Teachers, and the Council of Supervisory Associations. This
undermined the cooperation of various pro-decentralization factions, resulting in
grave peril to the school system. Based on primary and secondary sources; 58
notes. E. E. Beauregard

2320. Reiss, Albert J., Jr. POLICE BRUTALITY - ANSWERS TO KEY QUES-
TIONS. *Trans-action 1968 5(8): 10-19.* A survey made during the summer of
1966 in Boston, Chicago, and Washington, D.C., revealed that police brutality
was highly related to racial and economic class status. Brutality means the use of
profane and abusive language, stopping and questioning people, threats to use
force, the actual use of physical force, and prodding with the intention of using
force. The observations were made by investigators who accompanied police and
recorded police procedures. Citizens and police did not necessarily agree that the
methods used could be defined as police brutality. The author offers several
examples of each type of behavior. Police officials are sometimes more concerned
about reports of brutality than they are about the acts of brutality. Surprisingly,
the rate of white citizens who experienced excessive force exceeded that of blacks
by nearly two-to-one. The author does not contend that police select their victims
by race, but they do tend to operate against those from the lower class. Police
tend to use force in the situations they control, such as in the station house.
Disobedience of police by the citizen is often viewed as defiant or deviant behavior. The author concludes by stating that official police reports do not offer much
real information on police behavior or police brutality. Illus.

A. Erlebacher

2321. Reuther, Walter P. CHALLENGE TO FREEDOM IN A CHANGING WORLD. *Colorado Q. 1963 12(3): 230-246.* In our struggle with Communism, we must demonstrate the superiority of our system by solving our great problems of unemployment and racial discrimination. We must be willing to devote more money to education. "The American dream means that we go about the practical job of utilizing our advanced technology and our knowledge of nuclear energy to build a new world and a free world where poverty, ignorance, and disease are overcome and where all people enjoy freedom." A. Zilversmit

2322. Rinder, Irwin D. MINORITY ORIENTATIONS: AN APPROACH TO INTERGROUP RELATIONS THEORY THROUGH SOCIAL PSYCHOLOGY. *Phylon 1965 26(1): 5-17.* Explores the utility of studying "the interdependence or feedback between societal and social psychological phenomena in intergroup relations," and develops a concept of group self-hatred as a conceptual tool in the analysis of intergroup phenomena. The ideal of segregated pluralism which has arisen among American Negroes was fostered by group self-hatred yielding before environmental pressures to the demand for assimilation or secession. S. C. Pearson, Jr.

2323. Roberts, Launey F., Jr. MINORITY SELF-IDENTIFICATION THROUGH TEXTS: A STUDY OF PUBLICATION PROGRESS. *J. of Human Relations 1968 16(3): 356-367.* Reports the findings of two separate studies conducted in 1960 and 1966 "of selected textbook publishers for the purpose of ascertaining if there has been a distinct degree of change in the editorial, artistic, and over-all publishing views and practices regarding the use of multiracial pictures in elementary school textbooks." In 1960 "not one of the eleven firms who answered the inquiry included, in their publications, pictures of Negroes or Puerto Ricans with whites even when it might have been germane to the printed text." In 1966 "that thirteen, or 50 percent, of the twenty-six firms polled were attempting to show and portray a true picture of life in America in their printed texts and in their illustrations was significant and positively a sign of change." Based on a questionnaire mailed to textbooks publishers. D. J. Abramoske

2324. Rogin, M. POLITICS, EMOTION AND THE WALLACE VOTE. *British J. of Sociol. 1969 20(1): 27-49.* Analyzes the sources of support for George Wallace's presidential candidature to 1968, using voting returns in Maryland, Wisconsin, and Indiana, and interviews with politicians, journalists, and union officials in Baltimore, Milwaukee, Gary, and East Chicago. A comparison with the Goldwater vote of 1964 is added. The author concludes in general that Wallace sentiment was diffused throughout the urban population, largely racially motivated and hostile to recent tax increases. But it is suggested that support for Wallace was also a revolt of the population against its political leadership (which had sought to keep issues like race out of mass politics) and therefore should "serve as a reminder both of racist emotion in America and of the consequent failure of a pragmatic politics of race." 40 notes. D. H. Murdoch

2325. Rogin, Michael. WALLACE AND THE MIDDLE CLASS: THE WHITE BACKLASH IN WISCONSIN. *Public Opinion Q. 1966 30(1): 98-108.*

Finds that much of the political expression of white prejudice is centered among "middle- and upper-class conservatives." The article uses comparative studies of votes for George Wallace and former Senator Joseph McCarthy.

S. L. Banks

2326. Rose, Harold M. AN APPRAISAL OF THE NEGRO EDUCATOR'S SITUATION IN THE ACADEMIC MARKETPLACE. *J. of Negro Educ. 1966 35(1): 18-26.* On the basis of data drawn from several sources the author estimates that there were about six thousand Negroes teaching in colleges and universities in the United States in 1964 and that slightly less than three-fourths were employed in the South in schools created specifically for Negroes. This represents a decrease from 82 percent in 1960 and a corresponding increase in the number of Negro educators employed in the open market. However, the employment opportunities for Negro educators remain extremely limited. The role of recruitment policies and graduate schools in determining this situation is discussed.

S. C. Pearson, Jr.

2327. Rose, Harold M. THE DEVELOPMENT OF AN URBAN SUBSYSTEM: THE CASE OF THE NEGRO GHETTO. *Ann. of the Assoc. of Am. Geographers 1970 60(1): 1-17.* "The Negro ghetto represents an expanding residential spatial configuration in all of the major metropolitan areas in the United States. The process of ghetto development is essentially related to the refusal of Whites to share residential space with Blacks on a permanent basis, and to the search behavior employed by Blacks in seeking housing accommodations. An attempt has been made to predict the changing scale of the ghetto configuration in Milwaukee, Wisconsin from 1960-1970. A simulation model was developed for this purpose. The model employed can be described as a strict segregation model since all Negro housing demand is satisfied within contiguous space, described here as ghetto space. It is apparent from the results that the model includes some inherent weaknesses, but only a few are related to its conceptual base. In general the simulated pattern of Negro residential occupance in Milwaukee is characterized by general overprediction in a low income area along the eastern side of the ghetto and by underprediction along the northern margin of the ghetto. The actual pattern of Black residential-movement in Milwaukee demonstrated that the heaviest entry occurred in an area of more desirable housing."

J

2328. Rosen, Bruce. THE USE OF POTENTIALLY DISCRIMINATORY QUESTIONS ON COLLEGE APPLICATIONS IN THE SOUTHERN UNITED STATES. *J. of Negro Educ. 1969 38(2): 120-124.* A study to determine to what extent schools in the 11 States of the "Old South" use potentially discriminatory questions about race or religion on their applications for admission. Of the schools sampled, 36 percent ask for race, 80 percent ask about religious preference, and 58 percent require a photograph on the application form. Public State universities are least likely to ask potentially discriminatory questions on their applications. Questions of religion exceed all other categories of questions. Table, 4 notes.

B. D. Johnson

2329. Rosenberg, B. and Howton, F. W. ETHNIC LIBERALISM AND EM-PLOYMENT DISCRIMINATION IN THE NORTH. *Am. J. of Econ. and Sociol. 1967 26(4): 387-398.* Concerned with de facto segregation in employment in the North, discussing the image of the Negro as an employee. The authors concluded that whites are preferentially hired and upgraded.

D. F. Rossi

2330. Rowan, Carl T. NEW FRONTIERS IN RACE RELATIONS. *Colorado Q. 1967 16(2): 127-140.* Discusses the current U.S. racial problem. The vested interests of the United States perpetuate racism and its attendant problems. While racial progress exists, so does a concurrent resurgence of hate groups. One of the factors is the lack of real black leaders. Some exploiters exist, but responsible Negroes are deprived of the respect necessary to leadership. Yet the Negro 10 percent of the population can make life miserable for the white 90 percent of America. Racism is central to much anti-American propaganda abroad.

B. A. Storey

2331. Rowan, Richard L. DISCRIMINATION AND APPRENTICE REGU-LATION IN THE BUILDING TRADES. *J. of Business 1967 40(4): 435-447.* Examines interrelationships among those parties directly involved and concerned with the implementation of State and Federal regulations pertaining to nondiscrimination in employment in Philadelphia. Negroes have had to rely on the traditionally closed apprenticeship training program to get into the building industry unions. Title 29 (Nondiscrimination in Apprenticeship) was implemented in 1963 to eliminate barriers to entry. However, since implementation is usually administered by the same personnel as the old programs, not much has been done to eliminate discrimination. In Philadelphia not one of the four major craft unions meet all the requirements and standards established under the law. Part of the problem is the task of bridging the gap between broad policy and local union decisionmaking. Within the Bureau of Apprenticeship Training the qualification exam is too subjective to assure nondiscrimination in selection. The Philadelphia Human Rights Commission is hindered by a rapid turnover in personnel and by a lack of communication with the unions and the bureau. Federal agencies should learn more about the implementation of the programs and should develop a more specific plan of action for carrying out the law. Based mainly on secondary sources; 24 notes.

C. A. Gallacci

2332. Rowland, Monroe and Hill, Patricia. RACE, ILLUSTRATIONS, AND INTEREST IN MATERIALS FOR READING AND CREATIVE WRIT-ING. *J. of Negro Educ. 1965 34(1): 84-87.* The authors studied 14 Caucasian and 17 Negro children in a first grade class and found that their interest, as measured by their voluntary selections, in materials for reading and creative writing was influenced by the racial content of the materials and the race of the children. Negro children, however, showed greater ambivalence than Caucasian in selections and commitments. Suggests the desirability of increasing the production of materials illustrated with a variety of racial types.

S. C. Pearson, Jr.

2333. Rubin, Lillian. THE RACIST LIBERALS - AN EPISODE IN A COUNTY JAIL. *Trans-action 1968 5(9): 39-44.* Describes and analyzes racial relations among 70 women arrested in Alameda County, California, during an antiwar demonstration. Only one of the 70 women was black, although a large percentage of the prison's regular inmates were. The white demonstrators were anxious to prove their lack of racism toward black inmates by seeming to condone even their most aggressive actions, and they made demands on themselves that they would not make on blacks. The white demonstrators largely shied away from any of the physical contact that prevailed among the black prisoners. Tension increased between the one black demonstrator and a white demonstrator over the issue of a fast. There was a tendency on the part of some of the whites to explain away any antisocial behavior of the blacks. Many of the whites did not understand the subtle racial overtones of having lower expectations of blacks. There was a tendency to treat the single black demonstrator as "our nigger." The author concludes that the behavior described by Jonathan Kozol in *Death at an Early Age* prevailed here - an unawareness of one's own deep connection with the racist structure and with the attitudes of society. Photo.   A. Erlebacher

2334. Rubington, Earl. RACE RELATIONS IN A PSYCHIATRIC HOSPI-TAL. *Human Organization 1969 28(2): 128-132.* To study interracial behavior in a situation of involuntary racial association, the behavior of patients in a ward of a small psychiatric receiving hospital in a border State was observed. It was hypothesized that because of the nature of the subjects that the white and Negro patients would eat together because the hospital required it, regardless of their personal feelings. It was also hypothesized that roommates would select table-mates who have the same social characteristics as the roommates. The author observed the seating patterns in the ward dining room for 40 days. For the observed meals, 46.8 percent of the table groupings were mixed. The table group-ings were compared to room assignment and it was found that patients who had roommates of the opposite race were more likely to eat with one of the opposite race, and that if the bedroom was large, the tendency to mix was greater. Hospital organization does shape patient behavior, and even greater mixing would be achieved if room assignment were designed to promote mixing rather than occur-ring at random. 3 tables, 5 notes.   E. S. Johnson

2335. Saunders, Marie Simmons. THE GHETTO: SOME PERCEPTIONS OF A BLACK SOCIAL WORKER. *Social Work 1969 14(4): 84-88.* The black man's survival in the ghetto has depended on his understanding of and adaptation to a hostile white society. How can this understanding and adaptation become a two-way street, with the ultimate goal of eliminating hostility and the ghetto itself? An answer to this question is suggested along with the characteristics of the black ghetto and how it developed. 6 notes.   W. L. Willigan

2336. Schaffer, Ruth C. and Schaffer, Albert. SOCIALIZATION AND THE DEVELOPMENT OF ATTITUDES TOWARD NEGROES IN ALABAMA. *Phylon 1966 27(3): 274-285.* A study designed to discover some of the attributes of southern whites willing or unwilling to grant citizenship status to Negroes and to accept the premise of equality was conducted among 47 students at the University of Alabama. On the basis of ideas respecting rights and social distance, students were described as equalitarian (16), semiequalitarian (22), or antiequalitarian (9). The most important factor in determining attitudes was found to be the method and content of socialization employed by the parents. Antiequalitarian students learned their attitudes from parents while equalitarian and semiequalitarian students came usually from nondirective homes in which experience played a larger role. Such students generally were more equalitarian than their parents. Social stratification was also a factor as was sex with males and students from upper- or middle-class homes more equalitarian than others. Academic class also contributed to attitudes as did field of study. Upper-class students and arts and science students were least equalitarian. Neither the characteristics of home community nor personal interaction with Negroes was shown to be of consequence. 6 notes. S. C. Pearson, Jr.

2337. Schuler, Edgar A. and Green, Robert L. A SOUTHERN EDUCATOR AND SCHOOL INTEGRATION: AN INTERVIEW. *Phylon 1967 28(1): 28-40.* C. G. Gordon Moss, dean of Longwood College in Farmville, Virginia, and a native of that State, was interviewed in 1963 on the subject of the integration controversy in Prince Edward County. Moss traced the history of the school controversy and showed how the attitude of the white community toward the Negroes had changed from one of benevolent paternalism almost to hatred. Moss himself has been subjected to social and economic pressures from the white community because he supports the idea that a public school system must be maintained even if it must be integrated. He analyzes the effect that closing the schools has had on the county and upon relations between the races within the county. D. N. Brown

2338. Schurmann, Franz. CRISIS 1968. *Minority of One 1968 10(7/8): 9-13.* Discusses the liberal fascination with power. The liberals, since the 1930's, have worked through the machinery of the Democratic Party. The Democratic masses have supported the liberals in their program to maximize the powers of the Federal Government. But in 1968 the liberal dream went awry, both on the domestic and international fronts. The liberals face two challenges: the race war in American cities and the Vietnam War. Regarding the former, the liberals propose to contain social discontent through pragmatic legislation and funding. Abroad, the liberals have failed to obtain control by demanding total victory in Vietnam. The liberation movements in America's cities and in Vietnam have shattered the dream of the liberals. The basic shortcoming of the liberals is that they have no confidence in society or in the ability of men or nations to decide their own fate. P. W. Kennedy

2339. Seals, Alvin M. and Kolaja, Jiri. A STUDY OF NEGRO VOLUNTARY ORGANIZATIONS IN LEXINGTON, KENTUCKY. *Phylon 1964 25(1): 27-32.* The authors made a study of instrumental (goal-directed) and expressive (self-gratifying) voluntary organizations in the Negro community in Lexington, Kentucky, from 1958 to 1960. Noting the structural characteristics of these organizations which were significantly different from corresponding characteristics of white organizations the authors suggest that Lexington Negroes "are no longer segregated to the extent that they can develop their own community-wide integrative organizations" but that "they are not integrated to the extent that they feel that the white-dominated community organizations are also their organizations."

S. C. Pearson, Jr.

2340. Segal, Bernard E. RACIAL PERSPECTIVES AND ATTITUDES AMONG NEGRO AND WHITE DELINQUENT BOYS: AN EMPIRICAL EXAMINATION. *Phylon 1966 27(1): 27-39.* Reports findings of a study of Negro and white boys between the ages of 13 and 15 years at an eastern border-State boys training school. Negro boys were found to have a higher racial awareness than white boys. A higher proportion of Negro boys were substantive as opposed to technical delinquents. Substantive delinquents showed a higher racial awareness score, and white substantive delinquents had the highest prejudice scores. 22 notes.

S. C. Pearson, Jr.

2341. Selkow, Samuel. A VIEW FROM AFRICA OF AMERICAN RACE RELATIONS. *J. of Negro Educ. 1964 33(2): 201-202.* Problems encountered by Americans working in Africa are intensified by the African's concern about race relations in the United States.

S. C. Pearson, Jr.

2342. Sexton, Patricia Cayo. CITY SCHOOLS. *Ann. of the Am. Acad. of Pol. and Social Sci. 1964 352: 95-106.* "Though other issues exist, the basic issues and problems in city schools arise from a conflict of interests between haves and have-nots. Race appears as a subdimension of the larger problem. The major contours of this engagement are seen at the federal level where the power exists to make governing decisions about school financing and in state government where conservative and usually anticity interests dominate. It is seen in a dimmer but far more explosive form in the city itself where have-nots, mainly Negroes, are pressing demands for school equity. Class lines are somewhat redrawn within liberal city governments and school systems. Negro demands give the illusion that the issue is strictly racial although, in fact, the educational and political interests of other have-not and liberal leadership groups run parallel and converge more often than they diverge."

J

2343. Shannon, Barbara E. IMPLICATIONS OF WHITE RACISM FOR SOCIAL WORK PRACTICES. *Social Casework 1970 51(5): 270-276.* Offers examples of effects of white racism on social work practice. Negative stereotyping of Negroes is the most common indication of racism. The answer to the problem does not rest in black capitalism. If all Negroes had doctorates, they still could not live where they wanted; if all Negroes owned successful businesses, the national economy would still be dominated by a handful of industrialists who manipulate whites as well as Negroes. Suggests ways to deal with white racism, especially in social work practice. 13 notes.

M. A. Kaufman

2344. Shostak, Arthur. APPEALS FROM DISCRIMINATION IN FEDERAL EMPLOYMENT: A CASE STUDY. *Social Forces 1963 42(2): 174-178.* "Increased use by Federal employees of an appeals procedure in matters of suspected racial discrimination has given rise to controversy and concern. The writer, in the summer of 1962, examined the appeals records in 27 cases filed in the last 10 years in a Northeastern Federal manufacturing and repair center of 10,000 employees. Special attention was paid to the fact that 25 of 27 appellants were Negroes, most appeals involved failure to secure promotions, and only one appeal was decided in the appellants' favor. Analysis suggested that despite the official record of losses the procedure served the appellants in four ways: It provided a 'day in court.' It was a source of answers. It was a locus of hope. And it was an instrument of pressure. Similarly, the center found several uses for the procedure: It was a 'safety valve.' It was a spotlight on sources of friction. It was a device for correcting mis-impressions. And it was an effective check on the conduct of supervisory personnel. Overall, however, the writer concludes that the procedure is a limited tool with an essentially negative character. It must be supplemented by more positive measures if it is not to undo its own slim contribution to industrial race relations." J

2345. Simmons, Donald C. ANTI-ITALIAN-AMERICAN RIDDLES IN NEW ENGLAND. *J. of Am. Folklore 1966 79(313): 475-478.* Anecdotal tales denigrating Italians are widespread in New England; several examples are given. Only since about 1961 has the telling of anti-Italian riddles sprung up. The recentness of these riddles is probably due to the rise in status of the third and fourth generation Italian-American who is beginning to appear in "occupations formerly reserved for the traditional Yankee and, later, for the Irish-American." Such anecdotes are reported for the Irish in New York City by 1866 when they began to enter the profession of the law. The apparent infrequency of protest stories in the case of the Italian-American may be explained by the absence of a long history of oppressive denigratory tales; the "Italian-Americans have not been able, as the Jews and Negroes have, to fall back on their own folklore and defend themselves by telling tales which denigate the majority group." Gives 26 riddles, 4 notes. E. P. Stickney

2346. Singletary, Otis. HIGHER EDUCATION IN THE SOUTH: A CON-TEMPORARY VIEW. *South Atlantic Q. 1969 68(1): 86-95.* Despite impressive gains, the South still lags in higher education and is falling further behind. There is still no "truly *national* university in the South today." There are a number of hopeful signs, but many problems. It is too simplistic to blame southern lags in education on relative poverty. Other important considerations are racial preju-dice, the influences of southern religion on higher education, and political inter-ference. 12 notes. J. M. Bumsted

2347. Smith, Bob. NOTES TOWARD A NEW MODERACY. *Virginia Q. R. 1965 41(2): 207-216.* The author of a book on the Prince Edward County, Virginia, school closings argues for a new moderacy in racial affairs. An "unnatu-ral emphasis on color has led to many errors which are gradually being recog-nized, among them the idea that school integration alone, in time, will solve the Negro's educational problems." Moderacy must seek wider participation for the Negro in American society "but in such a way as to reduce the gulf of color obsession." We must achieve a universalization of the Prince Edward lesson:

"Uplift these people, white and black, because that is the way we do things in America and because their color does not keep them apart as much as their common plight unites them." E. P. Stickney

2348. Smith, Bob. THE CASE AGAINST BLACKTHINK. *Virginia Q. R. 1968 44(1): 43-50.* Insists that Americans have legally largely abolished racial segregation and are now in great danger of overemphasizing race. He pleads that, rather than thinking in racial terms ("blackthink"), Americans now turn to solving the great urban problems of air pollution, traffic, noise, squalor, and lack of privacy while improving the education and potential of all the poor. He insists that class, as much as race, excludes the Negro in American society and that "blackthink" is both dangerous and cruel for it adds to the hyperconsciousness of race which no longer should be the central concern. O. H. Zabel

2349. Smith, Paul M., Jr. and Pindle, Viola. THE CULTURALLY DISAD-VANTAGED PUPIL ON THE CUMULATIVE RECORD. *J. of Negro Educ. 1969 38(1): 78-81.* A study of elementary school pupils in the Piedmont section of North Carolina. The study showed that teachers tend to write more negative reports on the cumulative records of disadvantaged pupils, despite the achievement of these pupils on tests and despite other measures of intelligence shown. The authors suggest that such subjective reports should be on a temporary form and not on the permanent record of the student. They also suggest the use of a standardized checklist for such remarks. 2 tables, note. B. D. Johnson

2350. Smythe, Hugh H. and Murray, Walter I. HUMAN RELATIONS PER-SPECTIVE ON INTEGRATION IN THE U.S.A. *J. of Human Relations 1965 13(2): 247-265.* Surveys the progress made toward desegregation in the South. Efforts toward integration in the public schools have been "most unsatisfactory." Less than two percent of the Negro students are in integrated schools. Effort toward the integration of Negro teachers has been extremely limited. A State-by-State summary of this in the southern and border States is included. As for the desegregation of other public facilities, the picture is equally discouraging. The white community might think that compliance is being achieved, but there is much resistance, evasion, and delay. As a result, tension, resentment, and frustration intensifies within the Negro community. Colored people are learning "that never can they derive the full bounty of their American birthright through the white man's good will." D. J. Abramoske

2351. Stackhouse, Max L. REPARATIONS: A CALL TO REPENTANCE? *Lutheran Q. 1969 21(4): 358-380.* Analyzes the Black Manifesto, which demanded reparations as a sign of repentance from predominantly white churches. "We are...in the midst of a sustained cultural and religious shift which is shaking the foundations....A new formation now is aborning in the travail of institutional repentance by the bearers of the West's moral and spiritual traditions." 11 notes. D. H. Swift

2352. Stafford, Walter W. and Ladner, Joyce. COMPREHENSIVE PLAN-
NING AND RACISM. *J. of the Am. Inst. of Planners 1969 35(2): 68-74.* "The
largely unexplored linkages between comprehensive planning and racism are
examined in the light of the two major types of racism - *individual* and *institutional.* Examples are drawn from Model Cities programs and comprehensive
plans for Chicago, Boston, and Washington to illustrate the ineffectiveness of
most standard planning techniques in the face of institutional racism. Advocacy
planning is seen as a useful approach, especially in terms of political power and
accountability."   J

2353. Stein, Annie. STRATEGIES FOR FAILURE. *Harvard Educ. R. 1971
41(2): 158-204.* From 1954 to 1966 the strategy for maintaining a segregated, dual
school system in New York City was containment of the integration drive
through school zoning and transfer procedures, mechanisms for site selection and
construction, empty rhetoric, and blaming insufficient funds or uncooperative
parents. When the battle for community control began (1967) in response to the
ineffectiveness of the school board's policies, the strategy changed (with the help
of the United Federation of Teachers) to an espousal of integration and to a
rejection of black separatism. This strategy assured that community boards would
come under white, middle-class leadership. On another level, the strategy took
the form of feeding teachers false expectations based on a mystique of reading and
a myth of cultural deprivation to assure their failure in their attempts to teach
ghetto children. Tracking, a watered-down curriculum for the ghetto child, dropout and pushout policies, a teacher professionalism amounting to rejection of
teacher accountability, and compensatory and pacification programs all constitute yet another strategy that assures student failure. The remedy must come from
the victims themselves, the students and their parents, with some help given by
honest educators and social scientists. 51 notes.   J. Herbst

2354. Stevenson, Elizabeth. A PERSONAL HISTORY OF CHANGE IN AT-
LANTA. *Virginia Q. R. 1965 41(4): 580-595.* Suggests that Atlanta, whose recent
physical changes have been much like those of other cities, has remarkable traits
of imagination, vigor, and suppleness in dealing with complex human relations.
Atlanta's success, since 1960, in dealing with desegregation without violence can
be traced to the long-time willingness of Atlanta citizens to talk and argue frankly
about difficult problems which has accustomed people "to the fact that not
everyone took everything the same way." It helped deflate dangers and put
problems into perspective. Thus, "Atlanta has been in these years of change an
example of creativity."   O. H. Zabel

2355. Sudman, Seymour, Bradburn, Norman M. , and Gockel, Galen. THE
EXTENT AND CHARACTERISTICS OF RACIALLY INTEGRATED
HOUSING IN THE UNITED STATES. *J. of Business 1969 42(1): 50-92.*
Presents the results of a study which contradict the "widespread belief...that
stable racially integrated neighborhoods are a rare phenomenon." Provides "data
on the extent and characteristics of racially integrated housing in the United
States." The data are based on a study by the National Opinion Research Center
in 1966-67 designed to detail the characteristics of integrated as compared with

segregated neighborhoods and to study the factors influencing a family's decision to move into or to remain in a racially mixed area. Research strategy involved sampling integrated neighborhoods in the Nation, acquiring personal interviews to obtain neighborhood characteristics, and, finally, sampling households within neighborhoods and conducting further personal interviews. The results were reported in relation to types of integrated neighborhoods, estimates of housing integration for the United States, regional variation in integration, city size, the number of Negro households in integrated neighborhoods, level of integration, summary of estimates of extent of integration, the characteristics of housing and of the housing market in integrated neighborhoods, owners and renters, housing values, age of housing and of neighborhood, and single or multiple builders in neighborhood. Major "increases in integration may be achieved by the opening of segregated rental units to Negroes." This "lowers the pressures on substantially integrated neighborhoods by Negroes and makes it easier for them to remain stable." 17 tables, biblio., appendix.   C. A. Gallacci

2356. Sugg, Redding S., Jr. JOHN'S YOKNAPATAWPHA. *South Atlantic Q. 1969 68(3): 343-362.* John Wesley Faulkner III, the younger brother who also wrote, deserves a higher repute as a local colorist and humorist of north Mississippi hill-country life than he has received. Critical attention has been hampered by 1) his brother William's reputation, 2) the cheap and garish paperback form in which much of John's work has been published, and 3) the tendency to dismiss him as a stock reactionary, white segregationist Mississippian. But John Faulkner, whose high point was reached in *Cabin Road* (1951), "found his subject, developed the style appropriate to it, and thoroughly exploited both." He has developed dialects with a readable orthography and an authentic syntax. As a practitioner of Southwest humor John should rank high. 5 notes.

J. M. Bumsted

2357. Taylor, James S. JOHN M. PATTERSON AND THE 1958 ALABAMA GUBERNATORIAL RACE. *Alabama R. 1970 23(3): 226-234.* Patterson was a surprise winner of the Alabama governorship in 1958, defeating Circuit Judge George C. Wallace. Six reasons are given for his election victory: 1) the death of his father, Albert Patterson; 2) the priority of segregation as a campaign issue; 3) the alleged graft and corruption in the Folsom administration; 4) the failure of primary opponents to interpret accurately the mood of the electorate; 5) Patterson's use of the broadcast media; and 6) bloc voting by Alabama's senior citizens. 24 notes.

D. F. Henderson

2358. Teitel, B. and Demos, George D. EMOTIONAL ASPECTS OF DISCRIMINATION. *Indian J. of Social Res. [India] 1964 5(1): 1-6.* There is a gulf between the espoused ideals of democracy and the presence of racial prejudice and discrimination. This segregation stems from mutual feelings of inferiority. The Caucasian utilizes racial prejudice as a convenient defense mechanism which enables him to maintain a feeling of self-esteem and security and to repress any feelings of inferiority. For the Negro who has emotionally developed under the myth of inferiority, all motivation lies dormant. Solving the problems caused by emotions in race relations goes far in bridging the gap between democratic ideals and practice. Note.

G. R. Hess

2359. Thomas, Charles Walker. THE CHURCH CATCHES UP: PRES-BYTERIANS, U.S.A. ELECT ELDER G. HAWKINS. *Negro Hist. Bull. 1964 28(1): 19-20.* Reviews recent developments in American churches which reflect the revolution in race relations, with special emphasis on the significance of the choice of a Negro as moderator of the United Presbyterian Church in 1964.

L. Gara

2360. Thorburn, Neil. "STRANGE FRUIT" AND SOUTHERN TRADI-TION. *Midwest Q. 1971 12(2): 157-171.* Discusses Lillian Smith's 1944 novel *Strange Fruit* (New York: New American Library, 1954) and her 1949 nonfiction *Killers of the Dream* (New York: Doubleday and Co., 1963). Points out Smith's importance as a pioneer analyst of racism. This gracious and aristocratic southern lady posed basic questions for southern whites and shed light on the pervasiveness of southern racial tradition. Smith (1897-1966) questioned whether segregation was an outmoded custom that could be gradually eliminated. She reasoned that change must begin in the hearts of men and that white southerners must first admit the existence of their racial feelings. In her books she pointed out the need for the more sophisticated of them to drop their complacent tendency to blame everything anti-Negro on the poor whites, and to begin to improve race relations themselves. Biblio.

G. H. G. Jones

2361. Tillman, James A., Jr. THE CASE AGAINST DE FACTO SEGRE-GATED EDUCATION IN THE NORTH AND WEST: A CONTEMPO-RARY CASE STUDY. *J. of Negro Educ. 1964 33(4): 371-381.* This paper was prepared in 1962 for the Michigan University School Facilities Survey Team which was then surveying the future building needs of the Minneapolis public school system. The paper was designed "to sensitize the Survey Team to the need for including 'racially balanced schools' as one of the criteria for determining future building needs of the Minneapolis School System." The author documents the existence of de facto patterns of housing segregation and argues for school board programs to overcome de facto school segregation which results from housing segregation. He considers such possible programs as split school building use by grades, permissive bussing to the schools, open enrollments, and redistrict-ing and/or school relocation.

S. C. Pearson, Jr.

2362. Trachtenberg, Stephen J. WE MUST NOT DRAG ON THE CHAIN. *Catholic Educ. R. 1968 66(6): 361-375.* American schools have failed in accul-turating black Americans. Legal and practical attacks on de jure and de facto segregation have been increasing in scope and intensity, yet educational segrega-tion still affects the lives of Negroes. Many studies have pointed out the centrality of education to the achievement of real equality. Educators thus have a mandate to seek realistic solutions now.

J. M. McCarthy

2363. Tripp, Wendell. SOME LETTERS OF FESTUS MKUNI. *New York Hist.* *1967 48(1): 54-90.* A native of Zambia, Festus Mkuni attended Hobart College, Geneva, New York, from 1961 to 1964. His letters to family and friends relate his experiences in the United States, life on the campus, and his personal reaction to various aspects of American institutions and customs, especially race relations. 17 notes.   G. Kurland

2364. Troy, Leo. THE GROWTH OF UNION MEMBERSHIP IN THE SOUTH, 1939-1953. *Southern Econ. J. 1958 24(4): 407-420.* Organized labor has long regarded the South as a major source of potential members. Membership figures indicate that the relative growth of unions in the South from 1939 to 1953 was greater than for the country, but measured by the increase in the percentage of nonfarm employees organized, the South lagged behind the national average. Hypothetical figures of southern membership, based on the composition of industrial employment, show that the cause of low organization does not lie in the lack of organizable workers. Rather it is explained by historical and institutional factors. Some of these appear to be State and local law, employed opposition, an abundant labor supply, and racial problems. Based on Leo Troy's *Distribution of Union Membership Among the States, 1939-1953* (New York: National Bureau of Economic Research, Occasional Paper 56, 1957), articles, monographs, government documents, and newspapers.   A

2365. Tyack, David B. GROWING UP BLACK: PERSPECTIVES ON THE HISTORY OF EDUCATION IN NORTHERN GHETTOS. *Hist. of Educ. Q. 1969 9(3): 287-297.* Suggests that the historian ask why scholars and educators have defined Negro education chiefly as a southern problem, what effects bureaucratization and centralization of city schools had on black children, how schools respond to the low job ceiling for blacks, who favored intentionally segregated schools, and what was the effect of racism in textbooks. 76-item biblio.
                                                                                    J. Herbst

2366. Tyler, Lawrence L. THE PROTESTANT ETHIC AMONG THE BLACK MUSLIMS. *Phylon 1966 27(1): 5-14.* Suggests that the Max Weber thesis of the interdependence of ethical values and socioeconomic developments has a utility for the evaluation of contemporary society. After outlining and tracing the traditional applications of the Weber thesis, the author proposes that the Black Muslim ethic has effects, for its adherents, similar to the effects of the Protestant ethic upon its faithful. Based on published sources; 31 notes.
                                                                              S. C. Pearson, Jr.

2367. Vandiver, Frank E. "HARPER'S" INTERPRETS "THE SOUTH TODAY." *J. of Southern Hist. 1965 31(3): 318-323.* Reviews a supplement to the April 1965 issue of *Harper's Magazine* by 14 writers on "The South Today...100 Years After Appomattox." All the articles are more or less on the racial question, with changes and rights and dignities as the main threads of thought. The South is once again subjected to a poking, prodding, and pilloring but guilt should not blind one to a kind of victory that is coming. Articles mentioned are by C. Vann Woodward, historian; Jonathan Daniels, publisher; William Styron, novelist; D.

W. Brogan, British observer; James Kilpatrick, editor; Robert Cole, psychiatrist; Walker Percy, Mississippian; Louis Rubin, literary critic; and Arna Bontemps and Louis Lomax, Alabama and Georgia Negroes.　　　S. E. Humphreys

2368. Vanfossen, Beth E. VARIABLES RELATED TO RESISTANCE TO DESEGREGATION IN THE SOUTH. *Social Forces 1968 47(1): 39-44.* "Several theories of the causes of discrimination and resistance to interracial change are examined. The proportion of nonwhites in the state and the social class composition of nonwhites are found to be highly related to desegregation in southern states. The income of whites and indices of urbanization and industrialization show only a moderate relationship to desegregation, and education and occupational status of whites are slightly inversely related to desegregation."
J

2369. Vines, Kenneth N. FEDERAL DISTRICT JUDGES AND RACE RELATIONS CASES IN THE SOUTH. *J. of Pol. 1964 26(2): 337-357.* Examines all race relations cases decided in the Federal district courts of 11 States of the traditional South from May 1954 to October 1962 and correlates these decisions with the background and experience of the judges. The great majority of district judges are strongly tied to their districts by birth, residence, training, and experience. For example, pro-Negro decisions "are negatively co-related to the proportion of Negroes in the districts' population."　　　B. E. Swanson

2370. Vontress, Clemmont E. THE NEGRO AGAINST HIMSELF. *J. of Negro Educ. 1963 32(3): 237-242.* Observes that "several forces are operative in the American society to cause the Negro to devaluate himself and all things Negroid." The author discusses such factors as the failure of the white American to treat the Negro as a person and white reactions of horror, disgust, avoidance, indifference, or toleration in the presence of the Negro. Such factors lead the Negro to receive an unpleasant image of himself and with resultant self-destructive behavior.　　　S. C. Pearson, Jr.

2371. Wachman, Marvin. THE UNIVERSITY: PUTTING PRINCIPLES INTO PRACTICE. *J. of Human Relations 1968 16(1): 17-23.* A commencement address delivered at Central State University, Wilberforce, Ohio, 17 April 1966. The current pattern of race relations in the United States is discussed optimistically. Although Americans, both white and black, have not adequately lived up to their principles, "a great deal of progress has been made on many fronts." There has, for example, been an impressive increase in the number of employers seeking graduates of predominantly Negro colleges.　　　D. J. Abramoske

2372. Warshauer, Mary Ellen. GLEN COVE, NEW YORK: THE EVOLUTION OF A SCHOOL DESEGREGATION PLAN. *Urban R. 1968 2(4): 25-28.* In 1965 Glen Cove, a city of 25 thousand people on Long Island, decided to end segregation by eliminating its one predominately black elementary school and transferring those students to white elementary schools. To avoid having the decision forced upon them by State officials, the community assumed the initiative without causing a deep split between the black and white community. The relatively amicable way in which the community solved the problem should serve as a model for other communities.   H. B. Powell

2373. Watters, Pat. SOCIETY OF THE ABSURD: A LOOK AT THE NEW SOUTH. *Dissent 1970 17(1): 32-37.* Suggests that some aspects of the present Southern racial situation are absurd in the existential sense. Sees an element of ironic humor that is understood only by those blacks and whites who are part of the situation. Points out the relative lack of violent rioting by southern blacks as compared to those in the North and hopes that something constructive and purposeful will issue from the present confrontation.   W. L. Hogeboom

2374. Weatherby, W. J. LOOKING ON THE BLACK SIDE. *Twentieth Cent. [Great Britain] 1964 173(1022): 102-107.* The experiences of a journalist of the Manchester *Guardian* in Atlanta, Georgia. Despite Atlanta's recognition as a showcase for good race relations in the South, the author's description of the personal relationships between the races points out the serious inadequacies of "gradual integration" and of the integration achieved thus far.
                                                            L. Knafla

2375. Webster, Staten W. and Kroger, Marie N. A COMPARATIVE STUDY OF SELECTED PERCEPTIONS AND FEELINGS OF NEGRO ADOLESCENTS WITH AND WITHOUT WHITE FRIENDS IN INTEGRATED URBAN HIGH SCHOOLS. *J. of Negro Educ. 1966 35(1): 55-61.* Reports the findings of a study of 312 Negro adolescents in the San Francisco Bay Area school district. Subjects with white friends had more favorable self-images or concepts and expressed higher levels of aspiration for themselves. There was no significant difference between the two groups as to their levels of esteem for Negroes as a group. Testing procedure and measures are indicated, and the significance of the findings is discussed.   S. C. Pearson, Jr.

2376. Weimar, David R. BLACK REALITIES AND WHITE: THE CITY AND THE IMAGINATION GAP. *Southwest R. 1969 54(2): 105-119.* From his own experiences and involvement in a race riot and his studies of Negro literature, the author ponders the implications of black and white urban attitudes, observations, and conceptions of reality that frequently differ or are in conflict. Imagination is a principal ingredient of this dichotomy. Although most liberals still hope for "an eventual meeting of black and white minds on the bedrock of truth," the differences in imagination are of crucial importance. Black and white minds should stand apart, each preserving its own identity. Interaction is desirable, but melting into "a single, grayish imagination" is to be avoided.
                                                            D. L. Smith

2377. Welch, Finis. LABOR-MARKET DISCRIMINATION: AN INTERPRETATION OF INCOME DIFFERENCES IN THE RURAL SOUTH. *J. of Pol. Econ. 1967 75(3): 225-240.* An attempt to determine the economic effects of discrimination, concentrating on education as a distinct factor of production complementary to physical (unskilled) labor and capital. The most important conclusion "is that the market evidently discriminates much more heavily against a Negro's education than against his unskilled labor." Thus, relative to whites with similar schooling, Negro income declines as school completion increases.

W. Marina

2378. West, Earle H. and Daniel, Walter G. PROGRAMS IN THE SOUTH. *J. of Negro Educ. 1965 34(3): 310-318.* Surveys development of programs for the equalization of educational opportunity in the Southern States. Though progress in desegregation and in provision of compensatory education has been made, the goal of "complete integration at all educational levels on a system-wide basis" must be reached soon if equal educational opportunity is to be provided.

S. C. Pearson, Jr.

2379. Wilder, Emilia. AMERICA AS SEEN BY POLISH EXCHANGE STU-DENTS. *Public Opinion Q. 1964 28(2): 243-256.* In 1962 Polish publishers put out eight volumes on America written by "highly qualified observers": exchange scholars of which there had been over 1,500 in the preceding five years. These books were reviewed by a leading Polish party sociologist, Jerzy J. Wiatr, himself an exchangee. What influence they will have on the Poles at large is still conjec-tural, but they help the Communist rulers of Poland form new generalizations about capitalism with the result that they may act on the basis of expert knowl-edge. The books tend to show that the present Polish image does not reflect the real America but that false concepts are being removed as a result of contacts. To these observers "the intensity of cultural activities at the American universities is startling," counteracting the trends toward uniformity in American life. De-spite the Negro question there are areas of true democratization, one of which is the field of culture. 5 notes.

E. P. Stickney

2380. Wilhelm, Sidney M. RED MAN, BLACK MAN AND WHITE AMER-ICA: THE CONSTITUTIONAL APPROACH TO GENOCIDE. *Catalyst 1969 (4): 1-62.* "Racism is a basic component of American society, rising from the past, perpetuated in the present and assured for the future. The pattern of racism with its complementary myths now engulfs the Negro just as it foreclosed upon the Indians of yesterday. The white majority repudiates the black majority for the very qualities for which it must accept blame: poverty, ignorance, family disrup-tion, filth, crime, disease, substandard housing. The white strategy reflects the nation's earlier history when the ingenious plan evolved of first maddening the Indians into war and falling upon them with exterminating punishment." Photo.

P. A. Proett

2381. Williams, Frank. AMERICAN DOUBLE STANDARDS AND RACIAL BIGOTRY. *Pan-African J. 1969 2(4): 368-374.* American foreign and domestic affairs are inextricably interwoven because of racial considerations. America has a "bi-partisan foreign policy": one favoring largely white countries, the other negative toward predominantly nonwhite countries. This results from America acting as a white Anglo-Saxon Christian nation. Such white racism is evidenced by the words and deeds of Woodrow Wilson and is reinforced by present scholars who neglect Africa particularly and the problems of race generally in international affairs. Blacks must enter fully into the mainstream of American life so as to advance the United States domestically and externally; otherwise, the now advancing racism will isolate America. Based on primary and secondary sources.·

E. E. Beauregard

2382. Wirtz, Willard. COMMUNITY OR CHAOS. *Colorado Q. 1968 17(2): 117-127.* Two groups are pressing for increased participation - the disadvantaged and the universities. Four key factors must take place in this participation: people must work in local groups for racial equality, they must participate rather than merely receive if pride and self-respect are to be built up, there must be a national concept of "service" in such groups as VISTA (Volunteers in Service to America), and America must believe that man can shape the future and that a man cannot blame others for the faults of American society. Americans must take the responsibility and do something.

B. A. Storey

2383. Wood, James R. and Zald, Mayer N. ASPECTS OF RACIAL INTEGRATION IN THE METHODIST CHURCH: SOURCES OF RESISTANCE TO ORGANIZATIONAL POLICY. *Social Forces 1966 45(2): 255-265.* "Ideologies and social perspectives of the larger society penetrate large-scale organizations as well as affecting community life and politics. Such penetration confronts organizational policy makers with critical decisions. Evidence is presented indicating that attempts by The Methodist Church (at the national level) to initiate policies leading to racial integration of the church have led (in the southern subgroups) to unanticipated consequences counter to this policy. For instance, some churches have decreased or eliminated their race relations giving. Leadership at the local church and conference level has accommodated to the forces resisting such policies. The *extent* of resistance to policy is correlated with the percent of nonwhites in a district. The study indicates the difficulty of introducing policies with low consensus in a voluntary organization in which the leaders (both national and local) have a low balance of sanctions relative to the membership."

J

2384. Woodward, C. Vann. SOUTHERN MYTHOLOGY. *Commentary 1965 39(5): 60-63.* Primarily a review of Howard Zinn, *The Southern Mystique* (New York: Knopf, 1964) which claims that what most Americans, northern and southern, see as the basic and ineradicable difference of the South from the American norm is not so much a difference in kind as one of degree. The distinctive evils of the South, such as racism, fundamentalism, provincialism, and bigotry, are really universal American characteristics, brought to quintessence in the South. The prevalence of the myth that southern culture is something different, decadent, and ugly (and fascinating) is a predictable psychological response to seeing that which is worst in ourselves made obvious by exaggeration. The author agrees, pointing out, however, that southerners, both black and white, have a distinctive historical past, and no solutions to the problems of the South will be able to ignore that past.

A. K. Main

2385. Woodward, C. Vann. THE NORTH AND THE SOUTH OF IT. *Am. Scholar 1966 35(4): 647-658.* While living in borderstate Maryland, the author had come to view northern and southern differences over race as diminishing, the South at a greater pace than the North. But a move to Yale University in 1962, in the midst of struggles in the South over integration, led him to reassess. The polarity of region and race is one of many in America, but it is heightened by the fact that other dichotomies gradually becoming homogenized. Only Negroes and southerners remain unassimilated - the former by color, the latter by choice. The combination has meant that Negroes remain unwanted and unemployed. Indices of family income and segregation show a widening between black and white. Hope rests, perhaps, in the fact that Negroes who have recently moved cityward and northward will take with them the traits of courage and endurance which allowed them to survive in the South. T. R. Cripps

2386. Wright, Charles H. THE NEGRO PHYSICIAN IN DETROIT. *Negro Hist. Bull. 1964 27(5): 109-110.* Discusses the number and specialities of the Negro physicians in Detroit, where in recent years discrimination in medical practice has been narrowed down to certain private hospitals which refuse to make their facilities available to colored physicians. L. Gara

2387. Wright, N., Jr. ECONOMICS OF RACE. *Am. J. of Econ. and Sociol. 1967 26(1): 1-12.* An approach to American race relations from an economic point of view. Placing our own resources on the side of progress may hold the key to improved race relations. Three tables show comparisons of earning power for white and nonwhite heads of households for 1947-64. 5 notes. D. F. Rossi

2388. Yankauer, Marian P. and Sunderhauf, Milo B. HOUSING: EQUAL OPPORTUNITY TO CHOOSE WHERE ONE SHALL LIVE. *J. of Negro Educ. 1963 32(4): 402-414.*

2389. Young, I. JUIFS ET NOIRS A NEW YORK [The Jews and blacks in New York]. *Esprit [France] 1969 36(3): 510-516.* Views Negro-Jewish hostility in New York as seen in the *Jewish Press.* G. F. Jewsbury

2390. Zinn, Howard. THE SOUTHERN MYSTIQUE. *Am. Scholar 1963 33(1): 49-56.* The overwhelming majority of Atlanta's white people still considers Negroes inferior, and prefers segregation. The whites are numerous enough to have prevented most of the changes, by riots, elections, or boycotts. "A key to the...vault of prejudice locked inside the mind of the white Southerner [is that] he cares, but *not enough.*" He cares more about other things than segregation: monetary profit, political power, staying out of jail, approval of his peers, conformity to the dominant decision of the community. The author concludes that the "magical and omnipotent dispeller of the mystery...is *contact*" which must be massive and prolonged. E. P. Stickney

2391. --. CURRENT TRENDS IN NEGRO EDUCATION AND SHORTER PAPERS. *J. of Negro Educ. 1968 37(4): 432-451.*
Freeman, Donald, Kimbrough, Rollie, and Brother Zolili. THE MEANING OF EDUCATION, pp. 432-434. Extracted from a position paper presented to the Conference of Afro-American Educators, 6-9 June 1968, in Chicago. Proper education of Negroes requires completely independent black educational institutions in the black community.

Caplin, Morris D. SELF CONCEPT, LEVEL OF ASPIRATION, AND ACADEMIC ACHIEVEMENT, pp. 435-439. A study made of children in three elementary schools in a small city near New York City. Tests used were the Iowa Test of Basic Skills (Form 2); the California Test of Mental Maturity, 1957 edition, Level II, Long Form; and a self-concept scale developed at the Horace-Mann-Lincoln Institute of the School of Experimentation, Teachers College, Columbia University. The study results indicated that the apparent effect of desegregation was an initial upsurge in school-related self concept and level of aspiration of children from the segregated school, but that this eventually leveled to equal or even fell below that of the white children. "School climate" could have some effect on this self concept.

Harris, Edward E. PREJUDICE AND OTHER SOCIAL FACTORS IN SCHOOL SEGREGATION, pp. 440-443. Examines the amount of school segregation remaining in the South and the Border States in 1966. The author found that the major correlation lay between the ratio of Negro to white and the amount of segregation remaining. Urbanism and economic prosperity did not seem to be an important factor in the distribution of school segregation. Table.

McNamara, J. Regis. A PILOT PROGRAM FOR PRE-SCHOOL CULTURALLY DEPRIVED CHILDREN WITH LEARNING DISABILITIES, pp. 444-446. Nine retarded children were removed from the regular Head Start classes and placed in a special class with a teacher and two aides. At the end of seven months definite improvement was found. When compared with equally retarded children who had remained in the regular class, the special class made about two and one-half times the gain on total inventory scores than did the control group.

Kraft, Leonard E. and Kraft, Wilma R. SURVEY OF ATTITUDES OF RURAL DISADVANTAGED PUPILS TOWARD THEIR SCHOOL - A MODEL, pp. 447-451. Summarizes the methods and findings of a survey of student and teacher attitudes in a small rural community school system in southern Illinois.   B. D. Johnson

2392. --. PAPERS AND PROCEEDINGS OF A CONFERENCE ON NEGRO-JEWISH RELATIONS IN THE UNITED STATES. *Jewish Social Studies 1965 27(1): 3-66.*
Bond, Horace Mann. NEGRO ATTITUDES TOWARD JEWS, pp. 3-9. Provides anecdotes of the author's own experience.

Brotz, Howard. THE NEGRO-JEWISH COMMUNITY AND THE CONTEMPORARY RACE CRISIS, pp. 10-17. Analyzes a community in New York, and goes on to suggest that more emphasis ought to be given to the coincidence of class and race lines which tends to make more difficult assimilation and integration.

Duker, Abraham G. ON NEGRO-JEWISH RELATIONS - A CONTRI-BUTION TO A DISCUSSION, pp. 18-31. Stresses contributions of the Jewish community in aiding the Negro and suggests that work needs to be done on the weakening of Negro anti-Semitism.

Strole, Leo. REMARKS BY DISCUSSANT LEO SROLE, pp. 31-32. Comments variously on the preceding papers.

Rustin, Bayard. THE CIVIL RIGHTS STRUGGLE, pp. 33-36. Attacks Jewish criticism of Negro activists, pointing out that the Jewish struggle for acceptance came in an economically expanding society and simultaneously with other fights such as that for trade union organization, while the Negro struggle is coming with contracting job opportunities and with the "closed ghetto."

Halpern, Ben. ETHNIC AND RELIGIOUS MINORITIES: SUBCUL-TURES AND SUBCOMMUNITIES, pp. 37-44. Analyzes the differences between the Jewish and Negro communities in their interaction with the dominant Protestant culture.

Caplovitz, David. THE MERCHANT AND THE LOW-INCOME CON-SUMER, pp. 45-53. Reports the findings of a survey of two Harlem and one lower East Side communities. Stresses information regarding merchandizing, sales, and financing practices.

Robinson, Cleveland. REMARKS BY DISCUSSANT CLEVELAND ROBINSON, pp. 53-57. Discusses the tensions between Jews and Negroes in the trade unions and the need for a united front on their part against right-wing groups.

Schappes, Morris U. REMARKS BY DISCUSSANT MORRIS U. SCHAPPES, pp. 57-65. Comments variously upon the papers and commentaries of the day's session.

Diamond, Sigmund. SUMMATION, pp. 65-66. Provides a brief summation.
A. B. Rollins

2393. --. [RACE RELATIONS IN THE ARMY]. *Military R. 1970 50(7): 3-19.*
White, James S. RACE RELATIONS IN THE ARMY, pp. 3-12. The Armed Forces have led all sections of American society in providing equality of opportunity and treatment for all personnel without regard to race, color, creed, or national origin. However, in spite of its aggressive and determined actions to insure that all soldiers received equal and just treatment, the Army could not deal with the larger question of racial equality beyond the limits of its installations. Nor was it fully aware of the adverse effects which the root causes of racial friction in civilian society have on interpersonal relations within the Army. Before 1966, this approach did not present many serious problems; but since then, black racial pride, black and white racism, and the racial tensions of American civilian society have created racial tension in the military. Cites the seven major actions which the Army Chief of Staff directed to be taken in 1969 to cope with these problems.

Gibson, James M. SEMINAR ON RACIAL RELATIONS, pp. 13-19. Discusses the result of the Army Chief of Staff's order in the fall of 1969 that action be taken to identify and relieve the causes of racial tensions within the Army. One result was a number of seminars at all major continental U.S. installations. One of these seminars met at Fort Leavenworth, Kansas, in December 1969. Discusses the racial, professional, and rank composition of this seminar as well as some of its findings and conclusions.   G. E. Snow

The Social, Political, & Economic Situation

2394. Adler, Manfred. INTELLIGENCE TESTING OF THE CULTURALLY DISADVANTAGED: SOME PITFALLS. *J. of Negro Educ. 1968 37(4): 364-369.* States that many gifted persons are never identified as such and their potential is not used because they do not test well. Socioeconomic factors have a great effect on intelligence test performance. Klineberg found that Negro's test scores improved as their environment improved (Otto Klineberg, *Social Psychology*, rev. ed., New York: Holt, 1954). A double set of standards may be necessary in order to identify and develop these gifted people. 16 notes.
                                                                                            B. D. Johnson

2395. Aiken, Michael and Ferman, Louis A. THE SOCIAL AND POLITICAL REACTIONS OF OLDER NEGROES TO UNEMPLOYMENT. *Phylon 1966 27(4): 333-346.* Reports the findings of a study in which 314 former employees of Packard Motor Car Company were interviewed two years after the plant closed. Displaced Negro workers had less favorable labor market experiences than did whites. More Negroes than whites defined their life situations as having deteriorated. Negroes had slightly higher levels of economic deprivation as measured by reduced savings, increased debts, and cutbacks in spending for essentials. They also had lower participation rates with relatives and friends and evidenced a greater degree of political alienation and economic liberalism. The authors conclude that lower educational attainment and skill levels are significant in job discrimination and that the personal and political alienation of many Negroes stems from negative experiences in the labor market. 22 notes.
                                                                                            S. C. Pearson, Jr.

2396. Allen, Anne. THIS WAY OUT. *Am. Educ. 1967 3(7): 3-4, 28-29.* Considers the problems faced by students from subcultures who attend college. To illustrate, three students attending the University of California, Los Angeles were interviewed: a Mexican-American, a girl of Oriental ancestry, and a Negro from Watts. Problems common to all were identified as lack of encouragement to seek educational opportunities beyond the minimum State requirement and inability to finance a university education without substantial assistance from university, community, and Federal funds. 7 photos.   W. R. Boedecker

2397. Allen, Donald E. and Sandhu, Harjit S. A COMPARATIVE STUDY OF DELINQUENTS AND NON-DELINQUENTS: FAMILY EFFECT, RELIGION, AND PERSONAL INCOME. *Social Forces 1967 46(2): 263-269.* A test group of 179 delinquents is compared to a control group of 198 nondelinquents. The following areas were studied: alienation, Hedonism, life goals, and delinquency. Findings show that religious categories did not relate with delinquency. More delinquent boys are employed full time than nondelinquent. White delinquents are more hedonistic than white nondelinquents. The Negro delinquent has the poorest vision of life-goals. 4 tables, 12 notes. A. S. Freedman

2398. Allen, Irving L. SELECTING AN ECONOMIC PROBABILITY SAMPLE OF NEGRO HOUSEHOLDS IN A CITY. *J. of Negro Educ. 1969 38(1): 4-13.* Discusses methods of arriving at a probability sample of Negro households in cities in a reliable way. The methods discussed were arrived at while designing social surveys on school segregation in northern cities. 2 tables, 12 notes. B. D. Johnson

2399. Alston, Fannie C. and Williams, R. Ora. JOHNNY DOESN'T - DIDN'T HEAR. *J. of Negro Educ. 1964 33(2): 197-200.* Reports findings of a listening experiment conducted with students in the Morgan State College Basic Skills Program in 1959. S. C. Pearson, Jr.

2400. Amos, William E. and Perry, Jane. NEGRO YOUTH AND EMPLOYMENT OPPORTUNITIES. *J. of Negro Educ. 1963 32(4): 358-366.*

2401. Anderson, James E. POVERTY, UNEMPLOYMENT, AND ECONOMIC DEVELOPMENT: THE SEARCH FOR A NATIONAL ANTIPOVERTY POLICY. *J. of Pol. 1967 29(1): 70-93.* An examination of the antipoverty programs of the late 1950's and early 1960's in which the nature of poverty, the strategies of the antipoverty program, and the politics of poverty are covered. There is little agreement on what constitutes poverty or the number of people in this category. Only the middle-of-the-road approach of the Department of Health, Education and Welfare has enabled the Government to come to grips with the problem. Many strategies are available in the war on poverty, including the aggregationist, alleviative, curative, and efforts to create equal opportunity. These are interdependent and are currently being used in one form or another. Strategy selection is usually made on the basis of "existing policy objectives and traditional national values and beliefs." Poverty programs tend to create so many political differences that there is little agreement on any particular approach or its effectiveness; however, the best efforts have included aid to depressed areas, manpower development, and efforts to revive entire regions. The latter usually has the greatest political appeal, but many experts feel that manpower development is the only true solution to the problem of poverty. The author questions the reason for the current intensification of interest in poverty and offers as answers the desire of Presidents Kennedy and Johnson to be "recognized as great presidents," the increased volume of literature on the subject, the race situation, the hope that crime might be diminished, and the perplexing situation of poverty in the midst of plenty. Opposition to and support for antipoverty programs has been along liberal versus conservative lines. It has little to do with traditional pressure group and logrolling tactics. The recent antipoverty programs have been created through a combination of favorable public opinion, presidential support, party interests, and changing ideology. 36 notes.   A. R. Stoesen

2402. Antonovsky, Aaron. A STUDY OF SOME MODERATELY SUCCESS-FUL NEGROES IN NEW YORK CITY. *Phylon 1967 28(3): 246-260.* Examines the career patterns of 83 moderately successful Negroes by focusing on their backgrounds, processes of occupational selection, and some of their adult experiences, attitudes, and feelings. Of the respondents, most came from urban areas. More than half were born in the North, most came from stable family backgrounds, and slightly more than half had at least one parent in a middle-class occupation. Thus, the respondents were not typical of the Negroes of their generation. Their major achievement has been movement into the broader economic world, rather than upward mobility. The author maintains that the qualities and values which characterize their childhood and patterns of family life are more important than the objective facts of their background. They were raised in an atmosphere of what was called the religion of amounting to something. Consistent with their upbringing, the feelings of most about their work is inner-directed: the nature of the work rather than the responses of others because of their occupational status or the rewards it brings is what is important to them. The respondents wished little from life and their conception of success was moderate. They attribute their success to such personal characteristics as hard work and perseverance. Based on published sources and interviews; 3 tables, 9 notes.   D. N. Brown

2403. Antonovsky, Aaron. ASPIRATIONS, CLASS AND RACIAL-ETHNIC MEMBERSHIP. *J. of Negro Educ. 1967 36(4): 385-393.* A study of 378 boys and girls in the 10th grade in five high schools of a large city was conducted in 1958 to determine the relationship of their aspirations to class and racial-ethnic membership. Respondents were coded white, Negro, and Puerto Rican, and each ethnic group was divided into middle- and lower-class on the basis of the current occupation of the head of the household. Middle-class whites were found to have higher levels of aspiration and expectation, and a larger percentage of them were enrolled in academic programs and expressed negative feelings about remaining in the city. Lower-class Puerto Ricans had a relatively low aspiration level and fewer were in academic programs or were negative about staying in the city. A substantial similarity in patterns of response was found among the two Negro groups, lower-class whites, and middle-class Puerto Ricans. On a question of how they felt about 10 different occupations, middle-class white boys followed closely the order of national rating, while this was not true for the other groups with lower-class Puerto Ricans tending to be most different. The significance of the data and possible explanations are briefly discussed. 10 notes.

S. C. Pearson, Jr.

2404. Arnez, Nancy Levi. A LIBERAL EDUCATION FOR JUNIOR HIGH SCHOOL STUDENTS IN A CULTURALLY LIMITED AREA. *J. of Negro Educ. 1964 33(4): 436-440.* Reports an attempt to provide programs to "expand the cultural quotients and experiential backgrounds" of the students in Cherry

Hill Junior High School, a comparatively new school located in a Negro neighborhood in south Baltimore. Emphasis was placed on developing reading skills, interesting parents in enlarging community library facilities, encouraging students to use television as a learning tool, designing field trips, and using team teaching.   S. C. Pearson, Jr.

2405. Arnez, Nancy Levi. A STUDY OF ATTITUDES OF NEGRO TEACHERS AND PUPILS TOWARD THEIR SCHOOL. *J. of Negro Educ. 1963 32(3): 289-293.* A study of Houston Junior High School in Baltimore conducted in 1958 disclosed that the attitudes of both Negro teachers and Negro pupils were negative from the perspective of educational motivation. The author concluded that "what is needed are general programs of uplift educationally and culturally. The acquisition of subject matter must be blended with the acquisition of basic living standards and both of these must be harmonized with broadening experiences."   S. C. Pearson, Jr.

2406. Astre, G. A. RICHARD NIXON, SON GOUVERNMENT, SES PROBLEMES [The Nixon administration and its problems]. *Année Pol. et Econ. [France] 1969 42(209): 207-218.* Assesses the problems facing the Nixon administration. The "American dream" is deeply rooted in the national tradition, beginning with the original Puritan settlers of the 17th century. Lyndon B. Johnson raised extravagant hopes of the "Great Society," only to be faced with the harsh reality of the problems facing the United States, and only making a few token gestures toward their solution. The present administration is essentially the political arm of the privileged classes, which attempt to quell the demands of the underprivileged by the imposition of "law and order." The militant anticommunism which Nixon displayed during the McCarthy era does not seem to have lost either its simplicity or its virulence. The constant factors in American policy seem to be monopoly capitalism, imperialist expansion, racism, and comfort for the privileged. Despite this, the dollar is continually menaced and the flight of the Euro-dollar threatens the basis of the European economy. This is only counteracted by some attenuation of internal credit, which can only be a short-term solution. The demand for Black Power and general unrest can similarly not be silenced by the incarceration of a few Black Panthers. In short, the "realistic" measures of the new President have hitherto been too few, too cautious, and marked by traditionalism. The expensive compromises of the Nixon administration are in danger of pleasing nobody, and a fresh approach is only to be found among those of the Democratic Party in sympathy with the ideas of Robert Kennedy and Eugene McCarthy, who represent a break with the traditional Democratic ethos.   G. E. Orchard

2407. Bacon, Lloyd. POVERTY AMONG INTERREGIONAL RURAL-TO-URBAN MIGRANTS. *Rural Sociol. 1971 36(2): 125-140.* "Migration and residence data from the 1967 Survey of Economic Opportunity are used to examine the differential incidence of poverty among people of rural origins. Migration within and between the South and the North (the census Northeast, North Central, and West aggregated) is analyzed for Negro-white patterns of movement and associated proportions in poverty. Poverty status, the dependent variable, is operationally defined as a measure of how successfully adults in various residence and migration categories have coped with their environments. A social systems framework is utilized, and a set of theoretical propositions is induced from the findings. These propositions are statements of relationships between social distances traversed and differential selectivity operative in migration."

                                                                                          J

2408. Bailey, Beryl Loftman. TOWARD A NEW PERSPECTIVE IN NEGRO ENGLISH DIALECTOLOGY. *Am. Speech 1965 40(3): 171-177.* The author, a Jamaican, disagrees with the usual concept of American Negro dialect including that presented by Henry Louis Mencken in *The American Language.* He believes there is an underlying similarity between the various pidgin languages of the world (which are used in international commerce), Jamaican Creole, and American Negro dialect. By analyzing Negro dialect in a novel, he draws some comparisons between English, Jamaican Creole, and American Negro. The article is based on the author's own familiarity with the language and dialects under consideration. 8 notes.   R. W. Shoemaker

2409. Baldwin, James, Glazer, Nathan, Hook, Sidney, and Myrdal, Gunnar. LIBERALISM AND THE NEGRO: A ROUND-TABLE DISCUSSION. *Commentary 1964 37(3): 25-42.*

2410. Balfour, Nancy. NIXON'S THE ONE FOR AMERICA? *World Today [Great Britain] 1968 24(11): 467-475.* Analysis of the state of the 1968 American presidential campaign as of mid-October. There is particular discussion of the role which has been played in the campaign by the young and by black radicals. Richard Nixon's projected program is compared with that of Hubert Humphrey and is described as a central position which he feels is essential to unite both party and country when he becomes President. Note.   R. Howell

2411. Baratz, Stephen S. and Baratz, Joan C. EARLY CHILDHOOD INTERVENTION: THE SOCIAL SCIENCE BASE OF INSTITUTIONAL RACISM. *Harvard Educ. R. 1970 40(1): 29-50.* The authors contend that Head Start programs are based on an ethnocentric liberal ideology which, when denying cultural differences, sees the Negro as living in a state of social pathology. Such initial assumptions make for institutional racism and doom to failure a program like Head Start. The authors base their argument on the results of current linguistic and anthropological research. Far from verifying the pathological status of Negro children in regard to language, the authors find that linguistic data show that "many lower-class Negro children speak a well ordered, highly structural, but different, dialect...." Interventionist programs cannot afford to be built on the model of Negro pathology.   J. Herbst

2412. Barker, Gordon H. NEGRO DELINQUENTS IN PUBLIC TRAINING SCHOOLS IN THE WEST. *J. of Negro Educ. 1963 32(3): 294-300.* The author studied all Negro boys in Lookout Mountain School for Boys, for delinquent boys, in Golden, Colorado over a period of 18 months. He found family instability with a breakdown of parental role structures, particularly those of the male, in a majority of cases. He concluded that there are definite signs that "the boys have experienced a good deal of alienation from the families and their social structure."

S. C. Pearson, Jr.

2413. Batchelder, Alan B. DECLINE IN THE RELATIVE INCOME OF NEGRO MEN. *Q. J. of Econ. 1964 78(4): 525-548.* Based on decennial census data, between 1949 and 1959 the income of Negro men advanced more slowly than the income of white men in the North, in the West, and in the South. In contrast, the income of Negro women increased more rapidly than the income of white women.

T. Hočevar

2414. Bates, William M. NARCOTICS, NEGROES AND THE SOUTH. *Social Forces 1966 45(1): 61-67.* "Sociological literature for 30 years has shown an overrepresentation of Negroes in the known addict population. This study of addict admissions to the U.S.P.H. [U.S. Public Health] Service hospitals at Lexington and Fort Worth shows that there was a dramatic increase in Negro admissions in 1950. Although Negro narcotic addiction is almost entirely confined to northern metropolitan areas, what Negro addiction exists in the South is almost entirely from a few big cities. White addicts from the southern states, on the other hand, are chiefly from rural areas. Negro addicts from the South are younger than white addicts, but northern white and Negro addicts are the same age."

J

Bauman, John F. see abstract 2500

2415. Beard, Richard L. POPULAR CULTURE AND NEGRO EDUCATION. *J. of Negro Educ. 1969 38(1): 86-90.* Negro students should study the popular culture of the United States because this culture reflects the socioculture structure. After thorough study, the Negro student can know the imperatives of the culture in which he lives and can then deal with these imperatives, either by acceptance or rejection.

B. D. Johnson

2416. Bearwood, Roger. LA VERITE SUR LES GHETTOS NOIRS AUX ETATS-UNIS [The truth about the black ghettos of the United States]. *R. Pol. et Parlementaire [France] 1968 70(794): 62-80.* A translation of an article in *Fortune.* The author reviews the surplus of manual labor on southern farms, which has driven the unemployed blacks into the city. Without a lobby, unorganized, and faced with endemic hunger, the small farmer has been the victim of the large cultivator whose interests alone are represented by southern legislators on congressional committees which formulate policy. Cooperatives and loans have helped, but not enough to stem the flight to the cities where blacks represent a large percentage of the population. Thus, the frustrations found in the cities are born in the fields of the South.

T. D. Lockwood

2417. Bell, Robert Roy. LOWER CLASS NEGRO MOTHERS' ASPIRATIONS FOR THEIR CHILDREN. *Social Forces 1965 43(4): 493-500.* "The data given in this paper support the hypothesis that it is possible to distinguish different subgroups along the Negro lower class continuum. Given the importance of the Negro mother in the lower class Negro family, her values and aspirations for her children are very influential for her children's future. Significant differences were found in the responses of low status and high status lower class mothers to questions concerning their aspirations for their children."

J

2418. Benet, James. GOOGOL! *Am. Educ. 1967 3(9): 9-10.* An account of an Office of Education project called Special Elementary Education for the Disadvantaged (SEED) which employs an inductive approach to the teaching of mathematics in ghetto schools. The project operates on three tradition-violating principles: 1) the best time to introduce students to abstract mathematics is early childhood rather than high school; 2) disadvantaged children can successfully reason abstractly because they are not handicapped by their inadequate language skills; 3) the best way to help the disadvantaged is to offer the opportunity of success in a prestige subject, giving them pride in their abilities, rather than remedial instruction, which further damages self-image. Speculates that incorporation of this approach in other areas of the curriculum, introduced in model schools for the disadvantaged in major urban areas, would act as a powerful lever for school integration. Apparently based on interviews with members of the SEED staff; photo. W. R. Boedecker

2419. Berendt, Joachim E. DEN SCHWARZEN DER USA FEHLEN DIE POLITIKER [The blacks in the United States need politicians]. *Frankfurter Hefte [West Germany] 1970 25(5): 339-342.* Discusses the polarizing effects of Eldridge Cleaver and James Baldwin on the black community in the United States, and also the problem of sexual perceptions of whites and blacks. The author identifies the need for black politicians to articulate and focus black aspirations. R. W. Heywood

2420. Berkman, Dave. ADVERTISING IN "EBONY" AND "LIFE": NEGRO ASPIRATIONS VS. REALITY. *Journalism Q. 1963 40(1): 53-64.* Four issues of *Ebony,* a leading Negro magazine, were compared with four issues of *Life* magazine, published in the same months of 1960 and having approximately the same total column inches of advertising. They were nearly identical in layout, format and typography, but there was a basic socioeconomic difference which reflected the hard reality that the American Negro as a race has a long way to go before achieving real equality of status. Some advertising, reflecting the general middle-class status to which the Negro aspires, was almost identical, but other advertising was quite different. *Ebony* had far fewer advertisements for products whose purchase involves heavy expenditure and much more advertising of alcoholic beverages. Considerable patent medicine advertising and "money-making opportunities" appeared in *Ebony* and little of either category in *Life.* S. E. Humphreys

2421. Billings, Charles E. THE CHALLENGE OF AFRICA IN THE CURRICULUM. *Social Educ. 1971 35(2): 139-146, 153.* Deals with the importance of intelligent inquiry in the study of Africa. Part of the article is drawn from a paper given at a meeting of the Committee on Teaching About Africa of the

African Studies Association, and the rest develops the author's position on the question. Traces the history of the teaching of the American Negro, explores the ramifications and possibilities of today's stress on the study of African history, and looks at the scope and sequence of an African curriculum, the role of the teacher in fostering a spirit of inquiry, and the teachers' attitudes toward Africa. Teachers of African history must examine their own motives and purposes in including such materials in their curriculum. Teachers must act as guides in a project of learning together. Since so many questions about Africa are as yet unanswered, students and teachers can learn together. 3 illus.

N. E. Tutorow

2422. Blodgett, Emerson and Green, Robert Lee. A JUNIOR HIGH SCHOOL GROUP COUNSELING PROGRAM. *J. of Negro Educ. 1966 35(1): 11-17.* Reports a program conducted among failing ninth grade students in an Oakland, California, school in an interracial and economically underprivileged neighborhood. After the selection of prospects and the interpretation of the program to parents and students, 45 students met in groups of seven or eight with a guidance worker in weekly sessions over a period of five months. The leaders were permissive and nondirective, and the emphasis was on self-expression and group discussion. Self-expression resulted in the enunciation of complaints, at first about school and later about home situations. It became evident that much of the behavior of the students in the classroom was simply an effort to complain through negative, resistant behavior. Recognition of this fact led to specific recommendations to the school including the review of fighting and penalties for fighting, the encouragement of additional remedial programs, and the improvement of communication between counselors, teachers, and students regarding the latter's feelings, attitudes, and complaints.   S. C. Pearson, Jr.

2423. Blood, Robert O., Jr. and Wolfe, Donald M. NEGRO-WHITE DIFFERENCES IN BLUE-COLLAR MARRIAGES IN A NORTHERN METROPOLIS. *Social Forces 1969 48(1): 59-64.* "Representative samples of Negro and white blue-collar marriages in the Detroit Metropolitan Area show differences in marriage patterns even when comparisons are limited to low blue-collar or high blue-collar marriages only. Negro families are more often wife-dominant at the expense of equalitarianism in making major family decisions. The division of labor in Negro homes involves less sharing and flexibility despite a slightly higher proportion of working wives. Negro wives are more self-reliant in coping with their own emotional problems and emphasize their own contributions to the family welfare, rather than the husband's occupational prospects. Negro men are less companionable to their wives and are generally evaluated less favorably as marriage partners than white husbands of the same occupational level."

J

2424. Bluestein, Gene. FOLK TRADITION, INDIVIDUAL TALENT: A NOTE ON THE POETRY OF ROCK. *Massachusetts R. 1970 11(2): 373-384.* Contemporary rock and roll music is an authentic folk poetry blending the elements of the Afro-American and Anglo-Saxon musical heritage.

G. Kurland

2425. Bock, E. Wilbur. THE DECLINE OF THE NEGRO CLERGY: CHANGES IN FORMAL RELIGIOUS LEADERSHIP IN THE UNITED STATES IN THE TWENTIETH CENTURY. *Phylon 1968 29(1): 48-64.* A statistical study of the importance of the clergy as a profession for Negroes in the United States, covering the years 1930-60. The author has discovered that, while both whites and Negroes since 1930 have used the clergy less and less frequently as a means of achieving professional status, the decline has been greater for Negroes than whites; and, while the white clergy is increasing relative to the white population, the Negro clergy relative to the Negro population has decreased greatly since 1930. As Negroes have gained educational and occupational opportunities, they have been attracted into other professions, at the expense of the Negro churches. Based on secondary sources; 7 tables (statistics drawn from published Government census reports), 18 notes.   R. D. Cohen

2426. Bogan, Forrest A. and O'Boyle, Edward J. WORK EXPERIENCE OF THE POPULATION. *Monthly Labor R. 1968 91(1): 35-45.* Examines the following components of the labor force: part-time, unemployed, nonworker, Negro worker, and teenager. For the first time, the number of persons working full-time for an entire year (1966) reached 50 million. Forty-seven percent of the advance was among women, who constituted only 40 percent of the annual labor force. During 1966, part-time employment expanded to 16 million persons, an increase of 600 thousand over the previous year, and unemployment was reduced, with the greatest improvement observed among those who had been jobless for more than 15 weeks. Negro unemployment remained stable at 22 percent. 3 tables, 4 charts, 9 notes.   A. P. Young

2427. Bolden, Wiley S. TASKS FOR THE NEGRO TEACHER IN IMPROVING ACADEMIC ACHIEVEMENT OF NEGRO PUPILS IN THE SOUTH. *J. of Negro Educ. 1963 32(2): 173-178.* Tasks include understanding and maintaining an objective attitude to the pupil's problems, helping pupils and parents to understand, examining teaching effectiveness by the use of standardized tests, applying knowledge of the learning process in the classroom, and working at self-improvement.   S. C. Pearson, Jr.

2428. Boulware, Marcus H. J. FINLEY WILSON, FRATERNAL ORATOR. *Negro Hist. Bull. 1963 27(3): 67-68.* A laudatory obituary of Wilson (1921-63), "Grand Exalted Ruler of the Protective Order of the Elks of the World," a brilliant orator who "aroused pride in the black race" and ameliorated their lot. Illus.   S

2429. Bowman, Lewis and Boynton, G. R. COALITION AS PARTY IN A ONE-PARTY SOUTHERN AREA: A THEORETICAL AND CASE ANALYSIS. *Midwest J. of Pol. Sci. 1964 8(3): 277-297.* "This paper analyzes a situation in a southern arena in which the political aimlessness of the usual one-party stereotype has been relieved occasionally by coalitions serving party functions. A liberal coalition of local labor, Negro, academic, and progressive business factions - organized loosely under the rubric, Voters for Better Government - developed in Durham, North Carolina after World War II....The thesis of this paper is that one of the coalitions - the one more liberally inclined and centered around the Voters for Better Government - performed certain party functions over a considerable period of time....The liberal coalition served as party in the performance of all of the party functions investigated." B. W. Onstine

2430. Boyenton, William H. THE NEGRO TURNS TO ADVERTISING. *Journalism Q. 1965 42(2): 227-235.* Integration of Negroes into general advertising is complicated. Lack of faster progress need not be construed as segregationist or anti-Negro, but rather the result of business habits of seeking customers where they are known to be. Dispassionate economic information is lacking as to what the Negro is really like as a consumer and how to satisfy him.
S. E. Humphreys

2431. Bradford, M. E. FAULKNER, JAMES BALDWIN, AND THE SOUTH. *Georgia R. 1966 20(4): 431-443.* Defends William Faulkner from Baldwin's attack. Quoting Edmund Burke, the author shows the southern "community" and Faulkner's attachment to it. This gives a belief in "a definite order of status, function and place" and does not allow "for any but restorative reform....The product of a collective experience,...community is inveterately provincial." It is to be preserved so that the integrated Negro is integrated to the community from within, not by Federal law. Of Baldwin the author says, "it would seem most unlikely that he would understand community or the difference between change and progress within a communal framework." He "is monstrously inconsistent, ...his voice now heard nightly...crying love-in-hate on a thousand darkened streets." T. M. Condon

2432. Bradley, Gladyce H. FRIENDSHIPS AMONG STUDENTS IN DESEGREGATED SCHOOLS. *J. of Negro Educ. 1964 33(1): 90-92.* The author studied groups of Negro students in Morgan State College, Maryland, and in Baltimore high schools. She found that "more than twice as many of the college group and three times as many of the secondary school group indicated that their closest friend, ranked as number one, was a Negro, as indicated that their closest friend, similarly ranked, was white. The percent of Negro friends, among the five closest friends, exceeds that of white friends, even though the enrollment was predominantly white in some of the schools attended by these students."
S. C. Pearson, Jr.

2433. Bradley, Nolen E. THE NEGRO UNDERGRADUATE STUDENT: FACTORS RELATIVE TO PERFORMANCE IN PREDOMINANTLY WHITE STATE COLLEGES AND UNIVERSITIES IN TENNESSEE. *J. of Negro Educ. 1967 36(1): 15-23.* Reports results of a study of Negro undergraduate students in seven formerly all-white State colleges and universities in Tennessee. While desegregation is a well-established and accepted fact, integration is proceeding at a variable but slower pace. Minimal social integration was found. Negro students attend integrated schools because of lesser cost, convenience, and better educational opportunities. The schools provide inadequate noncredit remedial work and inadequate financial assistance. American College Test scores in English and mathematics are inadequate tools for predicting success of Negro students. The author suggests that student performance could be improved by interracial education at the primary and secondary levels, by enrollment of more middle-class Negroes, and by integration of faculties.   S. C. Pearson, Jr.

2434. Bragg, Emma W. CHANGES AND CHALLENGES IN THE '60'S. *J. of Negro Educ. 1963 32(1): 25-34.* Discusses the implications of the current American social and economic changes for the Negro teacher.   S. C. Pearson, Jr.

2435. Brazziel, William F. HIGHER HORIZONS IN SOUTHERN ELEMENTARY SCHOOLS. *J. of Negro Educ. 1964 33(4): 382-389.* Describes an effort in the Henry Clay School of Norfolk, an elementary school in a downtown urban renewal area, to implement a program modeled on New York City's Higher Horizons Program. The paper reports an optimistic appraisal of the program's success after three years.   S. C. Pearson, Jr.

2436. Brazziel, William F. MANPOWER TRAINING AND THE NEGRO WORKER. *J. of Negro Educ. 1966 35(1): 83-87.* Considers the necessity of increasing the rate of movement of Negroes into skilled and professional occupations and discusses the possibilities and limitations of the Manpower Development and Training Program inaugurated by Congress in 1962 "to promote and encourage the development of training programs designed to qualify for employment the many persons who cannot reasonably be expected to secure fulltime employment without such training." While this program offers great promise, other efforts are needed. The support of industry is particularly required.   S. C. Pearson, Jr.

2437. Brazziel, William F. and Gordon, Margaret. REPLICATIONS OF SOME ASPECTS OF THE HIGHER HORIZONS PROGRAM IN A SOUTHERN JUNIOR HIGH SCHOOL. *J. of Negro Educ. 1963 32(2): 107-113.* Concludes that "replications of the principles and procedures designed to help culturally disadvantaged children make better use of public education can, according to this study, be carried out in any school."   S. C. Pearson, Jr.

2438. Brimmer, Andrew F. BILDUNGSPROBLEME DER NEGER IN DEN VEREINIGTEN STAATEN [Educational problems of the Negroes in the United States]. *Politische Studien [West Germany] 1970 21(190): 151-154.* The educational level of the Negroes has been increasing although it still lags behind that of the whites. The higher educational level is directly related to the increases in black incomes. The serious gaps in Negro education need to be filled, not by Black Studies programs, but by remedial instruction in order to prepare Negroes for the realities of a competitive world.   R. V. Pierard

2439. Brodin, Nils-Eric. AMERIKAS NEGRER [America's Negroes]. *Svensk Tidskrift [Sweden] 1969 56(1): 31-37.* Describes progress recently made in the United States in improving the status of Negroes, especially in education and economic opportunities. Public opinion polls show that Negroes themselves perceive their situation to be improving. Such information corrects the false image often given in the Swedish press.   R. G. Selleck

2440. Brooks, Albert N. D. WORDS TO TEACHERS. *Negro Hist. Bull. 1964 27(8): 196.* Urges Negro teachers to join the American Teachers Association and to support the association's efforts to improve social studies teaching, especially as it relates to the role of Negroes in American life.   L. Gara

2441. Brooks, Michael P. and Stegman, Michael A. URBAN SOCIAL POLICY, RACE, AND THE EDUCATION OF PLANNERS. *J. of the Am. Inst. of Planners 1968 34(5): 275-286.* "This paper examines the impact of contemporary urban social problems, especially those related to race and the black ghetto, on the planning profession in general and the education of planners in particular. Several dimensions of the planner's role are discussed, leading to the making of a case for a greatly intensified effort in the training of social policy planners. Recommendations are made concerning the content and structure which should characterize such new training programs."   J

2442. Brown, Beulah E. "LEARNING IS FUN" WITH THE DICTAPHONE ELECTRONIC CLASSROOM - A DISCUSSION. *J. of Negro Educ. 1966 35(3): 246-251.* Discusses and encourages the use of the Dictaphone Electronic Classroom as an aid to learning. The author believes that this instrument is particularly valuable in teaching slow and reluctant learners.
S. C. Pearson, Jr.

2443. Brown, Charles I. THE MARRIED STUDENT AT BENNETT COLLEGE. *J. of Negro Educ. 1963 32(2): 183-187.* A study of 23 married students at Bennett College in 1960-62 which shows them to be emotionally mature and responsible individuals.   S. C. Pearson, Jr.

2444. Bryant, Lawrence C. A STUDY OF MUSIC PROGRAMS IN PUBLIC NEGRO COLLEGES. *J. of Negro Educ. 1963 32(2): 188-192.*

2445. Bryant, Lawrence C. ASSISTANCE DESIRED BY COUNSELORS FROM THE STATE DEPARTMENT OF EDUCATION. *J. of Negro Educ. 1965 34(2): 188-191.* Reports findings of a study of 145 Negro counselors working in the public schools of South Carolina. All counselors indicated a desire for help from the State Department of Education. Interest was expressed in receiving guidance materials, bulletins, directories, and personal assistance from the Guidance Supervisor.   S. C. Pearson, Jr.

2446. Buel, Ronald A. RACE, WELFARE, AND HOUSING IN ST. LOUIS. *Interplay 1969 3(3): 45-47.* The geographical position of St. Louis (between the South and the Midwest) has often meant the worst of both worlds - "Northern urban problems and old-line Southern racial attitudes." There has been no large-scale racial conflagration in St. Louis, partially because of the lack of the black following for a nonviolent nondisruptive rent strike aimed at St. Louis public housing. Analyzes who is striking and why, the problem of malnutrition, and the Federal and local policies that have created slums out of public housing. Federal actions have had little impact if resisted by local officials. 2 photos.

J. A. Zabel

2447. Burma, John H. INTERETHNIC MARRIAGE IN LOS ANGELES, 1948-1959. *Social Forces 1963 42(2): 156-165.* "Marriage license records of Los Angeles County were examined for the 1948-59 period for which data were available. Some 3,200 intermarriages were found. Negro-white and Filipino-white marriages were most common. Intermarriage rates at the end of the eleven year period were about triple the rates at the beginning of the period."

J

2448. Butts, Hugh F. SKIN COLOR PERCEPTION AND SELF-ESTEEM. *J. of Negro Educ. 1963 32(2): 122-128.* Reports a New York study supporting the hypothesis that "a group of Negro children with impaired self-esteem would perceive themselves less accurately in terms of skin color." S. C. Pearson, Jr.

2449. Cahalan, Don and Cisin, Ira H. AMERICAN DRINKING PRACTICES: SUMMARY OF FINDINGS FROM A NATIONAL PROBABILITY SAMPLE. *Q. J. of Studies on Alcohol 1968 29.*
I. EXTENT OF DRINKING BY POPULATION SUBGROUPS, (1): 130-151."Data were gathered by means of a random probability sample survey of 2,746 persons (1,177 men) representative of the adult household population of the continental U.S.A. (except Alaska, Hawaii), interviewed in late 1964 and early 1965. All interviewers were nonabstaining men. Drinking was found to be typical behavior; both total abstention and heavy drinking were atypical. Of the household population, 68 [percent] were drinkers (men 77 [percent], women 60 [percent]): 77 [percent] of the White and 79 [percent] of the Negro men, and 61 [percent] of the White and 49 [percent] of the Negro women, were drinkers. A Quantity-Frequency-Variability Drinking Index was constructed and showed that 32 [percent] of the respondents were abstainers, 15 [percent] infrequent drinkers (less than once a month), 28 [percent] light drinkers (no more than one or two drinks per occasion at least once a month), 13 [percent] moderate drinkers (no more than three or four drinks usually several times a month), 12 [percent] heavy drinkers (five or more drinks nearly every day or at least weekly). Half of the heavy drinkers were classified as escape drinkers on the basis of the answers they gave about their reasons for drinking (e.g., 'I drink when I want to forget everything,' or 'because I need it when tense and nervous'). Groups showing below-average numbers of drinkers were: women 40 years and older (52 [percent] drinkers); men 60 years and older (65 [percent]); respondents with family incomes below [six thousand dollars] (55 [percent]); farm owners (42 [percent]), service workers (61 [percent]), laborers (57 [percent]) and semiskilled operatives (62 [percent]); those who had not completed high school (57 [percent]); residents of the South Atlantic region (58 [percent]), East South Central (35 [percent]),

West South Central (62 [percent]), West North Central (66 [percent]), and Mountain states (58 [percent]); respondents living outside Standard Metropolitan Statistical Areas (51 [percent]); Baptists (47 [percent]) and members of other conservative Protestant denominations (36 [percent]); and those identifying their national origin as U.S. (46 [percent]), English or Scotch (60 [percent]), Scotch-Irish (50 [percent]), and Latin-American or Caribbean (63 [percent]). The prevalence of drinking varied directly by social status as measured by the Hollingshead Index of Social Position; a materially higher proportion of those of upper status (76 [percent] of highest and upper-middle) were drinkers. However, among those who drank at all, those of lower status had a slightly higher proportion of heavy drinkers (18 [percent] of lower-middle and lowest status). Four out of 10 of the respondents said they had either cut down or quit drinking, while 14 [percent] said they were now drinking more than previously. Retrospective responses and evidence from past studies indicate that the proportion of drinkers among women - especially younger women - is increasing. Multivariate analysis of the interaction of various factors is required to attain adequate understanding of the complex interrelationships in drinking behavior. Thus, while higher urbanization is usually associated with a higher proportion of heavy drinkers, the relationship is much more pronounced when sociocultural status and age are held constant: the greatest difference was found among men aged 45 or older of lower status, among whom 31 [percent] of those of higher urbanization were heavy drinkers, compared with 7 [percent] of men over 45 of lower status living in areas of lower urbanization. It is concluded that common sociological variables such as sex, age, socioeconomic status, religion, region and urbanization are sufficient to explain much of the variance in whether an individual drinks at all. In addition, certain measures of individual personality were useful in explaining the variance in heavy drinking: measures of psychological involvement with alcohol, alienation, and psychoneurotic tendencies."

II. MEASUREMENT OF MASSED VERSUS SPACED DRINKING, (3): 642-656. "A new Volume-Variability (V-V) index of drinking behavior consists of eight groups (ranging from abstainer to high-volume-high-maximum consumption) and two amount-per-occasion levels (five or more drinks at least occasionally vs always less than five) for each of three volume-per-month groups (high, medium and low volume). A comparison with the Quantity-Frequency-Variability index as described in Part I of this study...demonstrates the relative simplicity and freedom from arbitrary definitions offered by the V-V index, which also eliminates grouping as 'heavy drinkers' those who drink small amounts daily with those who drink large amounts sporadically. Data from the authors' 1964-1965 national survey of 2746 adults interpreted by the V-V index are tabulated in detail. When aggregate consumption was held constant, those who never drank as many as five drinks on an occasion, when compared with those who did, were older, of higher social status, better adapted to their environments and more successful and satisfied in achieving their life goals, as well as less likely to worry about their drinking or feel they would miss alcohol if forced to give it up, and less dependent upon drinking to cope with problems." J

2450. Caldwell, William. DEN NYE SVARTE INTELLEKTUELLE AMERIKANER [The new black intellectual American]. *Samtiden [Norway] 1968 77(4): 217-225.* The author is a native of the West Indies, a former resident of New York

City, and a present resident of Norway. The topic of his essay is the background of black nationalism. The author argues that the primary reason for the present racial confrontation in the United States is the economic exploitation of the Negro, as shown by the Federal budget for 1968, which allots "still fewer crumbs" to the black community than in the previous year. This interpretation is also supported with references to the emphasis on repressive measures in response to civil disorders. Only through higher economic standards for the black community can the present movement toward catastrophe or chaos be halted. The author also comments on the situation in Europe in terms of the views of left-wing intellectuals and their treatment of Negroes; the differences between Europe and the United States are a matter of degree rather than fundamental differences in attitudes.   P. O. Jonsson

2451. Caliguri, Joseph. STUDENT HUMAN RELATIONS COMMITTEE - TOKENISM OR NOT? *J. of Human Relations 1969 17(1): 95-103.* Evaluates a student human relations committee operating in a junior high school with an enrollment of about twelve hundred students and with a 40-60 Negro-white ratio. Negro students entering the school in the seventh grade from a segregated environment are often in dire need of help. Most of the committee members improved their self-perception and their perceptions of others. Committee members also made a contribution toward stopping student fights. It is concluded, however, that the existence of the committee represents human relations tokenism by school officials who did very little initial planning and on-going monitoring. Based on questionnaires; 4 notes.   D. J. Abramoske

2452. Cameron, Howard. A REVIEW OF RESEARCH AND AN INVESTIGATION OF EMOTIONAL DEPENDENCY AMONG NEGRO YOUTH. *J. of Negro Educ. 1967 36(2): 111-120.* Surveys research in the area of emotional overdependency particularly among Negroes and reports the results of a study conducted among 822 male and female Negro students between the ages of 18 and 22 from different regions of the United States. Regional differences in overdependency were found with the highest incidence among southern students. Where regional factors were controlled no significant differences were found between males and females. Techniques of parental discipline were perceived to be more physical and restrictive by overdependent students, and there appeared to be some type of emotional attachment exhibited by mothers of dependent children. Biblio.   S. C. Pearson, Jr.

2453. Campbell, Joel T. and Belcher, Leon. CHANGES IN NONWHITE EMPLOYMENT, 1960-1966. *Phylon 1967 28(4): 325-337.* Examines data compiled by the Bureau of the Census in an effort to determine if there has been any significant changes in nonwhite employment during the period characterized as that of the "Civil Rights Revolution." It is concluded that there has been a reasonably steady but slow increase in such employment in the higher - status professions, but that the proportion of nonwhites in the lower - status occupations declined, even though total employment showed a marked increase. The evidence shows that nonwhites in an occupational category earn lower average incomes than do whites in the same job. This can be partially explained by the fact that

proportionally more nonwhites were employed less than full time. Based on reports of the Bureau of the Census and other published sources; 10 tables, 17 notes.
D. N. Brown

2454. Cardoso, Jack J. GHETTO BLACKS AND COLLEGE POLICY. *Liberal Educ. 1969 55(3): 363-372.* College is irrelevant to blacks from the ghetto. The ghetto gave the blacks security and a common experience with other blacks. Colleges dominated by white males is a frightening experience; blacks face competition and are forced to leave if they do not succeed. The blacks respond by demanding separate courses, black teachers, and even black colleges. The author describes the effects of the blacks' demands on faculty and college administrators, and feels the college should take a stand to aid the blacks but not to accept outrageous demands. 3 notes.
C. G. Lauritsen

2455. Carey, George W., Macomber, Lenore, and Greenberg, Michael. EDUCATIONAL AND DEMOGRAPHIC FACTORS IN THE URBAN GEOGRAPHY OF WASHINGTON, D.C. *Geographical R. 1968 58(4): 515-537.* "Social patterns in the nation's capital are explored through the factor analysis of a set of demographic data and a set of educational data for elementary schools. The demographic factors highlight racial division and ghetto expansion along the fringe of Rock Creek Park, and indicate additional class polarization within the Negro population. These broad trends are counterpointed by the presence of blight, of centers of higher education, and of areas with rapid population increase. The educational factors, similarly, reflect the racial divisions in the city's schools, and the preference of all well-trained teachers - including Negro teachers - for positions elsewhere than in the core. Finally, the relationships between the demographic and educational factors are explored, and their interaction discussed."
J

2456. Carr, Leslie G. THE SROLE ITEMS AND ACQUIESCENCE. *Am. Sociol. R. 1971 36(2): 287-293.* "Twelve years ago Lenski and Leggett found that race and class factors produced a strong agreeing tendency to one of the Srole 'anomie' items. Many subsequent applications of the Srole items have failed to take into account the implications of their findings. Most of the research on the subject of acquiescence has been done on the F scale by psychologists who have explained it as a personality characteristic. The technique of comparing scale items to the same items in obverse form has been the principal research technique. The same technique is used here in a sociological perspective. One-half of a sample of poor Southern Negroes was given the Srole items and the other half was given the same items in an obverse form. Analysis shows a strong tendency to agree with both forms despite the fact that they had opposite meanings. The implications of this for the use of the Srole items and similar scales are examined."
J

2457. Carroll, James C. RETAIL STORE PATRONAGE DECISIONS AMONG COLLEGE-AGE NEGROES. *J. of the Alabama Acad. of Sci. 1969 40(2): 109-112.* Shows the rank orders assigned to six selected retail store operating characteristics, for each of four categories of retail stores, as given by 80 Negro students at Stillman College (Tuscaloosa, Alabama) in 1967. The rank orderings showed that retail price levels were the most powerful factor influencing store patronage among these Negroes, followed by the availability of nationally advertised brands and the employment of Negro personnel. Availability of credit was less significant than most merchants believed. Local newspaper and radio advertising ranked lowest of the factors. Makes tentative recommendations to retail merchants in view of the apparent differences between the manner in which they perceive Negro demand and that in which Negroes themselves perceive it. Table, 2 notes.

                                                                    Sr. A. Doyle

2458. Centers, Richard, Raven, Bertram H. , and Rodrigues, Aroldo. CONJU-
GAL POWER STRUCTURE: A RE-EXAMINATION. *Am. Sociol. R. 1971*
36(2): 264-278. "A representative sample of 776 husbands and wives in the Los
Angeles area were interviewed regarding the relative power of husbands and
wives in various decision areas, following the basic procedures utilized by Blood
and Wolfe in their 1959 study of wives only, in Detroit. Essentially, these results
paralleled those obtained by Blood and Wolfe, extending their findings to responses from husbands and in a different area. Husband power was greatest
among Oriental couples and least among Negro couples; it decreases with age,
with length of marriage, and is less where a second marriage is involved; husband
power increases with occupational status and educational level. The current study
questions the effects of sampling of conjugal decision areas. With a somewhat
more representative sampling of decisions, the distribution of power changes
dramatically. Husband dominant families tend to show high authoritarianism
scores for both husbands and wives. Least marital satisfaction is associated with
wife dominance. While the current investigation centers on power relationships
between husbands and wives, the basic approach can be extended to analysis in
other types of groups."   J

2459. Centra, John A. BLACK STUDENTS AT PREDOMINANTLY WHITE
COLLEGES: A RESEARCH DESCRIPTION. *Sociol. of Educ. 1970 43(3):*
325-339. "How do the background characteristics, activities, goals, and perceptions of black students at predominantly white colleges differ from those of their
white counterparts? In an attempt to answer these questions, this report analyzes
findings from several sources. Particular emphasis is upon data from the 'Questionnaire on Student and College Characteristics' (QSCC) which was administered to a sample of 249 black students at 83 traditionally white institutions in
1968. The similarities and differences between this group of black students and
a matched group of white students are discussed and related to other research
evidence."   J

2460. Chennareddy, Venkareddy. A REGRESSION ANALYSIS OF THE
RATE OF OFF-FARM MIGRATION OF FARM PEOPLE IN THE TEN-
NESSEE VALLEY REGION. *J. of the Ala. Acad. of Sci. 1969 40(1): 47-51.*
A statistical study of the relationships between off-farm migration rate and
five independent variables. Data used were based on the years 1950-60 in 19
State economic areas in the Tennessee Valley region. These findings were
compared with an earlier study based on State economic areas in the South-

east; the two studies showed the same direction of correlation, but with different magnitudes. Off-farm migration is negatively associated with per capita farm income and capital gains per acre; it is positively correlated with the off-farm experience of rural farm males, the percentage of farm people 10 to 24 years old, and the percentage of Negroes. The author concludes that actions generating higher farm income and capital gains may retard off-farm movements, while such things as vocational training and laws to inhibit discrimination against Negroes in urban areas may increase the rate of off-farm migration. 5 tables, biblio. Sr. A. Doyle

2461. Cismaru, Alfred. THE AMERICAN NEGRO IN POST-WAR FRENCH DRAMA. *Negro Hist. Bull. 1964 27(4): 77-78.*

2462. Clarizio, Harvey F. MATERNAL ATTITUDE CHANGE ASSOCIATED WITH INVOLVEMENT IN PROJECT HEAD START. *J. of Negro Educ. 1968 37(2): 106-113.* Reports the findings of a study designed to determine differences in maternal attitude toward schools and education following participation of children in Head Start projects. In one experimental group primary parental contact was through group meetings while in a second an individual counseling relationship was established. A control group was made up of mothers from similar socioeconomic circumstances whose children were not accepted for Head Start programs. Both a maternal attitude scale and a teacher rating scale were used to measure results. Differences among the groups were not statistically significant and suggested that the school-home aspect of Head Start programs has not modified the educational attitudes of lower-class mothers. 2 notes. S. C. Pearson, Jr.

2463. Clark, Blake. AN ENTERPRISING MINORITY. *Natl. Civic R. 1970 59(9): 477-481.* In 1968 the Arcata Investment Company was formed to help blacks become businessmen in California. The company was created from financing and counseling initiated by a white man, Robert O. Dehlendorf, and has been responsible for 46 minority-group members reaching their goal of ownership of business concerns. After 18 months of service only 3 of the 46 have failed. The Nixon administration, using Arcata as a model, has created the Minority Enterprise Small Business Investment Company (MESBIC) to attract other corporate executives into following Dehlendorf's example. The real drive in America is in the private sector. If businessmen get behind MESBIC, they can prove to the minority society that free enterprise works and the black community can be brought into the mainstream of free enterprise. H. S. Marks

2464. Clift, Virgil A. CURRICULUM STRATEGY BASED ON THE PERSONALITY CHARACTERISTICS OF DISADVANTAGED YOUTH. *J. of Negro Educ. 1969 38(2): 94-104.* Teachers must recognize certain character traits among disadvantaged youth. Lists 44 factors of personality, 72 factors of cognitive function, and 53 factors in relation to educational values. The teacher should watch for these characteristics and teach in a fashion that will reach these children. 3 notes. B. D. Johnson

2465. Cloward, Richard, Dentler, Robert, Ianni, Francis A. J., Kahn, Alfred J., Meyer, Carol H., Riessman, Frank, Rustin, Bayard, Weinstein, Gerald , and Wilcox, Preston. EDUCATING THE CHILDREN OF THE WELFARE POOR: A "RECORD" SYMPOSIUM. *Teachers Coll. Record 1968 69(4): 301-319.* Held at Teachers College on 3 November 1967, the symposium primarily centered around the problems of poverty, slums, political will, welfare, etc., as they relate to education. Some of the points made by the various discussants included a proposal to establish universally a family allowance, whether needed or not, in order to provide the 20th-century amenities of health and education (Kahn); a suggestion that we address ourselves to the whole issue of racism, not just to education and schooling for the blacks (Wilcox); and a suggestion that the blacks create a political movement to deal with housing, jobs, and the like, rather than concentrating on just the schools and inferior education obtained by Negroes (Rustin). C. P. McMahon

2466. Cobbs, Hamner. "GIVE ME THE BLACK BELT!" *Alabama R. 1964 17(3): 163-180.* Presidential address before the Alabama Historical Association 25 April 1964. Discusses first the total humor of the Negro and then Negro humor under four categories: 1) the humor of the Negro who refuses to accept white standards of life, 2) of the Negro who has an innate desire to be well-mannered, 3) the humor which comes from the practiced ear of the Negro, and 4) from the illiterate. D. F. Henderson

2467. Comer, James P. and Johnson, Samuel H. SUMMER STUDY-SKILLS PROGRAM: A CASE FOR STRUCTURE. *J. of Negro Educ. 1969 38(1): 38-45.* Survey of a program at Knoxville College, Tennessee, which teaches study and social skills to primarily southern Negro students for six-week periods following their 10th year of school. The program is very rigidly structured and traditional. The faculty is predominantly Negro. Results of follow-up studies have shown that the participants did benefit substantially from the training received; although they were usually the top students in their schools and from middle class and upper class families, they showed considerable improvement. Table. B. D. Johnson

2468. Conyers, James E. and Kennedy, T. H. REPORTED KNOWLEDGE NEGRO AND WHITE COLLEGE STUDENTS HAVE OF NEGROES WHO HAVE PASSED AS WHITES. *J. of Negro Educ. 1964 33(4): 454-459.* Deals with problems of gathering reliable statistics on the phenomenon of "passing" and relates the findings of a 1961 study in which 930 college students (404 Negro, 526 white) were questioned about their knowledge of Negroes who had passed as whites. One hundred and twenty Negro and 48 white respondents indicated knowledge of Negroes who had permanently passed as white, and 260 Negro and 105 white respondents indicated knowledge of Negroes who had temporarily passed as white. Negro respondents indicated that the large number of cases of which they had knowledge were females. Based on data in Conyers' unpublished Ph.D. dissertation, "Selected Aspects of the Phenomenon of Negro Passing" (Washington State U., 1962). S. C. Pearson, Jr.

2469. Cooke, Paul. DELINQUENCY PREVENTION THROUGH EDUCA-TIONAL INTERVENTION. *J. of Negro Educ. 1966 35(2): 151-160.* Reviews some of the educational projects of the District of Columbia public schools' Model School Division. While these projects - such as parent education, a program of assigning Teachers College students to work with potentially delinquent elementary school children, tutoring, preschools, teacher aides, after-school programs, and work-training and work-study programs - are designed to provide better education, they also tend to reduce delinquency.   S. C. Pearson, Jr.

2470. Cowhig, James D. and Beale, Calvin L. RELATIVE SOCIOECONOMIC STATUS OF SOUTHERN WHITES AND NONWHITES, 1950 AND 1960. *Southwestern Social Sci. Q. 1964 45(2): 113-124.* Objective: to answer the question whether widening of white-nonwhite socioeconomic status (SES) differences was characteristic of the southern urban and rural nonfarm populations. Four measures of SES were used: economic, educational, demographic, and housing. The conclusion, illustrated by four tables, was "that despite absolute improvement in most of the quantitative measures of SES, the relative position of nonwhites to whites in the South was generally lower in 1960 than in 1950."
D. F. Henderson

2471. Cowhig, James D. and Beale, Calvin L. SOCIOECONOMIC DIFFER-ENCES BETWEEN WHITE AND NONWHITE FARM POPULATIONS OF THE SOUTH. *Social Forces 1964 42(3): 354-362.* More nonwhites (53 percent) than whites (17 percent) are tenant farmers, with median income for the former only 45 percent of the latter. White farmers exceed nonwhites in completion of high school by 30 percent. Despite individual variation by States, nonwhite farmers exhibit wide gaps in comparison with white farmers. White southern farmers, on the other hand, are below standards in most respects when compared to national averages.   A. S. Freedman

2472. Cuban, Larry. "WHAT'S THE REAL STORY." *Social Studies 1965 56(1): 21-26.* Condemns stereotyped attitudes and thinking on the part of some teachers, as to socioeducational problems which exist in predominantly Negro schools in the urban areas of the United States with respect to levels of educational motivation, aspiration, achievement, and acceptable standards of decorum. The assumption of such stereotyped attitudes precludes objective and logical approaches to a solution of the problems that actually exist.
L. Raife

2473. D'Amico, Louis A. and Reed, Maenylie M. A COMPARISON OF TU-ITION-AND-FEE CHARGES IN NEGRO INSTITUTIONS WITH CHARGES IN INSTITUTIONS OF THE SOUTHEAST AND OF THE NA-TION: 1962-1963. *J. of Negro Educ. 1964 33(2): 186-190.*

2474. Daniel, Johnnie. NEGRO POLITICAL BEHAVIOR AND COMMU-NITY POLITICAL AND SOCIOECONOMIC STRUCTURAL FACTORS. *Social Forces 1969 47(3): 274-280.* "In analyzing Negro political mobilization and its relationship to the political and socioeconomic structure of Alabama communities, it was found that substantial changes have been made since the passage of the 1965 Voting Rights Act. Negro political mobilization has increased in practically every county of Alabama, being facilitated by the presence of candidates acceptable to Negroes and the presence of federal examiners. Traditional relationships between community socioeconomic structure and Negro political mobilization have been disrupted and new ones instituted. It is thought that these changes in Alabama reflect similar changes occurring in other southern states, and demand a reformulation of many generalizations concerning Negro political behavior."   J

2475. Daniel, Walter G. EDUCATION, RACE AND ECONOMIC OPPORTUNITY. *J. of Negro Educ. 1966 35(1): 1-4.* Reviews recent studies of the relation of education and race to economic opportunity with particular emphasis on the published papers of a conference on "Equal Opportunity - The Job Aspect" sponsored by the Labor Relations Council of the Wharton School of Finance and Commerce, the University of Pennsylvania. Educational reform is demanded, and encouragement is given educational institutions "promoting action, research, and publication in this area."   S. C. Pearson, Jr.

2476. Daniel, Walter G. NEEDED: A REEXAMINATION OF PLANS FOR DISADVANTAGED NEGRO YOUTH. *J. of Negro Educ. 1966 35(3): 199-203.* In this editorial comment the author suggests the need for reexamination of educational programs designed for disadvantaged youth. Such study should permit the identification of relevant and effective programs and educational planning designed to help all disadvantaged youth.   S. C. Pearson, Jr.

2477. Daniel, Walter G. PROBLEMS OF DISADVANTAGED YOUTH, URBAN AND RURAL. *J. of Negro Educ. 1964 33(3): 218-224.* The author deals with disadvantages of children of the inner city, rural school drop-outs, migrant children, and Negro children. He suggests that "the American economy needs all of the manpower available for its wholesome expansion" and that schools and communities must support efforts "for achieving economic, social and political participation of all elements in the population, and for attaining a significantly greater measure of equality in opportunity now."   S. C. Pearson, Jr.

2478. Daniel, Walter G. TEACHERS FOR AMERICA'S DISADVANTAGED WITH SPECIAL REFERENCE TO RACE. *J. of Negro Educ. 1965 34(4): 381-384.* In this editorial comment it is suggested that effective teacher education programs must provide "(a) a broad, general education, (b) competency in one or more specialized fields or scholarly disciplines, (c) the development of personal and social traits requisite to teaching success, and (d) teacher education experiences which focus on professional competence." Knowledge must be supplemented with a contagious enthusiasm born of concern for the student.
                                                            S. C. Pearson, Jr.

2479. Daniel, Walter G. THE RELATIVE EMPLOYMENT AND INCOME OF AMERICAN NEGROES. *J. of Negro Educ. 1963 32(4): 349-357.*

2480. De Mott, Benjamin. PROJECT FOR ANOTHER COUNTRY. *Am. Scholar 1963 32(3): 451-457.* Comments on the gloomy views taken on the Domestic Peace Corps project in central Harlem. The members of the project would serve for a year as "aides" in Harlem's understaffed welfare agencies. Such fresh evidence of the resources of leadership in the American Negro community should, it seems, have aroused a positive response. The chief reason for the apathy toward the project is that it was institution-oriented, and American faith in institutions has been in the process of breaking down. To believe in the efficiency of "modest, slow, molecular, definitive, social work" is to forego "audience appeal" and "to appear to minimize torment." But intensifications of the rage for reform testify "to a new access of belief in the possibility of change."
E. P. Stickney

2481. DeFriese, Gordon H. and Ford, W. Scott. OPEN OCCUPANCY - WHAT WHITES SAY, WHAT THEY DO. *Trans-action 1968 5(5): 53-56.* Studies how social pressures affect the stated attitudes of whites on the problems of open occupancy. More than half of the subjects changed their behavior toward Negroes from the stated attitudes. Most claimed it was because of social and cultural pressures placed on them. The authors found a definite connection between expressed attitudes on the issue and overt behavior. Only slightly more than one-third signed a statement favoring or opposing open housing. The authors concluded that a person's attitudes and the social pressures operating measured together were the better predicators of his future behavior than either aspect measured separately. Based on a survey taken by the authors; 2 tables.
A. Erlebacher

2482. Delco, Mrs. Exalton A., Jr., Matthews, George T., and Rogers, Robert W. OPPORTUNITIES AND RESPONSIBILITIES FOR DEVELOPING HUMAN RESOURCES. *Liberal Educ. 1969 55(2): 235-243.* The black students who attend college are divided into two groups: the predominantly ambitious and predominantly aggressive. Both groups share similar cultures. To meet the challenges that the Negro poses, universities must have a radical revision of methods and goals.
C. G. Lauritsen

2483. Derbyshire, Robert L. THE UNCOMPLETED NEGRO FAMILY: SUGGESTED RESEARCH UPON HIS OWN AND OTHER AMERICAN SEXUAL ATTITUDES AND BEHAVIOR. *J. of Human Relations 1967 15(4): 458-468.* Discusses the impact of caste and class upon American Negroes and their sexual behavior. Living under a caste system with two sets of behavior expectations is disruptive to U.S. identity for Negroes. Without a pragmatic ego-identity to minimize anxiety during the assimilation process in American cities, the Negro, "to a greater degree than other minorities, experiences personal and social disorganization, a result of the disintegrative function of identity conflict." A number of sexual patterns are noted among lower-class urban

Negroes. "Both males and females have sexual contact early in adolescence," for example. These sexual patterns may be explained by four hypotheses: the female status and freedom from anxiety hypothesis, the cultural negativism toward contraceptive hypothesis, the potency hypothesis, and the male hostility hypothesis. The disorganization of the urban Negro will be alleviated by the elimination of the Negro caste system. Based on recent studies of Negroes and other minorities; 21 notes.   D. J. Abramoske

2484. Derbyshire, Robert L. UNITED STATES NEGRO IDENTITY CONFLICT. *Sociol. and Social Res. 1966 51(1): 63-77.* "One hundred and two Negro college students were given an Osgood Semantic Differential Test which measures the meanings associated with a series of ethnic concepts. Data are presented in terms of the relationship between semantic distance and social distance. An insignificant rank-order correlation between social distance and semantic distance exhibited by these Negro college students for their own group as well as other minority and majority categories is interpreted as evidence of identity conflict."   J

2485. Deutsch, Martin. SOCIAL AND PSYCHOLOGICAL PERSPECTIVES ON THE DEVELOPMENT OF THE DISADVANTAGED LEARNER. *J. of Negro Educ. 1964 33(3): 232-244.* The author presents the thesis "that the behavioral scientist and the educator can facilitate the evolution of the educational institution for preparing all children for optimal social participation as the racial, social class, and sex gatekeepers become inoperative" and argues that the curriculum "should serve both for the primary prevention of the social deviancies associated with deprivation and for the stimulation of healthy growth and utilization of individual resources."   S. C. Pearson, Jr.

2486. Dilworth, Richardson. THE CHAOS OF OUR URBAN AREAS. *Pro. of the Am. Phil. Soc. 1968 112(6): 355-357.* Presents the author's views on current urban problems and their possible solution, especially as they relate to the Negro. Though recognizing the increased restiveness of the black community, the author insists that Negroes today have significantly improved economic and social opportunities. Frustration has arisen among blacks, however, largely because they have been unable to obtain the education required for the better jobs now open to them. There are basically two solutions to the problems: a systematic elimination of the ghetto and a substantial improvement in the educational systems of the large urban areas.   W. G. Morgan

2487. Dodd, John M. and Randall, Robert R. A COMPARISON OF NEGRO CHILDREN'S DRAWINGS OF A MAN AND A WOMAN. *J. of Negro Educ. 1966 35(3): 287-288.* Reports the findings of a study designed to determine whether the prekindergarten, culturally-deprived Negro children's drawings of men or women are more complete. Both boys and girls did draw more complete women than men, and, while the difference did not appear significant, the authors believe additional studies should be made.   S. C. Pearson, Jr.

2488. Doddy, Hurley H. THE PROGRESS OF THE NEGRO IN HIGHER EDUCATION. *J. of Negro Educ. 1963 32(4): 485-492.* Evaluates the quality of Negro higher education in the decade of the 1950's and suggests that in the present decade the institutions concerned may justify their continued existence by serving primarily a remedial function. S. C. Pearson, Jr.

2489. Dohrenwend, Bruce P. SOCIAL STATUS AND PSYCHOLOGICAL DISORDER: AN ISSUE OF SUBSTANCE AND AN ISSUE OF METHOD. *Am. Sociol. R. 1966 31(1): 14-34.* "The most consistent demographic finding reported in social psychiatric field studies is an inverse relation between social class and psychological disorder. This relationship has been interpreted on the one hand as evidence of social causation, with low status producing disorder, and on the other as evidence of social selection, with pre-existing disorder determining social status. This substantive issue could turn on a simple question of fact: whether Negroes and Puerto Ricans in New York City have higher or lower rates of disorder than their class counterparts in more advantaged ethnic groups. The facts, however, are not available from existing research. The results of field studies contain clues to group differences in modes of expressing distress, including some that involve problems of response bias, but the evidence is far from clear about the relation of the symptoms reported to the underlying psychiatric condition of individuals. It would seem that the substantive issue of social causation vs. social selection must yield precedence to resolution of the central unsolved problem of psychiatric epidemiology - the measurement of untreated psychological disorder." J

2490. Droettboom, Theodore, Jr., McAllister, Ronald J., Kaiser, Edward J. , and Butler, Edgar W. URBAN VIOLENCE AND RESIDENTIAL MOBILITY. *J. of the Am. Inst. of Planners 1971 37(5): 319-325.* "Data from a recently completed national longitudinal survey suggest, contrary to popular expectations, that individual perceptions of local violence have at best only a very moderate influence on significant changes in residential location, that concern with crime problems does not seem to result in a major exodus to the suburbs, and that what little effect urban crime has on mobility is stronger for the poor and black than for high and middle income whites. The findings are interpreted to indicate that those groups who are most affected by crime and violence, the poor and the black, are precisely those groups least able to escape the problem through residential relocation." J

2491. Dubey, Sumati N. and Grant, Morris L. POWERLESSNESS AMONG DISADVANTAGED BLACKS. *Social Casework 1970 51(5): 285-290.* Indicates the importance of Negroes' feelings of powerlessness, and suggests the implications for successful social work practice. For over 300 years, the social system has victimized the black American by denying him opportunities and advantages; in effect, society has suppressed the black's aggressive drive for self-assertion. Programs must be designed to help the black develop his sense of confidence, which means that blacks must participate in the formulation of programs, as well as in their implementation. 31 notes. M. A. Kaufman

2492. Dumas, W. Wayne and Lucas, Christopher. TEACHING ABOUT THE NEGRO'S STRUGGLE FOR SOCIAL EQUALITY IN INTEGRATED CLASSROOMS. *Social Studies 1970 61(1): 29-34.* Offers unique and elaborately organized plans for secondary instruction in interracial understanding, difficult to teach and test because of the controversial nature of such concepts as "social equality," "racial equality," "the same civil liberties," etc. The author includes suggestions for an instructional unit as well as guidelines for its implementation.

L. R. Raife

2493. Eatherly, Billy J. THE OCCUPATIONAL PROGRESS OF MISSISSIPPI NEGROES, 1940-1960. *Mississippi Q. 1968 21(1): 48-62.* Market segregation has been defined as the result of concentration of whites and Negroes in different skill categories so that the two racial groups do not effectively compete for comparable job levels. Using tables derived from U.S. census returns, this study concentrates on differences between the distribution among occupations of Mississippi Negroes and whites in order to assess the extent and effects of market segregation of the Negro labor force in Mississippi. Conclusions reached are that, between 1940 and 1960, the occupational position of male and female Negroes was lower in Mississippi than in the United States as a whole, and that they made much more progress in increasing their occupational position relative to whites in the United States as a whole than in Mississippi alone. The failure of previous indexes to consider female workers was a serious omission, since Negro females improved their relative occupational position much more rapidly than Negro males, both in the country as a whole and in Mississippi. Based mainly on published U.S. Census returns; 3 notes.

R. V. Calvert

2494. Edwards, G. Franklin. MARRIAGE AND FAMILY LIFE AMONG NEGROES. *J. of Negro Educ. 1963 32(4): 451-465.*

2495. Ekberg, Dennis and Ury, Claude. "EDUCATION FOR WHAT?" - A REPORT ON AN M.D.T.A. PROGRAM. *J. of Negro Educ. 1968 37(1): 15-22.* Problems encountered in conducting two 30-week sessions in a Manpower Development and Training Act program in Oakland, California, are discussed. Difficulties resulted from a conflict of values. The participants from the ghetto of West Oakland revealed family structures, a work ethic, and a failure orientation which militated against success in the program. It was concluded that the values being taught by MDTA - punctuality, responsibility, honesty - are in conflict with values held in the ghetto. The authors suggest that in such situations the values of middle-class society should be taught as if they were the characteristics of a foreign culture and that the ghetto community itself should be involved in shaping such programs. 15 notes.

S. C. Pearson, Jr.

2496. Elman, Richard M. NEAR WATTS: THE AMERICAN DREAM IN COMPTON, CAL. *Urban R. 1967 2(2): 5-9.* Compton, an upper-lower-class community of 75 thousand in southern Los Angeles County, was at one time considered a respectable town for housing both black and white people. With the trend in Los Angeles County for creating all white cities, one California editor predicted that Compton could become an all Negro city and found the possibility disquieting. The explosion in next door Watts caused many Negroes to move to this city, brought the black population to more than 50 percent, and accelerated the process of social degeneration. Nine of the city's citizens from various social, ethnic, and occupational backgrounds give brief impressions about the plight of the community. H. B. Powell

2497. Epps, Edgar G. SOCIOECONOMIC STATUS, RACE, LEVEL OF ASPIRATION AND JUVENILE DELINQUENCY: A LIMITED EMPIRICAL TEST OF MERTON'S CONCEPT OF DEVIATION. *Phylon 1967 28(1): 16-27.* Maintains that from Robert K. Merton's theory, expressed in *Social Theory and Social Structure* (New York: Macmillan, 1957), it can be assumed that juvenile delinquency is most prevalent in the lower socioeconomic strata, high aspirations for achieving success are held by individuals in all social strata, ethnic minorities because of limited access to legitimate avenues of achieving success have a high degree of delinquent behavior. To check these hypotheses, a test was administered to 346 juniors in a Seattle high school. Included in the sample were 159 white, 111 Negro, and 76 Oriental students. The findings do not support the hypotheses and the data secured do not uphold Merton's theory of deviant behavior. Based on a case study and published material; 21 notes. D. N. Brown

2498. Erskine, Hazel. THE POLLS: NEGRO FINANCES. *Public Opinion Q. 1969 33(2): 272-282.* A collection of public opinion polling questions based on nationwide samples of opinion taken between 1935 and 1967. Topics include "adequate income," "socioeconomic status," "satisfaction with income," "changes in financial status," "economic expectations," "financial resources," "family financial relationships," "attitude toward expenses," and "attitudes toward money." The majority of the findings derive from studies made by Elmo Roper for *Fortune* and the *Saturday Evening Post.* D. J. Trickey

2499. Fair, Daryl R. PENNSYLVANIA SUPREME COURT JUSTICES: A COLLECTIVE BIOGRAPHY, 1933-1963. *Pennsylvania Hist. 1968 35(3): 243-274.* This is a socioeconomic portrait of the 28 men who have served on the Pennsylvania Supreme Court from 1933 to 1963. All but 10 have been Republicans. Elected to 21-year terms, the mean length of service has been 11.5 years, with nine dying in office. The mean age of a new justice was 57.4 years. The average age of justices who die or resign from the court was 75.2. Twelve were born in cities, seven in small towns, and the rest were born in rural areas. All but five were of upper- or middle-class origins. Twenty-three were of Northern European background; no Negro has served on the court. Eighteen have specialized in the general practice of law, while five specialized in corporate law, one in criminal law, and two in property relations law. All but one have held public office, usually that of prosecutor or judge. Information is also given on their religions, military records, marital status, and educational backgrounds. Based on questionnaires sent to living judges and other sources; illus., 15 tables, 64 notes. D. C. Swift

2500. POVERTY IN THE URBAN GHETTO. *Current Hist. 1970 59(351): 283-289, 302.* The American city, with its blighted areas, can never be revitalized until it ceases to be a prison for the victims of poverty and racism. Today, urban poverty is primarily black poverty; urban crime is a related symptom of the disease of poverty. Opening suburbia to blacks, even locating attractive low-cost housing units in the suburbs and closer to the new industrial parks, will do as much to end poverty as billions spent for slum clearance and renewal.

B. D. Rhodes

2501. Fantini, Mario D. SCHOOL REFORM: EDUCATIONAL AGENDA FOR TOMORROW'S AMERICA. *Current Hist.* 1970 59(351): 267-272, 303-305. Urban school systems, once regarded as models of quality education, have been caught in a steadily worsening spiral of decline. During the 1960's, efforts to improve urban systems concentrated upon compensatory education, desegregation and integration, model subsystems, parallel systems, credit for tuition purposes, and participatory systems. Yet, we have been pouring money into an outdated system. In order to avoid some of the costly errors of the past, a new set of guiding assumptions must be developed for the 1970's and beyond.

B. D. Rhodes

2502. Farley, Reynolds and Hermalin, Albert I. FAMILY STABILITY: A COMPARISON OF TRENDS BETWEEN BLACKS AND WHITES. *Am. Sociol. R.* 1971 36(1): 1-17. "From the 1890s to the present, writers have commented upon the instability of Negro family life. Most have observed that discrimination in the job and housing markets have made it difficult for black men to support their wives and children. As a result, desertion occurs commonly. Family stability has been of interest because of the belief that children who grow up apart from their parents will be adversely affected. Indeed, some investigations imply that being raised in a home which did not have both parents is linked to lower rates of achievement in school, higher rates of delinquency and lower occupational status. While commentators have discussed family stability, there has been little consensus as to how this concept should be measured. Moreover, there are only a few demographic indicators available for operationalizing this concept, particularly if one desires to study long-term trends or to compare blacks and whites. The major portion of this paper examines Negro and white trends on a number of indicators related to a specific definition of family stability. This study concludes that (1) the majority of both blacks and whites are in the statuses indicative of family stability. Contrary to the images which are sometimes portrayed, most black families are husband-wife families, and the majority of black children live with both parents. (2) In every comparison, the proportion of people in the status indicative of family stability is greater among whites than among blacks. (3) In recent years there have been changes in family status, although most of them have been small. Some changes suggest a trend toward greater stability while others indicate a trend in the opposite direction."   J

2503. Fen, Sing-Nan. THE LEARNING OF SOCIAL RELATIONS IN SCHOOL. *J. of Negro Educ.* 1963 32(1): 87-91. The author draws from the published works of John Dewey to indicate that "intellectual learning should aim at socialization and socialization can be rationally redirected and expanded through appropriate intellectual studies. There is the relation between learning and socialization which constitutes another of Dewey's original contributions not only to philosophy of education but to social philosophy in general."

S. C. Pearson, Jr.

2504. Ferris, William R., Jr. RACIAL REPERTOIRES AMONG BLUES PERFORMERS. *Ethnomusicology 1970 14(3): 439-449.* "Black blues singers in Mississippi have 'racial repertoires' of music, the use of which is determined by whether the audience is white or black. Music performed for whites is characterized by concealment of racial protest and obscenity and by a musical style similar to white hillbilly music. James Thomas and Scott Dunbar are Mississippi blues singers who perform regularly for black and white audiences respectively. Their basically different repertoires reflect differing racial taste of black and white audiences. Thomas sings only traditional blues which are highly obscene and which sometimes deal with racial conflict. In contrast, over two-thirds of Dunbar's repertoire is sung and played in a non-blues style, relying heavily on songs recorded by white singers such as Eddy Arnold and Jimmy Davis. This research indicates that stylistic differences among black performers and their use or nonuse of narrative ballads and songs from the white tradition is a response to the racial taste of the singer's audience." AIA (2:1:102) I. J. Katz

2505. Fischer, Roger A. GHETTO AND GOWN: THE BIRTH OF BLACK STUDIES. *Current Hist. 1969 57(339): 290-294, 299-300.* As blacks discovered the potential of student power in the 1960's, they demanded the creation of programs in Black Studies. From the beginning, however, activists and academicians have clashed over how to define "Black Studies." To the traditionalist, Black Studies should emphasize historical subject matter; to the militant the stress should be upon advancing the black revolution in every facet of American life. Unless an equitable compromise is achieved, Black Studies will be damaged.

B. D. Rhodes

2506. Forbes, Gordon B. and Gipson, Marilyn. POLITICAL ATTITUDES AND OPINIONS, NEED FOR SOCIAL APPROVAL, DOGMATISM AND ANXIETY IN NEGRO AND WHITE COLLEGE STUDENTS. *J. of Negro Educ. 1969 38(1): 61-63.* Studies 20 Negro and 35 white college students in a midwestern university to test the stereotyped image of Negro students as strongly leftist politically, as dogmatic in their views, as highly anxious, and as low in need for middle-class social approval. It was found that the Negro students fit the stereotype (as compared to the white students) only in being more leftist politically and in having less need for social approval. Table, 6 notes.

B. D. Johnson

2507. Ford, Nick Aaron. THE FIRE NEXT TIME? A CRITICAL SURVEY OF BELLES LETTRES BY AND ABOUT NEGROES PUBLISHED IN 1963. *Phylon 1964 25(2): 123-134.* Reviews briefly James Baldwin's *The Fire Next Time* (1963); Gwendolyn Brook's *Selected Poems* (1963); Langston Hughes' *Five Plays;* William Gardner Smith's *The Stone Face;* John A. Williams' *Sissie;* Charles Wright's *The Messenger;* Mary Elizabeth Vroman's *Esther;* Gordon

Park's *The Learning Tree;* Richard Wright's *Lawd Today;* and Junior Edward's *If We Must Die;* Arna Bontemps' *American Negro Poetry;* and Herbert Hill's *Soon One Morning.*   S. C. Pearson, Jr.

2508. Form, William H. and Rytina, Joan. IDEOLOGICAL BELIEFS ON THE DISTRIBUTION OF POWER IN THE UNITED STATES. *Am. Sociol. R. 1969 34(1): 19-31.* "Although dominant ideologies represent a vindication of societal power arrangements, we hypothesized that specific belief systems vary by social strata. Annual family income, a major reward, was used as the chief indicator of stratal position. In a community study, we found that although the pluralistic model of power was selected most frequently as an accurate description of the way the system works, it was embraced most strongly by rich and middle-income strata. The poor and Negroes favored elitist and economic models of power more than other strata. When confronted with an interest-group model of power in Congress, all strata selected 'big business and the rich' as the most powerful groups. Yet the higher the income and education of the respondents, the less they believed that all groups *should* have equal political power. The poor and Negroes gave most normative support to political pluralism. These findings cast doubt on current theory concerning political authoritarianism of the poor and suggest that all strata differentially select existential and normative beliefs concerning the distribution of societal power. Stratal differences in such beliefs may play an important role in class political movements."   J

2509. Forslund, Morris A. STANDARDIZATION OF NEGRO CRIME RATES FOR NEGRO-WHITE DIFFERENCES IN AGE AND STATUS. *Rocky Mountain Social Sci. J. 1970 7(1): 151-160.* Since Negroes are overrepresented in the younger and young adult categories of population and in the lower socioeconomic levels, hypothesizes that the excess of Negro over white crime rate would be substantially reduced if crime rates were adjusted to take these differences into account. The author analyzed data from Stamford, Connecticut (1959-61), in testing the hypothesis. 4 tables, 19 notes.   R. F. Allen

2510. Fort, Edward B. DESEGREGATION AND THE BELGIAN CONGO SYNDROME. *Teachers Coll. Record 1968 69(6): 556-560.* By "Belgian Congo Syndrome" is meant the reluctance shown by middle-class Negroes who move into a newly desegregated neighborhood to challenge the status quo of educational practices in that area. The Negro fears that any interference on his part will cause the remaining whites to flee and more Negroes to move in, thus resulting in deterioration of the schools and the reappearance of the attitude of culture deprivation where none, in fact, may exist. The only hope to retain quality education in such cases is to exert pressure on administrative and teaching personnel to maintain educational standards. 8 notes.   C. P. McMahon

2511. Fredriksson, Conny. 1960-TALETS POLITISKA UTVECKLING I TENNESSEE [Political development in Tennessee in the 1960's]. *Statsvetenskaplig Tidskrift [Sweden] 1965 68(1): 389-409.* Examines shifting party voting patterns in Tennessee from 1960 through 1964, in both State level and presidential elections. Though Democrats dominate the national elections, Republicans are traditionally strong in the mountain areas of the east and southwest, and the strong Republican bids in 1964 senatorial races indicate a shift toward greater two-party competition in the State as a whole. In Memphis, new Republican strength rests on a white segregationist voting bloc, which has driven Negro, trade unionist, and liberal voters toward the liberal Democratic wing. Knoxville, with few Negro voters, shows no such clear realignment. Both Democrats and Republicans tend to split into conservative and moderate or liberal wings. Two-party competition is thus modified by a potential coalition between conservatives across party lines. Documented from newspapers, interviews, and printed statistics maps, charts.

R. G. Selleck

2512. Freedman, Alex S., ed. SYMPOSIUM: VIEWS ON AMERICAN POVERTY. *J. of Human Relations 1967 15(2): 146-168.*
Kaplan, Ben. THE CULTURE OF POVERTY: THE MORAL PERSPECTIVE, pp. 147-154. Presents "a brief descriptive profile of the culture of the poor," a culture for which we in America pay a heavy material and human price. "Poverty has its own language, its own color, its own odor, its own sounds, its own humor, its own sense of law and justice, its own interpretation of politics, religion and education, its own values regarding children and family life, and its own perspective of God and His universe." Poverty, in short, has its own culture, as culture lacking cohesiveness and generating nihilism. A paper presented at the annual meeting of the Louisiana Home Economics Association in September 1965.
Bertrand, Alvin L. POVERTY AS RELATIVE DEPRIVATION: A SOCIOLOGICAL VIEW, pp. 155-158. Defines poverty as "having too little of what is considered to be the basic necessities of life within our society." Various characteristics of poverty are discussed. A paper presented before a meeting of the University of Southwestern Louisiana Sociology Club in October 1965.
Siegmund, Peggy. POVERTY FROM BEHIND THE PLOW: THE RURAL GENERATION AND SPREAD OF AMERICAN POVERTY, pp. 158-168. Discusses rural poverty, finding that much of it is linked to the sharecropping system, mechanization, racial prejudice, and old age. The consequences of rural poverty include the very low level of education, the social isolation, and the degradation and distortion of the human personality. 11 notes.

D. J. Abramoske

2513. Friedman, S. Thomas, Pierce-Jones, John, Barron, W. E., and Caldwell, Bill S. PROJECT HEAD START: TEACHER INTEREST AND COMMITMENT. *Public Opinion Q. 1967 31(2): 279-284.* A comprehensive study of attitudes using autobiographical and opinion questionnaire data from 1,250 teachers to describe the teachers' initial attitude and expectations for the Head Start program. Factors studied were teachers' experience in working with children, volunteering for Head Start work, socioeconomic status, and ethnicity. Negro teachers evinced greater confidence in their abilities to be effective and in the program as a whole. Such factors as the socioeconomic origins of the teachers and the mode of entry into the project (volunteering) did not show basic influences on the attitudes of the various subgroups compared. Table, 3 notes.

D. H. Swift

2514. Friesema, H. Paul. BLACK CONTROL OF CENTRAL CITIES: THE HOLLOW PRIZE. *J. of the Am. Inst. of Planners 1969 35(2): 75-79.* "Given the distribution of power in the American political system, future control of central cities seems to offer Negroes very limited opportunities for gains. Some of the problems created by municipal dependence upon white state and federal legislatures are explored in this article, using alternate future scenarios as a prediction technique."   J

2515. Froe, Otis D. A COMPARATIVE STUDY OF A POPULATION OF "DISADVANTAGED" COLLEGE FRESHMEN. *J. of Negro Educ. 1968 37(4): 370-382.* Compares freshmen at Morgan State College (predominantly Negro) and freshmen at several other colleges which are predominantly white. The author found significant differences in their goals, family backgrounds, and attitudes. These variables indicate a need for more relevant college planning in dealing with these different groups. 4 tables.   B. D. Johnson

2516. Froe, Otis D. EDUCATIONAL PLANNING FOR DISADVANTAGED COLLEGE YOUTH. *J. of Negro Educ. 1964 33(3): 290-303.* Asserts that planning must be based on a careful analysis of student needs, characterizes "disadvantaged" college youth, and makes proposals which may be useful in assisting them in academic achievement.   S. C. Pearson, Jr.

2517. Fuller, Hoyt W. REVERBERATIONS FROM A WRITERS' CONFERENCE. *African Forum 1965 1(2): 78-84.* Views the basic problem confronting Negro writers: whether to depict truthfully the life they know and risk attack from critics or to pad and distort their views so as to appeal to a broader and more receptive public. "The deepening estrangement of the Negro writer from the so-called 'mainstream' of American literature was vividly illustrated" during a conference held in New York in 1965. Speakers at the conference included such literary figures as James Baldwin, John O. Killens, and LeRoi Jones. The conference stressed the widening gap between the critics and Negro writers and, as the critic refuses to acknowledge the writer, the public loses interest in Negro novels. The future lies in critical acceptance of Negro artists on the artists' own merits.
                                                                                                                              M. J. McBaine

2518. Funnye, Clarince. THE MILITANT BLACK SOCIAL WORKER AND THE URBAN HUSTLE. *Social Work 1970 15(2): 5-12.* Urges black social workers to develop militant and special responses to the problems of black people and to resist the divisionary urban repair and antipoverty programs as well as those social work theories and practices that are institutionalizing the new urban hustle, which exploits not only blacks, but all poverty-stricken minority groups. Urban research studies, model cities programs, and neighborhood manpower training projects are critically evaluated as major forms of the urban hustle. Guidelines for a new philosophical approach are presented. 16 notes.
                                                                                                                              W. L. Willigan

2519. Gallaway, Lowell E. THE NEGRO AND POVERTY. *J. of Business 1967 40(1): 27-35.* Evaluates the relative contribution to Negro poverty of 1) educational differences between Negroes and whites and 2) a composite of all other elements correlated with race. The process of income distribution was based on D. G. Champernowne's "A Model of Income Distribution," in *Economic Journal,* June 1953. Records of the Social Security Administration were used to gather pertinent data. From an analysis of the data considering factors affecting the one-period transition rates and the permanence of poverty, concludes that education and race factors equally are causes of poverty-level income. Poverty is also greater among workers with a prior history of poverty levels of income. While race factors are not as easily definable as those of education, both should be considered in determining policy. Based on secondary sources and the records of the Social Security Administration; 5 tables, 15 notes.   C. A. Gallacci

2520. Gass, Oscar. TENSIONS AND CONSERVATISM IN AMERICAN POLITICS. *Commentary 1966 42(5): 63-70.* A general survey of the progress and status of the Great Society in the fall of 1966. The early progress in Great Society programs has slowed down to an unexciting consolidating action, which, together with various failures in the program and "convictions of public injustice." have "distinctly tarnished" the "image of the Great Society." The situation of American Negroes is particularly unsatisfactory. The author presents a program for the substantial furthering of Great Society aspirations, "contained within the limits of American economic conservatism." Using only the projected increase of about 60 billion dollars in Federal revenue in 1970 (that is, without touching any present wealth or property) the following would be provided: a national system of unemployment; a rise in foreign aid to one percent of GNP; regular increases in benefit rates on old-age pensions and the like; a national program of minimum medical insurance; substantial reduction of income taxes for low-income groups; and substantial increase in Federal spending in all social welfare areas. Such a program would make the Great Society much closer to a reality for a large number of people while still not entailing any major changes in American economic or political life.   A. K. Main

2521. Gass, Oscar. THE POLITICAL ECONOMY OF THE GREAT SOCIETY. *Commentary 1965 40(4): 31-36.* After a brief review of the political forces which shaped the economy of the United States in the critical years of 1896 and 1932, the author points out that in 1964 Lyndon Baines Johnson broke decisively with the Roosevelt tradition of Democratic Party estrangement from the established leaders of the American business community. "What is new today is that many sophisticated businessmen believe that, in Washington, it is the Democratic party leadership which is the more skillful and useful. This belief may make 1964 as great a break with its political antecedents as were 1932 and 1896....In the summer of 1965,Lyndon Johnson heads the strongest political coalition since the New Deal....It has a near monopoly of the political Left - the trade unions, the Negroes, and the ethnic minorities.And it reaches deep into the political Right.... I believe it to be greatly unlikely that the demand managers, who act for the coalition, will now move deliberately toward full employment. Full employment is a condition which can be borne, in good health, only by societies that have other *effective* sources of restraint than the market....Our demand managers judge that American society cannot." D. D. Cameron

2522. Gayle, Addison, Jr. THE QUIET REVOLUTION: THE PRE-BAC-CALAUREATE PROGRAM OF THE CITY COLLEGE. *J. of Human Relations 1968 16(3): 301-314.* Discusses the program conducted by the City College of New York since the summer of 1965. Negro and Puerto Rican children lack motivation because an indifferent society has assumed that such children cannot learn. The first basic objective of the program is "to set up an educational situation in which the student has an opportunity to improve his scholarship to the level of standards he could not meet at the time of the initial application." The college has established what is in effect a protracted entrance process which may last a year or longer. The staff works closely with the students on a personal basis, employing a variety of pedagogical, administrative, and advisory services to develop in the student an attitude that will enable him to achieve academically and live with a reasonable expectation of attaining professional status after graduation. The program has been such a success that it may well "result in an overhaul of the archaic admissions and selective machinery of America's higher educational system." 9 notes. D. J. Abramoske

2523. Gersh, G. THE ECONOMIC ADVANCES OF THE AMERICAN NE-GRO. *Contemporary R. [Great Britain] 1965 207(1196): 134-139.* Assesses the improvements in the American Negro's economic position. Comparison with 1930 indicates that the incomes of Negroes in Houston, Texas, have doubled since 1940, reflecting an increase in wage-earners per household. Their spending patterns reflect both practical emulation of white luxury standards and social insecurity. Negroes in Atlanta, Georgia, live more segregated lives than in Houston, yet within this area Negro business (notably life insurance) has grown markedly. A general survey shows that the economic gulf between white and black is narrowing, that the Negro has been the chief beneficiary of the decline in immigration, and, though he may need more educational opportunities, the American Negro is not "dispossessed" in any real economic sense. D. H. Murdoch

2524. Gerson, Walter M. MASS MEDIA SOCIALIZATION BEHAVIOR: NE-GRO-WHITE DIFFERENCES. *Social Forces 1966 45(1): 40-50.* "This paper is a comparative analysis of differences between 351 Negro and 272 white adolescents in their uses of the mass media as an agency of socialization. Through the use of indexes to measure two socialization behaviors - media reinforcement and media norm-acquiring - it was possible to empirically differentiate between media socializees and non-media-socializees. The data indicate that, under almost every condition considered in the analysis, more Negro than white adolescents were media socializees. The interpretation of the data suggests that many Negro adolescents are using the mass media to learn how to behave like whites (i.e., behave in a socially acceptable way). An attempt is made to explain the findings by the consideration of a Negro subcommunity which is a partially bounded subsystem within the larger community system and which is the result of three types of mechanisms of maintenance: (1) ecological and social segregation of Negro-white interactions; (2) self-conceptions of Negro children; and (3) subcultural differences between white and Negro communities." J

2525. Geschwender, James A. SOCIAL STRUCTURE AND THE NEGRO REVOLT: AN EXAMINATION OF SOME HYPOTHESES. *Social Forces 1964 43(2): 248-256.* "An attempt is made to examine objective structural conditions in order to provide a sociological interpretation of the current Negro revolt. The sociological literature is examined and five structural hypotheses are derived. Data on the changing position of the nonwhite in the United States are examined. Nonwhites are found to be improving their position in terms of level of education, type of occupation, and amount of income. They are found to be improving their position relative to whites in level of education and in holding middle status occupations but not upper status occupations. They are falling further behind whites in income. It seems likely that the proportion of status inconsistents among Negroes is increasing. The data are inconsistent with two of the derived hypotheses and are consistent with the other three. These latter hypotheses are reconciled in terms of a single common denominator. Changes in objective conditions cause feelings of relative deprivation, which, in turn, produce a tendency toward protest and rebellion." J

2526. Gist, Noel P. and Bennett, William S., Jr. ASPIRATIONS OF NEGRO AND WHITE STUDENTS. *Social Forces 1963 42(1): 40-48.* Cognitive patterns of Negro students are similar to those for white students. Negroes in the sample studied had higher occupational mobility aspirations than whites. The matricentric family was a characteristic of the Negro group. However, mothers, both white and Negro, assume the major role for educational guidance in the family. In this study of 873 Negro and white students, the North-Hatt occupational prestige scale is used as modified by Leonard Reissman. 10 tables. A. S. Freedman

2527. Gittell, Marilyn. A PILOT STUDY OF NEGRO MIDDLE CLASS ATTITUDES TOWARD HIGHER EDUCATION IN NEW YORK. *J. of Negro Educ. 1965 34(4): 385-394.* In this study of one hundred Negro families in the Jamaica section of Queens every respondent indicated that he intended to send his children to college. Greater concern in selection of a college and in consideration of problems attendant to higher education was evidenced by the higher-income, college-educated, and northern-born parents than by lower-income, noncollege-educated, and southern-born parents. The latter group's attitude toward New York City colleges was more indifferent or negative than was that of the former group. S. C. Pearson, Jr.

2528. Glazer, Nathan. THE PUERTO RICANS. *Commentary 1963 36(1): 1-9.* Analyzes migration, assimilation, and adjustment patterns of Puerto Ricans who have settled in New York City, with emphasis on their family structure, housing, religion, voting habits, social and sexual mores, employment and business activities, organizational life, and relationships with other ethnic groups and with Puerto Rico. Though many of these newcomers live in a "veritable sea of misery" and present difficult problems for New York City's schools and welfare agencies, the migrants' experience has on the whole been "remarkably successful," following the path taken by earlier ethnic groups like the Jews and Italians rather than that of the American Negro. The Puerto Ricans' most significant contribution to New York may well turn out to be their indifference to the color bar which has marked American social behavior.   J. J. Appel

2529. Glenn, Norval D. NEGRO POPULATION CONCENTRATION AND NEGRO STATUS. _J. of Negro Educ. 1967 36(4): 353-361._ Examines the allegation that Negro population concentration and Negro status are inversely related through an analysis of 1960 census data for 179 urbanized areas. The data do not clearly support the hypothesis that Negro population concentration and Negro status are inversely related. In areas of high concentration there is some overflow of Negro workers into intermediate level occupations, but this gain is offset by lower income levels and higher unemployment rates in such areas. The study casts doubt on the theory that a more nearly even distribution of the Negro population in the United States would in itself appreciably aid Negro advancement.   S. C. Pearson, Jr.

2530. Glenn, Norval D. SOME CHANGES IN THE RELATIVE STATUS OF AMERICAN NONWHITES. 1940 TO 1960. _Phylon 1963 24(2): 109-122._ The following applies mainly to Negroes. Examination of changes relative to occupational, income, and educational status shows advance as greater in the 1940's than the 1950's. Nationwide gain was greater than in any one region, except the West. A major influence was a movement of nonwhites from the South, where their status was lowest. The greatest gains came from war-induced opportunities in both the 1940's and 1950's. Nonwhite employment opportunities were hurt by mechanization, which profited whites. Education of nonwhites improved more than income. In desirable occupations, nonwhites gained greatest in professional capacities, rather than managerial and proprietory capacities.
                                                                      L. Filler

2531. Globetti, Gerald. A COMPARATIVE STUDY OF WHITE AND NEGRO TEENAGE DRINKING IN TWO MISSISSIPPI COMMUNITIES. _Phylon 1967 28(2): 131-138._ Suggests that use of alcohol in America is a culturally defined pattern which varies according to subgroup affiliation and membership. In the South, Negro and white youth represent two distinct subgroups. Thus, it was assumed that varying drinking patterns would emerge. The study showed that, contrary to the belief by laymen that drinking is unrestrained in Negro society, consumption of alcohol among Negro students was governed more by adults than among whites. This suggests Negro adults regard teenage drinking as more acceptable than do white adults, and train their children for an adult role which will include the use of alcohol. With regard to the sociocultural factors that influence teenage drinking, Negro and white youth were virtually indistinguishable. Based on a study conducted by the Department of Sociology and Anthropology, Mississippi State University; 2 charts, 13 notes.   D. N. Brown

2532. Glock, Charles Y. IMAGES OF MAN AND PUBLIC OPINION. _Public Opinion Q. 1964 28(4): 539-546._ As social science defines more and more precisely the roles of free will and determinism in human behavior, man's concept of his own nature changes; consequently, his opinions change and political, economic, and social problems also change. The strains produced by these various images generate much of the social discord and political strife in contemporary America. The application of these varying views of man's ability to control his own fate is illustrated by the cases of the Negro and of socialized medicine. Address by the president at the annual conferences of the American Association for Public Opinion Research and the World Association for Public Opinion Research, 9 May 1964. E. P. Stickney

2533. Goldberg, Steven Brown. THE CONCEPT OF HIPNESS: THE SEARCH FOR A MEANINGFUL DEFINITION. *J. of Popular Culture 1968 2(4): 613-623.* Discusses the evolving meaning of "hipness" as a sociological concept. The term "hip" traditionally referred to persons - usually Negroes - whose life-styles were characterized by alienation and deviance from, coolness toward, awareness of, and criminality within the dominant social order. More recently, however, "hipness" has evolved away from violence and activism and toward "music, drugs, interpersonal relationships and introspection as sources of meaning." Based on secondary sources; 14 notes. B. A. Lohof

2534. Goldman, Ralph M. THE POLITICS OF POLITICAL INTEGRATION. *J. of Negro Educ. 1964 33(1): 26-34.* Discusses the integration of Negroes as citizens and as party politicians and the integration of their organized group interests. Concludes that when Negroes are randomly distributed in the "citizenry of a self-governing nation, within the political parties, and among the pressure groups - we shall be able to say that Negro political integration has taken place." S. C. Pearson, Jr.

2535. Goldsmith, Harold F. and Lee, S. Young. SOCIOECONOMIC STATUS WITHIN THE OLDER AND LARGER 1960 METROPOLITAN AREAS. *Rural Sociol. 1966 31(2): 207-215.* "The average socioeconomic status of the resident white and nonwhite populations of city, suburb, and fringe zones of the older and larger SMSAs [Standard Metropolitan Statistical Areas] in 1960 was investigated. The pattern most often observed was that suburbs had higher average levels than cities or fringe areas, and fringe areas had higher levels than cities. Only the magnitude of the differences between suburbs and cities was considered large. For the white population alone, the average status levels of cities and fringe areas were about equal and slightly below those of suburbs. For nonwhite residents, in contrast, the most consistently observed pattern was for cities to have higher SES [Socioeconomic Status] levels than suburbs which in turn had higher SES levels than fringe areas. Thus, systematic differences in socioeconomic status existed among the city, suburbs, and fringe zones of older and larger SMSAs. However, the differences were small when race was controlled." J

2536. Goldstein, Marcus S. LONGEVITY AND HEALTH STATUS OF THE NEGRO AMERICAN. *J. of Negro Educ. 1963 32(4): 337-348.*

2537. Gosnell, Harold F. and Martin, Robert E. THE NEGRO AS VOTER AND OFFICE-HOLDER. *J. of Negro Educ. 1963 32(4): 415-425.* Traces the impact of the Negro on politics in the United States from 1950 to 1960.

S. C. Pearson, Jr.

2538. Graebner, Norman A. AMERICAN NOMINATING POLITICS AND THE FAILURE OF CONSENSUS: 1968. *Australian J. of Pol. and Hist. 1968 14(3): 393-408.* Analyzes the presidential candidates of 1968 and draws a contrast between the "old" politics which gave Nixon and Humphrey the nominations and the "new" politics of Rockefeller, McCarthy, Kennedy, and McGovern, which revealed widespread opposition to the Johnson administration's Vietnam policy. The old New Deal coalition of labor, the South, the Negroes, the city and county bosses, and the urban intellectuals, held firm in the 1960's and maintained successful policies of containment. However, European stability, deterrence, detente with Russia, prosperity and full employment, the rise of the mass media, and the spread of higher education (all evidences of progress) caused a shift in interest from abundance to the quality of life. The new concern of the affluent middle classes for the economic and racial outcasts threatened the interests of the large new lower-middle class of white blue-collar workers who felt endangered by rising taxes, inflation and Negro demands. The Vietnam War accelerated these tendencies through its demand for men and material. The author discusses the actions of Johnson, McCarthy, Kennedy, Romney, Nixon, Rockefeller, Humphrey, Wallace, and McGovern, and stresses Humphrey's and Nixon's success in securing the party regulars. Documented from newspapers.   D. McIntyre

2539. Green, Edward. RACE, SOCIAL STATUS, AND CRIMINAL ARREST. *Am. Sociol. R. 1970 35(3): 476-490.* "The Negro-white arrest rate differential for selected years between 1942 and 1965 in a northern industrial community is analyzed with respect to age, sex, and the socioeconomic variables of employment status, occupation, and migration. Although the incidence of recorded Negro crime has greatly increased since 1942 owing to the increase in the Negro population, the rate of Negro crime has decreased. The magnitude of the excess of the Negro over the white arrest rate reflects the wider distribution among Negroes of the lower social class characteristics of unemployment, employment in unskilled and semiskilled occupations, and migration from the rural South. The findings do not support color-caste theories which interpret Negro criminal behavior as a response to racial proscriptions or which construe Negro criminality as a function of racially suppressive law enforcement tactics."

J

2540. Green, Philip. DECENTRALIZATION, COMMUNITY CONTROL, AND REVOLUTION. *Massachusetts R. 1970 11(3): 415-441.* Discusses the issues of the 1968 Ocean Hill-Brownsville school dispute, which closed the New York City public school system. Argues that American society accepts only that pluralism which makes no substantive changes in the institutional patterns of the majoritarian society. Contends that community control, which offers Negroes a viable alternative to a liberal pluralism which has been found sadly wanting, is a threat which the majoritarian power structure cannot abide. Sees the teachers of New York and their union, the United Federation of Teachers, as the agents of a coercive State power, using "due process of law" as a club to maintain their oppressive power over the city's schoolchildren. Concludes that the failure of community control will prove disastrous for the viability of a democratic social order. 13 notes.   G. Kurland

2541. Green, Robert L. and Hofmann, Louis J. A CASE STUDY OF THE EFFECTS OF EDUCATIONAL DEPRIVATION ON SOUTHERN RURAL NEGRO CHILDREN. *J. of Negro Educ. 1965 34(3): 327-341.* A study of the impact of extended educational deprivation upon the measured academic achievement and intelligence of Negro children in Prince Edward County, Virginia, both before and one year after the resumption of formal academic training. It was found that extended educational deprivation had a significant effect upon the development of academic achievement and measured intelligence which was not entirely compensated for by later education.   S. C. Pearson, Jr.

2542. Greenberg, Edward S. CHILDREN AND GOVERNMENT: A COMPARISON ACROSS RACIAL LINES. *Midwest J. of Pol. Sci. 1970 14(2): 249-275.* Investigates the differences between black and white children's evaluation and relation to government. "The greatest racial disparities appear in children's assessment of government benevolence," which shows a decline in black attitudes between the third and seventh grades, but an increase during junior high school. "Environment and political events thus seem to have a great impact on children's political orientations. Awareness of the deprivation around them but later information about favorable government activities seems to account for the pattern of decline and recovery." Based on a survey of 980 Philadelphia school children taken in 1968; 11 illus., 4 tables, 28 notes.   J. W. Thacker, Jr.

2543. Greene, Maxine. RETURN TO COMMUNITY? *Teachers Coll. Record 1968 69(5): 484-490.* The Bundy report, *Reconnection for Learning,* submitted to the Mayor of New York by his Advisory Panel on Decentralization of the New York City Schools, and subtitled "A Community School System for New York City," declares that New York's public school system is failing because large numbers of children are not learning adequately. Other urban centers are faced with the same dilemma - that of lost confidence by the people in the public schools, of disillusionment, of protests, etc. The remedy for this failure is the return of the schools to the control of the local community. Centralization has resulted in producing two school systems, with one (the black one) inferior to the other. A number of recent accounts of ghetto education, as well as thought-provoking essays and talks, has attested to this situation. It must also be remembered that parent participation in the running of the schools means power, and often racism. We need "liberating decentralization," but liberation from what? The answers may come with the deliberate creation of the community of tradition, the face-to-face community.   C. P. McMahon

2544. Greenstone, J. David. POLITICAL NORMS AND GROUP PROCESS IN PRIVATE GOVERNMENT: THE CASE OF A LOCAL UNION. *Midwest J. of Pol. Sci. 1965 9(4): 339-361.* Attempts to show that the political norms of industrial union Local 718 "are as important as its group structure in determining the union's prospects for democracy." This union, chosen for case study, is distinguished by Negro minority control. The author concludes that minority control is perpetuated because of the lack of "development of political leadership roles through factions and accountable steward representatives," and "a preference for direct rather than constitutional democracy." Illus., 3 tables, 31 notes.

J. W. Thacker, Jr.

2545. Greer, Colin. IMMIGRANTS, NEGROES AND THE PUBLIC SCHOOLS. *Urban R. 1969 3(3): 9-12.* It has been assumed that the public school has been the agency for upward mobility among immigrants in making the American "melting pot" work. Factories, unions, and ethnic communities instead of public schools have been the means of upward mobility. Getting a high school education for a majority of immigrant families has followed economic and social success. In contrast, Negroes have not been able to follow the traditional route of European immigrants into middle-class America.   H. B. Powell

2546. Grossack, Martin M. PSYCHOLOGICAL CONSIDERATIONS ESSENTIAL TO EFFECTIVE EDUCATIONAL INTEGRATION. *J. of Negro Educ. 1965 34(3): 278-287.* A psychotherapist suggests that educational integration must be accompanied by massive expenditures to transform conditions of Negro social life, that integration must be total, and that the mental health of the entire society depends upon such integration though it is not guaranteed by integration. The author champions the Freedom Clubs which are integrated groups in public schools designed for individual adjustment. It is advised that children be given mental health adjustment education including help for Negro children in dealing with their feelings about prejudice exhibited toward them by white children, about inferiority, and their fear of competition. Documented.

S. C. Pearson, Jr.

2547. Gulley, William H. RELATIVE EFFECTIVENESS IN NEGRO AND WHITE VOLUNTARY ASSOCIATIONS. *Phylon 1963 24(2): 172-183.* This exploratory study employed a small sample, not using random procedures. Negroes tended to be more critical of their organizations than were whites. They felt, more than did the latter, that soliciting financial support from the public was essential to their operations. An NAACP official pointed to the drain on finances by court actions and believed these were deliberately instigated by whites to bankrupt the NAACP. White voluntary organizations are much more adequately staffed than Negro, which are as large, and which seek to acquire voluntary workers. Contacts with the Negro community are impeded by illiteracy, fear of reprisal, and "lack of role definition." Lack of rewards may explain some voluntary worker inefficiency. Northern Negroes tend to pre-empt leadership, but there may be changes as a consequence of the "sit-in" movement.

L. Filler

2548. Gurin, Patricia and Epps, Edgar. SOME CHARACTERISTICS OF STUDENTS FROM POVERTY BACKGROUNDS ATTENDING PREDOMINANTLY NEGRO COLLEGES IN THE DEEP SOUTH. *Social Forces 1966*

45(1): 27-39. "This study examines the motivations and environmental influences of 3,112 Deep South Negro students who, despite severe obstacles, were attending predominantly Negro colleges in that area. The students range from a *severe poverty* level to a *comfortable income* level. Our data indicate that regardless of the intactness of the home, the lower the family income the greater is the influence of nonfamily figures, especially the high school teacher, in the decision to go to college. While the *severe poverty* and the *comfortable* groups differ in income, family structure, etc., they are strikingly similar in their motivations and in the values they attach to educational goals. They do differ, however, in their expectancies of reaching their goals. The data suggest that factors such as family structure and early socialization, which are usually considered crucial, are not necessarily so." J

2549. Hadden, Jeffrey K., Masotti, Louis H., and Thiessen, Victor. THE MAKING OF THE NEGRO MAYORS 1967. *Transaction 1968 5(3): 21-30.* A discussion of how Carl Stokes and Richard Hatcher became the first two Negro mayors of major cities in the United States. The bulk of the analysis deals with Stokes' victory in Cleveland. Stokes won in 1967 whereas he lost in 1965 because he increased his vote in the Negro wards as well as in the white wards and the mixed wards. A close inquiry is made into the reasons for his increase in each of these cases.Stokes' victory in Cleveland was much more biracial than Hatcher's in Gary. The authors feel that in both cases the margin of victory was narrow enough to force the victors to proceed with caution. Negroes elected to office must indicate to their Negro constituents that such election can make a change in their lives. Negro mayors must also continue to share power with white elements in the political structure. It is felt that at best these elections purchased some additional time in which to solve the complex problems of race and urban society. Based on personal observation and newspaper reports; 2 tables, illus.
A. Erlebacher

2550. Hadwiger, Don F. THE FREEMAN ADMINISTRATION AND THE POOR. *Agric. Hist. 1971 45(1): 21-32.* Discusses hunger, racism, and Department of Agriculture policy during the Kennedy and Johnson administrations, emphasizing the final two years of the period. Because of political priorities within the Democratic administration and the power of three Capitol Hill chairmen who opposed effective food distribution programs, Orville Lothrop Freeman, Secretary of Agriculture, and other liberals in the Department of Agriculture did not enlighten the Nation about hunger, poverty, and racism in rural America or work wholeheartedly to solve these problems. Instead, the department was an instrument in thwarting efforts to achieve substantial reforms within the system. Based primarily on government documents; 32 notes.
D. E. Brewster

2551. Haisch, H. M. DO CHILD LABOR LAWS PREVENT YOUTH EMPLOYMENT? *J. of Negro Educ. 1964 33(2): 182-185.* Criticizes the opinion that legal regulation of child labor is responsible for widespread unemployment of young people and that such legislation is no longer necessary. Insists that only better understanding of existing laws is needed.
S. C. Pearson, Jr.

2552. Hamilton, Charles V. RACE AND EDUCATION: A SEARCH FOR LEGITIMACY. *Harvard Educational R. 1968 38(4):669-684.* Black communities raise the problem of the legitimacy of the existing educational system and are not necessarily inclined to accept the counsel of experts who seek to improve the existing order. The author holds that it is more important today to understand the black critics than the experts. Black communities seek a new order for the schools in which black parents strive to participate in the education of their children and question the professionals. They ask to recognize and accept diverse views and secular political cultures, and may opt, where possible, for a comprehensive community institution, comprising welfare, credit unions, law enforcement, recreational programs, and schooling as a center for participation by all members of the community.   J. Herbst

2553. Hamilton, Homer. "THEY SPOKE OF THEIR FUTURES WITH HOPE." *J. of Negro Educ. 1965 34(2): 184-187.* A report on the "Young at Heart" project at Jackson State College, one of five summer enrichment projects for high school youth, conducted in 1964 and participated in by 100 Negro high school students.   S. C. Pearson, Jr.

2554. Hannerz, Ulf. WHAT NEGROES MEAN BY "SOUL." *Trans-action 1968 5(8): 57-61.* Inquires about the meaning of "soul" to Negroes. Simply, it signifies the central essence of being black. It is a folk concept most common to the urban slum dweller. The influence of religion on the Negro is reflected in it. It has strong connotations of racial pride. It manifests itself in the Negro's food and in his music, especially when it is given a sense of perfection of achievement. The author offers many examples of how "soul" enters the daily life of the Negro or how he uses it to describe his way of life. The author believes that the motive of soul is to produce a vocabulary which denotes superiority both to one's self as well as to others. There would be little agreement by Negroes on a precise and narrow definition of soul. Soul is a part of a "piecemeal rhetoric attempt to establish a satisfactory self-image." Photo.   A. Erlebacher

2555. Hare, Nathan. RECENT TRENDS IN THE OCCUPATIONAL MOBILITY OF NEGROES, 1930-1960: AN INTRACOHORT ANALYSIS. *Social Forces 1965 44(2): 166-172.* "An intracohort analysis of occupational trends produced more consistent results than did conventional approaches to the study of labor force change. There was a trend of convergence between the occupational distributions of white and Negro males from 1930 to 1940 and, especially, from 1940 to 1950, which did not hold, however, during the fifties. Figures for the South showed a trend of convergence similar to that of the country as a whole during the 1940's, but, in contrast to popular opinion, the Negro lost notable occupational ground in the South during the fifties. The factor of education was found to be of special importance for the Negro's mobility during periods of substantial occupational change."   J

2556. Hargrett, Andrew J. THE EDUCATION-UNEMPLOYMENT RELATIONSHIP IN CHICAGO AS REVEALED IN THE 1960 CENSUS. *J. of Negro Educ. 1965 34(2): 121-129.* The study grew out of an investigation of the community of Englewood in Chicago. It was found that neighborhoods of the same average grade level may vary widely in unemployment rates, reflecting such factors as race, socioeconomic status, extent of diversity of foreign language heritage, and geographic relation to industries. Thus the study suggests that while "there is a relationship of education to unemployment rates,...this relationship is not the strong factor which many...seem to believe to exist."

S. C. Pearson, Jr.

2557. Harris, Edward E. FAMILY AND STUDENT IDENTITIES: AN EX-PLORATORY STUDY IN SELF AND "WE-GROUP" ATTITUDES. *J. of Negro Educ. 1965 34(1): 17-22.* Explores the influence of race, sex, and the combined influence of race and sex on the presence and absence of family, self, and "we-group" attitudes. The family self-identity appeared more often among females and whites. Family "we-group" identities were found among a relatively small proportion of the respondents. Almost all respondents identified themselves in terms of a student self-identity. Studied were students from two midwestern universities, one predominantly white and one predominantly Negro.

S. C. Pearson, Jr.

2558. Harrison, E. C. WORKING AT IMPROVING THE MOTIVATIONAL AND ACHIEVEMENT LEVELS OF THE DEPRIVED. *J. of Negro Educ. 1963 32(3): 301-307.* Provides an account of the efforts of the Louisiana Education Association to encourage Negro schools in Louisiana to become concerned with raising the achievement levels of students. The author summarizes the proceedings of three conferences held for this purpose in 1960-61.

S. C. Pearson, Jr.

2559. Harrison, Ira E. THE STATE EMPLOYMENT SERVICE AND THE ATTITUDES OF "UNEMPLOYABLE" DROPOUTS. *J. of Negro Educ. 1966 35(2): 134-143.* Describes the attitudes of "unemployable" dropouts toward the Office of the State Employment Service in Syracuse, New York. Such attitudes are generally favorable (42.3 percent) or neutral or ambivalent (40.1 percent). However, dropouts want work which they can handle, and their attitudes toward the employment service become negative as they continue to experience failure. Proposals are made for fostering positive attitudes on the assumption that the service cannot help alienated youth who cease frequenting the employment office. Based on interviews with 60 boys under the age of 18. S. C. Pearson, Jr.

2560. Hart, Joe W. A STUDY OF THE EFFECTS OF EFFORTS TO IM-PROVE EMPLOYMENT OPPORTUNITIES OF NEGROES ON THE UTI-LIZATION OF NEGRO WORKERS. *J. of Human Relations 1964 12(3): 421-423.* A report on Negro employment in 10 types of establishments "in a large Southern city (Negro population, 35 per cent)." Truck lines and storage companies, for example, have a total of 555 employees including 164 Negroes. Brief comments describe the practices of each type of establishment in hiring Negroes. Based on interviews. D. J. Abramoske

2561. Hart, Joe W. EFFECTS OF AUTOMATION ON THE POSITION OF NEGROES IN A SOUTHERN INDUSTRIAL PLANT. *J. of Human Relations 1964 12(3): 419-421.* Describes the position of Negro production workers at a plant located "in a mid-Southern city in a metropolitan area of 750,000 people." The plant studied has approximately two thousand workers, of which six hundred are Negroes. They have done fairly well in this plant, but further improvement is difficult because of the effects of automation. The author concludes that adult education and retraining programs as well as more active Negro participation in labor union affairs would help. Based on "200 depth interviews" conducted in the workers' homes. D. J. Abramoske

2562. Hartman, Chester W. and Carr, Gregg. HOUSING AUTHORITIES RECONSIDERED. *J. of the Am. Inst. of Planners 1969 35(1): 10-21.* "The local public housing authority is a product of the 'good government' ethic of the 1920's and 1930's, which postulates that certain public welfare programs should be run by disinterested laymen - representing 'the best of the community' - who will keep these programs 'out of politics.' A nationwide survey of authority commissioners indicates widespread lack of knowledge about and sympathy with the housing programs they administer and the low-income families they serve. Inherent disparities between the commissioner group - who are white and of high socioeconomic status - and public housing clientele - largely low-income black families - are one possible source of this conflict. It is suggested that the housing authority system currently acts as a barrier to expanded and improved housing programs for the poor, and instead agencies, which will aggressively advocate the interests of those in need of decent low-cost housing, are needed. Possible alternatives to the quasi-independent housing authority include establishment of a department directly responsible to the elected chief executive, greater federal and/or state involvement, and decentralization of housing program administration to give greater control to community organizations." J

2563. Hastie, Elizabeth. A BATTLEFRONT IN THE WAR ON POVERTY. *New England Social Studies Bull. 1965 23(1): 13-18.* As a member of the staff, Miss Hastie provides a brief history of the origin and development, successes and failures of the St. James Pre-Kindergarten School in a Negro ghetto in Roxbury, Massachusetts. The school worked with parents as well as with children, and sought to coordinate all social services for the families involved. The great majority of the 30 children and 24 families demonstrated positive gains as a result of the one-year program. W. D. Metz

2564. Havighurst, Robert J. WHO ARE THE SOCIALLY DISADVANTAGED? *J. of Negro Educ. 1964 33(3): 210-217.* Socially disadvantaged children can be discovered at an early age. They "tend to come from families that are poor, and that are recent immigrants to the big cities," and they "need special attention in the schools and special help to assist them to overcome the disadvantages conferred on them by their families." S. C. Pearson, Jr.

2565. Hawkins, Thomas E. UTILIZING THE SERVICES OF THE ACADEMICALLY TALENTED STUDENTS. *J. of Negro Educ. 1965 34(1):*

93-95. Describes a volunteer tutorial program initiated at Hampton Institute in 1947 which enables the academically talented students "to be involved in a creative enterprise which is designed to give them an opportunity to develop a sense of belonging by rendering service to assist their fellow students to improve their scholarship." S. C. Pearson, Jr.

2566. Hayes, Edward Daniel and Monroe, Ethel M. IMPRESSIONS OF SHORT TERM COUNSELING INTERVIEWS AMONG 187 FRESHMEN STUDENTS AT GIBBS JUNIOR COLLEGE, ST. PETERSBURG, FLORIDA. *J. of Negro Educ. 1965 34(2): 192-194.* Reports the findings of a study by questionnaire of the effectiveness of the freshman counseling program. S. C. Pearson, Jr.

2567. Heald, Henry T. WITHIN THE NATION'S REACH. *South Atlantic Q. 1965 64(4): 457-464.* The established dogma of southern education has been resignation to second-best standards, with southern colleges and universities comparing and ranking themselves only with others in the region. This has been complicated by inferior education at all levels in the South, and by racial problems. But universities today must be public leaders, especially in educational terms, and they can cooperate with government and the private foundations to advance education in the region. J. M. Bumsted

2568. Henderson, George. BEYOND POVERTY OF INCOME. *J. of Negro Educ. 1967 36(1): 42-50.* Summarizes the author's unpublished dissertation "Aspirations and Social Class in Pockets of Poverty: A Study of Educational Obsolescence," at Wayne State University in 1965. The author examines some of the disadvantages of poverty other than lack of adequate income. He describes education as the single most important social institution for curbing and preventing the growth of subcultures of poverty. Educational needs of the culturally disadvantaged include the need not to be loved to death, the need to receive consistent sanctions, and the need to be accepted as a fellow human being. Raised aspirations must be accompanied by raised opportunities, and other social institutions must support the work of the schools if subcultures of poverty are to be reduced. Note. S. C. Pearson, Jr.

2569. Henderson, George. TWELFTH STREET: AN ANALYSIS OF A CHANGED NEIGHBORHOOD. *Phylon 1964 25(1): 91-96.* A Detroit neighborhood is traced in its transition from middle-class white to middle-class Negro (1950-57) and from middle-class Negro to lower-class Negro residence (1958-64). The area is described as a marginal environment in which "many have become the victims of aspirations they cannot achieve and hopes they cannot satisfy." S. C. Pearson, Jr.

2570. Henderson, Vivian W. UNIQUE PROBLEMS OF BLACK COLLEGES. *Liberal Educ. 1970 56(3): 373-383.* Discusses problems facing black colleges in 1970 and offers some solutions. The most pressing problem is that whites have long considered Negroes and their institutions inferior to whites and their institutions. Many whites now want black colleges phased out of existence or reduced to remedial status. Black colleges enroll over half of the black youth attending colleges. Whites must recognize the worth of black institutions. Makes specific recommendations on funds, faculty, and administration to improve black colleges.   C. G. Lauritsen

2571. Hero, Alfred O., Jr. AMERICAN NEGROES AND U.S. FOREIGN POLICY: 1937-1967. *J. of Conflict Resolution 1969 13(2): 220-251.* Large amounts of opinion-survey data have been collated for this study in order to obtain more accurate information about racial differences in foreign policy opinions in this country. Extensive tables are presented and discussed. Negro Americans have not differed consistently from whites during the 1960's in respect to resisting Communist aggression by force, if necessary, nor in their recent sentiments about military service and the cost of armaments. In recent years they have been at most only slightly more supportive than whites of the U.N. However, Negro Americans have been more favorably inclined recently to foreign aid, negotiation, and compromise to alleviate tensions concerning the Communist world, admission of mainland China to the U.N., intercultural exchanges, and liberalized trade and immigration. The author interprets the shift of Negro Americans from relative isolationism prior to the 1950's to relative liberalism on foreign policy in the 1960's. Changes in demographic, social, and political factors may account for some of this shift. Possibly more important are changes in the substance of U.S. relations with the rest of the world, the divergent connotations of those changes among the two races, and the differential significance of the domestic race issue. 13 tables, 20 notes.   F. Marzari

2572. Hersey, John. OUR ROMANCE WITH POVERTY. *Am. Scholar 1964 33(4): 525-536.* Describes two foundation-funded assaults on poverty, both in the field of education: the Prince Edward [County, Virginia] Free School Association - in effect a private school for Negroes; and the Community Progress, Incorporated, of New Haven, Connecticut. With only one full year of operation for each, certain principles emerge "for all succeeding school-based efforts to alleviate poverty." No single approach will suffice. A truly comprehensive attack requires new conditions and new educational techniques. Vocational training needs revamping. Leadership is a prerequisite and may have to be Federal, at least in terms of aid to education and for manpower training.   E. P. Stickney

2573. Herson, Phyllis. PERSONAL AND SOCIOLOGICAL VARIABLES ASSOCIATED WITH THE OCCUPATIONAL CHOICES OF NEGRO YOUTH: SOME IMPLICATIONS FOR GUIDANCE. *J. of Negro Educ. 1965 34(2): 147-151.* Reviews literature in the area of occupational choice of Negro youth and discusses the relationship to it of such variables as family background, community occupational patterns, intelligence, aptitudes, and interests. Some implications are suggested for school guidance programs.   S. C. Pearson, Jr.

2574. Herson, Phyllis F. AN ASSESSMENT OF CHANGES IN ACHIEVEMENT MOTIVATION AMONG UPWARD BOUND PARTICIPANTS AT THE UNIVERSITY OF MARYLAND. *J. of Negro Educ. 1968 37(4): 383-391.*

A study made of disadvantaged youths who attended the Upward Bound program (funded by the Office of Economic Opportunity) at the University of Maryland during the first summer of the program in 1966. The 30 boys, 25 Negro and five white, had just finished the 10th grade at inner-city high schools in Washington, D.C., and Baltimore, Maryland. A control group of 30 participants from the same schools was selected. After the program the participants were more inclined toward a college education than the control group, but no differences were found in the value orientations of the two groups. A full evaluation of Upward Bound would require follow-up studies of the participants over a long period of time. 2 tables, 14 notes.   B. D. Johnson

2575. Herzog, Elizabeth. SOME ASSUMPTIONS ABOUT THE POOR. *Social Service R. 1963 37(4): 389-402.* Concerns three assumptions about poor people. "There is a culture of poverty. The family and sex patterns of the poor differ from those of the middle class. The family and sex patterns of poor Negroes differ from those of whites on the same socioeconomic level." The "culture" of the poor in America, while real enough in certain respects, is lacking in other important aspects. Family patterns among the poor differ from those of the middle-class or rich, but distinctions between Negroes and whites seem more solidly based on economic levels than on race. Based on 46 studies; 5 notes.   M. W. Machan

2576. Hess, Jeffrey A. BLACK SETTLEMENT HOUSE, EAST GREENWICH, 1902-1914. *Rhode Island Hist. 1970 29(3/4): 113-127.* Traces the history of a Rhode Island welfare agency against the background of the national settlement-house movement. The East Greenwich Neighborhood Cottage at Scolloptown, Rhode Island, failed to become more than a charity organization devoted in the end to abolishing the very community it purported to serve, because its leaders despised existing social patterns in the Negro community. Based on newspapers, periodicals, census records, and secondary sources.
P. J. Coleman

2577. Hess, Robert D., Shipman, Virginia, and Jackson, David. SOME NEW DIMENSIONS IN PROVIDING EQUAL EDUCATIONAL OPPORTUNITY. *J. of Negro Educ. 1965 34(3): 220-231.* A reports of findings of research projects which support the contention "first, that the behavior which leads to social, educational, and economic poverty is socialized in early childhood, that is, it is learned; and, second, that the central quality involved in the effects of cultural deprivation is a lack of cognitive meaning in the mother-child communication system."   S. C. Pearson, Jr.

2578. Hickerson, Nathaniel. PHYSICAL INTEGRATION ALONE IS NOT ENOUGH. *J. of Negro Educ. 1966 35(2): 110-116.* Argues that physical integration is only the first step in solving the educational problems of Negro children. The author charges that "at present Negroes in physically integrated schools in the North are denied equal opportunity; they are discriminated against...; they are channeled out of academic courses by counselors...; they are evaluated as slow learners and herded into slow learning groups....They are declared slow learners on the basis of so-called intelligence and achievement tests, the validity of which has been challenged over and over again by educators and psychologists...; they are saddled with teachers and counselors who haven't the foggiest notion of Negro culture or conditioning; they are isolated from the social activities of the school...;they are defeated so long, so often and so continuously by the integrated American race-culture-perpetuating public school, that for the most part they reject education as a waste of time and effort." Proposals for remedying these problems are made.   S. C. Pearson, Jr.

2579. Hill, Beatrice M. and Burke, Nelson S. SOME DISADVANTAGED YOUTHS LOOK AT THEIR SCHOOLS. *J. of Negro Educ. 1968 37(2): 135-139.* Presents the findings of a study of 15 Neighborhood Youth Corps and Job Corps participants at a workshop in San Francisco in 1966. The participants felt that their schools had been unsatisfactory. They found the curriculum inadequate, the textbooks slanted, and the teachers biased. They felt that the schools were not helping Negroes acquire information about their past and that teachers showed little real interest in students. On the other hand, the participants felt that the NYC and the Job Corps had improved their learning ability and their sense of identity and personal worth. The authors conclude that the NYC and Job Corps programs may be useful in accomplishing the drastic reforms necessary in ghetto schools. 12 notes.   S. C. Pearson, Jr.

2580. Himmelfarb, Milton. ARE JEWS STILL LIBERALS? *Commentary 1967 43(4): 67-72.* The fact that the Jewish vote in the recent voting on a civilian review board for the police in New York City was only 50 percent favorable has been taken by some observers as evidence that American Jews are becoming "selfishly conservative" in their attitudes toward underprivileged groups such as Negroes and Puerto Ricans. On the contrary, the author points out that of all white votes on the question, the Jews as a group showed significantly more support for the idea than the other major white groups (Italians and Irish voted only 13-17 percent in favor), when they as a group had significantly less reason to care about the issue. The unfortunate fact was that civil rights groups made a major issue out of the civilian police review board, which would have accomplished very little real gain for the poor of New York and which alienated white groups, both middle and lower class, who fear a "breakdown of law and order."
                                                                            A. K. Main

2581. Hines, Ralph H. SOCIAL EXPECTATIONS AND CULTURAL DEPRIVATION. *J. of Negro Educ. 1964 33(2): 136-142.* Suggests that some aspects of the behavior of a culturally deprived group such as the American Negro develop out of the normative expectations of the larger society.
                                                                            S. C. Pearson, Jr.

2582. Hirsch, Paul M. AN ANALYSIS OF "EBONY": THE MAGAZINE AND ITS READERS. *Journalism Q. 1968 45(2): 261-270.* There has been little systematic study of the Negro middle class. Because it has been the policy of the editors of *Ebony* to be highly sensitive to the opinions and desires of their readers, a content analysis was made of *Ebony* magazine from its beginning in 1945 through spring 1966. *Ebony* readers are predominantly Negro middle class, with a sizable minority of lower status Negroes who may be undergoing "anticipatory socialization." The magazine's wide range and diversity of views are an attempt to please all segments of the audience. The presentation of success by hard work as a very desirable good is consistent. A shift in the attitudes toward civil rights seems to have closely followed the changing viewpoints of the majority of the readers. The presentation of protest and self-help side-by-side has affected the treatment of success. The study reveals within-class differences. 3 tables, 40 notes.

K. J. Puffer

2583. Hobart, Charles W. UNDERACHIEVEMENT AMONG MINORITY GROUP STUDENTS: AN ANALYSIS AND A PROPOSAL. *Phylon 1963 24(2): 184-196.* Puerto Rican, Negro, and Mexican children are affected by damaged self concepts, inadequate motivation, unawareness of employment opportunities for which they could train themselves, and resistance by peers and community to self-advancement. A unified program might combat these tendencies by encouraging achievement, recognizing individual capacities, and appealing to them. Enrichment procedures would inspire the underachievers. Giving them the status of an elite group would support their efforts. Summers should be utilized so as not to lose the gains of the regular school year. With proper administration, the enriched minority student should be at one with his Anglo peers by the time he is in senior high school.

L. Filler

2584. Hoffmann, Stanley. LA DEFAITE DE GOLDWATER [The defeat of Goldwater]. *Esprit [France] 1964 32(12): 1035-1041.* Analyzes the significance of Senator Goldwater's failure to win the presidential elections of 1964, especially noting the sophistication of the American electorate which was largely unmoved by threats of communism and racism and which split its ticket to get the candidates it wanted on both the national and local levels. This shows that the European stereotype of the unthinking American public is in need of revision. As a result of the 1964 victory, President Johnson has a good chance of enjoying the cooperation of a Democratic Congress which is predominantly liberal and moderate. He may meet with some disagreeable surprises in foreign affairs. Meanwhile the Republicans are badly divided and will probably move to a middle-of-the-road position in preparation for the next campaign.

Mother M. H. Quinlan

2585. Holloway, Harry. THE TEXAS NEGRO AS A VOTER. *Phylon 1963 24(2): 135-145.* As an example of city Negro political participation, Austin reveals that the Negro's turnout to elections is well below that of whites. Republican Party loyalties persist, as for Eisenhower in 1956, but city Negroes bloc-voted for liberal and/or Democratic candidates as do Negro voters in the north. They favored Negro candidates, when they were not "Uncle Toms." Rural Negro voters accept a humble status, vote as their patrons vote, or not at all, and are susceptible to corrupt influences and intimidation. NAACP chapters, unions, and local Negro colleges are affecting the pattern. The large potential of unused Negro suffrage makes it an important target for those with the will to cultivate it.

L. Filler

2586. Holloway, Harry and Olson, David M. ELECTORAL PARTICIPATION BY WHITE AND NEGRO IN A SOUTHERN CITY. *Midwest J. of Pol. Sci. 1966 10(1): 99-122.* Examines registration and voting in white and Negro precincts in Austin, Texas, from 1954 through 1964 in an attempt to determine the response of both white and Negro electorate to the changing conditions of this period. The voting trend shows a steady increase in the percentage of Negroes voting in local elections while, in the presidential and gubernatorial elections, there is a marked increase in Negro turnout. However, the Negro turnout is still well below that of the whites as there is some evidence of increased participation of both white and Negro. The author concludes that, from the available data, "the time when the Southern political system rests on a large mass electorate, both white and Negro, does not seem likely to occur overnight." 5 tables, 24 notes.
J. W. Thacker, Jr.

2587. Hoover, Dwight W. SOME COMMENTS ON RECENT UNITED STATES HISTORIOGRAPHY. *Am. Q. 1965 17(2, Part 2): 299-318.* Contends that since the 1950's, American historians have been captivated by the consensus school of historical interpretation. Where conflict and confrontation had hitherto been previously accepted as dominant forces in certain periods of American history, consensus historians have sought for revision. Although consensus history has its strengths, it overlooks vital areas of American history. Its middle-class orientation submerges awareness of lower-class movements. The new concern for poverty, the Negro, and the urban masses may make massive inroads on consensus theory. Documented.
R. S. Pickett

2588. Hope, John, II and Shelton, Edward E. THE NEGRO IN THE FEDERAL GOVERNMENT. *J. of Negro Educ. 1963 32(4): 367-374.*

2589. Houston, Laura Pires. BLACK PEOPLE, NEW CAREERS, AND HUMANE HUMAN SERVICES. *Social Casework 1970 51(5): 291-299.* The New Careers Program was developed in 1966 with the purpose of employing and training nonprofessionals for jobs in the public services. The program was intended to help the overburdened professionals and to bridge the gap between the agency and the community. The funds have not been sufficient to train large numbers of people, so the benefits have been limited. If it can be considered as an initial step, it can educate for the future, by helping the low-income black adult to improve community services as well as his own position. Blacks have been prevented from entering the human services professions largely by the credentials required by the professions. How essential are the existing credentials for human services jobs? It should be possible for people to enter the professions through other routes than the traditional educational paths. Describes the Talent Corps as a model which tries to deal with problems relevant to New Careers. 14 notes.
M. A. Kaufman

2590. Howe, Florence. MISSISSIPPI'S FREEDOM SCHOOLS: THE POLITICS OF EDUCATION. *Harvard Educ. R. 1965 35(2): 144-160.* A report and evaluation of teaching which centered on the awakening and strengthening of self-respect and self-awareness. This orientation led to self-help through social action and self-expression in the writing of poetry by Negro youths. Education as the act of freeing man's bodies and minds for creative growth and action is, above all, a political activity. J. Herbst

2591. Howell, Elmo. THE GRENVILLE WRITERS AND THE MISSISSIPPI COUNTRY PEOPLE. *Louisiana Studies 1969 8(4): 348-360.* A discussion of a group of Delta writers during the period 1945-65, many from Grenville, who reflect the culture of Mississippi. The writers are William Alexander Percy, David L. Cohn, Hodding Carter, Shelby Foote, Eudora Welty, and William Faulkner. The author analyzes their attitudes toward plantation aristocrats, yeoman farmers, poor whites, and Negroes, as expressed in writing. 34 notes.
G. W. McGinty

2592. Hyman, Herbert H. and Reed, John Shelton. "BLACK MATRIARCHY" RECONSIDERED: EVIDENCE FROM SECONDARY ANALYSIS OF SAMPLE SURVEYS. *Public Opinion Q. 1969 33(3): 346-354.* Finds no evidence for any pattern of matriarchy peculiar to the Negro family when viewed from the perspective of survey results for white families. Examines three surveys: a 1960 National Opinion Research Center sample of one thousand adults over 18, including 100 Negroes who were asked who made the decisions in their family; a 1951 Gallup Poll of 1,400 adults who were asked which parent had been most influential during their childhood; and a 1965 sample of 2,500 high school seniors, including 150 Negroes, whose parents had differing political loyalties, who were asked their political preferences. Table, 14 notes. D. J. Trickey

2593. Hyman, Herbert H. and Wright, Charles R. TRENDS IN VOLUNTARY ASSOCIATION MEMBERSHIPS OF AMERICAN ADULTS: REPLICATION BASED ON SECONDARY ANALYSIS OF NATIONAL SAMPLE SURVEYS. *Am. Sociol. R. 1971 36(2): 191-206.* "A small but noteworthy increase in the percentage of American adults who belong to voluntary associations has occurred since the mid-1950's (the date of an earlier study of this topic by the authors), as documented through several replications of national sample surveys. These same replications also confirm a major generalization of the earlier study that such membership is less common than had been assumed; indeed, voluntary association membership is not characteristic of the majority of American adults. Data from the replications confirm the previously demonstrated relationship between membership and major socioeconomic characteristics; but subgroup trends suggest that during the more recent period there has been a sharper growth in associational membership among the lower status groups. Although the findings are not completely consistent, there also seems to have been a sharper growth in association memberships on the part of Negroes. All of these findings, like those in the earlier study which has been replicated, are based on secondary analysis of national sample surveys. These social trends should be systematically measured and documented in the future by additional replications and new primary surveys." J

2594. Ingle, Dwight J. AIDS TO NEGRO ADVANCEMENT. *J. of Human Relations 1965 13(1): 40-48.* Considers the value of intensive programs of nursery and child care, youth guidance projects, subsidized good housing, birth control, voluntary sterilization, wise leadership, and the "scientific analyses of the origins of group bias rather than prejudice against prejudice." Discusses the meaning of the phrase, "substandard culture" in terms of the Negro slum and the "question of an average difference in the genetic endowment of Negroes, whites, and Asians." The evidence on both sides of this issue is thought to be flimsy. Based on a convocation address delivered at Central State College of Ohio.

D. J. Abramoske

2595. Irelan, Lola M., Moles, Oliver C. , and O'Shea, Robert M. ETHNICITY, POVERTY, AND SELECTED ATTITUDES: A TEST OF THE "CULTURE OF POVERTY" HYPOTHESIS. *Social Forces 1969 47(4): 405-413.* "It was hypothesized, to test an assumption implicit in the 'culture of poverty' concept, that poor respondents of three separate ethnic groups (Anglo, Negro, and Spanish-speaking Americans) would not differ significantly from each other in their responses to 8 attitude areas related to the concept. Each ethnic group was divided on the basis of receipt or nonreceipt of public assistance, providing two separate tests of the significance of ethnic determinants for each attitude area measured. It was found that in 14 out of 16 instances ethnic groups differed significantly from each other. The hypothesis was rejected. In addition, the data suggest that (1) the Spanish-speaking poor are more likely to express the values commonly assigned to the culture of poverty, and that (2) extreme economic deprivation affects their scores on these values less than it does the comparable scores of Negro- and Anglo-Americans." J

2596. Jackson, Luther P. NEEDED: THE TRUTH ABOUT HARLEM. *Negro Hist. Bull. 1964 28(1): 11-12.* Deplores the numerous newspaper accounts which picture all of Harlem as a jungle and suggests as an antidote to such distortion a study of available material on the history of Harlem as well as new research and scholarly writing on the subject. L. Gara

2597. Jackson, Miles M. SIGNIFICANT BELLES LETTRES BY AND ABOUT NEGROES PUBLISHED IN 1964. *Phylon 1965 26(3): 216-227.* Reviews 12 works marked by a perspective "directly related to the cultural realities of life for Negroes in the United States today." Biblio.

S. C. Pearson, Jr.

2598. Jeansonne, Glen. RACISM AND LONGISM IN LOUISIANA: THE 1959-60 GUBERNATORIAL ELECTIONS. *Louisiana Hist. 1970 11(3): 259-270.* Earl Long's mental breakdown and irrational antics in 1959 greatly discredited the Long candidates in the 1959 gubernatorial primary. William A. Rainach injected the segregation question into the campaign. Although Rainach failed to win, he endorsed James H. Davis in the runoff because Davis successfully exploited the race issue against New Orleans Mayor de Lesseps S. Morrison. Morrison charged that Davis' segregationism was insincere and pointed to his own segregationist record in New Orleans; however, his south Louisiana moderate strength was insufficient to offset the white racist vote of north Louisiana. The election ended the predominance of the Longs in State politics. Although all candidates supported the Long welfare program, it was no longer an issue. The race issue could not be ignored, as the Long machine had done successfully since 1928. In 1959-60 the race issue overtook the economic-class issue as the dominant theme in Louisiana politics. Based on published materials, interviews, and manuscript collections in the Tulane University Library (New Orleans) and at the Ed Reed Organization (Baton Rouge); 29 notes. R. L. Woodward

2599. Jemmings, M. Kent and Zeigler, Harmon. CLASS, PARTY, AND RACE IN FOUR TYPES OF ELECTIONS: THE CASE OF ATLANTA. *J. of Pol. 1966 28(2): 391-407.* An analysis of 16 elections: partisan (presidential and congressional); Democratic primaries (congressional and gubernatorial); nonpartisan local (general and mayoralty); and referenda. All were held in Atlanta between 1954 and 1964. The analysis was to determine the relationship between class, party, and race on electoral outcomes. The author concludes that class is the weakest variable in each type of election; party is more important in partisan elections than in referenda; racial composition is more important than party in the Democratic primary elections. A comparison is noted between Atlanta and Des Moines, where a similar but not identical study was made. A revised version of a paper presented to the Southern Political Science Association, 12-14 November 1964, in Durham, North Carolina; 2 tables, 14 notes. M. A. Burr

2600. Jennings, M. Kent and Zeigler, L. Harmon. A MODERATE'S VICTORY IN A SOUTHERN CONGRESSIONAL DISTRICT. *Public Opinion Q. 1964 28(4): 595-603.* Illustrates signs of change in the South (urbanization, increasing Negro political participation, growing Republicanism, and legislative redistricting) by a study of the 1962 congressional election in the Fifth District of Georgia (Fulton County, which includes Atlanta; suburban De Kalb County; and tiny, rural Rockdale County). The research shows that in the victory of the moderate candidate the support of predominantly Negro electorates was crucial; lower-class whites supported the conservative Democrat and higher-status whites the moderate. This may be typical, but the challenge from the right (conservative Democrats in primaries and Republicans in general elections) may be a serious one to the moderate, more nationally-oriented Southern Democrats. 2 tables, 8 notes. E. P. Stickney

2601. Jiobu, Robert M. and Marshall, Harvey H., Jr. URBAN STRUCTURE AND THE DIFFERENTIATION BETWEEN BLACKS AND WHITES. *Am. Sociol. R. 1971 36(4): 638-649.* "In this study some of the determinants of black assimilation into large United States cities are examined. Assimilation is treated as a multidimensional phenomenon, the various dimensions of which are attributes of organized populations. A structural model is developed and analyzed, using the technique of path analysis, in which other attributes of urban social structures are related to the various dimensions of assimilation. Analysis suggests that the dimensions of assimilation are causally interrelated, with educational assimilation a major determinant of income assimilation, both directly and indirectly through its effects upon occupational assimilation. However, other attributes of organized urban populations also make important direct and indirect contributions to assimilation. Of special importance is percent of the city's population that is black and the rate of black population growth. Surprisingly, ghettoization is not very important causally when compared with other variables in the system, a significant negative finding in view of current emphasis upon this factor. This analysis suggests that greater attention be paid to organizational dimensions of urban populations as a means of specifying the process underlying the assimilation of blacks."   J

2602. Johnson, G. Orville. ORGANIZING INSTRUCTION AND CUR-RICULUM PLANNING FOR THE SOCIALLY DISADVANTAGED. *J. of Negro Educ. 1964 33(3): 154-263.* The author suggests planning a program that has meaning, value, and purpose for the students and which utilizes the best pedagogical techniques possible. Children should be taught in the context of their own culture and should be able to perform assigned tasks though a large expenditure of effort may be involved.   S. C. Pearson, Jr.

2603. Johnson, Gerald W. AFTER FORTY YEARS - DIXIE. *Virginia Q.R. 1965 41(2): 192-201.* In 1963 and 1964 the southern Negro has demonstrated a high degree of political maturity. "If one-third...of all white Southerners are as mature politically as the mass of the Negroes, we have a numerical majority of the whole population against a reversion to barbarism." An effective group of the whites has estimated that cultural and economic advance for the Negroes would make them not only more formidable but also "more valuable cultural and economic assets; and they estimated that the increase in value would be greater than the increase in danger." The fact that some progress has been made in the past 40 years is shown conclusively by the "Negro Revolution" itself, since the utterly hopeless do not rebel.   E. P. Stickney

2604. Johnson, Jerald B. THE UNIVERSITY AS PROBLEM SOLVER: CRE-ATIVITY AND THE GHETTO. *Liberal Educ. 1968 54(3): 418-428.* The university ought to be a prime mover in the creation of a better society. This could be done but for the attitudes of Americans, both those of college graduates and of those without an advanced degree. The author gives many illustrations of what the university could do. It should employ more blacks. It should see that building contractors keep their nondiscrimination pledge. It must bring the youth of the ghetto to the university. Students, faculty, and alumni should be encouraged to use their talents to improve the ghetto. Finally, there must be a commitment on the part of the university. 18 notes.   C. G. Lauritsen

2605. Josey, E. J. READING IS WHAT'S HAPPENING. *Negro Hist. Bull. 1967 30(5): 14-17.* A summary of the reading habits of Negro students and their use of available library resources. Many young people are denied entrance to good colleges and universities because of improper preparation for higher education. Calls for outside reading by students to be well informed, to supplement the subject areas of study in college, and to meet the critical demands of a changing society. Note.   D. H. Swift

2606. Josey, E. J. READING: NEGRO YOUTHS' QUEST FOR CER-
TAINTY. *Negro Hist. Bull. 1964 27(7): 158-159, 172.* Suggests that wide reading
is the key to open the doors of job and educational opportunities for today's Negro
youths in the United States.   L. Gara

2607. Kain, John F. COPING WITH GHETTO UNEMPLOYMENT. *J. of the
Am. Inst. of Planners 1969 35(2): 80-89.* "This paper examines the rationale for
ghetto job creation and similar ghetto 'gilding' programs. Such policies accept
and strengthen the ghetto and are inefficient on narrow cost-effectiveness
grounds. Since a long-range solution to the problem of the ghetto and the metropolis requires the destruction of the ghetto, it is crucial that programs be consistent
with this long term objective. Several alternative programs consistent with the
long term objective are discussed. In particular, the paper outlines a wage subsidy
program that would weaken the constricting ties of the ghetto while providing
jobs for unemployed blacks at lower cost than ghetto job creation programs."
                                                                         J

2608. Kallen, D. J. and Miller, D. PUBLIC ATTITUDES TOWARD WEL-
FARE. *Social Work 1971 16(3): 83-90.* Compares the attitudes of 300 white and
300 black women in Baltimore (1964) toward welfare. A series of tables compares
the mean scale scores by education, percentage of antiwelfare responses expressed
by whites by item and education; the same percentage scale for blacks, and the
intercorrelations of attitude items. 4 tables, 5 notes.   W. L. Willigan

2609. Kaplan, Sidney J. and Coleman, A. Lee. THE STRATEGY OF
CHANGE: CONTRASTING APPROACHES TO TEACHER INTEGRA-
TION. *Social Sci. 1963 38(4): 218-221.* Analyzes the lag in teacher integration
as compared to pupil integration. The authors studied two separate contemporary
attempts in the State of Kentucky, one based upon placing Negro teachers in
social roles least vulnerable to white criticism (e.g., librarian), and the other based
upon selection for classroom positions of Negro teachers whose personalities
would elicit the most favorable reception. Finally, the authors suggest a theoretical model combining both approaches.   M. Small

2610. Katz, Loren B. SOME GUIDELINES IN TEACHING AMERICAN
NEGRO HISTORY. *Negro Hist. Bull. 1965 28(8): 190-191.* Quotes Martin
Luther King: "Before the Pilgrims landed at Plymouth, we were here." The
restoration of the Negro to his rightful place in history will serve not only the
cause of justice but of truth. The Negro's story is an integral part of all American
history, valid for all Americans. No drastic revision of the curriculum is needed
but rather the integration of the Negro contribution to the appropriate parts of
the curriculum. Negro life cannot be accurately taught only in terms of its leaders.
"Our heroes must not obscure our common people."   E. P. Stickney

2611. Kelley, Joseph B. RACIAL INTEGRATION POLICIES OF THE NEW
YORK CITY HOUSING AUTHORITY, 1958-61. *Social Service R. 1964 38(2):
153-162.* Describes the New York City Housing Authority's efforts from 1 May

1958 to 31 December 1961 to overcome racial segregation in the projects and to promote racial integration of the Negro into all phases of the community on the principle of equality. In public housing, the quantity and quality of housing are the welfare end, and racial integration is the status end. "In summary, the policies developed by the New York City Housing Authority to promote racial integration contain a mixture of status and welfare ends. That is, objectives concerned with racial integration were paralleled by objectives concerned with quantitative and qualitative aspects of housing. There were instances in which status and welfare goals were mutually reinforcing....The increase in the proportion of white families...is an indication of the influence of the policies directed at promoting racial integration." Based on reports issued by the New York City Housing Authority, 1957-60; 2 tables, 21 notes.   D. D. Cameron

2612. Kemble, Penn. THE DEMOCRATS AFTER 1968. *Commentary 1969 47(1): 35-41.* The old Roosevelt coalition did not stay with the Democratic Party in 1968, but a new coalition began to take shape. The South, the machines, and the liberal intellectuals gave half-hearted or no support to Hubert Humphrey, the trade unions and the Negroes providing his main props. Humphrey's unexpected showing has left him in a stronger position to affect the party's future than many had surmised. The author feels the Vietnam War will be brought to an end by 1972 and that the intellectual liberals will get together with unions and the Negroes to form a new coalition uncompromised by conservative or racist interest.   C. G. Lauritsen

2613. Kendrick, S. A. EXTENDING EDUCATIONAL OPPORTUNITY - PROBLEMS OF RECRUITMENT, ADMISSIONS, HIGH RISK STUDENTS.... *Liberal Educ. 1969 55(1): 12-17.* Reviews the history of the militant black student movement, then discusses four issues that arise with the recruitment and admission of black students to colleges. First, colleges must not promise that 11 percent of their student body will be black. Such a figure is fantasy. Second, colleges must confront the problem of race. Third, colleges must realize that to institute a program for the disadvantaged requires money which must come from the Federal Government. Fourth, the relationship of higher and lower educational institutions must be examined.   C. G. Lauritsen

2614. Kiernan, Irene R. and Daniels, Roy P. SIGNS OF SOCIAL CHANGE THROUGH AN EXPLORATORY STUDY OF 23 NEGRO STUDENTS IN A COMMUNITY COLLEGE. *J. of Negro Educ. 1967 36(2): 129-135.* Summarizes the findings on 23 Negro students between the ages of 18 and 24 who sought assistance from the counseling office of a community college. Students were from lower-class backgrounds and experienced a much higher dropout rate than the average. The authors conclude that social and cultural changes may take place at a rather slow pace for individuals and that the grip of subcultures looms significantly as a behavior determinant for many students. For the sample, the attempted transition from a lower- to a middle-class status involved value conflict, personal anxiety, bitterness, and hatred of self, group, and the group to which the sample aspired. 8 notes.   S. C. Pearson, Jr.

2615. Killingsworth, Charles. NEGRO UNEMPLOYMENT: CAUSES AND CURES. *Centennial R. 1966 10(2): 131-146.* Since the early 1950's unemployment among Negroes has increased steadily, a factor which tends to nullify Negro progress in other areas such as civil rights. More Negroes are unemployed in the North and West than in the South where Negroes tend to hold traditional jobs. The basic reasons for rising Negro unemployment include changes in technology as well as changing industrial growth patterns which have diminished opportunities for younger and better educated Negroes. The opposite was true during the forties and early fifties which were periods of war and postwar boom with a labor shortage. The passage of time will not improve this situation but will result in a greater economic disadvantage for the Negro. Some solutions to the problem include long-range plans to disperse ghetto populations and improvement of the quality of education available to Negroes. In the short run a special effort should be made to create jobs specifically for Negroes, and a program should be instituted in which the poor would train the poor. A special and costly effort should be mounted to assure the reality of economic equality for the Negro.
A. R. Stoesen

2616. Klein, Malcolm W. FACTORS RELATED TO JUVENILE GANG MEMBERSHIP PATTERNS. *Sociol. and Social Res. 1966 51(1): 49-62.* "Fifty-four judgmental items thought to distinguish between 'core' and 'fringe' members of juvenile gangs were applied by gang workers to 120 Negro and Mexican-American gang members. The items significantly differentiating between core and fringe members were submitted to a factor analysis which produced two major factors labeled Deficient-Aggressive and Group Involvement. Independently collected behavioral data provided empirical validation of the two factors as related to the core-fringe distinction and as predictive indices of gang-related behavior."
J

2617. Koch, Ejler. U.S.A.S VLAG NOVEMBER 1968 [USA's elections November 1968]. *Økonomi og Politik [Denmark] 1968 42(4): 397-411.* The problems of Vietnam, race riots, and growing unrest created unusual interest in the 1968 presidential election. Early candidates for the Republican nomination lost ground; Richard Nixon steadily won votes when George Romney bumbled and Nelson Rockefeller could not be accepted by the conservative wing. Nixon was the only choice by reason of his moderation and his apparent ability to draw the party together. Neither party presented a clear program, the Republicans by reason of Nixon's strategy and the Democrats because of Hubert Humphrey's association with the Johnson administration. The significance of the election lies in the moderate nature of the Nixon administration, the lack of a legislative reform program, the confusion of the Democratic Party, and the possibility that both parties must reckon with new conservative strength. The coalitions among diverse groups might be at an end. Because of the close popular vote, the question of electoral college reform is brought into focus. R. E. Lindgren

2618. Kochman, Thomas. "RAPPING" IN THE BLACK GHETTO. *Transaction 1969 6(4): 26-34.* Analyzes the uses of rapping and its variations as shown by examples recorded by the author in his analysis of the ethnography of black speech behavior. Rapping takes place mostly in the ghetto, but all Negroes have some acquaintance with it and its forms ("shucking," "giving," "running it down," etc.). Rapping has found a place in black literature as well as in the street. Ability with words is as highly prized as physical strength, and its use helps the person to achieve a status within the group or to achieve his goals in relationship to the outside community. It is another way in which the ghetto Negro has established his personality and found a way to manipulate people and control the situations into which he falls. 5 photos, biblio.   A. Erlebacher

2619. Kolosova, Iu. A. OSOBENNOSTI URBANIZATSII NEGRITIAN-SKOGO NASELENIIA SSHA [Features of the urbanization of the Negro population of the United States]. *Sovetskaia Etnografiia [USSR] 1968 (2): 46-55.* Discusses the urbanization of Negroes in the United States - its patterns and consequences. The author points out that Negro urbanization (73.2 percent) is higher than that of the rest of the population (69.9 percent). He traces the movement of Negroes out of the South (1910-60) and their ghettoization, using Harlem to illustrate the process. The occupational pattern of Negroes is discussed, income figures for blacks and whites as well as unemployment statistics are compared, and the lack of political rights for Negroes is explored. The author also discusses the ramifications of present conditions on the Negro family structure. Based on Government and other published sources; 4 maps, 29 notes.
D. J. MacIntyre

2620. Kornberg, Allan, Tepper, Elliot L., and Watson, George L. THE NATIONAL ELECTIONS AND COMPARATIVE POSITIONS OF NEGROES AND WHITES ON POLICY. *South Atlantic Q. 1968 67(3): 405-418.* Delineates policy positions of Negroes and whites on selected domestic and foreign issues, based on 1964 data and issues, to determine the extent to which variations in these positions are factors of racial or economic background and to suggest implications for partisan politics in the immediate future. On domestic issues (especially Government action in the welfare state), variations which are functions of race are greater than those which are functions of income. On foreign policy, Negroes are much less interventional than on domestic issues. The author predicts that, as far as the Negro electorate is concerned, the Democratic Party can do what it wants abroad so long as it is favorably linked with domestic social welfare issues. 13 notes.   J. M. Bumsted

2621. Kornberg, Leonard. SLUM CHILDREN AND NEW TEACHERS. *J. of Negro Educ. 1963 32(1): 74-80.* The author discusses personal experiences at Queens College as Project Director of BRIDGE (Building Resources of Instruction for Disadvantaged Groups in Education).   S. C. Pearson, Jr.

2622. Kosa, John and Nunn, Clyde Z. RACE, DEPRIVATION AND ATTITUDE TOWARD COMMUNISM. *Phylon 1964 25(4): 337-346.* Data were collected from 508 undergraduate students of a white college and a Negro college situated in neighboring cities of a Southern State in an attempt to ascertain whether comparable Negro and white groups differ in their attitude toward communism and, if so, whether the difference is a function of deprivation or of personality factors. Concludes that Negro students are more likely than white students to be intolerant toward communism and that such intolerance is a function of personality factors rather than of deprivation.   S. C. Pearson, Jr.

2623. Krass, Elaine M., Peterson, Claire, and Shannon, Lyle W. DIFFEREN-TIAL ASSOCIATION, CULTURAL INTEGRATION, AND ECONOMIC ABSORPTION AMONG MEXICAN-AMERICANS AND NEGROES IN A NORTHERN INDUSTRIAL COMMUNITY. *Southwestern Social Sci. Q. 1966 47(3): 349-353.* A partial report, using data compiled from 1959 to 1961, of differential association, cultural integration, and economic absorption among Mexican-Americans and Negroes. Coefficients of correlation were computed as measures of the interrelationship of a number of basic variables. It is concluded that the measured upward movement of Mexican-Americans and Negroes "is in reality an artifact of their movement from rural to urban or South and Southwest to the Northern industrial community." 4 tables.   D. F. Henderson

2624. Kuritz, Hyman. INTEGRATION ON NEGRO COLLEGE CAM-PUSES. *Phylon 1967 28(2): 121-130.* Contends that one dimension of Negro colleges which is rarely discussed but is of basic importance is that of integration of white students and faculty into the life of the college community. The author maintains that on Negro campuses in both the North and South there is an invisible wall dividing the races. A first indispensable step for those who live and work on the Negro college campus is to open lines of communication and expose all problems. There must be a conscious effort to narrow the gap between the two streams of life that keep white and Negro members of the faculty apart. Academic excellence demands an uninhibited and free exchange of ideas on all levels of life. This calls for an alteration in the institutional life as well as a transformation of attitudes and values between the races at Negro colleges.   D. N. Brown

2625. Kushnick, Louis. RACE, CLASS AND POWER: THE NEW YORK DECENTRALIZATION CONTROVERSY. *J. of Am. Studies [Great Britain] 1969 3(2): 201-219.* Discusses the struggle between the white - largely Jewish - educational establishment and Negroes over the decentralization of New York City's public schools, which have almost completely failed to educate the majority of black pupils. The collapse of desegregation plans has left 65 percent of the black children attending schools which are over 90 percent black. Given this situation, blacks turned from desegregation to questions of quality and local control. This shift in emphasis coincided with Mayor John Lindsay's attempt in 1967 to obtain more money from New York State for the city's schools by proposing the system's decentralization. The Ford Foundation at the same time agreed to finance three experimental demonstration districts, most importantly the Ocean Hill-Browns-ville district, which became the center of the fight over decentralization. Both the Board of Education and the United Federation of Teachers failed to cooperate with the Local Governing Board. Their opposition has been determined and unscrupulous in spite of the fact that the demonstration districts have improved the quality of education. The State Legislature in May 1969 passed a decentraliza-tion law which conceded virtually everything to the United Federation of Teachers. New York's blacks are still determined to control their own schools, however. Based on interviews and on both published and unpublished sources.

D. J. Abramoske

2626. Kuvlesky, William P. and Ohlendorf, George W. A RURAL-URBAN COMPARISON OF THE OCCUPATIONAL STATUS ORIENTATIONS OF NEGRO BOYS. *Rural Sociol. 1968 33(2): 141-152.* "This paper provides information about occupational status orientations of Negro youth through analysis of data obtained from a recent study of high school sophomores residing in Texas. The specific objective of the research was to explore rural and urban differences among Negro boys on the following aspects of occupational orientations: aspirations, expectations, and anticipatory deflection from goals. The findings indicated that both rural and urban Negro boys maintain generally high level goals and expectations. Given this broad similarity, the urbanboys had higher goal and expectation levels than the rural. Rural-urban differences were greater for goals than for expectations. Rural and urban respondents were found to experience very similar rates of anticipatory deflection from occupational goals, but differences were observed in reference to the nature of anticipatory deflection experienced."   J

2627. Lambert, Verdelle. NEGRO EXPOSURE IN "LOOK'S" EDITORIAL CONTENT. *Journalism Q. 1965 42(4): 657-659.* Two one-year periods of *Look* magazine issues, 1959-60 and 1963-64, were studied. An increased number of articles pertaining to Negroes, a more favorable treatment of the Negro and a greater tendency to treat him not as a Negro but as a member of society were noted. Notes.   S. E. Humphreys

2628. Lamott, Kenneth. A FEW HAZARDS OF THE GOOD LIFE. *Horizon 1969 11(2): 26-29.* Discusses the good life as practiced in Marin County, California. Marin County is one of the richest suburban counties in the United States. The author describes the strenuous efforts made by its inhabitants to attain a leisurely life. He goes on to discuss the Negro population (part of which lives in San Quentin Prison), the kids (with their hangups on drugs and sex), and the adults (with their hangups on alcohol and sex). The author contrasts the East, where men identify with their professions, to the West, where the profession is seen as a means to an end - the good life.   R. N. Alvis

2629. Landers, Jacob. THE RESPONSIBILITIES OF TEACHERS AND SCHOOL ADMINISTRATORS. *J. of Negro Educ. 1964 33(3): 318-332.* Schools must be organized and teachers trained to redress the social balance for the disadvantaged in order to extend to them a measure of equal opportunity.

S. C. Pearson, Jr.

2630. Landers, Jacob and Mercurio, Carmela. IMPROVING CURRICULUM AND INSTRUCTION FOR THE DISADVANTAGED MINORITIES. *J. of Negro Educ. 1965 34(3): 342-366.* Surveys present programs such as those in reading and language arts, guidance and motivation, cultural emphasis, community-school relations, pre-kindergarten and early childhood education, pre-service and in-service training, prevention of school dropouts, auxiliary programs, etc., as they are being developed in the largest American cities. S. C. Pearson, Jr.

2631. Landis, Judson R. MORAL VALUE STRUCTURE OF LABORERS AND PENITENTIARY INMATES: A RESEARCH NOTE. *Social Forces 1967 46(2): 269-274.* A 50-item questionnaire was administered to three different groups: white laborers, white penitentiary inmates, and Negro penitentiary inmates. The conclusions are that differences in subcultures are more important than racial differences. The criminal sample consisted of 335 Negro and white males in a penitentiary and the noncriminal sample was made up of 195 white laborers from industrial centers. The laborers are more conservative in their responses than the criminals. Secondary research based on the work of Paul Crissman and Salomon Rettig with Benjamin Pasamanick; 3 tables, 8 notes.
A. S. Freedman

2632. Lane, David A. AN ARMY PROJECT IN THE DUTY-TIME GENERAL EDUCATION OF NEGRO TROOPS IN EUROPE, 1947-51. *J. of Negro Educ. 1964 33(2): 117-124.* Traces the "inception, growth, and demise of a U.S. Army special educational program for Negro troops in Europe" in the period 1947-52. S. C. Pearson, Jr.

2633. Lassiter, Roy J., Jr. THE ASSOCIATION OF INCOME AND EDUCATION FOR MALES BY REGION, RACE AND AGE. *Southern Econ. J. 1965 32(1): 15-22.* An attempt to measure the statistical relationship by regression and correlation analysis between income and years of school completed for males in the South and in other areas of the United States, and to investigate the differing private incentives to invest in education by region and race. Using data from the 1960 Census of Population, the author found a relatively low positive, but statistically significant, relationship between income and education, by race and region. The difference in rates of return to investment in education by whites as against nonwhites may explain the former's greater incentive to undertake such investment, while the latter's failure to invest may be regarded as economically sound from a private standpoint. A. W. Coats

2634. Lauter, Paul. THE SHORT, HAPPY LIFE OF THE ADAMS-MORGAN COMMUNITY SCHOOL PROJECT. *Harvard Educ. R. 1968 38(2): 235-262.* This widely acclaimed community school project in Washington, D.C., suffered from a plethora of innovations attempted simultaneously: university participation (Antioch College), team-teaching, nongraded organization, open-ended curriculum, teacher training, and training of teacher-aids. Conflicting desires and claims to authority by college community, and school staff, insufficient financial resources, pressure of time combined with inexperience, and differing expectations of black and white parents all contributed to a tense and turbulent experience. The role of Antioch casts light on the problematic relationship of a middle-class institution to a lower-class community. Written as a report by the project director; 8 notes. J. Herbst

2635. Leggett, John C. ECONOMIC INSECURITY AND WORKING-CLASS CONSCIOUSNESS. *Am. Sociol. R. 1964 29(2): 226-234.* "The transition from early to late industrial society is accomplished by a general decline in economic crises, the class struggle, and class militance. Nevertheless, economic insecurity rooted in structural change continues to contribute to the formation of working-class consciousness. A recent study of workers in a modern industrial community reveals that the unemployed express more militant views than the employed, while a disproportionate number of Negro workers voice class-conscious opinions. Negroes who are unemployed generally do not acquire militant perspectives unless they belong to unions. Interpretative comments on this finding stress the impact of *industrial* unions, since almost all of the unionized unemployed Negroes belong to these organizations."   J

2636. Levine, Daniel U. ISSUES IN THE PROVISION OF EQUAL EDUCATIONAL OPPORTUNITY. *J. of Negro Educ. 1968 37(1): 4-14.* Suggests that the issue of homogeneous or heterogeneous grouping is central to broader problems of providing equal educational opportunity. The author suggests a policy of avoiding homogeneous grouping except for students who truly need remedial work and of limiting remedial classes to no more than 15 students. Ability grouping for instruction should normally take place within the class. The controversy over the relative merits of strengthening inner city schools and providing preschool programs is discussed. The author advocates greater attention to preschool programs but agrees that students presently in school are not expendable and must be assisted by massive improvement in the schools. Such improvement would not make inner city schools indistinguishable from middle-class schools but would recognize the unique problems of disadvantaged students and provide compensatory curricula. Cites recent literature on each topic discussed; 10 notes.
S. C. Pearson, Jr.

2637. Levinson, Boris M. A COMPARATIVE STUDY OF NORTHERN AND SOUTHERN NEGRO HOMELESS MEN. *J. of Negro Educ. 1966 35(2): 144-150.* Twenty-four pairs of northern and southern Negro homeless men in New York City were administered the Wechsler Adult Intelligence Scale and the scores were correlated with education. The author concluded that "apparently, the Skid Row has a differential effect on its denizens. While for the vast majority, it brings about a debilitation of potential and depression of intellectual aspirations it may become stimulating for some very culturally deprived individuals. It apparently stimulated and reawakened the latent intellectual abilities of some men. While for most men, living on the Skid Row means a descent in standard of living, for many Negroes it meant maintenance of previous standards, and possibly even an ascent to a higher level."   S. C. Pearson, Jr.

2638. Lewis, Peirce F. IMPACT OF NEGRO MIGRATION ON THE ELECTORAL GEOGRAPHY OF FLINT, MICHIGAN, 1932-1962: A CARTOGRAPHIC ANALYSIS. *Ann. of the Assoc. of Am. Geographers 1965 55(1): 1-25.* Uses detailed electoral maps to analyze voter behavior and indicates how such maps may be employed to detect spatial variations in the composition of populations. Illus., 8 maps, 48 notes.   W. R. Boedecker

2639. Liddle, Gordon P. THE ROLE OF PARENTS AND FAMILY LIFE. *J. of Negro Educ. 1964 33(3): 311-317.* Parental support is necessary for a successful school program for socially disadvantaged children and youth. School personnel must assume the initiative in communicating with parents and securing their interest. .S. C. Pearson, Jr.

2640. Liebow, Elliot. FATHERS WITHOUT CHILDREN. *Public Interest 1966 (5): 13-25.* Discusses the range of father-child relationships in the Tally's Corner area of a Washington, D.C., slum. Numerous cases are cited to indicate the forces influencing the relationships within the family in the Negro slum. Based on a chapter in a projected book entitled *Tally's Corner.* H. E. Cox

2641. Lindsay, Powell. WE STILL NEED NEGRO THEATRE IN AMERICA. *Negro Hist. Bull. 1964 27(5): 112.* Argues that until there is total racial integration in American life there is need for a Negro theater drawing upon the work of Negro playwrights and actors. L. Gara

2642. Lipset, M. L. BEYOND THE BACKLASH. *Encounter [Great Britain] 1964 23(134): 11-24.* "Backlash" politics is generated by groups declining in power and influence. From the beginning, conservative parties in the United States have repeatedly sought to widen the appeal of what is inherently a minority tendency by fostering nativism and other emotional issues. A discussion of class and economic factors in their relation to the sources of support and the policies of the conservative parties and an analysis of the dynamics of these factors explain the rise of Goldwater Republicanism. The evidence suggests that dogmatic conservatism, racial bigotry, and xenophobic nationalism are not becoming more popular in the United States. D. H. Murdoch

2643. Littig, Lawrence W. NEGRO PERSONALITY CORRELATES OF ASPIRATION TO TRADITIONALLY OPEN AND CLOSED OCCUPATIONS. *J. of Negro Educ. 1968 37(1): 31-36.* Reports the findings of a study of 70 male Negro undergraduates at Howard University designed to assess the relationships among achievement motivation, social class identification, and aspirations to traditionally open and traditionally closed occupations. Strong achievement motivation and working-class identification were related to aspiration to traditionally closed occupations whereas weak achievement motivation and middle-class identification were related to aspiration to traditionally open occupations. 19 notes. S. C. Pearson, Jr.

2644. Lloren, David. RAPSODI [sic] IN BLACK. *Am. Educ. 1968 4(10): 7-9.* Describes the program provided by Chicago's Center for Inner City Studies. The center seeks to bridge the gap between disadvantaged children and middle-class teachers. Its programs ignore tradition and focus on the reality which teachers encounter in the inner city. The center's operation has revealed the need for such a program as part of preservice training for inner-city teachers. Apparently based on an interview with the founder and first director of the center; 3 photos. W. R. Boedecker

2645. Lowe, Gilbert A., Jr. HOWARD UNIVERSITY STUDENTS AND THE COMMUNITY SERVICE PROJECT. *J. of Negro Educ. 1967 36(4): 368-376.* Howard University in collaboration with community churches sponsored a Community Service Project in Washington's second precinct, an impoverished and disorganized area south of the campus, from 1961 through 1966. The project sought to stimulate and guide positive social change as well as to advance the research and training activities of the university. Student participants fell into four categories: those who were assigned by their teachers or who voluntarily chose to do research in the second precinct for theses or term papers; those who volunteered to assist in the campus research office; those who volunteered to work in action programs, especially involving youth; and those paid by the project or assigned to it under the College Work-Study Program. Both research and service activities of students are enumerated and discussed by the author. Problems of matching student interest with programs, maintaining a high level of student motivation, using students with limited time, and working without a concrete administrative policy governing student involvement are discussed. The author concludes with suggestions for strengthening similar projects and with the observation that such programs can be very valuable to the community, the university, and the student.   S. C. Pearson, Jr.

2646. Lowry, Mark, II. POPULATION AND RACE IN MISSISSIPPI, 1940-1960. *Ann. of the Assoc. of Am. Geographers 1971 61(3): 576-588.* "The plural society of Mississippi, working through time, has produced two population geographies, with race the distinguisher. Whites and Negroes have significantly different distributions and trends of change at regional, local, and intermediate levels, and the geography of the total population is not closely representative of either race."   J

2647. Lowry, Mark, II. RACE AND SOCIOECONOMIC WELL-BEING: A GEOGRAPHICAL ANALYSIS OF THE MISSISSIPPI CASE. *Geographical R. 1970 60(4): 511-528.* "The plural society in Mississippi is manifest in spatial patterns and relative levels of socioeconomic well-being for Negroes and whites. Quantitative indexes of socioeconomic well-being exhibit significantly different patterns for each race. These indexes and the index for the socioeconomic well-being gap between the races show distinctive spatial relationships with the degree of urbanization, the racial composition of the population, and an array of economic phenomena. The pattern of socioeconomic well-being of the total population does not adequately represent the pattern for either race, and therefore the races must be considered separately. Interpretation of differences in patterns, levels, and spatial relationships must be made in the light of historical processes and of the biracial society characterized by rigid class membership."
J

2648. Lurie, Melvin and Rayack, Elton. RACIAL DIFFERENCES IN MIGRATION AND JOB SEARCH: A CASE STUDY. *Southern Econ. J. 1966 33(1): 81-95.* Previous studies of the causes of Negro underemployment and unemployment have neglected the role of the job hunting patterns of Negro and white workers, and in an attempt to counteract this the authors studied the

Middletown, Connecticut, labor market area in the summer of 1964. They found that reliance on informal methods of search tended to perpetuate existing patterns of employment, and that public employment services were especially important for Negroes. The authors therefore propose more vigorous action by the U.S. Employment Service backed by strong antidiscriminatory measures and an improvement in informal job information and placement provisions like the National Urban League's registry. The portion of migratory workers was also considered. A. W. Coats

2649. Lyda, W. J. and Copenny, Verline P. SOME SELECTED FACTORS ASSOCIATED WITH RURAL AND URBAN DROPOUTS IN LAURENS COUNTY, GEORGIA. *J. of Negro Educ. 1965 34(1): 96-98.* A study of dropouts in Laurens County Negro schools for the 1961-62 school year compared rural and urban dropouts with respect to such factors as age and sex, residence, socioeconomic status, intelligence, lack of interest in school work, school failures, adjustment problems, and vocational interest and problems. Significant differences were found with respect to these factors. S. C. Pearson, Jr.

2650. Lyons, Schley R. LABOR IN CITY POLITICS: THE CASE OF THE TOLEDO UNITED AUTO WORKERS. *Social Sci. Q. 1969 49(4): 816-828.* While workers approve of union involvement in local politics, endorsement of candidates does not deliver the votes. Those most clearly still influenced by union opinion were Negroes and older unionists still affiliated with the Democratic Party. Based on interviews with 314 workers during September and October 1967, as well as follow-ups, examines the following aspects of the problem: union political activities and membership support; the union and the transmission of political information; and the impact of United Automobile Workers' political endorsements on the rank-and-file. 6 tables, 8 notes. M. Hough

2651. Macklin, Fleming and Pollak, Louis. THE BLACK QUOTA AT YALE LAW SCHOOL. *Public Interest 1970 19: 44-52.* In an exchange of letters, Macklin questions the results of an arbitrary 10 percent quota of Negroes at the law school in terms of its effect on the school and on the future role of the black lawyer in society. Pollak states the case for the obligation of the law school to accept and train a larger number of minority students and at the same time to maintain a standard of professional excellence. Elizabeth C. Hyslop

2652. Maddox, G. L. and Williams, J. R. DRINKING BEHAVIOR OF NEGRO COLLEGIANS. *Q. J. of Studies on Alcohol 1968 29(1): 117-129.* "Evidence on the drinking behavior of American Negro men suggests that heavy drinking is prevalent, that social complications are commonly associated with this behavior, and that among middle-status Negroes self-disparagement is a prominent component of such complications. Data from a sample *(N* [equals] 262) consisting of all freshmen in a Negro college in North Carolina supported these generalizations. The subjects' median age was 18.7 years and 90 [percent] were residents of North Carolina; the position of the average family was on the margin between middle and lower socioeconomic status; 88 [percent] were Protestants (mostly Baptists), 9 [percent] Catholics; most were active religious participants.

A pretested interview schedule, administered by trained upperclassmen, obtained information on drinking patterns and self-esteem. Of the 262, 76 [percent] were drinking during their first semester in college, 27 [percent] of them heavily (Quantity-Frequency Index type 5: frequent use, medium or large amounts). This is the same proportion of drinkers as in Straus and Bacon's drinking in college study (whose subjects were, on the average, older), but about double the proportion of heavy drinkers. Almost half (48 [percent]) of the Negro collegians reported drinking for physiological effect, and 53 [percent] of those who drank reported being preoccupied with alcohol, a higher percentage than that reported in previous studies of adults. Only 3 [percent] of the 208 drinkers reported having had trouble with the police as a result of drinking; 56 [percent] had never been drunk, 84 [percent] had never passed out, 11 [percent] did not worry about their drinking; 20 [percent] reported social complications as a result of drinking and 26 [percent] 'warning signs' (e.g., blackouts); these percentages are lower than those found by Straus and Bacon in their older sample, but less favorable comparisons are expected in succeeding college years. On Mulford's preoccupation-with-alcohol scale 27 [percent] of the subjects were in scale types which have been found to be predictive of trouble with drinking. In this predominantly Protestant middle-class sample, 51 [percent] of the abstainers but 81 [percent] of the heavy drinkers scored low on a scale of self-esteem. The subjects have been followed through college and changes in patterns of drinking are being studied."

J

2653. Maddox, George L. ROLE-MAKING: NEGOTIATIONS IN EMERGENT DRINKING CAREERS. *Social Sci. Q. 1968 49(2): 331-349.* A study of the emergent patterns of drinking and abstinence among selected Negro males in college. Specifically, the objective was to "describe their behavior, to explore the stability and change in this behavior during their first year in college, and, insofar as possible, identify the factors" which underlay the observed patterns. 6 tables, 30 notes. D. F. Henderson

2654. Madron, Thomas W. SOME NOTES ON THE NEGRO AS A VOTER IN A SMALL SOUTHERN CITY. *Public Opinion Q. 1966 30(2): 279-284.* A study of the voting habits of the Negro population of Jackson, Tennessee. Jackson does not conform to V. O. Key's statement that "teachers, tradesmen, lawyers, businessmen, doctors, landowners compose a much larger proportion of Negro voters than of the Negro population." Based on published materials; 4 tables, 3 notes. S. L. Banks

2655. Marburger, Carl L. SCHOOL AND COMMUNITY ROLES IN EFFECTIVE PLANNING. *J. of Negro Educ. 1964 33(3): 304-310.* The author deals with the respective roles of school and community in planning for socially disadvantaged children and youth. S. C. Pearson, Jr.

2656. Marcell, David W. CRISIS IN POLITICS. *Colorado Q. 1968 17(2): 210-222.* In 1968 two aspects of American politics are notable: the failure of the parties to produce a widely popular leader, and the violence and militancy of some minor political groups. Since the death of John Fitzgerald Kennedy politics has become divergent, factional, and ideologically polarized. The problem rests in the ability of Americans to realistically approach the late 20th century. American thought, uniquely, has been formed on a basic consensus of the political and social good life. Now America faces problems which the consensus, created in agrarian America of the 17th and 18th centuries, cannot successfully confront. Two areas of special importance are urban problems and the problem of poverty and the Negro. B. A. Storey

2657. Marcus, Matityahu. RACIAL COMPOSITION AND HOME PRICE CHANGES: A CASE STUDY. *J. of the Am. Inst. of Planners 1968 34(5): 334-338.* "This case study of Plainfield, New Jersey, considered the hypothesis that the continuing entry of Negroes into a suburban community, surrounded by municipalities without Negro populations, will bring a decline in property values. Examination of price changes since 1955 turned up no evidence of either an absolute or relative adverse racial effect on home prices." J

2658. Marcus, Robert, Bispo, Edward, and Katuna, Irving. SOCIAL CHANGE AND CURRICULUM INNOVATION. *J. of Negro Educ. 1967 36(2): 121-128.* Describes a program developed at Benjamin Franklin High School in San Francisco, California, to help provide suitable adult images for lower-class minority group children. The program, called Cultural Profiles For All, brings successful community members of the minority group into the school. Curriculum materials are developed using biographical and vocational profiles of such persons and deliberately including minority group history. The article concludes with a discussion of The Franklin Plan, a proposal to deal with educational problems of core cities through a sister-school approach. A school in a disadvantaged area is united with one in a higher socioeconomic area. The two share facilities, faculty, experience, and students. S. C. Pearson, Jr.

2659. Marlar, Mary A. THE LIGHTS ARE ON. *Am. Educ. 1967 3(5): 21-24.* Describes the organization and operation of a special evening program called Operation REACH (Raising Educational Achievement of Child and Home) in a small, impoverished, all-Negro community. The project was designed not only to aid the children but also adults, and to provide a bridge between school and home. The most success has been in providing remedial tutorial assistance for secondary pupils. Illus. W. R. Boedecker

2660. Marvick, Dwaine. THE POLITICAL SOCIALIZATION OF THE AMERICAN NEGRO. *Ann. of the Am. Acad. of Pol. and Social Sci. 1965 361: 112-127.* "American Negroes perforce 'came to terms' historically with a locality-circumscribed political world. A huge northward migration has occurred, and the younger Negro has gradually become aware of metropolitan as well as national American political processes as they affect him. Opinion-survey evidence reveals clear contrasts by region and generation in Negro attitudes toward public officials; it also suggests that Negro evaluations of political opportunity sometimes approach parity with matched counterpart groups of underprivileged whites. A shift has also occurred in Negro leadership, away from accommodationist civic dignitaries, tapped by whites as liaison spokesmen for the Negro subcommunity, to Negro professional politicians, negotiating from positions of pivotal electoral power both in Southern localities and Northern metropolitan districts. The middle-class leadership of the National Association for the Advancement of Colored People (NAACP) and Urban League, moreover, has been supplemented...by [such] direct-action protest organizers [as] the Southern Christian Leadership Conference [and others]....Full...possession by Negroes of a reformulated place in American polity depends, however, on the proliferation of community-level opportunities to learn new skills and roles in civic affairs." 3 tables, 15 notes.

J

2661. Marx, Gary T. RELIGION: OPIUM OR INSPIRATION OF CIVIL RIGHTS MILITANCY AMONG NEGROES? *Am. Sociol. R. 1967 32(1): 64-72.* "The implications of religion for protest are somewhat contradictory. With their stake in the status quo, established religious institutions have generally fostered conservatism, although as the source of humanistic values they have occasionally inspired movements of protest. For a nationwide sample of Negroes, analysis of the effect of religiosity on protest attitudes indicates that the greater the religious involvement, the less the militancy. However, among the religious, religion does not seem to inhibit, and may even inspire, protest among those with a temporal as distinct from an otherworldly orientation. Still, until such time as religion loosens its hold, or comes to embody more of a temporal orientation, it may be seen as an important factor inhibiting black militancy."

J

2662. Marx, Gary T. THE WHITE NEGRO AND THE NEGRO WHITE. *Phylon 1967 28(2): 168-177.* Contends that in their striving for identity a part of the Negro middle class and some whites have reversed the roles traditionally assigned to people of their color. The author compares some Negroes and the whites who adhere to a beat philosophy of life and finds that in spite of obvious differences some important similarities may be noted. One is that as groups in transition both the Negroes and hippies have a distorted image of both the group they seek to identify with and the one they seek to leave. For example, the black bourgeoisie take a positive stand toward middle-class values and are very critical of average Negroes while the hippies reject middle-class values and take their cues for behavior from working-class Negroes. Both groups attempt to avoid identification with what they assume society regards as their past and both may take extreme steps to show that they are just the opposite. Both emphasize what they assume to be the customs and mores of the group with which they are attempting to identify. The result has been a misconception by Negroes of what it means to be middle-class white and a misconception by hippies of what it really means to be Negro. Based on published sources; 36 notes.   D. N. Brown

2663. Mathes, William. A NEGRO PEPYS. *Antioch R. 1965 25(3): 456-462.* A review of the novel *Manchild in the Promised Land* by Claude Brown (New York: Macmillan, 1965). The work, about the "first Northern urban generation of Negroes" is highly praised and Brown is compared to Samuel Pepys. He says that both give the "feeling of being alive in their respective milieus." The difference, however, is that Pepys' England is gone, while Brown's Harlem is a "contemporary tragedy." D. F. Rossi

2664. Mathewson, Kent. "LEFTOVER" CITIES REQUIRE REGIONAL PROBLEM SOLVING. *Natl. Civic R. 1971 60(5): 266-270.* Regional agencies are a key way to solve urban problems. The "institutional renewal" they need now is a renewal of faith. Regional agencies are not, as the Columbia University sociologists Frances F. Piven and Richard A. Cloward maintain, a ploy to rob Negroes of political power in cities where they are approaching majorities. 3 notes. H. S. Marks

2665. Matthews, Donald R. and Prothro, James W. POLITICAL FACTORS AND NEGRO VOTER REGISTRATION IN THE SOUTH. *Am. Pol. Sci. R. 1963 57(2): 355-367.* The authors have "attempted to determine the relationships between political and legal factors and variations in the rate of Negro voter registration in the Southern states. In order to control the substantial effects of social and economic factors on Negro registration, we employed a multiple-regression equation containing the typical relationships between 21 social and economic variables and Negro registration rates in the counties of the region." Data cover from 1900 to the present. "...it would appear that political variables [e.g. formal voter requirements, State factional systems, and extent of partisan competition] are nearly as important as socio-economic factors in explaining Negro registration in the South." B. W. Onstine

2666. Matthews, Donald R. and Prothro, James W. SOCIAL AND ECONOMIC FACTORS AND NEGRO VOTER REGISTRATIONS IN THE SOUTH. *Am. Pol. Sci. R. 1963 57(1): 24-44.* Makes a detailed "analysis of the relationships between variations in rate of Negro voter registration in southern counties (in the USA) and the social and economic characteristics of those counties." Data is principally drawn for 1950 from the U.S. Census and a wide variety of other sources, but also comparisons are made with 1900 and 1940. "The correlation between all of the social and economic variables and county registration rates of Negroes is .53, which explains about 28 percent (R2) of the variation in Negro registration." B. W. Onstine

2667. Mayer, Kurt B. CLASS AND STATUS IN THE UNITED STATES. *Q. R. [Great Britain] 1965 303(646): 450-459.* The American class system, whose gradations are denied by the American creed, is characterized by an unique brand of equalitarianism, gross inequities in income, wealth and power, and a racial caste system. The equalitarian ideology insists that each individual (white) be allowed to improve his economic and social position according to his personal capacity, with an implied moral obligation to avail himself of every available opportunity. The material inequities which continue to exist are mitigated by the high absolute level of income, which in blurring outer class distinctions of dress, education, residence and recreation is in turn leading to considerable inner "status anxiety." The remaining pockets of poverty are concentrated among groups of unskilled, migrant farm workers, broken families, aged, handicapped and, above all, Negroes who until recently have not been included in the ideology of equal opportunity. Their current militancy in this regard poses the most immediate challenge to the established class structure.   R. G. Schafer

2668. Mayo, Selz C. and Hamilton, C. Horace. THE RURAL NEGRO POPU-LATION OF THE SOUTH IN TRANSITION. *Phylon 1963 24(2): 160-171.* Negro population changes include growth rates and redistribution, changing residential composition, fertility and migration, and functional roles. Negro population is increasing in the Southeast, but declining relative to whites. During 1940-60, it increased 9.4 percent in the Southeast, 48.7 percent nationally. Negroes are now predominantly urban, as is the white population. The farm population has rapidly declined, the Negro "rural-nonfarm" population has increased. Fertility ratios for Negro women in all age classes are higher than whites. In the 1950's, the Southeast lost almost a million people by migration; about a million and a half departing Negroes were offset by only 381 thousand new white residents. Young Negro adults left in high proportions. Both Negro and white sharecroppers have largely disappeared. Negro employment has not kept pace with population. There have been rapidly rising indices in education, but the rural picture is dismal. Higher levels of educational attainment will affect the entire Negro fabric in the South.   L. Filler

2669. Mays, Nebraska. BEHAVIORAL EXPECTATIONS OF NEGRO AND WHITE TEACHERS ON RECENTLY DESEGREGATED PUBLIC SCHOOL FACULTIES. *J. of Negro Educ. 1963 32(3): 218-226.* The author concludes that "with regard to most of the behavioral activities studied in this investigation it seems that Negroes probably will express a much greater desire for freedom to participate in the activities than whites; however, it appears that they will differ little from whites with respect to expectations of how they will really behave."   S. C. Pearson, Jr.

2670. McAndrew, Gordon. EDUCATIONAL INNOVATION IN NORTH CAROLINA - A CASE STUDY. *J. of Negro Educ. 1967 36(2): 94-99.* Discusses the purposes, methods, and initial achievements of the North Carolina Advancement School, a project of the Learning Institute of North Carolina supported by Federal, State, and Carnegie Corporation funds. The school, established in 1964, enrolls 300 eighth-grade boys each quarter. The boys are nominated by their schools as of average or better ability but underachievers, and they have shown significant improvement as a result of their quarter in the residential Advancement School. The school also accepts 20 visiting teachers per quarter for training in working with such students. The permanent staff is concerned not only with these programs but also with research and development of methods and materials.   S. C. Pearson, Jr.

2671. McBride, Conrad L. THE 1964 ELECTION IN COLORADO. *Western Pol. Q. 1965 18(2, pt. 2): 475-480.* Colorado's politics are especially marked by a two-party tradition. In the span of six years, 1958-64 (four elections), the State experienced a complete cycle of political change. The details of these changes are offered; the 1964 elections were a climax insofar as the 1962 Republican victory was wiped out in a complete Democratic landslide - by far the largest victory by one party in the State's history - Johnson over Goldwater by 472,714 to 295,533 and in the congressional races Democrats won all four seats. Efforts at reapportionment undertaken by the Republican-dominated legislature after 1962 were undone by the U.S. Supreme Court and the results of a special session of the legislature had disoriented the Republican Party. The nomination of a Right candidate by the Republican Party, identified with "extremism," increased the disaffection in that party. The Democratic Party, on the other hand, was united - intensely so after President Kennedy's assassination. Note is made of the fact that urban centers are growing rapidly and that in them the Negro, Spanish, and Italian segments are particularly increasing. Where these groups lived the sweep of the Democratic Party was even more pronounced than elsewhere; and the weight of such minority strength in the State's politics seems sure to grow.

H. Aptheker

2672. McConahay, John B. ATTITUDES OF NEGROES TOWARD THE CHURCH FOLLOWING THE LOS ANGELES RIOT. *Sociol. Analysis 1970 31(1): 12-22.* "Data from a sample survey are presented bearing upon the hypotheses that following the Watts uprising (1) Negroes in Los Angeles were able to distinguish those persons, groups and institutions helping and supporting them from those hindering them, and (2) they regarded the church as an ally in their struggle. The data revealed that Negroes expressed great approval of the church, their attitudes were generally more favorable than those of a sample of suburban whites, they discriminated in their evaluations of political groups and leaders, they ranked the church third behind the Democratic party and the U.S. Congress in their evaluations of social institutions, and black clergymen were highly regarded as representatives of the Negro community. Among those less favorable in their attitude toward the church were males, the better educated, the urban socialized, and those identifying themselves as working class. Denominational affiliation was not related to evaluations of the church." J

2673. McDowell, Sophia. HOW ANTI-WHITE ARE NEGRO YOUTH? *Am. Educ. 1968 4(3): 2-4.* A summary of an investigation of interracial attitudes of Negro youth living in Washington, D.C. Questionnaire data were collected from 582 male and female high school students and dropouts between the ages of 16 and 19. Points which stand out in the study include, "First, Negro willingness to associate with whites is, in general, high, much higher than we expected. Second, this willingness is not extended equally to all whites or in all situations, but varies according to the kinds of whites and the kind of situation.... Standing in the margins of a white society that both invites and rejects, the Negro youth is frustrated by the incongruity. Hence anger. Hence violence. Only when he is assured of sincere acceptance by whites will he be able to demonstrate the findings of our study: his willingness to live together in interracial amity and good will." Based on the study entitled "Prejudice and Other Interracial Attitudes of Negro Youth" completed under a Cooperative Research contract with the U.S. Office of Education. Table. W. R. Boedecker

2674. McKenna, William J. THE NEGRO VOTE IN PHILADELPHIA ELEC-
TIONS. *Pennsylvania Hist. 1965 32(4): 406-415.* The strength of the Democratic
Party in Philadelphia lies in the voting behavior of the 17 predominately Negro
areas. The author examines this voting pattern and the factors that have in-
fluenced its development. There are six main factors influencing the voting behav-
ior of this Negro bloc: 1) Negroes have identified the Democratic Party with the
Roosevelt reform policies; 2) economically, the Negroes feel that their demands
for jobs, housing, and better education can be met by the Democrats and not the
Republicans; 3) the Democratic administration has been active in providing
Government jobs for Negroes; 4) there is a need for public housing and, since the
Democrats initiated the first improved housing bills, the Negroes feel that the
Democrats are more committed to housing needs; 5) they feel that the Democrats
are the best hope for the improvement of civil rights; and 6) in the 1963 mayoralty
campaign, the Negroes felt that the Republicans had merely " 'written off the
Negro vote' " and that they were conducting a "white" campaign. 4 tables, 24
notes.   M. J. McBaine

2675. Meeth, L. Richard. THE REPORT ON PREDOMINANTLY NEGRO
COLLEGES ONE YEAR LATER. *J. of Negro Educ. 1966 35(3): 204-209.*
Traces the background, method, conclusions, recommendations, and results of a
study financed by the Carnegie Corporation and conducted by the Institute of
Higher Education. The report prepared by Earl J. McGrath and published as
The Predominantly Negro Colleges and Universities in Transition called for
strengthening the Negro institutions. It has contributed in the year after its
publication to increased legislation in favor of Negro colleges, greater interest in
the problems of Negro colleges, extended research and consultation in the education of Negroes, and a more optimistic atmosphere for the Negro college.
                                                             S. C. Pearson, Jr.

2676.   Middlekauff, Robert M. , Edwards, Nelson Jack, and Wallen,
Saul. EMPLOYING THE DISADVANTAGED: THREE VIEW-
POINTS. *Arbitration J. 1969 24(3): 143-160.* "National policy and the public
conscience dictate that millions of Negroes and members of other minority groups
who were the victims of discrimination in employment be absorbed into the work
force without further delay. But the offer of a job on a nondiscriminatory basis
does not fulfill all obligations in the case of individuals who have been left ill
prepared for full participation in the industrial community. An AAA [American
Arbitration Association] educational program heard from spokesmen of management and labor, and from a professional arbitrator who was then the directing
head of the New York Urban Coalition on ways of righting the historical wrongs
within the framework of modern collective bargaining. Major excerpts of the
addresses are reproduced."   J

2677. Miller, Albert H. PROBLEMS OF THE MINORITY STUDENT ON
THE CAMPUS. *Liberal Educ. 1969 55(1): 18-23.* Elaborates on some of the
problems facing black students in today's universities. Rejection is the common

fact of a black's experiences. The militant black will not compromise on his demand for a share in decisions about college life, college rules, college curricula, and college administration.   C. G. Lauritsen

2678. Miller, Henry. SOCIAL WORK IN THE BLACK GHETTO: THE NEW COLONIALISM. *Social Work 1969 14(3): 65-76.* Social welfare's stance toward the Negro has been one of philanthropic colonialism, having two aspects: paternalism predicated on the assumption of cultural underdevelopment, and clinicalism founded on a presumption of psychological damage resulting from the Negro's history. A comparison is made of the values of cultural pluralism with those of the melting pot ideology. It is recommended that Americans try the great experiment to opt for the desirability of ethnicity, to provide a decent standard of living for minority groups and an opportunity to enter the American mainstream while at the same time maintaining their differences. 27 notes.
W. L. Willigan

2679. Mitchell, Melvin L., Mann, Lawrence Casey, II , and Jayson, Robert F. THE CASE FOR ENVIRONMENTAL PLANNING EDUCATION IN BLACK SCHOOLS. *J. of the Am. Inst. of Planners 1970 36(4): 279-284.* "Establishment of radically new professional-level environmental planning schools at a selected number of black urban based colleges and universities is an essential aspect of a larger strategy for rapidly increasing the supply of effective black planning professionals, while at the same time creating an American planning education process that is relevant to the ideal of a multiracial, urban, post-industrial society. The strategy of beginning new programs at black schools rests on two key assumptions: (1) black people themselves must evolve an urban theory of group power based on new realities - white people cannot supply them with such a theory; and (2) it is black people who are most desperately and immediately in need of functional mergers between the behavioral sciences and the 'manmade environment' professions - functional mergers which these professions seem incapable of taking beyond the level of 'interdisciplinary' rhetoric. Thus, it is black scholars, activists, professionals, and technicians at black urban institutions who must build the first generation models for relevant urban planning education throughout the American higher education system."
J

2680. Morgan, Gordon D. EXPLORATORY STUDY OF PROBLEMS OF ACADEMIC ADJUSTMENT OF NIGERIAN STUDENTS IN AMERICA. *J. of Negro Educ. 1963 32(3): 208-217.* Basing his article on responses to a questionnaire, the author concludes that "Nigerians expect instructors to show concern for their problems as individuals trying to succeed in the academic process. These problems cannot be divorced from concern for the roles they will play in the modernization of Nigeria."   S. C. Pearson, Jr.

2681. Morison, Robert S. FOUNDATIONS AND UNIVERSITIES. *Daedalus 1964 93(4): 1109-1141.* A study of foundations and their influence upon universities. In the early 20th century, the Carnegie Foundation played an important part in establishing more uniform standards of admission to colleges and universities, in systematizing their finances, in raising salaries, and in severing denominational ties. The General Education Board introduced the "matching" principle, earmarked large funds for Negro education, conducted a fellowship program, and gave substantial sums to "progressive" colleges and for experimental and honors programs. In the first decades of the century, foundations exercised a significant coordinating influence. In the succeeding decades they supported various "interdisciplinary" programs and area studies of Russia, Japan, China, and other "exotic" countries. The foundations have indirectly influenced universities by their support of such organizations as the National Research Council, the Social Science Research Council, the American Council of Learned Societies, the American Council on Education, the Institute of International Education, and others. The author concludes with an inquiry as to possible future developments, especially in the fields of the humanities, arts, and law. 15 notes.

E. P. Stickney

2682. Morrison, Joseph L. ILLEGITIMACY, STERILIZATION, AND RACISM: A NORTH CAROLINA CASE HISTORY. *Social Service R. 1965 39(1): 1-10.* A history and analysis of two bills which were presented to the General Assemblies of North Carolina: in 1957, an amendment (SB 321) to the Eugenic Sterilization Law, which made sterilization of sexually delinquent individuals permissible at State expense; and, in 1959, a still more stringent Sterilization Bill (SB 113) which provided for compulsory sterilization of grossly sexually delinquent persons. "Neither of these two bills became law, but the concerns that gave rise to such bizarre legislative 'solutions' remain latent and endemic. The illegitimacy-sterilization-racist mixture is strong medicine, which remains potentially dangerous." In North Carolina, the prevalence of illegitimacy among the lower-class Negro population created a particular difficulty for social agencies because the majority of these unmarried mothers had no means of support except through public assistance. "The Jolly-Davis Sterilization Bill was defeated not by the established welfare agencies...but by ordinary people offended in their religion and in their sense of humanity." 43 notes.   D. D. Cameron

2683. Moynihan, Daniel P. THE PROFESSORS AND THE POOR. *Commentary 1968 46(2): 19-29.* The war on poverty has transformed during the last five years from a program concerned generally with the poor to one concerned with Negroes. The war on poverty was the work of intellectuals. The author describes some of the influences on John F. Kennedy that made him eager to improve the lot of the poor. This work fit perfectly into the style of Lyndon B. Johnson. The author investigates some unproven generalities that were used in the 1960's and were the rationale for the poverty bill of 1964. The people who developed and administered the program knew little about Negro urban poverty. When violence broke out in the Negro cities, community-action programs were blamed. The author concludes with some of the questions that should be asked before beginning further programs.   C. G. Lauritsen

2684. Mullen, Patrick B. A NEGRO STREET PERFORMER: TRADITION AND INNOVATION. *Western Folklore 1970 29(2): 91-103.* Studies a street entertainer who reflects the general values of Negro culture. The man is George

"Bongo Joe" Coleman (b. 1928), who was studied in Galveston, Texas, in 1967. Discusses his performance, which combines several elements in the "soul" tradition. Within the traditional street singer format Coleman displays considerable innovation. To his music he adds spoken routines, generally comments on American society as a black man sees it. Through his act he can talk about racial subjects in a way that would not be permitted by southern whites under ordinary circumstances. Coleman is proud of his role as entertainer, a role which is given high status in Afro-American culture and thus allows him to express Negro values. 15 notes. R. A. Trennert

2685. Murphy, Judith and Gross, Ronald. CAN THE ARTS "TURN ON" POOR KIDS TO LEARNING? *Teachers Coll. Record 1968 69(6): 581-586.* Isolated examples of experiments with the arts as motivating forces in unlocking the minds and spirits of deprived youngsters can be seen in the Watts Towers Art Center in Los Angeles, in Dorothy Maynor's music school in Harlem, in the Arts-for-Living Program on the Lower East Side of Manhattan, and in the communication course at the North Carolina Advancement School in Winston-Salem. Now is the time to move the arts into the center of the school program for the deprived. Both public and private funds are becoming available for such programs. C. P. McMahon

2686. Murray, Al and McDarrah, Fred. IMAGE AND LIKENESS IN HARLEM. *Urban R. 1967 2(2): 12-17.* Harlem has presented different pictures to different people. The dominant image of it as a ghetto for pathological Negroes divorced from the mainstream of American life is not necessarily accurate. The authors maintain that this stereotype exists because of preconceived notions and distorted attitudes toward the place. Having lived there, the authors feel that Harlem has many positive assets which should be interpreted as signs of human health rather than as indications of psychological disorder. The beauty of Harlem's architecture is presented in a series of photographs. Harlem is depicted as a part of metropolitan New York. H. B. Powell

2687. Nabrit, James M., Jr. CRITICAL SUMMARY AND EVALUATION. *J. of Negro Educ. 1963 32(4): 507-516.* Surveys contributions to this issue dealing with various aspects of "The Relative Progress of the American Negro since 1950." S. C. Pearson, Jr.

2688. Nelson, Harold A. A NOTE ON EDUCATION AND THE NEGRO REVOLT. *J. of Negro Educ. 1965 34(1): 99-102.* Stress upon education for Negroes will greatly facilitate the accomplishment of the general aims of the Negro revolt. S. C. Pearson, Jr.

2689. Nelson, Harold A. CHARITY, POVERTY AND RACE. *Phylon 1968 29(3): 303-316.* Charity in America is based on the concept of voluntary compassion and is not considered to be a right of the recipients. The recipients are not allowed to ask for more or to complain about what is given them. "Further, the concept of charity as a part of the ideological framework acts as a buttress to the existing structure of the society." Charity is designed not to better significantly the life of the recipient, but to keep him at a constant low level of existence, and deals with effects rather than causes. The War on Poverty follows this same basic attitude toward charity and the poor, as does the recent concern for the Negro and civil rights - neither posed as a challenge to the system. "Until it is possible to go beyond charity to a direct confrontation with the presently structured social system, the abject poor, the subjugated and the powerless remain and the society will continue to fail to come to grips with the realities of the problems which beset it."   R. D. Cohen

2690. Newman, Lucile F. FOLKLORE OF PREGNANCY: WIVES' TALES IN CONTRA COSTA COUNTY, CALIFORNIA. *Western Folklore 1969 28(2): 112-135.* Examines birth folklore in both a general sense and in one California county. Beliefs and rules about pregnancy are still very prevalent; new beliefs are being introduced. The cultural meaning of wives' tales is not to impart useful instructions to the expectant mother, but to symbolize the status of pregnancy. Several differences appear in the pregnancy beliefs of Negro and white groups. Negro beliefs tend largely to magic and are mostly concerned with marking or death. White beliefs are largely signs for determining sex and avoiding pain. Discusses traditional beliefs and modern tales which talk in medical terms, but which are still presented as superstitions. Fear of the unknown keeps these beliefs alive. Lists 284 pregnancy beliefs collected in Contra Costa County. Based on secondary sources and questionnaires; 23 notes, appendix.
                                                                                      R. A. Trennert

2691. Newton, Eunice S. and West, Earle H. THE PROGRESS OF THE NEGRO IN ELEMENTARY AND SECONDARY EDUCATION. *J. of Negro Educ. 1963 32(4): 466-483.* Examines the availability and quality of education for the Negro during the 1950's.   S. C. Pearson, Jr.

2692. Newton, Eunice Shaed. PLANNING FOR THE LANGUAGE DEVELOPMENT OF DISADVANTAGED CHILDREN AND YOUTH. *J. of Negro Educ. 1964 33(3): 264-274.* The author suggests that "the language arts program for disadvantaged children and youth should be in a continuum of linguistic experiences from nursery school through grade 14,...the development of proficiency in reading should be the dominant concern of the language program,...experiencing should be the basic activity of the language program,...the thinking processes (relating, generalizing, classifying, modifying) should be an integral part of language activities,...many and varied audio-visual materials should be utilized in the language program to reinforce multi-sensory learning,...teachers of the verbally handicapped must avoid alienating the pupil from the teaching-learning experience,...the language teacher...must function as a prototype in all communicative stiuations," and "promising instructional innovations should be experimented with."   S. C. Pearson, Jr.

2693. Neyland, Leedell W. WHY NEGRO HISTORY IN THE JUNIOR AND SENIOR HIGH SCHOOLS? *Social Studies 1967 58(7): 315-321.* Offers a well-reasoned argument for inclusion of Negro history in the junior and senior high school curriculum. It is thought that Negroes, as a result of having been instructed in Negro history, will have a better appreciation of their contributions to civilization and to American society, and majority groups will better understand and appreciate the Negro. Textbooks have failed to portray significant aspects of Negro life, and many segments of American society have formed negative opinions of the Negro, largely because of inadequate or distorted information. 19 notes.   L. Raife

2694. North, George E. and Buchanan, O. Lee. MATERNAL ATTITUDES IN A POVERTY AREA. *J. of Negro Educ. 1968 37(4): 418-425.* A 1967 study of 4- and 5-year-old children and their mothers in a Negro poverty area of Phoenix. The authors used primarily the Parental Attitude Research Instrument and the Illinois Test of Psycholingual Ability. They found two distinct types of maternal authoritarianism: "disgruntled authoritarianism (disgusted and pushing kind of control) and self-sacrificing authoritarianism (martyred kind of control)." They found a strong relationship between authoritarian mothers and low social class or low educational level. The authors surmise that these authoritarian attitudes are a response of poor mothers to the burdens of too many children, lack of resources, and little economic or family security. Table, 19 notes.
                                                                 B. D. Johnson

2695. Ohlendorf, George W. and Kuvlevsky, William P. RACIAL DIFFERENCES IN THE EDUCATIONAL ORIENTATIONS OF RURAL YOUTHS. *Social Sci. Q. 1968 49(2): 274-283.* A survey to ascertain whether racial differences exist in reference to the following dimensions of educational status orientations: "aspirations, expectations, anticipatory deflection, intensity of aspiration and certainty of expectation." The data were obtained from 530 students residing in three rural east central Texas counties. It is concluded that rural Negro boys and girls have higher educational aspirations and expectations than rural white youth. 5 tables, 27 notes.   D. F. Henderson

2696. Olson, Marvin E. SOCIAL AND POLITICAL PARTICIPATION OF BLACKS. *Am. Sociol. R. 1970 35(4): 682-697.* "Recent research has suggested that although blacks often participate less actively than whites in voluntary associations and voting, when socioeconomic status is controlled this relationship is reversed, with blacks becoming more active than whites. The present study expands this line of research into a wide variety of social and political activities, and also adds age as a second control variable. The general tendency for blacks to be more active than whites under these controlled conditions is found to occur in every type of activity investigated. Comparison of data collected in 1957 and 1968 indicates that the tendency has become more pronounced in recent years. Myrdal's 'compensation' interpretation of this trend, which has been accepted by all previous writers on this topic, is challenged as inadequate, since it does not explain black participation in such realms as mass media exposure, community activities, partisan political activities, and contacts with the government. An alternative 'ethnic community' thesis is proposed, and is partially substantiated by the finding that blacks who identify as members of an ethnic minority tend to be more active than nonidentifiers."   J

2697. Ornstein, Allan C. TECHNIQUES AND FUNDAMENTALS FOR TEACHING THE DISADVANTAGED. *J. of Negro Educ. 1967 36(2): 136-145.* Examines the areas of discipline and classroom management and of motivation and student achievement as central to teaching the disadvantaged. Success in teaching the disadvantaged depends largely on establishing and maintaining rules and routine in the classroom. Student achievement is motivated by good teaching which is practical, concrete, interesting, and oriented toward the child's level of learning. The teacher's attitude and the development of rapport between the teacher and the class are also important. Many specific suggestions are provided for classroom teachers of disadvantaged youth.   S. C. Pearson, Jr.

2698. Ornstein, Allan C. THEORY PRACTICES FOR TEACHING DISADVANTAGED YOUTH. *J. of Negro Educ. 1969 38(1): 82-85.* The results of special compensatory programs for disadvantaged children have not been very successful. The author suggests the use of good classroom teachers as consultants and the formation of summer demonstration schools with disadvantaged children. Any good teacher should be able to teach the disadvantaged, but the "teacher training institutions do not prepare good teachers." The development of an effective theory of good teaching would give teachers a frame of reference in which to work. 12 notes.   B. D. Johnson

2699. Ornstein, Allen C. PROGRAM REVISION FOR CULTURALLY DISADVANTAGED CHILDREN. *J. of Negro Educ. 1966 35(2): 117-124.* Suggests changes for urban schools to meet the needs of disadvantaged children. Proposals discussed include maximum use of school facilities; smaller classes and more individual attention; preschool education to increase learning readiness; textbook modification to focus on the role of minority groups in American history and culture; improved methods for selection of principals and supervisors; exposure of students to the riches of culture; comprehensive reading programs; provision of psychological, social, and other community services; orientation programs for students changing schools or classes; talent discovery programs; individualized testing and scheduling of programs; improvement of vocational education; evening programs; and enlistment of community action and support.
          S. C. Pearson, Jr.

2700. Overacker, Louise. THE CHANGING PATTERN OF AMERICAN POLITICS. *Australian J. of Pol. and Hist. 1966 12(1): 32-42.* A general survey of 20th-century American politics, which suggests that party alignments and structures are changing. Instead of the loosely knit, regional combinations, cohesive organizations, capable of unified national programs, are emerging. The "solid south" is seen to have changed because it became less dependent on agriculture and because of population migration. Definite party differences are seen to exist. Democrats appealed to urban workers, racial and ethnic minorities, and lower-income groups. The Republicans attracted rural Protestants, Anglo-Saxons, middle- and upper-income groups. The parties are not doctrinaire, but the author suggests each has an "implicit doctrine." Democrats favor innovation, human rights, and responsibility on world affairs. Republicans are cautious, traditional, opposed to expanding Federal controls, and hesitant about overseas commitments. Documented from political science works.   D. McIntyre

2701. Palley, Howard A. THE MIGRANT LABOR PROBLEM - ITS STATE AND INTERSTATE ASPECTS. *J. of Negro Educ. 1963 32(1); 35-42.* Discusses forces which have produced a "migrant labor problem," reform movements and interests opposing reform, and the inability of the States to achieve independently a solution to the problem. Urges that the time for Federal reform legislation is long overdue.   S. C. Pearson, Jr.

2702. Palmer, Roderick. GENERAL EDUCATION AND THE PROFESSION-BOUND NEGRO STUDENT. *J. of Negro Educ. 1964 33(1): 86-89.* The Negro should receive a different type of academic general education to help him overcome the cultural disadvantages of often inferior elementary and secondary education. The author's approach to general education is instrumental (goal directed).   S. C. Pearson, Jr.

2703. Palmore, Erdman. INTEGRATION AND PROPERTY VALUES IN WASHINGTON, D.C. *Phylon 1966 27(1): 15-19.* Reports the findings of a survey of 772 real-estate sales in six census tracts in the northern tip of Washington between 1954 and 1963. Four tracts experienced a rapid increase in the percentage of Negro ownership while two remained essentially all white. Property values increased in each tract over the decade but in widely varying amounts. The author concludes that a combination of factors rather than the single factor of an increase in percentage of Negro population explains the variations in property value increase.   S. C. Pearson, Jr.

2704. Panepinto, W. C. and Higgins, M. J. KEEPING ALCOHOLICS IN TREATMENT; EFFECTIVE FOLLOW-THROUGH PROCEDURES. *Q. J. of Studies on Alcohol 1969 30(2): 414-419.* "The procedures which increased the length and stability of patient participation in the outpatient Alcohol Clinic of the State University of New York, Brooklyn, included making one social worker responsible for all follow-through procedures and writing letters to patients who missed appointments. The clinic has over 1000 active patients, most of whom are lower-class Negro (56 [percent]) men (75 [percent]). During the 7 weeks prior to instituting the procedures 51 [percent] of 79 new admissions dropped out after less than 4 visits compared with 28 [percent] of 92 during the 7 weeks after *(p* [less than] .01); 57 [percent] of 284 vs 22 [percent] of 221 failed to keep 2 consecutive appointments *(p* [less than] .001); 57 [percent] of 388 patients attending the clinic vs 22 [percent] of 161 made unscheduled visits to the clinic *(p* [less than] .001); 33 [percent] of 128 long-term patients vs 8 [percent] of 197 dropped out after a first missed appointment *(p* [less than] .001)."   J

2705. Parker, Franklin. HUMAN RELATIONS AND THE SCHOOL. *J. of Human Relations 1968 16(1): 24-31.* Discusses race relations in the United States since 1954 and the high cost of discrimination, "something teachers need to talk about honestly in the classroom." Life-expectancy rates are lower among Negroes. Their families have been forced into a matriarchal pattern, and their children have poor learning experiences. It should be emphasized that whites are not inherently more intelligent than Negroes and that racial differences are probably adaptive characteristics provided by nature to enable men to survive in different environments.   D. J. Abramoske

2706. Parker, James H. THE INTERACTION OF NEGROES AND WHITES IN AN INTEGRATED CHURCH SETTING. *Social Forces 1968 46(3): 359-366.* A study of racial integration between whites, Japanese, and Negroes in one Baptist Church in Chicago. The hypothesis is that a positive association exists between social class and interracial interaction. Racial composition of membership was 71 percent Negro, 25 percent white, and 4 percent Oriental. The "most active" members were the managerial or professional class (55 percent) as compared to the clerical workers (20 percent) and skilled or unskilled workers (25 percent). The church population was "selective" in that the members were not violently opposed to racial integration. There was more segregated seating at Sunday services than at Wednesday night suppers. Conclusion: that the people who are more involved in the life of the church are more racially integrated. Several secondary explanations are explored including areas of church location, status composition, history of leadership, and tradition of liberal interpretation of Christianity. Based on participant observation (608 observations on a group of 38 subjects); 4 tables.   A. S. Freedman

2707. Parks, Norman L. TENNESSEE POLITICS SINCE KEFAUVER AND REECE: A "GENERALIST" VIEW. *J. of Pol. 1966 28(1): 144-168.* Analyzes the political situation in Tennessee since the deaths of Senator Estes Kefauver (d. 1963) and Congressman Carroll Reece (d. 1961). "Instead of two one-party systems living under a *modus vivendi* of necessity and convenience, we have in 1964 two parties in a state-wide campaign involving issues and voter response as much or more like that of the nation than of the South. Instead of small, fragmented Negro groups under venal leaders voting with free poll tax receipts for white-man issues, there is a disciplined bloc oriented to Negro issues with the potential to swing state and local elections. Instead of a labor vote whose public endorsement was a hindrance rather than a help, there is a less disciplined but effective labor front carrying considerable weight in the industrial areas. And, finally, in the cities there has appeared the phenomenon of urban Republicanism and class voting like that of the North and East." The liberal Kefauver movement has survived his death and has stabilized itself as the dominant wing of the Democratic Party. Negroes and labor, working together, have become a political force to be reckoned with. A two-party system has emerged, with strong Republican machinery established in the Democratic sections of Tennessee. 4 figs., 3 tables, 25 notes.   D. D. Cameron

2708. Parris, Wendell A. A NEW APPROACH TO EDUCATING NEGRO CHILDREN IN GRAY AREA SCHOOLS. *Negro Hist. Bull. 1964 28(3): 61-64, (4): 91, 93.* Discusses the problems of making educational experiences in large city schools meaningful for Negro children living in lower income areas and suggests specific changes which should be introduced to reach this objective.

L. Gara

2709. Parsons, Cynthia and Welch, W. Bruce. MISSISSIPPI'S BEEHIVE COLLEGE. *Am. Educ. 1967 4(1): 19-22, 28.* Surveys the transformation of the small "predominantly Negro" Jackson State College in Mississippi from a struggling teacher training institution to one leading a revolution in the education of Negro teachers throughout the State. Financial assistance from a variety of private foundations as well as Federal agencies is credited for the college's rapid progress. The author concludes that not only the curriculum and faculty have been transformed, but "Students, too, are a different breed than those who came to the college 17 years ago. They are more determined, confident that they can succeed, and that they can speed the pace of change throughout the South. Not with bitterness - few if any Jackson State students were involved in last spring's riots in which a man was killed a few blocks from the campus, say college administrators." 6 photos.

W. R. Boedecker

2710. Pasca, Alyce E. A BUSINESS CAREER FOR THE NEGRO MALE (A COOPERATIVE VENTURE BETWEEN A UNIVERSITY AND BUSINESS). *J. of Negro Educ. 1969 38(1): 64-68.* Describes Roosevelt University's BOOST Program (Business Occupational Opportunities Scholarship Trainee Program) which provided to six young Negro men 4-year full tuition awards, a stipend, and opportunity to work summers with leading business firms. Today there are openings in business for Negroes, but there are few qualified for these positions. This program is one answer, but a great deal of training should be given to the counselors, teachers, and business executives involved to help them understand the behavior of lower status Negroes. The program is continuing at Roosevelt University, and expansion is planned. 4 notes.

B. D. Johnson

2711. Pascal, Anthony. BLACK GOLD AND BLACK CAPITALISM. *Public Interest 1970 19: 111-119.* Minority groups must dominate a specific industry or "turf" to enter the mainstream of economic and social life of the Nation. Although Negroes are increasingly entering the professions, and have established roles in sports and entertainment, what is needed is a sector of the private economy which is an integral part of society that can provide great numbers of skilled and unskilled jobs as well as management opportunities. Proposes the gas station business as such a possibility. This industry employs 400 thousand people, generates 25 billion dollars in sales, and (most importantly) requires a low investment for the initial expense. Encouragement for the entrance of Negroes into this field could be supported with public and private aid.

E. C. Hyslop

2712. Paschal, Billy J. THE ROLE OF SELF CONCEPT IN ACHIEVEMENT. *J. of Negro Educ. 1968 37(4): 392-396.* A study of 152 seventh graders of a junior high school in Dade County, Florida, using the Spivack Response Form. The subjects, 80 boys and 72 girls, were from 11 to 14 years old and lived in an urban, middle-class community. The study showed a relationship between the student's self concept and his grades in all major subjects except for the nonverbal subject of mathematics. It was also found that a disproportionate number of those in the Inadequate Self Concept category were younger siblings. The author extends these findings to the hypothesis that possibly the Negro student's self concept has a relationship to his grades. 2 tables, 9 notes.   B. D. Johnson

2713. Penn, Nolan. RACIAL INFLUENCE ON VOCATIONAL CHOICE. *J. of Negro Educ. 1966 35(1): 88-89.* Reports the findings of a study conducted among junior high school students in Compton, California. Students were asked, "Will your racial background help, hinder, neither, your getting the type of job you would like most to spend your whole life working at?" Students questioned were classified as Negro, white, Mexican, Chinese, Japanese, or Jewish. The results of the study suggest that the racial or ethnic background of boys included does have some influence on their vocational choices. This was less apparent with respect to the girls.   S. C. Pearson, Jr.

2714. Perry, Jane G. THE PREPARATION OF DISADVANTAGED YOUTH FOR EMPLOYMENT AND CIVIC RESPONSIBILITIES. *J. of Negro Educ. 1964 33(3): 275-281.* The author describes various programs designed to provide motivation, training and education, and professional help necessary in the preparation of disadvantaged youth for employment and civic responsibility.
                                                             S. C. Pearson, Jr.

2715. Perry, Jane Greverus. THE JOB OUTLOOK FOR NEGRO YOUTH. *J. of Negro Educ. 1964 33(2): 111-116.*

2716. Petrof, John V. BUSINESS ADMINISTRATION CURRICULA IN PREDOMINANTLY NEGRO COLLEGES. *J. of Negro Educ. 1966 35(3): 276-279.* Reports the findings of a study designed to measure the adequacy of business curricula in predominantly Negro colleges. Forty surveyed institutions offer 1,205 courses. Thirty-eight percent are in the field of accounting, 33 percent in the field of secretarial science, and 29 percent cover other functional areas. There has been virtually no curricula change since 1958. The study suggests that the majority of these institutions are not keeping up with changing times and are preparing students to fill clerical positions rather than to exercise business leadership. Critical examination and revision of programs is needed. 10 notes.
                                                             S. C. Pearson, Jr.

2717. Petrof, John V. READERSHIP STUDY OF THE INFLUENCE OF PRINTED COMMERCIAL MESSAGES ON NEGRO READERS IN AT-LANTA, GEORGIA. *Phylon 1967 28(4): 399-407.* The function of advertising is to provide a firm with a communications channel through which it can promote its goods or services to the public. Newspaper advertising is one of the cheapest forms of accomplishing this objective, but there are many factors which determine its effectiveness. Employers have accelerated integration in society by hiring Negroes for responsible positions, but they may be retarding integration by segregating Negroes as customers in the format of their advertisements and in their selection of advertising media. After examining advertisements in newspapers specifically aimed at Negro and white readers the author concluded that many firms purchase space in minority publications on the assumption that the message will have a better impact on the minority group. His conclusion is that this hypothesis lacks validity. Atlanta Negroes notice advertisements featuring exclusively Negro products and services better in the segregated medium. Advertisers featuring products and services of general use can communicate with Negro readers better if they beam their messages through general newspapers. Based on published sources; table, 2 figures, 12 notes.   D. N. Brown

2718. Pettigrew, Thomas F. NEGRO AMERICAN INTELLIGENCE: A NEW LOOK AT AN OLD CONTROVERSY. *J. of Negro Educ. 1964 33(1): 6-25.* Reviews the position of the "scientific racist" and the modern psychologist and concludes that intelligence "is a plastic product of inherited structure developed by environmental stimulation and opportunity, an alloy of endowment and experience" and that the mean differences observed between Negro and white children are largely the result of environmental rather than genetic factors.
S. C. Pearson, Jr.

2719. Phillips, Romeo Eldridge. STUDENT ACTIVITIES AND SELF-CONCEPT. *J. of Negro Educ. 1969 38(1): 32-37.* Reports on the results of a study made at a high school in Marquis, Michigan, to determine if there was a significant correlation between participation in student activities and scores on a self-concept measure. The students were 80 percent Negro, and only seniors who had been at the school since the ninth grade were subjects. The Osgood Semantic Differential was used to measure self-concept. A high correlation was found between participation and self-concept for boys, but there was no apparent relationship for girls. Eighty-five percent of the nonparticipants, however, had high self-concept scores, indicating that other variables were affecting positive self-concepts. A questionnaire on the activities students found most helpful showed they preferred those which gave public exposure, such as athletics and music. Table, 8 notes.   B. D. Johnson

2720. Pierre-Noel, Lois Jones. AMERICAN NEGRO ART IN PROGRESS. *Negro Hist. Bull. 1967 30(6): 6-9.* Summarizes the development of American Negro art. Mentions many prominent artists, of whom few earn their living directly from art. Most are teachers and commercial artists. 5 illus.
D. H. Swift

2721. Polansky, Norman A. POWERLESSNESS AMONG RURAL APPALACHIAN YOUTH. *Rural Sociol. 1969 34(2): 219-222.* Defines "felt powerlessness" as "the degree to which the individual believes that he has little control over his fate, but either is at the mercy of outside forces beyond his control, or his circumstances are due largely to chance, or both." Data for this study of powerlessness were collected from 120 white and 60 black students (under age 16) in grades nine and 10 who lived in rural or semirural areas of western North Carolina and northern Georgia. Concludes that a combination of race and class position produces a lower powerlessness score from those whites who have a high socioeconomic status. There is a distinct parallel between the phenomenon of felt powerlessness among disadvantaged groups in both urban slums and rural mountains. Although a sense of powerlessness may affect anyone, it is less likely to be as strong among youngsters who are white and whose life circumstances are more secure. 2 tables, note, biblio.   D. D. Cameron

2722. Pruitt, Shirley. ETHNIC AND RACIAL COMPOSITION OF SE-LECTED CLEVELAND NEIGHBORHOODS. *Social Sci. 1968 43(3): 171-174.* "The hypothesis is that neighborhoods in Cleveland, Ohio, which have contained and retained highly ethnic populations are neighborhoods which have been least affected by the growing Negro population in that city. Conversely, the least amount of resistance to Negro occupancy in a neighborhood has occurred in those neighborhoods which do not contain a large proportion of ethnic groups. When this hypothesis was tested, it was not substantiated. Negroes, in fact, live in neighborhoods which are highly ethnic. The proportion of any one ethnic group to the total area population does appear to be a factor in the proportion of Negroes residing in the area."   J

2723. Psencik, Leroy F. TEACHING ABOUT THE NEGRO IN SOCIAL STUDIES - A GUIDE TO SOURCES. *Social Studies 1970 61(5): 195-200.* Lists and summarizes the contents of authentic sources (i.e., general references, books, films, and records) relating to the study of instruction of Negro history and culture in America.   L. R. Raife

2724. Radford, Frederick. THE JOURNEY TOWARDS CASTRATION: IN-TERRACIAL SEXUAL STEREOTYPES IN ELLISON'S "INVISIBLE MAN." *J. of Am. Studies [Great Britain] 1971 4(2): 227-231.* Analyzes the sexual incidents in Ralph Ellison's novel (New York: Random House, 1952). With varying degrees of success, Ellison used the incidents to explode white stereotypes about Negro sexual behavior. He utilized his craft to vindicate Negroes and to exact "revenge" upon white tormentors. Ellison delved into black-white conflicts and explained them on the basis of Sigmund Freud's interpretations of human sexual taboos and desires. Based on the *Invisible Man,* the writings of Freud, and parallel commentaries by James Baldwin; 5 notes.   H. T. Lovin

2725. Radin, Norma and Kamii, Constance K. THE CHILD-REARING ATTI-TUDES OF DISADVANTAGED NEGRO MOTHERS AND SOME EDU-CATIONAL IMPLICATIONS. *J. of Negro Educ. 1965 34(2): 138-146.* Reports a study conducted in Ypsilanti, Michigan, in which 44 culturally deprived Negro mothers and 50 middle-class Caucasian mothers of children aged three to five, were investigated. The feelings of the disadvantaged group toward child rearing "shed light on why children from this socioeconomic group have such difficulty participating in our middle-class schools and ultimately in middle-class society." Such disadvantaged mothers fail to "conceive of children's potential for develop-ing inner control. Children are seen as objects to be carefully protected when young and helpless and then controlled, shielded, and suppressed as they grow older."   S. C. Pearson, Jr.

2726. Rakestraw, W. Vincent. FAMOUS HOTEL NOW COLLEGE DORM. *Negro Hist. Bull. 1964 27(6): 140-141.* Comments on Ohio University's Berry Hall which was originally a famous hotel, owned and operated by Edward Cornelius Berry, a highly gifted Negro businessman. L. Gara

2727. Rapping, Leonard A. UNIONISM, MIGRATION, AND THE MALE NONWHITE - WHITE UNEMPLOYMENT DIFFERENTIAL. *Southern Econ. J. 1966 32(3): 317-329.* Examines the role played by nonwhite and white migration patterns in the emergence of a regional difference in incidence of unemployment by race, based mainly on data for male unemployment in the census week of April 1960. The author concludes that the geographic pattern of migration flows plays only a small part in the regional unemployment differential, for nonwhites move both northward and southward. Unionism probably has some effect on the regional structure of unemployment by race through the operation of union seniority rules. A. W. Coats

2728. Rauch, Julia B. FEDERAL FAMILY PLANNING PROGRAMS: CHOICE OR COERCION? *Social Work 1970 15(4): 68-75.* Evaluates charges by blacks that "genocide" is inherent in Federal planning programs. Explicates individual and structural theories explaining poverty, as well as the argument for considering the access of the poor to family planning service as a medical, not a welfare, problem. 23 notes. W. L. Willigan

2729. Reed, Harold J. GUIDANCE AND COUNSELING. *J. of Negro Educ. 1964 33(3): 282-289.* The problems of disadvantaged youth may be creatively dealt with through group guidance and individual counseling. Such services need to be available to all youth with special services available to those with special problems including students of minority groups. S. C. Pearson, Jr.

2730. Reiss, Ira L. HOW AND WHY AMERICA'S SEX STANDARDS ARE CHANGING. *Transaction 1968 5(4): 26-32.* Contends that the contemporary notion that America is undergoing a sexual revolution is but a myth. Instead he asserts that young people are assuming more responsibility for their sexual behavior. In a study of fifteen hundred people above 21 and twelve hundred between the ages of 16 and 22, the author found wide differences on the acceptance of premarital sex among whites and Negroes of both sexes. The greater acceptance of this practice among Negroes the author traces mostly to the history of slavery and the effects of discrimination. Among other findings of significance is that the sexual attitudes of people are among the more reliable indicators of their behavior. He also concluded that "guilt feelings do not generally inhibit sexual behavior," and that two-thirds of students felt their sexual standards were similar to those of their parents. Also discussed is the degree of responsibility that young people feel toward sexual standards and how this influences their behavior. The extent of premarital sexual permissiveness is best correlated with the "general permissiveness in the adult cultural environment." Based on a survey conducted by the author; 2 tables, illus. A. Erlebacher

2731. Reiss, Ira L. PREMARITAL SEXUAL PERMISSIVENESS AMONG NEGROES AND WHITES. *Am. Sociol. R. 1964 29(5): 688-698.* "Results from a sample of 903 students and 1515 adults indicate that Negroes and whites differ considerably in the ways in which premarital sexual attitudes are produced and maintained. The white group is less permissive, and its permissiveness is inversely related to church attendance and belief in romantic love and positively related to the number of times in love. In the Negro group these associations were either absent or in the opposite direction. A similar pattern distinguished men from women within each racial group. The theory advanced to explain these findings proposes that the lower the traditional level of sexual permissiveness in a group, the greater the likelihood that social factors will alter individual levels of permissiveness."

J

2732. Rich, Leslie and Rich, Joan. IT TAKES COURAGE. *Am. Educ. 1966 2(6): 5-8.* Describes "Operation Reclaim," a program sponsored by the New York City schools and the U.S. Office of Education to recruit southern Negro teachers who lost their jobs when integration was enacted. The program developed around a National Defense Education Act institute designed to assist the displaced teachers to qualify for licenses as New York teachers. Illus.

W. R. Boedecker

2733. Riessman, Frank. THE OVERLOOKED POSITIVES OF DISADVANTAGED GROUPS. *J. of Negro Educ. 1964 33(3): 225-231.* The author suggests that disadvantaged youth bring to the educational process such positive characteristics as "co-operativeness and mutual aid that mark the extended family; the avoidance of the strain accompanying competitiveness and individualism; the equalitarianism, in informality and humor; the freedom from self-blame and parental over-protection; the children's enjoyment of each other's company and lessened sibling rivalry, the security found in the extended family and a traditional outlook; the enjoyment of music, games, sports and cards; the ability to express anger; the freedom from being word-bound; an externally oriented rather than an introspective outlook; a spatial rather than temporal perspective; an expressive orientation in contrast to an instrumental one; content-centered not a form-centered mental style; a problem-centered rather than an abstract-centered approach; and finally, the use of physical and visual style of learning."

S. C. Pearson, Jr.

2734. Rinder, Irwin D. A NOTE ON HUMOR AS AN INDEX OF MINORITY GROUP MORALE. *Phylon 1965 26(2): 117-121.* Reviews the research on humor which has been done in the field of the sociology of minorities and notes that characteristically the self-reference of the minority group involves both the conflict and control use of humor directed upon itself. The author sees the relative predominance of one or the other as the critical index of group self-acceptance or rejection and believes "a new mode of joking among Negroes about Negro assimilationists/passers [indicates] that the attempts to improve Negro self-attitudes, to enhance pride and respect of self, have been making progress."

S. C. Pearson, Jr.

2735. Rist, Ray C. STUDENT SOCIAL CLASS AND TEACHER EXPECTA-TIONS: THE SELF-FULFILLING PROPHECY IN GHETTO EDUCA-TION. *Harvard Educ. R. 1970 40(3): 411-451.* Describes the route of a group of ghetto children through kindergarten and the first two grades. The children were separated into three groups by the kindergarten teacher on the basis of subjective criteria related to the childrens' social class. These criteria gave rise to the expectations of academic success or failure, and the expectations took on the force of a self-fulfilling prophecy. Groupings in grades one and two continued this pattern, and were now based on the recorded past academic performance of the children. The public school system mirrors and maintains the class structure of society and with it the organizational perpetuation of poverty and unequal opportunity. J. Herbst

2736. Robbins, Lee N. NEGRO HOMICIDE VICTIMS - WHO WILL THEY BE? *Trans-action 1968 5(7): 15-19.* The homicide rate for Negro men is extremely high - 10 times that of whites. The highest rate is for Negro boys, who are most likely to die before their mid-30's. Is there any way to identify such potential homicides which might suggest remedial efforts by society? The records of 326 Negro boys from Saint Louis having at least average intelligence quotients suggest that truancy from school and academic problems combined into the highest predictable homicide rate. School factors predicted future homicides much more readily than the fact of coming from a broken or fatherless home. Negro children without school problems, even from low social status, revealed a death rate less than half of that in a comparable sample of white children. School problems also predicted deaths from causes other than homicide. The author contends such failures are not related to lack of intelligence but come from early evidence of childhood behavioral problems. Therefore such persons could easily be identified at an early time. Based on personal study; illus., 2 charts, table, biblio. A. Erlebacher

2737. Robertson, Leon S., Kosa, John, Alpert, Joel J., and Heagarty, Margaret C. RACE, STATUS, AND MEDICAL CARE. *Phylon 1967 28(4): 353-360.* A report on medical care of a selected group of families in Boston. The purpose of the study was to examine differences among Negroes and whites with respect to some medical care attitudes and usages. From the data compiled from persons bringing a child to the Medical Emergency Clinic of the Childrens Hospital Medical Center the authors concluded that Negroes are less likely than whites to have a usual physician for their children and are more likely to use public clinics for routine and acute illness care. They are less likely than whites to indicate that children get the best care from such clinics. It is concluded that the attitudes which generate the Negro-white differences are probably subtle results of the oppression of slavery and the caste-like discrimination which followed. Based on medical records, interviews, and published sources; 4 tables, 15 notes. D. N. Brown

2738. Robins, Lee N., Murphy, George E., and Breckenridge, Mary B. DRINK-ING BEHAVIOR OF YOUNG URBAN NEGRO MEN. *Q. J. of Studies on Alcohol 1968 29(3): 657-684.* "Drinking behavior was studied in 235 Negro men aged 30-36, born and reared in St. Louis, Mo., whose names had been selected from elementary-school records. Information about drinking was obtained by interview with 95 [percent] of the sample and by searching agency records. Of the 223, 61 [percent] were at some time heavy drinkers (7 or more drinks per week and 7 or more per occasion or 4 daily), 30 [percent] currently; 18 [percent] once distributive drinkers (7 or more drinks per week but less than 7 per occasion), 23 [percent] currently; 17 [percent] once light drinkers (less than 7 drinks per week), 37 [percent] currently; 4 [percent] once nondrinkers, 10 [percent] currently. The subjects began drinking at an early age and early drinking was associated with becoming a heavy drinker: 13 [percent] before age 11 (of whom 79 [percent] became heavy drinkers), 38 [percent] before age 15 (73 [percent] heavy drinkers), 66 [percent] before age 17 (69 [percent] heavy drinkers), 84 [percent] before age 19 (67 [percent] heavy drinkers). Heavy drinking was twice as common in these men as in a previously studied sample of White men similarly identified in the St. Louis school records[...], and problems from drinking were found to be more than 3 times as common: 20 [percent] had a public record of some drinking problem; 46 [percent] reported problems due to drinking and 53 [percent] reported personal concern about drinking excessively; 27 [percent] had a history of medical problems (6 [percent] alcoholic psychoses, 3 [percent] liver damage, 9 [percent] hospitalization for alcohol-related problems, 20 [percent] tremulousness, 2 [percent] gastritis); 44 [percent] had a history of social problems (20 [percent] arrests for alcohol-related offenses, 35 [percent] family complaints, 6 [percent] job difficulties). Recent (since age 30) medical or social problems due to drinking had been experienced by 30 [percent]. Such problems were most frequent in the heavy drinkers (69 [percent]). Heavy drinking was predicted by truancy and failure occurring together in elementary school (77 [percent] heavy drinkers), failure to graduate from high school (72 [percent]) and a first juvenile offense record after age 14 (79 [percent]). Failure to graduate together with late delinquency predicted that heavy drinkers (89 [percent]) would become problem drinkers (94 [percent] of heavy drinkers); 49 [percent] of high-school graduates without elementary-school problems became heavy drinkers, and of these 49 [percent] became problem drinkers. Father's presence in the home throughout elementary school, a conforming, successful father and a family with a middle-class life style all decreased the risk of heavy drinking, but did not significantly reduce the risk of problems if heavy drinking occurred: 10 [percent] became heavy drinkers of whom 25 [percent] became problem drinkers. Intelligence, guardian's occupation during elementary school and mother's religious affiliation showed little relationship to drinking behavior. Thus, heavy drinking is a common pattern among urban Negro men and usually leads to objective difficulties and personal worry. However, those few whose families lived like middle-class White families had as little excessive drinking as do White samples. Like White men previously studied, Negro men develop problems with alcohol when they have been brought up by inadequate parents and when they themselves have had a history of juvenile behavior problems."   J

2739. Robinson, Wilhelmena S. IN-SERVICE EDUCATION OF THE TEACHER OF AFRICAN HISTORY. *Negro Hist. Bull. 1964 28(2): 33-34, 38-39.* Points out the vast ignorance of African history and suggests that teachers should study recent scholarly writings and take advantage of African studies programs in order to teach adequately Negroes and others about the rich historical background of a part of our people.   L. Gara

2740. Roby, Pamela. INEQUALITY: A TREND ANALYSIS. *Ann. of the Am. Acad. of Pol. and Social Sci. 1969 385: 110-117.* "The attempt to grapple with poverty during the 1960's led to renewed recognition of the importance of inequality in affluent societies. This paper summarizes trends in the share of national income going to the bottom fifth of the population, ranked according to income, and in the composition of that bottom fifth over the past twenty years. Between 1947 and 1967, despite the decline in the share of total national income going to the top 5 percent, little progress was made in increasing the share of the bottom 20 percent. A specific timetable of income-redistribution is needed for the 1970's so that we can assess our programs in increasing the share of national goods going to the poor and to minorities. Over the next ten years, we should seek to expand the share of income going to families in the bottom 20 percent in 1967 to 7 or 8 percent in 1977. In the mid-1960's considerable progress was made in reducing inequality between blacks and whites: the ratio of nonwhite to white income increased from 53 percent in 1963 to 62 percent in 1967 - an increase of approximately 2.25 percent a year. This gain should continue, so that by 1979, a black income would be at least 89 percent of white income."

J

2741. Rogers, Tommy W. and Watson, Ora V. LOUISIANA POPULATION MIGRATION PATTERNS, 1950-1960. *Louisiana Studies 1969 8(4): 285-311.* Analyzes migration trends in Louisiana with emphasis on the decade 1950-60. The author notes the trend in births over deaths and discusses in detail the relevation of out-migration (the number and State of residence in 1960) of people born in Louisiana; in-migration (the number and State birth of people living in Louisiana in 1960). This is broken down for whites and nonwhites. The intra-State migration is also shown by race. 2 maps, 13 tables.   G. W. McGinty

2742. Rokeach, Milton and Parker, Seymour. VALUES AS SOCIAL INDICATORS OF POVERTY AND RACE RELATIONS IN AMERICA. *Ann. of the Am. Acad. of Pol. and Social Sci. 1970 388: 97-111.* "The purpose of this paper is to explore the usefulness of values as social indicators of underlying social problems. Using value choices of a national sample, an attempt was made to determine the extent and nature of cultural differences between groups differing in socioeconomic status and race. Since the publication of *The Negro Family* (the 'Moynihan Report'), there has been lively debate and invective about the issue of whether or not cultural differences exist between the poor and the rich and between Negro and white. The issue of whether those living in poverty, particularly the Negro poor, are characterized by a distinctive 'culture of poverty' has policy ramifications for programs of poverty-amelioration and community development. The findings reported here lend support to the idea that considerable value differences *do* distinguish the rich from the poor, but not Negroes from whites. For the most part, differences found between the latter disappear when socioeconomic position is controlled."   J

2743. Rosenberg, Bernard and Bensman, Joseph. SEXUAL PATTERNS IN THREE ETHNIC SUBCULTURES OF AN AMERICAN UNDERCLASS. *Ann. of the Am. Acad. of Pol. and Social Sci. 1968 376: 61-75.* "Three American ethnic subcultures, all consisting of transmigrated groups living in poverty, were studied and the sexual patterns of the youth described. The groups consisted of white Appalachians living in Chicago, Negroes in Washington, D.C., and Puerto Ricans in New York. Sharply differentiated patterns of sexual behavior, involving conquest, sex education, sex misinformation, attitudes toward females, responsibility, and affect were discovered, and these patterns are reflected in the language of the subcultures, particularly in their argot. The underclass sexual mores differ from those of the American middle class, but not more than they differ from each other among the three ethnic groups. Sexual practices are related to general life styles, and reflect ghettoization, subcultural isolation, and short-range hedonism in groups only recently transplanted from their rural areas of origin."

J

2744. Rosenblatt, S. M., Gross, M. M., Broman, M., Lewis, E., and Malenowski, B. PATIENTS ADMITTED FOR TREATMENT OF ALCOHOL WITHDRAWAL SYNDROMES; AN EPIDEMIOLOGICAL STUDY. *Q. J. of Studies on Alcohol 1971 32(1): 104-115.* "From July to December 1966, 567 men (222 Whites, 333 Negroes) were admitted for treatment of alcohol withdrawal syndromes to the Kings County Psychiatric Hospital, the only community facility for such treatment in Brooklyn, N.Y. The patients tended to cluster in definite areas; half came from 15 of the 116 health areas in the borough. In the zone of lowest density of patients the Negroes had over 12 times, and in the zone of highest density 3.5 times, the admission rate of Whites. The following sociocultural and demographic factors were significantly correlated with the number of admissions in a zone: overcrowded housing and high rates of aid to dependent children, venereal disease, juvenile delinquency, tuberculosis, unemployment and homicide; and low educational level, median income and residential stability. The highest correlation was with the rate of admissions to New York State mental hospitals in 1967. It is concluded that social-class and environmental factors are directly related to the incidence of alcohol withdrawal syndromes."

J

2745. Rousseve, Ronald J. COUNSELOR EDUCATION AND THE CULTURALLY ISOLATED: AN ALLIANCE FOR MUTUAL BENEFIT. *J. of Negro Educ. 1965 34(4): 395-403.* Suggests that "the field of guidance and the culturally isolated members of our society can perhaps best find fulfillment each in the other." For such fulfillment to take place guidance education must enable counselors to understand culturally alienated youth, must expose them more extensively to scientific findings in cultural anthropology and related fields which are concerned with intergroup prejudice and discrimination, and must seek to counteract tendencies toward impersonality and "scientific professionitis" in the field.   S. C. Pearson, Jr.

2746. Rousseve, Ronald J. TEACHERS OF CULTURALLY DISADVAN-
TAGED AMERICAN YOUTH. *J. of Negro Educ. 1963 32(2): 114-121.* En-
courages such teachers to "redefine our purposes and upgrade our competencies."
S. C. Pearson, Jr.

2747. Rubin, Lillian B. MAXIMUM FEASIBLE PARTICIPATION: THE
ORIGINS, IMPLICATIONS, AND PRESENT STATUS. *Ann. of the Am.
Acad. of Pol. and Social Sci. 1969 385: 14-29.* "Even among those who framed
the Economic Opportunity Act, there is little consensus about how the phrase
'maximum feasible participation' was formulated or about its intended meaning.
An analysis of the social history of the idea suggests that its roots lie in community development programs for underdeveloped nations. The civil rights movement, coupled with a growing disquietude with existing welfare policy, gave
impetus to translating community development notions to the domestic scene.
Several demonstration projects emphasizing the need for citizen participation
were precursors of CAP [Community Action Program]; some were already em-
broiled in heated conflicts. Yet, the revolutionary implications of what they were
proposing escaped the framers of the act, in part, because of the preconceptions
about poverty, race, and welfare that grip American thought and distort our
vision. The struggle over defining and implementing the participation clause
focused on policy-making and jobs. The most profound controversy settled
around the policy-making issue because it involved a redistribution of power.
Congress dealt with the conflict by both specifying the meaning of participation
and limiting local initiative. While CAP may not survive current OEO reorganization in any viable form, the idea of 'maximum feasible participation' has
captured the imagination of the urban poor, with the force of an idea whose time
has come; it will not die." J

2748. Rubington, E. THE CHANGING SKID ROW SCENE. *Q. J. of Studies
on Alcohol 1971 32(1): 123-135.* "Skid Row is a symbol of socialization failure
in general, failure to learn moderate drinking customs in particular. Its widespread symbolism has hidden more alcoholics than it has exposed and helped
other classes of alcoholics to rationalize their deviant drinking. As a social system,
Skid Row is a special urban territory for unattached men who perform casual
labor, use low-cost services and facilities, and share the designation of social
deviants. Abstainers, moderate drinkers and alcoholics constitute three social
segments on Skid Row, each avoiding the others and with its own status hierarchy. Surveys in Chicago, Minneapolis and Philadelphia all indicated that each
type represents about one-third of the Skid Row population. The alcoholics
resemble three of the Jellinek types: gamma, delta, and epsilon. The longer a
drinker remains in the system, the more likely his status will drop. Social changes
on Skid Row may make its false stereotype come true. Its population is declining,
composed increasingly of older Whites and younger Negroes, and its moral order
is atrophying while internal crime assumes more violent form. The characteristics
of the three segments and the relative proportion of types of alcoholics are
changing with the composition of the population. Alcoholics, once a minority,
now predominate. With decreased needs for casual labor, and improved health
and welfare services, there is a gradual disappearance of Skid Rows. Homeless-
ness will not disappear but the territory for its traditional style will go out of

existence. The consequences of these changes will take different forms for the caretakers, depending on whether they seek to help or control the various types of homeless alcoholics on or off Skid Row. These consequences suggest a paradox - that deviants assigned a territory are better controlled socially than when they are dispersed under conditions of competing therapeutic and punitive social definitions."   J

2749. Rustin, Bayard. THE LESSONS OF THE LONG HOT SUMMER. *Commentary 1967 44(4): 39-45.* The Joint Economic Committee of Congress has drawn up an inventory of urban needs projected to 1975. The author estimates unmet needs, projects what it will take to meet those needs, and notes the benefits of long-range employment opportunities. The author describes the needs in education, housing, health facilities, jobs, and race relations. The needs of the American population, and particularly of the Negro, have been neglected. Full employment, a two dollar minimum wage, and a guaranteed annual income are needed. The author mentions areas from which money for these programs should be obtained. Concludes that political will can effect the above changes if Negroes join with liberal whites and if the southern Negro is allowed to vote.
                                                                                    C. Grollman

2750. Sacadat, Evelyn. AROUSING PARENT INTEREST IN A PROGRAM FOR THE CULTURALLY DEPRIVED. *J. of Negro Educ. 1965 34(2): 195-196.* Reports the results of a program conducted in Quincy, Illinois to interest parents of a group of students in Jackson School in the academic and cultural development of their children.   S. C. Pearson, Jr.

2751. Salomone, Jerome J., and Parenton, Vernon J. SELECTED ATTITUDES OF MINISTERS TOWARD SOME ASPECTS OF THE FUNERAL INDUSTRY IN CALCASIEU PARISH, LOUISIANA. *Louisiana Studies 1968 7(2): 122-131.* A research report based on intensive taped interviews conducted in the summer of 1965, with 24 ministers, including 17 white and 7 Negroes. Seventeen different denominations, or sects, representing practically all the religious bodies in the parish are included. The clergymen's attitudes toward the wake and toward the cost of funerals were ascertained and analyzed. 13 notes.
                                                                                    G. W. McGinty

2752. Saurman, Kenneth P. AWAKENING STUDENTS TO SOCIETY THROUGH AN URBAN DIALOGUE. *Catholic Educ. R. 1965 63(7): 433-438.* Convinced that "forces of social change provide [urban] students with a living practicum, a humanities course that is alive and throbbing," the author feels that schools do not fulfill their responsibilities merely by offering formal course work in current affairs. Commuters in particular might benefit from the reinforcement and personal involvement available through visits to faculty homes. The article describes three "forums" hosted by Dean Saurman and his wife. These were loosely planned and each attended by a controversial or community figure (as a Negro civil rights leader). Benefits include student interest in social developments, including a greater sense of social responsibility, extension of knowledge of society and of learning as a whole (students were invited from a number of subject fields), and greater tolerance. The author suggests groups of less than 20 and extension of the pattern.   D. H. Broderick

2753. Sawyer, Broadus E. THE GRADUATE TRAINING OF TWENTY-ONE SELECTED COLLEGE FACULTIES. *J. of Negro Educ. 1963 32(2): 193-197.* Studies the degrees (and granting institutions) of faculty members in colleges attended and staffed primarily by Negroes and located in the South or close thereto.   S. C. Pearson, Jr.

2754. Schickel, Richard. THE COMPLETE AMERICAN PRAGMATIST. *Horizon 1969 11(1): 60-65.* Discusses the ideas of Daniel Patrick Moynihan (b. 1927). Moynihan is described as an American of the classic type, as described by Alexis de Tocqueville, who has an abiding faith in the long-term viability of our system and is impatient with ideologically based attempts to improve it, especially those that toy with revolutionary doctrines. The author centers on Moynihan's ideas concerning the urban Negro.   R. N. Alvis

2755. Schleifer, Carl, Derbyshire, Robert, and Brown, Jeffrey. SYMPTOMS AND SYMPTOM CHANGE IN HOSPITALIZED NEGRO AND WHITE MENTAL PATIENTS. *J. of Human Relations 1964 12(4): 476-485.* Reports the results of tests given to 64 patients in two of Maryland's mental institutions. The purpose of the study was "to determine their clinical pictures at the first and third day of hospitalization." Negro patients "presented a more disturbed clinical picture" than did whites. Female patients recovered "significantly faster" than did males. No difference was found between the races with regard to rate of recovery. Possible reasons for the results are discussed.   D. J. Abramoske

2756. Schoenthal, Klaus. DER NEGER-EINFLUSS AUF DIE PARTEIEN DER USA [The Negro influence on the parties of the United States]. *Aussenpolitik [West Germany] 1965 16(3): 192-201.* This examination of the American Negro's position in the national political life finds that he has achieved much but is still limited in important respects. The political control of the various civil rights organizations is, in contrast to earlier years, almost exclusively in Negro hands. With, theoretically, somewhat over 10 percent of the vote in national elections, the Negroes can swing the balance against any presidential candidate who does not appeal at least to a majority of them. In the seven most populous States they constitute the difference between a Democratic or a Republican majority. But they do not have the strength to improve their position by the vote alone. Furthermore, they are not represented in the organizations of either party except in preponderantly Negro areas of the North, and they do not have substantial positive representation in the Congress.   E. F. Ziemke

2757. Schrank, Robert and Stein, Susan. INDUSTRY IN THE BLACK COMMUNITY: IBM IN BEDFORD-STUYVESANT. *J. of the Am. Inst. of Planners 1969 35(5): 348-351.* "In 1968 IBM [International Business Machines] decided to locate a computer component assembly plant in New York City's Bedford-

Stuyvesant section. After one year of operation, the plant has expanded to a second product line and claims to have built production and performance records comparable to those at other new IBM facilities. While admittedly a small accomplishment, the plant may have important implications for industrial development in other ghetto areas. The IBM experience may also begin to lay to rest a few of the old shibboleths about center city locations and the disadvantaged work force."

J

2758. Schwartz, Jack. MEN'S CLOTHING AND THE NEGRO. *Phylon 1963 24(3): 224-232.* The study indicates "that hats and shoes are exhibited to and presumably consumed in greater proportions by Negroes than by whites" and that "men's clothing advertised to Negroes is also higher priced than that shown to whites." The author suggests that the individual Negro may seek to compensate for a position of social inferiority through clothing symbols.

S. C. Pearson, Jr.

2759. Schwartz, Michael. THE NORTHERN UNITED STATES NEGRO MATRIARCH: STATUS VERSUS AUTHORITY. *Phylon 1965 26(1): 18-24.* Reports the findings of a study based on interviews and observations in the city of Detroit. The matriarchal family pattern among lower-class Negroes does not result solely from the negative effects of restricted opportunities for exploiting one's life chances in a market. Much matriarchal family organization among lower-class Negroes is "maladaptive" in the sense that status and authority inhere in different persons. Questions the matriarchal system as a preferred and valued style of life among persons of this class.   S. C. Pearson, Jr.

2760. Seaman, John. DILEMMA: THE MYTHOLOGY OF RIGHT AND LEFT. *J. of Human Relations 1969 17(1): 43-57.* Analyzes the anti-Communist thought of Billy James Hargis, an ordained minister of the Disciples of Christ, who has written and lectured extensively on the Communist menace in the United States, and relates his individualistic mythology to the problems of racial minorities in the United States. "For Hargis, America is an Eden confronted by the Satanic presence of international communism." However exaggerated such views may be, there is something to be said for his acceptance of certain traditional myths about the way individual character develops strength and maturity. To be truly free a man has to be in command of himself. A minimum standard of living decreed by law may alleviate the marginal desperation of many Negroes and ease the threat of civil disorders, "but it will not in itself bestow the hope, morale, and respect that come with earning a living, managing one's own affairs, and feeling that life is a story with a point....The issue is crucial in a free society. The principles of inner restraint and self-discipline are indispensable; in fact, it is hard to envision how an open society can survive without it." Based on the writings of Hargis and other published sources; 26 notes.   D. J. Abramoske

2761. Sears, David O. BLACK ATTITUDES TOWARD THE POLITICAL SYSTEM IN THE AFTERMATH OF THE WATTS INSURRECTION. *Midwest J. of Pol. Sci. 1969 13(4): 515-544.* Using interviews conducted with two samples (one Negro and one white) of respondents in Los Angeles in 1965-66, the author explored the feelings of the black community in the aftermath of the Watts riot. It was discovered that the Negroes did not withdraw from national politics and still supported the Democratic Party, but they were distrustful of and disaffected by the local government officials. It was also found that racial partisanship toward black leadership and disaffection from white leadership (especially among the more racially partisan and politicized younger generation) were dominant attitudes. "The principle conclusion of the study is that racial partisanship, rather than estrangement from the political system, was dominant in the black community after the riot, and appears likely to remain so." 10 tables, 30 notes.   J. W. Thacker, Jr.

2762. Segal, Bernard E. RACIAL GROUP MEMBERSHIP AND JUVENILE DELINQUENCY. *Social Forces 1964 43(1): 70-81.* "Sixty Negro and forty white delinquent boys, interviewed while they were residents of a state training school, provided materials for a comparative analysis of relationships between racial membership and delinquency. The Negro boys tended to derive from lower-status families more than the white, and they were also more likely to have been sent to training school for having committed more serious offenses. Among the whites racial attitudes were associated with types of offenses, with more serious offenders showing more antipathy toward Negroes. Negro boys' racial attitudes varied less by offense category, but there was a strong tendency for those who committed less serious offenses to show more self-hatred than those whose offenses were more serious. These findings are interpreted in terms of social-structural theories of delinquency, notably those of Cohen and of Cloward and Ohlin."   J

2763. Segal, David R. and Schaffner, Richard. STATUS, PARTY AND NEGRO AMERICANS. *Phylon 1968 29(3): 224-230.* A study of Negro voting behavior in the 1964 elections to determine which of the following models is the most satisfactory: the economic determinist model, the class and status model, the "Black Bourgeoisie" model, or the assimilation approach model. The "data suggest the rejection of both economic determinist and Black Bourgeoisie explanations of the place of Negroes in American social structure, and their political behavior. It is clearly necessary to distinguish between the class of Negroes, in purely economic terms, and their status....Through increasing political participation, however, one may expect rates of social mobility among Negroes to increase, and once social structural integration is accomplished, one may expect that the Negro vote will become less coherent within the context of the American electorate." 7 tables, 13 notes.   R. D. Cohen

2764. Sekora, John. ON NEGRO COLLEGES: A REPLY TO JENCKS AND RIESMAN. *Antioch R. 1968 28(1): 5-26.* Sharply criticizes the article, "The American Negro College," in the *Harvard Educational Review* 1967 37(1): 3-60, by Christopher Jencks and David Riesman (see abstract 167). The author thinks these writers have not adequately proven their charges that the gross inadequacies of Negro colleges are the result of having been dominated by "Negroes who were incompetent, myopic, pedantic, cowardly, and defensive to the point of paranoia." He argues that the Riesman-Jencks statistics are inadequate, their understanding of the history of the colleges (particularly the enormous pressures from the white community) faulty, and their recommendations "unneeded, unoriginal, and misdirected." In a postscript he summarizes the reactions of Negro college presidents to the original article and finds the rejoinder by Jencks and Riesman, though moderate, still inadequate.   F. Harrold

2765. Sémidéi, Manuela. LA POLITIQUE AMERICAINE APRES LES ELEC-TIONS [American policy after the elections]. *R. Pol. et Parlementaire [France] 1968 70(794): 57-61.* The most interesting feature of the 1968 national election was George Wallace's candidature, a challenge to the established parties. Although the results brought Richard Nixon to the White House, the uncertainty of the electorate kept a Democratic majority in Congress. Nixon did, however, capture the strategic geographical areas. The author notes that blacks and Jews stayed with the Democratic Party, and concludes that the electoral college will be reorganized, that the "New Left" will revamp itself, and that the parties will realign themselves as Nixon governs through a center coalition.
                                                    T. D. Lockwood

2766. Shannon, Lyle W. THE PUBLIC'S PERCEPTION OF SOCIAL WEL-FARE AGENCIES AND ORGANIZATIONS IN AN INDUSTRIAL COM-MUNITY. *J. of Negro Educ. 1963 32(3): 276-285.* Basing his findings on a study conducted in Racine, Wisconsin, in 1961, the author concludes that "social service or welfare agencies and community organizations were quite differentially known and contacted by the sample from the larger white community as contrasted to the sample from the Negro community," and that "there are great differences in the extent to which people are favorably oriented toward the activities and personnel of agencies and organizations, and that whites are distributed on the continuum of favorable orientations quite differently than are Negroes."   S. C. Pearson, Jr.

2767. Shockley, Ann Allen. NEGRO LIBRARIANS IN PREDOMINANTLY NEGRO COLLEGES. *Coll. and Res. Lib. 1967 28(6): 423-426.* A survey of Negro librarians in predominantly Negro colleges examined their backgrounds and attitudes toward their profession. Negro librarians are in a minority because of the historical background of a society long operated on a dual pattern of segregation. Due to current trends and changing attitudes, Negro librarians are looking forward to broader avenues to occupational achievement and fulfillment. Note.   V. J. Carter

2768. Short, James F., Rivera, Ramen, and Marshall, Harvey. ADULT-ADOLESCENT RELATIONS AND GANG DELINQUENCY. *Pacific Sociol. R. 1964 7(2): 59-65.* A review of established theories about juvenile delinquency. Existing theories, although incomplete, are in agreement about the importance of relations between adolescents and adults to an understanding of the adolescent behavior. Data for the study were drawn from Chicago in cooperation with the YMCA of that city. Interviews of gang members were designed to describe nine adult roles on four three-point scales, including that of a "guy in politics," "teacher," and "policeman." Results show that politicians are seen as "right guys" but that policemen receive their lowest rating from gang boys. Theories of delinquency - gang delinquency in particular - receive little support from these data. Thus, Negro gang boys do not give lower ratings to adult roles than do white boys. Gang boys appear to have "weaker" relations with adults than do nongang boys, but they are not alienated from them. Conclusions are incomplete and await further verification. 5 tables, 2 figs., 21 notes.   A. S. Freedman

2769. Short, James F., Jr., Rivera, Ramon, and Tennyson, Ray A. PERCEIVED OPPORTUNITIES, GANG MEMBERSHIP, AND DELINQUENCY. *Am. Sociol. R. 1965 30(1): 56-67.* "Certain aspects of the opportunity structure paradigm were operationalized in a study of delinquent gangs in Chicago. Negro and white lower-class gang boys were compared with lower-class nongang boys from the same neighborhoods, and with middle-class boys of the same race. The ranking of the six race-by-class-by-gang status groups on official delinquency rates corresponded more closely to ranking on perceptions of legitimate opportunities than to ranking on perceptions of illegitimate opportunities, which is consistent with the assumption that illegitimate opportunities intervene after legitimate opportunities have been appraised and found wanting. Gang members perceived legitimate opportunities as available less often than nongang boys, lower-class boys, less often than middle-class, and Negro boys, less often than white. Differences in perceptions of illegitimate opportunities were in the reverse direction, as expected."   J

2770. Sigel, Irving E., Anderson, Larry M., and Shapiro, Howard. CATEGORIZATION BEHAVIOR OF LOWER- AND MIDDLE-CLASS NEGRO PRESCHOOL CHILDREN: DIFFERENCES IN DEALING WITH REPRESENTATION OF FAMILIAR OBJECTS. *J. of Negro Educ. 1966 35(3): 218-229.* Reports the findings of a study in which 12 familiar three-dimensional objects, colored pictures of such objects, and black and white pictures of them were shown to two groups of Negro nursery school children for identification and grouping. All children identified all objects and pictures. Considerable variation in ability to classify was discovered, and the variation seems related to other factors in addition to social class. Lower-class children showed important differences from their middle-class peers in having less ability to objectify or to deal representationally with material. It is concluded that lower-class children have not yet acquired adequate representation of familiar objects; the implications of this for education are presented. Biblio.   S. C. Pearson, Jr.

2771. Simons, Alfred E. and Burke, Nelson S. THE PROBABLE SYNDROME IN TERMS OF EDUCATIONAL EXPERIENCES WHICH PRECIPITATES DROPOUTS, DELINQUENCY, AND EVENTUAL INCARCERATION. *J. of Negro Educ. 1966 35(1): 27-34.* Reports the findings of a study conducted among youths confined at the Youth Center of the Department of Corrections of the District of Columbia. A strong positive relationship exists between school experiences, dropouts, and incarceration. "The inmate is most likely to be a poverty stricken, culturally deprived, Negro dropout from an unstable home situation who left school at the age of 16. His school record will reveal a history of poor adjustment, truancy, retentions, and mobility. There is evidence that he will be an under-achiever. Serious deficiencies in reading, communication skills, and arithmetic will be apparent despite average intelligence. He will have attained a grade level of 7, 8, or 9. The inmate will usually have a history of juvenile offenses and commitment to other institutions." Specific recommendations are given for schools in developing a program which will lead to the early internalization of an acceptable self-image by students from economically deprived circumstances. Biblio.   S. C. Pearson, Jr.

2772. Singell, Larry D. BARRIERS TO EARNING INCOME. *Q. R. of Econ. and Business 1968 8(2): 35-44.* "The purpose of this article is to survey generally the barriers to earning which result in or contribute to poverty. The author discusses the problem of defining poverty, examines the major socioeconomic characteristics of the poor, and discusses some of the causes of poverty. The causes which represent barriers to earning are classified in three main groups. The author concludes that poverty in the United States will decline significantly by 1980 if rapid economic growth and full employment are maintained, not only because expanding income and employment will pull people over the poverty line, but because these conditions tend to increase productivity and to reduce discrimination. Some groups, however, may be left in a backwash unless some of the barriers are eliminated or reduced."   J

2773. Singleton, Robert and Bullock, Paul. SOME PROBLEMS IN MINORITY-GROUP EDUCATION IN THE LOS ANGELES PUBLIC SCHOOLS. *J. of Negro Educ. 1963 32(2): 137-145.* Concludes that the long-run problems of minority-group education cannot be solved within the existing Anglo-oriented educational framework.   S. C. Pearson, Jr.

2774. Sisk, Glenn. NEGRO HEALTH IN ATLANTA. *Negro Hist. Bull. 1963 27(3): 65-66.*

2775. Sisk, Glenn. THE ECONOMIC CONDITION OF THE NEGRO IN ATLANTA. *Negro Hist. Bull. 1964 27(4): 87-90.* Documented.
                                                                          S

2776. Skolnick, Jerome H. COMMENT: THE GENERATION GAP. *Transaction 1968 6(10): 4-5.* Suggests that most youth are not rebelling, but rather trying to make their society relate to its stated values. Children who grew up in the 1950's did not witness a government which served as a positive and progressive force in society. The present generation is truly realistic since they are not willing to sacrifice for causes unless those causes are genuinely honorable. A revolutionary situation poses a real dilemma for a liberal since he sympathizes with the goals of the revolution but condemns the concomitant violence. We must recognize that blacks in the inner city are more concerned with real needs than with drawing abstractions about freedom. Today liberty costs more than eternal vigilance; it must include social knowledge and a will to social justice.
                                                                          A. Erlebacher

2777. Slaughter, Charles H. COGNITIVE STYLE: SOME IMPLICATIONS FOR CURRICULUM AND INSTRUCTIONAL PRACTICES AMONG NEGRO CHILDREN. *J. of Negro Educ. 1969 38(2): 105-111.* A major problem in teaching the disadvantaged in general and Negro children in particular is the difference in perception and cognitive style between the middle-class teacher and the lower-class youth. One teaching innovation to deal with this problem is Inquiry Training, first reported in 1962. Similar to the game of Twenty Questions, the technique rewards observation, hypothesizing, theorizing, and active participation. Negro youths also need to receive experiences in language development. 16 notes. B. D. Johnson

2778. Smith, Hughie Lee. THE NEGRO ARTIST IN AMERICA TODAY. *Negro Hist. Bull. 1964 27(5): 111-112.* Discusses the position of the Negro artist in American life, the problems confronting Negro artists, and the possibilty of future improvement based on the inspiration and impact of the civil rights revolution. L. Gara

2779. Smith, Paul M., Jr. A DESCRIPTIVE SELF-CONCEPT OF HIGH SCHOOL COUNSELORS. *J. of Negro Educ. 1963 32(2): 179-182.* Basing his findings on a 1961 study of 31 male and 31 female high school counselors, the author observes that the self concepts of high school counselors are generally positive and that the sex role is a dominant factor in framing such concepts. While many descriptive adjectives were chosen by both male and female counselors, men emphasized fair-minded and responsible while women emphasized kind and sympathetic as descriptive of themselves. S. C. Pearson, Jr.

2780. Smith, Paul M., Jr. THE REALISM OF COUNSELING FOR SCHOLARSHIP AID WITH FRESHMEN IN THE NEGRO COLLEGE. *J. of Negro Educ. 1964 33(1): 93-96.* Smith found that the catalogs of Negro colleges were exceptionally vague in indicating the amount of scholarship aid available to a student and the criteria used in awarding aid. He suggests that colleges make their catalog statements clear and precise and that counselors "inform their college-hopefuls with special talents that the expectation of receiving a full scholarship is slim and that although their chances are better for receiving partial assistance the competition is intense for these limited resources and therefore many who qualify will not obtain such aid." S. C. Pearson, Jr.

2781. Smith, Paul M., Jr. and Johnson, Norman C. ATTITUDES AND ACADEMIC STATUS OF FRESHMEN. *J. of Negro Educ. 1966 35(1): 95-99.* Reports the findings of a study of 217 freshman students at North Carolina College in 1962-63. Probation, average, and honor students had the same general pattern of responses to questions concerning classroom adjustment but differed in response to questions concerning personal relationships. Apparently the degree of positive feelings toward the self was in relative proportion to the level of academic success. S. C. Pearson, Jr.

2782. Smith, Stanley H. A CASE STUDY ON SOCIO-POLITICAL CHANGE. *Phylon 1968 29(4): 380-387.* Analyzes the "role of the ballot as a mechanism of change in the political institution of a rural social structure." Political power in the rural South has been dominated by a handful of whites, without broad participation by either whites or Negroes. Recent voting by Negroes, however, has brought about significant social changes in the Nation and in the South. Macon County, Alabama, is an example of such changes. Comprising 84 percent of the population, in 1964 Negroes for the first time outnumbered white voting registrants. This participation led to the election of a biracial local govenment, with corresponding social changes and increased opportunities for Negroes. The ballot can be an effective means of promoting change. 16 notes.

R. D. Cohen

2783. Smith, Wayne C. and Dean, K. Imogene. NEGRO BOYS IN THE YOUTH DEVELOPMENT CENTERS OF GEORGIA. *J. of Negro Educ. 1969 38(1): 69-73.* A study of 422 Negro boys in Georgia's two Youth Development Centers at Gracewood and Milledgeville. The authors wished to determine if there were any significant differences between rural and urban boys who had been judged delinquent. The boys were found to be quite similar, although the rural boys were more educationally retarded than those from urban areas. 3 tables, 9 notes.

B. D. Johnson

2784. Sorkin, Alan L. A COMPARISON OF QUALITY CHARACTERIS-TICS IN NEGRO AND WHITE PUBLIC COLLEGES AND UNIVERSI-TIES IN THE SOUTH. *J. of Negro Educ. 1968 38(2): 112-119.* Using data from James Cass and Max Birnbaum's *Comparative Guide to American Colleges* (New York: Harper and Row, 1969), compares 105 predominantly white State colleges in the Southern and border States with 29 Negro State colleges in these areas. Uses these characteristics in the study: the percentage of faculty with the Ph.D., the number of library books per student, the number of accredited professional programs, the student-faculty ratio, faculty salaries, and expenditure per student. The States are putting a disproportionate amount of money into the principal State universities and are neglecting the other colleges, both black and white. The gap between the Negro and other white colleges (other than the major university) is much smaller than originally assumed. Negro institutions, however, do have fewer accredited professional programs, fewer books per student, smaller classes, and lower expenditures per pupil than white institutions. Progress has occurred since 1947; Negro institutions have increased the proportion of faculty with a Ph.D., the number of library books per student, and the number of faculty members at a faster pace than have white institutions. 8 notes.

B. D. Johnson

2785. Sorkin, Alan L. EDUCATION, MIGRATION AND NEGRO UNEM-PLOYMENT. *Social Forces 1969 47(3): 265-274.* "The purpose of this paper is to provide an explanation concerning the behavior of the nonwhite/white unem-ployment ratio from 1930-66. Two factors are considered, namely the influence of education as measured by years of schooling, and the importance of nonwhite migration from the South. It is argued that while these factors appear to have relevance in a study of adult workers, neither factor can explain the teenage nonwhite/white unemployment ratio." J

2786. Spears, Harold and Pivnick, Isadore. HOW AN URBAN SCHOOL SYSTEM IDENTIFIES ITS DISADVANTAGED. *J. of Negro Educ. 1964 33(3): 245-253.* The authors suggest that disadvantaged youth may be identified through observation of academic achievement, transiency, language patterns, attendance, the image of the school in the community, discipline, dropouts, and student aspirations. They discuss San Francisco's methods of dealing with problems of the disadvantaged through the services of compensatory teachers, provision of additional counseling services, and involvement of other community agencies. S. C. Pearson, Jr.

2787. St. John, Nancy Hoyt. THE EFFECT OF SEGREGATION ON THE ASPIRATIONS OF NEGRO YOUTH. *Harvard Educ. R. 1966 36(3): 284-294.* Research in a middle-sized New England city did not confirm the hypothesis that a high average of Negro students in elementary and junior high school classrooms lowered the educational aspirations of Negro high school students. Segregation in early schooling did not produce different educational planning, whereas early residence in the South and subsequent migration to the North lowered aspirations. Yet for those who grew up in the North, de facto segregation heightened educational aspiration, regardless of social class of parents or of variations in school quality. It is suggested that self-esteem and motivation of Negro children is more threatened in an integrated than in a segregated school. J. Herbst

2788. Standley, Fred L. JAMES BALDWIN: THE CRUCIAL SITUATION. *South Atlantic Q. 1966 65(3): 371-381.* Baldwin has a type of religious devotion toward his vocation as writer. This means gaining an adequate perspective on modern man by digging beneath the surface, writing from one's own experience, and having a sense of personal and social responsiblity for furnishing himself and his fellow man with a vision of themselves as they are. Baldwin is particularly concerned with the impact on man (particularly in the lower socioeconomic strata) of urban life and society. He confronts his characters with a "crucial situation" - an inescapable position in which man must take a stand and make a decision because existence itself is threatened. This crucial situation frequently takes the form of a crisis of identity, and Baldwin's characters respond to this with love. 30 notes. J. M. Bumsted

2789. Stewart, Charles E. CORRECTING THE IMAGE OF NEGROES IN TEXTBOOKS. *Negro Hist. Bull. 1964 28(2): 29-30, 42-44.* Places the question of school textbooks which either omitted or distorted the contributions of Negroes in historical perspective and calls attention to recent educational trends which will, hopefully, correct the matter. L. Gara

2790. Stokes, Donald E. SPATIAL MODELS OF PARTY COMPETITION. *Am. Pol. Sci. R. 1963 57(2): 368-377.* Criticizes spatial models of party competition, particularly the one of Anthony Downs, *An Economic Theory of Democracy* (Harper, New York, 1957). An example of such a model would be "the conception of a liberal-conservatism dimension on which parties maneuver for the support of a public that is itself distributed from left to right." Using data drawn from the Survey Research Center's files at the University of Michigan, the author shows that American voting behavior has involved many dimensions such as domestic social-economic issues; foreign policy, particularly since 1952; and race relations. Such variables as these need to be considered in model building of party competition. Documented.   B. W. Onstine

2791. Sullivan, Leon H. NEW TRENDS IN THE DEVELOPMENT OF SELF-HELP IN THE INNER CITY. *Pro. of the Am. Phil. Soc. 1968 112(6): 358-361.* Discusses innovations in solving inner-city problems by self-help programs, with specific emphasis on the Opportunities Industrialization Centers of America and Adult Armchair Education, both established by the author. The answer to the urban Negro's problem must be in self-help programs rather than in projects imposed by the Government, though the Government should support the "people-developed" plans. The central goal is racial, economic emancipation by training members of the black community to qualify for the wider range of better jobs now available to them. The programs have been extremely successful.
W. G. Morgan

2792. Sullivan, William C. COMMUNISM AND THE AMERICAN NEGRO. *Religion in Life 1968 37(4): 591-601.* Although communism has selected the Negro as a primary target for activity, it has failed to attract Negroes to its membership in significant numbers. The trends toward lawlessness and violence have been exploited by Communists among the Negroes. A positive program of social equality attracts the Negro and leads to his advancement.
D. B. Melvin

2793. Surace, Samuel J. and Seeman, Melvin. SOME CORRELATES OF CIVIL RIGHTS ACTIVISM. *Social Forces 1967 46(2): 197-207.* Reports research on civil rights affairs based on expectation of success, ideological commitments, and alternative rewards derived from 350 questionnaires to college students and civil service personnel. The following variables were scaled and/or measured: contact, action and attitude, powerlessness, status concern, and liberalism-conservatism. Conclusions are tentative and weak. Contact differences appear to be more important for whites than for Negroes. The variables reviewed here seem to work better in predicting activism for whites than for Negroes. 7 tables.
A. S. Freedman

2794. Suttles, Gerald D. ANATOMY OF A CHICAGO SLUM. *Trans-action 1969 6(4): 16-25.* Explores social character of the slum, the "Addams Area." Concentrates on the social characteristics of the Italian population with some comparison to the characteristics of the other major groups in the slum: Mexicans, Puerto Ricans, and Negroes. The Italians are concerned with privacy and with settling most of their disputes among themselves, whereas the Negroes have confronted the public with their complaints. Analyzes the street gangs, their mores, and their relations with one another. The "Addams Area" is a more stable slum than many others and has its own internal unity and moral order. Excerpt from the author's *The Social Order of the Slum* (Chicago: U. of Chicago Press, 1970). 7 photos. A. Erlebacher

2795. Suval, Elizabeth M. and Hamilton, C. Horace. SOME NEW EVIDENCE ON EDUCATIONAL SELECTIVITY IN MIGRATION TO AND FROM THE SOUTH. *Social Forces 1965 43(4): 536-547.* "Analysis of the 1960 United States Census data on lifetime and recent migration confirms the general hypothesis that migration to and from the South is correlated with education. However, the correlation between migration and education varies by age, sex, and color. Gross migration, both to and from the South, is positively correlated with education and there is little difference between the educational level of in- and out-migrants. Adverse educational selectivity of net migration from the South is greatest among young people, among Negroes, and among males. Gross migration rates among the white population, both to and from the South, are greater than those among the nonwhite population at all educational levels; but *net* migration from the South is relatively greater in the nonwhite than in the white population because the gross movement of Negroes back to the South is relatively much less than that of white people. Regional differences in migration, in relation to education, reflect differences in industrialization and urbanization. Areas with large expanding metropolitan populations are attracting well-educated migrants, and rural areas of the South are continuing to lose more well-educated people than they gain." J

2796. Szwed, John F. MUSICAL STYLE AND RACIAL CONFLICT. *Phylon 1966 27(4): 358-366.* While noting that after World War II changes in jazz suggested the imminent total assimilation of serious music from Negro and white traditions, the author observes that the emergence of "funky" or "soul" music about 1957 marked a departure from the trend toward formalization and assimilation. Soul music is performed almost exclusively by young Negroes, makes a conscious effort to bring Negro church and folk music into the jazz repertoire, and has led to modification of existing jazz melodies along the same lines. This movement marks a new consciousness of and pride in race and a sensitivity to African nationalism. It draws an enthusiastic, quasi-religious response from Negro audiences. The author views the new style as a response of Negro musicians to existing social conditions and as an attempt of Negro Americans to find a place in society. 21 notes. S. C. Pearson, Jr.

2797. Taussig, H. C. AMERICA'S "FEW." *Eastern World [Great Britain] 1965 19(11): 5-6.* An Asian view of U.S. involvement in the Vietnamese war, as well as general American foreign policy, condemning both as manifestations of "American *Herrenvolk* mentality." Americans who have criticized their government's foreign policy, in defiance of majority public opinion and the extremes of feeling generated by the Vietnam conflict in particular, are praised for their stands, and it is noted that this vocal minority includes many figures of considerable national and international stature, such as Dr. Martin Luther King, "whose partisanship for another 'minority' has been honoured by the whole world." Some attention is focused on U.S. policy in the Western Hemisphere, particularly the American intervention in the Dominican Republic.   A. K. Main

2798. Thernstrom, Stephan. UP FROM SLAVERY. *Perspectives in Am. Hist. 1967 1: 434-439.* Reviews Gilbert Osofsky's *Harlem: The Making of a Ghetto; Negro New York, 1890-1930* (New York: Harper & Row, 1966), "a fascinating book...lively, perceptive, succinct, smoothly written, based on an impressive array of sources." It is also somewhat superficial and impressionistic. Its distortions, omissions, and missed opportunities are attributed to a failure to think comparatively and to compare the Negro community with other immigrant and minority groups. Admittedly, Osofsky might have devoted a lifetime to the task without fully meeting all this criticism; "workers in the vineyard of American urban history have barely begun to scratch the surface."   D. J. Abramoske

2799. Thompson, Daniel C. EVALUATION AS A FACTOR IN PLANNING PROGRAMS FOR THE CULTURALLY-DISADVANTAGED. *J. of Negro Educ. 1964 33(3): 333-340.* Explicit criteria are urgently needed to test the effectiveness of various experimental programs. Ideally, the criteria would measure immediate, intermediate, and future-oriented levels of progress.
S. C. Pearson, Jr.

2800. Tilly, Charles and Feagin, Joe. BOSTON'S EXPERIMENT WITH RENT SUBSIDIES. *J. of the Am. Inst. of Planners 1970 36(5): 323-329.* "Within the last few years several new housing programs for low-income families have been authorized by Congress. Before these low-income housing programs came into existence, an experimental rent subsidy program in Boston anticipated many of their features and characteristics. From 1964 to 1967, forty large, low-income families, who had been displaced by public action, paid the rents they normally would have paid in public housing for lodging in three newly constructed non-profit developments built mainly for middle income families. Evaluation showed that the experimental rent subsidy program met its objective - providing sound, attractive housing to low-income families without major difficulties and at moderate cost. Such rent sudsidy programs have important implications for certain persistent problems of housing policy - relocation, desegregation, economic integration, and code enforcement."   J

2801. Tomlinson, T. M., ed. CONTRIBUTING FACTORS IN BLACK POLITICS. *Psychiatry 1970 33(2): 137-281.*
Tomlinson, T. M. CONTRIBUTING FACTORS IN BLACK POLITICS: INTRODUCTION, pp. 139-144. Black politics is a set of shared attitudes about Negro life, and the political and social pressure being used to solve the problems of the black community. All the contributors to this issue are white, as black intellectuals were found to be "immersed in working with black students and their energy is consumed by local and national black political conflicts."
TenHouten, Warren D. THE BLACK FAMILY: MYTH AND REALITY, pp. 145-173. Examines Daniel Patrick Moynihan's report on the black

family. There is no evidence for Moynihan's conclusions that rates of illegitimacy, female-headed families, and unemployment indicate deterioration of the black family. A detailed analysis of Los Angeles male-headed black families indicates that black fathers are no less powerful than white fathers, and that black husbands are no weaker in their marital role than white husbands. 14 notes.

Laurence, Joan. WHITE SOCIALIZATION: BLACK REALITY, pp. 174-194. Analyzes political socialization of black and white children. Black children are more egalitarian and more committed to traditional democratic concepts at the start of their schooling, but as they grow older they begin to recognize that true democracy is lacking in the ghetto. 25 notes.

Dizard, Jan E. BLACK IDENTITY, SOCIAL CLASS, AND BLACK POWER, pp. 195-207. A sociological analysis of black social classes and attitudes. Self-esteem among blacks is rising in all classes, and a powerful black group consciousness is developing. This will have important implications for future relationships between the races; as black pride increases, militancy and solidarity also increase. 20 notes.

Crawford, Thomas and Naditch, Murray. RELATIVE DEPRIVATION, POWERLESSNESS, AND MILITANCY: THE PSYCHOLOGY OF SOCIAL PROTEST, pp. 208-223. An analysis and model typology for understanding the wave of civil unrest in the black community. Potential rioters are those who recognize a discrepancy between real-life conditions and ideal circumstances, and who see themselves at the mercy of outside forces. 4 notes.

Kelman, Herbert C. A SOCIAL-PSYCHOLOGICAL MODEL OF POLITICAL LEGITIMACY AND ITS RELEVANCE TO BLACK AND WHITE STUDENT PROTEST MOVEMENTS, pp. 224-246. Describes the attitudes of student protesters. Whites argue that the system's inability to uphold democratic values has destroyed the legitimacy of the system itself. Whites strive to restore the humanistic value structure of society, although some determine that the only salvation is in the destruction of what they consider a corrupt social and political structure. Black student protesters, on the other hand, want to improve their identity and gain easier access to power. As the system denies the black an acceptable identity, and as it fails to meet his economic needs, it is considered illegitimate. 4 notes.

Tomlinson, T. M. DETERMINANTS OF BLACK POLITICS: RIOTS AND THE GROWTH OF MILITANCY, pp. 247-264. A study of the relationship between political perceptions and behavior. Data from the 1965 Los Angeles Riot Study indicate that militants are more sophisticated and more skeptical about political issues than conservative or uncommitted blacks. The conservatives are well-informed, but are more content with the existing political structure. The uncommitted were poorly informed, but their sense of disillusionment with the political system is equal to that of the militants. "Given the current (1970) trends of reduced governmental responsivity and increased black militancy, this society may indeed have finally forfeited its last chance for 'peaceful' resolution of its racial problem." 6 notes.

Boesel, David. THE LIBERAL SOCIETY, BLACK YOUTHS, AND THE GHETTO RIOTS, pp. 264-281. Compares recent events in the black movement with past revolutionary activity. Early black protest movements were short-lived and doomed to failure because of the unified and repressive character of the white elite. Since the New Deal, the white elite unity began to falter, at the same time as changes in economic and social life altered the system of racial control.

Presents a case study of a riot in Plainfield, New Jersey, which indicates that "the riots may be giving way to more disciplined means of asserting black claims." 11 notes.

M. A. Kaufman

2802. Torrey, Jane W. ILLITERACY IN THE GHETTO. *Harvard Educ. R. 1970 40(2): 253-259.* The functional aspects of language are far more significant in problems arising from dialect differences between Afro-American and Standard English than the structural differences. Clear expression, logical thought, and artistic subtlety are just as characteristic of the Afro-American dialect as of the language taught in the schools. In education, it is the low-status stigma attached to the Afro-American dialect that has led to the rejection of black children by white teachers, and to the subsequent inability of black children to do well in school. The author suggests that Standard English be recognized as a second language, and he asks whether we cannot admit Afro-American dialect and culture as objects worthy of study in the schools. Biblio.

J. Herbst

2803. Trooboff, Benjamin M. EMPLOYMENT OPPORTUNITIES FOR NEGROES IN HEALTH RELATED OCCUPATIONS. *J. of Negro Educ. 1969 38(1): 22-31.* The Bureau of Labor Statistics has estimated that the health manpower needs of the Nation for the decade 1966-75 will increase by 44 percent. This is due to redistribution of population, better methods of paying for medical care, and such programs as Medicare and Medicaid. The health industry has also become more competitive in pay and hours. There are many opportunities for Negroes in these health related occupations. A lack of educational background has kept many Negroes from entering these occupations; but this is changing among the younger Negroes, and a real opportunity exists. 4 tables, 15 notes.

B. D. Johnson

2804. Trousdale, Marion. RITUAL THEATRE: "THE GREAT WHITE HOPE." *Western Humanities R. 1969 23(4): 295-303.* Howard Sackler's play *The Great White Hope,* based on the career of Jack Johnson, the first Negro heavyweight champion, opened in 1968 at the Alvin Theatre in New York. It was a hit, but won little acclaim among the drama critics because its producers, responding to the mood of the time, produced it as a sensational tract on the race question. In an earlier production, in 1967 at the Arena Theatre in Washington, the play was far more successful as drama. The series of episodes which provide its structure present aspects of our culture in a way to draw the audience into the plot and to make their response a part of the play itself. Thus, the performance approaches "ritual theatre."

A. Turner

2805. Tucker, G. Richard and Lambert, Wallace E. WHITE AND NEGRO LISTENERS' REACTIONS TO VARIOUS AMERICAN-ENGLISH DIALECTS. *Social Forces 1969 47(4): 463-468.* "Samples of the taped speech of representatives of six American-English dialect groups *(Network, Educated White Southern, Educated Negro Southern, Mississippi Peer, Howard University, New York Alumni)* were played to three groups of college students (one northern white, one southern white and one southern Negro), who were asked to listen to the recorded readings and evaluate certain characteristics of the speakers, using an adjective checklist developed for this purpose. It was found that both northern white and southern Negro judges rated the *Network* speakers most favorably, and the *Educated Negro Southern* speakers next. The southern white students also evaluated the *Network* speakers most favorably, but, in contrast, the *Educated White Southern* speakers next most favorably. On the other hand, both groups of white judges rated the *Mississippi Peer* speakers least favorably, while the Negro judges rated the *Educated White Southern* speakers least favorably. The theoretical and practical significance of the results are discussed."

J

2806. Ulansky, Gene. MBARI - THE MISSING LINK. *Phylon 1965 26(3): 247-254.* Discusses the Mbari clubs as an instrument of value to Negro Americans in their search for a sense of identity with Africa. The Mbari clubs emerged in Nigeria in 1961 and spread through Africa creating a "kind of Nigerian version of a Parisian coffee house atmosphere" drawing together artists and writers concerned with African artistic life of the past and present. Thus the clubs offer "Negro American artists and writers an opportunity to taste deeply of Africa and to make connections with both particular and universal aspects in the African tradition."

S. C. Pearson, Jr.

2807. Unsigned. AMERICAN TEACHERS ASSOCIATION PUSHES ACTIVITY IN TWO VITAL AREAS. *Negro Hist. Bull. 1964 27(6): 149-152.* Describes the work of a commission of the American Teachers Association which recommended changes in school and college textbooks, especially in their treatment of Negro history, and another commission assigned the task of helping to improve the quality of teaching in predominantly Negro schools.

L. Gara

2808. Unsigned. ELIZABETH DUNCAN KOONTZ - PRESIDENT OF THE NAT'L EDUCATION ASSN'S DEPT. OF CLASSROOM TEACHERS. *Negro Hist. Bull. 1964 28(3): 55-56.* Describes the educational contributions of Mrs. Koontz, a Negro educator, and excerpts a newspaper article about her.

L. Gara

2809. Unsigned. THREE NEGROES RECEIVE 1964 PRESIDENTIAL FREEDOM MEDAL. *Negro Hist. Bull. 1964 28(3): 58-59.* Brief profiles of the three Negro recipients of 1964 Presidential Freedom Medals: Dr. Lena F. Edwards, medical missionary; Leontyne Price, concert singer; and A. Philip Randolph, labor leader.

L. Gara

2810. Valentine, Charles A. DEFICIT, DIFFERENCE, AND BICULTURAL MODELS OF AFRO-AMERICAN BEHAVIOR. *Harvard Educ. R. 1971 41(2): 137-157.* Rejects the biologically and culturally based deficit models and the cultural difference and the culture-of-poverty models as inadequate for describing and analyzing Afro-American culture. Presents evidence that social workers, clinical psychologists, guidance counselors, and psychiatrists using these models do immense harm to those whom they are supposed to help. A bicultural model, taking into account that Afro-Americans are living in two cultures simultaneously, can be far more helpful. The two cultures are not mutually exclusive. To adopt the bicultural model requires a radical shift in the values embraced by the existing dominant institutions and in the power relationships that underlie these institutions. Reprinted, with adaptations, from the author's essay, "It's either Brain Damage or No Father," in Robert Buckout, ed., *Toward Social Change: A Handbook for Those Who Will* (New York: Harper and Row, 1971). 16 notes.   J. Herbst

2811. Valien, Preston. GENERAL DEMOGRAPHIC CHARACTERISTICS OF THE NEGRO POPULATION IN THE UNITED STATES. *J. of Negro Educ. 1963 32(4): 329-336.*

2812. Vanderbilt, Amy. BAD MANNERS IN AMERICA. *Ann. of the Am. Acad. of Pol. and Social Sci. 1968 378: 90-98.* "The widely held contention that American manners are uniformly bad is not tenable. The very mobility of American society brings into sharp focus the bad manners of the minority, thus making bad manners seem to be the norm. The sharp delineations between classes are less important as proponents of exemplary manners and mores. The changes in etiquette frequently come from other sources. Higher education does not necessarily result in culture. Education and social grace are today not necessarily synonymous. The decline of the mother's influence in the home has meant the decline of what was once known as 'ordinary' manners among America's children. Because of many economic pressures, we are living more simply, with less formality and a minimum restriction upon the family. The pattern of meal-taking has changed drastically. There is a blurring, too, of the difference between the sexes, with a resulting difference in our approach to manners between them. 'Society' has taken on many meanings and is influenced by geography. Reduction in service has been one of the most striking changes in our society, along with a great change in our attitude toward language, from which 'indelicacies' have virtually disappeared. The Negro revolution is making, and will continue to make, a great change in our manners and mores. The admission of new peoples into our social stream has made changes in our behavior. We have become increasingly forthright. Our etiquette is changing. When developing manners are deemed 'bad,' they are usually modified because bad manners make people uncomfortable."
J

2813. Verba, Sidney, Brody, Richard A., Parker, Edwin B., Nie, Norman H., Polsby, Nelson W., Ekman, Paul , and Black, Gordon S. PUBLIC OPINION AND THE WAR IN VIETNAM. *Am. Pol. Sci. R. 1967 61(2): 317-333.* A survey of American attitudes toward the Vietnam War in February and March 1966, by the National Opinion Research Center, which tested 1,495 adults. Among the conclusions: 1) "The public expressed concern about the war and was relatively informed about it." 2) "Though the preferences of respondents have internal structure, they are not related to the broad social groupings around which political and social attitudes often cluster." 3) More women and Negroes favor de-escalation than men and whites. 4) Policy preferences on this issue are possibly "patterned by the respondents' cognitive and affective relationship to the war itself." 5) The shape of opinion differs little between the informed, articulate population and the rest of the population. 6) The "data suggest a higher permissiveness for reduction of the war, but evidence from other polls since then suggests that the President's support increases no matter what he does - increase the war or talk of negotiations - as long as he does something." 15 tables, 30 notes.

D. D. Cameron

2814. Vishmevskii, S. FINAL "VELIKOGO OBSHCHESTVA" [Finale of the "Great Society"]. *Mezhdunarodnaia Zhizn [USSR] 1969 16(4): 51-58.* Discusses the "Great Society." That attempt to solve the social ills of America failed. Can the complex problems facing American society be solved by state monopoly capitalism? The war on poverty, the pressing question of the reconstruction of cities, and unemployment all remain unsolved. No change was effected in the position of the Negro. The dissatisfaction of the workers was manifested by numerous strikes. To remedy the ills troubling American society, it will be necessary to make important changes in the social structure of that society. 5 notes.

T. Yedlin

2815. Vittenson, Lillian K. AREAS OF CONCERN TO NEGRO COLLEGE STUDENTS AS INDICATED BY THEIR RESPONSES TO THE MOONEY PROBLEM CHECK LIST. *J. of Negro Educ. 1967 36(1): 51-57.* Reports the findings of a study of 100 Negro students in Illinois Teachers Colleges in Chicago. Most students indicated concern about their adjustment to college work. The second largest area of concern centered about the area of social and recreational activities. Comparisons of responses between sexes, freshmen and seniors, and age groups are provided. The author recommends early identification, encouragement, and guidance for the academically capable Negro student with placement in a college preparatory high school curriculum. She also suggests that Negro boys be placed in contact with Negro teenagers and adults who can serve as models with whom they can identify.

S. C. Pearson, Jr.

2816. Vontress, Clemmont E. COUNSELING NEGRO STUDENTS FOR COLLEGE. *J. of Negro Educ. 1968 37(1): 37-44.* Discusses counseling problems such as parental and student indifference and apathy which high school counselors are likely to encounter in urging Negro students to prepare for and seek admission to college. Counselors are encouraged to be aggressive in showing parents and students how they may and why they should attend college. Counselors are advised to help college admissions counselors understand the strengths and weaknesses of Negro students, and some sources of financial assistance for Negro students are enumerated. 5 notes.

S. C. Pearson, Jr.

2817. Vontress, Clemmont E. THE NEGRO PERSONALITY RECONSIDERED. *J. of Negro Educ. 1966 35(3): 210-217.* The Negro's status in American society has shaped his personality. This thesis is discussed in terms of self-hatred, desire to escape self, aggression, and masculine protest. Based on published materials; 50 notes.

S. C. Pearson, Jr.

2818. Vose, Clement E. INTEREST GROUPS, JUDICIAL REVIEW, AND LOCAL GOVERNMENT. *Western Pol. Q. 1966 19(1): 85-100.* Writing on judicial review of State and local government has concentrated upon structure, power, and policy but has tended to ignore process. Little examination has been made of the ways in which courts - passive instruments of government - have been stimulated into action. Much litigation originates with action organizations; there is great importance to group agitation for judicial review of State and municipal public policy. Examples cited are those emanating from such groups as the National Association for the Advancement of Colored People, National Institute of Municipal Law Officers, and the American Trial Lawyers Association. Evidence shows that judicial review must be thought of not only in terms of Supreme Court review of congressional acts and of State legislatures, but also laws and regulations emanating from local and municipal bodies. 62 notes.

H. Aptheker

2819. Walker, Bailus, Jr. IMPROVING COMMUNITY HEALTH THROUGH STUDENT PARTICIPATION. *J. of Negro Educ. 1965 34(1): 23-29.* Proposes developing a more favorable attitude toward community health through a program of in-school and extra-curricular activities directed toward school children.

S. C. Pearson, Jr.

2820. Walker, Jack. NEGRO VOTING IN ATLANTA: 1953-1961. *Phylon 1963 24(4): 379-387.* The author studied Negro voting behavior in a period during which the Negro precentage of the total electorate in Atlanta advanced from 4.0 to 34.0 and found that in certain elections Negroes voted in much larger percentages than whites.

S. C. Pearson, Jr.

2821. Warner, Sam Bass, Jr. and Burke, Colin B. CULTURAL CHANGE AND THE GHETTO. *J. of Contemporary Hist. [Great Britain] 1969 4(4): 173-187.* According to current analysis, the attitude and presumably the behavior of almost all urban Americans can be located on a matrix of four classes (upper class, middle class, working class, and lower class) and four socioreligious identifications (white Protestant, white Catholic, white Jewish, and Negro Protestant). The authors consider the dimensions of cultural change as dependent variables and economic class structure as the independent variable. The former literature on the ghetto process of cultural change has now been harnessed to the explanation of the history of the four-part socioreligious culture of today's metropolis. Although not enough research has been done to warrant new hypotheses to supplement the ghetto one, some illustrative, statistical material exists which helps to define the boundaries of the ghetto interpretation. The largest immigrant group, the Irish, were scattered throughout the city; the Germans were both scattered and had a strong cluster or clusters in each large city. If this analysis shows a representative situation, a ghetto interpretation of urban cultural change is hardly supported. The view of the ghetto as a limited case changes one's view of the ghetto itself to that of an agent of localized acculturation for the whole metropolitan area. 3 tables, 14 notes.

Sr. M. P. Trauth

2822. Warren, Paul B. GUIDELINES FOR THE FUTURE - AN EDUCA-
TIONAL APPROACH FOR THE CULTURALLY DISADVANTAGED. *J.
of Negro Educ. 1966 35(3): 283-286.* Advocates a program designed to integrate
culturally disadvantaged youth within the larger social structure socially, politically, and economically, and to eliminate barriers to meaningful interaction with
the society at large. Such a program should create a place for the culturally
disadvantaged in the immediate environment, a place for him within the larger
social framework, and sound psychological foundations for him within the school
environment. 3 notes. S. C. Pearson, Jr.

2823. Watson, Franklin J. A COMPARISON OF NEGRO AND WHITE POP-
ULATIONS, CONNECTICUT: 1940-1960. *Phylon 1968 29(2): 142-155.* A
number of socioeconomic and demographic indexes were used by the author to
study the comparison of white and Negro performances in Connecticut over the
period 1940-60. While both groups advanced, Negroes still lagged far behind
whites in educational achievement. The rate of educational improvement for
whites exceeded that of Negroes. In occupational achievement, the same was true;
while both groups advanced, whites advanced at a greater rate than Negroes. At
the same time, the youth dependency ratio increased more rapidly for Negroes
than for whites, as the Negro birthrate remained consistently higher than the
white rate. Concerning infant mortality, the Negro rate in 1960 was higher than
the white rate in 1940, although both have decreased over the years. In conclusion, the author stresses that Negroes in Connecticut in 1960 "were inhabitants
of a world from which whites have long since departed." 5 tables, 2 figs., 11 notes.
R. D. Cohen

2824. Weber, George H. and Motz, Annabelle B. SCHOOL AS PERCEIVED
BY THE DROPOUT. *J. of Negro Educ. 1968 37(2): 127-134.* Discusses the
perceptions of school personnel by dropouts as revealed in intensive interviews
with two groups of Negro males from an Eastern city. All school personnel were
seen as indifferent or punitive. Principals were inaccessible and failed to provide
leadership. Counselors were parent surrogates, disciplinarians, advisers, and gatekeepers but had little real interest in the student. Teachers were dull, uninspiring,
disinterested in student success, and punitive. School policemen were ineffective
in their protective role but shared the teachers' punitive function. In general the
dropouts felt that great social distance separates students and staff and that the
latter are united in opposition to the former. 7 notes. S. C. Pearson, Jr.

2825. Weber, Robert E. FEEDBACK AND THE JOB CORPS. *J. of Negro
Educ. 1968 37(1): 55-61.* Advocating the use of feedback techniques for program
evaluation and modification, the author presents the results of an interview with
three teenage Negro male Job Corpsmen. The youths expressed a strong and
warm appreciation of the Job Corps for its contribution to their sense of manliness, its nontraditional approach, its recognition of abilities and achievements, its
provision of interested staff members, and its increase in corpsmen's aspirations
and marketable skills. Criticisms dealt with inadequacies in administration and
operations, location of camps away from large cities, and failure to foster a
positive image of the corpsman. S. C. Pearson, Jr.

2826. Webster, Staten W. SOME CORRELATES OF REPORTED ACADEMICALLY SUPPORTIVE BEHAVIORS OF NEGRO MOTHERS TOWARD THEIR CHILDREN. *J. of Negro Educ. 1965 34(2): 114-120.* The author studied 311 Negro adolescents in three integrated high schools of a San Francisco Bay area high school district in an attempt to determine the role of maternal supportive behavior in the self-perceptions and levels of academic achievement of their offspring. Results indicate that academically supportive behavior encourages favorable self-perceptions, vocational aspirations, and predictions of educational attainment. However, such behavior was not found to be directly related to high school grades when the sex of the offspring was taken into consideration.   S. C. Pearson, Jr.

2827. Weinberg, Carl. SOCIAL ATTITUDES OF NEGRO AND WHITE STUDENT LEADERS. *J. of Negro Educ. 1966 35(2): 161-167.* Reports the findings of a study of 60 Negro and 88 white high school students who "responded to a questionnaire which elicited their responses to a number of controversial and not so controversial subjects. The responses to both kinds of questions were capable of being fitted into categories held to be *Conservative, Moderate,* or *Liberal.*" Negro student leaders were found to be "at least as conservative and other-directed as are white leaders, and, in some areas, appear to be even more so." Thus the hypothesis that the Negro, to attain and maintain middle-class status, must exaggerate the behaviors of the white middle class through social conservatism seemed supported.   S. C. Pearson, Jr.

2828. Wellman, David. THE "WRONG" WAY TO FIND JOBS FOR NEGROES. *Trans-action 1968 5(5): 9-18.* Analyzing the failure of a Federal-State program to train 47 young people for jobs, the study concludes that the young people did not care to "play-act" in situations such as filling out application forms, taking aptitude tests, and engaging in job interviews. Yet, when opportunities came for interviews for real jobs, the students seemed to take a serious attitude. The program was another attempt by the white community to inculcate white middle-class values in blacks. The students, mostly black, responded by "putting on" by simple passive noncooperation. Such treatment was even accorded to black leaders who spoke to the group. The author noted that Negro women reacted more positively toward the program than Negro men. The program did not meet the needs of the students as it asked them to stop being what they were. Based on the author's observation; illus., biblio.
                                                                A. Erlebacher

2829. Wheeler, James O. TRANSPORTATION PROBLEMS IN NEGRO GHETTOS. *Sociol. and Social Res. 1969 53(2): 171-179.* "The geographical mobility of urban Negroes is limited by the poor structure of transportation facilities and services connecting the ghetto with other areas of the city, and yet Negroes may be forced to travel as far or farther than whites in order to reach workplaces, at least in some cities. These problems are outlined with particular reference to work-trip data for Tulsa, Oklahoma, with emphasis on time and distance of travel. It is concluded that the unique geographical mobility pattern of Negroes is an interrelated function of inadequate transportation and residential segregation." J

2830. Whitten, Norman E., Jr. and Szwed, John. ANTHROPOLOGISTS LOOK AT AFRO-AMERICANS: INTRODUCTION. *Trans-action 1968 5(8): 49-56.* Reviews the ways in which anthropologists have looked at the Negro in America. The work of Melville J. Herskovits is emphasized. Herskovits and his followers concentrated on a search for "Africanisms." The authors describe a symposium held in 1966 in which a dozen anthropologists considered the studies of the Negro in the New World since the publication of Herskovits' *The Myth of the Negro Past* in 1941 (reprinted by Beacon Press in 1958). The emphasis in such studies has been on the social organization of Negro families. Three new concepts - exclusion from access to capital resources, economic marginality, and adaption to marginality - were considered. The symposium members agreed that certain common stylistic features of life did characterize New World Negroes. Among these are what Alan Lomax referred to as "cantometric analysis." Other participants in the symposium stressed the necessity for Negro scholars to emphasize the norms of their community, rather than those characteristics which are exotic or marginal. The symposium also attempted to define the extent of the African world. Illus., biblio. A. Erlebacher

2831. Wilcox, Preston. EDUCATION FOR BLACK LIBERATION. *New Generation 1969 51(1): 17-21.* Schools, unions, and businesses in America are racist for training blacks for outmoded vocations and excluding them from others. Education for blacks can never be relevant to their needs until whites no longer control it. Education for black ghetto dwellers must prepare them for life in the ghetto, where most of them will remain; education must not subject them to a constant barrage of white values. Continued failure to permit blacks to survive economically may lead to the undoing of white America. K. E. Hendrickson

2832. Wiley, Norbert. AMERICA'S UNIQUE CLASS POLITICS: THE INTERPLAY OF THE LABOR, CREDIT AND COMMODITY MARKETS. *Am. Sociol. R. 1967 32(4): 529-541.* "American political life, both historically and at present, has proven unusually resistant to economic interpretation, either by the Classical Liberal or the Marxist versions of economic determinism. Instead, political scholars have placed heavy reliance on a variety of noneconomic factors, the most recent being those of alienation, mass society and status protest. However, in this paper we argue that a great deal of American political life can be explained economically, in terms of class conflict, if revisions are made in class theory. Accordingly, a multi-dimensional theory of class conflict, based on the work of Max Weber, is presented, using the dimensions of the credit and commodity markets along with the usual dimension of the labor market. This theory is then applied to three political problems: (1) the relation between agrarian and labor protest in the 19th century; (2) the contemporary radical right; and (3) the current Negro protest movement." J

2833. Wilkerson, Doxey A. BIBLIOGRAPHY ON THE EDUCATION OF SOCIALLY DISADVANTAGED CHILDREN AND YOUTH. *J. of Negro Educ. 1964 33(3): 358-366.*

2834. Wilkerson, Doxey A. PREVAILING AND NEEDED EMPHASIS IN RESEARCH ON THE EDUCATION OF DISADVANTAGED CHILDREN AND YOUTH. *J. of Negro Educ. 1964 33(3): 346-357.* Preoccupation with the assessment of children should give way to much increased evaluation of the school, more studies should be conducted of the characteristics and developmental patterns of disadvantaged young people, and increased attention should be devoted to the needs of a society which creates and maintains vast numbers of socially disadvantaged children and youth. S. C. Pearson, Jr.

2835. Williams, Murat W. VIRGINIA POLITICS: WINDS OF CHANGE. *Virginia Q. R. 1966 42(2): 177-188.* Insists Virginians have traditionally prided themselves on conservative State policies and the obstruction of national liberal movements. However, conservative power is declining as a result of population mobility and new voters, including many Negroes. The new voters look to the future and are interested less in State economy than in cultural, educational, recreational, and social services. Many younger Virginia politicians understand both the new voter's desires and the necessity of a shift in political position from that represented by Senator Harry F. Byrd. Aroused voters can bring about the change. O. H. Zabel

2836. Williams, Robert L. and Cole, Spurgeon. SCHOLASTIC ATTITUDES OF SOUTHERN NEGRO STUDENTS. *J. of Negro Educ. 1969 38(1): 74-77.* A study of 11th grade students in the deep South to assess the academic attitudes of Negro students in segregated and integrated schools and to compare their academic orientations with those of Caucasian students in the same geographic areas. The authors found that the Negro students have poorer academic morale in recently integrated schools than in segregated schools and that they are less interested in scholarship than white students in the same regions. Mere physical integration will apparently not remedy the background of scholastic apathy. Attitudes of white teachers and students could affect these results, however. The sample used in the study was smaller than the authors wish. Table, 8 notes. B. D. Johnson

2837. Willie, Charles V. ANTI-SOCIAL BEHAVIOR AMONG DISADVANTAGED YOUTH: SOME OBSERVATIONS ON PREVENTION FOR TEACHERS. *J. of Negro Educ. 1964 33(2): 176-181.*

2838. Willie, Charles V., Gershenovitz, Anita, Levine, Myrna, Glazer, Sulochana, and Jones, Roy J. RACE AND DELINQUENCY. *Phylon 1965 26(3): 240-246.* Reports the findings of a study of juveniles referred to Juvenile Court in Washington, D.C., from July 1959 through March 1962. The authors found that "(1) socio-economic status is related to juvenile delinquency - the lower the socio-economic status level of a neighborhood, the higher the juvenile delinquency rate; (2) family composition is related to juvenile delinquency - the higher the proportion of broken families in a neighborhood, the greater the juvenile delinquency rate; and (3) any association between race and juvenile delinquency may be explained by differences in the socio-economic status and family composition of white and nonwhite populations." S. C. Pearson, Jr.

2839. Willner, Milton. FAMILY DAY CARE: AN ESCAPE FROM POVERTY. *Social Work 1971 16(2): 30-35.* Analysis of a three-year research study of 203 Negro working mothers in New York City who sought child care arrangements reveals the need for sufficient day-care facilities, properly supervised service, and built-in safeguards to guarantee the total development of children. 11 notes. W. L. Willigan

2840. Wilson, James Q. "THE FLAMBOYANT MR. POWELL." *Commentary 1966 41(1): 31-35.* Adam Clayton Powell has achieved his tremendous successes by means of minority appeal. That he is quite corrupt is admitted by everybody, even Powell; he owes his overwhelming support in Harlem to the fact that he can admit it, even make jokes about it, and get away with it. Other minority-group politicians, such as James Michael Curley of the Boston Irish, have made use of this kind of tactic to win; the tragedy of Powell is that that is all he does. Curley used his power to the advantage of his Irish electorate and Boston as a whole; Powell, however, has not used his power to gain anything for Negroes in Harlem or elsewhere, but only for his personal advantage. He is seen primarily as a product of New York of the 1930's and 1940's, in which an honest and restrained Negro politican, playing by the rules, would not have been able to win in the city's dirty politics. The author expects that as more Negro communities become "politically as volatile as Harlem in the 1930's," the new Negro politicians will have "a bit of Adam in them," though they will probably be more responsible. A. K. Main

2841. Wilson, James Q. THE WAR ON CITIES. *Public Interest 1966 (3): 27-44.* Discusses government efforts to resolve the problems of the American cities. The author argues that the government policy has no concrete goals or clear priorities and that government agencies have been in conflict over the proper approach to the problems at hand. Conditions in the cities have improved on the whole, but certain problems still cause serious difficulty, such as the increase of expectations at a more rapid rate than achievements in urban society, technical problems associated with high density living, and the problem of the urban Negro. A program is outlined whereby the Federal Government could assist in the solution of these problems. H. E. Cox

2842. Wish, Harvey. NEGRO EDUCATION AND THE PROGRESSIVE MOVEMENT. *J. of Negro Hist. 1964 49(3): 184-200.* Presents a dismal picture of Negro education during the Progressive Era. In the South race prejudice, poverty, and the leadership of Booker T. Washington operated to keep all educational opportunities for Negroes except industrial training at a bare minimum. Among the factors at work to better conditions were the contributions of a group of outstanding Negro educators, the work of W. E. B. Du Bois, the founding of the National Association for the Advancement of Colored People, the shocked reactions of whites to race riots and other injustices, and the improvement of standards and teaching in Negro schools.   L. Gara

2843. Wolf, Eleanor P. THE BAXTER AREA: A NEW TREND IN NEIGH-BORHOOD CHANGE? *Phylon 1965 26(4): 344-353.* Describes a study conducted by field observation and home interviews in two neighborhoods of Detroit. One, identified as Russell Woods, received its first Negro household in 1955, was 20 percent Negro two years later, and was 75 percent Negro by 1961. The other, identified as Baxter, received its first recognized Negro household in 1960 and was only about one percent Negro two years later. An attempt was made to determine the cause for greater stability in the latter area, and it was attributed to a combination of factors: "general market conditions unfavorable to residential mobility, and a population which includes a substantial number of households with low mobility inclinations....Reluctance to leave appears to be associated with certain demographic characteristics, especially the large percentage of older people, rather than with any differences, or changes, in attitudes toward interracial housing."   S. C. Pearson, Jr.

2844. Wolfe, Deborah P. WHAT THE ECONOMIC OPPORTUNITY ACT MEANS TO THE NEGRO. *J. of Negro Educ. 1965 34(1): 88-92.* Observing that the Economic Opportunity Act of 1964 (H. R. 11377) is of crucial significance to the American Negro, the author summarizes the provisions of the six titles of this act and urges that they be used to the fullest extent by Negroes.

S. C. Pearson, Jr.

2845. Woolfolk, E. O. and Smith, L. S. CHEMICAL EDUCATION IN NEGRO COLLEGES. *Negro Hist. Bull. 1967 30(2): 7-11.* Compares the educational programs of the chemistry departments and chemistry instructors of 54 colleges which have chapters of the Beta Kappa Chi Scientific Society and the chemistry departments of 54 colleges among predominantly white colleges which do not have chapters of Beta Kappa Chi, an honor society in the natural sciences and mathematics to foster high scholarship and scientific achievement at Negro colleges. The rate at which the Negro college has moved to its present position over the past 75 years, in a segregated society, should serve as a yardstick in evaluating its potential for operating in an open society. 2 tables, 4 figs.

D. H. Swift

2846. Yarmolinsky, Adam. DAS PROBLEM DER NEGERGETTOS IN DEN AMERIKANISCHEN GROSSTÄDTEN [The problem of the Negro ghettos in large American cities]. *Europa-Archiv [West Germany] 1968 23(7): 251-256.* Summarizes the origins and the extent of the problem of the Negro ghetto, suggesting that this is the greatest problem that American society currently faces. The author proposes several means of helping to solve the problem, with particular emphasis on relations between police and ghetto residents. The author also emphasizes the importance of employment and housing and, finally, the constructive role of the black community itself.   L. H. Legters

2847. Youmans, E. Grant, Grigsby, S. E. , and King, H. SOCIAL CHANGE, GENERATION, AND RACE. *Rural Sociol. 1969 34(3): 305-312.* "This paper focuses on one aspect of social change - changes in value orientations which reflect relationships between self and society. Two questions are examined: What differences in value orientations exist between younger and older generations of Negroes and whites in a rural area? What are the implications of the differences to social change in the United States? Data were collected in 1962 from younger and older generations of Negroes and of whites living in three rural counties in northern Florida. The younger generations included 411 Negro and white 12th graders and the older generations included their parents. Generational differences in value orientations - in achievement, in anomia, and in family identification - were more pronounced among Negroes than among whites. These generational differences among rural Negroes suggest an orientation to life for young Negroes which enables them to identify easily with movements for change in race relations in the United States." J

2848. Young, Harding B. NEGRO PARTICIPATION IN AMERICAN BUSINESS. *J. of Negro Educ. 1963 32(4): 390-401.* Traces recent progress of Negro owned and operated business which is termed "both real and unprecedented" but concludes that Negroes must gain "total integration into the mainstream of American business life." S. C. Pearson, Jr.

2849. --. [EDUCATION AND SOUTHERN MIGRATION.] *Southern Econ. J. 1965 32(1, part 2): 106-128.*
Fein, Rashi. EDUCATIONAL PATTERNS IN SOUTHERN MIGRATION, pp. 106-124. Most of those who leave the South are poorly educated. While among whites the least educated leave in disproportionate numbers, it is the better educated Negroes who tend to leave. Although the best trained and best educated white southerners leave in large numbers, equally well educated persons come in and the balance is not especially adverse, especially as mobility may help to erode some institutional differences unfavorable to growth. There are, however, important regional differences within the South. Data from the 1960 census.
Parker, William N. COMMENT, pp. 125-128. Emphasizes the regional differences within the South. A. W. Coats

2850. --. HIGHER EDUCATION OF NEGRO AMERICANS: PROSPECTS AND PROGRAMS. *J. of Negro Educ. 1967 36(3): 187-347.*
Daniel, Walter G. EDITORIAL COMMENT, pp. 187-191. Provides an overview of this 36th yearbook which includes the principal papers delivered at a conference 16-18 April 1967 commemorating the centennial of the opening of Howard University.
Unsigned. PROGRAM OF THE CONFERENCE ON "THE HIGHER EDUCATION OF NEGRO AMERICANS: PROSPECTS AND PROGRAMS," pp. 192-195.
Clark, Kenneth B. HIGHER EDUCATION FOR NEGROES: CHALLENGES AND PROSPECTS, pp. 196-203. Though early efforts of Negro colleges were successful, these colleges gradually capitulated to American racism. They are academically inferior because they reflect the cumulative inferiority of

segregated primary and secondary education. But white colleges and universities are morally inferior because they have allowed education to become contaminated by racism. Since segregated education will not quickly be eradicated, Negro colleges should be made as good as possible.

Unsigned. SYMPOSIUM ON THE HIGHER EDUCATION OF NEGRO AMERICANS, pp. 204-215. Reproduces the panel discussion of the Clark paper which followed its presentation.

Dyer, Henry S. TOWARD MORE EFFECTIVE RECRUITMENT AND SELECTION OF NEGROES FOR COLLEGE, pp. 216-229. Discusses recruitment practices and suggests a need for reform if recruitment is to accomplish its stated purposes.

Plaut, Richard L. PROSPECTS FOR THE ENTRANCE AND SCHOLASTIC ADVANCEMENT OF NEGROES IN HIGHER EDUCATIONAL INSTITUTIONS, pp. 230-237. Discusses the merits of several recent public and private programs designed to encourage the entrance and success of Negroes in interracial institutions.

Valien, Preston. IMPROVING PROGRAMS IN GRADUATE EDUCATION FOR NEGROES, pp. 238-248. Discusses the graduate programs and faculties provided in 24 predominantly Negro institutions and concludes with proposals for improvement.

Kirk, Grayson. CHANGING PATTERNS OF PUBLIC AND PRIVATE SUPPORT FOR HIGHER EDUCATION, pp. 249-257. Suggests that both public and private institutions face a major financial crisis, reviews past sources of support, and evaluates potential sources of future support with emphasis on public sources.

Bressler, Marvin. WHITE COLLEGES AND NEGRO HIGHER EDUCATION, pp. 258-265. Considers some of the ways in which predominantly white colleges may serve the educational needs of Negroes.

Henderson, Vivian W. THE ROLE OF THE PREDOMINANTLY NEGRO INSTITUTIONS, pp. 266-273. While encouraging liberal arts education, the author points to the need for specialized education to meet contemporary needs and suggests that Negro colleges might provide such education.

Pettigrew, Thomas F. A SOCIAL PSYCHOLOGICAL VIEW OF THE PREDOMINANTLY NEGRO COLLEGE, pp. 274-285. After tracing the past contributions of Negro colleges in producing a Negro elite, the author suggests the urgency of vigorous participation by such colleges in the current struggle for an integrated and democratic America.

Bayton, James A. and Lewis, Harold O. REFLECTIONS AND SUGGESTIONS FOR FURTHER STUDY CONCERNING THE HIGHER EDUCATION OF NEGROES, pp. 286-294. Suggests the need to place specific problems in a broader context, to investigate problems in greater depth and with objectivity, and to consider the administrative organization of education. Suggestions resulting from the conference are also enumerated.

Thompson, Charles H. THE HIGHER EDUCATION OF NEGRO AMERICANS: PROSPECTS AND PROGRAMS - A CRITICAL SUMMARY, pp. 295-314. Provides a critical review of papers presented at the conference.

Boney, J. Don. SOME DYNAMICS OF DISADVANTAGED STUDENTS IN LEARNING SITUATIONS, pp. 315-319. Reports "that nonwhite students tend to assign a disproportionate amount of importance to the evaluations of whites with reference to their role expectations." The author encourages teachers "to reward more assertiveness which would be enhancing to learning and social and emotional development."

McClain, Edwin W. PERSONALITY CHARACTERISTICS OF NEGRO COLLEGE STUDENTS IN THE SOUTH — A RECENT APPRAISAL, pp. 320-325. Reports the results of a study of undergraduate students in two Southern schools, a private liberal arts college for Negroes and a state university for Negroes. 99 males and 198 females were tested with Cattell's Sixteen Personality Factor Questionnaire. The study suggests that Negro students "are far from able to enter on an equal footing with their white age-mates into the educational, social, or vocational life of the country."

Codwell, John E. THE EDUCATION IMPROVEMENT PROJECT OF THE SOUTHERN ASSOCIATION OF COLLEGES AND SCHOOLS - A FOCUS ON IMPROVING THE PERFORMANCE OF DISADVANTAGED PUPILS, pp. 326-333. Describes the programs of the Southern Association in providing special education for the disadvantaged.

Unsigned. PREDOMINANTLY NEGRO COLLEGES AND UNIVERSITIES IN THE UNITED STATES, 1963-1964, WITH ENROLLMENT FIGURES FOR FALL 1964 (APPENDIX I), pp. 334-343.

Unsigned. EXCERPTS FROM FORD FOUNDATION RELEASE OF JULY 1967 (APPENDIX II), pp. 344-347.   S. C. Pearson, Jr.

2851. --. [ISSUES OF THE PRESIDENTIAL ELECTION]. *Current Hist. 1968 55(326): 193-233, 239-245.*

Seligman, Ben B. AMERICAN POVERTY: RURAL AND URBAN, pp. 193-198, 239-240. Until President Lyndon Johnson began his War on Poverty in 1964 few politicians became excited over the issue. Subsequently, the Social Security Administration estimated that America harbored 30 million poor people or 9 million poor families. Most of the heads of poor families are employed but cannot earn enough to sustain themselves or their families. The most conspicuous groups mired in poverty include the Negro, the elderly, the youthful, and the rural. Largely due to congressional parsimony and political infighting, the War on Poverty has been unable to reach more than 15 percent of the poor. Only continued frustration will result unless a broad and adequately supported antipoverty program is initiated.

Sindler, Allan P. NEGROES, ETHNIC GROUPS AND AMERICAN POLITICS, pp. 207-212, 242-243. To a limited extent the experience of the American Negro is comparable to that of earlier ethnic groups seeking acceptance and status in American society. However, the Negroes' task is more difficult than that faced by earlier immigrants due to his belated entry on the political and economic scene, in addition to the rejection and repression of the Negro by white society. The Black Power movement, which is as much mood as doctrine, signifies that Negroes have correctly digested the American experience with regard to ethnic groups and have now embarked upon that short-run separation which has proved in the past to be the necessary transition to integration and assimilation.

B. D. Rhodes

2852. --. [SOUTHERN UNDERDEVELOPMENT.] *Southern Econ. J. 1965 32(1, part 2): 73-105.*

Bowman, Mary Jean. HUMAN INEQUALITIES AND SOUTHERN UNDERDEVELOPMENT. pp. 73-102. Uses data concerning education, income, and occupations (mainly in the period 1950-60) to show the distributional relationships in the southern socioeconomic structure and to explore the recent pace of change. The results show the concentration of the South's problems in its undereducated of both races and in its racial inequalities. The differences for whites between that region and the rest of the Nation lie at the lower end of the scale. The spread between high and low incomes is greater for southern whites than for northern, as is also the rate at which incomes fall off with lower levels of educational achievement. The distribution of income among Negroes also shows a relatively steeper income-education gradient than in the North, though it is lower than the distribution curve for whites at all levels. Hence "there is an emptiness at the heart of the social and economic structures that sets men apart, both within and between races."

Rivlin, Alice M. COMMENT, pp. 103-105. Argues that the Bowman paper gives too depressing a picture.   A. W. Coats

2853. --. STUDIES IN THE HIGHER EDUCATION OF NEGRO AMERICANS. *J. of Negro Educ. 1966 35(4): 293-513.*

Daniel, Walter G. EDITORIAL COMMENT, pp. 293-298. Provides an overview of the contents of this yearbook.

Clement, Rufus E. THE HISTORICAL DEVELOPMENT OF HIGHER EDUCATION FOR NEGRO AMERICANS, pp. 299-305.

Badger, Henry G. COLLEGES THAT DID NOT SURVIVE, pp. 306-312.

Bindman, Aaron M. PRE-COLLEGE PREPARATION OF NEGRO COLLEGE STUDENTS, pp. 313-321. A study of Negro male undergraduates in a large midwestern State university indicated that Negro students were proportionately less adequately prepared for college-level work than their white counterparts even when they had attended integrated high schools.

Fichter, Joseph H. CAREER PREPARATION AND EXPECTATIONS OF NEGRO COLLEGE SENIORS, pp. 322-335. Focuses on part of the data of a National Opinion Research Center survey of career plans of graduating seniors in 50 predominantly Negro colleges in 1954.

Gurin, Patricia. SOCIAL CLASS CONSTRAINTS ON THE OCCUPATIONAL ASPIRATIONS OF STUDENTS ATTENDING SOME PREDOMINANTLY NEGRO COLLEGES, pp. 336-350. Social class effects are seen only with freshman students at the point of entering college. By the time students are seniors most of the class differences and effects of parental influence on students' occupational aspirations have disappeared.

Harris, Edward E. SOME COMPARISONS AMONG NEGRO-WHITE COLLEGE STUDENTS: SOCIAL AMBITION AND ESTIMATED SOCIAL MOBILITY, pp. 351-368. Assesses the distribution of social ambition among Negroes and whites, its relation to their estimated mobility, and some interrelations among its phenomena.

Abraham, Ansley A. and Simmons, Gertrude L. THE EDUCATIONAL OUTLOOK FOR NONWHITES IN FLORIDA, pp. 369-380. Elements contributing to a negative outlook are considered, and suggestions are provided for making the outlook more promising.

Huyck, Earl E. FACULTY IN PREDOMINANTLY WHITE AND PREDOMINANTLY NEGRO HIGHER INSTITUTIONS, pp. 381-392. A comparison of faculties and institutions concluding with proposals for strengthening Negro colleges and their faculties. Biblio.

Plaut, Richard L. PLANS FOR ASSISTING NEGRO STUDENTS TO ENTER AND TO REMAIN IN COLLEGE, pp. 393-399.

Love, Theresa R. NEEDS AND APPROACHES FOR DEVELOPING LINGUISTIC ABILITIES, pp. 400-408. Discusses problems of teaching English in Negro colleges and approaches for dealing with the problems through linguistics, descriptive grammar, oral activities, and theme writing.

Hurst, Charles G., Jr. and Jones, Wallace L. PSYCHOSOCIAL CONCOMITANTS OF SUB-STANDARD SPEECH, pp. 409-421. Describes a study conducted among Howard University students which suggests a profound relationship between speech behavior and personality and between speech proficiency and certain psychological characteristics considered essential for social, academic, and economic success. Biblio.

Froe, Otis D. MEETING THE NEEDS OF COLLEGE YOUTH: THE MORGAN STATE COLLEGE PROGRAM, pp. 422-429. Describes a program in which three separate curricula are offered to meet the needs of students with varying scholastic aptitudes.

Wiggins, Sam P. DILEMMAS IN DESEGREGATION IN HIGHER EDUCATION, pp. 430-438. Suggests problems in providing education for disadvantaged students which remain after desegregation is achieved.

Cleary, Robert E. THE ROLE OF GUBERNATORIAL LEADERSHIP IN DESEGREGATION IN PUBLIC HIGHER EDUCATION, pp. 439-444. Suggests that gubernatorial leadership is an important element in determining the speed and degree of desegregation in public schools.

Cohen, Arthur M. THE PROCESS OF DESEGREGATION: A CASE STUDY, pp. 445-451. Examines the integration of the student body and faculty at Miami-Dade Junior College as an illustration of the thesis that such integration requires that the school boards demonstrate clearly their intent to desegregate, that the intent be made known to all persons directly concerned with the affected schools, and that all school personnel be willing to work toward the established goal.

Allen, Leroy B. THE POSSIBILITIES OF INTEGRATION FOR PUBLIC COLLEGES FOUNDED FOR NEGROES, pp. 452-458.

Ware, Gilbert and Determan, Dean W. THE FEDERAL DOLLAR, THE NEGRO COLLEGE, AND THE NEGRO STUDENT, pp. 459-468. Suggests that very little Federal assistance goes to Negro colleges and that in effect the Federal Government is giving the Negro student a better chance of going to college while denying him an adequate college to attend. The authors believe that a more adequate amount of assistance can be provided.

Branson, Herman R. INTERINSTITUTIONAL PROGRAMS FOR PROMOTING EQUAL HIGHER EDUCATIONAL OPPORTUNITIES FOR NEGROES, pp. 469-476. Reports the findings of a survey conducted to determine the extent of participation in interinstitutional programs such as the Cornell-Hampton program.

Patterson, Frederick D. COOPERATION AMONG THE PREDOMINANTLY NEGRO COLLEGES AND UNIVERSITIES, pp. 477-484.

Miller, Carroll L. ISSUES AND PROBLEMS IN THE HIGHER EDU-
CATION OF NEGRO AMERICANS, pp. 485-493. Summarizes issues emerging from yearbook articles.

Meeth, L. Richard. THE TRANSITION OF THE PREDOMINANTLY
NEGRO COLLEGE, pp. 494-505. Describes both negative and positive results
of rapid transition for the Negro college and suggests a present need for restructuring change so that such colleges may lead their students to equal education.

Wright, Stephen J. PROBLEMS, DEVELOPMENTS AND ISSUES IN-
CIDENT TO EQUALITY OF OPPORTUNITY IN THE HIGHER EDUCA-
TION OF NEGROES: A CRITICAL SUMMARY OF THE 1966
YEARBOOK, pp. 506-513.   S. C. Pearson, Jr.

2854. --. THE AMERICAN SOUTH: 1950-1970. *J. of Pol. 1964 26(1): 3-240.*
Dunbar, Leslie W. THE CHANGING MIND OF THE SOUTH: THE
EXPOSED NERVE, pp. 3-21.

Nicholls, William H. THE SOUTH AS A DEVELOPING AREA, pp.
22-40.

Durisch, Lawrence L. SOUTHERN REGIONAL PLANNING AND
DEVELOPMENT, pp. 41-59.

Connery, Robert H. and Leach, Richard H. SOUTHERN METROPOLIS:
CHALLENGE TO GOVERNMENT, pp. 60-91.

Matthews, Donald K. and Prothro, James. SOUTHERN IMAGES OF
POLITICAL PARTIES: AN ANALYSIS OF WHITE AND NEGRO ATTI-
TUDES, pp. 92-111.

Clubok, Alfred, DeGrone, John, and Farris, Charles. THE MANIPU-
LATED NEGRO VOTE: PRECONDITIONS AND CONSEQUENCES, pp.
112-129.

Cook, Samuel DuBois. POLITICAL MOVEMENTS AND ORGANIZA-
TIONS, pp. 130-153.

Spicer, George W. THE FEDERAL JUDICIARY AND POLITICAL
CHANGE IN THE SOUTH, pp. 154-176.

Jewell, Malcolm E. STATE LEGISLATURES IN SOUTHERN POLI-
TICS, pp. 177-196.

Ransome, Coleman B. POLITICAL LEADERSHIP IN THE GOVER-
NOR'S OFFICE, pp. 197-220.

Weeks, D. Douglas. THE SOUTH IN NATIONAL POLITICS, pp. 221-
240.

A broad survey of the effects of economic and social developments upon
southern politics and judiciary system.   B. E. Swanson

Black Cultural Ideas & Movements

2855. Anderson, Jervis. PANTHERS: BLACK MEN IN EXTREMES. *Dissent
1970 17(2): 120-123.* Throughout most of American history, it was difficult and

dangerous enough to *be* black. Therefore, recent attempts to *act* black with some degree of pride and dignity have only heightened the perilousness of the situation. The current extreme example of this is the Black Panther party with its talk of war on whites. In reaction, white society in the form of the police, the F.B.I., and the Vice President have declared verbal and sometimes physical war on the Panthers. The Panthers should have expected no less, given their rhetoric and actions, and they know full well the price that they are paying. However, the Panthers do represent to some degree the frustrations and fears of young blacks. While at present they are accomplishing little more than martyrdom, they have some notion of achieving more. W. L. Hogeboom

2856. Anderson, Jervis. RACE, RAGE & ELDRIDGE CLEAVER. *Commentary 1968 46(6): 63-69. Soul On Ice* (New York: McGraw Hill, 1968) is an autobiography of Eldridge Cleaver's political, spiritual, and intellectual development in the decade after 1954. The book shows the alienation of a black nationalist from the United States. He has departed from the tradition of Ralph Ellison, James Baldwin, and Richard Wright in becoming a spokesman and partisan in political rebellion and revolution. The author considers Cleaver's attacks on Baldwin as unjust and concludes that, although Cleaver is a talented writer, his vision is narrow and racially determined. C. Grollman

2857. Arbeiter, Solomon. A WHITE, JEWISH LIBERAL DISCOURSES WITH THE YOUNG BLACK PEOPLE. *Social Studies 1971 62(2): 51-55.* Black racists are in error in their move toward separatism. Integration must come if the Nation is to remain strong and true to its democratic ideals. 5 notes. L. R. Raife

2858. Arnez, Nancy Levi and Anthony, Clara B. CONTEMPORARY NEGRO HUMOR AS SOCIAL SATIRE. *Phylon 1968 29(4): 339-346.* There have been three distinct stages of Negro humor: 1) "an oral tradition in which the group pokes fun at its customs, its idioms, its folkways" - totally in-group humor; 2) a public humor perpetuated by outsiders using "minority group, Negroes, as the brunt of half-truth caricatures"; and 3) today's self-conscious humor, which is image-creating. "Now the group permits a sharing of its humor with the outside group, while continuing to perpetuate and enrich its own private in-group humor." Using the humor of Dick Gregory, Moms Mabley, Flip Wilson, and Godfrey Cambridge, the authors illustrate the third stage. The study of current black humor can be very valuable in understanding black attitudes in America. 6 notes. R. D. Cohen

2859. Becker, William H. BLACK POWER IN CHRISTOLOGICAL PERSPECTIVE. *Religion in Life 1969 38(3): 404-414.* There are two models of manhood: the sufferer and the rebel. The Black Power movement takes the second as its model of behavior in reaction to the former which has been the traditional role of the black. The correct model for today's black is a combination of the two. The example of Christ is used to show the validity of this approach. 16 notes. D. Brockway

2860. Benosky, Alan L. MINORITY GROUPS AND THE TEACHING OF AMERICAN HISTORY. *Social Studies 1971 62(2): 60-63.* True historical scholarship cannot be sacrificed for the sake of yielding to demands about how black history should be interpreted by historians. 7 notes.   L. R. Raife

2861. Benz, Ernst. DER "SCHWARZE ISLAM" [Black Muslims]. *Zeitschrift für Religions- und Geistesgeschichte [West Germany] 1967 19(2): 97-113.* Describes the founding and doctrines of the Black Muslims, emphasizing the influence of Wallace D. Fard, Elijah Muhammed, and Malcolm X. There is an analysis of the revelation allegedly made to Fard that the black race once ruled the world, possessed a superior culture, and were tricked out of their hegemony by the whites who were culturally and physically inferior to the blacks and who will return to their status of inferiority. Malcolm X accentuated the trend toward separatism by stressing the possibility of gaining all the benefits of bourgeois America for the blacks. The author concludes that the Black Muslims who accent separatism are a danger to American society in case of disillusionment of the black middle class. Based on two books: C. Eric Lincoln's *The Black Muslims in America* (Boston: Beacon Press, 1961) and Essien Udom's *Black Nationalism* (Chicago, 1962).   S. J. Miller

2862. Berger, Morroe. THE BLACK MUSLIMS. *Horizon 1964 6(1): 49-65.* Spokesmen for the Black Muslims insist that the original religion of Negroes was Islam and that they had a distinctively African culture. The link connecting the Negroes and the Moslems in America was the slave trade, though it is not known how many Moslems came to America. Three ethnologists (Theodore Dwight, William Brown Hodgson, and James Hamilton Couper) before the Civil War uncovered the story of six individual Moslem slaves. Fundamentally the Black Muslim movement today is a reaction to the white stereotype of the Negro. The "pragmatic mixture of traditional Islam, Judaism, and Christianity is designed to encourage pride in blackness." Illus.   E. P. Stickney

2863. Bibb, Leon Douglas. A NOTE ON THE BLACK MUSLIMS: THEY PREACH BLACK TO BE THE IDEAL. *Negro Hist. Bull. 1965 28(6): 132-133.* A description of the basic religious teaching and social practices of the Black Muslims.   L. Gara

2864. Blake, J. Herman. BLACK NATIONALISM. *Ann. of the Am. Acad. of Pol. and Social Sci. 1969 382: 15-25.* "Black nationalism has been one of the most militant and strident protest movements in the Afro-American community since the early nineteenth century. In its earliest manifestations, political nationalism sought to separate black people from the United States; economic nationalism sought to break down racial barriers through developing economic strength in the black community; while cultural nationalism sought the same goal through the development of racial solidarity and black consciousness. The various strands were brought together into an integral form of nationalism by Marcus Garvey after World War I. The Nation of Islam continued the emphasis on integral nationalism under the leadership of Elijah Muhammad but added a significant religious component. Contemporary trends in black nationalism reflect the pro-

found influence of the late El-Hajj Malik El-Shabazz. Political nationalism has been expanded to include a new and unique emphasis upon land, as well as emphasis upon self-determination for black communities and accountability of black leaders. The growing strength of cultural nationalism is seen in the new manifestations of black consciousness. The nature of the current trends indicates that black people see themselves as part of the American society even though they feel very much separated from it. Future trends in black nationalism may be significantly affected by the most persistent racial barrier in America - the color line."
J

2865. Blassingame, John W. BLACK STUDIES: AN INTELLECTUAL CRISIS. *Am. Scholar 1969 38(4): 548-561.* A general survey of new "black studies" programs in American universities, an estimate of their "relevance" (including an attempt to precisely define relevance), an analysis of their worst forms created by cynical administrators, and an expression of alarm over the possibility of taking false and dangerous directions in the future. The author's solutions call for rigorous courses and programs, and for planning which is as deep and intensive as any other academic discipline and which is realistically tied to community needs. Any other choice will produce superficial, redundant courses and a mere pretense at community involvement.
T. R. Cripps

2866. Blassingame, John W. "SOUL" OR SCHOLARSHIP: AN EXAMINATION OF BLACK STUDIES SO FAR; WHAT STUDENTS LEARN ABOUT HISTORY. *Smithsonian 1970 1(1): 58-64.* A discussion of the efforts to create a Black Studies program at the University of Maryland. Includes some analysis of courses and their content as well as of the nature of "soul" courses - those designed for blacks only. Photos.
J. M. Hawes

2867. Bone, Robert. RALPH ELLISON AND THE USES OF IMAGINATION. *Tri-Q. 1966 (6): 39-54.* As a Negro writer, Ralph Waldo Ellison explores "the relationship of Negro folk culture to American culture as a whole, and the responsibility of the Negro artist to his ethnic group." For the black man, Negro folk culture is a monument to the national past. Ellison expresses his obligation to his ethnic group through the imagination rather than through politics. Thus he has steered a middle course between assimilation and Negro nationalism, both of which involve "a maiming of the self." While Ellison has aesthetic roots in American transcendentalism, he has borrowed from Negro folk culture the devices of masking and naming. Moreover, his background in jazz and blues has "left a permanent mark upon his style." Photo, note.
W. H. Agee

2868. Brimmer, Andrew F. THE BLACK REVOLUTION AND THE ECONOMIC FUTURE OF NEGROES IN THE UNITED STATES. *Am. Scholar 1969 38(4): 629-643.* Reviews Negro economic gains in the 1960's in most sectors of the economy, which the author rates considerably greater than white growth. Projections for the future seem about as sanguine, with a continuing burden on the system to provide jobs for what will be an increasingly younger labor force. "Sadly," however, the author finds a few "digressions" in the path of this fruitful change, the most noteworthy being a movement to establish separate black studies programs in a number of white universities. He finds this dangerous on the grounds that separate programs can never be equal, that separation will deny blacks the incentive and competition they need with whites, and that such curricula will encourage courses that are soft and distant from the real concerns of American society. Thus, if the projections are to be manifest, Negroes must acquire the techniques with which to deal with them.   T. R. Cripps

2869. Brooks, Thomas R. DRUMBEATS IN DETROIT. *Dissent 1970 17(1): 16-25.* Many unions are faced with the task of admitting more minority group members, but the United Auto Workers (UAW) in Detroit, the membership of which is nearly 40 percent Negro, faces a strong internal challenge, the Dodge Revolutionary Union Movement (DRUM). DRUM began a movement among militant black auto workers to gain more power in union decisionmaking. The movement spread to General Motors, Ford, and others. While it represents only a small minority of black auto workers, the movement has forced the leadership of the UAW and the auto industry to be more responsive to blacks. Concludes that the movement is an awakening of ethnic class-consciousness, and cannot reasonably be expected to be moderate.   W. L. Hogeboom

2870. Brower, Brock. OF NOTHING BUT FACTS. *Am. Scholar 1964 33(4): 613-618.* Comments on the tendency of imaginative prose fiction to rework the lowly magazine article into books that might commence a literature of fact, e.g., James Baldwin's *The Fire Next Time* (1963) or Theodore White's *The Making of the President 1960* (1961), "a work of political reportage that closely parallels the novel." The appetite for reality, whetted by facts, "now seeks to be satisfied with a prose that has that taste of actual existence in it."   E. P. Stickney

2871. Caldwell, Wallace E. A SURVEY OF ATTITUDES TOWARD BLACK MUSLIMS IN PRISON. *J. of Human Relations 1968 16(2): 220-238.* Reports the results of a survey of the opinions of prison officials and chaplains of Black Muslims. A random sample of 71 wardens and superintendents of penal institutions were asked if they experienced Black Muslim activities among their prison inmates and whether the sect should be accorded the same recognition as other religions. The Black Muslim movement presents difficult discipline problems for prison administrators, particularly in Federal institutions and prisons located in Northern and Western States with large Negro populations. In southern prisons the movement has not made much headway. Muslims affect a distinctive behavior and strive for separate status within prison communities - a status largely built around the principle of black racial supremacy. While many officials thought that Black Muslims could not safely be treated like followers of other religions, in some prisons they are recognized, although, as with other religious groups, proselytizing is prohibited, regularly scheduled meetings are supervised, and the ministry must be provided from the outside. 10 notes.   D. J. Abramoske

2872. Caldwell, Wallace F. BLACK MUSLIMS BEHIND BARS. *Res. Studies 1966 34(4): 185-204.* Examines conduct of members of the Black Muslim sect in Federal and State penitentiaries, their demands for religious rights and privileges, Federal and State legal responses to these demands, attitudes of prison wardens, and administrative and constitutional problems flowing from the detention of Black Muslims. Three legal views have been established in Federal and State courts: Black Islam is a religion; other considerations affect the right of Black Muslims to practice their faith in prison; Black Islam is not exclusively a religion. Although there is not always a positive correlation between their presence and violence, prison administrators tend to believe that, generally speaking, Muslim activities promote agitation which tends to lead to prison violence. Some wardens maintain that prison converts cause overt trouble; convicts who were Muslims before imprisonment cause covert trouble. Black Muslims tend to cause security problems particularly in Federal institutions and in prisons located in Northern and Western States with large, urban Negro populations. The crux of the problem is to give Black Muslim prisoners constitutional recognition and protection of their religious rights while maintaining adequate prison security and discipline. Based on Federal and State court decisions, surveys of Federal and State prison wardens, secondary sources; 47 notes.   D. R. Picht

2873. Cassidy, Rita M. BLACK HISTORY: SOME BASIC READINGS. *Hist. Teacher 1969 2(4): 36-39.* Teachers have a responsibility "to make sure that the traditions and interpretations and values they pass on to their students reflect the total American past rather than a whitened summary....The teacher who would do a good job of incorporating the black experience into the total American experience must be prepared to read widely and deeply.." Biblio.
D. J. Engler

2874. Chalasinski, Jozef. MURZYNSKA AMERYKA, MURZYNSKA IN-TELIGENCJA I PROBLEM AMERYKANSKIEJ SWIADOMOSCI NARODOWEJ [American Negroes, their intelligentsia and the problem of American nationality].*Przegląd Socjologiczny [Poland] 1960 14(2): 30-63.* The emerging Negro intelligentsia is one of the most interesting developments to attract the attention of foreign observers. Since World War II the ever increasing number of Negroes with higher education has coincided with their ideological transformation. The new intelligentsia combines the fight against discrimination with a revolt against leadership in the Negro community by the black profession-als and businessmen. Martin Luther King, Jr. is perhaps the best example of this new type of Negro leader. Rediscovery of Africa has played a very important role in the present-day American Negro movement. Conversely, the African Negro intelligentsia looks to Negro America as a source of inspiration, exemplified by Leopold S. Senghor's poem "To New York." American cultural pluralism is considered to be a good vehicle for the social aspirations of Negroes and other minorities, as well as for their recognition and prestige. 45 notes.
T. N. Cieplak

2875. Clark, Kenneth B. THE PRESENT DILEMMA OF THE NEGRO. *J. of Negro Hist. 1968 53(1): 1-11.* Negro Americans have accepted the moral and ethical aspirations of America but have been denied the opportunity to enjoy them. The doctrine of segregation and discrimination led Negroes to accept, as well, an inferior status in society. In answer to continued frustration at every level the cry "Black Power" arose as a defiant response. Though "Black Power" is self-defeating and a retreat from integration it is an understandable answer to continued white resistance and an actual worsening of conditions in the Negro ghettos. The key to the future and to America's survival is the response of Negro intellectuals who, by identifying the real enemies of progress as "human irrationality, ignorance, superstition, rigidity, and arbitrary cruelty" may yet contribute to the survival of America.   L. Gara

2876. Comer, James P. INDIVIDUAL DEVELOPMENT AND BLACK REBELLION: SOME PARALLELS. *Midway 1968 9(1): 33-48.* No applicable historical model exists for understanding the nature of the black movement in the United States. The African colonial experience, often used for this purpose, is different in fundamental ways. A better model is that of individual development, for while individual development and the development of an Afro-American community are not identical phenomena, there are striking parallels. For the emergence of the black community, a response which compensates for previous unjust denial and enables that community to establish an equal peer relationship is the only move that will adequately reduce the level of racial conflict in the Nation.   R. Howell

2877. Epstein, Joseph. DOWN THE LINE. *Commentary 1965 40(4): 101-105.* Discusses the significance of *Who Speaks for the Negro?* (New York: Random, 1965) by Robert Penn Warren, the author of *Segregation: The Inner Conflict of the South* (New York: Random, 1956). "As in *Segregation,* Warren continues to be interested in philosophies of social change, but now he puts his questions exclusively to Negroes: to civil-rights leaders and rank-and-filers, to writers and artists, civil servants and businessmen, college presidents and students - to a variety of people who, as the saying goes, have been down the line. And...for the first time Negroes are now in a position to exert a major influence on decisions affecting their future in this country." Among the Negro leaders whose interviews with Warren were tape recorded are Roy Wilkins, Whitney Young, James Forman, James Farmer, and Martin Luther King, Jr. "Thus far the civil-rights movement...has not in any serious or definite way addressed itself to the question of what is to be done once discrimination will no longer be the major issue....Up to now the biggest single victory the Negro has won, as Warren's book makes amply clear, is the moral strength to speak for himself."   D. D. Cameron

2878. Fairlie, Henry. MARTIN LUTHER KING. *Encounter [Great Britain] 1968 30(177): 3-6.* A brief tribute to Martin Luther King, Jr., a man who embodied the qualities of the South, rejected the reactionism of the Black Power movement, and was, in the most real sense, a free man.   D. H. Murdoch

2879. Felt, Jeremy P. BLACK HISTORY: THE QUESTION OF "OBJECTIVITY." *Social Studies 1972 63(2): 51-54.* There is a national necessity for black history. Deterrents to instruction in black history hinge upon deep-rooted pedagogical debate and upon revelations which would not support American ideals of fair play. 4 notes.   L. R. Raife

2880. Fuller, Hoyt W. CONTEMPORARY NEGRO FICTION. *Southwest R. 1965 50(4): 321-334.* Discusses the branding of novels by Negro writers as protest literature. Not only the better known authors such as Ralph Ellison, Richard Wright, and James Baldwin, but also the lesser known such as Owen Dodson, William Demby, and Chester Himes are considered. The "authors hear the siren call of the critics urging them to enter 'the mainstream of American literature,' but they remain unswayed."   D. F. Henderson

2881. Glazer, Joseph. WER SPRICHT FÜR DEN AMERIKANISCHEN NE-GER? [Who speaks for the American Negro?]. *Politische Studien [West Germany] 1968 19(181): 574-576.* A description of six major Negro organizations and their aims for the information of a German reading audience. Many smaller groups also exist with aims more vague than the better known organizations. The young Negroes are impatient with the slow progress being made and they stress the need for "black power."   R. V. Pierard

2882. Goldman, Martin S. BLACK ARRIVAL IN AMERICAN HISTORY: A HISTORIOGRAPHICAL LOOK AT THE SIXTIES. *Social Studies 1971 62(5): 209-219.* Cites a preponderance of evidence of "Black Arrival" in American history by reference to significant manuscripts written by Negroes about Negroes, or by others about Negroes. Gives reasons for the neglect of Negroes' participation in American life: southern pressures on publishers, and racist myths which have permeated American scholarship, including the historical profession. Cites probable danger in using Black Studies for purposes other than academic inquiry. 48 notes.   L. R. Raife

2883. Gorlier, Claudio. MOTIVAZIONI RELIGIOSE DELLA RIVOLTA NE-GRA NEGLI STATI UNITI [Religious roots of the Negro revolution in the United States]. *R. Storica Italiana 1968 80(3): 516-537.* Churches helped maintain segregation and white power structure by encouraging Negroes to seek heavenly rewards. At the same time, they created strong bonds necessary to challenge white oppression. Emigration from the South and the rise of a Negro bourgeoisie caused a chasm between established churches and independent groups. Marcus Garvey, Wallace D. Fard, Elijah Muhammad, and Malcolm X symbolize the need for distinct Negro traditions viable for social and political change. Martin Luther King's Southern Christian Leadership Conference, tied to established churches, successfully challenged southern rural segregation but failed in urban ghettos. The Student Non-Violent Coordinating Committee renounced passivity, facing the problem of institutionalized violence. Militancy encouraged whites, especially in the South, to woo conservative Negro religious leaders. 29 notes.   C. M. Lovett

2884. Graham, Hugh Davis. THE STORM OVER BLACK POWER. *Virginia Q. R. 1967 43(4): 545-565.* Analyzes the crisis in the civil rights movement resulting from the breakup of liberal support and the rise of Black Power. After more than 12 years a reappraisal has occurred on the part of white liberals questioning whether real integration is either possible (Is the American melting-pot a myth?) or desirable (Do subcommunities have a right to exist?). At the same time many Negro intellectuals have seen white racism in the liberal Moynihan Report which found the fundamental cause of the Negro's situation in his family structure. Black Power envisages a racially based quest for political and economic power and has international implications. It is attacked by some Negro critics as suicidal, appealing to only a small Negro minority and as destructive of the civil rights coalition. White liberals now may need to accept "negritude," recognize a distinction between civil rights and the Negro movement, and support major social legislation such as a "Freedom Budget" and a guaranteed minimum income.   O. H. Zabel

2885. Grisevich, George W. RETHINKING VALUES IN THE NEW SOCIAL STUDIES. *Hist. Teacher 1969 2(4): 31-35.* "The growing emphasis upon and concern with Afro-American History, if correctly directed, can be usefully employed as a vehicle in our quest for reevaluation." 2 photos, 7 notes.
                                                                D. J. Engler

2886. Gross, Theodore L. OUR MUTUAL ESTATE: THE LITERATURE OF THE AMERICAN NEGRO. *Antioch R. 1968 28(3): 293-303.* The author points out that the field of black culture in America is "parochial and chauvinistic and disorganized." Giving the critiques of Richard Wright as an example, he points out the dangers of parochialism, especially now that Negro studies are moving into the forefront. He urges rejection of the argument that only blacks can evaluate black literature.   F. Harrold

2887. Halpern, Ben. THE ETHNIC REVOLT. *Midstream 1971 17(1): 3-16.* Discusses the impact of dissent and civil disobedience on Negroes and Jews, and treats the minority experience in America. Draws on historical experience and environmental causes to suggest reasons for the growing ethnic and radical movements in America. Compares radical American Negroes to radicals among the Eastern European Jewish and Israeli communities. The success of the Jewish experience in American society and the Jews' ability to maintain their identity makes the possibility of a widespread Jewish radical base unlikely. The black revolutionary experience grew out of the early civil rights and integration leadership of persons such as the late Martin Luther King, Jr. The quest for black identity and manliness are prerequisites for success such as Jewish and other ethnic immigrants experienced earlier in the 20th century. Discusses the impact of the processes and ideology of the Negro revolt on the black and Jewish communities in America. From the author's *Jews and Blacks* (New York: Herder and Herder, 1971).   G. E. Frakes

2888. Hare, Nathan. WHAT SHOULD BE THE ROLE OF AFRO-AMERICAN EDUCATION IN THE UNDERGRADUATE CURRICULUM? *Liberal Educ. 1969 55(1): 42-50.* Racism must be eliminated from America's schools. Education must prepare black youths for power in the community and the Nation. Black studies must be taught from a black perspective and black education must be black-community centered.   C. G. Lauritsen

2889. Herman, Reg. POWER AND PREJUDICE: A SURVEY AND A HYPOTHESIS. *J. of Human Relations 1969 17(1): 1-11.* Reviews several scholarly theories developed on the dynamics of prejudice and discusses their relevance to the current Separatist movement in French Canada and the Black Power movement in the United States. "The sanction of ethnic prejudice originates in any community in the upper class, and the individual response to prejudice takes two essentially different forms - authoritarianism and conformity....The liberal has the existentialist choice: to choose to do nothing or to choose absolute commitment to this place and this time." If he chooses engagement "he must come down hard on the side of the outgroups, riots included. Nothing less is acceptable, because nothing less will help." 18 notes.   D. J. Abramoske

2890. Himmelfarb, Milton. NEGROES, JEWS, AND MUZHIKS. *Commentary 1966 42(4): 83-86.* Examines the relationship between Jews and muzhiks (peasants) in pre-World War II Eastern Europe, finding some parallels with the relationship between Jews and Negroes in the United States. "The Jews of the Pale of Settlement thought themselves superior to the muzhiks, feared them, felt guilty about them, pitied them, envied them, and, while distrusting them, wanted to see their lot bettered." The muzhik to the Jew was the essence of the Gentile: physically strong, uncultured, illogical, dirty, and tending to violence. There are elements of these ideas in the relation of Jews to Negroes in modern America, but here the Negroes are only a part of the larger group of uncultured plebeians who often tend to think with their emotions and to be led to violence, like the muzhiks who were led to pogroms in the 19th century. The tendency toward populist emotionalism, which almost certainly leads to anti-Semitism, has been shown among American Negroes by such leaders as Malcolm X and some proponents of "black power" ideology. Black Power, however, represents not only the ideology of populist violence, but also the ideal of auto-emancipation, with which American Jews are certainly familiar and in sympathy.   A. K. Main

2891. Hoover, Dwight W. THE BLACK PAST AS A REFLECTION OF THE AMERICAN PRESENT. *Michigan Academician 1970 2(3): 49-62.* There are two kinds of historiography about African Americans. One is black history, still in the process of being created, which honors radical critics of American society and creates myths for the purpose of achieving a sense of black cohesiveness and pride. Negro history, on the other hand, has its origins in the beginning of the 20th century and is based on the idea that historical traditions are important in building nationalism and group pride. Discusses specific examples. 32 notes.
                              E. M. Gersman

2892. Isaacs, Harold R. GROUP IDENTITY AND POLITICAL CHANGE. *Survey 1968 (69): 76-98.* Discusses the search for man's basic group identity, i.e., man's ethnic being, family and group name, color and physical characteristics, culture-past, etc. Any group's identity is shaped by all these; political considerations are the most decisive. Discusses the untouchables of India trying to find their identity by becoming "Indians," the problems of the American Jew settling in Israel, the Chinese trying to become Malaysians (the English-educated are more successful), the postcolonial Filipinos looking back into the past for something uniquely Filipino, post-World War II Japan seeking something in the ruins of the Meiji State, and the Black Nationalists in the United States. The importance of the latter may lie in that they have succeeded in sparking a profound revolution in the way Negro Americans see themselves as blacks.

R. S. Valliant

2893. Jackson, Maurice. TOWARD A SOCIOLOGY OF BLACK STUDIES. *J. of Black Studies 1970 1(2): 131-140.* Discusses possible approaches to teaching black studies in colleges and universities. Defines black studies as being concerned with the role of blacks in man's development in society. Black studies programs should give insights into the historical and contemporary roles of black people, but at the same time these programs should not treat blacks as ethnic minorities or focus entirely on race relations. Black studies assumes that the United States is a black man's country and that the black man's contributions to the country should be studied and acknowledged. Black studies also means that blacks should be studied as subjects with goals, hopes, aspirations, etc., rather than as objects, i.e., victims of slavery, segregation, or whatever. While currently there is a dispute over whites teaching black studies, the real concern should be to solidify the black studies programs and to encourage more blacks to participate. Biblio.

K. Butcher

2894. Johnson, Gerald W. A QUESTION OF MEASUREMENTS. *Virginia Q. R. 1970 46(2): 227-239.* Contrasts the philosophy of the typical American in 1925 and in 1969. The author insists that "in 1925 the typical American was superbly convinced that his political ideas were manifestly superior to all other political ideas whatsoever and were bound eventually to prevail, to the greatly increased happiness of all mankind." A decade of depression, a great war, minor wars, and "a series of revolts by dissident elements" have battered the typical American. Many current problems are related to the failure of politics (philosophy) to keep up with technology. Desperately needed are reinterpretations of the concepts of individualism and free enterprise and liberty under law in a technological society. The author insists that "Vietnam, Red Russia, Black Power, the cities, and the students all sink to the level of minor troubles by comparison with the terrible danger that the ordinary American may come to believe that control of the republic itself has passed into other hands, and he no longer has a voice in it." This loss of the republic, "then, is the measure of the philosophical distance from Coolidge to Nixon." However, the author suggests that "faith in our own and our country's destiny" may reassert itself.

O. H. Zabel

2895. Jones, Major J. BLACK AWARENESS: THEOLOGICAL IMPLICATIONS OF THE CONCEPT. *Religion in Life 1969 38(3): 389-403.* The concept of black awareness has expanded. This raises many questions as to what it means for both white and black communities. Self-identity, self-acceptance, black liberation, and black messiahs are examined critically. 13 notes.

D. Brockway

2896. Jovanovich, William. THE AMERICAN TEXTBOOK: AN UNSCIENTIFIC PHENOMENON - QUALITY WITHOUT CONTROL. *Am. Scholar 1969 38(2): 227-239.* Traces the shift in American textbook publishing from the turn of the century to the present, during which time the industry moved from a laissez-faire position to one more involved with Federal funds, mass education of a specialized nature, technological advances, and changing priorities of the growing American educational system. The publishing industry formerly produced a basic list of titles, to be sold to "systems," for high volume profits. The schools had no control over the product. Since Russian technological achievements in the 1950's, the American education system has responded with new goals of excellence and sophisticated specialized technical training. The result has been a change in textbook economics. Another important factor stimulating change has been increasing stress on Negro studies. Also, the tradition of local control over schools has been under assault by Federal budgeting procedures providing direct aid to public schools. At the same time, television and other technology continue to affect teaching methods.   T. R. Cripps

2897. Kaplan, H. M. THE BLACK MUSLIMS AND THE NEGRO AMERICAN'S QUEST FOR COMMUNION. A CASE STUDY IN THE GENESIS OF NEGRO PROTEST MOVEMENTS. *British J. of Sociol. 1969 20(2): 164-176.* A historical analysis of the Black Muslim movement, its origins, character, and the nature of its appeal, applying the concepts of German sociologist Schmalenbach. The author concludes that protest movements like that of the Black Muslims will arise as long as their social organizational courses exist, but all movements will be "confronted with the internal contradiction between a communion foundation and the ultimate triumph of that foundation's volatility." 37 notes.   D. H. Murdoch

2898. Kirman, Joseph M. THE CHALLENGE OF THE BLACK MUSLIMS. *Social Educ. 1963 27(7): 365-368.* Reviews the history of the Black Muslims in America and analyzes their appeal to underprivileged Negroes, particularly adolescents. The author describes his own classroom response to the Muslims' challenge.   M. Small

2899. Kirschenmann, Frederick. THE DANGER AND NECESSITY OF BLACK SEPARATISM. *Lutheran Q. 1969 21(4): 352-357.* Discusses the rationale for Negroes to have the freedom to discover their own identity, to test their link as individuals with the values inherent in Afro-American culture and history. The dangers of separation "lead to fanaticism and violence, to inhibit communication, to harbor a narrow, group narcissism, to breed a dangerous idolatry, and to prevent identity development and self-actualization." Lists seven ways for the white community to respond to separatism. "If we want black separatism to be the positive movement which will eventually lead to the establishment of a healthy, integrated society, then whites had best discover [that] the problem of the Negro is really the white man's problem."   D. H. Swift

2900. Ladner, Joyce. THE NEW NEGRO IDEOLOGY...WHAT "BLACK POWER" MEANS TO NEGROES IN MISSISSIPPI. *Transaction 1967 5(1): 7-15.* A discussion of the various directions that Black Power has taken in recent years in Mississippi. The author interviewed 30 Black Power advocates and divided them into local and cosmopolitan groups depending on their backgrounds, goals, and attitudes. Each group has its own heroes, each has its own political goals, and each has its own sources of strength. Each group defines Black Power according to its own needs and goals. Frustration with the existing situation drew members to both concepts of Black Power. The long-range aims of both are the same. The locals are more prudent while the cosmopolitans are focusing more attention on black self-consciousness. The future success of the movements will depend upon how many organizers they can put into the field and how they use their resources. Based on interviews; illus.   A. Erlebacher

2901. Laue, James H. A CONTEMPORARY REVITALIZATION MOVE-MENT IN AMERICAN RACE RELATIONS: THE BLACK MUSLIMS. *Social Forces 1964 42(3): 315-323.* An attempt to develop a new culture, black nationalism has met with failure in the past. Membership estimates vary between 5,000 and 100,000. Members are mostly male. The movement is geared to an ideology that states: "The white man has robbed you of your name, your language, your culture, and your religion." Appeals strongly to the disillusioned Negro in America.   A. Freedman

2902. Lindberg, John. DISCOVERING BLACK LITERATURE. *North Am. R. 1969 6(3): 51-56.* The author describes how he approached preparation for, and the teaching of, a black literature course. He began by examining his and others' attitudes about such courses and decided that skin color as a criterion for including authors would be racist. However, he further decided that cultural identity is an important enough factor to validate the separation of black from other literature. He then began to structure his material, not by genre, but by dealing with sources, backgrounds, schools, and influences. He first read material on historical and cultural backgrounds. The article includes many authors and titles helpful to the study and provides locations of three bookstores in America where black materials may be found. The author found five main themes in the black literature he read. First is source, from African heritage until emancipation. Next is struggle, which deals with the shifting attitudes of blacks toward whites. Autobiography is third, and includes the realization of a minority group as they live within a repressive society. The fourth theme is selfhood, primarily represented by contemporaries sympathetic to black nationalism. Fantasy is the final theme, in which day-dream, hero-worship, wish fulfillment, and free association of ideas occur. The author felt that his course was successful. He saw students come to a fuller understanding of literature, discovering that an intellectual tradition as well as a moral commitment is necessary. The course was pure discovery for himself, as well.   S. L. McNeel

2903. Mackey, James. A RATIONALE FOR BLACK STUDIES. *Social Studies 1970 61(7): 323-325.* Proposes an urgent need for a rationale on which to base the Black Studies Program. Black Studies, an explosive issue, is beset with confusion and untenable assumptions. Asks who should teach and who should receive instruction in such a course. Proposes salient points to consider in determining structure, quality, and objective methods of procedure. Student planning is needed. Blacks should not be the only students allowed to attend such courses. 5 notes.   L. R. Raife

2904. Maldonado-Denis, Manuel. THE PUERTO RICANS: PROTEST OR SUBMISSION? *Ann. of the Am. Acad. of Pol. and Social Sci. 1969 382: 26-31.* "The situation of Puerto Ricans in the United States cannot be seen as abstracted from that of those living in Puerto Rico. Puerto Rico has been a colony of the United States since 1898, and the most pervasive characteristic of its population - both in the Island and in the Mainland - is its colonialist mentality or world view: hence, the attitude of submission and acquiescence characteristic of the Puerto Ricans. The only forces in Puerto Rico that represent Puerto Rican protest against the perpetuation of colonialism in Puerto Rico are the proindependence groups. In this respect, their goal is similar to that of the Black Power advocates in the United States, because both groups are faced with a similar situation. Only when Puerto Ricans have achieved decolonization, both psychologically and politically, will they be able to come of age as a true protest movement. Otherwise they run the risk of a total destruction of Puerto Rican nationality, and cultural assimilation by the United States." J

2905. Materassi, Mario. MITO E REALTA DEL NEGRO AMERICANO [Myth and reality regarding the American Negro]. *Il Ponte [Italy] 1966 22(7): 951-961.* Discusses some of the historic myths that have developed over the centuries in the United States regarding the Negro and delineates some of the trends in the civil rights movement during the past decade; e.g., the role of the Black Muslims and black nationalism. C. F. Delzell

2906. McCollum, M. G., Jr. ROBERT EARL TIDWELL AND PUBLIC EDUCATION IN ALABAMA. *Paedagogica Historica [Belgium] 1968 8(1): 81-107.* A description and evaluation of the educational career of Robert Earl Tidwell and his role in the introduction of educational reforms into the institutions of the State of Alabama. Tidwell's professional positions ranged from that of high school principal to director of the University of Alabama's Extension Division. For four years (1913-17) he was engaged as superintendent of a unique system of education, subsidized by the Tennessee Coal, Iron and Railroad Company, established to provide a quality education for the children of the company's employees. He later played a key role in improving teacher certification in Alabama and in developing educational radio and television within that State. Upon retiring in 1954, he continued his interest in education as assistant to the president of all-black Stillman College and was instrumental in the school's meeting the membership standards of the Southern Association of Secondary Schools and Colleges. Based on printed sources and 3 personal interviews; 34 notes. E. R. Beauchamp

2907. McNall, Scott Grant. THE SECT MOVEMENT. *Pacific Sociol. R. 1963 6(2): 60-64.* Black Muslims are a movement, a racist sect, a cult of black hatred, and a social movement. Membership is characteristic of young, lower-class black males who are mostly former Christians. In attempting to develop a typology, the author questions whether or not the movement is a religion, a sect, or a cult. There is some consensus that the Black Muslims attempt to be a separate "subculture." Black Muslims are compared to the Freedom Center (an American rightist organization); both fit into the sect movement category. 20 notes.

A. S. Freedman

2908. Menard, Orville D. AMERICA'S EMERGING NATION. *Midwest Q.
1971 12(2): 137-144.* American race relations have entered a new era, the era of equal status for white and black communities. A new racial relationship is emerging, based on participation and cooperation between equals, not on white paternalism, condescension, and integration. The nationalistic recognition of belonging to a nation of brothers, of sharing a common heritage of ethnic identity, and the demand for the right to determine one's own life, are reflected in the slogan, "Black is Beautiful", "Afro" haircuts, and opposition to integration in favor of self-determination. Calls attention to the semicolonial status of Negroes and argues for some form of self-determination and self-rule for this emerging nation within a nation.   G. H. G. Jones

2909. Monteil, Vincent. LA RELIGION DES BLACK MUSLIMS [The religion of the Black Muslims]. *Esprit [France] 1964 32(10): 601-629.* Analyzes the religious aspect of the Black Muslim movement. Islamic features of the movement are identification of Wallace Fard with Allah, Mr. Elijah Muhammad (born Robert Poole) with the Great Prophet Mohammed, alimentary laws paralleling the fast of Ramadan, profession of faith, high standards of moral conduct, and generous money donations to the movement. The interest in the Arabic origins of Islam continues in the main body of the movement, but an emphasis on the African roots of Negro culture marks the branch established by Malcolm X. Uses as sources the works of Beynon (1938), C. Eric Lincoln (1956) who gave the name to the movement, Louis Lomax (1962), and James Baldwin (1963) among others.

Mother M. H. Quinlan

2910. Moriarty, Thomas F. THE "TRUTH TELLER" AND IRISH AMERICANA OF THE 1820'S. *Records of the Am. Catholic Hist. Soc. 1964 75(1): 39-52.* The *Truth Teller* was the most important newspaper of Irish Americans in the 1820's and as such is a valuable source of information about the Irish of the pre-famine years, being widely read by the literate among them. It played a role in shaping the American Irish character. "The similarities of the minority mentality of the American Irish of the 1820's to the minority mentality of the American Negro of the 1960's are striking and obvious. Thus an understanding and appreciation of Irish Americana in the 1820's cannot but increase our understanding and appreciation of Negro Americana in the 1960's." 71 notes.

E. P. Stickney

2911. Moss, James A. THE NEGRO CHURCH AND BLACK POWER. *J. of Human Relations 1969 17(1): 119-128.* Discusses the concept of Black Power and the current plight of the Negro in America. Perhaps the most insightful statement on Black Power was made in 1966 by a group of Negro churchmen. These leaders cautioned that the principle threat to our Nation "comes neither from riots erupting in our big cities, nor from the disagreements among the leaders of the civil rights movement, nor even from the mere raising of the cry of 'black power.'"

The basic causes of these eruptions stem from the "silent and covert violence which white middle class America inflicts upon the victims of the inner city." Based on the *Congressional Record,* newspapers, and magazines; 21 notes.

D. J. Abramoske

2912. Muhammad, Elijah. THE DEMANDS AND BELIEFS OF THE BLACK MUSLIMS IN AMERICA. *Islamic R. [Great Britain] 1964 52(10): 25-27.* Exposition of what the Black Muslims of America believe and want, along with a statement of their distinctive characteristics.   P. D. Thomas

2913. Neuwirth, G. A WEBERIAN OUTLINE OF A THEORY OF A COMMUNITY: ITS APPLICATION TO THE "DARK GHETTO." *British J. of Sociol. 1969 20(2): 148-163.* Reviews the Weberian approach to a theory of community and its application to "the current predicament of the economically and socially deprived Negro American (the residents of the Dark Ghetto)." Ethnic labels hide the basic struggle for economic, political, and social advantages in American society, and serve also to conceal status differences. An analysis of ghetto communities and the Black Power movement permits a fruitful application of the Weberian framework. 32 notes.   D. H. Murdoch

2914. Newman, R. THE AMERICAN RACIAL CRISIS. *Contemporary R. [Great Britain] 1968 213(1232): 121-124.* Asserting that Black Power is a bridge between the old Civil Rights movement and the new Black nationalism, the author examines the characteristics of Negro militancy. Black violence is the product of poverty and humiliation, and the assassination of men committed to help the Negro betrays "the fear and anxiety of the society, the ideational and bureaucratic paralysis of an officialdom at least a generation behind the country's new radicalism, and the recalcitrant unwillingness of a prosperous majority to alter its way of life."   D. H. Murdoch

2915. O'Brien, David J. BLACK HISTORY AND COLOR BLIND MEN. *Catholic World 1968 208(1243): 29-32.* Arguing that history is "a tool for the preservation of the present rather than a lever for prying open the door to the future," the author sees a special role for black history. Just as white America maintains itself on the basis of a "mythology essentially historical in character," so black history must give black Americans a "mythology for its unity and its desire for freedom." If black people decide that they want to be free and to be one people, they can learn from history that there are limits to the possibilities before men but that within these limits men can make their own future. To do so they must commit themselves to the future and not to the past, they must free black history from the confines of racial history of those men who happen to be black. By so doing, black history based on the commitment to freedom and equality may end by freeing all races.   Sr. M. Campion Kuhn

2916. Obiechina, Emmanuel. THREE NEW NOVELS BY NEGRO AMERICANS. *African Forum 1966 1(3): 107-111.* Reviews three new books: William Demby's *The Catacombs* (New York: Pantheon Books, 1965), William Melvin

Kelley's *A Drop of Patience* (New York: Doubleday, 1965), and Henry Van Dyke's *Ladies of the Rachmaninoff Eyes* (New York: Farrar, Straus, and Giroux, 1965). These writers, plus many others of whom James Baldwin is the most prominent, form a new generation of Negro writers. They have rejected the standard protest novel and emphasize the hidden emotional and psychological motives behind their characters. The author compares the basic themes and actions of these three books and shows how they are representative of this new generation of Negro writers. M. J. McBaine

2917. Olorunsola, Victor A. INTERACTION BETWEEN AFRICANS AND BLACK AMERICANS. *Pan-African J. 1969 2(1): 64-68.* The long history of black-American interest in Africa has been poorly rewarding. Several factors are responsible: on the black-American side, the small number of people seriously involved, the paternalistic attitude of educated black Americans, and the attitude of the communications media toward Africa; on the other side, most Africans are uninformed about black America because few Africans visited America before World War II, and, when in the 1950's a new generation of Africans visited America, many displayed paternalism to black Americans. Now, although the black Power idea makes some Africans uneasy, it has heightened interest in African culture. Africans and black Americans must have constant, efficient communication to facilitate their selective acculturation and cooperation. E. E. Beauregard

2918. Paetel, Karl O. DER "NEUE NEGER" IN DEN VEREINIGTEN STAATEN [The "new Negro" in the United States]. *Dokumente [West Germany] 1963 19(4): 269-282.* The significance of John F. Kennedy's civil rights legislation is examined against the historical background of the Negro question in America. The "new Negro," characterized as young, of lower-class origin, and insisting on immediate and full emancipation, is contrasted with the older, more intellectual, and upper middle-class type which makes up the National Association for the Advancement of Colored People. Ever increasing numbers of the "new Negro" are filling the ranks of the "Gandhist" movement of Martin Luther King and CORE (Congress of Racial Equality) or the more uncompromising "Apartheid" movement of the Black Muslims in order to make the Negroes' cause, as expressed by James Baldwin, the acid test of the American nation. G. P. Bassler

2919. Paetel, Karl O. USA - NEUE LINKE UND BLACK POWER [USA - The new Left and Black Power]. *Aussenpolitik [West Germany] 1969 20(11): 693-699.* The unrest of youth, particularly students, is international, but in each instance specific national characteristics also must be considered. In the United States the student movements began with opposition to the Vietnam War and concern over the problem of ethnic minorities, primarily the black minority. Today, among such groups as the Students for Democratic Society, the Progressive Labor Party, and the Youth International Party, what began as rebellion on the campuses has developed into an effort to achieve outright revolution. The radicals no longer seek change within the system but aspire to destroy the system. The same has been true of the black movements. Earlier they sought equality for the Negro in white society. The Black Panthers and the Black Muslims want separateness, not equality; hence, they want revolution rather than change. In the past the white radicals and the black radicals have cooperated at times. Their mutual dedication to revolution has brought them together on method; but the question now is whether they will also find a theoretical common ground. E. F. Ziemke

2920. Peavy, Charles D. THE BLACK ART OF PROPAGANDA: THE CULTURAL ARM OF THE BLACK POWER MOVEMENT. *Rocky Mountain Social Sci. J. 1970 7(1): 9-16.* Discusses the activities of black artists and writers as a function of the ideology and goals of the Black Power movement. Ron Karenga and LeRoi Jones are quoted to define black art and the revolutionary role of the black artist. 14 notes. R. F. Allen

2921. Pickens, William G. TEACHING NEGRO CULTURE IN HIGH SCHOOLS - IS IT WORTHWHILE? *J. of Negro Educ. 1965 34(2): 106-113.* "Cultural training" is important for social and educational adjustment, and curriculum changes should be introduced in the secondary school in order that all Americans might be more cognizant of the history of Negroes in America and Africa. S. C. Pearson, Jr.

2922. Record, Wilson. AMERICAN RACIAL IDEOLOGIES AND ORGANIZATIONS IN TRANSITION. *Phylon 1965 26(4): 315-329.* Deals primarily with the National Association for the Advancement of Colored People. The author believes that the American Negro is not attracted by Communist ideology or Negro separatism (e.g., Black Muslims) but is interested in the attainment of a better life in the existing society through removal of barriers of segregation and discrimination. Developments in the post-World War II period have produced new Negro organizations such as the Southern Christian Leadership Conference, the Congress of Racial Equality, and the Student Non-Violent Coordinating Committee. No insurmountable obstacle is seen to cooperation between these groups and the NAACP, but the latter organization must carefully reassess the present situation and propose programs for the future if it is to retain its position among Negro organizations. S. C. Pearson, Jr.

2923. Redding, Saunders. THE BLACK YOUTH MOVEMENT. *Am. Scholar 1969 38(4): 584-587.* A brief survey of "the black youth movement" from its earliest southern days of sit-ins in Greensboro, idealizing Martin Luther King, Jr., to the day when Stokely Carmichael replaced James Forman as head of the Student Non-Violent Coordinating Committee in 1965. Then the movement became black and racially exclusive, a course which the author deplores as "self-defeating extremism." It emerged out of the feelings of inadequacy created by a neglectful white racist educational system; but the author feels that, as a movement toward black studies, it could prove to perpetuate the conditions that created it. People like Rap Brown, Leroi Jones, and other leaders of the quest for "ethnic integrity," hire white lawyers, produce their plays for white audiences, write for white publishers, in effect accept the fact of the very Western culture they vigorously condemn. They are living proof that the goal of all racial movements ought to be "a completely rewarding participation in American life."

T. R. Cripps

2924. Reid, Inez Smith. AN ANALYSIS OF BLACK STUDIES PROGRAMS. *Pan-African J. 1969 2(3): 284-298.* Black Studies programs are needed to correct historical and cultural myths, to assist teachers in knowing their black students, to fulfill a psychological need of black students, and to further resocialization of Americans. Perhaps the best program is a double major - one in Black Studies, the other in a traditional discipline. Alternative ways include a Black Studies Department and its offering a major, drawing together a listing of existent courses, establishing a permanent Institute of Afro-American Studies, having a system of visiting professors, or revising present curricula to emphasize contributions of blacks. Colleges also might introduce special black cultural affairs programs such as poetry readings, theater productions, musical and dance companies, art exhibitions, or a black arts festival. Black Studies must aim to advance the entire society, this being crucial for the "humanism of man." Undocumented. E. E. Beauregard

2925. Relyea, Harold C. "BLACK POWER": THF GENESIS AND FUTURE OF A REVOLUTION. *J. of Human Relations 1968 16(4): 502-513.* Defines the ideology of black power and discusses its history. The antecedents of this ideology can be traced to Richard Wright's *Black Power* (New York: Harper and Brothers, 1954), "a chronicle of the emergence of modern Africa from colonial rule and white oppression....For most Americans 'black power' immediately entered their purview in the summer of 1966." The ideology was created by Stokely Carmichael and transformed by Martin Luther King, Jr. Basic is the principle of race consciousness. "Being the extension of Pan-Africanism that it is, this concept of race consciousness, or *Negritude,* is a positive statement of racial identity and pride." And "just as there is a strong anticolonial sentiment in Pan-Africanism, so too is there opposition to the 'colonialist' white power structure in the 'black power' ideology." Black power proposes the practice of participatory democracy. It supports the concept of "counter-communities" or "parallel institutions." It seeks to replace existing institutions with more equitable institutions but through orderly procedures. It is "the nationalism of a subculture, the reform program of an oppressed people." Based on newspapers and other published sources; 30 notes. D. J. Abramoske

2926. Relyea, Harold C. BLACK POWER AS AN URBAN IDEOLOGY. *Social Studies 1969 60(6): 243-260.* Explores the theories of Black Power and attempts to define the underlying factors which give it meaning and force. Disillusionment, frustration, and similar factors arising from deprived socioeconomic conditions of inner-city decay, help to give it motivating force. Through this theory, meaning and value attach themselves to the lives of black people. 34 notes. L. Raife

2927. Relyea, Harold C. THE THEOLOGY OF BLACK POWER. *Religion in Life 1969 38(3): 415-420.* Describes the development of the theology of Black Power, attending to its origins as well as its present expression.
D. Brockway

2928. Riesman, David. SOME RESERVATIONS ABOUT BLACK POWER. *Transaction 1967 5(1): 20-22.* Some white American students remind the author of the Japanese *Zengakuren,* a leftist student union similar to other such organizations around the world. These students feel that America has now reached the zenith of corruption and racism. Yet the contention is that conditions in the South have considerably improved over the last 10 to 20 years. The frustration results from a feeling that the improvement has not come fast enough. The protests themselves are a symbol of improvement. The author fears that if whites are totally rejected from the Black Power movement it may lead to their spiritual rejection. Since the blacks will never be a majority, they must seek issues on which they can unite with others. These might very well be economic issues. Black Power is helping the Negro to reshape self-definition. Eventually the Negroes will develop a complex of self-help organizations which may serve as a kind of mystique.
A. Erlebacher

2929. Rosovsky, Henry. BLACK STUDIES AT HARVARD: PERSONAL REFLECTIONS CONCERNING RECENT EVENTS. *Am. Scholar 1969 38(4): 562-572.* As part of a worldwide "crisis of authority," the author reflects on "black studies" as a case study of the phenomenon. He discusses his coming to Harvard University and his success in agitating for a committee to recruit black students, which was much like the informal quota system used for recruiting and admitting foreign students. By the spring of 1968 and after the assassination of Martin Luther King, the program had begun to develop into an Afro-American Studies program. But events proceeded in such a way as to polarize faculty into radical and conservative groups with an admixture of the fearful and the confused. The result of student demonstrations, demands, and implied threats was that the original proposals for an academically based program were replaced by an activist program with a large involvement by black undergraduates with some influence over appointments and tenure. The author feels that a faculty decision of such a nature while under pressure was bad for Harvard, black students, the program, and the future of the black community.
T. R. Cripps

2930. Roucek, Joseph S. THE RISE OF "BLACK POWER" IN THE UNITED STATES. *Contemporary R. [Great Britain] 1968 212(1224): 31-39.* Surveys the rise of Black Power from Negro revolutionary movements in America. Until recently, the Negro revolt has used "freedom" as its battle-cry, but "Freedom Road had taken a disconcerting new turn by the time the James H. Meredith March arrived, 12,000 strong, at the steps of the Mississippi State capital at Jackson during the summer of 1966"; the slogan "Black Power" had arisen and was becoming a reality. Examines the contributions of Stokely Carmichael and Malcolm X. Black Power is not exclusive; whites are allowed to join on the student committee's terms. The philosophy of "Black Power" is that white society has failed and the Negro's only salvation is to seize political power. However, there is fragmentation within the Negro communities. Some exclude all whites, desiring a Negro exodus to Africa, while the other extreme tolerates (to the extent of marrying) whites and wants Harlem as a separate city. Concludes that "the increasingly obvious confluence of racial, caste and class factors may set the spark of a new movement. But there is little chance of such a movement effecting progressing social change without a profound reorganisation of American politics."

L. Brown

2931. Sanders, Charles L. GROWTH OF THE ASSOCIATION OF BLACK SOCIAL WORKERS. *Social Casework 1970 51(5): 277-284.* The failure of integration and the existence of a separate black America encouraged the formation of the Association of Black Social Workers. In addition, the black revolution's emphasis on black organization and solidarity provided an important impulse to the founders of the association. The racist social system was attacked by blacks at the May 1968 National Conference on Social Welfare and a drive for a black social work organization began there. The National Conference on Social Welfare has agreed to all of the black demands except one, and a joint committee has been established to make recommendations. Describes the problems faced in the association, including the need to be democratic, pluralistic, and sensitive to the opinions of others, especially in reply to the American blacks' history of disappointment and denial. 12 notes.   M. A. Kaufman

2932. Satter, David. BLACK POWER. *Chicago Today 1967 4(3): 37-39.* Interprets remarks by Stokely Carmichael, leader of the Student Non-Violent Coordinating Committee (SNCC), on the topic "black power." The phrase is defined in different terms for specific audiences; thus, warring gangs in Chicago were told they were fighting the wrong people, white college students were told SNCC wanted political power, and poor Negroes were told it meant economic power. The author views the trend as conservative, despite the violent, antiwhite rhetoric. Black Power could eventually be the same as Jewish, or Polish, or Irish power - a unifying force in the community, a base for group pride, and perhaps for group social change.   M. W. Machan

2933. Schroth, Raymond A. THE REDEMPTION OF MALCOLM X. *Catholic World 1967 205(1230): 346-352.* Applies to Malcolm X (Al Hajj Malik Shabazz, originally Malcolm Little) the principle that "it is possible for a man to be open to Christ, and so be redeemed in Christ, even though his own personal creed contains a vehement denial of Christianity," by tracing "the pattern of sin, grace, and redemption in his life."   K. A. Chauvin

2934. Scnulze-Wilde, Harry. MALCOLM X UND ELIJAH MUHAMMED - DIE RELIGIÖSEN WURZELN DER AMERIKANISCHEN RASSEN-KÄMPFE [Malcolm X and Elijah Muhammad - the religious roots of American racial strife]. *Frankfurter Hefte [West Germany] 1967 22(5): 333-348.* The Black Muslim movement is described as the religious dimension of racial strife in the United States. Christianity has been identified with the white society, Islam is the religion of the colored - not only the Negro, but the Arab, the Indonesian, and the Chinese. The author's discussion of the problem includes the earlier role of

Marcus Aurelius Garvey (1887-1940) who assumed the title "Leader of the Negro Peoples of the World," James Baldwin, and Elijah Muhammad. Late 19th-century Protestant factors in the Black Muslim movement, and the idea of a "black homeland" are considered. Space is devoted to the pronouncements of Elijah Muhammad and Malcolm X.   R. W. Heywood

2935. Seigel, J. E. ON FRANTZ FANON. *Am. Scholar 1968/69 38(1): 84-96.* Reexamines the work of Frantz Fanon, a Negro-French-Martinique psychiatrist who wrote three books after the Algerian War: *The Wretched of the Earth* (New York: Grove, 1968), *A Dying Colonialism* (New York: Grove, 1967), and *Black Skin, White Masks* (New York: Grove, 1967). These books provided an ideology for black revolutionaries and nationalists in America. The violent and urgent tone is found to mask an essential humanism and dignity, and Fanon's own life is seen as a drift from neurosis toward a universal linkage with mankind. What he calls for is not the destruction of man, but the destruction of racism, of the myths of black inferiority, of the symbols of colonialism. Fanon's work is also read as part of the French intellectual scene of Jean-Paul Sartre's *Orphée Noir,* Leopold Senghor's concept of "négritude," and western psychiatric theory. Finally, the author finds Fanon wanting as a rhetoretician for black American radicals, both because of his unnoticed humanism and because of the false analogy between America and Algeria.   T. R. Cripps

2936. Thompson, William Irwin. LOS ANGELES: REFLECTIONS AT THE EDGE OF HISTORY. *Antioch R. 1968 28(3): 261-275.* Los Angeles fascinates the author who sees it as the prototype of America's future megalopolises. Los Angeles' "idea of history is a shattered landscape in which the individual moves through a world of discontinuities...." Because the megalopolis is too vast to be perceived meaningfully, "the individual projects, against the chaos of his world, a new mythopoetic simplification of reality..." such as right-wing paranoia and black nationalism. The connecting tissue of traditional family and society is missing. Watts found its image as the result of the riots and seems to be becoming a genuine community.   F. Harrold

2937. Tinker, Irene. NATIONALISM IN A PLURAL SOCIETY: THE CASE OF THE AMERICAN NEGRO. *Western Pol. Q. 1966 19(1): 112-122.* Sees an inherent conflict between nationalism and unity in a plural society such as the United States and especially the the southern United States. The author sees the Negro civil rights movement as part of a worldwide phenomenon of nationalism, marked with divisions of color, class, occupation, and culture among Negroes themselves. To succeed Negro nationalism requires unity of conservative middle classes with Negro masses. Eduard Franklin Frazier's concept of *Black Bourgeoisie* (New York: Macmillan, 1957) is valuable as a tool but inaccurate, for the black bourgeoisie is neither black nor really bourgeois. Emphasizing matriarchal structure in the family, some of its sources are explained while denying the presence of real Negro leadership in terms of an entire people. Growing radicalization of demands as is true in worldwide nationalistic movements is seen. The drawing of stronger lines between the Negro minority and the white majority forces reconsideration of minority rights in a democracy. The author suggests some accommodation for guaranteed minority representation to help preserve some consensus - especially in the South - in what he sees as a troubled transition period before achievement of first-class citizenship. 31 notes, including references to African and Asian literature.   H. Aptheker

2938. Turner, Floyd. THE STUDENT MOVEMENT AS A FORCE FOR EDUCATIONAL CHANGE. *Liberal Educ. 1970 56(1): 39-50.* The student movement has four distinct sources: the antiwar movement; the increasingly militant Black Power movement; the educational reformists, who oppose educational "processing" but have largely failed to gain real reform; and the hippy-cultural revolutionists, who have created significant new forms of life and culture. Protesting students tend to be above average academically, and from good schools. They hold intellectual, humanistic, and democratic values, and subscribe more to the ethic of spontaneity than to the Protestant ethic of order, rationality, and worldly ambition. They have well-internalized principles rather than conventional "good-boy" or law-and-order morality. Their family background is humanistic rather than authoritarian, and they are less in revolt against their families than against the failings of society. Philosophically they are most influenced by Marx and Freud, who offered new definitions of man's political, economic, and psychological self. Gandhi and the Nuremberg trials have been lesser influences, the one giving an alternative to violent revolution, and the other both a precedent for antiwar and civil rights activity, and the argument that acquiescence is equivalent to guilt. The "depression mentality" of the students' parents, and their desire for economic stability and security, have led students to search for a missing psychological stability in communal living. Basic values have not changed, but traditional institutional forms do not serve the end of a humane society. College must respond with more complete efforts to educate the whole man with less-specialized, more integrated programs. Note.   P. M. Olson

2939. Unsigned. IDEOLOGICAL STATEMENT BY CONGRESS OF AFRICAN PEOPLE. *Pan-African J. 1971 4(1): 1-7.* The Coordinating Committee and Workshop Coordinators of the Congress of African People, meeting at Atlanta, Georgia, in September 1970, set four goals of Black Power for Africans all over the world: self-determination, self-sufficiency, self-respect, and self-defense. This means that all Africans are bound together racially, historically, culturally, politically, and emotionally. Workshops reflected 11 major areas of black concern: political liberation, economic autonomy, creativity and the arts, religious system, education, history, law and justice, black technology, communications and system analysis, social organization, and community organization. The congress attempts to appeal to the widest possible spectrum of black people so that nationalist ideology can sooner become the philosophy of the people.
                                                    E. E. Beauregard

2940. Vermeer, Donald E. AFRICAN STUDIES IN THE UNITED STATES. *Social Studies 1970 61(7): 333-338.* Surveys the African Studies program in the United States and gives a brief historical account of the noteworthy programs in the university and other academically oriented and scholarly associations in the United States. Suggests a tie-in of African Studies with Afro-American Studies, which programs should complement each other. 12 notes.   L. R. Raife

2941. Walker, Jack L. and Aberbach, Joel D. THE MEANINGS OF BLACK POWER: A COMPARISON OF WHITE AND BLACK INTERPRETA-TIONS OF A POLITICAL SLOGAN. *Am. Pol. Sci. R. 1970 64(2): 367-388.* Describes the difference of interpretations of "black power" among blacks and whites. Of the whites interviewed in Detroit, Michigan, in 1967-68, 40 percent thought the term means blacks will rule; nine percent of the blacks thought so. Many whites associate riots and violence with the term. Some 42 percent of the blacks associate the term with "fair share." This survey did not find black power to be a lower class or youth movement, but found birth in Michigan as opposed to a migrant status to be significantly related to supporters of black power. City life in Detroit was more important than southern culture. Black power is an ideology though it is narrow in conception and not a world view. 12 tables, 54 notes.   L. H. Grothaus

2942. Walters, Ronald. CRITICAL ISSUES ON BLACK STUDIES. *Pan-African J. 1970 3(3): 127-139.* The Black Studies Movement must uproot the every-day oppression of black people. This requires education and programing from two areas - white institutions under whatever black framework blacks can construct, and independent black centers and systems. The objective must be "to reconstruct the black intellectual tradition from the standpoint of black history and culture." Such structuring must be based on interaction between Black Studies programs and the immediate black community, i.e., "the construction of systems of learning out of the traditional mode of operation." A "wholistic" approach should be used to evaluate these new methods. Imaginative financial support will be demanded for the varied innovative programs. Black efforts must be coordinated to guard against control by the white establishment of Black Studies. The Black Studies Movement gains strength by black caucuses of political scientists, sociologists, historians, and others launching attacks upon white professional organizations such as the African Studies Association.   E. E. Beauregard

2943. Watson, Edward A. THE NOVELS AND ESSAYS OF JAMES BALD-WIN. *Queen's Q. [Canada] 1965 72(2): 385-402.* The literary importance of Baldwin's work has been overshadowed unjustly, in the author's opinion, by its sociological significance.   M. Abrash

2944. Weiss, Samuel A. THE ORDEAL OF MALCOLM X. *South Atlantic Q. 1968 67(1): 53-63.* As demonstrated by his *Autobiography* (New York: Grove Press, 1966), Malcolm X spent his life on the edge of violence. Denounced as a racist and fomenter of violence, Malcolm never led a violent demonstration. He emphasized the conscious reconstruction of an independent self-reliant black community. The danger of this reconstruction was that a new set of illusions could be fostered which would disappoint the Negro just as the older "liberal" ones had. Malcolm recognized the explosiveness of the ghetto as few before him had done.   J. M. Bumsted

2945. Wolf, Edmund. DIE SIEBEN SCHWARZEN WEGE [The seven paths of the blacks]. *Monat [West Germany] 1970 22(256): 44-50.* Discusses American Negroes, organizations such as the Black Panthers, National Urban League, and the NAACP, and the varying views of such Negro leaders as Leroi Jones, Huey P. Newton, Eldridge Cleaver, Stokely Carmichael, Roy Wilkins, Whitney Young, and Dr. Daniel Hare. Discusses the Negroes' situation in the United States, their somewhat improved status, and their varying aims, hopes, aspirations, and methods of obtaining them. Based on interviews, especially in Newark, New Jersey.
                                                                            A. E. Cornebise

2946. Woodward, C. Vann. CLIO WITH SOUL. *J. of Am. Hist. 1969 56(1): 5-20.* In this presidential address to the Organization of American Historians, the author discusses the benefits and possible pitfalls of an overdue recognition of black history in America. A valuable corrective to the neglect and distortion of the role of blacks in our history can be anticipated, and a new pride in the achievements of Africans may give positive identity to the Afro-Americans, revealing as well a filiopietism characteristic of other American ethnic groups. However, historians must oppose the idea that only blacks write or teach the black experience, and must hope that those who write and teach will be dissuaded from an indulgence in compensatory exaggeration, black ethnocentrism, or gratification of the white liberals' masochistic cravings. Based on secondary sources; 41 notes.   K. B. West

2947. Wright, Nathan, Jr. BLACK POWER. *Catholic World 1966 204(1,219): 46-51.* The theme of "black power" is an old one in America, but to see in it a vision of armed conflict between two opposing and unequal adversaries indicates a failure to understand the dynamics of social and moral progress. Black Power is a necessity because, like all individuals who grow into responsible adulthood, the Negro must assert his own inherent sense of worth. The movement can broaden America's national outlook, help solve problems caused by urbanization, extend our understanding of the meaning of equality, and create a changed racial situation.   Sr. M. Campion

2948. --. [A POLITICS OF REPRESSION?]. *Current 1970 115: 33-45.*
   Ferry, W. H. THE POLICE STATE, AMERICAN MODE, pp. 33-36. Argues that a police state is emerging, accelerated and directed by white apathy and insecurity toward the black ghetto. The author detects blatant intimations of Hitler in police relations with the Black Panthers.
   Kopkind, Andrew and Lang, Frances. HOW FAR REPRESSION? pp. 36-38. Argue that repression is widespread, seen equally in the reorganization of the Justice Department and the "emerging Republican majority" of fear-ridden social groups. The authors especially point to repression of the Black Panthers, but note that the administration seeks to stifle opposition by giving it partial, lesser gains.
   Unsigned. A CONSPIRACY AGAINST THE BLACK PANTHERS? pp. 39-40. Concludes that "the climate of anger and the specific cases of police harassment against the Black Panther Party warrant intensive investigation."

Unsigned. WARPED PERCEPTIONS, pp. 40-42. A reprinted editorial from *The Wall Street Journal* which disclaims assertions of 28 Black Panthers killed by police and notes that the thorough Federal put-down of the right-wing Minutemen ought to suggest caution in accepting Panther claims of being persecuted.

Cox, Harvey. PREVENTIVE WAR AGAINST THE BLACK PANTHERS, p. 42. Claims the existence of "a collective determination to wipe out the Panthers as an effective political force."

Unsigned. THE PERSECUTION AND ASSASSINATION OF THE BLACK PANTHER PARTY AS DIRECTED BY GUESS WHO, pp. 43-44. A reprinted editorial from the *National Review* which sees lines between lawful protest and the intent to overthrow the Government drawn between true liberal dissenters and the Black Panthers, placing the latter beyond the pale of usual legal restraints.

Stone, I. F. THE REBIRTH OF FREEDOM - OR OF FASCISM? pp. 44-45. Sees present political leadership, goals, and tactics leading away from freedom. The author pleads for the education of America in humanism and for an army of youth to put it into practice.   C. A. Newton

2949. --. DIRECTIONS IN BLACK STUDIES. *Massachusetts R. 1969 10(4): 701-756.*

Chametzky, Jules. A LETTER, pp. 701-702. Reprints the letter that invited the comments below.

Thelwell, Mike. BLACK STUDIES: A POLITICAL PERSPECTIVE, pp. 703-712. Since blacks will have to attend oppressive white colleges or go without higher education, black studies programs must be instituted to rescue them from the intellectual colonialism of the white-controlled university. Black studies must be autonomous and free from the control of white college administrators. 2 notes.

Unsigned. PURPOSE AND PROGRAM, pp. 713-717. A statement by the Institute of the Black World, in Atlanta, Georgia. The institute is "an experiment with scholarship in the context of struggle." It will encourage research and develop new techniques of teaching the black experience.

Kilson, Martin. ANATOMY OF THE BLACK STUDIES MOVEMENT, pp. 718-725. Contemporary black studies advocates are ignorant of and intellectually inferior to their predecessors. Scholars such as Carter G. Woodson, William Edward Burghardt Du Bois, and John Hope Franklin were objective researchers who sought to increase understanding of the black experience. Their present-day successors lack scholarly perspective and objectivity. Too many black studies programs are controlled by lower-class militants who propose pseudosolutions and whose programs are not intellectually valid. Black studies should resemble other disciplines. 73 notes.

Cruse, Harold. TWO FUNDAMENTAL PROBLEMS, p. 726. Black studies programs suffer from the lack of qualified personnel to teach black-oriented courses, and the lack of consensus on what constitutes an adequate program of black studies. Only time can overcome these difficulties; excessive haste will produce academically invalid programs.

Hare, Nathan. QUESTIONS AND ANSWERS ABOUT BLACK STUDIES, pp. 727-736. Such studies are "based ideally on the ideology of revolutionary nationalism,...nationalistic, not separatist." It must be relevant to blacks, build their pride, and destroy white racism. Black studies must be controlled by "the black community" but should be open to white students. Offers a sample black studies curriculum.

Wilson, William J. THE QUEST FOR MEANINGFUL BLACK EXPERIENCE ON WHITE CAMPUSES, pp. 737-746. Black studies departments should have black chairmen who "organize the curricula and screen out those professors, white or black, who do not have a proper orientation." 8 notes.

Stuckey, Sterling. CONTOURS OF BLACK STUDIES: THE DIMENSION OF AFRICAN AND AFRO-AMERICAN RELATIONSHIPS, pp. 747-756. Afro-American culture is strongly influenced by African cultural patterns. Black studies scholars must intensively study the African past and the crucial interrelationships between African and American culture.   G. Kurland

2950. --. [OF ANGELA DAVIS]. *Midstream 1971 17.*
Katz, Shlomo. AN OPEN LETTER TO JAMES BALDWIN, (4): 3-5. Discusses an open letter that James Baldwin wrote to Angela Davis likening her to the Jewish mother on her way to Dachau. The author strongly takes exception to that comparison, enunciates differences between the two, and condemns Davis for not speaking out against her Communist supporters in Russia on behalf of the Russian Jews who are victims of Soviet tyranny.

Baldwin, James and Katz, Shlomo. OF ANGELA DAVIS AND "THE JEWISH HOUSEWIFE HEADED FOR DACHAU," (6): 3-7. Baldwin answers Katz, who had challenged his comparison of the aloneness of Angela Davis to that of "the Jewish housewife...headed for Dachau." Katz then gives a rejoinder to Baldwin's reply, emphasizing the amount of anti-Semitism among present Negro leaders.   R. J. Wechman

2951. --. [STOKELY CARMICHAEL SPEAKS]. *Southern Speech J. 1967 33(2): 77-92.*
Jefferson, Pat. THE MAGNIFICENT BARBARIAN AT NASHVILLE, pp. 77-87. Evaluates the rhetorical abilities of Stokely Carmichael (b. 1942), "the Magnificent Barbarian," executive chairman of the Student Nonviolent Coordinating Committee, who gave the main address at Impact '67 in the Memorial Gymnasium at Vanderbilt University (Nashville, Tennessee) on 8 April 1967. "Carmichael devoted three fourths of his speech to an explanation of SNCC's position in the civil-rights movement. His discussion of black power illustrated a rationally articulated plan. If the auditor accepted his basic premise - the white man's responsibility for the victimization of the Negro - all other statements sounded reasonable and logical....Climaxing the address with an effective utilization of the either-or dichotomy, he gave 'white America' a choice between 'concentration camps...' or 'organized and powerful communities able to make constructive contributions to the total society." As predicted by the local press, "Four hours after Carmichael's speech, riots broke out in the Negro section of Nashville." 40 notes.

Phifer, Elizabeth Flory and Taylor, Dencil R. CARMICHAEL IN TALLAHASSEE, pp. 88-92. The authors, two white members of a predominantly Negro audience who heard Stokely Carmichael speak at the Tabernacle Baptist Church in Tallahassee, Florida, on 16 April 1967, record their reactions to Carmichael's extemporaneous talk. Phifer concludes, "Perhaps many in the audience did not understand or agree with the black-power movement; but I doubt if anyone who heard its leading spokesman in Tallahassee would underestimate his power with an audience." Taylor observes, Carmichael's oratorical style is dynamic, but based on emotional appeals with "little logical support...." Note.

D. D. Cameron

2952. --. [THE AFRO-AMERICAN STUDIES INSTITUTE PROGRAM AT ANTIOCH COLLEGE]. *Antioch R. 1969 29(2): 145-154.*

Clark, Kenneth B. A CHARADE OF POWER: BLACK STUDENTS AT WHITE COLLEGES, pp. 145-148. A trustee who resigned from the board of Antioch College because of his disapproval of the college's recognition of the Afro-American Studies Institute and its activities on campus, the author states his case against such programs. He argues that "a university could not surrender to student control of Black Studies Institute with exclusionary characteristics and without even minimal academic standards if it truly valued the humanity of blacks. If the university does not insist that Negroes be as rigorously trained as whites to compete in the arena of real power, or that studies of racism be as roughly and systematically pursued as nuclear physics, one must question whether it is really serious." He further argues that whites have greater need of black studies than blacks and that their exclusion from the program robs it of some of its value.

Lythcott, Stephen. THE CASE FOR BLACK STUDIES, pp. 149-154. Declares that Clark condemned the Afro-American Studies Institute program at Antioch College without really investigating it. Tha author says that to admit whites to the program would be a hindrance because their "subtle inbred racism" would slow down the classes and would prevent frank discussion by blacks of the schisms within the race and of their own prejudices. He defends the academic integrity of the program, pointing out the use of black Ph.D. candidates from neighboring institutions as instructors. He explains the relevance of the AASI maintaining a garage and gas station in Cincinnati and indicates a hope of establishing headquarters in West Dayton away from the "ivory tower." Undocumented.

F. Harrold

2953. --. THE NEGRO INTELLECTUAL. *Midcontinent Am. Studies J. 1963 4(2): 3-27.*

Levant, Howard. ASPIRALING WE SHOULD GO, pp. 3-20. Discusses the Negro's search for identity, particularly the work of two of the more significant writers of the present, James Baldwin and Ralph Ellison. "They share an evident intention to let the (Caucasian) reader *feel* what it means to be a Negro." The author hopes that Baldwin does communicate; "we need him much more desperately than he needs us." 28 notes.

Horowitz, Floyd R. RALPH ELLISON'S MODERN VERSION OF BRER BEAR AND BRER RABBIT IN "INVISIBLE MAN" (1963), pp. 21-27. "Mr. Ellison's Invisible Man is an intelligent young Negro attuned to what he considers the clarion philosophy of the white world - 'keep this nigger boy running.' At first we find him like a bear, by his own admission, hibernation." Horowitz analyzes this one theme in the book, and considers it "a psychological study, impressionistically told."

E. P. Stickney

REFERENCE MATTER

INDEX

This is a combined index of author, biographical, geographical, and subject entries. Biographical entries are followed by an asterisk. Autobiographical entries are followed by two asterisks. Personal names without asterisks are authors of articles.

H

LIST OF PERIODICALS

This list contains the titles of the periodicals surveyed for abstracts in AFRO-AMERICAN HISTORY. The titles are arranged in alphabetical order by journal title.

The frequency of publication, years of coverage, and the code of the country of publication follow the title of the periodical.

Example:

Alabama Historical Quarterly	Q	1963-	US
Deutsche Aussenpolitik	BM	1961-	EG
History Today	M	1954-	GB
Revue de Défense Nationale	M	1955-	FR

Abbreviations and explanation:

A	annual		Q	quarterly
B	biennial		SA	semiannual
BM	bimonthly		SM	semimonthly
BW	biweekly		3	3 times a year
I	irregular		T	triennial
M	monthly		W	weekly

Persons interested in further information concerning the journals are referred to HISTORICAL PERIODICALS (Santa Barbara: Clio Press, 1961) and ULRICH'S INTERNATIONAL PERIODICALS DIRECTORY 1969/70, thirteenth edition (New York: R. R. Bowker, 1969).

Other frequencies of publication are indicated by a number such as "3."

Alphabetical list of country codes and countries:

AU	Australia	GB	Great Britain	RU	Rumania
BE	Belgium	HU	Hungary	SR	Senegal
BR	Brazil	ID	India	SU	Union of Soviet
CA	Canada	IT	Italy		Socialist Republics
CU	Cuba	JA	Japan	SW	Sweden
CZ	Czechoslovakia	KE	Kenya	SZ	Switzerland
DE	Denmark	MX	Mexico	TZ	Tanzania
EG	German	NE	Netherlands	US	United States
	Democratic	NO	Norway	WI	West Indies
	Republic	PH	Philippines	WG	German
FI	Finland	PO	Poland		Federal
FR	France	PU	Puerto Rico		Republic

A

AAUP Bulletin	Q	1969-	US
African Affairs	Q	1959-	GB
African Forum (ceased pub 1967)	Q	1965-67	US
Agricultural History	Q	1954-	US
Alabama Historical Quarterly	Q	1963-	US
Alabama Review	Q	1963-	US
American Anthropologist	BM	1963-	US
American Benedictine Review	Q	1967-	US
American Economic Review	5	1954-	US
American Education	10	1965-	US
American-German Review	BW	1955-	US
American Heritage	BM	1955-	US
American Historical Review	5	1954-	US
American History Illustrated	10	1966-	US
American Jewish Archives	SA	1954-	US
American Jewish Historical Quarterly	Q	1954-	US
American Journal of Economics and Sociology	Q	1963-	US
American Journal of Legal History	Q	1957-	US
American Literature	Q	1963-	US
American Neptune	Q	1954-	US
American Political Science Review	Q	1954-	US
American Quarterly	Q	1954-	US
American Scholar	Q	1963-	US
American Sociological Review	BM	1963-	US
American Speech	Q	1963-	US
American Studies	3	1965-	US
American West	BM	1964-	US
Américas	M	1969-	US
Americas, The	Q	1954-	US

Annales Africaines	A	1956-	SR
Annales: Économies, Sociétés, Civilisations	BM	1954-	FR
Annals of Iowa	Q	1963-	US
Annals of the American Academy of Political and Social Science	BM	1954-	US
Annals of the Association of American Geographers	Q	1963-	US
Année Politique et Économique	BM	1954-	FR
Antioch Review	Q	1963-	US
Arbitration Journal	Q	1969-	US
Arizona and the West	Q	1963-	US
Arizona Quarterly	Q	1963-	US
Arizoniana (old title, see Journal of Arizona History)	Q	1963-	US
Arkansas Historical Quarterly	Q	1963-	US
Art in America	BM	1963-	US
Atenea	Q	1965-	PU
Atlantic	M	1954-56	US
Aussenpolitik	M	1954-	WG
Australian Journal of Politics and History	3	1956-	AU

B

Baptist Quarterly	Q	1955-	GB
Beiträge zur Geschichte der Deutschen Arbeiterbewegung	BM	1959-	EG
British Association for American Studies Bulletin (old title, see Journal of American Studies)	SA	1963-	GB
British Journal of Sociology	Q	1955-	GB
Bulletin of the Friends Historical Association (old title, see Quaker History)	SA	1954-	US
Bulletin of the History of Medicine	BM	1963-	US
Bulletin of the New York Public Library	10	1966-	US
Bulletin of the United Church of Canada	I	1963-	CA
Business History Review	Q	1954-	US

C

California Council for the Social Studies Review	Q	1963-	US
California Historical Society Quarterly	Q	1954-	US
California Social Science Review (old title, see California Council for the Social Studies)	Q	1963-	US
Canadian Historical Review	Q	1954-	CA
Canadian Journal of Economics and Political Science (old title, see Canadian Journal of Political Science)	Q	1954-	CA
Canadian Journal of History	3	1966-	CA
Canadian Journal of Political Science	Q	1954-	CA
Caribbean Studies	Q	1961-	PU
Casa de las Americas	BM	1961-	CU
Catalyst	SA	1969-	US
Catholic Educational Review (suspended pub 1969)	9	1954-69	US
Catholic Historical Review	Q	1954-	US

Catholic World (old title, see New Catholic World)	M	1966-70	US
Centennial Review	Q	1963-	US
Československý Časopis Historický	BM	1954-	CZ
Chicago History	SA	1963-	US
Chicago Today (ceased pub 1968)	3	1966-68	US
Christian Century	W	1954-59	US
Chronicles of Oklahoma	Q	1963-	US
Church History	Q	1954-	US
Cincinnati Historical Society Bulletin	Q	1963-	US
Civil War History	Q	1955-	US
Civil War Times Illustrated	10	1962-	US
College and Research Libraries	BM	1964-	US
Colorado Magazine	Q	1964-	US
Colorado Quarterly	Q	1963-	US
Commentary	M	1955-	US
Comparative Studies in Society and History	Q	1958-	US
Concordia Historical Institute Quarterly	Q	1962-	US
Connecticut Historical Society Bulletin	Q	1963-	US
Contemporary Review	M	1954-	GB
Cornell Library Journal	3	1966-	US
Cotton History Review (old title, see Textile History Review)	Q	1960-65	US
Crisis	10	1969-	US
Current	M	1969-	US
Current History	M	1954-	US

D

Daedalus	Q	1963-	US
Dalhousie Review	Q	1954-	CA
Delaware History	SA	1963-	US
Deutsche Aussenpolitik	BM	1961-	EG
Deutsche Rundschau (ceased pub 1963)	M	1954-63	WG
Diogenes	Q	1955-	IT
Dissent	BM	1968-	US
Dokumente	BM	1959-	WG
Duquesne Review	SA	1962-	US

E

Eastern World	BM	1955-	GB
Economic History Review	3	1954-	GB
Encounter	M	1955-	GB
Esprit	M	1955-	FR
Essex Institute Historical Collections	Q	1963-	US
Ethnomusicology	3	1970-	US
Études	M	1955-	FR
Europa-Archiv	BW	1955-	WG
Explorations in Economic History	Q	1955-	US

F

Florida Historical Quarterly	Q	1954-	US
FOCUS Midwest	BM	1966-	US
Forest History	Q	1963-	US
Frankfurter Hefte	M	1954-	WG
Freedom and Union	M	1955-57	US

G

Geographical Review	Q	1963-	US
Georgia Historical Quarterly	Q	1955-	US
Georgia Review	Q	1963-	US
Geschichte in Wissenschaft und Unterricht	M	1954-	WG

H

Harvard Educational Review	Q	1963-	US
Hispanic American Historical Review	Q	1954-	US
Historiallinen Aikakauskirja	Q	1954-	FI
Historiallinen Arkisto	I	1953-	FI
Historian	Q	1953-	US
Historica Judaica (old title, see Revue des Etudes Juives)	Q	1955-	FR
Historical Bulletin	Q	1957-59	PH
Historical Magazine of the Protestant Episcopal Church	Q	1954-	US
Historical New Hampshire	Q	1963-	US
Historie a Vojenstvi	BM	1963-	CZ
Historisches Jahrbuch	SA	1954-	WG
History	3	1954-	GB
History of Education Journal (old title, see History of Education Quarterly)	Q	1954-	US
History of Education Quarterly	Q	1954-	US
History Teacher	Q	1968-	US
History Today	M	1954-	GB
Horizon	BM	1958-	US
Horizons: The Marxist Quarterly (ceased pub 1968)	Q	1967-68	CA
Human Organization	Q	1963-	US

I

Il Ponte	M	1955-	IT
Indian Journal of Social Research	3	1962	ID
Indiana History Bulletin	M	1963-	US
Indiana Magazine of History	Q	1963-	US
Indo-Asian Culture	Q	1955-	ID
Information Historique	5	1955-	FR
Internasjonal Politikk	BM	1954-	NO
International Organization	Q	1955-	US
International Review of Social History	3	1954-	NE
International Social Science Journal	Q	1955-	FR

Interplay	10	1967-	US
Islamic Review	M	1959-	GB

J

Jahrbuch für Amerikastudien	A	1959-	WG
Jahrbücher für Geschichte Osteuropas	Q	1954-	WG
Jewish Social Studies	Q	1954-	US
Journal: Division of Higher Education United Church of Christ (old title, see Journal of Current Social Issues)	I	1968-	US
Journal of African History	Q	1960-	GB
Journal of American Folklore	Q	1965-	US
Journal of American History	Q	1954-	US
Journal of American Studies	3	1963-	GB
Journal of Arizona History	Q	1963-	US
Journal of Black Studies	Q	1970-	US
Journal of Business	Q	1967-	US
Journal of Church and State	3	1963-	US
Journal of Conflict Resolution	Q	1957-	US
Journal of Contemporary History	Q	1966-	US
Journal of Current Social Issues	I	1968-	US
Journal of Economic History	Q	1954-	US
Journal of Historical Studies (ceased pub 1970)	Q	1967-70	US
Journal of Human Relations	Q	1963-	US
Journal of Inter-American Studies (old title, see Journal of Inter-American Studies and World Affairs)	Q	1954-	US
Journal of Inter-American Studies and World Affairs	Q	1954-	US
Journal of Library History (old title, see Journal of Library History, Philosophy, and Comparative Librarianship)	Q	1966-	US
Journal of Library History, Philosophy, and Comparative Librarianship	Q	1966-	US
Journal of Long Island History	SA	1963-	US
Journal of Mississippi History	Q	1963-	US
Journal of Modern African Studies	Q	1963-	GB
Journal of Negro Education	Q	1963-	US
Journal of Negro History	Q	1954-	US
Journal of Philosophy	BW	1952-70	US
Journal of Political Economy	BM	1954-	US
Journal of Politics	Q	1964-	US
Journal of Popular Culture	Q	1967-	US
Journal of Presbyterian History	Q	1954-	US
Journal of Social History	Q	1967-	US
Journal of Social Issues	Q	1971-	US
Journal of Southern History	Q	1954-	US
Journal of the Alabama Academy of Science	Q	1964-	US
Journal of the American Institute of Planners	BM	1967-	US
Journal of the Folklore Institute	3	1964-	US
Journal of the Friends' Historical Society	3	1957-	GB
Journal of the History of Ideas	Q	1954-	US

Journal of the History of Medicine and Allied Sciences	Q	1954-	US
Journal of the Illinois State Historical Society	Q	1963-	US
Journal of the Lancaster County Historical Society	Q	1963-	US
Journal of the Presbyterian Historical Society (old title, see Journal of Presbyterian History)	Q	1954-	US
Journal of the Rutgers University Library	SA	1955-	US
Journal of the United Service Institution of India	Q	1955-	ID
Journal of the West	Q	1963-	US
Journalism Quarterly	Q	1954-	US

K

Kansas Historical Quarterly	Q	1963-	US
Kentucky Folklore Record	Q	1963-	US
Kleio	10	1963-	NE
Kokka Gakkai Zasshi	BM	1954-	JA
Kroeber Anthropological Society Papers	SA	1963-	US
Kwartalnik Historyczny	Q	1954-	PO

L

Labor History	Q	1960-	US
Liberal Education	Q	1963-	US
Library Quarterly	Q	1963-	US
Lincoln Herald	Q	1955-	US
Long Island Forum	M	1969-	US
Louisiana Historical Quarterly (old title, see Louisiana History)	Q	1955-	US
Louisiana History	Q	1955-	US
Louisiana Studies	Q	1963-	US
Lutheran Quarterly	Q	1963-	US

M

Mankind	BM	1967-	US
Maryland Historian	SA	1970-	US
Maryland Historical Magazine	Q	1963-	US
Massachusetts Historical Society Proceedings	A	1953-	US
Massachusetts Review	Q	1968-	US
Mennonite Life	Q	1962-	US
Methodist History	Q	1962-	US
Mezhdunarodnaia zhizn'	M	1965-	SU
Michigan Academician	Q	1971-	US
Michigan History	Q	1963-	US
Mid-America	Q	1954-	US

Midcontinent American Studies Journal (old title, see American Studies)	3	1965-	US
Midstream	M	1971-	US
Midway	Q	1967-	US
Midwest Journal of Political Science	Q	1957-	US
Midwest Quarterly	Q	1963-	US
Military Affairs	Q	1955-	US
Military Review	M	1963-	US
Minnesota History	Q	1963-	US
Minority of One	M	1968	US
Mississippi Quarterly	Q	1963-	US
Mississippi Valley Historical Review (old title, see Journal of American History)	Q	1954-	US
Missouri Historical Review	Q	1962-	US
Missouri Historical Society Bulletin	Q	1962-	US
Monat	M	1954-	WG
Montana	Q	1955-	US
Monthly Labor Review	M	1967-	US
Moravian Historical Society Transactions	A	1963-	US
Myśl Filozoficzna	Q	1955-	PO

N

National Civic Review	11	1970-	US
Naval War College Review	10	1969-	US
Nebraska History	Q	1963-	US
Negro History Bulletin	8	1954-	US
Nevada Historical Society Quarterly	Q	1963-	US
New Catholic World	M	1966-70	US
New-England Galaxy	Q	1963-	US
New England Quarterly	Q	1954-	US
New England Social Studies Bulletin	A	1954-	US
New Generation	Q	1969-	US
New Jersey History	Q	1963-	US
New Mexico Historical Review	Q	1954-	US
New World Review	Q	1969-	US
New York Historical Society Quarterly	Q	1963-	US
New York History	Q	1955-	US
New York Times Magazine	W	1954-61	US
North American Review	Q	1968-	US
North Carolina Historical Review	Q	1963-	US
North Dakota Quarterly	Q	1963-	US
Northwest Ohio Quarterly	Q	1963-	US
Northwestern Report	Q	1967-	US
Novaia i Noveishaia Istoriia	BM	1957-	SU
Nowe Drogi	M	1954-	PO

O

Ohio History	Q	1958-	US
Ohio History Quarterly (old title, see Ohio History)	Q	1958-	US

Økonomi og Politik	Q	1954-	DE
Ontario History	Q	1963-	CA
Organon	3	1969-	US

P

Pacific Historical Review	Q	1954-	US
Pacific Northwest Quarterly	Q	1955-	US
Pacific Sociological Review	Q	1963-	US
Paedagogica Historica	SA	1968-	BE
Pan-African Journal	Q	1969-	KE
Panoramas (ceased pub 1965)	BM	1963-65	MX
Państwo i Prawo	M	1956-	PO
Past and Present	I	1954-	GB
Pennsylvania Folklife	Q	1963-	US
Pennsylvania Magazine of History and Biography	Q	1955-	US
Pensée	BM	1954-	FR
Perspectives in American History	A	1967-	US
Phylon	Q	1954-	US
Polish Review	Q	1956-	US
Political Science Quarterly	Q	1954-	US
Politique Étrangère	BM	1954-	FR
Politische Studien	BM	1954-	WG
Population Studies	3	1955-	GB
Prepodavanie Istorii v Shkole	BM	1954-	SU
Princeton University Library Chronicle	3	1963-	US
Proceedings of the American Antiquarian Society	SA	1954-	US
Proceedings of the American Philosophical Society	BM	1955-	US
Proceedings of the British Academy	A	1953-	GB
Proceedings of the South Carolina Historical Association	A	1963-	US
Przegląd Socjologiczny	A	1957-	PO
Psychiatry	Q	1969-	US
Public Administration	Q	1955-	GB
Public Interest	Q	1966-	US
Public Opinion Quarterly	Q	1963-	US

Q

Quaker History	SA	1954-	US
Quarterly Journal of Economics	Q	1960-	US
Quarterly Journal of Speech	Q	1964-	US
Quarterly Journal of Studies on Alcohol	Q	1968-	US
Quarterly Journal of the Library of Congress	Q	1963-	US
Quarterly Review (ceased pub 1967)	Q	1954-67	GB
Quarterly Review of Economics and Business	Q	1966-	US
Queen's Quarterly	Q	1954-	CA

R

Records of the American Catholic Historical Society of Philadelphia	Q	1954-	US

Register of the Kentucky Historical Society	Q	1963-	US
Religion in Life	Q	1954-	US
Research Studies	Q	1964-	US
Review of Politics	Q	1954-	US
Revista de Historia de América	SA	1955-	MX
Revista do Instituto de Estudos Brasileiros	I	1966-	BR
Revue de Défense Nationale	M	1955-	FR
Revue des Études Juives	Q	1955-	FR
Revue des Travaux de l'Academie des Sciences Morales et Politiques et Comptes Rendus de ses Séances	SA	1954-	FR
Revue Politique et Parlimentaire	M	1954-	FR
Revue Roumaine d'Histoire	BM	1962-	RU
Rhode Island History	Q	1963-	US
Rivista Storica Italiana	Q	1954-	IT
Rochester History	Q	1963-	US
Rocky Mountain Social Science Journal	SA	1966-	US
Rural Sociology	Q	1963-	US

S

Samtiden	10	1954-	NO
Schweizer Monatshefte	M	1955-	SZ
Science and Society	Q	1963-	US
Shirin	BM	1955-	JA
Smithsonian	M	1970-	US
Social and Economic Studies	Q	1957-	WI
Social Casework	10	1970-	US
Social Education	8	1963-	US
Social Forces	Q	1963-	US
Social Science	Q	1963-	US
Social Science Quarterly	Q	1963-	US
Social Service Review	Q	1963-	US
Social Studies	7	1963-	US
Social Work	Q	1964-	US
Society	M	1967	US
Sociological Analysis	Q	1967-	US
Sociological Quarterly	Q	1967-	US
Sociology and Social Research	Q	1966-	US
Sociology of Education	Q	1968-	US
South Atlantic Quarterly	Q	1954-	US
South Carolina Historical Magazine	Q	1963-	US
Southern California Quarterly	Q	1962-	US
Southern Economic Journal	Q	1954-	US
Southern Folklore Quarterly	Q	1959-	US
Southern Literary Journal	SA	1968-	US
Southern Quarterly	Q	1963-	US
Southern Review	Q	1967-	US
Southern Speech Journal	Q	1963-	US
Southwest Review	Q	1963-	US
Southwestern Historical Quarterly	Q	1955-	US

Southwestern Social Science Quarterly (old title, see Social Science Quarterly)	Q	1963-	US
Sovetskaia Etnografiia	BM	1968-	SU
Speech Monographs	Q	1965-	US
Statsvetenskaplig Tidskrift	Q	1954-	SW
Survey	Q	1958-	GB
Svensk Tidskrift	10	1954-	SW
Swedish Pioneer Historical Quarterly	Q	1963-	US
Századok	BM	1954-	HU

T

Tanganyika Notes and Records (old title, see Tanzania Notes and Records)	SA	1963-	TZ
Tanzania Notes and Records	SA	1963-	TZ
Tarsadalmi Szemle	M	1964-	HU
Teachers College Record	I	1967-	US
Tennessee Historical Quarterly	Q	1963-	US
Texana	Q	1964-	US
Textile History Review (ceased pub 1965)	Q	1960-65	US
Thought	Q	1963-	US
Tijdschrift voor Geschiedenis	Q	1954-	NE
Trans-Action (old title, see Society)	M	1967-	US
Tri Quarterly	3	1966-	US
Twentieth Century	Q	1954-	GB

U

United Asia	BM	1955-	ID
Urban and Social Change Review	SA	1970-	US
Urban Review	I	1967-	US
Utah Historical Quarterly	Q	1963-	US

V

Vermont History	Q	1963-	US
Victorian Studies	Q	1957-	US
Virginia Cavalcade	Q	1963-	US
Virginia Law Review	8	1966-	US
Virginia Magazine of History and Biography	Q	1955-	US
Virginia Quarterly Review	Q	1954-	US
Voprosy Istorii	M	1954-	SU

W

Washington Monthly	M	1971-	US
West Virginia History	Q	1963-	US
Western Folklore	Q	1963-	US
Western Historical Quarterly	Q	1970-	US
Western Humanities Review	Q	1963-	US

Western Political Quarterly	Q	1955-	US
William and Mary Quarterly	Q	1954-	US
Winterthur Portfolio	A	1964-	US
Wisconsin Magazine of History	Q	1962-	US
Wisconsin Then and Now	M	1963-	US
World Today	M	1967-	GB

Z

Zeitschrift für Geschichtswissenschaft	M	1954-	EG
Zeitschrift für Politik	Q	1954-	WG
Zeitschrift für Religions- und Geistesgeschichte	Q	1954-	WG

FESTSCHRIFTS

Diplomacy in the Age of Nationalism: Essays in Honor of Lynn Marshall Case (The Hague, Neth.: Martinus Nijhoff, 1971).

Essays in American Historiography (Westport, Conn.: Greenwood Press, Inc., 1973).

Essays on American Literature in Honor of Jay B. Hubbell (Durham, N.C.: Duke U. Press).

Essays on the American Constitution: A Commemorative Volume in Honor of Alpheus T. Mason (Englewood Cliffs, N.J.: Prentice-Hall, Inc., 1964).

Folklore and Society: Essays in Honor of Benjamin A. Botkin (Hatboro, Pa.: Folklore Associates, Inc., 1966).

In the Trek of the Immigrants: Essays Presented to Carl Wittke (Rock Island, Ill.: Augustana College Library, 1964).

Studies in History and the Social Sciences: Essays in Honor of John A. Kinneman (Normal, Ill.: Illinois State U., 1965).

Writing Southern History: Essays in Historiography in Honor of Fletcher M. Green (Baton Rouge, La.: Louisiana State U. Press, 1967).

LIST OF ABSTRACTERS

A

Abramoske, D.J.
Abrash, M.
Adams, G.R.
Adolphus, L.
Agee, W.H.
Allen, C.R., Jr.
Allen, R.F.
Alvis, R.N.
Appel, J.J.
Aptheker, H.
Arkel, D. van
Armstrong, W.M.
Athey, L.L.

B

Banks, S.L.
Bardsley, V.E.
Bardsley, V.O.
Bassett, T.D.S.
Bassler, G.P.
Bauer, K.J.
Beauchamp, E.R.
Beauregard, E.E.
Bedford, H.F.
Berman, M.
Birkos, A.S.
Blum, G.P.
Boedecker, W.R.
Bottorff, W.K.
Bowers, W.L.
Boykin, J.H.

Brady, J.M.
Brandes, J.
Brescia, A.M.
Brewster, D.E.
Brockman, N.C.
Brockway, D.
Broderick, D.H.
Brown, D.N.
Brown, L.
Brown, T.H.
Buckman, W.A.
Bumsted, J.M.
Burke, R.S.
Burns, R.S.
Burr, M.A.
Bushnell, D.
Butcher, K.

C

Calkin, H.L.
Callahan, N.
Calvert, R.V.
Cameron, D.D.
Campbell, R.F.
Campion, Sr. M.
Carter, V.J.
Casada, J.A.
Case, L.M.
Chand, R.
Chauvin, K.A.
Cieplak, T.N.
Coates, W.H.
Coats, A.W.

Cohen, R.D.
Coleman, P.J.
Collins, R.O.
Colwell, J.L.
Comegys, R.G.
Condon, T.M.
Cook, J.F.
Cornebise, A.E.
Costello, E.P.
Counelis, J.S.
Cox, H.E.
Crane, J.K.
Crapster, B.L.
Cripps, T.R.
Crowe, J.C.

D

Davis, D.
Davis, G.H.
Davis, K.P.
Davis, T.B.
Davison, S.R.
Dawson, J.F.
Dehmelt, B.K.
Delaney, R.W.
Delzell, C.F.
Deutsch, H.C.
Doyle, G.D.
Doyle, Sr. A.
Drescher, N.M.
Drummond, B.A.
Dubay, R.W.
Duff, J.B.

Duquid, S.R.
Dutra, F.A.

E

Earnhart, H.G.
Eichelberger, C.L.
Eid, L.V.
Eilerman, R.
Ekrut, V.S.
Elkins, W.
Eminhizer, E.E.
Engler, D.J.
English, J.C.
Erickson, J.
Erlebacher, A.
Eyman, D.H.

F

Farnham, T.J.
Feldman, E.
Fiala, R.D.
Filipiak, J.D.
Filler, L.
Findlay, J.
Flack, J.K.
Fleener, C.J.
Flynn, J.J.
Fox, W.L.
Frakes, G.E.
Frazier, J.
Freedman, A.S.
Frykenberg, R.E.
Furman, D.M.

G

Gagnon, G.O.
Gallacci, C.A.
Gallagher, D.P.
Gara, L.
Gassner, J.S.

Geiger, L.G.
Gersman, E.M.
Goodman, D.B.
Gorchels, C.C.
Graham, H.J.
Grant, C.L.
Grattan, W.J.
Gregory, T.E.
Gressley, G.M.
Griffin, W.R.
Grob, G.N.
Grollman, C.
Grothaus, L.H.

H

Halstead, J.P.
Hanks, R.J.
Harlan, L.R.
Harper, J.
Harris, B.
Harrold, F.L.
Hathaway, E.W.
Hawes, J.M.
Hayes, M.A.
Helmreich, J.E.
Henderson, D.F.
Hendrickson, K.E.
Herbst, J.
Hess, G.R.
Heywood, R.W.
Hillje, J.W.
Hines, J.
Hočevar, T.
Hoff, C.J.
Hogeboom, W.L.
Hollyday, F.B.M.
Hopping, A.
Hough, M.
Houston, D.
Howell, R.
Hudson, J.A.
Hull, G.W.
Humphreys, S.E.
Humphreys, S.R.
Hyman, R.
Hyslop, E.C.

I

Iggers, G.
Imai, H.

J

James, D.C.
Jewsbury, G.F.
Johnson, B.D.
Johnson, E.C.
Johnson, E.D.
Johnson, E.S.
Jones, G.H.G.
Jones, S.L.
Jonsson, P.O.
Jordan, H.D.
Joynt, C.B.
Judd, J.

K

Kanin, M.M.
Kantor, H.
Katz, I.J.
Kaufman, M.A.
Kennedy, C.W.
Kennedy, P.W.
Kerley, R.
Kittell, A.H.
Klutts, W.A.
Knafla, L.A.
Krenkel, J.H.
Krichmar, A.
Kuhn, Sr. M.
Kuntz, N.A.
Kurland, G.
Kurland, N.D.

L

Lampe, A.B.
Lange, R.B.
Latour, C.F.
Lauritsen, C.G.

Legters, L.H.
LeGuin, C.
Leonard, I.M.
Liersch, G.
Lindgren, R.E.
Lockwood, T.D.
Lohof, B.A.
Loose, J.W.W.
Lovett, C.M.
Lovin, H.T.
Lowitt, R.
Lycan, G.L.
Lydon, J.G.

M

März, E.
Machan, M.W.
MacIntyre, D.J.
Maciuika, B.V.
Mahoney, J.F.
Main, A.K.
Marina, W.
Marion, R.J.
Marks, H.S.
Marzari, F.
Mathews, T.
Mayo, D.E.
McAuley, Sr. M.
McBaine, M.J.
McBane, R.L.
McCain, P.M.
McCarthy, J.M.
McCornack, R.B.
McCusker, J.J.
McCutcheon, J.
McDonald, F.J.
McGinty, G.W.
McIntyre, W.D.
McMahon, C.P.
McNeel, S.L.
Melamed, R.S.
Melvin, D.B.
Metz, W.D.
Millar, D.R.
Miller, R.M.
Miller, S.J.

Miller, W.B.
Miyake, T.
Moen, N.W.
Mohl, R.A.
Moir, T.L.
Moore, R.J.
Morgan, W.G.
Morrison, B.M.
Mueller, R.
Murdoch, D.H.
Murdock, E.C.
Murphy, L.R.

N

Naidis, M.
Negaard, H.A.
Newton, C.A.
Nix, R.L.
Noppen, I.W. Van
Norton, D.H.

O

O'Brien, E.J.
Oberholzer, E., Jr.
Ogilvie, C.F.
Ohrvall, C.W.
Olson, P.M.
Onstine, B.W.
Orchard, G.E.

P

Pearson, S.C., Jr.
Peltier, D.P.
Pennington, J.G.
Peterson, N.L.
Peterson, W.F.
Petrie, M.
Picht, D.R.
Pickett, R.S.
Pierard, R.V.
Pliska, S.R.

Podjed, P.
Powell, H.B.
Proett, P.A.
Proschansky, H.
Puffer, K.J.
Pula, J.S.
Pusateri, C.J.

Q

Quinlan, Mother M.H.
Quinten, B.T.

R

Raack, R.C.
Raife, R.C.
Rasmussen, W.D.
Ratliff, W.E.
Rehder, G.
Reilly, G.L.A.
Rhodes, B.D.
Richards, E.B.
Richardson, D.R.
Roberts, S.E.
Roddy, E.G.
Rollins, A.B.
Roon, G. van
Rosenthal, F.
Ross, D.R.B.
Rossi, D.F.
Rossi, F.J.
Rotondaro, F.

S

Scaccia, J.F.
Schafer, R.G.
Schoebe, G.
Selleck, R.G.
Shoemaker, R.W.
Silveri, L.D.
Silverman, H.J.
Simon, W.M.

Small, M.
Smith, D.L.
Snow, G.E.
Soady, F.W., Jr.
Soroka, W.W.
Spector, S.D.
Spurgin, C.R.
Stelzner, H.G.
Stickney, E.P.
Stoesen, A.R.
Stokes, D.A.
Stone, R.
Storey, B.A.
Strahan, M.J.
Strain, R.
Strausbaugh, M.R.
Swanson, B.E.
Swift, D.C.
Swift, D.H.

T

Thacker, J.W., Jr.
Thomas, J.R.
Thomas, P.D.
Thompson, A.W.
Tietz, G.
Tracy, A.P.

Trauth, Sr. M.P.
Trennert, R.A.
Trickey, D.J.
Turner, A.
Turner, J.G.
Tutorow, N.E.

U

Upton, L.F.S.
Usher, J.M.E.

V

Valliant, R.B.
Valliant, R.S.
Vatter, B.A.
Vignery, J.R.
Visser, D.
Volgyes, I.

W

Wagner, F.
Waldstein, B.
Ward, H.M.

Warnock, J.
Warren, C.N.
Warren, H.G.
Wechman, R.J.
Weltsch, R.E.
West, K.B.
White, L.J.
Wight, W.E.
Wilkins, B.
Williamson, M.M.
Willigan, W.L.
Wilson, R.E.
Winks, R.W.
Wollert, E.
Woodward, R.L., Jr.

Y

Yedlin, T.
Young, A.P.

Z

Zabel, J.A.
Zabel, O.H.
Ziemke, E.F.
Zilversmit, A.
Zornow, W.F.